The Principles of Chemistry (Volume I)

CW01090942

Dmitry Ivanovich Mendeleyev, (Editor: T. A. Lawson),
(Translator: George Kamensky)

Alpha Editions

This edition published in 2024

ISBN 9789362515155

Design and Setting By
Alpha Editions
www.alphaedis.com
Email - info@alphaedis.com

Contents

CHAPTER XIV THE VALENCY AND SPECIFIC HEAT OF THE METALS. MAGNESIUM. CALCIUM, STRONTIUM, BARIUM, AND BERYLLIUM

PREFACE TO THE
ENGLISH TRANSLATION

The first English edition of this work was published in 1891, and that a second edition is now called for is, we think, a sufficient proof that the enthusiasm of the author for his science, and the philosophical method of his teaching, have been duly appreciated by English chemists.

In the scientific work to which Professor Mendeléeff's life has been devoted, his continual endeavour has been to bring the scattered facts of chemistry within the domain of law, and accordingly in his teaching he endeavours to impress upon the student the *principles* of the science, the generalisations, so far as they have been discovered, under which the facts naturally group themselves.

Of those generalisations the periodic law is perhaps the most important that has been put forward since the establishment of the atomic theory. It is therefore interesting to note that Professor Mendeléeff was led to its discovery in preparing the first Russian edition of this book.

It is natural, too, that the further application and development of that generalisation should be the principal feature of this, the latest edition.

There are special difficulties in rendering the Russian language into good English, and we are conscious that these have not been entirely overcome. Doubtless also there are errors of statement which have escaped correction, but we believe that the present edition will be found better in both respects than its predecessor. We have thought it our duty as translators to give as far as possible a faithful reproduction of Professor Mendeléeff's work—the sixth Russian edition—without amplifying or modifying his statements, and in this we have the author's approval.

Although other duties have prevented Mr. Greenaway from undertaking the care of the present edition, he has been kind enough to give us the benefit of his suggestions on several points. We also wish to thank the Managers of the Royal Institution for permission to reprint the lecture delivered at the Royal Institution by Professor Mendeléeff (Appendix I.), and to the Council of the Chemical Society for permission to reprint the Faraday lecture which forms Appendix II.

In conclusion, we are indebted to Mr. F. Evershed, who has given us much valuable assistance in revising the sheets for the press.

G. K.
T. A. L.

August 1897

AUTHOR'S PREFACE
TO THE SIXTH RUSSIAN EDITION

This work was written during the years 1868–1870, its object being to acquaint the student not only with the methods of observation, the experimental facts, and the laws of chemistry, but also with the insight given by this science into the unchangeable substratum underlying the varying forms of matter.

If statements of fact themselves depend upon the person who observes them, how much more distinct is the reflection of the personality of him who gives an account of methods and of philosophical speculations which form the essence of science! For this reason there will inevitably be much that is subjective in every objective exposition of science. And as an individual production is only significant in virtue of that which has preceded and that which is contemporary with it, it resembles a mirror which in reflecting exaggerates the size and clearness of neighbouring objects, and causes a person near it to see reflected most plainly those objects which are on the side to which it is directed. Although I have endeavoured to make my book a true mirror directed towards the whole domain of chemical changes, yet involuntarily those influences near to me have been the most clearly reflected, the most brightly illuminated, and have tinted the entire work with their colouring. In this way the chief peculiarity of the book has been determined. Experimental and practical data occupy their place, but the philosophical principles of our science form the chief theme of the work. In former times sciences, like bridges, could only be built up by supporting them on a few broad buttresses and long girders. In addition to the exposition of the principles of chemistry, it has been my desire to show how science has now been built up like a suspension bridge, supported by the united strength of a number of slender, but firmly-fixed, chains, which individually are of little strength, and has thus been carried over difficulties which before appeared insuperable. In comparing the science of the past, the present, and the future, in placing the particulars of its restricted experiments side by side with its aspirations after unbounded and infinite truth, and in restraining myself from yielding to a bias towards the most attractive path, I have endeavoured to incite in the reader a spirit of inquiry, which, dissatisfied with speculative reasonings alone, should subject every idea to experiment, encourage the habit of stubborn work, and excite a search for fresh chains of evidence to complete the bridge over the bottomless unknown. History proves that it is possible by this means to avoid two equally pernicious extremes, the Utopian—a visionary contemplation which proceeds from a current of thought only—and the stagnant realism which is content with bare facts. Sciences like chemistry, which deal with ideas as well as with material substances, and create a possibility of immediately verifying that which has been or may be discovered or assumed, demonstrate at every step that the work of the past has availed much, and that without it it would be impossible to advance into the ocean of the unknown. They also show the possibility of becoming acquainted with fresh portions of this unknown, and compel us, while duly respecting the teachings of history, to cast aside classical illusions, and to engage in a work which not only gives mental satisfaction but is also practically useful to all our fellow-creatures.[1]

Thus the desire to direct those thirsting for truth to the pure source of the science of the forces acting throughout nature forms the first and most important aim of this book. The time has arrived when a knowledge of physics and chemistry forms as important a part of education as that of the classics did two centuries ago. In those days the nations which excelled in classical learning stood foremost, just as now the most advanced are those which are superior in the knowledge of the natural sciences, for they form the strength and characteristic of our times. In following the above and chief aim, I set myself a second object: to furnish a text-book for an elementary knowledge of chemistry and so satisfy a want which undoubtedly exists among students and those who have recourse to chemistry either as a source of truth or welfare.[2] Hence, although the fundamental object of this work was to express and embrace the general chemical teaching of the present day from a personal point of view, I have nevertheless striven throughout to maintain such a level as would render the 'Principles of Chemistry' accessible to the beginner. Many aspects of this work are determined by this combination of requirements which frequently differ widely. An issue was only possible under one condition, *i.e.* not to be carried away by what appears to be a plausible theory in explaining individual facts and to always endeavour to transmit the simple truth of a given fact, extracting it from the vast store of the literature of the subject and from tried personal experience. In publishing a new edition of this work I have striven to add any facts of importance recently discovered[3] and to revise the former edition in the above spirit. With this object I have entirely gone over this edition, and a comparison of it with the former one will show that the additions and alterations have cost as much labour as many chapters of the work. I also wished to show in an elementary treatise on chemistry the striking advantages gained by the application of the periodic law, which I first saw in its entirety in the year 1869 when I was engaged in writing the first edition of this book, in which, indeed, the law was first enunciated. At that time, however, this law was not established so firmly as now, when so many of its consequences have been verified by the researches of numerous chemists, and especially by Roscoe, Lecoq de Boisbaudran, Nilson, Brauner, Thorpe, Carnelley, Laurie, Winkler, and others. The, to me, unexpectedly rapid success with which the teaching of the periodicity of the elements has spread in our science, and perhaps also, the perseverance with which I collected in this work, and upon a new plan, the most important data respecting the elements and their mutual relations, explained sufficiently the fact that the former (5th, 1889) edition of my work has been translated into English[4] and German[5] and is being translated into French.[6] Deeply touched by the favourable opinions expressed by English men of science upon my book, I ascribe them chiefly to the periodic law placed at the basis of my treatise and especially of the second part of the book, which contains a large amount of data having a special and sometimes quite unexpected, bearing from the point of view of this law. As the entire scheme of this work is subordinated to the law of periodicity, which may be illustrated in a tabular form by placing the elements in series, groups, and periods, two such tables are given at the end of this preface.

In this the sixth edition I have not altered any essential feature of the original work, and have retained those alterations which were introduced into the fifth edition.[7] I have, however, added many newly discovered facts, and in this respect it is necessary to say a few words. Although all aspects of the simplest chemical relations are as far as possible equally developed in this book, yet on looking back I see that I have, nevertheless, given most attention to the so-called indefinite compounds examples of which may be seen in solutions. I recur repeatedly to them, and to all the latest data respecting them, for in them I see a starting point for the future progress of our science and to them I affiliate numerous instances of definite compounds, beginning with alloys and silicates and ending with complex acids. There are two reasons for this. In the first place, this subject has deeply interested me from my youth; I have devoted a portion of my own researches to it, and therefore it occupied an important position even in the first edition of my book; besides which all that has been subsequently accomplished in our science, especially during the last five or six years, shows that at the present day an interest in these questions plays an important part in the minds of a large circle of contemporary workers in chemistry. This personal attachment, if I may so call it, to the question of solutions and such indefinite compounds, must involuntarily have impressed itself upon my work, and in the later editions I have even had to strive not to give this subject a greater development than previously, so great was the material accumulated, which however does not yet give us the right to consider even the most elementary questions respecting solutions as solved. Thus, we cannot yet say what a solution really is. My own view is that a solution is a homogeneous liquid system of unstable dissociating compounds of the solvent with the substance dissolved. But although such a theory explains much to me, I cannot consider my opinion as proved, and therefore give it with some reserve as one of several hypotheses.[8] As a subject yet far from solved, I might naturally have ignored it, or only mentioned it cursorily, but such a treatment of solutions, although usual in elementary treatises on chemistry, would not have answered my views upon the subject of our science, and I wished that the reader might find in my book beyond everything an expression of all that a study of the subject built up for me. If in solutions I see and can frequently prove distinct evidences of the existence of those definite compounds which form the more generalised province of chemical data, I could not refrain from going into certain details respecting solutions; otherwise, there would have remained no trace of that general idea, that in them we have only a certain instance of ordinary definite or atomic compounds, subject to Dalton's laws. Having long had this idea, I wished to impress it upon the reader of my book, and it is this desire which forms the second of those chief reasons why I recur so frequently to solutions in this work. At present, my ideas respecting solutions are shared by few, but I trust that by degrees the instances I give will pave the way for their general recognition, and it is my hope that they may find adherents among those of my readers who are in a position to work out by experiment this difficult but highly interesting problem.

In conclusion, I desire to record my thanks to V. D. Sapogenikoff, who has corrected the proofs of the whole of this edition and compiled the indexes which greatly facilitate the search for those details which are scattered throughout the work.

D. MENDELÉEFF.

Footnotes:

[1] Chemistry, like every other science, is at once a means and an end. It is a means of attaining certain practical results. Thus, by its assistance, the obtaining of matter in its various forms is facilitated; it shows new possibilities of availing ourselves of the forces of nature, indicates the methods of preparing many substances, points out their properties, &c. In this sense chemistry is closely connected with the work of the manufacturer and the artisan, its sphere is active, and is a means of promoting general welfare. Besides this honourable vocation, chemistry has another. With it, as with every other elaborated science, there are many lofty aspirations, the contemplation of which serves to inspire its workers and adherents. This contemplation comprises not only the principal data of the science, but also the generally-accepted deductions, and also hypotheses which refer to phenomena as yet but imperfectly known. In this latter sense scientific

contemplation varies much with times and persons, it bears the stamp of creative power, and embraces the highest forms of scientific progress. In that pure enjoyment experienced on approaching to the ideal, in that eagerness to draw aside the veil from the hidden truth, and even in that discord which exists between the various workers, we ought to see the surest pledges of further scientific progress. Science thus advances, discovering new truths, and at the same time obtaining practical results. The edifice of science not only requires material, but also a plan, and necessitates the work of preparing the materials, putting them together, working out the plans and the symmetrical proportions of the various parts. To conceive, understand, and grasp the whole symmetry of the scientific edifice, including its unfinished portions, is equivalent to tasting that enjoyment only conveyed by the highest forms of beauty and truth. Without the material, the plan alone is but a castle in the air—a mere possibility; whilst the material without a plan is but useless matter. All depends on the concordance of the materials with the plan and execution, and the general harmony thereby attained. In the work of science, the artisan, architect, and creator are very often one and the same individual; but sometimes, as in other walks of life, there is a difference between them; sometimes the plan is preconceived, sometimes it follows the preparation and accumulation of the raw material. Free access to the edifice of science is not only allowed to those who devised the plan, worked out the detailed drawings, prepared the materials, or piled up the brickwork, but also to all those who are desirous of making a close acquaintance with the plan, and wish to avoid dwelling in the vaults or in the garrets where the useless lumber is stored.

Knowing how contented, free, and joyful is life in the realm of science, one fervently wishes that many would enter its portals. On this account many pages of this treatise are unwittingly stamped with the earnest desire that the habits of chemical contemplation which I have endeavoured to instil into the minds of my readers will incite them to the further study of science. Science will then flourish in them and by them, on a fuller acquaintance not only with that little which is enclosed within the narrow limits of my work, but with the further learning which they must imbibe in order to make themselves masters of our science and partakers in its further advancement.

Those who enlist in the cause of science have no reason to fear when they remember the urgent need for practical workers in the spheres of agriculture, arts, and manufacture. By summoning adherents to the work of theoretical chemistry, I am confident that I call them to a most useful labour, to the habit of dealing correctly with nature and its laws, and to the possibility of becoming truly practical men. In order to become actual chemists, it is necessary for beginners to be well and closely acquainted with three important branches of chemistry—analytical, organic, and theoretical. That part of chemistry which is dealt with in this treatise is only the groundwork of the edifice. For the learning and development of chemistry in its truest and fullest sense, beginners ought, in the first place, to turn their attention to the practical work of analytical chemistry; in the second place, to practical and theoretical acquaintance with some special chemical question, studying the original treatises of the investigators of the subject (at first, under the direction of experienced teachers), because in working out particular facts the faculty of judgment and of correct criticism becomes sharpened; in the third place, to a knowledge of current scientific questions through the special chemical journals and papers, and by intercourse with other chemists. The time has come to turn aside from visionary contemplation, from platonic aspirations, and from classical verbosity, and to enter the regions of actual labour for the common weal, to prove that the study of science is not only air excellent education for youth, but that it instils the virtues of industry and veracity, and creates solid national wealth, material and mental, which without it would be unattainable. Science, which deals with the infinite, is itself without bounds.

[2] I recommend those who are commencing the study of chemistry with my book *to first read only what is printed in the large type*, because in that part I have endeavoured to concentrate all the fundamental, indispensable knowledge required for that study. In the footnotes, printed in small type (which should be read only after the large text has been mastered), certain details are discussed; they are either further examples, or debatable questions on existing ideas which I thought useful to lay before those entering into the sphere of science, or certain historical and technical details which might be withdrawn from the fundamental portion of the book. Without intending to attain in my treatise to the completeness of a work of reference, I have still endeavoured to express the principal developments of science as they concern the chemical elements viewed in that aspect in which they appeared to me after long continued study of the subject and participation in the contemporary advance of knowledge.

I have also placed my personal views, suppositions, and arguments in the footnotes, which are chiefly designed for details and references. But I have endeavoured to avoid here, as in the text, not only all that I consider doubtful, but also those details which belong either to special branches of chemistry (for instance, to analytical, organic, physical, theoretical, physiological, agricultural, or technical chemistry), or to different branches of natural science which are more and more coming into closer and closer contact with chemistry. Chemistry, I am convinced, must occupy a place among the natural sciences side by side with mechanics; for mechanics treats of matter as a system of ponderable points having scarcely any individuality and only standing in a certain state of mobile equilibrium. For chemistry, matter is an entire world of life, with an infinite variety of individuality both in the elements and in their combinations. In studying the general uniformity from a mechanical point of view, I think that the highest point of knowledge of nature cannot be attained without taking into account the individuality of things in which chemistry is set to seek for general higher laws. Mechanics may be likened to the science of statesmanship, chemistry to the sciences of jurisprudence and sociology. The general universe could not be built up without the particular individual universe, and would be a dry abstract were it not enlivened by the real variety of the individual world. Mechanics forms the classical basis of natural philosophy, while chemistry, as a comparatively new and still young science, already strives to—and will, in the future introduce a new, living aspect into the philosophy of nature; all the more as chemistry alone is never at rest or anywhere dead—its vital action has universal sway, and inevitably determines the general aspect of the universe. Just as the microscope and telescope enlarge the scope of vision, and discover life in seeming immobility, so chemistry, in discovering and striving to discern the life of the invisible world of atoms and molecules and their ultimate limit of divisibility, will clearly introduce new and important problems into our conception of nature. And I think that its *rôle*, which is now considerable, will increase more and more in the future; that is, I think that in its further development it will occupy a place side by side with mechanics for the comprehension of the secrets of nature. But here we require some second Newton; and I have no doubt that he will soon appear.

[3] I was much helped in gathering data from the various chemical journals of the last five years by the abstracts made for me by Mr. Y. V. Kouriloff, to whom I tender my best thanks.

[4] The English translation was made by G. Kamensky, and edited by A. J. Greenaway; published by Longmans, Green & Co.

[5] The German translation was made by L. Jawein and A. Thillot; published by Ricker (St. Petersburg).

[6] The French translation has been commenced by E. Achkinasi and H. Carrion from the fifth edition, and is published by Tignol (Paris).

[7] The fifth edition was not only considerably enlarged, compared with the preceding, but also the foundations of the periodic system of the elements were placed far more firmly in it than in the former editions. The subject-matter was also divided into text and footnotes, which contained details unnecessary for a first acquaintance with chemistry. The fifth edition sold out sooner than I expected, so that instead of issuing supplements

(containing the latest discoveries in chemistry), as I had proposed, I was obliged to publish the present entirely new edition of the work.

[8] This hypothesis is not only mentioned in different parts of this book, but is partly (from the aspect of the specific gravity of solutions) developed in my work, *The Investigation of Solutions from their Specific Gravity*, 1887.

TABLE I
Distribution of the Elements in Groups and Series

Group	I.	II.	III.	IV.	V.	VI.	VII.	VIII.			
Series 1	H	—	—	—	—	—	—				
„ 2	Li	Be	B	C	N	O	F				
„ 3	Na	Mg	Al	Si	P	S	Cl				
„ 4	K	Ca	Sc	Ti	V	Cr	Mn	Fe	Co	Ni	Cu
„ 5	(Cu)	Zn	Ga	Ge	As	Se	Br				
„ 6	Rb	Cr	Y	Zr	Nb	Mo	—	Ru	Rh	Pd	Ag
„ 7	(Ag)	Cd	In	Sn	Sb	Te	I				
„ 8	Cs	Ba	La	Ce	Di?	—	—	—	—	—	—
„ 9	—	—	—	—	—	—	—				
„ 10	—	—	Yb	—	Ta	W	—	Os	Ir	Pt	Au

,, 1/1	(Au)	Hg	Tl	Pb	Bi	—	—	
,, 1/2	—	—	—	Th	—	U	—	
	R_2O	R_2O_2	R_2O_3	R_2O_4	R_2O_5	R_2O_6	R_2O_7	Higher oxides
	—	RO	—	RO_2	—	RO_3	—	RO_4
	—	—	—	RH_4	RH_3	RH_2	RH	Hydrogen compounds

TABLE II
Periodic System and Atomic Weights of the Elements
(Giving the pages on which they are described)

		2nd Series, Typical elements	4th Series	6th Series	8th Series	10th Series	12th Series
I.		Li 7	K 89	Rb 86	Cs 133	—	—
		vol. i. 574	vol. i. 558	vol. i. 576	vol. i. 576		
II.		Be 9	Ca 40	Sr 88	Ba 137	—	—
		vol. i. 618	vol. i. 590	vol. i. 614	vol. i. 614		
III.		B 11	Sc 44	Y 89	La 138	Yb 173	—
		vol. ii. 60	vol. ii. 94	vol. ii. 93	vol. ii. 93	vol. ii. 93	
IV.		C 12	Ti 48	Zr 91	Ce 140	? 178	Th 232
		vol. i. 338	vol. ii. 144	vol. ii. 146	vol. ii. 93		vol. ii. 148

		3rd Series	5th Series	7th Series	9th Series	11th Series
V.		N 14	V 51	Nb 94	?Di 142	Ta 183	—
		vol. i. 223	vol. ii. 194	vol. ii. 197	vol. ii. 93	vol. ii. 197	
VI.		O 16	Cr 52	Mo 96	—	W 184	U 239
		vol. i. 155	vol. ii. 276	vol. ii. 290		vol. ii. 290	vol. ii. 297
VII.		F 19	Mn 55	? 99	—	—	—
		vol. i. 489	vol. ii. 303				
			Fe 56	Ru 102	—	Os 192	
			vol. ii. 317	vol. ii. 369		vol. ii. 369	
VIII.			Co 59	Rh 103	—	Ir 193	
			vol. ii. 353	vol. ii. 369		vol. ii. 369	
			Ni 59·5	Pd 106	—	Pt 196	
			vol. ii. 353	vol. ii. 369		vol. ii. 369	
			3rd Series	5th Series	7th Series	9th Series	11th Series
I.	H 1	Na 23	Cu 64	Ag 108	—	Au 197	
	vol. i. 129	vol. i. 533	vol. ii. 398	vol. ii. 415		vol. ii. 442	
II.		Mg 24	Zn 65	Cd 112	—	Hg 200	
		vol. i. 590	vol. ii. 39	vol. ii. 47		vol. ii. 48	
III.		Al 27	Ga 70	In 114	—	Tl 204	
		vol. ii. 70	vol. ii. 90	vol. ii. 91		vol. ii. 91	

IV.	Si 28	Ge 72	Sn 119	—	Pb 207
	vol. ii. 99	vol. ii. 124	vol. ii. 125		vol. ii. 134
V.	P 31	As 75	Sb 120	—	Bi 209
	vol. ii. 149	vol. ii. 179	vol. ii. 186		vol. ii. 189
VI.	S 32	Se 79	Te 125	—	—
	vol. ii. 200	vol. ii. 270	vol. ii. 270		
VII.	Cl 35·5	Br 80	I 127	—	—
	vol. i. 459	vol. i. 494	vol. i. 496		

Note.—Two lines under the elements indicate those which are very widely distributed in nature; one line indicates those which, although not so frequently met with, are of general use in the arts and manufactures.

PRINCIPLES OF CHEMISTRY

INTRODUCTION

The study of natural science, whose rapid development dates from the days of Galileo (†1642) and Newton (†1727), and its closer application to the external universe[1] led to the separation of Chemistry as a[2] particular branch of natural philosophy, not only owing to the increasing store of observations and experiments relating to the mutual transformations of substances, but also, and more especially, because in addition to gravity, cohesion, heat, light and electricity it became necessary to recognise the existence of particular internal forces in the ultimate parts of all substances, forces which make themselves manifest in the transformations of substances into one another, but remain hidden (latent) under ordinary circumstances, and whose existence cannot therefore be directly apprehended, and so for a long time remained unrecognised. The primary object of chemistry is the study of the homogeneous substances[2] of which all the objects of the universe are made up, with the transformations of these substances into each other, and with the phenomena[3] which accompany such transformations. Every chemical change or reaction,[4] as it is called, can only take place under a condition of most intimate and close contact of the re-acting substances,[5] and is determined by the forces proper to the smallest invisible particles (molecules) of matter. We must distinguish three chief classes of chemical transformations.

1. *Combination* is a reaction in which the union of two substances yields a new one, or in general terms, from a given number of substances, a lesser number is obtained. Thus, by heating a mixture of iron and sulphur[6] a single new substance is produced, iron sulphide, in which the constituent substances cannot be distinguished even by the highest magnifying power. Before the reaction, the iron could be separated from the mixture by a magnet, and the sulphur by dissolving it in certain oily liquids;[7] in general, before combination they might be mechanically separated from each other, but after combination both substances penetrate into each other, and are then neither mechanically separable nor individually distinguishable. As a rule, reactions of direct combination are accompanied by an evolution of heat, and the common case of combustion, evolving heat, consists in the combination of combustible substances with a portion (oxygen) of the atmosphere, the gases and vapours contained in the smoke being the products of combination.

2. Reactions of *decomposition* are cases the reverse of those of combination, that is, in which one substance gives two—or, in general, a given number of substances a greater number. Thus, by heating wood (and also coal and many animal or vegetable substances) without access to air, a combustible gas, a watery liquid, tar, and carbon are obtained. It is in this way that tar, illuminating gas, and charcoal are prepared on a large scale.[8] All limestones, for example, flagstones, chalk, or marble, are decomposed by heating to redness into lime and a peculiar gas called carbonic anhydride. A similar decomposition, taking place, however, at a much lower temperature, proceeds with the green copper carbonate which is contained in natural malachite. This example will be studied more in detail presently. Whilst heat is evolved in the ordinary reactions of combination, it is, on the contrary, absorbed in the reactions of decomposition.

3. The third class of chemical reactions—where the number of re-acting substances is equal to the number of substances formed—may[5] be considered as a simultaneous decomposition and combination. If, for instance, two compounds A and B are taken and they react on each other to form the substances C and D, then supposing that A is decomposed into D and E, and that E combines with B to form C, we have a reaction in which two substances A, or D E, and B were taken and two others C, or E B, and D were produced. Such reactions ought to be placed under the general term of reactions of '*rearrangement*,' and the particular case where two substances give two fresh ones, reactions of '*substitution*.'[9] Thus, if a piece of iron be immersed in a solution of blue vitriol (copper sulphate), copper is formed—or, rather, separated out, and green vitriol (iron sulphate, which only differs from the blue vitriol in that the iron has replaced the copper) is obtained in solution. In this manner iron may be coated with copper, so also copper with silver; such reactions are frequently made use of in practice.

The majority of the chemical changes which occur in nature and are made use of technically are very complicated, as they consist of an association of many separate and simultaneous combinations, decompositions, and replacements. It is chiefly due to this natural complexity of chemical phenomena that for so many centuries chemistry did not exist as an exact science; that is so say, that although many chemical changes were known and made use of,[10] yet their real nature was unknown, nor could they be predicted or directed at will. Another reason for the tardy progress of chemical knowledge is the participation of gaseous substances, especially air, in many reactions. The true comprehension of air as a ponderable substance, and of gases in general as peculiar elastic and dispersive states of matter, was only arrived at in the sixteenth and seventeenth centuries, and it was only after this that the transformations of substances could form a science. Up to that time, without understanding the invisible and yet ponderable gaseous and vaporous states of substances, it was impossible to obtain any fundamental chemical evidence, because gases escaped from notice[6] between the reacting and resultant substances. It is easy from the impression conveyed to us by the phenomena we observe to form the opinion that matter is created and destroyed: a whole mass of trees burn, and there only remains a little charcoal and ash, whilst from one small seed there grows little by little a majestic tree. In one case matter seems to be destroyed, and in the other to be created. This conclusion is arrived at because the formation or consumption of gases, being under the circumstances invisible to the eye, is not observed. When wood burns it undergoes a chemical change into gaseous products, which escape as smoke. A very simple experiment will prove this. By collecting the smoke it may be observed that it contains gases which differ entirely from air, being incapable of supporting combustion or respiration. These gases may be weighed, and it will then be seen that their weight exceeds that of the wood taken. This increase in weight arises from the fact that, in burning, the component parts of the wood combine with a portion of the air; in like manner iron increases in weight by rusting. In burning gunpowder its substance is not destroyed, but only converted into gases and smoke. So also in the growth of a tree; the seed does not increase in mass of itself and from itself, but grows because it absorbs gases from the atmosphere and sucks water and substances dissolved therein from the earth through its roots. The sap and solid substances which give plants their form are produced from these absorbed gases and liquids by complicated chemical processes. The gases and liquids are converted into solid substances by the plants themselves. Plants not only do not increase in size, but die, in a gas which does not contain the constituents of air. When moist substances dry they decrease in weight; when water evaporates we know that it does not disappear, but will return from the atmosphere as rain, dew, and snow. When water is absorbed by the earth, it does not disappear there for ever, but accumulates somewhere underground, from whence it afterwards flows forth as a spring. Thus matter does not disappear and is not created, but only undergoes various physical and chemical transformations—that is to say, changes its locality and form. Matter remains on the earth in the same quantity as before; in a word it is, so far as we are concerned, everlasting. It was difficult to submit this simple and primary truth of chemistry to investigation, but when once made clear it rapidly spread, and now seems as natural and simple as many truths which have been acknowledged for ages. Mariotte and other savants of the seventeenth century already suspected the existence of the law of the indestructibility of matter, but they made no efforts to express it or to apply it to the requirements of science. The experiments by[7] means of which this simple law was arrived at were made during the latter half of the last century by the founder of modern chemistry, LAVOISIER, the French Academician and tax farmer. The numerous experiments of this savant were conducted with the aid of the balance, which is the only means of directly and accurately determining the quantity of matter.

Lavoisier found, by weighing all the substances, and even the apparatus, used in every experiment, and then weighing the substances obtained after the chemical change, that the sum of the weights of the substances formed was always equal to the sum of the weights of the substances taken; or, in other words: MATTER IS NOT CREATED AND DOES NOT DISAPPEAR, or that, *matter is everlasting*. This expression naturally includes a hypothesis, but our only aim in using it is to concisely express the following lengthy period—That in all experiments, and in all the investigated phenomena of nature, it has never been observed that the weight of the substances formed was less or greater (as far as accuracy of weighing permits[11]) than the weight of the substances originally taken, and as weight is proportional to mass[11 bis] or quantity of matter, it follows that no one has ever succeeded in observing a disappearance of matter or its appearance in fresh quantities. The law of the indestructibility of matter endows all chemical investigations with exactitude, as, on its basis, an equation may be formed for every chemical reaction. If in any reaction the weights of the substances taken be designated by the letters A, B, C, &c., and the weights of the substances formed by the letters M, N, O, &c., then

$$A + B + C + \ldots \ldots \ldots = M + N + O + \ldots \ldots \ldots$$

Therefore, should the weight of one of the re-acting or resultant substances be unknown, it may be determined by solving the equation.[8] The chemist, in applying the law of the indestructibility of matter, and in making use of the chemical balance, must never lose sight of any one of the re-acting or resultant substances. Should such an over-sight be made, it will at once be remarked that the sum of the weights of the substances taken is unequal to the sum of the weights of the substances formed. All the progress made by chemistry during the end of the last, and in the present, century is entirely and immovably founded on the law of the indestructibility of matter. It is absolutely necessary in beginning the study of chemistry to become familiar with the simple truth which is expressed by this law, and for this purpose several examples elucidating its application will now be cited.

1. It is well known that iron rusts in damp air,[12] and that when heated to redness in air it becomes coated with scoria (oxide), having, like rust, the appearance of an earthy substance resembling some of the iron ores from which metallic iron is extracted. If the iron is weighed before and after the formation of the scoria or rust, it will be found that the metal has increased

in weight during the operation.[13] It can easily be proved that this increase in weight is accomplished at the expense of the atmosphere, and mainly, as Lavoisier proved, at the expense of that portion which is called oxygen. In fact, in a vacuum, or in gases which do not contain oxygen, for instance, in hydrogen or nitrogen, the iron neither rusts nor becomes coated with scoria. Had the iron not been weighed, the participation of the oxygen of the atmosphere in its transformation into an earthy substance might have easily passed unnoticed, as was formerly the case, when phenomena like the above were, for this reason, misunderstood. It is evident from the[9] law of the indestructibility of matter that as the iron increases in weight in its conversion into rust, the latter must be a more complex substance than the iron itself, and its formation is due to a reaction of combination. We might form an entirely wrong opinion about it, and might, for instance, consider rust to be a simpler substance than iron, and explain the formation of rust as the removal of something from the iron. Such, indeed, was the general opinion prior to Lavoisier, when it was held that iron contained a certain unknown substance called 'phlogiston,' and that rust was iron deprived of this supposed substance.

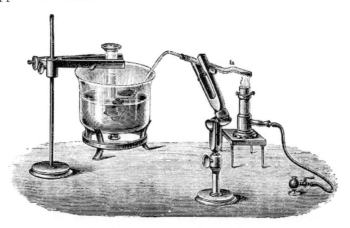

FIG. 1.—Apparatus for the decomposition of red mercury oxide.

2. Copper carbonate (in the form of a powder, or as the well-known green mineral called 'malachite,' which is used for making ornaments, or as an ore for the extraction of copper) changes into a black substance called 'copper oxide' when heated to redness.[14] This black substance is also obtained by heating copper to redness in air—that is, it is the scoria or oxidation product of copper. The weight of the black oxide of copper left is less than that of the copper carbonate originally taken, and therefore we consider the reaction which occurred to have been one of decomposition, and that by it something was separated from the green copper carbonate, and, in fact, by closing the orifice of the vessel in which the copper

carbonate is heated with a well-fitting cork, through which a gas delivery tube[15] passes whose end is immersed under water, it will be observed that on heating, a gas is formed which bubbles through the water. This gas can be easily collected, as will presently be described, and it will be found to essentially[10] differ from air in many respects; for instance, a burning taper is extinguished in it as if it had been plunged into water. If weighing had not proved to us that some substance had been separated, the formation of the gas might easily have escaped our notice, for it is colourless and transparent like air, and is therefore evolved without any striking feature. The carbonic anhydride evolved may be weighed,[16] and it will be seen that the sum of the weights of the black copper oxide and carbonic anhydride is equal to the weight of the copper carbonate[17] originally taken, and thus by carefully following out the[11] various stages of all chemical reactions we arrive at a confirmation of the law of the indestructibility of matter.

3. Red mercury oxide (which is formed as mercury rust by heating mercury in air) is decomposed like copper carbonate (only by heating more slowly and at a somewhat higher temperature), with the formation of the peculiar gas, oxygen. For this purpose the mercury oxide is placed in a glass tube or retort,[18] to which a gas delivery tube is attached by means of a cork. This tube is bent downwards, as shown in the drawing (Fig. 1). The open end of the gas delivery tube is immersed in a vessel filled with water, called a pneumatic trough.[19] When[12] the gas begins to be evolved in the retort it is obliged, having no other outlet, to escape through the gas delivery tube into the water in the pneumatic trough, and therefore its evolution will be rendered visible by the bubbles coming from this tube. In heating the retort containing the mercury oxide, the air contained in the apparatus is first partly expelled, owing to its expansion by heat, and then the peculiar gas called 'oxygen' is evolved, and may be easily collected as it comes off. For this purpose a vessel (an ordinary cylinder, as in the drawing) is filled quite full with water and its mouth closed; it is then inverted and placed in this position under the water in the trough; the mouth is then opened. The cylinder will remain full of water—that is, the water will remain at a higher level in it than in the surrounding vessel, owing to the atmospheric pressure. The atmosphere presses on the surface of the water in the trough, and prevents the water from flowing out of the cylinder. The mouth of the cylinder is placed over the end of the gas delivery tube,[20] and the bubbles issuing from it will rise into the cylinder and displace the water contained in it. Gases are generally collected in this manner. When a sufficient quantity of gas has accumulated in the cylinder it can be clearly shown that it is not air, but another gas which is distinguished by its capacity for vigorously supporting combustion. In order to show this, the cylinder is closed, under water, and removed from the bath; its mouth is then turned upwards, and a smouldering taper

plunged into it. As is well known, a smouldering taper will be extinguished in air, but in the gas which is given off from red mercury oxide it burns clearly and vigorously, showing the property possessed by this gas for supporting combustion more energetically than air, and thus enabling it to be distinguished from the latter. It may be observed in this experiment that, besides the formation of oxygen, metallic mercury is formed, which, volatilising at the high temperature required for the reaction, condenses on the cooler parts of the retort as a mirror or in globules. Thus two substances,[13] mercury and oxygen, are obtained by heating red mercury oxide. In this reaction, from one substance, two new substances are produced—that is, a decomposition has taken place. The means of collecting and investigating gases were known before Lavoisier's time, but he first showed the real part they played in the processes of many chemical changes which before his era were either wrongly understood (as will be afterwards explained) or were not explained at all, but only observed in their superficial aspects. This experiment on red mercury oxide has a special significance in the history of chemistry contemporary with Lavoisier, because the oxygen gas which is here evolved is contained in the atmosphere, and plays a most important part in nature, especially in the respiration of animals, in combustion in air, and in the formation of rusts or scoriæ (earths, as they were then called) from metals—that is, of earthy substances, like the ores from which metals are extracted.

4. In order to illustrate by experiment one more example of chemical change and the application of the law of the indestructibility of matter, we will consider the reaction between common table salt and lunar caustic, which is well known from its use in cauterising wounds. By taking a clear solution of each and mixing them together, it will at once be observed that a solid white substance is formed, which settles to the bottom of the vessel, and is insoluble in water. This substance may be separated from the solution by filtering; it is then found to be an entirely different substance from either of those taken originally in the solutions. This is at once evident from the fact that it does not dissolve in water. On evaporating the liquid which passed through the filter, it will be found to contain a new substance unlike either table salt or lunar caustic, but, like them, soluble in water. Thus table salt and lunar caustic, two substances soluble in water, produced, by their mutual chemical action, two new substances, one insoluble in water, and the other remaining in solution. Here, from two substances, two others are obtained, consequently there occurred a reaction of substitution. The water served only to convert the re-acting substances into a liquid and mobile state. If the lunar caustic and salt be dried[21] and weighed, and if about 58½ grams[22] of[14] salt and 170 grams of lunar caustic be taken, then 143½ grams of insoluble silver chloride and 85 grams of sodium nitrate will be obtained. The sum of the weights of the re-acting

and resultant substances are seen to be similar and equal to 228½ grams, which necessarily follows from the law of the indestructibility of matter.

Accepting the truth of the above law, the question naturally arises as to whether there is any limit to the various chemical transformations, or are they unrestricted in number—that is to say, is it possible from a given substance to obtain an equivalent quantity of any other substance? In other words, does there exist a perpetual and infinite change of one kind of material into every other kind, or is the cycle of these transformations limited? This is the second essential problem of Chemistry, a question of quality of matter, and one, it is evident, which is more complicated than the question of quantity. It cannot be solved by a mere superficial glance at the subject. Indeed, on seeing how all the varied forms and colours of plants are built up from air and the elements of the soil, and how metallic iron can be transformed into colours such as inks and Prussian blue, we might be led to think that there is no end to the qualitative changes to which matter is susceptible. But, on the other hand, the experiences of everyday life compel us to acknowledge that food cannot be made out of a stone, or gold out of copper. Thus a definite answer can only be looked for in a close and diligent study of the subject, and the problem has been resolved in different way at different times. In ancient times the opinion most generally held was that everything visible was composed of four elements—Air, Water, Earth, and Fire. The origin of this doctrine can be traced far back into the confines of Asia, whence it was handed down to the Greeks, and most fully expounded by Empedocles, who lived before 460 B.C. This doctrine was not the result of exact research, but apparently owes its origin to the clear division of bodies into gases (like air), liquids (like water), and solids (like the earth). The Arabs appear to have been the first who attempted to solve the question by experimental methods, and they introduced, through Spain, the taste for the study of similar problems into Europe, where from that time there appear many adepts in chemistry, which was considered as an unholy art, and called 'alchemy.' As the alchemists were ignorant of any exact law which[15] could guide them in their researches, they obtained most anomalous results. Their chief service to chemistry was that they made a number of experiments, and discovered many new chemical transformations; but it is well known how they solved the fundamental problem of chemistry. Their view may be taken as a positive acknowledgment of the infinite transmutability of matter, for they aimed at discovering the Philosopher's Stone, capable of converting everything into gold and diamonds, and of making the old young again. This solution of the question was afterwards completely overthrown, but it must not, for this reason, be thought that the hopes held by the alchemists were only the fruit of their imaginations. The first chemical experiments might well lead them to their conclusions. They took, for instance, the bright metallic mineral galena, and extracted metallic lead from it. Thus they saw that from a metallic substance which is unfitted for use they could obtain another metallic substance which is ductile and valuable for many technical purposes. Furthermore, they took this lead and obtained silver, a still more valuable metal, from it. Thus they might easily conclude that it was possible to ennoble metals by means of a whole series of transmutations—that is to say, to obtain from them those which are more and more precious. Having got silver from lead, they assumed that it would be possible to obtain gold from silver. The mistake they made was that they never weighed or measured the substances used or produced in their experiments. Had they done so, they would have learnt that the weight of the lead was much less than that of the galena from which it was obtained, and the weight of the silver infinitesimal compared with that of the lead. Had they looked more closely into the process of the extraction of the silver from lead (and silver at the present time is chiefly obtained from the lead ores) they would have seen that the lead does not change into silver, but that it only contains a certain small quantity of it, and this amount having once been separated from the lead it cannot by any further operation give more. The silver which the alchemists extracted from the lead was in the lead, and was not obtained by a chemical change of the lead itself. This is now well known from experiment, but the first view of the nature of the process was very likely to be an erroneous one.[23] The methods of research adopted[16] by the alchemists could give but little success, for they did not set themselves clear and simple questions whose answers would aid them to make further progress. Thus though they did not arrive at any exact law, they left nevertheless numerous and useful experimental data as an inheritance to chemistry; they investigated, in particular, the transformations proper to metals, and for this reason chemistry was for long afterwards entirely confined to the study of metallic substances.

In their researches, the alchemists frequently made use of two chemical processes which are now termed 'reduction' and 'oxidation.' The rusting of metals, and in general their conversion from a metallic into an earthy form, is called 'oxidation,' whilst the extraction of a metal from an earthy substance is called 'reduction.' Many metals—for instance, iron, lead, and tin—are oxidised by heating in air alone, and may be again reduced by heating with carbon. Such oxidised metals are found in the earth, and form the majority of metallic ores. The metals, such as tin, iron, and copper, may be extracted from these ores by heating them together with carbon. All these processes were well studied by the alchemists. It was afterwards shown that all earths and minerals are formed of similar metallic rusts or oxides, or of their combinations. Thus the alchemists knew of two forms of chemical changes: the oxidation of metals and the reduction of the oxides so formed into metals. The explanation of the nature of these two classes of chemical phenomena was the means for the discovery of the most important chemical laws. The first hypothesis on their nature is due to Becker, and more particularly to Stahl, a surgeon to the King of Prussia. Stahl writes in his 'Fundamenta Chymiæ,' 1723, that all substances consist of an imponderable fiery substance called 'phlogiston' (materia aut principium ignis non ipse ignis), and of another element having particular properties for each substance. The greater the capacity of a body for oxidation, or the more combustible it is, the richer it is in phlogiston. Carbon contains it in great abundance. In oxidation or combustion phlogiston is emitted, and in reduction it is consumed or enters into combination. Carbon reduces earthy substances because it is rich in phlogiston, and gives up a[17] portion of its phlogiston to the substance reduced. Thus Stahl supposed metals to be compound substances consisting of phlogiston and an earthy substance or oxide. This hypothesis is distinguished for its very great simplicity, and for this and other reasons it acquired many supporters.[24]

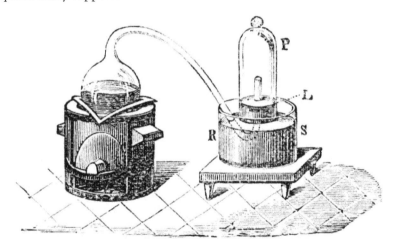

FIG. 3.—Lavoisier's apparatus for determining the composition of air and the reason of metals increasing in weight when they are calcined in air.

Lavoisier proved by means of the balance that every case of rusting of metals or oxidation, or of combustion, is accompanied by an increase in weight at the expense of the atmosphere. He formed, therefore, the natural opinion that the heavier substance is more complex than the lighter one.[25] Lavoisier's celebrated experiment, made in 1774,[18] gave indubitable support to his opinion, which in many respects was contradictory to Stahl's doctrine. Lavoisier poured four ounces of pure mercury into a glass retort (fig. 3), whose neck was bent as shown in the drawing and dipped into the vessel R S, also full of mercury. The projecting end of the neck was covered with a glass bell-jar P. The weight of all the mercury taken, and the volume of air remaining in the apparatus, namely, that in the upper portion of the retort, and under the bell-jar, were determined before beginning the experiment. It was most important in this experiment to know the volume of air in order to learn what part it played in the oxidation of the mercury, because, according to Stahl, phlogiston is emitted into the air, whilst, according to Lavoisier, the mercury in oxidising absorbs a portion of the air; and consequently it was absolutely necessary to determine whether the amount of air increased or decreased in the oxidation of the metal. It was, therefore, most important to measure the volume of the air in the apparatus both before and after the experiment. For this purpose it was necessary to know the total capacity of the retort, the volume of the mercury poured into it, the volume of the bell-jar above the level of the mercury, and also the temperature and pressure of the air at the time of its measurement. The volume of air contained in the apparatus and isolated from the surrounding atmosphere could be determined from these data. Having arranged his apparatus in this manner, Lavoisier heated the retort holding the mercury for a period of twelve days at a temperature near the boiling point of mercury. The mercury became covered with a quantity of small red[19] scales; that is, it was oxidised or converted into an earth. This substance is the same mercury oxide which has already been mentioned (example 3). After the lapse of twelve days the apparatus was cooled, and it was then seen that the volume of the air in the apparatus had diminished during the time of the experiment. This result was in exact contradiction to Stahl's hypothesis. Out of 50 cubic inches of air originally taken, there only remained 42. Lavoisier's experiment led to other equally important results. The weight of the air taken decreased by as much as the weight of the mercury increased in oxidising; that is, the portion of the air was not destroyed, but only combined with mercury. This portion of the air may be again separated from the mercury oxide and has, as we saw (example 3), properties different from those of air. It is called 'oxygen.' That portion of the air which remained in the apparatus and did not combine with the mercury does not oxidise metals, and cannot support either combustion or respiration, so that a lighted taper is immediately extinguished if it be dipped into the gas which remains in the bell-jar. 'It is extinguished in the residual gas as if it had been plunged into water,' writes Lavoisier in his memoirs. This gas is called 'nitrogen.' Thus air is not a simple substance, but consists of two gases, oxygen and nitrogen, and therefore the opinion that air is an elementary substance is erroneous. The oxygen of the air is absorbed in combustion and the oxidation of metals, and the earths produced by the oxidation of metals are substances composed of oxygen and a metal. By mixing the oxygen with the nitrogen the same air as was originally taken is re-formed. It has also been shown by direct experiment that on reducing an oxide with carbon, the oxygen contained in the oxide is transferred to the carbon, and gives the same gas that is obtained by the combustion of carbon in air. Therefore this gas is a compound of carbon and oxygen, just as the earthy oxides are composed of metals and oxygen.

The many examples of the formation and decomposition of substances which are met with convince us that the majority of substances with which we have to deal are compounds made up of several other substances. By heating chalk (or else copper carbonate, as in the second example) we obtain lime and the same carbonic acid gas which is produced by the combustion of carbon. On bringing lime into contact with this gas and water, at the ordinary temperature, we again obtain the compound, carbonate of lime, or chalk. Therefore chalk is a compound. So also are those substances from which it may be built up. Carbonic anhydride is formed by the combination of carbon and oxygen; and lime is produced by the oxidation of a certain metal[20] called 'calcium.' By resolving substances in this manner into their component parts, we arrive at last at such as are indivisible into two or more substances by any means whatever, and which cannot be formed from other substances. All we can do is to make such substances combine together to act on other substances. Substances which cannot be formed from or decomposed into others are termed *simple substances* (elements). Thus all homogeneous substances may be classified into simple and compound substances. This view was introduced and established as a scientific fact during the lifetime of Lavoisier. The number of these elements is very small in comparison with the number of compound substances which are formed by them. At the present time, only seventy elements are known with certainty to exist. Some of them are very rarely met with in nature, or are found in very small quantities, whilst the existence of others is still doubtful. The number of elements with whose compounds we commonly deal in everyday life is very small. Elements cannot be transmuted into one another—at least up to the present not a single case of such a transformation has been met with; it may therefore be said that, as yet, it is impossible to transmute one metal into another. And as yet, notwithstanding the number of attempts which have been made in this direction, no fact has been discovered which could in any way support the idea of the complexity of such well-known elements[26] as oxygen, iron, sulphur, &c. Therefore, from its very conception, an element is not susceptible to reactions of decomposition.[27]

[21]

The quantity, therefore, of each element remains constant in all chemical changes: a fact which may be deduced as a consequence of the law of the indestructibility of matter, and of the conception of elements themselves. Thus the equation expressing the law of the indestructibility of matter acquires a new and still more important signification. If we know the quantities of the elements which occur in the re-acting substances, and if from these substances there proceed, by means of chemical changes, a series of new compound substances, then the latter will together contain the same quantity of each of the elements as there originally existed in the re-acting substances. The essence of chemical change is embraced in the study of how, and with what substances, each element is combined before and after change.

In order to be able to express various chemical changes by equations, it has been agreed to represent each element by the first or some two letters of its (Latin) name. Thus, for example, oxygen is represented by the letter O; nitrogen by N; mercury (hydrargyrum) by Hg; iron (ferrum) by Fe; and so on for all the elements, as is seen in the tables on page 24. A compound substance is represented by placing the symbols representing the elements of which it is made up side by side. For example, red mercury oxide is represented by HgO, which shows that it is composed of oxygen and mercury. Besides this, the symbol of every element corresponds with a certain relative quantity of it by weight, called its 'combining' weight, or the weight of an atom; so that the chemical formula of a compound substance not only designates the nature of the elements of which it is composed, but also their quantitative proportion. Every chemical process may be expressed by an equation composed of the formulæ corresponding with those substances which take part in it and are produced by it. The amount by weight of the elements in every chemical equation must be equal on both sides of the equation, since no element is either formed or destroyed in a chemical change.

On pages 24, 25, and 26 a list of the elements, with their symbols and combining or atomic weights, is given, and we shall see afterwards on what basis the atomic weights of elements are determined. At present we will only point out that a compound containing the elements A and B is designated by the formula An Bm, where m and n are the coefficients or multiples in which the combining weights of the elements enter into the composition of the substance. If we represent[22] the combining weight of the substance A by a and that of the substance B by b, then the composition of the substance An Bm will be expressed thus: it contains na parts by weight of the substance A and mb parts by weight of the substance B, and consequently 100 parts of our compound contain $na\ 100 \dfrac{}{na + mb}$ percentage parts by weight of the substance A and $mb\ 100 \dfrac{}{na + mb}$ of the substance B. It is evident that as a formula shows the relative amounts of all the elements contained in a compound, the actual weights of the elements contained in a given weight of a compound may be calculated from its formula. For example, the formula NaCl of table salt shows (as Na = 23 and Cl = 35·5) that 58·5 lbs. of salt contain 23 lbs. of sodium and 35·5 lbs. of chlorine, and that 100 parts of it contain 39·3 per cent. of sodium and 60·7 per cent. of chlorine.

What has been said above clearly limits the province of chemical changes, because from substances of a given kind there can be obtained only such as contain the same elements. Even with this limitation, however, the number of possible combinations is infinitely great. Only a comparatively small number of compounds have yet been described or subjected to research, and any one working in this direction may easily discover new compounds which had not before been obtained. It often happens, however, that such newly-discovered compounds were foreseen by chemistry, whose object is the apprehension of that uniformity which rules over the multitude of compound substances, and whose aim is the comprehension of those laws which govern their formation and properties. The conception of elements having been established, the next objects of chemistry were: the determination of the properties of compound substances on the basis of the determination of the quantity and kind of elements of which they are composed; the investigation of the elements themselves; the determination of what compound substances can be formed from each element and the properties which these compounds show; and the apprehension of the nature of the connection between the elements in different compounds. An element thus serves as the starting point, and is taken as the primary conception on which all other substances are built up.

When we state that a certain element enters into the composition of a given compound (when we say, for instance, that mercury oxide contains oxygen) we do not mean that it contains oxygen as a gaseous substance, but only desire to express those transformations which mercury oxide is capable of making; that is, we wish to say that it is possible to obtain oxygen from mercury oxide, and that it can give[23] up oxygen to various other substances; in a word, we desire only to express those transformations of which mercury oxide is capable. Or, more concisely, it may be said that the *composition* of a compound is the expression of those transformations of which it is capable. It is useful in this sense to make a clear distinction between the conception of an element as a *separate* homogeneous substance, and as a *material* but invisible *part* of a compound. Mercury oxide does not contain two simple bodies, a gas and a metal, but two elements, mercury and oxygen, which, when free, are a gas and a metal. Neither mercury as a metal nor oxygen as a gas is contained in mercury oxide; it only contains the substance of these elements, just as steam only contains the substance of ice, but not ice itself, or as corn contains the substance of the seed, but not the seed itself. The existence of an element may be recognised without knowing it in the uncombined state, but only from an investigation of its combinations, and from the knowledge that it gives, under all possible conditions, substances which are unlike other known combinations of substances. Fluorine is an example of this kind. It was for a long time unknown in a free state, and nevertheless was recognised as an element because its combinations with other elements were known, and their difference from all other similar compound substances was determined. In order to grasp the difference between the conception of the visible form of an element as we know it in the free state, and of the intrinsic element (or 'radicle,' as Lavoisier called it) contained in the visible form, it should be remarked that compound substances also combine together forming yet more complex compounds, and that they evolve heat in the process of combination. The original compound may often be extracted from these new compounds by exactly the same methods as elements are extracted from their corresponding combinations. Besides, many elements exist under various visible forms whilst the intrinsic element contained in these various forms is something which is not subject to change. Thus carbon appears as charcoal, graphite, and diamond, but yet the element carbon alone, contained in each, is one and the same. Carbonic anhydride contains carbon, and not charcoal, or graphite, or the diamond.

Elements alone, although not all of them, have the peculiar lustre, opacity, malleability, and the great heat and electrical conductivity which are proper to metals and their mutual combinations. But elements are far from all being *metals*. Those which do not possess the physical properties of metals are called *non-metals* (or *metalloids*). It is, however, impossible to draw a strict line of demarcation between metals and non-metals, there being many intermediary substances.[24] Thus graphite, from which pencils are manufactured, is an element with the lustre and other properties of a metal; but charcoal and the diamond, which are composed of the same substance as graphite, do not show any metallic properties. Both classes of elements are clearly distinguished in definite examples, but in particular cases the distinction is not clear and cannot serve as a basis for the exact division of the elements into two groups.

The conception of elements forms the basis of chemical knowledge, and in giving a list of them at the very beginning of our work, we wish to tabulate our present knowledge on the subject. Altogether about seventy elements are now authentically known, but many of them are so rarely met with in nature, and have been obtained in such small quantities, that we possess but a very insufficient knowledge of them. The substances most widely distributed in nature contain a very small number of elements. These elements have been more completely studied than the others, because a greater number of investigators have been able to carry on experiments and observations on them. The elements most widely distributed in nature are:—

Hydrogen,	$H = 1.$	In water, and in animal and vegetable organisms.
Carbon,	$C = 12.$	In organisms, coal, limestones.
Nitrogen,	$N = 14.$	In air and in organisms.
Oxygen,	$O = 16.$	In air, water, earth. It forms the greater part of the mass of the earth.
Sodium,	$Na = 23.$	In common salt and in many minerals.
Magnesium,	$Mg = 24.$	In sea-water and in many minerals.
Aluminium,	$Al = 27.$	In minerals and clay.
Silicon,	$Si = 28.$	In sand, minerals, and clay.
Phosphorus,	$P = 31.$	In bones, ashes of plants, and soil.
Sulphur,	$S = 32.$	In pyrites, gypsum, and in sea-water.
Chlorine,	$Cl = 35 \cdot 5.$	In common salt, and in the salts of sea-water.
Potassium,	$K = 39.$	In minerals, ashes of plants, and in nitre.
Calcium,	$Ca = 40.$	In limestones, gypsum, and in organisms.
Iron,	$K = 56.$	In the earth, iron ores, and in organisms.

Besides these, the following elements, although not very largely distributed in nature, are all more or less well known from their applications to the requirements of everyday life or the arts, either in a free state or in their compounds:—

Lithium,	$Li = 7.$	In medicine (Li_2CO_3), and in photography (LiBr).
Boron,	$B = 11.$	As borax, $B_4Na_2O_7$, and as boric anhydride, B_2O_3.[25]
Fluorine,	$F = 19.$	As fluor spar, CaF_2, and as hydrofluoric acid, HF.
Chromium,	$Cr = 52.$	As chromic anhydride, CrO_3, and potassium dichromate, $K_2Cr_2O_7$.
Manganese,	$Mn = 55.$	As manganese peroxide, MnO_2, and potassium permanganate, $MnKO_4$.

Cobalt,   Co = 59·5.   In smalt and blue glass.

Nickel,   Ni = 59·5.   For electro-plating other metals.

Copper,   Cu = 63.   The well-known red metal.

Zinc,   Zn = 65.   Used for the plates of batteries, roofing, &c.

Arsenic,   As = 75.   White arsenic (poison), As_2O_3.

Bromine,   Cu = 80.   A brown volatile liquid; sodium bromide, NaBr.

Strontium,   Sr = 87.   In coloured fires (SrN_2O_6).

Silver,   Ag = 109.   The well-known white metal.

Cadmium,   Cd = 112.   In alloys. Yellow paint (CdS).

Tin,   Sn = 119.   The well-known metal.

Antimony,   Sb = 120.   In alloys such as type metal.

Iodine,   I = 127.   In medicine and photography; free, and as KI.

Barium,   Ba = 137.   "Permanent white," and as an adulterant in white lead, and in heavy spar, $BaSO_4$.

Platinum,   Pt = 196.

Gold,   Au = 197.
                          Well-known metals.
Mercury,   Hg = 200.

Lead,   Pb = 207.

Bismuth,   Bi = 209.   In medicine and fusible alloys.

Uranium,   U = 239.   In green fluorescent glass.

The compounds of the following metals and semi-metals have fewer applications, but are well known, and are somewhat frequently met with in nature, although in small quantities:—

Beryllium,	Be = 9.	Palladium,	Pd = 107.
Titanium,	Ti = 48.	Cerium,	Ce = 140.
Vanadium,	V = 51.	Tungsten,	W = 184.
Selenium,	Se = 79.	Osmium,	Os = 192.
Zirconium,	Zr = 91.	Iridium,	Ir = 193.

Molybdenum, Mo = 96.   Thallium,   Tl = 204.

The following rare metals are still more seldom met with in nature, but have been studied somewhat fully:—

Scandium,   Sc = 44.   Germanium, Ge = 72.

Gallium,   Ga = 70.   Rubidium,   Rb = 86.

Yttrium,   Y = 89.   Cæsium,   Cs = 133.[26]

Niobium,   Nb = 94.   Lanthanum, La = 138.

Ruthenium, Ru = 102.   Didymium,   Di = 142.

Rhodium,   Rh = 103.   Ytterbium,   Yb = 173.

Indium,   In = 114.   Tantalum,   Ta = 183.

Tellurium,   Te = 125.   Thorium,   Th = 232.

Besides these 66 elements there have been discovered:—Erbium, Terbium, Samarium, Thullium, Holmium, Mosandrium, Phillipium, and several others. But their properties and combinations, owing to their extreme rarity, are very little known, and even their existence as independent substances[28] is doubtful.

It has been incontestably proved from observations on the spectra of the heavenly bodies that many of the commoner elements (such as H, Na, Mg, Fe) occur on the far distant stars. This fact confirms the belief that those forms of matter which appear on the earth as elements are widely distributed over the entire universe. But we do not yet know why, in nature, the mass of some elements should be greater than that of others.[28 bis]

The capacity of each element to combine with one or another element, and to form compounds with them which are in a greater or less degree prone to give new and yet more complex substances, forms the fundamental character of each element. Thus sulphur easily combines with the metals, oxygen, chlorine, or carbon, whilst gold and silver enter into combinations with difficulty, and form unstable compounds, which are easily decomposed by heat. The cause or force which induces the elements to enter into chemical change must be considered, as also the cause which holds different substances in combination—that is, which endues the substances formed with their particular degree of stability. This cause or force is called *affinity* (*affinitas, affinité, Verwandtschaft*), or chemical affinity.[29] Since this force must[27] be regarded as exclusively an attractive force, like gravity, many writers (for instance, Bergmann at the end of the last, and Berthollet at the beginning of this, century) supposed affinity to be essentially similar to the universal force of gravity, from which it only differs in that the latter acts at observable distances whilst affinity only evinces itself at the smallest possible distances. But chemical affinity cannot be entirely identified with the universal attraction of gravity, which acts at appreciable distances and is dependent only on mass and distance, and not on the quality of the material on which it acts, whilst it is by the quality of matter that affinity is most forcibly influenced. Neither can it be entirely identified with cohesion, which gives to homogeneous solid substances their crystalline form, elasticity, hardness, ductility, and other properties, and to liquids their surface tension, drop formation, capillarity, and other properties, because affinity acts between the component parts of a substance and cohesion on a substance in its homogeneity, although both act at imperceptible distances (by contact) and have much in common. Chemical force, which makes one substance penetrate into another, cannot be entirely identified with even those attracting forces which make different substances adhere to each other, or hold together (as when two plane-polished surfaces of solid substances are brought into close contact), or which cause liquids to soak into solids, or adhere to their surfaces, or gases and vapours to condense on the surfaces of solids. These forces must not be confounded with chemical forces, which cause one substance to penetrate into the substance of another and to form a new substance, which is never the case with cohesion. But it is evident that the forces which determine cohesion form a connecting-link between mechanical and chemical forces, because they only act by intimate contact. For a long time, and especially during the first half of this century, chemical attraction and chemical forces were identified with electrical forces. There is certainly an intimate relation between them, for electricity is evolved in chemical reactions, and has also a powerful influence on chemical processes—for instance, compounds are decomposed by the action of an electrical current. And the exactly similar relation which exists between chemical phenomena and the phenomena of heat (heat being developed by chemical phenomena, and heat being able to decompose compounds) only proves the unity of the forces of nature, the capability of one force to produce and to be transformed into others. For this reason the identification of chemical force with electricity will[28] not bear experimental proof.[30] As of all the (molecular) phenomena of nature which act on substances at immeasurably small distances, the phenomena of heat are at present the best (comparatively) known, having been reduced to the simplest fundamental principles of mechanics (of energy, equilibrium, and movement), which, since Newton, have been subjected to strict mathematical analysis, it is quite natural that an effort, which has been particularly pronounced during recent years, should have been made to bring chemical phenomena into strict correlation with the already investigated phenomena of heat, without, however, aiming at any identification of chemical with heat phenomena. The true nature of chemical force is still a secret to us, just as is the nature of the universal force of gravity, and yet without knowing what gravity really is, by applying mechanical conceptions, astronomical phenomena have been subjected not only to exact generalisation but to the detailed prediction of a number of particular facts; and so, also, although the true nature of chemical affinity may be unknown, there is reason to hope for considerable progress in chemical science by applying the laws of mechanics to chemical phenomena by means of the mechanical theory of heat. As yet this portion of chemistry has been but little worked at, and therefore, while forming a current problem of the science, it is treated more fully in that particular field which is termed either 'theoretical' or 'physical' chemistry, or, more correctly, *chemical mechanics*. As this province of chemistry requires a knowledge not only of the various homogeneous[29] substances which have yet been obtained and of the chemical transformations which they undergo, but also of the phenomena (of heat and other kinds) by which these transformations are accompanied, it is only possible to enter on the study of chemical mechanics after an acquaintance with the fundamental chemical conceptions and substances which form the subject of this book.[31]

As the chemical changes to which substances are liable proceed from internal forces proper to these substances, as chemical phenomena certainly consist of motions of material parts (from the laws of the indestructibility of matter and of elements), and as the investigation of mechanical and physical phenomena proves the law of the *indestructibility of forces*, or the conservation of energy—that is, the possibility of the transformation of one kind of motion into another (of visible or mechanical into invisible or physical)—we are inevitably obliged to acknowledge the presence in substances (and especially in the elements of which all others are composed) of a store of *chemical energy* or invisible motion inducing them to enter into combinations. If heat be evolved in a reaction, it means that a portion of chemical energy is[30] transformed into heat;[32] if heat be absorbed in a reaction,[33] that it is partly transformed (rendered latent) into chemical energy. The store of force or energy going to the formation of new compounds may, after several combinations, accomplished with an absorption of heat, at last diminish to such a degree that indifferent compounds will be obtained, although these sometimes, by combining with energetic elements or compounds, give more complex compounds, which may be capable of entering into chemical combination. Among elements, gold, platinum, and nitrogen have but little energy, whilst potassium, oxygen, and chlorine have a very marked degree of energy. When dissimilar substances enter into combination they often form substances of diminished energy. Thus sulphur and potassium when heated easily burn in air, but when combined together their compound is neither inflammable nor burns in air like its component parts. Part of the energy of the potassium and of the sulphur was evolved in their combination in the form of heat. Just as in the passage of substances from one physical state into another a portion of their store of heat is absorbed or evolved, so in combinations or decompositions and in every chemical[31] process, there occurs a change in the store of chemical energy, and at the same time an evolution or absorption of heat.[34]

For the comprehension of chemical phenomena as mechanical processes—*i.e.*, the study of the *modus operandi* of chemical phenomena—it is most important to consider: (1) the facts gathered from stoïchiometry, or that part of chemistry which treats of the quantitative relation, by weight or volume, of the reacting substances; (2) the distinction between the different forms and classes of chemical reactions; (3) the study of the changes in properties produced by alteration in composition; (4) the study of the phenomena which accompany chemical transformation; (5) a generalisation of the conditions under which reactions occur. As regards stoïchiometry, this branch of chemistry has been worked out most thoroughly, and comprises laws (of Dalton, Avogadro-Gerhardt, and others) which bear so deeply on all parts of chemistry that at the present time the chief problem of chemical research consists in the application of general stoïchiometrical laws to concrete examples, *i.e.*, the quantitative (volumetric or gravimetric) composition of substances. All other branches of chemistry are clearly subordinate to this most important portion of chemical knowledge. Even the very signification of reactions of combination, decomposition, and rearrangement, acquired, as we shall see, a particular and new character under the influence of the progress of exact ideas concerning the quantitative relations of substances entering into chemical changes. Furthermore, in this sense there arose a new—and, till then, unknown— division of compound substances into *definite* and *indefinite* compounds. Even at the beginning of this century, Berthollet had not made this distinction. But Prout showed that a number of compounds contain the substances of which they are composed and into which they break up, in exact definite proportions by weight, which are unalterable under any conditions. Thus, for example, red mercury oxide always contains sixteen parts by weight of oxygen for every 200 parts by weight of mercury, which is expressed by the formula HgO. But in an alloy of copper and silver one or the other metal may be added at will, and in an aqueous solution of sugar, the relative proportion of the sugar and water may be altered and nevertheless a homogeneous whole with the sum of the independent[32] properties will be obtained—*i.e.*, in these cases there was indefinite chemical combination. Although in nature and chemical practice the formation of indefinite compounds (such as alloys and solutions) plays as essential a part as the formation of definite chemical compounds, yet, as the stoïchiometrical laws at present apply chiefly to the latter, all facts concerning indefinite compounds suffer from inexactitude, and it is only during recent years that the attention of chemists has been directed to this province of chemistry.

In chemical mechanics it is, from a qualitative point of view, very important to clearly distinguish at the very beginning between *reversible* and *non-reversible reactions*. Substances capable of reacting on each other at a certain temperature produce substances which at the same temperature either can or cannot give back the original substances. For example, salt dissolves in water at the ordinary temperature, and the solution so obtained is capable of breaking up at the same temperature, leaving salt and separating the water by evaporation. Carbon bisulphide is formed from sulphur and carbon at about the same temperature at which it can be resolved into sulphur and carbon. Iron, at a certain temperature, separates hydrogen from water, forming iron oxide, which, in contact with hydrogen at the same temperature, is able to produce iron and water. It is evident that if two substances, A and B, give two others C and D, and the reaction be reversible, then C and D will form A and B, and, consequently, by taking a definite mass of A and B, or a corresponding mass of C and D, we shall obtain, in each case, all four substances—that is to say, there will be a state of *chemical equilibrium* between the reacting substances. By increasing the mass of one of the substances we obtain a new condition of equilibrium, so that reversible reactions present a means of studying the *influence of mass* on the *modus operandi* of chemical changes. Many of those reactions which occur with very complicated compounds or mixtures may serve as examples of non-reversible reactions. Thus many of the compound substances of animal and vegetable organisms are broken up by heat, but cannot be re-formed from their products of decomposition at any temperature. Gunpowder, as a mixture of sulphur, nitre, and carbon, on being exploded, forms gases from which the original substances cannot be re-formed at any temperature. In order to obtain them, recourse must be had to an indirect method *of combination at the moment of separation*. If A does not under any circumstances combine directly with B, it does not follow that it cannot give a compound A B. For A can often combine with C and B with D, and if C has a great affinity for D, then the reaction of A C or B D produces not only C D, but also A B. As on the formation of C D,[33] the substances A and B (previously in A C and B D) are left in a peculiar state of separation, it is supposed that their mutual combination occurs because they meet together in this *nascent state* at the moment of separation (*in statu nascendi*). Thus chlorine does not directly combine with charcoal, graphite, or diamond; there are, nevertheless, compounds of chlorine with carbon, and many of them are distinguished by their stability. They are obtained in the action of chlorine on hydrocarbons, as the separation products from the direct action of chlorine on hydrogen. Chlorine takes up the hydrogen, and the carbon liberated at the moment of its separation, enters into combination with another portion of the chlorine, so that in the end the chlorine is combined with both the hydrogen and the carbon.[35]

As regards those phenomena which accompany chemical action, the most important circumstance in reference to chemical mechanics is that not only do chemical processes produce a mechanical displacement (a motion of particles), heat, light, electrical potential and current; but that all these agents are themselves capable of changing and governing chemical transformations. This reciprocity or reversibility naturally depends on the fact that all the phenomena of nature are only different kinds and forms of visible and invisible (molecular) motions. First sound, and then light, was shown to consist of vibratory motions, as the laws of physics have proved and developed beyond a doubt. The connection between heat and mechanical motion and work has ceased to be a supposition, but has become an accepted fact, and the mechanical equivalent of heat (425 kilogrammetres of mechanical work correspond with one kilogram unit of heat or Calorie) gives a mechanical measure for thermal phenomena. Although the mechanical theory of electrical phenomena cannot be considered so fully developed as the theory of heat, both statical and dynamical electricity are[34] produced by mechanical means (in common electrical machines or in Gramme or other dynamos), and conversely, a current (in electric motors) can produce mechanical motion. Thus by connecting a current with the poles of a Gramme dynamo it may be made to revolve, and, conversely, by rotating it an electrical current is produced, which demonstrates the reversibility of electricity into mechanical motion. Accordingly chemical mechanics must look for the fundamental lines of its advancement in the correlation of chemical with physical and mechanical phenomena. But this subject, owing to its complexity and comparative novelty, has not yet been expressed by a harmonious theory, or even by a satisfactory hypothesis, and therefore we shall avoid lingering over it.

A chemical change in a certain direction is accomplished not only by reason of the difference of masses, the composition of the substances concerned, the distribution of their parts, and their affinity or chemical energy, but also by reason of the *conditions* under which the substances occur. In order that a certain chemical reaction may take place between substances which are capable of reacting on each other, it is often necessary to have recourse to conditions which are sometimes very different from those in which the substances usually occur in nature. For example, not only is the presence of air (oxygen) necessary for the combustion of charcoal, but the latter must also be heated to redness. The red-hot portion

of the charcoal burns—*i.e.* combines with the oxygen of the atmosphere—
and in so doing evolves heat, which raises the temperature of the adjacent
parts of charcoal, so that they burn. Just as the combustion of charcoal is
dependent on its being heated to redness, so also every chemical reaction
only takes place under certain physical, mechanical, or other conditions.
The following are the chief conditions which exert an influence on the
progress of chemical reactions.

(*a*) *Temperature.*—Chemical reactions of combination only take place
within certain definite limits of temperature, and cannot be accomplished
outside these limits. We may cite as examples not only that the combustion
of charcoal begins at a red heat, but also that chlorine and salt only
combine with water at a temperature below 0°. These compounds cannot
be formed at a higher temperature, for they are then wholly or partially
broken up into their component parts. A certain rise in temperature is
necessary to start combustion. In certain cases the effect of this rise may be
explained as causing one of the reacting bodies to change from a solid into
a liquid or gaseous form. The transference into a fluid form facilitates the
progress of the reaction, because it aids the intimate contact of the
particles[35] reacting on each other. Another reason, and to this must be
ascribed the chief influence of heat in exciting chemical action, is that the
physical cohesion, or the internal chemical union, of homogeneous particles
is thereby weakened, and in this way the separation of the particles of the
original substances, and their transference into new compounds, is
rendered easier. When a reaction absorbs heat—as in decomposition—the
reason why heat is necessary is self-evident.

At the present day it may be asserted upon the basis of existing data,
respecting the action of high temperature, that all compound bodies are
decomposed at a more or less high temperature. We have already seen
examples of this in describing the decomposition of mercury oxide into
mercury and oxygen, and the decomposition of wood under the influence
of heat. Many substances are decomposed at a very moderate temperature;
for instance, the fulminating salt which is employed in cartridges is
decomposed at a little above 120°. The majority of those compounds which
make up the mass of animal and vegetable tissues are decomposed at 200°.
On the other hand, there is reason to think that at a very low temperature
no reaction whatever can take place. Thus plants cease to carry on their
chemical processes during the winter. Raoul Pictet (1892), employing the
very low temperatures (as low as -200°C.) obtained by the evaporation of
liquefied gases (*see* Chap. II.), has recently again proved that at temperatures
below -120°, even such reactions as those between sulphuric acid and
caustic soda or metallic sodium do not take place, and even the coloration
of litmus by acids only commences at temperatures above -80°. If a given

reaction does not take place at a certain low temperature, it will at first only proceed slowly with a rise of temperature (even if aided by an electric discharge), and will only proceed rapidly, with the evolution of heat, when a certain definite temperature has been reached. Every chemical reaction requires certain limits of temperature for its accomplishment, and, doubtless, many of the chemical changes observed by us cannot take place in the sun, where the temperature is very high, or on the moon, where it is very low.

The influence of heat on reversible reactions is particularly instructive. If, for instance, a compound which is capable of being reproduced from its products of decomposition be heated up to the temperature at which decomposition begins, the decomposition of a mass of the substance contained in a definite volume is not immediately completed. Only a certain fraction of the substance is decomposed, the other portion remaining unchanged, and if the temperature be raised, the quantity of the substance decomposed increases; furthermore, for a given volume, the ratio between the part decomposed and the part unaltered[36] corresponds with each definite rise in temperature until it reaches that at which the compound is entirely decomposed. This partial decomposition under the influence of heat is called *dissociation*. It is possible to distinguish between the temperatures at which dissociation begins and ends. Should dissociation proceed at a certain temperature, yet should the product or products of decomposition not remain in contact with the still undecomposed portion of the compound, then decomposition will go on to the end. Thus limestone is decomposed in a limekiln into lime and carbonic anhydride, because the latter is carried off by the draught of the furnace. But if a certain mass of limestone be enclosed in a definite volume—for instance, in a gun barrel—which is then sealed up, and heated to redness, then, as the carbonic anhydride cannot escape, a certain proportion only of the limestone will be decomposed for every increment of heat (rise in temperature) higher than that at which dissociation begins. Decomposition will cease when the carbonic anhydride evolved presents a maximum *dissociation pressure* corresponding with each rise in temperature. If the pressure be increased by increasing the quantity of gas, then combination begins afresh; if the pressure be diminished decomposition will recommence. Decomposition in this case is exactly similar to evaporation; if the steam given off by evaporation cannot escape, its pressure will reach a maximum corresponding with the given temperature, and then evaporation will cease. Should steam be added it will be condensed in the liquid; if its quantity be diminished—*i.e.* if the pressure be lessened, the temperature being constant—then evaporation will go on. We shall afterwards discuss more fully these phenomena of dissociation, which were first discovered by Henri St. Claire Deville. We will only remark that the products of decomposition re-combine with greater facility the nearer their temperature is to that at which dissociation begins, or, in other words, that the initial temperature of dissociation is near to the initial temperature of combination.

(*b*) *The influence of an electric current*, and of electricity in general, on the progress of chemical transformations is very similar to the influence of heat. The majority of compounds which conduct electricity are decomposed by the action of a galvanic current, and as there is great similarity in the conditions under which decomposition and combination proceed, combination often proceeds under the influence of electricity. Electricity, like heat, must be regarded as a peculiar form of molecular motion, and all that refers to the influence of heat also refers to the phenomena produced by the action of an electrical current, with this difference, only that a substance can be separated into its component parts with much greater ease by electricity,[37] since the process goes on at the ordinary temperature. The most stable compounds may be decomposed by this means, and a most important fact is then observed—namely, that the component parts appear at the different poles of electrodes by which the current passes through the substance. Those substances which appear at the positive pole (anode) are called 'electro-negative,' and those which appear at the negative pole (cathode, that in connection with the zinc of an ordinary galvanic battery) are called 'electro-positive.' The majority of non-metallic elements, such as chlorine, oxygen, &c., and also acids and substances analogous to them, belong to the first group, whilst the metals, hydrogen, and analogous products of decomposition appear at the negative pole. Chemistry is indebted to the decomposition of compounds by the electric current for many most important discoveries. Many elements have been discovered by this method, the most important being potassium and sodium. Lavoisier and the chemists of his time were not able to decompose the oxygen compounds of these metals, but Davy showed that they might be decomposed by an electric current, the metals sodium and potassium appearing at the negative pole. Now that the dynamo gives the possibility of producing an electric current by the combustion of fuel, this method of Sir H. Davy is advantageously employed for obtaining metals, &c. on a large scale, for instance, sodium from fused caustic soda or chlorine from solutions of salt.

(*c*) Certain unstable compounds are also decomposed by *the action of light*. Photography is based on this property in certain substances (for instance, in the salts of silver). The mechanical energy of those vibrations which determine the phenomena of light is very small, and therefore only certain, and these generally unstable, compounds can be decomposed by light—at least under ordinary circumstances. But there is one class of chemical phenomena dependent on the action of light which forms as yet an unsolved problem in chemistry—these are the processes accomplished in plants under the influence of light. Here there take place most unexpected decompositions and combinations, which are often unattainable by artificial means. For instance, carbonic anhydride, which is so stable under the influence of heat and electricity, is decomposed and evolves oxygen in plants under the influence of light. In other cases, light decomposes unstable compounds, such as are usually easily decomposed by heat and other agents. Chlorine combines with hydrogen under the influence of light, which shows that combination, as well as decomposition, can be determined by its action, as was likewise the case with heat and electricity.

[38]

(d) *Mechanical causes* exert, like the foregoing agents, an action both on the process of chemical combination and of decomposition. Many substances are decomposed by friction or by a blow—as, for example, the compound called iodide of nitrogen (which is composed of iodine, nitrogen, and hydrogen), and silver fulminate. Mechanical friction causes sulphur to burn at the expense of the oxygen contained in potassium chlorate. Pressure affects both the physical and chemical state of the reacting substances, and, together with the temperature, determines the state of a substance. This is particularly evident when the substance occurs in an elastic-gaseous form since the volume, and hence also the number of points of encounter between the reacting substances is greatly altered by a change of pressure. Thus, under equal conditions of temperature, hydrogen when compressed acts more powerfully upon iodine and on the solutions of many salts.

(e) Besides the various conditions which have been enumerated above, the progress of chemical reactions is accelerated or retarded by the *condition of contact* in which the reacting bodies occur. Other conditions remaining constant, the rate of progress of a chemical reaction is accelerated by increasing the number of points of contact. It will be enough to point out the fact that sulphuric acid does not absorb ethylene under ordinary conditions of contact, but only after continued shaking, by which means the number of points of contact is greatly increased. To ensure complete action between solids, it is necessary to reduce them to very fine powder and to mix them as thoroughly as possible. M. Spring, the Belgian chemist, has shown that finely powdered solids which do not react on each other at the ordinary temperature may do so under an increased pressure. Thus, under a pressure of 6,000 atmospheres, sulphur combines with many metals at the ordinary temperature, and mixtures of the powders of many metals form alloys. It is evident that an increase in the number of points or surfaces must be regarded as the chief cause producing reaction, which is doubtless accomplished in solids, as in liquids and gases, in virtue of an internal motion of the particles, which motion, although in different degrees and forms, must exist in all the states of matter. It is very important to direct attention to the fact that the internal motion or condition of the parts of the particles of matter must be different on the surface of a substance from what it is inside; because in the interior of a substance similar particles are acting on all sides of every particle, whilst at the surface they act on one side only. Therefore, the condition of a substance at its surfaces of contact with other substances must be more or less modified by them—it may be in a manner similar to that caused by an elevation of temperature.[39] These considerations throw some light on the action in the large class of *contact reactions*; that is, such as appear to proceed from the mere presence (contact) of certain special substances. Porous or powdery substances are very prone to act in this way, especially spongy platinum and charcoal. For example, sulphurous anhydride does not combine directly with oxygen, but this reaction takes place in the presence of spongy platinum.[36]

The above general and introductory chemical conceptions cannot be thoroughly grasped in their true sense without a knowledge of the particular facts of chemistry to which we shall now turn our attention. It was, however, absolutely necessary to become acquainted on the very threshold with such fundamental principles as the laws of the indestructibility of matter and of the conservation of energy, since it is only by their acceptance, and under their direction and influence, that the examination of particular facts can give practical and fruitful results.

Footnotes:

[1] The investigation of a substance or a natural phenomenon consists (*a*) in determining the relation of the object under examination to that which is already known, either from previous researches, or from experiment, or from the knowledge of the common surroundings of life— that is, in determining and expressing the quality of the unknown by the aid of that which is known; (*b*) in measuring all that which can be subjected to measurement, and thereby denoting the quantitative relation of that under investigation to that already known and its relation to the categories of time, space, temperature, mass, &c.; (*c*) in determining the position held by the object under investigation in the system of known objects guided by both qualitative and quantitative data; (*d*) in determining, from the quantities which have been measured, the empirical (visible) dependence (function, or 'law,' as it is sometimes termed) of variable factors—for instance, the dependence of the composition of the substance on its properties, of temperature on time, of time on locality, &c.; (*e*) in framing hypotheses or propositions as to the actual cause and true nature of the relation between that studied (measured or observed) and that which is

known or the categories of time, space, &c.; (*f*) in verifying the logical consequences of the hypotheses by experiment; and (*g*) in advancing a theory which shall account for the nature of the properties of that studied in its relations with things already known and with those conditions or categories among which it exists. It is certain that it is only possible to carry out these investigations when we have taken as a basis some incontestable fact which is self-evident to our understanding; as, for instance, number, time, space, motion, or mass. The determination of such primary or fundamental conceptions, although not excluded from the possibility of investigation, frequently does not subject itself to our present mode of scientific generalisation. Hence it follows that in the investigation of anything, there always remains something which is accepted without investigation, or admitted as a known factor. The axioms of geometry may be taken as an example. Thus in the science of biology it is necessary to admit the faculty of organisms for multiplying themselves, as a conception whose meaning is as yet unknown. In the study of chemistry, too, the notion of elements must be accepted almost without any further analysis. However, by first investigating that which is visible and subject to direct observation by the organs of the senses, we may hope that in the first place hypotheses will be arrived at, and afterwards theories of that which has now to be placed at the basis of our investigations. The minds of the ancients strove to seize at once the very fundamental categories of investigation, whilst all the successes of recent knowledge are based on the above-cited method of investigation without the determination of 'the beginning of all beginnings.' By following this inductive method, the *exact sciences* have already succeeded in becoming accurately acquainted with much of the invisible world, which directly is imperceptible to the organs of sense (for example, the molecular motion of all bodies, the composition of the heavenly luminaries, the paths of their motion, the necessity for the existence of substances which cannot be subjected to experiment, &c.), and have verified the knowledge thus obtained, and employed it for increasing the interests of humanity. It may therefore be safely said that *the inductive method of investigation* is a more perfect mode of acquiring knowledge than the deductive method alone (starting from a little of the unknown accepted as incontestable to arrive at the much which is visible and observable) by which the ancients strove to embrace the universe. By investigating the universe by an inductive method (endeavouring from the much which is observable to arrive at a little which may be verified and is indubitable) the new science refuses to recognise dogma as truth, but through *reason*, by a slow and laborious method of investigation, strives for and attains to true deductions.

[2] A substance or material is that which occupies space and has weight; that is, which presents a mass attracted by the earth and by other masses of

material, and of which the *objects* of nature are composed, and by means of which the motions and *phenomena* of nature are accomplished. It is easy to discover by examining and investigating, by various methods, the objects met with in nature and in the arts, that some of them are homogeneous, whilst others are composed of a mixture of several homogeneous substances. This is most clearly apparent in solid substances. The metals used in the arts (for example, gold, iron, copper) must be homogeneous, otherwise they are brittle and unfit for many purposes. Homogeneous matter exhibits similar properties in all its parts. By breaking up a homogeneous substance we obtain parts which, although different in form, resemble each other in their properties. Glass, pure sugar, marble, &c., are examples of homogeneous substances. Examples of non-homogeneous substances are, however, much more frequent in nature and the arts. Thus the majority of the rocks are not homogeneous. In porphyries bright pieces of a mineral called 'orthoclase' are often seen interspersed amongst the dark mass of the rock. In ordinary red granite it is easy to distinguish large pieces of orthoclase mixed with dark semi-transparent quartz and flexible laminæ of mica. Similarly, plants and animals are non-homogeneous. Thus, leaves are composed of a skin, fibre, pulp, sap, and a green colouring matter. As an example of those non-homogeneous substances which are produced artificially, gunpowder may be cited, which is prepared by mixing together known proportions of sulphur, nitre, and charcoal. Many liquids, also, are not homogeneous, as may be observed by the aid of the microscope, when drops of blood are seen to consist of a colourless liquid in which red corpuscles, invisible to the naked eye owing to their small size, are floating about. It is these corpuscles which give blood its peculiar colour. Milk is also a transparent liquid, in which microscopical drops of fat are floating, which rise to the top when milk is left at rest, forming cream. It is possible to extract from every non-homogeneous substance those homogeneous substances of which it is made up. Thus orthoclase may he separated from porphyry by breaking it off. So also gold is extracted from auriferous sand by washing away the mixture of clay and sand. Chemistry deals only with the homogeneous substances met with in nature, or extracted from natural or artificial non-homogeneous substances. The various mixtures found in nature form the subjects of other natural sciences—as geognosy, botany, zoology, anatomy, &c.

[3] All those events which are accomplished by substances in time are termed 'phenomena.' Phenomena in themselves form the fundamental subject of the study of physics. Motion is the primary and most generally understood form of phenomenon, and therefore we endeavour to reason about other phenomena as clearly as when dealing with motion. For this reason mechanics, which treats of motion, forms the fundamental science of natural philosophy, and all other sciences endeavour to reduce the

phenomena with which they are concerned to mechanical principles. Astronomy was the first to take to this path of reasoning, and succeeded in many cases in reducing astronomical to purely mechanical phenomena. Chemistry and physics, physiology and biology are proceeding in the same direction. One of the most important questions of all natural science, and one which has been handed down from the philosophers of classic times, is, whether the comprehension of all that is visible can be reduced to motion? Its participation in all, from the 'fixed' stars to the most minute parts of the coldest bodies (Dewar, in 1894 showed that many substances cooled to -180° fluoresce more strongly than at the ordinary temperature; *i.e.* that there is a motion in them which produces light) must now be recognised as undoubtable from direct experiment and observation, but it does not follow from this that by motion alone can all be explained. This follows, however, from the fact that we cannot apprehend motion otherwise than by recognising matter in a state of motion. If light and electricity be understood as particular forms of motion, then we must inevitably recognise the existence of a peculiar luminiferous (universal) ether as a material, transmitting this form of motion. And so, under the present state of knowledge, it is inevitably necessary to recognise the particular categories, motion and matter, and as chemistry is more closely concerned with the various forms of the latter, it should, together with mechanics or the study of motion, lie at the basis of natural science.

[4] The verb 'to react' means to act or change chemically.

[5] If a phenomenon proceeds at visible or measurable distances (as, for instance, magnetic attraction or gravity), it cannot be described as chemical, since these phenomena only take place at distances immeasurably small and undistinguishable to the eye or the microscope; that is to say, they are purely molecular.

[6] For this purpose a piece of iron may be made red hot in a forge, and then placed in contact with a lump of sulphur, when iron sulphide will be obtained as a molten liquid, the combination being accompanied by a visible increase in the glow of the iron. Or else iron filings are mixed with powdered sulphur in the proportion of 5 parts of iron to 3 parts of sulphur, and the mixture placed in a glass tube, which is then heated in one place. Combination does not commence without the aid of external heat, but when once started in any portion of the mixture it extends throughout the entire mass, because the portion first heated evolves sufficient heat in forming iron sulphide to raise the adjacent parts of the mixture to the temperature required for starting the reaction. The rise in temperature thus produced is so high as to soften the glass tube.

[7] Sulphur is slightly soluble in many thin oils; it is very soluble in carbon bisulphide and in some other liquids. Iron is insoluble in carbon bisulphide, and the sulphur therefore can be dissolved away from the iron.

[8] Decomposition of this kind is termed 'dry distillation,' because, as in distillation, the substance is heated and vapours are given off which, on cooling, condense into liquids. In general, decomposition, in absorbing heat, presents much in common to a physical change of state—such as, for example, that of a liquid into a gas. Deville likened complete decomposition to boiling, and compared partial decomposition, when a portion of a substance is not decomposed in the presence of its products of decomposition (or dissociation), to evaporation.

[9] A reaction of rearrangement may in certain cases take place with one substance only; that is to say, a substance may by itself change into a new isomeric form. Thus, for example, if hard yellow sulphur be heated to a temperature of 250° and then poured into cold water it gives, on cooling, a soft, brown variety. Ordinary phosphorus, which is transparent, poisonous, and phosphorescent in the dark (in the air), gives, after being heated at 270° (in an atmosphere incapable of supporting combustion, such as steam), an opaque, red, and non-poisonous isomeric variety, which is not phosphorescent. Cases of isomerism point out the possibility of an internal rearrangement in a substance, and are the result of an alteration in the grouping of the same elements, just as a certain number of balls may be grouped in figures and forms of different shapes.

[10] Thus the ancients knew how to convert the juice of grapes containing the saccharine principle (glucose) into wine or vinegar, how to extract metals from the ores which are found in the earth's crust, and how to prepare glass from earthy substances.

[11] The experiments conducted by Staas (described in detail in Chap. XXIV. on Silver) form some of the accurate researches, proving that the weight of matter is not altered in chemical reactions, because he accurately weighed (introducing all the necessary corrections) the reacting and resultant substances. Landolt (1893) carried on various reactions in inverted and sealed glass U-tubes, and on weighing the tubes before reaction (when the reacting solutions were separated in each of the branches of the tubes), and after (when the solutions had been well mixed together by shaking), found that either the weight remained perfectly constant or that the variation was so small (for instance, 0·2 milligram in a total weight of about a million milligrams) as to be ascribed to the inevitable errors of weighing.

[11 bis] The idea of the mass of matter was first shaped into an exact form by Galileo (died 1642), and more especially by Newton (born 1643, died 1727), in the glorious epoch of the development of the principles of

inductive reasoning enunciated by Bacon and Descartes in their philosophical treatises. Shortly after the death of Newton, Lavoisier, whose fame in natural philosophy should rank with that of Galileo and Newton, was born on August 26, 1743. The death of Lavoisier occurred during the Reign of Terror of the French Revolution, when he, together with twenty-six other chief farmers of the revenue, was guillotined on May 8, 1794, at Paris; but his works and ideas have made him immortal.

[12] By covering iron with an enamel, or varnish, or with unrustable metals (such as nickel), or a coating of paraffin, or other similar substances, it is protected from the air and moisture, and so kept from rusting.

[13] Such an experiment may easily be made by taking the finest (unrusted) iron filings (ordinary filings must be first washed in ether, dried, and passed through a very fine sieve). The filings thus obtained are capable of burning directly in air (by oxidising or forming rust), especially when they hang (are attracted) on a magnet. A compact piece of iron does not burn in air, but spongy iron glows and smoulders like tinder. In making the experiment, a horse-shoe magnet is fixed, with the poles downwards, on one arm of a rather sensitive balance, and the iron filings are applied to the magnet (on a sheet of paper) so as to form a beard about the poles. The balance pan should be exactly under the filings on the magnet, in order that any which might fall from it should not alter the weight. The filings, having been weighed, are set light to by applying the flame of a candle; they easily take fire, and go on burning by themselves, forming rust. When the combustion is ended, it will be clear that the iron has increased in weight; from 5½ parts by weight of iron filings taken, there are obtained, by complete combustion, 7½ parts by weight of rust.

[14] For the purpose of experiment, it is most convenient to take copper carbonate, which may be prepared by the experimenter himself, by adding a solution of sodium carbonate to a solution of copper sulphate. The precipitate (deposit) so formed is collected on a filter, washed, and dried. The decomposition of copper carbonate into copper oxide is effected by so moderate a heat that it may be performed in a glass vessel heated by a lamp. For this purpose a thin glass tube, closed at one end, and called a 'test tube,' may be employed, or else a vessel called a 'retort.' The experiment is carried on, as described in example three on p. 11, by collecting the carbonic anhydride over water, as will be afterwards explained.

[15] Gas delivery tubes are usually made of glass tubing of various diameters and thicknesses. If of small diameter and thickness, a glass tube is easily bent by heating in a gas jet or the flame of a spirit lamp, and it may also be easily divided at a given point by making a deep scratch with a file

and then breaking the tube at this point with a sharp jerk. These properties, together with their impermeability, transparency, hardness, and regularity of bore, render glass tubes most useful in experiments with gases. Naturally they might be replaced by straws, india-rubber, metallic, or other tubes, but these are more difficult to fix on to a vessel, and are not entirely impervious to gases. A glass gas delivery tube may be hermetically fixed into a vessel by fitting it into a perforated cork, which should be soft and free from flaws, and fixing the cork into the orifice of the vessel. To protect the cork from the action of gases it is sometimes previously soaked in paraffin, or it may be replaced by an india-rubber cork.

[16] Gases, like all other substances, may be weighed, but, owing to their extreme lightness and the difficulty of dealing with them in large masses, they can only be weighed by very sensitive balances; that is, in such as, with a considerable load, indicate a very small difference in weight—for example, a centigram or a milligram with a load of 1,000 grams. In order to weigh a gas, a glass globe furnished with a tight-fitting stop-cock is first of all exhausted of air by an air-pump (a Sprengel pump is the best). The stop-cock is then closed, and the exhausted globe weighed. If the gas to be weighed is then let into the globe, its weight can be determined from the increase in the weight of the globe. It is necessary, however, that the temperature and pressure of the air about the balance should remain constant for both weighings, as the weight of the globe in air will (according to the laws of hydrostatics) vary with its density. The volume of the air displaced, and its weight, must therefore be determined by observing the temperature, density, and moisture of the atmosphere during the time of experiment. This will be partly explained later, but may be studied more in detail by physics. Owing to the complexity of all these operations, the mass of a gas is usually determined from its volume and density, or from the weight of a known volume.

[17] The copper carbonate should be dried before weighing, as otherwise—besides copper oxide and carbonic anhydride—water will be obtained in the decomposition. Water forms a part of the composition of malachite, and has therefore to be taken into consideration. The water produced in the decomposition may be all collected by absorbing it in sulphuric acid or calcium chloride, as will be described further on. In order to dry a salt it must be heated at about 100° until its weight remains constant, or be placed under an air pump over sulphuric acid, as will also be presently described. As water is met with almost everywhere, and as it is absorbed by many substances, the possibility of its presence should never be lost sight of.

[18] As the decomposition of red oxide of mercury requires so high a temperature, near redness, as to soften ordinary glass, it is necessary for this

experiment to take a retort (or test tube) made of hard glass, which is able to stand high temperatures without softening. For the same reason, the lamp used must give a strong heat and a large flame, capable of embracing the whole bottom of the retort, which should be as small as possible for the convenience of the experiment.

[19] The pneumatic trough may naturally be made of any material (china, earthenware, or metal, &c.), but usually a glass one, as shown in the drawing, is used, as it allows the progress of the experiment to be better observed. For this reason, as well as the ease with which they are kept clean, and from the fact also that glass is not acted on by many substances which affect other materials (for instance, metals), glass vessels of all kinds—such as retorts, test tubes, cylinders, beakers, flasks, globes, &c.— are preferred to any other for chemical experiments. Glass vessels may be heated without any danger if the following precautions be observed: 1st, they should be made of thin glass, as otherwise they are liable to crack from the bad heat-conducting power of glass; 2nd, they should be surrounded by a liquid or with sand (Fig. 2), or sand bath as it is called; or else should stand in a current of hot gases without touching the fuel from which they proceed, or in the flame of a smokeless lamp. A common candle or lamp forms a deposit of soot on a cold object placed in their flames. The soot interferes with the transmission of heat, and so a glass vessel when covered with soot often cracks. And for this reason spirit lamps, which burn with a smokeless flame, or gas burners of a peculiar construction, are used. In the Bunsen burner the gas is mixed with air, and burns with a non-luminous and smokeless flame. On the other hand, if an ordinary lamp (petroleum or benzine) does not smoke it may be used for heating a glass vessel without danger, provided the glass is placed well above the flame in the current of hot gases. In all cases, the heating should be begun very carefully by raising the temperature by degrees.

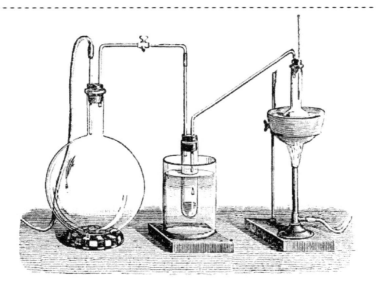

FIG. 2.—Apparatus for distilling under a diminished pressure liquids which decompose at their boiling points under the ordinary pressure. The apparatus in which the liquid is distilled is connected with a large globe from which the air is pumped out; the liquid is heated, and the receiver cooled.

[20] In order to avoid the necessity of holding the cylinder, its open end is widened (and also ground so that it may be closely covered with a ground-glass plate when necessary), and placed on a stand below the level of the water in the bath. This stand is called 'the bridge.' It has several circular openings cut through it, and the gas delivery tube is placed under one of these, and the cylinder for collecting the gas over it.

[21] Drying is necessary in order to remove any water which may be held in the salts (*see* Note 17, and Chapter I., Notes 13 and 14).

[22] The exact weights of the re-acting and resulting substances are determined with the greatest difficulty, not only from the possible inexactitude of the balance (every weighing is only correct within the limits of the sensitiveness of the balance) and weights used in weighing, not only from the difficulty in making corrections for the weight of air displaced by the vessels holding the substances weighed and by the weights themselves, but also from the hygroscopic nature of many substances (and vessels) causing absorption of moisture from the atmosphere, and from the difficulty in not losing any of the substance to be weighed in the several operations (filtering, evaporating, and drying, &c.) which have to be performed before arriving at a final result. All these circumstances have to

be taken into consideration in exact researches, and their elimination requires very many special precautions which are impracticable in preliminary experiments.

[23] Besides which, in the majority of cases, the first explanation of most subjects which do not repeat themselves in everyday experience under various aspects, but always in one form, or only at intervals and infrequently, is usually wrong. Thus the daily evidence of the rising of the sun and stars evokes the erroneous idea that the heavens move and the earth stands still. This apparent truth is far from being the real truth, and, as a matter of fact, is contradictory to it. Similarly, an ordinary mind and everyday experience concludes that iron is incombustible, whereas it burns not only as filings, but even as wire, as we shall afterwards see. With the progress of knowledge very many primitive prejudices have been obliged to give way to true ideas which have been verified by experiment. In ordinary life we often reason at first sight with perfect truth, only because we are taught a right judgment by our daily experience. It is a necessary consequence of the nature of our minds to reach the attainment of truth through elementary and often erroneous reasoning and through experiment, and it would be very wrong to expect a knowledge of truth from a simple mental effort. Naturally, experiment itself cannot give truth, but it gives the means of destroying erroneous representations whilst confirming those which are true in all their consequences.

[24] It is true that Stahl was acquainted with a fact which directly disproved his hypothesis. It was already known (from the experiments of Geber, and more especially of Ray, in 1630) that metals increase in weight by oxidation, whilst, according to Stahl's hypothesis, they should decrease in weight, because phlogiston is separated by oxidation. Stahl speaks on this point as follows:—'I am well aware that metals, in their transformation into earths, increase in weight. But not only does this fact not disprove my theory, but, on the contrary, confirms it, for phlogiston is lighter than air, and, in combining with substances, strives to lift them, and so decreases their weight; consequently, a substance which has lost phlogiston must be heavier.' This argument, it will be seen, is founded on a misconception of the properties of gases, regarding them as having no weight and as not being attracted by the earth, or else on a confused idea of phlogiston itself, since it was first defined as imponderable. The conception of imponderable phlogiston tallies well with the habit and methods of the last century, when recourse was often had to imponderable fluids for explaining a large number of phenomena. Heat, light, magnetism, and electricity were explained as being peculiar imponderable fluids. In this sense the doctrine of Stahl corresponds entirely with the spirit of his age. If heat be now regarded as motion or energy, then phlogiston also should be considered in

this light. In fact, in combustion, of coals for instance, heat and energy are evolved, and not combined in the coal, although the oxygen and coal do combine. Consequently, the doctrine of Stahl contains the essence of a true representation of the evolution of energy, but naturally this evolution is only a consequence of the combination occurring between the coal and oxygen. As regards the history of chemistry prior to Lavoisier, besides Stahl's work (to which reference has been made above), Priestley's *Experiments and Observations on Different Kinds of Air*, London, 1790, and also Scheele's *Opuscula Chimica et Physica*, Lips., 1788–89, 2 vols., must be recommended as the two leading works of the English and Scandinavian chemists showing the condition of chemical learning before the propagation of Lavoisier's views, and containing also many important observations which lie at the basis of the chemistry of our times. A most interesting memoir on the history of phlogiston is that of Rodwell, in the *Philosophical Magazine*, 1868, in which it is shown that the idea of phlogiston dates very far back, that Basil Valentine (1394–1415), in the *Cursus Triumphalis Antimonii*, Paracelsus (1493–1541), in his work, *De Rerum Natura*, Glauber (1604–1668), and especially John Joachim Becher (1625–1682), in his *Physica Subterranea*, all referred to phlogiston, but under different names.

[25] An Englishman, named Mayow, who lived a whole century before Lavoisier (in 1666), understood certain phenomena of oxidation in their true aspect, but was not able to develop his views with clearness, or support them by conclusive experiments; he cannot therefore be considered, like Lavoisier, as the founder of contemporary chemical learning. Science is a universal heritage, and therefore it is only just to give the highest honour in science, not to those who first enunciate a certain truth, but to those who are first able to convince others of its authenticity and establish it for the general welfare. But scientific discoveries are rarely made all at once; as a rule, the first teachers do not succeed in convincing others of the truth they have discovered; with time, however, a true herald comes forward, possessing every means for making the truth apparent to all, but it must not be forgotten that such are entirely indebted to the labours and mass of data accumulated by many others. Such was Lavoisier, and such are all the great founders of science. They are the enunciators of all past and present learning, and their names will always be revered by posterity.

[26] Many of the ancient philosophers assumed the existence of one elementary form of matter. This idea still appears in our times, in the constant efforts which are made to reduce the number of the elements; to prove, for instance, that bromine contains chlorine or that chlorine contains oxygen. Many methods, founded both on experiment and theory,

have been tried to prove the compound nature of the elements. All labour in this direction has as yet been in vain, and the assurance that elementary matter is not so homogeneous (single) as the mind would desire in its first transport of rapid generalisation is strengthened from year to year. All our knowledge shows that iron and other elements remain, even at such a high temperature as there exists in the sun, as different substances, and are not converted into one common material. Admitting, even mentally, the possibility of one elementary form of matter, a method must be imagined by which it could give rise to the various elements, as also the *modus operandi* of their formation from one material. If it be said that this diversitude only takes place at low temperatures, as is observed with isomerides, then there would be reason to expect, if not the transition of the various elements into one particular and more stable form, at least the mutual transformation of some into others. But nothing of the kind has as yet been observed, and the alchemist's hope to manufacture (as Berthollet puts it) elements has no theoretical or practical foundation.

[27] The weakest point in the idea of elements is the negative character of the determinative signs given them by Lavoisier, and from that time ruling in chemistry. They do *not* decompose, they do *not* change into one another. But it must be remarked that elements form the limiting horizon of our knowledge of matter, and it is always difficult to determine a positive side on the borderland of what is known. Besides, there is no doubt (from the results of spectrum analysis) that the elements are distributed as far as the most distant stars, and that they support the highest attainable temperatures without decomposing.

[28] Possibly some of their compounds are compounds of other already-known elements. Pure and incontestably independent compounds of these substances are unknown, and some of them have not even been separated, but are only supposed to exist from the results of spectroscopic researches. There can be no mention of such contestable and doubtful elements in a short general handbook of chemistry.

[28 bis] Clark in America made an approximate calculation of the amount of the different elements contained in the earth's crust (to a depth of 15 kilometres), and found that the chief mass (over 50 per cent.) is composed of oxygen; then comes silicon, &c.; while the amount of hydrogen is less than 1 per cent., carbon scarcely $0 \cdot 25$ per cent., nitrogen even less than $0 \cdot 03$ per cent. The relative masses of such metals as Cu, Ni, Au is minute. Judging from the density (see Chapter VIII.) of the earth, a large proportion of its mass must be composed of iron.

[29] This word, first introduced, if I mistake not, into chemistry by Glauber, is based on the idea of the ancient philosophers that combination

can only take place when the substances combining have something in common—a medium. As is generally the case, another idea evolved itself in antiquity, and has lived until now, side by side with the first, to which it is exactly contradictory; this considers union as dependent on contrast, on polar difference, on an effort to fill up a want.

[30] Especially conclusive are those cases of so-called metalepsis (Dumas, Laurent). Chlorine, in combining with hydrogen, forms a very stable substance called 'hydrochloric acid,' which is split up by the action of an electrical current into chlorine and hydrogen, the chlorine appearing at the positive and the hydrogen at the negative pole. Hence electro-chemists considered hydrogen to be an electro-positive and chlorine an electro-negative element, and that they are held together in virtue of their opposite electrical charges. It appears, however, from metalepsis, that chlorine can replace hydrogen (and, inversely, hydrogen can replace chlorine) in its compounds without in any way changing the grouping of the other elements, or altering their chief chemical properties. For instance, acetic acid in which hydrogen has been replaced by chlorine is still capable of forming salts. It must be observed, whilst considering this subject, that the explanation suggesting electricity as the origin of chemical phenomena is unsound, since it attempts to explain one class of phenomena whose nature is almost unknown by another class which is no better known. It is most instructive to remark that together with the electrical theory of chemical attraction there arose and survives a view which explains the galvanic current as being a transference of chemical action through the circuit—*i.e.*, regards the origin of electricity as being a chemical one. It is evident that the connection is very intimate, although both phenomena are independent and represent different forms of molecular (atomic) motion, whose real nature is not yet understood. Nevertheless, the connection between the phenomena of both categories is not only in itself very instructive, but it extends the applicability of the general idea of the unity of the forces of nature, conviction of the truth of which has held so important a place in the science of the last ten years.

[31] I consider that in an elementary text-book of chemistry, like the present, it is only possible and advisable to mention, in reference to chemical mechanics, a few general ideas and some particular examples referring more especially to gases, whose mechanical theory must be regarded as the most complete. The molecular mechanics of liquids and solids is as yet in embryo, and contains much that is disputable; for this reason, chemical mechanics has made less progress in relation to these substances. It may not be superfluous here to remark, with respect to the conception of chemical affinity, that up to the present time gravity, electricity, and heat have all been applied to its elucidation. Efforts have

also been made to introduce the luminiferous ether into theoretical chemistry, and should that connection between the phenomena of light and electricity which was established by Maxwell be worked out more in detail, doubtless these efforts to elucidate all or a great deal by the aid of luminiferous ether will again appear in theoretical chemistry. An independent chemical mechanics of the material particles of matter, and of their internal (atomic) changes, would, in my opinion, arise as the result of these efforts. Two hundred years ago Newton laid the foundation of a truly scientific theoretical mechanics of external visible motion, and on this foundation erected the edifice of celestial mechanics. One hundred years ago Lavoisier arrived at the first fundamental law of the internal mechanics of invisible particles of matter. This subject is far from having been developed into a harmonious whole, because it is much more difficult, and, although many details have been completely investigated, it does not possess any starting points. Newton only came after Copernicus and Kepler, who had discovered empirically the exterior simplicity of celestial phenomena. Lavoisier and Dalton may, in respect to the chemical mechanics of the molecular world, be compared to Copernicus and Kepler. But a Newton has not yet appeared in the molecular world; when he does, I think that he will find the fundamental laws of the mechanics of the invisible motions of matter more easily and more quickly in the chemical structure of matter than in physical phenomena (of electricity, heat, and light); for these latter are accomplished by particles of matter already arranged, whilst it is now clear that the problem of chemical mechanics mainly lies in the apprehension of those motions which are invisibly accomplished by the smallest atoms of matter.

[32] The theory of heat gave the idea of a store of internal motion or energy, and therefore with it, it became necessary to acknowledge chemical energy, but there is no foundation whatever for identifying heat energy with chemical energy. It may be supposed, but not positively affirmed, that heat motion is proper to molecules and chemical motion to atoms, but that as molecules are made up of atoms, the motion of the one passes to the other, and that for this reason heat strongly influences reaction and appears or disappears (is absorbed) in reactions. These relations, which are apparent and hardly subject to doubt on general lines, still present much that is doubtful in detail, because all forms of molecular and atomic motion are able to pass into each other.

[33] The reactions which take place (at the ordinary or at a high temperature) directly between substances may be clearly divided into exothermal, which are accompanied by an evolution of heat, and endothermal, which are accompanied by an absorption of heat. It is evident that the latter require a source of heat. They are determined either by the

directly surrounding medium (as in the formation of carbon bisulphide from charcoal and sulphur, or in decompositions which take place at high temperatures), or else by a secondary reaction proceeding simultaneously, or by some other form of energy (light, electricity). So, for instance, hydrogen sulphide is decomposed by iodine in the presence of water at the expense of the heat which is evolved by the solution in water of the hydrogen iodide produced. This is the reason why this reaction, as exothermal, only takes place in the presence of water; otherwise it would be accompanied by a cooling effect. As in the combination of dissimilar substances, the bonds existing between the molecules and atoms of the homogeneous substances have to be broken asunder, whilst in reactions of rearrangement the formation of any one substance proceeds simultaneously with the formation of another, and, as in reactions, a series of physical and mechanical changes take place, it is impossible to separate the heat directly depending on a given reaction from the total sum of the observed heat effect. For this reason, thermochemical data are very complex, and cannot by themselves give the key to many chemical problems, as it was at first supposed they might. They ought to form a part of chemical mechanics, but alone they do not constitute it.

[34] As chemical reactions are effected by heating, so the heat absorbed by substances before decomposition or change of state, and called 'specific heat,' goes in many cases to the preparation, if it may be so expressed, of reaction, even when the limit of the temperature of reaction is not attained. The molecules of a substance A, which is not able to react on a substance B below a temperature t, by being heated from a somewhat lower temperature to t, undergoes that change which had to be arrived at for the formation of A B.

[35] It is possible to imagine that the cause of a great many of such reactions is, that substances taken in a separate state, for instance, charcoal, present a complex molecule composed of separate atoms of carbon which are fastened together (united, as is usually said) by a considerable affinity; for atoms of the same kind, just like atoms of different kinds, possess a mutual affinity. The affinity of chlorine for carbon, although unable to break this bond asunder, may be sufficient to form a stable compound with atoms of carbon, which are already separate. Such a view of the subject presents a hypothesis which, although dominant at the present time, is without sufficiently firm foundation. It is evident, however, that not only does chemical reaction itself consist of motions, but that in the compound formed (in the molecules) the elements (atoms) forming it are in harmonious stable motion (like the planets in the solar system), and this motion will affect the stability and capacity for reaction, and therefore the mechanical side of chemical action must be exceedingly complex. Just as

there are solid, physically constant non-volatile substances like rock, gold, charcoal, &c., so are there stable and chemically constant bodies; while corresponding to physically volatile substances there are bodies like camphor, which are chemically unstable and variable.

[36] Contact phenomena are separately considered in detail in the work of Professor Konovaloff (1884). In my opinion, it must be held that the state of the internal motions of the atoms in molecules is modified at the points of contact of substances, and this state determines chemical reactions, and therefore, that reactions of combination, decomposition, and rearrangement are accomplished by contact. Professor Konovaloff showed that a number of substances, under certain conditions of their surfaces, act by contact; for instance, finely divided silica (from the hydrate) acts just like platinum, decomposing certain compound ethers. As reactions are only accomplished under close contact, it is probable that those modifications in the distribution of the atoms in molecules which come about by contact phenomena prepare the way for them. By this the *rôle* of contact phenomena is considerably extended. Such phenomena should explain the fact why a mixture of hydrogen and oxygen yields water (explodes) at different temperatures, according to the kind of heated substance which transmits this temperature. In chemical mechanics, phenomena of this kind have great importance, but as yet they have been but little studied. It must not be forgotten that contact is a necessary condition for every chemical reaction.

[40]

CHAPTER I

ON WATER AND ITS COMPOUNDS

Water is found almost everywhere in nature, and in all three physical states. As vapour, water occurs in the atmosphere, and in this form it is distributed over the entire surface of the earth. The vapour of water in condensing, by cooling, forms snow, rain, hail, dew, and fog. One cubic metre (or 1,000,000 cubic centimetres, or 1,000 litres, or 35·316 cubic feet) of air can contain at 0° only 4·8 grams of water, at 20° about 17·0 grams, at 40° about 50·7 grams; but ordinary air only contains about 60 per cent. of this maximum. Air containing less than 40 per cent. is felt to be dry, whilst air which contains more than 80 per cent. of the same maximum is considered as distinctly damp.[1] Water in the liquid state, in falling as rain and snow, soaks into the[41] soil and collects together into springs, lakes, rivers, seas, and oceans. It is absorbed from the soil by the roots of plants, which,   when   fresh,[42]

[43]

[44] contain from 40 to 80 per cent. of water by weight. Animals contain about the same amount of water. In a solid state, water appears as snow, ice, or in an intermediate form between these two, which is seen on mountains covered with perpetual snow. The water of rivers,[2] springs, oceans and seas, lakes, and wells contains various substances in solution mostly salt,—that is, substances resembling common table salt in their physical properties and chief chemical transformations. Further, the quantity and nature of these salts differ in different waters.[3] Everybody knows that there are salt, fresh, iron, and other waters. The presence of about   3½   per   cent.[45]

[46] of salts renders sea-water[4] bitter to the taste and increases its specific gravity. Fresh water also contains salts, but only in a comparatively small quantity. Their presence may be easily proved by simply evaporating water in a vessel. On evaporation the water passes away as vapour, whilst the salts are left behind. This is why a crust (incrustation), consisting of salts, previously in solution, is deposited on the insides of kettles or boilers, and other vessels in which water is boiled. Running water (rivers, &c.) is charged with salts, owing to its being formed from the collection of rain water percolating through the soil. While percolating, the water dissolves certain parts of the soil. Thus water which filters or passes through saline or calcareous soils becomes charged with salts or contains calcium carbonate (chalk). Rain water and snow are much purer than river or spring water.

Nevertheless, in passing through the atmosphere, rain and snow succeed in catching the dust held in it, and dissolve air, which is found in every water. The dissolved gases of the atmosphere are partly disengaged, as bubbles from water on heating, and water after long boiling is quite freed from them.

In general terms water is called pure when it is clear and free from insoluble particles held in suspension and visible to the naked eye, from[47] which it may be freed by filtration through charcoal, sand, or porous (natural or artificial) stones, and when it possesses a clean fresh taste. It depends on the absence of any taste, decomposing organic matter, on the quantity of air[5] and atmospheric gases in solution, and on the presence of mineral substances to the amount of about 300 grams per ton (or 1000 kilograms per cubic metre, or, what is the same, 300 milligrams to a kilogram or a litre of water), and of not more than 100 grams of organic matter.[6] Such water is suitable for drinking and[48] every practical application, but evidently it is not pure in a chemical sense. A *chemically pure water* is necessary not only for scientific purposes, as an independent substance having constant and definite properties, but also for many practical purposes—for instance, in photography and in the preparation of medicines—because many properties of substances in solution are changed by the impurities of natural waters. Water is usually purified by distillation, because the solid substances in solution are not transformed into vapours in this process. Such *distilled* water is prepared by chemists and in laboratories by boiling water in closed metallic boilers or stills, and causing the steam produced to pass into a condenser—that is, through tubes (which should be made of tin, or, at all events, tinned, as water and its impurities do not act on tin) surrounded by cold water, and in which the steam, being cooled, condenses into water which is collected[7] in a receiver. By standing exposed to the atmosphere, however, the water in time absorbs air, and dust carried in the air. Nevertheless, in distillation, water retains, besides air, a certain quantity of volatile impurities (especially organic) and the walls of the distillation apparatus are partly[49] corroded by the water, and a portion, although small, of their substance renders the water not entirely pure, and a residue is left on evaporation.[8]

For certain physical and chemical researches, however, it is necessary to have perfectly pure water. To obtain it, a solution of potassium permanganate is added to distilled water until the whole is a light rose colour. By this means the organic matter in the water is destroyed (converted into gases or non-volatile substances). An excess of potassium permanganate does no harm, because in the next distillation it is left behind in the distillation apparatus. The second distillation should take place in a platinum retort with a platinum receiver. Platinum is a metal which is not acted on either by air or water, and therefore nothing passes from it into the water. The water obtained in the receiver still contains air. It must then be boiled for a long time, and afterwards cooled in a vacuum under the receiver of an air pump. Pure water does not leave any residue on evaporation; does not in the least change, however long it be kept; does not decompose like water only[50] once distilled or impure; and it does not give bubbles of gas on heating, nor does it change the colour of a solution of potassium permanganate.

Water, purified as above described, has constant *physical* and *chemical* *properties*. For instance, it is of such water only that one cubic centimetre weighs one gram at 4° C.—*i.e.* it is only such pure water whose specific gravity equals 1 at 4° C.[9] Water in a solid state[51] [52] forms crystals of the hexagonal system[10] which are seen in snow, which generally consists of star-like clusters of several crystals, and also in the half-melted scattered ice floating on rivers in spring time. At this time of the year the ice splits up into spars or prisms, bounded by angles proper to substances crystallising in the hexagonal system.

The temperatures at which water passes from one state to another are taken as fixed points on the thermometer scale; namely, the zero corresponds with the temperature of melting ice, and the temperature of the steam disengaged from water boiling at the normal barometric pressure (that is 760 millimetres measured at 0°, at the latitude of 45°, at the sea level) is taken as 100° of the Celsius scale. Thus, the fact that water liquefies at 0° and boils at 100° is taken as one of its properties as a definite chemical compound. The weight of a litre of water at 4° is 1,000 grams, at 0° it is 999·8 grams. The weight of a litre of ice at 0° is less—namely, 917 grams; the weight of the same cubic measure of water vapour at 760 mm. pressure and 100° is only 0·60 gram; the density of the vapour compared with air = 0·62, and compared with hydrogen = 9.

These data briefly characterise the physical properties of water as a separate substance. To this may be added that water is a mobile liquid, colourless, transparent, without taste or smell, &c. Its latent heat of vaporisation is 534 units, of liquefaction 79 units of heat.[11] The large amount of heat stored up in water vapour and also in[53] liquid water (for its specific heat is greater than that of other liquids) renders it available in both forms for heating purposes. The chemical[54] [55] [56] reactions which water undergoes, and by means of which it is formed, are so numerous, and so closely allied to the reactions of many other substances, that it is impossible to describe the majority of them at this early stage of chemical exposition. We shall become acquainted with many of them afterwards, but at present we shall only cite certain compounds formed by water. In order to see clearly the nature of the various kinds of compounds formed by water we will begin with the most feeble, which are determined by purely mechanical superficial properties of the reacting substances.[12]

Water is mechanically attracted by many substances; it adheres to their surfaces just as dust adheres to objects, or one piece of polished glass adheres to another. Such attraction is termed 'moistening,' 'soaking,' or 'absorption of water.' Thus water moistens clean glass and adheres to its surface, is absorbed by the soil, sand, and clay, and does not flow away from them, but lodges itself between their particles. Similarly, water soaks into a sponge, cloth, hair, or paper, &c., but fat and greasy substances in general are not moistened. Attraction of this kind does not alter the physical or chemical properties of water. For instance, under these circumstances water, as is known from everyday experience, may be expelled from objects by drying. Water which is in any way held mechanically may be dislodged by mechanical means, by friction, pressure, centrifugal force, &c. Thus water is squeezed from wet cloth by pressure or centrifugal machines. But objects which in practice are called dry (because they do not feel wet) often still contain moisture, as may be proved by heating the object in a glass tube closed at one end. By placing a piece of paper, dry earth, or any similar object (especially porous substances) in such a glass tube, and heating that part of the tube where the object is situated, it will be remarked that water condenses on the cooler portions of the tube. The presence of such absorbed, or 'hygroscopic,' water is generally best detected in non-volatile substances by drying them at 100°, or under the receiver of an air-pump and over substances which[57] attract water chemically. By weighing a substance before and after drying, it is easy to determine the amount of hygroscopic water from the loss in weight.[13] Only in this case the amount of water must be[58] judged with care, because the loss in weight may sometimes proceed from the decomposition of the substance itself, with disengagement of gases or vapour. In making exact weighings the hygroscopic capacity of substances—that is, their capacity to absorb moisture—must be continually kept in view, as otherwise the weight will be untrue from the presence of moisture. The quantity of moisture absorbed depends on the degree of moisture of the atmosphere (that is, on the tension of the aqueous vapour in it) in which a substance is situated. In an entirely dry atmosphere, or in a vacuum, the hygroscopic water is expelled, being converted into vapour; therefore, substances containing hygroscopic water may be completely dried by placing them in a dry atmosphere or in a vacuum. The process is aided by heat, as it increases the tension of the aqueous vapour. Phosphoric anhydride (a white powder), liquid sulphuric acid, solid and porous calcium chloride, or the white powder of ignited copper sulphate, are most generally employed in drying gases. They absorb the moisture contained in air and all gases to a considerable, but not unlimited, extent. Phosphoric anhydride and calcium chloride deliquesce, become damp, sulphuric acid changes from an oily thick liquid into a more mobile liquid, and ignited copper sulphate becomes blue; after which changes these substances partly lose their capacity of holding water, and can, if it be in excess, even give up their water to the atmosphere. We may remark that the order in which these substances are placed above corresponds with the order in which they stand in respect to their capacity for absorbing moisture. Air dried by calcium chloride still contains a certain amount of moisture, which it can give up to sulphuric acid. The most complete desiccation takes place with phosphoric anhydride. Water is also removed from many substances by placing them in a dish over a vessel containing a substance absorbing water under a glass bell jar.[14] The bell jar,[59] like the receiver of an air pump, should be hermetically closed. In this case desiccation takes place; because sulphuric acid, for instance, first dries the air in the bell jar by absorbing its moisture, the substance to be dried then parts with its moisture to the dry air, from which it is again absorbed by the sulphuric acid, &c. Desiccation proceeds still better under the receiver of an air pump, for then the aqueous vapour is formed more quickly than in a bell jar full of air.

From what has been said above, it is evident that the transference of moisture to gases and the absorption of hygroscopic moisture present great resemblance to, but still are not, chemical combinations with water. Water, when combined as hygroscopic water, does not lose its properties and does not form new substances.[15]

The attraction of water for substances which dissolve in it is of a different character. In the solution of substances in water there proceeds a peculiar kind of indefinite combination; a new homogeneous substance is formed from the two substances taken. But here also the bond connecting the substances is very unstable. Water containing different substances in solution boils at a temperature near to its usual boiling point. From the solution of substances which are lighter than water itself, there are obtained solutions of a less density than water—as, for example, in the solution of alcohol in water; whilst a heavier substance in dissolving in water gives it a higher specific gravity. Thus salt water is heavier than fresh.[16]

We will consider *aqueous solutions* somewhat fully, because, among other reasons, solutions are constantly being formed on the earth and in the waters of the earth, in plants and in animals, in chemical processes and in the arts, and these solutions play an important part in the chemical transformations which are everywhere taking place, not[60] only because water is everywhere met with, but chiefly because a substance in solution presents the most favourable conditions for the process of chemical changes, which require a mobility of parts and a possible distension of parts. In dissolving, a solid substance acquires a mobility of parts, and a gas loses its elasticity, and therefore reactions often take place in solutions which do not proceed in the undissolved substances. Further, a substance, distributed in water, evidently breaks up—that is, becomes more like a gas and acquires a greater mobility of parts. All these considerations require that in describing the properties of substances, particular attention should be paid to their relation to water as a solvent.

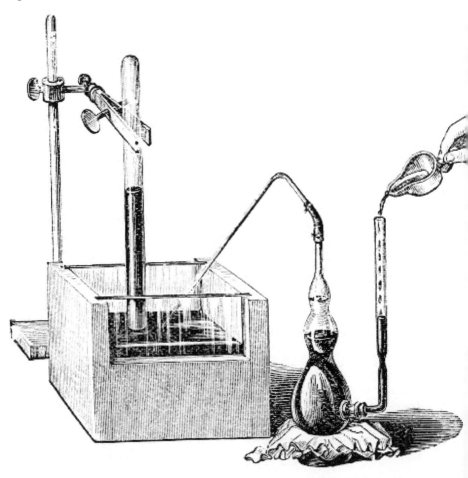

FIG. 14.—Method of transferring a gas into a cylinder filled with mercury and whose open end is immersed under the mercury in a bath having two glass sides. The apparatus containing the gas is represented on the right. Its upper extremity is furnished with a tube extending under the cylinder. The lower part of the vessel communicates with a vertical tube. If mercury be poured into this

tube, the pressure of the gas in the apparatus is increased, and it passes through the gas-conducting tube into the cylinder, where it displaces the mercury, and can be measured or subjected to the action of absorbing agents, such as water.

It is well known that water dissolves many substances. Salt, sugar, alcohol, and a number of other substances, dissolve in water and form homogeneous liquids with it. To demonstrate the solubility of gases in water, a gas should be taken which has a high co-efficient of solubility—for instance, ammonia. This is introduced into a bell jar (or cylinder, as in fig. 14), which is previously filled with mercury and stands in a mercury bath. If water be then introduced into the[61] cylinder, the mercury will rise, owing to the water dissolving the ammonia gas. If the column of mercury be less than the barometric column, and if there be sufficient water to dissolve the gas, all the ammonia will be absorbed by the water. The water is introduced into the cylinder by a glass pipette, with a bent end. The bent end is put into water, and the air is sucked out from the upper end. When full of water, its upper end is closed with the finger, and the bent end placed in the mercury bath under the orifice of the cylinder. On blowing into the pipette the water will rise to the surface of the mercury in the cylinder owing to its lightness. The solubility of a gas like ammonia may be demonstrated by taking a flask full of the gas, and closed by a cork with a tube passing through it. On placing the tube under water, the water will rise into the flask (this may be accelerated by previously warming the flask), and begin to play like a fountain inside it. Both the rising of the mercury and the fountain clearly show the considerable affinity of water for ammonia gas, and the force acting in this dissolution is rendered evident. A certain period of time is required both for the homogeneous intermixture of gases (diffusion) and the process of solution, which depends, not only on the surface of the participating substances, but also on their nature. This is seen from experiment. Solutions of different substances heavier than water, such as salt or sugar, are poured into tall jars. Pure water is then very carefully poured into these jars (through a funnel) on to the top of the solutions, so as not to disturb the lower stratum, and the jars are then left undisturbed. The line of demarcation between the solution and the pure water will be visible, owing to their different co-efficients of refraction. Notwithstanding that the solutions taken are heavier than water, after some time complete intermixture will ensue. Gay Lussac convinced himself of this fact by this particular experiment, which he conducted in the cellars under the Paris Astronomical Observatory. These cellars are well known as the locality where numerous interesting researches have been conducted, because, owing to their depth under ground, they have a uniform temperature during the whole year; the temperature does not change during the day, and this was indispensable for the experiments on the diffusion of solutions, in order that no doubt as to the results should arise from a daily change of temperature (the experiment lasted several months), which would set up currents in the liquids and intermix their strata. Notwithstanding the uniformity of the temperature, the substance in solution in time ascended into the water and distributed itself uniformly through it, proving that there exists between water and a substance dissolved in it a particular kind of attraction or striving for[62] mutual interpenetration in opposition to the force of gravity. Further, this effort, or rate of diffusion, is different for salt or sugar or for various other substances.[16 bis] It follows therefore that a peculiar force acts in solution, as in actual chemical combinations, and solution is determined by a particular kind of motion (by the chemical energy of a substance) which is proper to the substance dissolved and to the solvent.

Graham made a series of experiments similar to those above described, and showed that the *rate of diffusion*[17] in water is very variable—that is, a uniform distribution of a substance in the water dissolving it is attained in different periods of time with different solutions. Graham compared diffusive capacity with volatility. There are substances which diffuse easily, and there are others which diffuse with difficulty, just as there are more or less volatile substances. Seven hundred cubic centimetres of water were poured into a jar, and by means of a syphon (or a pipette) 100 cub. centimetres of a solution containing 10 grams of a substance were cautiously poured in so as to occupy the lower portion of the jar. After a lapse of several days, successive layers of 50 cubic centimetres were taken from the top downwards, and the quantity of substance dissolved in the different layers determined. Thus, common table salt, after fourteen days, gave the following amounts (in milligrams) in the respective layers, beginning from the top: 104, 120, 126, 198, 267, 340, 429, 535, 654, 766, 881, 991, 1,090, 1,187, and 2,266 in the remainder; whilst albumin in the same time gave, in the first seven layers, a very small amount, and beginning from the eighth layer, 10, 15, 47, 113, 343, 855, 1,892, and in the remainder 6,725 milligrams. Thus, the diffusive power of a solution depends on time and on the nature of the substance dissolved, which fact may serve, not only for explaining the process of solution, but also for distinguishing one substance from another. Graham showed that substances which rapidly diffuse through liquids[63] are able to rapidly pass through membranes and crystallise, whilst substances which diffuse slowly and do not crystallise are *colloids*, that is, resemble glue, and penetrate through a membrane slowly, and form jellies; that is, occur in insoluble forms,[18] as will be explained in speaking of silica.

[64]

Hence, if it be desired to increase the rate of solution, recourse must be had to stirring, shaking, or some such mechanical motion. But if once a uniform solution is formed, it will remain uniform, no matter how heavy the dissolved substance is, or how long the solution be left at rest, which fact again shows the presence of a force holding together the particles of the body dissolved and of the solvent.[19]

[65]

In the consideration of the process of solution, besides the conception of diffusion, another fundamental conception is necessary—namely, that of the *saturation of solutions*.

[66]
[67]

Just as moist air may be diluted with any desired quantity of dry air, so also an indefinitely large quantity of a liquid solvent may be taken, and yet a uniform solution will be obtained. But more than a definite quantity of aqueous vapour cannot be introduced into a certain volume of air at a certain temperature. The excess above the point of saturation will remain in the liquid state.[20] The relation between water and substances dissolved in it is similar. More than a definite quantity of a substance cannot, at a certain temperature, dissolve in a given quantity of water; the excess does not unite with the water. Just as air or a gas becomes saturated with vapour, so water becomes saturated with a substance dissolved in it. If an excess of a substance be added to water which is already saturated with it, it will remain in its original state, and will not diffuse through the water. The quantity of a substance (either by volume with gases, or by weight with solids and liquids) which is capable of saturating 100 parts of water is called the *coefficient of solubility* or the *solubility*. In 100 grams of water[68] [69] at 15°, there can be dissolved not more than 35·86 grams of common salt. Consequently, its solubility at 15° is equal to 35·86.[21] It is most important to turn attention to the *existence of the solid insoluble substances of nature*, because on them depends the shape of the substances of the earth's surface, and of plants and animals. There is so much water on the earth's surface, that were the surface of substances formed of soluble matters it would constantly change, and[70] however substantial their forms might be, mountains, river banks and sea shores, plants and animals, or the habitations and coverings of men, could not exist for any length of time.[22]

Substances which are easily soluble in water bear a certain resemblance to it. Thus sugar and salt in many of their superficial features[71] remind one of ice. Metals, which are not soluble in water, have no points in common with it, whilst on the other hand they dissolve each other in a molten state, forming alloys, just as oily substances dissolve each other; for example, tallow is soluble in petroleum and in olive oil, although they are all insoluble in water. From this it is evident that the *analogy of substances forming a solution* plays an important part, and as aqueous and all other solutions are liquids, there is good reason to believe that in the process of solution solid and gaseous substances change in a physical sense, passing into a liquid state. These considerations elucidate many points of solution—as, for instance, the variation of the co-efficient of solubility with the temperature and the evolution or absorption of heat in the formation of solutions.

The solubility—that is, the quantity of a substance necessary for saturation—*varies with the temperature*, and, further, with an increase in temperature the solubility of solid substances generally increases, and that of gases decreases; this might be expected, as solid substances by heating, and gases by cooling, approach to a liquid or dissolved state.[23] A graphic method is often employed to express the variation of solubility with temperature. On the axis of abscissæ or on a horizontal line, temperatures are marked out and perpendiculars are raised corresponding with each temperature, whose length is determined by the solubility of the salt at that temperature—expressing, for instance, one part by weight of a salt in 100 parts of water by one unit of length, such as a millimetre. By joining the summits of the perpendiculars, a curve is obtained which expresses the degree of solubility at different temperatures. For solids, the curve is generally an ascending one—*i.e.* recedes from the horizontal line with the rise in temperature. These curves clearly show by their inclination the degree of rapidity of increase in solubility with the temperature. Having determined several points of a curve—that is, having made a determination of the solubility for several temperatures—the solubility at intermediary temperatures may be determined from the form of the curve so obtained; in this way the empirical law of solubility may be examined.[24] The results of[72] research have shown that the solubility of certain salts—as, for example, common table salt—varies comparatively little with the temperature; whilst for other substances the solubility increases by equal amounts for equal increments of temperature. Thus, for example, for the saturation of 100 parts of water by potassium chloride there is required at 0°, 29·2 parts, at 20°, 34·7, at 40°, 40·2, at 60°, 45·7; and so on, for every 10° the solubility increases by 2·75 parts by weight of the salt. Therefore the solubility of the potassium chloride in water may be expressed by a direct equation: $a = 29\cdot2 + 0\cdot275t$, where a represents the solubility at $t°$. For other salts, more complicated equations are required. For example, for nitre: $a = 13\cdot3 + 0\cdot574t + 0\cdot01717t^2 + 0\cdot0000036t^3$, which shows that when $t = 0°$ $a = 13\cdot3$, when $t = 10°$ $a = 20\cdot8$, and when $t = 100°$ $a = 246\cdot0$.

Curves of solubility give the means of estimating the *amount of salt separated* by the cooling to a known extent of a solution saturated[73] at a given temperature. For instance, if 200 parts of a solution of potassium chloride in water saturated at a temperature of 60° be taken, and it be asked how much of the salt will be separated by cooling the solution to 0°, if its solubility at 60° = 45·7 and at 0° = 29·2? The answer is obtained in the following manner: At 60° a saturated solution contains 45·7 parts of potassium chloride per 100 parts by weight of water, consequently 145·7 parts by weight of the solution contain 45·7 parts, or, by proportion, 200 parts by weight of the solution contain 62·7 parts of the salt. The amount of salt remaining in solution at 0° is calculated as follows; In 200 grams taken there will be 137·3 grams of water; consequently, this amount of water is capable of holding only 40·1 grams of the salt, and therefore in lowering the temperature from 60° to 0° there should separate from the solution 62·7 - 40·1 = 22·6 grams of the dissolved salt.

The difference in the solubility of salts, &c., with a rise or fall of temperature is often taken advantage of, especially in technical work, for the separation of salts, in intermixture from each other. Thus a mixture of potassium and sodium chlorides (this mixture is met with in nature at Stassfurt) is separated from a saturated solution by subjecting it alternately to boiling (evaporation) and cooling. The sodium chloride separates out in proportion to the amount of water expelled from the solution by boiling, and is removed, whilst the potassium chloride separates out on cooling, as the solubility of this salt rapidly decreases with a lowering in temperature. Nitre, sugar, and many other soluble substances are purified (refined) in a similar manner.

Although in the majority of cases the solubility of solids increases with the temperature, yet there are some solid substances whose solubilities decrease on heating. Glauber's salt, or sodium sulphate, forms a particularly instructive example of the case in question. If this salt be taken in an ignited state (deprived of its water of crystallisation), then its solubility in 100 parts of water varies with the temperature in the following manner: at 0°, 5 parts of the salt form a saturated solution; at 20°, 20 parts of the salt, at 33° more than 50 parts. The solubility, as will be seen, increases with the temperature, as is the case with nearly all salts; but starting from 33° it suddenly diminishes, and at a temperature of 40°, less than 50 parts of the salt dissolve, at 60° only 45 parts of the salt, and at 100° about 43 parts of the salt in 100 parts of water. This phenomenon may be traced to the following facts: Firstly, that this salt forms various compounds with water, as will be afterwards explained; secondly, that at 33° the compound Na_2SO_4 + $10H_2O$ formed from the solution at lower temperatures, melts; and thirdly, that on evaporation at a[74] temperature above 33° an anhydrous salt, Na_2SO_4 separates out. It will be seen from this example how complicated such an apparently simple phenomenon as solution really is; and all data concerning solutions lead to the same conclusion. This complexity becomes evident in investigating the *heat of solution*. If solution consisted of a physical change only, then in the solution of gases there would be evolved—and in the solution of solids, there would be absorbed—just that amount of heat corresponding to the change of state; but in reality a large amount of heat is always evolved in solution, depending on the fact that in the process of solution chemical combination takes place accompanied by an evolution of heat. Seventeen grams of ammonia (this weight corresponds with its formula NH_3), in passing from a gaseous into a liquid state, evolve 4,400 units of heat (latent heat); that is, the quantity of heat necessary to raise the temperature of 4,400 grams of water 1°. The same quantity of ammonia, in dissolving in an excess of water, evolves twice as much heat—namely 8,800 units—showing that the combination with water is accompanied by the evolution of 4,400 units of heat. Further, the chief part of this heat is separated in dissolving in small quantities of water, so that 17 grams of ammonia, in dissolving in 18 grams of water (this weight corresponds with its composition H_2O), evolve 7,535 units of heat, and therefore the formation of the solution $NH_3 + H_2O$ evolves 3,135 units of heat beyond that due to the change of state. As in the solution of gases, the heat of liquefaction (of physical change of state) and of chemical combination with water are both positive (+), therefore in the *solution of gases* in water a *heat effect* is always observed. This phenomenon is different in the solution of solid substances, because their passage from a solid to a liquid state is accompanied by an absorption of heat (negative,- heat), whilst their chemical combination with water is accompanied by an evolution of heat (+ heat); consequently, their sum may either be a cooling effect, when the positive (chemical) portion of heat is less than the negative (physical), or it may be, on the contrary, a heating effect. This is actually the case. 124 grams of sodium thiosulphate (employed in photography) $Na_2S_2O_3,5H_2O$ in melting (at 48°) absorbs 9,700 units of heat, but in dissolving in a large quantity of water at the ordinary temperature it absorbs 5,700 units of heat, which shows the evolution of heat (about + 4,000 units), notwithstanding the cooling effect observed in the process of solution, in the act of the chemical combination of the salt with water.[25] But in most cases solid substances[75] in dissolving in water evolve heat, notwithstanding the passage into a liquid state, which indicates so considerable an evolution of (+) heat[76] in the act of combination with water that it exceeds the absorption of (-) heat dependent on the passage into a liquid state, Thus, for instance, calcium chloride, $CaCl_2$, magnesium sulphate, $MgSO_4$, and many other salts evolve heat in dissolving; for example, 60 grams of magnesium sulphate evolve about 10,000 units of heat. Therefore, *in the solution of solid bodies* either a cooling[26] or a heating[27] effect is produced, according to the difference of the reacting affinities. When they are considerable—that is, when water is with difficulty separated from the resultant solution, and only with a rise of temperature (such substances absorb water vapour)—then much heat is evolved in the process of solution, just as in many reactions of direct combination, and therefore a considerable heating of the solution is observed. Of such a kind, for instance, is the solution of sulphuric acid (oil of vitriol H_2SO_4), and of caustic soda (NaHO), &c., in water.[28]

Solution is a reversible reaction; for, if the water be expelled from a solution, the substance originally taken is obtained again. But it must be borne in mind that the expulsion of the water taken for solution is not always accomplished with equal facility, because water has different degrees of chemical affinity for the substance dissolved. Thus, if a solution of sulphuric acid, which mixes with water in all proportions, be heated, it will be found that very different degrees of heat are required to expel the water. When it is in a large excess,[77] water is given off at a temperature slightly above 100°, but if it be in but a small proportion there is such an affinity between it and the sulphuric acid that at 120°, 150°, 200°, and even at 300°, water is still retained by the sulphuric acid. The bond between the remaining quantity of water and the sulphuric acid is evidently stronger than the bond between the sulphuric acid and the excess of water. The force acting in solutions is consequently of different intensity, starting from so feeble an attraction that the properties of water—as, for instance, its power of evaporation—are but very little changed, and ending with cases of strong attraction between the water and the substance dissolved in or chemically combined with it. In consideration of the very important significance of the phenomena, and of the cases of the breaking up of solutions with separation of water or of the substance dissolved from them, we shall further discuss them separately, after[78] having acquainted ourselves with certain peculiarities of the solution of gases and of solid bodies.

The solubility of gases, which is usually measured by the volume of gas[29] (at 0° and 760 mm. pressure) per 100 volumes of water, varies not only with the nature of the gas (and also of the solvent), and with the temperature, but also with the pressure, because gases themselves change their volume considerably with the pressure. As might be expected, (1) gases which are easily liquefied (by pressure and cold) are more soluble than those which are liquefied with difficulty. Thus, in 100 volumes of water only two volumes of hydrogen dissolve at 0° and 760 mm., three volumes of carbonic oxide, four volumes of oxygen, &c., for these are gases which are liquefied with difficulty; whilst there dissolve 180 volumes of carbonic anhydride, 130 of nitrous oxide, and 437 of sulphurous anhydride, for these are gases which are rather easily liquefied. (2) The solubility of a gas is diminished by heating, which is easily intelligible from what has been said previously—the elasticity of a gas becomes greater, it is removed further from a liquid state. Thus 100 volumes of water at 0° dissolve 2·5 volumes of air, and at 20° only 1·7 volume. For this reason cold water, when brought into a warm room, parts with a portion of the gas dissolved in it.[30] (3) The quantity of the gas dissolved varies directly with the pressure. This rule is called the *law of Henry and Dalton*, and is applicable to those gases which are little soluble in water. Therefore a gas is separated from its solution in water in a vacuum, and water saturated with a gas under great pressure parts with it if the pressure[79] be diminished. Thus many mineral springs are saturated underground with carbonic anhydride under the great pressure of the column of water above them. On coming to the surface, the water of these springs boils and foams on giving up the excess of dissolved gas. Sparkling wines and aërated waters are saturated under pressure with the same gas. They hold the gas so long as they are in a well-corked vessel. When the cork is removed and the liquid comes in contact with air at a lower pressure, part of the gas, unable to remain in solution at a lower pressure, is separated as froth with the hissing sound familiar to all. It must be remarked that the law of Henry and Dalton belongs to the class of *approximate laws*, like the laws of gases (Gay-Lussac's and Mariotte's) and many others—that is, it expresses only a portion of a complex phenomenon, the limit towards which the phenomenon aims. The matter is rendered complicated from the influence of the degree of solubility and of affinity of the dissolved gas for water. Gases which are little soluble—for instance, hydrogen, oxygen, and nitrogen—follow the law of Henry and Dalton the most closely. Carbonic anhydride exhibits a decided deviation from the law, as is seen from the determinations of Wroblewski (1882). He showed that at 0° a cubic centimetre of water absorbs 1·8 cubic centimetre of the gas under a pressure of one atmosphere; under 10 atmospheres, 16 cubic centimetres (and not 18, as it should be according to the law); under 20 atmospheres,[80] 26·6 cubic centimetres (instead of 36), and under 30 atmospheres, 33·7 cubic centimetres.[31] However, as the researches of Sechenoff show, the absorption of carbonic anhydride within certain limits of change of pressure, and at the ordinary temperature, by water—and even by solutions of salts which are not chemically changed by it, or do not form compounds with it—very closely follows the law of Henry and Dalton, so that the chemical bond between this gas and water is so feeble that the breaking up of the solution with separation of the gas is accomplished by a decrease of pressure alone.[32] The case is different if a considerable affinity exists between the dissolved gas and water. Then it might even be expected that the gas would not be entirely separated from water in a vacuum, as should be the case with gases according to the law of Henry and Dalton. Such gases—and, in general, all those which are very soluble—exhibit a distinct deviation from the law of Henry and Dalton. As examples, ammonia and hydrochloric acid gas may be taken. The former is separated by boiling and decrease of pressure, while the latter is not, but they both deviate distinctly from the law.

Pressure in mm. of mercury	Ammonia dissolved in 100 grams of water at 0°	Hydrochloric acid gas dissolved in 100 grams of water at 0°
	Grams	Grams
100	28·0	65·7
500	69·2	78·2
1,000	112·6	85·6
1,500	165·6	—

It will be remarked, for instance, from this table that whilst the[81] pressure increased 10 times, the solubility of ammonia only increased 4½ times.

A number of examples of such cases of the absorption of gases by liquids might be cited which do not in any way, even approximately, agree with the laws of solubility. Thus, for instance, carbonic anhydride is absorbed by a solution of caustic potash in water, and if sufficient caustic potash be present it is not separated from the solution by a decrease of pressure. This is a case of more intimate chemical combination. A correlation less completely studied, but similar and clearly chemical, appears in certain cases of the solution of gases in water, and we shall afterwards find an example of this in the solution of hydrogen iodide; but we will first stop to consider a remarkable application of the law of Henry and Dalton[33] in the case of the solution of a mixture of two gases, and this we must do all the more because the phenomena which there take place cannot be foreseen without a clear theoretical representation of the nature of gases.[34]

[82]

The law of partial pressures is as follows:—The solubility of gases in intermixture with each other does not depend on the influence of the total pressure acting on the mixture, but on the influence of that portion of the total pressure which is due to the volume of each given gas in the mixture. Thus, for instance, if oxygen and carbonic anhydride were mixed in equal volumes and exerted a pressure of 760 millimetres, then water would dissolve so much of each of these gases as would be dissolved if each separately exerted a pressure of half an atmosphere, and in this case, at 0° one cubic centimetre of water would dissolve 0·02 cubic centimetre of oxygen and 0·90 cubic centimetre of carbonic anhydride. If the pressure of a gaseous mixture equals h, and in n volumes of the mixture there be a volumes of a given gas,[83] then its solution will proceed as though this gas were dissolved under a pressure $h \times a \boxed{n}$. That portion of the pressure under influence of which the solution proceeds is termed the 'partial' pressure.

In order to clearly understand the cause of the law of partial pressures, an explanation must be given of the fundamental properties of gases. Gases are elastic and disperse in all directions. We are led from what we know of gases to the assumption that these fundamental properties of gases are due to a rapid progressive motion, in all directions, which is proper to their smallest particles (molecules).[35] These molecules in impinging against an obstacle produce a pressure. The greater the number of molecules impinging against an obstacle in a given time, the greater the pressure. The pressure of a separate gas or of a gaseous mixture depends on the sum of the pressures of all the molecules, on the number of blows in a unit of time on a unit of surface, and on the mass and velocity (or the *vis viva*) of the impinging molecules. The nature of the different molecules is of no account; the obstacle is acted on by a pressure due to the sum of their *vis viva*. But, in a chemical action such as the solution of gases, the nature of the impinging molecules plays, on the contrary, the most important part. In impinging against a liquid, a portion of the gas enters into the liquid itself, and is held by it so long as other gaseous molecules impinge against the liquid—exert a pressure on it. As regards the solubility of a given gas, for the number of blows it makes on the surface of a liquid, it is immaterial whether other molecules of gases[84] impinge side by side with it or not. Hence, the solubility of a given gas will be proportional, not to the total pressure of a gaseous mixture, but to that portion of it which is due to the given gas separately. Moreover, the saturation of a liquid by a gas depends on the fact that the molecules of gases that have entered into a liquid do not remain at rest in it, although they enter in a harmonious kind of motion with the molecules of the liquid, and therefore they throw themselves off from the surface of the liquid (just like its vapour if the liquid be volatile). If in a unit of time an equal number of molecules penetrate into (leap into) a liquid and leave (or leap out of) a liquid, it is saturated. It is a case of mobile equilibrium, and not of rest. Therefore, if the pressure be diminished, the number of molecules departing from the liquid will exceed the number of molecules entering into the liquid, and a fresh state of mobile equilibrium only takes place under a fresh equality of the number of molecules departing from and entering into the liquid. In this manner the main features of the solution are explained, and furthermore of that special (chemical) attraction (penetration and harmonious motion) of a gas for a liquid, which determines both the measure of solubility and the degree of stability of the solution produced.

The consequences of the law of partial pressures are exceedingly numerous and important. All liquids in nature are in contact with the atmosphere, which, as we shall afterwards see more fully, consists of an intermixture of gases, chiefly four in number—oxygen, nitrogen, carbonic anhydride, and aqueous vapour. 100 volumes of air contain, approximately, 78 volumes of nitrogen, and about 21 volumes of oxygen; the quantity of carbonic anhydride, by volume, does not exceed 0·05. Under ordinary circumstances, the quantity of aqueous vapour is much greater than this, but it varies of course with climatic conditions. We conclude from these numbers that the solution of nitrogen in a liquid in contact with the atmosphere will proceed under a partial pressure of $(78/100) \times 760$ mm. if the atmospheric pressure equal 760 mm.; similarly, under a pressure of 600 mm. of mercury, the solution of oxygen will proceed under a partial pressure of about 160 mm., and the solution of carbonic anhydride only under the very small pressure of 0·4 mm. As, however, the solubility of oxygen in water is twice that of nitrogen, the ratio of O to N dissolved in water will be greater than the ratio in air. It is easy to calculate what quantity of each of the gases will be contained in water, and taking the simplest case we will calculate what quantity of oxygen, nitrogen, and carbonic anhydride will be dissolved from air having the above composition at 0° and 760 mm. pressure. Under a pressure of 760 mm.[85] 1 cubic centimetre of water dissolves 0·0203 cubic centimetre of nitrogen or under the partial pressure of 600 mm. it will dissolve $0·0203 \times 600 \boxed{700}$ or 0·0160 cubic centimetre; of oxygen $0·0411 \times 160 \boxed{760}$, or 0·0086 cubic centimetre; of carbonic anhydride $1·8 \times 0·4 \boxed{760}$ or 0·00095 cubic centimetre: hence, 100 cubic centimetres of water will contain at 0° altogether 2·55 cubic centimetres of atmospheric gases, and 100 volumes of air dissolved in water will contain about 62 p.c. of nitrogen, 34 p.c. of oxygen, and 4 p.c. of carbonic anhydride. The water of rivers, wells, &c. usually contains more carbonic anhydride. This proceeds from the oxidation of organic substances falling into the water. The amount of oxygen, however, dissolved in water appears to be actually about ⅓ the dissolved gases, whilst air contains only ⅕ of it by volume.

According to the law of partial pressures, whatever gas be dissolved in water will be expelled from the solution in an atmosphere of another gas. This depends on the fact that gases dissolved in water escape from it in a vacuum, because the pressure is nil. An atmosphere of another gas acts like a vacuum on a gas dissolved in water. Separation then proceeds, because the molecules of the dissolved gas no longer impinge upon the liquid, are not dissolved in it, and those previously held in solution leave the liquid in virtue of their elasticity.[36] For the[86] same reason a gas may be entirely expelled from a gaseous solution by boiling—at least, in many cases when it does not form particularly stable compounds with water. In fact the surface of the boiling liquid will be occupied by aqueous vapour, and therefore all the pressure acting on the gas will be due to the aqueous vapour. On this account, the partial pressure of the dissolved gas will be very inconsiderable, and this is the sole reason why *a gas separates from a solution on boiling the liquid containing it.* At the boiling point of water the solubility of gases in water is still sufficiently great for a considerable quantity of a gas to remain in solution. The gas dissolved in the liquid is carried away, together with the aqueous vapour; if boiling be continued for a long time, all the gas will finally be separated.[37]

It is evident that the conception of the partial pressures of gases should be applied not only to the formations of solutions, but also to all cases of chemical action of gases. Especially numerous are its applications to the physiology of respiration, for in these cases it is only the oxygen of the atmosphere that acts.[38]

[87]

The solution of *solids*, whilst depending only in a small measure on the pressure under which solution takes place (because solids and liquids are almost incompressible), is very clearly dependent on the temperature. In the great majority of cases the solubility of solids in water increases with the temperature; and further, the rapidity of solution increases also. The latter is determined by the rapidity of diffusion of the solution formed into the remainder of the water. The solution of a solid in water, although it is as with gases, a physical passage into a liquid state, is determined, however, by its chemical affinity for water; this is clearly shown from the fact that in solution there occurs a diminution in volume, a change in the boiling point of water, a change in the tension of its vapour, in the freezing point, and in many similar properties. If solution were a physical, and not a chemical, phenomenon, it would naturally be accompanied by an increase and not by a diminution of volume, because generally in melting a solid increases in volume (its density diminishes). *Contraction* is the usual phenomenon accompanying solution and takes place even in the addition of solutions to water,[39] and in the solution of liquids in water,[40] just as happens in the combination of substances when[88] evidently new substances are produced.[41] The contraction which takes place in solution is, however, very small, a fact which depends on the small compressibility of solids and liquids, and on the insignificance of the compressing force acting in solution.[42] The change of volume which takes place in the solution of solids and liquids, or the alteration in specific gravity[43] corresponding with it, depends on peculiarities of the dissolving substances, and of water, and, in the majority of cases, is not proportional to the quantity of the substance dissolved,[44] showing the[89] existence of a chemical force between the solvent and the substance dissolved which is of the same nature as in all other forms of chemical reaction.[45]

The feeble development of the chemical affinities acting in solutions of solids becomes evident from those multifarious methods by which[90] *their solutions are decomposed*, whether they be saturated or not. On heating (absorption of heat), on cooling, and by internal forces alone, aqueous solutions in many cases separate into their components or their definite compounds with water. The water contained in solutions is removed from them as vapour, or, by freezing, in the form of ice,[46] but the *tension of the vapour of water*[47] held in solution is less than that of water in a free state, and the *temperature of the formation of ice* from solutions is lower than 0°. Further, both the diminution of vapour tension and the lowering of the freezing point proceed, in dilute solutions, almost in proportion to the amount of a substance dissolved.[48] Thus, if[91] per 100 grams of water there be in solution 1, 5, 10 grams of common salt (NaCl), then at 100° the vapour tension of the solutions decreases by 4, 21, 43 mm. of the barometric column, against 760 mm., or the vapour tension of water, whilst the freezing points are -0·58°, -2·91°, and -6·10° respectively. The above figures[49] are almost proportional[92] [93] to the amounts of salt in solution (1, 5, and 10 per 100 of water). Furthermore, it has been shown by experiment that the ratio of the diminution of vapour tension to the vapour tension of water at different temperatures in a given solution is an almost constant quantity,[50] and that for every (dilute) solution the ratio between the diminution of vapour tension and of the freezing point is also a tolerably constant quantity.[51]

[94]

The diminution of the vapour tension of solutions explains the rise in boiling point due to the solution of solid non-volatile bodies in water. The temperature of a vapour is the same as that of the solution from which it is generated, and therefore it follows that the aqueous vapour given off from a solution will be superheated. A saturated solution of common salt boils at 108·4°, a solution of 335 parts of nitre in 100 parts of water at 115·9°, and a solution of 325 parts of potassium chloride in 100 parts of water at 179°, if the temperature of ebullition be determined by immersing the thermometer bulb in the liquid itself. This is another proof of the bond which exists between water and the substance dissolved. And this bond is seen still more clearly in those cases (for example, in the solution of nitric or formic acid in water) where the solution boils at a higher temperature than either water or the volatile substance dissolved in it. For this reason the solutions of certain gases—for instance, hydriodic or hydrochloric acid—boil above 100°.

The separation of ice from solutions[52] explains both the phenomenon, well known to sailors, that the ice formed from salt water gives fresh water, and also the fact that by freezing, just as by evaporation, a solution is obtained which is richer in salts than before. This is taken advantage of in cold countries for obtaining a liquor from sea water, which is then evaporated for the extraction of salt.

On the removal of part of the water from a solution (by evaporation or the separation of ice), a saturated solution should be obtained, and then the solid substance dissolved should separate out. Solutions saturated at a certain temperature should also separate out a corresponding portion of the substance dissolved if they be reduced, by cooling,[53] to a temperature at which the water can no longer hold the former quantity of the substance in solution. If this separation, by cooling a saturated[95] solution or by evaporation, take place slowly, *crystals* of the substance dissolved are in many cases formed; and this is the method by which crystals of soluble salts are usually obtained. Certain solids very easily separate out from their solutions in perfectly formed crystals, which may attain very large dimensions. Such are nickel sulphate, alum, sodium carbonate, chrome-alum, copper sulphate, potassium ferricyanide, and a whole series of other salts. The most remarkable circumstance in this is that many solids in separating out from an aqueous solution retain a portion of water, forming crystallised solid substances which contain water. A portion of the water previously in the solution remains in the separated crystals. The water which is thus retained is called the *water of crystallisation*. Alum, copper sulphate, Glauber's salt, and magnesium sulphate contain such water, but neither sal-ammoniac, table salt, nitre, potassium chlorate, silver nitrate, nor sugar, contains any water of crystallisation. One and the same substance may separate out from a solution with or without water of crystallisation, according to the temperature at which the crystals are formed. Thus common salt in crystallising from its solution in water at the ordinary or at a higher temperature does not contain water of crystallisation. But if its separation from the solution takes place at a low temperature, namely below -5°, then the crystals contain 38 parts of water in 100 parts. Crystals of the same substance which separate out at different temperatures may contain different amounts of water of crystallisation. This proves to us that a solid dissolved in water may form various compounds with it, differing in their properties and composition, and capable of appearing in a solid separate form like many ordinary definite compounds. This is indicated by the numerous properties and phenomena connected with solutions, and gives reason for thinking that there exist in solutions themselves such compounds of the substance dissolved, and the solvent or compounds similar to them, only in a liquid partly decomposed form. Even the *colour of solutions* may often confirm this opinion. Copper sulphate forms crystals having a blue colour and containing water of crystallisation. If the water of crystallisation be removed by heating the crystals to redness, a colourless anhydrous substance is obtained (a white powder). From this it may be seen that the blue colour belongs to the compound of the copper salt with water. Solutions of copper sulphate are all blue, and consequently they contain a compound similar to the compound formed by[96] the salt with its water of crystallisation. Crystals of cobalt chloride when dissolved in an anhydrous liquid—like alcohol, for instance—give a blue solution, but when they are dissolved in water a red solution is obtained. Crystals from the aqueous solution, according to Professor Potilitzin, contain six times as much water ($CoCl_2,6H_2O$) for a given weight of the salt, as those violet crystals ($CoCl_2,H_2O$) which are formed by the evaporation of an alcoholic solution.

That solutions contain particular compounds with water is further shown by the phenomena of supersaturated solutions, of so-called cryohydrates, of solutions of certain acids having constant boiling points, and the properties of compounds containing water of crystallisation whose data it is indispensable to keep in view in the consideration of solutions.

Supersaturated solutions exhibit the following phenomena:—On the refrigeration of a saturated solution of certain salts,[54] if the liquid be brought under certain conditions, the excess of the solid may sometimes remain in solution and not separate out. A great number of substances, and more especially sodium sulphate, Na_2SO_4, or Glauber's salt, easily form supersaturated solutions. If boiling water be saturated with this salt, and the solution be poured off from any remaining undissolved salt, and, the boiling being still continued, the vessel holding the solution be well closed by cotton wool, or by fusing up the vessel, or by covering the solution with a layer of oil, then it will he found that this saturated solution does not separate out any Glauber's salt whatever on cooling down to the ordinary or even to a much lower temperature; although without the above precautions a salt separates out on cooling, in the form of crystals, which contain $Na_2SO_4,10H_2O$—that is, 180 parts of water for 142 parts of anhydrous salt. The supersaturated solution may be moved about or shaken inside the vessel holding it, and no crystallisation will take place; the salt remains in the solution in as large an amount as at a higher temperature. If the vessel holding the supersaturated solution be opened and a crystal of Glauber's salt be thrown in, crystallisation suddenly takes place.[55] A considerable rise in temperature is noticed during this[97] rapid separation of crystals, which is due to the fact that the salt, previously in a liquid state, passes into a solid state. This bears some resemblance to the fact that water maybe cooled below 0° (even to -10°) if it be left at rest, under certain circumstances, and evolves heat in suddenly crystallising. Although from this point of view there is a resemblance, yet in reality the phenomenon of supersaturated solutions is much more complicated. Thus, on cooling, a saturated solution of Glauber's salt deposits crystals containing $Na_2SO_4,7H_2O,$[56] or 126 parts[98] of water per 142 parts of anhydrous salt, and not 180 parts of water, as in the above-mentioned salt. The crystals containing $7H_2O$ are distinguished for their instability; if they stand in contact not only with crystals of $Na_2SO_4,10H_2O$, but with many other substances, they immediately become opaque, forming a mixture of anhydrous and deca-hydrated salts. It is evident that between water and a soluble substance there may be established different kinds of greater or less stable equilibrium, of which solutions form a particular case.[57]

[99]

Solutions of salts on refrigeration below 0° deposit ice or crystals (which then frequently contain water of crystallisation) of the salt dissolved, and on reaching a certain degree of concentration they solidify in their entire mass. These solidified masses are termed *cryohydrates*. My researches on solutions of common salt (1868) showed that its solution solidifies when it reaches a composition $NaCl + 10H_2O$ (180 parts of water per 58·5 parts of salt), which takes place at about -23°. The solidified solution melts at the same temperature, and both the portion melted and the remainder preserve the above composition. Guthrie (1874–1876) obtained the cryohydrates of many salts, and he showed that certain of them are formed like the above at comparatively low temperatures, whilst others (for instance, corrosive sublimate, alums, potassium chlorate, and various colloids) are formed on a slight cooling, to -2° or even before.[58] In the case of common salt, the cryohydrate with 10 molecules of water, and in the case of sodium nitrate, the cryohydrate[59] with 7 molecules of water (*i.e.* 126 parts of water per 85 of salt) should be accepted as established substances, capable of passing from a solid to a liquid state and conversely; and therefore it may be thought that in cryohydrates we have solutions which are not only undecomposable by cold, but also have a definite composition which would present a fresh case of definite equilibrium between the solvent and the substance dissolved.

The formation of definite but unstable compounds in the process of[100] solution becomes evident from the phenomena of a marked decrease of vapour tension, or from the rise of the temperature of ebullition which occurs in the solution of certain volatile liquids and gases in water. As an example, we will take hydriodic acid, HI, a gas which liquefies, giving a liquid which boils at -20°. A solution of it containing 57 p.c. of hydriodic acid is distinguished by the fact that if it be heated the hydriodic acid volatilises together with the water in the same proportions as they occur in the solution, therefore such a solution may be distilled unchanged. The solution boils at a higher temperature than water, at 127°. A portion of the physical properties of the gas and water have in this case already disappeared—a new substance is formed, which has its definite boiling point. To put it more correctly, this is not the temperature of ebullition, but the temperature at which the compound formed decomposes, forming the vapours of the products of dissociation, which, on cooling, re-combine. Should a less amount of hydriodic acid be dissolved in water than the above, then, on heating such a solution, water only at first distils over, until the solution attains the above-mentioned composition; it will then distil over unaltered. If more hydriodic acid be passed into such a solution a fresh quantity of the gas will dissolve, but it passes off with great ease, like air from water. It must not, however, be thought that those forces which determine the formation of ordinary gaseous solutions play no part whatever in the formation of a solution having a definite boiling point; that they do react is shown from the fact that such constant gaseous solutions vary in their composition under different pressures.[60] It is not, therefore, at every, but only at the ordinary,[101] atmospheric pressure that a constant boiling solution of hydriodic acid will contain 57 p.c. of the gas. At another pressure the proportion of water and hydriodic acid will be different. It varies, however, judging from observations made by Roscoe, very little for considerable variations of pressure. This variation in composition directly indicates that pressure exerts an influence on the formation of unstable chemical compounds which are easily dissociated (with formation of a gas), just as it influences the solution of gases, only the latter is influenced to a more considerable degree than the former.[61] Hydrochloric, nitric, and other acids form *solutions having definite boiling points*, like that of hydriodic acid. They show further the common property, if containing but a small proportion of water, that they *fume in air*. Strong solutions of nitric, hydrochloric, hydriodic, and other gases are even termed[102] 'fuming acids.' The fuming liquids contain a definite compound whose temperature of ebullition (decomposition) is higher than 100°, and contain also an excess of the volatile substance dissolved, which exhibits a capacity to combine with water and form a hydrate, whose vapour tension is less than that of aqueous vapour. On evaporating in air, this dissolved substance meets the atmospheric moisture and forms a visible vapour (fumes) with it, which consists of the above-mentioned compound. The attraction or affinity which binds, for instance, hydriodic acid with water is evinced not only in the evolution of heat and the diminution of vapour tension (rise of boiling point), but also in many purely chemical relations. Thus hydriodic acid is produced from iodine and hydrogen sulphide in the presence of water, but unless water is present this reaction does not take place.[62]

Many compounds containing water of crystallisation are solid substances (when melted they are already solutions—*i.e.* liquids); furthermore, they are capable of being formed from solutions, like ice or aqueous vapour. They may be called *crystallo-hydrates*. Inasmuch as the direct presence of ice or aqueous vapour cannot be admitted in solutions (for these are liquids), although the presence of water may be, so also there is no basis for acknowledging the presence in solutions of crystallo-hydrates, although they are obtained from solutions as such.[63] It is evident that such substances present one of the many forms of equilibrium between water and a substance dissolved in it. This form, however, reminds one, in all respects, of solutions—that is, aqueous compounds which are more or less easily decomposed, with separation of water and the formation of a less aqueous or an anhydrous compound. In fact, there are not a few crystals containing water which lose a part of their water at the ordinary temperature. Of such a kind, for instance, are the crystals of soda, or sodium carbonate, which, when separated from an aqueous solution at the ordinary temperature, are quite transparent; but when left exposed to air, lose[103] a portion of their water, becoming opaque, and, in the process, lose their crystalline appearance, although preserving their original form. This process of the separation of water at the ordinary temperature is termed the *efflorescence* of crystals. Efflorescence takes place more rapidly under the receiver of an air pump, and especially at a gentle heat. This breaking up of a crystal is dissociation at the ordinary temperature. Solutions are decomposed in exactly the same manner.[64] The tension of the aqueous vapour which is given off from crystallo-hydrates is naturally, as with solutions, less than the vapour tension of water itself[65] at the same temperature, and therefore many anhydrous salts which are capable of combining with water absorb aqueous vapour[104] from moist air; that is, they act like a cold body on which water is deposited from steam. It is on this that the desiccation of gases is based, and it must further be remarked in this respect that certain substances—for instance, potassium carbonate (K_2CO_3) and calcium chloride ($CaCl_2$)—not only absorb the water necessary for the formation of a solid crystalline compound, but also give solutions, or *deliquesce*, as it is termed, in moist air. Many crystals do not effloresce in the least at the ordinary temperature; for example, copper sulphate, which may be preserved for an indefinite length of time without efflorescing, but when placed under the receiver of an air pump, if efflorescence be once started, it goes on at the ordinary temperature. The temperature at which the complete separation of water from crystals takes place varies considerably, not only for different substances, but also for different portions of the contained water. Very often the temperature at which dissociation begins is very much higher than the boiling point of water. So, for example, copper sulphate, which contains 36 p.c. of water, gives up 28·8 p.c. at 100°, and the remaining quantity, namely 7·2 p.c., only at 240°. Alum, out of the 45·5 p.c. of water which it contains, gives up 18·9 p.c. at 100°, 17·7 p.c. at 120°, 7·7 p.c. at 180°, and 1 p.c. at 280°; it only loses the last quantity (1 p.c.) at its temperature of decomposition. These examples clearly show that the annexation of water of crystallisation is accompanied by a rather profound, although, in comparison with instances which we shall consider later, still inconsiderable, change of its properties. In certain cases the water of crystallisation is only given off when the solid form of the substance is destroyed: when the crystals melt on heating. The crystals are then said *to melt in their water of crystallisation*. Further, after the separation of the water, a solid substance remains behind, so that by further heating it acquires a solid form. This is seen most clearly in crystals of sugar of lead or lead acetate, which melt in their water of crystallisation at a temperature of 56·25°, and in so doing begin to lose water. On reaching a temperature of 100° the sugar of lead solidifies, having lost all its water; and then at a temperature of 280°, the anhydrous and solidified salt again melts.[65 bis]

It is most important to recognise in respect to the water of crystallisation that its ratio to the quantity of the substance with which it is combined is always a constant quantity. However often we may[105] prepare copper sulphate, we shall always find 36·14 p.c. of water in its crystals, and these crystals always lose four-fifths of their water at 100°, and one-fifth of the whole amount of the water contained remains in the crystals at 100°, and is only expelled from them at a temperature of about 240°. What has been said about crystals of copper sulphate refers also to crystals of every other substance, which contain water of crystallisation. It is impossible in any of these cases to increase either the relative proportion of the salt or of the water, without changing the homogeneity of the substance. If once a portion of the water be lost—for instance, if once efflorescence takes place—a mixture is obtained, and not a homogeneous substance, namely a mixture of a substance deprived of water with a substance which has not yet lost water—*i.e.* decomposition has already commenced. This constant ratio is an example of the fact that in chemical compounds the quantity of the component parts is quite definite; that is, it is an example of the so-called *definite chemical compounds*. They may be distinguished from solutions, and from all other so-called indefinite chemical compounds, in that at least one, and sometimes both, of the component parts may be added in a large quantity to an indefinite chemical compound, without destroying its homogeneity, as in solutions, whilst it is impossible to add any one of the component parts to a definite chemical compound without destroying the homogeneity of the entire mass. Definite chemical compounds only decompose at a certain rise in temperature; on a lowering in temperature they do not, at least with very few exceptions, yield their components like solutions which form ice or compounds with water of crystallisation. This leads to the assumption that solutions contain water as water,[66] although it may sometimes be in a very small quantity. Therefore solutions which are capable of solidifying completely (for instance, crystallo-hydrates capable of melting) such as the compound of $84\frac{1}{2}$ parts of sulphuric acid, H_2SO_4, with $15\frac{1}{2}$ parts of water, H_2O, or H_2SO_4,H_2O (or H_4SO_5), appear as true definite chemical compounds. If, then, we imagine such a definite compound in a liquid state, and admit that it partially decomposes in this state, separating water—not as ice or vapour (for then the system would be heterogeneous, including substances in different physical states), but in a liquid form, when the system will be homogeneous—we[106] shall form an idea of a solution as an unstable, dissociating fluid state of equilibrium between water and the substance dissolved. Moreover, it should be remarked that, judging by experiment, many substances give with water not one but *diverse* compounds,[67] which is seen in the capacity of one substance to form with water many various *crystallo-hydrates*, or compounds with water of crystallisation, showing diverse and independent properties. From these considerations, *solutions*[68] *may be regarded as fluid, unstable, definite chemical compounds in a state of dissociation.*[69]

[107]

In regarding solutions from this point of view they come under the head of those definite compounds with which chemistry is mainly concerned.[70]

We saw above that copper sulphate loses four-fifths of its water at 100° and the remainder at 240°. This means that there are two definite[108] compounds of water with the anhydrous salt. Washing soda or carbonate of sodium, Na_2CO_3 separates out as crystals, $Na_2CO_3,10H_2O$, containing $62\cdot9$ p.c. of water by weight, from its solutions at the ordinary temperature. When a solution of the same salt deposits crystals at a low temperature, about -20°, then these crystals contain $71\cdot8$ parts of water per $28\cdot2$ parts of anhydrous salt. Further, the crystals are obtained together with ice, and are left behind when it melts. If ordinary soda, with $62\cdot9$ p.c. of water, be cautiously melted in its own water of crystallisation, there remains a salt, in a solid state, containing only $14\cdot5$ p.c. of water, and a liquid is obtained which contains the solution of a salt which separates out crystals at 34°, which contain 46 p.c. of water and do not effloresce in air. Lastly, if a supersaturated solution of soda be prepared, then at temperatures below 8° it deposits crystals containing $54\cdot3$ p.c. of water. Thus as many as five compounds of anhydrous soda with water are known; and they are dissimilar in their properties and crystalline form, and even in their solubility. It is to be observed that the greatest amount of water in the crystals corresponds with a temperature of -20°, and the smallest to the highest temperature. There is apparently no relation between the above quantities of water and the salts, but this is only because in each case the amount of water and anhydrous salt was given in percentages; but if it be calculated for one and the same quantity of anhydrous salt, or of water, a great regularity will be observed in the amounts of the component parts in all these compounds. It appears that for 106 parts of anhydrous salt in the crystals separated out at -20° there are 270 parts of water; in the crystals obtained at 15° there are 180 parts of water; in the crystals obtained from a supersaturated solution 126 parts, in the crystals which separate out at 34°, 90 parts, and the crystals with the smallest amount of water, 18 parts. On comparing these quantities of water it may easily be seen that they are in simple proportion to each other, for they are all divisible by 18, and are in the ratio 15 : 10 : 7 : 5 : 1. Naturally, direct experiment, however carefully it be conducted, is hampered with errors, but taking these unavoidable experimental errors into consideration, it will be seen that for a given quantity of an anhydrous substance there occur, in several of its compounds with water, quantities of water which are in very simple multiple proportion. This is observed in, and is common[109] to, all definite chemical compounds. This rule is called *the law of multiple proportions*. It was discovered by Dalton, and will be evolved in further detail subsequently in this work. For the present we will only state that the law of definite composition enables the composition of substances to be expressed by formulæ, and the law of multiple proportions permits the application of whole numbers as coefficients of the symbols of the elements in these formulæ. Thus the formula $Na_2CO_3,10H_2O$ shows directly that in this crystallo-hydrate there are 180 parts of water to 106 parts by weight of the anhydrous salt, because the formula of soda, Na_2CO_3, directly answers to a weight of 106, and the formula of water to 18 parts, by weight, which are here taken 10 times.

In the above examples of the combinations of water, we saw the gradually increasing intensity of the bond between water and a substance with which it forms a homogeneous compound. There is a series of such compounds with water, in which the water is held with very great force, and is only given up at a very high temperature, and sometimes cannot be separated by any degree of heat without the entire decomposition of the substance. In these compounds there is generally no outward sign whatever of their containing water. A perfectly new substance is formed from an anhydrous substance and water, in which sometimes the properties of neither one nor the other substance are observable. In the majority of cases, a considerable amount of heat is evolved in the formation of such compounds with water. Sometimes the heat evolved is so intense that a red heat is produced and light is emitted. It is hardly to be wondered at, after this, that stable compounds are formed by such a combination. Their decomposition requires great heat; a large amount of work is necessary to separate them into their component parts. All such compounds are definite, and, generally, completely and clearly definite. The number of such definite compounds with water or *hydrates*, in the narrow sense of the word, is generally inconsiderable for each anhydrous substance; in the greater number of cases, there is formed only one such combination of a substance with water, one hydrate, having so great a stability. The water contained in these compounds is often called *water of constitution—i.e.* water which enters into the structure or composition of the given substance. By this it is desired to express, that in other cases the molecules of water are, as it were, separate from the molecules of that substance with which it is combined. It is supposed that in the formation of hydrates this water, even in the smallest particles, forms one complete whole with the anhydrous substance. Many examples of the formation of such hydrates might be cited. The most familiar[110] example in practice is the hydrate of lime, or so-called 'slaked' lime. Lime is prepared by burning limestone, by which the carbonic anhydride is expelled from it, and there remains a white stony mass, which is dense, compact, and rather tenacious. Lime is usually sold in this form, and bears the name of 'quick' or 'unslaked' lime. If water be poured over such lime, a great rise in temperature is remarked either directly, or after a certain time. The whole mass becomes hot, part of the water is evaporated, the stony mass in absorbing water crumbles into powder, and if the water be taken in sufficient quantity and the lime be pure and well burnt, not a particle of the original stony mass is left—it all crumbles into powder. If the water be in excess, then naturally a portion of it remains and forms a solution. This process is called 'slaking' lime. Slaked lime is used in practice in intermixture with sand as mortar. Slaked lime is a definite hydrate of lime. If it is dried at 100° it retains 24·3 p.c. of water. This water can only be expelled at a temperature above 400°, and then quicklime is re-obtained. The heat evolved in the combination of lime with water is so intense that it can set fire to wood, sulphur, gunpowder, &c. Even on mixing lime with ice the temperature rises to 100°. If lime be moistened with a small quantity of water in the dark, a luminous effect is observed. But, nevertheless, water may still be separated from this hydrate.[71] If phosphorus be burnt in dry air, a white substance called 'phosphoric anhydride' is obtained. It combines with water with such energy, that the experiment must be conducted with great caution. A red heat is produced in the formation of the compound, and it is impossible to separate the water from the resultant hydrate at any temperature. The hydrate formed by phosphoric anhydride is a substance which is totally undecomposable into its original component parts by the action of heat. Almost as energetic a combination occurs when sulphuric anhydride, SO_3, combines with water, forming its hydrate, sulphuric acid, H_2SO_4. In both cases definite compounds are produced, but the latter substance, as a liquid, and capable of decomposition by heat, forms an evident link with solutions. If 80 parts of sulphuric anhydride retain 18 parts of water, this water cannot be separated from the anhydride, even at a temperature of 300°. It is only by the addition of phosphoric anhydride, or by a series of chemical transformations, that this water can be separated from its compound with sulphuric anhydride. Oil of vitriol, or sulphuric acid, is such a compound.[111] If a larger proportion of water be taken, it will combine with the H_2SO_4; for instance, if 36 parts of water per 80 parts of sulphuric anhydride be taken, a compound is formed which crystallises in the cold, and melts at +8°, whilst oil of vitriol does not solidify even at -30°. If still more water be taken, the oil of vitriol will dissolve in the remaining quantity of water. An evolution of heat takes place, not only on the addition of the water of constitution, but in a less degree on further additions of water.[72] And therefore there is no distinct boundary, but only a gradual transition, between those chemical phenomena which are expressed in the formation of solutions and those which take place in the formation of the most stable hydrates.[73]

[112]

We have thus considered many aspects and degrees of combination of various substances with water, or instances of the compounds of water, when it and other substances form new homogeneous substances, which in this case will evidently be complex—*i.e.* made up of different substances— and although they are homogeneous, yet it must be admitted that in them there exist those component parts which entered into their composition, inasmuch as these parts may be re-obtained from them. It must not be imagined that water really exists in hydrate of lime, any more than that ice or steam exists in water. When we say that water occurs in the composition of a certain hydrate, we only wish to point out that there are chemical transformations in which it is possible to obtain that hydrate by means of water, and other transformations in which this water may be separated out from the hydrate. This is all simply expressed by the words, that water enters into the composition of this hydrate. If a hydrate be formed by feeble bonds, and be decomposed even at the ordinary temperature, and be a liquid, then the water appears as one of the products of dissociation, and this gives an idea of what solutions are, and forms the fundamental distinction between them and other hydrates in which the water is combined with greater stability.

Footnotes:

[1] In practice, the chemist has to continually deal with gases, and gases are often collected over water; in which case a certain amount of water

passes into vapour, and this vapour mixes with the gases. It is therefore most important that he should be able to calculate the amount of water or of *moisture in air and other gases*. Let us imagine a cylinder standing in a mercury bath, and filled with a dry gas whose volume equals v, temperature $t°$, and pressure or tension h mm. (h millimetres of the column of mercury at 0°). We will introduce water into the cylinder in such a quantity that a small part remains in the liquid state, and consequently that the gas will be saturated with aqueous vapour; the volume of the gas will then increase (if a larger quantity of water be taken some of the gas will he dissolved in it, and the volume may therefore he diminished). We will further suppose that, after the addition of the water, the temperature remains constant; then since the volume increases, the mercury in the cylinder falls, and therefore the pressure as well as the volume is increased. In order to investigate the phenomenon we will artificially increase the pressure, and reduce the volume to the original volume v. Then the pressure or tension will be greater than h, namely $h + f$, which means that by the introduction of aqueous vapour the pressure of the gas is increased. The researches of Dalton, Gay-Lussac, and Regnault showed that this increase is equal to the maximum pressure which is proper to the aqueous vapour at the temperature at which the observation is made. The maximum pressure for all temperatures may be found in the tables made from observations on the pressure of aqueous vapour. The quantity f will be equal to this maximum pressure of aqueous vapour. This may be expressed thus: the maximum tension of aqueous vapour (and of all other vapours) saturating a space in a vacuum or in any gas is the same. This rule is known as *Dalton's law*. Thus we have a volume of dry gas v, under a pressure h, and a volume of moist gas, saturated with vapour, under a pressure $h + f$. The volume v of the dry gas under a pressure $h + f$ occupies, from Boyle's law, a volume $\dfrac{vh}{h + f}$, consequently the volume occupied by the aqueous vapour under the pressure $h + f$ equals $v - \dfrac{vh}{h + f}$, or $\dfrac{vf}{h + f}$. Thus the volumes of the dry gas and of the moisture which occurs in it, at a pressure $h + f$, are in the ratio $f : h$. And, therefore, if the aqueous vapour saturates a space at a pressure n, the volumes of the dry air and of the moisture which is contained in it are in the ratio $(n - f) : f$, where f is the pressure of the vapour according to the tables of vapour tension. Thus, if a volume N of a gas saturated with moisture be measured at a pressure H, then the volume of the gas, when dry, will be equal to $N \dfrac{H - f}{H}$. In fact, the entire volume N must be to the volume of dry gas x as H is to H - f; therefore, $N : x = H : H - f$, from which $x = N \dfrac{H - f}{H}$. Under any other pressure—for instance, 760 mm.—The volume of dry gas will be $\dfrac{xH}{760}$, or $\dfrac{H - f}{760}$, and we thus obtain the following practical rule: If a volume of a gas saturated with aqueous vapour be measured at a pressure H mm., then the volume of dry gas contained in it will be obtained by finding the volume corresponding to the pressure H, less the pressure due to the aqueous vapour at the temperature observed. For example, 37·5 cubic centimetres of air saturated with aqueous vapour were measured at a temperature of 15·3°, and under a pressure of 747·3 mm. of mercury (at 0°). What will be the volume of dry gas at 0° and 760 mm.?

The pressure of aqueous vapour corresponding to 15·3° is equal to 12·9 mm., and therefore the volume of dry gas at 15·3° and 747·3 mm. is equal to $37·5 \times \dfrac{747·3 - 12·9}{747·3}$; at 760 mm. it will be equal to $37·5 \times \dfrac{734·4}{760}$; and at 0° the volume of dry gas will be $37·5 \times \dfrac{734·4}{760} \times \dfrac{273}{273 + 15·3} = 34·31$ c.c.

From this rule may also be calculated what fraction of a volume of gas is occupied by moisture under the ordinary pressure at different temperatures; for instance, at 30° C. $f = 31·5$, consequently 100 volumes of a moist gas or air, at 760 mm., contain a volume of aqueous vapour $100 \times \dfrac{31·5}{760}$, or 4·110; it is also found that at 0° there is contained 0·61 p.c. by volume, at 10° 1·21 p.c., at 20° 2·29 p.c., and at 50° up to 12·11 p.c. From this it may be judged how great an error might be made in the measurement of gases by volume if the moisture were not taken into consideration. From this it is also evident how great are the variations in volume of the atmosphere when it loses or gains aqueous vapour, which again explains a number of atmospheric phenomena (winds, variation of pressure, rainfalls, storms, &c.)

If a gas is not saturated, then it is indispensable that the degree of moisture should be known in order to determine the volume of dry gas from the volume of moist gas. The preceding ratio gives the maximum quantity of water which can be held in a gas, and the degree of moisture shows what fraction of this maximum quantity occurs in a given case, when the vapour does not saturate the space occupied by the gas. Consequently, if the degree of moisture equals 50 p.c.—that is, half the maximum—then the volume of dry gas at 760 mm. is equal to the volume of dry gas at 760 mm. multiplied by $\dfrac{h - 0·5f}{760}$, or, in general, by $\dfrac{h - rf}{760}$ where r is the degree of moisture. Thus, if it is required to measure the volume of a moist gas, it must either be thoroughly dried or quite saturated with moisture, or else the degree of moisture determined. The first and last methods are inconvenient, and therefore recourse is usually had to the second. For this purpose water is introduced into the cylinder holding the gas to be measured; it is left for a certain time so that the gas may become saturated, the precaution being taken that a portion of the water remains in a liquid state; then the volume of the moist gas is determined, from which that of the dry gas may be calculated. In order to find the *weight of the aqueous vapour* in a gas it is necessary to know the weight of a cubic measure at 0° and 760 mm. Knowing that one cubic centimetre of air in these circumstances weighs 0·001293 gram, and that the density of aqueous vapour is 0·62, we find that one cubic centimetre of aqueous vapour at 0° and 760 mm. weighs 0·0008 gram, and at a temperature $t°$ and pressure h the weight of one cubic centimetre will be $0·0008 × h \boxed{760} × 273 \boxed{273 + t}$. We already know that v volumes of a gas at a temperature $t°$ pressure h contain $v × f \boxed{h}$ volumes of aqueous vapour which saturate it, therefore the weight of the aqueous vapour held in v volumes of a gas will be

$$v \text{ x } 0·0008 × f \boxed{760} × 273 \boxed{273 + t}$$

Accordingly, the weight of water which is contained in one volume of a gas depends only on the temperature and not on the pressure. This also signifies that evaporation proceeds to the same extent in air as in a vacuum, or, in general terms (this is *Dalton's law*), vapours and gases diffuse into each other as if into a vacuum. In a given space, at a given temperature, a constant quantity of vapour enters, whatever be the pressure of the gas filling that space.

From this it is clear that if the weight of the vapour contained in a given volume of a gas be known, it is easy to determine the degree of moisture $r = p \boxed{v × 0·0008} × 760 \boxed{h} × 273 + t \boxed{273}$. On the is founded the very exact determination of the degree of moisture of air by the weight of water contained in a given volume. It is easy to calculate from the preceding formula the number of grams of water contained at any pressure in one cubic metre or million cubic centimetres of air saturated with vapour at various temperatures; for instance, at $30° f = 31·5$, hence $p = 29·84$ grams.

The laws of Mariotte, Dalton, and Gay-Lussac, which are here applied to gases and vapours, are not entirely exact, but are approximately true. If they were quite exact, a mixture of several liquids, having a certain vapour pressure, would give vapours of a very high pressure, which is not the case. In fact the pressure of aqueous vapour is slightly less in a gas than in a vacuum, and the weight of aqueous vapour held in a gas is slightly less than it should be according to Dalton's law, as was shown by the experiments of Regnault and others. This means that the tension of the vapour is less in air than in a vacuum. The difference does not, however, exceed 5 per cent. of the total pressure of the vapours. This *decrement in vapour tension* which occurs in the intermixture of vapours and gases, although small, indicates that there is then already, so to speak, a beginning of chemical change. The essence of the matter is that in this case there occurs, as on contact (see preceding footnote), an alteration in the motions of the atoms in the molecules, and therefore also a change in the motion of the molecules themselves.

In the uniform intermixture of air and other gases with aqueous vapour, and in the capacity of water to pass into vapour and form a uniform mixture with air, we may perceive an instance of a physical phenomenon which is analogous to chemical phenomena, forming indeed a transition from one class of phenomena to the other. Between water and dry air there exists a kind of affinity which obliges the water to saturate the air. But such a homogeneous mixture is formed (almost) independently of the nature of the gas in which evaporation takes place; even in a vacuum the phenomenon occurs in exactly the same way as in a gas, and therefore it is not the property of the gas, nor its relation to water, but the property of the water itself, which compels it to evaporate, and therefore in this case chemical affinity is not yet operative—at least its action is not clearly pronounced. That it does, however, play a certain part is seen from the deviation from Dalton's law.

[2] In falling through the atmosphere, water dissolves the gases of the atmosphere, nitric acid, ammonia, organic compounds, salts of sodium, magnesium, and calcium, and mechanically washes out a mixture of dust and microbes which are suspended in the atmosphere. The amount of these and certain other constituents is very variable. Even in the beginning and end of the same rainfall a variation which is often very considerable may be remarked. Thus, for example, Bunsen found that rain collected at the beginning of a shower contained $3 \cdot 7$ grams of ammonia per cubic metre, whilst that collected at the end of the same shower contained only $0 \cdot 64$ gram. The water of the entire shower contained an average of $1 \cdot 47$ gram of ammonia per cubic metre. In the course of a year rain supplies an acre of ground with as much as 5½ kilos of nitrogen in a combined form. Marchand found in one cubic metre of snow water $15 \cdot 63$, and in one cubic metre of rain water $10 \cdot 07$, grams of sodium sulphate. Angus Smith showed that after a thirty hours' fall at Manchester the rain still contained $34 \cdot 3$ grams of salts per cubic metre. A considerable amount of organic matter, namely 25 grams per cubic metre, has been found in rain water. The total amount of solid matter in rain water reaches 50 grams per cubic metre. Rain water generally contains very little carbonic acid, whilst river water contains a considerable quantity of it. In considering the nourishment of plants it is necessary to keep in view the substances which are carried into the soil by rain.

River water, which is accumulated from springs and sources fed by atmospheric water, contains from 50 to 1,600 parts by weight of salts in 1,000,000 parts. The amount of solid matter, per 1,000,000 parts by weight, contained in the chief rivers is as follows:—the Don 124, the Loire 135, the St. Lawrence 170, the Rhone 182, the Dnieper 187, the Danube from 117 to 234, the Rhine from 158 to 317, the Seine from 190 to 432, the Thames at London from 400 to 450, in its upper parts 387, and in its lower parts up to 1,617, the Nile 1,580, the Jordan 1,052. The Neva is characterised by the remarkably small amount of solid matter it contains. From the investigations of Prof. G. K. Trapp, a cubic metre of Neva water contains 32 grams of incombustible and 23 grams of organic matter, or altogether about 55 grams. This is one of the purest waters which is known in rivers. The large amount of impurities in river water, and especially of organic impurity produced by pollution with putrid matter, makes the water of many rivers unfit for use.

The chief part of the soluble substances in river water consists of the calcium salts. 100 parts of the solid residues contain the following amounts of calcium carbonate—from the water of the Loire 53, from the Thames about 50, the Elbe 55, the Vistula 65, the Danube 65, the Rhine from 55 to 75, the Seine 75, the Rhone from 82 to 94. The Neva contains 40 parts of calcium carbonate per 100 parts of saline matter. The considerable amount of calcium carbonate which river water contains is very easily explained from the fact that water which contains carbonic acid in solution easily dissolves calcium carbonate, which occurs all over the earth. Besides calcium carbonate and sulphate, river water contains magnesium, silica, chlorine, sodium, potassium, aluminium, nitric acid, iron and manganese. The presence of salts of phosphoric acid has not yet been determined with exactitude for all rivers, but the presence of nitrates has been proved with certainty in almost all kinds of well-investigated river water. The quantity of calcium phosphate does not exceed 0·4 gram in the water of the Dnieper, and the Don does not contain more than 5 grams. The water of the Seine contains about 15 grams of nitrates, and that of the Rhone about 8 grams. The amount of ammonia is much less; thus in the water of the Rhine about 0·5 gram in June, and 0·2 gram in October; the water of the Seine contains the same amount. This is less than in rain water. Notwithstanding this insignificant quantity, the water of the Rhine alone, which is not so very large a river, carries 16,245 kilograms of ammonia into the ocean every day. The difference between the amount of ammonia in rain and river water depends on the fact that the soil through which the rain water passes is able to retain the ammonia. (Soil can also absorb many other substances, such as phosphoric acid, potassium salts, &c.)

The waters of springs, rivers, wells, and in general of those localities from which it is taken for drinking purposes, may be injurious to health if it contains much organic pollution, the more so as in such water the lower organisms (bacteria) may rapidly develop, and these organisms often serve as the carriers or causes of infectious diseases. For instance, certain pathogenic (disease-producing) bacteria are known to produce typhoid, the Siberian plague, and cholera. Thanks to the work of Pasteur, Metchnikoff,

Koch, and many others, this province of research has made considerable progress. It is possible to investigate the number and properties of the germs in water. In bacteriological researches a gelatinous medium in which the germs can develop and multiply is prepared with gelatin and water, which has previously been heated several times, at intervals, to 100° (it is thus rendered sterile—that is to say, all the germs in it are killed). The water to be investigated is added to this prepared medium in a definite and small quantity (sometimes diluted with sterilised water to facilitate the calculation of the number of germs), it is protected from dust (which contains germs), and is left at rest until whole families of lower organisms are developed from each germ. These families (colonies) are visible to the naked eye (as spots), they may be counted, and by examining them under the microscope and observing the number of organisms they produce, their significance may be determined. The majority of bacteria are harmless, but there are decidedly pathogenic bacteria, whose presence is one of the causes of malady and of the spread of certain diseases. The number of bacteria in one cubic centimetre of water sometimes attains the immense figures of hundreds of thousands and millions. Certain well, spring, and river waters contain very few bacteria, and are free from disease-producing bacteria under ordinary circumstances. By boiling water, the bacteria in it are killed, but the organic matter necessary for their nourishment remains in the water. The best kinds of water for drinking purposes do not contain more than 300 bacteria in a cubic centimetre.

The amount of gases dissolved in river water is much more constant than that of its solid constituents. One litre, or 1,000 c.c., of water contains 40 to 55 c.c. of gas measured at normal temperature and pressure. In winter the amount of gas is greater than in summer or autumn. Assuming that a litre contains 50 c.c. of gases, it may be admitted that these consist, on an average, of 20 vols. of nitrogen, 20 vols of carbonic anhydride (proceeding in all likelihood from the soil and not from the atmosphere), and of 10 vols. of oxygen. If the total amount of gases be less, the constituent gases are still in about the same proportion; in many cases, however, carbonic anhydride predominates. The water of many deep and rapid rivers contains less carbonic anhydride, which shows their rapid formation from atmospheric water, and that they have not succeeded, during a long and slow course, in absorbing a greater quantity of carbonic anhydride. Thus, for instance, the water of the Rhine, near Strasburg, according to Deville, contains 8 c.c. of carbonic anhydride, 16 c.c. of nitrogen, and 7 c.c. of oxygen per litre. From the researches of Prof. M. R. Kapoustin and his pupils, it appears that in determining the quality of a water for drinking purposes, it is most important to investigate the composition of the dissolved gases, more especially oxygen.

[3] *Spring water* is formed from rain water percolating through the soil. Naturally a part of the rain water is evaporated directly from the surface of the earth and from the vegetation on it. It has been shown that out of 100 parts of water falling on the earth only 36 parts flow to the ocean; the remaining 64 are evaporated, or percolate far underground. After flowing underground along some impervious strata, water comes out at the surface in many places as springs, whose temperature is determined by the depth from which the water has flowed. Springs penetrating to a great depth may become considerably heated, and this is why hot mineral springs, with a temperature of up to 30° and higher, are often met with. When a spring water contains substances which endow it with a peculiar taste, and especially if these substances are such as are only found in minute quantities in river and other flowing waters, then the spring water is termed a *mineral water*. Many such waters are employed for medicinal purposes. Mineral waters are classed according to their composition into—(*a*) saline waters, which often contain a large amount of common salt; (*b*) alkaline waters, which contain sodium carbonate; (*c*) bitter waters, which contain magnesia; (*d*) chalybeate waters, which hold iron carbonate in solution; (*e*) aërated waters, which are rich in carbonic anhydride; (*f*) sulphuretted waters, which contain hydrogen sulphide. Sulphuretted waters may be recognised by their smell of rotten eggs, and by their giving a black precipitate with lead salts, and also by their tarnishing silver objects. Aërated waters, which contain an excess of carbonic anhydride, effervesce in the air, have a sharp taste, and redden litmus paper. Saline waters leave a large residue of soluble solid matter on evaporation, and have a salt taste. Chalybeate waters have an inky taste, and are coloured black by an infusion of galls; on being exposed to the air they usually give a brown precipitate. Generally, the character of mineral waters is mixed. In the table below the analyses are given of certain mineral springs which are valued for their medicinal properties. The quantity of the substances is expressed in millionths by weight.

	Calcium salts	Sodium chloride	Sodium sulphate	Sodium carbonate	Potassium iodide and bromide	Other potassium salts	Iron carbonate	Magnesium salts	Silica	Carbonic anhydride	Sulphuretted hydrogen	Total solid contents
I.	1,928	—	152	—	—	24	—	448	152	1,300	80	2,609

II.	816	386	1,239	26	—	43	9	257	46	1,485	—	2,812
III.	1,085	1,430	1,105	—	4	90	—	187	65	1,326	11	3,950
IV.	343	3,783	16	3,431	—	14	—	251	112	2,883	—	7,950
V.	3,406	15,049	—	—	2	—	17	1,587	229	—	76	20,290
VI.	352	3,145	—	95	35	50	1	260	11	20	—	3,970
VII.	308	1,036	2,583	1,261	—	—	4	178	75	—	—	5,451
VIII.	1,726	9,480	—	—	40	120	26	208	40	—	—	11,790
IX.	551	2,040	1,150	999	—	1	30	209	50	2,749	—	4,070
X.	285	558	279	3,813	—	—	7	45	45	2,268	—	5,031
XI.	340	910	Iron and aluminium sulphates: 1,020 / 1,660					940	190	2,550 / 330		Sulphuric and hydrochloric acids

I. Sergieffsky, a sulphur water, Gov. of Samara (temp. 8° C.), analysis by Clause. II. Geléznovodskya water source No. 10, near Patigorsk, Caucasus (temp. 22·5°), analysis by Fritzsche. III. Aleksandroffsky, alkaline-sulphur source, Patigorsk (temp. 46·5°), average of analyses by Herman, Zinin and Fritzsche. IV. Bougountouksky, alkaline source, No. 17, Essentoukah, Caucasus (temp. 21·6°), analysis by Fritzsche. V. Saline water, Staro-Russi,

Gov. of Novgorod, analysis by Nelubin. VI. Water from artesian well at the factory of state papers, St. Petersburg, analysis by Struve. VII. Sprüdel, Carlsbad (temp. 83·7°), analysis by Berzelius. VIII. Kreuznach spring (Elisenquelle), Prussia (temp. 8·8°), analysis by Bauer. IX. Eau de Seltz, Nassau, analysis by Henry. X. Vichy water, France, analysis by Berthier and Puvy. XI. Paramo de Ruiz, New Granada, analysis by Levy; it is distinguished by the amount of free acids.

[4] *Sea water* contains more non-volatile saline constituents than the usual kinds of fresh water. This is explained by the fact that the waters flowing into the sea supply it with salts, and whilst a large quantity of vapour is given off from the surface of the sea, the salts remain behind. Even the specific gravity of sea water differs considerably from that of pure water. It is generally about 1·02, but in this and also in respect of the amount of salts contained, samples of sea water from different localities and from different depths offer rather remarkable variations. It will be sufficient to point out that one cubic metre of water from the undermentioned localities contains the following quantity in grams of solid constituents:—Gulf of Venice, 19,122; Leghorn Harbour 24,312; Mediterranean, near Cetta, 37,665; the Atlantic Ocean from 32,585 to 35,695,; the Pacific Ocean from 35,233 to 34,708. In closed seas which do not communicate, or are in very distant communication, with the ocean, the difference is often still greater. Thus the Caspian Sea contains 6,300 grams; the Black Sea and Baltic 17,700. Common salt forms the chief constituent of the saline matter of sea or ocean water; thus in one cubic metre of sea water there are 25,000–31,000 grams of common salt, 2,600–6,000 grams of magnesium chloride, 1,200–7,000 grams of magnesium sulphate, 1,500–6,000 grams of calcium sulphate, and 10–700 grams of potassium chloride. The small amount of organic matter and of the salts of phosphoric acid in sea water is very remarkable. Sea water (the composition of which is partially discussed in Chapter X.) contains, in addition to salts of common occurrence, a certain and sometimes minute amount of the most varied elements, even gold and silver, and as the mass of water of the oceans is so enormous these 'traces' of rare substances amount to large quantities, so that it may be hoped that in time methods will be found to extract even gold from sea water, which by means of the rivers forms a vast reservoir for the numerous products of the changes taking place on the earth's surface. The works of English, American, German, Russian, Swedish, and other navigators and observers prove that a study of the composition of sea water not only explains much in the history of the earth's life, but also gives the possibility (especially since the researches of C. O. Makaroff of the St. Petersburg Academy) of fixing one's position in the ocean in the absence of other means, for instance, in a fog, or in the dark.

[5] The taste of water is greatly dependent on the quantity of dissolved gases it contains. These gases are given off on boiling, and it is well known that, even when cooled, boiled water has, until it has absorbed gaseous substances from the atmosphere, quite a different taste from fresh water containing a considerable amount of gas. The dissolved gases, especially oxygen and carbonic anhydride, have an important influence on the health. The following instance is very instructive in this respect. The Grenelle artesian well at Paris, when first opened, supplied a water which had an injurious effect on men and animals. It appeared that this water did not contain oxygen, and was in general very poor in gases. As soon as it was made to fall in a cascade, by which it absorbed air, it proved quite fit for consumption. In long sea voyages fresh water is sometimes not taken at all, or only taken in a small quantity, because it spoils by keeping, and becomes putrid from the organic matter it contains undergoing decomposition. Fresh water may he obtained directly from sea-water by distillation. The distilled water no longer contains sea salts, and is therefore fit for consumption, but it is very tasteless and has the properties of boiled water. In order to render it palatable certain salts, which are usually held in fresh water, are added to it, and it is made to flow in thin streams exposed to the air in order that it may become saturated with the component parts of the atmosphere—that is, absorb gases.

[6] *Hard water* is such as contains much mineral matter, and especially a large proportion of calcium salts. Such water, owing to the amount of lime it contains, does not form a lather with soap, prevents vegetables boiled in it from softening properly, and forms a large amount of incrustation on vessels in which it is boiled. When of a high degree of hardness, it is injurious for drinking purposes, which is evident from the fact that in several large cities the death-rate has been found to decrease after introducing a soft water in the place of a hard water. *Putrid water* contains a considerable quantity of decomposing organic matter, chiefly vegetable, but in populated districts, especially in towns, chiefly animal remains. Such water acquires an unpleasant smell and taste, by which stagnant bog water and the water of certain wells in inhabited districts are particularly characterised. Water of this kind is especially injurious at a period of epidemic. It may be partially purified by being passed through charcoal, which retains the putrid and certain organic substances, and also certain mineral substances. Turbid water may be purified to a certain extent by the addition of alum, which aids, after standing some time, the formation of a sediment. Condy's fluid (potassium permanganate) is another means of purifying putrid water. A solution of this substance, even if very dilute, is of a red colour; on adding it to a putrid water, the permanganate oxidises and destroys the organic matter. When added to water in such a quantity as to impart to it an almost imperceptible rose colour it destroys much of the

organic substances it contains. It is especially salutary to add a small quantity of Condy's fluid to impure water in times of epidemic.

The presence in water of one gram per litre, or 1,000 grams per cubic metre, of any substance whatsoever, renders it unfit and even injurious for consumption by animals, and this whether organic or mineral matter predominates. The presence of 1 p.c. of chlorides makes water quite salt, and produces thirst instead of assuaging it. The presence of magnesium salts is most unpleasant; they have a disagreeable bitter taste, and, in fact, impart to sea water its peculiar taste. A large amount of nitrates is only found in impure water, and is usually injurious, as they may indicate the presence of decomposing organic matter.

[7]

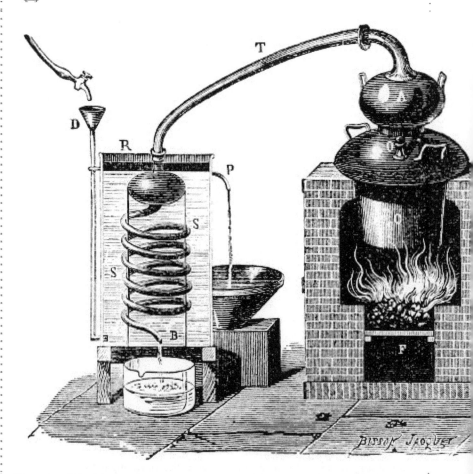

FIG. 4.—Distillation by means of a metallic still. The liquid in C is heated by the fire F. The vapours rise through the head A and pass

by the tube T to the worm S placed in a vessel R, through which a current of cold water flows by means of the tubes D and P.

Distilled water may be prepared, or distillation in general carried on, either in a metal still with worm condenser (fig. 4) or on a small scale in the laboratory in a glass retort (fig. 5) heated by a lamp. Fig. 5 illustrates the main parts of the usual glass laboratory apparatus used for distillation. The steam issuing from the retort (on the right-hand side) passes through a glass tube surrounded by a larger tube, through which a stream of cold water passes, by which the steam is condensed, and runs into a receiver (on the left-hand side).

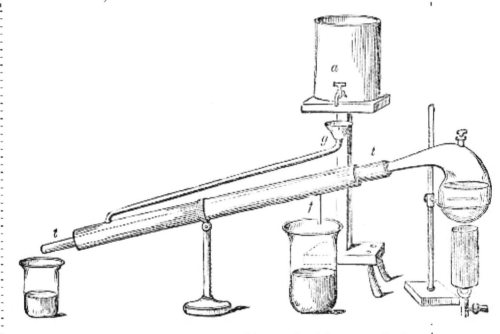

FIG. 5.—Distillation from a glass retort. The neck of the retort fits into the inner tube of the Liebig's condenser. The space between the inner and outer tube of the condenser is filled with cold water, which enters by the tube *g* and flows out at *f*.

[8] One of Lavoisier's first memoirs (1770) referred to this question. He investigated the formation of the earthy residue in the distillation of water in order to prove whether it was possible, as was affirmed, to convert water into earth, and he found that the residue was produced by the action of water on the sides of the vessel containing it, and not from the water itself. He proved this to be the case by direct weighing.

[9] Taking the generally-accepted specific gravity of water at its greatest density—*i.e.* at 4° as one—it has been shown by experiment that the specific gravity of water at different temperatures is as follows:

At   0° 0·99987   At 30° 0·99574

„ +10° 0·99974   „ 40° 0·99233

„   15° 0·99915   „ 50° 0·98817

„   20° 0·99827   „ 100° 0·95859

A comparison of all the data at present known shows that the variation of the specific gravity S_t with the temperature t (determined by the mercurial thermometer) maybe expressed (Mendeléeff 1891) by the formula

$$S_t = 1 - (t - 4)^2 \boxed{(94 \cdot 1 + t) (703 \cdot 51 - t) 1 \cdot 9}$$

t° C. according to the mercurial thermometer	Sp. gr. S_t (at 4° = 1,000,000)	Variation of sp. gr. with a rise of		Volume taking vol. at 4° = 1
		Temp. per 1° C. or ds/dt	Pressure per 1 atmosphere or ds/dp	
-10	998,281	+264	+54	1,001,722
0	999,873	+65	+50	1,000,127
10	999,738	-85	+47	1,000,262
20	998,272	-203	+45	1,001,731
30	995,743	-299	+43	1,004,276
50	988,174	-450	+40	1,011,967
70	977,948	-569	+39	1,022,549
90	965,537	-670	+41	1,035,692
100	958,595	-718	+42	1,043,194
120	943,814	-819	+43	1,060,093
160	907,263	-995	+55	1,102,216

| 200 | 863,473 | -1,200 | +73 | 1,158,114 |

If the temperature be determined by the hydrogen thermometer, whose indications between 0° and 100° are slightly lower than the mercurial (for example, about 0·1° C. at 20°), then a slightly smaller sp. gr. will be obtained for a given *t*. Thus Chappuis (1892) obtained 0·998233 for 20°. Water at 4° is taken as the basis for reducing measures of length to measures of weight and volume. The *metric, decimal, system* of measures of weights and volumes is generally employed in science. The starting point of this system is the metre (39·37 inches) divided into decimetres (= 0·1 metre), centimetres (= 0·01 metre), millimetres (= 0·001 metre), and micrometres (= one millionth of a metre). A cubic decimetre is called a *litre*, and is used for the measurement of volumes. The weight of a litre of water at 4° in a vacuum is called a kilogram. One thousandth part of a kilogram of water weighs one *gram*. It is divided into decigrams, centigrams, and milligrams (= 0·001 gram). An English pound equals 453·59 grams. The great advantage of this system is that it is a decimal one, and that it is universally adopted in science and in most international relations. *All the measures cited in this work are metrical.* The units most often used in science are:—Of length, the centimetre; of weight, the gram; of time, the second; of temperature, the degree Celsius or Centigrade. According to the most trustworthy determinations (Kupfer in Russia 1841, and Chaney in England 1892), the weight of a c. dcm. of water at 4° in vacuo is about 999·9 grms. For ordinary purposes the weight of a c. dcg. may be taken as equal to a kg. Hence the litre (determined by the weight of water it holds) is slightly greater than a cubic decimetre.

[10] As solid substances appear in independent, regular, crystalline forms which are dependent, judging from their cleavage or lamination (in virtue of which mica breaks, up into laminae, and Iceland spar, &c., into pieces bounded by faces inclined to each other at angles which are definite for each substance), on an inequality of attraction (cohesion, hardness) in different directions which intersect at definite angles the determination of crystalline form therefore affords one of the most important characteristics for identifying definite chemical compounds. The elements of crystallography which comprise a special science should therefore he familiar to all who desire to work in scientific chemistry. In this work we shall only have occasion to speak of a few crystalline forms, some of which are shown in figs. 6 to 12.

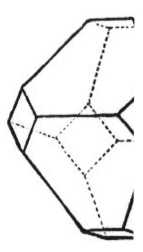

FIG. 6.—Example of the form belonging to the regular system. Combination of an octahedron and a cube. The former predominates. Alum, fluor spar, suboxide of copper, and others.

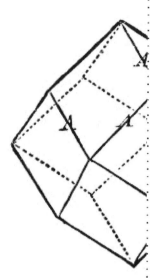

FIG. 7.—Rhombic Dodecahedron of the regular system. Garnet.

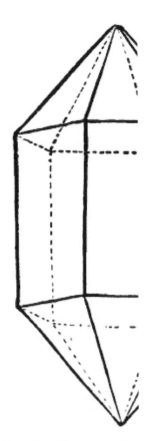

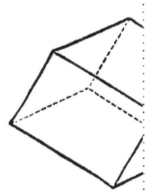

FIG. 9.—
Rhombohedron. Calc
spar, &c.

FIG. 8.—Hexagonal
prism terminated by
hexagonal pyramids.
Quartz, &c.

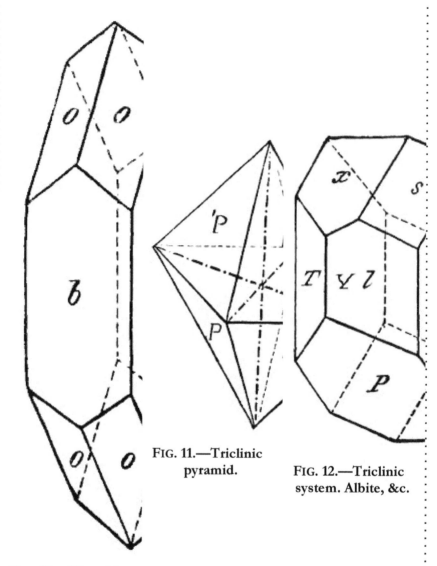

FIG. 11.—Triclinic
pyramid.

FIG. 12.—Triclinic
system. Albite, &c.

FIG. 10.—Rhombic
system. Desmine.

[11] Of all known liquids, water exhibits the greatest *cohesion* of particles. Indeed, it ascends to a greater height in capillary tubes than other liquids; for instance, two and a half times as high as alcohol, nearly three times as high as ether, and to a much greater height than oil of vitriol, &c. In a tube one mm. in diameter, water at 0° ascends 15·3 mm., measuring from the height of the liquid to two-thirds of the height of the meniscus, and at 100° it rises 12·5 mm. The cohesion varies very uniformly with the temperature;

thus at 50° the height of the capillary column equals 13·9 mm.—that is, the mean between the columns at 0° and 100°. This uniformity is not destroyed even at temperatures near the freezing point, and hence it may be assumed that at high temperatures cohesion will vary as uniformly as at ordinary temperatures; that is, the difference between the columns at 0° and 100° being 2·8 mm., the height of the column at 500° should be 15·2 - (5 × 2·8) = 1·2 mm.; or, in other words, at these high temperatures the cohesion between the particles of water would he almost *nil*. Only certain solutions (sal ammoniac and lithium chloride), and these only with a great excess of water, rise higher than pure water in capillary tubes. The great cohesion of water doubtless determines many of both its physical and chemical properties.

The quantity of heat required to raise the temperature of one part by weight of water from 0° to 1°, *i.e.* by 1° C., is called the *unit of heat* or calorie; the *specific heat of liquid water* at 0° is taken as equal to unity. The variation of this specific heat with a rise in temperature is inconsiderable in comparison with the variation exhibited by the specific heats of other liquids. According to Ettinger, the specific heat of water at 20° = 1·016, at 50° = 1·039, and at 100° = 1·073. The specific heat of water is greater than that of any other known liquid; for example, the specific heat of alcohol at 0° is 0·55—*i.e.* the quantity of heat which raises 55 parts of water 1° raises 100 parts of alcohol 1°. The specific heat of oil of turpentine at 0° is 0·41, of ether 0·53, of acetic acid 0·5274, of mercury 0·033. Hence water is the best condenser or absorber of heat. This property of water has an important significance in practice and in nature. Water prevents rapid cooling or heating, and thus tempers cold and heat. The specific heats of ice and aqueous vapour are much less than that of water; namely, that of ice is 0·504, and of steam 0·48.

With an increase in pressure equal to one atmosphere, the compressibility of water (*see* Note 9) is 0·000047, of mercury 0·00000352, of ether 0·00012 at 0°, of alcohol at 13° 0·000095. The addition of various substances to water generally decreases both its compressibility and cohesion. The compressibility of other liquids increases with a rise of temperature, but for water it decreases up to 53° and then increases like other liquids.

The *expansion of water* by heat (Note 9) also exhibits many peculiarities which are not found in other liquids. The expansion of water at low temperatures is very small compared with other liquids; at 4° it is almost zero, and at 100° it is equal to 0·0008; below 4° it is negative—*i.e.* water on cooling then expands, and does not decrease in volume. In passing into a solid state, the specific gravity of water decreases; at 0° one c.c. of water weighs 0·999887 gram, and one c.c. of ice at the same temperature weighs only 0·9175 gram. The ice formed, however, contracts on cooling like the majority of other substances. Thus 100 volumes of ice are produced from 92 volumes of water—that is, water expands considerably on freezing, which fact determines a number of natural phenomena. The freezing point of water falls with an increase in pressure (0·007° per atmosphere), because in freezing water expands (Thomson), whilst with substances which contract in solidifying the melting point rises with an increase in pressure; thus, paraffin under one atmosphere melts at 46°, and under 100 atmospheres at 49°.

When liquid water passes into vapour, the cohesion of its particles must be destroyed, as the particles are removed to such a distance from each other that their mutual attraction no longer exhibits any influence. As the cohesion of aqueous particles varies at different temperatures, the quantity of heat which is expended in overcoming this cohesion—or the *latent heat of evaporation*—will for this reason alone be different at different temperatures. The quantity of heat which is consumed in the transformation of one part by weight of water, at different temperatures, into vapour was determined by Regnault with great accuracy. His researches showed that one part by weight of water at 0°, in passing into vapour having a temperature t, consumes $606·5 + 0·305t$ units of heat, at 50° 621·7, at 100° 637·0, at 150° 652·2, and at 200° 667·5. But this quantity includes also the quantity of heat required for heating the water from 0° to t—*i.e.* besides the latent heat of evaporation, also that heat which is used in heating the water in a liquid state to a temperature t. On deducting this amount of heat, we obtain the latent heat of evaporation of water as 606·5 at 0°, 571 at 50°, 534 at 100°, 494 at 150°, and only 453 at 200°, which shows that the conversion of water at different temperatures into vapour at a constant temperature requires very different quantities of heat. This is chiefly dependent on the difference of the cohesion of water at different temperatures; the cohesion is greater at low than at high temperatures, and therefore at low temperatures a greater quantity of heat is required to overcome the cohesion. On comparing these quantities of heat, it will be observed that they decrease rather uniformly, namely their difference between 0° and 100° is 72, and between 100° and 200° is 81 units of heat. From this we may conclude that this variation will be approximately the same for high temperatures also, and therefore that no heat would be required for the conversion of water into vapour at a temperature of about 400°. At this temperature, water passes into vapour whatever be the pressure (see Chap. II. The absolute boiling point of water, according to Dewar, is 370°, the critical pressure 196 atmospheres). It must here be remarked that water, in presenting a greater cohesion, requires a larger quantity of heat for its conversion into vapour than other liquids. Thus alcohol consumes 208, ether 90, turpentine 70, units of heat in their conversion into vapour.

The whole amount of heat which is consumed in the conversion of water into vapour is not used in overcoming the cohesion—that is, in internal accomplished in the liquid. A part of this heat is employed in moving the aqueous particles; in fact, aqueous vapour at 100° occupies a volume 1,659 times greater than that of water (at the ordinary pressure), consequently a portion of the heat or work is employed in lifting the aqueous particles, in overcoming pressure, or in external work, which may be usefully employed, and which is so employed in steam engines. In order to determine this work, let us consider the variation of the maximum *pressure* or *vapour tension of steam* at different temperatures. The observations of Regnault in this respect, as on those preceding, deserve special attention from their comprehensiveness and accuracy. The pressure or tension of aqueous vapour at various temperatures is given in the adjoining table, and is expressed in millimetres of the barometric column reduced to 0°.

Temperature	Tension	Temperature	Tension
-20°	0·9	70°	233·3
-10°	2·1	90°	525·4
0°	4·6	100°	760·0
+10°	9·1	105°	906·4
15°	12·7	110°	1075·4
20°	17·4	115°	1269·4
25°	23·5	120°	1491·3
30°	31·5	150°	3581·0
50°	92·0	200°	11689·0

The table shows the boiling points of water at different pressures. Thus on the summit of Mont Blanc, where the average pressure is about 424 mm., water boils at 84·4°. In a rarefied atmosphere water boils even at the ordinary temperature, but in evaporating it absorbs heat from the neighbouring parts, and therefore it becomes cold and may even freeze if the pressure does not exceed 4·6 mm., and especially if the vapour be rapidly absorbed as it is formed. Oil of vitriol, which absorbs the aqueous vapour, is used for this purpose. Thus ice may be obtained artificially at the ordinary temperature with the aid of an air-pump. This table of the tension of aqueous vapour also shows the temperature of water contained in a closed boiler if the pressure of the steam formed be known. Thus at a pressure of five atmospheres (a pressure of five times the ordinary atmospheric pressure—*i.e.* 5 × 760 = 3,800 mm.) the temperature of the water would be 152°. The table also shows the pressure produced on a given surface by steam on issuing from a boiler. Thus steam having a temperature of 152° exerts a pressure of 517 kilos on a piston whose surface equals 100 sq. cm., for the pressure of one atmosphere on one sq. cm. equals 1,033 kilos, and steam at 152° has a pressure of five atmospheres. As a column of mercury 1 mm. high exerts a pressure of 1·35959 grams on a surface of 1 sq. cm., therefore the pressure of aqueous vapour at 0° corresponds with a pressure of 6·25 grams per square centimetre. The pressures for all temperatures may be calculated in a similar way, and it will be found that at 100° it is equal to 1,033·28 grams. This means that if a cylinder be taken whose sectional area equals 1 sq. cm., and if water be poured into it and it be closed by a piston weighing 1,033 grams, then on heating it in a vacuum to 100° no steam will be formed, because the steam cannot overcome the pressure of the piston; and if at 100° 534 units of heat be transmitted to each unit of weight of water, then the whole of the water will be converted into vapour having the same temperature; and so also for every other temperature. The question now arises, to what height does the piston rise under these circumstances? that is, in other words, What is the volume occupied by the steam under a known pressure? For this we must know the weight of a cubic centimetre of steam at various temperatures. It has been shown by experiment that the density of steam, which does not saturate a space, varies very inconsiderably at all possible pressures, and is nine times the density of hydrogen under similar conditions. Steam which saturates a space varies in density at different temperatures, but this difference is very small, and its average density with reference to air is 0·64. We will employ this number in our calculation, and will calculate what volume the steam occupies at 100°. One cubic centimetre of air at 0° and 760 mm. weighs 0·001293 gram, at 100° and under the same pressure it will weigh 0·001293 $\boxed{1\cdot368}$ or about 0·000946 gram, and consequently one cubic centimetre of steam whose density is 0·64 will weigh 0·000605 gram at 100°, and therefore one gram of aqueous vapour will occupy a volume of about 1·653 c.c. Consequently, the piston in the cylinder of 1 sq. cm. sectional area, and in which the water occupied a height of 1 cm., will be raised 1,653 cm. on the conversion of this water into steam. This piston, as has been mentioned, weighs 1,033 grams, therefore the *external work of the steam*—that is, that work which the water does in its conversion into steam at 100°—is equal to lifting a piston weighing 1,033 grams to a height of 1,653 cm., or 17·07 kilogram-metres of work—*i.e.* is capable of lifting 17 kilograms 1 metre, or 1 kilogram 17 metres. One gram of water requires for its conversion into steam 534 gram units of heat or 0·534 kilogram unit of heat—*i.e.* the quantity of heat absorbed in the evaporation of one gram of water is equal to the quantity of heat which is capable of heating 1 kilogram of water 0·534°. Each unit of heat, as has been shown by accurate experiment, is capable of doing 424 kilogram-metres of work. Hence, in evaporating, one gram of water expends 424 × 0·534 = (almost) 227 kilogram-metres of work. The external work was found to be only 17 kilogram-metres, therefore 210 kilogram-metres are expended in overcoming the internal cohesion of the aqueous particles, and consequently about 92 p.c. of the total heat or work is consumed in overcoming the internal cohesion. The following figures are thus calculated approximately:—

Temperature	Total work of evaporation in kilogram-metres	External work of vapour in kilogram-metres	Internal work of vapour
0°	255	13	242
50°	242	15	227
100°	226	17	209
150°	209	19	190
200°	192	20	172

The work necessary for overcoming the internal cohesion of water in its passage into vapour decreases with the rise in temperature—that is, corresponds with the decrease of cohesion; and, in fact, the variations which take place in this case are very similar to those which are observed in the heights to which water rises in capillary tubes at different temperatures. It is evident, therefore, that the amount of external—or, as it is termed, useful—work which water can supply by its evaporation is very small compared with the amount which it expends in its conversion into vapour.

In considering certain physico-mechanical properties of water, I had in view not only their importance for theory and practice, but also their purely chemical significance; for it is evident from the above considerations that even in a physical change of state the greatest part of the work done is employed in overcoming cohesion, and that an enormous amount of internal energy must be expended in overcoming chemical cohesion or affinity.

[12] When it is necessary to heat a considerable mass of liquid in different vessels, it would be very uneconomical to make use of metallic

vessels and to construct a separate furnace for each; such cases are continually met with in practice. Steam from a boiler is introduced into the liquid, or, in general, into the vessel which it is required to heat. The steam, in condensing and passing into a liquid state, parts with its latent heat, and as this is very considerable a small quantity of steam will produce a considerable heating effect. If it be required, for instance, to heat 1,000 kilos of water from 20° to 50°, which requires approximately 30,000 units of heat, steam at 100° is passed into the water from a boiler. Each kilogram of water at 50° contains about 50 units of heat, and each kilogram of steam at 100° contains 637 units of heat; therefore, each kilogram of steam in cooling to 50° gives up 587 units of heat, and consequently 52 kilos of steam are capable of heating 1,000 kilos of water from 20° to 50°. Water is very often applied for heating in chemical practice. For this purpose metallic vessels or pans, called 'water-baths,' are made use of. They are closed by a cover formed of concentric rings lying on each other. The vessels—such as beakers, evaporating basins, retorts, &c.—containing liquids, are placed on these rings, and the water in the bath is heated. The steam given off heats the bottom of the vessels to be heated, and thus effects the evaporation or distillation.

[13]

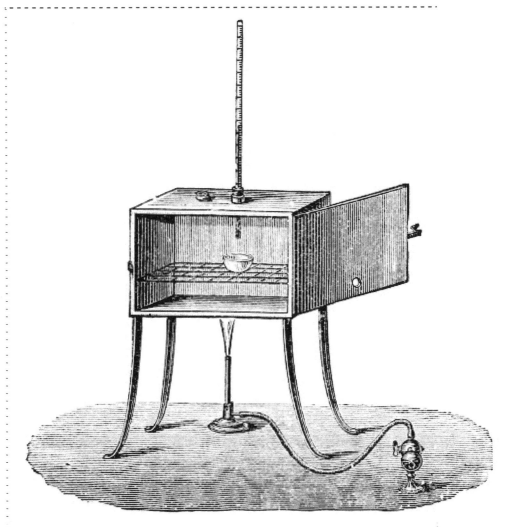

FIG. 13.—Drying oven, composed of brazed copper. It is heated by a lamp. The object to be dried is placed on the gauze inside the oven. The thermometer indicates the temperature.

In order to dry any substance at about 100°—that is, at the boiling point of water (hygroscopic water passes off at this temperature)—an apparatus called a 'drying-oven' is employed. It consists of a double copper box; water is poured into the space between the internal and external boxes, and the oven is then heated over a stove or by any other means, or else steam from a boiler is passed between the walls of the two boxes. When the water boils, the temperature inside the inner box will be approximately 100° C. The substance to be dried is placed inside the oven, and the door is closed.

Several holes are cut in the door to allow the free passage of air, which carries off the aqueous vapour by the chimney on the top of the oven. Often, however, desiccation is carried on in copper ovens heated directly over a lamp (fig. 13). In this case any desired temperature may be obtained, which is determined by a thermometer fixed in a special orifice. There are substances which only part with their water at a much higher temperature than 100°, and then such air baths are very useful. In order to determine directly the amount of water in a substance which does not part with anything except water at a red heat, the substance is placed in a bulb tube. By first weighing the tube empty and then with the substance to be dried in it, the weight of the substance taken may be found. The tube is then connected on one side with a gas-holder full of air, which, on opening a stop-cock, passes first through a flask containing sulphuric acid, and then into a vessel containing lumps of pumice stone moistened with sulphuric acid. In passing through these vessels the air is thoroughly dried, having given up all its moisture to the sulphuric acid. Thus dry air will pass into the bulb tube, and as hygroscopic water is entirely given up from a substance in dry air even at the ordinary temperature, and still more rapidly on heating, the moisture given up by the substance in the tube will be carried off by the air passing through it. This damp air then passes through a U-shaped tube full of pieces of pumice stone moistened with sulphuric acid, which absorbs all the moisture given off from the substance in the bulb tube. Thus all the water expelled from the substance will collect in the U tube, and so, if this be weighed before and after, the difference will show the quantity of water expelled from the substance. If only water (and not any gases) come over, the increase of the weight of the U tube will be equal to the decrease in the weight of the bulb tube.

[14] Instead of under a glass bell jar, drying over sulphuric acid is often carried on in a desiccator consisting of a shallow wide-mouthed glass vessel, closed by a well-fitting ground-glass cover. Sulphuric acid is poured over the bottom of the desiccator, and the substance to be dried is placed on a glass stand above the acid. A lateral glass tube with a stop-cock is often fused into the desiccator in order to connect it with an air pump, and so allow drying under a diminished pressure, when the moisture evaporates more rapidly. The fact that in the usual form of desiccator the desiccating substance (sulphuric acid) is placed beneath the substance to be dried has the disadvantage that the moist air being lighter than dry air distributes itself in the upper portion of the desiccator and not below. Hempel, in his desiccator (1891), avoids this by placing the absorbent above the substance to be dried. The process of desiccation can be further accelerated by cooling the upper portion of the desiccator, and so inducing ascending and descending currents of air within the apparatus.

[15] Chappuis, however, determined that in wetting 1 gram of charcoal with water 7 units of heat are evolved, and on pouring carbon bisulphide over 1 gram of charcoal as much as 24 units of heat are evolved. Alumina (1 gram), when moistened with water, evolves 2½ calories. This indicates that in respect to evolution of heat moistening already presents a transition towards exothermal combinations (those evolving heat in their formation).

[16] Strong acetic acid ($C_2H_4O_2$), whose specific gravity at 15° is 1·055, does not become lighter on the addition of water (a lighter substance, sp. gr. = 0·999), but heavier, so that a solution of 80 parts of acetic acid and 20 parts of water has a specific gravity of 1·074, and even a solution of equal parts of acetic acid and water (50 p.c.) has a sp. gr. of 1·065, which is still greater than that of acetic acid itself. This shows the high degree of contraction which takes place on solution. In fact, solutions—and, in general, liquids—on mixing with water, decrease in volume.

[16 bis] Graham, in the jelly formed by gelatine, and De Vries in gelatinous silica (Chapter XVIII.) most frequently employed coloured (tinted) substances, for instance, $K_2Cr_2O_7$, which showed the rate of diffusion with very great clearness. Prof. Oumoff employed the method described in Chapter X., Note 17, for this purpose.

[17] The researches of Graham, Fick, Nernst, and others showed that the quantity of a dissolved substance which is transmitted (rises) from one stratum of liquid to another in a vertical cylindrical vessel is not only proportional to the time and to the sectional area of the cylinder, but also to the amount and nature of the substance dissolved in a stratum of liquid, so that each substance has its corresponding co-efficient of diffusion. The cause of the diffusion of solutions must be considered as essentially the same as the cause of the diffusion of gases—that is, as dependent on motions which are proper to their molecules; but here most probably those purely chemical, although feebly-developed, forces, which incline the substances dissolved to the formation of definite compounds, also play their part.

[18]

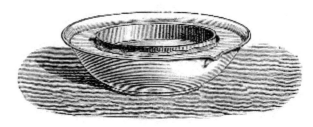

FIG. 15.—Dialyser. Apparatus for the separation of substances which pass through a membrane from those which do not. Description in text.

The rate of diffusion—like the rate of transmission—through membranes, or *dialysis* (which plays an important part in the vital processes of organisms and also in technical processes), presents, according to Graham's researches, a sharply defined change in passing from such crystallisable substances as the majority of salts and acids to substances which are capable of giving jellies (gum, gelatin, &c.) The former diffuse into solutions and pass through membranes much more rapidly than the latter, and Graham therefore distinguishes between *crystalloids*, which diffuse rapidly, and *colloids*, which diffuse slowly. On breaking solid colloids into pieces, a total absence of cleavage is remarked. The fracture of such substances is like that of glue or glass. It is termed a 'conchoidal' fracture. Almost all the substances of which animal and vegetable bodies consist are colloids, and this is, at all events, partly the reason why animals and plants have such varied forms, which have no resemblance to the crystalline forms of the majority of mineral substances. The colloid solid substances in organisms—that is, in animals and plants—almost always contain water, and take most peculiar forms, of networks, of granules, of hairs, of mucous, shapeless masses, &c., which are quite different from the forms taken by crystalline substances. When colloids separate out from solutions, or from a molten state, they present a form which is similar to that of the liquid from which they were formed. Glass may he taken as the best example of this. Colloids are distinguishable from crystalloids, not only by the absence of crystalline form, but by many other properties which admit of clearly distinguishing both these classes of solids, as Graham showed. Nearly all colloids are capable of passing, under certain circumstances, from a soluble into an insoluble state. The best example is shown by white of eggs (albumin) in the raw and soluble form, and in the hard-boiled and insoluble form. The majority of colloids, on passing into an insoluble form in the presence of water, give substances having a gelatinous appearance, which is familiar to every one in starch, solidified glue, jelly, &c. Thus gelatin, or common carpenter's glue, when soaked in water, swells up into an insoluble jelly. If this jelly be heated, it melts, and is then soluble in water, but on cooling it again forms a jelly which is insoluble in water. One of the properties which distinguish colloids from crystalloids is that the former pass very slowly through a membrane, whilst the latter penetrate very rapidly. This may be shown by taking a cylinder, open at both ends, and by covering its lower end with a bladder or with vegetable parchment (unsized paper immersed for two or three minutes in a mixture of sulphuric acid and half its volume of water, and then washed), or any other membranous substance (all such substances are themselves colloids in an insoluble form). The membrane must be firmly tied to the cylinder, so as not to leave any opening. Such an apparatus is called a *dialyser* (fig. 15), and the process of separation of crystalloids from colloids by means of such a membrane is termed *dialysis*. An aqueous solution of a crystalloid or colloid, or a mixture of both, is poured into the dialyser, which is then placed in a vessel containing water, so that the bottom of the membrane is covered with water. Then, after a certain period of time, the crystalloid passes through the membrane, whilst the colloid, if it does pass through at all, does so at an incomparably slower rate. The crystalloid naturally passes through into the water until the solution attains the same strength on both sides of the membrane. By replacing the outside water with fresh water, a fresh quantity of the crystalloid may be separated from the dialyser. While a crystalloid is passing through the membrane, a colloid remains almost entirely in the dialyser, and therefore a mixed solution of these two kinds of substances may be separated from each other by a dialyser. The study of the properties of colloids, and of the phenomena of their passage through membranes, should elucidate much respecting the phenomena which are accomplished in organisms.

[19] The formation of solutions may be considered in two aspects, from a physical and from a chemical point of view, and it is more evident in solutions than in any other department of chemistry how closely these provinces of natural science are allied together. On the one hand solutions form a particular case of a physico-mechanical interpenetration of homogeneous substances, and a juxtaposition of the molecules of the substance dissolved and of the solvent, similar to the juxtaposition which is exhibited in homogeneous substances. From this point of view this diffusion of solutions is exactly similar to the diffusion of gases, with only this difference, that the nature and store of energy are different in gases from what they are in liquids, and that in liquids there is considerable

friction, whilst in gases there is comparatively little. The penetration of a dissolved substance into water is likened to evaporation, and solution to the formation of vapour. This resemblance was clearly expressed even by Graham. In recent years the Dutch chemist, Van't Hoff, has developed this view of solutions in great detail, having shown (in a memoir in the *Transactions of the Swedish Academy of Science*, Part 21, No. 17, 'Lois de l'équilibre chimique dans l'état dilué, gazeux ou dissous,' 1886), that for dilute solutions the *osmotic pressure* follows the same laws of Boyle, Mariotte, Gay-Lussac, and Avogadro-Gerhardt as for gases. The osmotic pressure of a substance dissolved in water is determined by means of membranes which allow the passage of water, but not of a substance dissolved in it, through them. This property is found in animal protoplasmic membranes and in porous substances covered with an amorphous precipitate, such as is obtained by the action of copper sulphate on potassium ferrocyanide (Pfeffer, Traube). If, for instance, a one p.c. solution of sugar he placed in such a vessel, which is then closed and placed in water, the water passes through the walls of the vessel and increases the pressure by 50 mm. of the barometric column. If the pressure be artificially increased inside the vessel, then the water will be expelled through the walls. De Vries found a convenient means of determining *isotonic* solutions (those presenting a similar osmotic pressure) in the cells of plants. For this purpose a portion of the soft part of the leaves of the *Tradescantis discolor*, for instance, is cut away and moistened with the solution of a given salt and of a given strength. If the osmotic pressure of the solution taken be less than that of the sap contained in the cells they will change their form or shrink; if, on the other hand, the osmotic pressure be greater than that of the sap, then the cells will expand, as can easily be seen under the microscope. By altering the amount of the different salts in solution it is possible to find for each salt the strength of solution at which the cells begin to swell, and at which they will consequently have an equal osmotic pressure. As it increases in proportion to the amount of a substance dissolved per 100 parts of water, it is possible, knowing the osmotic pressure of a given substance—for instance, sugar at various degrees of concentration of solution—and knowing the composition of isotonic solutions compared with sugar, to determine the osmotic pressure of all the salts investigated. The osmotic pressure of dilute solutions determined in this manner directly or indirectly (from observations made by Pfeffer and De Vries) was shown to follow the same laws as those of the pressure of gases; for instance, by doubling or increasing the quantity of a salt (in a given volume) n times, the pressure is doubled or increases n times. So, for example, in a solution containing one part of sugar per 100 parts of water the osmotic pressure (according to Pfeffer) = 58·5 cm. of mercury, if 2 parts of sugar = 101·6, if 4 parts = 208·2 and so on, which proves that the ratio is true within the limits of experimental error. (2) Different substances for equal strengths of solutions, show very different osmotic pressures, just as gases for equal parts by weight in equal volumes show different tensions. (3) If, for a given dilute solution at 0°, the osmotic pressure equal $p°$, then at p it will be greater and equal to $p°(1 + 0·00367t)$, $i.e.$ it increases with the temperature in exactly the same manner as the tension of gases increases. (4) If in dilute solutions of such substances as do not conduct an electric current (for instance, sugar, acetone, and many other organic bodies) the substances be taken in the ratio of their molecular weights (expressed by their formulæ, see Chapter VII.), then not only will the osmotic pressure be equal, but its magnitude will be determined by that tension which would be proper to the vapours of the given substances when they would be contained in the space occupied by the solution, just as the tension of the vapours of molecular quantities of the given substances will be equal, and determined by the laws of Gay-Lussac, Mariotte, and Avogadro-Gerhardt. Those formulæ (Chapter VII., Notes 23 and 24) by which the gaseous state of matter is determined, may also be applied in the present case. So, for example, the osmotic pressure p, in centimetres of mercury, of a one per cent. solution of sugar, may be calculated according to the formula for gases:

$$Mp = 6200s(273 + t),$$

where M is the molecular weight, s the weight in grams of a cubic centimetre of vapour, and t its temperature. For sugar M = 342 (because its molecular composition is $C_{12}H_{22}O_{11}$). The specific gravity of the solution of sugar is 1·003, hence the weight of sugar s contained in a 1 per cent. solution = 0·01003 gram. The observation was made at $t = 14°$. Hence, according to the formula, we find $p = 52·2$ centimetres. And experiments carried on at 14° gave 53·5 centimetres, which is very near to the above. (5) For the solutions of salts, acids, and similar substances, which conduct an electric current, the calculated pressure is usually (but not always in a definite or multiple number of times) less than the observed by i times, and this i for dilute solutions of $MgSO_4$ is nearly 1, for $CO_2 = 1$, for KCl, NaCl, KI, KNO_3 greater than 1, and approximates to 2, for $BaCl_2$, $MgCl_2$, K_2CO_3, and others between 2 and 3, for HCl, H_2SO_4, $NaNO_3$, CaN_2O_6, and others nearly 2 and so on. It should be remarked that the above deductions are only applicable (and with a certain degree of accuracy) to dilute solutions, and in this respect resemble the generalisations of Michel and Kraft (see Note 44). Nevertheless, the arithmetical relation found by Van't Hoff between the formation of vapours and the transition into dilute solutions forms an important scientific discovery, which should facilitate the explanation of the nature of solutions, while the osmotic pressure of solutions already forms a very important aspect of the study of solutions.

In this respect it is necessary to mention that Prof. Konovaloff (1891, and subsequently others also) discovered the dependence (and it may be a sufficient explanation) of the osmotic pressure upon the differences of the tensions of aqueous vapours and aqueous solutions; this, however, already enters into a special province of physical chemistry (certain data are given in Note 49 and following), and to this physical side of the question also belongs one of the extreme consequences of the resemblance of osmotic pressure to gaseous pressure, which is that the concentration of a uniform solution varies in parts which are heated or cooled. Soret (1881) indeed observed that a solution of copper sulphate containing 17 parts of the salt at 20° only contained 14 parts after heating the upper portion of the tube to 80° for a long period of time. This aspect of solution, which is now being very carefully and fully worked out, may be called the *physical* side. Its other aspect is purely *chemical*, for solution does not take place between any two substances, but requires a special and particular attraction or affinity between them. A vapour or gas permeates any other vapour or gas, but a salt which dissolves in water may not be in the least soluble in alcohol, and is quite insoluble in mercury. In considering solutions as a manifestation of chemical force (and of chemical energy), it must be acknowledged that they are here developed to so feeble an extent that the definite compounds (that is, those formed according to the law of multiple proportions) formed between water and a soluble substance dissociate even at the ordinary temperature, forming a homogeneous system—that is, one in which both the compound and the products into which it decomposes (water and the aqueous compound) occur in a liquid state. The chief difficulty in the comprehension of solutions depends on the fact that the mechanical theory of the structure of liquids has not yet been so fully developed as the theory of gases, and solutions are liquids. The conception of solutions as liquid dissociated definite chemical compounds is based on the following considerations: (1) that there exist certain undoubtedly definite chemical crystallised compounds (such as H_2SO_4,H_2O; or $NaCl,2H_2O$; or $CaCl_2,6H_2O$; &c.) which melt on a certain rise of temperature, and then form true solutions; (2) that metallic alloys in a molten condition are real solutions, but on cooling they often give entirely distinct and definite crystallised compounds, which are recognised by the properties of alloys; (3) that between the solvent and the substance dissolved there are formed, in a number of cases, many undoubtedly definite compounds, such as compounds with water of crystallisation; (4) that the physical properties of solutions, and especially their specific gravities (a property which can be very accurately determined), vary with a change in composition, and in such a manner as would be required by the formation of one or more definite but dissociating compounds. Thus, for example, on adding water to fuming sulphuric acid its density is observed to decrease until it attains the definite composition H_2SO_4, or $SO_3 + H_2O$, when the specific gravity increases, although on further diluting with water it again falls. Moreover (Mendeléeff, *The Investigation of Aqueous Solutions from their Specific Gravities*, 1887), the increase in specific gravity (*ds*), varies in all well-known solutions with the proportion of the substance dissolved (*dp*), and this dependence can be expressed by a formula (ds $\boxed{dp}$ = A + Bp) between the limits of definite compounds whose existence in solutions must be admitted, and this is in complete accordance with the dissociation hypothesis. Thus, for instance, from H_2SO_4 to $H_2SO_4 + H_2O$ (both these substances exist as definite compounds in a free state), the fraction ds $\boxed{dp}$ = 0·0729 - 0·000749p (where p is the percentage amount of H_2SO_4). For alcohol C_2H_6O, whose aqueous solutions have been more accurately investigated than all others, the definite compound $C_2H_6O + 3H_2O$, and others must be acknowledged in its solutions.

The two aspects of solution above mentioned, and the hypotheses which have as yet been applied to the examination of solutions, although they have somewhat different starting points, will doubtless in time lead to a general theory of solutions, because the same common laws govern both physical and chemical phenomena, inasmuch as the properties and motions of molecules, which determine physical properties, depend on the motions and properties of atoms, which determine chemical reactions. For details of the questions dealing with theories of solution, recourse must now be had to special memoirs and to works on theoretical (physical) chemistry; for this subject forms one of special interest at the present epoch of the development of our science. In working out chiefly the chemical side of solutions, I consider it to be necessary to reconcile the two aspects of the question; this seems to me to be all the more possible, as the physical side is limited to dilute solutions only, whilst the chemical side deals mainly with strong solutions.

[20] A system of (chemically or physically) re-acting substances in different states of aggregation—for instance, some solid, others liquid or gaseous—is termed a heterogeneous system. Up to now it is only systems of this kind which can be subjected to detailed examination in the sense of the mechanical theory of matter. Solutions (*i.e.* unsaturated ones) form fluid homogeneous systems, which at the present time can only be investigated with difficulty.

In the case of limited solution of liquids in liquids, *the difference between the solvent and the substance dissolved* is clearly seen. The former (that is, the solvent) may be added in an unlimited quantity, and yet the solution obtained will always be uniform, whilst only a definite saturating proportion of the substance dissolved can be taken, We will take water and common (sulphuric) ether. On shaking the ether with the water, it will be remarked that a portion of it dissolves in the water. If the ether be taken in such a quantity that it saturates the water and a portion of it remains undissolved, then this remaining portion will act as a solvent, and water will diffuse through it and also form a saturated solution of water in the ether taken. Thus two saturated solutions will be obtained. One solution will contain ether dissolved in water, and the other solution will contain water dissolved in ether. These two solutions will arrange themselves in two layers, according to their density; the ethereal solution of water will be on the top. If the upper ethereal solution be poured off from the aqueous solution, any quantity of ether may be added to it; this shows that the dissolving substance is ether. If water be added to it, it is no longer dissolved in it; this shows that water saturates the ether—here water is the substance dissolved. If we act in the same manner with the lower layer, we shall find that water is the solvent and ether the substance dissolved. By taking different amounts of ether and water, the degree of solubility of ether in water, and of water in ether, may be easily determined. Water approximately dissolves $\frac{1}{10}$ of its volume of ether, and ether dissolves a very small quantity of water. Let us now imagine that the liquid poured in dissolves a considerable amount of water, and that water dissolves a considerable amount of the liquid. Two layers could not be formed, because the saturated solutions would resemble each other, and therefore they would intermix in all proportions. This is, consequently, a case of a phenomenon where two liquids present considerable co-efficients of solubility in each other, but where it is impossible to say what these co-efficients are, because it is impossible to obtain a saturated solution.

[21]

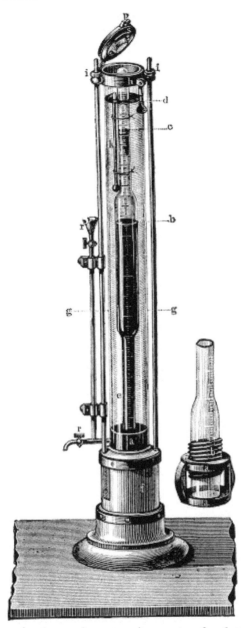

FIG. 16.—Bunsen's absorptiometer. Apparatus for determining the solubility of gases in liquids.

The solubility, or co-efficient of solubility, of a substance is determined by various methods. Either a solution is expressly prepared with a clear excess of the soluble substance and saturated at a given temperature, and the quantity of water and of the substance dissolved in it determined by evaporation, desiccation, or other means; or else, as is done with gases, definite quantities of water and of the soluble substance are taken and the amount remaining undissolved is determined.

The solubility of a gas in water is determined by means of an apparatus called an *absorptiometer* (fig. 16). It consists of an iron stand *f*, on which an india-rubber ring rests. A wide glass tube is placed on this ring, and is pressed down on it by the ring *h* and the screws *i i*. The tube is thus firmly fixed on the stand. A cock *r*, communicating with a funnel *r*, passes into the lower part of the stand. Mercury can be poured into the wide tube through this funnel, which is therefore made of steel, as copper would be affected by the mercury. The upper ring *h* is furnished with a cover *p*, which can be firmly pressed down on to the wide tube, and hermetically closes it by means of an india-rubber ring. The tube *r r* can be raised at will, and so by pouring mercury into the funnel the height of the column of mercury, which produces pressure inside the apparatus, can be increased. The pressure can also be diminished at will, by letting mercury out through the cock *r*. A graduated tube *e*, containing the gas and liquid to be experimented on, is placed inside the wide tube. This tube is graduated in millimetres for determining the pressure, and it is calibrated for volume, so that the number of volumes occupied by the gas and liquid dissolving it can be easily calculated. This tube can also be easily removed from the apparatus. The lower portion of this tube when removed from the apparatus is shown to the right of the figure. It will be observed that its lower end is furnished with a male screw *b*, fitting in a nut *a*. The lower surface of the nut *a* is covered with india-rubber, so that on screwing up the tube its lower end presses upon the india-rubber, and thus hermetically closes the whole tube, for its upper end is fused up. The nut *a* is furnished with arms *c c*, and in the stand *f* there are corresponding spaces, so that when the screwed-up internal tube is fixed into stand *f*, the arms *c c* fix into these spaces cut in *f*. This enables the internal tube to be fixed on to the stand *f*. When the internal tube is fixed in the stand, the wide tube is put into its right position, and mercury and water are poured into the space between the two tubes, and communication is opened between the inside of the tube *e* and the mercury between the interior and exterior tubes. This is done by either revolving the interior tube *e*, or by a key turning the nut about the bottom part of *f*. The tube *e* is filled with gas and water as follows: the tube is removed from the apparatus, filled with mercury, and the gas to be experimented on is passed into it. The volume of the gas is measured, the temperature and pressure determined, and the volume it would occupy at 0° and 760 mm. calculated. A known volume of water is then introduced into the tube. The water must be previously boiled, so as to be quite freed from air in solution. The tube is then closed by screwing it down on to the india-rubber on the nut. It is then fixed on to the stand f, mercury and water are poured into the intervening space between it and the exterior tube, which is then screwed up and closed by the cover p, and the whole apparatus is left at rest for some time, so that the tube e, and the gas in it, may attain the same temperature as that of the surrounding water, which is marked by a thermometer k tied to the tube e. The interior tube is then again closed by turning it in the nut, the cover p again shut, and the whole apparatus is shaken in order that the gas in the tube e may entirely saturate the water. After several shakings, the tube e is again opened by turning it in the nut, and the apparatus is left at rest for a certain time; it is then closed and again shaken, and so on until the volume of gas does not diminish after a fresh shaking—that is, until saturation ensues. Observations are then made of the temperature, the height of the mercury in the interior tube, and the level of the water in it, and also of the level of the mercury and water in the exterior tube. All these data are necessary in order to calculate the pressure under which the solution of the gas takes place, and what volume of gas remains undissolved, and also the quantity of water which serves as the solvent. By varying the temperature of the surrounding water, the amount of gas dissolved at various temperatures may be determined. Bunsen, Carius, and many others determined the solution of various gases in water, alcohol, and certain other liquids, by means of this apparatus. If in a determination of this kind it is found that n cubic centimetres of water at a pressure h dissolve m cubic centimetres of a given gas, measured at 0° and 760 mm., when the temperature under which solution took place was $t°$, then it follows that at the temperature t *the coefficient of solubility of the gas* in 1 volume of the liquid will be equal to $m \frac{}{n} \times 760 \frac{}{h}$.

This formula is very clearly understood from the fact that the coefficient of solubility of gases is that quantity measured at 0° and 760 mm., which is absorbed at a pressure of 760 mm. by one volume of a liquid. If n cubic centimetres of water absorb m cubic centimetres of a gas, then one cubic centimetre absorbs $m \frac{}{n}$. If $m \frac{}{n}$ c.c. of a gas are absorbed under a pressure of h mm., then, according to the law of the variation of solubility of a gas with the pressure, there would he dissolved, under a pressure of 760 mm., a quantity varying in the same ratio to m/n as 760 : h. In determining the residual volume of gas its moisture (note 1) must be taken into consideration.

Below are given the number of grams of several substances saturating 100 grams of water—that is, their co-efficients of solubility by weight at three different temperatures:—

	At 0°	At 20°	At 100°

Gases	Oxygen, O_2	6 |1000|	4 |1000|	—
	Carbonic anhydride, CO_2	35 |100|	18 |100|	—
	Ammonia, NH_3	90·0	51·8	7·3
Liquids	Phenol, C_6H_6O	4·9	5·2	∞
	Amyl alcohol, $C_5H_{12}O$	4·4	2·9	—
	Sulphuric acid, H_2SO_4	∞	∞	∞
Solids	Gypsum, $CaSO_4,2H_2O$	⅕	¼	⅕
	Alum, $AlKS_2O_8,12H_2O$	3·3	15·4	357·5
	Anhydrous sodium sulphate, Na_2SO_4	4·5	20	43
	Common Salt, $NaCl$	35·7	36·0	39·7
	Nitre, KNO_3	13·3	31·7	246·0

Sometimes a substance is so slightly soluble that it may be considered as insoluble. Many such substances are met with both in solids and liquids, and such a gas as oxygen, although it does dissolve, does so in so small a proportion by weight that it might be considered as zero did not the solubility of even so little oxygen play an important part in nature (as in the respiration of fishes) and were not an infinitesimal quantity of a gas by weight so easily measured by volume. The sign ∞, which stands on a line with sulphuric acid in the above table, indicates that it intermixes with water in all proportions. There are many such cases among liquids, and everybody knows, for instance, that spirit (absolute alcohol) can be mixed in any proportion with water.

[22] Just as the existence must he admitted of substances which are completely undecomposable (chemically) at the ordinary temperature—and of substances which are entirely non-volatile at such a temperature (as wood and gold), although capable of decomposing (wood) or volatilising (gold) at a higher temperature—so also the existence must be admitted of substances which are totally insoluble in water without some degree of change in their state. Although mercury is partially volatile at the ordinary temperature, there is no reason to think that it and other metals are soluble in water, alcohol, or other similar liquids. However, mercury forms solutions, as it dissolves other metals. On the other hand, there are many substances found in nature which are so very slightly soluble in water, that in ordinary practice they may be considered as insoluble (for example, barium sulphate). For the comprehension of that general plan according to which a change of state of substances (combined or dissolved, solid, liquid,

or gaseous) takes place, it is very important to make a distinction at this boundary line (on approaching zero of decomposition, volatility, or solubility) between an insignificant amount and zero, but the present methods of research and the data at our disposal at the present time only just touch such questions (by studying the electrical conductivity of dilute solutions and the development of micro-organisms in them). It must be remarked, besides, that water in a number of cases does not dissolve a substance as such, but acts on it chemically and forms a soluble substance. Thus glass and many rocks, especially if taken as powder, are chemically changed by water, but are not directly soluble in it.

[23] Beilby (1883) experimented on paraffin, and found that one litre of solid paraffin at 21° weighed 874 grams, and when liquid, at its melting-point 38°, 783 grams, at 49°, 775 grams, and at 60°, 767 grams, from which the weight of a litre of liquefied paraffin would be 795·4 grams at 21° if it could remain liquid at that temperature. By dissolving solid paraffin in lubricating oil at 21° Beilby found that 795·6 grams occupy one cubic decimetre, from which he concluded that the solution contained liquefied paraffin.

[24] Gay-Lussac was the first to have recourse to such a graphic method of expressing solubility, and he considered, in accordance with the general opinion, that by joining up the summits of the ordinates in one harmonious curve it is possible to express the entire change of solubility with the temperature. Now, there are many reasons for doubting the accuracy of such an admission, for there are undoubtedly critical points in curves of solubility (for example, of sodium sulphate, as shown further on), and it may be that definite compounds of dissolved substances with water, in decomposing within known limits of temperature, give critical points more often than would be imagined; it may even be, indeed, that instead of a continuous curve, solubility should be expressed—if not always, then not unfrequently—by straight or broken lines. According to Ditte, the solubility of sodium nitrate, $NaNO_3$, is expressed by the following figures per 100 parts of water:—

0°   4°   10°   15°   21°   29°   36°   51°   68°

66·7 71·0 76·3 80·6 85·7 92·9 99·4 113·6 125·1

In my opinion (1881) these data should be expressed with exactitude by a straight line, $67·5 + 0·87t$, which entirely agrees with the results of experiment. According to this the figure expressing the solubility of salt at 0° exactly coincides with the composition of a definite chemical compound—$NaNO_3,7H_2O$. The experiments made by Ditte showed that all saturated solutions between 0° and -15·7° have such a composition, and that at the latter temperature the solution completely solidifies into one homogeneous whole. Between 0° and -15·7° the solution $NaNO_3,7H_2O$ does not deposit either salt or ice. Thus the solubility of sodium nitrate is expressed by a broken straight line. In recent times (1888) Étard discovered a similar phenomenon in many of the sulphates. Brandes, in 1830, shows a diminution in solubility below 100° for manganese sulphate. The percentage by weight (*i.e.* per 100 parts of the solution, and not of water) of saturation for ferrous sulphate, $FeSO_4$, from -2° to +65° = 13·5 + 0·3784t—that is, the solubility of the salt increases. The solubility remains constant from 65° to 98° (according to Brandes the solubility then increases; this divergence of opinion requires proof), and from 98° to 150° it falls as = 104·35 - 0·6685t. Hence, at about +156° the solubility should = 0, and this has been confirmed by experiment. I observe, on my part, that Étard's formula gives 38·1 p.c. of salt at 65° and 38·8 p.c. at 92°, and this maximum amount of salt in the solution very nearly corresponds with the composition $FeSO_4,14H_2O$, which requires 37·6 p.c. From what has been said, it is evident that the data concerning solubility require a new method of investigation, which should have in view the entire scale of solubility— from the formation of completely solidified solutions (cryohydrates, which we shall speak of presently) to the separation of salts from their solutions, if this is accomplished at a higher temperature (for manganese and cadmium sulphates there is an entire separation, according to Étard), or to the formation of a constant solubility (for potassium sulphate the solubility, according to Étard, remains constant from 163° to 220° and equals 24·9 p.c.) (See Chapter XIV., note 50, solubility of $CaCl_2$.)

[25] The latent heat of fusion is determined at the temperature of fusion, whilst solution takes place at the ordinary temperature, and one must think that at this temperature the latent heat would be different, just as the latent heat of evaporation varies with the temperature (see Note 11). Besides which, in dissolving, disintegration of the particles of both the solvent and the substance dissolved takes place, a process which in its mechanical aspect resembles evaporation, and therefore must consume much heat. The heat emitted in the solution of a solid must therefore be considered (Personne) as composed of three factors—(1) positive, the effect of combination; (2) negative, the effect of transference into a liquid state; and (3) negative, the effect of disintegration. In the solution of a liquid by a liquid the second factor is removed; and therefore, if the heat evolved in combination is greater than that absorbed in disintegration a heating effect is observed, and in the reverse case a cooling effect; and, indeed, sulphuric acid, alcohol, and many liquids evolve heat in dissolving in each other. But the solution of chloroform in carbon bisulphide (Bussy and Binget), or of phenol (or aniline) in water (Alexéeff), produces cold. In the solution of a small quantity of water in acetic acid (Abasheff), or hydrocyanic acid (Bussy

and Binget), or amyl alcohol (Alexéeff), cold is produced, whilst in the solution of these substances in an excess of water heat is evolved.

The relation existing between the solubility of solid bodies and the heat and temperature of fusion and solution has been studied by many investigators, and more recently (1893) by Schröder, who states that in the solution of a solid body in a solvent which does not act chemically upon it, a very simple process takes place, which differs but little from the intermixture of two gases which do not react chemically upon each other. The following relation between the heat of solution Q and the heat of fusion p may then be taken: $P\ \boxed{T_0} = Q\ \boxed{T}$ = constant, where T_0 and T are the absolute (from -273°) temperatures of fusion and saturation. Thus, for instance, in the case of naphthalene the calculated and observed magnitudes of the heat of solution differ but slightly from each other.

The fullest information concerning the solution of liquids in liquids has been gathered by W. T. Alexéeff (1883–1885); these data are, however, far from being sufficient to solve the mass of problems respecting this subject. He showed that two liquids which dissolve in each other, intermix together in all proportions at a certain temperature. Thus the solubility of phenol, C_6H_6O, in water, and the converse, is limited up to 70°, whilst above this temperature they intermix in all proportions. This is seen from the following figures, where p is the percentage amount of phenol and t the temperature at which the solution becomes turbid—that is, that at which it is saturated:—

p = 7·12 10·20 15·31 26·15 28·55 36·70 48·86 61·15 71·97

t = 1°   45°   60°   67°   67°.   67°   65°   53°   20°

It is exactly the same with the solution of benzene, aniline, and other substances in molten sulphur. Alexéeff discovered a similar complete intermixture for solutions of secondary butyl alcohol in water at about 107°; at lower temperatures the solubility is not only limited, but between 50° and 70° it is at its minimum, both for solutions of the alcohol in water and for water in the alcohol; and at a temperature of 5° both solutions exhibit a fresh change in their scale of solubility, so that a solution of the alcohol in water which is saturated between 5° and 40° will become turbid when heated to 60°. In the solution of liquids in liquids, Alexéeff observed a lowering in temperature (an absorption of heat) and an absence of change in specific heat (calculated for the mixture) much more frequently than had been done by previous observers. As regards his hypothesis (in the sense of a mechanical and not a chemical representation of solutions) that substances in solution preserve their physical states (as gases, liquids, or

- 125 -

solids), it is very doubtful, for it would necessitate admitting the presence of ice in water or its vapour.

From what has been said above, it will be clear that even in so very simple a case as solution, it is impossible to calculate the heat emitted by chemical action alone, and that the chemical process cannot be separated from the physical and mechanical.

[26] The cooling effect produced in the solution of solids (and also in the expansion of gases and in evaporation) is applied to the *production of low temperatures*. Ammonium nitrate is very often used for this purpose; in dissolving in water it absorbs 77 units of heat per each part by weight. On evaporating the solution thus formed, the solid salt is re-obtained. The application of the various *freezing mixtures* is based on the same principle. Snow or broken ice frequently enters into the composition of these *mixtures*, advantage being taken of its latent heat of fusion in order to obtain the lowest possible temperature (without altering the pressure or employing heat, as in other methods of obtaining a low temperature). For laboratory work recourse is most often had to a mixture of three parts of snow and one part of common salt, which causes the temperature to fall from 0° to -21° C. Potassium thiocyanate, KCNS, mixed with water (¾ by weight of the salt) gives a still lower temperature. By mixing ten parts of crystallised calcium chloride, $CaCl_2,6H_2O$, with seven parts of snow, the temperature may even fall from 0° to -55°.

[27] The heat which is evolved in solution, or even in the dilution of solutions, is also sometimes made use of in practice. Thus caustic soda (NaHO), in dissolving or on the addition of water to a strong solution of it, evolves so much heat that it can replace fuel. In a steam boiler, which has been previously heated to the boiling point, another boiler is placed containing caustic soda, and the exhaust steam is made to pass through the latter; the formation of steam then goes on for a somewhat long period of time without any other heating. Norton makes use of this for smokeless street locomotives.

[28]

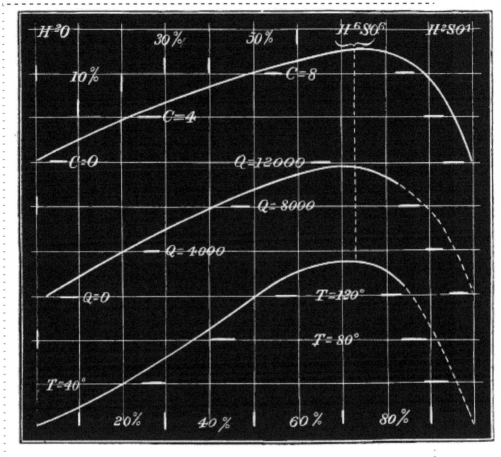

FIG. 17.—Curves expressing the contraction, quantity of heat, and rises of temperature produced by mixing sulphuric acid with water. Percentage of H_2SO_4 is given along the axis of abscissae.

The temperatures obtained by mixing monohydrated sulphuric acid, H_2SO_4, with different quantities of water, are shown on the lowest curve in fig. 17, the relative proportions of both substances being expressed in percentages by weight along the horizontal axis. The greatest rise of temperature is 149°. It corresponds with the greatest evolution of heat (given on the middle curve) corresponding with a definite volume (100 c.c.) of the solution produced. The top curve expresses the degree of contraction, which also corresponds with 100 volumes of the solution produced. The greatest contraction, as also the greatest rise of temperature, corresponds with the formation of a trihydrate, $H_2SO_4,2H_2O$ (= 73·1 p.c. H_2SO_4), which very likely repeats itself in a similar form in other solutions, although all the phenomena (of contraction, evolution of heat, and rise of temperature) are very complex and are dependent on many circumstances. One would think, however, judging from the above examples, that all other influences are feebler in their action than chemical attraction, especially when it is so considerable as between sulphuric acid and water.

[29] If a volume of gas v be measured under a pressure of h mm. of mercury (at 0°) and at a temperature t Centigrade, then, according to the combined laws of Boyle, Mariotte, and of Gay-Lussac, its volume at 0° and 760 mm. will equal the product of v into 760 divided by the product of h into $1 + at$, where a is the co-efficient of expansion of gases, which is equal to 0·00367. The weight of the gas will be equal to its volume at 0° and 760 mm. multiplied by its density referred to air and by the weight of one volume of air at 0° and 760 mm. The weight of one litre of air under these conditions being = 1·293 gram. If the density of the gas be given in relation to hydrogen this must be divided by 14·4 to bring it in relation to air. If the gas be measured when saturated with aqueous vapour, then it must be reduced to the volume and weight of the gas when dry, according to the rules given in Note 1. If the pressure be determined by a column of mercury having a temperature t, then by dividing the height of the column by $1 + 0·00018t$ the corresponding height at 0° is obtained. If the gas be enclosed in a tube in which a liquid stands above the level of the mercury, the height of the column of the liquid being = H and its density = D, then the gas will be under a pressure which is equal to the barometric pressure less HD $\boxed{13·59}$, where 13·59 is the density of mercury. By these methods the *quantity of a gas* is determined, and its observed volume reduced to normal conditions or to parts by weight. The physical data concerning vapours and gases must be continually kept in sight in dealing with and measuring gases. The student must become perfectly familiar with the calculations relating to gases.

[30] According to Bunsen, Winkler, Timofeeff, and others, 100 vols. of water under a pressure of one atmosphere absorb the following volumes of gas (measured at 0° and 760 mm.):—

	1	2	3	4	5	6	7	8	9	10	11
0°	4·82	2·35	2·15	179·7	3·54	130·5	437·1	688·6	5·4	104960	7·38
20°	3·10	1·54	1·83	90·1	2·32	67·0	290·5	362·2	3·5	65400	4·71

1, oxygen; 2, nitrogen; 3, hydrogen; 4, carbonic anhydride; 5, carbonic oxide; 6, nitrous oxide; 7, hydrogen sulphide; 8, sulphurous anhydride; 9, marsh gas; 10, ammonia; 11, nitric oxide. The decrease of solubility with a rise of temperature varies for different gases; it is greater, the greater the molecular weight of the gas. It is shown by calculation that this decrease varies (Winkler) as the cube root of the molecular weight of the gas. This is seen from the following table:

Decrease of solubility per 20° in per cent.		Cube root of molecular weight.	Ratio between decrease and cube root of mol. wt.
H_2	15·32	1·259	12·17
N_2	34·33	3·037	11·30
CO	34·44	3·037	11·34
NO	36·24	3·107	11·66
O_2	36·55	3·175	11·51

The decrease in the coefficient of absorption with the temperature must be connected with a change in the physical properties of the water. Winkler (1891) remarked a certain relation between the internal friction and the coefficient of absorption at various temperatures.

[31] These figures show that the co-efficient of solubility decreases with an increase of pressure, notwithstanding that the carbonic anhydride approaches a liquid state. As a matter of fact, liquefied carbonic anhydride does not intermix with water, and does not exhibit a rapid increase in solubility at its temperature of liquefaction. This indicates, in the first place, that solution does not consist in liquefaction, and in the second place that the solubility of a substance is determined by a peculiar attraction of water for the substance dissolving. Wroblewski even considered it possible to admit that a dissolved gas retains its properties as a gas. This he deduced from experiments, which showed that the rate of diffusion of gases in a solvent is, for gases of different densities, inversely proportional to the square roots of their densities, just as the velocities of gaseous molecules (see Note 34). Wroblewski showed the affinity of water, H_2O, for carbonic anhydride, CO_2, from the fact that on expanding moist compressed carbonic anhydride (compressed at 0° under a pressure of 10 atmospheres) he obtained (a fall in temperature takes place from the expansion) a very unstable definite crystalline compound, $CO_2 + 8H_2O$.

[32] As, according to the researches of Roscoe and his collaborators, ammonia exhibits a considerable deviation at low temperatures from the law of Henry and Dalton, whilst at 100° the deviation is small, it would appear that the dissociating influence of temperature affects all gaseous solutions; that is, at high temperatures, the solutions of all gases will follow the law, and at lower temperatures there will in all cases be a deviation from it.

[33] The ratio between the pressure and the amount of gas dissolved was discovered by Henry in 1805, and Dalton in 1807 pointed out the adaptability of this law to cases of gaseous mixtures, introducing the conception of partial pressures which is absolutely necessary for a right comprehension of Dalton's law. The conception of partial pressures essentially enters into that of the diffusion of vapours in gases (footnote 1); for the pressure of damp air is equal to the sum of the pressures of dry air and of the aqueous vapour in it, and it is admitted as a corollary to Dalton's law that evaporation in dry air takes place as in a vacuum. It is, however, necessary to remark that the volume of a mixture of two gases (or vapours) is only approximately equal to the sum of the volumes of its constituents (the same, naturally, also refers to their pressures)—that is to say, in mixing gases a change of volume occurs, which, although small, is quite apparent when carefully measured. For instance, in 1888 Brown showed that on mixing various volumes of sulphurous anhydride (SO_2) with carbonic anhydride (at equal pressures of 760 mm. and equal temperatures) a decrease of pressure of 3·9 millimetres of mercury was observed. The possibility of a chemical action in similar mixtures is evident from the fact that equal volumes of sulphurous and carbonic anhydrides at -19° form, according to Pictet's researches in 1888, a liquid which may be regarded as an unstable chemical compound, or a solution similar to that given when sulphurous anhydride and water combine to an unstable chemical whole.

[34] The origin of the kinetic theory of gases now generally accepted, according to which they are animated by a rapid progressive motion, is very ancient (Bernouilli and others in the last century had already developed a similar representation), but it was only generally accepted after the mechanical theory of heat had been established, and after the work of Krönig (1855), and especially after its mathematical side had been worked out by Clausius and Maxwell. The pressure, elasticity, diffusion, and internal friction of gases, the laws of Boyle, Mariotte, and of Gay-Lussac and Avogadro-Gerhardt are not only explained (deduced) by the kinetic theory of gases, but also expressed with perfect exactitude; thus, for example, the magnitude of the internal friction of different gases was foretold with exactitude by Maxwell, by applying the theory of probabilities to the impact of gaseous particles. The kinetic theory of gases must therefore be considered as one of the most brilliant acquisitions of the latter half of the present century. The velocity of the progressive motion of the particles of a gas, one cubic centimetre of which weighs d grams, is found, according to the theory, to be equal to the square root of the product of $3pDq$ divided by d, where p is the pressure under which d is determined expressed in centimetres of the mercury column, D the weight of a cubic centimetre of mercury in grams ($D = 13\cdot59$, $p = 76$, consequently the normal pressure = 1,033 grams on a sq. cm.), and g the

acceleration of gravity in centimetres ($g = 980\cdot5$, at the sea level and long. 45° = 981·92 at St. Petersburg; in general it varies with the longitude and altitude of the locality). Therefore, at 0° the velocity of hydrogen is 1,843, and of oxygen 461, metres per second. This is the average velocity, and (according to Maxwell and others) it is probable that the velocities of individual particles are different; that is, they occur in, as it were, different conditions of temperature, which it is very important to take into consideration in investigating many phenomena proper to matter. It is evident from the above determination of the velocity of gases, that different gases at the same temperature and pressure have average velocities, which are inversely proportional to the square roots of their densities; this is also shown by direct experiment on the flow of gases through a fine orifice, or through a porous wall. This *dissimilar velocity of flow* for different gases is frequently taken advantage of in chemical researches (see Chap. II. and also Chap. VII.) in order to separate two gases having different densities and velocities. The difference of the velocity of flow of gases also determines the phenomenon cited in the following footnote for demonstrating the existence of an internal motion in gases.

If for a certain mass of a gas which fully and exactly follows the laws of Mariotte and Gay-Lussac the temperature t and the pressure p be changed simultaneously, then the entire change would be expressed by the equation $pv = C(1 + at)$, or, what is the same, $pv = RT$, where $T = t + 273$ and C and R are constants which vary not only with the units taken but with the nature of the gas and its mass. But as there are discrepancies from both the fundamental laws of gases (which will be discussed in the following chapter), and as, on the one hand, a certain attraction between the gaseous molecules must be admitted, while on the other hand the molecules of gases themselves must occupy a portion of a space, hence for ordinary gases, within any considerable variation of pressure and temperature, recourse should be had to Van der Waal's formula—

$$(p + a\, v^2)(v - p) = R(1 + at)$$

where a is the true co-efficient of expansion of gases.

The formula of Van der Waals has an especially important significance in the case of the passage of a gas into a liquid state, because the fundamental properties of both gases and liquids are equally well expressed by it, although only in their general features.

The further development of the questions referring to the subjects here touched on, which are of especial interest for the theory of solutions, must be looked for in special memoirs and works on theoretical and physical chemistry. A small part of this subject will be partially considered in the footnotes of the following chapter.

[35] Although the actual motion of gaseous molecules, which is accepted by the kinetic theory of gases, cannot be seen, yet its existence may be rendered evident by taking advantage of the difference in the velocities undoubtedly belonging to different gases which are of different densities under equal pressures. The molecules of a light gas must move more rapidly than the molecules of a heavier gas in order to produce the same pressure. Let us take, therefore, two gases—hydrogen and air; the former is 14·4 times lighter than the latter, and hence the molecules of hydrogen must move almost four times more quickly than air (more exactly 3·8, according to the formula given in the preceding footnote). Consequently, if a porous cylinder containing air is introduced into an atmosphere of hydrogen, then in a given time the volume of hydrogen which succeeds in entering the cylinder will be greater than the volume of air leaving the cylinder, and therefore the pressure inside the cylinder will rise until the gaseous mixture (of air and hydrogen) attains an equal density both inside and outside the cylinder. If now the experiment be reversed and air surround the cylinder, and hydrogen be inside the cylinder, then more gas will leave the cylinder than enters it, and hence the pressure inside the cylinder will be diminished. In these considerations we have replaced the idea of the number of molecules by the idea of volumes. We shall learn subsequently that equal volumes of different gases contain an equal number of molecules (the law of Avogadro-Gerhardt), and therefore instead of speaking of the number of molecules we can speak of the number of volumes. If the cylinder be partially immersed in water the rise and fall of the pressure can be observed directly, and the experiment consequently rendered self-evident.

[36] Here two cases occur; either the atmosphere surrounding the solution may be limited, or it may be proportionally so vast as to be unlimited, like the earth's atmosphere. If a gaseous solution be brought into an atmosphere of another gas which is limited—for instance, as in a closed vessel—then a portion of the gas held in solution will be expelled, and thus pass over into the atmosphere surrounding the solution, and will produce its partial pressure. Let us imagine that water saturated with carbonic anhydride at $0°$ and under the ordinary pressure is brought into an atmosphere of a gas which is not absorbed by water; for instance, that 10 c.c. of an aqueous solution of carbonic anhydride is introduced into a vessel holding 10 c.c. of such a gas. The solution will contain 18 c.c. of carbonic anhydride. The expulsion of this gas proceeds until a state of equilibrium is arrived at. The liquid will then contain a certain amount of carbonic anhydride, which is retained under the partial pressure of that gas which has been expelled. Now, how much gas will remain in the liquid and how much will pass over into the surrounding atmosphere? In order to solve this problem, let us suppose that x cubic centimetres of carbonic

anhydride are retained in the solution. It is evident that the amount of carbonic anhydride which passed over into the surrounding atmosphere will be 18 - x, and the total volume of gas will be 10 + 18 - x or 28 - x cubic centimetres. The partial pressure under which the carbonic anhydride is then dissolved will be (supposing that the common pressure remains constant the whole time) equal to $18 - x \boxed{28 - x}$, hence there is not in solution 18 c.c. of carbonic anhydride (as would be the case were the partial pressure equal to the atmospheric pressure), but only $18 \ 18 - x \boxed{28 - x}$, which is equal to x, and we therefore obtain the equation $18 \ 18 - x \boxed{28 - x} = x$, hence $x = 8 \cdot 69$. Again, where the atmosphere into which the gaseous solution is introduced is not only that of another gas but also unlimited, then the gas dissolved will, on passing over from the solution, diffuse into this atmosphere, and produce an infinitely small pressure in the unlimited atmosphere. Consequently, no gas can be retained in solution under this infinitely small pressure, and it will be entirely expelled from the solution. For this reason water saturated with a gas which is not contained in air, will be entirely deprived of the dissolved gas if left exposed to the air. Water also passes off from a solution into the atmosphere, and it is evident that there might be such a case as a constant proportion between the quantity of water vaporised and the quantity of a gas expelled from a solution, so that not the gas alone, but the entire gaseous solution, would pass off. A similar case is exhibited in solutions which are not decomposed by heat (such as those of hydrogen chloride and iodide), as will afterwards be considered.

[37] However, in those cases when the variation of the co-efficient of solubility with the temperature is not sufficiently great, and when a known quantity of aqueous vapour and of the gas passes off from a solution at the boiling point, an atmosphere may be obtained having the same composition as the liquid itself. In this case the amount of gas passing over into such an atmosphere will not be greater than that held by the liquid, and therefore such a gaseous solution will distil over unchanged. The solution will then represent, like a solution of hydriodic acid in water, a liquid which is not altered by distillation, while the pressure under which this distillation takes place remains constant. Thus in all its aspects solution presents gradations from the most feeble affinities to examples of intimate chemical combination. The *amount of heat* evolved in the solution of equal volumes of different gases is in distinct relation with these variations of stability and solubility of different gases. $22 \cdot 3$ litres of the following gases (at 760 mm. pressure) evolve the following number of (gram) units of heat in dissolving in a large mass of water; carbonic anhydride 5,600, sulphurous anhydride 7,700, ammonia 8,800, hydrochloric acid 17,400, and hydriodic acid 19,400. The two last-named gases, which are not expelled from their

solution by boiling, evolve approximately twice as much heat as gases like ammonia, which are separated from their solutions by boiling, whilst gases which are only slightly soluble evolve very much less heat.

[38] Among the numerous researches concerning this subject, certain results obtained by Paul Bert are cited in Chapter III., and we will here point out that Prof. Sechenoff, in his researches on the absorption of gases by liquids, very fully investigated the phenomena of the solution of carbonic anhydride in solutions of various salts, and arrived at many important results, which showed that, on the one hand, in the solution of carbonic anhydride in solutions of salts on which it is capable of acting chemically (for example, sodium carbonate, borax, ordinary sodium phosphate), there is not only an increase of solubility, but also a distinct deviation from the law of Henry and Dalton; whilst, on the other hand, that solutions of salts which are not acted on by carbonic anhydride (for example, the chlorides, nitrates, and sulphates) absorb less of it, owing to the 'competition' of the salt already dissolved, and follow the law of Henry and Dalton, but at the same time show undoubted signs of a chemical action between the salt, water, and carbonic anhydride. Sulphuric acid (whose co-efficient of absorption is 92 vols. per 100), when diluted with water, absorbs less and less carbonic anhydride, until the hydrate H_2SO_4,H_2O (co-eff. of absorption then equals 66 vols.) is formed; then on further addition of water the solubility again rises until a solution of 100 p.c. of water is obtained.

[39] Kremers made this observation in the following simple form:—He took a narrow-necked flask, with a mark on the narrow part (like that on a litre flask which is used for accurately measuring liquids), poured water into it, and then inserted a funnel, having a fine tube which reached to the bottom of the flask. Through this funnel he carefully poured a solution of any salt, and (having removed the funnel) allowed the liquid to attain a definite temperature (in a water bath); he then filled the flask up to the mark with water. In this manner two layers of liquid were obtained, the heavy saline solution below and water above. The flask was then shaken in order to accelerate diffusion, and it was observed that the volume became less if the temperature remained constant. This can be proved by calculation, if the specific gravity of the solutions and water be known. Thus at 15° one c.c. of a 20 p.c. solution of common salt weighs 1·1500 gram, hence 100 grams occupy a volume of 86·96 c.c. As the sp. gr. of water at 15° = 0·99916, therefore 100 grams of water occupy a volume of 100·08 c.c. The sum of the volumes is 187·04 c.c. After mixing, 200 grams of a 10 p.c. solution are obtained. Its specific gravity is 1·0725 (at 15° and referred to water at its maximum density), hence the 200 grams will occupy a volume of 186·48 c.c. The contraction is consequently equal to 0·56 c.c.

[40] The contractions produced in the case of the solution of sulphuric acid in water are shown in the diagram Fig. 17 (page 77). Their maximum is 10·1 c.c. per 100 c.c. of the solution formed. A maximum contraction of 4·15 at 0°, 3·78 at 15°, and 3·50 at 30°, takes place in the solution of 46 parts by weight of anhydrous alcohol in 54 parts of water. This signifies that if, at 0°, 46 parts by weight of alcohol be taken per 54 parts by weight of water, then the sum of their separate volumes will he 104·15, and after mixing their total volume will be 100.

[41] This subject will be considered later in this work, and we shall then see that the contraction produced in reactions of combination (of solids or liquids) is very variable in its amount, and that there are, although rarely, reactions of combination in which contraction does not take place, or when an increase of volume is produced.

[42] The compressibility of solutions of common salt is less, according to Grassi, than that of water. At 18° the compression of water per million volumes = 48 vols. for a pressure of one atmosphere; for a 15 p.c. solution of common salt it is 32, and for a 24 p.c. solution 26 vols. Similar determinations were made by Brown (1887) for saturated solutions of sal ammoniac (38 vols.), alum (46 vols.), common salt (27 vols.), and sodium sulphate at +1°, when the compressibility of water = 47 per million volumes. This investigator also showed that substances which dissolve with an evolution of heat and with an increase in volume (as, for instance, sal ammoniac) are partially separated from their saturated solutions by an increase of pressure (this experiment was particularly conclusive in the case of sal ammoniac), whilst the solubility of substances which dissolve with an absorption of heat or diminution in volume increases, although very slightly, *with an increase of pressure.* Sorby observed the same phenomenon with common salt (1863).

[43] The most trustworthy data relating to the variation of the specific gravity of solutions with a change of their composition and temperature, are collected and discussed in my work cited in footnote 19. The practical (for the amount of a substance in solution is determined by the aid of the specific gravities of solutions, both in works and in laboratory practice) and the theoretical (for specific gravity can be more accurately observed than other properties, and because a variation in specific gravity governs the variation of many other properties) interest of this subject, besides the strict rules and laws to which it is liable, make one wish that this province of data concerning solutions may soon be enriched by further observations of as accurate a nature as possible. Their collection does not present any great difficulty, although requiring much time and attention. Pickering in London and Tourbaba in Kharkoff must be ranked first among those who have pursued problems of this nature during recent years.

[44] Inasmuch as the degree of change exhibited in many properties on the formation of solutions is not large, so, owing to the insufficient accuracy of observations, a proportionality between this change and a change of composition may, in a first rough approximation and especially within narrow limits of change of composition, easily be imagined in cases where it does not even exist. The conclusion of Michel and Kraft is particularly instructive in this respect; in 1854, on the basis of their incomplete researches, they supposed that the increment of the specific gravity of solutions was proportional to the increment of a salt in a given volume of a solution, which is only true for determinations of specific gravity which are exact to the second decimal place—an accuracy insufficient even for technical determinations. Accurate measurements do not confirm a proportionality either in this case or in many others where a ratio has been generally accepted; as, for example, for the rotatory power (with respect to the plane of polarisation) of solutions, and for their capillarity, &c. Nevertheless, such a method is not only still made use of, but even has its advantages when applied to solutions within a limited scope—as, for instance, very weak solutions, and for a first acquaintance with the phenomena accompanying solution, and also as a means for facilitating the application of mathematical analysis to the investigation of the phenomenon of solution. Judging by the results obtained in my researches on the specific gravity of solutions, I think that in many cases it would be nearer the truth to take the change of properties as proportional, not to the amount of a substance dissolved, but to the product of this quantity and the amount of water in which it is dissolved; the more so since many chemical relations vary in proportion to the reacting masses, and a similar ratio has been established for many phenomena of attraction studied by mechanics. This product is easily arrived at when the quantity of water in the solutions to be compared is constant, as is shown in investigating the fall of temperature in the formation of ice (*see* footnote 49, p. 91).

[45] All the different forms of chemical reaction may be said to take place in the process of solution. (1) *Combinations* between the solvent and the substance dissolved, which are more or less stable (more or less dissociated). This form of reaction is the most probable, and is that most often observed. (2) Reactions of *substitution* or of *double decomposition* between the molecules. Thus it may be supposed that in the solution of sal ammoniac, NH_4Cl, the action of water produces ammonia, NH_4HO, and hydrochloric acid, HCl, which are dissolved in the water and simultaneously attract each other. As these solutions and many others do indeed exhibit signs, which are sometimes indisputable, of similar double decompositions (thus solutions of sal-ammoniac yield a certain amount of ammonia), it is probable that this form of reaction is more often met with

than is generally thought. (3) Reactions of *isomerism* or *replacement* are also probably met with in solution, all the more as here molecules of different kinds come into intimate contact, and it is very likely that the configuration of the atoms in the molecules under these influences is somewhat different from what it was in its original and isolated state. One is led to this supposition especially from observations made on solutions of substances which rotate the plane of polarisation (and observations of this kind are very sensitive with respect to the atomic structure of molecules), because they show, for example (according to Schneider, 1881), that strong solutions of malic acid rotate the plane of polarisation to the right, whilst its ammonium salts in all degrees of concentration rotate the plane of polarisation to the left. (4) Reactions of *decomposition* under the influences of solution are not only rational in themselves, but have in recent years been recognised by Arrhenius, Ostwald, and others, particularly on the basis of electrolytic determinations. If a portion of the molecules of a solution occur in a condition of decomposition, the other portion may occur in a yet more complex state of combination, just as the velocity of the motion of different gaseous molecules may be far from being the same (*see* Note 34, p. 81).

It is, therefore, very probable that the reactions taking place in solution vary both quantitatively and qualitatively with the mass of water in the solution, and the great difficulty in arriving at a definite conclusion as to the nature of the chemical relations which take place in the process of solution will be understood, and if besides this the existence of a physical process, like the sliding between and interpenetration of two homogeneous liquids, be also recognised in solution, then the complexity of the problem as to the actual nature of solutions, which is now to the fore, appears in its true light. However, the efforts which are now being applied to the solution of this problem are so numerous and of such varied aspect that they will afford future investigators a vast mass of material towards the construction of a complete theory of solution.

For my part, I am of opinion that the study of the physical properties of solutions (and especially of weak ones) which now obtains, cannot give any fundamental and complete solution of the problem whatever (although it should add much to both the provinces of physics and chemistry), but that, parallel with it, should be undertaken the study of the influence of temperature, and especially of low temperatures, the application to solutions of the mechanical theory of heat, and the comparative study of the chemical properties of solutions. The beginning of all this is already established, but it is impossible to consider in so short an exposition of chemistry the further efforts of this kind which have been made up to the present date.

[46] If solutions are regarded as being in a state of dissociation (*see* footnote 19, p. 64) it would be expected that they would contain free molecules of water, which form one of the products of the decomposition of those definite compounds whose formation is the cause of solution. In separating as ice or vapour, water makes, with a solution, a heterogeneous system (made up of substances in different physical states) similar, for instance, to the formation of a precipitate or volatile substance in reactions of double decomposition.

[47] If the substance dissolved is non-volatile (like salt or sugar), or only slightly volatile, then the whole of the tension of the vapour given off is due to the water, but if a solution of a volatile substance—for instance, a gas or a volatile liquid—evaporates, then only a portion of the pressure belongs to the water, and the whole pressure observed consists of the sum of the pressures of the vapours of the water and of the substance dissolved. The majority of researches bear on the first case, which will be spoken of presently, and the observations of D. P. Konovaloff (1881) refer to the second case. He showed that in the case of two volatile liquids, mutually soluble in each other, forming two layers of saturated solutions (for example, ether and water, Note 20, p. 67), both solutions have an equal vapour tension (in the case in point the tension of both is equal to 431 mm. of mercury at 19·8°). Further, he found that for solutions which are formed in all proportions, the tension is either greater (solutions of alcohol and water) or less (solutions of formic acid) than that which answers to the rectilinear change (proportional to the composition) from the tension of water to the tension of the substance dissolved; thus, the tension, for example, of a 70 p.c. solution of formic acid is less, at all temperatures, than the tension of water and of formic acid itself. In this case the tension of a solution is never equal to the sum of the tensions of the dissolving liquids, as Regnault already showed when he distinguished this case from that in which a mixture of liquids, which are insoluble in each other, evaporates. From this it is evident that a mutual action occurs in solution, which diminishes the vapour tensions proper to the individual substances, as would be expected on the supposition of the formation of compounds in solutions, because the elasticity then always diminishes.

[48] This amount is usually expressed by the weight of the substance dissolved per 100 parts by weight of water. Probably it would be better to express it by the quantity of the substance in a definite volume of the solution—for instance, in a litre—or by the ratios of the number of molecules of water and of the substance dissolved.

[49] The variation of the vapour tension of solutions has been investigated by many. The best known researches are those of Wüllner in Germany (1858–1860) and of Tamman in Russia (1887). The researches on

the temperature of the formation of ice from various solutions are also very numerous; Blagden (1788), Rüdorff (1861), and De Coppet (1871) established the beginning, but this kind of investigation takes its chief interest from the work of Raoult, begun in 1882 on aqueous solutions, and afterwards continued for solutions in various other easily frozen liquids— for instance, benzene, C_6H_6 (melts at $4·96°$), acetic acid, $C_2H_4O_2$ ($16·75°$), and others. An especially important interest is attached to these cryoscopic investigations of Raoult in France on the depression of the freezing point, because he took solutions of many well-known carbon-compounds and discovered a simple relation between the molecular weight of the substances and the temperature of crystallisation of the solvent, which enabled this kind of research to be applied to the investigation of the nature of substances. We shall meet with the application of this method later on (*see also* Chapter VII.), and at present will only cite the deduction arrived at from these results. The solution of one-hundredth part of that molecular gram weight which corresponds with the formula of a substance dissolved (for example, $NaCl = 58·5$, $C_2H_6O = 46$, &c.) in 100 parts of a solvent lowers the freezing point of its solution in water $0·185°$, in benzene $0·49°$, and in acetic acid $O·39°$, or twice as much as with water. And as in weak solutions the depression or fall of freezing point is proportional to the amount of the substance dissolved, it follows that the fall of freezing point for all other solutions may be calculated from this rule. So, for instance, the weight which corresponds with the formula of acetone, C_3H_6O is 58; a solution containing $2·42$, $6·22$, and $12·35$ grams of acetone per 100 grams of water, forms ice (according to the determinations of Beckmann) at $0·770°$, $1·930°$, and $3·820°$, and these figures show that with a solution containing $0·58$ gram of acetone per 100 of water the fall of the temperature of the formation of ice will be $0·185°$, $0·180°$, and $0·179°$. It must be remarked that the law of proportionality between the fall of temperature of the formation of ice, and the composition of a solution, is in general only approximate, and is only applicable to weak solutions (Pickering and others).

We will here remark that the theoretical interest of this subject was strengthened on the discovery of the connection existing between the fall of tension, the fall of the temperature of the formation of ice, of osmotic pressure (Van't Hoff, Note 19), and of the electrical conductivity of solutions, and we will therefore supplement what we have already said on the subject by some short remarks on the method of cryoscopic investigations, although the details of the subject form the subject of more special works on physical chemistry (such as Ostwald's *Lehrbuch der allgemeinen Chemie*, 1891–1894, 2 vols.)

In order to determine the *temperature of the formation of ice* (or of crystallisation of other solvents), a solution of known strength is prepared and poured into a cylindrical vessel surrounded by a second similar vessel, leaving a layer of air between the two, which, being a bad conductor, prevents any rapid change of temperature. The bulb of a sensitive and corrected thermometer is immersed in the solution, and also a bent platinum wire for stirring the solution; the whole is then cooled (by immersing the apparatus in a freezing mixture), and the temperature at which ice begins to separate observed. If the temperature at first falls slightly lower, it nevertheless becomes constant when ice begins to form. By then allowing the liquid to get just warm, and again observing the temperature of the formation of ice, an exact determination may be arrived at. It is still better to take a large mass of solution, and induce the formation of the first crystals by dropping a small lump of ice into the solution already partially over-cooled. This only imperceptibly changes the composition of the solution. The observation should be made at the point of formation of only a very small amount of crystals, as otherwise the composition of the solution will become altered from their separation. Every precaution must be taken to prevent the access of moisture to the interior of the apparatus, which might also alter the composition of the solution or properties of the solvent (for instance, when using acetic acid).

With respect to the depression of dilute solutions it is known—(1) That the depression increases in almost direct proportion to the amount of the substance in solution (always per 100 parts of water), for example, for KCl when the solution contains 1 part of salt (per 100 parts of water) the depression $= 0.45°$, when the solution contains 2 parts of salt $= 0.90°$, with 10 parts of salt $= 4.4°$. (2) The greater the molecular weight expressed by the formula (see Chapter VII.), and designated by M, the less, under other similar conditions, will be the depression d, and therefore if the concentration of a solution (the amount by weight of substance dissolved per 100 parts of water) be designated by p, then the fraction M d p or the molecular depression for a given class of substances will be a constant quantity; for example, in the case of methyl alcohol in water 17.3, for acetone about 18.0, for sugar about 18.5. (3) In general the molecular depression for substances whose solutions do not conduct an electric current is about 18.5, while for acids, salts, and such like substances whose solutions do conduct electricity, it is i times greater; for instance, for HCl, KI, HNO_3, KHO, &c., about 36 (i is nearly 2), for borax about 66, and so on where i varies in the same manner as it does in the case of the osmotic pressure of solutions (Note 19). (4) Different solvents (water, acetic acid, benzene, &c.) have each their corresponding constants of molecular depression (which have a certain remote connection with their molecular weight); for example, for acetic acid the molecular depression is about 39 and not 19 (as it is for water), for benzene 49, for methyl alcohol about 17, &c. (5) If the molecular weight M of a substance be unknown, then in the case of non-conductors of electricity or for a given group, it may be found by determining the depression, d, for a given concentration, p; for example, in the case of peroxide of hydrogen, which is a non-conductor of electricity, the molecular weight, M, was found to be nearly 34, *i.e.* equal to H_2O_2.

Similar results have also been found for the fall in the vapour tension of solutions (Note 51), and for the rise of their boiling points (hence these data may also serve for determining the molecular weight of a substance in solution, as is shortly described in Chapter VII., Note 27 bis). And as these conclusions are also applicable in the case of osmotic pressure (Note 19), and a variation in the magnitude of i, in passing from solutions which do not conduct an electric current to those which do conduct electricity is everywhere remarked, so it was natural to here seek that causal connection which Arrhenius (1888), Ostwald, and others expected to find in the supposition that a portion of the substance of the electrolyte is already decomposed in the very act of solution, into its ions (for example, NaCl into Na and Cl), or into the atoms of those individual substances which make their appearance in electrolysis, and in this way to explain the fact that i is greater for those bodies which conduct an electric current. We will not consider here this supposition, known as the hypothesis of 'electrolytic dissociation,' not only because it wholly belongs to that special branch— physical chemistry, and gives scarcely any help towards explaining the chemical relations of solutions (particularly their passage into definite compounds, their reactions, and their very formation), but also because— (1) all the above data (for constant depression, osmotic pressure, &c.) only refer to dilute solutions, and are not applicable to strong solutions; whilst the chemical interest in strong solutions is not less than in dilute solutions, and the transition from the former into the latter is consecutive and inevitable; (2) because in all homogeneous bodies (although it may be insoluble and not an electrolyte) a portion of the atoms may he supposed (Clausius) to be passing from one particle to another (Chapter X., Note 28), and as it were dissociated, but there are no reasons for believing that such a phenomenon is proper to the solutions of electrolytes only; (3) because no essential mark of difference is observed between the solution of electrolytes and non-conductors, although it might be expected there would be according to Arrhenius' hypothesis; (4) because it is most reasonable to suppose the formation of new, more complex, but unstable and easily dissociated compounds in the act of solution, than a decomposition, even partial, of the substances taken; (5) because if Arrhenius' hypothesis be accepted it becomes necessary to admit the existence in solutions of free ions, like the atoms Cl or Na, without any apparent expenditure of the energy necessary for their disruption, and if in this case it can be explained why i then $= 2$, it is not at all clear why solutions of $MgSO_4$ give $i = 1$, although the solution does conduct an electric current; (6) because in dilute solutions, the approximative proportionality between the depression and concentration may be recognised, while admitting the formation of hydrates, with as much right as in admitting the solution of anhydrous substances, and if the formation of hydrates be recognised it is easier to admit that a portion of these hydrates is decomposed than to accept the breaking-up into ions; (7) because the best conductors of electricity are solutions like the sulphates in which it is necessary to recognise the formation of associated systems or hydrates; (8) because the cause of electro-conductivity can be sooner looked for in this affinity and this combination of the substance dissolved with the solvent, as is seen from the fact, that (D. P. Konovaloff) neither aniline nor acetic acid alone conduct an electric current, a solution of aniline in water conducts it badly (and here the affinity is very small), while a solution of aniline in acetic acid forms a good electrolyte, in which, without doubt, chemical forces are acting, bringing aniline, like ammonia, into combination with the acetic acid; which is evident from the researches made by Prof. Konovaloff upon mixtures (solutions) of aniline and other amines; and, lastly, (9) because I, together with many of the chemists of the present day, cannot regard the hypothesis of electrolytic dissociation in the form given to it up to now by Arrhenius and Ostwald, as answering to the sum total of the chemical data respecting solutions and dissociation in general. Thus, although I consider it superfluous to discuss further the evolution of the above theory of solutions, still I think that it would he most useful for students of chemistry to consider all the data referring to this subject, which can be found in the *Zeitschrift für physikalische Chemie*, 1888–1894.

[50] This fact, which was established by Gay-Lussac, Pierson, and v. Babo, is confirmed by the latest observations, and enables us to express not only the fall of tension $(p - p')$ itself, but its ratio to the tension of water ($p - p'$ $\frac{p'}{p}$). It is to be remarked that in the absence of any chemical action, the fall of pressure is either very small, or does not exist at all (note 33), and is not proportional to the quantity of the substance added. As a rule, the tension is then equal, according to the law of Dalton, to the sum of the tensions of the substances taken. Hence liquids which are insoluble in each other (for example, water and chloride of carbon) present a tension equal to the sum of their individual tensions, and therefore such a mixture boils at a lower temperature than the more volatile liquid (Magnus, Regnault).

[51] If, in the example of common salt, the fall of tension be divided by the tension of water, a figure is obtained which is nearly 105 times less than the magnitude of the fall of temperature of formation of ice. This correlation was theoretically deduced by Goldberg, on the basis of the application of the mechanical theory of heat, and is repeated by many investigated solutions.

[52] Fritzsche showed that solutions of certain colouring matters yield colourless ice, which clearly proves the passage of water only into a solid state, without any intermixture of the substance dissolved, although the possibility of the admixture in certain other cases cannot be denied.

[53] As the solubility of certain substances (for example, coniine, cerium sulphate, and others) decreases with a rise of temperature (between certain limits—see, for example, note 24), so these substances do not separate from their saturated solutions on cooling but on heating. Thus a solution of manganese sulphate, saturated at 70°, becomes cloudy on further heating. The point at which a substance separates from its solution with a change of temperature gives an easy means of determining the co-efficient of solubility, and this was taken advantage of by Prof. Alexéeff for determining the solubility of many substances. The phenomenon and method of observation are here essentially the same as in the determination of the temperature of formation of ice. If a solution of a substance which separates out on heating be taken (for example, the sulphate of calcium or manganese), then at a certain fall of temperature ice will separate out from it, and at a certain rise of temperature the salt will separate out. From this example, and from general considerations, it is clear that the separation of a substance dissolved from a solution should present a certain analogy to the separation of ice from a solution. In both cases, a heterogeneous system of a solid and a liquid is formed from a homogeneous (liquid) system.

[54] Those salts which separate out with water of crystallisation and give several crystallohydrates form supersaturated solutions with the greatest facility, and the phenomenon is much more common than was previously imagined. The first data were given in the last century by Loewitz, in St. Petersburg. Numerous researches have proved that supersaturated solutions do not differ from ordinary solutions in any of their essential properties. The variations in specific gravity, vapour tension, formation of ice, &c., take place according to the ordinary laws.

[55] Inasmuch as air, as has been shown by direct experiment, contains, although in very small quantities, minute crystals of salts, and among them sodium sulphate, air can bring about the crystallisation of a supersaturated solution of sodium sulphate in an open vessel, but it has no effect on saturated solutions of certain other salts; for example, lead acetate.

According to the observations of De Boisbaudran, Gernez, and others, isomorphous salts (analogous in composition) are capable of inducing crystallisation. Thus, a supersaturated solution of nickel sulphate crystallises by contact with crystals of sulphates of other metals analogous to it, such as those of magnesium, cobalt, copper, and manganese. The crystallisation of a supersaturated solution, set up by the contact of a minute crystal, starts from it in rays with a definite velocity, and it is evident that the crystals as they form propagate the crystallisation in definite directions. This phenomenon recalls the evolution of organisms from germs. An attraction of similar molecules ensues, and they dispose themselves in definite similar forms.

[56] At the present time a view is very generally accepted, which regards supersaturated solutions as homogeneous systems, which pass into heterogeneous systems (composed of a liquid and a solid substance), in all respects exactly resembling the passage of water cooled below its freezing point into ice and water, or the passage of crystals of rhombic sulphur into monoclinic crystals, and of the monoclinic crystals into rhombic. Although many phenomena of supersaturation are thus clearly understood, yet the spontaneous formation of the unstable hepta-hydrated salt (with $7H_2O$), in the place of the more stable deca-hydrated salt (with mol. $10H_2O$), indicates a property of a saturated solution of sodium sulphate which obliges one to admit that it has a different structure from an ordinary solution. Stcherbacheff asserts, on the basis of his researches, that a solution of the deca-hydrated salt gives, on evaporation, without the aid of heat, the deca-hydrated salt, whilst after heating above 33° it forms a supersaturated solution and the hepta-hydrated salt. But in order that this view should be accepted, some facts must be discovered distinguishing solutions (which are, according to this view, isomeric) containing the hepta-hydrated salt from those containing the deca-hydrated salt, and all efforts in this direction (the study of the properties of the solutions) have given negative results. As some crystallohydrates of salts (alums, sugar of lead, calcium chloride) melt straightway (without separating out anything), whilst others (like $Na_2SO_4,10H_2O$) are broken up, then it may be that the latter are only in a state of equilibrium at a higher temperature than their melting point. It may here be observed that in melting crystals of the deca-hydrated salt, there is formed, besides the solid anhydrous salt, a saturated solution giving the hepta-hydrated salt, so that this passage from the deca-to the hepta-hydrated salt, and the reverse, takes place with the formation of the anhydrous (or, it may be, monohydrated) salt.

Moreover, supersaturation (Potilitzin, 1889) only takes place with those substances which are capable of giving several modifications or several crystallohydrates, *i.e.* supersaturated solutions separate out, besides the stable normal crystallohydrate, hydrates containing less water and also the anhydrous salt. This degree of saturation acts upon the substance dissolved in a like manner to heat. Sulphate of nickel in a solution at 15° to 20° separates out rhombic crystals with $7H_2O$, at 30° to 40° cubical crystals, with $6H_2O$, at 50° to 70° monoclinic crystals, also containing $6H_2O$. Crystals of the same composition separate out from supersaturated solutions at one temperature (17° to 19°), but at different degrees of saturation, as was shown by Lecoq de Boisbaudran. The capacity to voluntarily separate out slightly hydrated or anhydrous salts by the introduction of a crystal into the solution is common to all supersaturated solutions. If a salt forms a supersaturated solution, then one would expect, according to this view, that it should exist in the form of several hydrates or in several modifications. Thus Potilitzin concluded that chlorate of strontium, which easily gives supersaturated solutions, should be capable of forming several hydrates, besides the anhydrous salt known; and he succeeded in discovering the existence of two hydrates, $Sr(ClO_3)_2,3H_2O$ and apparently $Sr(ClO_3)_2,8H_2O$. Besides this, three modifications of the common anhydrous salt were obtained, differing from each other in their crystalline form. One modification separated out in the form of rhombic octahedra, another in oblique plates, and a third in long brittle prisms or plates. Further researches showed that salts which are not capable of forming supersaturated solutions such as the bromates of calcium, strontium, and barium, part with their water of hydration with difficulty (they crystallise with $1H_2O$), and decompose very slowly in a vacuum or in dry air. In other words the tension of dissociation is very small in this class of hydrates. As the hydrates characterised by a small dissociation tension are incapable of giving supersaturated solutions, so conversely supersaturated solutions give hydrates whose tension of dissociation is great (Potilitzin, 1893).

[57] *Emulsions*, like milk, are composed of a solution of glutinous or similar substances, or of oily liquids suspended in a liquid in the form of drops, which are clearly visible under a microscope, and form an example of a mechanical formation which resembles solution. But the difference from solutions is here evident. There are, however, solutions which approach very near to emulsions in the facility with which the substance dissolved separates from them. It has long been known, for example, that a particular kind of Prussian blue, $KFe_2(CN)_6$, dissolves in pure water, but, on the addition of the smallest quantity of either of a number of salts, it coagulates and becomes quite insoluble. If copper sulphide (CuS), cadmium sulphide (CdS), arsenic sulphide (As_2S_5) (the experiments with these substances proceed with great ease, and the solution obtained is comparatively stable), and many other metallic sulphides, be obtained by a method of double decomposition (by precipitating salts of these metals by

hydrogen sulphide), and be then carefully washed (by allowing the precipitate to settle, pouring off the liquid, and again adding sulphuretted hydrogen water), then, as was shown by Schulze, Spring, Prost, and others, the previously insoluble sulphides pass into transparent (for mercury, lead, and silver, reddish brown; for copper and iron, greenish brown; for cadmium and indium, yellow; and for zinc, colourless) solutions, which may be preserved (the weaker they are the longer they keep) and even boiled, but which, nevertheless, in time coagulate—that is, separate in an insoluble form, and then sometimes become crystalline and quite incapable of re-dissolving. Graham and others observed the power shown by colloids (*see* note 18) of forming similar *hydrosols or solutions of gelatinous colloids*, and, in describing alumina and silica, we shall again have occasion to speak of such solutions.

In the existing state of our knowledge concerning solution, such solutions may be looked on as a transition between emulsion and ordinary solutions, but no fundamental judgment can be formed about them until a study has been made of their relations to ordinary solutions (the solutions of even soluble colloids freeze immediately on cooling below $0°$, and, according to Guthrie, do not form cryohydrates), and to supersaturated solutions, with which they have certain points in common.

[58] Offer (1880) concludes, from his researches on cryohydrates, that they are simple mixtures of ice and salts, having a constant melting point, just as there are alloys having a constant point of fusion, and solutions of liquids with a constant boiling point (*see* note 60). This does not, however, explain in what form a salt is contained, for instance, in the cryohydrate $NaCl + 10H_2O$. At temperatures above $-10°$ common salt separates out in anhydrous crystals, and at temperatures near $-10°$, in combination with water of crystallisation, $NaCl + 2H_2O$, and, therefore, it is very improbable that at still lower temperatures it would separate without water. If the possibility of the solidified cryohydrate containing $NaCl + 2H_2O$ and ice be admitted, then it is not clear why one of these substances does not melt before the other. If alcohol does not extract water from the solid mass, leaving the salt behind, this does not prove the presence of ice, because alcohol also takes up water from the crystals of many hydrated substances (for instance, from $NaCl + 2H_2O$) at about their melting-points. Besides which, a simple observation on the cryohydrate, $NaCl + 10H_2O$, shows that with the most careful cooling it does not on the addition of ice deposit ice, which would occur if ice were formed on solidification intermixed with the salt.

I may add with regard to cryohydrates that many of the solutions of acids solidify completely on prolonged cooling (for example, H_2SO_4,H_2O), and then form perfectly definite compounds. For the solutions of sulphuric acid (*see* Chapter X.) Pickering obtained, for instance, a hydrate, $H_2SO_4,4H_2O$ at -25°. Hydrochloric, nitric, and other acids also give similar crystalline hydrates, melting at low temperatures and presenting many similarities with the cryohydrates.

[59] *See* note 24.

[60] For this reason (the want of entire constancy of the composition of constant boiling solutions with a change of pressure), the existence of definite hydrates formed by volatile substances—for instance, by hydrochloric acid and water—is frequently denied. It is generally argued as follows: If there did exist a constancy of composition, then it would be unaltered by a change of pressure. But the distillation of constant boiling hydrates is undoubtedly accompanied (judging by the vapour densities determined by Bineau), like the distillation of sal ammoniac, sulphuric acid, &c., by a complete decomposition of the original compound—that is, these substances do not exist in a state of vapour, but their products of decomposition (hydrochloric acid and water) are gases at the temperature of volatilisation, which dissolve in the volatilised and condensed liquids; but the solubility of gases in liquids depends on the pressure, and, therefore, the composition of constant boiling solutions may, and even ought to, vary with a change of pressure, and, further, the smaller the pressure and the lower the temperature of volatilisation, the more likely is a true compound to be obtained. According to the researches of Roscoe and Dittmar (1859), the constant boiling solution of hydrochloric acid proved to contain 18 p.c. of hydrochloric acid at a pressure of 3 atmospheres, 20 p.c. at 1 atmosphere, and 23 p.c. at $\frac{1}{10}$ of an atmosphere. On passing air through the solution until its composition became constant (*i.e.* forcing the excess of aqueous vapour or of hydrochloric acid to pass away with the air), then acid was obtained containing about 20 p.c. at 100°, about 23 p.c. at 50°, and about 25 p.c. at 0°. From this it is seen that by decreasing the pressure and lowering the temperature of evaporation one arrives at the same limit, where the composition should be taken as $HCl + 6H_2O$, which requires 25·26 p.c. of hydrochloric acid. Fuming hydrochloric acid contains more than this.

In the case already considered, as in the case of formic acid in the researches of D. P. Konovaloff (note 47), the constant boiling solution corresponds with a minimum tension—that is, with a boiling point higher than that of either of the component elements. But there is another case of constant boiling solutions similar to the case of the solution of propyl alcohol, C_3H_8O, when a solution, undecomposed by distillation, boils at a lower point than that of the more volatile liquid. However, in this case also, if there be solution, the possibility of the formation of a definite compound in the form $C_3H_8O + H_2O$ cannot be denied, and the tension of the solution is not equal to the sum of tensions of the components. There are possible cases of constant boiling mixtures even when there is no solution nor any loss of tension, and consequently no chemical action, since the amount of liquids that are volatilised is determined by the product of the vapour densities into their vapour tensions (Wanklyn), in consequence of which liquids whose boiling point is above 100°—for instance, turpentine and ethereal oils in general—when distilled with aqueous vapour, pass over at a temperature below 100°. Consequently, it is not in the constancy of composition and boiling point (temperature of decomposition) that evidence of a distinct chemical action is to be found in the above-described solutions of acids, but in the great loss of tension, which completely resembles the loss of tension observed, for instance, in the perfectly-definite combinations of substances with water of crystallisation (see later, note 65). Sulphuric acid, H_2SO_4, as we shall learn later, is also decomposed by distillation, like $HCl + 6H_2O$, and exhibits, moreover, all the signs of a definite chemical compound. The study of the variation of the specific gravities of solutions as dependent on their composition (see note 19) shows that phenomena of a similar kind, although of different dimensions, take place in the formation of both H_2SO_4 from H_2O and SO_3, and of HCl $+ 6H_2O$ (or of aqueous solutions analogous to it) from HCl and H_2O.

[61] The essence of the matter may he thus represented. A gaseous or easily volatile substance A forms with a certain quantity of water, nH_2O, a definite complex compound AnH_2O, which is stable up to a temperature t° higher than 100°. At this temperature it is decomposed into two substances, $A + H_2O$. Both boil below $t°$ at the ordinary pressure, and therefore at $t°$ they distil over and re-combine in the receiver. But if a part of the substance AnH_2O is decomposed or volatilised, a portion of the undecomposed liquid still remains in the vessel, which can partially dissolve one of the products of decomposition, and that in quantity varying with the pressure and temperature, and therefore the solution at a constant boiling point will have a slightly different composition at different pressures.

[62] For solutions of hydrochloric acid in water there are still greater differences in reactions. For instance, strong solutions decompose antimony sulphide (forming hydrogen sulphide, H_2S), and precipitate common salt from its solutions, whilst weak solutions do not act thus.

[63] Supersaturated solutions give an excellent proof in this respect. Thus a solution of copper sulphate generally crystallises in penta-hydrated crystals, $CuSO_4 + 5H_2O$, and its saturated solution gives such crystals if it be brought into contact with the minutest possible crystal of the same kind. But, according to the observations of Lecoq de Boisbaudran, if a crystal of ferrous sulphate (an isomorphous salt, *see* note 55), $FeSO_4 + 7H_2O$, be placed in a saturated solution of copper sulphate, then crystals of hepta-

hydrated salt, $CuSO_4 + 7H_2O$, are obtained. It is evident that neither the penta- nor the hepta-hydrated salt is contained as such in the solution. The solution presents its own particular liquid form of equilibrium.

[64] Efflorescence, like every evaporation, proceeds from the surface. In the interior of crystals which have effloresced there is usually found a non-effloresced mass, so that the majority of effloresced crystals of washing soda show, in their fracture, a transparent nucleus coated by an effloresced, opaque, powdery mass. It is a remarkable circumstance in this respect that efflorescence proceeds in a completely regular and uniform manner, so that the angles and planes of similar crystallographic character effloresce simultaneously, and in this respect the crystalline form determines those parts of crystals where efflorescence starts, and the order in which it continues. In solutions evaporation also proceeds from the surface, and the first crystals which appear on its reaching the required degree of saturation are also formed at the surface. After falling to the bottom the crystals naturally continue to grow (*see* Chapter X.).

[65] According to Lescœur (1883), at 100° a concentrated solution of barium hydroxide, BaH_2O_2, on first depositing crystals (with $+ H_2O$) has a tension of about 630 mm. (instead of 760 mm., the tension of water), which decreases (because the solution evaporates) to 45 mm., when all the water is expelled from the crystals, $BaH_2O_2 + H_2O$, which are formed, but they also lose water (dissociate, effloresce at 100°), leaving the hydroxide, BaH_2O_2, which is perfectly undecomposable at 100°—that is, does not part with water. At 73° (the tension of water is then 265 mm.) a solution, containing $33H_2O$, on crystallising has a tension of 230 mm.; the crystals, $BaH_2O_2 + 8H_2O$, which separate out, have a tension of 160 mm.; on losing water they give $BaH_2O_2 + H_2O$. This substance does not decompose at 73°, and therefore its tension $= 0$. In those crystallohydrates which effloresce at the ordinary temperature, the tension of dissociation nearly approximates to that of the aqueous vapour, as Lescœur (1891) showed. To this category of compounds belong $B_2O_3(3 + x)H_2O$, $C_2O_4H_2(2 + x)H_2O$, $BaO(9 + x)H_2O$, and $SrO(9 + x)H_2O$. And a still greater tension is possessed by $Na_2SO_410H_2O$, $Na_2CO_310H_2O$, and $MgSO_4(7 + x)H_2O$. Müller-Erzbach (1884) determines the tension (with reference to liquid water) by placing tubes of the same length with water and the substances experimented with in a desiccator, the rate of loss of water giving the relative tension. Thus, at the ordinary temperature, crystals of sodium phosphate, $Na_2HPO_4 + 12H_2O$, present a tension of 0·7 compared with water, until they lose $5H_2O$, then 0·4 until they lose $5H_2O$ more, and on losing the last equivalent of water the tension falls to 0·04 compared with water. It is clear that the different molecules of water are held by an unequal force. Out of the five molecules of water in copper sulphate the

two first are comparatively easily separated even at the ordinary temperature (but only after several days in a desiccator, according to Latchinoff); the next two are more difficultly separated, and the last equivalent is retained even at 100°. This is another indication of the capacity of $CuSO_4$ to form three hydrates, $CuSO_45H_2O$, $CuSO_43H_2O$, and $CuSO_4H_2O$. The researches of Andreae on the tension of dissociation of hydrated sulphate of copper showed (1891) the existence of three provinces, characterised at a given temperature by a constant tension: (1) between 3–5, (2) between 1–3, and lastly (3) between 0–1 molecule of water, which again confirms the existence of three hydrates of the above composition for this salt.

[65 bis] Sodium acetate ($C_2H_3O_2Na,3H_2O$) melts at 58°, but re-solidifies only on contact with a crystal, otherwise it may remain liquid even at 0°, and may be used for obtaining a constant temperature. According to Jeannel, the latent heat of fusion is about 28 calories, and according to Pickering the heat of solution 35 calories. When melted this salt boils at 123°—that is, the tension of the vapour given off at that temperature equals the atmospheric pressure.

[66] Such a phenomenon frequently presents itself in purely chemical action. For instance, let a liquid substance A give, with another liquid substance B, under the conditions of an experiment, a mere minute quantity of a solid or gaseous substance C. This small quantity will separate out (pass away from the sphere of action, as Berthollet expressed it), and the remaining masses of A and B will again give C; consequently, under these conditions action will go on to the end. Such, it seems to me, is the action in solutions when they yield ice or vapour indicating the presence of water.

[67] Certain substances are capable of forming together only one compound, others several, and these of the most varied degrees of stability. The compounds of water are instances of this kind. In solutions the existence of several different definite compounds must be acknowledged, but many of these have not yet been obtained in a free state, and it may be that they cannot be obtained in any other but a liquid form—that is, dissolved; just as there are many undoubted definite compounds which only exist in one physical state. Among the hydrates such instances occur. The compound $CO_2 + 8H_2O$ (*see* note 31), according to Wroblewski, only occurs in a solid form. Hydrates like $H_2S + 12H_2O$ (De Forcrand and Villard), $HBr + H_2O$ (Roozeboom), can only be accepted on the basis of a decrease of tension, but present themselves as very transient substances, incapable of existing in a stable free state. Even sulphuric acid, H_2SO_4, itself, which undoubtedly is a definite compound, fumes in a liquid form, giving off the anhydride, SO_3—that is, it exhibits a very unstable

equilibrium. The crystallo-hydrates of chlorine, $Cl_2 + 8H_2O$, of hydrogen sulphide, $H_2S + 12H_2O$ (it is formed at $0°$, and is completely decomposed at $+1°$, as then 1 vol. of water only dissolves 4 vols. of hydrogen sulphide, while at $0·1°$ it dissolves about 100 vols.), and of many other gases, are instances of hydrates which are very unstable.

[68] Of such a kind are also other indefinite chemical compounds; for example, metallic alloys. These are solid substances or solidified solutions of metals. They also contain definite compounds, and may contain an excess of one of the metals. According to the experiments of Laurie (1888), the alloys of zinc with copper in respect to the electro-motive force in galvanic batteries behave just like zinc if the proportion of copper in the alloy does not exceed a certain percentage—that is, until a definite compound is attained—for in that case particles of free zinc are present; but if a copper surface be taken, and it be covered by only one-thousandth part of its area of zinc, then only the zinc will act in a galvanic battery.

[69] According to the above supposition, the condition of solutions in the sense of the kinetic hypothesis of matter (that is, on the supposition of an internal motion of molecules and atoms) may be represented in the following form:—In a homogeneous liquid—for instance, water—the molecules occur in a certain state of, although mobile, still stable, equilibrium. When a substance A dissolves in water, its molecules form with several molecules of water, systems AnH_2O, which are so unstable that when surrounded by molecules of water they decompose and re-form, so that A passes from one mass of molecules of water to another, and the molecules of water which were at this moment in harmonious motion with A in the form of the system AnH_2O, in the next instant may have already succeeded in getting free. The addition of water or of molecules of A may either only alter the number of free molecules, which in their turn enter into systems AnH_2O, or they may introduce conditions for the possibility of building up new systems AmH_2O, where m is either greater or less than n. If in the solution the relation of the molecules be the same as in the system AmH_2O, then the addition of fresh molecules of water or of A would be followed by the formation of new molecules AnH_2O. The relative quantity, stability, and composition of these systems or definite compounds will vary in one or another solution. I adopted this view of solutions (1887, Pickering subsequently put forward a similar view) after a most intimate study of the variation of their specific gravities, to which my book, cited in note 19, is devoted. Definite compounds, Am_1H_2O and Am_1H_2O, existing in a free—for instance, solid—form, may in certain cases be held in solutions in a dissociated state (although but partially); they are similar in their structure to those definite substances which are formed in solutions, but it is not necessary to assume that such systems as $Na_2SO_4 +$

$10H_2O$, or $Na_2SO_4 + 7H_2O$, or Na_2SO_4, are contained in solutions. The comparatively more stable systems An_1H_2O which exist in a free state and change their physical state must present, although within certain limits of temperature, an entirely harmonious kind of motion of A with n_1H_2O; the property also and state of systems AnH_2O and AmH_2O, occurring in solutions, is that they are in a liquid form, although partially dissociated. Substances A_1, which give solutions, are distinguished by the fact that they can form such unstable systems AnH_2O, but besides them they can give other much more stable systems An_1H_2O. Thus ethylene, C_2H_4, in dissolving in water, probably forms a system $C_2H_4nH_2O$, which easily splits up into C_2H_4 and H_2O, but it also gives the system of alcohol, C_2H_4,H_2O or C_2H_6O, which is comparatively stable. Thus oxygen can dissolve in water, and it can combine with it, forming peroxide of hydrogen. Turpentine, $C_{10}H_{16}$, does not dissolve in water, but it combines with it as a comparatively stable hydrate. In other words, the chemical structure of hydrates, or of the definite compounds which are contained in solutions, is distinguished not only by its original peculiarities but also by a diversity of stability. A similar structure to hydrates must be acknowledged in crystallo-hydrates. On melting they give actual (real) solutions. As substances which give crystallo-hydrates, like salts, are capable of forming a number of diverse hydrates, and as the greater the number of molecules of water (n) they (AnH_2O) contain, the lower is the temperature of their formation, and as the more easily they decompose the more water they hold, therefore, in the first place, the isolation of hydrates holding much water existing in aqueous solutions may be soonest looked for at low temperatures (although, perhaps, in certain cases they cannot exist in the solid state); and, secondly, the stability also of such higher hydrates will be at a minimum under the ordinary circumstances of the occurrence of liquid water. Hence a further more detailed investigation of cryohydrates may help to the elucidation of the nature of solutions. But it may be foreseen that certain cryohydrates will, like metallic alloys, present solidified mixtures of ice with the salts themselves and their more stable hydrates, and others will be definite compounds.

[70] The above representation of solutions, &c., considering them as a particular state of definite compounds, excludes the independent existence of indefinite compounds; by this means that unity of chemical conception is obtained which cannot be arrived at by admitting the physico-mechanical conception of indefinite compounds. The gradual transition from typical solutions (as of gases in water, and of weak saline solutions) to sulphuric acid, and from it and its definite, but yet unstable and liquid, compounds, to clearly defined compounds, such as salts and their crystallo-hydrates, is so imperceptible, that in denying that solutions pertain to the number of definite but dissociating compounds, we risk denying the definiteness of

the atomic composition of such substances as sulphuric acid or of molten crystallo-hydrates. I repeat, however, that for the present the theory of solutions cannot be considered as firmly established. The above opinion about them is nothing more than a hypothesis which endeavours to satisfy those comparatively limited data which we have for the present about solutions, and of those cases of their transition into definite compounds. By submitting solutions to the Daltonic conception of atomism, I hope that we may not only attain to a general harmonious chemical doctrine, but also that new motives for investigation and research will appear in the problem of solutions, which must either confirm the proposed theory or replace it by another fuller and truer one; and I for my part cannot consider this to be the case with any of the other present doctrines of solutions (note 49).

[71] In combining with water one part by weight of lime evolves 245 units of heat. A high temperature is obtained, because the specific heat of the resulting product is small. Sodium oxide, Na_2O, in reacting on water, H_2O, and forming caustic soda (sodium hydroxide), NaHO, evolves 552 units of heat for each part by weight of sodium oxide.

[72] The diagram given in note 28 shows the evolution of heat on the mixture of sulphuric acid, or monohydrate (H_2SO_4, *i.e.* $SO_3 + H_2O$), with different quantities of water per 100 vols. of the resultant solution. Every 98 grams of sulphuric acid (H_2SO_4) evolve, on the addition of 18 grams of water, 6,379 units of heat; with twice or three times the quantity of water 9,418 and 11,137 units of heat, and with an infinitely large quantity of water 17,860 units of heat, according to the determinations of Thomsen. He also showed that when H_2SO_4 is formed from SO_3 (= 80) and H_2O (= 18), 21,308 units of heat are evolved per 98 parts by weight of the resultant sulphuric acid.

[73] Thus, for different hydrates the stability with which they hold water is very dissimilar. Certain hydrates hold water very loosely, and in combining with it evolve little heat. From other hydrates the water cannot be separated by any degree of heat, even if they are formed from anhydrides (*i.e.* anhydrous substances) and water with little evolution of heat; for instance, acetic anhydride in combining with water evolves an inconsiderable amount of heat, but the water cannot then be expelled from it. If the hydrate (acetic acid) formed by this combination be strongly heated it either volatilises without change, or decomposes into new substances, but it does not again yield the original substances—*i.e.*, the anhydride and water, at least in a liquid form. Here is an instance which gives the reason for calling the water entering into the composition of the hydrate, water of constitution. Such, for example, is the water entering into the so-called caustic soda or sodium hydroxide (*see* note 71). But there are

hydrates which easily part with their water; yet this water cannot be considered as water of crystallisation, not only because sometimes such hydrates have no crystalline form, but also because, in perfectly analogous cases, very stable hydrates are formed, which are capable of particular kinds of chemical reactions, as we shall subsequently learn. Such, for example, is the unstable hydrated oxide of copper, which is not formed from water and oxide of copper, but which is obtained just like far more stable hydrates, for example, the hydrated oxide of barium BaH_2O_2 equal to $BaO + H_2O$, by the double decomposition of the solution of salts with alkalies. In a word, there is no distinct boundary either between the water of hydrates and of crystallisation, or between solution and hydration.

It must be observed that in separating from an aqueous solution, many substances, without having a crystalline form, hold water in the same unstable state as in crystals; only this water cannot be termed 'water of crystallisation' if the substance which separates out has no crystalline form. The hydrates of alumina and silica are examples of such unstable hydrates. If these substances are separated from an aqueous solution by a chemical process, then they always contain water. The formation of a new chemical compound containing water is here particularly evident, for alumina and silica in an anhydrous state have chemical properties differing from those they show when combined with water, and do not combine directly with it. The entire series of colloids on separating from water form similar compounds with it, which have the aspect of solid gelatinous substances. Water is held in a considerable quantity in solidified glue or boiled albumin. It cannot be expelled from them by pressure; hence, in this case there has ensued some kind of combination of the substance with water. This water, however, is easily separated on drying; but not the whole of it, a portion being retained, and this portion is considered to belong to the hydrate, although in this case it is very difficult, if not impossible, to obtain definite compounds. The absence of any distinct boundary lines between solutions, crystallo-hydrates, and ordinary hydrates above referred to, is very clearly seen in such examples.

[113]

CHAPTER II

THE COMPOSITION OF WATER, HYDROGEN

The question now arises, Is not *water* itself a *compound substance?* Cannot it be formed by the mutual combination of some component parts? Cannot it be broken up into its component parts? There cannot be the least doubt that if it does split up, and if it is a compound, then it is a *definite* one characterised by the stability of the union between those component parts from which it is formed. From the fact alone that water passes into all physical states as a homogeneous whole, without in the least varying chemically in its properties and without splitting up into its component parts (neither solutions nor many hydrates can be distilled—they are split up), we must conclude, from this fact alone, that if water is a compound then it is a stable and definite chemical compound capable of entering into many other combinations. Like many other great discoveries in the province of chemistry, it is to the end of the last century that we are indebted for the important discovery that water is not a simple substance, that it is composed of two substances like a number of other compound substances. This was proved by two of the methods by which the compound nature of bodies may be directly determined; by analysis and by synthesis—that is, by a method of the decomposition of water into, and of the formation of water from, its component parts. In 1781 Cavendish first obtained water by burning hydrogen in oxygen, both of which gases were already known to him. He concluded from this that water was composed of two substances. But he did not make more accurate experiments, which would have shown the relative quantities of the component parts in water, and which would have determined its complex nature with certainty. Although his experiments were the first, and although the conclusion he drew from them was true, yet such novel ideas as the complex nature of water are not easily recognised so long as there is no series of researches which entirely and indubitably proves the truth of such a conclusion. The fundamental experiments which proved the complexity of water by the method of synthesis, and[114] of its formation from other substances, were made in 1789 by Monge, Lavoisier, Fourcroy, and Vauquelin. They obtained four ounces of water by burning hydrogen, and found that water consists of 15 parts of hydrogen and 85 parts of oxygen. It was also proved that the weight of water formed was equal to the sum of the weights of the component parts entering into its composition; consequently, water contains all the matter entering into oxygen and hydrogen. The complexity of water was proved in this manner by a method of synthesis. But we will turn to its analysis—*i.e.* to its decomposition into its component parts. The analysis may be more or less complete. Either both component parts may be obtained in a separate state, or else only one is separated and the other is converted into a new compound in which its amount may be determined by weighing. This will be a reaction of substitution, such as is often taken advantage of for analysis. The first analysis of water was thus conducted in 1784 by Lavoisier and Meusnier. The apparatus they arranged consisted of a glass retort containing water previously purified, and of which the weight had been determined. The neck of the retort was inserted into a porcelain tube, placed inside an oven, and heated to a red heat by charcoal. Iron filings, which decompose water at a red heat, were placed inside this tube. The end of the tube was connected with a worm, for condensing any water which might pass through the tube undecomposed. This condensed water was collected in a separate flask. The gas formed by the decomposition was collected over water in a bell jar. The aqueous vapour in passing over the red-hot iron was decomposed, and a gas was formed from it whose weight could be determined from its volume, its density being known. Besides the water which passed through the tube unaltered, a certain quantity of water disappeared in the experiment, and this quantity, in the experiments of Lavoisier and Meusnier, was equal to the weight of gas which was collected in the bell jar plus the increase in weight of the iron filings. Hence the water was decomposed into a gas, which was collected in the bell jar, and a substance, which combined with the iron; consequently, it is composed of these two component parts. This was the first analysis of water ever made; but here only one (and not both) of the gaseous component parts of water was collected separately. Both the component parts of water can, however, be simultaneously obtained in a free state. For this purpose the decomposition is brought about by a galvanic current or by heat, as we shall learn directly.[1]

[115]

Water is a bad conductor of electricity—that is, pure water does not transmit a feeble current; but if any salt or acid be dissolved in it, then its conductivity increases, and *on the passage of a current* through acidified water *it is decomposed* into its component parts. Some sulphuric acid is generally added to the water. By immersing platinum plates (electrodes) in this water (platinum is chosen because it is not acted on by acids, whilst many other metals are chemically acted on by acids), and connecting them with a galvanic battery, it will be observed that bubbles of gas appear on these plates. The gas which separates is called *detonating gas*,[2] because, on ignition, it very easily explodes.[3] What takes place is as follows:—First, the water, by the action of the current, is decomposed into two gases. The mixture of these gases forms detonating gas. When detonating gas is brought into contact with an incandescent substance—for instance, a lighted taper—the gases re-combine, forming water, the combination being accompanied by a great evolution of heat, and therefore the vapour of the water formed expands considerably, which it does very rapidly, and as a consequence, an explosion takes place—that is, sound and increase of pressure, and atmospheric disturbance, as in the explosion of gunpowder.

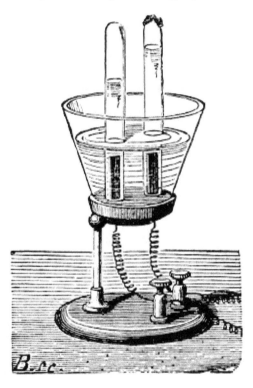

FIG. 18.—Decomposition of water by the galvanic current, for determining the relation between the volumes of hydrogen and oxygen.

In order to discover what gases are obtained by the decomposition of water, the gases which separate at each electrode must be collected separately. For this purpose a V-shaped tube is taken; one of its ends is open and the other fused up. A platinum wire, terminating inside the tube in a plate, is fused into the closed end; the closed end[116] is entirely filled with water[4] acidified with sulphuric acid, and another platinum wire, terminating in a plate, is immersed in the open end. If a current from a galvanic battery be now passed through the wires an evolution of gases will be observed, and the gas which is obtained in the open branch passes into the air, while that in the closed branch accumulates above the water. As this gas accumulates it displaces the water, which continues to descend in the closed and ascend into the open branch of the tubes. When the water, in this way, reaches the top of the open end, the passage of the current is stopped, and the gas which was evolved from one of the electrodes only is obtained in the apparatus. By this means it is easy to prove that a particular gas appears at each electrode. If the closed end be connected with the negative pole—*i.e.* with that joined to the zinc—then the gas collected in the apparatus is capable of burning. This may be demonstrated by the following experiment:—The bent tube is taken off the stand, and its open end stopped up with the thumb and inclined in such a manner that the gas passes from the closed to the open end. It will then be found, on applying a lighted lamp or taper, that the gas burns. This combustible gas is *hydrogen*. If the same experiment be carried on with a current passing in the opposite direction—that is, if the closed end be joined up with the positive pole (*i.e.* with the carbon, copper, or platinum), then the gas which is evolved from it does not itself burn, but it supports combustion very vigorously, so that a smouldering taper in it immediately bursts into flame. This gas, which is collected at the anode or positive pole, is *oxygen*, which is obtained, as we saw before (in the Introduction), from mercury oxide and is contained in air.

Thus in the decomposition of water oxygen appears at the positive pole and hydrogen at the negative pole,[4 bis] so that detonating gas will be a mixture of both. Hydrogen burns in air from the fact that in doing so it re-forms water, with the oxygen of the air. Detonating gas[117] explodes from the fact that the hydrogen burns in the oxygen mixed with it. It is very easy to measure the relative quantities of one and the other gas which are evolved in the decomposition of water. For this purpose a funnel is taken, whose orifice is closed by a cork through which two platinum wires pass. These wires are connected with a battery. Acidified water is poured into the funnel, and a glass cylinder full of water is placed over the end of each wire (fig. 18). On passing a current, hydrogen and oxygen collect in these cylinders, and it will easily be seen that two volumes of hydrogen are evolved for every one volume of oxygen. This signifies that, in decomposing, water gives two volumes of hydrogen and one volume of oxygen.

Water is also decomposed into its component parts by *the action of heat*. At the melting point of silver (960°), and in its presence, water is decomposed and the oxygen absorbed by the molten silver, which dissolves it so long as it is liquid. But directly the silver solidifies the oxygen is expelled from it. However, this experiment is not entirely convincing; it might be thought that in this case the decomposition of the water did not proceed from the action of heat, but from the action of the silver on water—that silver decomposes water, taking up the oxygen. If steam be passed through a red-hot tube, whose internal temperature attains 1,000°, then a portion[5] of the water decomposes into its component parts, forming detonating gas. But on passing into the cooler portions of the apparatus this detonating gas again reunites and forms water. The hydrogen and oxygen obtained combine together at a lower temperature.[6] Apparently the problem—to show the decomposability of water at high temperatures—is unattainable.[118] It was considered as such before Henri Sainte-Claire Deville (in the fifties) introduced the conception of dissociation into chemistry, as of a change of chemical state resembling evaporation, if decomposition be likened to boiling, and before he had demonstrated the decomposability of water by the action of heat in an experiment which will presently be described. In order to demonstrate clearly the *dissociation* of water, or its decomposability by heat, at a temperature approaching that at which it is formed, it was necessary to separate the hydrogen from the oxygen at a high temperature, without allowing the mixture to cool. Deville took advantage of the difference between the densities of hydrogen and oxygen.

FIG. 19.—Decomposition of water by the action of heat, and the separation of the hydrogen formed by its permeating through a porous tube.

A wide porcelain tube P (fig. 19) is placed in a furnace, which can be raised to a high temperature (it should be heated with small pieces of good coke). In this tube there is inserted a second tube T, of smaller diameter, made of unglazed earthenware and therefore porous.[119] The ends of the tube are luted to the wide tube, and two tubes, C and C', are inserted into the ends, as shown in the drawing. With this arrangement it is possible for a gas to pass into the annular space between the walls of the two tubes, from whence it can be collected. Steam from a retort or flask is passed through the tube D, into the inner porous tube T. This steam on entering the red-hot space is decomposed into hydrogen and oxygen. The densities of these gases are very different, hydrogen being sixteen times lighter than oxygen. Light gases, as we saw above, penetrate through porous surfaces very much more rapidly than denser gases, and therefore the hydrogen passes through the pores of the tube into the annular space very much more rapidly than the oxygen. The hydrogen which separates out into the annular space can only be collected when this space does not contain any oxygen. If any air remains in this space, then the hydrogen which separates out will combine with its oxygen and form water. For this reason a gas incapable of supporting combustion—for instance, nitrogen or carbonic anhydride—is previously passed into the annular space. Thus the carbonic anhydride is passed through the tube C, and the hydrogen, separated from the steam, is collected through the tube C', and will be partly mixed with carbonic anhydride. A certain portion of the carbonic anhydride will penetrate through the pores of the unglazed tube into the interior of the tube T. The oxygen will remain in this tube, and the volume of the remaining oxygen will be half that of the volume of hydrogen which separates out from the annular space.[6 bis]

The decomposition of water is effected much more easily by a method of substitution, taking advantage of the affinity of substances for the oxygen or the hydrogen of water. If a substance be added to[120] water, which takes up the oxygen and replaces the hydrogen—then we shall obtain the latter gas from the water. Thus with sodium, water gives hydrogen, and with chlorine, which takes up the hydrogen, oxygen is obtained.

Hydrogen is evolved from water by many metals, which are capable of forming oxides in air—that is, which are capable of burning or combining with oxygen. The capacity of metals for combining with oxygen, and therefore for decomposing water, or for the evolution of hydrogen, is very dissimilar.[7] Among metals, potassium and sodium exhibit considerable energy in this respect. The first occurs in potash,[121] the second in soda. They are both lighter than water, soft, and easily change in air. By bringing one or the other of them in contact with water at the ordinary temperature,[8] a quantity of hydrogen, corresponding with the amount of the metal taken, may be directly obtained. One gram of hydrogen, occupying a volume of 11·16 litres at 0° and 760 mm., is evolved from every 39 grams of potassium, or 23 grams of sodium. The phenomenon may be observed in the following way: a solution of sodium in mercury—or 'sodium amalgam,' as it is generally called—is poured into a vessel containing water, and owing to its weight sinks to the bottom; the sodium held in the mercury then acts on the water like pure sodium, liberating hydrogen. The mercury does not act here, and the same amount of it as was taken for dissolving the sodium is obtained in the residue. The hydrogen is evolved gradually in the form of bubbles, which pass through the liquid.

Beyond the hydrogen evolved and a solid substance, which remains in solution (it may be obtained by evaporating the resultant solution) no other products are here obtained. Consequently, from the two substances (water and sodium) taken, the same number of new substances (hydrogen and the substance dissolved in water) have been obtained, from which we may conclude that the reaction which here takes place is a reaction of double decomposition or of substitution. The resultant solid is nothing else but the so-called caustic soda (sodium hydroxide), which is made up of sodium, oxygen, and half of the hydrogen contained in the water. Therefore, the substitution took place between the hydrogen and the sodium, namely half of the hydrogen in the water was replaced by the sodium, and was evolved in a free state. Hence the reaction which takes place here may be expressed by the equation[122] $H_2O + Na = NaHO + H$; the meaning of this is clear from what has already been said.[9]

Sodium and potassium act on water at the ordinary temperature. Other heavier metals only act on it with a rise of temperature, and then not so rapidly or vigorously. Thus magnesium and calcium only liberate hydrogen from water at its boiling point, and zinc and iron only a red heat, whilst a whole series of heavy metals, such as copper, lead, mercury, silver, gold, and platinum, do not in the least decompose water at any temperature, and do not replace its hydrogen.

From this it is clear that hydrogen may be obtained by the decomposition of steam by the action of iron (or zinc) with a rise of temperature. The experiment is conducted in the following manner: pieces of iron (filings, nails, &c.), are placed in a porcelain tube, which is then subjected to a strong heat and steam passed through it. The steam,[123] coming into contact with the iron, gives up its oxygen to it, and thus the hydrogen is set free and passes out at the other end of the tube together with undecomposed steam. This method, which is historically very significant,[10] is practically inconvenient, as it requires a rather high temperature. Further, this reaction, as a reversible one (a red-hot mass of iron decomposes a current of steam, forming oxide and hydrogen; and a mass of oxide of iron, heated to redness in a stream of hydrogen, forms iron and steam), does not proceed in virtue of the comparatively small difference between the affinity of oxygen for iron (or zinc) and for hydrogen, but only because the hydrogen escapes, as it is formed, in virtue of its elasticity.[11] If the oxygen compounds—that is, the oxides—which are obtained from the iron or zinc, be able to pass into solution, then the affinity acting in solution is added, and the reaction may become non-reversible, and proceed with comparatively much greater facility.[12] As the oxides of iron and zinc, by themselves[124] insoluble in water, are capable of combining with (have an affinity for) acid oxides (as we shall afterwards fully consider), and form saline and soluble substances, with acids, or hydrates having acid properties, hence by the action of such hydrates, or of their aqueous solutions,[13] iron and zinc are able to liberate hydrogen with great ease at the ordinary temperature—that is, they act on solutions of acids just as sodium acts on water.[14] Sulphuric acid, H_2SO_4, is usually chosen for this purpose; the hydrogen is displaced from it by many metals with much greater facility than directly from water, and such a displacement is accompanied by the evolution of a large amount of heat.[15] When the hydrogen in[125] sulphuric acid is replaced by a metal, a substance is obtained which is called a salt of sulphuric acid or a sulphate. Thus, by the action of zinc on sulphuric acid, hydrogen and zinc sulphate $ZnSO_4$,[15 bis] are obtained. The latter is a solid substance, soluble in water. In order that the action of the metal on the acid should go on regularly, and to the end, it is necessary that the acid should be diluted with water, which dissolves the salt as it is formed; otherwise the salt covers the metal, and hinders the acid from attacking it. Usually the acid is diluted with from three to five times its volume of water, and the metal is covered with this solution. In order that the metal should act rapidly on the acid, it should present a large surface, so that a maximum amount of the reacting substances may come into contact in a given time. For this purpose the zinc is used as strips of sheet zinc, or in the granulated form (that is, zinc which has been poured from a certain height, in a molten state, into water). The iron should be in the form of wire, nails, filings, or cuttings.

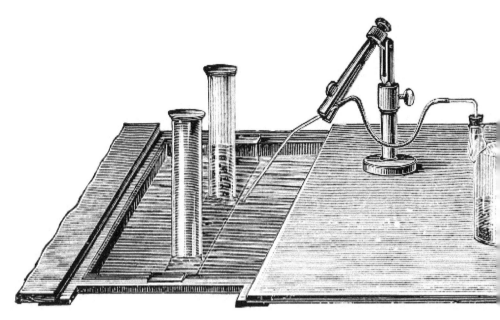

FIG. 20.—**Apparatus for the preparation of hydrogen from zinc and sulphuric acid.**

[126]

The usual method of obtaining hydrogen is as follows:—A certain quantity of granulated zinc is put into a double-necked, or Woulfe's, bottle. Into one neck a funnel is placed, reaching to the bottom of the bottle, so that the liquid poured in may prevent the hydrogen from escaping through it. The gas escapes through a special gas conducting tube, which is firmly fixed, by a cork, into the other neck, and ends in a water bath (fig. 20), under the orifice of a glass cylinder full of water.[16] If sulphuric acid be now poured into the Woulfe's bottle it will soon be seen that bubbles of a gas are evolved, which is hydrogen. The first part of the gas evolved should not be collected, as it is mixed with the air originally in the apparatus. This precaution should be taken in the preparation of all gases. Time must be allowed[127] for the gas evolved to displace all the air from the apparatus, otherwise in testing the combustibility of the hydrogen an explosion may occur[128] from the formation of detonating gas (the mixture of the oxygen of the air with the hydrogen).[17]

[129]

Hydrogen, besides being contained in water, is also contained in many other substances,[18] and may be obtained from them. As examples of this, it may be mentioned (1) that a mixture of formate of sodium, $CHNaO_2$, and caustic soda, NaHO, when heated to redness, forms sodium carbonate, Na_2CO_3, and hydrogen, H_2;[19] (2) that a number of organic substances are decomposed at a red heat, forming hydrogen, among other gases, and thus it is that hydrogen is contained in ordinary coal gas.

Charcoal itself liberates hydrogen from steam at a high temperature;[20] but the reaction which here takes place is distinguished by a certain complexity, and will therefore be considered later.

The properties of hydrogen.—Hydrogen presents us with an example of a gas which at first sight does not differ from air. It is not surprising, therefore, that Paracelsus, having discovered that an aëriform substance is obtained by the action of metals on sulphuric acid, did not determine exactly its difference from air. In fact, hydrogen, like air, is[130] colourless, and has no smell;[21] but a more intimate acquaintance with its properties proves it to be entirely different from air. The first sign which distinguishes hydrogen from air is its combustibility. This property is so easily observed that it is the one to which recourse is usually had in order to recognise hydrogen, if it is evolved in a reaction, although there are many other combustible gases. But before speaking of the combustibility and other chemical properties of hydrogen, we will first describe the physical properties of this gas, as we did in the case of water. It is easy to show that it is one of the lightest gases.[22] If passed into the bottom of a flask full of air, hydrogen will not remain in it, but, owing to its lightness, rapidly escapes and mixes with the atmosphere. If, however, a cylinder whose orifice is turned downwards be filled with hydrogen, it will not escape, or, more correctly, it will only slowly mix with the atmosphere. This may be demonstrated by the fact that a lighted taper sets fire to the hydrogen at the orifice of the cylinder, and is itself extinguished inside the cylinder. Hence, hydrogen, being itself combustible, does not support combustion. The great lightness of hydrogen is taken advantage of for balloons. Ordinary coal gas, which is often also used for the same purpose, is only about twice as light as air, whilst hydrogen is[131] 14½ times lighter than air. A very simple experiment with soap bubbles very well illustrates the application of hydrogen for filling balloons. Charles, of Paris, showed the lightness of hydrogen in this way, and constructed a balloon filled with hydrogen almost simultaneously with Montgolfier. One litre of pure and dry hydrogen[23] at[132] 0° and 760 mm. pressure weighs 0·08986 gram; that is, hydrogen is almost 14½ (more exactly, 14·39) times lighter than air. It is the lightest of all gases. The small density of hydrogen determines many remarkable properties which it shows; thus, hydrogen passes exceedingly rapidly through fine orifices, its molecules (Chapter I.) being endued with the greatest velocity.[24] At pressures somewhat higher than the atmospheric pressure, all other gases exhibit a greater compressibility and co-efficient of expansion than they should according to the laws of Mariotte and Gay-Lussac; whilst hydrogen, on the contrary, is compressed to a less degree than it should be from the law of Mariotte,[25] and with a rise of pressure it expands slightly[133] less than at the atmospheric pressure.[26] However, hydrogen, like air and many other gases which are permanent at the ordinary temperature,[134] does not pass into a liquid state under a very considerable pressure,[27] but is compressed into a lesser volume than would follow[135] from Mariotte's law.[28] From this it may be concluded that the absolute boiling point of hydrogen, and of gases resembling it,[29] lies very much below the ordinary temperature; that is, that the liquefaction of[136] [137]

[138] this *gas* is only possible at low temperatures, and under great pressures.[30] This conclusion was verified (1877) by the experiments of Pictet and Cailletet.[31] They compressed gases at a very low temperature, and then allowed them to expand, either by directly decreasing the pressure or by allowing them to escape into the air, by which means the temperature fell still lower, and then, just as steam when rapidly rarefied[32][139] deposits liquid water in the form of a fog, hydrogen in expanding forms a fog, thus indicating its passage into a liquid state. But as yet it has been impossible to preserve this liquid, even for a short time, to determine its properties, notwithstanding the employment of a temperature of -200° and a pressure of 200 atmospheres,[33] although by[140] these means the gases of the atmosphere may be kept in a liquid state for a long time. This is due to the fact that the absolute boiling point of hydrogen lies lower than that of all other known gases, which also depends on the extreme lightness of hydrogen.[34]

[141]
[142]

Although a substance which passes with great difficulty into a liquid state by the action of physico-mechanical forces, hydrogen loses its gaseous state (that is, its elasticity, or the physical energy of its molecules, or their rapid progressive motion) with comparative ease under the influence of chemical attraction,[35] which is not only shown from the fact that hydrogen and oxygen (two permanent gases) form liquid water, but also from many phenomena of the absorption of hydrogen.

Hydrogen is vigorously condensed by certain solids; for example, by charcoal and by spongy platinum. If a piece of freshly ignited charcoal be introduced into a cylinder full of hydrogen standing in a mercury bath, then the charcoal absorbs as much as twice its volume of hydrogen. Spongy platinum condenses still more hydrogen. But *palladium*, a grey metal which occurs with platinum, absorbs more hydrogen than any other metal. Graham showed that when heated to a red heat and cooled in an atmosphere of hydrogen, palladium retains as much as 600 volumes of hydrogen. When once absorbed it retains[143] the hydrogen at the ordinary temperature, and only parts with it when heated to a red heat.[36] This capacity of certain dense metals for the absorption of hydrogen explains the property of hydrogen of passing through metallic tubes.[37] It is termed *occlusion*, and presents a similar phenomenon to solution; it is based on the capacity of metals of forming unstable easily dissociating compounds[38] with hydrogen, similar to those which salts form with water.

At the ordinary temperature hydrogen very feebly and rarely enters[144] into chemical reaction. The capacity of gaseous hydrogen for reaction becomes evident only under a change of circumstances—by compression, heating, or the action of light, or at the moment of its evolution. However, under these circumstances it *combines* directly with only a very few of the elements. Hydrogen combines directly with oxygen, sulphur, carbon, potassium, and certain other elements, but it does not combine directly with either the majority of the metals or with nitrogen, phosphorus, &c. Compounds of hydrogen with certain elements on which it does not act directly are, however, known; they are not obtained by a direct method, but by reactions of decomposition, or of double decomposition, of other hydrogen compounds. The property of hydrogen of combining with oxygen at a red heat determines its combustibility. We have already seen that hydrogen easily takes fire, and that it then burns with a pale—that is, non-luminous—flame.[39] Hydrogen does not combine with the oxygen of the atmosphere at the ordinary temperature; but this combination takes place at a red heat,[40] and is accompanied by the evolution of much heat. The product of this combination is water—that is, a compound of oxygen and hydrogen. This is the *synthesis of water*, and we have already noticed its analysis or decomposition into its component parts. The synthesis of water may be very easily observed if a cold glass bell jar be placed over a burning hydrogen flame, and, better still, if the hydrogen flame be lighted in the tube of a condenser. The water will condense in drops as it is formed on the walls of the condenser and trickle down.[41]

[145]

Light does not aid the combination of hydrogen and oxygen, so that a mixture of these two gases does not change when exposed to the action of light; but an electric spark acts just like a flame, and this is taken advantage of for inflaming a mixture of oxygen and hydrogen, or detonating gas, inside a vessel, as will be explained in the following chapters. As hydrogen (and oxygen also) is condensed by spongy platinum, by which a rise of temperature ensues, and as platinum acts by contact (Introduction), therefore hydrogen also combines with oxygen, under the influence of platinum, as Döbereiner showed. If spongy platinum be thrown into a mixture of hydrogen and oxygen, an explosion takes place. If a mixture of the gases be passed over spongy platinum, combination also ensues, and the platinum becomes red-hot.[42]

Although gaseous hydrogen does not act directly[43] on many substances, yet in a *nascent state* reaction often takes place. Thus, for instance, water on which sodium amalgam is acting contains hydrogen in a nascent state. The hydrogen is here evolved from a liquid, and at the first moment of its formation must be in a condensed[146] state.[44] In this condition it is capable of reacting on substances on which it does not act in a gaseous state.[44 bis] Reactions of substitution or displacement of metals by hydrogen at the moment of its formation are particularly numerous.[45]

Metals, as we shall afterwards see, are in many cases able to replace each other; they also, and in some cases still more easily, replace and are replaced by hydrogen. We have already seen examples of this in the formation of hydrogen from water, sulphuric acid, &c. In all these[147] cases the metals sodium, iron, or zinc displace the hydrogen which occurs in these compounds. Hydrogen may be displaced from many of its compounds by metals in exactly the same manner as it is displaced from water; so, for example, hydrochloric acid, which is formed directly by the combination of hydrogen with chlorine, gives hydrogen by the action of a great many metals, just as sulphuric acid does. Potassium and sodium also displace hydrogen from its compounds with nitrogen; it is only from its compounds with carbon that hydrogen is not displaced by metals. Hydrogen, in its turn, is able to replace metals; this is accomplished most easily on heating, and with those metals which do not themselves displace hydrogen. If hydrogen be passed over the compounds of many metals with oxygen at a red heat, it takes up the oxygen from the metals and displaces them just as it is itself displaced by metals. If hydrogen be passed over the compound of oxygen with copper at a red heat, then metallic copper and water are obtained— $CuO + H_2 = H_2O + Cu$. This kind of double decomposition is called *reduction* with respect to the metal, which is thus reduced to a metallic state from its combination with oxygen. But it must be recollected that all metals do not displace hydrogen from its compound with oxygen, and, conversely, hydrogen is not able to displace all metals from their compounds with oxygen; thus it does not displace potassium, calcium, or aluminium from its compounds with oxygen. If the metals be arranged in the following series: K, Na, Ca, Al ... Fe, Zn, Hg ... Cu, Pb, Ag, Au, then the first are able to take up oxygen from water—that is, displace hydrogen—whilst the last do not act thus, but are, on the contrary, reduced by hydrogen—that is, have, as is said, a less affinity for oxygen than hydrogen, whilst potassium, sodium, and calcium have more. This is also expressed by the amount of heat evolved in the act of combination with oxygen (*see* Note 7), and is shown by the fact that potassium and sodium and other similar metals evolve heat in decomposing water; but copper, silver, and the like do not do this, because in combining with oxygen they evolve less heat than hydrogen does, and therefore it happens that when hydrogen reduces these metals heat is evolved. Thus, for example, if 16 grams of oxygen combine with copper, 38,000 units of heat are evolved; and when 16 grams of oxygen combine with hydrogen, forming water, 69,000 units of heat are evolved; whilst 23 grams of sodium, in combining with 16 grams of oxygen, evolve 100,000 units of heat. This example clearly shows that chemical reactions which proceed directly and unaided evolve heat. Sodium decomposes water and hydrogen reduces copper, because they are *exothermal* reactions, or those which evolve heat; copper does not decompose water,[148] because such a reaction would be accompanied by an absorption (or secretion) of heat, or belongs to the class of *endothermal* reactions in which heat is absorbed; and such reactions do not generally proceed directly, although they may take place with the aid of energy (electrical, thermal, &c.) borrowed from some foreign source.[46]

The reduction of metals by hydrogen is taken advantage of for *determining the exact composition of water by weight*. Copper oxide is usually chosen for this purpose. It is heated to redness in hydrogen, and the quantity of water thus formed is determined, when the quantity of oxygen which occurs in it is found from the loss of weight of the copper oxide. The copper oxide must be weighed immediately before and after the experiment. The difference shows the weight of the oxygen which entered into the composition of the water formed. In this manner only solids have to be weighed, which is a very great gain in the accuracy of the results obtained.[47] Dulong and Berzelius (1819) were the first to determine the composition of water by this method, and they found that water contains 88·91 of oxygen and 11·09 of hydrogen in 100 parts by weight, or 8·008 parts of oxygen per one part of hydrogen. Dumas (1842) improved on this method,[48] and found that[149] water contains 12·575 parts of hydrogen per 100 parts of oxygen—that is, 7·990 parts of oxygen per 1 part of hydrogen—and therefore it is usually[150] accepted that *water contains eight parts by weight of oxygen* to one *part by weight of hydrogen*. By whatever method water be obtained, it will[151] always present the same composition. Whether it be taken from nature and purified, or whether it be obtained from hydrogen by oxidation, or whether it be separated from any of its compounds, or obtained by some double decomposition—it will in every case contain one part by weight of hydrogen and eight parts of oxygen. This is because water is a definite chemical compound. Detonating gas, from which it may be formed, is a simple mixture of oxygen and hydrogen, although a mixture of the same composition as water. All the properties of both constituent gases are preserved in detonating gas. Either one or the other gas may be added to it without destroying its homogeneity. The fundamental properties of oxygen and hydrogen are not found in water, and neither of the gases can be directly combined with it. But they may be evolved from it. In the formation of water there is an evolution of heat; for the decomposition of water heat is required. All this is expressed by the words, *Water is a definite chemical compound of hydrogen with oxygen.* Taking the symbol of hydrogen, H, as expressing a unit quantity by weight of this substance, and expressing 16 parts by weight of oxygen by O, we can formulate all the above statements by the chemical symbol of water, H_2O. As only definite chemical compounds are denoted by formulæ, having denoted the formula of a compound substance we express by it the entire series of properties which go to make up our conception of a definite compound, and at the same time the quantitative composition of the substance by weight. Further, as we shall afterwards see, formulæ express the volume of the gases contained in a substance. Thus the formula of water shows that it contains two volumes of hydrogen and one volume of oxygen. Besides which, we shall learn that the formula expresses the density of the vapour of a compound, and on this many properties of substances depend, and, as we shall learn, determine the quantities of the bodies entering into reactions. This vapour density we shall find also determines the quantity of a substance entering into a reaction. Thus the letters H_2O tell the chemist the entire history of the substance. This is an international language, which endows chemistry with a simplicity, clearness, stability, and trustworthiness founded on the investigation of the laws of nature.

Footnotes:

[1] The first experiments of the synthesis and decomposition of water did not afford, however, an entirely convincing proof that water was composed of hydrogen and oxygen only. Davy, who investigated the decomposition of water by the galvanic current, thought for a long time that, besides the gases, an acid and alkali were also obtained. He was only convinced of the fact that water contains nothing but hydrogen and oxygen by a long series of researches, which showed him that the appearance of an acid and alkali in the decomposition of water proceeds from the presence of impurities (especially from the presence of ammonium nitrate) in water. A final comprehension of the composition of water is obtained from the accurate determination of the quantities of the component parts which enter into its composition. It will be seen from this how many data are necessary for proving the composition of water—that is, of the transformations of which it is capable. What has been said of water refers to all other compounds; the investigation of each one, the entire proof of its composition, can only be obtained by the accumulation of a large mass of data referring to it.

[2] This gas is collected in a voltameter.

[3] In order to observe this explosion without the slightest danger, it is best to proceed in the following manner. Some soapy water is prepared, so that it easily forms soap bubbles, and it is poured into an iron trough. In this water, the end of a gas-conducting tube is immersed. This tube is connected with any suitable apparatus, in which detonating gas is evolved. Soap bubbles, full of this gas, are then formed. If the apparatus in which the gas is produced be then removed (otherwise the explosion might travel into the interior of the apparatus), and a lighted taper be brought to the soap bubbles, a very sharp explosion takes place. The bubbles should be small to avoid any danger; ten, each about the size of a pea, suffice to give a sharp report, like a pistol shot.

[4] In order to fill the tube with water, it is turned up, so that the closed end points downwards and the open end upwards, and water acidified with sulphuric acid is poured into it.

[4 bis] Owing to the gradual but steady progress made during the last twenty-five years in the production of an electric current from the dynamo and its transmission over considerable distances, the electrolytic decomposition of many compound bodies has acquired great importance, and the use of the electric current is making its way into many chemical manufactures. Hence, Prof. D. A. Lachinoff's proposal to obtain hydrogen and oxygen (both of which have many applications) by means of electrolysis (either of a 10 to 15 per cent. solution of caustic soda or a 15 per cent. solution of sulphuric acid) may find a practical application, at all events in the future. In general, owing to their simplicity, electrolytic methods have a great future, but as yet, so long as the production of an electric current remains so costly, their application is limited. And for this reason, although certain of these methods are mentioned in this work, they are not specially considered, the more so since a profitable and proper use of the electric current for chemical purposes requires special electro-technical knowledge which beginners cannot he assumed to have, and therefore, an exposition of the principles of electrotechnology as applied, to the production of chemical transformations, although referred to in places, does not come within the scope of the present work.

[5] As water is formed by the combination of oxygen and hydrogen, with a considerable evolution of heat, and as it can also be decomposed, this reaction is a reversible one (*see* Introduction), and consequently at a high temperature the decomposition of water cannot be complete—it is limited by the opposite reaction. Strictly speaking, it is not known how much water is decomposed at a given temperature, although many efforts (Bunsen, and others) have been made in various directions to solve this

question. Not knowing the coefficient of expansion, and the specific heat of gases at such high temperatures, renders all calculations (from observations of the pressure on explosion) doubtful.

[6] Grove, in 1847, observed that a platinum wire fused in the oxyhydrogen flame—that is, having acquired the temperature of the formation of water—and having formed a molten drop at its end which fell into water, evolved detonating gas—that is, decomposed water. It therefore follows that water already decomposes at the temperature of its formation. At that time, this formed a scientific paradox; this we shall unravel only with the development of the conceptions of dissociation, introduced into science by Henri Sainte-Claire Deville, in 1857. These conceptions form an important epoch in science, and their development is one of the problems of modern chemistry. The essence of the matter is that, at high temperatures, water exists but also decomposes, just as a volatile liquid, at a certain temperature, exists both as a liquid and as a vapour. Similarly as a volatile liquid saturates a space, attaining its maximum tension, so also the products of dissociation have their maximum tension, and once that is attained decomposition ceases, just as evaporation ceases. Under like conditions, if the vapour be allowed to escape (and therefore its partial pressure be diminished), evaporation recommences, so also if the products of decomposition be removed, decomposition again continues. These simple conceptions of dissociation introduce infinitely varied consequences into the mechanism of chemical reactions, and therefore we shall have occasion to return to them very often. We may add that Grove also concluded that water was decomposed at a white heat, from the fact that he obtained detonating gas by passing steam through a tube with a wire heated strongly by an electric current, and also by passing steam over molten oxide of lead, he obtained, on the one hand, litharge (= oxide of lead and oxygen), and on the other, metallic lead formed by the action of hydrogen.

[6 bis] Part of the oxygen will also penetrate through the pores of the tube; but, as was said before, a much smaller quantity than the hydrogen, and as the density of oxygen is sixteen times greater than that of hydrogen, the volume of oxygen which passes through the porous walls will be four times less than the volume of hydrogen (the quantities of gases passing through porous walls are inversely proportional to the square roots of their densities). The oxygen which separates out into the annular space will combine, at a certain fall of temperature, with the hydrogen; but as each volume of oxygen only requires two volumes of hydrogen, whilst at least four volumes of hydrogen will pass through the porous walls for every volume of oxygen that passes, therefore, part of the hydrogen will remain free, and can be collected from the annular space. A corresponding

quantity of oxygen remaining from the decomposition of the water can be collected from the internal tube.

[7] In order to demonstrate the difference of the affinity of oxygen for different elements, it is enough to compare the amounts of heats which are evolved in their combination with 16 parts by weight of oxygen; in the case of sodium (when Na_2O is formed, or 46 parts of Na combine with 16 parts of oxygen, according to Beketoff) 100,000 calories (or units of heat), are evolved, for hydrogen (when water, H_2O, is formed) 69,000 calories, for iron (when the oxide FeO is formed) 69,000, and if the oxide Fe_2O_3 is formed, 64,000 calories, for zinc (ZnO is formed) 86,000 calories, for lead (when PbO is formed) 51,000 calories, for copper (when CuO is formed) 38,000 calories, and for mercury (HgO is formed) 31,000 calories.

These figures cannot correspond directly with the magnitude of the affinities, for the physical and mechanical side of the matter is very different in the different cases. Hydrogen is a gas, and, in combining with oxygen, gives a liquid; consequently it changes its physical state, and, in doing so, evolves heat. But zinc and copper are solids, and, in combining with oxygen, give solid oxides. The oxygen, previously a gas, now passes into a solid or liquid state, and, therefore, also must have given up its store of heat in forming oxides. As we shall afterwards see, the degree of contraction (and consequently of mechanical work) was different in the different cases, and therefore the figures expressing the heat of combination cannot directly depend on the affinities, on the loss of internal energy previously in the elements. Nevertheless, the figures above cited correspond, in a certain degree, with the order in which the elements stand in respect to their affinity for oxygen, as may be seen from the fact that the mercury oxide, which evolves the least heat (among the above examples), is the least stable is easily decomposed, giving up its oxygen; whilst sodium, the formation of whose oxide is accompanied by the greatest evolution of heat, is able to decompose all the other oxides, taking up their oxygen. In order to generalise the connection between affinity and the evolution and the absorption of heat, which is evident in its general features, and was firmly established by the researches of Favre and Silbermann (about 1840), and then of Thomsen (in Denmark) and Berthelot (in France), many investigators, especially the one last mentioned, established the *law of maximum work*. This states that only those chemical reactions take place of their own accord in which the greatest amount of chemical (latent, potential) energy is transformed into heat. But, in the first place, we are not able, judging from what has been said above, to distinguish that heat which corresponds with purely chemical action from the sum total of the heat observed in a reaction (in the calorimeter); in the second place, there are evidently endothermal reactions which proceed under the same circumstances as exothermal (carbon burns in the vapour of sulphur with absorption of heat, whilst in oxygen it evolves heat); and, in the third place, there are reversible reactions, which when taking place in one direction evolve heat, and when taking place in the opposite direction absorb it; and, therefore, the principle of maximum work in its elementary form is not supported by science. But the subject continues to be developed, and will probably lead to a general law, such as thermal chemistry does not at present possess.

[8] If a piece of metallic sodium be thrown into water, it floats on it (owing to its lightness), keeps in a state of continual motion (owing to the evolution of hydrogen on all sides), and immediately decomposes the water, evolving hydrogen, which can be lighted. This experiment may, however, lead to an explosion should the sodium stick to the walls of the vessel, and begin to act on the limited mass of water immediately adjacent to it (probably in this case NaHO forms with Na, Na_2O, which acts on the water, evolving much heat and rapidly forming steam), and the experiment should therefore be carried on with caution. The decomposition of water by sodium may he better demonstrated, and with greater safety, in the following manner. Into a glass cylinder filled with mercury, and immersed in a mercury bath, water is first introduced, which will, owing to its lightness, rise to the top, and then a piece of sodium wrapped in paper is introduced with forceps into the cylinder. The metal rises through the mercury to the surface of the water, on which it remains, and evolves hydrogen, which collects in the cylinder, and may be tested after the experiment has been completed. The safest method of making this experiment is, however, as follows. The sodium (cleaned from the naphtha in which it is kept) is either wrapped in fine copper gauze and held by forceps, or else held in forceps at the end of which a small copper cage is attached, and is then held under water. The evolution of hydrogen goes on quietly, and it may he collected in a bell jar and then lighted.

[9] This reaction is vigorously exothermal, $i.e.$ it is accompanied by the evolution of heat. If a sufficient quantity of water be taken the whole of the sodium hydroxide, NaHO, formed is dissolved, and about 42,500 units of heat are evolved per 23 grams of sodium taken. As 40 grams of sodium hydroxide are produced, and they in dissolving, judging from direct experiment, evolve about 10,000 calories; therefore, without an excess of water, and without the formation of a solution, the reaction would evolve about 32,500 calories. We shall afterwards learn that hydrogen contains in its smallest isolable particles H_2 and not H, and therefore it follows that the reaction should be written thus—$2Na + 2H_2O = H_2 + 2NaOH$, and it then corresponds with an evolution of heat of +65,000 calories. And as N. N. Beketoff showed that Na_2O, or anhydrous oxide of sodium, forms the

hydrate, or sodium hydroxide (caustic soda), 2NaHO, with water, evolving about 35,500 calories, therefore the reaction $2Na + H_2O = H_2 + Na_2O$ corresponds to 29,500 calories. This quantity of heat is less than that which is evolved in combining with water, in the formation of caustic soda, and therefore it is not to be wondered at that the hydrate, NaHO, is always formed and not the anhydrous substance Na_2O. That such a conclusion, which agrees with facts, is inevitable is also seen from the fact that, according to Beketoff, the anhydrous sodium oxide, Na_2O, acts directly on hydrogen, with separation of sodium, $Na_2O + H = NaHO + Na$. This reaction is accompanied by an evolution of heat equal to about 3,000 calories, because $Na_2O + H_2O$ gives, as we saw, 35,500 calories and $Na + H_2O$ evolves 32,500 calories. However, an opposite reaction also takes place—$NaHO + Na = Na_2O + H$ (both with the aid of heat)—consequently, in this case heat is absorbed. In this we see an example of calorimetric calculations and the limited application of the law of maximum work for the general phenomena of reversible reactions, to which the case just considered belongs. But it must be remarked that all reversible reactions evolve or absorb but little heat, and the reason of the law of maximum work, not being universal must first of all be looked for in the fact that we have no means of separating the heat which corresponds with the purely chemical process from the sum total of the heat observed, and as the structure of a number of substances is altered by heat and also by contact, we can scarcely hope that the time approaches when such a distinction will be possible. A heated substance, in point of fact, has no longer the original energy of its atoms—that is, the act of heating not only alters the store of motion of the molecules but also of the atoms forming the molecules, in other words, it makes the beginning of or preparation for chemical change. From this it must be concluded that thermochemistry, or the study of the heat accompanying chemical transformations, cannot he identified with chemical mechanics. Thermo-chemical data form a part of it, but they alone cannot give it.

[10] The composition of water, as we saw above, was determined by passing steam over red-hot iron; the same method has been used for making hydrogen for filling balloons. An oxide having the composition Fe_3O_4 is formed in the reaction, so that it is expressed by the equation $3Fe + 4H_2O = Fe_3O_4 + 8H$.

[11] The reaction between iron and water (note 10) is reversible. By heating the oxide in a current of hydrogen, water and iron are obtained. From this it follows, from the principle of chemical equilibria, that if iron and hydrogen be taken, and also oxygen, but in such a quantity that it is insufficient for combination with both substances, then it will divide itself between the two; part of it will combine with the iron and the other part

with the hydrogen, but a portion of both will remain in an uncombined state.

Therefore, if iron and water be placed in a closed space, decomposition of the water will proceed on heating to the temperature at which the reaction $3Fe + 4H_2O = Fe_3O_4 + 8H$ commences; but it ceases, does not go on to the end, because the conditions for a reverse reaction are attained, and a state of equilibrium will ensue after the decomposition of a certain quantity of water. Here again (*see* note 9) the reversibility is connected with the small heat effect, and again both reactions (direct and reverse) proceed at a red heat. But if, in the above-described reaction, the hydrogen escapes as it is evolved, then its partial pressure does not increase with its formation, and therefore all the iron can he oxidised by the water. In this we see the elements of that influence of mass to which we shall have occasion to return later. With copper and lead there will be no decomposition, either at the ordinary or at a high temperature, because the affinity of these metals for oxygen is much less than that of hydrogen.

[12] In general, if reversible as well as non-reversible reactions can take place between substances acting on each other, then, judging by our present knowledge, the non-reversible reactions take place in the majority of cases, which obliges one to acknowledge the action, in this case, of comparatively strong affinities. The reaction, $Zn + H_2SO_4 = H_2 + ZnSO_4$, which takes place in solutions at the ordinary temperature, is scarcely reversible under these conditions, but at a certain high temperature it becomes reversible, because at this temperature zinc sulphate and sulphuric acid split up, and the action must take place between the water and zinc. From the preceding proposition results proceed which are in some cases verified by experiment. If the action of zinc or iron on a solution of sulphuric acid presents a non-reversible reaction, then we may by this means obtain hydrogen in a very compressed state, and compressed hydrogen will not act on solutions of sulphates of the above-named metals. This is verified in reality as far as was possible in the experiments to keep up the compression or pressure of the hydrogen. Those metals which do not evolve hydrogen with acids, on the contrary, should, at least at an increase of pressure, be displaced by hydrogen. And in fact Brunner showed that gaseous hydrogen displaces platinum and palladium from the aqueous solutions of their chlorine compounds, but not gold, and Beketoff succeeded in showing that silver and mercury, under a considerable pressure, are separated from the solutions of certain of their compounds by means of hydrogen. Reaction already commences under a pressure of six atmospheres, if a weak solution of silver sulphate be taken; with a stronger solution a much greater pressure is required, however, for the separation of the silver.

[13] For the same reason, many metals in acting on solutions of the alkalis displace hydrogen. Aluminium acts particularly clearly in this respect, because its oxide gives a soluble compound with alkalis. For the same reason tin, in acting on hydrochloric acid, evolves hydrogen, and silicon does the same with hydrofluoric acid. It is evident that in such cases the sum of all the affinities plays a part; for instance, taking the action of zinc on sulphuric acid, we have the affinity of zinc for oxygen (forming zinc oxide, ZnO), the affinity of its oxide for sulphuric anhydride, SO_3 (forming zinc sulphate, $ZnSO_4$), and the affinity of the resultant salt, $ZnSO_4$, for water. It is only the first-named affinity that acts in the reaction between water and the metal, if no account is taken of those forces (of a physico-mechanical character) which act between the molecules (for instance, the cohesion between the molecules of the oxide) and those forces (of a chemical character) which act between the atoms forming the molecule, for instance, between the atoms of hydrogen giving the molecule H_2 containing two atoms. I consider it necessary to remark, that the hypothesis of the affinity or endeavour of heterogeneous atoms to enter into a common system and in harmonious motion (*i.e.* to form a compound molecule) must inevitably be in accordance with the hypothesis of forces including homogeneous atoms to form complex molecules (for instance, H_2), and to build up the latter into solid or liquid substances, in which the existence of an attraction between the homogeneous particles must certainly be admitted. Therefore, those forces which bring about solution must also be taken into consideration. These are all forces of one and the same series, and in this may be seen the great difficulties surrounding the study of molecular mechanics and its province—chemical mechanics.

[14] It is acknowledged that zinc itself acts on water, even at the ordinary temperature, but that the action is confined to small masses and only proceeds at the surface. In reality, zinc, in the form of a very fine powder, or so-called 'zinc dust,' is capable of decomposing water with the formation of oxide (hydrated) and hydrogen. The oxide formed acts on sulphuric acid, water then dissolves the salt produced, and the action continues because one of the products of the action of water on zinc, zinc oxide, is removed from the surface. One might naturally imagine that the reaction does not proceed directly between the metal and water, but between the metal and the acid, but such a simple representation, which we shall cite afterwards, hides the mechanism of the reaction, and does not permit of its actual complexity being seen.

[15] According to Thomsen the reaction between zinc and a very weak solution of sulphuric acid evolves about 38,000 calories (zinc sulphate being formed) per 65 parts by weight of zinc; and 56 parts by weight of iron—which combine, like 65 parts by weight of zinc, with 16 parts by

weight of oxygen—evolve about 25,000 calories (forming ferrous sulphate, FeSO$_4$). Paracelsus observed the action of metals on acids in the seventeenth century; but it was not until the eighteenth century that Lémery determined that the gas which is evolved in this action is a particular one which differs from air and is capable of burning. Even Boyle confused it with air. Cavendish determined the chief properties of the gas discovered by Paracelsus. At first it was called 'inflammable air'; later, when it was recognised that in burning it gives water, it was called hydrogen, from the Greek words for water and generator.

[15 bis] If, when the sulphuric acid is poured over the zinc, the evolution of the hydrogen proceed too slowly, it may be greatly accelerated by adding a small quantity of a solution of CuSO$_4$ or PtCl$_4$ to the acid. The reason of this is explained in Chap. XVI., note 10 bis.

[16]

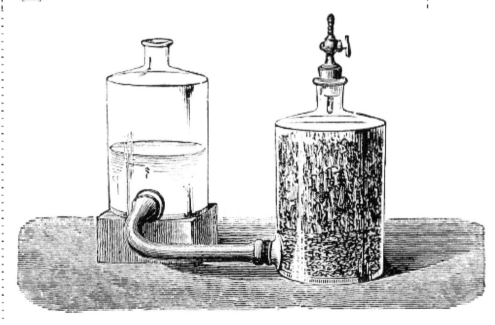

FIG. 21.—A very convenient apparatus for the preparation of gases obtained without heat. It may also replace an aspirator or gasometer.

As laboratory experiments with gases require a certain preliminary knowledge, we will describe certain *practical methods for the collection and preparation of gases*. When in laboratory practice an intermittent supply of hydrogen (or other gas which is evolved without the aid of heat) is required the apparatus represented in fig. 21 is the most convenient. It consists of two bottles, having orifices at the bottom, in which corks with tubes are placed, and these tubes are connected by an india-rubber tube (sometimes furnished with a spring clamp). Zinc is placed in one bottle, and dilute sulphuric acid in the other. The neck of the former is closed by a cork, which is fitted with a gas-conducting tube with a stopcock. If the two bottles are connected with each other and the stopcock be opened, the acid will flow to the zinc and evolve hydrogen. If the stopcock be closed, the hydrogen will force out the acid from the bottle containing the zinc, and the action will cease. Or the vessel containing the acid may be placed at a lower level than that containing the zinc, when all the liquid will flow into it, and in order to start the action the acid vessel may be placed on a higher level than the other, and the acid will flow to the zinc. It can also be employed for collecting gases (as an aspirator or gasometer).

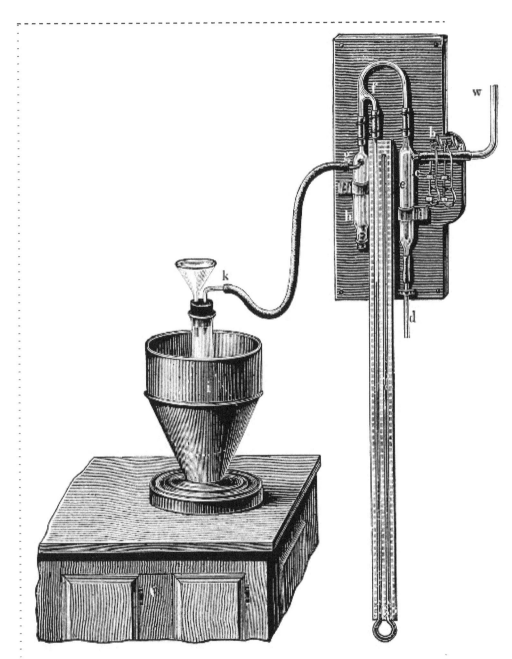

FIG. 22.—Continuous aspirator. The tube d should be more than 32 feet long.

In laboratory practice, however, other forms of apparatus are generally employed for exhausting, collecting, and holding gases. We will here cite the most usual forms. An *aspirator* usually consists of a vessel furnished with a stopcock at the bottom. A stout cork, through which a glass tube passes, is fixed into the neck of this vessel. If the vessel be filled up with water to the cork and the bottom stopcock is opened, then the water will run out and draw gas in. For this purpose the glass tube is connected with the apparatus from which it is desired to pump out or exhaust the gas.

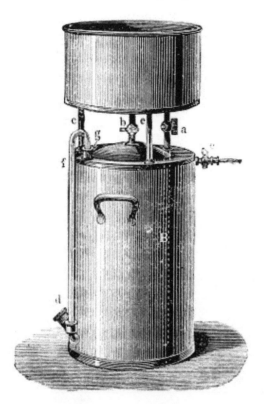

FIG. 23.—Gasholder.

The aspirator represented in fig. <u>22</u> may be recommended for its continuous action. It consists of a tube *d* which widens out at the top, the lower part being long and narrow. In the expanded upper portion *c*, two tubes are sealed; one, *e*, for drawing in the gas, whilst the other, *b*, is connected to the water supply *w*. The amount of water supplied through the tube *b* must be less than the amount which can be carried off by the tube *d*. Owing to this the water in the tube *d* will flow through it in cylinders alternating with cylinders of gas, which will be thus carried away. The gas which is drawn through may be collected from the end of the tube *d*, but this form of pump is usually employed where the air or gas aspirated is not to be collected. If the tube *d* is of considerable length, say 40 ft. or more, a very fair vacuum will be produced, the amount of which is shown by the gauge g; it is often used for filtering under reduced pressure, as shown in the figure. If water be replaced by mercury, and the length of the tube d be greater than 760 mm., the aspirator may be employed as an air-pump, and all the air may be exhausted from a limited space; for instance, by connecting g with a hollow sphere.

Gasholders are often used for collecting and holding gases. They are made of glass, copper, or tin plate. The usual form is shown in fig. 23. The lower vessel B is made hermetically tight—*i.e.*, impervious to gases—and is filled with water. A funnel is attached to this vessel (on several supports). The vessel B communicates with the bottom of the funnel by a stopcock b and a tube a, reaching to the bottom of the vessel B. If water be poured into the funnel and the stopcocks a and b opened, the water will run through a, and the air escape from the vessel B by b. A glass tube f runs up the side of the vessel B, with which it communicates at the top and bottom, and shows the amount of water and gas the gasholder contains. In order to fill the gasholder with a gas, it is first filled with water, the cocks a, b and e are closed, the nut d unscrewed, and the end of the tube conducting the gas from the apparatus in which it is generated is passed into d. As the gas fills the gasholder, the water runs out at d. If the pressure of a gas be not greater than the atmospheric pressure and it be required to collect it in the gasholder, then the stopcock e is put into communication with the space containing the gas. Then, having opened the orifice d, the gasholder acts like an aspirator; the gas will pass through e, and the water run out at d. If the cocks be closed, the gas collected in the gasholder may be easily preserved and transported. If it be desired to transfer this gas into another vessel, then a gas-conducting tube is attached to e, the cock a opened, b and d closed, and the gas will then pass out at e, owing to its pressure in the apparatus being greater than the atmospheric pressure, due to the pressure of the water poured into the funnel. If it be required to fill a cylinder or flask with the gas, it is filled with water and inverted in the funnel, and the stopcocks b and a opened. Then water will run through a, and the gas will escape from the gasholder into the cylinder through b.

[17] When it is required to prepare hydrogen in large quantities for filling balloons, copper vessels or wooden casks lined with lead are employed; they are filled with scrap iron, over which dilute sulphuric acid is poured. The hydrogen generated from a number of casks is carried through lead pipes into special casks containing water (in order to cool the gas) and lime (in order to remove acid fumes). To avoid loss of gas all the joints are made hermetically tight with cement or tar. In order to fill his gigantic balloon (of 25,000 cubic metres capacity), Giffard, in 1878, constructed a complicated apparatus for giving a continuous supply of hydrogen, in which a mixture

of sulphuric acid and water was continually run into vessels containing iron, and from which the solution of iron sulphate formed was continually drawn off. When coal gas, extracted from coal, is employed for filling balloons, it should be as light, or as rich in hydrogen, as possible. For this reason, only the last portions of the gas coming from the retorts are collected, and, besides this, it is then sometimes passed through red-hot vessels, in order to decompose the hydrocarbons as much as possible; charcoal is deposited in the red-hot vessels, and hydrogen remains as gas. Coal gas may be yet further enriched in hydrogen, and consequently rendered lighter, by passing it over an ignited mixture of charcoal and lime.

L. Mond (London) proposes to manufacture hydrogen on a large scale from water gas (*see infra*, and Chapters VIII. and IX.), which contains a mixture of oxide of carbon (CO) and hydrogen, and is produced by the action of steam upon incandescent coke ($C + H_2O = CO + H_2$). He destroys the oxide of carbon by converting it into carbon and carbonic anhydride ($2CO = C + CO_2$), which is easily done by means of incandescent, finely-divided metallic nickel; the carbon then remains with the nickel, from which it may be removed by burning it in air, and the nickel can then be used over again (*see* Chapter IX., Note 24 bis). The CO_2 formed is removed from the hydrogen by passing it through milk of lime. This process should apparently give hydrogen on a large scale more economically than any of the methods hitherto proposed.

[18] Of the metals, only a very few combine with hydrogen (for example, sodium), and give substances which are easily decomposed. Of the non-metals, the halogens (fluorine, chlorine, bromine, and iodine) most easily form hydrogen compounds; of these the hydrogen compound of chlorine, and still more that of fluorine, is stable, whilst those of bromine and iodine are easily decomposed, especially the latter. The other non-metals—for instance, sulphur, carbon, and phosphorus—give hydrogen compounds of different composition and properties, but they are all less stable than water. The number of the carbon compounds of hydrogen is enormous, but there are very few among them which are not decomposed, with separation of the carbon and hydrogen, at a red heat.

[19] The reaction expressed by the equation $CNaHO_2 + NaHO = CNa_2O_3 + H_2$ may be effected in a glass vessel, like the decomposition of copper carbonate or mercury oxide (*see* Introduction); it is non-reversible, and takes place without the presence of water, and therefore Pictet (*see* later) made use of it to obtain hydrogen under great pressure.

[20] The reaction between charcoal and superheated steam is a double one—that is, there may be formed either carbonic oxide, CO (according to the equation $H_2O + C = H_2 + CO$), or carbonic anhydride CO_2 (according

to the equation $2H_2O + C = 2H_2 + CO_2$), and the resulting mixture is called *water-gas*; we shall speak of it in Chapter IX.

[21] Hydrogen obtained by the action of zinc or iron on sulphuric acid generally smells of hydrogen sulphide (like rotten eggs), which it contains in admixture. As a rule such hydrogen is not so pure as that obtained by the action of an electric current or of sodium on water. The impurity of the hydrogen depends on the impurities contained in the zinc, or iron, and sulphuric acid, and on secondary reactions which take place simultaneously with the main reaction. Impure hydrogen may be easily freed from the impurities it contains: some of them—namely, those having acid properties—are absorbed by caustic soda, and therefore may be removed by passing the hydrogen through a solution of this substance; another series of impurities is absorbed by a solution of mercuric chloride; and, lastly, a third series is absorbed by a solution of potassium permanganate. If absolutely *pure hydrogen* be required, it is sometimes obtained by the decomposition of water (previously boiled to expel all air, and mixed with pure sulphuric acid) by the galvanic current. Only the gas evolved at the negative electrode is collected. Or else, an apparatus like that which gives detonating gas is used, the positive electrode, however, being immersed under mercury containing zinc in solution. The oxygen which is evolved at this electrode then immediately, at the moment of its evolution, combines with the zinc, and this compound dissolves in the sulphuric acid and forms zinc sulphate, which remains in solution, and therefore the hydrogen generated will be quite free from oxygen.

[22] An inverted beaker is attached to one arm of the beam of a tolerably sensitive balance, and its weight counterpoised by weights in the pan attached to the other arm, If the beaker be then filled with hydrogen it rises, owing to the air being replaced by hydrogen. Thus, at the ordinary temperature of a room, a litre of air weighs about 1·2 gram, and on replacing the air by hydrogen a decrease in weight of about 1 gram per litre is obtained. Moist hydrogen is heavier than dry—for aqueous vapour is nine times heavier than hydrogen. In filling balloons it is usually calculated that (it being impossible to have perfectly dry hydrogen or to obtain it quite free from air) the lifting force due to the difference between the weights of equal volumes of hydrogen and air is equal to 1 kilogram (= 1,000 grams) per cubic metre (= 1,000 litres).

[23] The density of hydrogen in relation to the air has been repeatedly determined by accurate experiments. The first determination, made by Lavoisier, was not very exact; taking the density of air as unity, he obtained 0·0769 for that of hydrogen—that is, hydrogen as thirteen times lighter than air. More accurate determinations are due to Thomsen, who obtained the figure 0·0693; Berzelius and Dulong, who obtained 0·0688; and Dumas

and Boussingault, who obtained 0·06945. Regnault, and more recently Le Duc (1892), took two spheres of considerable capacity, which contained equal volumes of air (thus avoiding the necessity of any correction for weighing them in air). Both spheres were attached to the scale pans of a balance. One was sealed up, and the other first weighed empty and then full of hydrogen. Thus, knowing the weight of the hydrogen filling the sphere, and the capacity of the sphere, it was easy to find the weight of a litre of hydrogen; and, knowing the weight of a litre of air at the same temperature and pressure, it was easy to calculate the density of hydrogen. Regnault, by these experiments, found the average density of hydrogen to be 0·06926 in relation to air; Le Duc, 0·06948 (with a possible error of ±0·00001), and this latter figure must now be looked upon as near to the truth.

In this work I shall always refer the densities of all gases to hydrogen, and not to air; I will therefore give, for the sake of clearness, the weight of a litre of dry pure hydrogen in grams at a temperature $t°$ and under a pressure H (measured in millimetres of mercury at 0°, in lat. 45°). The weight of a litre of hydrogen

$$= 0·08986 \times H \boxed{760} \times 1 \boxed{1 + 0·00367t} \text{ gram.}$$

For aëronauts it is very useful to know, besides this, the weight of the air at different heights, and I therefore insert the adjoining table, constructed on the basis of Glaisher's data, for the temperature and moisture of the atmospheric strata in clear weather. All the figures are given in the metrical system—1,000 millimetres = 39·37 inches, 1,000 kilograms = 2204·3375 lbs., 1,000 cubic metres = 35,316·6 cubic feet. The starting temperature at the earth's surface is taken as = 15° C., its moisture 60 p.c., pressure 760 millimetres. The pressures are taken as indicated by an *aneroid barometer*, assumed to be corrected at the sea level and at lat. 45° C. If the height above the level of the sea equal z kilometres, then the weight of 1 cubic metre of air may be approximately taken as $1·222 - 0·12z + 0·00377z^2$ kilogram.

Pressure	Temperature	Moisture	Height	Weight of the air	
760 mm.	15° C.	60 p.c.	0 metres	1222 kilos.	
700 „	11·0° „	64 „	690 „	1141 „	1,000 cubic metres
650 „	7·6° „	64 „	1200 „	1073 „	
600 „	4·3° „	63 „	1960 „	1003 „	

550	„	- 1·0°	„	62	„	2660	„	931	„
500	„	- 2·4°	„	58	„	3420	„	857	„
450	„	- 5·8°	„	52	„	4250	„	781	„
400	„	- 9·1°	„	44	„	5170	„	703	„
350	„	-12·5°	„	36	„	6190	„	624	„
300	„	-15·9°	„	27	„	7360	„	542	„
250	„	-19·2°	„	18	„	8720	„	457	„

Although the figures in this table are calculated with every possible care from average data, yet they can only be taken approximately, for in every separate case the conditions, both at the earth's surface and in the atmosphere, will differ from those here taken. In calculating the height to which a balloon can ascend, it is evident that the density of gas in relation to air must be known. This density for ordinary coal gas is from 0·6 to 0·35, and for hydrogen with its ordinary contents of moisture and air from 0·1 to 0·15.

Hence, for instance, it may be calculated that a balloon of 1,000 cubic metres capacity filled with pure hydrogen, and weighing (the envelope, tackle, people, and ballast) 727 kilograms, will only ascend to a height of about 4,250 metres.

[24] If a cracked flask be filled with hydrogen and its neck immersed under water or mercury, then the liquid will rise up into the flask, owing to the hydrogen passing through the cracks about 3·8 times quicker than the air is able to pass through these cracks into the flask. The same phenomenon may be better observed if, instead of a flask, a tube be employed, whose end is closed by a porous substance, such as graphite, unglazed earthenware, or a gypsum plate.

[25] According to Boyle and Mariotte's law, for a given gas at a constant temperature the volume decreases by as many times as the pressure increases; that is, this law requires that the product of the volume v and the

pressure p for a given gas should be a constant quantity: $pv = C$, a constant quantity which does not vary with a change of pressure. This equation does very nearly and exactly express the observed relation between the volume and pressure, but only within comparatively small variations of pressure, density, and volume. If these variations be in any degree considerable, the quantity pv proves to be dependent on the pressure, and it either increases or diminishes with an increase of pressure. In the former case the compressibility is less than it should he according to Mariotte's law, in the latter case it is greater. We will call the first case a positive discrepancy (because then $d(pv)/d(p)$ is greater than zero), and the second case a negative discrepancy (because then $d(pv)/d(p)$ is less than zero). Determinations made by myself (in the seventies), M. L. Kirpicheff, and V. A. Hemilian showed that all known gases at low pressures—*i.e.* when considerably rarefied—present positive discrepancies. On the other hand, it appears from the researches of Cailletet, Natterer, and Amagat that all gases under great pressures (when the volume obtained is 500–1,000 times less than under the atmospheric pressure) also present positive discrepancies. Thus under a pressure of 2,700 atmospheres air is compressed, not 2,700 times, but only 800, and hydrogen 1,000 times. Hence the positive kind of discrepancy is, so to say, normal to gases. And this is easily intelligible. If a gas followed Mariotte's law, or if it were compressed to a greater extent than is shown by this law, then under great pressures it would attain a density greater than that of solid and liquid substances, which is in itself improbable and even impossible by reason of the fact that solid and liquid substances are themselves but little compressible. For instance, a cubic centimetre of oxygen at 0° and under the atmospheric pressure weighs about 0·0014 gram, and at a pressure of 3,000 atmospheres (this pressure is attained in guns) it would, if it followed Mariotte's law, weigh 4·2 grams—that is, would be about four times heavier than water—and at a pressure of 10,000 atmospheres it would be heavier than mercury. Besides this, positive discrepancies are probable because the molecules of a gas themselves must occupy a certain volume. Considering that Mariotte's law, strictly speaking, applies only to the intermolecular space, we can understand the necessity of positive discrepancies. If we designate the volume of the molecules of a gas by b (like van der Waals, *see* Chap. I., Note 34), then it must be expected that $p(v - b) = C$. Hence $pv = C + bp$, which expresses a positive discrepancy. Supposing that for hydrogen $pv = 1,000$, at a pressure of one metre of mercury, according to the results of Regnault's, Amagat's, and Natterer's experiments, we obtain b as approximately 0·7 to 0·9.

Thus the increase of pv with the increase of pressure must be considered as the normal law of the compressibility of gases. Hydrogen presents such a positive compressibility at all pressures, for it presents positive discrepancies from Mariotte's law, according to Regnault, at all pressures above the atmospheric pressure. Hence hydrogen is, so to say, a perfect gas. No other gas behaves so simply with a change of pressure. All other gases at pressures from 1 to 30 atmospheres present negative discrepancies—that is, they are then compressed to a greater degree than should follow from Mariotte's law, as was shown by the determinations of Regnault, which were verified when repeated by myself and Boguzsky. Thus, for example, on changing the pressure from 4 to 20 metres of mercury—that is, on increasing the pressure five times—the volume only decreased 4·93 times when hydrogen was taken, and 5·06 when air was taken.

The positive discrepancies from the law at low pressures are of particular interest, and, according to the above-mentioned determinations made by myself, Kirpicheff, and Hemilian, and verified (by two methods) by K. D. Kraevitch and Prof. Ramsay (London, 1894), they are proper to all gases (even to those which are easily compressed into a liquid state, such as carbonic and sulphurous anhydrides). These discrepancies approach the case of a very high rarefaction of gases, where a gas is near to a condition of maximum dispersion of its molecules, and perhaps presents a passage towards the substance termed 'luminiferous ether' which fills up interplanetary and interstellar space. If we suppose that gases are rarefiable to a definite limit only, having attained which they (like solids) do not alter in volume with a decrease of pressure, then on the one hand the passage of the atmosphere at its upper limits into a homogeneous ethereal medium becomes comprehensible, and on the other hand it would be expected that gases would, in a state of high rarefaction (*i.e.* when small masses of gases occupy large volumes, or when furthest removed from a liquid state), present positive discrepancies from Boyle and Mariotte's law. Our present acquaintance with this province of highly rarefied gases is very limited (because direct measurements are exceedingly difficult to make, and are hampered by possible errors of experiment, which may be considerable), and its further development promises to elucidate much in respect to natural phenomena. To the three states of matter (solid, liquid, and gaseous) it is evident a fourth must yet be added, the ethereal or ultra-gaseous (as Crookes proposed), understanding by this, matter in its highest possible state of rarefaction.

[26] The law of Gay-Lussac states that all gases in all conditions present one coefficient of expansion 0·00367; that is, when heated from 0° to 100° they expand like air; namely, a thousand volumes of a gas measured at 0° will occupy 1367 volumes at 100°. Regnault, about 1850, showed that Gay-Lussac's law is not entirely correct, and that different gases, and also one and the same gas at different pressures, have not quite the same

coefficients of expansion. Thus the expansion of air between 0° and 100° is 0·367 under the ordinary pressure of one atmosphere, and at three atmospheres it is 0·371, the expansion of hydrogen is 0·366, and of carbonic anhydride 0·37. Regnault, however, did not directly determine the change of volume between 0° and 100°, but measured the variation of tension with the change of temperature; but since gases do not entirely follow Mariotte's law, the change of volume cannot be directly judged by the variation of tension. The investigations carried on by myself and Kayander, about 1870, showed the variation of volume on heating from 0° to 100° under a constant pressure. These investigations confirmed Regnault's conclusion that Gay-Lussac's law is not entirely correct, and further showed (1) that the expansion per volume from 0° to 100° under a pressure of one atmosphere, for air = 0·368, for hydrogen = 0·367, for carbonic anhydride = 0·373, for hydrogen bromide = 0·386, &c.; (2) that for gases which are more compressible than should follow from Mariotte's law the expansion by heat increases with the pressure—for example, for air at a pressure of three and a half atmospheres, it equals 0·371, for carbonic anhydride at one atmosphere it equals 0·373, at three atmospheres 0·389, and at eight atmospheres 0·413; (3) that for gases which are less compressible than should follow from Mariotte's law, the expansion by heat decreases with an increase of pressure—for example, for hydrogen at one atmosphere 0·367, at eight atmospheres 0·369, for air at a quarter of an atmosphere 0·370, at one atmosphere 0·368; and hydrogen like *air* (and all gases) is less compressed *at low pressures* than should follow from Mariotte's law (*see* Note 25). Hence, hydrogen, starting from zero to the highest pressures, exhibits a gradually, although only slightly, varying coefficient of expansion, whilst for air and other gases at the atmospheric and higher pressures, the coefficient of expansion increases with the increase of pressure, so long as their compressibility is greater than should follow from Mariotte's law. But when at considerable pressures, this kind of discrepancy passes into the normal (*see* Note 25), then the coefficient of expansion of all gases decreases with an increase of pressure, as is seen from the researches of Amagat. The difference between the two coefficients of expansion, for a constant pressure and for a constant volume, is explained by these relations. Thus, for example, for air at a pressure of one atmosphere the true coefficient of expansion (the volume varying at constant pressure) = 0·00368 (according to Mendeléeff and Kayander) and the variation of tension (at a constant volume, according to Regnault) = 0·00367.

[27] Permanent gases are those which cannot be liquefied by an increase of pressure alone. With a rise of temperature, all gases and vapours become permanent gases. As we shall afterwards learn, carbonic anhydride becomes

a permanent gas at temperatures above 31°, and at lower temperatures it has a maximum tension, and may be liquefied by pressure alone.

The liquefaction of gases, accomplished by Faraday (*see* Ammonia, Chapter VI.) and others, in the first half of this century, showed that a number of substances are capable, like water, of taking all three physical states, and that there is no essential difference between vapours and gases, the only distinction being that the boiling points (or the temperature at which the tension = 760 mm.) of liquids lie above the ordinary temperature, and those of liquefied gases below, and consequently a gas is a superheated vapour, or vapour heated above the boiling point, or removed from saturation, rarefied, having a lower tension than that maximum which is proper to a given temperature and substance. We will here cite the *maximum tensions* of certain liquids and gases *at various temperatures*, because they may be taken advantage of for obtaining constant temperatures by changing the pressure at which boiling or the formation of saturated vapours takes place. (I may remark that the dependence between the tension of the saturated vapours of various substances and the temperature is very complex, and usually requires three or four independent constants, which vary with the nature of the substance, and are found from the dependence of the tension p on the temperature t given by experiment; but in 1892 K. D. Kraevitch showed that this dependence is determined by the properties of a substance, such as its density, specific heat, and latent heat of evaporation.) The temperatures (according to the air thermometer) are placed on the left, and the tension in millimetres of mercury (at 0°) on the right-hand side of the equations. Carbon bisulphide, CS_2, 0° = 127·9; 10° = 198·5; 20° = 298·1; 30° = 431·6; 40° = 617·5; 50° = 857·1. Chlorobenzene, C_6H_5Cl, 70° = 97·9; 80° = 141·8; 90° = 208·4; 100° = 292·8; 110° = 402·6; 120° = 542·8; 130° = 719·0. Aniline, C_6H_7N, 150° = 283·7; 160° = 387·0; 170° = 515·6; 180° = 677·2; 185° = 771·5. Methyl salicylate, $C_8H_8O_3$, 180° = 294·4; 190° = 330·9; 200° = 432·4; 210° = 557·5; 220° = 710·2; 224° = 779·9. Mercury, Hg, 300° = 246·8; 310° = 304·9; 320° = 373·7; 330° = 454·4; 340° = 548·6; 350° = 658·0; 359° = 770·9. Sulphur, S, 395° = 300; 423° = 500; 443° = 700; 452° = 800; 459° = 900. These figures (Ramsay and Young) show the possibility of obtaining constant temperatures in the vapours of boiling liquids by altering the pressure. We may add the following boiling points under a pressure of 760 mm. (according to the air thermometer by Collendar and Griffiths, 1891): aniline, 184° = 13; naphthalene, 217° = 94; benzophenone, 305° = 82; mercury, 356° = 76; triphenyl-methane, 356° = 44; sulphur, 444° = 53. And melting points: tin, 231° = 68; bismuth, 269° = 22; lead, 327° = 69; and zinc, 417° = 57. These data may be used for obtaining a constant temperature and for verifying thermometers. The same object may be attained by the melting points of certain salts, determined according to the air thermometer by V. Meyer and Riddle (1893): NaCl, 851°; NaBr, 727°; NaI, 650°; KCl, 760°; KBr, 715°; KI, 623°; K_2CO_3, 1045°; Na_2CO_3, 1098°; $Na_2B_4O_7$, 873°; Na_2SO_4, 843°; K_2SO_4, 1073°. The tension of liquefied gases is expressed in atmospheres. Sulphurous anhydride, SO_2, -30° = 0·4; -20° = 0·6; -10° = 1; 0° = 1·5; +10° = 2·3; 20° = 3·2; 30° = 5·3. Ammonia, NH_3, -40° = 0·7; -30° = 1·1; -20° = 1·8; -10° = 2·8; 0° = 4·2; +10° = 6·0; 20° = 8·4. Carbonic anhydride, CO_2, -115° = 0·033; -80° = 1; -70° = 2·1; -60° = 3·9; -50° = 6·8; -40° = 10; -20° = 23; 0° = 35; +10° = 46; 20° = 58. Nitrous oxide, N_2O, -125° = 0·033; -92° = 1; -80° = 1·9; -50° = 7·6; -20° = 23·1; 0° = 36·1; +20° = 55·3. Ethylene, C_2H_4, -140° = 0·033; -130° = 0·1; -103° = 1; -40° = 13; -1° = 42. Air, -191° = 1; -158° = 14; -140° = 39. Nitrogen, N_2, -203° = 0·085; -193° = 1; -160° = 14; -146° = 32. The methods of liquefying gases (by pressure and cold) will be described under ammonia, nitrous oxide, sulphurous anhydride, and in later footnotes. We will now turn our attention to the fact that the evaporation of volatile liquids, under various, and especially under low, pressures, gives an easy means for obtaining *low temperatures*. Thus liquefied carbonic anhydride, under the ordinary pressure, reduces the temperature to -80°, and when it evaporates in a rarefied atmosphere (under an air-pump) to 25 mm. (= 0·033 atmosphere) the temperature, judging by the above-cited figures, falls to -115° (Dewar). Even the evaporation of liquids of common occurrence, under low pressures easily attainable with an air-pump, may produce low temperatures, which may be again taken advantage of for obtaining still lower temperatures. Water boiling in a vacuum becomes cold, and under a pressure of less than 4·5 mm. it freezes, because its tension at 0° is 4·5 mm. A sufficiently low temperature may be obtained by forcing fine streams of air through common ether, or liquid carbon bisulphide, CS_2, or methyl chloride, CH_3Cl, and other similar volatile liquids. In the adjoining table are given, for certain gases, (1) the number of atmospheres necessary for their liquefaction at 15°, and (2) the boiling points of the resultant liquids under a pressure of 760 mm.

	C_2H_4	N_2O	CO_2	H_2S	AsH_3	NH_3	HCl	CH_3Cl	C_2N_2	SO_2
(1)	42	31	52	10	8	7	25	4	4	3
(2)	-103°	-92°	-80°	-74°	-58°	-38°	-35°	-24°	-21°	-10°

[28] Natterer's determinations (1851–1854), together with Amagat's results (1880–1888), show that the compressibility of hydrogen, under high pressures, may be expressed by the following figures:—

p = 1   100   1000   2500

v = 1 0·0107 0·0019 0·0013

pv = 1   1·07   1·9   3·25

s = 0·11   10·3   58   85

where p = the pressure in metres of mercury, v = the volume, if the volume taken under a pressure of 1 metre = 1, and s the weight of a litre of hydrogen at 20° in grams. If hydrogen followed Mariotte's law, then under a pressure of 2,500 metres, one litre would contain not 85, but 265 grams. It is evident from the above figures that the weight of a litre of the gas approaches a limit as the pressure increases, which is doubtless the density of the gas when liquefied, and therefore the weight of a litre of liquid hydrogen will probably be near 100 grams (density about 0·1, being less than that of all other liquids).

[29] Cagniard de Latour, on heating ether in a closed tube to about 190°, observed that at this temperature the liquid is transformed into vapour occupying the original volume—that is, having the same density as the liquid. The further investigations made by Drion and myself showed that every liquid has such an *absolute boiling point*, above which it cannot exist as a liquid and is transformed into a dense gas. In order to grasp the true signification of this absolute boiling temperature, it must be remembered that the liquid state is characterised by a cohesion of its particles which does not exist in vapours and gases. The cohesion of liquids is expressed in their capillary phenomena (the breaks in a column of liquid, drop formation, and rise in capillary tubes, &c.), and the product of the density of a liquid into the height to which it rises in a capillary tube (of a definite diameter) may serve as the measure of the magnitude of cohesion. Thus, in a tube of 1 mm. diameter, water at 15° rises (the height being corrected for the meniscus) 14·8 mm., and ether at $t°$ to a height $5·35 - 0·028t°$ mm. The cohesion of a liquid is lessened by heating, and therefore the capillary heights are also diminished. It has been shown by experiment that this decrement is proportional to the temperature, and hence by the aid of capillary observations we are able to form an idea that at a certain rise of temperature the cohesion may become = 0. For ether, according to the above formula, this would occur at 191°. If the cohesion disappear from a liquid it becomes a gas, for cohesion is the only point of difference between these two states. A liquid in evaporating and overcoming the force of cohesion absorbs heat. Therefore, the absolute boiling point was defined by me (1861) as that temperature at which (*a*) a liquid cannot exist as a liquid, but forms a gas which cannot pass into a liquid state under any pressure whatever; (*b*) cohesion = 0; and (*c*) the latent heat of evaporation = 0.

This definition was but little known until Andrews (1869) explained the matter from another aspect. Starting from gases, he discovered that carbonic anhydride cannot be liquefied by any degree of compression at temperatures above 31°, whilst at lower temperatures it can be liquefied. He called this temperature the *critical temperature*. It is evident that it is the same as the absolute boiling point. We shall afterwards designate it by *tc*. At low temperatures a gas which is subjected to a pressure greater than its maximum tension (Note <u>27</u>) is transformed into a liquid, which, in evaporating, gives a saturated vapour possessing this maximum tension; whilst at temperatures above tc the pressure to which the gas is subjected may increase indefinitely. However, under these conditions the volume of the gas does not change indefinitely but approaches a definite limit (*see* Note <u>28</u>)—that is, it resembles in this respect a liquid or a solid which is altered but little in volume by pressure. The volume which a liquid or gas occupies at *tc* is termed the *critical volume*, and corresponds with the *critical pressure*, which we will designate by *pc* and express in atmospheres. It is evident from what has been said that the discrepancies from Mariotte and Boyle's law, the absolute boiling point, the density in liquid and compressed gaseous states, and the properties of liquids, must all he intimately connected together. We will consider these relations in one of the following notes. At present we will supplement the above observations by the values of *tc* and *pc* for certain liquids and gases which have been investigated in this respect—

	tc	pc		tc	pc
N_2	- 146°	33	H_2S	+ 108°	92
CO	- 140°	39	CH_2N_2	+ 124°	62
O_2	- 119°	50	NH_3	+ 131°	114
CH_4	- 100°	50	CH_3Cl	+ 141°	73
NO	- 93°	71	SO_2	+ 155°	79
C_2H_4	+ 10°	51	C_5H_{10}	+ 192°	34
CO_2	+ 32°	77	$C_4H_{10}O$	+ 193°	40
N_2O	+ 53°	75	$CHCl_3$	+ 268°	55
C_2H_2	+ 37°	68	CS_2	+ 278°	78
HCl	+ 52°	86	C_6H_6	+ 292°	60

H₂O	+ 365°	200	C₆H₅F	+ 287°	45
CH₃OH	+ 240°	79	C₆H₅Cl	+ 360°	45
C₂H₅OH	+ 243°	63	C₆H₅Br	+ 397°	45
CH₃COOH	+ 322°	57	C₆H₅I	+ 448°	45

Young and Guy (1891) showed that *tc* and *pc* clearly depend upon the composition and molecular weight.

[30] I came to this conclusion in 1870 (*Ann. Phys. Chem.* 141, 623).

[31]

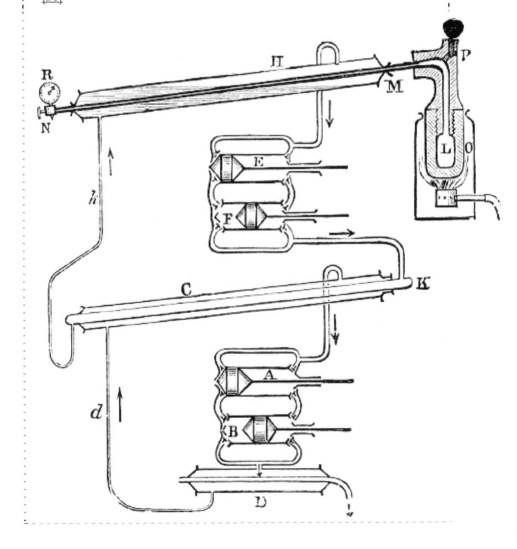

FIG. 24.—General arrangement of the apparatus employed by Pictet for liquefying gases.

Pictet, in his researches, effected the direct liquefaction of many gases which up to that time had not been liquefied. He employed the apparatus used for the manufacture of ice on a large scale, employing the vaporisation of liquid sulphurous anhydride, which may be liquefied by pressure alone. This anhydride is a gas which is transformed into a liquid at the ordinary temperature under a pressure of several atmospheres (*see* Note 27), and boils at -10° at the ordinary atmospheric pressure. This liquid, like all others, boils at a lower temperature under a diminished pressure, and by continually pumping out the gas which comes off by means of a powerful air-pump its boiling point falls as low as -75°. Consequently, if on the one hand we force liquid sulphurous anhydride into a vessel, and on the other hand pump out the gas from the same vessel by powerful air-pumps, then the liquefied gas will boil in the vessel, and cause the temperature in it to fall to -75°. If a second vessel is placed inside this vessel, then another gas may be easily liquefied in it at the low temperature produced by the boiling liquid sulphurous anhydride. Pictet in this manner easily liquefied carbonic anhydride, CO_2 (at -60° under a pressure of from four to six atmospheres). This gas is more refractory to liquefaction than sulphurous anhydride, but for this reason it gives on evaporating a still lower temperature than can be attained by the evaporation of sulphurous anhydride. A temperature of -80° may be obtained by the evaporation of liquid carbonic anhydride at a pressure of 760 mm., and in an atmosphere rarefied by a powerful pump the temperature falls to -140°. By employing such low temperatures, it was possible, with the aid of pressure, to liquefy the majority of the other gases. It is evident that special pumps which are capable of rarefying gases are necessary to reduce the pressure in the chambers in which the sulphurous and carbonic anhydride boil; and that, in order to re-condense the resultant gases into liquids, special force pumps are required for pumping the liquid anhydrides into the refrigerating chamber. Thus, in Pictet's apparatus (fig. 24), the carbonic anhydride was liquefied by the aid of the pumps E F, which compressed the gas (at a pressure of 4–6 atmospheres) and forced it into the tube K, vigorously cooled by being surrounded by boiling liquid sulphurous anhydride, which was condensed in the tube C by the pump B, and rarefied by the pump A. The liquefied carbonic anhydride flowed down the tube K into the tube H, in which it was subjected to a low pressure by the pump E, and thus gave a very low temperature of about -140°. The pump E carried off the vapour of the carbonic anhydride, and conducted it to the pump F, by which it was again liquefied. The carbonic anhydride thus made an entire circuit—that is, it passed from a rarefied vapour of small tension and low temperature into a compressed and cooled gas, which was transformed into a liquid, which again vaporised and produced a low temperature.

Inside the wide inclined tube H, where the carbonic acid evaporated, was placed a second and narrow tube M containing hydrogen, which was generated in the vessel L from a mixture of sodium formate and caustic soda ($CHO_2Na + NaHO = Na_2CO_3 + H_2$). This mixture gives hydrogen on heating the vessel L. This vessel and the tube M were made of thick copper, and could withstand great pressures. They were, moreover, hermetically connected together and closed up. Thus the hydrogen which was evolved had no outlet, accumulated in a limited space, and its pressure increased in proportion to the amount of it evolved. This pressure was recorded on a metallic manometer R attached to the end of the tube M. As the hydrogen in this tube was submitted to a very low temperature and a powerful pressure, all the necessary conditions were present for its liquefaction. When the pressure in the tube H became steady—*i.e.* when the temperature had fallen to -140° and the manometer R indicated a pressure of 650 atmospheres in the tube M—then this pressure did not rise with a further evolution of hydrogen in the vessel L. This served as an indication that the tension of the vapour of the hydrogen had attained a maximum corresponding with -140°, and that consequently all the excess of the gas was condensed to a liquid. Pictet convinced himself of this by opening the cock N, when the liquid hydrogen rushed out from the orifice. But, on leaving a space where the pressure was equal to 650 atmospheres, and coming into contact with air under the ordinary pressure, the liquid or powerfully compressed hydrogen expanded, began to boil, absorbed still more heat, and became still colder. In doing so a portion of the liquid hydrogen, according to Pictet, passed into a solid state, and did not fall in drops into a vessel placed under the outlet N, but as pieces of solid matter, which struck against the sides of the vessel like shot and immediately vaporised. Thus, although it was impossible to see and keep the liquefied hydrogen, still it was clear that it passed not only into a liquid, but also into a solid state. Pictet in his experiments obtained other gases which had not previously been liquefied, especially oxygen and nitrogen, in a liquid and solid state. Pictet supposed that liquid and solid hydrogen has the properties of a metal, like iron.

[32]

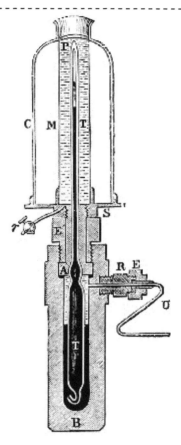

FIG. 25.—Cailletet's apparatus for liquefying gases.

At the same time (1879) as Pictet was working on the liquefaction of gases in Switzerland, Cailletet, in Paris, was occupied on the same subject, and his results, although not so convincing as Pictet's, still showed that the majority of gases, previously unliquefied, were capable of passing into a liquid state. Cailletet subjected gases to a pressure of several hundred atmospheres in narrow thick-walled glass tubes (fig. 25); he then cooled the compressed gas as far as possible by surrounding it with a freezing mixture; a cock was then rapidly opened for the outlet of mercury from the tube containing the gas, which consequently rapidly and vigorously expanded. This rapid expansion of the gas would produce great cold, just as the rapid compression of a gas evolves heat and causes a rise in temperature. This cold was produced at the expense of the gas itself, for in rapidly expanding its particles were not able to absorb heat from the walls of the tube, and in cooling a portion of the expanding gas was transformed into liquid. This was seen from the formation of cloud-like drops like a fog which rendered the gas opaque. Thus Cailletet proved the possibility of the liquefaction of gases, but he did not isolate the liquids. The method of Cailletet allows the passage of gases into liquids being observed with greater facility and simplicity than Pictet's method, which requires a very complicated and expensive apparatus.

The methods of Pictet and Cailletet were afterwards improved by Olszewski, Wroblewski, Dewar, and others. In order to obtain a still lower temperature they employed, instead of carbonic acid gas, liquid ethylene or nitrogen and oxygen, whose evaporation at low pressures produces a much lower temperature (to -200°). They also improved on the methods of determining such low temperatures, but the methods were not essentially altered; they obtained nitrogen and oxygen in a liquid, and nitrogen even in a solid, state, but no one has yet succeeded in seeing hydrogen in a liquid form.

The most illustrative and instructive results (because they gave the possibility of maintaining a very low temperature and the liquefied gas, even air, for a length of time) were obtained in recent years by Prof. Dewar in the Royal Institution of London, which is glorified by the names of Davy, Faraday, and Tyndall. Dewar, with the aid of powerful pumps, obtained many kilograms of oxygen and air (the boiling point under the atmospheric pressure = -190°) in a liquid state and kept them in this state for a length of time by means of open glass vessels with double walls, having a vacuum between them, which prevented the rapid transference of heat, and so gave the possibility of maintaining very low temperatures inside the vessel for a long period of time. The liquefied oxygen or air can be poured from one vessel into another and used for any investigations. Thus in June 1894, Prof. Dewar showed that at the low temperature produced by liquid oxygen many substances become phosphorescent (become self-luminous; for instance, oxygen on passing into a vacuum) and fluoresce (emit light after being illuminated; for instance, paraffin, glue, &c.) much more powerfully than at the ordinary temperature; also that solids then greatly alter in their mechanical properties, &c. I had the opportunity (1894) at Prof. Dewar's of seeing many such experiments in which open vessels containing pounds of liquid oxygen were employed, and in following the progress made in researches conducted at low temperatures, it is my firm impression that the study of many phenomena at low temperatures should widen the horizon of natural science as much as the investigation of phenomena made at the highest temperatures attained in the voltaic arc.

[33] The investigations of S. Wroblewski in Cracow give reason to believe that Pictet could not have obtained liquid hydrogen in the interior of his apparatus, and that if he did obtain it, it could only have been at the

moment of its outrush due to the fall in temperature following its sudden expansion. Pictet calculated that he obtained a temperature of -140°, but in reality it hardly fell below -120°, judging from the latest data for the vaporisation of carbonic anhydride under low pressure. The difference lies in the method of determining low temperatures. Judging from other properties of hydrogen (*see* Note 34), one would think that its absolute boiling point lies far below -120°, and even -140° (according to the calculation of Sarrau, on the basis of its compressibility, at -174°). But even at -200° (if the methods of determining such low temperatures be correct) hydrogen does not give a liquid even under a pressure of several hundred atmospheres. However, on expansion a fog is formed and a liquid state attained, but the liquid does not separate.

[34] After the idea of the absolute temperature of ebullition (*tc*, Note 29) had been worked out (about 1870), and its connection with the deviations from Mariotte's law had become evident, and especially after the liquefaction of permanent gases, general attention was turned to the development of the fundamental conceptions of the gaseous and liquid states of matter. Some investigators directed their energies to the further study of vapours (for instance, Ramsay and Young), gases (Amagat), and liquids (Zaencheffsky, Nadeschdin, and others), especially to liquids near *tc* and *pc*; others (Konovaloff and De Heen) endeavoured to discover the relation between liquids under ordinary conditions (removed from *tc* and *pc*) and gases, whilst a third class of investigators (van der Waals, Clausius, and others), starting from the generally-accepted principles of the mechanical theory of heat and the kinetic theory of gases, and assuming in gases the existence of those forces which certainly act in liquids, deduced the connection between the properties of one and the other. It would be out of place in an elementary handbook like the present to enunciate the whole mass of conclusions arrived at by this method, but it is well to give an idea of the results of van der Waals' considerations, for they explain the gradual uninterrupted passage from a liquid into a gaseous state in the simplest manner, and, although the deduction cannot be considered as complete and decisive (*see* Note 25), nevertheless it penetrates so deeply into the essence of the matter that its signification is not only reflected in a great number of physical investigations, but also in the province of chemistry, where instances of the passage of substances from a gaseous to a liquid state are so common, and where the very processes of dissociation, decomposition, and combination must be identified with a change of physical state of the participating substances, which has been elaborated by Gibbs, Lavenig, and others.

For a *given quantity* (weight, mass) *of a definite substance*, its state is expressed by three variables—volume *v*, pressure (elasticity, tension) *p*, and temperature *t*. Although the compressibility—[*i.e.*, $d(v)/d(p)$]—of liquids is small, still it is clearly expressed, and varies not only with the nature of liquids but also with their pressure and temperature (at *tc* the compressibility of liquids is very considerable). Although gases, according to Mariotte's law, with small variations of pressure, are uniformly compressed, nevertheless the dependence of their volume *v* on *t* and *p* is very complex. This also applies to the coefficient of expansion [= $d(v)/d(t)$, or $d(p)/d(t)$], which also varies with *t* and *p*, both for gases (*see* Note 26), and for liquids (at *tc* it is very considerable, and often exceeds that of gases, 0·00367). Hence, the *equation of condition* must include three variables, *v*, *p*, and *t*. For a so-called perfect (ideal) gas, or for inconsiderable variations of density, the elementary expression $pv = Ra(1 + at)$, or $pv = R(273 + t)$ should be accepted, where *R* is a constant varying with the mass and nature of a gas, as expressing this dependence, because it includes in itself the laws of Gay-Lussac and Mariotte, for at a constant pressure the volume varies proportionally to $1 + at$, and when *t* is constant the product of *tv* is constant. In its simplest form the equation may be expressed thus:

$$pv = RT;$$

where *T* denotes what is termed the absolute temperature, or the ordinary temperature + 273—that is, $T = t + 273$.

Starting from the supposition of the existence of an attraction or internal pressure (expressed by *a*) proportional to the square of the density (or inversely proportional to the square of the volume), and of the existence of a real volume or diminished length of path (expressed by *b*) for each gaseous molecule, van der Waals gives for gases the following more complex equation of condition:—

$$(p + a\ \boxed{v^2})(v - b) = 1 + 0·00367t;$$

if at 0° under a pressure $p = 1$ (for example, under the atmospheric pressure), the volume (for instance, a litre) of a gas or vapour he taken as 1, and therefore *v* and *b* be expressed by the same units as *p* and *a*. The deviations from both the laws of Mariotte and Gay-Lussac are expressed by the above equation. Thus, for hydrogen *a* must be taken as infinitely small, and $b = 0·0009$, judging by the data for 1,000 and 2,500 metres pressure (Note 28). For other permanent gases, for which (Note 28) I showed (about 1870) from Regnault's and Natterer's data, a decrement of *pv*, followed by an increment, which was confirmed (about 1880) by fresh determinations made by Amagat, this phenomena may be expressed in definite magnitudes of *a* and *b* (although van der Waals' formula is not applicable in the case of very small pressures) with sufficient accuracy for contemporary requirements. It is evident that van der Waals' formula can also express the difference of the coefficients of expansion of gases with a change of pressure, and according to the methods of determination (Note 26). Besides this, van der Waals' formula shows that at temperatures above 273(8a $\boxed{27b}$ -1) only one actual volume (gaseous) is possible, whilst at lower temperatures, by varying the pressure, three different volumes—liquid, gaseous, and partly liquid, partly saturated-vaporous—are possible. It is evident that the above temperature is the absolute boiling point—that is (tc) = 273(8a $\boxed{27b}$ - 1). It is found under the condition that all three possible volumes (the three roots of van der Waals' cubic equation) are then similar and equal (vc = 3b). The pressure in this case (pc) = a $\boxed{27b^2}$. These ratios between the constants a and b and the conditions of *critical state*—*i.e.* (tc) and (pc)—give the possibility of determining the one magnitude from the other. Thus for ether (Note 29), (tc) = 193°, (tp) = 40, hence a = 0·0307, b = 0·00533, and (vc) = 0·016. That mass of ether which at a pressure of one atmosphere at 0° occupies one volume—for instance, a litre—occupies, according to the above-mentioned condition, this critical volume. And as the density of the vapour of ether compared with hydrogen = 37, and a litre of hydrogen at 0° and under the atmospheric pressure weighs 0·0896 gram, then a litre of ether vapour weighs 3·32 grams; therefore, in a critical state (at 193° and 40 atmospheres) 3·32 grams occupy 0·016 litre, or 16 c.c.; therefore 1 gram occupies a volume of about 5 c.c., and the weight of 1 c.c. of ether will then be 0·21. According to the investigations of Ramsay and Young (1887), the critical volume of ether was approximately such at about the absolute boiling point, but the compressibility of the liquid is so great that the slightest change of pressure or temperature has a considerable effect on the volume. But the investigations of the above savants gave another indirect demonstration of the truth of van der Waals' equation. They also found for ether that the isochords, or the lines of equal volumes (if both t and p vary), are generally straight lines. Thus the volume of 10 c.c. for 1 gram of ether corresponds with pressures (expressed in metres of mercury) equal to $0·135t - 3·3$ (for example, at 180° the pressure = 21 metres, and at 280° it = 34·5 metres). The rectilinear form of the isochord (when $v = a$ constant quantity) is a direct result of van der Waals' formula.

When, in 1883, I demonstrated that the specific gravity of liquids decreases in proportion to the rise of temperature [$S_t = S_0 - Kt$ or $S_t = S_0(1 - Kt)$], or that the volumes increase in inverse proportion to the binomial $1 - Kt$, that is, $V_t = V_0(1-Kt)^{-1}$, where K is the modulus of expansion, which varies with the nature of the liquid, then, in general, not only does a connection arise between gases and liquids with respect to a change of volume, but also it would appear possible, by applying van der Waals' formula, to judge, from the phenomena of the expansion of liquids, as to their transition into vapour, and to connect together all the principal properties of liquids, which up to this time had not been considered to be in direct dependence. Thus Thorpe and Rücker found that $2(tc) + 273 = 1/K$, where K is the modulus of expansion in the above-mentioned formula. For example, the expansion of ether is expressed with sufficient accuracy from 0° to 100° by the equation $S_t = 0·736/(1 - 0·00154t)$, or $V_t = 1/(1 - 0·00154t)$, where 0·00154 is the modulus of expansion, and therefore $(tc) = 188°$, or by direct observation 193°. For silicon tetrachloride, $SiCl_4$, the modulus equals 0·00136, from whence $(tc) = 231°$, and by experiment 230°. On the other hand, D. P. Konovaloff, admitting that the external pressure p in liquids is insignificant when compared with the internal (a in van der Waals' formula), and that the work in the expansion of liquids is proportional to their temperature (as in gases), directly deduced, from van der Waals' formula, the above-mentioned formula for the expansion of liquids, $V_t = 1/(1 - Kt)$, and also the magnitude of the latent heat of evaporation, cohesion, and compressibility under pressure. In this way van der Waals' formula embraces the gaseous, critical, and *liquid states* of substances, and shows the connection between them. On this account, although van der Waals' formula cannot be considered as perfectly general and accurate, yet it is not only very much more exact than $pv = RT$, but it is also more comprehensive, because it applies both to gases and liquids. Further research will naturally give a closer proximity to truth, and will show the connection between composition and the constants (a and b); but a great scientific progress is seen in this form of the equation of state.

Clausius (in 1880), taking into consideration the variability of a, in van der Waals' formula, with the temperature, gave the following equation of condition:—

$$(p + a \boxed{T(v + c)^2})(v - b) = RT.$$

Sarrau applied this formula to Amagat's data for hydrogen, and found $a = 0·0551$, $c = -0·00043$, $b = 0·00089$, and therefore calculated its absolute boiling point as -174°, and $(pc) = 99$ atmospheres. But as similar calculations for oxygen (-105°), nitrogen (-124°), and marsh gas (-76°) gave tc higher than it really is, the absolute boiling point of hydrogen must lie below -174°.

[35] This and a number of similar cases clearly show how great are the internal chemical forces compared with physical and mechanical forces.

[36] The property of palladium of absorbing hydrogen, and of increasing in volume in so doing, may be easily demonstrated by taking a sheet of palladium varnished on one side, and using it as a cathode. The hydrogen which is evolved by the action of the current is retained by the unvarnished surface, as a consequence of which the sheet curls up. By attaching a

pointer (for instance, a quill) to the end of the sheet this bending effect is rendered strikingly evident, and on reversing the current (when oxygen will be evolved and combine with the absorbed hydrogen, forming water) it may be shown that on losing the hydrogen the palladium regains its original form.

[37] Deville discovered that iron and platinum become pervious to hydrogen at a red heat. He speaks of this in the following terms:—'The permeability of such homogeneous substances as platinum and iron is quite different from the passage of gases through such non-compact substances as clay and graphite. The permeability of metals depends on their expansion, brought about by heat, and proves that metals and alloys have a certain porosity.' However, Graham proved that it is only hydrogen which is capable of passing through the above-named metals in this manner. Oxygen, nitrogen, ammonia, and many other gases, only pass through in extremely minute quantities. Graham showed that at a red heat about 500 c.c. of hydrogen pass per minute through a surface of one square metre of platinum $1 \cdot 1$ mm. thick, but that with other gases the amount transmitted is hardly perceptible. Indiarubber has the same capacity for allowing the transference of hydrogen through its substance (*see* Chapter III.), but at the ordinary temperature one square metre, $0 \cdot 014$ mm. thick, transmits only 127 c.c. of hydrogen per minute. In the experiment on the decomposition of water by heat in porous tubes, the clay tube may be exchanged for a platinum one with advantage. Graham showed that by placing a platinum tube containing hydrogen under these conditions, and surrounding it by a tube containing air, the transference of the hydrogen may be observed by the decrease of pressure in the platinum tube. In one hour almost all the hydrogen (97 p.c.) had passed from the tube, without being replaced by air. It is evident that the occlusion and passage of hydrogen through metals capable of occluding it are not only intimately connected together, but are dependent on the capacity of metals to form compounds of various degrees of stability with hydrogen—like salts with water.

[38] It appeared on further investigation that palladium gives a definite compound, Pd_2H (*see* further) with hydrogen; but what was most instructive was the investigation of sodium hydride, Na_2H, which clearly showed that the origin and properties of such compounds are in entire accordance with the conceptions of dissociation.

Since hydrogen is a gas which is difficult to condense, it is little soluble in water and other liquids. At $0°$ a hundred volumes of water dissolve $1 \cdot 9$ volume of hydrogen, and alcohol $6 \cdot 9$ volumes measured at $0°$ and 760 mm. Molten iron absorbs hydrogen, but in solidifying, it expels it. The solution of hydrogen by metals is to a certain degree based on its affinity for metals, and must be likened to the solution of metals in mercury and to the formation of alloys. In its chemical properties hydrogen, as we shall see later, has much of a metallic character. Pictet (*see* Note 31) even affirms that liquid hydrogen has metallic properties. The metallic properties of hydrogen are also evinced in the fact that it is a good conductor of heat, which is not the case with other gases (Magnus).

[39] If it be desired to obtain a perfectly colourless hydrogen flame, it must issue from a platinum nozzle, as the glass end of a gas-conducting tube imparts a yellow tint to the flame, owing to the presence of sodium in the glass.

[40] Let us imagine that a stream of hydrogen passes along a tube, and let us mentally divide this stream into several parts, consecutively passing out from the orifice of the tube. The first part is lighted—that is, brought to a state of incandescence, in which state it combines with the oxygen of the atmosphere. A considerable amount of heat is evolved in the combination. The heat evolved then, so to say, ignites the second part of hydrogen coming from the tube, and, therefore, when once ignited, the hydrogen continues to burn, if there be a continual supply of it, and if the atmosphere in which it burns be unlimited and contains oxygen.

[41] The combustibility of hydrogen may be shown by the direct decomposition of water by sodium. If a pellet of sodium be thrown into a vessel containing water, it floats on the water and evolves hydrogen, which may be lighted. The presence of sodium imparts a yellow tint to the flame. If potassium be taken, the hydrogen bursts into flame spontaneously, because sufficient heat is evolved in the reaction to ignite the hydrogen. The flame is coloured violet by the potassium. If sodium be thrown not on to water, but on to an acid, it will evolve more heat, and the hydrogen will then also burst into flame. These experiments must be carried on with caution, as, sometimes towards the end, a mass of sodium oxide (Note 8) is produced, and flies about; it is therefore best to cover the vessel in which the experiment is carried on.

[42] This property of spongy platinum is made use of in the so-called hydrogen cigar-lighter. It consists of a glass cylinder or beaker, inside which there is a small lead stand (which is not acted on by sulphuric acid), on which a piece of zinc is laid. This zinc is covered by a bell, which is open at the bottom and furnished with a cock at the top. Sulphuric acid is poured into the space between the bell and the sides of the outer glass cylinder, and will thus compress the gas in the bell. If the cock of the cylinder be opened the gas will escape by it, and will be replaced by the acid, which, coming into contact with the zinc, evolves hydrogen, and it will escape through the cock. If the cock be closed, then the hydrogen evolved will increase the pressure of the gas in the bell, and thus again force the acid

into the space between the bell and the walls of the outer cylinder. Thus the action of the acid on the zinc may be stopped or started at will by opening or shutting the cock, and consequently a stream of hydrogen may be always turned on. Now, if a piece of spongy platinum be placed in this stream, the hydrogen will take light, because the spongy platinum becomes hot in condensing the hydrogen and inflames it. The considerable rise in temperature of the platinum depends, among other things, on the fact that the hydrogen condensed in its pores comes into contact with previously absorbed and condensed atmospheric oxygen, with which hydrogen combines with great facility in this form. In this manner the hydrogen cigar-lighter gives a stream of burning hydrogen when the cock is open. In order that it should work regularly it is necessary that the spongy platinum should be quite clean, and it is best enveloped in a thin sheet of platinum foil, which protects it from dust. In any case, after some time it will be necessary to clean the platinum, which may be easily done by boiling it in nitric acid, which does not dissolve the platinum, but clears it of all dirt. This imperfection has given rise to several other forms, in which an electric spark is made to pass before the orifice from which the hydrogen escapes. This is arranged in such a manner that the zinc of a galvanic element is immersed when the cock is turned, or a small coil giving a spark is put into circuit on turning the hydrogen on.

[43] Under conditions similar to those in which hydrogen combines with oxygen it is also capable of combining with chlorine. A mixture of hydrogen and chlorine explodes on the passage of an electric spark through it, or on contact with an incandescent substance, and also in the presence of spongy platinum; but, besides this, the action of light alone is enough to bring about the combination of hydrogen and chlorine. If a mixture of equal volumes of hydrogen and chlorine be exposed to the action of sunlight, complete combination rapidly ensues, accompanied by a report. Hydrogen does not combine directly with carbon, either at the ordinary temperature or by the action of heat and pressure. But if an electric current be passed through carbon electrodes at a short distance from each other (as in the electric light or voltaic arc), so as to form an electric arc in which the particles of carbon are carried from one pole to the other, then, in the intense heat to which the carbon is subjected in this case, it is capable of combining with hydrogen. A gas of peculiar smell called acetylene, C_2H_2, is thus formed from carbon and hydrogen.

[44] There is another explanation of the facility with which hydrogen reacts in a nascent state. We shall afterwards learn that the molecule of hydrogen contains two atoms, H_2, but there are elements the molecules of which only contain one atom—for instance, mercury. Therefore, every reaction of gaseous hydrogen must be accompanied by the disruption of

that bond which exists between the atoms forming a molecule. At the moment of evolution, however, it is supposed that free atoms exist, and in this condition, according to the hypothesis, act energetically. This hypothesis is not based upon facts, and the idea that hydrogen is condensed at the moment of its evolution is more natural, and is in accordance with the fact (Note 12) that compressed hydrogen displaces palladium and silver (Brunner, Beketoff)—that is, acts as at the moment of its liberation.

[44 bis] There is a very intimate and evident relation between the phenomena which take place in the action of spongy platinum and the phenomena of the action in a nascent state. The combination of hydrogen with aldehyde may be taken as an example. Aldehyde is a volatile liquid with an aromatic smell, boiling at 21°, soluble in water, and absorbing oxygen from the atmosphere, and in this absorption forming acetic acid—the substance which is found in ordinary vinegar. If sodium amalgam be thrown into an aqueous solution of aldehyde, the greater part of the hydrogen evolved combines with the aldehyde, forming alcohol—a substance also soluble in water, which forms the principle of all spirituous liquors, boils at 78°, and contains the same amount of oxygen and carbon as aldehyde, but more hydrogen. The composition of aldehyde is C_2H_4O, that of alcohol C_2H_6O.

[45] When, for instance, an acid and zinc are added to a salt of silver, the silver is reduced; but this may be explained as a reaction of the zinc, and not of the hydrogen at the moment of its formation. There are, however, examples to which this explanation is entirely inapplicable; thus, for instance, hydrogen, at the moment of its liberation easily takes up oxygen from its compounds with nitrogen if they be in solution, and converts the nitrogen into its hydrogen-compound. Here the nitrogen and hydrogen, so to speak, meet at the moment of their liberation, and in this state combine together.

It is evident from this that the elastic gaseous state of hydrogen fixes the limit of its energy: prevents it from entering into those combinations of which it is capable. In the nascent state we have hydrogen which is not in a gaseous state, and its action is then much more energetic. At the moment of evolution that heat, which would be latent in the gaseous hydrogen, is transmitted to its molecules, and consequently they are in a state of strain, and can hence act on many substances.

[46] Several numerical data and reflections bearing on this matter are enumerated in Notes 7, 9, and 11. It must be observed that the action of iron or zinc on water is reversible. But the reaction $CuO + H_2 = Cu + H_2O$ is not reversible; the difference between the degrees of affinity is very

great in this case, and, therefore, so far as is at present known, no hydrogen is liberated even in the presence of a large excess of water. It is to be further remarked, that under the conditions of the dissociation of water, copper is not oxidised by water, because the oxide of copper is reduced by free hydrogen. If a definite amount of a metal and acid be taken and their reaction be carried on in a closed space, then the evolution of hydrogen will cease, when its tension equals that at which compressed hydrogen displaces the metal. The result depends upon the nature of the metal and the strength of the solution of acid. Tammann and Nernst (1892) found that the metals stand in the following order in respect to this limiting tension of hydrogen:—Na, Mg, Zn, Al, Cd, Fe, Ni.

[47] This determination may be carried on in an apparatus like that mentioned in Note 13 of Chapter I.

[48] We will proceed to describe Dumas' method and results. For this determination pure and dry copper oxide is necessary. Dumas took a sufficient quantity of copper oxide for the formation of 50 grams of water in each determination. As the oxide of copper was weighed before and after the experiment, and as the amount of oxygen contained in water was determined by the difference between these weights, it was essential that no other substance besides the oxygen forming the water should be evolved from the oxide of copper during its ignition in hydrogen. It was necessary, also, that the hydrogen should be perfectly pure, and free not only from traces of moisture, but from any other impurities which might dissolve in the water or combine with the copper and form some other compound with it. The bulb containing the oxide of copper (fig. 26), which was heated to redness, should be quite free from air, as otherwise the oxygen in the air might, in combining with the hydrogen passing through the vessel, form water in addition to that formed by the oxygen of the oxide of copper. The water formed should be entirely absorbed in order to accurately determine its quantity. The hydrogen was evolved in the three-necked bottle. The sulphuric acid, for acting on the zinc, is poured through funnels into the middle neck. The hydrogen evolved in the Woulfe's bottle passes through U tubes, in which it is purified, to the bulb, where it comes into contact with the copper oxide, forms water, and reduces the oxide to metallic copper; the water formed is condensed in the second bulb, and any passing off is absorbed in the second set of U tubes. This is the general arrangement of the apparatus. The bulb with the copper oxide is weighed before and after the experiment. The loss in weight shows the quantity of oxygen which entered into the composition of the water formed, the weight of the latter being shown by the gain in weight of the absorbing apparatus. Knowing the amount of oxygen in the water formed, we also know the quantity of hydrogen contained in it, and consequently we

determine the composition of water by weight. This is the essence of the determination. We will now turn to certain particulars. In one neck of the three-necked bottle a tube is placed dipping under mercury. This serves as a safety-valve to prevent the pressure inside the apparatus becoming too great from the rapid evolution of hydrogen. If the pressure rose to any considerable extent, the current of gases and vapours would be very rapid, and, as a consequence, the hydrogen would not be perfectly purified, or the water entirely absorbed in the tubes placed for this purpose. In the third neck of the Woulfe's bottle is a tube conducting the hydrogen to the purifying apparatus, consisting of eight U tubes, destined for the purification and testing of the hydrogen. The hydrogen, evolved by zinc and sulphuric acid, is purified by passing it first through a tube full of pieces of glass moistened with a solution of lead nitrate next through silver sulphate; the lead nitrate retains sulphuretted hydrogen, and arseniuretted hydrogen is retained by the tube with silver sulphate. Caustic potash in the next U tube retains any acid which might come over. The two following tubes are filled with lumps of dry caustic potash in order to absorb any carbonic anhydride and moisture which the hydrogen might contain. The next two tubes, to remove the last traces of moisture, are filled with phosphoric anhydride, mixed with lumps of pumice-stone. They are immersed in a freezing mixture. The small U tube contains hygroscopic substances, and is weighed before the experiment: this is in order to know whether the hydrogen passing through still retains any moisture. If it does not, then the weight of this tube will not vary during the whole experiment, but if the hydrogen evolved still retains moisture, the tube will increase in weight. The copper oxide is placed in the bulb, which, previous to the experiment, is dried with the copper oxide for a long period of time. The air is then exhausted from it, in order to weigh the oxide of copper in a vacuum and to avoid the need of a correction for weighing in air. The bulb is made of infusible glass, that it may be able to withstand a lengthy (20 hours) exposure to a red heat without changing in form. The weighed bulb is only connected with the purifying apparatus after the hydrogen has passed through for a long time, and after experiment has shown that the hydrogen passing from the purifying apparatus is pure and does not contain any air. On passing from the condensing bulb the gas and vapour enter into an apparatus for absorbing the last traces of moisture. The first U tube contains pieces of ignited potash, the second and third tubes phosphoric anhydride or pumice-stone moistened with sulphuric acid. The last of the two is employed for determining whether all the moisture is absorbed, and is therefore weighed separately. The final tube only serves as a safety-tube for the whole apparatus, in order that the external moisture should not penetrate into it. The glass cylinder contains sulphuric acid, through which the excess of hydrogen passes; it enables the rate at which the hydrogen is evolved to be judged, and whether its amount should be decreased or increased.

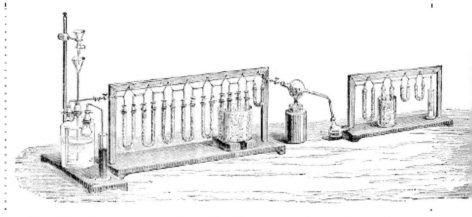

FIG. 26.—Apparatus employed by Dumas for determining the composition of water. Described in text.

When the apparatus is fitted up it must be seen that all its parts are hermetically tight before commencing the experiment. When the previously weighed parts are connected together and the whole apparatus put into communication, then the bulb containing the copper oxide is heated with a spirit lamp (reduction does not take place without the aid of heat), and the reduction of the copper oxide then takes place, and water is formed. When nearly all the copper oxide is reduced the lamp is removed and the apparatus allowed to cool, the current of hydrogen being kept up all the time. When cool, the drawn-out end of the bulb is fused up, and the hydrogen remaining in it is exhausted, in order that the copper may be again weighed in a vacuum. The absorbing apparatus remains full of hydrogen, and would therefore present a less weight than if it were full of air, as it was before the experiment, and for this reason, having disconnected the copper oxide bulb, a current of dry air is passed through it until the gas passing from the glass cylinder is quite free from hydrogen. The condensing bulb and the two tubes next to it are then weighed, in order to determine the quantity of water formed. Dumas repeated this experiment many times. The average result was that water contains 1253·3 parts of hydrogen per 10,000 parts of oxygen. Making a correction for the amount of air contained in the sulphuric acid employed for producing the hydrogen, Dumas obtained the average figure 1251·5, between the extremes 1247·2 and 1256·2. This proves that per 1 part of hydrogen water contains 7·9904 parts of oxygen, with a possible error of not more than $\frac{1}{250}$, or 0·03, in the amount of oxygen per 1 part of hydrogen.

Erdmann and Marchand, in eight determinations, found that per 10,000 parts of oxygen water contains an average of 1,252 parts of hydrogen, with a difference of from 1,258·5 to 1,248·7; hence per 1 part of hydrogen there would be 7·9952 of oxygen, with an error of at least 0·05.

Keiser (1888), in America by employing palladium hydride, and by introducing various fresh precautions for obtaining accurate results, found the composition of water to be 15·95 parts of oxygen per 2 of hydrogen.

Certain of the latest determinations of the composition of water, as also those made by Dumas, always give less than 8, and on the average 7·98, of oxygen per 1 part of hydrogen. However, not one of these figures is to be entirely depended on, and for ordinary accuracy it may be considered that $O = 16$ when $H = 1$.

[152]

CHAPTER III

OXYGEN AND THE CHIEF ASPECTS OF ITS SALINE COMBINATIONS

On the earth's surface there is no other element which is so widely distributed as oxygen in its various compounds.[1] It makes up eight-ninths of the weight of water, which occupies the greater part of the earth's surface. Nearly all earthy substances and rocks consist of compounds of oxygen with metals and other elements. Thus, the greater part of sand is formed of silica, SiO_2, which contains 53 p.c. of oxygen; clay contains water, alumina (formed of aluminium and oxygen), and silica. It may be considered that earthy substances and rocks contain up to one-third of their weight of oxygen; animal and vegetable substances are also very rich in oxygen. Without counting the water present in them, plants contain up to 40, and animals up to 20 p.c. by weight of oxygen. Thus, oxygen compounds predominate on the earth's surface. Besides this, a portion exists in a free state, and is contained in admixture with nitrogen in the atmosphere, forming about one-fourth of its mass, or one-fifth of its volume.

Being so widely distributed in nature, oxygen plays a very important part in it, for a number of the phenomena which take place before us are mainly dependent on it. *Animals breathe* air in order to obtain only *oxygen* from it, the oxygen entering into their respiratory organs (the lungs of human beings and animals, the gills of fishes, and the trachæ of insects); they, so to say, drink in air in order to absorb the oxygen. The oxygen of the air (or dissolved in water) passes through the membranes of the respiratory organs into the blood, is retained in it by the blood corpuscles, is transmitted by their means to all parts of the body, aids their transformations, bringing about chemical processes in them, and chiefly extracting carbon from them in the form of carbonic anhydride, the greater part of which passes into the blood, is dissolved by it, and is thrown off by the lungs during[153] the absorption of the oxygen. Thus, in the process of respiration carbonic anhydride (and water) is given off, and the oxygen of the air absorbed, by which means the blood is changed from a red venous to a dark-red arterial blood. The cessation of this process causes death, because then all those chemical processes, and the consequent heat and work which the oxygen introduced into the system brought about, cease. For this reason suffocation and death ensue in a vacuum, or in a gas which does not contain free oxygen, *i.e.* which does not support combustion. If an animal be placed in an atmosphere of free oxygen, at first its movements are very active and a general invigoration is remarked, but a reaction soon sets in, and death may ensue. The oxygen of the air when it enters the lungs is diluted with four volumes of nitrogen, which is not absorbed into the system, so that the blood absorbs but a small quantity of oxygen from the air, whilst in an atmosphere of pure oxygen a large quantity of oxygen would be absorbed, and would produce a very rapid change of all parts of the organism, and destroy it. From what has been said, it will be understood that oxygen may be employed in respiration, at any rate for a limited time, when the respiratory organs suffer under certain forms of suffocation and impediment to breathing.[2]

The combustion of organic substances—that is, substances which make up the composition of plants and animals—proceeds in the same manner as the combustion of many inorganic substances, such as sulphur, phosphorus, iron, &c., from the combination of these substances with oxygen, as was described in the Introduction. The decomposition, rotting, and similar transformations of substances, which proceed around us, are also very often dependent on the action of the oxygen of the air, and also reduce it from a free to a combined state. The[154] majority of the compounds of oxygen are, like water, very stable, and do not give up their oxygen under the ordinary conditions of nature. As these processes are taking place everywhere, it might be expected that the amount of free oxygen in the atmosphere should decrease, and this decrease should proceed somewhat rapidly. This is, in fact, observed where combustion or respiration proceeds in a closed space. Animals suffocate in a closed space because in consuming the oxygen the air remains unfit for respiration. In the same manner combustion, after a time, ceases in a closed space, which may be proved by a very simple experiment. An ignited substance—for instance, a piece of burning sulphur—has only to be placed in a glass flask, which is then closed with a stout cork to prevent the access of the external air; combustion will proceed for a certain time, so long as the flask contains any free oxygen, but it will cease when the oxygen of the enclosed air has combined with the sulphur. From what has been said, it is evident that regularity of combustion or respiration requires a constant renewal of air— that is, that the burning substance or respiring animal should have access to a fresh supply of oxygen. This is attained in dwellings by having many windows, outlets, and ventilators, and by the current of air produced by fires and stoves. As regards the air over the entire earth's surface its amount of oxygen hardly decreases, because in nature there is a process going on which renews the supply of free oxygen. *Plants*, or rather their leaves, during daytime,[3] under the influence of light, absorb carbonic anhydride CO_2, and *evolve free oxygen*. Thus the loss of oxygen which occurs in consequence of the respiration of animals and of combustion is made good by plants. If a leaf be placed in a bell jar containing water, and carbonic anhydride (because this gas is absorbed and oxygen evolved from it by plants) be passed into the bell, and the whole apparatus placed in sunlight, then oxygen will accumulate in the bell jar. This experiment was first made by Priestley at the end of the last century. Thus the life of plants on the earth not only serves for the formation of food for animals, but also for keeping up a constant percentage of oxygen in the atmosphere. In the long period of the life of the earth an equilibrium has been attained between the processes absorbing and evolving oxygen, by which a definite quantity of free oxygen is preserved in the entire mass of the atmosphere.[4]

[155]

Oxygen was obtained as an independent gas in 1774 by Priestley in England and in the same year by Scheele in Sweden, but its nature and great importance were only perfectly elucidated by Lavoisier.

Free oxygen may be obtained by one or other method from all the substances in which it occurs. Thus, for instance, the oxygen of many substances may be transferred into water, from which, as we have already seen, oxygen may be obtained.[5] We will first consider the methods of extracting oxygen from air as being a substance everywhere distributed. The separation of oxygen from it is, however, hampered by many difficulties.

From air, which contains a *mixture* of oxygen and nitrogen, the nitrogen alone cannot be removed, because it has no inclination to combine directly or readily with any substance; and although it does combine with certain substances (boron, titanium), these substances combine simultaneously with the oxygen of the atmosphere.[6] However,[156] [157] oxygen may be separated from air by causing it to combine with substances which may be easily decomposed by the action of heat, and, in so doing, give up the oxygen absorbed—that is, by making use of reversible reactions. Thus, for instance, the oxygen of the atmosphere may be made to oxidise sulphurous anhydride, SO_2 (by passing directly over ignited spongy platinum), and to form sulphuric anhydride, or sulphur trioxide, SO_3; and this substance (which is a solid and volatile, and therefore easily separated from the nitrogen and sulphurous anhydride), on further heating, gives oxygen and sulphurous anhydride. Caustic soda or lime extracts (absorbs) the sulphurous anhydride from this mixture, whilst the oxygen is not absorbed, and thus it is isolated from the air. On a large scale in works, as we shall afterwards see, sulphurous anhydride is transformed into hydrate of sulphuric trioxide, or sulphuric acid, H_2SO_4; if this is allowed to drop on to red-hot flagstones, water, sulphurous anhydride, and oxygen are obtained. The oxygen is easily isolated from this mixture by passing the gases over lime. The extraction of oxygen from oxide of mercury (Priestley, Lavoisier), which is obtained from mercury and the oxygen of the atmosphere, is also a reversible reaction by which oxygen may be obtained from the atmosphere. So also, by passing dry air through a red-hot tube containing barium oxide, it is made to combine with the oxygen of the air. In this reaction the so-called barium peroxide, BaO_2, is formed from the barium oxide, BaO, and at a higher temperature the former evolves the absorbed oxygen, and leaves the barium oxide originally taken.[7]

[158]

Oxygen is evolved with particular ease by a whole series of unstable oxygen compounds, of which we shall proceed to take a general survey, remarking that many of these reactions, although not all, belong to the number of reversible reactions;[8] so that in order to obtain many of these substances (for instance, potassium chlorate) rich in oxygen, recourse must be had to indirect methods (see Introduction) with which we shall become acquainted in the course of this book.

1. *The compounds of oxygen* with certain metals, and especially with the so-called noble metals—that is, mercury, silver, gold, and platinum—having once been obtained, retain their oxygen at the ordinary temperature, but part with it at a red heat. The compounds are solids, generally amorphous and infusible, and are easily decomposed by heat into the metal and oxygen. We have seen an example of this in[159] speaking of the decomposition of mercury oxide. Priestley, in 1774, obtained pure oxygen for the first time by heating mercury oxide by means of a burning-glass, and clearly showed its difference from air. He showed its characteristic property of supporting combustion 'with remarkable vigour,' and named it dephlogisticated air.

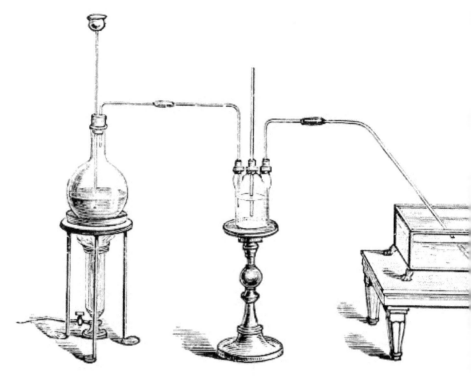

FIG. 29.—Preparation of oxygen from manganese peroxide and sulphuric acid. The gas evolved is passed through a Woulfe's bottle containing caustic potash.

2. The substances called *peroxides*[9] evolve oxygen at a greater or less heat (and also by the action of many acids). They usually contain metals combined with a large quantity of oxygen. Peroxides are the highest oxides of certain metals; those metals which form them generally give several compounds with oxygen. Those of the lowest degrees of oxidation, containing the least amount of oxygen, are generally substances which are capable of easily reacting with acids—for instance, with sulphuric acid. Such low oxides are called bases. Peroxides contain more oxygen than the bases formed by the same metals. For example, lead oxide contains 7·1 parts of oxygen in 100 parts, and is basic, but lead peroxide contains 13·3 parts of oxygen in 100 parts. *Manganese peroxide* is a similar substance, and is a solid of a dark colour, which occurs in nature. It is employed for technical purposes under the name of black oxide of manganese (in German, 'Braunstein,' the pyrolusite of the mineralogist). Peroxides are able to evolve oxygen at a more or less elevated temperature. They do not then part with all their oxygen, but with only a portion of it, and are converted into a lower oxide or base. Thus, for example, lead peroxide, on heating,

gives oxygen and lead oxide. The decomposition of this peroxide proceeds tolerably easily on heating, even in a glass vessel, but manganese peroxide only evolves oxygen at a strong red heat, and therefore oxygen can only be obtained from it in iron, or other metallic, or clay vessels. This was formerly the method for obtaining oxygen. Manganese peroxide only parts with one-third of its oxygen (according to the equation $3MnO_2 = Mn_3O_4 + O_2$), whilst two-thirds remain in the solid substance which forms the residue after heating. Metallic peroxides are also capable of evolving oxygen on heating with sulphuric acid. They then evolve just that amount of oxygen which is in excess of that necessary for the formation of the base, the latter reacting on the sulphuric acid forming a compound (salt) with it. Thus barium peroxide, when heated with sulphuric acid, forms oxygen and barium oxide, which gives a compound with sulphuric acid termed barium sulphate ($BaO_2 + H_2SO_4 = BaSO_4 + H_2O + O$).[9 bis] This reaction usually[160] proceeds with greater ease than the decomposition of peroxides by heat alone. For the purposes of experiment powdered manganese peroxide is usually taken and mixed with strong sulphuric acid in a flask, and the apparatus set up as shown in Fig. 28. The gas which is evolved is passed through a Woulfe's bottle containing a solution of caustic potash, to purify it from carbonic anhydride and chlorine, which accompany the evolution of oxygen from commercial manganese peroxide, and the gas is not collected until a thin smouldering taper placed in front of the escape orifice bursts into flame, which shows that the gas coming off is oxygen. By this method of decomposition of the manganese peroxide by sulphuric[161] acid there is evolved, not, as in heating, one-third, but one-half of the oxygen contained in the peroxide ($MnO_2 + H_2SO_4 = MnSO_4 + H_2O + O$)—that is, from 50 grams of peroxide about 7⅙ grams, or about 5½ litres, of oxygen,[10] whilst by heating only about 3½ litres are obtained. The chemists of Lavoisier's time generally obtained oxygen by heating manganese peroxide. At the present time more convenient methods are known.

3. A third source to which recourse may be had for obtaining oxygen is represented in *acids* and *salts* containing much oxygen, which are capable, by parting with a portion or all of their oxygen, of being converted into other compounds (lower products of oxidation) which are more difficultly decomposed. These acids and salts (like peroxides) evolve oxygen either on heating alone, or only when in the presence of some other substance. Sulphuric acid may be taken as an example of an acid which is decomposed by the action of heat alone,[11] for it breaks up at a red heat into water, sulphurous anhydride, and oxygen, as was mentioned before. Priestley, in 1772, and Scheele, somewhat later, obtained oxygen by heating nitre to a red heat. The best examples of the formation of oxygen by the heating of

salts is given in *potassium chlorate*, or Berthollet's salt, so called after the French chemist who discovered it. Potassium chlorate is a salt composed of the elements potassium, chlorine, and oxygen, $KClO_3$. It occurs as transparent colourless plates, is soluble in water, especially in hot water, and resembles common table salt in some of its reactions and physical properties; it melts on heating, and in melting begins to decompose, evolving oxygen gas. This decomposition ends in all the oxygen being evolved from the potassium chlorate, potassium chloride being left as a residue, according to the equation $KClO_3 = KCl + O_3$.[12] This[162] decomposition proceeds at a temperature which allows of its being conducted in a glass vessel. However, in decomposing, the molten potassium chlorate swells up and boils, and gradually solidifies, so the evolution of the oxygen is not regular, and the glass vessel may crack. In order to overcome this inconvenience, the potassium chlorate is crushed and mixed with a powder of a substance which is infusible, incapable of combining with the oxygen evolved, and is a good conductor of heat. Usually it is mixed with manganese peroxide.[13] The decomposition of the potassium chlorate is then considerably facilitated, and proceeds at a lower temperature (because the entire mass is then better heated, both externally and internally), without swelling up, and this method is therefore more convenient than the decomposition of the salt alone. This method for the preparation of oxygen is very convenient; it is generally employed when a small quantity of oxygen is required. Further, potassium chlorate is easily obtained pure, and it evolves much oxygen. 100 grams of the salt give as much as 39 grams, or 30 litres, of oxygen. This method is so simple and easy,[14] that a course of practical chemistry is often commenced by the preparation of oxygen by this method, and of hydrogen by the aid of zinc and sulphuric acid, since by means of these gases many interesting and striking experiments may be performed.[15]

A solution of *bleaching powder*, which contains calcium hypochlorite, $CaCl_2O_2$, evolves oxygen on gently heating when a small quantity of certain oxides is added—for instance, cobalt oxide, which in this case acts by contact (*see* Introduction). When heated by itself, a solution of bleaching powder does not evolve oxygen, but it oxidises the cobalt oxide to a higher degree of oxidation; this higher oxide of cobalt in contact with the bleaching powder decomposes into oxygen and lower[163] oxidation products, and the resultant lower oxide of cobalt with bleaching powder again gives the higher oxide, which again gives up its oxygen, and so on.[16] The calcium hypochlorite is here decomposed according to the equation $CaCl_2O_2 = CaCl_2 + O_2$. In this manner a small quantity of cobalt oxide[17] is sufficient for the decomposition of an indefinitely large quantity of bleaching powder.

The properties of oxygen.[18]—It is a permanent *gas*—that is, it cannot be liquefied by pressure at the ordinary temperature, and further, is only liquefied with difficulty (although more easily than hydrogen) at temperatures below -120°, because this is its absolute boiling point. As its critical pressure[19] is about 50 atmospheres, it can be easily liquefied under pressures greater than 50 atmospheres at temperatures below -120°. According to Dewar, the density of oxygen in a critical[164] state is 0·65 (water = 1), but, like all other substances in this state,[20] it varies considerably in density with a change of pressure and temperature, and therefore many investigators who made their observations under high pressures give a greater density, as much as 1·1. Liquefied oxygen is an exceedingly mobile transparent liquid, with a faint blue tint and boiling (tension = 1 atmosphere) about -180°. Oxygen, like all gases, is transparent, and like the majority of gases, colourless. It has no smell or taste, which is evident from the fact of its being a component of air. The weight of one litre of oxygen gas at 0° and 760 mm. pressure is 1·4298 gram; it is therefore slightly denser than air. Its density in respect to air = 1·1056 and in respect to hydrogen = 16.[21]

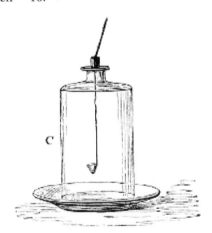

FIG. 29.—Mode of burning sulphur, phosphorus, sodium, &c., in oxygen.

In its chemical properties oxygen is remarkable from the fact that it very easily—and, in a chemical sense, vigorously—reacts on a number of substances, forming oxygen compounds. However, only a few substances and mixtures of substances (for example, phosphorus, copper with ammonia, decomposing organic matter, aldehyde, pyrogallol with an alkali, &c.) combine directly with oxygen at the ordinary temperature, whilst many substances easily combine with oxygen at a red heat, and often this combination presents a rapid chemical reaction accompanied by the evolution of a large quantity of heat. Every reaction which takes place rapidly, if it be accompanied by so great an evolution of heat as to produce incandescence, is termed *combustion.* Thus combustion ensues when many metals are plunged into chlorine, or oxide of sodium or barium into carbonic anhydride, or when a spark falls on gunpowder. A great many substances are combustible in oxygen, and, owing to its presence, in air also. In order to start[165] combustion it is generally necessary[22] that the combustible substance should be brought to a state of incandescence. The continuation of the process does not require the aid of fresh external heat, because sufficient heat[23] is evolved to raise the temperature of the remaining parts of the combustible substance to the required degree. Examples of this are familiar to all from every-day experience. Combustion proceeds in oxygen with greater rapidity, and is accompanied by a more powerful incandescence, than in ordinary air. This may be demonstrated by a number of very convincing experiments. If a piece of charcoal, attached to a wire and previously brought to red-heat, be plunged into a flask full of oxygen, it burns rapidly at a white heat—*i.e.* it combines with the oxygen, forming a gaseous product of combustion called carbonic anhydride, or carbonic acid gas, CO_2. This is the same gas that is evolved in the act of respiration, for charcoal is one of the substances which is obtained by the decomposition of all organic substances which contain it, and in the process of respiration part of the constituents of the body, so to speak, slowly burn. If a piece of burning sulphur be placed in a small cup attached to a wire and introduced into a flask full of oxygen, then the sulphur, which burns in air with a very feeble flame, burns in the oxygen with a violet flame, which, although pale, is much larger than in air. If the sulphur be exchanged for a piece of phosphorus,[24] then, unless the phosphorus be heated, it combines very slowly with the oxygen; but, if heated, although on only one spot, it burns with an exceedingly brilliant white flame. In order to heat the phosphorus inside the flask, the simplest way is to bring a red-hot wire into contact with it. Before the charcoal can burn, it must be brought to a state of incandescence. Sulphur[166] also will not burn under 100°, whilst phosphorus inflames at 40°. Phosphorus which has been already lighted in air cannot so well be introduced into the flask, because it burns very rapidly and with a large flame in air. If a small lump of metallic *sodium* be put in a small cup made of lime,[25] melted, and ignited,[26] it burns very feebly in air. But if burning sodium be introduced into oxygen, the combustion is invigorated and is accompanied by a brighter yellow flame. Metallic *magnesium*, which burns brightly in air, continues to burn with still greater vigour in oxygen, forming a white powder, which is a compound of magnesium with oxygen (magnesium oxide; magnesia). A strip of *iron* or steel does not burn in air, but an iron wire or steel spring may be easily burnt in oxygen.[27] The combustion of steel or iron in oxygen is not accompanied by a flame, but sparks of oxide fly in all directions from the burning portions of the iron.[28]

FIG. 30.—Mode of burning a steel spring in oxygen.

In order to demonstrate by experiment the *combustion of hydrogen* in oxygen, a gas-conducting tube, bent so as to form a convenient jet, is led from the vessel evolving hydrogen. The hydrogen is first set light to in air, and then the gas-conducting tube is let down into a flask containing oxygen. The combustion in oxygen will be similar to that in air; the flame remains pale, notwithstanding the fact that its temperature rises considerably. It is[167] instructive to remark that oxygen may burn in hydrogen, just as hydrogen in oxygen. In order to show the combustion of oxygen in hydrogen, a tube bent vertically upwards and ending in a fine orifice is attached to the stopcock of a gas-holder full of oxygen. Two wires, placed at such a distance from each other as to allow the passage of a constant series of sparks from a Ruhmkorff's coil, are fixed in front of the orifice of the tube. This is in order to ignite the oxygen, which may also be done by attaching tinder round the orifice, and burning it. When the wires are arranged at the orifice of the tube, and a series of sparks passes between them, then an inverted (because of the lightness of the hydrogen) jar full of hydrogen is placed over the gas-conducting tube. When the jar covers the orifice of the gas-conducting tube (and not before, as otherwise an explosion might take place) the cock of the gasometer is opened, and the oxygen flows into the hydrogen and is set light to by the sparks. The flame obtained is similar to that formed by the combustion of hydrogen in oxygen.[29] From this it is evident that the flame is the locality where the oxygen combines with the hydrogen, therefore a flame of burning oxygen can be obtained as well as a flame of burning hydrogen.

If, instead of hydrogen, any other combustible gas be taken—for example, ordinary coal gas—then the phenomenon of combustion will be exactly the same, only a bright flame will be obtained, and the products of combustion will be different. However, as coal gas contains a considerable amount of free and combined hydrogen, it will also form a considerable quantity of water in its combustion.

[168]

If hydrogen be mixed with oxygen in the proportion in which they form water—*i.e.* if two volumes of hydrogen be taken for each volume of oxygen—then the mixture will be the same as that obtained by the decomposition of water by a galvanic current—detonating gas.

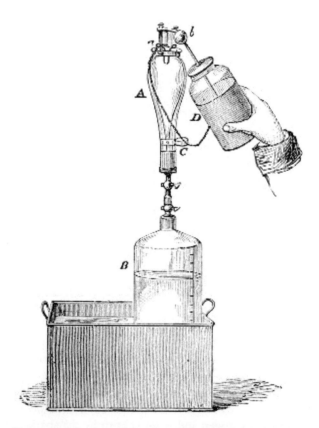

FIG. 31.—Cavendish's apparatus for exploding detonating gas. The bell jar standing in the bath is filled with a mixture of two volumes of hydrogen and one volume of oxygen, and the thick glass vessel A is then screwed on to it. The air is first pumped out of this vessel, so that when the stopcock C is opened, it becomes filled

with detonating gas. The stopcock is then re-closed, and the explosion produced by means of a spark from a Leyden jar. After the explosion has taken place the stopcock is again opened, and the water rises into the vessel A.

FIG. 32.—Eudiometer

We have already mentioned in the last chapter that the combination of these gases, or their explosion, may be brought about by the action of an electric spark, because the spark heats the space through which it passes, and acts consequently in a manner similar to ignition by means of contact with an incandescent or burning substance.[29 bis] Cavendish made this experiment on the ignition of detonating gas, at the end of the last century, in the apparatus shown in fig. 31. Ignition by the aid of the electric spark is convenient, for the reason that it may then be brought about in a closed vessel, and hence chemists still employ this method when it is required to ignite a mixture of oxygen with a combustible gas in a closed vessel. For this purpose, especially since Bunsen's time,[30] an *eudiometer* is employed. It consists of a thick glass tube graduated along its length in millimetres (for indicating the height of the mercury column), and calibrated for a definite volume (weight of mercury). Two platinum wires are[169] fused into the upper closed end of the tube, as shown in fig. 32.[31] By the aid of the eudiometer we may not only determine the volumetric composition of water,[32] and the quantitative contents of oxygen in[170] air,[33] but also make a number of experiments explaining the phenomenon of combustion.

Thus, for example, it may be demonstrated, by the aid of the eudiometer, that for the ignition of detonating gas, a *definite temperature* is required. If the temperature be below that required, combination will not take place, but if at any spot within the tube it rises to the temperature of inflammation, then combination will ensue at that spot, and evolve enough heat for the ignition of the adjacent portions of the detonating mixture. If to 1 volume of detonating gas there be added 10 volumes of oxygen, or 4 volumes of hydrogen, or 3 volumes of carbonic anhydride, then we shall not obtain an explosion by passing a spark through the diluted mixture. This depends on the fact that the temperature falls with the dilution of the detonating gas by another gas, because the heat evolved by the combination of the small quantity of hydrogen and oxygen brought to incandescence by the spark is not only transmitted to the water proceeding from the combination, but also to the foreign substance mixed with the detonating gas.[34] The necessity of a definite temperature for the ignition of detonating gas is also seen from the fact that pure detonating gas explodes in the presence of a red-hot iron wire, or of charcoal heated to 275°, but with a lower degree of incandescence there is not any explosion. It may also be brought about by rapid compression, when, as is known, heat is evolved.[35][171]

[172] Experiments made in the eudiometer showed that the ignition of detonating gas takes place at a temperature between 450° and 560°.[36]

The combination of hydrogen with oxygen is accompanied by the evolution of a very considerable amount of heat; according to the determinations of *Favre* and *Silbermann*,[37] 1 part by weight of hydrogen[173] in forming water evolves 34,462 units of heat. Many of the most recent determinations are very close to this figure, so that it may be taken that in the formation of 18 parts of water (H_2O) there are evolved 69 major calories, or 69,000 units of heat.[38] *If the specific heat of*[174] *aqueous vapour* (0·48) *remained constant from the ordinary temperature to that at which the combustion of detonating gas takes place* (but there is now no doubt that it increases), were the combustion concentrated at one point[39] (but it occurs in the whole region of a flame), were there no loss from radiation and heat conduction, and *did dissociation not take place*—that is, did not a state of equilibrium between the hydrogen, oxygen, and water come about—*then it would be possible to calculate the temperature of the flame of detonating gas.* It would then be 8,000°.[40] In reality it is very much lower, but it is nevertheless higher than the temperature attained in furnaces and flames, and is as high as 2,000°. The explosion of detonating gas is explained by this high temperature, because the aqueous vapour formed must occupy a volume at least 5 times greater than that occupied by the detonating gas at the ordinary temperature. Detonating gas emits a sound, not only as a consequence of the commotion which occurs from the rapid expansion of the heated vapour, but also because it is immediately followed by a cooling effect, the conversion of the vapour into water, and a rapid contraction.[41]

[175]

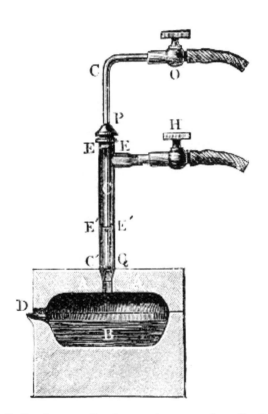

FIG. 34.—Safety burner for detonating gas, described in text.

Mixtures of hydrogen and of various other gases with oxygen are taken advantage of for obtaining high temperatures. By the aid of such high temperatures metals like platinum may be melted on a large scale, which cannot be performed in furnaces heated with charcoal and fed by a current of air. The burner, shown in fig. 34, is constructed for the application of detonating gas to the purpose. It consists of two brass tubes, one fixed inside the other, as shown in the drawing. The internal central tube C C conducts oxygen, and the outside, enveloping, tube E' E' conducts hydrogen. Previous to their egress the gases do not mix together, so that there can be no explosion inside the apparatus. When this burner is in use C is connected with a gas-holder containing oxygen, and E with a gas-holder containing hydrogen (or sometimes coal-gas). The flow of the gases can be easily regulated by the stopcocks O H. The flame is shortest and evolves the greatest heat when the gases burning are in the proportion of 1 volume of oxygen to 2 volumes of hydrogen. The degree of heat may be easily judged from the fact that a thin platinum wire placed in the flame of a properly proportioned mixture easily melts. By placing the burner in the orifice of a hollow piece of lime, a crucible A B is obtained in which the platinum may be easily melted, even in large quantities if the current of oxygen and hydrogen be sufficiently great (Deville). The flame of detonating gas may also be used for illuminating purposes. It is by itself very pale, but owing to its high temperature it may serve for rendering infusible objects incandescent, and at the very high temperature produced by the detonating gas the incandescent[176] substance gives a most intense light. For this purpose lime, magnesia, or oxide of zirconium are used, as they are not fusible at the very high temperature evolved by the detonating gas. A small cylinder of lime placed in the flame of detonating gas, if regulated to the required point, gives a very brilliant white light, which was at one time proposed for illuminating lighthouses. At present in the majority of cases the electric light, owing to its constancy and other advantages, has replaced it for this purpose. The light produced by the incandescence of lime in detonating gas is called the *Drummond light* or *limelight*.

The above cases form examples of the combustion of elements in oxygen, but exactly similar phenomena are observed in the *combustion of compounds*. So, for instance, the solid, colourless, shiny substance, naphthalene, $C_{10}H_8$, burns in the air with a smoky flame, whilst in oxygen it continues to burn with a very brilliant flame. Alcohol, oil, and other substances burn brilliantly in oxygen on conducting the oxygen by a tube to the flame of lamps burning these substances. A high temperature is thus evolved, which is sometimes taken advantage of in chemical practice.

In order to understand why combustion in oxygen proceeds more rapidly, and is accompanied by a more intense heat effect, than combustion in air, it must be recollected that air is oxygen diluted with nitrogen, which does not support combustion, and therefore fewer particles of oxygen flow to the surface of a substance burning in air than when burning in pure oxygen, besides which the reason of the intensity of combustion in oxygen is the high temperature acquired by the substance burning in it.[41 bis]

[177]

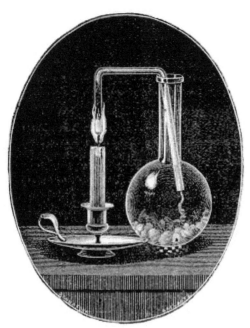

**FIG. 35.—Faraday's experiment for investigating the different parts
of a candle flame.**

Among the phenomena accompanying the combustion of certain
substances, the *phenomenon of flame* attracts attention. Sulphur, phosphorus,
sodium, magnesium, naphthalene, &c., burn like hydrogen with a flame,
whilst in the combustion of other substances no flame is observed, as, for
instance, in the combustion of iron and of charcoal. The appearance of
flame depends on the capacity of the combustible substance to yield gases
or vapours at the temperature of combustion. At the temperature of
combustion, sulphur, phosphorus, sodium, and naphthalene pass into
vapour, whilst wood, alcohol, oil, &c., are decomposed into gaseous and
vaporous substances. The combustion of gases and vapours forms flames,
and therefore *a flame is composed of the hot and incandescent gases and vapours
produced by combustion.* It may easily be proved that the flames of such non-
volatile substances as wood contain volatile and combustible substances
formed from them, by placing a tube in the flame connected with an
aspirator. Besides the products of combustion, combustible gases and
liquids, previously in the flame as vapours, collect in the aspirator. For this
experiment to succeed—*i.e.* in order to really extract combustible gases and
vapours from the flame it is necessary that the suction tube should be
placed *inside* the flame. The combustible gases and vapours can only remain
unburnt inside the flame, for at the surface of the flame they come into
contact with the oxygen of the air and burn.[42] Flames are of different

degrees of *brilliancy*, according to whether *solid* incandescent particles occur in the combustible gas or vapour, or not. Incandescent gases and vapours emit but little light by themselves, and therefore give a paler flame.[43] If a flame does not contain solid particles it is transparent,[178] pale, and emits but little light.[44] The flames of burning alcohol, sulphur, and hydrogen are of this kind. A pale flame may be rendered luminous by placing fine particles of solid matter in it. Thus, if a very fine platinum wire be placed in the pale flame of burning alcohol—or, better still, of hydrogen—the flame emits a bright light. This is still better seen by sifting the powder of an incombustible substance, such as fine sand, into the flame, or by placing a bunch of asbestos threads in it. Every brilliant flame always contains some kind of solid particles, or at least some very dense vapour. The flame of sodium burning in oxygen has a brilliant yellow colour, from the presence of particles of solid sodium oxide. The flame of magnesium is brilliant from the fact that in burning it forms solid magnesia, which becomes white hot, and similarly the brilliancy of the Drummond light is due to the heat of the flame raising the solid non-volatile lime to a state of incandescence. The flames of a candle, wood, and similar substances are brilliant, because they contain particles of charcoal or soot. It is not the flame itself which is luminous, but the incandescent soot it contains. These particles of charcoal which occur in flames may be easily observed by introducing a cold object, like a knife, into the flame.[45] The particles of charcoal burn at the outer surface of the flame if the supply of air be sufficient, but if the supply of air—that is,[179] of oxygen—be insufficient for their combustion the flame smokes, because the unconsumed particles of charcoal are carried off by the current of air.[46]

[180]

The combination of various substances with oxygen may not present any signs of combustion—that is, the temperature may rise but inconsiderably. This may either proceed from the fact that the reaction of the substance (for example, tin, mercury, lead at a high temperature, or a mixture of pyrogallol with caustic potash at the ordinary temperature) evolves but little heat, or that the heat evolved is transmitted to good conductors of heat, like metals, or that the combination with oxygen takes place so slowly that the heat evolved succeeds in passing to the surrounding objects. Combustion is only a particular, intense, and evident case of combination with[181] oxygen. Respiration is also an act of combination with oxygen; it also serves, like combustion, for the development of heat by those chemical processes which accompany it (the transformation of oxygen into carbonic anhydride). Lavoisier enunciated this in the lucid expression, 'respiration is slow combustion.'

Reactions involving slow combination of substances with oxygen are termed *oxidations*. Combination of this kind (and also combustion) often results in the formation of acid substances, and hence the name *oxygen* (*Sauerstoff*). Combustion is only rapid oxidation. Phosphorus, iron, and wine may be taken as examples of substances which slowly oxidise in air at the ordinary temperature. If such a substance be left in contact with a definite volume of air or oxygen, it absorbs the oxygen little by little, as may be seen by the decrease in volume of the gas. This slow oxidation is not often accompanied by a sensible evolution of heat; an evolution of heat really does occur, only it is not apparent to our senses owing to the small rise in temperature which takes place; this is owing to the slow rate of the reaction and to the transmission of the heat formed as radiant heat, &c. Thus, in the oxidation of wine and its transformation into vinegar by the usual method of preparation of the latter, the heat evolved cannot be observed because it extends over several weeks, but in the so-called rapid process of the manufacture of vinegar, when a large quantity of wine is comparatively rapidly oxidised, the evolution of heat is quite apparent.

Such slow processes of oxidation are always taking place in nature by the action of the atmosphere. Dead organisms and the substances obtained from them—such as bodies of animals, wood, wool, grass, &c.—are especially subject to this action. They *rot* and *decompose*—that is, their solid matter is transformed into gases, under the influence of moisture and atmospheric oxygen, and generally under the influence of other organisms, such as moulds, worms, micro-organisms (bacteria), and the like. These are processes of slow combustion, of slow combination with oxygen. It is well known that manure rots and develops heat, that stacks of damp hay, damp flour, straw, &c., become heated and are changed in the process.[47] In all these transformations the same chief products of combustion are formed as those which are contained in smoke; the carbon gives carbonic anhydride, and the hydrogen water. Hence these processes require oxygen just like combustion. This is the reason why the entire prevention of access of[182] air hinders these transformations,[48] and an increased supply of air accelerates them. The mechanical treatment of arable lands by the plough, harrow, and other similar means has not only the object of facilitating the spread of roots in the ground, and of making the soil more permeable to water, but it also serves to facilitate the access of the air to the component parts of the soil; as a consequence of which the organic remains of soil rot—so to speak, breathe air and evolve carbonic anhydride. One acre of good garden land in the course of a summer evolves more than sixteen tons of carbonic anhydride.

It is not only vegetable and animal substances which are subject to slow oxidation in the presence of water. Some metals even rust under these conditions. Copper very easily absorbs oxygen in the presence of acids. Many metallic sulphides (for example, pyrites) are very easily oxidised with access of air and moisture. Thus processes of slow oxidation proceed throughout nature. However, there are many elements which do not under any circumstances combine directly with gaseous oxygen; nevertheless their compounds with oxygen may be obtained. Platinum, gold, iridium, chlorine, and iodine are examples of such elements. In this case recourse is had to a so-called *indirect method*—*i.e.* the given substance is combined with another element, and by a method of double decomposition this element is replaced by oxygen. Substances which do not directly combine with oxygen, but form compounds with it by an indirect method, often readily lose the oxygen which they had absorbed by double decomposition or at the moment of its evolution. Such, for example, are the compounds of oxygen with chlorine, nitrogen, and platinum, which evolve oxygen on heating—that is, they may be used as oxidising agents. In this respect *oxidising agents*, or those compounds of oxygen which are employed in chemical and technical practice for transferring oxygen to other substances, are especially remarkable. The most important among these is nitric acid or *aqua fortis*—a substance rich in oxygen, and capable of evolving it when heated, which easily oxidises a great number of substances. Thus nearly all metals and organic substances containing carbon and hydrogen are more or less oxidised when heated[183] with nitric acid. If strong nitric acid be taken, and a piece of burning charcoal be immersed in the acid, it continues to burn. Chromic acid acts like nitric acid; alcohol burns when mixed with it. Although the action is not so marked, even water may oxidise with its oxygen. Sodium is not oxidised in perfectly dry oxygen at the ordinary temperature, but it burns very easily in water and aqueous vapour. Charcoal can burn in carbonic anhydride—a product of combustion—forming carbonic oxide. Magnesium burns in the same gas, separating carbon from it. Speaking generally, combined oxygen can pass from one compound to another.

The products of combustion or oxidation—and in general the definite compounds of oxygen—are termed *oxides*. Some oxides are not capable of combining with other oxides—or combine with only a few, and then with the evolution of very little heat; others, on the contrary, enter into combination with very many other oxides, and in general have remarkable chemical energy. The oxides incapable of combining with others, or only showing this quality in a small degree, are termed *indifferent oxides*. Such are the peroxides, of which mention has before been made.

The class of oxides capable of entering into mutual combination we will term *saline oxides*. They fall into two chief groups—at least, as regards the most extreme members. The members of one group combine with the members of the other group with particular ease. As representative of one group may be taken the oxides of the metals, magnesium, sodium, calcium, &c. Representatives of the other group are the oxides formed by the non-metals, sulphur, phosphorus, carbon. Thus, if we take the oxide of calcium, or lime, and bring it into contact with oxides of the second group, combination very readily ensues. For instance, if we mix calcium oxide with oxide of phosphorus they combine with great facility and with the evolution of much heat. If we pass the vapour of sulphuric anhydride, obtained by the combination of sulphurous oxide with oxygen, over pieces of lime heated to redness, the sulphuric anhydride is absorbed by the lime with the formation of a substance called calcium sulphate. The oxides of the first kind, which contain metals, are termed *basic oxides* or *bases*. Lime is a familiar example of this class. The oxides of the second group, which are capable of combining with the bases, are termed *anhydrides of the acids* or *acid oxides*. Sulphuric anhydride, SO_3, may be taken as a type of the latter group. It is a compound of sulphur with oxygen formed not directly but by the addition of a fresh quantity of oxygen to sulphurous anhydride, SO_2, by passing it together with oxygen over incandescent spongy platinum. Carbonic[184] anhydride (often termed 'carbonic acid'), CO_2, phosphoric anhydride, sulphurous anhydride, are all acid oxides, for they can combine with such oxides as lime or calcium oxide, magnesia or magnesium oxide, MgO, soda or sodium oxide, Na_2O, &c.

If a given element form but one basic oxide, it is termed the *oxide*; for example, calcium oxide, magnesium oxide, potassium oxide. Some indifferent oxides are also called 'oxides' if they have not the properties of peroxides, and at the same time do not show the properties of acid anhydrides—for example, carbonic oxide, of which mention has already been made. If an element forms two basic oxides (or two indifferent oxides not having the characteristics of a peroxide) then that of the lower degree of oxidation is called a *suboxide*—that is, suboxides contain less oxygen than oxides. Thus, when copper is heated to redness in a furnace it increases in weight and absorbs oxygen, until for 63 parts of copper there is absorbed not more than 8 parts of oxygen by weight, forming a red mass, which is suboxide of copper; but if the roasting be prolonged, and the draught of air increased, 63 parts of copper absorb 16 parts of oxygen, and form black oxide of copper. Sometimes to distinguish between the degrees of oxidation a change of suffix is made in the oxidised element, *-ic* oxide denoting the higher degree of oxidation, and *-ous* oxide the lower degree. Thus ferrous oxide and ferric oxide are the same as suboxide of iron and oxide of iron. If an element forms one anhydride only, then it is named by an adjective formed from the name of the element made to end in *-ic* and the word *anhydride*. When an element forms two anhydrides, then the suffixes *-ous* and *-ic* are used to distinguish them: *-ous* signifying less oxygen than -*ic*; for example, sulphurous and sulphuric anhydrides.[49] When several oxides are formed from the same element, the prefixes *mon*, *di*, *tri*, *tetra* are used, thus: chlorine monoxide,[185] chlorine dioxide, chlorine trioxide, and chlorine tetroxide or chloric anhydride.

The oxides themselves rarely undergo chemical transformations, and in the few cases where they are subject to such changes a particularly important part is played by their combinations with water. The majority of, if not all, basic and acid oxides combine with water, either by a direct or an indirect method forming *hydrates*—that is, compounds which split up into water and an oxide of the same kind only. It is well known that many substances are capable of combining with water. Oxides possess this property in the highest degree. We have already seen examples of this (Chapter I.) in the combination of lime, and of sulphuric and phosphoric anhydrides, with water. The resulting combinations are basic and acid hydrates. Acid hydrates are called *acids* because they have an acid taste when dissolved in water (or saliva), for then only can they act on the palate. Vinegar, for example, has an acid taste because it contains acetic acid dissolved in water. Sulphuric acid, to which we have frequently referred, because it is the acid of the greatest importance both in practical chemistry and for its technical applications, is really a hydrate formed by the combination of sulphuric anhydride with water. Besides their acid taste, dissolved acids or acid hydrates have the property of changing the blue colour of certain vegetable dyes to red. Of these dyes *litmus* is particularly remarkable and much used. It is the blue substance extracted from certain lichens, and is used for dyeing tissues blue; it gives a blue infusion with water. This infusion, on the addition of an acid, *changes from blue to red*.[50]

[186]

Basic oxides, in combining with water, form hydrates, of which, however, very few are soluble in water. Those which are soluble in water have an alkaline taste like that of soap or of water in which wood ashes have been boiled, and are called *alkalis*. Further, alkalis have the property of restoring the blue colour to litmus which has been reddened by the action of acids. The hydrates of the oxides of sodium and potassium, NaHO and KHO, are examples of basic hydrates easily soluble in water. They are true alkalis, and are termed *caustic*, because they act very powerfully on the skin of animals and plants. Thus NaHO is called 'caustic' soda.

The saline oxides are capable of combining together and with water. Water itself is an oxide, and not an indifferent one, for it can, as we have seen, combine with basic and acid oxides; it is a representative of a whole series of saline oxides, *intermediate oxides*, capable of combining with both basic and acid oxides. There are many such oxides, which, like water, combine with basic and acid anhydrides—for instance, the oxides of aluminium and tin, &c. From this it may be concluded that all oxides might be placed, in respect to their capacity for combining with one another, in one uninterrupted series, at one extremity of which would stand those oxides which do not combine with the bases—that is, the alkalis—while at the other end would be the acid oxides, and in the interval those oxides which combine with one another and with both the acid and basic oxides. The further apart the members of this series are, the more stable are the compounds they form together, the more energetically do they act on each other, the greater the quantity of heat evolved in their reaction, and the more marked is their saline chemical character.

We said above that basic and acid oxides combine together, but rarely react on each other; this depends on the fact that the majority of them are solids or gases—that is, they occur in the state least prone[187] to chemical reaction. The gaseo-elastic state is with difficulty destroyed, because it necessitates overcoming the elasticity proper to the gaseous particles. The solid state is characterised by the immobility of its particles; whilst chemical action requires contact, and hence a displacement and mobility. If solid oxides be heated, and especially if they be melted, then reaction proceeds with great ease. But such a change of state rarely occurs in nature or in practice. Only in a few furnace processes is this the case. For example; in the manufacture of glass, the oxides contained in it combine together in a molten state. But when oxides combine with water, and especially when they form hydrates soluble in water, then the mobility of their particles increases to a considerable extent, and their reaction is greatly facilitated. Reaction then takes place at the ordinary temperature—easily and rapidly; so that this kind of reaction belongs to the class of those which take place with unusual facility, and are, therefore, very often taken advantage of in practice, and also have been and are going on in nature at every step. We will now consider the reactions of oxides in the state of hydrates, not losing sight of the fact that water is itself an oxide with definite properties, and has, therefore, no little influence on the course of those changes in which it takes part.

If we take a definite quantity of an acid, and add an infusion of litmus to it, it turns red; the addition of an alkaline solution does not immediately alter the red colour of the litmus, but on adding more and more of the alkaline solution a point is reached when the red colour changes to violet, and then the further addition of a fresh quantity of the alkaline solution changes the colour to blue. This change of the colour of the litmus is a consequence of the formation of a new compound. This reaction is termed the *saturation* or *neutralisation* of the acid by the base, or *vice versâ*. The solution in which the acid properties of the acid are saturated by the alkaline properties of the base is termed a *neutral* solution. Such a solution, although derived from the mixture of a base with an acid, does not exhibit either the acid or basic reaction on litmus, yet it preserves many other signs of the acid and alkali. It is observed that in such a definite admixture of an acid with an alkali, besides the changes in the colour of litmus there is a heating effect—*i.e.* an evolution of heat—which is alone sufficient to prove that there was chemical action. And, indeed, if the resultant violet solution be evaporated, there separates out, not the acid or the alkali originally taken, but a substance which has neither acid nor alkaline properties, but is usually solid and crystalline, having a saline appearance; this is a *salt* in the chemical sense of the word. Hence a salt is derived from the reaction of an acid on[188] an alkali, in a certain definite proportion. The water here taken for solution plays no other part than merely facilitating the progress of the reaction. This is seen from the fact that the anhydrides of the acids are able to combine with basic oxides, and give the same salts as do the acids with the alkalis or hydrates. Hence, a salt is a compound of definite quantities of an acid with an alkali. In the latter reaction, water is separated out if the substance formed be the same as is produced by the combination of anhydrous oxides together.[51] Examples of the formation of salts from acids and bases are easily observed, and are very often applied in practice. If we take, for instance, insoluble magnesium oxide (magnesia) it is easily dissolved in sulphuric acid, and on evaporation gives a saline substance, bitter, like all the salts of magnesium, and familiar to all under the name of Epsom salts, used as a purgative. If a solution of caustic soda—which is obtained, as we saw, by the action of water on sodium oxide—be poured into a flask in which charcoal has been burnt; or if carbonic anhydride, which is produced under so many circumstances, be passed through a solution of caustic soda, then sodium carbonate or soda, Na_2CO_3, is obtained, of which we have spoken several times, and which is prepared on a large scale and often used in manufactures. This reaction is expressed by the equation, $2NaHO + CO_2 = Na_2CO_3 + H_2O$. Thus, the various bases and acids form an innumerable number of different salts.[52] Salts constitute an[189] example of definite chemical compounds, and both in the history and practice of science are most often cited as confirming the conception of definite chemical compounds. Indeed, all the indications of a definite chemical combination are clearly seen in the formation and properties of salts. Thus, they are produced with a definite proportion of oxides, heat is evolved in their formation,[53] and the chemical character of the oxides and many of the physical properties become hidden in their salts. For example, when gaseous carbonic anhydride combines with a base[190] to form a solid salt, the elasticity of the gas quite disappears in its passage into the salt.[54]

Judging from the above, a salt is a compound of basic and acid oxides, or the result of the action of hydrates of these classes on each other with separation of water. But salts may be obtained by other methods. It must not be forgotten that basic oxides are formed by metals, and acid oxides usually by non-metals. But metals and non-metals are capable of combining together, and a salt is frequently formed by the oxidation of such a compound. For example, iron very easily combines with sulphur, forming iron sulphide FeS (as we saw in the Introduction); this in air, and especially moist air, absorbs oxygen, with the formation of the same salt $FeSO_4$, that may be obtained by the combination of the oxides of iron and sulphur, or of the hydrates of these oxides. Hence, it cannot be said or supposed that a salt has the properties of the oxides, or must necessarily contain two kinds of oxides in itself. The derivation of salts from oxides is merely one of the methods of their preparation. We saw, for instance, that in sulphuric acid it was possible to replace the hydrogen by zinc, and that by this means zinc sulphate was formed; so likewise the hydrogen in many other acids may be replaced by zinc, iron, potassium, sodium, and a whole series of similar metals, corresponding salts being obtained. The hydrogen of the acid, in all these cases, is exchanged for a metal, and a salt is obtained from the hydrate. Regarding a salt from this point of view, it may be said that *a salt is an acid in which hydrogen is replaced by a metal.* This definition shows that a salt and an acid are essentially compounds of the same series, with the difference that the latter contains hydrogen and the former a metal. Such a definition is more exact than the first definition of salts, inasmuch as it likewise includes those acids which do not contain oxygen, and, as we shall afterwards learn, there is a series of such acids. Such elements as chlorine and bromine form compounds with hydrogen in which the hydrogen may be replaced by a metal, forming substances which, in their reactions and external characters, resemble the salts formed from oxides. Table salt, $NaCl$, is an example of this. It may[191] be obtained by the replacement of hydrogen in hydrochloric acid, HCl, by the metal sodium, just as sulphate of sodium, Na_2SO_4, may be obtained by the replacement of hydrogen in sulphuric acid, H_2SO_4, by sodium. The exterior appearance of the resulting products, their neutral reaction, and even their saline taste, show their resemblance to one another.

To the fundamental properties of salts yet another must be added—namely, that they are more or less *decomposed by the action of a galvanic current.* The results of this decomposition are very different according to whether the salt be taken in a fused or dissolved state. But the decomposition may generally be so represented, that the metal appears at the electro-negative pole or cathode (like hydrogen in the decomposition of water, or its mixture with sulphuric acid), and the remaining parts of the salt appear at the electro-positive pole or anode (where the oxygen of water appears). If, for instance, an electric current acts on an aqueous solution of sodium sulphate, then the sodium appears at the negative pole, and oxygen and the anhydride of sulphuric acid at the positive pole. But in the solution itself the result is different, for sodium, as we know, decomposes water with evolution of hydrogen, forming caustic soda; consequently hydrogen will be evolved, and caustic soda appear at the negative pole: while at the positive pole the sulphuric anhydride immediately combines with water and forms sulphuric acid, and therefore oxygen will be evolved and sulphuric acid formed round this pole.[55] In other cases, when the metal separated is not able to decompose water, it will be deposited in a free state. Thus, for example, in the decomposition of copper sulphate, copper separates out at the cathode, and oxygen and sulphuric acid appear at the anode, and if a copper plate be attached to the positive pole, then the oxygen evolved will oxidise the copper, and the oxide of copper will dissolve and be deposited at the negative pole—that is, a transfer of copper from the positive to the negative pole ensues. The galvanoplastic art (electro-typing) is based on this principle.[56] Therefore the most radical and general properties of salts (including also such salts as table salt, which[192] contain no oxygen) may be expressed by representing the salt as composed of a metal M and a haloid X—that is, by expressing the salt by MX. In common table salt the metal is sodium, and the haloid an elementary body, chlorine. In sodium sulphate, Na_2SO_4, sodium is again the metal, but the complex group, SO_4, is the haloid. In sulphate of copper, $CuSO_4$, the metal is copper and the haloid the same as in the preceding salt. Such a representation of salts expresses with great simplicity the *capacity of every salt to enter into saline double decompositions with other salts*; consisting in the mutual replacement of the metals in the salts. This exchange of their metals is the fundamental property of salts. In the case of two salts with different metals and haloids, which are in solution or fusion, or in any other manner brought into contact, the metals of these salts will always partially or wholly exchange places. If we designate one salt by MX, and the other by NY, then we either partially or wholly obtain from them new salts, MY and NX. Thus we saw in the Introduction, that on mixing solutions of table salt, NaCl, and silver nitrate, $AgNO_3$, a white insoluble precipitate of silver chloride, AgCl, is formed and a new salt, sodium nitrate, $NaNO_3$, is obtained in solution. If the metals of salts exchange places in reactions of double decomposition, it is clear that metals themselves, taken in a separate state, are able to act on salts, as zinc evolves hydrogen from acids, and as iron separates copper from copper sulphate. When, to what extent, and which metals displace each other, and how the metals are distributed between the haloids, will be discussed in Chapter X., where we shall be guided by those reflections and deductions which Berthollet introduced into the science at the beginning of this century.

According to the above observations, an acid is nothing more than a salt of hydrogen. Water itself may be looked on as a salt in which the hydrogen is combined with either oxygen or the aqueous radicle, OH; water will then be HOH, and alkalis or basic hydrates, MOH. The group OH, or the *aqueous radicle*, otherwise called *hydroxyl*, may be looked on as a haloid like the chlorine in table salt, not only because the element Cl and the group OH very often change places, and combine with one and the same element, but also because free chlorine is very similar in many properties and reactions to peroxide of hydrogen, which is the same in composition as the aqueous radicle, as we shall afterwards see in Chapter IV. Alkalis and basic hydrates are also[193] salts consisting of a metal and hydroxyl—for instance, caustic soda, NaOH; this is therefore termed *sodium hydroxide*. According to this view, *acid salts* are those in which a portion only of the hydrogen is replaced by a metal, and a portion of the hydrogen of the acid remains. Thus sulphuric acid (H_2SO_4) not only gives the normal salt Na_2SO_4, with sodium, but also an acid salt, $NaHSO_4$. A *basic salt* is one in which the metal is combined not only with the haloids of acids, but also with the aqueous radicale of basic hydrates—for example, bismuth gives not only a normal salt of nitric acid, $Bi(NO_3)_3$, but also basic salts like $Bi(OH)_2(NO_3)$.

As basic and acid salts of the oxygen acids contain hydrogen and oxygen, they are able to part with these as water and to give anhydro-salts, which it is evident will be compounds of normal salts with anhydrides of the acids or with bases. Thus the above-mentioned acid sodium sulphate corresponds with the anhydro-salt, $Na_2S_2O_7$, equal to $2NaHSO_4$, less H_2O. The loss of water is here, and frequently in other cases, brought about by heat alone, and therefore such salts are frequently termed *pyro-salts*—for instance, the preceding is sodium pyrosulphate ($Na_2S_2O_7$), or it may be regarded as the normal salt Na_2SO_4 + sulphuric anhydride, SO_3. *Double* salts are those which contain either two metals, $KAl(SO_4)_2$, or two haloids.[57][194]

Inasmuch as oxygen compounds predominate in nature, it should be expected from what has been said above, that salts, rather than acids[195] or bases, would occur most frequently in nature, for these latter would always tend to combine forming salts, especially through the medium[196] of the all-pervading water. And, as a matter of fact, salts are found everywhere in nature. They occur in animals and plants, although in but small quantity, because, as forming the last stage of chemical reaction, they are capable of only a few chemical transformations. And organisms are bodies in which a series of uninterrupted, varied, and active chemical transformations proceed, whilst salts, which only enter into double decompositions between each other, are little prone to such changes. But organisms always contain salts. Thus, for instance, bones contain calcium phosphate, the juice of grapes potassium tartrate (cream of tartar), certain lichens calcium oxalate, and the shells of mollusca calcium carbonate, &c. As regards water and soil, portions of the earth in which the chemical processes are less active, they are full of salts. Thus the waters of the oceans, and all others (Chap. I.), abound in salts, and in the soil, in the rocks of the earth's crust, in the upheaved lavas, and in the falling meteorites the salts of silicic acid, and especially its double salts, predominate. Saline substances also make up the composition of those limestones which often form mountain chains and whole thicknesses of the earth's strata, these consisting of calcium carbonate, $CaCO_3$.

Thus we have seen oxygen in a free state and in various compounds of different degrees of stability, from the unstable salts, like Berthollet's salt and nitre, to the most stable silicon compounds, such as exist in granite. We saw an entirely similar gradation of stability in the compounds of water and of hydrogen. In all its aspects oxygen, as an element, or single substance, remains the same however varied its chemical states, just as a substance may appear in many different physical states of aggregation. But our notion of the immense variety of the chemical states in which oxygen can occur would not be completely[197] understood if we did not make ourselves acquainted with it in the form in which it occurs in ozone and peroxide of hydrogen. In these it is most active, its energy seems to have increased. They illustrate fresh aspects of chemical correlations, and the variety of the forms in which matter can appear stand out clearly. We will therefore consider these two substances somewhat in detail.

Footnotes:

[1] As regards the interior of the earth, it probably contains far less oxygen compounds than the surface, judging by the accumulated evidences of the earth's origin, of meteorites, of the earth's density, &c. (see Chapter VIII., Note 58, and Chapter XXII., Note 2).

[2] It is evident that the partial pressure (see Chapter I.) acts in respiration. The researches of Paul Bert showed this with particular clearness. Under a pressure of one-fifth of an atmosphere consisting of oxygen only, animals and human beings remain under the ordinary conditions of the partial pressure of oxygen, but organisms cannot support air rarefied to one-fifth, for then the partial pressure of the oxygen falls to one-twenty-fifth of an atmosphere. Even under a pressure of one-third of an atmosphere the regular life of human beings is impossible, by reason of the impossibility of respiration (because of the decrease of solubility of oxygen in the blood), owing to the small partial pressure of the oxygen, and not from any mechanical effect of the decrease of pressure. Paul Bert

illustrated all this by many experiments, some of which he conducted on himself. This explains, among other things, the discomfort felt in the ascent of high mountains or in balloons when the height reached exceeds eight kilometres, and at pressures below 250 mm. (Chapter II., Note 23). It is evident that an artificial atmosphere has to be employed in the ascent to great heights, just as in submarine work. The cure by compressed and rarefied air which is practised in certain illnesses is based partly on the mechanical action of the change of pressure, and partly on the alteration in the partial pressure of the respired oxygen.

[3] At night, without the action of light, without the absorption of that energy which is required for the decomposition of carbonic anhydride into free oxygen and carbon (which is retained by the plants) they breathe like animals, absorbing oxygen and evolving carbonic anhydride. This process also goes on side by side with the reverse process in the daytime, but it is then far feebler than that which gives oxygen.

[4] The earth's surface is equal to about 510 million square kilometres, and the mass of the air (at a pressure of 760 mm.) on each kilometre of surface is about $10\frac{1}{3}$ thousand millions of kilograms, or about $10\frac{1}{3}$ million tons; therefore the whole weight of the atmosphere is about 5,100 million million ($= 51 \times 10^{14}$) tons. Consequently there are about 2×10^{15} tons of free oxygen in the earth's atmosphere. The innumerable series of processes which absorb a portion of this oxygen are compensated for by the plant processes. Assuming that 100 million tons of vegetable matter, containing 40 p.c. of carbon, formed from carbonic acid, are produced (and the same process proceeds in water) per year on the 100 million square kilometres of dry land (ten tons of roots, leaves, stems, &c., per hectare, or 1 $\boxed{100}$ of a square kilometre), we find that the plant life of the dry land gives about 100,000 tons of oxygen, which is an insignificant fraction of the entire mass of the oxygen of the air.

[5] The extraction of oxygen from water may be effected by two processes: either by the decomposition of water into its constituent parts by the action of a galvanic current (Chapter II.), or by means of the removal of the hydrogen from water. But, as we have seen and already know, hydrogen enters into direct combination with very few substances, and then only under special circumstances; whilst oxygen, as we shall soon learn, combines with nearly all substances. Only gaseous chlorine (and, especially, fluorine) is capable of decomposing water, taking up the hydrogen from it, without combining with the oxygen. Chlorine is soluble in water, and if an aqueous solution of chlorine, so-called chlorine water, be poured into a flask, and this flask be inverted in a basin containing the same chlorine water, then we shall have an apparatus by means of which

oxygen may be extracted from water. At the ordinary temperature, and in the dark, chlorine does not act on water, or only acts very feebly; but under the action of direct sunlight chlorine decomposes water, with the evolution of oxygen. The chlorine then combines with the hydrogen, and gives hydrochloric acid, which dissolves in the water, and therefore free oxygen only will be separated from the liquid, and it will only contain a small quantity of chlorine in admixture, which can be easily removed by passing the gas through a solution of caustic potash.

[6]

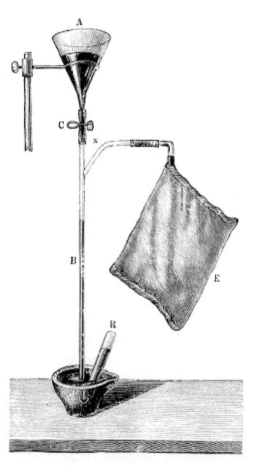

FIG. 27.—Graham's apparatus for the decomposition of air by pumping it through india-rubber.

A difference in the physical properties of both gases cannot be here taken advantage of, because they are very similar in this respect. Thus the density of oxygen is 16 times and of nitrogen 14 times greater than the density of hydrogen, and therefore porous vessels cannot be here employed—the difference between the times of their passage through a porous surface would be too insignificant.

Graham, however, succeeded in enriching air in oxygen by passing it through india-rubber. This may be done in the following way:—A common india-rubber cushion, E (Fig. 27), is taken, and its orifice hermetically connected with an air-pump, or, better still, a mercury aspirator (the Sprengel pump is designated by the letters A, C, B). When the aspirator (Chapter II., Note 16) has pumped out the air, which will be seen by the mercury running out in an almost uninterrupted stream, and from its standing approximately at the barometric height, then it may be clearly observed that gas passes through the india-rubber. This is also seen from the fact that bubbles of gas continually pass along with the mercury. A minus pressure may be constantly maintained in the cushion by pouring mercury into the funnel A, and screwing up the pinchcock C, so that the stream flowing from it is small, and then a portion of the air passing through the india-rubber will be carried along with the mercury. This air may be collected in the cylinder, R. Its composition proves to be about 42 volumes of oxygen with 57 volumes of nitrogen, and one volume of carbonic anhydride, whilst ordinary air contains only 21 volumes of oxygen in 100 volumes. A square metre of india-rubber surface (of the usual thickness) passes about 45 c.c. of such air per hour. This experiment clearly shows that india-rubber is permeable to gases. This may, by the way, be observed in common toy balloons filled with coal-gas. They fall after a day or two, not because there are holes in them, but because air penetrates into, and the gas from, their interior, through the surface of the india-rubber of which they are made. The rate of the passage of gases through india-rubber does not, as Mitchell and Graham showed, depend on their densities, and consequently its permeability is not determined by orifices. It more resembles dialysis—that is, the penetration of liquids through colloid surfaces. Equal volumes of gases penetrate through india-rubber in periods of time which are related to each other as follows:—carbonic anhydride, 100; hydrogen, 247; oxygen, 532; marsh gas, 633; carbonic oxide, 1,220; nitrogen, 1,358. Hence nitrogen penetrates more slowly than oxygen, and carbonic anhydride more quickly than other gases. 2·556 volumes of oxygen and 13·585 volumes of carbonic anhydride penetrate in the same time as one volume of nitrogen. By multiplying these ratios by the amounts of these gases in air, we obtain figures which are in almost the same proportion as the volumes of the gases penetrating from air through india-rubber. If the process of dialysis be repeated on the air which has already passed through india-rubber, then a mixture containing 65 p.c. by volume of oxygen is obtained. It may be thought that the cause of this phenomenon is the absorption or occlusion (*see* Chap. II., Note 37) of gases by india-rubber and the evolution of the gas dissolved in a vacuum; and, indeed, india-rubber does absorb gases, especially carbonic anhydride. Graham called the above method of the decomposition of air *atmolysis*.

[7] The preparation of oxygen by this method, which is due to Boussingault, is conducted in a porcelain tube, which is placed in a stove heated by charcoal, so that its ends project beyond the stove. Barium oxide (which may be obtained by igniting barium nitrate, previously dried) is placed in the tube, one end of which is connected with a pair of bellows, or a gas-holder, for keeping up a current of air through it. The air is previously passed through a solution of caustic potash, to remove all traces of carbonic anhydride, and it is very carefully dried (for the hydrate BaH_2O_2 does not give the peroxide). At a *dark-red heat* (500–600°) the oxide of barium absorbs oxygen from the air, so that the gas leaving the tube consists almost entirely of nitrogen. When the absorption ceases, the air will pass through the tube unchanged, which may be recognised from the fact that it supports combustion. The barium oxide is converted into peroxide under these circumstances, and eleven parts of barium oxide absorb about one part of oxygen by weight. When the absorption ceases, one end of the tube is closed, a cork with a gas-conducting tube is fixed into the other end, and the heat of the stove is increased to a *bright-red heat* (800°). At this temperature the barium peroxide gives up all that oxygen which it acquired at a dark-red heat—*i.e.* about one part by weight of oxygen is evolved from twelve parts of barium peroxide. After the evolution of the oxygen there remains the barium oxide which was originally taken, so that air may be again passed over it, and thus the preparation of oxygen from one and the same quantity of barium oxide may be repeated many times. Oxygen has been produced one hundred times from one mass of oxide by this method; all the necessary precautions being taken, as regards the temperature of the mass and the removal of moisture and carbonic acid from the air. Unless these precautions be taken, the mass of oxide soon spoils.

As oxygen may become of considerable technical use, from its capacity for giving high temperatures and intense light in the combustion of substances, its preparation directly from air by practical methods forms a problem whose solution many investigators continue to work at up to the present day. The most practical methods are those of Tessié du Motay and Kassner. The first is based on the fact that a mixture of equal weights of manganese peroxide and caustic soda at an incipient red heat (about 350°) absorbs oxygen from air, with the separation of water, according to the equation $MnO_2 + 2NaHO + O = Na_2MnO_4 + H_2O$. If superheated steam, at a temperature of about 450°, be then passed through the mixture, the manganese peroxide and caustic soda originally taken are regenerated, and the oxygen held by them is evolved, according to the reverse equation $Na_2MnO_4 + H_2O = MnO_2 + 2NaHO + O$. This mode of preparing oxygen may be repeated for an infinite number of times. The oxygen in combining liberates water, and steam, acting on the resultant substance, evolves oxygen. Hence all that is required for the preparation of oxygen by this method is fuel and the alternate cutting off the supply of air and steam. In Kassner's process (1891) a mixture of oxide of lead and lime (PbO + 2CaO) is heated to redness in the presence of air, oxygen is then absorbed and calcium plumbate, Ca_2PbO_4, formed. The latter is of a chocolate colour, and on further heating evolves oxygen and gives the original mixture PbO + 2CaO—that is, the phenomenon is essentially the same as in Boussingault's process (with BaO), but according to Le Chatelier (1893) the dissociation tension of the oxygen evolved from Ca_2PbO_4 is less than with BaO_2 at equal temperatures; for instance, at 940°, 112 mm. of mercury for the first, and for the latter 210 mm. at 720°, and 670 mm. at 790°, while for Ca_2PbO_4 this tension is only reached at 1,080°. However, in Kassner's process the oxygen is absorbed more rapidly, and the influence of the presence of moisture and CO_2 in the air is not so marked, so that this process, like that of Tessié du Motay, deserves consideration.

[8] Even the decomposition of manganese peroxide is reversible, and it may be re-obtained from that suboxide (or its salts), which is formed in the evolution of oxygen (Chap. XI., Note 6). The compounds of chromic acid containing the trioxide CrO_3 in evolving oxygen give chromium oxide, Cr_2O_3, but they re-form the salt of chromic acid when heated to redness in air with an alkali.

[9] We shall afterwards see that it is only substances like barium peroxide (which give hydrogen peroxide) which should be counted as true peroxides, and that MnO_2, PbO_2, &c., should be distinguished from them (they do not give hydrogen peroxide with acids), and therefore it is best to call them dioxides.

[9 bis]Peroxide of barium also gives oxygen at the ordinary temperature in the presence of the solutions of many substances in a higher degree of oxidation. In this respect we may mention that Kassner (1890) proposes to obtain oxygen for laboratory purposes by mixing BaO_2 with $FeK_3(CN)_6$ (red prussiate of potash, Chapter XXII.): the reaction proceeds with the evolution of oxygen even on the addition of a very small quantity of water. In order to ensure a gradual evolution of gas the author proposes to introduce both substances into the reaction, little by little, instead of all at once, which may be done with the following arrangement (Gavaloffsky): finely powdered peroxide of barium is placed in an ordinary flask and sufficient water is added to fill the flask one-third full. The cork closing the flask has three holes; (1) for the gas-conducting tube; (2) for a rod to stir

the BaO_2; and (3) for a glass rod terminating in a perforated glass vessel containing crystals of $FeK_3(CN)_6$. When it is desired to start the evolution of the oxygen, the vessel is lowered until it is immersed in the liquid in the flask, and the BaO_2 is stirred with the other rod. The reaction proceeds according to the equation, $BaO_2 + 2FeK_3(CN)_6 = FeK_4(CN)_6 + FeK_2Ba(CN)_6 + O_2$. The double salt, $FeBa_2(CN)_6$, crystallises out from the mother liquor. To understand the course of the reaction, it must be remembered BaO_2 is of a higher degree of oxidation, and that it parts with oxygen and gives the base BaO which enters into the complex salt $FeK_2Ba(CN)_6 = Fe(CN)_2 + 2KCN + Ba(CN)_2$, and this latter $= BaO + 2HCN - H_2O$. Moreover, $FeK_3(CN)_6$ contains the salt $Fe_2(CN)_6$ which also corresponds to the higher degree of oxidation of iron, Fe_2O_3, whilst after the reaction a salt is obtained which contains $Fe(CN)_2$, and corresponds to the lower degree of oxidation, FeO, so that (in the presence of water) oxygen is also set free on this side also, *i.e.* the reaction gives lower degrees of oxidation and oxygen.

[10] Scheele, in 1785, discovered the method of obtaining oxygen by treating manganese peroxide with sulphuric acid.

[11] All acids rich in oxygen, and especially those whose elements form lower oxides, evolve oxygen either directly at the ordinary temperature (for instance, ferric acid), or on heating (nitric, manganic, chromic, chloric, and others), or if basic lower oxides are formed from them, by heating with sulphuric acid. Thus the salts of chromic acid (for example, potassium dichromate, $K_2Cr_2O_7$) give oxygen with sulphuric acid; first potassium sulphate, K_2SO_4, is formed, and then the chromic acid set free gives a sulphuric acid salt of the lower oxide, Cr_2O_3.

[12] This reaction is not reversible, and is exothermal—that is, it does not absorb heat, but, on the contrary, evolves 9,713 calories per molecular weight $KClO_3$, equal to 122 parts of salt (according to the determination of Thomsen, who burnt hydrogen in a calorimeter either alone or with a definite quantity of potassium chlorate mixed with oxide of iron). It does not proceed at once, but first forms perchlorate, $KClO_4$ (*see* Chlorine and Potassium). It is to be remarked that potassium chloride melts at 766°, potassium chlorate at 359°, and potassium perchlorate at 610°. (Concerning the decomposition of $KClO_3$, *see* Chapter II., Note 47.)

[13] The peroxide does not evolve oxygen in this case. It may be replaced by many oxides—for instance, by oxide of iron. It is necessary to take the precaution that no combustible substances (such as bits of paper, splinters, sulphur, &c.) fall into the mixture, as they might cause an explosion.

[14] The decomposition of a mixture of fused and well-crushed potassium chlorate with powdered manganese peroxide proceeds at so low a temperature (the salt does not melt) that it may be effected in an ordinary glass flask. The apparatus is arranged in the same manner as in the decomposition of mercury oxide (Introduction), or as shown in the last drawing. As the reaction is exothermal, the decomposition of potassium chlorate with the formation of oxygen may probably be accomplished, under certain conditions (for example, under contact action), at very low temperatures. Substances mixed with the potassium chlorate probably act partially in this manner.

[15] Many other salts evolve oxygen by heat, like potassium chlorate, but they only part with it either at a very high temperature (for instance, common nitre) or else are unsuited for use on account of their cost (potassium manganate), or evolve impure oxygen at a high temperature (zinc sulphate at a red heat gives a mixture of sulphurous anhydride and oxygen), and are not therefore used in practice.

[16] Such is, at present, the only possible method of explaining the phenomenon of contact action. In many cases, such as the present one, it is supported by observations based on facts. Thus, for instance, it is known, as regards oxygen, that often two substances rich in oxygen retain it so long as they are separate, but directly they come into contact free oxygen is evolved from both of them. Thus, an aqueous solution of hydrogen peroxide (containing twice as much oxygen as water) acts in this manner on silver oxide (containing silver and oxygen). This reaction takes place at the ordinary temperature, and the oxygen is evolved from both compounds. To this class of phenomena may be also referred the fact that a mixture of barium peroxide and potassium manganate with water and sulphuric acid evolves oxygen at the ordinary temperature (Note 9). It would seem that the essence of phenomena of this kind is entirely and purely a property of contact; the distribution of the atoms is changed by contact, and if the equilibrium be unstable it is destroyed. This is more especially evident in the case of those substances which change exothermally—that is, for those reactions which are accompanied by an evolution of heat. The decomposition $CaCl_2O_2 = CaCl_2 + O_2$ belongs to this class (like the decomposition of potassium chlorate).

[17] Generally a solution of bleaching powder is alkaline (contains free lime), and therefore, a solution of cobalt chloride is added directly to it, by which means the oxide of cobalt required for the reaction is formed.

[18] It must be remarked that in all the reactions above mentioned the formation of oxygen may be prevented by the admixture of substances capable of combining with it—for example, charcoal, many carbon

(organic) compounds, sulphur, phosphorus, and various lower oxidation products, &c. These substances absorb the oxygen evolved, combine with it, and a compound containing oxygen is formed. Thus, if a mixture of potassium chlorate and charcoal be heated, no oxygen is obtained, but an explosion takes place from the rapid formation of gases resulting from the combination of the oxygen of the potassium chlorate with the charcoal and the evolution of gaseous CO_2.

The oxygen obtained by any of the above-described methods is rarely pure. It generally contains aqueous vapour, carbonic anhydride, and very often small traces of chlorine. The oxygen may be freed from these impurities by passing it through a solution of caustic potash, and by drying it. If the potassium chlorate be dry and pure, it gives almost pure oxygen. However, if the oxygen be required for respiration in cases of sickness, it should be washed by passing it through a solution of caustic alkali and through water. The best way to obtain pure oxygen directly is to take potassium perchlorate ($KClO_4$), which can be well purified and then evolves pure oxygen on heating.

[19] With regard to the absolute boiling point, critical pressure, and the critical state in general, *see* Chapter II., Notes 29 and 34.

[20] Judging from what has been said in Note 34 of the last chapter, and also from the results of direct observation, it is evident that all substances in a critical state have a large coefficient of expansion, and are very compressible.

[21] As water consists of 1 volume of oxygen and 2 volumes of hydrogen, and contains 16 parts by weight of oxygen per 2 parts by weight of hydrogen, it therefore follows directly that oxygen is 16 times denser than hydrogen. Conversely, the composition of water by weight may be deduced from the densities of hydrogen and oxygen, and the volumetric composition of water. This method of mutual and reciprocal correction strengthens the practical data of the exact sciences, whose conclusions require the greatest possible exactitude and variety of corrections.

It must he observed that the specific heat of oxygen at constant pressure is 0·2175, consequently it is to the specific heat of hydrogen (3·409) as 1 is to 15·6. Hence, the specific heats are inversely proportional to the weights of equal volumes. This signifies that equal volumes of both gases have (nearly) equal specific heats—that is, they require an equal quantity of heat for raising their temperature by 1°. We shall afterwards consider the specific heat of different substances more fully in Chap. XIV.

Oxygen, like the majority of difficultly-liquefiable gases, is but slightly soluble in water and other liquids. The solubility is given in Note 30, Chap.

I. From this it is evident that water standing in air must absorb—*i.e.* dissolve—oxygen. This oxygen serves for the respiration of fishes. Fishes cannot exist in boiled water, because it does not contain the oxygen necessary for their respiration (*see* Chap. I.)

[22] Certain substances (with which we shall afterwards become acquainted), however, ignite spontaneously in air; for example, impure phosphuretted hydrogen, silicon hydride, zinc ethyl, and pyrophorus (very finely divided iron, &c.)

[23] If so little heat is evolved that the adjacent parts are not heated to the temperature of combustion, then combustion will cease.

[24] The phosphorus must be dry; it is usually kept in water, as it oxidises in air. It should be cut under water, as otherwise the freshly-cut surface oxidises. It must be dried carefully and quickly by wrapping it in blotting-paper. If damp, it splutters on burning. A small piece should be taken, as otherwise the iron spoon will melt. In this and the other experiments on combustion, water should be poured over the bottom of the vessel containing the oxygen, to prevent it from cracking. The cork closing the vessel should not fit tightly, in order to allow for the expansion of the gas due to the heat of the combustion.

[25] An iron cup will melt with sodium in oxygen.

[26] In order to rapidly heat the lime crucible containing the sodium, it is heated in the flame of a blowpipe described in Chap. VIII.

[27] In order to burn a watch spring, a piece of tinder (or paper soaked in a solution of nitre, and dried) is attached to one end. The tinder is lighted, and the spring is then plunged into the oxygen. The burning tinder heats the end of the spring, the heated part burns, and in so doing heats the further portions of the spring, which then burns completely if sufficient oxygen be present.

[28] The sparks of rust are produced, owing to the fact that the volume of the oxide of iron is nearly twice that of the volume of the iron, and as the heat evolved is not sufficient to entirely melt the oxide or the iron, the particles must be torn off and fly about. Similar sparks are formed in the combustion of iron, in other cases also. We saw the combustion of iron filings in the Introduction. In the welding of iron small iron splinters fly off in all directions and burn in the air, as is seen from the fact that whilst flying through the air they remain red hot, and also because, on cooling, they are seen to be no longer iron, but a compound of it with oxygen. The same thing takes place when the hammer of a gun strikes against the flint. Small scales of steel are heated by the friction, and glow and burn in the air. The combustion of iron is still better seen by taking it as a very fine

powder, such as is obtained by the decomposition of certain of its compounds—for instance, by heating Prussian blue, or by the reduction of its compounds with oxygen by hydrogen; when this fine powder is strewn in air, it burns by itself, even without being previously heated (it forms a pyrophorus). This obviously depends on the fact that the powder of iron presents a larger surface of contact with air than an equal weight in a compact form.

[29] The experiment may be conducted without the wires, if the hydrogen be lighted in the orifice of an inverted cylinder, and at the same time the cylinder be brought over the end of a gas-conducting tube connected with a gas-holder containing oxygen. Thomsen's method may be adopted for a lecture experiment. Two glass tubes, with platinum ends, are passed through orifices, about 1–1½ centimetre apart, in a cork. One tube is connected with a gas-holder containing oxygen, and the other with a gas-holder full of hydrogen. Having turned on the gases, the hydrogen is lighted, and a common lamp glass, tapering towards the top, is placed over the cork. The hydrogen continues to burn inside the lamp glass, at the expense of the oxygen. If the current of oxygen be then decreased little by little, a point is reached when, owing to the insufficient supply of oxygen, the flame of the hydrogen increases in size, disappears for several moments, and then reappears at the tube supplying the oxygen. If the flow of oxygen be again increased, the flame reappears at the hydrogen tube. Thus the flame may be made to appear at one or the other tube at will, only the increase or decrease of the current of gas must take place by degrees and not suddenly. Further, air may be taken instead of oxygen, and ordinary coal-gas instead of hydrogen, and it will then be shown how air burns in an atmosphere of coal-gas, and it can easily be proved that the lamp glass is full of a gas combustible in air, because it may be lighted at the top.

[29 bis] In fact, instead of a spark a fine wire may be taken, and an electric current passed through it to bring it to a state of incandescence; in this case there will be no sparks, but the gases will inflame if the wire be fine enough to become red hot by the passage of the current.

[30] Now, a great many other different forms of apparatus, sometimes designed for special purposes, are employed in the laboratory for the investigation of gases. Detailed descriptions of the methods of gas analysis, and of the apparatus employed, must be looked for in works on analytical and applied chemistry.

[31] They must be sealed into the tube in such a manner as to leave no aperture between them and the glass. In order to test this, the eudiometer is filled with mercury, and its open end inverted into mercury. If there be the

smallest orifice at the wires, the external air will enter into the cylinder and the mercury will fall, although not rapidly if the orifice be very fine.

[32]The eudiometer is used for determining the composition of combustible gases. A detailed account of *gas analysis* would be out of place in this work (*see* Note 30), but, as an example, we will give a short description of the determination of the composition of water by the eudiometer.

Pure and dry oxygen is first introduced into the eudiometer. When the eudiometer and the gas in it acquire the temperature of the surrounding atmosphere—which is recognised by the fact of the meniscus of the mercury not altering its position during a long period of time—then the heights at which the mercury stands in the eudiometer and in the bath are observed. The difference (in millimetres) gives the height of the column of mercury in the eudiometer. It must be reduced to the height at which the mercury would stand at 0° and deducted from the atmospheric pressure, in order to find the pressure under which the oxygen is measured (*see* Chap. I. Note 29). The height of the mercury also shows the volume of the oxygen. The temperature of the surrounding atmosphere and the height of the barometric column must also be observed, in order to know the temperature of the oxygen and the atmospheric pressure. When the volume of the oxygen has been measured, pure and dry hydrogen is introduced into the eudiometer, and the volume of the gases in the eudiometer again measured. They are then exploded. This is done by a Leyden jar, whose outer coating is connected by a chain with one wire, so that a spark passes when the other wire, fused into the eudiometer, is touched by the terminal of the jar. Or else an electrophorus is used, or, better still, a Ruhmkorff's coil, which has the advantage of working equally well in damp or dry air, whilst a Leyden jar or electrical machine does not act in damp weather. Further, it is necessary to close the lower orifice of the eudiometer before the explosion (for this purpose the eudiometer, which is fixed in a stand, is firmly pressed down from above on to a piece of india-rubber placed at the bottom of the bath), as otherwise the mercury and gas would be thrown out of the apparatus by the explosion. It must also be remarked that to ensure complete combustion the proportion between the volumes of oxygen and hydrogen must not exceed twelve of hydrogen to one volume of oxygen, or fifteen volumes of oxygen to one volume of hydrogen, because no explosion will take place if one of the gases be in great excess. It is best to take a mixture of one volume of hydrogen with several volumes of oxygen. The combustion will then be complete. It is evident that water is formed, and that the volume (or tension) is diminished, so that on opening the end of the eudiometer the mercury will rise in it. But the tension of the aqueous vapour is now added to the tension of the gas remaining after the explosion. This must be taken into account (Chap. I. Note 1). If but little gas remain, the water which is formed will be sufficient for its saturation with aqueous vapour. This may be learnt from the fact that drops of water are visible on the sides of the eudiometer after the mercury has risen in it. If there be none, a certain quantity of water must be introduced into the eudiometer. Then the number of millimetres expressing the pressure of the vapour corresponding with the temperature of the experiment must be subtracted from the atmospheric pressure at which the remaining gas is measured, otherwise the result will be inaccurate (Chap. I. Note 1).

This is essentially the method of the determination of the composition of water which was made for the first time by Gay-Lussac and Humboldt with sufficient accuracy. Their determinations led them to the conclusion that water consists of two volumes of hydrogen (more exactly 2·003, Le Duc 1892), and one volume of oxygen. Every time they took a greater quantity of oxygen, the gas remaining after the explosion was oxygen. When they took an excess of hydrogen, the remaining gas was hydrogen; and when the oxygen and hydrogen were taken in exactly the above proportion, neither one nor the other remained. The composition of water was thus definitely confirmed.

[33] Concerning this application of the eudiometer, see the chapter on Nitrogen. It may be mentioned as illustrating the various uses of the eudiometer that Prof. Timeraseeff employed microscopically small eudiometers to analyse the bubbles of gas given off from the leaves of plants.

[34] Thus ¼ volume of carbonic oxide, an equal volume of marsh gas, two volumes of hydrogen chloride or of ammonia, and six volumes of nitrogen or twelve volumes of air added to one volume of detonating gas, prevent its explosion.

[35] If the compression be brought about slowly, so that the heat evolved succeeds in passing to the surrounding space, then the combination of the oxygen and hydrogen does not take place, even when the mixture is compressed by 150 times; for the gases are not heated. If paper soaked with a solution of platinum (in aqua regia) and sal ammoniac be burnt, then the ash obtained contains very finely-divided platinum, and in this form it is best fitted for igniting hydrogen and detonating gas. Platinum wire requires to be heated, but platinum in so finely divided a state as it occurs in this ash inflames hydrogen, even at -20°. Many other metals, such as palladium (175°), iridium, and gold, act with a slight rise of temperature, like platinum; but mercury, at its boiling point, does not inflame detonating gas, although the slow formation of water then begins

at 305°. All data of this kind show that the explosion of detonating gas presents one of the many cases of contact phenomena. This conclusion is further confirmed by the researches of V. Meyer (1892). He showed that only a very slow formation of steam begins at 448°, and that it only proceeds more rapidly at 518°. The temperature of the explosion of detonating gas, according to the same author, varies according as to whether the explosion is produced in open vessels or in closed tubes. In the first case the temperature of explosion lies between 530°–606°, and in the second between 630°–730°. In general it may be remarked that the temperature of explosion of gaseous mixtures is always lower in closed vessels than when the detonating mixture flows freely through tubes. According to Freyer and V. Meyer, the following gases when mixed with the requisite amount of oxygen explode at the following temperatures:

	When flowing freely	In closed vessels
H_2	630°–730°	530°–606°
CH_4	650°–730°	606°–650°
C_2H_6	606°–650°	530°–606°
C_2H_4	606°–650°	530°–606°
CO	650°–730°	650°–730°
H_2S	315°–320°	250°–270°
$H_2 + Cl_2$	430°–440°	240°–270°

The velocity of the transmission of explosion in gaseous mixtures is as characteristic a quantity for gaseous systems as the velocity of the transmission of sound. Berthelot showed that this velocity depends neither upon the pressure nor upon the size of the tubes in which the gaseous mixture is contained, nor upon the material out of which the tube is made. Dixon (1891) determined the magnitude of these velocities for various mixtures, and his results proved very near to those previously given by Berthelot. For comparison we give the velocities expressed in metres per second:

	Dixon	Berthelot
$H_2 + O$	2,821	2,810
$H_2 + N_2O$	2,305	2,284

CH$_4$ + 4O	2,322	2,287
C$_2$H$_2$ + 6O	2,364	2,210
C$_2$H$_2$ + 5O	2,391	2,482
C$_2$H$_2$ + 4O	2,321	2,195

The addition of oxygen to detonating gas lowers the velocity of the transmission of explosion almost as much as the introduction of nitrogen. An excess of hydrogen on the contrary raises the velocity of transmission. It is remarked that the explosion of mixtures of oxygen with marsh gas, ethylene and cyanogen is transmitted more quickly if the oxygen be taken in such a proportion that the carbon should burn to oxide of carbon, *i.e.* the velocity of the explosion is less if the oxygen be taken in sufficient quantity to form carbonic anhydride. Observations upon liquid and solid explosives (Berthelot) show that in this case the velocity of transmission of explosion is dependent upon the material of the tube. Thus the explosion of liquid nitro-methyl ether in glass tubes travels at the rate (in dependence upon the diam., from 1 mm.–45 mm.) of from 1,890 to 2,482 metres, and in tubes of Britannia metal (3 mm. in diam) at the rate of 1,230 metres. The harder the tube the greater the velocity of transmission of explosion. The following are the velocities for certain bodies:

metres

Nitro-glycerine 1,300

Dynamite 2,500

Nitro-mannite 7,700

Picric acid 6,500

In conclusion we may add that Mallard and Le Chatelier (1882) observed that in the explosion of a mixture of 1 volume of detonating gas with n volumes of an inert gas, the pressure is approximately equal to $9 \cdot 2 - 0 \cdot 9n$ atmospheres.

[36] From the very commencement of the promulgation of the idea of dissociation, it might have been imagined that reversible reactions of combination (the formation of H$_2$ and O belongs to this number) commence at the same temperature as that at which dissociation begins. And in many cases this is so, but not always, as may be seen from the facts (1) that at 450–560°, when detonating gas explodes, the density of aqueous vapour not only does not vary (and it hardly varies at higher temperatures, probably because the amount of the products of dissociation is small), but

there are not, as far as is yet known, any traces of dissociation; (2) that under the influence of contact the temperature at which combination takes place falls even to the ordinary temperature, when water and similar compounds naturally are not dissociated and, judging from the data communicated by D. P. Konovaloff (Introduction, Note 39) and others, it is impossible to escape the phenomena of contact; all vessels, whether of metal or glass, show the same influence as spongy platinum, although to a much less degree. The phenomena of contact, judging from a review of the data referring to it, must be especially sensitive in reactions which are powerfully exothermal, and the explosion of detonating gas is of this kind.

[37]

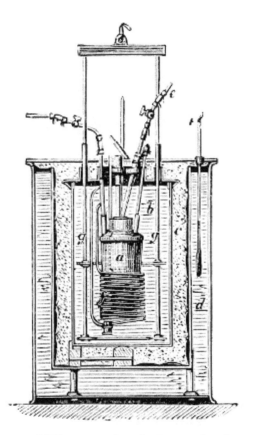

FIG. 33.—Favre and Silbermann's calorimeter for determining the heat evolved in combustion.

The amount of heat evolved in the combustion of a known weight (for instance, 1 gram) of a given substance is determined by the rise in temperature of water, to which the whole of the heat evolved in the combustion is transmitted. A *calorimeter*, for example that shown in fig. 33, is employed for this purpose. It consists of a thin (in order that it may absorb less heat), polished (that it should transmit a minimum of heat) metallic vessel, surrounded by down (*c*), or some other bad conductor of heat, and an outer metallic vessel. This is necessary in order that the least possible amount of heat should be lost from the vessels; nevertheless, there is always a certain loss, whose magnitude is determined by preliminary experiment (by taking warm water, and determining its fall in temperature after a definite period of time) as a correction for the results of observations. The water to which the heat of the burning substance is transmitted is poured into the vessel. The stirrer *g* allows of all the layers of water being brought to the same temperature, and the thermometer serves for the determination of the temperature of the water. The heat evolved passes, naturally, not to the water only, but to all the parts of the apparatus. The quantity of water corresponding to the whole amount of those objects (the vessels, tubes, &c.) to which the heat is transmitted is previously determined, and in this manner another most important correction is made in the calorimetric determinations. The combustion itself is carried on in the vessel *a*. The ignited substance is introduced through the tube at the top, which closes tightly. In fig. 33 the apparatus is arranged for the combustion of a gas, introduced by a tube. The oxygen required for the combustion is led into *a* by the tube *e*, and the products of combustion either remain in the vessel *a* (if liquid or solid), or escape by the tube *f* into an apparatus in which their quantity and properties can easily be determined. Thus the heat evolved in combustion passes to the walls of the vessel *a*, and to the gases which are formed in it, and these transmit it to the water of the calorimeter.

[38] This quantity of heat corresponds with the formation of liquid water at the ordinary temperature from detonating gas at the same temperature. If the water be as vapour the heat evolved = 58 major calories; if as ice = 70·4 major calories. A portion of this heat is due to the fact that 2 vols. of hydrogen and 1 vol. of oxygen give 2 vols. of aqueous vapour—that is to say, contraction ensues—and this evolves heat. This quantity of heat may be calculated, but it cannot be said how much is expended in the separation of the atoms of oxygen from each other, and, therefore, strictly speaking, we do not know the quantity of heat which is evolved in the reaction alone, although the number of units of heat evolved in the combustion of detonating gas is accurately known.

The construction of the calorimeter and even the method of determination vary considerably in different cases. Since the beginning of the nineties, a large number of determinations of the heat of combustion have been conducted in closed bombs containing compressed oxygen. The greatest number of calorimetric determinations were made by Berthelot and Thomsen. They are given in their works *Essai de mécanique chimique fondée sur la thermochimie*, by M. Berthelot, 1879 (2 vols.), and *thermochemische Untersuchungen*, by J. Thomsen, 1886 (4 vols.) The most important methods of recent thermochemistry, and all the trustworthy results of experiment, are given in Prof. P. F. Louginin's *Description of the Different Modes of Determining the Heat of Combustion of Organic Compounds*, Moscow, 1894. The student must refer to works on theoretical and physical chemistry for a description of the elements and methods of *thermochemistry*, into the details of which it is impossible to enter in this work. One of the originators of thermochemistry, Hess, was a member of the St. Petersburg Academy of Sciences. Since 1870 a large amount of research has been carried out in this province of chemistry, especially in France and Germany, after the investigations of the French Academician, Berthelot, and Professor Thomsen, of Copenhagen. Among Russians, Beketoff, Louginin, Cheltzoff, Chroustchoff, and others are known by their thermochemical researches. The present epoch of thermochemistry must be considered rather as a collective one, wherein the material of facts is amassed, and the first consequences arising from them are noticed. In my opinion two essential circumstances prevent the possibility of deducing any exact consequences, of importance to chemical mechanics, from the immense store of thermochemical data already collected: (1) The majority of the determinations are conducted in weak aqueous solutions, and, the heat of solution being known, are referred to the substances in solution; yet there is much (Chapter I.) which leads to the conclusion that in solution water does not play the simple part of a diluting medium, but of itself acts independently in a chemical sense on the substance dissolved. (2) Physical and mechanical changes (decrease of volume, diffusion, and others) invariably proceed side by side with chemical changes, and for the present it is impossible, in a number of cases, to distinguish the thermal effect of the one and the other kind of change. It is evident that the one kind of change (chemical) is essentially inseparable and incomprehensible without the other (mechanical and physical); and therefore it seems to me that thermochemical data will only acquire their true meaning when the connection between the phenomena of both kinds (on the one hand chemical and atomic, and on the other hand mechanical and molecular or between entire masses) is explained more clearly and fully than is at present the case. As there is no doubt that the simple mechanical contact, or the action of heat alone, on substances sometimes causes an evident and always a latent (incipient) chemical change—that is, a different distribution or motion of the atoms in the molecules—it follows that purely chemical phenomena are inseparable from physical and mechanical phenomena. A mechanical change may be imagined without a physical change, and a physical without a chemical change, but it is impossible to imagine a chemical change without a physical and mechanical one, for without the latter we should not be able to recognise the former, and it is by their means that we are enabled to do so.

[39] The flame, or locality where the combustion of gases and vapours takes place, is a complex phenomenon, 'an entire factory,' as Faraday says, and therefore we will consider flame in some detail in one of the following notes.

[40] If 34,500 units of heat are evolved in the combustion of 1 part of hydrogen, and this heat is transmitted to the resulting 9 parts by weight of aqueous vapour, then we find that, taking the specific heat of the latter as 0·475, each unit of heat raises the temperature of 1 part by weight of aqueous vapour $2°·1$ and 9 parts by weight $(2·1 \div 9)$ $0°·23$; hence the 34,500 units of heat raise its temperature 7,935°. If detonating gas is converted into water in a closed space, then the aqueous vapour formed cannot expand, and therefore, in calculating the temperature of combustion, the specific heat at a constant volume must be taken into consideration; for aqueous vapour it is 0·36. This figure gives a still higher temperature for the flame. In reality it is much lower, but the results given by different observers are very contradictory (from 1,700° to 2,400°), the discrepancies depending on the fact that flames of different sizes are cooled by radiation to a different degree, but mainly on the fact that the methods and apparatus (pyrometers) for the determination of high temperatures, although they enable relative changes of temperature to be judged, are of little use for determining their absolute magnitude. By taking the temperature of the flame of detonating gas as 2,000°, I give, I think, the average of the most trustworthy determinations and calculations based upon the determination of the variation of the specific heat of aqueous vapour and other gases (*see* Chapter XLI.)

[41] It is evident that not only hydrogen, but every other combustible gas, will give an explosive mixture with oxygen. For this reason coal-gas mixed with air explodes when the mixture is ignited. The pressure obtained in the explosions serves as the *motive power of gas engines*. In this case advantage is taken, not only of the pressure produced by the explosion, but also of that contraction which takes place after the explosion. On this is based the construction of several motors, of which Lenoir's was formerly, and Otto's is now, the best known. The explosion is usually produced by coal-gas and air, but of late the vapours of combustible liquids (kerosene, benzene) are also being employed in place of gas (Chapter IX.) In Lenoir's engine a mixture of coal-gas and air is ignited by means of sparks from a Ruhmkorff's coil, but in the most recent machines the gases are ignited by the direct action of a gas jet, or by contact with the hot walls of a side tube.

[41 bis] Let us consider as an example the combustion of sulphur in air and in oxygen. If 1 gram of sulphur burns in air or oxygen it evolves in either case 2250 units of heat—*i.e.* evolves sufficient heat for heating 2,250 grams of water 1° C. This heat is first of all transmitted to the sulphurous anhydride, SO_2, formed by the combination of sulphur with oxygen. In its combustion 1 gram of sulphur forms 2 grams of sulphurous anhydride—*i.e.* the sulphur combines with 1 gram of oxygen. In order that 1 gram of sulphur should have access to 1 gram of oxygen in air, it is necessary that 3·4 grams of nitrogen should simultaneously reach the sulphur, because air contains seventy-seven parts of nitrogen (by weight) per twenty-three parts of oxygen. Thus in the combustion of 1 gram of sulphur, the 2,250 units of heat are transmitted to 2 grams of sulphurous oxide and to at least 3·4 grams of nitrogen. As 0·155 unit of heat is required to raise 1 gram of sulphurous anhydride 1° C., therefore 2 grams require 0·31 unit. So also 3·4 grams of nitrogen require 3·4 × 0·244 or 0·83 unit of heat, and therefore in order to raise both gases 1° C. 0·31 + 0·83 or 1·14 unit of heat is required; but as the combustion of the sulphur evolves 2,250 units of heat, therefore the gases might be heated (if their specific heats remained constant) to 2250 $\boxed{1·14}$ or 1,974° C. That is, the maximum possible temperature of the flame of the sulphur burning in air will be 1,974° C. In the combustion of the sulphur in oxygen the heat evolved (2,250 units) can only pass to the 2 grams of sulphurous anhydride, and therefore the highest possible temperature of the flame of the sulphur in oxygen will be = 2250 $\boxed{0·31}$ or 7258°. In the same manner it may be calculated that the temperature of charcoal burning in air cannot exceed 2,700°, while in oxygen it may attain 10,100° C. For this reason the temperature in oxygen will always be higher than in air, although (judging from what has been said respecting detonating gas) neither one temperature nor the other will ever approximate to the theoretical amount.

[42] Faraday proved this by a very convincing experiment on a candle flame. If one arm of a bent glass tube be placed in a candle flame above the wick in the dark portion of the flame, then the products of the partial combustion of the stearin will pass up the tube, condense in the other arm, and collect in a flask placed under it (fig. 35) as heavy white fumes which burn when lighted. If the tube be raised into the upper luminous portion of the flame, then a dense black smoke which will not inflame accumulates in the flask. Lastly, if the tube be let down until it touches the wick, then little but stearic acid condenses in the flask.

[43] All transparent substances which transmit light with great ease (that is, which absorb but little light) are but little luminous when heated; so also substances which absorb but few heat rays, when heated transmit few rays of heat.

[44] There is, however, no doubt but that very heavy dense vapours or gases under pressure (according to the experiments of Frankland) are luminous when heated, because, as they become denser they approach a liquid or solid state. Thus detonating gas when exploded under pressure gives a brilliant light.

[45] If hydrogen gas be passed through a volatile liquid hydrocarbon— for instance, through benzene (the benzene may be poured directly into the vessel in which hydrogen is generated)—then its vapour burns with the hydrogen and gives a very bright flame, because the resultant particles of carbon (soot) become incandescent. Benzene, or platinum gauze, introduced into a hydrogen flame may be employed for illuminating purposes.

[46] In *flames* the separate parts may be distinguished with more or less distinctness. That portion of the flame whither the combustible vapours or gases flow, is not luminous because its temperature is still too low for the process of combustion to take place in it. This is the space which in a candle surrounds the wick, or in a gas jet is immediately above the orifice from which the gas escapes. In a candle the combustible vapours and gases which are formed by the action of heat on the melted tallow or stearin rise in the wick, and are heated by the high temperature of the flame. By the action of the heat, the solid or liquid substance is here, as in other cases, decomposed, forming products of dry distillation. These products occur in the central portion of the flame of a candle. The air travels to it from the outside, and is not able to intermix at once with the vapours and gases in all parts of the flame equally; consequently, in the outer portion of the flame the amount of oxygen will be greater than in the interior portions. But, owing to diffusion, the oxygen, of course mixed with nitrogen, flowing towards the combustible substance, does finally penetrate to the interior of the flame (when the combustion takes place in ordinary air). The combustible vapours and gases combine with this oxygen, evolve a considerable amount of heat, and bring about that state of incandescence which is so necessary both for keeping up the combustion and also for the uses to which the flame is applied. Passing from the colder envelope of air through the interior of the flame, to the source of the combustible vapours (for instance, the wick), we evidently first traverse layers of higher and higher temperature, and then portions which are less and less hot, in which the combustion is less complete, owing to the limited supply of oxygen.

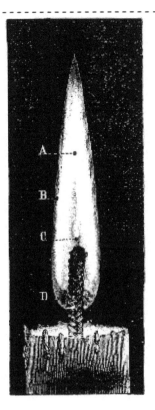

FIG. 36.—In the candle flame the portion C contains the vapours and products of decomposition; in the bright zone A the combustion has commenced, and particles of carbon are emitted; and in the pale zone B the combustion is completed.

Thus unburnt products of the decomposition of organic substances occur in the interior of the flame. But there is always free hydrogen in the interior of the flame, even when oxygen is introduced there, or when a mixture of hydrogen and oxygen burns, because the temperature evolved in the combustion of hydrogen or the carbon of organic matter is so high that the products of combustion are themselves partially decomposed—that is, dissociated—at this temperature. Hence, in a flame a portion of the hydrogen and of the oxygen which might combine with the combustible substances must always be present in a free state. If a hydrocarbon burns, and we imagine that a portion of the hydrogen is in a free state, then a portion of the carbon must also occur in the same form in the flame, because, other conditions being unchanged, carbon burns after hydrogen, and this is actually observed in the combustion of various hydrocarbons. Charcoal, or the soot of a common flame, arises from the dissociation of organic substances contained in the flame. The majority of hydrocarbons, especially those containing much carbon—for instance, naphthalene—burn, even in oxygen, with separation of soot. In that portion of the flame where the hydrogen burns the carbon remains unburnt, or at least partly so. It is this free carbon which causes the brilliancy of the flame. That the interior of the flame contains a mixture which is still capable of combustion may be proved by the following experiment: A portion of the gases may be withdrawn by an aspirator from the central portion of the flame of carbonic oxide, which is combustible in air. For this purpose Deville passed water through a metallic tube having a fine lateral orifice, which is placed in the flame. As the water flows along the tube portions of the gases of the flame enter, and, passing along the tube alternately with cylinders of water, are carried away into an apparatus where they can be investigated. It appears that all portions of the flame obtained by the combustion of a mixture of carbonic oxide and oxygen contain a portion of this mixture still unburnt. The researches of Deville and Bunsen showed that in the explosion of a mixture of hydrogen and of carbonic oxide with oxygen in a closed space, complete combustion does not ever take place immediately. If two volumes of hydrogen and one volume of oxygen be confined in a closed space, then on explosion the pressure does not attain that magnitude which it would were there immediate and complete combustion. It may be calculated that the pressure should attain twenty-six atmospheres. In reality, it does not exceed nine and a half atmospheres.

Hence the admixture of the products of combustion with an explosive mixture prevents the combustion of the remaining mass, although capable of burning. The admixture of carbonic anhydride prevents carbonic oxide from burning. The presence of any other foreign gas interferes in the same manner. This shows that every portion of a flame must contain combustible, burning, and already burnt substances—*i.e.* oxygen, carbon, carbonic oxide, hydrogen, hydrocarbons, carbonic anhydride, and water. Consequently, *it is impossible to attain instantaneous complete combustion*, and this is one of the reasons of the phenomenon of flame. A certain space is required, and the temperature must be unequal in different parts of it. In this space different quantities of the component parts are successively subjected to combustion, or are cooled under the influence of adjacent objects, and combustion only ends where the flame ends. If the combustion could be concentrated at one spot, then the temperature would be incomparably higher than it is under the actual circumstances.

The various regions of the flame have formed the frequent subject of experimental research, and the experiments conducted by Smithells and Ingle (1892) are particularly instructive; they show that the reducing (interior) and oxidising (exterior) portions of the flame of a burning gas may be divided by taking a Bunsen burner and surrounding the flame of the gas burnt in it, by another wider tube (without the access of air to the annular space or allowing only a small current of air to pass), when a gaseous mixture, containing oxide of carbon and capable of further combustion, will issue from this enveloping tube, so that a second flame, corresponding to the exterior (oxidising) portion of an ordinary flame, may be obtained above the enveloping tube. This division of the flame into two portions is particularly clear when cyanogen C_2N_2 is burnt, because the interior portion (where CO is chiefly formed according to the equation $C_2N_2 + O_2 = 2CO + N_2$, but a portion of the nitrogen is oxidised) is of a rose colour, while the exterior portion (where the CO burns into CO_2 at the expense of a fresh quantity of oxygen and of the oxides of nitrogen proceeding from the interior portions) is of a bluish-grey colour.

[47] Cotton waste (used in factories for cleaning machines from lubricating oil) soaked in oil and lying in heaps is self-combustible, being oxidised by the air.

[48] When it is desired to preserve a supply of vegetable and animal food, the access of the oxygen of the atmosphere (and also of the germs of organisms present in the air) is often prevented. With this object articles of food are often kept in hermetically closed vessels, from which the air has been withdrawn; vegetables are dried and soldered up while hot in tin boxes; sardines are immersed in oil, &c. The removal of water from substances is also sometimes resorted to with the same object (the drying of hay, corn, fruits), as also is saturation with substances which absorb oxygen (such as sulphurous anhydride), or which hinder the growth of organisms forming the first cause of putrefaction, as in processes of smoking, embalming, and in the keeping of fishes and other animal specimens in spirit, &c.

[49] It must be remarked that certain elements form oxides of all three kinds—*i.e.* indifferent, basic, and acid; for example, manganese forms manganous oxide, manganic oxide, peroxide of manganese, red oxide of manganese, and manganic anhydride, although some of them are not known in a free state but only in combination. The basic oxides contain less oxygen than the peroxides, and the peroxides less than the acid anhydrides. Thus they must be placed in the following general normal order with respect to the amount of oxygen entering into their composition—(1) basic oxides, suboxides, and oxides; (2) peroxides; (3) acid anhydrides. The majority of elements, however, do not give all three kinds of oxides, some giving only one degree of oxidation. It must further be remarked that there are oxides formed by the combination of acid anhydrides with basic oxides, or, in general, of oxides with oxides. For every oxide having a higher and a lower degree of oxidation, it might be

said that the intermediate oxide was formed by the combination of the higher with the lower oxide. But this is not true in all cases—for instance, when the oxide under consideration forms a whole series of independent compounds—for oxides which are really formed by the combination of two other oxides do not give such independent compounds, but in many cases decompose into the higher and lower oxides.

[50] Blotting or unsized paper, soaked in a solution of litmus, is usually employed for detecting the presence of acids. This paper is cut into strips, and is called *test paper*; when dipped into acid it immediately turns red. This is a most sensitive reaction, and may be employed for testing for the smallest traces of acids. If 10,000 parts by weight of water be mixed with 1 part of sulphuric acid, the coloration is distinct, and it is even perceptible on the addition of ten times more water. Certain precautions must, however, be taken in the preparation of such very sensitive litmus paper. Litmus is sold in lumps. Take, say, 100 grams of it; powder it, and add it to cold pure water in a flask; shake and decant the water. Repeat this three times. This is done to wash away easily-soluble impurities, especially alkalis. Transfer the washed litmus (it is washed with absolute alcohol to remove the non-sensitive reddish colouring matter) to a flask, and pour in 600 c.c. of water, heat, and allow the hot infusion to remain for some hours in a warm place. Then filter, and divide the filtrate into two parts. Add a few drops of nitric acid to one portion, so that a faint red tinge is obtained, and then mix the two portions. Add spirit to the mixture, and keep it in a stoppered bottle (it soon spoils if left open to the air). This infusion may be employed directly; it reddens in the presence of acids, and turns blue in the presence of alkalis. If evaporated, a solid mass is obtained which is soluble in water, and may be kept unchanged for any length of time. The test paper may be prepared as follows:—Take a strong infusion of litmus, and soak blotting-paper with it; dry it, and cut it into strips, and use it as test-paper for acids. For the detection of alkalis, the paper must be soaked in a solution of litmus just reddened by a few drops of acid; if too much acid be taken, the paper will not be sensitive. Such acids as sulphuric acid colour litmus, and especially its infusion, a brick-red colour, whilst more feeble acids, such as carbonic, give a faint red-wine tinge. Test-paper of a yellow colour is also employed; it is dyed by an infusion of turmeric roots in spirit. In alkalis it turns brown, but regains its original hue in acids. Many blue and other vegetable colouring matters may be used for the detection of acids and alkalis; for example, infusions of cochineal, violets, log-wood, &c. Certain artificially prepared substances and dyes may also be employed. Thus rosolic acid, $C_{20}H_{16}O_3$ and phenolphthaleïn, $C_{20}H_{14}O_4$ (it is used in an alcoholic solution, and is not suitable for the detection of ammonia), are colourless in an acid, and red in an alkaline, solution. Cyanine is also colourless in the presence of acids, and gives a blue coloration with alkalis.

Methyl-orange (yellow in an aqueous solution) is not altered by alkalis but becomes pink with acids (weak acids have no action), &c. These are very sensitive tests. Their behaviour in respect to various acids, alkalis, and salts sometimes give the means of distinguishing substances from each other.

[51] That water really is separated in the reaction of acid on alkaline hydrates, may be shown by taking some other intermediate hydrate—for example, alumina—instead of water. Thus, if a solution of alumina in sulphuric acid be taken, it will have, like the acid, an acid reaction, and will therefore colour litmus red. If, on the other hand, a solution of alumina in an alkali—say, potash—be taken, it will have an alkaline reaction, and will turn red litmus blue. On adding the alkaline to the acid solution until neither an alkaline nor an acid reaction is produced, a salt is formed, consisting of sulphuric anhydride and potassium oxide. In this, as in the reaction of hydrates, an intermediate oxide is separated out—namely, alumina. Its separation will be very evident in this case, as alumina is insoluble in water.

[52] The mutual interaction of hydrates, and their capacity of forming salts, may be taken advantage of for determining the character of those hydrates which are insoluble in water. Let us imagine that a given hydrate, whose chemical character is unknown, is insoluble in water. It is therefore impossible to test its reaction on litmus. It is then mixed with water, and an acid—for instance, sulphuric acid—is added to the mixture. If the hydrate taken be basic, reaction will take place, either directly or by the aid of heat, with the formation of a salt. In certain cases, the resultant salt is soluble in water, and this will at once show that combination has taken place between the insoluble basic hydrate and the acid, with the formation of a soluble saline substance. In those cases where the resultant salt is insoluble, still the water loses its acid reaction, and therefore it may he ascertained, by the addition of an acid, whether a given hydrate has a basic character, like the hydrates of oxide of copper, lead, &c. If the acid does not act on the given insoluble hydrate (at any temperature), then it has not a basic character, and it should be tested as to whether it has an acid character. This is done by taking an alkali, instead of the acid, and by observing whether the unknown hydrate then dissolves, or whether the alkaline reaction disappears. Thus it may he proved that hydrate of silica is acid, because it dissolves in alkalis and not in acids. If it be a case of an insoluble intermediate hydrate, then it will be observed to react on both the acid and alkali. Hydrate of alumina is an instance in question, which is soluble both in caustic potash and in sulphuric acid.

The *degree of affinity* or chemical *energy* proper to oxides and their hydrates is very dissimilar; some extreme members of the series possess it to a great extent. When acting on each other they evolve a large quantity of heat, and when acting on intermediate hydrates they also evolve heat to a considerable degree, as we saw in the combination of lime and sulphuric anhydride with water. When extreme oxides combine they form stable salts, which are decomposed with difficulty, and often show characteristic properties. The compounds of the intermediate oxides with each other, or even with basic and acid oxides, present a very different case. However much alumina we may dissolve in sulphuric acid, we cannot saturate the acid properties of the sulphuric acid, the resulting solution will always have an acid reaction. So also, whatever quantity of alumina is dissolved in an alkali, the resulting solution will always present an alkaline reaction.

[53] In order to give an idea of the quantity of heat evolved in the formation of salts I append a table of data for *very dilute aqueous solutions* of acids and alkalis, according to the determinations of Berthelot and Thomsen. The figures are given in major calories—that is, in thousands of units of heat. For example, 49 grams of sulphuric acid, H_2SO_4, taken in a dilute aqueous solution, when mixed with such an amount of a weak solution of caustic soda, NaHO, that a neutral salt is formed (when all the hydrogen of the acid is replaced by the sodium), evolves 15,800 units of heat.

	49 parts of H_2SO_4	63 parts of HNO_3		49 parts of H_2SO_4	63 parts of HNO_3
NaHO	15·8	13·7	MgO	15·6	13·8
KHO	15·7	13·8	FeO	12·5	10·7(?)
NH_3	14·5	12·5	ZnO	11·7	9·8
CaO	15·6	13·9	Fe_2O_3	5·7	5·9
BaO	18·4	13·9			

These figures cannot be considered as the heat of neutralisation, because the water here plays an important part. Thus, for instance, sulphuric acid and caustic soda in dissolving in water evolve very much heat, and the resultant sodium sulphate very little; consequently, the amount of heat evolved in an anhydrous combination will be different from that evolved in a hydrated combination. Those acids which are not energetic in combining with the same quantity of alkalis required for the formation of normal salts of sulphuric or nitric acids always, however, give less heat. For instance, with caustic soda: carbonic acid gives 10·2, hydrocyanic, 2·9, hydrogen sulphide, 3·9 major calories. And as feeble bases (for example, Fe_2O_3) also evolve less heat than those which are more powerful, so a certain general correlation between thermochemical data and the degree of affinity shows itself here, as in other cases (*see* Chapter II., Note 7); this does not, however, give any reason for measuring the affinity which binds the elements of salts by the heat of their formation in dilute solutions. This is very clearly demonstrated by the fact that water is able to decompose many salts, and is separated in their formation.

[54] Carbonic anhydride evolves heat in dissolving in water. The solution easily dissociates and evolves carbonic anhydride, according to the law of Henry and Dalton (*see* Chapter I.) In dissolving in caustic soda, it either gives a normal salt, Na_2CO_3, which does not evolve carbonic anhydride, or an acid salt, $NaHCO_3$ which easily evolves carbonic anhydride when heated. The same gas, when dissolved in solutions of salts, acts in one or the other manner (*see* Chapter II., Note 38). Here it is seen what a successive series of relations exists between compounds of a different order, between substances of different degrees of stability. By making a distinction between the phenomena of solutions and chemical compounds, we overlook those natural transitions which in reality exist.

[55] This kind of decomposition may be easily observed by pouring a solution of sodium sulphate into a U-shaped tube and inserting electrodes in the two branches. If the solution be coloured with an infusion of litmus, it will easily be seen that it turns blue at the cathode, owing to the formation of sodium hydroxide, and red at the electro-positive pole, from the formation of sulphuric acid.

[56] In other cases the decomposition of salts by the electric current may be accompanied by much more complex results. Thus, when the metal of the salt is capable of a higher degree of oxidation, such a higher oxide may be formed at the positive pole by the oxygen which is evolved there. This takes place, for instance, in the decomposition of salts of silver and manganese by the galvanic current, peroxides of these metals being formed. Thus in the electrolysis of a solution of KCl, $KClO_3$ is formed, and of sulphuric acid (corresponding to SO_3) persulphuric acid, corresponding to S_2O_7. But all the phenomena as yet known may be expressed by the above law—that the current decomposes salts into metals, which appear at the negative pole, and into the remaining component parts, which appear at the positive pole.

[57] The above-enunciated generalisation of the conception of salts as compounds of the metals (simple, or compound like ammonium, NH_4), with the haloids (simple, like chlorine, or compound, like cyanogen, CN, or the radical of sulphuric acid, SO_4), capable of entering into double saline decomposition, which is in accordance with the general data respecting salts, was only formed little by little after a succession of most varied propositions as to the chemical structure of salts.

Salts belong to the class of substances which have been known since very early times, and have long been investigated in many directions. At first, however, no distinction was made between salts, acids, and bases. Glauber prepared many artificial salts during the latter half of the seventeenth century. Up to that time the majority of salts were obtained from natural sources, and that salt which we have referred to several times—namely, sodium sulphate—was named Glauber's salt after this chemist. Rouelle distinguished normal, acid, and basic salts, and showed their action on vegetable dyes, still he confounded many salts with acids (even now every acid salt ought to be regarded as an acid, because it contains hydrogen, which may be replaced by metals—that is, it is the hydrogen of an acid). Baumé disputed Rouelle's opinion concerning the subdivision of salts, contending that normal salts only are true salts, and that basic salts are simple mixtures of normal salts with bases and acid salts with acids, considering that washing alone could remove the base or acid from them. Rouelle, in the middle of the last century, however, rendered a great service to the study of salts and the diffusion of knowledge respecting this class of compounds in his attractive lectures. He, like the majority of the chemists of that period, did not employ the balance in his researches, but satisfied himself with purely qualitative data. The first quantitative researches on salts were carried on about this time by Wenzel, who was the director of the Freiburg mines, in Saxony. Wenzel studied the double decomposition of salts, and observed that in the double decomposition of neutral salts a neutral salt was always obtained. He proved, by a method of weighing, that this is due to the fact that the saturation of a given quantity of a base requires such relative quantities of different acids as are capable of saturating every other base. Having taken two neutral salts—for example, sodium sulphate and calcium nitrate—let us mix their solutions together. Double decomposition takes place, because calcium sulphate is formed, which is almost insoluble. However much we might add of each of the salts, the neutral reaction will still be preserved, consequently the neutral character of the salts is not destroyed by the interchange of metals; that is to say, that quantity of sulphuric acid which saturated the sodium is sufficient for the saturation of the calcium, and that amount of nitric acid which saturated the calcium is enough to saturate the sodium contained in combination with sulphuric acid in sodium sulphate. Wenzel was even convinced that matter does not disappear in nature, and on this principle he corrects, in his *Doctrine of Affinity*, the results of his experiments when he found that he obtained less than he had originally taken. Although Wenzel deduced the law of the double decomposition of salts quite correctly, he did not determine those quantities in which acids and bases act on each other. This was carried out at the end of the last century by Richter. He determined the quantities by weight of the bases which saturate acids and of the acids which saturate bases, and obtained comparatively correct results, although his conclusions were not correct, for he states that the quantity of a base saturating a given acid varies in arithmetical progression, and the quantity of an acid saturating a given base in geometrical progression. Richter studied the deposition of metals from their salts by other metals, and observed that the neutral reaction of the solution is not destroyed by this exchange. He also determined the quantities by weight of the metals replacing one another in salts. He showed that copper displaces silver from its salt, and that zinc displaces copper and a whole series of other metals. Those quantities of metals which were capable of replacing one another were termed equivalents.

Richter's teaching found no followers, because, although he fully believed in the discoveries of Lavoisier, yet he still held to the phlogistic reasonings which rendered his expositions very obscure. The works of the Swedish savant Berzelius freed the facts discovered by Wenzel and Richter from the obscurity of former conceptions, and led to their being explained in accordance with Lavoisier's views, and in the sense of the law of multiple proportions which had already been discovered by Dalton. On applying to salts those conclusions which Berzelius arrived at by a whole series of researches of remarkable accuracy, we arrive at the following law of equivalents—*one part by weight of hydrogen in an acid is replaced by the corresponding equivalent weight of any metal*; and, therefore, when metals replace each other their weights are in the same ratio as their equivalents. Thus, for instance, one part by weight of hydrogen is replaced by 23 parts of sodium, 39 parts of potassium, 12 parts of magnesium, 20 parts of calcium, 28 parts of iron, 108 parts of silver, 33 parts of zinc, &c.; and, therefore, if zinc replaces silver, then 33 parts of zinc will take the place of 108 parts of silver, or 33 parts of zinc will he substituted by 23 parts of sodium, &c.

The doctrine of equivalents would be precise and simple did every metal only give one oxide or one salt. It is rendered complicated from the fact that many metals form several oxides, and consequently offer different equivalents in their different degrees of oxidation. For example, there are oxides containing iron in which its equivalent is 28—this is in the salts formed by the suboxide; and there is another series of salts in which the equivalent of iron equals 18⅔—which contain less iron, and consequently more oxygen, and correspond with a higher degree of oxidation—ferric oxide. It is true that the former salts are easily formed by the direct action of metallic iron on acids, and the latter only by a further oxidation of the compound formed already; but this is not always so. In the case of copper, mercury, and tin, under different circumstances, salts are formed which correspond with different degrees of oxidation of these metals, and many metals have two equivalents in their different salts—that is, in salts

- 265 -

corresponding with the different degrees of oxidation. Thus it is impossible to endow every metal with one definite equivalent weight. Hence the conception of equivalents, while playing an important part from an historical point of view, appears, with a fuller study of chemistry, to be but subordinate to a higher conception, with which we shall afterwards become acquainted.

The fate of the theoretical views of chemistry was for a long time bound up with the history of salts. The clearest representation of this subject dates back to Lavoisier, and was systematically developed by Berzelius. This representation is called the *binary* theory. All compounds, and especially salts, are represented as consisting of two parts. Salts are represented as compounds of a basic oxide (a base) and an acid (that is, an anhydride of an acid, then termed an acid), whilst hydrates are represented as compounds of anhydrous oxides with water. Such an expression was employed not only to denote the most usual method of formation of these substances (where it would be quite true), but also to express that internal distribution of the elements by which it was proposed to explain all the properties of these substances. Copper sulphate was supposed to contain two most intimate component parts—copper oxide and sulphuric anhydride. This is an hypothesis. It arose from the so-called *electro-chemical hypothesis*, which supposed the two component parts to be held in mutual union, because one component (the anhydride of the acid) has electro-negative properties, and the other (the base in salts) electro-positive. The two parts are attracted together, like substances having opposite electrical charges. But as the decomposition of salts in a state of fusion by an electric current always gives a metal, that representation of the constitution and decomposition of salts called the *hydrogen theory* of acids is nearer the truth than that which considers salts as made up of a base and an anhydride of an acid. But the hydrogen theory of acids is also a binary hypothesis, and does not contradict the electro-chemical hypothesis, but is rather a modification of it. The binary theory dates from Rouelle and Lavoisier, the electro-chemical aspect was zealously developed by Berzelius, and the hydrogen theory of acids is due to Davy and Liebig.

These hypothetical views simplified and generalised the study of a complicated subject, and served to support further arguments, but when salts were in question it was equally convenient to follow one or the other of these hypotheses. But these theories were brought to bear on all other substances, on all compound substances. Those holding the binary and electro-chemical hypotheses searched for two anti-polar component parts, and endeavoured to express the process of chemical reactions by electro-chemical and similar differences. If zinc replaces hydrogen, they concluded that it is more electro-positive than hydrogen, whilst they forgot that hydrogen may, under different circumstances, displace zinc—for instance, at a red heat. Chlorine and oxygen were considered as being of opposite polarity to hydrogen because they easily combine with it, nevertheless both are capable of replacing hydrogen, and, what is very characteristic, in the replacement of hydrogen by chlorine in carbon compounds not only does the chemical character often remain unaltered, but even the external form may remain unchanged, as Laurent and Dumas demonstrated. These considerations undermine the binary, and more especially the electro-chemical theory. An explanation of known reactions then began to be sought for not in the difference of the polarity of the different substances, but in the joint influences of all the elements on the properties of the compound formed. This is the reverse of the preceding hypothesis.

This reversal was not, however, limited to the destruction of the tottering foundations of the preceding theory; it proposed a new doctrine, and laid the foundation for the modern course of our science. This doctrine may be termed the unitary theory—that is, it strictly acknowledges the joint influences of the elements in a compound substance, denies the existence of separate and contrary components in them, regards copper sulphate, for instance, as a strictly definite compound of copper, sulphur, and oxygen; then seeks for compounds which are analogous in their properties, and, placing them side by side, endeavours to express the influence of each element in determining the united properties of its compound. In the majority of cases it arrives at conclusions similar to those which are obtained by the above-mentioned hypotheses, but in certain special cases the conclusions of the unitary theory are in entire opposition to those of the binary theory and its corollaries. Cases of this kind are most often met with in the consideration of compounds of a more complex nature than salts, especially organic compounds containing hydrogen. But it is not in this change from an artificial to a natural system, important as it is, that the chief service and strength of the unitary doctrine lies. By a simple review of the vast store of data regarding the reactions of typical substances, it succeeded from its first appearance in establishing a new and important law, it introduced a new conception into science—namely, the conception of molecules, with which we shall soon become acquainted. The deduction of the law and of the conception of molecules has been verified by facts in a number of cases, and was the cause of the majority of chemists of our times deserting the binary theory and accepting the unitary theory, which forms the basis of the present work. Laurent and Gerhardt must be considered as the founders of this doctrine.

[198]

CHAPTER IV

OZONE AND HYDROGEN PEROXIDE— DALTON'S LAW

VAN MARUM, during the last century, observed that oxygen in a glass tube, when subjected to the action of a series of electric sparks, acquired a peculiar smell, and the property of combining with mercury at the ordinary temperature. This was afterwards confirmed by a number of fresh experiments. Even in the simple revolution of an electrical machine, when electricity diffuses into the air or passes through it, the peculiar and characteristic smell of ozone, proceeding from the action of the electricity on the oxygen of the atmosphere, is recognised. In 1840 Prof. Schönbein, of Basle, turned his attention to this odoriferous substance, and showed that it is also formed, with the oxygen evolved at the positive pole, in the decomposition of water by the action of a galvanic current; in the oxidation of phosphorus in damp air, and also in the oxidation of a number of substances, although it is distinguished for its instability and capacity for oxidising other substances. The characteristic smell of this substance gave it its name, from the Greek ὄζω, 'I emit an odour.' Schönbein pointed out that *ozone* is capable of oxidising many substances on which oxygen does not act at the ordinary temperature. It will be sufficient to point out for instance that it oxidises silver, mercury, charcoal, and iron with great energy at the ordinary temperature. It might be thought that ozone was some new compound substance, as it was at first supposed to be; but careful observations made in this direction have long led to the conclusion that ozone is nothing but oxygen altered in its properties. This is most strikingly proved by the complete transformation of oxygen containing ozone into ordinary oxygen when it is passed through a tube heated to 250°. Further, at a low temperature pure oxygen gives ozone when electric sparks are passed through it (Marignac and De la Rive). Hence it is proved both by synthesis and analysis that ozone is that same oxygen with which we are already acquainted, only endowed with particular properties and in a particular state. However, by whatever method it be obtained, the[199] amount of it contained in the oxygen is inconsiderable, generally only a few fractions per cent., rarely 2 per cent., and only under very propitious circumstances as much as 20 per cent. The reason of this must be looked for first in the fact that *ozone in its formation from oxygen absorbs heat.* If any substance be burnt in a calorimeter at the expense of ozonised oxygen, then more heat is evolved than when it is burnt in ordinary oxygen, and

Berthelot showed that this difference is very large—namely, 29,600 heat units correspond with every forty-eight parts by weight of ozone. This signifies that the transformation of forty-eight parts of oxygen into ozone is accompanied by the absorption of this quantity of heat, and that the reverse process evolves this quantity of heat. Therefore the passage of ozone into oxygen should take place easily and fully (as an exothermal reaction), like combustion; and this is proved by the fact that at 250° ozone entirely disappears, forming oxygen. Any rise of temperature may thus bring about the breaking up of ozone, and as a rise of temperature takes place in the action of an electrical discharge, there are in an electric discharge the conditions both for the preparation of ozone and for its destruction. Hence it is clear that the transformation of oxygen into ozone *as a reversible reaction* has a limit when a state of equilibrium is arrived at between the products of the two opposite reactions, that the phenomena of this transformation accord with the phenomena of *dissociation*, and that a fall of temperature should aid the formation of a large quantity of ozone.[1] Further, it is evident, from what has been said, that the best way of preparing ozone is not by electric sparks,[2] which raise the temperature, but by the employment of a continual discharge or flow of electricity—that is, by the action of a *silent discharge*.[3] For this[200] reason all *ozonisers* (which are of most varied construction), or forms of apparatus for the preparation of ozone from oxygen (or air) by the action of electricity, now usually consist of sheets of metal—for instance, tinfoil—a solution of sulphuric acid mixed with chromic acid, &c. separated by thin glass surfaces placed at short distances from each other, and between which the oxygen or air to be ozonised is introduced and subjected to the action of a silent discharge.[4] Thus in Siemens' apparatus (fig. 37) the exterior of the tube *a* and the interior of the tube *b c* are coated with tinfoil and connected with the poles of a source of electricity (with the terminals of a Ruhmkorff's coil). A silent discharge passes through the thin walls of the glass cylinders *a* and *b c*[201] over all their surfaces, and consequently, if oxygen be passed through the apparatus by the tube *d*, fused into the side of *a*, it will be ozonised in the annular space between *a* and *b c*. The ozonised oxygen escapes by the tube *e*, and may be introduced into any other apparatus.[5]

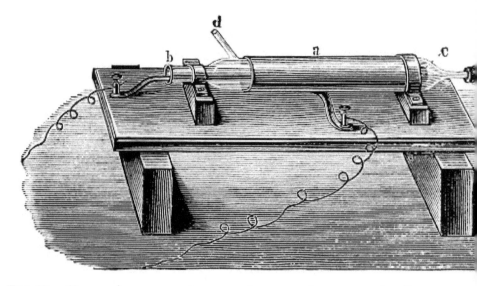

FIG. 37.—Siemens' apparatus for preparing ozone by means of a silent discharge.

The properties of ozone obtained by such a method[6] distinguish it in many respects from oxygen. Ozone very rapidly decolorises indigo, litmus, and many other dyes by oxidising them. Silver is oxidised by it at the ordinary temperature, whilst oxygen is not able to oxidise silver even at high temperatures; a bright silver plate rapidly turns black (from oxidation) in ozonised oxygen. It is rapidly absorbed by mercury, forming oxide; it transforms the lower oxides into higher—for instance, sulphurous anhydride into sulphuric, nitrous oxide into nitric, arsenious anhydride (As_2O_3) into arsenic anhydride (As_2O_5) &c.[7] But what is especially characteristic in ozone is the decomposing action[202] it exerts on potassium iodide. Oxygen does not act on it, but ozone passed into a solution of potassium iodide *liberates iodine*, whilst the potassium is obtained as caustic potash, which remains in solution, $2KI + H_2O + O = 2KHO + I_2$. As the presence of minute traces of free iodine may be discovered by means of starch paste, with which it forms a very dark blue-coloured substance, a mixture of potassium iodide with starch paste will detect the presence of very small traces of ozone.[8] Ozone is destroyed or converted into ordinary oxygen not only by heat, but also by long keeping, especially in the presence of alkalis, peroxide of manganese, chlorine, &c.

Hence *ozone*, although it has the same *composition as oxygen*, differs from it in stability, and by the fact that it oxidises a number of substances very energetically at the ordinary temperature. In this respect ozone resembles the oxygen of certain unstable compounds, or oxygen at the moment of its liberation.[8 bis]

In ordinary oxygen and ozone we see an example of one and the same substance, in this case an element, appearing in two states. This indicates that the properties of a substance, and even of an element, may vary without its composition varying. Very many such cases are known. Such cases of a chemical transformation which determine a difference in the properties of one and the same element are termed[203] cases of isomerism. The cause of isomerism evidently lies deep within the essential conditions of a substance, and its investigation has already led to a number of results of unexpected importance and of immense scientific significance. It is easy to understand the difference between substances containing different elements or the same elements in different proportions. That a difference should exist in these cases necessarily follows, if, as our knowledge compels us, we admit that there is a radical difference in the simple bodies or elements. But when the composition—*i.e.* the quality and quantity of the elements in two substances is the same and yet their properties are different, then it becomes clear that the conceptions of diverse elements and of the varying composition of compounds, alone, are insufficient for the expression of all the diversity of properties of matter in nature. Something else, still more profound and internal than the composition of substances, must, judging from isomerism, determine the properties and transformation of substances.

On what are the isomerism of ozone and oxygen, and the peculiarities of ozone, dependent? In what, besides the extra store of energy, which is one of the peculiarities of ozone, resides the cause of its difference from oxygen? These questions for long occupied the minds of investigators, and were the motive for the most varied, exact, and accurate researches, which were chiefly directed to the study of the volumetric relations exhibited by ozone. In order to acquaint the reader with the previous researches of this kind, I cite the following from a memoir by Soret, in the 'Transactions of the French Academy of Sciences' for 1866:

'Our present knowledge of the volumetric relations of ozone may be expressed in the following manner:

'1. "Ordinary oxygen in changing into ozone under the action of electricity shows a diminution in volume." This was discovered by Andrews and Tait.

'2. "In acting on ozonised oxygen with potassium iodide and other substances capable of being oxidised, we destroy the ozone, but the volume of the gas remains unchanged." For the researches of Andrews, Soret, v. Babo, and others showed that the proportion of ozonised oxygen absorbed by the potassium iodide is equal to the original contraction of volume of the oxygen—that is, in the absorption of the ozone the volume of the gas remains unchanged. From this it might be imagined that ozone, so to say, does not occupy any space—is indefinitely dense.

'3. "By the action of heat ozonised oxygen increases in volume, and is transformed into ordinary oxygen. This increase in volume[204] corresponds with the quantity of ozonised oxygen which is given up to the potassium iodide in its decomposition" (the same observers).

'4. These unquestionable experimental results lead to the conclusion that ozone is denser than oxygen, and that in its oxidising action it gives off that portion of its substance to which is due its extra density distinguishing it from ordinary oxygen.'

If we imagine (says Weltzien) that n volumes of ozone consist of n volumes of oxygen combined with m volumes of the same substance, and that ozone in oxidising gives up m volumes of oxygen and leaves n volumes of ordinary oxygen gas, then all the above facts can be explained; otherwise it must be supposed that ozone is infinitely dense. 'In order to determine the density of ozone' (we again cite Soret) 'recourse cannot be had to the direct determination of the weight of a given volume of the gas, because ozone cannot be obtained in a pure state. It is always mixed with a very large quantity of oxygen. It was necessary, therefore, to have recourse to such substances as would absorb ozone without absorbing oxygen and without destroying the ozone. Then the density might be deduced from the decrease of volume produced in the gas by the action of this solvent in comparison with the quantity of oxygen given up to potassium iodide. Advantage must also be taken of the determination of the increase of volume produced by the action of heat on ozone, if the volume occupied by the ozone before heating be known.' Soret found two such substances, turpentine and oil of cinnamon. 'Ozone disappears in the presence of turpentine. This is accompanied by the appearance of a dense vapour, which fills a vessel of small capacity (0·14 litre) to such an extent that it is impenetrable to direct solar-rays. On leaving the vessel at rest, it is observed that the cloud of vapour settles; the clearing is first remarked at the upper portion of the vessel, and the brilliant colours of the rainbow are seen on the edge of a cloud of vapour.' Oil of cinnamon—that is, the volatile or essential oil of the well-known spice, cinnamon—gives under similar circumstances the same kind of vapours, but they are much less voluminous. On measuring the gaseous volume before and after the action of both volatile oils, a considerable decrease is remarked. On applying all the necessary corrections (for the solubility of oxygen in the oily liquids named above, for the tension of their vapour, for the change of pressure, &c.) and making a series of comparative determinations, Soret obtained the following result: two volumes of ozone capable of being dissolved, when changed to ordinary (by heating a wire to a red-heat by a galvanic current) increase by one volume. Hence it is evident that in the formation of ozone three volumes of oxygen give two volumes of ozone—that is, its density (referred to hydrogen) = 24.

[205]

The observations and determinations of Soret showed that ozone is heavier than oxygen, and even than carbonic anhydride (because ozonised oxygen passes through fine orifices more slowly than oxygen and than its mixtures with carbonic anhydride), although lighter than chlorine (it flows more rapidly through such orifices than chlorine), and they indicated that *ozone is one and a half times denser than oxygen*, which may be expressed by designating a molecule of oxygen by O_2 and of ozone by O_3, and hence ozone OO_2 is comparable with compound substances[9] formed by oxygen, as for instance CO_2, SO_2, NO_2, &c. This explains the chief differences between ozone and oxygen and the cause of the isomerism, and at the same time leads one to expect[10] that ozone, being a gas which is denser than oxygen, would be liquefied much more easily. This was actually shown to be the case in 1880, by Chappuis and Hautefeuille in their researches on the *physical properties of ozone*. Its boiling point under a pressure of 760 mm. is about -106°, and consequently compressed and refrigerated ozone when rapidly expanded forms drops, *i.e.* is liquefied. Liquid and compressed[11] ozone is[206] blue. In dissolving in water ozone partly passes into oxygen. It explodes violently when suddenly compressed and heated, changing into ordinary oxygen and evolving, like all explosive substances,[12] that extra heat which distinguishes it from oxygen.

Thus, judging by what has been said above, ozone should he formed in nature not only in the many processes of oxidation which go on, but also by the condensation of atmospheric oxygen. The significance of ozone in nature has often arrested the attention of observers. There is a series of ozonometrical observations which show the different amounts of ozone in the air at different localities, at different times of the year, and under different circumstances. But the observations made in this direction cannot be considered as sufficiently exact, because the methods in use for determining ozone were not quite accurate. It is however indisputable[13] that the amount of ozone in the atmosphere is subject to variation; that the air of dwellings contains no ozone (it disappears in oxidising organic matter); that the air of fields and forests always contains ozone, or substances (peroxide of hydrogen) which act like it (on iodised starch paper &c.)[13 bis]; that the amount of ozone increases after storms; and that miasms, &c., are destroyed by ozonising the atmosphere. It easily oxidises organic substances, and miasms are produced by organic substances and the germs of organisms, all of which are easily changed and oxidised. Indeed, many miasms—for instance, the volatile substance of decomposing organisms—are clearly destroyed or changed not only by ozone, but also by many other powerfully oxidising substances, such as chlorine water, potassium permanganate, and the like.[14] All that is now known respecting the presence of ozone in the air may be[207] summed up in the following words: A small quantity of an oxidising substance, resembling ozone in its reactions, has undoubtedly been observed and determined in the atmosphere, especially in fresh air, for instance after a storm, and it is very likely that this substance contains a mixture of such oxidising substances as ozone, peroxide of hydrogen, and the lower oxides of nitrogen (especially nitrous acid and its ammonia salt) produced from the elements of the atmosphere by oxidation and by the action of electrical discharges.

Thus in ozone we see (1) the capacity of elements (and it must be all the more marked in compounds) of changing in properties without altering in composition; this is termed isomerism;[15] (2) the capacity of certain elements for condensing themselves into molecules of different densities; this forms a special case of isomerism called *polymerism*; (3) the capacity of oxygen for appearing in a still more active and energetic chemical state than that in which it occurs in ordinary gaseous oxygen; and (4) the formation of unstable equilibria, or chemical states, which are illustrated both by the ease with which ozone acts as an oxidiser and by its capacity for decomposing with explosion.[16]

Hydrogen peroxide.—Many of those properties which we have seen in ozone belong also to a peculiar substance containing oxygen and hydrogen and called hydrogen peroxide or oxygenated water. This substance was discovered in 1818 by Thénard. When heated it is decomposed into water and oxygen, evolving as much oxygen as is contained in the water remaining after the decomposition. That portion of oxygen by which hydrogen peroxide differs from water behaves in a number of cases just like the active oxygen in ozone, which distinguishes it from ordinary oxygen. In H_2O_2, and in O_3, one atom of oxygen acts as a powerful oxidiser, and on separating out it leaves H_2O or O_2, which do not act so energetically, although they still contain oxygen.[17] Both H_2O_2 and O_3 contain the oxygen in a compressed state, so to speak, and when freed from pressure by the forces (internal) of the elements in another substance, this oxygen is easily evolved, and therefore acts as oxygen does at the moment of its liberation.[208] Both substances in decomposing, with the separation of a portion of their oxygen, *evolve* heat, whilst decomposition is usually accompanied by an absorption of heat.

Hydrogen peroxide is formed under many circumstances by combustion and oxidation, but in very limited quantities; thus, for instance, it is sufficient to shake up zinc with sulphuric acid, or even with water, to observe the formation of a certain quantity of hydrogen peroxide in the water.[18] From this cause, probably, a series of diverse oxidation processes are accomplished in nature, and according to Prof. Schöne of Moscow, hydrogen peroxide occurs in the atmosphere, although in variable and small quantities, and probably its formation is connected with ozone, with which it has much in common. The usual mode of the formation of hydrogen peroxide, and the method by which it may be indirectly obtained,[19] is by the double decomposition of an acid and the[209] peroxides of certain metals, especially those of potassium, calcium, and barium.[20] We saw when speaking of Oxygen (Chap. III.) that it is only necessary to heat the anhydrous oxide of barium to a red heat in a current of air or oxygen (or, better still, to heat it with potassium chlorate, and then to wash away the potassium chloride formed) to obtain peroxide of barium.[21] Barium peroxide gives hydrogen peroxide by the action of acids in the cold.[22] The process of decomposition is very clear in this case; the hydrogen of the acid replaces the barium of the peroxide, a barium salt of the acid being formed, while the hydrogen peroxide formed in the reaction remains in solution.[23]

[210]

The reaction is expressed by the equation $BaO_2 + H_2SO_4 = H_2O_2 + BaSO_4$. It is best to take a weak cold solution of sulphuric acid and to almost saturate it with barium peroxide, so that a small excess of acid remains; insoluble barium sulphate is formed. A more or less dilute aqueous solution of hydrogen peroxide is obtained. This solution may be concentrated in a vacuum over sulphuric acid. In this way the water may even be entirely evaporated from the solution of the hydrogen peroxide; only in this case it is necessary to work at a low temperature, and not to keep the peroxide for long in the rarefied atmosphere, as otherwise it decomposes.[23 bis] A solution of peroxide of hydrogen (mixed with the solution of a salt of sodium NaX) is used for bleaching (especially silk and wool) on a large scale, and is now usually prepared from peroxide of sodium Na_2O_2 by the action of acids. $Na_2O_2 + 2HX = 2NaX + H_2O_2$[24].

When pure, hydrogen peroxide is a colourless liquid, without smell, and having a very unpleasant taste—such as belongs to the salts of many metals—the so-called 'metallic' taste. Water stored in zinc vessels has this taste, which is probably due to its containing hydrogen peroxide. The tension of the vapour of hydrogen peroxide is less than that of aqueous vapour; this enables its solutions to be concentrated in a vacuum. The specific gravity of anhydrous hydrogen peroxide is 1·455. Hydrogen peroxide decomposes, with the evolution of oxygen, when heated even to 20°. But the more dilute its aqueous solution the more stable it is. Very weak solutions may be distilled without decomposing the hydrogen peroxide. It decolorises solutions of litmus and turmeric, and acts in a similar manner on many colouring matters of organic origin (for which reason it is employed for bleaching tissues).[24 bis]

Many substances decompose hydrogen peroxide, forming water and oxygen, without apparently suffering any change. In this case substances[211] in a state of fine division show a much quicker action than compact masses, from which it is evident that the action is here based on contact (*see* Introduction). It is sufficient to bring hydrogen peroxide into contact with charcoal, gold, the peroxide of manganese or lead, the alkalis, metallic silver, and platinum, to bring about the above decomposition.[25] Besides which, hydrogen peroxide forms water and parts with its oxygen with great ease to a number of substances which are capable of being oxidised or of combining with oxygen, and in this respect is very like ozone and other *powerful oxidisers*.[26] To the class of contact phenomena, which are so characteristic of hydrogen peroxide as a substance which is unstable and easily decomposable with the evolution of heat, must be referred the following—that in the presence of many substances containing oxygen it evolves, not only its own oxygen, but also that of the substances which are brought into contact with it—that[212] is, *it acts in a reducing manner.* It behaves thus with ozone, the oxides of silver, mercury, gold and platinum, and lead peroxide. The oxygen in these substances is not stable, and therefore the feeble influence of contact is enough to destroy its position. Hydrogen peroxide, especially in a concentrated form, in contact with these substances, evolves an immense quantity of oxygen, so that an explosion takes place and an exceedingly powerful evolution of heat is observed if hydrogen peroxide in a concentrated form be made to drop upon these substances in dry powder. Slow decomposition also proceeds in dilute solutions.[27]

Just as a whole series of metallic compounds, and especially the oxides and their hydrates, correspond with water, so also there are many substances analogous to hydrogen peroxide. Thus, for instance, calcium peroxide is related to hydrogen peroxide in exactly the same way as calcium oxide or lime is related to water. In both cases the hydrogen is replaced by a metal—namely, by calcium.[27 bis] But it is most important to remark that the nearest approach to the properties of hydrogen peroxide is afforded by a non-metallic element, chlorine;[213] its action on colouring matters, its capacity for oxidising, and for evolving oxygen from many oxides, is analogous to that exhibited by hydrogen peroxide. Even the very formation of chlorine is closely analogous to the formation of peroxide of hydrogen; chlorine is obtained from manganese peroxide, MnO_2, and hydrochloric acid, HCl, and hydrogen peroxide from barium peroxide, BaO_2, and the same acid. The result in one case is essentially water, chlorine, and manganese chloride; and in the other case barium chloride and hydrogen peroxide are produced. Hence water + chlorine corresponds with hydrogen peroxide, and the action of chlorine in the presence of water is analogous to the action of hydrogen peroxide. This analogy between chlorine and hydrogen peroxide is expressed in the conception of an aqueous radicle, which (Chapter III.) has been already mentioned. *This aqueous radicle* (or hydroxyl) is that which is left from water if it be imagined as deprived of half of its hydrogen. According to this method of expression, caustic soda will be a compound of sodium with the aqueous radicle, because it is formed from water with the evolution of half the hydrogen. This is expressed by the following formulæ: water, H_2O, caustic soda, $NaHO$, just as hydrochloric acid is HCl and sodium chloride $NaCl$. Hence the aqueous radicle HO is a compound radicle, just as chlorine, Cl, is a simple radicle. They both give hydrogen compounds, HHO, water, and HCl, hydrochloric acid; sodium compounds, $NaHO$ and $NaCl$, and a whole series of analogous compounds. Free chlorine in this sense will be $ClCl$, and hydrogen peroxide $HOHO$, which indeed expresses its composition, because it contains twice as much oxygen as water does.[28]

Thus in ozone and hydrogen peroxide we see examples of very unstable, easily decomposable (by time, spontaneously, and on contact) substances, full of the energy necessary for change,[28 bis] capable of being easily reconstituted (in this case decomposing with the evolution of heat); they are therefore examples of *unstable chemical equilibria*. If a substance exists, it signifies that it already presents a certain form of equilibrium between those elements of which it is built up. But[214] chemical, like mechanical, equilibria exhibit different degrees of stability or solidity.[29]

Besides this, hydrogen peroxide presents another side of the subject which is not less important, and is much clearer and more general.

Hydrogen unites with oxygen in two degrees of oxidation: water or hydrogen oxide, and oxygenated water or hydrogen peroxide; for a given quantity of hydrogen, the peroxide contains twice as much oxygen as does water. This is a fresh example confirming the correctness of the law of multiple proportions, to which we have already referred in speaking of the water of crystallisation of salts. We can now formulate this law—*the law of multiple proportions. If two substances A and B (either simple or compound), unite together to form several compounds, A_nB_m, A_qB_r ..., then having expressed the compositions of all these compounds in such a way that the quantity (by weight or volume) of one of the component parts will be a constant quantity A, it will be observed that in all the compounds AB_a, AB_b ... the quantities of the other component part, B, will always be in commensurable relation: generally in simple multiple proportion—that is, that a : b ..., or m/n is to r/q as whole numbers, for instance as 2 : 3 or 3 : 4....*

The analysis of water shows that in 100 parts by weight it contains 11·112 parts by weight of hydrogen and 88·888 of oxygen, and the analysis of peroxide of hydrogen shows that it contains 94·112 parts of oxygen to 5·888 parts of hydrogen. In this the analysis is expressed,[215] as analyses generally are, in percentages; that is, it gives the amounts of the elements in a hundred parts by weight of the substance. The direct comparison of the percentage compositions of water and hydrogen peroxide does not give any simple relation. But such a relation is immediately apparent if we calculate the composition of water and of hydrogen peroxide, having taken either the quantity of oxygen or the quantity of hydrogen as a constant quantity—for instance, as unity. The most simple proportions show that in water there are contained eight parts of oxygen to one part of hydrogen, and in hydrogen peroxide sixteen parts of oxygen to one part of hydrogen; or one-eighth part of hydrogen in water and one-sixteenth part of hydrogen in hydrogen peroxide to one part of oxygen. Naturally, the analysis does not give these figures with absolute exactness—it gives them within a certain degree of error—but they approximate, as the error diminishes, to that limit which is here given. The comparison of the quantities of hydrogen and oxygen in the two substances above named, taking one of the components as a constant quantity, gives an example of the application of the law of multiple proportions, because water contains eight parts and hydrogen peroxide sixteen parts of oxygen to one part of hydrogen, and these figures are commensurable and are in the simple proportion of 1 : 2.

An exactly similar multiple proportion is observed in the composition of all other well-investigated definite chemical compounds,[30][216] and therefore the law of multiple proportions is accepted in chemistry as the starting point from which other considerations proceed.

The law of multiple proportions was discovered at the beginning of this century by John Dalton, of Manchester, in investigating the compounds of carbon with hydrogen. It appeared that two gaseous compounds of these substances—marsh gas, CH_4, and olefiant gas, C_2H_4, contain for one and the same quantity of hydrogen, quantities of carbon which stand in multiple proportion; namely, marsh gas contains relatively half as much carbon as olefiant gas. Although the analysis of that time was not exact, still the accuracy of this law, recognised by Dalton, was further confirmed by more accurate investigations. On establishing the law of multiple proportions, Dalton gave a hypothetical explanation for it. This explanation is based on the atomic theory of matter. In fact, the law of multiple proportions may be very easily understood by admitting the atomic structure of matter.

The essence of the atomic theory is that matter is supposed to consist of an agglomeration of small and indivisible parts—atoms—which do not fill up the whole space occupied by a substance, but stand apart from each other, as the sun, planets, and stars do not fill up the whole space of the universe, but are at a distance from each other. The form and properties of substances are determined by the position of their atoms in space and by their state of motion, whilst the reactions accomplished by substances are understood as redistributions of the relative positions of atoms and changes in their motion. The atomic representation of matter arose in very ancient times,[31] and up to recent[217] times was at variance with the dynamical hypothesis, which considers matter as only a manifestation of forces. At the present time, however, the majority of scientific men uphold the atomic hypothesis,[218] although the present conception of an atom is quite different from that of the ancient philosophers. An atom at the present day is regarded rather as an individual or unit which is indivisible by physical[32] and chemical forces, whilst the atom of the ancients was actually mechanically and geometrically indivisible. When Dalton (1804) discovered the law of multiple proportions, he pronounced himself in favour of the atomic doctrine, because it enables this law to be very easily understood. If the divisibility of every element has a limit, namely the atom, then the atoms of elements are the extreme limits of all divisibility, and if they differ from each other in their nature, the formation of a compound from elementary matter must consist in the aggregation of several different atoms into one whole or system of atoms, now termed *particles or molecules*. As atoms can only combine in their entire masses, it is evident that not only the law of definite composition, but also that of multiple proportions, must apply to the combination of atoms with one another; for one atom of a substance can combine with one, two, or three atoms of another substance, or in general one, two, three atoms of one substance are able to combine with one, two, or three atoms of another; this being the essence of the law of multiple proportions. Chemical and physical data are very well explained by the aid of the atomic theory. The displacement of one element by another follows the law of equivalency. In this case one or several atoms of a given element take the place of one or several atoms of another element in its compounds. The atoms of different substances can be mixed together in the same sense as sand can be mixed with clay. They do not unite into one whole—*i.e.* there is not a perfect blending in the one or other case, but only a juxtaposition, a homogeneous whole being formed from individual parts. This is the first and most simple method of applying the atomic theory to the explanation of chemical phenomena.[33]

[219]
[220]
[221]

A certain number of atoms *n* of an element A in combining with several atoms *m* of another element B give a compound $A_n B_m$, each molecule of which will contain the atoms of the elements A and B in this ratio, and therefore the compound will present a *definite composition*, expressed by the formula A_nB_m, where A and B are the weights of the atoms and n and m their relative number. If the same elements A and B, in addition to A_nB_m, also yield another compound A_rB_q, then by expressing the composition of the first compound by $A_{nr}B_{mr}$ (and this is the same composition as A_nB_m), and of the second compound by A_mB_{qn}, we have the law of multiple proportions, because for a given quantity of the first element, A_m, there occur quantities of the second element bearing the same ratio to each other as mr is to qn; and as m, r, q, and n are whole numbers, their products are also whole numbers, and this is expressed by the law of multiple proportion. Consequently the atomic theory is in accordance with and evokes the first laws of definite chemical compounds: the law of definite composition and the law of multiple proportions.

So, also, is the relation of the atomic theory to the third law of definite chemical compounds, the *law of reciprocal combining weights*, which is as follows:—If a certain weight of a substance C combine with a weight *a* of a substance A, and with a weight *b* of a substance B, then, also, the substances A and B will combine together in quantities *a* and *b* (or in multiples of them). This should be the case from the conception of atoms. Let A, B, and C be the weights of the atoms of the three substances, and for simplicity of reasoning suppose that combination takes place between single atoms. It is evident that if the substance gives AC and BC, then the substances A and B will give a compound AB, or their multiple, A_nB_m. And so it is in reality in nature.

Sulphur combines with hydrogen and with oxygen. Sulphuretted hydrogen contains thirty-two parts by weight of sulphur to two parts by weight of hydrogen; this is expressed by the formula H_2S. Sulphur dioxide, SO_2, contains thirty-two parts of sulphur and thirty-two parts of oxygen, and therefore we conclude, from the law of combining weights, that oxygen and hydrogen will combine in the proportion of two parts of hydrogen and thirty-two parts of oxygen, or multiple numbers of them. And we have seen this to be the case. Hydrogen peroxide contains thirty-two parts of oxygen, and water sixteen parts, to two parts of hydrogen; and so it is in all other cases. This consequence of the atomic theory is in accordance with nature, with the results of analysis, and is one of the most important laws of chemistry. It is a law, because it indicates the *relation between* the weights of substances entering into chemical combination. Further, it is an[222] eminently exact law, and not an approximate one. The law of combining weights is a law of nature, and by no means an hypothesis, for even if the entire theory of atoms be refuted, still the laws of multiple proportions and of combining weights will remain, inasmuch as they deal with facts. They may be guessed at from the sense of the atomic theory, and historically the law of combining weights is intimately connected with this theory; but they are not identical, but only connected, with it. The law of combining weights is formulated with great ease, and is an immediate consequence of the atomic theory; without it, it is even difficult to understand. Data for its evolution existed previously, but it was not formulated until those data were interpreted by the atomic theory, an hypothesis which up to the present time has contradicted neither experiment nor fact, and is useful and of general application. Such is the nature of hypotheses. They are indispensable to science; they bestow an order and simplicity which are difficultly attainable without their aid. The whole history of science is a proof of this. And therefore it may be truly said that it is better to hold to an hypothesis which may afterwards prove untrue than to have none at all. Hypotheses facilitate scientific work and render it consistent. In the search for truth, like the plough of the husbandman, they help forward the work of the labourer.

Footnotes:

[1] This conclusion, deduced by me as far back as 1878 (*Moniteur Scientifique*) by conceiving the molecules of ozone (see later) as more complex than those of oxygen, and ozone as containing a greater quantity of heat than oxygen, has been proved experimentally by the researches of Mailfert (1880), who showed that the passage of a silent discharge through a litre of oxygen at 0° may form up to 14 milligrams of ozone, and at -30° up to 60 milligrams; but best of all in the determinations of Chappuis and Hautefeuille (1880), who found that at a temperature of -25° a silent discharge converted 20 p.c. of oxygen into ozone, whilst at 20° it was impossible to obtain more than 12 p.c., and at 100° less than 2 p.c. of ozone was obtained.

[2] A series of electric sparks may be obtained by an ordinary electrical machine, the electrophorus machines of Holtz and Teploff, &c., Leyden jars, Ruhmkorff coils, or similar means, when the opposite electricities are able to accumulate at the terminals of conductors, and a discharge of sufficient electrical intensity passes through the non-conductors air or oxygen.

[3] A silent discharge is such a combination of opposite statical (potential) electricities as takes place (generally between large surfaces) regularly, without sparks, slowly, and quietly (as in the dispersion of electricity). The discharge is only luminous in the dark; there is no observable rise of temperature, and therefore a larger amount of ozone is formed. But, nevertheless, on continuing the passage of a silent discharge through ozone it is destroyed. For the action to be observable a large

surface is necessary, and consequently a source of electricity at a high potential. For this reason the silent discharge is best produced by a Ruhmkorff coil, as the most convenient means of obtaining a considerable potential of statical electricity with the employment of the comparatively feeble current of a galvanic battery.

[4] *v. Babo's apparatus* was one of the first constructed for ozonising oxygen by means of a silent discharge (and it is still one of the best). It is composed of a number (twenty and more) of long, thin capillary glass tubes closed at one end. A platinum wire, extending along their whole length, is introduced into the other end of each tube, and this end is then fused up round the wire, the end of which protrudes outside the tube. The protruding ends of the wires are arranged alternately in two sides in such a manner that on one side there are ten closed ends and ten wires. A bunch of such tubes (forty should make a bunch of not more than 1 c.m. diameter) is placed in a glass tube, and the ends of the wires are connected with two conductors, and are fused to the ends of the surrounding tube. The discharge of a Ruhmkorff coil is passed through these ends of the wires, and the dry air or oxygen to be ozonised is passed through the tube. If oxygen be passed through, ozone is obtained in large quantities, and free from oxides of nitrogen, which are partially formed when air is acted on. At low temperatures ozone is formed in large quantities. As ozone acts on corks and india-rubber, the apparatus should be made entirely of glass. With a powerful Ruhmkorff coil and forty tubes the ozonation is so powerful that the gas when passed through a solution of iodide of potassium not only sets the iodine free, but even oxidises it to potassium iodate, so that in five minutes the gas-conducting tube is choked up with crystals of the insoluble iodate.

[5] In order to connect the ozoniser with any other apparatus it is impossible to make use of india-rubber, mercury, or cements, &c., because they are themselves acted on by, and act on, ozone. All connections must, as was first proposed by Brodie, be hermetically closed by sulphuric acid, which is not acted on by ozone. Thus, a cork is passed over the vertical end of a tube, over which a wide tube passes so that the end of the first tube protrudes above the cork; mercury is first poured over the cork (to prevent its being acted on by the sulphuric acid), and then sulphuric acid is poured over the mercury. The protruding end of the first tube is covered by the lower end of a third tube immersed in the sulphuric acid.

[6] The method above described is the only one which has been well investigated. The admixture of nitrogen, or even of hydrogen, and especially of silicon fluoride, appears to aid the formation and preservation of ozone. Amongst other methods for preparing ozone we may mention the following: 1. In the action of oxygen on phosphorus at the ordinary

temperature a portion of the oxygen is converted into ozone. At the ordinary temperature a stick of phosphorus, partially immersed in water and partially in air in a large glass vessel, causes the air to acquire the odour of ozone. It must further be remarked that if the air be left for long in contact with the phosphorus, or without the presence of water, the ozone formed is destroyed by the phosphorus. 2. By the action of sulphuric acid on peroxide of barium. If the latter be covered with strong sulphuric acid (the acid, if diluted with only one-tenth of water, does not give ozone), then at a low temperature the oxygen evolved contains ozone, and in much greater quantities than in that ozone is obtained by the action of electric sparks or phosphorus. 3. Ozone may also be obtained by decomposing strong sulphuric acid by potassium manganate especially with the addition of barium peroxide.

[7] Ozone takes up the hydrogen from hydrochloric acid; chlorine is liberated, and can dissolve gold. Iodine is directly oxidised by ozone, but not by oxygen. Ammonia, NH_3, is oxidised by ozone into ammonium nitrite (and nitrate), $2NH_3 + O_3 = NH_4NO_2 + H_2O$, and therefore a drop of ammonia, on falling into the gas, gives a thick cloud of the salts formed. Ozone converts lead oxide into peroxide, and suboxide of thallium (which is colourless) into oxide (which is brown), so that this reaction is made use of for detecting the presence of ozone. Lead sulphide, PbS (black), is converted into sulphate, $PbSO_4$ (colourless), by ozone. A neutral solution of manganese sulphate gives a precipitate of manganese peroxide, and an acid solution may be oxidised into permanganic acid, $HMnO_4$. With respect to the oxidising action of ozone on organic substances, it may be mentioned that with ether, $C_4H_{10}O$, ozone gives ethyl peroxide, which is capable of decomposing with explosion (according to Berthelot), and is decomposed by water into alcohol, $2C_2H_6O$, and hydrogen peroxide, H_2O_2.

[8] This reaction is the one usually made use of for detecting the presence of ozone. In the majority of cases paper is soaked in solutions of potassium iodide and starch. Such *ozonometrical* or iodised starch-paper when damp turns blue in the presence of ozone, and the tint obtained varies considerably, according to the length of time it is exposed and to the amount of ozone present. The amount of ozone in a given gas may even to a certain degree he judged by the shade of colour acquired by the paper, if preliminary tests be made.

Test-paper for ozone is prepared in the following manner:—One gram of neutral potassium iodide is dissolved in 100 grams of distilled water; 10 grams of starch are then shaken up in the solution, and the mixture is boiled until the starch is converted into a jelly. This jelly is then smeared over blotting-paper and left to dry. It must always he remembered, however, that the colour of iodised starch-paper is changed not only by the action of ozone, but of many other oxidisers; for example, by the oxides of nitrogen (especially N_2O_3) and hydrogen peroxide. Houzeau proposed soaking common litmus-paper with a solution of potassium iodide, which in the presence of iodine would turn blue, owing to the formation of KHO. In order to determine if the blue colour is not produced by an alkali (ammonia) in the gas, a portion of the paper is not soaked in the potassium iodide, but moistened with water; this portion will then also turn blue if ammonia be present. A reagent for distinguishing ozone from hydrogen peroxide with certainty is not known, and therefore these substances in very small quantities (for instance, in the atmosphere) may easily he confounded. Until recent years the mistake has frequently been made of ascribing the alteration of iodised starch-paper in the air to the presence of ozone; at the present time there is reason to believe that it is most often due to the presence of nitrous acid (Ilosva, 1889).

[8 bis] Fluorine (Chap. XI.), acting upon water at the ordinary temperature, takes up the hydrogen, and evolves the oxygen in the form of ozone (Moissan, 1889), and therefore the reaction must be expressed thus:—$3H_2O + 3F_2 = 6HF + O_3$.

[9] Ozone is, so to say, an oxide of oxygen, just as water is an oxide of hydrogen. Just as aqueous vapour is composed of two volumes of hydrogen and one volume of oxygen, which on combining condense into two volumes of aqueous vapour, so also two volumes of oxygen are combined in ozone with one volume of oxygen to give two volumes of ozone. In the action of ozone on different substances it is only that additional portion of its molecule by which it differs from ordinary oxygen that combines with other bodies, and that is why, under these circumstances, the volume of the ozonised oxygen does not change. Starting with two volumes of ozone, one-third of its weight is parted with, and two volumes of oxygen remain.

The above observations of Soret on the capacity of turpentine for dissolving ozone, together with Schönbein's researches on the formation of ozone in the oxidation of turpentine and of similar volatile vegetable oils (entering into the composition of *perfumes*), also explain the action of this ethereal oil on a great many substances. It is known that turpentine oil, when mixed with many substances, promotes their oxidation. In this case it probably not only itself promotes the formation of ozone, but also dissolves ozone from the atmosphere, and thus acquires the property of oxidising many substances. It bleaches linen and cork, decolorises indigo, promotes the oxidation and hardening of boiled linseed oil, &c. These properties of turpentine oil are made use of in practice. Dirty linen and many stained materials are easily cleaned by turpentine, not only because it dissolves the grease, but also because it oxidises it. The admixture of turpentine with drying (boiled) oil, oil-colours, and lacs aids their rapid drying because it attracts ozone. Various oils occurring in plants, and entering into the composition of perfumes and certain scent extracts, also act as oxidisers. They act in the same manner as oil of turpentine and oil of cinnamon. This perhaps explains the refreshing influence they have in scents and other similar preparations, and also the salubrity of the air of pine forests. Water upon which a layer of turpentine oil has been poured acquires, when left standing in the light, the disinfecting and oxidising properties in general of ozonised turpentine (is this due to the formation of H_2O_2?).

[10] The densest, most complex, and heaviest particles of matter should, under equal conditions, evidently be less capable of passing into a state of gaseous motion, should sooner attain a liquid state, and have a greater cohesive force.

[11] The blue colour proper to ozone may be seen through a tube one metre long, filled with oxygen, containing 10 p.c. of ozone. The density of liquid ozone has not, so far as I am aware, been determined.

[12] All explosive bodies and mixtures (gunpowder, detonating gas, &c.) evolve heat in exploding—that is, the reactions which accompany explosions are exothermal. In this manner ozone in decomposing evolves latent heat, although generally heat is absorbed in decomposition. This shows the meaning and cause of explosion.

[13] In Paris it has been found that the further from the centre of the town the greater the amount of ozone in the air. The reason of this is evident: in a city there are many conditions for the destruction of ozone. This is why we distinguish country air as being fresh. In spring the air contains more ozone than in autumn; the air of fields more than the air of towns.

[13 bis] The question of the presence of ozone in the air has not yet been fully elucidated, as those reactions by which ozone is generally detected are also common to nitrous acid (and its ammonia salt). Ilosvay de Ilosva (1889), in order to exclude the influence of such bodies, passed air through a 40 per cent. solution of caustic soda, and then through a 20 per cent. solution of sulphuric acid (these solutions do not destroy ozone), and tested the air thus purified for the presence of ozone. As no ozone was then detected the author concludes that all the effects which were formerly ascribed to ozone should be referred to nitrous acid. But this conclusion requires more careful verification, since the researches of Prof. Schönbein on the presence of peroxide of hydrogen in the atmosphere.

[14] The oxidising action of ozone may be taken advantage of for technical purposes; for instance, for destroying colouring matters. It has even been employed for bleaching tissues and for the rapid preparation of vinegar, although these methods have not yet received wide application.

[15] Isomerism in elements is termed *allotropism*.

[16] A number of substances resemble ozone in one or other of these respects. Thus cyanogen, C_2N_2, nitrogen chloride, &c., decompose with an explosion and evolution of heat. Nitrous anhydride, N_2O_3, forms a blue liquid like ozone, and in a number of cases oxidises like ozone.

[17] It is evident that there is a want of words here for distinguishing oxygen, O, as an ultimate *element*, from oxygen, O_2, as a *free element*. The latter should be termed oxygen gas, did not custom and the length of the expression render it inconvenient.

[18] Schönbein states that the formation of hydrogen peroxide is to be remarked in every oxidation in water or in the presence of aqueous vapour. According to Struve, hydrogen peroxide is contained in snow and in rain-water, and its formation, together with ozone and ammonium nitrate, is even probable in the processes of respiration and combustion. A solution of tin in mercury, or liquid tin amalgam, when shaken up in water containing sulphuric acid, produces hydrogen peroxide, whilst iron under the same circumstances does not give rise to its formation. The presence of small quantities of hydrogen peroxide in these and similar cases is recognised by many reactions. Amongst them, its action on *chromic acid* in the presence of ether is very characteristic. Hydrogen peroxide converts the chromic acid into a higher oxide, Cr_2O_7, which is of a dark-blue colour and dissolves in ether. This ethereal solution is to a certain degree stable, and therefore the presence of hydrogen peroxide may be recognised by mixing the liquid to be tested with ether and adding several drops of a solution of chromic acid. On shaking the mixture the ether dissolves the higher oxide of chromium which is formed, and acquires a blue colour. The formation of hydrogen peroxide in the combustion and oxidation of substances containing or evolving hydrogen must be understood in the light of the conception, to be considered later, of molecules occupying equal volumes in a gaseous state. At the moment of its evolution a molecule H_2 combines with a molecule O_2, and gives H_2O_2. As this substance is unstable, a large proportion of it is decomposed, a small amount only remaining unchanged. If it is obtained, water is easily formed from it; this reaction evolves heat, and the reverse action is not very probable. Direct determinations show that the reaction $H_2O_2 = H_2O + O$ evolves 22,000 heat units. From this it will be understood how easy is the decomposition of hydrogen peroxide, as well as the fact that a number of substances which are not directly oxidised

by oxygen are oxidised by hydrogen peroxide and by ozone, which also evolves heat on decomposition. Such a representation of the origin of hydrogen peroxide has been developed by me since 1870. Recently (1890) Traube has pronounced a similar opinion, stating that Zn under the action of water and air gives, besides ZnH_2O_2, also H_2O_2.

[19] The formation of hydrogen peroxide from barium peroxide by a method of double decomposition is an instance of a number of *indirect methods of preparation*. A substance A does not combine with B, but A B is obtained from A C in its action on B D (see Introduction) when C D is formed. Water does not combine with oxygen, but as a hydrate of acids it acts on the compound of oxygen with barium oxide, because this oxide gives a salt with an acid anhydride; or, what is the same thing, hydrogen with oxygen does not directly form hydrogen peroxide, but when combined with a haloid (for example, chlorine), under the action of barium peroxide, BaO_2, it leads to the formation of a salt of barium and H_2O_2. It is to be remarked that the passage of barium oxide, BaO, into the peroxide, BaO_2, is accompanied by the *evolution* of 12,100 heat units per 16 parts of oxygen by weight combined, and the passage of H_2O into the peroxide H_2O_2 does not proceed directly, because it would be accompanied by the *absorption* of 22,000 units of heat by 16 parts by weight of oxygen combined. Barium peroxide, in acting on an acid, evidently evolves less heat than the oxide, and it is this difference of heat that is absorbed in the hydrogen peroxide. Its energy is obtained from that evolved in the formation of the salt of barium.

[20] Peroxides of lead and manganese, and other analogous peroxides (see Chap. III., Note 9), do not give hydrogen peroxide under these conditions, but yield chlorine with hydrochloric acid.

[21] The impure barium peroxide obtained in this manner may be easily purified. For this purpose it is dissolved in a dilute solution of nitric acid. A certain quantity of an insoluble residue always remains, from which the solution is separated by filtration. The solution will contain not only the compound of the barium peroxide, but also a compound of the barium oxide itself, a certain quantity of which always remains uncombined with oxygen. The acid compounds of the peroxide and oxide of barium are easily distinguishable by their stability. The peroxide gives an unstable compound, and the oxide a stable salt. By adding an aqueous solution of barium oxide to the resultant solution, the whole of the peroxide contained in the solution may be precipitated as a pure aqueous compound (Kouriloff, 1889, obtained the same result by adding an excess of BaO_2). The first portions of the precipitate will consist of impurities—for instance, oxide of iron. The barium peroxide then separates out, and is collected on a filter and washed; it forms a substance having a definite composition,

$BaO_2,8H_2O$, and is very pure. Pure hydrogen peroxide should always be prepared from such purified barium peroxide.

[22] In the cold, strong sulphuric acid with barium peroxide gives ozone; when diluted with a certain amount of water it gives oxygen (see Note 6), and hydrogen peroxide is only obtained by the action of very weak sulphuric acid. Hydrochloric, hydrofluoric, carbonic, and hydrosilicofluoric acids, and others, when diluted with water also give hydrogen peroxide with barium peroxide. Professor Schöne, who very carefully investigated hydrogen peroxide, showed that it is formed by the action of many of the above-mentioned acids on barium peroxide. In preparing peroxide of hydrogen by means of sulphuric acid, the solution must be kept cold. A solution of maximum concentration may be obtained by successive treatments with sulphuric acid of increasing strength. In this manner a solution containing 2 to 3 grams of pure peroxide in 100 c.c. of water may be obtained (V. Kouriloff).

[23] With the majority of acids, that salt of barium which is formed remains in solution; thus, for instance, by employing hydrochloric acid, hydrogen peroxide and barium chloride remain in solution. Complicated processes would be required to obtain pure hydrogen peroxide from such a solution. It is much more convenient to take advantage of the action of carbonic anhydride on the pure hydrate of barium peroxide. For this purpose the hydrate is stirred up in water, and a rapid stream of carbonic anhydride is passed through the water. Barium carbonate, insoluble in water, is formed, and the hydrogen peroxide remains in solution, so that it may be separated from the carbonate by filtering only. On a large scale hydrofluosilicic acid is employed, its barium salt being also insoluble in water.

[23 bis] Hydrogen peroxide may be extracted from very dilute solutions by means of ether, which dissolves it, and when mixed with it the hydrogen peroxide may even be distilled. A solution of hydrogen peroxide in water may be strengthened by cooling it to a low temperature, when the water crystallises out—that is, is converted into ice—whilst the hydrogen peroxide remains in solution, as it only freezes at very low temperatures. It must be observed that hydrogen peroxide, in a strong solution in a pure state, is exceedingly unstable even at the ordinary temperature, and therefore it must be preserved in vessels always kept cold, as otherwise it evolves oxygen and forms water.

[24] Peroxide of sodium (Chap. XII., Note 49) is prepared by burning sodium in dry air.

[24 bis] Peroxide of hydrogen should apparently find an industrial application in the arts, for instance, (1) as a bleaching agent, it having the

important advantage over chloride of lime, SO₂, &c., of not acting upon the material under treatment. It may be used for bleaching feathers, hair, silk, wool, wood, &c., it also removes stains of all kinds, such as wine, ink, and fruit stains; (2) it destroys bacteria like ozone without having any injurious effect upon the human body. It can also be used for washing all kinds of wounds, for purifying the air in the sick room, &c., and (3) as a preserving agent for potted meats, &c.

[25] As the result of careful research, certain of the *catalytic* or contact phenomena have been subjected to exact explanation, which shows the participation of a substance present in the process of a reaction, whilst, however, it does not alter the series of changes proceeding from mechanical actions only. Professor Schöne, of the Petroffsky Academy, has already explained a number of reactions of hydrogen peroxide which previously were not understood. Thus, for instance, he showed that with hydrogen peroxide, alkalis give peroxides of the alkaline metals, which combine with the remaining hydrogen peroxide, forming unstable compounds which are easily decomposed, and therefore alkalis evince a decomposing (catalytic) influence on solutions of hydrogen peroxide. Only acid solutions of hydrogen peroxide, and then only dilute ones, can be preserved well.

[26] *Hydrogen peroxide,* as a substance containing much oxygen (namely, 16 parts to one part by weight of hydrogen), exhibits many *oxidising reactions.* Thus, it oxidises arsenic, converts lime into calcium peroxide, the oxides of zinc and copper into peroxides; it parts with its oxygen to many sulphides, converting them into sulphates, &c. So, for example, it converts black lead sulphide, PbS, into white lead sulphate, PbSO₄, copper sulphide into copper sulphate, and so on. The restoration of old oil paintings by hydrogen peroxide is based on this action. Oil colours are usually admixed with white lead, and in many cases the colour of oil-paints becomes darker in process of time. This is partly due to the sulphuretted hydrogen contained in the air, which acts on white lead, forming lead sulphide, which is black. The intermixture of the black colour darkens the rest. In cleaning a picture with a solution of hydrogen peroxide, the black lead sulphide is converted into white sulphate, and the colours brighten owing to the disappearance of the black substance which previously darkened them. Hydrogen peroxide oxidises with particular energy substances containing hydrogen and capable of easily parting with it to oxidising substances. Thus it decomposes hydriodic acid, setting the iodine free and converting the hydrogen it contains into water; it also decomposes sulphuretted hydrogen in exactly the same manner, setting the sulphur free. Starch paste with potassium iodide is not, however, directly coloured by peroxide of hydrogen in the entire absence of free acids; but the addition of a small

quantity of iron sulphate (green vitriol) or of lead acetate to the mixture is enough to entirely blacken the paste. This is a very sensitive reagent (test) for peroxide of hydrogen, like the test with chromic acid and ether (*see* Note 8).

[27] To explain the phenomenon, an hypothesis has been put forward by Brodie, Clausius, and Schönbein which supposes ordinary oxygen to be an electrically neutral substance, composed, so to speak, of two electrically opposite kinds of oxygen—positive and negative. It is supposed that hydrogen peroxide contains one kind of such polar oxygen, whilst in the oxides of the above-named metals the oxygen is of opposite polarity. It is supposed that in the oxides of the metals the oxygen is electro-negative, and in hydrogen peroxide electro-positive, and that on the mutual contact of these substances ordinary neutral oxygen is evolved as a consequence of the mutual attraction of the oxygens of opposite polarity. Brodie admits the polarity of oxygen in combination, but not in an uncombined state, whilst Schönbein supposes uncombined oxygen to be polar also, considering ozone as electro-negative oxygen. The supposition that the oxygen of ozone is different from that of hydrogen peroxide is contradicted by the fact that in acting on barium peroxide strong sulphuric acid forms ozone, and dilute acid forms hydrogen peroxide.

[27 bis] It should be mentioned that Schiloff (1893) on taking a 3 per cent. solution of H_2O_2, adding soda to it, and then extracting the peroxide of hydrogen from the mixture by shaking it with ether, obtained a 50 per cent. solution of H_2O_2, which, although perfectly free from other acids, gave a distinctly acid reaction with litmus. And here attention should first of all be turned to the fact that the peroxides of the metals correspond to H_2O_2, like salts to an acid, for instance, Na_2O_2 and BaO_2, &c. Furthermore, it must be remembered that O is an analogue of S (Chapters XV. and XX.), and sulphur gives H_2S, H_2SO_3, and H_2SO_4. And sulphurous acid, H_2SO_3, is unstable as a hydrate, and gives water and the anhydride SO_2. If the sulphur be replaced by oxygen, then instead of H_2SO_3 and SO_2, we have H_2OO_3 and OO_2. The latter is ozone, while the salt K_2O_4 (peroxide of potassium) corresponds to the hydrate H_2O_4 as to an acid. And between H_2O and H_2O_4 there may exist intermediate acid compounds, the first of which would be H_2O_2, in which, from analogy to the sulphur compounds, one would expect acid properties. Besides which we may mention that for sulphur, besides H_2S (which is a feeble acid), H_2S_2, H_2S_3, H_2S_5 are known. Thus in many respects H_2O_2 offers points of resemblance to acid compounds, and as regards its qualitative (reactive) analogies, it not only resembles Na_2O_2, BaO_2, &c., but also persulphuric acid HSO_4 (to which the anhydride S_2O_7 corresponds) and Cu_2O_7, &c., which will be subsequently described.

[28] Tamman and Carrara (1892) showed by determining the depression (fall of the temperature of the formation of ice, Chapters I. and VII.) that the molecule of peroxide of hydrogen contains H_2O_2, and not HO or H_3O_3.

[28 bis] The lower oxides of nitrogen and chlorine and the higher oxides of manganese are also formed with the absorption of heat, and therefore, like hydrogen peroxide, act in a powerfully oxidising manner, and are not formed by the same methods as the majority of other oxides. It is evident that, being endowed with a richer store of energy (acquired in combination or by absorption of heat), such substances, compared with others poorer in energy, will exhibit a greater diversity of cases of chemical action with other substances.

[29] If the point of support of a body lies in a vertical line below the centre of gravity, it is in unstable equilibrium. If the centre of gravity lies below the point of support; the state of equilibrium is very stable, and a vibration may take place about this position of stable equilibrium, as in a pendulum or balance, when finally the body assumes a position of stable equilibrium. But if, keeping to the same mechanical example, the body be supported not on a point, in the geometrical sense of the word, but on a small plane, then the state of unstable equilibrium may be preserved, unless destroyed by external influences. Thus a man stands upright supported on the plane, or several points of the surfaces of his feet, having the centre of gravity above the points of support. Vibration is then possible, but it is limited, otherwise on passing outside the limit of possible equilibrium another more stable position is attained about which vibration becomes more possible. A prism immersed in water may have several more or less stable positions of equilibrium. The same is also true with the atoms in molecules. Some molecules present a state of more stable equilibrium than others. Hence from this simple comparison it will be at once evident that the stability of molecules may vary considerably, that one and the same elements, taken in the same number, may give isomerides of different stability, and, lastly, that there may exist states of equilibria which are so unstable, so ephemeral, that they will only arise under particularly special conditions—such, for example, as certain hydrates mentioned in the first chapter (see Notes 57, 67, and others). And if in one case the instability of a given state of equilibrium is expressed by its instability with a change of temperature or physical state, then in other cases it is expressed by the facility with which it decomposes under the influence of contact or of the chemical influence of other substances.

[30] When, for example, any element forms several oxides, they are subject to the law of multiple proportions. For a given quantity of the non-metal or metal the quantities of oxygen in the different degrees of

oxidation will stand as 1 : 2, or as 1 : 3, or as 2 : 3, or as 2 : 7, and so on. Thus, for instance, copper combines with oxygen in at least two proportions, forming the oxides found in nature, and called the suboxide and the oxide of copper, Cu_2O and CuO; the oxide contains twice as much oxygen as the suboxide. Lead also presents two degrees of oxidation, the oxide and peroxide, and in the latter there is twice as much oxygen as in the former, PbO and PbO_2. When a base and an acid are capable of forming several kinds of salts, normal, acid, basic, and anhydro-, it is found that they also clearly exemplify the law of multiple proportions. This was demonstrated by Wollaston soon after the discovery of the law in question. We saw in the first chapter that salts show different degrees of combination with water of crystallisation, and that they obey the law of multiple proportions. And, more than this, the indefinite chemical compounds existing as solutions may, as we saw in the same chapter, be brought under the law of multiple proportions by the hypothesis that solutions are unstable hydrates formed according to the law of multiple proportions, but occurring in a state of dissociation. By means of this hypothesis the law of multiple proportions becomes still more general, and all the aspects of chemical compounds are subject to it. The direction of the whole contemporary state of chemistry was determined by the discoveries of Lavoisier and Dalton. By endeavouring to prove that in solutions we have nothing else than the liquid products of the dissociation of definite hydrates, it is my aim to bring also this category of indefinite compounds under the general principle enunciated by Dalton; just as astronomers have discovered a proof and not a negation of the laws of Newton in perturbations.

[31] Leucippus, Democritus, and especially Lucretius, in the classical ages, represented matter as made up of atoms—that is, of parts incapable of further division. The geometrical impossibility of such an admission, as well as the conclusions which were deduced by the ancient atomists from their fundamental propositions, prevented other philosophers from following them, and the atomic doctrine, like very many others, lived, without being ratified by fact, in the imaginations of its followers. Between the present atomic theory and the doctrine of the above-named ancient philosophers there is naturally a remote historical connection, as between the doctrine of Pythagoras and Copernicus, but they are essentially different. For us the atom is indivisible, not in the geometrical abstract sense, but only in a physical and chemical sense. It would be better to call the atoms indivisible *individuals*. The Greek atom = the Latin individual, both according to the etymology and original sense of the words, but in course of time these two words have acquired a different meaning. The individual is mechanically and geometrically divisible, and only indivisible in a special sense. The earth, the sun, a man or a fly are individuals, although

geometrically divisible. Thus the 'atoms' of contemporary science, indivisible in a chemical sense, form those units with which we are concerned in the investigation of the natural phenomena of matter, just as a man is an indivisible unit in the investigation of social relations, or as the stars, planets, and luminaries serve as units in astronomy. The formation of the vortex hypothesis, in which, as we shall afterwards see, atoms are entire whirls mechanically complex, although physico-chemically indivisible, clearly shows that the scientific men of our time in holding to the atomic theory have only borrowed the word and form of expression from the ancient philosophers, and not the essence of their atomic doctrine. It is erroneous to imagine that the contemporary conceptions of the atomists are nothing but the repetition of the metaphysical reasonings of the ancients. To show the true meaning of the atomism of the ancient philosophers, and the profound difference between their points of argument and those of contemporary men of science, I cite the following fundamental propositions of Democritus (B.C. 470–380) as the best expounder of the atomic doctrine of the ancients:—(1) Nothing can proceed from nothing, nothing that exists can disappear or be destroyed (and hence matter), and every change only consists of a combination or separation. (2) Nothing is accidental, there is a reason and necessity for everything. (3) All except atoms and vacua is reason and not existence. (4) The atoms, which are infinite in number and form, constitute the visible universe by their motion, impact, and consequent revolving motion. (5) The variety of objects depends only upon a difference in the number, form, and order of the atoms of which they are formed, and not upon a qualitative difference of their atoms, which only act upon each other by pressure and impact. (6) The spirit, like fire, consists of minute, spherical, smooth, and very mobile and all-penetrating atoms, whose motion forms the phenomenon of life. These Democritian, chiefly metaphysical, principles of atomism are so essentially different from the principles of the present atomic doctrine, which is exclusively applied to explaining the phenomena of the external world, that it may be useful to mention the essence of the atomic propositions of Boscovitch, a Slav who lived in the middle of the eighteenth century, and who is regarded as the founder of the modern atomic doctrines which, however, did not take hold upon the minds of scientific men, and were rarely applied prior to Dalton—*i.e.* until the beginning of the nineteenth century. The doctrine of Boscovitch was enunciated by him in 1758–1764 in his '*Philosophiæ naturalis theoria reducta ad unicam legem virium in natura existentium.*' Boscovitch considers matter to be composed of atoms, and the atoms to be the points or centres of forces (just as the stars and planets may be considered as points of space), acting between bodies and their parts. These forces vary with the distance, so that beyond a certain very small distance all atoms, and hence also their aggregates, are attracted according to Newton's law, but at less distances, there alternate wave-like spheres of gradually decreasing attraction and increasing (as the distance decreases) repulsion, until at last at a minimum distance only the repellent action remains. Atoms, therefore, cannot merge into each other. Consequently, the atoms are held at a certain distance from each other, and therefore occupy space. Boscovitch compares the sphere of repulsion surrounding the atoms to the spheres of action of firing of a detachment of soldiers. According to his doctrine, atoms are indestructible, do not merge into each other, have mass, are everlasting and mobile under the action of the forces proper to them. Maxwell rightly calls this hypothesis the 'extreme' among those existing to explain matter, but many aspects of Boscovitch's doctrine repeat themselves in the views of our day, with this essential difference, that instead of a mathematical point furnished with the properties of mass, the atoms are endowed with a corporality, just as the stars and planets are corporal, although in certain aspects of their interaction they may be regarded as mathematical points. In my opinion, the atomism of our day must first of all be regarded merely as a convenient method for the investigation of ponderable matter. As a geometrician in reasoning about curves represents them as formed of a succession of right lines, because such a method enables him to analyse the subject under investigation, so the scientific man applies the atomic theory as a method of analysing the phenomena of nature. Naturally there are people now, as in ancient times, and as there always will be, who apply reality to imagination, and therefore there are to be found atomists of extreme views; but it is not in their spirit that we should acknowledge the great services rendered by the atomic doctrine to all science, which, while it has been essentially independently developed, is, if it be desired to reduce all ideas to the doctrines of the ancients, a union of the ancient dynamical and atomic doctrines.

[32] Dalton and many of his successors distinguished the atoms of elements and compounds, in which they clearly symbolised the difference of their opinion from the representations of the ancients. Now only the individuals of the elements, indivisible by physical and chemical forces, are termed atoms, and the individuals of compounds indivisible under physical changes are termed molecules; these are divisible into atoms by chemical forces.

[33] In the present condition of science, either the atomic or the dynamical hypothesis is inevitably obliged to admit the existence of an invisible and imperceptible motion in matter, without which it is impossible to understand either light or heat, or gaseous pressure, or any of the mechanical, physical, or chemical phenomena. The ancients saw vital motion in animals only, but to us the smallest particle of matter, endued

with *vis viva*, or energy in some degree or other, is incomprehensible without self-existent motion. Thus motion has become a conception inseparably knit with the conception of matter, and this has prepared the ground for the revival of the dynamical hypothesis of the constitution of matter. In the atomic theory there has arisen that generalising idea by which the world of atoms is constructed, like the universe of heavenly bodies, with its suns, planets, and meteors, endued with everlasting force of motion, forming molecules as the heavenly bodies form systems, like the solar system, which molecules are only relatively indivisible in the same way as the planets of the solar system are inseparable, and stable and lasting as the solar system is lasting. Such a representation, without necessitating the absolute indivisibility of atoms, expresses all that science can require for an hypothetical representation of the constitution of matter. In closer proximity to the dynamical hypothesis of the constitution of matter is the oft-times revived *vortex hypothesis*. Descartes first endeavoured to raise it; Helmholtz and Thomson (Lord Kelvin) gave it a fuller and more modern form; many scientific men applied it to physics and chemistry. The idea of vortex rings serves as the starting point of this hypothesis; these are familiar to all as the rings of tobacco smoke, and may be artificially obtained by giving a sharp blow to the sides of a cardboard box having a circular orifice and filled with smoke. Phosphuretted hydrogen, as we shall see later on, when bubbling from water always gives very perfect vortex rings in a still atmosphere. In such rings it is easy to observe a constant circular motion about their axes, and to notice the stability the rings possess in their motion of translation. This unchangeable mass, endued with a rapid internal motion, is likened to the atom. In a medium deprived of friction, such a ring, as is shown by theoretical considerations of the subject from a mechanical point of view, would be perpetual and unchangeable. The rings are capable of grouping together, and in combining, without being absolutely indivisible, remain indivisible. The vortex hypothesis has been established in our times, but it has not been fully developed; its application to chemical phenomena is not clear, although not impossible; it does not satisfy a doubt in respect to the nature of the space existing between the rings (just as it is not clear what exists between atoms, and between the planets), neither does it tell us what is the nature of the moving substance of the ring, and therefore for the present it only presents the germ of an hypothetical conception of the constitution of matter; consequently, I consider that it would be superfluous to speak of it in greater detail. However, the thoughts of investigators are now (and naturally will be in the future), as they were in the time of Dalton, often turned to the question of the limitation of the mechanical division of matter, and the atomists have searched for an answer in the most diverse spheres of nature. I select one of the methods attempted, which does not in any way refer to chemistry, in order to show how closely all the provinces of natural science are bound together. Wollaston proposed the investigation of the *atmosphere of the heavenly bodies* as a means for confirming the existence of atoms. If the divisibility of matter be infinite, then air must extend throughout the entire space of the heavens as it extends all over the earth by its elasticity and diffusion. If the infinite divisibility of matter be admitted, it is impossible that any portion of the whole space of the universe can be entirely void of the component parts of our atmosphere. But if matter be divisible up to a certain limit only—namely, up to the atom—then there *can exist* a heavenly body void of an atmosphere; and if such a body be discovered, it would serve as an important factor for the acceptation of the validity of the atomic doctrine. The moon has long been considered as such a luminary and this circumstance, especially from its proximity to the earth, has been cited as the best proof of the validity of the atomic doctrine. This proof is apparently (Poisson) deprived of some of its force from the possibility of the transformation of the component parts of our atmosphere into a solid or liquid state at immense heights above the earth's surface, where the temperature is exceedingly low; but a series of researches (Pouillet) has shown that the temperature of the heavenly space is comparatively not so very low, and is attainable by experimental means, so that at the low existing pressure the liquefaction of the gases of the atmosphere cannot he expected even on the moon. Therefore the absence of an atmosphere about the moon, if it were not subject to doubt, would be counted as a forcible proof of the atomic theory. As a proof of the absence of a lunar atmosphere, it is cited that the moon, in its independent motion between the stars, when eclipsing a star— that is, when passing between the eye and the star—does not show any signs of refraction at its edge; the image of the star does not alter its position in the heavens on approaching the moon's surface, consequently there is no atmosphere on the moon's surface capable of refracting the rays of light. Such is the conclusion by which the absence of a lunar atmosphere is acknowledged. But this conclusion is most feeble, and there are even facts in exact contradiction to it, by which the existence of a lunar atmosphere may be proved. The entire surface of the moon is covered with a number of mountains, having in the majority of cases the conical form natural to volcanoes. The volcanic character of the lunar mountains was confirmed in October 1866, when a change was observed in the form of one of them (the crater Linnea). These mountains must be on the edge of the lunar disc. Seen in profile, they screen one another and interfere with observations on the surface of the moon, so that when looking at the edge of the lunar disc we are obliged to make our observations not on the moon's surface, but at the summits of the lunar mountains. These mountains are higher than those on our earth, and consequently at their summits the lunar atmosphere must he exceedingly rarefied even if it possess an observable density at the surface. Knowing the mass of the moon to be eighty-two times less than the mass of the earth, we are able to determine approximately that our atmosphere at the moon's surface would be about twenty-eight times lighter than it is on the earth, and consequently at the very surface of the moon the refraction of light by the lunar atmosphere must he very slight, and at the heights of the lunar mountains it must be imperceptible, and would be lost within the limits of experimental error. Therefore the absence of refraction of light at the edge of the moon's disc cannot yet be urged in favour of the absence of a lunar atmosphere. There is even a series of observations obliging us to admit the existence of this atmosphere. These researches are due to Sir John Herschel. This is what he writes: 'It has often been remarked that during the eclipse of a star by the moon there occurs a peculiar optical illusion; it seems as if the star before disappearing passed over the edge of the moon and is seen through the lunar disc, sometimes for a rather long period of time. I myself have observed this phenomenon, and it has been witnessed by perfectly trustworthy observers. I ascribe it to optical illusion, but it must be admitted that the star might have been seen on the lunar disc through some deep ravine on the moon.' Geniller, in Belgium (1856), following the opinion of Cassini, Eiler, and others, gave an explanation of this phenomenon: he considers it due to the refraction of light in the valleys of the lunar mountains which occur on the edge of the lunar disc. In fact, although these valleys do not probably present the form of straight ravines, yet it may sometimes happen that the light of a star is so refracted that its image might he seen, notwithstanding the absence of a direct path for the light-rays. He then goes on to remark that the density of the lunar atmosphere must be variable in different parts, owing to the very long nights on the moon. On the dark, or non-illuminated portion, owing to these long nights, which last thirteen of our days and nights, there must be excessive cold, and hence a denser atmosphere, while, on the contrary, on the illuminated portion the atmosphere must be much more rarefied. This variation in the temperature of the different parts of the moon's surface explains also the absence of clouds, notwithstanding the possible presence of air and aqueous vapour, on the visible portion of the moon. The presence of an atmosphere round the sun and planets, judging from astronomical observations, may be considered as fully proved. On Jupiter and Mars even bands of clouds may be distinguished. Thus the atomic doctrine, admitting a finite mechanical divisibility only, must he, as yet at least, only accepted as a means, similar to that means which a mathematician employs when he breaks up a continuous curvilinear line into a number of straight lines. There is a simplicity of representation in atoms, but there is no absolute necessity to have recourse to them. The conception of the individuality of the parts of matter exhibited in chemical elements only is necessary and trustworthy.

[223]

CHAPTER V

NITROGEN AND AIR

Gaseous *nitrogen* forms about four-fifths (by volume) of the atmosphere; consequently the air contains an exceedingly large mass of it. Whilst entering in so considerable a quantity into the composition of air, nitrogen does not seem to play any active part in the atmosphere, the chemical action of which is mainly dependent on the oxygen it contains. But this is not an entirely correct idea, because animal life cannot exist in pure oxygen, in which animals pass into an abnormal state and die; and the nitrogen of the air, although slowly, forms diverse compounds, many of which play a most important part in nature, especially in the life of organisms. However, neither plants[1] nor animals directly absorb the nitrogen of the air, but take it up from already prepared nitrogenous compounds; further, plants are nourished by the nitrogenous substances contained in the soil and water, and animals by the nitrogenous substances contained in plants and in other animals. Atmospheric electricity is capable of aiding the passage of gaseous nitrogen into nitrogenous compounds, as we shall afterwards see, and the resultant substances are carried to the soil by rain, where they serve for the nourishment of plants. Plentiful harvests, fine crops of hay, vigorous growth of trees—other conditions being equal—are only obtained when the soil contains *ready prepared nitrogenous compounds*, consisting either of those which occur in air and water, or of the residues of the decomposition of other plants or animals (as in manure). The nitrogenous substances contained in animals have their origin in those substances which are formed in plants. Thus the nitrogen of the atmosphere is the origin of all the nitrogenous substances occurring in animals and plants, although not directly so, but after first combining with the other elements of air.

The nitrogenous compounds which enter into the composition of plants and animals are of primary importance; no vegetable or animal cell—that is, the elementary form of organism—exists without containing a nitrogenous[224] substance, and moreover organic life manifests itself primarily in these nitrogenous substances. The germs, seeds, and those parts by which cells multiply themselves abound in nitrogenous substances; the sum total of the phenomena which are proper to organisms depend primarily on the chemical properties of the nitrogenous substances which enter into their composition. It will be sufficient, for instance, to point out the fact that vegetable and animal organisms, clearly distinguishable as such, are characterised by a different degree of energy in their nature, and at the same time by a difference in the amount of nitrogenous substances they contain. In plants, which compared with animals possess but little activity, being incapable of independent movement, &c., the amount of nitrogen is very much less than in animals, whose tissues are almost exclusively formed of nitrogenous substances. It is remarkable that the nitrogenous parts of plants, chiefly of the lower orders, sometimes present both forms and properties which approach to those of animal organisms; for example, the zoospores of sea-weeds, or those parts by means of which the latter multiply themselves. These zoospores on leaving the sea-weed in many respects resemble the lower orders of animal life, having, like the latter, the property of moving. They also approach the animal kingdom in their composition, their outer coating containing nitrogenous matter. Directly the zoospore becomes covered with that non-nitrogenous or cellular coating which is proper to all the ordinary cells of plants, it loses all resemblance to an animal organism and becomes a small plant. It may be thought from this that the cause of the difference in the vital processes of animals and plants is the different amount of nitrogenous substances they contain. The nitrogenous substances which occur in plants and animals appertain to a series of exceedingly complex and very changeable chemical compounds; their elementary composition alone shows this; besides nitrogen, they contain carbon, hydrogen, oxygen, and sulphur. Being distinguished by a very great instability under many conditions in which other compounds remain unchanged, these substances are fitted for those perpetual changes which form the first condition of vital activity. These complex and changeable nitrogenous substances of the organism are called *proteïd substances*. The white of eggs is a familiar example of such a substance. They are also contained in the flesh of animals, the curdy elements of milk, the glutinous matter of wheaten flour, or so-called gluten, which forms the chief component of macaroni, &c.

Nitrogen occurs in the earth's crust, in compounds either forming the remains of plants and animals, or derived from the nitrogen of the atmosphere as a consequence of its combination with the other component[225] parts of the air. It is not found in other forms in the earth's crust; so that nitrogen must be considered, in contradistinction to oxygen, as an element which is purely superficial, and does not extend to the depths of the earth.[1 bis]

Nitrogen is liberated in a free state in the decomposition of the *nitrogenous organic substances* entering into the composition of organisms—for instance, on their combustion. All organic substances burn when heated to redness with oxygen (or substances readily yielding it, such as oxide of copper); the oxygen combines with the carbon, sulphur, and hydrogen, and the nitrogen is evolved in a free state, because at a high temperature it does not form any stable compound, but remains uncombined. Carbonic anhydride and water are formed from the carbon and hydrogen respectively, and therefore to obtain pure nitrogen it is necessary to remove the carbonic anhydride from the gaseous products obtained. This may be done very easily by the action of alkalis—for instance, caustic soda. The amount of nitrogen in organic substances is determined by a method founded on this.

It is also very easy to obtain *nitrogen from air*, because oxygen combines with many substances. Either phosphorus or metallic copper is usually employed for removing the oxygen from air, but, naturally, a number of other substances may also be used. If a small saucer on which a piece of phosphorus is laid be placed on a cork floating on water, and the phosphorus be lighted, and the whole covered with a glass bell jar, then the air under the jar will be deprived of its oxygen, and nitrogen only will remain, owing to which, on cooling, the water will rise to a certain extent in the bell jar. The same object (procuring nitrogen from air) is attained much more conveniently and perfectly by passing air through a red-hot tube containing copper filings. At a red heat, metallic copper combines with oxygen and gives a black powder of copper oxide. If the layer of copper be sufficiently long and the current of air slow, all the oxygen will be absorbed, and nitrogen alone will pass from the tube.[2]

[226]

Nitrogen may also be procured from many of its *compounds with oxygen*[3] *and hydrogen*,[4] but the best fitted for this purpose is a saline mixture containing, on the one hand, a compound of nitrogen with oxygen, termed nitrous anhydride, N_2O_3, and on the other hand, ammonia, NH_3—that is, a compound of nitrogen with hydrogen. By heating such a mixture, the oxygen of the nitrous anhydride combines with the hydrogen of the ammonia, forming water, and gaseous nitrogen is evolved, $2NH_3 + N_2O_3 = 3H_2O + N_4$. Nitrogen is procured by this method in the following manner:—A solution of caustic potash is saturated with nitrous anhydride, by which means potassium nitrite is formed. On the other hand, a solution of hydrochloric acid saturated with ammonia is prepared; a saline substance called sal-ammoniac, NH_4Cl, is thus formed in the solution. The two solutions thus prepared are mixed together and heated. Reaction takes place according to the equation $KNO_2 + NH_4Cl = KCl + 2H_2O + N_2$. This reaction proceeds in virtue of the fact that potassium nitrite and ammonium chloride are salts which, on interchanging their metals, give potassium chloride and ammonium nitrite, NH_4NO_2, which breaks up into water and nitrogen. This reaction does not take place without the aid of heat, but it proceeds very easily at a moderate temperature. Of the resultant substances, the nitrogen only is gaseous. Pure nitrogen may be obtained by drying the resultant gas and passing it through a solution of sulphuric acid (to absorb a certain quantity of ammonia which is evolved in the reaction).[4 bis]

[227]

Nitrogen is a gaseous substance which does not differ much in physical properties from air; its density, referred to hydrogen, is approximately equal to 14—that is, it is slightly lighter than air, its density referred to air being 0·972; one litre of nitrogen weighs 1·257 gram. Nitrogen mixed with oxygen, which is slightly heavier than air, forms air. It is a gas which, like oxygen and hydrogen, is liquefied with difficulty, and is but little soluble in water and other liquids. Its absolute boiling point[5] is about -140°; above this temperature it is not liquefiable by pressure, and at lower temperatures it remains a gas at a pressure of 50 atmospheres. Liquid nitrogen boils at -193°, so that it may be employed as a source of great cold. At about -203°, in vaporising under a decrease of pressure, nitrogen solidifies into a colourless snow-like mass. Nitrogen does not burn,[5 bis] does not support combustion, is not absorbed by any of the reagents used in gas analysis, at least at the ordinary temperature—in a word, it presents a whole series of negative chemical properties; this is expressed by saying that this element has no energy for combination. Although it is capable of forming compounds both with oxygen and hydrogen as well as with carbon, yet these compounds are only formed under particular circumstances, to which we will directly turn our attention. At a red heat nitrogen combines with boron, titanium, and silicon, barium, magnesium, &c., forming very stable nitrogenous compounds,[6] whose properties are entirely different from those of nitrogen with hydrogen, oxygen and carbon. However, the combination of nitrogen with carbon, although it does not take place directly between the elements at a red heat, yet proceeds with comparative ease by heating a mixture of charcoal with an alkaline carbonate, especially potassium carbonate or barium carbonate,[228] to redness, carbo-nitrides or cyanides of the metals being formed; for instance, $K_2CO_3 + 4C + N_2 = 2KCN + 3CO$.[7]

Nitrogen is found with oxygen in the air, but they do not readily combine. Cavendish, however, in the last century, showed that *nitrogen combines with oxygen under the influence of a series of electric sparks*. Electric sparks in passing through a moist[8] mixture of nitrogen and oxygen cause these elements to combine, forming reddish-brown fumes of oxides of nitrogen,[9] which form nitric acid,[10] NHO_3. The presence of the latter is easily recognised, not only from its reddening litmus paper, but also from its acting as a powerful oxidiser even of mercury. Conditions similar to these occur in nature, during a[229] thunderstorm or in other electrical discharges which take place in the atmosphere; whence it may be taken for granted that air and rain-water always contain traces of nitric and nitrous acids.[11] Besides which Crookes (1892) showed that under certain circumstances and when electricity of high potential[11 bis] passes through the air, the combination of nitrogen with oxygen is accompanied by the formation of a true flame. This was also observed previously (1880) during the passage of electrical discharges through the air.

Further observations showed that under the influence of electrical discharges,[12] silent as well as with sparks, nitrogen is able to enter into many reactions with hydrogen and with many hydrocarbons; although these reactions cannot be effected by exposure to a red heat. Thus, for instance, a series of electric sparks passed through a mixture of nitrogen and hydrogen causes them to combine and *form ammonia*[13] or nitrogen hydride, NH_3, composed of one volume of nitrogen and three volumes of hydrogen. This combination is limited to the formation of 6 per cent. of ammonia, because ammonia is decomposed, although not entirely (94 $\boxed{100}$) by electric sparks. This signifies that under the influence of an electrical discharge the reaction $NH_3 = N + 3H$ is reversible, consequently it is a dissociation, and in it a state of equilibrium is arrived at. The equilibrium may be destroyed by the addition of gaseous hydrochloric acid, HCl, because with ammonia it forms a solid saline compound, sal-ammoniac, NH_4Cl, which (being formed from a gaseous mixture of 3H, N, and HCl) fixes the ammonia. The remaining mass of nitrogen and hydrogen, under the action of the[230] sparks, again forms ammonia, and in this manner *solid sal-ammoniac is obtained to the end by the action of a series of electric sparks on a mixture of gaseous* N, H_3, *and* HCl.[14] Berthelot (1876) showed that under the action of a silent discharge many non-nitrogenous organic substances (benzene, C_6H_6, cellulose in the form of paper, resin, glucose, $C_6H_{10}O_5$, and others) absorb nitrogen and form complex nitrogenous compounds, which are capable, like albuminous substances, of evolving their nitrogen as ammonia when heated with alkalis.[15]

By such indirect methods does the gaseous nitrogen of the atmosphere yield its primary compounds, in which form it enters into plants, and is elaborated in them into complex albuminous substances.[15 bis] But, starting from a given compound of nitrogen with[231] hydrogen or oxygen, we may, without the aid of organisms, obtain, as will afterwards be partially indicated, most diverse and complex nitrogenous substances, which cannot by any means be formed directly from gaseous nitrogen. In this we see an example not only of the difference between an element in the free state and an intrinsic element, but also of those circuitous or *indirect methods* by which substances are formed in nature. The discovery, prognostication, and, in general, the study of such indirect methods of the preparation and formation of substances forms one of the existing problems of chemistry. From the fact that A does not act at all on B, it must not be concluded that a compound AB is not to be formed. The substances A and B contain atoms which occur in AB, but their state or the nature of their motion may not be at all that which is required for the formation of AB, and in this substance the chemical state of the elements may be as different as the state of the atoms of oxygen in ozone and in water. Thus free nitrogen is inactive; but in its compounds it very easily enters into changes and is distinguished by great activity. An acquaintance with the compounds of nitrogen confirms this. But, before entering on this subject, let us consider air as a mass containing free nitrogen.

Judging from what has been already stated, it will be evident that *atmospheric air*[16] contains a mixture of several gases and vapours. Some of them are met with in it in nearly constant proportions, whilst others, on the contrary, are very variable in their amount. The chief[232] component parts of air, placed in the order of their relative amounts, are the following: nitrogen,[16 bis] oxygen, aqueous vapour, carbonic anhydride, nitric acid, salts of ammonia, oxides of nitrogen, and also ozone, hydrogen peroxide, and complex organic nitrogenous substances. Besides these, air generally contains water, as spray, drops, and snow, and particles of solids, perhaps of cosmic origin in certain instances, but in the majority of cases proceeding from the mechanical translation of solid particles from one locality to another by the wind. These small solid and liquid particles (having a large surface in proportion to their weight) are suspended in air as solid matter is suspended in turbid water; they often settle on the surface of the earth, but the air is never entirely free from them because they are never in a state of complete rest. Then, air not unfrequently contains incidental traces of various substances as everyone knows by experience. These incidental substances sometimes belong to the order of those which act injuriously, the germs of lower organisms—for instance of moulds—and the class of carriers of infectious diseases.

In the air of the various countries of the earth, at different longitudes and at different altitudes above its surface, on the ocean or on the dry land—in a word, in the air of most diverse localities of the earth—the oxygen and nitrogen are found everywhere to be in a constant ratio. This is, moreover, self-evident from the fact that the air constantly diffuses (intermixes by virtue of the internal motion of the gaseous particles) and is also put into motion and intermixed by the wind, by which processes it is equalised in its composition over the entire surface of the earth. In those localities where the air is subject to change, and is in a more or less enclosed space, or, at any rate, in an unventilated space, it may alter very considerably in its composition. For this reason the air in dwellings, cellars, and wells, in which there are substances absorbing oxygen, contains less of this gas, whilst the air on[233] the surface of standing water, which abounds in the lower orders of plant life evolving oxygen, contains an excess of this gas.[17] The constant composition of air over the whole surface of the earth has been proved by a number of most careful researches.[18]

The analysis of air is effected by converting the oxygen into a non-gaseous compound, so as to separate it from the air. The original[234] volume of the air is first measured, and then the volume of the remaining nitrogen. The quantity of oxygen is calculated either from the difference between these volumes or by the weight of the oxygen compound formed. All the volumetric measurements have to be corrected for pressure, temperature, and moisture (Chapters I. and II.) The medium employed for converting the oxygen into a non-gaseous substance should enable it to be taken up from the nitrogen to the very end without evolving any gaseous substance. So, for instance,[19] a mixture of pyrogallol, $C_6H_6O_3$, with a solution of a caustic alkali absorbs oxygen with great ease at the ordinary temperature (the solution turns black), but it is unsuited for accurate analysis because it requires an aqueous solution of an alkali, and it alters the composition of the air by acting on it as a solvent.[20] However, for approximate determinations this simple method gives results which are entirely satisfactory.

The determinations in a eudiometer (Chapter III.) give more exact results, if all the necessary corrections for changes of pressure, temperature, and moisture be taken into account. This determination is carried out essentially as follows:—A certain amount of air is introduced into the eudiometer, and its volume is determined. About an equal volume of dry hydrogen is then passed into the eudiometer, and the volume again determined. The mixture is then exploded, in the way described for the determination of the composition of water. The remaining volume of the gaseous mixture is again measured; it will be less than the second of the previously measured volumes. Out of three volumes which have disappeared, one belonged to the oxygen and two to the hydrogen, consequently one-third of the loss of volume indicates the amount of oxygen contained in the air.[21]

The most complete method for the analysis of air, and one which is[235] accompanied by the least amount of error, consists in the direct weighing, as far as is possible, of the oxygen, nitrogen, water, and carbonic anhydride contained in it. For this purpose the air is first passed through an apparatus for retaining the moisture and carbonic anhydride (which will be considered presently), and is then led through a tube which contains shavings of metallic copper and has been previously weighed. A long layer of such copper heated to redness absorbs all the oxygen from the air, and leaves pure nitrogen, whose weight must be determined. This is done by collecting it in a weighed and exhausted globe, while the amount by weight of oxygen is shown by the increase in weight of the tube with the copper after the experiment.

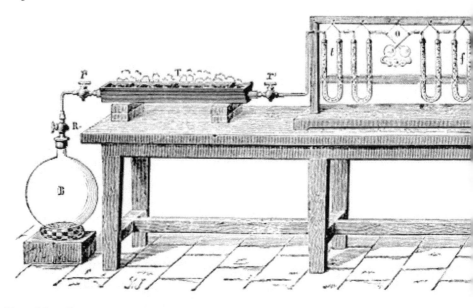

FIG. 38.—Dumas and Boussingault's apparatus for the analysis of air by weight. The globe B contains 10–15 litres. The air is first pumped out of it, and it is weighed empty. The tube T connected with it is filled with copper, and is weighed empty of air. It is heated in a charcoal furnace. When the copper has become red-hot, the stopcock r (near R) is slightly opened, and the air passes through the vessels L, containing a solution of potash, f, containing solutions and pieces of caustic potash, which remove the carbonic anhydride from the air, and then through o and t, containing sulphuric acid (which has been previously boiled to expel dissolved air) and pumice-stone, which removes the moisture from the air. The pure air then gives up its oxygen to the copper in T. When the air passes into T the stopcock R of the globe B is opened, and it becomes filled with nitrogen. When the air ceases to flow in, the stopcocks are closed, and the globe B and tube T weighed. The nitrogen is then pumped out of the tube and it is weighed again. The increase in weight of the tube shows the amount of oxygen, and the difference of the second and third weighings of the tube, with the increase in weight of the globe, gives the weight of the nitrogen.

Air free from moisture and carbonic anhydride[22] contains 20·95 to[236] 20·88[23] parts by volume of oxygen; the mean amount of oxygen will therefore be 20·92 ± 0·05 per cent. Taking the density of air = 1 and of oxygen = 1·105 and nitrogen 0·972 the composition of air by weight will be 23·12 per cent. of oxygen and 76·88 per cent. of nitrogen.[24]

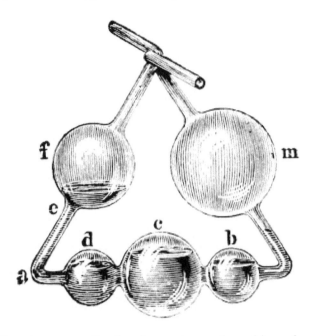

FIG. 39.—Apparatus for the absorption and washing of gases, known as Liebig's bulbs. The gas enters *m*, presses on the absorptive liquid, and passes from m into *b*, *c*, *d*, and *e* consecutively, and escapes through *f*.

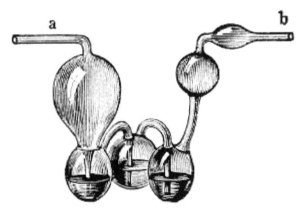

FIG. 40.—Geisler's potash bulbs. The gas enters at *a*, and passes through a solution of potash in the lower bulbs, where the carbonic anhydride is absorbed, and the gas escapes from *b*. The

lower bulbs are arranged in a triangle, so that the apparatus can stand without support.

FIG. 41.—Tube for the absorption of carbonic acid. A plug of cotton wool is placed in the bulb to prevent the powder of soda-lime being carried off by the gas. The tube contains soda-lime and chloride of calcium.

The possibility of the composition of air being altered by the mere action of a solvent very clearly shows that the component parts of air are in a state of mixture, in which any gases may occur; they do not in this case form a definite compound, although the composition of the atmosphere does appear constant under ordinary conditions. The fact that its composition varies under different conditions confirms the truth of this conclusion, and therefore the constancy of the composition of air must not be considered as in any way dependent on the nature of the gases entering into its composition, but only as proceeding from cosmic phenomena co-operating towards this constancy. It must be admitted, therefore, that the processes evolving oxygen, and chiefly the processes of the respiration of plants, are of equal force with those processes which absorb oxygen over the entire surface of the earth.[25]

[237]

Air always contains more or less moisture[26] and *carbonic anhydride* produced by the respiration of animals and the combustion of carbon and carboniferous compounds. The latter shows the properties of an acid anhydride. In order to determine the amount of carbonic anhydride in air, substances are employed which absorb it—namely, alkalis either in solution or solid. A solution of caustic potash, KHO, is poured into light glass vessels, through which the air is passed, and the amount of carbonic anhydride is determined by the increase in weight of the vessel. But it is best to take a solid porous alkaline mass such as soda-lime.[27] With a slow current of air a layer of soda-lime 20 cm. in length is sufficient to completely deprive 1 cubic metre of air of the carbonic anhydride it contains. A series of tubes containing calcium chloride for absorbing the moisture[28] is placed before the apparatus for the absorption of the carbonic anhydride, and a measured mass of air is passed through the whole apparatus by means of an aspirator. In this manner the determination of the moisture is combined with the[238] absorption of the carbonic anhydride. The arrangement shown in fig. 38 is such a combination.

The amount of carbonic anhydride[29] in free air is incomparably more constant than the amount of moisture. The average amount in 100 volumes of dry air is approximately 0·03 volume—that is, 10,000 volumes of air contain about three volumes of carbonic anhydride, most frequently about 2·95 volumes. As the specific gravity of carbonic anhydride referred to air = 1·52, it follows that 100 parts by weight of air contain 0·045 part by weight of carbonic anhydride. This quantity varies according to the time of year (more in winter), the altitude above the level of the sea (less at high altitudes), the proximity to forests and fields (less) or cities (greater), &c. But the variation is small and rarely exceeds the limits of 2½ to 4 ten-thousandths by volume.[30] As there are many natural local influences which either increase the amount of carbonic anhydride in the air (respiration, combustion, decomposition, volcanic eruptions, &c.), or diminish it (absorption by plants and water), the reason of the great constancy in the amount of this gas in the air must be looked for, in the first place, in the fact that the wind mixes the air of various localities together, and, in the second place, in the fact that the waters of the ocean, holding carbonic acid in solution,[31] form an immense reservoir for regulating the amount of this gas in the atmosphere. Immediately the partial[239] pressure of the carbonic anhydride in the air decreases, the water evolves it, and when the partial pressure increases, it absorbs it, and thus nature supplies the conditions for a natural state of moving equilibrium in this as in so many other instances.[32]

Besides nitrogen, oxygen, moisture, and carbonic acid, all the other substances occurring in air are found in infinitesimally small quantities by weight, and therefore the *weight of a cubic measure of air* depends, to a sensible degree, on the above-named components alone. We have already mentioned that at 0° and 760 mm. pressure the weight of a cubic litre of air is 1·293 gram. This weight varies with the acceleration of gravity, g, so that if g be expressed in metres the weight of a litre of air, $e = g \times 0 \cdot 131844$ gram. For St. Petersburg g is about $9 \cdot 8188$, and therefore e is about $1 \cdot 2946$,[33] the air being understood to be dry and free from carbonic anhydride. Taking the amount of the latter as $0 \cdot 03$ per 100 volumes, we obtain a greater weight; for example, for St. Petersburg $e = 1 \cdot 2948$ instead of $1 \cdot 2946$ gram. The weight of one litre of moist air in which the tension[34] of the aqueous vapour (partial pressure) $= f$ mm., at a pressure (total) of air of H[240] millimetres, at a temperature t, will be (*i.e.*, if at 0° and 760 mm. the weight of dry air $= e$) equal to $e \boxed{1 + 0 \cdot 00367t} \times \text{H} - 0 \cdot 38f \boxed{760}$. For instance, if H = 730 mm., $t = 20°$, and $f = 10$ mm. (the moisture is then slightly below 60 p.c.), the weight of a litre of air at St. Petersburg = $1 \cdot 1527$ gram.[35]

The presence of ammonia, a compound of nitrogen and hydrogen, in the air, is indicated by the fact that all acids exposed to the air absorb ammonia from it after a time. De Saussure observed that aluminium sulphate is converted by air into a double sulphate of ammonium and aluminium, or the so-called ammonia alum. Quantitative determinations have shown that the amount of ammonia[36] contained in air varies at different periods. However, it may be accepted that 100 cubic metres of air do not contain less than 1 or more than 5 milligrams of ammonia. It is remarkable that mountain air contains more ammonia than the air of valleys. The air in those places where animal substances undergoing change are accumulated, and especially that of stables, generally contains a much greater quantity of this gas. This is the reason of the peculiar pungent smell noticed in such places. Moreover ammonia, as we shall learn in the following chapter, combines with acids, and should therefore be found in air in the form of such combinations, since air contains carbonic and nitric acids.

The presence of nitric acid in air is proved without doubt by the fact that rain-water contains an appreciable amount of it.

Further (as already mentioned in Chapter IV.), air contains ozone[241] and hydrogen peroxide and nitrous acid (and its ammonia salt), *i.e.* substances having a direct oxidising action (for instance, upon iodized starch-paper), but they are present in very small quantities.[37]

Besides substances in a gaseous or vaporous state,[38] there is always found a more or less considerable quantity of substances which are not known in a state of vapour. These substances are present in the air as *dust*. If a linen surface, moistened with an acid, be placed in perfectly pure air, then the washings are found to contain sodium, calcium, iron, and potassium.[39] Linen moistened with an alkali absorbs carbonic, sulphuric, phosphoric, and hydrochloric acids. Further, the presence of organic substances in air has been proved by a similar experiment. If a glass globe be filled with ice and placed in a room where are a number of people, then the presence of organic substances, like albuminous substances, may be proved in the water which condenses on the surface of the globe. It may be that the miasmas causing infection in marshy localities, hospitals, and in certain epidemic illnesses proceed from the presence of such substances in the air (and especially in water, which contains many micro-organisms), as well as from the presence of germs of lower organisms in the air as a minute dust. Pasteur proved the existence of such germs in the air by the following experiment:—He placed gun-cotton (pyroxylin), which has the appearance of ordinary cotton, in a glass tube. Gun-cotton is soluble in a mixture of ether and alcohol, forming the so-called collodion. A current of air[242] was passed through the tube for a long period of time, and the gun-cotton was then dissolved in a mixture of ether and alcohol. An insoluble residue was thus obtained which actually contained the germs of organisms, as was shown by microscopical observations, and by their capacity to develop into organisms (mould, &c.) under favourable conditions. The presence of these germs determines the property of air of bringing about the processes of putrefaction and fermentation—that is the fundamental alteration of organic substances, which is accompanied by an entire change in their properties. The appearance of lower organisms, both vegetable and animal, is always to be remarked in these processes. Thus, for instance, in the process of fermentation, when, for example, wine is procured from the sweet juice of grapes, a sediment separates out which is known under the name of lees, and contains peculiar yeast organisms. Germs are required before these organisms can appear.[40] They are floating in the air, and fall into the sweet fermentable liquid from it. Finding themselves under favourable conditions, the germs develop into organisms; they are nourished at the expense of the organic substance, and during growth change and destroy it, and bring about fermentation and putrefaction. This is why, for instance, the juice of the grape when contained in the skin of the fruit, which allows access of the air but is impenetrable to the germs, does not ferment, does not alter so long as the skin remains intact. This is also the reason why animal substances when kept from the access of air may be preserved for a great length of time. Preserved foods for long sea voyages are kept in this way.[41] Hence it is evident that however infinitesimal the quantity of germs carried in the atmosphere may be, still they have an immense significance in nature.[42]

Thus we see that air contains a great variety of substances. The nitrogen, which is found in it in the largest quantity, has the least[243] influence on those processes which are accomplished by the action of air. The oxygen, which is met with in a lesser quantity than the nitrogen, on the contrary takes a very important part in a number of reactions; it supports combustion and respiration, it brings about decomposition and every process of slow oxidation. The part played by the moisture of air is well known. The carbonic anhydride, which is met with in still smaller quantities, has an immense significance in nature, inasmuch as it serves for the nourishment of plants. The importance of the ammonia and nitric acid is very great, because they are the sources of the nitrogenous substances comprising an indispensable element in all living organisms. And, lastly, the infinitesimal quantity of germs also have a great significance in a number of processes. Thus it is not the quantitative but the qualitative relations of the component parts of the atmosphere which determine its importance in nature.[43]

Air, being a mixture of various substances, may suffer considerable *changes* in consequence of incidental circumstances. It is particularly necessary to remark those changes in the composition of air which take place in dwellings and in various localities where human beings have to remain during a lengthy period of time. The respiration of human beings and animals alters the air.[44] A similar deterioration of air is produced by the influence of decomposing organic substances, and especially of substances burning in it.[45] Hence it is necessary to have[244] regard to the purification of the air of dwellings. The renewal of air, the replacing of respired by fresh air, is termed 'ventilation,'[46] and the[245] removal of foreign and injurious admixtures from the air is called 'disinfection.'[47] The accumulation of all kinds of impurities in the air of dwellings and cities is the reason why the air of mountains, forests, seas, and non-marshy localities, covered with vegetation or snow, is distinguished for its freshness, and, in all respects, beneficial action.

Footnotes:

[1] See Note 15 bis.

[1 bis] The reason why there are no other nitrogenous substances within the earth's mass beyond those which have come there with the remains of organisms, and from the air with rain-water, must be looked for in two circumstances. In the first place, in the instability of many nitrogenous compounds, which are liable to break up with the formation of gaseous nitrogen; and in the second place in the fact that the salts of nitric acid, forming the product of the action of air on many nitrogenous and especially organic compounds, are very soluble in water, and on penetrating into the depths of the earth (with water) give up their oxygen. The result of the changes of the nitrogenous organic substances which fall into the earth is without doubt frequently, if not invariably, the formation of gaseous nitrogen. Thus the gas evolved from coal always contains much nitrogen (together with marsh gas, carbonic anhydride, and other gases).

[2] Copper (best as turnings, which present a large surface) absorbs oxygen, forming CuO, at the ordinary temperature in the presence of solutions of acids, or, better still, in the presence of a solution of ammonia, when it forms a bluish-violet solution of oxide of copper in ammonia. Nitrogen is very easily procured by this method. A flask filled with copper turnings is closed with a cork furnished with a funnel and stopcock. A solution of ammonia is poured into the funnel, and caused to drop slowly upon the copper. If at the same time a current of air be slowly passed through the flask (from a gasholder), then all the oxygen will be absorbed from it and the nitrogen will pass from the flask. It should be washed with water to retain any ammonia that may be carried off with it.

[3] The oxygen compounds of nitrogen (for example, N_2O, NO, NO_2) are decomposed at a red heat by themselves, and under the action of red-hot copper, iron, sodium, &c., they give up their oxygen to the metals, leaving the nitrogen free. According to Meyer and Langer (1885), nitrous oxide, N_2O, decomposes below 900°, although not completely.

[4] Chlorine and bromine (in excess), as well as bleaching powder (hypochlorites), take up the hydrogen from ammonia, NH_3, leaving nitrogen. Nitrogen is best procured from ammonia by the action of a solution of sodium hypobromite on solid sal-ammoniac.

[4 bis] Lord Rayleigh in 1894, when determining the weight of a volume of carefully purified nitrogen by weighing it in one and the same globe, found that the gas obtained from air, by the action of incandescent copper (or iron or by removing the oxygen by ferrous oxide) was always $\frac{1}{200}$ heavier than the nitrogen obtained from its compounds, for instance, from the oxide or suboxide of nitrogen, decomposed by incandescent pulverulent iron or from the ammonia salt of nitrous acid. For the nitrogen procured from air, he obtained, at 0° and 760·4 mm. pressure, a weight = 2·310 grms., while for the nitrogen obtained from its compounds, 2·299 grms. This difference of about $\frac{1}{200}$ could not be explained by the nitrogen not having been well purified, or by inaccuracy of experiment, and was the means for the remarkable discovery of the presence of a heavy gas in air, which will be mentioned in Note 16 bis.

[5] See Chapter II. Note 29.

[5 bis] See Note 11 bis.

[6] The combination of boron with nitrogen is accompanied by the evolution of sufficient heat to raise the mass to redness; titanium combines so easily with nitrogen that it is difficult to obtain it free from that element; magnesium easily absorbs nitrogen at a red heat. It is a remarkable and instructive fact that these compounds of nitrogen are very stable and non-

volatile. Carbon (C = 12) with nitrogen gives cyanogen, C_2N_2, which is gaseous and very unstable, and whose molecule is not large, whilst boron (B = 11) forms a nitrogenous compound which is solid, non-volatile, and very stable. Its composition, BN, is similar to that of cyanogen, but its molecular weight, B_nN_n, is probably greater. Its composition, like that of N_2Mg_3, NNa_3, N_2Hg_3 and of many of the metallic nitrides, corresponds to ammonia with the substitution of all its hydrogen by a metal. In my opinion, a detailed study of the transformations of the nitrides now known, should lead to the discovery of many facts in the history of nitrogen.

[7] This reaction, so far as is known, does not proceed beyond a certain limit, probably because cyanogen, CN, itself breaks up into carbon and nitrogen.

[8] Frémy and Becquerel took dry air, and observed the formation of brown vapours of oxides of nitrogen on the passage of sparks.

[9] If a mixture of one volume of nitrogen and fourteen volumes of hydrogen be burnt, then water and a considerable quantity of nitric acid are formed. It may be partly due to this that a certain quantity of nitric acid is produced in the slow oxidation of nitrogenous substances in an excess of air. This is especially facilitated by the presence of an alkali with which the nitric acid formed can combine. If a galvanic current be passed through water containing the nitrogen and oxygen of the air in solution, then the hydrogen and oxygen set free combine with the nitrogen, forming ammonia and nitric acid.

When copper is oxidised at the expense of the air at the ordinary temperature in the presence of ammonia, oxygen is absorbed, not only for combination with the copper, but also for the formation of nitric acid.

The combination of nitrogen with oxygen, even, for example, by the action of electric sparks, is not accompanied by an explosion or rapid combination, as in the action of a spark on a mixture of oxygen and hydrogen. This is explained by the fact that heat is not evolved in the combination of nitrogen with oxygen, but is absorbed—an expenditure of energy is required, there is no evolution of energy. In fact, there will not be the transmission of heat from particle to particle which occurs in the explosion of detonating gas. Each spark will aid the formation of a certain quantity of the compound of oxygen and nitrogen, but will not excite the same in the neighbouring particles. In other words, the combination of hydrogen with oxygen is an exothermal reaction, and the combination of nitrogen with oxygen an endothermal reaction.

A condition particularly favourable for the oxidation of nitrogen is the explosion of detonating gas and air if the former be *in excess*. If a mixture of two volumes of detonating gas and one volume of air be exploded, then one-tenth of the air is converted into nitric acid, and consequently after the explosion has taken place there remain only nine-tenths of the volume of air originally taken. If a large proportion of air be taken—for instance, four volumes of air to two volumes of detonating gas—then the temperature of the explosion is lowered, the volume of air taken remains unchanged, and no nitric acid is formed. This gives a rule to be observed in making use of the eudiometer—namely that to weaken the force of the explosion not less than an equal volume of air should be added to the explosive mixture. On the other hand a large excess must not be taken as no explosion would then ensue (*see* Chapter III. Note 34). Probably in the future means will be found for obtaining compounds of nitrogen on a large industrial scale by the aid of electric discharges, and by making use of the inexhaustible mass of nitrogen in the atmosphere.

[10] In reality nitric oxide, NO, is first formed, but with oxygen and water it gives (brown fumes) nitrous anhydride, which, as we shall afterwards learn, in the presence of water and oxygen gives nitric acid.

[11] The nitric acid contained in the soil, river water (Chapter I., Note 2), wells, &c., proceeds (like carbonic anhydride) from the oxidation of organic compounds which have fallen into water, soil, &c.

[11 bis] Crookes employed a current of 15 ampères and 65 volts, and passed it through an induction coil with 330 vibrations per second, and obtained a flame between the poles placed at a distance of 46 mm. which after the appearance of the arc and flame could be increased to 200 mm. A platinum wire fused in the flame.

[12] This property of nitrogen, which under normal conditions is inactive, leads to the idea that under the influence of an electric discharge gaseous nitrogen changes in its properties; if not permanently like oxygen (electrolysed oxygen or ozone does not react on nitrogen, according to Berthelot), it may be temporarily at the moment of the action of the discharge, just as some substances under the action of heat are permanently affected (that is, when once changed remain so—for instance, white phosphorus passes into red, &c.), whilst others are only temporarily altered (the dissociation of S_6 into S_2 or of sal-ammoniac into ammonia and hydrochloric acid). Such a proposition is favoured by the fact that nitrogen gives two kinds of spectra, with which we shall afterwards become acquainted. It may be that the molecules N_2 then give less complex molecules, N containing one atom, or form a complex molecule N_3, like oxygen in passing into ozone. Probably under a silent discharge the molecules of oxygen, O_2, are partly decomposed and the individual atoms O combine with O_2, forming ozone, O_3.

[13] This reaction, discovered by Chabrié and investigated by Thénard, was only rightly understood when Deville applied the principles of dissociation to it.

[14] The action of nitrogen on acetylene (Berthelot) resembles this reaction. A mixture of these gases under the influence of a silent discharge gives hydrocyanic acid, $C_2H_2 + N_2 = 2CNH$. This reaction cannot proceed beyond a certain limit because it is reversible.

[15] Berthelot successfully employed electricity of even feeble potential in these experiments, which fact led him to think that in nature, where the action of electricity takes place very frequently, a part of the complex nitrogenous substances may proceed from the gaseous nitrogen of the air by this method.

As the nitrogenous substances of organisms play a very important part in them (organic life cannot exist without them), and as the nitrogenous substances introduced into the soil are capable of invigorating its crops (of course in the presence of the other nourishing principles required by plants), the question of the means of converting the atmospheric nitrogen into the nitrogenous compounds of the soil, or into *assimilable nitrogen* capable of being absorbed by plants and of forming complex (albuminous) substances in them, is one of great theoretical and practical interest. The artificial (technical) conversion of the atmospheric nitrogen into nitrogenous compounds, notwithstanding repeated attempts, cannot yet be considered as fulfilled in a practical remunerative manner although its possibility is already evident. Electricity will probably aid in solving this very important practical problem. When the theoretical side of the question is further advanced, then without doubt an advantageous means will be found for the manufacture of nitrogenous substances from the nitrogen of the air; and this is needed, before all, for the agriculturist, to whom nitrogenous fertilisers form an expensive item, and are more important than all other manures.

One thousand tons of farmyard manure do not generally contain more than four tons of nitrogen in the form of complex nitrogenous substances, and this amount of nitrogen is contained in twenty tons of ammonium sulphate, therefore the effect of a mass of farmyard manure in respect to the introduction of nitrogen may be produced by small quantities of artificial nitrogenous fertilisers (*see* Note 15 bis).

[15 bis] Although the numerous, and as far as possible accurate and varied researches made in the physiology of plants have proved that the higher forms of plants are not capable of directly absorbing the nitrogen of the atmosphere and converting it into complex albuminous substances, still it has been long and repeatedly observed that the amount of nitrogenous

substances in the soil is increased by the cultivation of plants of the bean (leguminous) family such as pea, acacia, &c. A closer study of these plants has shown that this is connected with the formation of peculiar nodular swellings in their roots caused by the growth of peculiar micro-organisms (bacteria) which cohabit the soil with the roots, and are capable of absorbing nitrogen from the air, *i.e.* of converting it into assimilated nitrogen. This branch of plant physiology, which forms another proof of the important part played by micro-organisms in nature, cannot be discussed in this work, but it should be mentioned, since it is of great theoretical and practical interest, and, moreover, phenomena of this kind, which have recently been discovered, promise to explain, to some extent at least, certain of the complex problems concerning the development of life on the earth.

[16] Under the name of atmospheric air the chemist and physicist understand ordinary air containing nitrogen and oxygen only, notwithstanding that the other component parts of air have a very important influence on the living matter of the earth's surface. That air is so represented in science is based on the fact that only the two components above-named are met with in air in a constant quantity, whilst the others are variable. The solid impurities may be separated from air required for chemical or physical research by simple filtration through a long layer of cotton-wool placed in a tube. Organic impurities are removed by passing the air through a solution of potassium permanganate. The carbonic anhydride contained in air is absorbed by alkalis—best of all, soda-lime, which in a dry state in porous lumps absorbs it with exceeding rapidity and completeness. Aqueous vapour is removed by passing the air over calcium chloride, strong sulphuric acid, or phosphoric anhydride. Air thus purified is accepted as containing only nitrogen and oxygen, although in reality it still contains a certain quantity of hydrogen and hydrocarbons, from which it may be purified by passing over copper oxide heated to redness. The copper oxide then oxidises the hydrogen and hydrocarbons— it burns them, forming water and carbonic anhydride, which may be removed as above described. When it is said that in the determination of the density of gases the weight of air is taken as unity, it is understood to be such air, containing only nitrogen and oxygen.

[16 bis] Thanks to the remarkable discovery made in the summer of 1894 by Lord Rayleigh and Prof. Ramsay, the well-known component elements of air must now he supplemented by 1 p.c. (by volume) of a heavy gas (density about 19, H = 1), inactive like nitrogen, which was discovered in the researches made by Lord Rayleigh on the density of nitrogen as mentioned in note 4 bis. Up to the present time this gas has been always determined together with nitrogen, because it combines with

neither the hydrogen in the eudiometer nor with the copper in the gravimetric method of determining the composition of air, and therefore has always remained with the nitrogen. It has been possible to separate it from nitrogen since magnesium absorbs nitrogen at a red heat, while this gas remains unabsorbed, and was found to have a density nearly one and a half time greater than that of nitrogen (is it not a polymer of nitrogen, N_3?). It is now known also that this gas gives a luminous spectrum, which contains the bright blue line observed in the spectrum of nitrogen. Owing to the fact that it is an exceedingly inert substance, even more so than nitrogen, it has been termed Argon. Further reference will be made to it in the Appendix.

[17] As a further proof of the fact that certain circumstances may change the composition of air, it will be enough to point out that the air contained in the cavities of glaciers contains only up to 10 p.c. of oxygen. This depends on the fact that at low temperatures oxygen is much more soluble in snow-water and snow than nitrogen. When shaken up with water the composition of air should change, because the water dissolves unequal quantities of oxygen and nitrogen. We have already seen (Chapter I.) that the air boiled off from water saturated at about 0° contains about thirty-five volumes of oxygen and sixty-five volumes of nitrogen, and we have considered the reason of this.

[18] The analysis of air by weight conducted by Dumas and Boussingault in Paris, which they repeated many times between April 27 and September 22, 1841, under various conditions of weather, showed that the amount by weight of oxygen only varies between 22·89 p.c. and 23·08 p.c., the average amount being 23·07 p.c. Brunner, at Bern in Switzerland, and Bravais, at Faulhorn in the Bernese Alps, at a height of two kilometres above the level of the sea, Marignac at Geneva, Lewy at Copenhagen, and Stas at Brussels, have analysed the air by the same methods, and found that its composition does not exceed the limits determined for Paris. The most recent determinations (with an accuracy of ±0·05 p.c.) confirm the conclusion that the composition of the atmosphere is constant.

As there are some grounds (which will be mentioned shortly) for considering that the composition of the air at great altitudes is slightly different from that at attainable heights—namely, that it is richer in the lighter nitrogen—several fragmentary observations made at Munich (Jolly, 1880) gave reason for thinking that in the upward currents (that is in the region of minimum barometric pressure or at the centres of meteorological cyclones) the air is richer in oxygen than in the descending currents of air (in the regions of anticyclones or of barometric maxima); but more carefully conducted observations showed this supposition to be incorrect. Improved methods for the analysis of air have shown that certain slight variations in its composition do actually occur, but in the first place they depend on incidental local influences (on the passage of the air over mountains and large surfaces of water, regions of forest and herbage, and the like), and in the second place are limited to quantities which are scarcely distinguishable from possible errors in the analyses. The researches made by Kreisler in Germany (1885) are particularly convincing.

The considerations which lead to the supposition that the atmosphere at great altitudes contains less oxygen than at the surface of the earth are based on the law of partial pressures (Chapter I.) According to this law, the equilibrium of the oxygen in the strata of the atmosphere is not dependent on the equilibrium of the nitrogen, and the variation in the densities of both gases with the height is determined by the pressure of each gas separately. Details of the calculations and considerations here involved are contained in my work *On Barometric Levellings*, 1876, p. 48.

On the basis of the law of partial pressure and of hypsometrical formulæ, expressing the laws of the variation of pressures at different altitudes, the conclusion may be deduced that at the upper strata of the atmosphere the proportion of the nitrogen with respect to the oxygen increases, but the increase will not exceed a fraction per cent., even at altitudes of four and a half to six miles, the greatest height within the reach of men either by climbing mountains or by means of balloons. This conclusion is confirmed by the analyses of air collected by Welch in England during his aëronautic ascents.

[19] The complete absorption of the oxygen may be attained by introducing moist phosphorus into a definite volume of air; the occurrence of this is recognised by the fact of the phosphorus becoming non-luminous in the dark. The amount of oxygen may be determined by measuring the volume of nitrogen remaining. This method however cannot give accurate results, owing to a portion of the air being dissolved in the water, to the combination of some of the nitrogen with oxygen and to the necessity of introducing and withdrawing the phosphorus, which cannot be accomplished without introducing bubbles of air.

[20] For rapid and approximate analyses (technical and hygienic), such a mixture is very suitable for determining the amount of oxygen in mixtures of gases from which the substances absorbed by alkalis have first been removed. According to certain observers, this mixture evolves a certain (small) quantity of carbonic oxide after absorbing oxygen.

[21] Details of eudiometrical analysis must, as was pointed out in Chap. III., Note 32, be looked for in works on analytical chemistry. The same remark applies to the other analytical methods mentioned in this work.

They are only described for the purpose of showing the diversity of the methods of chemical research.

[22] Air free from carbonic anhydride indicates after explosion the presence of a small quantity of carbonic anhydride, as De Saussure remarked, and air free from moisture, after being passed over red-hot copper oxide, appears invariably to contain a small quantity of water, as Boussingault has observed. These observations lead to the assumption that air always contains a certain quantity of gaseous hydrocarbons, like marsh gas, which, as we shall afterwards learn, is evolved from the earth, marshes, &c. Its amount, however, does not exceed a few hundredths per cent.

[23] The analyses of air are accompanied by errors, and there are variations of composition attaining hundredths per cent.; the average normal composition of air is therefore only correct to the first decimal place.

[24] These figures express the mean composition of air from an average of the most accurate determinations; they are accurate within $\pm 0\cdot05$ p.c.

[25] In Chapter III., Note 4, an approximate calculation is made for the determination of the balance of oxygen in the entire atmosphere; it may therefore he supposed that the composition of air will vary from time to time, the relation between vegetation and the oxygen absorbing processes changes; but as the atmosphere of the earth can hardly have a definite limit and we have already seen (Chapter IV., Note 33) that there are observations confirming this, it follows that our atmosphere should vary in its component parts with the entire heavenly space, and therefore it must he supposed that any variation in the composition by weight of the air can only take place exceedingly slowly, and in a manner imperceptible by experiment.

[26] The amount of moisture contained in the air is considered in greater detail in the study of physics and meteorology and the subject has been mentioned above, in Chapter I., Note 1, where the methods of absorbing moisture from gases were pointed out.

[27] Soda-lime is prepared in the following manner:—Unslaked lime is finely powdered and mixed with a slightly warmed and very strong solution of caustic soda. The mixing should be done in an iron dish, and the materials should be well stirred together until the lime begins to slake. When the mass becomes hot, it boils, swells up, and solidifies, forming a porous mass very rich in alkali and capable of rapidly absorbing carbonic anhydride. A lump of caustic soda or potash presents a much smaller surface for absorption and therefore acts much less rapidly. It is necessary to place an apparatus for absorbing water after the apparatus for absorbing

the carbonic anhydride, because the alkali in absorbing the latter gives off water.

[28] It is evident that the calcium chloride employed for absorbing the water should be free from lime or other alkalis in order that it may not retain carbonic anhydride. Such calcium chloride may be prepared in the following manner: A perfectly neutral solution of calcium chloride is prepared from lime and hydrochloric acid; it is then carefully evaporated first on a water-bath and then on a sand-bath. When the solution attains a certain strength a scum is formed, which solidifies at the surface. This scum is collected, and will be found to be free from caustic alkalis. It is necessary in any case to test it before use, as otherwise a large error may be introduced into the results, owing to the presence of free alkali (lime). It is best to pass carbonic anhydride through the tube containing the calcium chloride for some time before the experiment, in order to saturate any free alkali that may remain from the decomposition of a portion of the calcium chloride by water, $CaCl_2 + 2H_2O = CaOH_2O + 2HCl$.

[29] Recourse is had to special methods when the determination only takes note of the carbonic anhydride of the air. For instance, it is absorbed by an alkali which does not contain carbonates (by a solution of baryta or caustic soda mixed with baryta), and then the carbonic anhydride is expelled by an excess of an acid, and its amount determined by the volume given off. A rapid method of determining CO_2 (for hygienic purposes) is given by the fall of tension produced by the introduction of an alkali (the air having been either brought to dryness or saturated with moisture). Dr. Schidloffsky's apparatus is based upon this principle. The question as to the amount of carbonic anhydride present in the air has been submitted to many voluminous and exact researches, especially those of Reiset, Schloesing, Müntz, and Aubin, who showed that the amount is not subject to such variations as at first announced on the basis of incomplete and insufficiently accurate determinations.

[30] It is a different case in enclosed spaces, in dwellings, cellars, wells, caves, and mines, where the renewal of air is impeded. Under these circumstances large quantities of carbonic anhydride may accumulate. In cities, where there are many conditions for the evolution of carbonic anhydride (respiration, decomposition, combustion), its amount is greater than in free air, yet even in still weather the difference does not often exceed one ten-thousandth (that is, rarely attains 4 instead of 2·9 vols. in 10000 vols. of air).

[31] In the sea as well as in fresh water, carbonic acid occurs in two forms, directly dissolved in the water, and combined with lime as calcium bicarbonate (hard waters sometimes contain very much carbonic acid in

this form). The tension of the carbonic anhydride in the first form varies with the temperature, and its amount with the partial pressure, and that in the form of acid salts is under the same conditions, for direct experiments have shown a similar dependence in this case, although the quantitative relations are different in the two cases.

[32] In studying the phenomena of nature the conclusion is arrived at that the universally reigning state of mobile equilibrium forms the chief reason for that harmonious order which impresses all observers. It not unfrequently happens that we do not see the causes regulating the order and harmony; in the particular instance of carbonic anhydride, it is a striking circumstance that in the first instance a search was made for an harmonious and strict uniformity, and in incidental (insufficiently accurate and fragmentary) observations conditions were even found for concluding it to be absent. When, later, the rule of this uniformity was confirmed, then the causes regulating such order were also discovered. The researches of Schloesing were of this character. Deville's idea of the dissociation of the acid carbonates of sea-water is suggested in them. In many other cases also, a correct interpretation can only follow from a detailed investigation.

[33] The difference of the weight of a litre of dry air (free from carbonic anhydride) at 0° and 760 mm., at different longitudes and altitudes, depends on the fact that the force of gravity varies under these conditions, and with it the pressure of the barometrical column also varies. This is treated in detail in my works *On the Elasticity of Gases* and *On Barometric Levellings*, and 'The Publications of the Weights and Measures Department' (*Journal of the Russian Physico-Chemical Society*, 1894).

In reality the weight is not measured in absolute units of weight (in pressure—refer to works on mechanics and physics), but in relative units (grams, scale weights) whose mass is invariable, and therefore the variation of the weight of the weights itself with the change of gravity must not be here taken into account, for we are here dealing with weights proportional to masses, since with a change of locality the weight of the weights varies as the weight of a given volume of air does. In other words: the mass of a substance always remains constant, but the pressure produced by it varies with the acceleration of gravity: the gram, pound, and other units of weight are really units of mass.

[34] The tension of the aqueous vapour in the air is determined by hygrometers and other similar methods. It may also be determined by analysis (*see* Chapter I., Note 1).

[35] For rapid calculation the weight of a litre of air (in a room) in St. Petersburg, may under these conditions (H, t, and f) be obtained by the formula $e = 1 \cdot 20671 + 0 \cdot 0016$ [H_1 - 755 + $2 \cdot 6(18° - t°)$] where H_1 = H -

$0.38f$. In determining the weight of small and heavy objects (crucibles, &c. in analysis, and in determining the specific gravities of liquids, &c.) *a correction may be introduced for the loss of weight* in the air of the room, by taking the weight of a litre of air displaced as 1.2 gram, and consequently 0.0012 gram for every cubic centimetre. But if gases or, in general, large vessels are weighed, and the weighings require to be accurate, it is necessary to take into account all the data for the determination of the density of the air (t, H, and f), because sensitive balances can determine the possible variations of the weight of air, as in the case of a litre the weight of air varies in centigrams, even at a constant temperature, with variations of H and f. Some time ago (1859) I proposed the following method and applied it for this purpose. A large light and closed vessel is taken, and its volume and weight in a vacuum are accurately determined, and verified from time to time. On weighing it we obtain the weight in air of a given density, and by subtracting this weight from its absolute weight and dividing by its volume we obtain the density of the air.

[36] Schloesing studied the equilibrium of the ammonia of the atmosphere and of the rivers, seas, &c., and showed that the amount of the gas is interchangeable between them. The ratio between the amount of ammonia in a cubic metre of air and a litre of water at $0° = 0.004$, at $10° = 0.010$, at $25° = 0.040$ to 1, and therefore in nature there is a state of equilibrium in the amount of ammonia in the atmosphere and waters.

[37] Whilst formed in the air these oxidising substances (N_2O_3, ozone and hydrogen peroxide) at the same time rapidly disappear from it by oxidising those substances which are capable of being oxidised. Owing to this instability their amounts vary considerably, and, as would be expected, they are met with to an appreciable amount in pure air, whilst their amount decreases to zero in the air of cities, and especially in dwellings where there is a maximum of substances capable of oxidisation and a minimum of conditions for the formation of such bodies. There is a causal connection between the amount of these substances present in the air and its purity— that is, the amount of foreign residues of organic origin liable to oxidation present in the air. Where there is much of such residues their amount must be small. When they are present the amount of organic substances must be small, as otherwise they would be destroyed. For this reason efforts have been made to apply ozone for purifying the air by evolving it by artificial means in the atmosphere; for instance, by passing a series of electrical sparks through the ventilating pipes conveying air into a building. Air thus ozonised destroys by oxidation—that is, brings about the combustion of— the organic residues present in the air, and thus will serve for purifying it. For these reasons the air of cities contains less ozone and such like oxidising agents than country air. This forms the distinguishing feature of

country air. However, animal life cannot exist in air containing a comparatively large amount of ozone.

[38] Amongst them we may mention iodine and alcohol, C_2H_6O, which Müntz found to be always present in air, the soil, and water, although in minute traces only.

[39] A portion of the atmospheric dust is of cosmic origin; this is undoubtedly proved by the fact of its containing metallic iron as do meteorites. Nordenskiöld found iron in the dust covering snow, and Tissandier in every kind of air, although naturally in very small quantities.

[40] The idea of the spontaneous growth of organisms in a suitable medium, although still upheld by many, has since the work of Pasteur and his followers (and to a certain extent of his predecessors) been discarded, because it has been proved how, when, and whence (from the air, water, &c.) the germs appear; that fermentation as well as infectious diseases cannot take place without them; and chiefly because it has been shown that any change accompanied by the development of the organisms introduced may be brought about at will by the introduction of the germs into a suitable medium.

[41] In further confirmation of the fact that putrefaction and fermentation depend on germs carried in the air, we may cite the circumstance that poisonous substances destroying the life of organisms stop or hinder the appearance of the above processes. Air which has been heated to redness or passed through sulphuric acid no longer contains the germs of organisms, and loses the faculty of producing fermentation and putrefaction.

[42] Their presence in the air is naturally due to the diffusion of germs into the atmosphere, and owing to their microscopical dimensions, they, as it were, hang in the air in virtue of their large surfaces compared to their weight. In Paris the amount of dust suspended in the air equals from 6 (after rain) to 23 grams per 1,000 c.m. of air.

[43] We see similar cases everywhere. For example, the predominating mass of sand and clay in the soil takes hardly any chemical part in the economy of the soil in respect to the nourishment of plants. The plants by their roots search for substances which are diffused in comparatively small quantities in the soil. If a large quantity of these nourishing substances are removed, then the plants will not develop in the soil, just as animals die in oxygen.

[44] A man in breathing burns about 10 grams of carbon per hour—that is, he produces about 880 grams, or (as 1 cub.m. of carbonic anhydride weighs about 2,000 grams) about $\frac{5}{12}$ c.m. of carbonic anhydride. The air

coming from the lungs contains 4 p.c. of carbonic anhydride by volume. The exhaled air acts as a direct poison, owing to this gas and to other impurities.

[45] For this reason candles, lamps, and gas change the composition of air almost in the same way as respiration. In the burning of 1 kilogram of stearin candles, 50 cubic metres of air are changed as by respiration—that is, 4 p.c. of carbonic anhydride will be formed in this volume of air. The respiration of animals and exhalations from their skins, and especially from the intestines and the excrements and the transformations taking place in them, contaminate the air to a still greater extent, because they introduce other volatile substances besides carbonic anhydride into the air. At the same time that carbonic anhydride is formed the amount of oxygen in the air decreases, and there is noticed the appearance of miasmata which occur in but small quantity, but which are noticeable in passing from fresh air into a confined space full of such adulterated air. The researches of Schmidt and Leblanc and others show that even with 20·6 p.c. of oxygen (instead of 20·9 p.c.), when the diminution is due to respiration, air becomes noticeably less fit for respiration, and that the heavy feeling experienced in such air increases with a lesser percentage of oxygen. It is difficult to remain for a few minutes in air containing 17·2 p.c. of oxygen. These observations were chiefly obtained by observations on the air of different mines, at different depths below the surface. The air of theatres and buildings full of people also proves to contain less oxygen; it was found on one occasion that at the end of a theatrical representation the air in the stalls contained 20·75 p.c. of oxygen, whilst the air at the upper part of the theatre contained only 20·36 p.c. The amount of carbonic anhydride in the air may be taken as a measure of its purity (Pettenkofer). When it reaches 1 p.c. it is very difficult for human beings to remain long in such air, and it is necessary to set up a vigorous ventilation for the removal of the adulterated air. In order to keep the air in dwellings in a uniformly good state, it is necessary to introduce at least 10 cubic metres of fresh air per hour per person. We saw that a man exhales about five-twelfths of a cubic metre of carbonic anhydride per day. Accurate observations have shown that air containing one-tenth p.c. of exhaled carbonic anhydride (and consequently also a corresponding amount of the other substances evolved together with it) is not felt to be oppressive; and therefore the five-twelfth cubic metres of carbonic anhydride should be diluted with 420 cubic metres of fresh air if it be desired to keep not more than one-tenth p.c. (by volume) of carbonic anhydride in the air. Hence a man requires 420 cubic metres of air per day, or 18 cubic metres per hour. With the introduction of only 10 cubic metres of fresh air per person, the amount of carbonic anhydride may reach one-fifth p.c., and the air will not then be of the requisite freshness.

[46] The *ventilation* of inhabited buildings is most necessary, and is even indispensable in hospitals, schools, and similar buildings. In winter it is carried on by the so-called calorifiers or stoves heating the air before it enters. The best kind of calorifiers in this respect are those in which the fresh cold air is led through a series of pipes heated by the hot gases coming from a stove. In ventilation, particularly during winter, care is taken that the incoming air shall be moist, because in winter the amount of moisture in the air is very small. Ventilation, besides introducing fresh air into a dwelling-place, must also withdraw the air already spoilt by respiration and other causes—that is, it is necessary to construct channels for the escape of the bad air, besides those for the introduction of fresh air. In ordinary dwelling-places, where not many people are congregated, the ventilation is conducted by natural means, in the heating by fires, through crevices, windows, and various orifices in walls, doors, and windows. In mines, factories, and workrooms ventilation is of the greatest importance.

Animal vitality may still continue for a period of several minutes in air containing up to 30 p.c. of carbonic anhydride, if the remaining 70 p.c. consist of ordinary air; but respiration ceases after a certain time, and death may even ensue. The flame of a candle is very easily extinguished in an atmosphere containing from 5 to 6 p.c. of carbonic anhydride, but animal vitality can be sustained in it for a somewhat long time, although the effect of such air is exceedingly painful even to the lower animals. There are mines in which a lighted candle easily goes out from the excess of carbonic anhydride, but in which the miners have to remain for a long time. The presence of 1 p.c. of carbonic oxide is deadly even to cold-blooded animals. The air in the galleries of a mine where blasting has taken place, is known to produce a state of insensibility resembling that produced by charcoal fumes. Deep wells and vaults not unfrequently contain similar substances, and their atmosphere often causes suffocation. The atmospheres of such places cannot be tested by lowering a lighted candle into it, as these poisonous gases would not extinguish the flame. This method only suffices to indicate the amount of carbonic anhydride. If a candle keeps alight, it signifies that there is less than 6 p.c. of this gas. In doubtful cases it is best to lower a dog or other animal into the air to be tested. If CO_2 be very carefully added to air, the flame of a candle is not extinguished (although it becomes very much smaller) even when the gas amounts to 12 p.c. of air. Researches made by F. Clowes (1894) show that the flames (in every case ¾ in. long) of different combustible substances are extinguished by the gradual addition of different percentages of nitrogen and carbonic acid to the air; the percentage sufficient to extinguish the flame being as follows (the percentage of oxygen is given in parenthesis):

	p.c. CO_2	p.c. N.
Absolute alcohol	14 (18·1)	21 (16·6)
Candle	14 (18·1)	22 (16·4)
Hydrogen	58 (8·8)	70 (6·3)
Coal gas	33 (14·1)	46 (11·3)
Carbonic oxide	24 (16·0)	28 (15·1)
Methane	10 (18·9)	17 (17·4)

The flames of all solid and liquid substances is extinguished by almost the same percentage of CO_2 or N_2, but the flames of different gases vary in this respect, and hydrogen continues to burn in mixtures which are far poorer in oxygen than those in which the flames of other combustible gases are extinguished; the flame of methane CH_4 is the most easily extinguished. The percentage of nitrogen may be greater than that of CO_2. This, together with the fact that, under the above circumstances, the flame of a gas before going out becomes fainter and increases in size, seems to indicate that the chief reason for the extinction of the flame is the fall in its temperature.

[47] Different so-called disinfectants purify the air, and prevent the injurious action of certain of its components by changing or destroying them. Disinfection is especially necessary in those places where a considerable amount of volatile substances are evolved into the air, and where organic substances are decomposed; for instance, in hospitals, closets, &c. The numerous disinfectants are of the most varied nature. They may be divided into oxidising, antiseptic, and absorbent substances. To the oxidising substances used for disinfection belong chlorine, and various substances evolving it, because chlorine in the presence of water oxidises the majority of organic substances, and this is why chlorine is used as a disinfectant for Siberian plagues. Further, to this class belong the permanganates of the alkalis and peroxide of hydrogen, as substances easily oxidising matters dissolved in water; these salts are not volatile like chlorine, and therefore act much more slowly, and in a much more limited sphere. Antiseptic substances are those which convert organic substances into such as are little prone to change, and prevent putrefaction and fermentation. They most probably kill the germs of organisms occurring in miasmata. The most important of these substances are creosote and phenol (carbolic acid), which occur in tar, and act in preserving smoked meat. Phenol is a substance little soluble in water, volatile, oily, and having the characteristic smell of smoked objects. Its action on animals in

considerable quantities is injurious, but in small quantities, used in the form of a weak solution, it prevents the change of animal matter. The smell of privies, which depends on the change of excremental matter, may be easily removed by means of chlorine or phenol. Salicylic acid, thymol, common tar, and especially its solution in alkalis as proposed by Nensky, &c., are also substances having the same property. Absorbent substances are of no less importance, especially as preventatives, than the preceding two classes of disinfectants, inasmuch as they are innocuous. They are those substances which absorb the odoriferous gases and vapours emitted during putrefaction, which are chiefly ammonia, sulphuretted hydrogen, and other volatile compounds. To this class belong charcoal, certain salts of iron, gypsum, salts of magnesia, and similar substances, as well as peat, mould, and clay. Questions of disinfection and ventilation appertain to the most serious problems of common life and hygiene. These questions are so vast that we are here able only to give a short outline of their nature.

[246]

CHAPTER VI

TTHE COMPOUNDS OF NITROGEN WITH HYDROGEN AND OXYGEN

FIG. 42.—The dry distillation of bones on a large scale. The bones are heated in the vertical cylinders C (about 1½ metre high and 30 centimetres in diameter). The products of distillation pass through the tubes T, into the condenser B, and receiver F. When the distillation is completed the trap H is opened, and the burnt bones are loaded into trucks V. The roof M is then opened, and the cylinders are charged with a fresh quantity of bones. The ammonia water is preserved, and goes to the preparation of ammoniacal salts, as described in the following drawing.

In the last chapter we saw that nitrogen does not directly combine with hydrogen, but that a mixture of these gases in the presence of hydrochloric acid gas, HCl, forms ammonium chloride, NH_4Cl, on the passage of a series of electric sparks.[1] In ammonium chloride, HCl is combined with NH_3, consequently N with H_3 forms ammonia.[2] Almost all the *nitrogenous substances of plants and animals* evolve ammonia when heated with an alkali. But even without the presence of an alkali the majority of nitrogenous substances, when decomposed or heated with a limited supply of air, evolve their nitrogen, if not entirely, at all events partially, in the form of ammonia. When animal substances such as skins, bones, flesh, hair, horns, &c., are heated without access of[247] air in iron retorts—they undergo what is termed dry distillation. A portion of the resultant substances remains in the retort and forms a carbonaceous residue, whilst the other portion, in virtue of its volatility, escapes through the tube leading from the retort. The vapours given off, on cooling, form a liquid which separates into two layers; the one, which is oily, is composed of the so-called animal oils (*oleum animale*): the other, an aqueous layer, contains a solution of ammonia salts. If this solution be mixed with lime and heated, the lime takes up the elements of carbonic acid from the ammonia salts, and ammonia is evolved as a gas.[3] In ancient times ammonia compounds were imported into Europe from Egypt, where they were prepared from the soot obtained in the employment of camels' dung as fuel in the locality of the temple of Jupiter Ammon (in Lybia), and therefore the salt obtained was called 'sal-ammoniacale,' from which the name of ammonia is derived. At the present time ammonia is obtained exclusively, on a large scale, either from the products of the dry distillation of animal or[248] vegetable refuse, from urine, or from the ammoniacal liquors collected in the destructive distillation of coal for the preparation of coal gas. This ammoniacal liquor is placed in a retort with lime and heated; the ammonia is then evolved together with steam.[4] In the arts, only a small amount of ammonia is used in a free state—that is, in an aqueous solution; the greater portion of it is converted into different salts having technical uses, especially sal-ammoniac, NH_4Cl, and ammonium sulphate, $(NH_4)_2SO_4$. They are saline substances which are formed because ammonia, NH_3, combines with all acids, HX, forming ammonia salts, NH_4X. Sal-ammoniac, NH_4Cl, is a compound of ammonia with hydrochloric acid. It is prepared by passing the vapours of ammonia and water, evolved, as above described, from ammoniacal liquor, into an aqueous solution of hydrochloric acid, and on evaporating the solution sal-ammoniac is obtained in the form of soluble crystals[5][249] resembling common salt in appearance and properties. Ammonia may be very easily prepared *from* this *sal-ammoniac*, NH_4Cl, as from any other ammoniacal salt, by heating it with lime. Calcium hydroxide, CaH_2O_2, as an alkali takes up the acid and sets free the ammonia, forming calcium chloride, according to the equation $2NH_4Cl + CaH_2O_2 = 2H_2O + CaCl_2 + 2NH_3$. In this reaction the ammonia is evolved as a gas.[6]

FIG. 43,—Method of abstracting ammonia, on a large scale, from ammonia water obtained at gas works by the dry distillation of coal, or by the fermentation of urine, &c. This water is mixed with lime and poured into the boiler C", and from thence into C' and C consecutively. The last boiler is heated directly over a furnace, and hence no ammonia remains in solution after the liquid has been boiled in it. The liquid is therefore then thrown away. The ammonia vapour and steam pass from the boiler C, through the tube T, into the boiler C', and then into C", so that the solution in C' becomes stronger than that in C, and still stronger in C". The boilers are furnished with stirrers A, A', and A" to prevent the lime settling. From C" the ammonia and steam pass through the tube T" into worm condensers surrounded with cold water, thence into the Woulfe's bottle P, where the solution of ammonia is collected, and finally the still uncondensed ammonia vapour is led into the flat vessel R, containing acid which absorbs the last traces of ammonia.

It must be observed that all the complex nitrogenous substances of plants, animals, and soils are decomposed when heated with an excess of sulphuric acid, the whole of their nitrogen being converted into ammonium sulphate, from which it may be liberated by treatment with an excess of alkali. This reaction is so complete that it forms the basis of Kjeldahl's method for estimating the amount of nitrogen in its compounds.

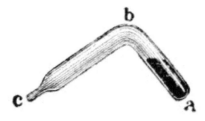

FIG. 45.—The liquefaction of ammonia in a thick bent glass tube. A compound of chloride of silver and ammonia is placed in the end *a*, and the end *c* is then sealed up.

Ammonia is a colourless gas, resembling those with which we are already acquainted in its outward appearance, but clearly distinguishable from any other gas by its very characteristic and pungent smell. It irritates the eyes, and it is positively impossible to inhale it. Animals die in it. Its density, referred to hydrogen, is 8·5; hence it is lighter than air. It belongs to the class of gases which are easily liquefied.[7][250] Faraday employed the following method for liquefying ammonia. Ammonia when passed over dry silver chloride, AgCl, is absorbed by it to a considerable extent, especially at low temperatures.[8] The solid[251] compound $AgCl,3NH_3$ thus obtained is introduced into a bent tube (fig. 45), whose open end c is then fused up. The compound is then slightly heated at *a*, and the ammonia comes off, owing to the easy dissociation of the compound. The other end of the tube is immersed in a freezing mixture. The pressure of the gas coming off, combined with the low temperature at one end of the tube, causes the ammonia evolved to condense into a liquid, in which form it collects at the cold end of the tube. If the heating be stopped, the silver chloride again absorbs the ammonia. In this manner one tube may serve for repeated experiments. Ammonia may also be liquefied by the ordinary methods— that is, by means of pumping dry ammonia gas into a refrigerated space. Liquefied ammonia is a colourless and very mobile liquid,[9] whose specific gravity at 0° is 0·63 (E. Andréeff). At the temperature (about -70°) given by a mixture of liquid carbonic anhydride and ether, liquid ammonia crystallises, and in this form its odour is feeble, because at so low a temperature its vapour tension is very inconsiderable. The boiling point (at a pressure of 760 mm.) of liquid ammonia is about -32°. Hence this temperature may be obtained at the ordinary pressure by the evaporation of liquefied ammonia.

Ammonia, containing, as it does, much hydrogen, is *capable of combustion*; it does not, however, burn steadily, and sometimes not at all, in ordinary atmospheric air. In pure oxygen it burns with a greenish-yellow flame,[10] forming water, whilst the nitrogen set free[252] gives its oxygen compounds—that is, oxides of nitrogen. The decomposition of ammonia into hydrogen and nitrogen not only takes place at a red heat and under the action of electric sparks, but also by means of many oxidising substances; for instance, by passing ammonia through a tube containing red-hot copper oxide. The water thus formed may be collected by substances absorbing it, and the quantity of nitrogen may be measured in a gaseous form, and thus the composition of ammonia determined. In this manner it is very easy to prove that ammonia contains 3 parts by weight of hydrogen to 14 parts by weight of nitrogen; and, by volume, 3 vols. of hydrogen and 1 vol. of nitrogen form 2 vols. of ammonia.[11]

Ammonia is capable of combining with a number of substances, forming, like water, substances of various degrees of stability. It is more soluble than any of the gases yet described, both in water and in many aqueous solutions. We have already seen, in the first chapter, that one volume of water, at the ordinary temperature, dissolves about 700 vols. of ammonia gas. The great solubility of ammonia enables it to be always kept ready for use in the form of an aqueous solution,[12][253] which is commercially known as *spirits of hartshorn*. Ammonia water is continually evolving ammoniacal vapour, and so has the characteristic smell of ammonia itself. It is a very characteristic and important fact that ammonia has an alkaline reaction, and colours litmus paper blue, just like caustic potash or lime; it is therefore sometimes called *caustic ammonia* (volatile alkali). Acids may be saturated by ammonia water or gas in exactly the same way as by any other alkali. In this process *ammonia combines directly with acids*, and this forms the most essential[254] chemical reaction of this substance. If sulphuric, nitric, acetic, or any other acid be brought into contact with ammonia it absorbs it, and in so doing evolves a large amount of heat and forms a compound having all the properties of a salt. Thus, for example, sulphuric acid, H_2SO_4, in absorbing ammonia, forms (on evaporating the solution) two salts, according to the relative quantities of ammonia and acid. One salt is formed from $NH_3 + H_2SO_4$, and consequently has the composition NH_5SO_4, and the other is formed from $2NH_3 + H_2SO_4$, and its composition is therefore $N_2H_8SO_4$. The former has an acid reaction and the latter a neutral reaction, and they are called respectively acid ammonium sulphate (ammonium hydrogen sulphate), and normal ammonium sulphate, or simply ammonium sulphate. The same takes place in the action of all other acids; but certain of them are able to form normal ammonium salts only, whilst others give both acid and normal ammonium salts. This depends on the nature of the acid and not on the ammonia, as we shall afterwards see. Ammonium salts are very similar in appearance and in many of their properties to metallic salts; for instance, sodium chloride, or table salt, resembles sal-ammoniac, or ammonium chloride, not only in its outward appearance but even in crystalline form, in its property of giving precipitates with silver salts, in its solubility in water, and in its evolving hydrochloric acid when heated with sulphuric acid—in a word, a most perfect analogy is to be remarked in an entire series of reactions. An analogy in composition is seen if sal-ammoniac, NH_4Cl, be compared with table salt, $NaCl$; and the ammonium hydrogen sulphate, NH_4HSO_4, with the sodium hydrogen sulphate, $NaHSO_4$; or ammonium nitrate, NH_4NO_3, with sodium nitrate, $NaNO_3$.[13] It is seen, on comparing the above compounds, that the part which sodium takes in the sodium salts is played in ammonium salts by a group NH_4, which is called *ammonium*. If table salt be[255] called 'sodium chloride,' then sal-ammoniac should be and is called 'ammonium chloride.'

The hypothesis that ammoniacal salts correspond with a complex metal ammonium bears the name of the *ammonium theory*. It was enunciated by the famous Swedish chemist Berzelius after the proposition made by Ampère. The analogy admitted between ammonium and metals is probable, owing to the fact that mercury is able to form an amalgam with ammonium similar to that which it forms with sodium or many other metals. The only difference between ammonium amalgam and sodium amalgam consists in the instability of the ammonium, which easily decomposes into ammonia and hydrogen.[14] Ammonium amalgam may be prepared from sodium amalgam. If the latter be shaken up with a strong solution of sal-ammoniac, the mercury swells up violently and loses its mobility whilst preserving its metallic appearance. In so doing, the mercury dissolves ammonium—that is, the sodium in the mercury is replaced by the ammonium, and replaces it in the sal-ammoniac,[256] forming sodium chloride, $NH_4Cl + HgNa = NaCl + HgNH_4$. Naturally, the formation of ammonium amalgam does not entirely prove the existence of ammonium itself in a separate state; but it shows the possibility of this substance existing, and its analogy with the metals, because only metals dissolve in mercury.[15] Ammonium amalgam crystallises in cubes, three times heavier than water; it is only stable in the cold, and particularly at very low temperatures. It begins to decompose at the ordinary temperature, evolving ammonia and hydrogen in the proportion of two volumes of ammonia and one volume of hydrogen, $NH_4 = NH_3 + H$. By the action of water, ammonium amalgam gives hydrogen and ammonia water, just as sodium amalgam gives hydrogen and sodium hydroxide; and therefore, in accordance with the ammonium theory, ammonia water must be looked on as containing ammonium hydroxide, NH_4OH,[16] just as an aqueous solution of sodium hydroxide, contains $NaOH$. The ammonium hydroxide, like ammonium itself, is an unstable substance, which easily dissociates, and can only exist in a free state at low temperatures.[17] Ordinary solutions of ammonia must be looked on as the products of the dissociation of this hydroxide, inasmuch as $NH_4OH = NH_3 + H_2O$.

All ammoniacal salts *decompose at a red heat* into ammonia and an acid, which, on cooling in contact with each other, re-combine together. If the acid be non-volatile, the ammoniacal salt, when heated, evolves the ammonia, leaving the non-volatile acid behind; if the acid be volatile, then, on heating, both the acid and ammonia volatilise together, and on cooling re-combine into the salt which originally served for the formation of their vapours.[18]

[257]

Ammonia is not only capable of combining with acids, but also with many salts, as was seen from its forming definite compounds, $AgCl,3NH_3$ and $2AgCl,3NH_3$, with silver chloride. Just as ammonia is absorbed by various oxygen salts of the metals, so also is it absorbed by the chlorine, iodine, and bromine compounds of many metals, and in so doing evolves heat. Certain of these compounds part with their ammonia even when left exposed to the air, but others only do so at a red heat; many give up their ammonia when dissolved, whilst others dissolve without decomposition, and when evaporated separate from their solutions unchanged. All these facts only indicate that ammoniacal, like aqueous, compounds dissociate with greater or lesser facility.[19] Certain metallic oxides also absorb ammonia and are dissolved in ammonia water. Such are, for instance, the oxides of zinc, nickel, copper, and many others; the majority of such compounds are unstable. The property of ammonia of combining with certain oxides explains its action on certain metals.[20] By reason of such action, copper vessels are not suitable for holding liquids containing ammonia. Iron is not acted on by such liquids.

The similarity between the relation of ammonia and water to salts and other substances is more especially marked in those cases in which the salt is capable of combining with both ammonia and water. Take, for example, copper sulphate, $CuSO_4$. As we saw in Chapter I., it gives with water blue crystals, $CuSO_4,5H_2O$; but it also absorbs ammonia in the same molecular proportion, forming a blue substance, $CuSO_4,5NH_3$, and therefore the ammonia combining with salts may be termed *ammonia of crystallisation*.

Such are the *reactions of combination* proper to ammonia. Let us now turn our attention to the reactions of substitution proper to this substance. If ammonia be passed through a heated tube containing metallic sodium, hydrogen is evolved, and a compound is obtained[258] containing ammonia in which one atom of hydrogen is replaced by an atom of sodium, NH_2Na

(according to the equation $NH_3 + Na = NH_2Na + H$). This body is termed sodium amide. We shall afterwards see that iodine and chlorine are also capable of directly displacing hydrogen from ammonia, and of replacing it. In fact, the hydrogen of ammonia may be replaced in many ways by different elements. If in this replacement NH_2 remains, the resultant substances NH_2R are called *amides*, whilst the substitution products, NHR_2, in which only NH remains, are called *imides*,[20 bis] and those in which none of the ammoniacal hydrogen remains, NR_3, are known as *nitrides*. Free amidogen, N_2H_4, is now known in a state of hydration under the name of hydrazine;[21] it combines[259] with acids and resembles ammonia in this respect. In the action of different substances on ammonia it is the *hydrogen that is substituted*, whilst the nitrogen remains in the resultant compound, so to say, untouched. The same phenomenon is to be observed in the action of various substances on water. In the majority of cases the reactions of water consist in the hydrogen being evolved, and in its being replaced by different elements. This also takes place, as we have seen, in acids in which the hydrogen is easily displaced by metals. This chemical mobility of hydrogen is perhaps connected with the great lightness of the atoms of this element.

In practical chemistry[21 bis] ammonia is often employed, not only for saturating acids, but also for effecting reactions of double decomposition[260] with salts, and especially for separating insoluble basic hydroxides from soluble salts. Let MHO stand for an insoluble basic hydroxide and HX for an acid. The salt formed by them will have a composition $MHO + XH - H_2O = MX$. If aqueous ammonia, NH_4OH, be added to a solution of this salt, the ammonia will change places with the metal M, and thus form the insoluble basic hydroxide, or, as it is said, give a precipitate.

$$MX \quad + \quad NH_4(OH) \quad = \quad NH_4X \quad + \quad MHO$$

Salt of the metal.   Aqueous ammonia.   Ammonium salt.   Basic hydrate.
   In solution   In solution   In solution   As precipitate

Thus, for instance, if aqueous ammonia is added to a solution of a salt of aluminium, then alumina hydrate is separated out as a colourless gelatinous precipitate.[22]

In order to grasp the relation between ammonia and the oxygen compounds of nitrogen it is necessary to recognise the general *law of substitution*, applicable to all cases of substitution between elements,[23] and therefore showing what may be the cases of substitution between oxygen and hydrogen as component parts of water. The law of substitution may be deduced from mechanical principles if the molecule be conceived as a system of elementary atoms occurring in a certain chemical and mechanical equilibrium. By likening the molecule to a system of bodies in a state of motion—for instance, to the sum total of the sun, planets, and satellites, existing in conditions of mobile equilibrium—then we should expect the action of one part, in this system, to be equal and opposite to the other, according to Newton's third law of mechanics. Hence, given a molecule of a compound, for instance, H_2O, NH_3, NaCl, HCl, &c., its every two parts must in a chemical sense[261] represent two things somewhat alike in force and properties, and therefore *every two parts into which a molecule of a compound may be divided are capable of replacing each other*. In order that the application of the law should become clear it is evident that among compounds the most stable should be chosen. We will therefore take hydrochloric acid and water as the most stable compounds of hydrogen.[24] According to the above law of substitution, if the elements H and Cl are able to form a molecule, HCl, and a stable one, they are able to replace each other. And, indeed, we shall afterwards see (Chapter XI.) that in a number of instances a substitution between hydrogen and chlorine can take place. Given RH, then RCl is possible, because HCl exists and is stable. The molecule of water, H_2O, may be divided in two ways, because it contains 3 atoms: into H and (HO) on the one hand, and into H_2 and O on the other. Consequently, being given RH, its substitution products will be R(HO) according to the first form, and R_2O according to the second; being given RH_2, its corresponding substitution products will be RH(OH), $R(OH)_2$, RO, $(RH)_2O$, &c. The group (OH) is the same hydroxyl or aqueous radicle which we have already mentioned in the third chapter as a component part of hydroxides and alkalis—for instance, Na(OH), $Ca(OH)_2$, &c. It is evident, judging from H(HO) and HCl, that (OH) can be substituted by Cl, because both are replaceable by H; and this is of common occurrence in chemistry, because metallic chlorides—for example, NaCl and NH_4Cl—correspond with hydroxides of the alkalis Na(OH) or $NH_4(OH)$. In hydrocarbons—for instance, C_2H_6—the hydrogen is replaceable by chlorine and by hydroxyl. Thus ordinary alcohol is C_2H_6, in which one atom of H is replaced by (OH); that is, $C_2H_5(OH)$. It is evident that the replacement of hydrogen by hydroxyl essentially forms the phenomenon of oxidation, because RH gives R(OH), or RHO. Hydrogen peroxide may in this sense be regarded as water in which the hydrogen is replaced by hydroxyl; H(OH) gives $(OH)_2$ or H_2O_2. The other form of substitution—namely, that of O in the place of H_2—is also a common chemical phenomenon. Thus alcohol, C_2H_6O, or $C_2H_5(OH)$, when oxidising in the air, gives acetic acid, $C_2H_4O_2$, or $C_2H_3O(OH)$, in which H_2 is replaced by O.

In the further course of this work we shall have occasion to refer to the law of substitution for explaining many chemical phenomena and relations.

We will now apply these conceptions to ammonia in order to see its relation to the oxygen compounds of nitrogen. It is evident that many substances should be obtainable from ammonia, NH_3, or aqueous ammonia, $NH_4(OH)$, by substituting their hydrogen by hydroxyl, or H_2 by oxygen. And such is the case. The two extreme cases of such substitution will be as follows: (1) One atom of H in NH_3 is substituted by (OH), and $NH_2(OH)$ is produced. Such a substance, still containing much hydrogen, should have many of the properties of ammonia. It is known under the name of *hydroxylamine*,[25] and, in fact, is capable, like[263] ammonia, of giving salts with acids; for example, with hydrochloric acid, $NH_3(OH)Cl$— which is a substance corresponding to sal-ammoniac, in which one atom of hydrogen is replaced by hydroxyl.[25 bis] (2) The[264] other extreme case of substitution is that given by ammonium hydroxide, $NH_4(OH)$, when the whole of the hydrogen of the ammonium is replaced by oxygen; and, as ammonium contains 4 atoms of hydrogen, the highest oxygen compound should be $NO_2(OH)$, or NHO_3, as we find to be really the case, for NHO_3 is nitric acid, exhibiting the highest degree of oxidation of nitrogen.[26] If instead of the two extreme aspects of substitution we take an intermediate one, we obtain the intermediate oxygen compounds of nitrogen. For instance, $N(OH)_3$ is orthonitrous acid,[27] to which corresponds nitrous acid, $NO(OH)$, or NHO_2, equal to $N(OH)_3 - H_2O$, and nitrous anhydride, $N_2O_3 = 2N(OH)_3 - 3H_2O$. Thus nitrogen gives a series of oxygen compounds, which we will proceed to describe. We will, however, first show by two examples that in the first place the passage of ammonia into the oxygen compounds of nitrogen up to nitric acid, as well as the converse preparation of ammonia (and consequently of the intermediate compounds also) from nitric acid, are reactions which proceed directly and easily under many circumstances, and in the second place that the above general principle of substitution gives the possibility of understanding many, at first sight unexpected and complex, relations and transformations, such as the preparation of hydronitrous acid, HN_3. In nature the matter is complicated by a number of influences and circumstances,[265] but in the law the relations are presented in their simplest aspect.

1. It is easy to prove the possibility of the oxidation of ammonia into nitric acid by passing a mixture of ammonia and air over heated spongy platinum. This causes the oxidation of the ammonia, nitric acid being formed, which partially combines with the excess of ammonia.

The converse passage of nitric acid into ammonia is effected by the action of hydrogen at the moment of its evolution.[28] Thus metallic aluminium, evolving hydrogen from a solution of caustic soda, is able to completely convert nitric acid added to the mixture (as a salt, because the alkali gives a salt with the nitric acid) into ammonia, $NHO_3 + 8H = NH_3 + 3H_2O$.

2. In 1890 Curtius in Germany obtained a gaseous substance of the composition HN_3 (hydrogen trinitride), having the distinctive properties of an acid, and giving, like hydrochloric acid, salts; for example, a sodium salt, NaN_3; ammonium salt, $NH_4N_3 = N_4H_4$; barium salt, $Ba(N_3)_2$, &c., which he therefore named hydronitrous acid, HN_3.[28 bis][266] The extraordinary composition of the compound (ammonia, NH_3, contains one N atom and three H atoms; in HN_3, on the contrary, there are three N atoms and one H atom), the facile decomposition of its salts with an explosion, and above all its distinctly acid character (an aqueous solution shows a strong acid reaction to litmus), not only indicated the importance of this unexpected discovery, but at first gave rise to some perplexity as to the nature of the substance obtained, for the relations in which HN_3 stood to other simple compounds of nitrogen which had long been known was not at all evident, and the scientific spirit especially requires that there should be a distinct bond between every innovation, every fresh discovery, and that which is already firmly established and known, for upon this basis is founded that apparently paradoxical union in science of a conservative stability with an irresistible and never-ceasing improvement. This missing, connection between the newly discovered hydronitrous acid, HN_3, and the long known ammonia, NH_3, and nitric acid, HNO_3, may be found in the law of substitution, starting from the well-known properties and composition of nitric acid and ammonia, as I mentioned in the 'Journal of the Russian Physico-Chemical Society' (1890). The essence of the matter lies in the fact that to the hydrate of ammonium, or caustic ammonia, NH_4OH, there should correspond, according to the law of substitution, an ortho-nitric acid (*see* Note 27), $H_3NO_4 = NO(OH)_3$, which equals $NH_4(OH)$ with the substitution in it of (*a*) two atoms of hydrogen by oxygen ($O—H_2$) and (*b*) two atoms of hydrogen by the aqueous radicle ($OH—H$). Ordinary or meta-nitric acid is merely this ortho-nitric acid minus water. To ortho-nitric acid there should correspond the ammoniacal salts: mono-substituted, $H_2NH_4NO_4$; bi-substituted, $H(NH_4)_2NO_4$; and tri-substituted, $(NH_4)_3NO_4$. These salts, containing as they do hydrogen and oxygen, like many similar ammoniacal salts (see, for instance, Chapter IX.—Cyanides), are[267] able to part with them in the form of water. Then from the first salt we have $H_2NH_4NO_4 - 4H_2O = N_2O$—nitrous oxide, and from the second $H(NH_4)_2NO4 - 4H_2O = HN_3$—hydronitrous acid, and from the third $(NH_4)_3NO - 4H_2O = N_4H_4$—the ammonium salt of the same acid. The composition of HN_3 should be thus understood, whilst its acid properties are explained by the fact that the water ($4H_2O$) from $H(NH_4)_2N\_O_4$ is formed at the expense of the hydrogen of the ammonium and oxygen of the nitric acid, so that there remains the same hydrogen as in nitric acid, or

that which may be replaced by metals and give salts. Moreover, nitrogen undoubtedly belongs to that category of metalloids which give acids, like chlorine and carbon, and therefore, under the influence of three of its atoms, one atom of hydrogen acquires those properties which it has in acids, just as in HCN (hydrocyanic acid) the hydrogen has received these properties under the influence of the carbon and nitrogen (and HN_3 may be regarded as HCN where C has been replaced by N_2). Moreover, besides explaining the composition and acid properties of HN_3, the above method gives the possibility of foretelling the closeness of the bond between hydronitrous acid and nitrous oxide, for $N_2O + NH_3 = HN_3 + H_2O$. This reaction, which was foreseen from the above considerations, was accomplished by Wislicenus (1892) by the synthesis of the sodium salt, by taking the amide of sodium, NH_2Na (obtained by heating Na in a current of NH_3), and acting upon it (when heated) with nitrous oxide, N_2O, when $2NH_2Na + N_2O = NaN_3 + NaHO + NH_3$. The resultant salt, NaN_3, gives hydronitrous acid when acted upon by sulphuric acid, $NaN_3 + H_2SO_4 = NaHSO_4 + HN_3$. The latter gives, with the corresponding solutions of their salts, the insoluble (and easily explosive) salts of silver, AgN_3 (insoluble, like AgCl or AgCN), and lead, $Pb(N_3)_2$.

The compounds of nitrogen with oxygen present an excellent example of the law of multiple proportions, because they contain, for 14 parts by weight of nitrogen, 8, 16, 24, 32, and 40 parts respectively by weight of oxygen. The composition of these compounds is as follows:—

N_2O, nitrous oxide; hydrate NHO.

N_2O_2, nitric oxide, NO.

N_2O_3, nitrous anhydride; hydrate NHO_2.

N_2O_4, peroxide of nitrogen, NO_2.

N_2O_5, nitric anhydride; hydrate NHO_3.

Of these compounds,[29] nitrous and nitric oxides, peroxide of nitrogen,[268] and nitric acid, NHO_3, are characterised as being the most stable. *The lower oxides, when coming into contact with the higher, may give the intermediate forms*; for instance, NO and NO_2 form N_2O_3, *and the intermediate oxides may, in splitting up, give a higher and lower oxide.* So N_2O_4 gives N_2O_3 and N_2O_5, or, in the presence of water, their hydrates.

We have already seen that, under certain conditions, nitrogen combines with oxygen, and we know that ammonia may he oxidised. In these cases various oxidation products of nitrogen are formed, but in the presence of water and an excess of oxygen they always give nitric acid. Nitric acid, as corresponding with the highest oxide, is able, in deoxidising, to give the lower oxides; it is the only nitrogen acid whose salts occur somewhat widely in nature, and it has many technical uses, for which reason we will begin with it.

Nitric acid, NHO₃, is likewise known as aqua fortis. In a free state it is only met with in nature in small quantities, in the air and in rain-water after storms; but even in the atmosphere nitric acid does not long remain free, but combines with ammonia, traces of which are always found in air. On falling on the soil and into running water, &c., the nitric acid everywhere comes into contact with bases (or their carbonates), which easily act on it, and therefore it is converted into the nitrates of these bases. Hence nitric acid is always met with in the form of salts in nature. The soluble salts of nitric acid are called *nitres*. This name is derived from the Latin *sal nitri*. The potassium salt, KNO_3, is common nitre, and the sodium salt, $NaNO_3$, Chili saltpetre, or cubic nitre. Nitres are formed in the soil when a nitrogenous[269] substance is slowly oxidised in the presence of an alkali by means of the oxygen of the atmosphere. In nature there are very frequent instances of such oxidation. For this reason certain soils and rubbish heaps—for instance, lime rubbish (in the presence of a base)—lime contain a more or less considerable amount of nitre. One of these nitres—sodium nitrate—is extracted from the earth in large quantities in Chili, where it was probably formed by the oxidation of animal refuse. This kind of nitre is employed in practice for the manufacture of nitric acid and the other oxygen compounds of nitrogen. Nitric acid is obtained from *Chili saltpetre* by heating it with *sulphuric acid*. The hydrogen of the sulphuric acid replaces the sodium in the nitre. The sulphuric acid then forms either an acid salt, $NaHSO_4$, or a normal salt, Na_2SO_4, whilst nitric acid is formed from the nitre and is volatilised. The decomposition is expressed by the equations: (1) $NaNO_3 + H_2SO_4 = HNO_3 + NaHSO_4$, if the acid salt be formed, and (2) $2NaNO_3 + H_2SO_4 = Na_2SO_4 + 2HNO_3$, if the normal sodium sulphate is formed. With an excess of sulphuric acid, at a moderate heat, and at the commencement of the reaction, the decomposition proceeds according to the first equation; and on further heating with a sufficient amount of nitre according to the second, because the acid salt $NaHSO_4$ itself acts like an acid (its hydrogen being replaceable as in acids), according to the equation $NaNO_3 + NaHSO_4 = Na_2SO_4 + HNO_3$.

The sulphuric acid, as it is said, here displaces the nitric acid from its compound with the base.[29 bis] Thus, in the reaction of sulphuric[270] acid on nitre there is formed a non-volatile salt of sulphuric acid, which remains, together with an excess of this acid, in the distilling apparatus, and nitric acid, which is converted into vapour, and may be condensed, because it is a liquid and volatile substance. On a small scale, this reaction may be carried on in a glass retort with a glass condenser. On a large scale, in chemical works, the process is exactly similar, only iron retorts are employed for holding the mixture of nitre and sulphuric acid, and earthenware three-necked bottles are used instead of a condenser,[30] as shown in fig. 47.

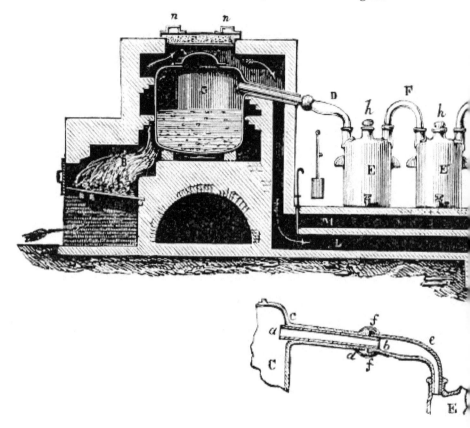

FIG. 47.—Method of preparing nitric acid on a large scale. A cast-iron retort, C, is fixed into the furnace, and heated by the fire, B. The flame and products of combustion are at first led along the flue, M (in order to heat the receivers), and afterwards into L. The retort is charged with Chili saltpetre and sulphuric acid, and the cover is luted on with clay and gypsum. A clay tube, *a*, is fixed into the neck of the retort (in order to prevent the nitric acid from corroding the cast iron), and a bent glass tube, D, is luted on to it. This tube carries the vapours into a series of earthenware receivers, E. Nitric acid mixed with sulphuric acid collects in the first. The purest nitric acid is procured from the second, whilst that which condenses in the third receiver contains hydrochloric acid, and that in the fourth nitrous oxide. Water is poured into the last receiver in order to condense the residual vapours.

Nitric acid so obtained always contains water. It is extremely difficult to deprive it of all the admixed water without destroying a portion of the acid itself and partially converting it into lower oxides, because without the presence of an excess of water it is very unstable. When rapidly distilled a portion is decomposed, and there are obtained free oxygen and lower oxides of nitrogen, which, together with the water, remain in solution with the nitric acid. Therefore it is necessary to work with great care in order to obtain a pure hydrate of nitric acid, HNO_3, and especially to mix the nitric acid obtained from nitre, as above described, with sulphuric acid, which takes up the water, and to distil it at the lowest possible temperature—that is, by placing the retort holding the mixture in a water or oil bath and carefully heating it. The first portion of the nitric acid thus distilled boils at 86°, has a specific gravity at 15° of 1·526, and solidifies at -50°; it is very unstable at higher temperatures. This is the normal hydrate, HNO_3, which corresponds with the salts, NMO_3, of nitric acid. When diluted with water nitric acid presents a higher boiling point, not only as compared with that of the nitric acid itself, but also with that of water; so that, if very dilute nitric acid be distilled, the first portions passing over will consist of almost pure water, until the boiling point in the vapours reaches 121°. At this temperature a compound of nitric acid with water, containing about 70 p.c. of nitric acid,[31] distils over; its[272] specific gravity at 15° = 1·421. If the solution contain less than 25 p.c. of water, then, the specific gravity of the solution being above 1·44, HNO_3 evaporates off and fumes in the air, forming the above hydrate, whose vapour tension is less than that of water. Such solutions form *fuming nitric acid.* On distilling it gives monohydrated acid,[32] HNO_3; it is a hydrate boiling at 121°, so that it is obtained from both weak and strong solutions. Fuming nitric acid, under the action not only of organic substances, but even of heat, loses a portion of its oxygen, forming lower oxides of nitrogen, which impart a *red-brown colour* to it;[33] the pure acid is colourless.

[273]

Nitric acid, as an *acid hydrate,* enters into reactions of double decomposition with bases, basic hydrates (alkalis), and with salts. In all these cases a salt of nitric acid is obtained. An alkali and nitric acid give water and a salt; so, also, a basic oxide with nitric acid gives a salt and water; for instance, lime, $CaO + 2HNO_3 = Ca(NO_3)_2 + H_2O$. Many of these salts are termed nitres.[34] The composition of the ordinary salts of nitric acid may be expressed by the general formula $M(NO_3)_n$, where M indicates a metal replacing the hydrogen in one or several (n) equivalents of nitric acid. We shall find afterwards that the atoms M of metals are equivalent to one (K, Na, Ag) atom of hydrogen, or two (Ca, Mg, Ba), or three (Al, In), or, in general, *n* atoms of hydrogen. *The salts of nitric acid* are especially characterised by being all *soluble in water*.[35] From the property common to all these salts of entering into double decompositions, and owing to the volatility of nitric acid, they evolve nitric acid when heated with sulphuric acid. They all, like the acid itself, are capable of evolving oxygen when heated, and consequently of acting as oxidising substances; they therefore, for instance, deflagrate with ignited carbon, the carbon burning at the expense of the oxygen of the salt and forming gaseous products of combustion.[36]

[274]

Nitric acid also enters into double decompositions with a number of hydrocarbons not in any way possessing alkaline characters and not reacting with other acids. Under these circumstances the nitric acid gives water and a new substance termed a *nitro-compound.* The chemical character of the nitro-compound is the same as that of the original substance; for example, if an indifferent substance be taken, then the nitro compound obtained from it will also be indifferent; if an acid be taken, then an acid is obtained also.[36 bis] Benzene, C_6H_6, for instance, acts according to the equation $C_6H_6 + HNO_3 = H_2O + C_6H_5NO_2$. Nitrobenzene is produced. The substance taken, C_6H_6, is a liquid hydrocarbon having a faint tarry smell, boiling at 80°, and lighter than water; by the action of nitric acid nitrobenzene is obtained, which is a substance boiling at about 210°, heavier than water, and having an almond-like odour: it is employed in large quantities for the preparation of aniline and aniline dyes.[37] As the nitro-compounds[275] contain both combustible elements (hydrogen and carbon), as well as oxygen in unstable combination with nitrogen, in the form of the radicle NO_2 of nitric acid, they decompose with an explosion when ignited or even struck, owing to the pressure of the vapours and gases formed—free nitrogen, carbonic anhydride, CO_2, carbonic oxide, CO, and aqueous vapour. In the explosion of nitro compounds[37 bis] much heat is[276] evolved, as in the combustion of gunpowder or detonating gas, and in this case the force of explosion in a closed space is great, because from a solid or liquid nitro-compound occupying a small space there proceed vapours and gases whose elasticity is great not only from the small space in which they are formed, but owing to the high temperature corresponding to the combustion of the nitro-compound.[38]

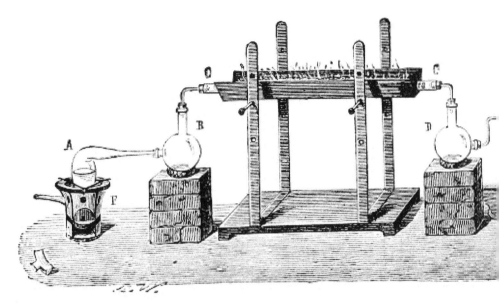

FIG. 48.—The method of decomposition of nitrous anhydride, also applicable to the other oxides of nitrogen, and to their analysis. NO_2 is generated from nitrate of lead in the retort A. Nitric acid and other less volatile products are condensed in B. The tube C C contains copper, and is heated from below. Undecomposed volatile products (if any are formed) are condensed in D, which is cooled. If the decomposition be incomplete, brown fumes make their appearance in this receiver. The gaseous nitrogen is collected in the cylinder E.

If the vapour of nitric acid is passed through an even moderately heated glass tube, the formation of dark-brown fumes of the lower oxides of nitrogen and the separation of free oxygen may be observed, $2NHO_3 = H_2O + 2NO_2 + O$. The decomposition is complete at a white heat—that is, nitrogen is formed, $2NHO_3 = H_2O + N_2 + O_5$. Hence it is easily understood that nitric acid may part with its oxygen to a number of substances capable of being oxidised.[39] It is consequently[277] an *oxidising agent*. Charcoal, as we have already seen, burns in nitric acid; phosphorus, sulphur, iodine, and the majority of metals also decompose nitric acid, some on heating and others even at the ordinary temperature: the substances taken are oxidised and the nitric acid is deoxidised, yielding compounds containing less oxygen. Only a few metals, such as gold and platinum, do not act on nitric acid, but the majority decompose it; in so doing, an oxide of the metal is formed, which, if it has the character of a base, acts on the remaining nitric acid; hence, with the majority of metals the result of the reaction is usually not an oxide of the metal, but the corresponding salt[278] of nitric acid, and, at the same time, one of the lower oxides of nitrogen. The resulting salts of the metals are soluble, and hence it is said that nitric acid *dissolves* nearly all metals.[40] This case is termed the solution of metals by acids, although it is not a case of simple solution, but a complex chemical change of the substances taken. When treated with this acid, those metals whose oxides do not combine with nitric acid yield the oxide itself, and not a salt; for example, tin acts in this manner on nitric acid, forming a hydrated oxide, SnH_2O_3, which is obtained in the form of a white powder, $Sn + 4NHO_3 = H_2SnO_3 + 4NO_2 + H_2O$. Silver is able to take up still more oxygen, and to convert a large portion of nitric acid into nitrous anhydride, $4Ag + 6HNO_3 = 4AgNO_3 + N_2O_3 + 3H_2O$. Copper takes up still more oxygen from nitric acid, converting it into nitric oxide, and, by the action of zinc, nitric acid is able to give up a still further quantity of nitrogen, forming nitrous oxide, $4Zn + 10NHO_3 = 4Zn(NO_3)_2 + N_2O + 5H_2O$.[41] Sometimes, and especially with dilute solutions of nitric acid, the deoxidation proceeds as far as the formation of hydroxylamine and ammonia, and sometimes it leads to the formation of nitrogen itself. The formation of one or other nitrogenous substance from nitric acid is[279] determined, not only by the nature of the reacting substances, but also by the relative mass of water and nitric acid, and also by the temperature and pressure, or the sum total of the conditions of reaction; and as in a given mixture even these conditions vary (the temperature and the relative mass vary), it not unfrequently happens that a mixture of different products of the deoxidation of nitric acid is formed.

Thus the action of nitric acid on metals consists in their being oxidised, whilst the acid itself is converted, according to the temperature, concentration in which it is taken, and the nature of the metal, &c., into lower oxides, ammonia, or even into nitrogen.[42] Many compounds are oxidised by nitric acid like metals and other elements; for instance, lower oxides are converted into higher oxides. Thus, arsenious acid is converted into arsenic acid, suboxide of iron into oxide, sulphurous acid into sulphuric acid, the sulphides of the metals, M_2S, into sulphates, M_2SO_4, &c.; in a word, nitric acid brings about oxidation, its oxygen is taken up and transferred to many other substances. Certain substances are oxidised by strong nitric acid so rapidly and with so great an evolution of heat that they deflagrate and burst into flame. Thus turpentine, $C_{10}H_{16}$, bursts into flame when poured into fuming nitric acid. In virtue of its oxidising property, nitric acid *removes the hydrogen* from many substances. Thus it decomposes hydriodic acid, separating the iodine and forming water; and if fuming nitric acid be poured into a flask containing gaseous hydriodic acid, then a rapid[280] reaction takes place, accompanied by flame and the separation of violet vapours of iodine and brown fumes of oxides of nitrogen.[43]

As nitric acid is very easily decomposed with the separation of oxygen, it was for a long time supposed that it was not capable of forming the corresponding *nitric anhydride*, N_2O_5; but Deville first and subsequently Weber and others, discovered the methods of its formation. Deville obtained nitric anhydride by decomposing silver nitrate by chlorine under the influence of a moderate heat. Chlorine acts on the above salt at a temperature of 95° ($2AgNO_3 + Cl_2 = 2AgCl + N_2O_5 + O$), and when once the reaction is started, it continues by itself without further heating. Brown fumes are given off, which are condensed in a tube surrounded by a freezing-mixture. A portion condenses in this tube and a portion remains in a gaseous state. The latter contains free oxygen. A crystalline mass and a liquid substance are obtained in the tube; the liquid is poured off, and a current of dry carbonic acid gas is passed through the apparatus in order to remove all traces of volatile substances (liquid oxides of nitrogen) adhering to the crystals of nitric anhydride. These form a voluminous mass of rhombic crystals (density 1·64), which sometimes are of rather large size; they melt at about 30° and distil at about 47°. In distilling, a portion of the substance is decomposed. With water these crystals give nitric acid. Nitric anhydride is also obtained by the action of phosphoric anhydride, P_2O_5, on cold pure nitric acid (below 0°). During the very careful distillation of equal parts by weight of these two substances a portion of the acid decomposes, giving a liquid compound, $H_2O,2N_2O_5 = N_2O_5,2HNO_3$, whilst the greater part of the nitric acid gives the anhydride according to the equation $2NHO_3 + P_2O_5 = 2PHO_3 + N_2O_5$. On heating, nitric anhydride decomposes with an explosion, or gradually, into nitric peroxide and oxygen, $N_2O_5 = N_2O_4 + O$.

Nitrogen peroxide, N_2O_4, and *nitrogen dioxide*, NO_2, express one[281] and the same composition, but they should be distinguished like ordinary oxygen and ozone, although in this case their mutual conversion is more easily effected and takes place on vaporisation; also, O_3 loses heat in passing into O_2, whilst N_2O_4 absorbs heat in forming NO_2.

Nitric acid in acting on tin and on many organic substances (for example, starch) gives brown vapours, consisting of a mixture of N_2O_3 and NO_2. A purer product is obtained by the decomposition of lead nitrate by heat, $Pb(NO_3)_2 = 2NO_2 + O + PbO$, when non-volatile lead oxide, oxygen gas, and nitrogen peroxide are formed. The latter condenses, in a well-cooled vessel, to a brown liquid, which boils at about 22°. The purest peroxide of nitrogen, solidifying at -9°, is obtained by mixing dry oxygen in a freezing-mixture with twice its volume of dry nitric oxide, NO, when transparent prisms of nitrogen peroxide are formed in the receiver: they melt into a colourless liquid at about -10°. When the temperature of the receiver is above -9°, the crystals melt,[44] and at 0° give a reddish yellow liquid, like that obtained in the decomposition of lead nitrate. The vapours of nitrogen peroxide have a characteristic odour, and at the ordinary temperature are of a dark-brown colour, but at lower temperatures the colour of the vapour is much fainter. When heated, especially above 50°, the colour becomes a very dark brown, so that the vapours almost lose their transparency.

The causes of these peculiarities of nitrogen peroxide were not clearly understood until Deville and Troost determined the density and dissociation of the vapour of this substance at different temperatures, and showed that the density varies. If the density be referred to that of hydrogen at the same temperature and pressure, then it is found to vary from 38 at the boiling point, or about 27°, to 23 at 135°, after which the density remains constant up to those high temperatures at which the oxides of nitrogen are decomposed. As on the basis of the laws enunciated in the following chapter, the density 23 corresponds with the compound NO_2 (because the weight corresponding with this molecular formula = 46, and the density referred to hydrogen as unity is equal to half the molecular weight); therefore at temperatures above 135° the existence of nitrogen dioxide only must be recognised. It is this gas which is of a brown colour. At a lower temperature it forms[282] nitrogen peroxide, N_2O_4, whose molecular weight, and therefore density, is twice that of the dioxide. This substance, which is isomeric with nitrogen dioxide, as ozone is isomeric with oxygen, and has twice as great a vapour density (46 referred to hydrogen), is formed in greater quantity the lower the temperature, and crystallises at -10°. The reasons both of the variation of the colour of the gas (N_2O_4 gives colourless and transparent vapours, whilst those of NO_2 are brown and opaque) and the variation of the vapour density with the variation of temperature are thus made quite clear; and as at the boiling point a density 38 was obtained, therefore at that temperature the vapours consist of a mixture of 79 parts by weight of N_2O_4 with 21 parts by weight of NO_2.[45] It is evident that a decomposition here takes place the peculiarity of which consists in the fact that the product of decomposition, NO_2, is polymerised (*i.e.* becomes denser, combines with itself) at a lower temperature; that is, the reaction

$$N_2O_4 = NO_2 + NO_2$$

is a reversible reaction, and consequently the whole phenomenon represents a *dissociation* in a homogeneous gaseous medium, where the original substance, N_2O_4, and the resultant, NO_2, are both gases. The *measure of dissociation* will be expressed if we find the proportion of the quantity of the substance decomposed to the whole amount of the substance. At the boiling point, therefore, the measure of the decomposition of nitrogen peroxide will be 21 p.c.; at 135° it = 1, and at

10° it = 0; that is, the N_2O_4 is not then decomposable. Consequently the limits of dissociation here are -10° and 135° at the atmospheric pressure.[46] Within the limits of these temperatures[283] the vapours of nitrogen peroxide have not a constant density, but, on the other hand, above and below these limits definite substances exist. Thus above 135° N_2O_4 has ceased to exist and NO_2 alone remains. It is evident that at the ordinary temperature there is a partially dissociated system or mixture of nitrogen peroxide, N_2O_4, and nitrogen dioxide, NO_2. In the brown liquid boiling at 22° probably a portion of the N_2O_4 has already passed into NO_2, and it is only the colourless liquid and crystalline substance at -10° that can be considered as pure nitrogen peroxide.[47]

The above explains the action of nitrogen peroxide on water at low temperatures. N_2O_4 then acts on water like a mixture of the anhydrides of nitrous and nitric acids. The first, N_2O_3, may be looked on as water in which each of the two atoms of hydrogen is replaced by the radicle NO, while in the second each hydrogen is replaced by the radicle NO_2, proper to nitric acid; and in nitrogen peroxide one atom of the hydrogen of water is replaced by NO and the other by NO_2, as is seen from the formulæ—

$$\left.\begin{array}{c}H\\H\end{array}\right\}O; \quad \left.\begin{array}{c}NO\\NO\end{array}\right\}O; \quad \left.\begin{array}{c}NO\\NO_2\end{array}\right\}O; \quad \left.\begin{array}{c}NO_2\\NO_2\end{array}\right\}O;$$

or $H_2O \quad N_2O_3 \quad N_2O_4 \quad N_2O_5$

In fact, nitrogen peroxide at low temperatures gives with water (ice) both nitric, HNO_3, and nitrous, HNO_2, acids. The latter, as we shall afterwards see, splits up into water and the anhydride, N_2O_3. If, however, warm water act on nitrogen peroxide, only nitric acid and monoxide of nitrogen are formed: $3NO_2 + H_2O = NO + 2NHO_3$.

Although NO_2 is not decomposed into N and O even at 500°, still in many cases it acts as an oxidising agent. Thus, for instance, it oxidises mercury, converting it into mercurous nitrate, $2NO_2 + Hg[284] = HgNO_3 + NO$, being itself deoxidised into nitric oxide, into which the dioxide in many other instances passes, and from which it is easily formed.[48]

Nitrous anhydride, N_2O_3, corresponds[49] to nitrous acid, NHO_2, which forms a series of salts, the nitrites—for example, the sodium salt $NaNO_2$, the potassium salt KNO_2, the ammonium salt $(NH_4)NO_2$,[50] the silver salt $AgNO_2$,[51] &c. Neither the anhydride nor the hydrate of the acid is known in a perfectly pure state. The anhydride has only been obtained as a very unstable substance, and has not yet been fully investigated; and on attempting to obtain the acid NHO_2 from its salts, it always gives water and the anhydride, whilst the latter, as an intermediate oxide, partially or wholly splits up into $NO + NO_2$. But the salts of nitrous acid are distinguished for their great stability. Potassium nitrate, KNO_3, may be converted into potassium nitrite by[285] depriving it of a portion of its oxygen; for instance, by fusing it (at not too high a temperature) with metals, such as lead, $KNO_3 + Pb = KNO_2 + PbO$.[51 bis] The resultant salt is soluble in water, whilst the oxide of lead is insoluble. With sulphuric and other acids the solution of potassium nitrite[52] immediately evolves a brown gas, nitrous anhydride: $2KNO_2 + H_2SO_4 = K_2SO_4 + N_2O_3 + H_2O$. The same gas ($N_2O_3$) is obtained by passing nitric oxide at $0°$ through liquid peroxide of nitrogen,[53] or by heating starch with nitric acid of sp. gr. $1·3$. At a very low temperature it condenses into a blue liquid boiling below $0°$,[54] but then partially decomposing into $NO + NO_2$. Nitrous anhydride possesses a remarkable capacity for oxidising. Ignited bodies burn in it, nitric acid absorbs it, and then acquires the property of acting on silver and other metals, even when diluted. *Potassium iodide* is oxidised by this gas just as it is by ozone (and by peroxide of hydrogen, chromic and other acids, but not by dilute nitric acid nor by sulphuric acid), with the *separation of iodine*. This iodine may he recognised (*see* Ozone, Chapter IV.) by its turning starch blue. Very small traces of nitrites may be easily detected by this method. If, for example, starch and potassium iodide are added to a solution of potassium nitrite (at first there will be no change, there being no free nitrous acid), and then sulphuric acid be added, the nitrous acid (or its anhydride) immediately set free liberates iodine, which produces a blue colour with the starch. Nitric acid does not act in this manner, but in the presence of zinc the coloration takes place, which proves the formation of nitrous acid in the deoxidation of nitric acid.[55] Nitrous acid acts[286] directly on ammonia, forming nitrogen and water, $HNO_2 + NH_3 = N_2 + 2H_2O$.[56]

As nitrous anhydride easily splits up into $NO_2 + NO$, so, like NO_2, with warm water it gives nitric acid and nitric oxide, according to the equation $3N_2O_3 + H_2O = 4NO + 2NHO_3$.

Being in a lower degree of oxidation than nitric acid, nitrous acid and its anhydride are oxidised in solutions by many oxidising substances—for example, by potassium permanganate—into nitric acid.[57]

Nitric oxide, NO.—This permanent gas[58] (that is, unliquefiable by pressure without the aid of cold) may be obtained from all the above-described compounds of nitrogen with oxygen. The deoxidation of nitric acid by metals is the usual method employed for its preparation. Dilute nitric acid (sp. gr. $1·18$, but not stronger, as then N_2O_3 and NO_2 are produced) is poured into a flask containing metallic copper.[59][287] The reaction commences at the ordinary temperature. Mercury and silver also give nitric oxide with nitric acid. In these reactions with metals one portion of the nitric acid is employed in the oxidation of the metal, whilst the other, and by far the greater, portion combines with the metallic oxide so obtained, with formation of the nitrate corresponding with the metal taken. The first action of the copper on the nitric acid is thus expressed by the equation

$$2NHO_3 + 3Cu = H_2O + 3CuO + 2NO.$$

The second reaction consists in the formation of copper nitrate—

$$6NHO_3 + 3CuO = 3H_2O + 3Cu(NO_3)_2.$$

Nitric oxide is a colourless gas which is only slightly soluble in water ($1 \over 20$ of a volume at the ordinary temperature). Reactions of double decomposition in which nitric oxide readily takes part are not known—that is to say, it is an indifferent, not a saline, oxide. Like the other oxides of nitrogen, it is decomposed into its elements at a red heat (starting from 900°, at 1,200° 60 per cent. give N_2 and $2N_2O_3$, but complete decomposition into N_2 and O_2 only takes place at the melting point of platinum, Emich 1892). The most characteristic property of nitric oxide is its capacity for directly and easily combining with oxygen (owing to the evolution of heat in the combination). With oxygen it forms nitrous anhydride and nitrogen peroxide, $2NO + O = N_2O_3$, $2NO + O_2 = 2NO_2$. If nitric oxide is mixed with oxygen and immediately shaken up with caustic potash, it is almost entirely converted into potassium nitrite; whilst after a certain time, when the formation of nitric peroxide has already commenced, a mixture of potassium nitrite and nitrate is obtained. If oxygen is passed into a bell jar filled with nitric oxide, brown fumes of nitrous anhydride and nitric peroxide are formed, even in the absence of moisture; these in the presence of water give, as we already know, nitric acid and nitric oxide, so that in the presence of an excess of water and oxygen the whole of the nitric oxide is easily and directly converted into nitric acid. This reaction of the re-formation of nitric acid from nitric oxide, air, and water, $2NO + H_2O + O_3 = 2HNO_3$, is frequently made use of in practice. The experiment showing the conversion of nitric oxide into nitric acid is very striking and instructive. As the intermixture of the oxygen with the oxide of nitrogen proceeds, the nitric acid formed dissolves in water, and if an excess of oxygen has not been added the whole of the gas (nitric oxide), being converted[288] into HNO_3, is absorbed, and the water entirely fills the bell jar previously containing the gas.[60] It is evident that nitric oxide[61] in combining with oxygen has a strong tendency to give the higher types of nitrogen compounds, which we see in nitric acid, HNO_3 or $NO_2(OH)$, in nitric anhydride, N_2O_5 or $(NO_2)_2O$, and in ammonium chloride, NH_4Cl. If X stand for an atom of hydrogen, or its equivalents, chlorine, hydroxyl, &c., and if O, which is, according to the law of substitution, equivalent to H_2, be indicated by X_2, then the three compounds of nitrogen above named should be considered as compounds of the type or form NX_5. For example, in nitric acid $X_5 = O_2 + (OH)$, where $O_2 = X_4$, and $OH = X$; whilst nitric oxide is a compound of the form NX_2. Hence this lower form, like lower forms in general, strives by combination to attain to the higher forms proper to the compounds of a given element. NX_2 passes consecutively into NX_3—namely, into N_2O_3 and NHO_2, NX_4 (for instance NO_2) and NX_5.

As the decomposition of nitric oxide begins at temperatures above 900°, many substances burn in it; thus, ignited phosphorus continues to burn in nitric oxide, but sulphur and charcoal are extinguished in it. This is due to the fact that the heat evolved in the combustion of these two substances is insufficient for the decomposition of the nitric[289] oxide, whilst the heat developed by burning phosphorus suffices to produce this decomposition. That nitric oxide really supports combustion, owing to its being decomposed by the action of heat, is proved by the fact that strongly ignited charcoal continues to burn in the same nitric oxide[62] in which a feebly incandescent piece of charcoal is extinguished.

The compounds of nitrogen with oxygen which we have so far considered may all be prepared from nitric oxide, and may themselves be converted into it. Thus nitric oxide stands in intimate connection with them.[63] The passage of nitric oxide into the higher degrees of oxidation and the converse reaction is employed in practice as a means for *transferring* the oxygen of the air to substances capable of being oxidised. Starting with nitric oxide, it may easily be converted, with the aid of the oxygen of the atmosphere and water, into nitric acid, nitrous anhydride, and nitric peroxide, and by their means employed to oxidise other substances. In this oxidising action nitric oxide is again formed, and it may again be converted into nitric acid, and so on continuously, if only oxygen and water be present. Hence the fact, which at first appears to be a paradox, that by means of a small quantity of nitric oxide in the presence of oxygen and water it is possible to oxidise[290] an indefinitely large quantity of substances which cannot be directly oxidised either by the action of the atmospheric oxygen or by the action of nitric oxide itself. The sulphurous anhydride, SO_2, which is obtained in the combustion of sulphur and in roasting many metallic sulphides in the air is an example of this kind. In practice this gas is obtained by burning sulphur or iron pyrites, the latter being thereby converted into oxide of iron and sulphurous anhydride. In contact with the oxygen of the atmosphere this gas does not pass into the higher degree of oxidation, sulphuric anhydride, SO_3, and if it does form sulphuric acid with water and the oxygen of the atmosphere, $SO_2 + H_2O + O = H_2SO_4$, it does so very slowly. With nitric acid (and especially with nitrous acid, but not with nitrogen peroxide) and water, sulphurous anhydride, on the contrary, very easily forms sulphuric acid, and especially so when slightly heated (about 40°), the nitric acid (or, better still, nitrous acid) being converted into nitric oxide—

$$3SO_2 + 2NHO_3 + 2H_2O = 2H_2SO_4 + 2NO.$$

The presence of water is absolutely indispensable here, otherwise sulphuric anhydride is formed, which combines with the oxides of nitrogen (nitrous anhydride), forming a crystalline substance containing oxides of nitrogen (*chamber crystals*, which will be described in Chapter XX.) Water destroys this compound, forming sulphuric acid and separating the oxides of nitrogen. The water must be taken in a greater quantity than that required for the formation of the hydrate H_2SO_4, because the latter absorbs oxides of nitrogen. With an excess of water, however, solution does not take place. If, in the above reaction, only water, sulphurous anhydride, and nitric or nitrous acid be taken in a definite quantity, then a definite quantity of sulphuric acid and nitric oxide will be formed, according to the preceding equation; but there the reaction ends and the excess of sulphurous anhydride, if there be any, will remain unchanged. But if we add air and water, then the nitric oxide will unite with the oxygen to form nitrogen peroxide, and the latter with water to form nitric and nitrous acids, which again give sulphuric acid from a fresh quantity of sulphurous anhydride. Nitric oxide is again formed, which is able to start the oxidation afresh if there be sufficient air. Thus it is possible with a definite quantity of nitric oxide to convert an indefinitely large quantity of sulphurous anhydride into sulphuric acid, water and oxygen only being required.[64][291] This may be easily demonstrated by an experiment on a small scale, if a certain quantity of nitric oxide be first introduced into a flask, and sulphurous anhydride, steam, and oxygen be then continually passed in. Thus the above-described reaction may be expressed in the following manner:—

$$nSO_2 + nO + (n + m)H_2O + NO = nH_2SO_4, mH_2O + NO$$

if we consider only the original substances and those finally formed. In this way a definite quantity of nitric oxide may serve for the conversion of an indefinite quantity of sulphurous anhydride, oxygen, and water into sulphuric acid. In reality, however, there is a limit to this, because air, and not pure oxygen, is employed for the oxidation, so that it is necessary to remove the nitrogen of the air and to introduce a fresh quantity of air. A certain quantity of nitric oxide will pass away with this nitrogen, and will in this way be lost.[65]

The preceding series of changes serve as the basis of the *manufacture of sulphuric acid* or so-called *chamber acid.* This acid is prepared on a very large scale in chemical works because it is the cheapest acid whose action can be applied in a great number of cases. It is therefore used in immense quantities.

[292]

The process is carried on in a series of chambers (or in one divided by partitions as in fig. 50, which shows the beginning and end of a chamber) constructed of sheet lead. These chambers are placed one against the other, and communicate by tubes or special orifices so placed that the inlet tubes are in the upper portion of the chamber, and the outlet in the lower and opposite end. The current of steam and gases necessary for the preparation of the sulphuric acid passes through these chambers and tubes. The acid as it is formed falls to the bottom of the chambers or runs down their walls, and flows from chamber to chamber (from the last towards the first), to permit of which the partitions do not reach to the bottom. The floor and walls of the chambers should therefore be made of a material on which the sulphuric acid will not act. Among the ordinary metals lead is the only one suitable.[65 bis]

FIG. 50.—Section of sulphuric acid chambers, the first and last chambers only being represented. The tower to the left is called the Glover's tower, and that on the right the Gay-Lussac's tower. Less than 1 $\boxed{10}$ th of the natural size.

For the formation of the sulphuric acid it is necessary to introduce[293] sulphurous anhydride, steam, air, and nitric acid, or some oxide of nitrogen, into the chambers. The sulphurous anhydride is produced by burning sulphur or iron pyrites. This is carried on in the furnace with four hearths to the left of the drawing. Air is led into the chambers and furnace through orifices in the furnace doors. The current of air and oxygen is regulated by opening or closing these orifices to a greater or less extent. The ingoing draught in the chambers is brought about by the fact that heated gases and vapours pass into the chambers, whose temperature is further raised by the reaction itself, and also by the remaining nitrogen being continually withdrawn from the outlet (above the tower K) by a tall chimney situated near the chambers. Nitric acid is prepared from a mixture of sulphuric acid and Chili saltpetre, in the same furnaces in which the sulphurous anhydride is evolved (or in special furnaces). Not more than 8 parts of nitre are taken to 100 parts of sulphur burnt. On leaving the furnace the vapours of nitric acid and oxides of nitrogen mixed with air and sulphurous anhydride first pass along the horizontal tubes T into the receiver B B, which is partially cooled by water flowing in on the right-hand side and running out on the left by *o*, in order to reduce the temperature of the gases entering the chamber. The gases then pass up a tower filled with coke, and shown to the left of the drawing. In this tower are placed lumps of coke (the residue from the dry distillation of coal), over which sulphuric acid trickles from the reservoir M. This acid has absorbed in the end tower K the oxides of nitrogen escaping from the chamber. This end tower is also filled with coke, over which a stream of strong sulphuric acid trickles from the reservoir M. The acid spreads over the coke, and, owing to the large surface offered by the latter, absorbs the greater part of the oxides of nitrogen escaping from the chambers. The sulphuric acid in passing down the tower becomes saturated with the oxides of nitrogen, and flows out at *h* into a special receiver (in the drawing situated by the side of the furnaces), from which it is forced up the tubes *h' h'* by steam pressure into the reservoir M, situated above the first tower. The gases passing through this tower (hot) from the furnace on coming into contact with the sulphuric acid take up the oxides of nitrogen contained in it, and these are thus returned to the chamber and again participate in the reaction. The sulphuric acid left after their extraction flows into the chambers. Thus, on leaving the first coke tower the sulphurous anhydride, air, and vapours of nitric acid and of the oxides of nitrogen pass through the upper tube *m* into the chamber. Here they come into contact with steam introduced by lead tubes into various parts of the chamber. The reaction takes place in the presence of water, the sulphuric acid falls to the bottom of the chamber, and the same process[294] takes place in the following chambers until the whole of the sulphurous anhydride is consumed. A somewhat greater proportion of air than is strictly necessary is passed in, in order that no sulphurous anhydride should be left unaltered for want of sufficient oxygen. The presence of an excess of oxygen is shown by the colour of the gases escaping from the last chamber. If they be of a pale colour it indicates an insufficiency of air (and the presence of sulphurous anhydride), as otherwise peroxide of nitrogen would be formed. A very dark colour shows an excess of air, which is also disadvantageous, because it increases the inevitable loss of nitric oxide by increasing the mass of escaping gases.[66]

Nitrous oxide, N_2O,[67] is similar to water in its volumetric composition. Two volumes of nitrous oxide are formed from two volumes of[295] nitrogen and one volume of oxygen, which may be shown by the ordinary method for the analysis of the oxides of nitrogen (by passing them over red-hot copper or sodium). In contradistinction to the other oxides of nitrogen, it is not directly oxidised by oxygen, but it may be obtained from the higher oxides of nitrogen by the action of certain deoxidising substances; thus, for example, a mixture of two volumes of nitric oxide and one volume of sulphurous anhydride if left in contact with water and spongy platinum is converted into sulphuric acid and nitrous oxide, $2NO + SO_2 + H_2O = H_2SO_4 + N_2O$. Nitric acid, also, under the action of certain metals—for instance, of zinc[68]—gives nitrous oxide, although in this case mixed with nitric oxide. The usual method of preparing nitrous oxide consists in the decomposition of ammonium nitrate by the aid of heat, because in this case only water and nitrous oxide are formed, $NH_4NO_3 = 2H_2O + N_2O$ (a mixture of NH_4Cl and KNO_3 is sometimes taken). The decomposition[69] proceeds very easily in an apparatus like that used for the preparation of ammonia or oxygen—that is, in a retort or flask with a gas-conducting tube. The decomposition must, however, be carried on carefully, as otherwise nitrogen is formed from the decomposition of the nitrous oxide.[70]

[296]

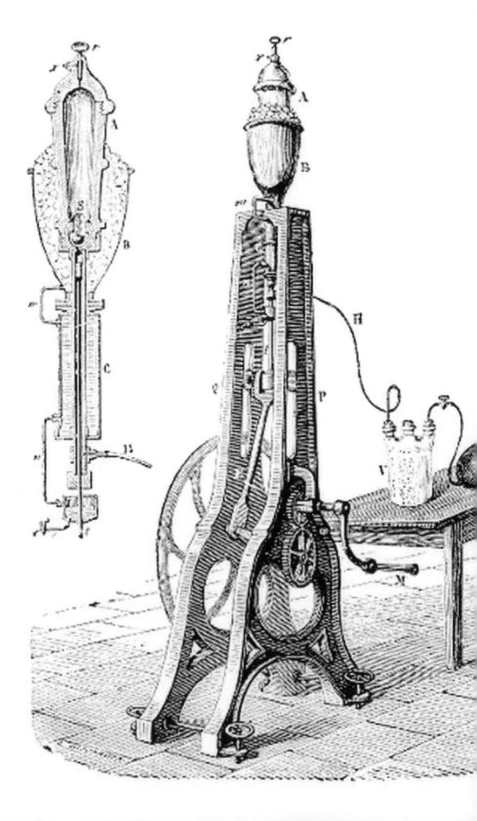

FIG. 51.—Natterer's apparatus for the preparation of liquid nitrous oxide and carbonic anhydride. The gas first passes though the vessel V, for drying, and then into the pump (a section of the upper part of the apparatus is given on the left). The piston t of the force pump is moved by the crank E and fly-wheel turned by hand. The gas is pumped into the iron chamber A, where it is liquefied. The valve S allows the gas to enter A, but not to escape from it. The chamber and pump are cooled by the jacket B, filled with ice. When the gas is liquefied the vessel A is unscrewed from the pump, and the liquid may be poured from it by inverting it and unscrewing the valve v, when the liquid runs out of the tube x.

Nitrous oxide is not a permanent gas (absolute boiling point $+36°$); it is easily liquefied by the action of cold under a high pressure; at $15°$ it may be liquefied by a pressure of about 40 atmospheres. This gas is usually liquefied by means of the force pump[71] shown in fig. 51. As it is liquefied with comparative ease, and as the cold produced by its vaporisation is very considerable,[72] it (as also liquid carbonic anhydride) is often employed in investigations requiring a low temperature. Nitrous oxide forms a very mobile, colourless liquid, which acts on the skin, and is incapable in a cold state of oxidising either metallic potassium, phosphorus, or carbon; its specific gravity is slightly less than that of water ($0° = 0·910$, $10° = 0·856$, $35° = 0·60$, $39° = 0·45$, Villard, 1894). When evaporated under the receiver of an air-pump, the temperature falls to $-100°$, and the liquid solidifies into a snow-like mass, and partially forms transparent crystals. Both these substances are solid nitrous oxide. Mercury is immediately solidified in contact with evaporating liquid nitrous oxide.[73]

When introduced into the respiratory organs (and consequently into the blood also) nitrous oxide produces a peculiar kind of intoxication accompanied by spasmodic movements, and hence this gas, discovered by Priestley in 1776, received the name of 'laughing gas.' On a prolonged respiration it produces a state of insensibility (it is an anæsthetic like chloroform), and is therefore employed in dental and surgical operations.

Nitrous oxide is easily decomposed into nitrogen and oxygen by the action of heat, or a series of electric sparks; and this explains why a number of substances which cannot burn in nitric oxide do so with great ease in nitrous oxide. In fact, when nitric oxide gives some oxygen on decomposition, this oxygen immediately unites with a fresh portion of the gas to form nitric peroxide, whilst nitrous oxide does not possess this capacity for further combination with oxygen.[74] A mixture of nitrous oxide with hydrogen explodes like detonating[298] gas, gaseous nitrogen being formed, $N_2O + H_2 = H_2O + N_2$. The volume of the remaining nitrogen is equal to the original volume of nitrous oxide, and is equal to the volume of hydrogen entering into combination with the oxygen; hence in this reaction equal volumes of nitrogen and hydrogen replace each other. Nitrous oxide is also very easily decomposed by red-hot metals; and sulphur, phosphorus, and charcoal burn in it, although not so brilliantly as in oxygen. A substance in burning in nitrous oxide evolves more heat than an equal quantity burning in oxygen; which most clearly shows that in the formation of nitrous oxide by the combination of nitrogen with oxygen there was not an evolution but an absorption of heat, there being no other source for the excess of heat in the combustion of substances in nitrous oxide (*see* Note 29). If a given volume of nitrous oxide be decomposed by a metal—for instance, sodium—then there remains, after cooling and total decomposition, a volume of nitrogen, exactly equal to that of the nitrous oxide taken; consequently the oxygen is, so to say, distributed between the atoms of nitrogen without producing an increase in the volume of the nitrogen.

Footnotes:

[1] The ammonia in the air, water, and soil proceeds from the decomposition of the nitrogenous substances of plants and animals, and also probably from the reduction of nitrates. Ammonia is always formed in the rusting of iron. Its formation in this case depends in all probability on the decomposition of water, and on the action of the hydrogen at the moment of its evolution on the nitric acid contained in the air (Cloez), or on the formation of ammonium nitrite, which takes place under many circumstances. The evolution of vapours of ammonia compounds is sometimes observed in the vicinity of volcanoes. At a red heat nitrogen combines directly with B Ca Mg, and with many other metals, and these compounds, when heated with a caustic alkali, or in the presence of water, give ammonia (*see* Chapter XIV., Note 14, and Chapter XVII., Note 12). These are examples of the indirect combination of nitrogen with hydrogen.

[2] If a silent discharge or a series of electric sparks be passed through ammonia gas, it is decomposed into nitrogen and hydrogen. This is a phenomenon of dissociation; therefore, a series of sparks do not totally decompose the ammonia, but leave a certain portion undecomposed. One volume of nitrogen and three volumes of hydrogen are obtained from two volumes of ammonia decomposed. Ramsay and Young (1884) investigated the decomposition of NH_3 under the action of heat, and showed that at 500°, 1½ p.c. is decomposed, at 600° about 18 p.c., at 800° 65 p.c., but these results were hardly free from the influence of 'contact.' The *presence* of free ammonia—that is, ammonia not combined with acids—in a gas or aqueous solution may be recognised by its characteristic smell. But many ammonia salts do not possess this smell. However, on the addition of an

alkali (for instance, caustic lime, potash, or soda), they evolve ammonia gas, especially when heated. The presence of ammonia may be made visible by introducing a substance moistened with strong hydrochloric acid into its neighbourhood. A white cloud, or visible white vapour, then makes its appearance. This depends on the fact that both ammonia and hydrochloric acid are volatile, and on coming into contact with each other produce solid sal-ammoniac, NH_4Cl, which forms a cloud. This test is usually made by dipping a glass rod into hydrochloric acid, and holding it over the vessel from which the ammonia is evolved. With small amounts of ammonia this test is, however, untrustworthy, as the white vapour is scarcely observable. In this case it is best to take paper moistened with mercurous nitrate, $HgNO_3$. This paper turns black in the presence of ammonia, owing to the formation of a black compound of ammonia with mercurous oxide. The smallest traces of ammonia (for instance, in river water) may be detected by means of the so-called Nessler's reagent, containing a solution of mercuric chloride and potassium iodide, which forms a brown coloration or precipitate with the smallest quantities of ammonia. It will be useful here to give the thermochemical data (in thousands of units of heat, according to Thomsen), or the quantities of heat *evolved* in the formation of ammonia and its compounds in quantities expressed by their formulæ. Thus, for instance, $(N + H_3)$ 26·7 indicates that 14 grams of nitrogen in combining with 3 grams of hydrogen develop sufficient heat to raise the temperature of 26·7 kilograms of water 1°. $(NH_3 + nH_2O)$ 8·4 (heat of solution); $(NH_3,nH_2O + HCl,nH_2O)$ 12·3; $(N + H_4 + Cl)$ 90·6; $(NH_3 + HCl)$ 41·9.

[3] The same ammonia water is obtained, although in smaller quantities, in the dry distillation of plants and of coal, which consists of the remains of fossil plants. In all these cases the ammonia proceeds from the destruction of the complex nitrogenous substances occurring in plants and animals. The ammonia salts employed in the arts are prepared by this method.

[4] The technical methods for the preparation of ammonia water, and for the extraction of ammonia from it, are to a certain extent explained in the figures accompanying the text.

[5] Usually these crystals are sublimed by heating them in crucibles or pots, when the vapours of sal-ammoniac condense on the cold covers as a crust, in which form the salt comes into the market.

[6] On a small scale ammonia may be prepared in a glass flask by mixing equal parts by weight of slaked lime and finely-powdered sal-ammoniac, the neck of the flask being connected with an arrangement for drying the gas obtained. In this instance neither calcium chloride nor sulphuric acid can be used for drying the gas, since both these substances absorb ammonia, and therefore solid caustic potash, which is capable of retaining the water,

is employed. The gas-conducting tube leading from the desiccating apparatus is introduced into a mercury bath, if dry gaseous ammonia be required, because water cannot be employed in collecting ammonia gas. Ammonia was first obtained in this dry state by Priestley, and its composition was investigated by Berthollet at the end of the last century. Oxide of lead mixed with sal-ammoniac (Isambert) evolves ammonia with still greater ease than lime. The cause and process of the decomposition are almost the same, $2PbO + 2NH_4Cl = Pb_2OCl_2 + H_2O + 2NH_3$. Lead oxychloride is (probably) formed.

[7]

FIG. 44.—Carré's apparatus. Described in text.

This is evident from the fact that its absolute boiling point lies at about +130° (Chapter II., Note 29). It may therefore be liquefied by pressure alone at the ordinary, and even at much higher temperatures. The latent heat of evaporation of 17 parts by weight of ammonia equals 4,400 units of heat, and hence liquid ammonia may be employed for the production of cold. Strong aqueous solutions of ammonia, which in parting with their ammonia act in a similar manner, are not unfrequently employed for this purpose. Suppose a saturated solution of ammonia to be contained in a closed vessel furnished with a receiver. If the ammoniacal solution be heated, the ammonia, with a small quantity of water, will pass off from the solution, and in accumulating in the apparatus will produce a considerable pressure, and will therefore liquefy in the cooler portions of the receiver. Hence liquid ammonia will be obtained in the receiver. The heating of the vessel containing the aqueous solution of ammonia is then stopped. After having been heated it contains only water, or a solution poor in ammonia. When once it begins to cool the ammonia vapours commence dissolving in it, the space becomes rarefied, and a rapid vaporisation of the liquefied ammonia left in the receiver takes place. In evaporating in the receiver it will cause the temperature in it to fall considerably, and will itself pass into the aqueous solution. In the end, the same ammoniacal solution as originally taken is re-obtained. Thus, in this case, on heating the vessel the pressure increases by itself, and on cooling it diminishes, so that here heat directly replaces mechanical work. This is the principle of the simplest forms of *Carré's ice-making machines*, shown in fig. 44. C is a vessel made of boiler plates into which the saturated solution of ammonia is poured; m is a tube conducting the ammonia vapour to the receiver A. All parts of the apparatus should be hermetically joined together, and should be able to withstand a pressure reaching ten atmospheres. The apparatus should be freed from air, which would otherwise hinder the liquefaction of the ammonia. The process is carried on as follows:—The apparatus is first so inclined that any liquid remaining in A may flow into C. The vessel C is then placed upon a stove F, and heated until the thermometer *t* indicates a temperature of 130° C. During this time the ammonia has been expelled from C, and has liquefied in A. In order to facilitate the liquefaction, the receiver A should be immersed in a tank of water R (*see* the left-hand drawing in fig. 44). After about half an hour, when it may be supposed that the ammonia has been expelled, the fire is removed from under C, and this is now immersed in the tank of water R. The apparatus is represented in this position in the right-hand drawing of fig. 44. The liquefied ammonia then evaporates, and passes over into the water in C. This causes the temperature of A to fall considerably. The substance to be refrigerated is placed in a vessel G, in the cylindrical space inside the receiver A. The refrigeration is also kept on for about half an hour, and with an apparatus of ordinary dimensions (containing about two litres of ammonia solution), five kilograms of ice are produced by the consumption of one kilogram of coal. In industrial works more complicated types of Carré's machines are employed.

[8] Below 15° (according to Isambert), the compound $AgCl,3NH_3$ is formed, and above 20° the compound $2AgCl,3NH_3$. The tension of the ammonia evolved from the latter substance is equal to the atmospheric pressure at 68°, whilst for $AgCl,3NH_3$ the pressures are equal at about 20°;

consequently, at higher temperatures it is greater than the atmospheric pressure, whilst at lower temperatures the ammonia is absorbed and forms this compound. Consequently, all the phenomena of dissociation are here clearly to be observed. Joannis and Croisier (1894) investigated similar compounds with AgBr, AgI, AgCN and AgNO$_3$, and found that they all give definite compounds with NH$_3$, for instance AgBr,3NH$_3$, 2AgBr,3NH$_3$ and AgBr,2NH$_3$; they are all colourless, solid substances which decompose under the atmospheric pressure at +3·5, +34° and +51°.

[9] The liquefaction of ammonia may be accomplished without an increase of pressure, by means of refrigeration alone, in a carefully prepared mixture of ice and calcium chloride (because the absolute boiling point of NH$_3$ is high, about +130°). It may even take place in the severe frosts of a Russian winter. The application of liquid ammonia as a motive power for engines forms a problem which has to a certain extent been solved by the French engineer Tellier.

[10] The combustion of ammonia in oxygen may be effected by the aid of platinum. A small quantity of an aqueous solution of ammonia, containing about 20 p.c. of the gas, is poured into a wide-necked beaker of about one litre capacity. A gas-conducting tube about 10 mm. in diameter, and supplying oxygen, is immersed in the aqueous solution of ammonia. But before introducing the gas an incandescent platinum spiral is placed in the beaker; the ammonia in the presence of the platinum is oxidised and burns, whilst the platinum wire becomes still more incandescent. The solution of ammonia is heated, and oxygen passed through the solution. The oxygen, as it bubbles off from the ammonia solution, carries with it a part of the ammonia, and this mixture explodes on coming into contact with the incandescent platinum. This is followed by a certain cooling effect, owing to the combustion ceasing, but after a short interval this is renewed, so that one feeble explosion follows after another. During the period of oxidation without explosion, white vapours of ammonium nitrite and red-brown vapours of oxides of nitrogen make their appearance, while during the explosion there is complete combustion and consequently water and nitrogen are formed.

[11] This may be verified by their densities. Nitrogen is 14 times denser than hydrogen, and ammonia is 8½ times. If 3 volumes of hydrogen with 1 volume of nitrogen gave 4 volumes of ammonia, then these 4 volumes would weigh 17 times as much as 1 volume of hydrogen; consequently 1 volume of ammonia would be 4¼ times heavier than the same volume of hydrogen. But if these 4 volumes only give 2 volumes of ammonia, the latter will be 8½ times as dense as hydrogen, which is found to be actually the case.

[12] Aqueous solutions of ammonia are lighter than water, and at 15°, taking water at 4° = 10,000, their specific gravity, as dependent on p, or the percentage amount (by weight) of ammonia, is given by the expression $s = 9{,}992 - 42 \cdot 5p + 0 \cdot 21p^2$; for instance, with 10 p.c. $s = 9{,}587$. If t represents the temperature between the limits of $+10°$ and $+20°$, then the expression $(15 - t)(1 \cdot 5 + 0 \cdot 14p)$ must be added to the formula for the specific gravity. Solutions containing more than 24 p.c. have not been sufficiently investigated in respect to the variation of their specific gravity. It is, however, easy to obtain more concentrated solutions, and at 0° solutions approaching NH_3,H_2O (48·6 p.c. NH_3) in their composition, and of sp. gr. 0·85, may be prepared. But such solutions give up the bulk of their ammonia at the ordinary temperature, so that more than 24 p.c. NH_3 is rarely contained in solution. Ammoniacal solutions containing a considerable amount of ammonia give ice-like crystals which seem to contain ammonia at temperatures far below 0° (for instance, an 8 p.c. solution at -14°, the strongest solutions at -48°). The whole of the ammonia may be expelled from a solution by heating, even at a comparatively low temperature; hence on heating aqueous solutions containing ammonia a very strong solution of ammonia is obtained in the distillate. Alcohol, ether, and many other liquids are also capable of dissolving ammonia. Solutions of ammonia, when exposed to the atmosphere, give off a part of their ammonia in accordance with the laws of the solution of gases in liquids, which we have already considered. But the ammoniacal solutions at the same time absorb carbonic anhydride from the air, and ammonium carbonate remains in the solution.

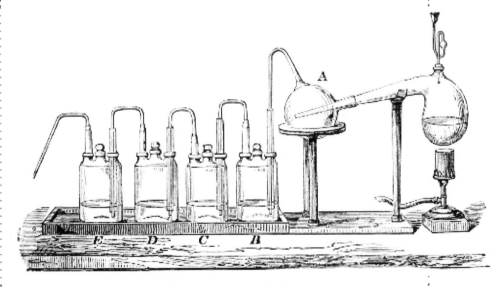

FIG. 46.—Apparatus for preparing solutions of ammonia.

Solutions of ammonia are required both for laboratory and factory operations, and have therefore to be frequently prepared. For this purpose the arrangement shown in fig. 46 is employed in the laboratory. In works the same arrangement is used, only on a larger scale (with earthenware or metallic vessels). The gas is prepared in the retort, from whence it is led into the two-necked globe A, and then through a series of Woulfe's bottles, B, C, D, E. The impurities spurting over collect in A, and the gas is dissolved in B, but the solution soon becomes saturated, and a purer (washed) ammonia passes over into the following vessels, in which only a pure solution is obtained. The bent funnel tube in the retort preserves the apparatus from the possibility both of the pressure of the gas evolved in it becoming too great (when the gas escapes through it into the air), and also from the pressure incidentally falling too low (for instance, owing to a cooling effect, or from the reaction stopping). If this takes place, the air passes into the retort, otherwise the liquid from B would be drawn into A. The safety tubes in each Woulfe's bottle, open at both ends, and immersed in the liquid, serve for the same purpose. Without them, in case of an accidental stoppage in the evolution of so soluble a gas as ammonia, the solution would be sucked from one vessel to another—for instance, from E into D, &c. In order to clearly see the necessity for *safety tubes* in a gas apparatus, it must be remembered that the *gaseous pressure* in the interior of the arrangement must exceed the atmospheric pressure by the height of the sum of the columns of liquid through which the gas has to pass.

[13] The analogy between the ammonium and sodium salts might seem to be destroyed by the fact that the latter are formed from the alkali or oxide and an acid, with the separation of water, whilst the ammonium salts are directly formed from ammonia and an acid, without the separation of water; but the analogy is restored if we compare soda to ammonia water, and liken caustic soda to a compound of ammonia with water. Then the very preparation of ammonium salts from such a hydrate of ammonia will completely resemble the preparation of sodium salts from soda. We may cite as an example the action of hydrochloric acid on both substances.

$$NaHO \quad + \quad HCl \quad = H_2O + \quad NaCl$$

Sodium hydroxide   Hydrochloric acid   Water   Table salt

$$NH_4HO \quad + \quad HCl \quad = H_2O + \quad NH_4Cl$$

Ammonium hydroxide   Hydrochloric acid   Water   Sal-ammoniac

Just as in soda the hydroxyl or aqueous radicle OH is replaced by chlorine, so it is in ammonia hydrate.

[14] Weyl (1864) by subjecting sodium to the action of ammonia at the ordinary temperature and under considerable pressures, obtained a liquid, which was subsequently investigated by Joannis (1889), who confirmed the results obtained by Weyl. At 0° and the atmospheric pressure the composition of this substance is $Na + 5\cdot3NH_3$. The removal (at 0°) of ammonia from the liquid gives a solid copper-red body having the composition NH_3Na. The determination of the molecular weight of this substance by the fall of the tension of liquid ammonia gave $N_2H_6Na_2$. It is, therefore, free ammonium in which one H is replaced by Na. The compound with potassium, obtained under the same conditions, proved to have an analogous composition. By the decomposition of NH_3Na at the ordinary temperature, Joannis (1891) obtained hydrogen and sodium-amide NH_2Na in small colourless crystals which were soluble in water. The addition of liquid ammonia to metallic sodium and a saturated solution of sodium chloride, gives NH_2Na_2Cl, and this substance is sal-ammoniac, in which H_2 is replaced by Na_2.

If pure oxygen be passed through a solution of these compounds in ammonia at a temperature of about -50°, it is seen that the gas is rapidly absorbed. The liquid gradually loses its dark red colour and becomes lighter, and when it has become quite colourless a gelatinous precipitate is thrown down. After the removal of the ammonia, this precipitate dissolves easily in water with a considerable evolution of heat, but without giving off any gaseous products. The composition of the sodium compound thus obtained is NH_2Na_2HO, which shows that it is a hydrate of bisodium-ammonium. Thus, although free ammonium has not been obtained, still a sodium substitution product of it is known which corresponds to it as a salt to a hydrate. Ammonium amalgam was originally obtained in exactly the same way as sodium amalgam (Davy); namely, a piece of sal-ammoniac was taken, and moistened with water (in order to render it a conductor of electricity). A cavity was made in it, into which mercury was poured, and it was laid on a sheet of platinum connected with the positive pole of a galvanic battery, while the negative pole was put into connection with the mercury. On passing a current the mercury increased considerably in volume, and became plastic, whilst preserving its metallic appearance, just as would be the case were the sal-ammoniac replaced by a lump of a sodium salt or of many other metals. In the analogous decomposition of common metallic salts, the metal contained in a given salt separates out at the negative pole, immersed in mercury, by which the metal is dissolved. A similar phenomenon is observed in the case of sal-ammoniac; the elements of ammonium, NH_4, in this case are also collected in the mercury, and are retained by it for a certain time.

[15] We may mention, however, that under particular conditions hydrogen is also capable of forming an amalgam resembling the amalgam of ammonium. If an amalgam of zinc be shaken up with an aqueous solution of platinum chloride, without access of air, then a spongy mass is formed which easily decomposes, with the evolution of hydrogen.

[16] We saw above that the solubility of ammonia in water at low temperatures attains to the molecular ratio $NH_3 + H_2O$, in which these substances are contained in caustic ammonia, and perhaps it may be possible at exceedingly low temperatures to obtain ammonium hydroxide, NH_4HO, in a solid form. Regarding solutions as dissociated definite compounds, we should see a confirmation of this view in the property shown by ammonia of being extremely soluble in water, and in so doing of approaching to the limit NH_4HO.

[17] In confirmation of the truth of this conclusion we may cite the remarkable fact that there exist, in a free state and as comparatively stable compounds, a series of alkaline hydroxides, NR_4HO, which are perfectly analogous to ammonium hydroxide, and present a striking resemblance to it and to sodium hydroxide, with the only difference that the hydrogen in NH_4HO is replaced by complex groups, $R = CH_3$, C_2H_5, &c., for instance $N(CH_3)_4HO$. Details will be found in organic chemistry.

[18] The fact that ammoniacal salts are decomposed when ignited, and not simply sublimed, may be proved by a direct experiment with sal-ammoniac, NH_4Cl, which in a state of vapour is decomposed into ammonia, NH_3, and hydrochloric acid, HCl, as will be explained in the following chapter. The readiness with which ammonium salts decompose is seen from the fact that a solution of ammonium oxalate is decomposed with the evolution of ammonia even at -1°. Dilute solutions of ammonium salts, when boiled give aqueous vapour having an alkaline reaction, owing to the presence of free ammonia given off from the salt.

[19] Isambert studied the dissociation of ammoniacal compounds, as we have seen in Note 8, and showed that at low temperatures many salts are able to combine with a still greater amount of ammonia, which proves an entire analogy with hydrates; and as in this case it is easy to isolate the definite compounds, and as the least possible tension of ammonia is greater than that of water, therefore the ammoniacal compounds present a great and peculiar interest, as a means for explaining the nature of aqueous solutions and as a confirmation of the hypothesis of the formation of definite compounds in them; for these reasons we shall frequently refer to these compounds in the further exposition of this work.

[20] Chapter V., Note 2.

[20 bis] Imide, NH, has not been obtained in a free state, but its hydrochloric acid salt, NHHCl, has apparently been obtained (1890) by Maumené by igniting the double bichloride of platinum and ammonium chloride, $PtCl_2NH_4Cl = Pt + 2HCl + NHHCl$. It is soluble in water, and crystallises from its solution in hexagonal rhombic prisms. It gives a double salt with $FeCl_3$ of the composition $FeCl_3 3NHHCl$. The salt NHHCl is similar (isomeric) with the first possible product of the metalepsis of ammonia, NH_2Cl, although it does not resemble it in any of its properties.

[21] Free *amidogen* or *hydrazine*, N_2H_4, or $2NH_2$, was prepared by Curtius (1887) by means of ethyl diazoacetate, or triazoacetic acid. Curtius and Jay (1889) showed that triazoacetic acid, $CHN_2.COOH$ (the formula should be tripled), when heated with water or a mineral acid, gives (quantitatively) oxalic acid and amidogen (hydrazine), $CHN_2.COOH + 2H_2O = C_2O_2(OH)_2 + N_2H_4$—*i.e.* (empirically), the oxygen of the water replaces the nitrogen of the azoacetic acid. The amidogen is thus obtained in the form of a salt. With acids, amidogen forms very stable salts of the two types N_2H_4HX and $N_{[2]}H_4H_2X_2$, as, for example, with HCl, H_2SO_4, &c. These salts are easily crystallised; in acid solutions they act as powerful reducing agents, evolving nitrogen; when ignited they are decomposed into ammoniacal salts, nitrogen, and hydrogen; with nitrites they evolve nitrogen. The sulphate N_2H_4,H_2SO_4 is sparingly soluble in cold water (3 parts in 100 of water), but is very soluble in hot water; its specific gravity is 1·378, it fuses at 254° with decomposition. The hydrochloride $N_2H_4,2HCl$ crystallises in octahedra, is very soluble in water, but not in alcohol; it fuses at 198°, evolving hydrogen chloride and forming the salt N_2H_4HCl; when rapidly heated it decomposes with an explosion; with platinic chloride it immediately evolves nitrogen, forming platinous chloride. By the action of alkalis the salts $N_2H_4,2HX$ give *hydrate of amidogen*, N_2H_4,H_2O, which is a fuming liquid (specific gravity 1·03), boiling at 119°, almost without odour, and whose aqueous solution corrodes glass and india-rubber, has an alkaline taste and poisonous properties. The reducing capacities of the hydrate are clearly seen from the fact that it reduces the metals platinum and silver from their solutions. With mercuric oxide it explodes. It reacts directly with the aldehydes RO, forming N_2R_2 and water; for example, with benzaldehydes it gives the very stable insoluble *benzalazine* $(C_6H_5CHN)_2$ of a yellow colour. We may add that hydrazine often forms double salts; for example, $MgSO_4N_2H_4H_2SO_4$ or $KClN_2H_4HCl$, and that it is also formed by the action of nitrous acid upon aldehyde-ammonia. The products of the substitution of the hydrogen in hydrazine by hydrocarbon groups R (R = CH_3, C_2H_5, C_6H_5, &c.) were obtained before hydrazine itself; for example, $NHRNH_2$, NR_2NH_2, and $(NRH)_2$.

The heat of solution of the sulphuric acid salt (1 part in 200 and 300 parts of water at 10°·8) is equal to -8·7 C. According to Berthelot and Matigon (1892), the heat of neutralisation of hydrazine by sulphuric acid is +5·5 C and by hydrochloric acid +5·2 C. Thus hydrazine is a very feeble base, for its heat of saturation is not only lower than that of ammonia (+12·4 C. for HCl), but even below that of hydroxylamine (+9·3 C.) The heat of formation from the elements of hydrated hydrazine -9·5 C was deduced from the heat of combustion, determined by burning $N_2H_4H_2SO_4$ in a calorimetric bomb, +127·7 C. Thus hydrazine is an endothermal compound; its passage into ammonia by the combination of hydrogen is accompanied by the evolution of 51·5 C. In the presence of an acid these figures were greater by +14·4 C. Hence the direct converse passage from ammonia into hydrazine is impossible. As regards the passage of hydroxylamine into hydrazine, it would be accompanied by the evolution of heat (+21·5 C.) in an aqueous solution.

Amidogen must be regarded as a compound which stands to ammonia in the same relation as hydrogen peroxide stands to water. Water, H(OH), gives, according to the law of substitution, as was clearly to be expected, (OH)(OH)—that is, peroxide of hydrogen is the free radicle of water (hydroxyl). So also ammonia, H(NH₂), forms hydrazine, (NH₂)(NH₂)—that is, the free radicle of ammonia, NH₂, or amidogen. In the case of phosphorus a similar substance, as we shall afterwards see, has long been known under the name of liquid phosphuretted hydrogen, P_2H_4.

[21 bis] In practice, the applications of ammonia are very varied. The use of ammonia as a stimulant, in the forms of the so-called 'smelling salts' or of spirits of hartshorn, in cases of faintness, &c., is known to everyone. The volatile carbonate of ammonium, or a mixture of an ammonium salt with an alkali, is also employed for this purpose. Ammonia also produces a well-known stimulating effect when rubbed on the skin, for which reason it is sometimes employed for external applications. Thus, for instance, the well-known volatile salve is prepared from any liquid oil shaken up with a solution of ammonia. A portion of the oil is thus transformed into a soapy substance. The solubility of greasy substances in ammonia, which proceeds from the formation both of emulsions and soaps, explains its use in extracting grease spots. It is also employed as an external application for stings from insects, and for bites from poisonous snakes, and in general in medicine. It is also remarkable that in cases of drunkenness a few drops of ammonia in water taken internally rapidly renders a person sober. A large quantity of ammonia is used in dyeing, either for the solution of certain dyes—for example, carmine—or for changing the tints of others, or else for neutralising the action of acids. It is also employed in the manufacture of artificial pearls. For this purpose the small scales of a peculiar small fish

are mixed with ammonia, and the liquid so obtained is blown into small hollow glass beads shaped like pearls.

In nature and the arts, however, ammonium salts, and not free ammonia, are most frequently employed. In this form a portion of that *nitrogen* which is necessary for the formation of albuminous substances is *supplied to plants*. Owing to this, a large quantity of ammonium sulphate is now employed as a fertilising substance. But the same effect may be produced by nitre, or by animal refuse, which in decomposing gives ammonia. For this reason, an ammoniacal (hydrogen) compound may be introduced into the soil in the spring which will be converted into a nitrate (oxygen salt) in the summer.

[22] As certain basic hydrates form peculiar compounds with ammonia, in some cases it happens that the first portions of ammonia added to a solution of a salt produce a precipitate, whilst the addition of a fresh quantity of ammonia dissolves this precipitate if the ammoniacal compound of the base be soluble in water. This, for example, takes place with the copper salts. But alumina does not dissolve under these circumstances.

[23] When the element chlorine, as we shall afterwards more fully learn, replaces the element hydrogen, the reaction by which such an exchange is accomplished proceeds as a substitution, $AH + Cl_2 = ACl + HCl$, so that two substances, AH and chlorine, react on each other, and two substances, ACl and HCl, are formed; and further, two molecules react on each other, and two others are formed. The reaction proceeds very easily, but the substitution of one element, A, by another, X, does not always proceed with such ease, clearness, or simplicity. The substitution between oxygen and hydrogen is very rarely accomplished by the reaction of the free elements, but the substitution between these elements, one for another, forms the most common case of oxidation and reduction. In speaking of the law of substitution, I have in view the substitution of the elements one by another, and not the direct reaction of substitution. The law of substitution determines the cycle of the combinations of a given element, if a few of its compounds (for instance, the hydrogen compounds) be known. A development of the conceptions of the law of substitution may be found in my lecture given at the Royal Institution in London, 1889.

[24] If hydrogen peroxide be taken as a starting point, then still higher forms of oxidation than those corresponding with water should be looked for. They should possess the properties of hydrogen peroxide, especially that of parting with their oxygen with extreme ease (even by contact). Such compounds are known. Pernitric, persulphuric, and similar acids present these properties, as we shall see in describing them.

[25] The compound of hydroxylamine with hydrochloric acid has the composition $NH_2(OH)HCl = NH_4ClO$—that is, it is as it were oxidised sal-ammoniac. It was prepared by Lossen in 1865 by the action of tin and hydrochloric acid in the presence of water on a substance called ethyl nitrate, in which case the hydrogen liberated from the hydrochloric acid by the tin acts upon the elements of nitric acid—

$$C_2H_5\cdot NO_3 + \quad 6H \quad + HCl = \quad NH_4OCl \quad + H_2O + C_2H_5\cdot OH$$

| Ethyl nitrate | Hydrogen from HCl and Sn | Hydroxylamine + HCl | Water | Alcohol |

Thus in this case the nitric acid is deoxidised, not directly into nitrogen, but into hydroxylamine. Hydroxylamine is also formed by passing nitric oxide, NO, into a mixture of tin and hydrochloric acid—that is, by the action of the hydrogen evolved on the nitric oxide, $NO + 3H + HCl = NH_4OCl$—and in many other cases. According to Lossen's method, a mixture of 30 parts of ethyl nitrate, 120 parts of tin, and 40 parts of a solution of hydrochloric acid of sp. gr. 1·06 are taken. After a certain time the reaction commences spontaneously. When the reaction has ceased the tin is separated by means of hydrogen sulphide, the solution is evaporated, and a large amount of sal-ammoniac is thus obtained (owing to the further action of hydrogen on the hydroxylamine compound, the hydrogen taking up oxygen from it and forming water); a solution ultimately remains containing the hydroxylamine salt; this salt is dissolved in anhydrous alcohol and purified by the addition of platinum chloride, which precipitates any ammonium salt still remaining in the solution. After concentrating the alcoholic solution the hydroxylamine hydrochloride separates in crystals. This substance melts at about 150°, and in so doing decomposes into nitrogen, hydrogen chloride, water, and sal-ammoniac. A sulphuric acid compound of hydroxylamine may be obtained by mixing a solution of the above salt with sulphuric acid. The sulphate is also soluble in water like the hydrochloride; this shows that hydroxylamine, like ammonia itself, forms a series of salts in which one acid may be substituted for another. It might he expected that by mixing a strong solution of a hydroxylamine salt with a solution of a caustic alkali hydroxylamine itself would be liberated, just as an ammonia salt under these circumstances evolves ammonia; but the liberated hydroxylamine is immediately decomposed with the formation of nitrogen and ammonia (and probably nitrous oxide), $3NH_3O = NH_3 + 3H_2O + N_2$. Dilute solutions give the same reaction, although very slowly, but by decomposing a solution of the sulphate with barium hydroxide a certain amount of hydroxylamine is obtained in solution (it is partly decomposed). Hydroxylamine in aqueous solution, like ammonia, precipitates basic hydrates, and it deoxidises the oxides of copper, silver, and other metals. Free hydroxylamine was obtained by Lobry de Bruyn (1891). It is a solid, colourless, crystalline substance, without odour, which does not melt below 27°. It has the property of dissolving metallic salts; for instance, sodium chloride. Hydroxylamine, when rapidly heated with platinum, decomposes with a flash and the formation of a yellow flame. It is almost insoluble in ordinary solvents like chloroform, benzine, acetic ether, and carbon bisulphide. Its aqueous solutions are tolerably stable, contain up to 60 per cent. (sp. gr. $1 \cdot 15$ at 20°), and may be kept for many weeks without undergoing any change. Lobry de Bruyn used the hydrochloric salt to prepare pure hydroxylamine. The salt was first treated with sodium methylate (CH_3NaO), and then methyl alcohol was added to the mixture. The precipitated sodium chloride was separated from the solution by filtration. (The methyl alcohol is added to prevent the precipitated chloride of sodium from coating the insoluble hydrochloric salt of hydroxylamine.) The methyl alcohol was driven off under a pressure 150–200 mm., and after extracting a further portion of methyl alcohol by ether and several fractional distillations, a solution was obtained containing 70 per cent. of free hydroxylamine, 8 per cent. water, $9 \cdot 9$ per cent. chloride of sodium, and $12 \cdot 1$ per cent. of the hydrochloric salt of hydroxylamine. Pure free hydroxylamine, NH_3O, is obtained by distilling under a pressure of 60 mm.; it then boils at 70°, and solidifies in a condenser cooled to 0° in the form of long needles. It melts at 33°, boils at 58° under a pressure of 22 mm., and has a sp. gr. of about $1 \cdot 235$ (Brühl). Under the action of NaHO it gives NH_3 and NHO_2 or N_2O, and forms nitric acid (Kolotoff, 1893) under the action of oxidising agents. Hydroxylamine is obtained in a great number of cases, for instance by the action of tin on dilute nitric acid, and also by the action of zinc on ethyl nitrate and dilute hydrochloric acid, &c. The relation between hydroxylamine, $NH_2(OH)$, and nitrous acid, $NO(OH)$, which is so clear in the sense of the law of substitutions, becomes a reality in those cases when reducing agents act on salts of nitrous acid. Thus Raschig (1888) proposed the following method for the preparation of the hydroxylamine sulphate. A mixture of strong solutions of potassium nitrite, KNO_2, and hydroxide, KHO, in molecular proportions, is prepared and cooled. An excess of sulphurous anhydride is then passed into the mixture, and the solution boiled for a long time. A mixture of the sulphates of potassium and hydroxylamine is thus obtained: $KNO_2 + KHO + 2SO_2 + 2H_2O = NH_2(OH),H_2SO_4 + K_2SO_4$. The salts may be separated from each other by crystallisation.

[25 bis] In order to illustrate the application of the law of substitution to a given case, and to show the connection between ammonia and the oxides of nitrogen, let us consider the possible products of an oxygen and

hydroxyl substitution in caustic ammonia, $NH_4(OH)$. It is evident that the substitution of H by OH can give: (1) $NH_3(OH)_2$; (2) $NH_2(OH)_3$; (3) $NH(OH)_4$; and (4) $N(OH)_5$. They should all, like caustic ammonia itself, easily part with water and form products (hydroxylic) of the oxidation of ammonia. The first of them is the hydrate of hydroxylamine, $NH_2(OH)$ + H_2O; the second, $NH(OH)_2$ + H_2O (and also the substance $NH(OH)_4$ or NH_3O_2), containing, as it does, both hydrogen and oxygen, is able to part with all its hydrogen in the form of water (which could not be done by the first product, since it contained too little oxygen), forming, as the ultimate product, $2NH_2(OH)_3$ - $5H_2O$ = N_2O—that is, it corresponds with nitrous oxide, or the lower degree of the oxidation of nitrogen. So, also, nitrous anhydride corresponds with the third of the above products, $2NH(OH)_4$ - $5H_2O$ = N_2O_3, and nitric anhydride with the fourth, $2N(OH)_5$ - $5H_2O$ = N_2O_5. As, in these three equations, two molecules of the substitution products ($-5H_2O$) are taken, it is also possible to combine two different products in one equation. For instance, the third and fourth products: $NH(OH)_4$ + $N(OH)_5$ - $5H_2O$ corresponds to N_2O_4 or $2NO_2$, that is, to peroxide of nitrogen. Thus all the five (see later) oxides of nitrogen, N_2O, NO, N_2O_3, NO_2, and N_2O_5, may be deduced from ammonia. The above may be expressed in a general form by the equation (it should be remarked that the composition of all the substitution products of caustic ammonia may be expressed by NH_3O_{5-a}, where a varies between 0 and 4):

$$NH_5O_{5-a} + NH_5O_{5-b} - 5H_2O = N_2O_{5-(a+b)},$$

where $a + b$ can evidently be not greater than 5; when $a + b$ = 5 we have N_2—nitrogen, when = 4 we have N_2O nitrous oxide; when $a + b$ = 3 we have N_2O_2 or NO—nitric oxide, and so on to N_2O_5, when $a + b$ = 0. Besides which it is evident that intermediate products may correspond with (and hence also break up into) different starting points; for instance, N_2O is obtained when $a + b$ = 2, and this may occur either when a = 0 (nitric acid), and b = 2 (hydroxylamine), or when $a = b = 1$ (the third of the above substitution products).

[26] Nitric acid corresponds with the anhydride N_2O_5, which will afterwards be described, but which must be regarded as the highest saline oxide of nitrogen, just as Na_2O (and the hydroxide $NaHO$) in the case of sodium, although sodium forms a peroxide possessing the property of parting with its oxygen with the same ease as hydrogen peroxide, if not on heating, at all events in reactions—for instance, with acids. So also nitric acid has its corresponding peroxide, which may be called pernitric acid. Its composition is not well known—probably NHO_4—so that its corresponding anhydride would be N_2O_7. It is formed by the action of a silent discharge on a mixture of nitrogen and oxygen, so that a portion of its oxygen is in a state similar to that in ozone. The instability of this

substance (obtained by Hautefeuille, Chappuis, and Berthelot), which easily splits up with the formation of nitric peroxide, and its resemblance to persulphuric acid, which we shall afterwards describe, will permit our passing over the consideration of the little that is further known concerning it.

[27] Phosphorus (Chapter XIX.) gives the hydride PH_3, corresponding with ammonia, NH_3, and forms phosphorous acid, PH_3O_3, which is analogous to nitrous acid, just as phosphoric acid is to nitric acid; but phosphoric (or, better, orthophosphoric) acid, PH_3O_4, is able to lose water and give pyro-and meta-phosphoric acids. The latter is equal to the ortho-acid minus water $= PHO_3$, and therefore nitric acid, NHO_3, is really meta-nitric acid. So also nitrous acid, HNO_2, is meta-nitrous (anhydrous) acid, and thus the ortho-acid is $NH_3O_3 = N(OH)_3$. Hence for nitric acid we should expect to find, besides the ordinary or meta-nitric acid, HNO_3 ($= \frac{1}{2}N_2O_3,H_2O$), and ortho-nitric acid, H_3NO_4 ($= \frac{1}{2}N_2O_3,3H_2O$), an intermediate pyro-nitric acid, $N_2H_4O_7$, corresponding to pyrophosphoric acid, $P_2H_4O_7$. We shall see (for instance, in Chapter XVI., Note 21) that in nitric acid there is indeed an inclination of the ordinary salts (of the meta-acid), MNO_3, to combine with bases M_2O, and to approximate to the composition of ortho-compounds which are equal to meta-compound and bases ($MNO_3 + M_2O = M_3NO_4$).

[28] The formation of ammonia is observed in many cases of oxidation by means of nitric acid. This substance is even formed in the action of nitric acid on tin, especially if dilute acid be employed in the cold. A still more considerable amount of ammonia is obtained if, in the action of nitric acid, there are conditions directly tending to the evolution of hydrogen, which then reduces the acid to ammonia; for instance, in the action of zinc on a mixture of nitric and sulphuric acids.

[28 bis] Curtius started with benzoylhydrazine, $C_6H_5CONHNH_2$ (hydrazine, see Note 20 bis). (This substance is obtained by the action of hydrated hydrazine on the compound ether of benzoic acid). Benzoylhydrazine under the action of nitrous acid gives benzoylazoimide and water:

$$C_6H_5CONHNH_2 + NO_2H = C_6H_5CON_3 + 2H_2O.$$

Benzoylazoimide when treated with sodium alcoholate gives the sodium salt of hydronitrous acid:

$$C_6H_5CON_3 + C_2H_3ONa = C_6H_5O_2C_2H_3 + NaN_3.$$

The addition of ether to the resultant solution precipitates the NaN_3, and this salt when treated with sulphuric acid gives gaseous hydronitrous acid, HN_3. It has an acrid smell, and is easily soluble in water. The aqueous solution exhibits a strongly acid reaction. Metals dissolve in this solution and give the corresponding salts. With hydronitrous acid gaseous ammonia forms a white cloud, consisting of the salt of ammonium, NH_4N_3. This salt separates out from an alcoholic solution in the form of white lustrous scales. The salts of hydronitrous acid are obtained by a reaction of substitution with the sodium or ammonium salts. In this manner Curtius obtained and studied the salts of silver (AgN_3), mercury (HgN_3), lead (PbN_6), barium (BaN_6). With hydrazine, N_2H_4, hydronitrous acid forms saline compounds in the composition of which there are one or two particles of N_3H per one particle of hydrazine; thus N_5H_5 and N_8H_6. The first was obtained in an almost pure form. It crystallises from an aqueous solution in dense, volatile, lustrous prisms (up to 1 in. long), which fuse at 50°, and deliquesce in the air; from a solution in boiling alcohol it separates out in bright crystalline plates. This salt, N_5H_5, has the same empirical composition, NH, as the ammonium salt of hydronitrous acid, N_4H_4, and imide; but their molecules and structure are different. Curtius also obtained (1893) hydronitrous acid by passing the vapour of N_2O_5 (evolved by the action of HNO_3 on As_2O_3) into a solution of hydrazine, N_2H_4. Similarly Angeli, by acting upon a saturated solution of silver nitrite with a strong solution of hydrazine, obtained the explosive AgN_3 in the form of a precipitate, and this reaction, which is based upon the equation $N_2H_4 + NHO_2 = HN_3 + 2H_2O$, proceeds so easily that it forms an experiment for the lecture table. A thermal investigation of hydronitrous acid by Berthelot and Matignon gave the following figures for the heat of solution of the ammonium salt N_3HNH_3 (1 grm. in 100 parts of water) -708 C., and for the heat of neutralisation by barium hydrate +10·0 C., and by ammonia +8·2 C. The heat of combustion of N_4H_4 (+163·8 C. at a constant vol.) gives the heat of formation of the salt N_4H_4 (solid) as - 25·3 C. and (solution) - 32·3 C.; this explains the explosive nature of this compound. In its heat of formation from the elements N_3H = -62·6 C., this compound differs from all the hydrogen compounds of nitrogen in having a maximum absorption of heat, which explains its instability.

[29] According to the thermochemical determinations of Favre, Thomsen, and more especially of Berthelot, it follows that, in the formation of such quantities of the oxides of nitrogen as express their formulæ, if gaseous nitrogen and oxygen be taken as the starting points, and if the compounds formed be also gaseous, the following amounts of heat, expressed in thousands of heat units, are *absorbed* (hence a minus sign):—

N_2O	N_2O_2	N_2O_3	N_2O_4	N_2O_5
-21	-43	-22	-5	-1

-22	+21	+17	+4

The difference is given in the lower line. For example, if N_2, or 28 grams of nitrogen, combine with O—that is, with 16 grams of oxygen—then 21,000 units of heat are absorbed, that is, sufficient heat to raise 21,000 grams of water through 1°. Naturally, direct observations are impossible in this case; but if charcoal, phosphorus, or similar substances are burnt both in nitrous oxide and in oxygen, and the heat evolved is observed in both cases, then the difference (more heat will be evolved in burning in nitrous oxide) gives the figures required. If N_2O_2, by combining with O_2, gives N_2O_4, then, as is seen from the table, heat should be developed, namely, 38,000 units of heat, or NO + O = 19,000 units of heat. The differences given in the table show that the maximum absorption of heat corresponds with nitric oxide, and that the higher oxides are formed from it with evolution of heat. If liquid nitric acid, NHO_3, were decomposed into N + O_3 + H, then 41,000 heat units would be required; that is, an evolution of heat takes place in its formation from the gases. It should be observed that the formation of ammonia, NH_3, from the gases N + H_3 evolves 12·2 thousand heat units.

[29 bis] This often gives rise to the supposition that sulphuric acid possesses a considerable degree of affinity or energy compared with nitric acid, but we shall afterwards see that the idea of the relative degree of affinity of acids and bases is, in many cases, exceedingly unbiassed; it need not be accepted so long as it is possible to explain the observed phenomena without admitting any supposition whatever of the degree of the force of affinity, because the latter cannot be measured. The action of sulphuric acid upon nitre may be explained by the fact alone that the resultant nitric acid is volatile. The nitric acid is the only one of all the substances partaking in the reaction which is able to pass into vapour; it alone is volatile, while the remainder are non-volatile, or, more strictly speaking, exceedingly difficultly volatile substances. Let us imagine that the sulphuric acid is only able to set free a small quantity of nitric acid from its salt, and this will suffice to explain the decomposition of the whole of the nitre by the sulphuric acid, because once the nitric acid is separated it passes into vapour when heated, and passes away from the sphere of action of the remaining substances; then the free sulphuric acid will set free a fresh small quantity of nitric acid, and so on until it drives off the entire quantity. It is evident that, in this explanation, it is essential that the sulphuric acid should be in excess (although not greatly) throughout the reaction; according to the equation expressing the reaction, 98 parts of sulphuric acid are required per 85 parts of Chili nitre; but if this proportion be maintained in practice the nitric acid is not all disengaged by the sulphuric acid; an excess of the latter must be taken, and generally 80 parts

of Chili nitre are taken per 98 parts of acid, so that a portion of the sulphuric acid remains free to the very end of the reaction.

[30] It must be observed that sulphuric acid, at least when undiluted (60° Baumé), corrodes cast iron with difficulty, so that the acid may be heated in cast-iron retorts. Nevertheless, both sulphuric and nitric acids have a certain action on cast iron, and therefore the acid obtained will contain traces of iron. In practice sodium nitrate (Chili saltpetre) is usually employed because it is cheaper, but in the laboratory it is best to take potassium nitrate, because it is purer and does not froth up so much as sodium nitrate when heated with sulphuric acid. In the action of an excess of sulphuric acid on nitre and nitric acid a portion of the latter is decomposed, forming lower oxides of nitrogen, which are dissolved in the nitric acid. A portion of the sulphuric acid itself is also carried over as spray by the vapours of the nitric acid. Hence sulphuric acid occurs as an impurity in commercial nitric acid. A certain amount of hydrochloric acid will also be found to be present in it, because sodium chloride is generally found as an impurity in nitre, and under the action of sulphuric acid it forms hydrochloric acid. Commercial acid further contains a considerable excess of water above that necessary for the formation of the hydrate, because water is first poured into the earthenware vessels employed for condensing the nitric acid in order to facilitate its cooling and condensation. Further, the acid of composition HNO_3 decomposes with great ease, with the evolution of oxides of nitrogen. Thus the commercial acid contains a great number of impurities, and is frequently purified in the following manner:—Lead nitrate is first added to the acid because it forms non-volatile and almost insoluble (precipitated) substances with the free sulphuric and hydrochloric acids, and liberates nitric acid in so doing, according to the equations $Pb(NO_3)_2 + 2HCl = PbCl_2 + 2NHO_3$ and $Pb(NO_3)_2 + H_2SO_4 = PbSO_4 + 2NHO_3$. Potassium chromate is then added to the impure nitric acid, by which means oxygen is liberated from the chromic acid, and this oxygen, at the moment of its evolution, oxidises the lower oxides of nitrogen and converts them into nitric acid. A pure nitric acid, containing no impurities other than water, may be then obtained by carefully distilling the acid, treated as above described, and particularly if only the middle portions of the distillate are collected. Such acid should give no precipitate, either with a solution of barium chloride (a precipitate shows the presence of sulphuric acid) or with a solution of silver nitrate (a precipitate shows the presence of hydrochloric acid), nor should it, after being diluted with water, give a coloration with starch containing potassium iodide (a coloration shows the admixture of other oxides of nitrogen). The oxides of nitrogen may be most easily removed from impure nitric acid by heating for a certain time with a small quantity of pure charcoal. By the action of nitric acid on the charcoal carbonic anhydride is evolved, which

carries off the lower oxides of nitrogen. On redistilling, pure acid is obtained. The oxides of nitrogen occurring in solution may also be removed by passing air through the nitric acid.

[31] Dalton, Smith, Bineau, and others considered that the hydrate of constant boiling point (see Chapter I., Note 60) for nitric acid was the compound $2HNO_3,3H_2O$, but Roscoe showed that its composition changes with a variation of the pressure and temperature under which the distillation proceeds. Thus, at a pressure of 1 atmosphere the solution of constant boiling point contains 68·6 p.c., and at one-tenth of an atmosphere 66·8 p.c. Judging from what has been said concerning solutions of hydrochloric acid, and from the variation of specific gravity, I think that the comparatively large decrease in the tensions of the vapours depends on the formation of a hydrate, $NHO_3,2H_2O$ (= 63·6 p.c.). Such a hydrate may be expressed by $N(HO)_5$, that is, as $NH_4(HO)$, in which all the equivalents of hydrogen are replaced by hydroxyl. The constant boiling point will then be the temperature of the decomposition of this hydrate.

The variation of the specific gravity at 15° from water ($p = 0$) to the hydrate $NHO_3,5H_2O$ (41·2 p.c. HNO_3) is expressed by $s = 9992 + 57·4p + 0·16p^2$, if water = 10,000 at 4°. For example, when $p = 30$ p.c., $s = 11,860$. For more concentrated solutions, at least, the above-mentioned hydrate, $HNO_3,2H_2O$, must be taken, up to which the specific gravity $s = 9570 + 84·18p - 0·240p^2$; but perhaps (since the results of observations of the specific gravity of the solutions are not in sufficient agreement to arrive at a conclusion) the hydrate $HNO_3,3H_2O$ should be recognised, as is indicated by many nitrates (Al, Mg, Co, &c.), which crystallise with this amount of water of crystallisation. From $HNO_3,2H_2O$ to HNO_3 the specific gravity of the solutions (at 15°) $s = 10,652 + 62·08p - 0·160p^2$. The hydrate $HNO_3,2H_2O$ is recognised by Berthelot on the basis of the thermochemical data for solutions of nitric acid, because on approaching to this composition there is a rapid change in the amount of heat evolved by mixing nitric acid with water. Pickering (1892) by refrigeration obtained the crystalline hydrates: HNO_3,H_2O, melting at -37° and $HNO_3,3H_2O$, melting at -18°. A more detailed study of the reactions of hydrated nitric acid would no doubt show the existence of change in the process and rapidity of reaction in approaching these hydrates.

[32] The normal hydrate HNO_3, corresponding with the ordinary salts, may be termed the monohydrated acid, because the anhydride N_2O_5 with water forms this normal nitric acid. In this sense the hydrate $HNO_3,2H_2O$ is the pentahydrated acid.

[33] For technical and laboratory purposes recourse is frequently had to *red fuming nitric acid*—that is, the normal nitric acid, HNO_3, containing lower

oxides of nitrogen in solution. This acid is prepared by decomposing nitre with half its weight of strong sulphuric acid, or by distilling nitric acid with an excess of sulphuric acid. The normal nitric acid is first obtained, but it partially decomposes, and gives the lower oxidation products of nitrogen, which are dissolved by the nitric acid, to which they impart its usual pale-brown or reddish colour. This acid fumes in the air, from which it attracts moisture, forming a less volatile hydrate. If carbonic anhydride be passed through the red-brown fuming nitric acid for a long period of time, especially if, assisted by a moderate heat, it expels all the lower oxides, and leaves a colourless acid free from these oxides. It is necessary, in the preparation of the red acid, that the receivers should be kept quite cool, because it is only when cold that nitric acid is able to dissolve a large proportion of the oxides of nitrogen. The strong red fuming acid has a specific gravity 1·56 at 20°, and has a suffocating smell of the oxides of nitrogen. When the red acid is mixed with water it turns green, and then of a bluish colour, and with an excess of water ultimately becomes colourless. This is owing to the fact that the oxides of nitrogen in the presence of water and nitric acid are changed, and give coloured solutions.

Markleffsky (1892) showed that the green solutions contain (besides HNO_3) HNO_2 and N_2O_4, whilst the blue solutions only contain HNO_2 (see Note 48).

The action of red fuming nitric acid (or a mixture with sulphuric acid) is in many cases very powerful and rapid, and it sometimes acts differently from pure nitric acid. Thus iron becomes covered with a coating of oxides, and insoluble in acids; it becomes, as is said, passive. Thus chromic acid (and potassium dichromate) gives oxide of chromium in this red acid—that is, it is deoxidised. This is owing to the presence of the lower oxides of nitrogen, which are capable of being oxidised—that is, of passing into nitric acid like the higher oxides. But, generally, the action of fuming nitric acid, both red and colourless, is powerfully oxidising.

[34] Hydrogen is not evolved in the action of nitric acid (especially strong) on metals, even with those metals which evolve hydrogen under the action of other acids. This is because the hydrogen at the moment of its separation reduces the nitric acid, with formation of the lower oxides of nitrogen, as we shall afterwards see.

[35] Certain basic salts of nitric acid, however (for example, the basic salt of bismuth), are insoluble in water; whilst, on the other hand, all the normal salts are soluble, and this forms an exceptional phenomenon among acids, because all the ordinary acids form insoluble salts with one or another base. Thus, for sulphuric acid the salts of barium, lead, &c., for

hydrochloric acid the salts of silver, &c., are insoluble in water. However, the normal salts of acetic and certain other acids are all soluble.

[36] *Ammonium nitrate*, NH_4NO_3, is easily obtained by adding a solution of ammonia or of ammonium carbonate to nitric acid until it becomes neutral. On evaporating this solution, crystals of the salt are formed which contain no water of crystallisation. It crystallises in prisms like those formed by common nitre, and has a refreshing taste; 100 parts of water at $t°$ dissolve $54 + 0·61t$ parts by weight of the salt. It is soluble in alcohol, melts at 160°, and is decomposed at about 180°, forming water and nitrous oxide, $NH_4NO_3 = 2H_2O + N_2O$. If ammonium nitrate be mixed with sulphuric acid, and the mixture be heated to about the boiling point of water, then nitric acid is evolved, and ammonium hydrogen sulphate remains in solution; but if the mixture be heated rapidly to 160°, then nitrous oxide is evolved. In the first case the sulphuric acid takes up ammonia, and in the second place water. Ammonium nitrate is employed in practice for the artificial production of cold, because in dissolving in water it lowers the temperature very considerably. For this purpose it is best to take equal parts by weight of the salt and water. The salt must first be reduced to a powder and then rapidly stirred up in the water, when the temperature will fall from +15° to -10°, so that the water freezes.

Ammonium nitrate absorbs ammonia, with which it forms unstable compounds resembling compounds containing water of crystallisation. (Divers 1872, Raoult 1873.) At -10° $NH_4NO_3,2NH_3$ is formed: it is a liquid of sp. gr. 1·15, which loses all its ammonia under the influence of heat. At +28° NH_4NO_3,NH_3 is formed: it is a solid which easily parts with its ammonia when heated, especially in solution.

Troost (1882) investigated the tension of the dissociation of the compounds formed, and came to the conclusion that a definite compound corresponding to the formula $2NH_4NO_3,3NH_3$ is formed, because the tension of dissociation remains constant in the decomposition of such a compound at 0°. Y. Kouriloff (1893), however, considers that the constancy of the tension of the ammonia evolved is due to the decomposition of a saturated solution, and not of a definite compound. During decomposition the system is composed of a liquid and a solid; the tension only becomes constant from the moment the solid falls down. The composition $2NH_4NO_3,3NH_3$ corresponds to a saturated solution at 0°, and the solubility of NH_4NO_3 in NH_3 increases with a rise of temperature.

[36 bis] This is explained by saying that in true nitro-compounds the residue of nitric acid NO_2 takes the place of the hydrogen in the hydrocarbon group. For example, if C_6H_5OH be given, then $C_6H_4(NO_2)OH$ will be a true nitro-compound having the radical properties

of C_6H_5OH. If, on the other hand, the NO_2 replace the hydrogen of the aqueous radicle ($C_6H_5ONO_2$), then the chemical character varies, as in the passage of KOH into $KONO_2$ (nitre) (*see* Note 37 and Organic Chemistry).

[37] The compound ethers of nitric acid in which the hydrogen of the aqueous radicle (OH) is replaced by the residue of nitric acid (NO_2) are frequently called nitro-compounds. But in their chemical character they differ from true nitro-compounds (for details *see* Organic Chemistry) and do not burn like them.

The action of nitric acid on cellulose, $C_6H_{10}O_5$, is an example. This substance, which forms the outer coating of all plant cells, occurs in an almost pure state in cotton, in common writing-paper, and in flax, &c.; under the action of nitric acid it forms water and nitrocellulose (like water and KNO_3 from KHO), which, although it has the same appearance as the cotton originally taken, differs from it entirely in properties. It explodes when struck, bursts into flame very easily under the action of sparks, and acts like gunpowder, whence its name of pyroxylin, or gun-cotton. The composition of gun-cotton is $C_6H_7N_3O_{11} = C_6H_{10}O_5 + 3NHO_3 - 3H_2O$. The proportion of the group NO_2 in nitrocellulose may be decreased by limiting the action of the nitric acid and compounds obtained with different properties; for instance, the (impure) well-known *collodion cotton*, containing from 11 to 12 per cent. of nitrogen, and *pyro-collodion* (Mendeléeff, 1890), containing 12·4 per cent. of nitrogen. Both these products are soluble in a mixture of alcohol and ether (in collodion a portion of the substance is soluble in alcohol), and the solution when evaporated gives a transparent film, which is insoluble in water. A solution of collodion is employed in medicine for covering wounds, and in wet-plate photography for giving on glass an even coating of a substance into which the various reagents employed in the process are introduced. Extremely fine threads (obtained by forcing a gelatinous mixture of collodion, ether, and alcohol through capillary tubes in water) of collodion form artificial silk.

[37 bis] The property possessed by nitroglycerin (occurring in dynamite), nitrocellulose, and the other nitro-compounds, of burning with an explosion, and their employment for smokeless powder and as explosives in general, depends on the reasons in virtue of which a mixture of nitre and charcoal deflagrates and explodes; in both cases the elements of the nitric acid occurring in the compound are decomposed, the oxygen in burning unites with the carbon, and the nitrogen is set free; thus a very large volume of gaseous substances (nitrogen and oxides of carbon) is rapidly formed from the solid substances originally taken. These gases occupy an incomparably larger volume than the original substance, and therefore produce a powerful pressure and explosion. It is evident that in exploding

with the development of heat (that is, in decomposing, not with the absorption of energy, as is generally the case, but with the evolution of energy) the nitro-compounds form stores of energy which are easily set free, and that consequently their elements occur in a state of particularly energetic motion, which is especially strong in the group NO_2: this group is common to all nitro-compounds, and all the oxygen compounds of nitrogen are unstable, easily decomposable, and (Note 29) absorb heat in their formation. On the other hand, the nitro-compounds are instructive as an example and proof of the fact that the elements and groups forming compounds are united in definite order in the molecules of a compound. A blow, concussion, or rise of temperature is necessary to bring the combustible elements C and H into the most intimate contact with NO_2, and to distribute the elements in a new order in new compounds.

As regards the composition of the nitro-compounds, it will be seen that the hydrogen of a given substance is replaced by the complex group NO_2 of the nitric acid. The same is observed in the passage of alkalis into nitrates, so that the reactions of substitution of nitric acid—that is, the formation of salts and nitro-compounds—may be expressed in the following manner. In these cases the hydrogen is replaced by the so-called *radicle of nitric acid* NO_2, as is evident from the following table:—

Caustic potash KHO.	Glycerin $C_3H_5H_3O_3$.
Nitre $K(NO_2)O$.	Nitroglycerin $C_3H_5(NO_2)_3O_3$.
Hydrate of lime CaH_2O_2	Phenol C_6H_5OH.
Calcium nitrate $Ca(NO_2)_2O_2$.	Picric acid $C_6H_2(NO_2)_3OH$, &c.

The difference between the salts formed by nitric acid and the nitro-compounds consists in the fact that nitric acid is very easily separated from the salts of nitric acid by means of sulphuric acid (that is, by a method of double saline decomposition), whilst nitric acid is not displaced by sulphuric acid from true nitro-compounds; for instance, nitrobenzene, $C_6H_5 \cdot NO_2$. As nitro-compounds are formed exclusively from hydrocarbons, they are described with them in organic chemistry.

The group NO_2 of nitro-compounds in many cases (like all the oxidised compounds of nitrogen) passes into the ammonia group or into the ammonia radicle NH_2. This requires the action of reducing substances evolving hydrogen: $RNO_2 + 6H = RNH_3 + 2H_2O$. Thus Zinin converted nitrobenzene, $C_6H_5 \cdot NO_2$, into aniline, $C_6H_5 \cdot NH_2$, by the action of hydrogen sulphide.

Admitting the existence of the group NO_2, as replacing hydrogen in various compounds, then nitric acid may be considered as water in which half the hydrogen is replaced by the radical of nitric acid. In this sense nitric acid is nitro-water, NO_2OH, and its anhydride dinitro-water, $(NO_2)_2O$. In nitric acid the radical of nitric acid is combined with hydroxyl, just as in nitrobenzene it is combined with the radical of benzene.

It should here be remarked that the group NO_3 may be recognised in the salts of nitric acid, because the salts have the composition $M(NO_3)_n$, just as the metallic chlorides have the composition MCl_n. But the group NO_3 does not form any other compounds beyond the salts, and therefore it should he considered as hydroxyl, HO, in which H is replaced by NO_2.

[38] The nitro-compounds play a very important part in mining and artillery. Detailed accounts of them must be looked for in special works, among which the works of A. R. Shuliachenke and T. M. Chelletsoff occupy an important place in the Russian literature on this subject, although historically the scientific works of Abel in England and Berthelot in France stand pre-eminent. The latter elucidated much in connection with explosive compounds by a series of both experimental and theoretical researches. Among explosives a particularly important place from a practical point of view is occupied by ordinary or black gunpowder (Chapter XIII., Note 16), fulminating mercury (Chapter XVI., Note 26), the different forms of gun-cotton (Chapter VI., Note 37), and nitro-glycerine (Chapter VIII., Note 45, and Chapter XII., Note 33). The latter when mixed with solid pulverulent substances, like magnesia, tripoli, &c., forms dynamite, which is so largely used in quarries and mines in driving tunnels, &c. We may add that the simplest true nitro-compound, or marsh gas, CH_4, in which all the hydrogens are replaced by NO_2 groups has been obtained by L. N. Shishkoff, $C(NO_2)_4$, as well as nitroform, $CH(NO_2)_3$.

[39]

FIG. 49.—Decomposition of nitrous oxide by sodium.

Nitric acid may be entirely decomposed by passing its vapour over highly incandescent copper, because the oxides of nitrogen first formed give up their oxygen to the red-hot metallic copper, so that water and nitrogen gas alone are obtained. This forms a means for determining the composition both of nitric acid and of all the other compounds of nitrogen with oxygen, because by collecting the gaseous nitrogen formed it is possible to calculate, from its volume, its weight and consequently its amount in a given quantity of a nitrogenous substance, and by weighing the copper before and after the decomposition it is possible to determine the amount of oxygen by the increase in weight. The complete decomposition of nitric acid is also accomplished by passing a mixture of hydrogen and nitric acid vapours through a red-hot tube. Sodium also decomposes the oxides of nitrogen at a red-heat, taking up all the oxygen. This method is sometimes used for determining the composition of the oxides of nitrogen.

[40] The application of this acid for etching copper or steel in engraving is based on this fact. The copper is covered with a coating of wax, resin, &c. (etching ground), on which nitric acid does not act, and then the ground is removed in certain parts with a needle, and the whole is washed in nitric acid. The parts coated remain untouched, whilst the uncovered portions are eaten into by the acid. Copper plates for etchings, aquatints, &c., are prepared in this manner.

[41] The formation of such complex equations as the above often presents some difficulty to the beginner. It should be observed that if the reacting and resultant substances be known, it is easy to form an equation

for the reaction. Thus, if we wish to form an equation expressing the reaction that nitric acid acting on zinc gives nitrous oxide, N_2O, and zinc nitrate, $Zn(NO_3)_2$, we must reason as follows:—Nitric acid contains hydrogen, whilst the salt and nitrous oxide do not; hence water is formed, and therefore it is as though anhydrous nitric acid, N_2O_5, were acting. For its conversion into nitrous oxide it parts with four equivalents of oxygen, and hence it is able to oxidise four equivalents of zinc and to convert it into zinc oxide, ZnO. These four equivalents of zinc oxide require for their conversion into the salt four more equivalents of nitric anhydride; consequently five equivalents in all of the latter are required, or ten equivalents of nitric acid. Thus ten equivalents of nitric acid are necessary for four equivalents of zinc in order to express the reaction in whole equivalents. It must not be forgotten, however, that there are very few such reactions which can be entirely expressed by simple equations. The majority of equations of reactions only express the chief and ultimate products of reaction, and thus none of the three preceding equations express all that in reality occurs in the action of metals on nitric acid. In no one of them is only one oxide of nitrogen formed, but always several together or consecutively—one after the other, according to the temperature and strength of the acid. And this is easily intelligible. The resulting oxide is itself capable of acting on metals and of being deoxidised, and in the presence of the nitric acid it may change the acid and be itself changed. The equations given must be looked on as a systematic expression of the main features of reactions, or as a limit towards which they tend, but to which they only attain in the absence of disturbing influences.

[42] Montemartini endeavours to show that the products evolved in the action of nitric acid upon metals (and their amount) is in direct connection with both the concentration of the acid and the capacity of the metals to decompose water. Those metals which only decompose water at a high temperature give, under the action of nitric acid, NO_2, N_2O_4, and NO; whilst those metals which decompose water at a lower temperature give, besides the above products, N_2O, N, and NH_3; and, lastly, the metals which decompose water at the ordinary temperature also evolve hydrogen. It is observed that concentrated nitric acid oxidises many metals with much greater difficulty than when diluted with water; iron, copper, and tin are very easily oxidised by dilute nitric acid, but remain unaltered under the influence of monohydrated nitric acid or of the pure hydrate NHO_3. Nitric acid diluted with a large quantity of water does not oxidise copper, but it oxidises tin; dilute nitric acid also does not oxidise either silver or mercury; but, on the addition of nitrous acid, even dilute acid acts on the above metals. This naturally depends on the smaller stability of nitrous acid, and on the fact that after the commencement of the action the nitric acid is itself converted into nitrous acid, which continues to act on the silver and

mercury. Veley (Oxford 1891) made detailed researches on the action of nitric acid upon Cu, Hg, and Bi, and showed that nitric acid of 30 p.c. strength does not act upon these metals at the ordinary temperature if nitrous acid (traces are destroyed by urea) and oxidising agents such as H_2O_2, $KClO_3$, &c. be entirely absent; but in the presence of even a small amount of nitrous acid the metals form nitrites, which, with HNO_3, form nitrates and the oxides of nitrogen, which re-form the nitrous acid necessary for starting the reaction, because the reaction $2NO + HNO_3 + H_2O = 3HNO_2$ is reversible. The above metals are quickly dissolved in a 1 p.c. solution of nitrous acid. Moreover, Veley observed that nitric acid is partially converted into nitrous acid by gaseous hydrogen in the presence of the nitrates of Cu and Pb.

[43] When nitric acid acts on many organic substances it often happens that not only is hydrogen removed, but also oxygen is combined; thus, for example, nitric acid converts toluene, C_7H_8, into benzoic acid, $C_7H_6O_2$. In certain cases, also, a portion of the carbon contained in an organic substance burns at the expense of the oxygen of the nitric acid. So, for instance, phthalic acid, $C_8H_6O_4$, is obtained from naphthalene, $_{10}H_8$. Thus the action of nitric acid on the hydrocarbons is often most complex; not only does nitrification take place, but also separation of carbon, displacement of hydrogen, and combination of oxygen. There are few organic substances which can withstand the action of nitric acid, and it causes fundamental changes in a number of them. It leaves a yellow stain on the skin, and in a large quantity causes a wound and entirely eats away the membranes of the body. The membranes of plants are eaten into with the greatest ease by strong nitric acid in just the same manner. One of the most durable blue vegetable dyes employed in dyeing tissues is *indigo*; yet it is easily *converted into a yellow substance* by the action of nitric acid, and small traces of free nitric acid may be recognised by this means.

[44] According to certain investigations, if a brown liquid is formed from the melted crystals by beating above -9°, then they no longer solidify at -10°, probably because a certain amount of N_2O_3 (and oxygen) is formed, and this substance remains liquid at -30°, or it may be that the passage from $2NO_2$ into N_2O_4 is not so easily accomplished as the passage from N_2O_4 into $2NO_2$.

Liquid nitrogen peroxide (that is, a mixture of NO_2 and N_2O_4) is employed in admixture with hydrocarbons as an explosive.

[45] Because if x equal the amount by weight of N_2O_4, its volume will $=$ $x/46$, and the amount of NO_2 will $= 100 - x$, and consequently its volume will $= (100 - x)/23$. But the mixture, having a density 38, will weigh 100;

consequently its volume will = 100/38. Hence $x/46$ + $(100 - x)/23$ = 100/38, or $x = 79 \cdot 0$.

[46] The phenomena and laws of dissociation, which we shall consider only in particular instances, are discussed in detail in works on theoretical chemistry. Nevertheless, in respect to nitrogen peroxide, as an historically important example of dissociation in a homogeneous gaseous medium, we will cite the results of the careful investigations (1885–1880) of E. and L. Natanson, who determined the densities under various conditions of temperature and pressure. The degree of dissociation, expressed as above (it may also he expressed otherwise—for example, by the ratio of the quantity of substance decomposed to that unaltered), proves to increase at all temperatures as the pressure diminishes, which would he expected for a homogeneous gaseous medium, as a decreasing pressure aids the formation of the lightest product of dissociation (that having the least density or largest volume). Thus, in the Natansons' experiments the degree of dissociation at 0° increases from 10 p.c. to 30 p.c., with a decrease of pressure of from 251 to 38 mm.; at 49°·7 it increases from 49 p.c. to 93 p.c., with a fall of pressure of from 498 to 27 mm., and at 100° it increases from 89·2 p.c. to 99·7 p.c., with a fall of pressure of from 732·5 to 11·7 mm. At 130° and 150° the decomposition is complete—that is, only NO_2 remains at the low pressures (less than the atmospheric) at which the Natansons made their determinations; but it is probable that at higher pressures (of several atmospheres) molecules of N_2O_4 would still be formed, and it would be exceedingly interesting to trace the phenomena under the conditions of both very considerable pressures and of relatively large volumes.

[47] Liquid nitrogen peroxide is said by Geuther to boil at 22°–26°, and to have a sp. gr. at 0° = 1·494 and at 15° = 1·474. It is evident that, in the liquid as in the gaseous state, the variation of density with the temperature depends, not only on physical, but also on chemical changes, as the amount of N_2O_4 decreases and the amount of NO_2 increases with the temperature, and they (as polymeric substances) should have different densities, as we find, for instance, in the hydrocarbons C_5H_{10} and $C_{10}H_{20}$.

It may not be superfluous to mention here that the measurement of the specific heat of a mixture of the vapours of N_2O_4 and NO_2 enabled Berthelot to determine that the transformation of $2NO_2$ into N_2O_4 is accompanied by the evolution of about 13,000 units of heat, and as the reaction proceeds with equal facility in either direction, it will be exothermal in the one direction and endothermal in the other; and this clearly demonstrates the possibility of reactions taking place in either direction, although, as a rule, reactions evolving heat proceed with greater ease.

[48] Nitric acid of sp. gr. 1·51 in dissolving nitrogen peroxide becomes brown, whilst nitric acid of sp. gr. 1·32 is coloured greenish blue, and acid of sp. gr. below 1·15 remains colourless after absorbing nitrogen peroxide (Note 33).

[49] Nitrogen peroxide as a mixed substance has no corresponding independent salts, but Sabatier and Senderens (1892) showed that under certain conditions NO_2 combines directly with some metals—for instance, copper and cobalt—forming Cu_2NO_2 and $CoNO_2$ as dark brown powders, which do not, however, exhibit the reactions of salts. Thus by passing gaseous nitrogen dioxide over freshly reduced (from the oxides by heating with hydrogen) copper at 25°–30°, Cu_2NO_2 is directly formed. With water it partly gives off NO_2 and partly forms nitrite of copper, leaving metallic copper and its suboxide. The nature of these compounds has not yet been sufficiently investigated.

[50] Ammonium nitrite may be easily obtained in solution by a similar method of double decomposition (for instance, of the barium salt with ammonium sulphate) to the other salts of nitrous acid, but it decomposes with great ease when evaporated, with evolution of gaseous nitrogen, as already mentioned (Chapter V.) If the solution, however, be evaporated at the ordinary temperature under the receiver of an air-pump, a solid saline mass is obtained, which is easily decomposed when heated. The dry salt even decomposes with an explosion when struck, or when heated to about 70°—$NH_4NO_2 = 2H_2O + N_2$. It is also formed by the action of aqueous ammonia on a mixture of nitric oxide and oxygen, or by the action of ozone on ammonia, and in many other instances. Zörensen (1894) prepared NH_4NO_2 by the action of a mixture of N_2O_3 and other oxides of nitrogen on lumps of ammonium carbonate, extracting the nitrite of ammonium formed with absolute alcohol, and precipitating it from this solution by ether. This salt is crystalline, dissolves in water with absorption of heat, and attracts moisture from the air. The solid salt and its concentrated solutions decompose with an explosion when heated to 50°–80°, especially in the presence of traces of foreign acids. Decomposition also proceeds at the ordinary temperature, but more slowly; and in order to preserve the salt it should be covered with a layer of pure dry ether.

[51] Silver nitrite, $AgNO_2$, is obtained as a very slightly soluble substance, as a precipitate, on mixing solutions of silver nitrate, $AgNO_3$, and potassium nitrite, KNO_2. It is soluble in a large volume of water, and this is taken advantage of to free it from silver oxide, which is also present in the precipitate, owing to the fact that potassium nitrite always contains a certain amount of oxide, which with water gives the hydroxide, forming oxide of silver with silver nitrate. The solution of silver nitrite gives, by double decomposition with metallic chlorides (for instance, barium

chloride), insoluble silver chloride and the nitrite of the metal taken (in this case, barium nitrite, $Ba(NO_2)_2$).

[51 bis] Leroy (1889) obtained KNO_2 by mixing powdered KNO_3 with BaS, igniting the mixture in a crucible and washing the fused salts; $BaSO_4$ is then left as an insoluble residue, and KNO_2 passes into solution: $4KNO_3 + BaS = 4KNO_2 + BaSO_4$.

[52] Probably potassium nitrite, KNO_2, when strongly heated, especially with metallic oxides, evolves N and O, and gives potassium oxide, K_2O, because nitre is liable to such a decomposition; but it has, as yet, been but little investigated.

[53] There are many researches which lead to the conclusion that the reaction $N_2O_3 = NO_2 - NO$ is reversible, *i.e.* resembles the conversion of N_2O_4 into NO_2. The brown colour of the fumes of N_2O_3 is due to the formation of NO_2.

If nitrogen peroxide be cooled to -20°, and half its weight of water be added to it drop by drop, then the peroxide is decomposed, as we have already said, into nitrous and nitric acids; the former does not then remain as a hydrate, but straightway passes into the anhydride, and, hence, if the resultant liquid be slightly warmed vapours of nitrous anhydride, N_2O_3, are evolved, and condense into a blue liquid, as Fritzsche showed. This method of preparing nitrous anhydride apparently gives the purest product, but it easily dissociates, forming NO and NO_2 (and therefore also nitric acid in the presence of water).

[54] According to Thorpe, N_2O_3 boils at +18°. According to Geuther, at +3°·5, and its sp. gr. at 0° = 1·449.

[55] In its oxidising action nitrous anhydride gives nitric oxide, $N_2O_3 = 2NO + O$. Thus its analogy to ozone becomes still more marked, because in ozone it is only one-third of the oxygen that acts in oxidising; from O_3 there is obtained O, which acts as an oxidiser, and common oxygen O_2. In a physical aspect the relation between N_2O_3 and O_3 is revealed in the fact that both substances are of a blue colour when in the liquid state.

[56] This reaction is taken advantage of for converting the amides, NH_2R (where R is an element or a complex group) into hydroxides, RHO. In this case $NH_2R + NHO_2$ forms $2N + H_2O + RHO$; NH_2, is replaced by HO, the radicle of ammonia by the radicle of water. This reaction is employed for transforming many nitrogenous organic substances having the properties of amides into their corresponding hydroxides. Thus aniline, $C_6H_5 \cdot NH_2$, which is obtained from nitrobenzene, $C_6H_5 \cdot NO_2$ (Note 37), is converted by nitrous anhydride into phenol, $C_6H_5 \cdot OH$, which occurs in the creosote extracted from coal tar. Thus the H of the benzene is successively

replaced by NO_2, NH_2, and HO; a method which is suitable for other cases also.

[57] The action of a solution of potassium permanganate, $KMnO_4$, on nitrous acid in the presence of sulphuric acid is determined by the fact that the higher oxide of manganese, Mn_2O_7, contained in the permanganate is converted into the lower oxide, MnO, which as a base forms manganese sulphate, $MnSO_4$, and the oxygen serves for the oxidation of the N_2O_3 into N_2O_5, or its hydrate. As the solution of the permanganate is of a red colour, whilst that of manganese sulphate is almost colourless, this reaction is clearly seen, and may be employed for the detection and determination of nitrous acid and its salts.

[58] The absolute boiling point = -93° (*see* Chapter II., Note 29).

[59] Kammerer proposed preparing nitric oxide, NO, by pouring a solution of sodium nitrate over copper shavings, and adding sulphuric acid drop by drop. The oxidation of ferrous salts by nitric acid also gives NO. One part of strong hydrochloric acid is taken and iron is dissolved in it ($FeCl_2$), and then an equal quantity of hydrochloric acid and nitre is added to the solution. On heating, nitric oxide is evolved. In the presence of an excess of sulphuric acid and mercury the conversion of nitric acid into nitric oxide is complete (that is, the reaction proceeds to the end and the nitric oxide is obtained without other products), and upon this is founded one of the methods for determining nitric acid (in nitrometers of various kinds, described in text-books of analytical chemistry), as the amount of NO can be easily and accurately measured volumetrically. The amount of nitrogen in gun-cotton, for instance, is determined by dissolving it in sulphuric acid. Nitrous acid acts in the same manner. Upon this property Emich (1892) founds his method for preparing pure NO. He pours mercury into a flask, and then covers it with sulphuric acid, in which a certain amount of $NaNO_2$ or other substance corresponding to HNO_2 or HNO_3 has been dissolved. The evolution of NO proceeds at the ordinary temperature, being more rapid as the surface of the mercury is increased (if shaken, the reaction proceeds very rapidly). If the gas be passed over KHO, it is obtained quite pure, because KHO does not act upon NO at the ordinary temperature (if heated, KNO_2 and N_2O or N_2, are formed).

[60] This transformation of the permanent gases nitric oxide and oxygen into liquid nitric acid in the presence of water, and with the evolution of heat, presents a most striking instance of liquefaction produced by the action of chemical forces. They perform with ease the work which physical (cooling) and mechanical (pressure) forces effect with difficulty. In this the motion, which is so distinctively the property of the gaseous molecules, is apparently destroyed. In other cases of chemical action it is apparently

created, arising, no doubt, from latent energy—that is, from the internal motion of the atoms in the molecules.

[61] Nitric oxide is capable of entering into many characteristic combinations; it is absorbed by the solutions of many acids, for instance, tartaric, acetic, phosphoric, sulphuric, and metallic chlorides (for example, $SbCl_5$, $BiCl_3$, &c., with which it forms definite compounds; Besson 1889), and also by the solutions of many salts, especially those formed by suboxide of iron (for instance, ferrous sulphate). In this case a brown compound is formed which is exceedingly unstable, like all the analogous compounds of nitric oxide. The amount of nitric oxide combined in this manner is in atomic proportion with the amount of the substance taken; thus ferrous sulphate, $FeSO_4$, absorbs it in the proportion of NO to $2FeSO_4$. Ammonia is obtained by the action of a caustic alkali on the resultant compound, because the oxygen of the nitric oxide and water are transferred to the ferrous oxide, forming ferric oxide, whilst the nitrogen combines with the hydrogen of the water. According to the investigations of Gay (1885), the compound is formed with the evolution of a large quantity of heat, and is easily dissociated, like a solution of ammonia in water. It is evident that oxidising substances (for example, potassium permanganate, $KMnO_4$, Note 57) are able to convert it into nitric acid. If the presence of a radicle NO_2, composed like nitrogen peroxide, must be recognised in the compounds of nitric acid, then a radicle NO, having the composition of nitric oxide, may be admitted in the compounds of nitrous acid. The compounds in which the radicle NO is recognised are called *nitroso-compounds*. These substances are described in Prof. Bunge's work (Kief, 1868).

[62] A mixture of nitric oxide and hydrogen is inflammable. If a mixture of the two gases be passed over spongy platinum the nitrogen and hydrogen even combine, forming ammonia. A mixture of nitric oxide with many combustible vapours and gases is very inflammable. A very characteristic flame is obtained in burning a mixture of nitric oxide and the vapour of the combustible carbon bisulphide, CS_2. The latter substance is very volatile, so that it is sufficient to pass the nitric oxide through a layer of the carbon bisulphide (for instance, in a Woulfe's bottle) in order that the gas escaping should contain a considerable amount of the vapours of this substance. This mixture continues to burn when ignited, and the flame emits a large quantity of the so-called ultra-violet rays, which are capable of inducing chemical combinations and decompositions, and therefore the flame may be employed in photography in the absence of sufficient daylight (magnesium light and electric light have the same property). There are many gases (for instance, ammonia) which when mixed with nitric oxide explode in a eudiometer.

[63] The oxides of nitrogen naturally do not proceed directly from oxygen and nitrogen by contact alone, because their formation is accompanied by the absorption of a large quantity of heat, for (*see* Note 29) about 21,500 heat units are absorbed when 16 parts of oxygen and 14 parts of nitrogen combine; consequently the decomposition of nitric oxide into oxygen and nitrogen is accompanied by the evolution of this amount of heat; and therefore with nitric oxide, as with all explosive substances and mixtures, the reaction once started is able to proceed by itself. In fact, Berthelot remarked the decomposition of nitric oxide in the explosion of fulminate of mercury. This decomposition does not take place spontaneously; substances even burn with difficulty in nitric oxide, probably because a certain portion of the nitric oxide in decomposing gives oxygen, which combines with another portion of nitric oxide, and forms nitric peroxide, a somewhat more stable compound of nitrogen and oxygen. The further combinations of nitric oxide with oxygen all proceed with the evolution of heat, and take place spontaneously by contact with air alone. It is evident from these examples that the application of thermochemical data is limited.

[64] The instance of the action of a small quantity of NO in inducing a definite chemical reaction between large masses (SO_2 + O + H_2O = H_2SO_4) is very instructive, because the particulars relating to it have been studied, and show that intermediate forms of reaction may be discovered in the so-called contact or catalytic phenomena. The essence of the matter here is that A (= SO_2) reacts upon B (= O and H_2O) in the presence of C, because it gives BC, a substance which forms AB with A, and again liberates C. Consequently C is a medium, a transferring substance, without which the reaction does not proceed. Many similar phenomena may be found in other departments of life. Thus the merchant is an indispensable medium between the producer and the consumer; experiment is a medium between the phenomena of nature and the cognisant faculties, and language, customs, and laws are media which are as necessary for the exchanges of social intercourse as nitric oxide for those between sulphurous anhydride and oxygen and water.

[65] If the sulphurous anhydride be prepared by roasting iron pyrites, FeS_2, then each equivalent of pyrites (equivalent of iron, 56, of sulphur 32, of pyrites 120) requires six equivalents of oxygen (that is 96 parts) for the conversion of its sulphur into sulphuric acid (for forming $2H_2SO_4$ with water), besides 1½ equivalents (24 parts) for converting the iron into oxide, Fe_2O_3; hence the combustion of the pyrites for the formation of sulphuric acid and ferric oxide requires the introduction of an equal weight of oxygen (120 parts of oxygen to 120 parts of pyrites), or five times its weight of air, whilst four parts by weight of nitrogen will remain inactive, and in the

removal of the exhausted air will carry off the remaining nitric oxide. If not all, at least a large portion of the nitric oxide may be collected by passing the escaping air, still containing some oxygen, through substances which absorb oxides of nitrogen. Sulphuric acid itself may be employed for this purpose if it be used in the form of the hydrate H_2SO_4, or containing only a small amount of water, because such sulphuric acid dissolves the oxides of nitrogen. They may be easily expelled from this solution by heating or by dilution with water, as they are only slightly soluble in aqueous sulphuric acid. Besides which, sulphurous anhydride acts on such sulphuric acid, being oxidised at the expense of the nitrous anhydride, and forming nitric oxide from it, which again enters into the cycle of action. For this reason the sulphuric acid which has absorbed the oxides of nitrogen escaping from the chambers in the tower K (*see* fig. 50) is led back into the first chamber, where it comes into contact with sulphurous anhydride, by which means the oxides of nitrogen are reintroduced into the reaction which proceeds in the chambers. This is the use of the towers (Gay-Lussac's and Glover's) which are erected at either end of the chambers.

[65 bis] Other metals, iron, copper, zinc, are corroded by it; glass and china are not acted upon, but they crack from the variations of temperature taking place in the chambers, and besides they are more difficult to join properly than lead; wood, &c., becomes charred.

[66] By this means as much as 2,500,000 kilograms of chamber acid, containing about 60 per cent. of the hydrate H_2SO_4 and about 40 per cent. of water, may be manufactured per year in one plant of 5,000 cubic metres capacity (without stoppages). This process has been brought to such a degree of perfection that as much as 300 parts of the hydrate H_2SO_4 are obtained from 100 parts of sulphur, whilst the theoretical amount is not greater than 306 parts. The acid parts with its excess of water on heating. For this purpose it is heated in lead vessels. However, the acid containing about 75 per cent. of the hydrate (60° Baumé) already begins to act on the lead when heated, and therefore the further removal of water is conducted by evaporating in glass or platinum vessels, as will he described in Chapter XX. The aqueous acid (50° Baumé) obtained in the chambers is termed chamber acid. The acid concentrated to 60° Baumé is more generally employed, and sometimes the hydrate (66° Baumé) termed vitriol acid is also used. In England alone more than 1,000 million kilograms of chamber acid are produced by this method. The formation of sulphuric acid by the action of nitric acid was discovered by Drebbel, and the first lead chamber was erected by Roebuck, in Scotland, in the middle of the last century. The essence of the process was only brought to light at the beginning of this century, when many improvements were introduced into practice.

[67] If the hydrate HNO_3 corresponds to N_2O_4, the hydrate HNO, *hyponitrous acid*, corresponds to N_2O, and in this sense N_2O is *hyponitrous anhydride*. Hyponitrous acid, corresponding with nitrous oxide (as its anhydride), is not known in a pure state, but its salts (Divers) are known. They are prepared by the reduction of nitrous (and consequently of nitric) salts by sodium amalgam. If this amalgam he added to a cold solution of an alkaline nitrite until the evolution of gas ceases, and the excess of alkali saturated with acetic acid, an insoluble yellow precipitate of silver hyponitrite, $NAgO$, will he obtained on adding a solution of silver nitrate. This hyponitrite is insoluble in cold acetic acid, and decomposes when heated, with the evolution of nitrous oxide. If rapidly heated it decomposes with an explosion. It is dissolved unchanged by weak mineral acids, whilst the stronger acids (for example, sulphuric and hydrochloric acids) decompose it, with the evolution of nitrogen, nitric and nitrous acids remaining in solution. Among the other salts of hyponitrous acid, HNO, the salts of lead, copper, and mercury are insoluble in water. Judging by the bond between hyponitrous acid and the other compounds of nitrogen, there is reason for thinking that its formula should he doubled, $N_2H_2O_2$. For instance, Thoune (1893) on gradually oxidising hydroxylamine, $NH_2(OH)$, into nitrous acid, $NO(OH)$ (Note 25), by means of an alkaline solution of $KMnO_4$, first obtained hyponitrous acid, $N_2H_2O_2$, and then a peculiar intermediate acid, $N_2H_2O_3$, which, by further oxidation, gave nitrous acid. On the other hand, Wislicenus (1893) showed that in the action of the sulphuric acid salt of hydroxylamine upon nitrite of sodium, there is formed, besides, nitrous oxide (according to V. Meyer, $NH_3O,H_2SO_4 + NaNO_2 = NaHSO_4 + 2H_2O + N_2O$), a small amount of hyponitrous acid which may be precipitated in the form of the silver salt; and this reaction is most simply expressed by taking the doubled formula of hyponitrous acid, $NH_2(OH) + NO(OH) = H_2O + N_2H_2O_2$. The best argument in favour of the doubled formula is the property possessed by hyponitrous acid of forming acid salts, $HNaN_2O_2$ (Zorn).

According to Thoune, the following are the properties of hyponitrous acid. When liberated from the dry silver salt by the action of dry sulphuretted hydrogen, hyponitrous acid is unstable, and easily explodes even at low temperatures. But when dissolved in water (having been formed by the action of hydrochloric acid upon the silver salt), it is stable even when boiled with dilute acids and alkalis. The solution is colourless and has a strongly acid reaction. In the course of time, however, the aqueous solution also decomposes into nitrous oxide and water. The complete oxidation by permanganate of potash proceeds according to the following equation: $5H_2N_2O_2 + 8KMnO_4 + 12H_2SO_4 = 10HNO_3 + 4K_2SO_4 + 8MnSO_4 + 12H_2O$. In an alkaline solution, $KMnO_4$ only oxidises hyponitrous acid into nitrous and not into nitric acid. Nitrous acid has a decomposing action upon hyponitrous acid, and if the aqueous solutions of the two acids be mixed together they immediately give off oxides of nitrogen. Hyponitrous acid does not liberate CO_2 from its salts, but on the other hand it is not displaced by CO_2.

[68] It is remarkable that electro-deposited copper powder gives nitrous oxide with a 10 p.c. solution of nitric acid, whilst ordinary copper gives nitric oxide. It is here evident that the physical and mechanical structure of the substance affects the course of the reaction—that is to say, it is a case of contact-action.

[69] This decomposition is accompanied by the evolution of about 25,000 calories per molecular quantity, NH_4NO_3, and therefore takes place with ease, and sometimes with an explosion.

[70] In order to remove any nitric oxide that might be present, the gas obtained is passed through a solution of ferrous sulphate. As nitrous oxide is very soluble in cold water (at 0°, 100 volumes of water dissolve 130 volumes of N_2O; at 20°, 67 volumes), it must be collected over warm water. The nitrous oxide is much more soluble than nitric oxide, which is in agreement with the fact that nitrous oxide is much more easily liquefied than nitric oxide. Villard obtained a crystallohydrate, $N_2O,6H_2O$, which was tolerably stable at 0°.

[71] Faraday obtained liquid nitrous oxide by the same method as liquid ammonia, by beating dry ammonium nitrate in a closed bent tube, one arm of which was immersed in a freezing mixture. In this case two layers of liquid are obtained at the cooled end, a lower layer of water and an upper layer of nitrous oxide. This experiment should be conducted with great care, as the pressure of the nitrous oxide in a liquid state is considerable, namely (according to Regnault), at +10° = 45 atmospheres, at 0° = 36 atmospheres, at -10° = 29 atmospheres, and at -20° = 23 atmospheres. It boils at -92°, and the pressure is then therefore = 1 atmosphere (*see* Chapter II., Note 27).

[72] Liquid nitrous oxide, in vaporising at the same pressure as liquid carbonic anhydride, gives rise to almost equal or even slightly lower temperatures. Thus at a pressure of 25 mm. carbonic anhydride gives a temperature as low as -115°, and nitrous oxide of -125° (Dewar). The similarity of these properties and even of the absolute boiling point (CO_2 + 32°, N_2O +36°) is all the more remarkable because these gases have the same molecular weight = 44 (Chapter VII.)

[73] A very characteristic experiment of simultaneous combustion and intense cold may be performed by means of liquid nitrous oxide; if liquid nitrous oxide be poured into a test tube containing some mercury the

mercury will solidify, and if a piece of red-hot charcoal be thrown upon the surface of the nitrous oxide it will continue to burn very brilliantly, giving rise to a high temperature.

[74] In the following chapter we shall consider the volumetric composition of the oxides of nitrogen. It explains the difference between nitric and nitrous oxide. Nitrous oxide is formed with a diminution of volumes (contraction), nitric oxide without contraction, its volume being equal to the sum of the volumes of the nitrogen and oxygen of which it is composed. By oxidation, if it could be directly accomplished, two volumes of nitrous oxide and one volume of oxygen would not give three but four volumes of nitric oxide. These facts must be taken into consideration in comparing the calorific equivalents of formation, the capacity for supporting combustion, and other properties of nitrous and nitric oxides, N_2O and NO.

[299]

CHAPTER VII

MOLECULES AND ATOMS. THE LAWS OF GAY-LUSSAC AND AVOGADRO-GERHARDT

Hydrogen combines with oxygen in the proportion of two volumes to one. The composition by volume of nitrous oxide is exactly similar—it is composed of two volumes of nitrogen and one volume of oxygen. By decomposing ammonia by the action of an electric spark it is easy to prove that it contains one volume of nitrogen to three volumes of hydrogen. So, similarly, it is found, whenever a compound is decomposed and the volumes of the gases proceeding from it are measured, that the volumes of the gases or vapours entering into combination are in a very simple proportion to one another. With water, nitrous oxide, &c., this may be proved by direct observation; but in the majority of cases, and especially with substances which, although volatile—that is, capable of passing into a gaseous (or vaporous) state—are liquid at the ordinary temperature, such a direct method of observation presents many difficulties. But, then, if the densities of the vapours and gases be known, the same simplicity in their ratio is shown by calculation. The volume of a substance is proportional to its weight, and inversely proportional to its density, and therefore by dividing the amount by weight of each substance entering into the composition of a compound by its density in the gaseous or vaporous state we shall obtain factors which will be in the same proportion as the volumes of the substances entering into the composition of the compound.[1] So, for example,[300] water contains eight parts by weight of oxygen to one part by weight of hydrogen, and their densities are 16 and 1, consequently their volumes (or the above-mentioned factors) are 1 and ½, and therefore it is seen without direct experiment that water contains two volumes of hydrogen for every one volume of oxygen. So also, knowing that nitric oxide contains fourteen parts of nitrogen and sixteen parts of oxygen, and knowing that the specific gravities of these last two gases are fourteen and sixteen, we find that the volumes in which nitrogen and oxygen combine for the formation of nitric oxide are in the proportion of 1 : 1. We will cite another example. In the last chapter we saw that the density of NO_2 only becomes constant and equal to twenty-three (referred to hydrogen) above 135°, and as a matterof fact a method of direct observation of the volumetric composition of this substance would be very difficult at so high a temperature. But it may be easily calculated. NO_2, as is seen from its formula and analysis, contains thirty-two parts by weight of oxygen to fourteen parts by weight of nitrogen, forming forty-six parts by weight of NO_2, and knowing the densities of these gases we find that one volume of nitrogen with two volumes of oxygen gives two volumes of nitrogen peroxide. Therefore, knowing the amounts by weight of the substances participating in a reaction or forming a given substance, and knowing the density of the gas or vapour,[2] the volumetric relations of the substances acting in a[301] reaction or entering into the composition of a compound, may be also determined.

[302]
[303]
[304]

Such an investigation (either direct, or by calculation from the densities and composition) of every chemical reaction, resulting in the formation of definite chemical compounds, shows that the volumes of the reacting substances in a gaseous or vaporous state are either equal or are in simple multiple proportion.[3] This forms the *first law* of those discovered by *Gay-Lussac*. It may be formulated as follows: *The amounts of substances entering into chemical reaction occupy under similar physical conditions, in a gaseous or vaporous state, equal or simple multiple volumes.* This law refers not only to elements, but also to compounds entering into mutual chemical combination; thus, for example, one volume of ammonia gas combines with one volume of hydrogen chloride. For in the formation of sal-ammoniac, NH_4Cl, there enter into reaction 17 parts by weight of ammonia, NH_3, which is $8 \cdot 5$ times denser than hydrogen, and $36 \cdot 5$ parts by weight of hydrogen chloride, whose vapour density is $18 \cdot 25$ times that of hydrogen, as has been proved by direct experiment. By dividing the weights by the respective densities we find that the volume of ammonia, NH_3, is equal to two, and so also the volume of hydrogen chloride. Hence the volumes of the compounds which here combine together are equal to each other. Taking into consideration that the law of Gay-Lussac holds good, not only for elements, but also for compounds, it should be expressed as follows: *Substances interact with one another in commensurable volumes of their vapours.*[4]

[305]

The law of combining volumes and the law of multiple proportion were discovered independently of each other—the one in France by Gay-Lussac, the other in England by Dalton—almost simultaneously. In the language of the atomic hypothesis it may be said that atomic quantities of elements occupy equal or multiple volumes.

The first law of Gay-Lussac expresses the relation between the volumes of the component parts of a compound. Let us now consider the relation existing between the volumes of the component parts and of the compounds which proceed from them. This may sometimes be determined by direct observation. Thus the volume occupied by water, formed by two volumes of hydrogen and one volume of oxygen, may be determined by the aid of the apparatus shown in fig. 56. The long glass tube is closed at the top and open at the bottom, which is immersed in a cylinder containing mercury. The closed end is furnished with wires like a eudiometer. The tube is filled with mercury, and then a certain volume of detonating gas is introduced. This gas is obtained from the decomposition of water, and therefore in every three volumes contains two volumes of hydrogen and one volume of oxygen. The tube is surrounded by a second and wider glass tube, and the vapour of a substance boiling above 100°—that is, whose boiling point is higher than that of water—is passed through the annular space between them. Amyl alcohol, whose boiling point is 132°, may be taken for this purpose. The amyl alcohol is boiled in the vessel to the right hand and its vapour passed between the walls of the two tubes. In the case of amyl alcohol the outer glass tube should be connected with a condenser to prevent the escape into the air of the unpleasant-smelling vapour. The detonating gas is thus heated up to a temperature of 132°. When its volume becomes constant it is measured, the height of the column of mercury in the tube above the level of the mercury in the cylinder being noted. Let this volume equal v, it will therefore contain $\frac{1}{3} v$ of oxygen and $\frac{2}{3} v$ of hydrogen. The current of vapour is then stopped, and the gas exploded; water is formed, which condenses into a liquid. The volume occupied by the vapour of the water formed has now to be determined. For this purpose the vapour of the amyl alcohol is again passed between the tubes, and thus the whole of the water formed is converted into vapour at the same temperature as that at which the detonating gas was measured; and the cylinder of mercury being raised until the column of mercury in the tube stands at the same height above the surface of the mercury in the cylinder as it did before the explosion, it is found that the volume of the water formed is equal to $\frac{2}{3} v$—that is, it is equal to the volume of the hydrogen contained[306]

[307] in it. Consequently the volumetric composition of water is expressed in the following terms: Two volumes of hydrogen combine with one volume of oxygen to form two volumes of aqueous vapour. For substances which are gaseous at the ordinary temperature, this direct method of observation is sometimes very easily conducted; for instance, with ammonia, nitric and nitrous oxides. Thus to determine the composition by volume of nitrous oxide, the above-described apparatus may be employed. Nitrous oxide is introduced into the tube, and after measuring its volume electric sparks are passed through the gas; it is then found that two volumes of nitrous oxide have given three volumes of gases—namely, two volumes of nitrogen and one volume of oxygen. Consequently the composition of

nitrous oxide is similar to that of water; two volumes of nitrogen and one volume of oxygen give two volumes of nitrous oxide. By decomposing ammonia it is found to be composed in such a manner that two volumes give one volume of nitrogen and three volumes of hydrogen; also two volumes of nitric oxide are formed by the union of one volume of oxygen with one volume of nitrogen. The same relations may be proved by calculation from the vapour densities, as was described above.

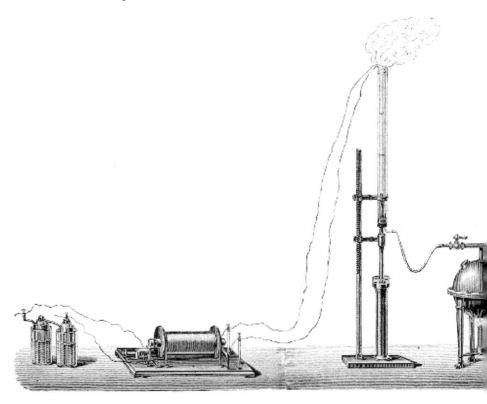

FIG. 56.—Apparatus for demonstrating the volume occupied by the steam formed from the explosion of detonating gas.

Comparisons of various results made by the aid of direct observations or calculation, an example of which has just been cited, led Gay-Lussac to the conclusion that *the volume of a compound in a gaseous or vaporous state is always in simple multiple proportion to the volume of each of the component parts of which it is formed* (and consequently to the sum of the volumes of the elements of which it is formed). This is the *second law of Gay-Lussac*; it extends the simplicity of the volumetric relations to compounds, and is of the same nature as that presented by the elements entering into mutual combination. Hence not only the substances forming a given compound, but also the substances formed, exhibit a simple relation of volume when measured as vapour or gas.[5]

When a compound is formed from two or more components, there may or may not be a contraction; the volume of the reacting substances is in this case either equal to or greater than the volume of the resultant[308] compound. The reverse is naturally observed in the case of decompositions, when from one substance there are produced several of simpler nature. Therefore in the future we shall term *combination* a reaction in which a contraction is observed—that is, a diminution in the volume of the component bodies in a state of vapour or gas; and we shall term *decomposition* a reaction in which an expansion is produced; while those reactions in which the volumes in a gaseous or vaporous state remain constant (the volumes being naturally compared at the same temperature and pressure) we shall term reactions of *substitution* or of double decomposition. Thus the transition of oxygen into ozone is a reaction of combination, the formation of nitrous oxide from oxygen and nitrogen will also be a combination, the formation of nitric oxide from the same will be a reaction of substitution, the action of oxygen on nitric oxide a combination, and so on.

The degree of contraction produced in the formation of chemical compounds not unfrequently leads to the possibility of distinguishing the degree of change which takes place in the chemical character of the components when combined. In those cases in which a contraction occurs, the properties of the resultant compound are very different from the properties of the substances of which it is composed. Thus ammonia bears no resemblance in its physical or chemical properties to the elements from which it is derived; a contraction takes place in a state of vapour, indicating a proximation of the elements—the distance between the atoms is diminished, and from gaseous substances there is formed a liquid substance, or at any rate one which is easily liquefied. For this reason nitrous oxide formed by the condensation of two permanent gases is a substance which is somewhat easily converted into a liquid; again, nitric acid, which is formed from elements which are permanent gases, is a liquid, whilst, on the contrary, nitric oxide, which is formed without contraction and is decomposed without expansion, remains a gas which is as difficult to liquefy as nitrogen and oxygen. In order to obtain a still more complete idea of the dependence of the properties of a compound on the properties of the component substances, it is further necessary to know the quantity of heat which is developed in the formation of the compound. If this quantity be large—as, for example, in the formation of water—then the amount of energy in the resultant compound will be considerably less than the energy of the elements entering into its composition; whilst, on the contrary, if the amount of heat evolved in the formation of a compound be small, or if there even be an absorption of heat, as in the formation of nitrous oxide, then the energy of the elements is[309] not destroyed, or is only altered to a slight extent; hence, notwithstanding the contraction (compression) involved in its formation, nitrous oxide supports combustion.

The preceding laws were deduced from purely experimental and empirical data and as such evoke further consequences, as the law of multiple proportions gave rise to the atomic theory and the law of equivalents (Chapter IV.) In view of the atomic conception of the constitution of substances, the question naturally arises as to what, then, are the relative volumes proper to those physically indivisible molecules which chemically react on each other and consist of the atoms of elements. The simplest possible hypothesis in this respect would be that the volumes of the molecules of substances are equal; or, what is the same thing, to suppose that equal volumes of vapours and gases contain an equal number of molecules. This proposition was first enunciated by the Italian savant *Avogadro* in 1810. It was also admitted by the French physico-mathematician *Ampère* (1815) for the sake of simplifying all kinds of physico-mathematical conceptions respecting gases. But Avogadro and Ampère's propositions were not generally received in science until Gerhardt in the forties had applied them to the generalisation of chemical reactions, and had demonstrated, by aid of a series of phenomena, that the reactions of substances actually take place with the greatest simplicity, and more especially that such reactions take place between those quantities of substances which occupy equal volumes, and until he had stated the hypothesis in an exact manner and deduced the consequences that necessarily follow from it. Following Gerhardt, Clausius, in the fifties, placed this hypothesis of the equality of the number of molecules in equal volumes of gases and vapours on the basis of the kinetic theory of gases. At the present day the hypothesis of Avogadro and Gerhardt lies at the basis of contemporary physical, mechanical, and chemical conceptions; the consequences arising from it have often been subject to doubt, but in the end have been verified by the most diverse methods; and now, when all efforts to refute those consequences have proved fruitless, the hypothesis must be considered as verified,[6] and the *law of Avogadro-Gerhardt* must be spoken of as fundamental, and as of great importance for the comprehension of the phenomena of nature. The[310] law may now be formulated from two points of view. In the first place, from a physical aspect: *equal volumes of gases* (or vapours) at equal temperatures and pressures *contain the same number of molecules*—or of particles of matter which are neither mechanically nor physically divisible—previous to chemical change. In the second place, from a chemical aspect, the same law may be expressed thus: *the quantities of substances entering into chemical reactions occupy, in a state of vapour, equal volumes.* For our purpose the chemical aspect is the most important, and therefore, before developing the law and its consequences, we will consider the chemical phenomena from which the law is deduced or which it serves to explain.

When two isolated substances interact with each other directly and easily—as, for instance, an alkali and an acid—then it is found that the reaction is accomplished between quantities which in a gaseous state occupy equal volumes. Thus ammonia, NH_3, reacts directly with hydrochloric acid, HCl, forming sal-ammoniac, NH_4Cl, and in this case the 17 parts by weight of ammonia occupy the same volume as the 36·5 parts by weight of hydrochloric acid.[7] Ethylene, C_2H_4, combines with chlorine, Cl_2, in only one proportion, forming ethylene dichloride, $C_2H_4Cl_2$, and this combination proceeds directly and with great facility, the reacting quantities occupying equal volumes. Chlorine reacts with hydrogen in only one proportion, forming hydrochloric acid, HCl, and in this case equal volumes interact with each other. If an equality of volumes is observed in cases of combination, it should be even more frequently encountered in cases of decomposition, taking place in substances which split up into two others. Indeed, acetic acid breaks up into marsh gas, CH_4, and carbonic anhydride, CO_2, and in the proportions in which they are formed from acetic acid they occupy equal volumes. Also from phthalic acid, $C_8H_6O_4$, there may be obtained benzoic acid, $C_7H_6O_2$, and carbonic anhydride, CO_2, and as all the elements of phthalic acid enter into the composition of these substances, it follows that, although[311] they cannot re-form it by their direct action on each other (the reaction is not reversible), still they form the direct products of its decomposition, and they occupy equal volumes. But benzoic acid, $C_7H_6O_2$, is itself composed of benzene, C_6H_6, and carbonic anhydride, CO_2, which also occupy equal volumes.[8] There is an immense number of similar examples among those organic substances to whose study Gerhardt consecrated his whole life and work, and he did not allow such facts as these to escape his attention. Still more frequently in the phenomena of substitution, when two substances react on one another, and two are produced without a change of volume, it is found that the two substances acting on each other occupy equal volumes as well as each of the two resultant substances. Thus, in general, reactions of substitution take place between volatile acids, HX, and volatile alcohols, R(OH), with the formation of ethereal salts, RX, and water, H(OH), and the volume of the vapour of the reacting quantities, HX, R(OH), and RX, is the same as that of water H(OH), whose weight, corresponding with the formula, 18, occupies 2 volumes, if 1 part by weight of hydrogen occupy 1 volume and the density of aqueous vapour referred to hydrogen is 9. Such general examples, of which there are many,[9] show that the reaction of equal volumes forms a chemical phenomenon of frequent occurrence, indicating the necessity for acknowledging the law of Avogadro-Gerhardt.

But the question arises, What is the relation of volumes if the reaction of two substances takes place in more than one proportion, according to the law of multiple proportions? A definite answer can only be given in cases which have been very thoroughly studied. Thus chlorine, in acting on marsh gas, CH_4, forms four compounds, CH_3Cl, CH_2Cl_2, $CHCl_3$, and CCl_4, and it may be established by direct experiment that the substance CH_3Cl (methylic chloride) precedes the remainder, and that the latter proceed from it by the further action of chlorine. And this substance, CH_3Cl, is formed by the reaction of equal volumes of[312] marsh gas, CH_4, and chlorine, Cl_2, according to the equation $CH_4 + Cl_2 = CH_3Cl + HCl$. A great number of similar cases are met with amongst organic—that is, carbon—compounds. Gerhardt was led to the discovery of his law by investigating many such reactions, and by observing that in them the reaction of equal volumes precedes all others.

But if nitrogen or hydrogen give several compounds with oxygen, the question proposed above cannot be answered with complete clearness, because the successive formations of the different combinations cannot be so strictly defined. It may be supposed, but neither definitely affirmed nor experimentally confirmed, that nitrogen and oxygen first give nitric oxide, NO, and only subsequently the brown vapours N_2O_3 and NO_2. Such a sequence in the combination of nitrogen with oxygen can only be supposed on the basis of the fact that NO forms N_2O_3 and NO_2 directly with oxygen. If it be admitted that NO (and not N_2O or NO_2) be first formed, then this instance would also confirm the law of Avogadro-Gerhardt, because nitric oxide contains equal volumes of nitrogen and oxygen. So, also, it may be admitted that, in the combination of hydrogen with oxygen, hydrogen peroxide is first formed (equal volumes of hydrogen and oxygen), which is decomposed by the heat evolved into water and oxygen. This explains the presence of traces of hydrogen peroxide (Chapter IV.) in almost all cases of the combustion or oxidation of hydrogenous substances; for it cannot be supposed that water is first formed and then the peroxide of hydrogen, because up to now such a reaction has not been observed, whilst the formation of H_2O from H_2O_2 is very easily reproduced.[10]

Thus a whole series of phenomena show that the chemical reaction of substances actually takes place, as a rule, between equal volumes, but this does not preclude the possibility of the frequent reaction of unequal[313] volumes, although, in this case, it is often possible to discover a preceding reaction between equal volumes.[11]

The law of Avogadro-Gerhardt may also be easily expressed in an algebraical form. If the weight of a molecule, or of that quantity of a substance which enters into chemical reaction and occupies in a state[314] of vapour, according to the law, a volume equal to that occupied by the molecules of other bodies, be indicated by the letters M_1, M_2 ... or, in general, M, and if the letters D_1, D_2, ... or, in general, D, stand for the density or weight of a given volume of the gases or vapours of the corresponding substances under certain definite conditions of temperature and pressure, then the law requires that

$$M_1 \boxed{D_1} = M_2 \boxed{D_2} \cdots = M \boxed{D} = C$$

where C is a certain constant. This expression shows directly that the volumes corresponding with the weights M_1, M_2 ... M, are equal to a certain constant, because the volume is proportional to the weight and inversely proportional to the density. The magnitude of C is naturally conditioned by and dependent on the units taken for the expression of the weights of the molecules and the densities. The weight of a molecule (equal to the sum of the atomic weights of the elements forming it) is usually expressed by taking the weight of an atom of hydrogen as unity, and hydrogen is now also chosen as the unit for the expression of the densities of gases and vapours; it is therefore only necessary to find the magnitude of the constant for any one compound, as it will be the same for all others. Let us take water. Its reacting mass is expressed (conditionally and relatively) by the formula or molecule H_2O, for which M = 18, if H = 1, as we already know from the composition of water. Its vapour density, or D, compared to hydrogen = 9, and consequently for water C = 2, and therefore and in general for the molecules of all substances M $\boxed{D}$ = 2.

Consequently the weight of a molecule is equal to twice its vapour density expressed in relation to hydrogen, and conversely *the density of a gas is equal to half the molecular weight referred to hydrogen.*

The truth of this may be seen from a very large number of observed vapour densities by comparing them with the results obtained by calculation. As an illustration, we may point out that for ammonia, NH_3, the weight of the molecule or quantity of the reacting substance, as well as the composition and weight corresponding with the formula, is expressed by the figures 14 + 3 = 17. Consequently M = 17. Hence, according to the law, D = 8·5. And this result is also obtained by experiment. The density, according to both formula and experiment, of nitrous oxide, N_2O, is 22, of nitric acid 15, and of nitric peroxide 23. In the case of nitrous anhydride, N_2O_3, as a substance which dissociates into NO + NO_2, the density should vary between 38 (so long as the[315] N_2O_3 remains unchanged) and 19 (when NO + NO_2 is obtained). There are no figures of constant density for

H₂O₂, NHO₃, N₂O₄, and many similar compounds which are either wholly or partially decomposed in passing into vapour. Salts and similar substances either have no vapour density because they do not pass into vapour (for instance, potassium nitrate, KNO_3) without decomposition, or, if they pass into vapour without decomposing, their vapour density is observed with difficulty only at very high temperatures. The practical determination of the vapour density at these high temperatures (for example, for sodium chloride, ferrous chloride, stannous chloride, &c.) requires special methods which have been worked out by Sainte-Claire Deville, Crafts, Nilson and Pettersson, Meyer, Scott, and others. Having overcome the difficulties of experiment, it is found that the law of Avogadro-Gerhardt holds good for such salts as potassium iodide, beryllium chloride, aluminium chloride, ferrous chloride, &c.—that is, the density obtained by experiment proves to be equal to half the molecular weight—naturally within the limits of experimental error or of possible deviation from the law.

Gerhardt deduced his law from a great number of examples of volatile carbon compounds. We shall become acquainted with certain of them in the following chapters; their entire study, from the complexity of the subject, and from long-established custom, forms the subject of a special branch of chemistry termed 'organic' chemistry. With all these substances the observed and calculated densities are very similar.

When the consequences of a law are verified by a great number of observations, it should be considered as confirmed by experiment. But this does not exclude the possibility of *apparent* deviations. They may evidently be of two kinds: the fraction $\frac{M}{D}$ may be found to be either greater or less than 2—that is, the calculated density may be either greater or less than the observed density. When the difference between the results of experiment and calculation falls within the possible errors of experiment (for example, equal to hundredths of the density), or within a possible error owing to the laws of gases having an only approximate application (as is seen from the deviations, for instance, from the law of Boyle and Mariotte), then the fraction $\frac{M}{D}$ proves but slightly different from 2 (between 1·9 and 2·2), and such cases as these may be classed among those which ought to be expected from the nature of the subject. It is a different matter if the quotient of $\frac{M}{D}$ be several times, and in general a multiple, *greater* or less than 2.[316] The application of the law must then be explained or it must be laid aside, because the laws of nature admit of no exceptions. We will therefore take two such cases, and first one in which the *quotient* $\frac{M}{D}$ *is greater than 2, or the density obtained by experiment is less than is in accordance with the law.*

It must be admitted, as a consequence of the law of Avogadro-Gerhardt, that there is a decomposition in those cases where the volume of the vapour corresponding with the weight of the amount of a substance entering into reaction is greater than the volume of two parts by weight of hydrogen. Suppose the density of the vapour of water to be determined at a temperature above that at which it is decomposed, then, if not all, at any rate a large proportion of the water will be decomposed into hydrogen and oxygen. The density of such a mixture of gases, or of detonating gas, will be less than that of aqueous vapour; it will be equal to 6 (compared with hydrogen), because 1 volume of oxygen weighs 16, and 2 volumes of hydrogen 2; and, consequently, 3 volumes of detonating gas weigh 18 and 1 volume 6, while the density of aqueous vapour = 9. Hence, if the density of aqueous vapour be determined after its decomposition, the quotient M $\boxed{\text{D}}$ would be found to be 3 and not 2. This phenomenon might be considered as a deviation from Gerhardt's law, but this would not be correct, because it may be shown by means of diffusion through porous substances, as described in Chapter II., that water is decomposed at such high temperatures. In the case of water itself there can naturally be no doubt, because its vapour density agrees with the law at all temperatures at which it has been determined.[12] But there are many substances which decompose with great ease directly they are volatilised, and therefore only exist as solids or liquids, and not in a state of vapour. There are, for example, many salts of this kind, besides all definite solutions having a constant boiling point, all the compounds of ammonia for example, all ammonium salts—&c. Their vapour densities, determined by Bineau, Deville, and others, show that they do not agree with Gerhardt's law. Thus the vapour density of sal-ammoniac,[317] NH_4Cl, is nearly 14 (compared with hydrogen), whilst its molecular weight is not less than 53·5, whence the vapour density should be nearly 27, according to the law. The molecule of sal-ammoniac cannot be less than NH_4Cl, because it is formed from the molecules NH_3 and HCl, and contains single atoms of nitrogen and chlorine, and therefore cannot be divided; it further never enters into reactions with the molecules of other substances (for instance, potassium hydroxide, or nitric acid) in quantities of less than 53·5 parts by weight, &c. The calculated density (about 27) is here double the observed density (about 13·4); hence M $\boxed{\text{D}}$ = 4 and not 2. For this reason the vapour density of sal-ammoniac for a long time served as an argument for doubting the truth of the law. But it proved otherwise, after the matter had been fully investigated. The low density depends on the decomposition of sal-ammoniac, on volatilising, into ammonia and hydrogen chloride. The observed density is not that of sal-ammoniac, but of a mixture of NH_3 and HCl, which should be nearly 14, because the density of NH_3 = 8·5 and of HCl = 18·2, and therefore the density of their mixture (in equal volumes) should be about 13·4.[13] The actual decomposition of the vapours of sal-ammoniac was demonstrated by Pebal and Than by the same method as the decomposition of water, by passing the vapour of sal-ammoniac through a porous substance. The experiment demonstrating the decomposition during volatilisation of sal-ammoniac may be made very easily, and is a very instructive point in the history of the law of Avogadro-Gerhardt, because without its aid it would never have been imagined that sal-ammoniac decomposed in volatilising, as this decomposition bears all the signs of simple sublimation; consequently the knowledge of the decomposition itself was forestalled by the law. The whole aim and practical use of the discovery of the laws of nature consists in, and is shown by, the fact that they enable the unknown to be foretold, the unobserved to be foreseen. The arrangement of the experiment is based on the following reasoning.[14] According to the law and to experiment, the density of ammonia, NH_3, is $8\frac{1}{2}$, and of hydrochloric[318] acid, HCl, $18\frac{1}{4}$, if the density of hydrogen $= 1$. Consequently, in a mixture of NH_3 and HCl, the ammonia will penetrate much more rapidly through a porous mass, or a fine orifice, than the heavier hydrochloric acid, just as in a former experiment the hydrogen penetrated more rapidly than the oxygen. Therefore, if the vapour of sal-ammoniac comes into contact with a porous mass, the ammonia will pass through it in greater quantities than the hydrochloric acid, and this excess of ammonia may be detected by means of moist red litmus paper, which should be turned blue. If the vapour of sal-ammoniac were not decomposed, it would pass through the porous mass as a whole, and the colour of the litmus paper would not be altered, because sal-ammoniac is a neutral salt. Thus, by testing with litmus the substances passing through the porous mass, it may be decided whether the sal-ammoniac is decomposed or not when passing into vapour. Sal-ammoniac volatilises at so moderate a temperature that the experiment may be conducted in a glass tube heated by means of a lamp, an asbestos plug being placed near the centre of the tube.[15] The asbestos forms a porous mass, which is unaltered at a high temperature. A piece of dry sal-ammoniac is placed at one side of the asbestos plug, and is heated by a Bunsen burner. The vapours formed are driven by a current of air forced from a gasometer or bag through two tubes containing pieces of moist litmus paper, one blue and one red paper in each. If the sal-ammoniac be heated, then the ammonia appears on the opposite side of the asbestos plug, and the litmus there turns blue. And as an excess of hydrochloric acid remains on the side where the sal-ammoniac is heated, it turns the litmus at that end red. This proves that the sal-ammoniac, when converted into vapour, splits up into ammonia and hydrochloric acid, and at the same time gives an instance of the possibility of correctly conjecturing a fact on the basis of the law of Avogadro-Gerhardt.[15 bis]

So also the fact of a decomposition may be proved in the other instances where $\frac{M}{D}$ proved greater than 2, and hence the apparent deviations appear in reality as an excellent proof of the general application and significance of the law of Avogadro-Gerhardt.

[319]

In those cases where the *quotient* $\frac{M}{D}$ proves to be *less* than 2, or the observed density *greater* than that calculated, by a multiple number of times, the matter is evidently more simple, and the fact observed only indicates that the weight of the molecule is as many times greater as that taken as the quotient obtained is less than 2. So, for instance, in the case of ethylene, whose composition is expressed by CH_2, the density was found by experiment to be 14, and in the case of amylene, whose composition is also CH_2, the density proved to be 35, and consequently the quotient for ethylene = 1, and for amylene = ⅖. If the molecular weight of ethylene be taken, not as 14, as might be imagined from its composition, but as twice as great—namely, as 28—and for amylene as five times greater—that is as 70—then the molecular composition of the first will be C_2H_4, and of the second C_5H_{10}, and for both of them $\frac{M}{D}$ will be equal to 2. This application of the law, which at first sight may appear perfectly arbitrary, is nevertheless strictly correct, because the amount of ethylene which reacts—for example, with sulphuric and other acids—is not equal to 14, but to 28 parts by weight. Thus with H_2SO_4, Br_2, or HI, &c., ethylene combines in a quantity C_2H_4, and amylene in a quantity C_5H_{10}, and not CH_2. On the other hand, ethylene is a gas which liquefies with difficulty (absolute boiling point = $+10°$), whilst amylene is a liquid boiling at $35°$ (absolute boiling point = $+192°$), and by admitting the greater density of the molecules of amylene ($M = 70$) its difference from the lighter molecules of ethylene ($M = 28$) becomes clear. Thus, the smaller quotient $\frac{M}{D}$ is *an indication of polymerisation*, as the larger quotient is of decomposition. The difference between the densities of oxygen and ozone is a case in point.

On turning to the elements, it is found in certain cases, especially with metals—for instance, mercury, zinc, and cadmium—that that weight of the atoms which must be acknowledged in their compounds (of which mention will be afterwards made) appears to be also the molecular weight. Thus, the atomic weight of mercury must be taken as = 200, but the vapour density = 100, and the quotient = 2. Consequently the *molecule of mercury contains one atom*, Hg. It is the same with sodium, cadmium, and zinc. This is the simplest possible molecule, which necessarily is only possible in the case of elements, as the molecule of a compound must contain at least two atoms. However, the molecules of many of the elements prove to be complex—for instance, the weight of an atom of oxygen = 16, and its density = 16, so that its[320] molecule must contain two atoms, O_2, which might already be concluded by comparing its density with that of ozone, whose molecule contains O_3 (Chapter IV.) So also the molecule of hydrogen equals H_2, of chlorine Cl_2, of nitrogen N_2, &c. If chlorine react with hydrogen, the volume remains unaltered after the formation of hydrochloric acid, $H_2 + Cl_2 = HCl + HCl$. It is a case of substitution between the one and the other, and therefore the volumes remain constant. There are elements whose molecules are much more complex—for instance, sulphur, S_6—although, by heating, the density is reduced to a third, and S_2 is formed. Judging from the vapour density of phosphorus (D = 62) the molecule contains four atoms P_4. Hence many elements when polymerised appear in molecules which are more complex than the simplest possible. In carbon, as we shall afterwards find, a very complex molecule must be admitted, as otherwise its non-volatility and other properties cannot be understood. And if compounds are decomposed by a more or less powerful heat, and if polymeric substances are depolymerised (that is, the weight of the molecule diminishes) by a rise of temperature, as N_2O_4 passes into NO_2, or ozone, O_3, into ordinary oxygen, O_2, then we might expect to find the splitting-up of the complex molecules of elements into the simplest molecule containing a single atom only—that is to say, if O_2 be obtained from O_3, then the formation of O might also be looked for. The possibility but not proof of such a proposition is indicated by the vapour of iodine. Its normal density = 127 (Dumas, Deville, and others), which corresponds with the molecule I_2. At temperatures above 800° (up to which the density remains almost constant), this density distinctly decreases, as is seen from the verified results obtained by Victor Meyer, Crafts, and Troost. At the ordinary pressure and 1,000° it is about 100, at 1,250° about 80, at 1,400° about 75, and apparently it strives to reduce itself to one-half—that is, to 63. Under a reduced pressure this splitting-up, or depolymerisation, of iodine vapour actually reaches a density[16] of 66, as Crafts demonstrated by reducing the pressure to 100 mm. and raising the temperature to 1,500°. From this it may be concluded that at high temperatures and low pressures the molecule I_2 gradually passes into the molecule I containing one atom like mercury, and that something similar occurs with other elements at a considerable rise of temperature, which tends to bring about the disunion of compounds and the decomposition of complex molecules.[17]

[321]

Besides these cases of apparent discrepancy from the law of Avogadro-Gerhardt there is yet a third, which is the last, and is very instructive. In the investigation of separate substances they have to be isolated in the purest possible form, and their chemical and physical properties, and among them the vapour density, then determined. If it be normal—that is, if D =

M/2—it often serves as a proof of the purity of the substance, *i.e.* of its freedom from all foreign matter. If it be abnormal—that is, if D be not equal to M/2—then for those who do not believe in the law it appears as a new argument against it and nothing more; but to those who have already grasped the important significance of the law it becomes clear that there is some error in the observation, or that the density was determined under conditions in which the vapour does not follow the laws of Boyle or Gay-Lussac, or else that the substance has not been sufficiently purified, and contains other substances. The law of Avogadro-Gerhardt in that case furnishes convincing evidence of the necessity of a fresh and more exact research. And as yet the causes of error have always been found. There are not a few examples in point in the recent history of chemistry. We will cite one instance. In the case of pyrosulphuryl chloride, $S_2O_5Cl_2$, M = 215, and consequently D should $= 107 \cdot 5$, instead of which Ogier and others obtained $53 \cdot 8$—that is, a density half as great; and further, Ogier (1882) demonstrated clearly that the substance is not dissociated by distillation into SO_3 and SO_2Cl_2, or any other two products, and[322] thus the abnormal density of $S_2O_5Cl_2$ remained unexplained until D. P. Konovaloff (1885) showed that the previous investigators were working with a mixture (containing SO_3HCl), and that pyrosulphuryl chloride has a normal density of approximately 107. Had not the law of Avogadro-Gerhardt served as a guide, the impure liquid would have still passed as pure; the more so since the determination of the amount of chlorine could not aid in the discovery of the impurity. Thus, by following a true law of nature we are led to true deductions.

All cases which have been studied confirm the law of Avogadro-Gerhardt, and as by it a deduction is obtained, from the determination of the vapour density (a purely physical property), as to the weight of the molecule or quantity of a substance entering into chemical reaction, this law links together the two provinces of learning—physics and chemistry—in the most intimate manner. Besides which, the law of Avogadro-Gerhardt places the conceptions of *molecules* and *atoms* on a firm foundation, which was previously wanting. Although since the days of Dalton it had become evident that it was necessary to admit the existence of the elementary atom (the chemical individual indivisible by chemical or other forces), and of the groups of atoms (or molecules) of compounds, indivisible by mechanical and physical forces; still the relative magnitude of the molecule and atom was not defined with sufficient clearness. Thus, for instance, the atomic weight of oxygen might be taken as 8 or 16, or any multiple of these numbers, and nothing indicated a reason for the acceptation of one rather than another of these magnitudes;[18] whilst as regards the weights of the molecules of elements and compounds there was no trustworthy knowledge whatever. With the establishment of Gerhardt's law the idea of the molecule was fully defined, as well as the relative magnitude of the elementary atom.

The chemical particle or *molecule must be considered as the*[323] *quantity of a substance which enters into chemical reaction with other molecules, and occupies in a state of vapour the same volume as two parts by weight of hydrogen.*

The molecular weight (which has been indicated by M) of a substance is determined by its composition, transformations, and vapour density.

The molecule is not divisible by the mechanical and physical changes of substances, but in chemical reaction it is either altered in its properties, or quantity, or structure, or in the nature of the motion of its parts.

An agglomeration of molecules, which are alike in all chemical respects, makes up the masses of homogeneous substances in all states.[19]

Molecules consist of atoms in a certain state of distribution and motion, just as the solar system[20] is made up of inseparable parts (the sun, planets, satellites, comets, &c.) The greater the number of atoms in a molecule, the more complex is the resultant substance. The equilibrium between the dissimilar atoms may be more or less stable, and may for this reason give more or less stable substances. Physical and mechanical transformations alter the velocity of the[324] motion and the distances between the individual molecules, or of the atoms in the molecules, or of their sum total, but they do not alter the original equilibrium of the system; whilst chemical changes, on the other hand, alter the molecules themselves, that is, the velocity of motion, the relative distribution, and the quality and quantity of the atoms in the molecules.

Atoms are the smallest quantities or chemically indivisible masses *of the elements forming the molecules* of elements and compounds.

Atoms have weight, the sum of their weights forms the weight of the molecule, and the sum of the weights of the molecules forms the weight of masses, and is the cause of gravity, and of all the phenomena which depend on the mass of a substance.

The elements are characterised, not only by their independent existence, their incapacity of being converted into each other, &c., but also by the weight of their atoms.

Chemical and physical properties depend on the weight, composition, and properties of the molecules forming a substance, and on the weight and properties of the atoms forming the molecules.

This is the substance of those principles of molecular mechanics which lie at the basis of all contemporary physical and chemical constructions since the establishment of the law of Avogadro-Gerhardt. The fecundity of the principles enunciated is seen at every step in all the particular cases forming the present store of chemical data. We will here cite a few examples of the application of the law.

As the weight of an atom must be understood as the minimum quantity of an element entering into the composition of all the molecules formed by it, therefore, in order to find the weight of an atom of oxygen, let us take the molecules of those of its compounds which have already been described, together with the molecules of certain of those carbon compounds which will be described in the following chapter:

	Molecular Weight	Amount of Oxygen		Molecular Weight	Amount of Oxygen
H_2O	18	16	HNO_3	63	48
N_2O	44	16	CO	28	16
NO	30	16	CO_2	44	32
NO_2	46	32			

The number of substances taken might be considerably increased, but the result would be the same—that is, the molecules of the compounds of oxygen would never be found to contain less than 16 parts by weight of this element, but always $n16$, where n is a whole number.[325] The molecular weights of the above compounds are found either directly from the density of their vapour or gas, or from their reactions. Thus, the vapour density of nitric acid (as a substance which easily decomposes above its boiling point) cannot be accurately determined, but the fact of its containing one part by weight of hydrogen, and all its properties and reactions, indicate the above molecular composition and no other. In this manner it is very easy to find the atomic weight of all the elements, knowing the molecular weight and composition of their compounds. It may, for instance, be easily proved that less than $n12$ parts of carbon never enters into the molecules of carbon compounds, and therefore C must be taken as 12, and not as 6 which was the number in use before Gerhardt. In a similar manner the atomic weights now accepted for the elements oxygen, nitrogen, carbon, chlorine, sulphur, &c., were found and indubitably established, and they are even now termed the Gerhardt atomic weights. As regards the metals, many of which do not give a single volatile compound, we shall afterwards see that there are also methods by which their atomic weights may be established, but nevertheless the law of Avogadro-Gerhardt is here also ultimately resorted to, in order to remove any doubt which may be encountered. Thus, for instance, although much that was known concerning the compounds of beryllium necessitated its atomic weight being taken as Be = 9—that is, the oxide as BeO and the chloride $BeCl_2$—still certain analogies gave reason for considering its atomic weight to be Be = 13·5, in which case its oxide would be expressed by the composition Be_2O_3, and the chloride by $BeCl_3$.[21] It was then found that the vapour density of beryllium chloride was approximately 40, when it became quite clear that its molecular weight was 80, and as this satisfies the formula $BeCl_2$, but does not suit the formula $BeCl_3$, it therefore became necessary to regard the atomic weight of Be as 9 and not as 13½.

[326]

With the establishment of a true conception of molecules and atoms, chemical formulæ became direct expressions, not only of composition,[22] but also of molecular weight or *vapour density*, and consequently of a series of fundamental chemical and physical data, inasmuch as a number of the properties of substances are dependent on their[327] vapour density, or molecular weight and composition. The vapour density D = M/2. For instance, the formula of ethyl ether is $C_4H_{10}O$, corresponding with the molecular weight 74, and the vapour density 37, which is the fact. Therefore, the density of vapours and gases has ceased to be an empirical magnitude obtained by experiment only, and has acquired a rational meaning. It is only necessary to remember that 2 grams of hydrogen, or the molecular weight of this primary gas in grams, occupies, at 0° and 760 mm. pressure, a volume of 22·3 litres (or 22,300 cubic centimetres), in order to directly determine the weights of cubical measures of gases and vapours from their formulæ, because *the molecular weights in grams of all other vapours at 0° and 760 mm. occupy the same volume, 22·3 litres.* Thus, for example, in the case of carbonic anhydride, CO_2, the molecular weight M = 44, hence 44 grams of carbonic anhydride at 0° and 760 mm. occupy a volume of 22·3 litres—consequently, a litre weighs 1·97 gram. By combining the laws of gases—Gay-Lussac's, Mariotte's, and Avogadro-Gerhardt's—we obtain[23] a general formula for gases

$$6200s(273 + t) = Mp$$

where s is the weight in grams of a cubic centimetre of a vapour or gas at a temperature t and pressure p (expressed in centimetres of mercury) if the molecular weight of the gas = M. Thus, for instance, at 100° and 760 millimetres pressure (*i.e.* at the atmospheric pressure) the weight of a cubic centimetre of the vapour of ether (M = 74) is s = 0·0024.[24]

[328]

As the molecules of many elements (hydrogen, oxygen, nitrogen, chlorine, bromine, sulphur—at least at high temperatures) are of uniform composition, the formulæ of the compounds formed by them directly indicate the composition by volume. So, for example, the formula HNO_3 directly shows that in the decomposition of nitric acid there is obtained 1 vol. of hydrogen, 1 vol. of nitrogen, and 3 vols. of oxygen.

And since a great number of mechanical, physical, and chemical properties are directly dependent on the elementary and volumetric composition, and on the vapour density, the accepted system of atoms and molecules gives the possibility of simplifying a number of most complex relations. For instance, it may be easily demonstrated *that the vis viva of the molecules of all vapours and gases is alike.* For it is proved by mechanics that the *vis viva* of a moving mass $= (\frac{1}{2})\ mv^2$, where m is the mass and v the velocity. For a molecule, $m = M$, or the molecular weight, and the velocity of the motion of gaseous molecules = a constant which we will designate by C, divided by the square root of the density of the gas[25] $= C/\sqrt{D}$, and as $D = M/2$, the *vis viva* of molecules $= C^2$—that is, a constant for all molecules. *Q.E.D.*[26] The specific heat of gases (Chapter XIV.), and many other of their properties, are determined by their density, and consequently by their molecular weight. Gases and vapours in passing into a liquid state evolve the so-called *latent heat*, which also proves to be in connection with the molecular weight. The observed latent heats[329] of carbon bisulphide, CS_2 = 90, of ether, $C_4H_{10}O$, = 94, of benzene, C_6H_6, = 109, of alcohol, C_2H_6O, = 200, of chloroform, $CHCl_3$, = 67, &c., show the amount of heat expended in converting one part by weight of the above substances into vapour. A great uniformity is observed if the measure of this heat he referred to the weight of the molecule. For carbon bisulphide the formula CS_2 expresses a weight 76, hence the latent heat of evaporation referred to the molecular quantity CS_2 = 76 x 90 = 6,840, for ether = 9,656, for benzene = 8,502, for alcohol = 9,200, for chloroform = 8,007, for water = 9,620, &c. That is, for molecular quantities, the latent heat varies comparatively little, from 7,000 to 10,000 heat units, whilst for equal parts by weight it is ten times greater for water than for chloroform and many other substances.[27]

Generalising from the above, the weight of the molecule determines the properties of a substance *independently of its composition—i.e.* of the number and quality of the atoms entering into the molecule—whenever the substance is in a gaseous state (for instance, the density of gases and vapours, the velocity of sound in them, their specific heat, &c.), or passes into that state, as we see in the latent heat of evaporation. This is intelligible from the point of view of the atomic theory in its present form, for, besides a rapid motion proper to the molecules of gaseous bodies, it is further necessary to postulate that these molecules are dispersed in space (filled throughout with the luminiferous ether) like the heavenly bodies distributed throughout the universe. Here, as there, it is only the degree of removal (the distance) and the masses of substances which take effect, while those peculiarities of a substance which are expressed in chemical transformations, and only come into action on near approach or on contact, are in abeyance by reason of the dispersal. Hence it is at once obvious,[330] in the first place, that in the case of solids and liquids, in which the molecules are closer together than in gases and vapours, a greater complexity is to be expected, *i.e.* a dependence of all the properties not only upon the weight of the molecule but also upon its composition and quality, or upon the properties of the individual chemical atoms forming the molecule; and, in the second place, that, in the case of a small number of molecules of any substance being disseminated through a mass of another substance—for example, in the formation of weak (dilute) solutions (although in this case there is an act of chemical reaction—*i.e.* a combination, decomposition, or substitution)—the dispersed molecules will alter the properties of the medium in which they are dissolved, almost in proportion to the molecular weight and almost independently of their composition. The greater the number of molecules disseminated—*i.e.* the stronger the solution—the more clearly defined will those properties become which depend upon the composition of the dissolved substance and its relation to the molecules of the solvent, for the distribution of one kind of molecules in the sphere of attraction of others cannot but be influenced by their mutual chemical reaction. These general considerations give a starting point for explaining why, since the appearance of Van't Hoff's memoir (1886), 'The Laws of Chemical Equilibrium in a Diffused Gaseous or Liquid State' (*see* Chapter I., Note 19), it has been found more and more that *dilute* (weak) solutions exhibit such variations of properties as depend wholly upon the weight and number of the molecules and not upon their composition, and even give the means of determining the weight of molecules by studying the variations of the properties of a solvent on the introduction of a small quantity of a substance passing into solution. Although this subject has been already partially considered in the first chapter (in speaking of solutions), and properly belongs to a special (physical) branch of chemistry, we touch upon it here because the meaning and importance of molecular weights are seen in it in a new and peculiar light, and because it gives a method for determining them whenever it is possible to obtain dilute solutions. Among the numerous properties of dilute solutions which have been investigated (for instance, the osmotic pressure, vapour tension, boiling point, internal friction, capillarity, variation with change of temperature, specific heat, electroconductivity, index of refraction, &c.) we will select one—the 'depression' or fall of the temperature of freezing (Raoult's cryoscopic method), not only because this method has been the most studied, but also because it is the most easily carried out and most frequently applied for determining the weight of the molecules of substances in solution, although here, owing to the novelty of the subject there are[331] also many experimental discrepancies which cannot as yet be explained by theory.[27 bis]

[332]
[333]

If 100 gram-molecules of water, *i.e.* 1,800 grms, be taken and n gram-molecules of sugar, $C_{12}H_{22}O_{11}$, *i.e.* n 342 grms., be dissolved in them, then the depression d, or fall (counting from $0°$) of the temperature of the formation of ice will be (according to Pickering)

$n = 0 \quad 0·010 \quad 0·025 \quad 0·100 \quad 0·250 \quad 1·000$

$d = 0° \quad 0°·0103 \quad 0°·0280 \quad 0°·1115 \quad 0°·2758 \quad 1°·1412$

which shows that for high degrees of dilution (up to $0·25n$) d approximately (estimating the possible errors of experiment at $\pm 0°·005$) $= n1·10$, because then $d = 0°$, $0°·0110$, $0°·0275$, $0°·1100$, $0°·2750$, $1°·1000$, and the difference between these figures and the results of experiment for very dilute solutions is less than the possible errors of experiment (for $n = 1$ the difference is already greater) and therefore for dilute solutions of sugar it may be said that n molecules of sugar in dissolving in 100 molecules of water give a depression of about $1°·1n$. Similar data for acetone (Chapter I., Note 49) give a depression of $1°·006n$ for n molecules of acetone per 100 molecules of water. And in general, for indifferent substances (the majority of organic bodies) the depression per $100H_2O$ is *nearly* $n1°·1$ to $n1°·0$ (ether, for instance, gives the last number), and consequently in dissolving in 100 grms. of water it is about $18°·0n$ to $19°·0n$, taking this rule to apply to the case of a small number of n (not over $0·2n$). If instead of water, other liquid or fused solvents (for example, benzene, acetic acid, acetone, nitrobenzene or molten naphthaline, metals, &c.) be taken and in the proportion of 100 molecules of the solvent to n molecules of a dissolved indifferent (neither acid nor saline) substance, then the depression is found to be equal to from $0°·62n$ to $0°·65n$ and in general Kn. If the molecular weight of the solvent $= m$, then 100 gram-molecules will weigh $100m$ grms., and the depression will be approximately (taking $0·63n$) equal to $m0·63n$ degrees for n molecules of the substance dissolved in 100 grms. of the solvent, or in general the depression for 100 grms. of a given solvent $= kn$ where k is almost a constant quantity (for water nearly 18, for acetone nearly 37, &c.) for all dilute solutions. Thus, having found a convenient solvent for a given substance and prepared a definite (by weight) solution (*i.e.* knowing how many grms. r of the solvent there are to q grms. of the substance dissolved) and having determined the depression d—*i.e.* the fall in temperature of freezing for the solvent—it is possible to determine the molecular weight of the substance dissolved, because $d = kn$ where d is found by experiment and k is determined by the nature of the solvent, and therefore n or the number of molecules of the[334] substance dissolved can be found. But if r grms. of the solvent and q grms. of the substance dissolved are taken, then there are $100q/r$ of the latter per 100 grms. of the former, and this quantity $= nX$, where n is found from the depression and $= d \dfrac{}{k}$ and X is the molecular weight of the substance dissolved. Hence X $= 100qk \dfrac{}{rd}$, which gives the molecular weight, naturally only approximately, but still with sufficient accuracy to easily indicate, for instance, whether in peroxide of hydrogen the molecule contains HO or H_2O_2 or H_3O_3, &c. (H_2O_2 is obtained). Moreover, attention should be drawn to the fact that a great many substances taken as solvents give per 100 molecules a depression of about $0·63n$, whilst water gives about $1·05n$, i.e. a larger quantity, as though the molecules of liquid water were more complex than is expressed by the formula H_2O.[28] A similar phenomenon which repeats itself in the osmotic pressure, vapour tension of the solvent, &c. (see Chapter I., Notes 19 and 49), i.e. a variation of the constant (k for 100 grms. of the solvent or K for 100 molecules of it), is also observed in passing from indifferent substances to saline (to acids, alkalis and salts) both in aqueous and other solutions as we will[335] show (according to Pickering's data 1892) for solutions of NaCl and $CuSO_4$ in water. For

$$n = 0·01 \ 0·03 \ 0·05 \ 0·1 \ 0·5$$

molecules of NaCl the depression is

$$d = 0°·0177 \ 0°·0598 \ 0°·0992 \ 0°·1958 \ 0°·9544$$

which corresponds to a depression per molecule

$$K = 1·77 \ 1·96 \ 1·98 \ 1·96 \ 1·91$$

i.e. here in the most dilute solutions (when n is nearly 0) d is obtained about $1·7n$, while in the case of sugar it was about $1·1n$. For $CuSO_4$ for the same values of n, experiment gave:

$$d = \ 0°·0164 \ 0°·0451 \ 0°·0621 \ 0°·1321 \ 0°·5245$$

$$K = \ 1·64 \quad 1·50 \quad 1·44 \quad 1·32 \quad 1·05$$

i.e. here again d for very dilute solutions is nearly $1·7n$, but the value of K falls as the solution becomes more concentrated, while for NaCl it at first increased and only fell for the more concentrated solutions. The value of K in the solution of n molecules of a body in $100H_2O$, when $d = Kn$, for very dilute solutions of $CaCl_2$ is nearly $2·6$, for $Ca(NO_3)_2$ nearly $2·5$, for HNO_3, KI and KHO nearly $1·9–2·0$, for borax $Na_2B_4O_7$ nearly $3·7$, &c., while for sugar and similar substances it is, as has been already mentioned, nearly $1 \cdot 0$–$1 \cdot 1$. Although these figures are very different[28 bis] still k and K may be considered constant for analogous substances, and therefore the weight of the molecule of the body in solution can be found from d. And as the vapour tension of solutions and their boiling points (*see* Note 27 bis and Chapter I., Note 51) vary in the same manner as the freezing point depression, so they also may serve as means for determining the molecular weight of a substance in solution.[29]

Thus not only in vapours and gases, but also in dilute solutions of solid and liquid substances, we see that if not all, still many properties[336] are wholly dependent upon the molecular weight and not upon the quality of a substance, and that this gives the possibility of determining the weight of molecules by studying these properties (for instance, the vapour density, depression of the freezing point, &c.) It is apparent from the foregoing that the physical and even more so the chemical properties of homogeneous substances, more especially solid and liquid, do not depend exclusively upon the weights of their molecules, but that many are in definite (*see* Chapter XV.) dependence upon the weights of the atoms of the elements entering into their composition, and are determined by their quantitative and individual peculiarities. Thus the density of solids and liquids (as will afterwards be shown) is chiefly determined by the weights of the atoms of the elements entering into their composition, inasmuch as dense elements (in a free state) and compounds are only met with among substances containing elements with large atomic weights, such as gold, platinum, and uranium. And these elements themselves, in a free state, are the heaviest of all elements. Substances containing such light elements as hydrogen, carbon, oxygen and nitrogen (like many organic substances) never have a high specific gravity; in the majority of cases it scarcely exceeds that of water. The density generally decreases with the increase of the amount of hydrogen, as the lightest element, and a substance is often obtained lighter than water. The refractive power of substances also entirely depends on the composition and the properties of the component elements.[29 bis] The history[337] of chemistry presents a striking example in point—Newton foresaw from the high refractive index of the diamond that it would contain a combustible substance since so many combustible oils have a high refractive power. We shall afterwards see (Chapter XV.) that many of those properties of substances which are in direct dependence not upon the weight of the molecules but upon their composition, or, in other words, upon the properties and quantities of the elements entering into them, stand in a peculiar (periodic) dependence upon the atomic weight of the elements; that is, the mass (of molecules and atoms), proportional to the weight, determines the properties of substances as it also determines (with the distance) the motions of the heavenly bodies.

Footnotes:

[1] If the weight be indicated by P, the density by D, and the volume by V, then

$$P \boxed{D} = KV$$

where K is a coefficient depending on the system of the expressions P, D, and V. If D be the weight of a cubic measure of a substance referred to the weight of the same measure of water—if, as in the metrical system (Chapter I., Note 2), the cubic measure of one part by weight of water be taken as a unit of volume—then $K = 1$. But, whatever it be, it is cancelled in dealing with the comparison of volumes, because comparative and not absolute measures of volumes are taken. In this chapter, as throughout the book, the weight P is given in grams in dealing with absolute weights; and if comparative, as in the expression of chemical composition, then the weight of an atom is taken as unity. The density of gases, D, is also taken in reference to the density of hydrogen, and the volume V in metrical units (cubic centimetres), if it be a matter of absolute magnitudes of volumes, and if it be a matter of chemical transformations—that is, of relative volumes—then the volume of an atom of hydrogen, or of one part by weight of hydrogen, is taken as unity, and all volumes are expressed according to these units.

[2] As the volumetric relations of vapours and gases, next to the relations of substances by weight, form the most important province of chemistry, and a most important means for the attainment of chemical conclusions, and inasmuch as these volumetric relations are determined by the densities of gases and vapours, necessarily the methods of determining the densities of vapours (and also of gases) are important factors in chemical research. These methods are described in detail in works on physics and physical and analytical chemistry, and therefore we here only touch on the general principles of the subject.

FIG. 52.—Apparatus for determining the vapour density by Dumas' method. A small quantity of the liquid whose vapour density is to be determined is placed in the glass globe, and heated in a water or oil bath to a temperature above the boiling point of the liquid. When all the liquid has been converted into vapour and has displaced all the air from the globe, the latter is sealed up and weighed. The capacity of the globe is then measured, and in this manner the volume occupied by a known weight of vapour at a known temperature is determined.

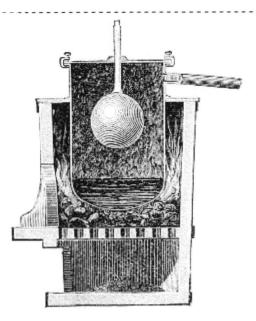

FIG. 53.—Deville and Troost's apparatus for determining the
vapour densities, according to Dumas' method, of substances
which boil at high temperatures. A porcelain globe containing the
substance whose vapour density is to be determined is heated in
the vapour of mercury (350°), sulphur (410°), cadmium (850°), or
zinc (1,040°). The globe is sealed up in an oxyhydrogen flame.

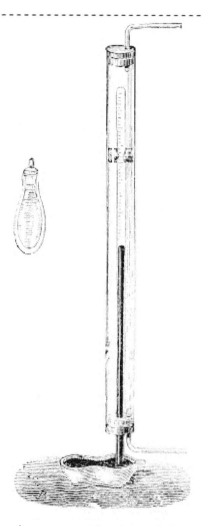

FIG. 54.—Hofmann's apparatus for determining vapour densities.
The internal tube, about one metre long, which is calibrated and
graduated, is filled with mercury and inverted in a mercury bath. A
small bottle (depicted in its natural size on the left) containing a
weighed quantity of the liquid whose vapour density is to be
determined, is introduced into the Torricellian vacuum. Steam, or
the vapour of amyl alcohol, &c., is passed through the outer tube,
and heats the internal tube to the temperature t, at which the
volume of vapour is measured.

FIG. 55.—Victor Meyer's apparatus for determining vapour
densities. The tube *b* is heated in the vapour of a liquid of
constant boiling point. A glass tube, containing the liquid to be

experimented upon, is caused to fall from d. The air displaced is collected in the cylinder e, in the trough f.

If we know the weight p and volume v, occupied by the vapour of a given substance at a temperature t and pressure h, then its density may be directly obtained by dividing p by the weight of a volume v of hydrogen (if the density be expressed according to hydrogen, *see* Chapter II., Note 23) at t and h. Hence, the methods of determining the density of vapours and gases are based on the determination of p, v, t, and h. The two last data (the temperature t and pressure h) are given by the thermometer and barometer and the heights of mercury or other liquid confining the gas, and therefore do not require further explanation. It need only be remarked that: (1) In the case of easily volatile liquids there is no difficulty in procuring a bath with a constant temperature, but that it is nevertheless best (especially considering the inaccuracy of thermometers) to have a medium of absolutely constant temperature, and therefore to take either a bath in which some substance is melting—such as melting ice at $0°$ or crystals of sodium acetate, melting at $+56°$—or, as is more generally practised, to place the vessel containing the substance to be experimented with in the vapour of a liquid boiling at a definite temperature, and knowing the pressure under which it is boiling, to determine the temperature of the vapour. For this purpose the boiling points of water at different pressures are given in Chapter I., Note 11, and the boiling points of certain easily procurable liquids at various pressures are given in Chapter II., Note 27. (2) With respect to temperatures above $300°$ (below which mercurial thermometers may be conveniently employed), they are most simply obtained constant (to give time for the weight and volume of a substance being observed in a given space, and to allow that space to attain the calculated temperature t) by means of substances boiling at a high temperature. Thus, for instance, at the ordinary atmospheric pressure the temperature t of the vapour of sulphur is about $445°$, of phosphorus pentasulphide $518°$, of tin chloride $606°$, of cadmium $770°$, of zinc $930°$ (according to Violle and others), or $1040°$ (according to Deville), &c. (3) The indications of the hydrogen thermometer must be considered as the most exact (but as hydrogen diffuses through incandescent platinum, nitrogen is usually employed). (4) The temperature of the vapours used as the bath should in every case be several degrees higher than the boiling point of the liquid whose density is to be determined, in order that no portion should remain in a liquid state. But even in this case, as is seen from the example of nitric peroxide (Chapter VI.), the vapour density does not always remain constant with a change of t, as it should were the law of the expansion of gases and vapours absolutely exact (Chapter II., Note 26). If variations of a chemical and physical nature similar to that which we saw in nitric peroxide take place in the vapours, the main interest is centred in *constant* densities, which do not vary with *t*, and therefore the possible effect of *t* on the density must always be kept in mind in having recourse to this means of investigation. (5) Usually, for the sake of convenience of observation, the vapour density is determined at the atmospheric pressure which is read on the barometer; but in the case of substances which are volatilised with difficulty, and also of substances which decompose, or, in general, vary at temperatures near their boiling points, it is best or even indispensable to conduct the determination at low pressures, whilst for substances which decompose at low pressures the observations have to be conducted under a more or less considerably increased pressure. (6) In many cases it is convenient to determine the vapour density of a substance in admixture with other gases, and consequently under the partial pressure, which may be calculated from the volume of the mixture and that of the intermixed gas (*see* Chapter I., Note 1). This method is especially important for substances which are easily decomposable, because, as shown by the phenomena of dissociation, a substance is able to remain unchanged in the atmosphere of one of its products of decomposition. Thus, Wurtz determined the density of phosphoric chloride, PCl_5, in admixture with the vapour of phosphorous chloride, PCl_3. (7) It is evident, from the example of nitric peroxide, that a change of pressure may alter the density and aid decomposition, and therefore identical results are sometimes obtained (if the density be variable) by raising *t* and lowering *h*; but if the density does not vary under these variable conditions (at least, to an extent appreciably exceeding the limits of experimental error), then this *constant* density indicates the *gaseous* and *invariable* state of a substance. The laws hereafter laid down refer only to such vapour densities. But the majority of volatile substances show such a constant density at a certain degree above their boiling points up to the starting point of decomposition. Thus, the density of aqueous vapour does not vary for *t* between the ordinary temperature and 1000° (there are no trustworthy determinations beyond this) and for pressures varying from fractions of an atmosphere up to several atmospheres. If, however, the density does vary considerably with a variation of *h* and *t*, the fact may serve as a guide for the investigation of the chemical changes which are undergone by the substance in a state of vapour, or at least as an indication of a deviation from the laws of Boyle, Mariotte, and Gay-Lussac (for the expansion of gases with *t*). In certain cases the separation of one form of deviation from the other may be explained by special hypotheses.

With respect to the means of determining *p* and *v*, with a view to finding the vapour density, we may distinguish three chief methods: (*a*) by weight, by ascertaining the weight of a definite volume of vapour; (*b*) by volume, by measuring the volume occupied by the vapour of a definite weight of a substance; and (*c*) by displacement. The last-mentioned is essentially volumetric, because a known weight of a substance is taken, and the volume of the air displaced by the vapour at a given t and h is determined.

The method by weight (*a*) is the most trustworthy and historically important. *Dumas' method* is typical. An ordinary spherical glass or porcelain vessel, like those shown respectively in figs. 52 and 54, is taken, and an excess of the substance to be experimented upon is introduced into it. The vessel is heated to a temperature t higher than the boiling point of the liquid: this gives a vapour which displaces the air, and fills the spherical space. When the air and vapour cease escaping from the sphere, it is fused up or closed by some means; and when cool, the weight of the vapour remaining in the sphere is determined (either by direct weighing of the vessel with the vapour and introducing the necessary corrections for the weight of the air and of the vapour itself, or the weight of the volatilised substance is determined by chemical methods), and the volume of the vapour at t and the barometric pressure h are then calculated.

The volumetric method (*b*) originally employed by Gay-Lussac and then modified by Hofmann and others is based on the principle that a weighed quantity of the liquid to be experimented with (placed in a small closed vessel, which is sometimes fused up before weighing, and, if quite full of the liquid, breaks when heated in a vacuum) is introduced into a graduated cylinder heated to t, or simply into a Torricellian vacuum, as shown in fig. 54, and the number of volumes occupied by the vapour noted when the space holding it is heated to the desired temperature t.

The method of displacement (*c*) proposed by Victor Meyer is based on the fact that a space b is heated to a constant temperature t (by the surrounding vapours of a liquid of constant boiling point), and the air (or other gas enclosed in this space) is allowed to attain this temperature, and when it has done so a glass bulb containing a weighed quantity of the substance to be experimented with is dropped into the space. The substance is immediately converted into vapour, and displaces the air into the graduated cylinder *e*. The amount of this air is calculated from its volume, and hence the volume at t, and therefore also the volume occupied by the vapour, is found. The general arrangement of the apparatus is given in fig. 55.

[3] Vapours and gases, as already explained in the second chapter, are subject to the same laws, which are, however, only approximate. It is evident that for the deduction of the laws which will presently be enunciated it is only possible to take into consideration a perfect gaseous state (far removed from the liquid state) and chemical invariability in which the *vapour density is constant*—that is, the volume of a given gas or vapour varies like a volume of hydrogen, air, or other gas, with the pressure and temperature.

It is necessary to make this statement in order that it may be clearly seen that the laws of gaseous volumes, which we shall describe presently, are in the most intimate connection with the laws of the variations of volumes with pressure and temperature. And as these latter laws (Chapter II.) are not infallible, but only approximately exact, the same, therefore, applies to the laws about to be described. And as it is possible to find more exact laws (a second approximation) for the variation of v with p and t (for example, van der Waals' formula, Chapter II., Note 33), so also a more exact expression of the relation between the composition and the density of vapours and gases is also possible. But to prevent any doubt arising at the very beginning as to the breadth and general application of the laws of volumes, it will be sufficient to mention that the density of such gases as oxygen, nitrogen, and carbonic anhydride is already known to *remain constant* (within the limits of experimental error) between the ordinary temperature and a white heat; whilst, judging from what is said in my work on the 'Tension of Gases' (vol. i. p. 9), it may be said that, as regards pressure, the relative density remains very constant, even when the deviations from Mariotte's law are very considerable. However, in this respect the number of data is as yet too small to arrive at an exact conclusion.

[4] We must recollect that this law is only approximate, like Boyle and Mariotte's law, and that, therefore, like the latter, a more exact expression may be found for the exceptions.

[5] This second law of volumes may be considered as a consequence of the first law. The first law requires simple ratios between the volumes of the combining substances A and B. A substance AB is produced by their combination. It may, according to the law of multiple proportion, combine, not only with substances C, D, &c., but also with A and with B. In this new combination the volume of AB, combining with the volume of A, should be in simple multiple proportion with the volume of A; hence the volume of the compound AB is in simple proportion to the volume of its component parts. Therefore only one law of volumes need be accepted. We shall afterwards see that there is a third law of volumes embracing also the two first laws.

[6] It must not be forgotten that Newton's law of gravity was first a hypothesis, but it became a trustworthy, perfect theory, and acquired the qualities of a fundamental law owing to the concord between its deductions and actual facts. All laws, all theories, of natural phenomena, are at first hypotheses. Some are rapidly established by their consequences exactly agreeing with facts; others only take root by slow degrees; and there are many which are destined to be refuted owing to their consequences being found to be at variance with facts.

[7] This is not only seen from the above calculations, but may be proved by experiment. A glass tube, divided in the middle by a stopcock, is taken and one portion filled with *dry* hydrogen chloride (the dryness of the gases is very necessary, because ammonia and hydrogen chloride are both very soluble in water, so that a small trace of water may contain a large amount of these gases in solution) and the other with dry ammonia, under the atmospheric pressure. One orifice (for instance, of that portion which contains the ammonia) is firmly closed, and the other is immersed under mercury, and the cock is then opened. Solid sal-ammoniac is formed, but if the volume of one gas be greater than that of the other, some of the first gas will remain. By immersing the tube in the mercury in order that the internal pressure shall equal the atmospheric pressure, it may easily be shown that the volume of the remaining gas is equal to the difference between the volumes of the two portions of the tube, and that this remaining gas is part of that whose volume was the greater.

[8] Let us demonstrate this by figures. From 122 grams of benzoic acid there are obtained (*a*) 78 grams of benzene, whose density referred to hydrogen = 39, hence the relative volume = 2; and (*b*) 44 grams of carbonic anhydride, whose density = 22, and hence the volume = 2. It is the same in other cases.

[9] A large number of such generalised reactions, showing reaction by equal volumes, occur in the case of the hydrocarbon derivatives, because many of these compounds are volatile. The reactions of alkalis on acids, or anhydrides on water, &c., which are so frequent between mineral substances, present but few such examples, because many of these substances are not volatile and their vapour densities are unknown. But essentially the same is seen in these cases also; for instance, sulphuric acid, H_2SO_4, breaks up into the anhydride, SO_3, and water, H_2O, which exhibit an equality of volumes. Let us take another example where three substances combine in equal volumes: carbonic anhydride, CO_2, ammonia, NH_3, and water, H_2O (the volumes of all are equal to 2), form acid ammonium carbonate, $(NH_4)HCO_3$.

[10] This opinion which I have always held (since the first editions of this work), as to the primary origin of hydrogen peroxide and of the formation of water by means of its decomposition, has in latter days become more generally accepted, thanks more especially to the work of Traube. Probably it explains most simply the necessity for the presence of traces of water in many reactions, as, for instance, in the explosion of carbonic oxide with oxygen, and perhaps the theory of the explosion of detonating gas itself and of the combustion of hydrogen will gain in clearness and truth if we take into consideration the preliminary formation of hydrogen peroxide and its decomposition. We may here point out the

fact that Ettingen (at Dorpat, 1888) observed the existence of currents and waves in the explosion of detonating gas by taking photographs, which showed the periods of combustion and the waves of explosion, which should be taken into consideration in the theory of this subject. As the formation of H_2O_2 from O_2 and H_2 corresponds with a less amount of heat than the formation of water from H_2 and O, it may be that the temperature of the flame of detonating gas depends on the pre-formation of hydrogen peroxide.

[11] The possibility of reactions between unequal volumes, notwithstanding the general application of the law of Avogadro-Gerhardt, may, in addition to what has been said above, depend on the fact that the participating substances, at the moment of reaction, undergo a preliminary modification, decomposition, isomeric (polymeric) transformation, &c. Thus, if NO_2, seems to proceed from N_2O_4, if O_2 is formed from O_3, and the converse, then it cannot be denied that the production of molecules containing only one atom is also possible—for instance, of oxygen—as also of higher polymeric forms—as the molecule N from N_2, or H_3 from H_2. In this manner it is obviously possible, by means of a series of hypotheses, to explain the cases of the formation of ammonia, NH_3, from 3 vols. of hydrogen and 1 vol. of nitrogen. But it must be observed that perhaps our information in similar instances is, as yet, far from being complete. If hydrazine or diamide N_2H_4 (Chapter VI. Note 20 bis) is formed and the imide N_2H_2 in which 2 vols. of hydrogen are combined with 2 vols. of nitrogen, then the reaction here perhaps first takes place between equal volumes. If it be shown that diamide gives nitrogen and ammonia ($3N_2H_4 = N_2 + 4NH_3$) under the action of sparks, heat, or the silent discharge, &c., then it will be possible to admit that it is formed before ammonia. And perhaps the still less stable imide N_2H_2, which may also decompose with the formation of ammonia, is produced before the amide N_2H_4.

I mention this to show that the fact of apparent exceptions existing to the law of reactions between equal volumes does not prove the impossibility of their being included under the law on further study of the subject. Having put forward a certain law or hypothesis, consequences must be deduced from it, and if by their means clearness and consistency are attained—and especially, if by their means that which could not otherwise be known can be predicted—then the consequences verify the hypothesis. This was the case with the law now under discussion. The mere simplicity of the deduction of the weights proper to the atoms of the elements, or the mere fact that having admitted the law it follows (as will afterwards be shown) that the *vis viva* of the molecules of all gases is a constant quantity, is quite sufficient reason for retaining the hypothesis, if not for believing in it as a fact beyond doubt. And such is the whole doctrine of atoms. And since by the acceptance of the law it became possible to foretell even the properties and atomic weights of elements which had not yet been discovered, and these predictions afterwards proved to be in agreement with the actual facts, it is evident that the law of Avogadro-Gerhardt penetrates deeply into the nature of the chemical relation of substances. This being granted, it is possible at the present time to exhibit and deduce the truth under consideration in many ways, and in every case, like all that is highest in science (for example, the laws of the indestructibility of matter, of the conservation of energy, of gravity, &c.), it proves to be not an empirical conclusion from direct observation and experiment, not a direct result of analysis, but a creation, or instinctive penetration, of the inquiring mind, guided and directed by experiment and observation—a synthesis of which the exact sciences are capable equally with the highest forms of art. Without such a synthetical process of reasoning, science would only be a mass of disconnected results of arduous labour, and would not be distinguished by that vitality with which it is really endowed when once it succeeds in attaining a synthesis, or concordance of outward form with the inner nature of things, without losing sight of the diversities of individual parts; in short, when it discovers by means of outward phenomena, which are apparent to the sense of touch, to observation, and to the common mind, the internal signification of things—discovering simplicity in complexity and uniformity in diversity. And this is the highest problem of science.

[12] As the density of aqueous vapour remains constant within the limits of experimental accuracy, even at 1,000°, when dissociation has certainly commenced, it would appear that only a very small amount of water is decomposed at these temperatures. If even 10 p.c. of water were decomposed, the density would be 8·57 and the quotient $M/D = 2·1$, but at the high temperatures here concerned the error of experiment is not greater than the difference between this quantity and 2. And probably at 1,000° the dissociation is far from being equal to 10 p.c. *Hence the variation in the vapour density of water does not give us the means of ascertaining the amount of its dissociation.*

[13] This explanation of the vapour density of sal-ammoniac, sulphuric acid, and similar substances which decompose in being distilled was the most natural to resort to as soon as the application of the law of Avogadro-Gerhardt to chemical relations was begun; it was, for instance, given in my work on *Specific Volumes*, 1856, p. 99. The formula, $M/D = 2$, which was applied later by many other investigators, had already been made use of in that work.

[14] The beginner must remember that an experiment and the mode in which it is carried out must be determined by the principle or fact which it is intended to illustrate, and not *vice versa*, as some suppose. The idea which determines the necessity of an experiment is the chief consideration.

[15] It is important that the tubes, asbestos, and sal-ammoniac should be dry, as otherwise the moisture retains the ammonia and hydrogen chloride.

[15 bis] Baker (1894) showed that the decomposition of NH_4Cl in the act of volatilising only takes place in the presence of water, traces of which are amply sufficient, but that in the total absence of moisture (attained by carefully drying with P_2O_5) there is no decomposition, and the vapour density of the sal-ammoniac is found to be normal, *i.e.*, nearly 27. It is not yet quite clear what part the trace of moisture plays here, and it must be presumed that the phenomenon belongs to the category of electrical and contact phenomena, which have not yet been fully explained (*see* Chapter IX., Note 29).

[16] Just as we saw (Chapter VI. Note 46) an increase of the dissociation of N_2O_4 and the formation of a large proportion of NO_2, with a decrease of pressure. The decomposition of I_2 into $I + I$ is a similar dissociation.

[17] Although at first there appeared to be a similar phenomenon in the case of chlorine, it was afterwards proved that if there is a decrease of density it is only a small one. In the case of bromine it is not much greater, and is far from being equal to that for iodine.

As in general we very often involuntarily confuse chemical processes with physical, it may be that a physical process of change in the coefficient of expansion with a change of temperature participates with a change in molecular weight, and partially, if not wholly, accounts for the decrease of the density of chlorine, bromine, and iodine. Thus, I have remarked (Comptes Rendus, 1876) that the coefficient of expansion of gases increases with their molecular weight, and (Chapter II., Note 26) the results of direct experiment show the coefficient of expansion of hydrobromic acid (M = 81) to be 0·00386 instead of 0·00367, which is that of hydrogen (M = 2). Hence, in the case of the vapour of iodine (M = 254) a very large coefficient of expansion is to be expected, and from this cause alone the relative density would fall. As the molecule of chlorine Cl_2 is lighter (= 71) than that of bromine (= 160), which is lighter than that of iodine (= 254), we see that the order in which the decomposability of the vapours of these haloids is observed corresponds with the expected rise in the coefficient of expansion. Taking the coefficient of expansion of iodine vapour as 0·004, then at 1,000° its density would be 116. Therefore the dissociation of iodine may be only an apparent phenomenon. However, on the other hand, the heavy vapour of mercury (M = 200, D = 100) scarcely decreases in density at a temperature of 1,500° (D = 98, according to Victor Meyer); but it must not be forgotten that the molecule of mercury contains only one atom, whilst that of iodine contains two, and this is very important. Questions of this kind which are difficult to decide by experimental methods must long remain without a certain explanation, owing to the difficulty, and sometimes impossibility, of distinguishing between physical and chemical changes.

[18] And so it was in the fifties. Some took O = 8, others O = 16. Water in the first case would be HO and hydrogen peroxide HO_2, and in the second case, as is now generally accepted, water H_2O and hydrogen peroxide H_2O_2 or HO. Disagreement and confusion reigned. In 1860 the chemists of the whole world met at Carlsruhe for the purpose of arriving at some agreement and uniformity of opinion. I was present at this Congress, and well remember how great was the difference of opinion, and how a compromise was advocated with great acumen by many scientific men, and with what warmth the followers of Gerhardt, at whose head stood the Italian professor, Canizzaro, followed up the consequences of the law of Avogadro. In the spirit of scientific freedom, without which science would make no progress, and would remain petrified as in the middle ages, and with the simultaneous necessity of scientific conservatism, without which the roots of past study could give no fruit, a compromise was not arrived at, nor ought it to have been, but instead of it truth, in the form of the law of Avogadro-Gerhardt, received by means of the Congress a wider development, and soon afterwards conquered all minds. Then the new so-called Gerhardt atomic weights established themselves, and in the seventies they were already in general use.

[19] A bubble of gas, a drop of liquid, or the smallest crystal, presents an agglomeration of a number of molecules, in a state of continual motion (like the stars of the Milky Way), distributing themselves evenly or forming new systems. If the aggregation of all kinds of heterogeneous molecules be possible in a gaseous state, where the molecules are considerably removed from each other, then in a liquid state, where they are already close together, such an aggregation becomes possible only in the sense of the mutual reaction between them which results from their chemical attraction, and especially in the aptitude of heterogeneous molecules for combining together. Solutions and other so-called indefinite chemical compounds should be regarded in this light. According to the principles developed in this work we should regard them as containing both the compounds of the heterogeneous molecules themselves and the products of their decomposition, as in peroxide of nitrogen, N_2O_4 and NO_2. And we must consider that those molecules A, which at a given moment are combined with B in AB, will in the following moment become free in order to again

enter into a combined form. The laws of chemical equilibrium proper to dissociated systems cannot be regarded in any other light.

[20] This strengthens the fundamental idea of the unity and harmony of type of all creation and is one of those ideas which impress themselves on man in all ages, and give rise to a hope of arriving in time, by means of a laborious series of discoveries, observations, experiments, laws, hypotheses, and theories, at a comprehension of the internal and invisible structure of concrete substances with that same degree of clearness and exactitude which has been attained in the visible structure of the heavenly bodies. It is not many years ago since the law of Avogadro-Gerhardt took root in science. It is within the memory of many living scientific men, and of mine amongst others. It is not surprising, therefore, that as yet little progress has been made in the province of molecular mechanics; but the theory of gases alone, which is intimately connected with the conception of molecules, shows by its success that the time is approaching when our knowledge of the internal structure of matter will be defined and established.

[21] If Be = 9, and beryllium chloride be $BeCl_2$, then for every 9 parts of beryllium there are 71 parts of chlorine, and the molecular weight of $BeCl_2$ = 80; hence the vapour density should be 40 or $n40$. If Be = 13·5, and beryllium chloride be $BeCl_3$, then to 13·5 of beryllium there are 106·5 of chlorine; hence the molecular weight would be 120, and the vapour density 60 or $n60$. The composition is evidently the same in both cases, because 9 : 71 :: 13·5 : 106·5. Thus, if the symbol of an element designate different atomic weights, apparently very different formulæ may equally well express both the percentage composition of compounds, and those properties which are required by the laws of multiple proportions and equivalents. The chemists of former days accurately expressed the composition of substances, and accurately applied Dalton's laws, by taking H = 1, O = 8, C = 6, Si = 14, &c. The Gerhardt equivalents are also satisfied by them, because O = 16, C = 12, Si = 28, &c., are multiples of them. The choice of one or the other multiple quantity for the atomic weight is impossible without a firm and concrete conception of the molecule and atom, and this is only obtained as a consequence of the law of Avogadro-Gerhardt, and hence the modern atomic weights are the results of this law (*see* Note 28).

[22] The percentage amounts of the elements contained in a given compound may be calculated from its formula by a simple proportion. Thus, for example, to find the percentage amount of hydrogen in hydrochloric acid we reason as follows:—HCl shows that hydrochloric acid contains 35·5 of chlorine and 1 part of hydrogen. Hence, in 36·5 parts of hydrochloric acid there is 1 part by weight of hydrogen, consequently 100 parts by weight of hydrochloric acid will contain as many more units of hydrogen as 100 is greater than 36·5; therefore, the proportion is as

follows—$x : 1 :: 100 : 36·5$ or $x = 100 \boxed{36·5} = 2·739$. Therefore 100 parts of hydrochloric acid contain 2·739 parts of hydrogen. In general, when it is required to transfer a formula into its percentage composition, we must replace the symbols by their corresponding atomic weights and find their sum, and knowing the amount by weight of a given element in it, it is easy by proportion to find the amount of this element in 100 or any other quantity of parts by weight. If, on the contrary, it be required to find the formula from a given percentage composition, we must proceed as follows: Divide the percentage amount of each element entering into the composition of a substance by its atomic weight, and compare the figures thus obtained—they should be in simple multiple proportion to each other. Thus, for instance, from the percentage composition of hydrogen peroxide, 5·88 of hydrogen and 94·12 of oxygen, it is easy to find its formula; it is only necessary to divide the amount of hydrogen by unity and the amount of oxygen by 16. The numbers 5·88 and 5·88 are thus obtained, which are in the ratio 1 : 1, which means that in hydrogen peroxide there is one atom of hydrogen to one atom of oxygen.

The following is a proof of the practical rule given above *that to find the ratio of the number of atoms from the percentage composition, it is necessary to divide the percentage amounts by the atomic weights of the corresponding substances, and to find the ratio which these numbers bear to each other.* Let us suppose that two radicles (simple or compound), whose symbols and combining weights are A and B, combine together, forming a compound composed of x atoms of A and y atoms of B. The formula of the substance will be AxBy. From this formula we know that our compound contains xA parts by weight of the first element, and yB of the second. In 100 parts of our compound there will be (by proportion) $100.x$A $\boxed{xA + yB}$ of the first element, and $100.y$B $\boxed{xA + yB}$ of the second. Let us divide these quantities, expressing the percentage amounts by the corresponding combining weights; we then obtain $100x \boxed{xA + yB}$ for the first element and $100y \boxed{xA + yB}$ for the second element. And these numbers are in the ratio $x : y$—that is, in the ratio of the number of atoms of the two substances.

It may be further observed that even the very language or nomenclature of chemistry acquires a particular clearness and conciseness by means of the conception of molecules, because then the names of substances may directly indicate their composition. Thus the term 'carbon dioxide' tells more about and expresses CO_2 better than carbonic acid gas, or even carbonic anhydride. Such nomenclature is already employed by many. But expressing the composition without an indication or even hint as to the properties, would be neglecting the advantageous side of the present nomenclature. Sulphur dioxide, SO_2, expresses the same as barium dioxide, BaO_2, but sulphurous anhydride indicates the acid properties of SO_2.

Probably in time one harmonious chemical language will succeed in embracing both advantages.

[23] This formula (which is given in my work on 'The Tension of Gases,' and in a somewhat modified form in the 'Comptes Rendus,' Feb. 1876) is deduced in the following manner. According to the law of Avogadro-Gerhardt, M = 2D for all gases, where M is the molecular weight and D the density referred to hydrogen. But it is equal to the weight s_0 of a cubic centimetre of a gas in grams at 0° and 76 cm. pressure, divided by 0·0000898, for this is the weight in grams of a cubic centimetre of hydrogen. But the weight s of a cubic centimetre of a gas at a temperature t and under a pressure p (in centimetres) is equal to $s_0 p/76(1 + at)$. Therefore, $s_0 = s.76(1 + at)/p$; hence D = $76.s(1 + at)/0·0000898p$, whence M = $152s(1 + at)/0·0000898p$, which gives the above expression, because $1/a = 273$, and 152 multiplied by 273 and divided by 0·0000898 is nearly 6200. In place of s, m/v may be taken, where m is the weight and v the volume of a vapour.

[24] The above formula may be directly applied in order to ascertain the molecular weight from the data; weight of vapour m grms., its volume v c.c., pressure p cm., and temperature t°; for s = the weight of vapour m, divided by the volume v, and consequently M = $6,200m(273 + t)/pv$. Therefore, instead of the formula (*see* Chapter II., Note 34), pv = R(273 + t), where R varies with the mass and nature of a gas, we may apply the formula pv = $6,200(m/M)(273 + t)$. These formulæ simplify the calculations in many cases. For example, required the volume v occupied by 5 grms. of aqueous vapour at a temperature $t = 127$° and under a pressure $p = 76$ cm. According to the formula M = $6,200m(273 + t)/pv$, we find that $v = 9,064$ c.c., as in the case of water M = 18, m in this instance = 5 grms. (These formulæ, however, like the laws of gases, are only approximate.)

[25] Chapter I., Note 34.

[26] *The velocity of the transmission of sound through gases and vapours* closely bears on this. It = $\sqrt{(Kpg)}/D(1 + at)$, where K is the ratio between the two specific heats (it is approximately 1·4 for gases containing two atoms in a molecule), p the pressure of the gas expressed by weight (that is, the pressure expressed by the height of a column of mercury multiplied by the density of $a = 0·00367$, and t the temperature. Hence, if K be known, and as D can he found from the composition of a gas, we can calculate the velocity of the transmission of sound in that gas. Or if this velocity be known, we can find K. The relative velocities of sound in two gases can he easily determined (Kundt).

If a horizontal glass tube (about 1 metre long and closed at both ends) be full of a gas, and be firmly fixed at its middle point, then it is easy to bring the tube and gas into a state of vibration, by rubbing it from centre to end with a damp cloth. The vibration of the gas is easily rendered visible, if the interior of the tube be dusted with lycopodium (the yellow powder-dust or spores of the lycopodium plant is often employed in medicine), before the gas is introduced and the tube fused up. The fine lycopodium powder arranges itself in patches, whose number depends on the velocity of sound in the gas. If there be 10 patches, then the velocity of sound in the gas is ten times slower than in glass. It is evident that this is an easy method of comparing the velocity of sound in gases. It has been demonstrated by experiment that the velocity of sound in oxygen is four times less than in hydrogen, and the square roots of the densities and molecular weights of hydrogen and oxygen stand in this ratio.

[27] If the conception of the molecular weights of substances does not give an exact law when applied to the latent heat of evaporation, at all events it brings to light a certain uniformity in figures, which otherwise only represent the simple result of observation. Molecular quantities of liquids appear to expend almost equal amounts of heat in their evaporation. It may be said that the latent heat of evaporation of molecular quantities is approximately constant, because the *vis viva* of the motion of the molecules is, as we saw above, a constant quantity. According to thermodynamics the latent heat of evaporation is equal to $t + 273$ $\boxed{xA + yB}$ $(n' - n)$ dp $\boxed{dT}$ × 13·59, where t is the boiling point, n' the specific volume (*i.e.* the volume of a unit of weight) of the vapour, and n the specific volume of the liquid, dp/dT the variation of the tension with a rise of temperature per 1°, and 13·89 the density of the mercury according to which the pressure is measured. Thus the latent heat of evaporation increases not only with a decrease in the vapour density (*i.e.* the molecular weight), but also with an increase in the boiling point, and therefore depends on different factors.

[27 bis] The osmotic pressure, vapour tension of the solvent, and several other means applied like the cryoscopic method to dilute solutions for determining the molecular weight of a substance in solution, are more difficult to carry out in practice, and only the method of *determining the rise of the boiling point* of dilute solutions can from its facility be placed parallel with the cryoscopic method, to which it bears a strong resemblance, as in both the solvent changes its state and is partially separated. In the boiling point method it passes off in the form of a vapour, while in cryoscopic determinations it separates out in the form of a solid body.

Van't Hoff, starting from the second law of thermodynamics, showed that the dependence of the rise of pressure (dp) upon a rise of temperature (dT) is determined by the equation $dp = (kmp/2T^2)dT$, where k is the latent heat of evaporation of the solvent, m its molecular weight, p the tension of the saturated vapour of the solvent at T, and T the absolute temperature (T

= 273 + t), while Raoult found that the quantity $(p - p')/p$ (Chapter I., Note 50) or the measure of the relative fall of tension (p the tension of the solvent or water, and p' of the solution) is found by the ratio of the number of molecules, n of the substance dissolved, and N of the solvent, so that $(p - p')/p = Cn/(N + n)$ where C is a constant. With very dilute solutions $p - p'$ may be taken as equal to dp, and the fraction $n/(N + n)$ as equal to n/N (because in that case the value of N is very much greater than n), and then, judging from experiment, C is nearly unity—hence: $dp/p = n/N$ or $dp = np/N$, and on substituting this in the above equation we have $(kmp/2T^2)dT = np/N$. Taking a weight of the solvent $m/N = 100$, and of the substance dissolved (per 100 of the solvent) q, where q evidently $= nM$, if M be the molecular weight of the substance dissolved, we find that $n/N = qm/100M$, and hence, according to the preceding equation, we have $M = 0 \cdot 02T^2 \boxed{k} \cdot q$ $\boxed{dT}$, that is, by taking a solution of q grms. of a substance in 100 grms. of a solvent, and determining by experiment the rise of the boiling point dT, we find the molecular weight M of the substance dissolved, because the fraction $0 \cdot 02T^2/k$ is (for a given pressure and solvent) a constant; for water at 100° (T = 373°) when $k = 534$ (Chapter I., Note 11), it is nearly 5·2, for ether nearly 21, for bisulphide of carbon nearly 24, for alcohol nearly 11·5, &c. As an example, we will cite from the determinations made by Professor Sakurai, of Japan (1893), that when water was the solvent and the substance dissolved, corrosive sublimate, $HgCl_2$, was taken in the quantity $q = 8 \cdot 978$ and $4 \cdot 253$ grms., the rise in the boiling point dT was $= O° \cdot 179$ and $0° \cdot 084$, whence M = 261 and 263, and when alcohol was the solvent, $q = 10 \cdot 873$ and $8 \cdot 765$ and $dT = 0° \cdot 471$ and $0° \cdot 380$, whence M = 266 and 265, whilst the actual molecular weight of corrosive sublimate = 271, which is very near to that given by this method. In the same manner for aqueous solutions of sugar (M = 342), when q varied from 14 to 2·4, and the rise of the boiling point from $0° \cdot 21$ to $0° \cdot 035$, M was found to vary between 339 and 364. For solutions of iodine I_2 in ether, the molecular weight was found by this method to be between 255 and 262, and $I_2 = 254$. Sakurai obtained similar results (between 247 and 262) for solutions of iodine in bisulphide of carbon.

We will here remark that in determining M (the molecular weight of the substance dissolved) at small but increasing concentrations (per 100 grms. of water), the results obtained by Julio Baroni (1893) show that the value of M found by the formula may either increase or decrease. An increase, for instance, takes place in aqueous solutions of $HgCl_2$ (from 255 to 334 instead of 271), KNO_3 (57–66 instead of 101), $AgNO_3$ (104–107 instead of 170), K_2SO_4 (55–89 instead of 174), sugar (328–348 instead of 342), &c. On the contrary the calculated value of M decreases as the concentration increases, for solutions of KCl (40–39 instead of 74·5), NaCl (33–28 instead of 58·5), NaBr (60–49 instead of 103), &c. In this case (as also for LiCl, NaI, C₂H₃NaO₂, &c.) the value of i (Chapter I., Note 49), or the ratio between the actual molecular weight and that found by the rise of the boiling point, was found to increase with the concentration, *i.e.* to be greater than 1, and to differ more and more from unity as the strength of the solution becomes greater. For example, according to Schlamp (1894), for LiCl, with a variation of from 1·1 to 6·7 grm. LiCl per 100 of water, i varies from 1·63 to 1·89. But for substances of the first series (HgCl₂, &c.), although in very dilute solutions i is greater than 1, it approximates to 1 as the concentration increases, and this is the normal phenomenon for solutions which do not conduct an electric current, as, for instance, of sugar. And with certain electrolytes, such as HgCl₂, MgSO₄, &c., i exhibits a similar variation; thus, for HgCl₂ the value of M is found to vary between 255 and 334; that is, i (as the molecular weight = 271) varies between 1·06 and 0·81. Hence I do not believe that the difference between i and unity (for instance, for CaCl₂, i is about 3, for KI about 2, and decreases with the concentration) can at present be placed at the basis of any general chemical conclusions, and it requires further experimental research. Among other methods by which the value of i is now determined for dilute solutions is the study of their electroconductivity, admitting that $i = 1 + a(k - 1)$, where a = the ratio of the molecular conductivity to the limiting conductivity corresponding to an infinitely large dilution (*see* Physical Chemistry), and k is the number of ions into which the substance dissolved can split up. Without entering upon a criticism of this method of determining i, I will only remark that it frequently gives values of i very close to those found by the depression of the freezing point and rise of the boiling point; but that this accordance of results is sometimes very doubtful. Thus for a solution containing 5·67 grms. CaCl₂ per 100 grms. of water, i, according to the vapour tension = 2·52, according to the boiling point = 2·71, according to the electroconductivity = 2·28, while for solutions in propyl alcohol (Schlamp 1894) i is near to 1·33. In a word, although these methods of determining the molecular weight of substances in solution show an undoubted progress in the general chemical principles of the molecular theory, there are still many points which require explanation.

We will add certain general relations which apply to these problems. Isotonic (Chapter I., Note 19) solutions exhibit not only similar osmotic pressures, but also the same vapour tension, boiling point and freezing temperature. The osmotic pressure bears the same relation to the fall of the vapour tension as the specific gravity of a solution does to the specific gravity of the vapour of the solvent. The general formulæ underlying the whole doctrine of the influence of the molecular weight upon the properties of solutions considered above, are: 1. Raoult in 1886–1890 showed that

$$p - p' \boxed{p} \cdot 100 \boxed{a} \cdot M \boxed{m} = \text{a constant } C$$

where p and p' are the vapour tensions of the solvent and substance dissolved, a the amount in grms. of the substance dissolved per 100 grms. of solvent, M and m the molecular weights of the substance dissolved and solvent. 2. Raoult and Recoura in 1890 showed that the constant above C = the ratio of the actual vapour density d of the solvent to the theoretical density d calculated according to the molecular weight. This deduction may now be considered proved, because both the fall of tension and the ratio of the vapour densities d/d give, for water 1·03, for alcohol 1·02, for ether 1·04, for bisulphide of carbon 1·00, for benzene 1·02, for acetic acid 1·63. 3. By applying the principles of thermodynamics and calling L_1 the latent heat of fusion and T_1 the absolute ($= t + 273$) temperature of fusion of the solvent, and L_2 and T_2 the corresponding values for the boiling point, Van't Hoff in 1886–1890 deduced:—

$$\dfrac{\text{Depression of freezing point}}{\boxed{\text{Rise of boiling point}}} = L_2 \boxed{L_1} \cdot T_1{}^2 \boxed{T_2{}^2}$$

$$\text{Depression of freezing point} = AT_1{}^2 a \boxed{L_1 M_1}$$

$$\text{Rise of boiling point} = AT_2{}^2 a \boxed{L_2 M_1}$$

where $A = 0\cdot01988$ (or nearly $0\cdot02$ as we took it above), a is the weight in grms. of the substance dissolved per 100 grms. of the solvent, M_1 the molecular weight of the dissolved substance (in the solution), and M the molecular weight of this substance according to its composition and vapour density, then $i = M/M_1$. The experimental data and theoretical considerations upon which these formulæ are based will be found in text-books of physical and theoretical chemistry.

[28] A similar conclusion respecting the molecular weight of liquid water (*i.e.* that its molecule in a liquid state is more complex than in a gaseous state, or polymerized into H_8O_4, H_6O_3 or in general into nH_2O) is frequently met in chemico-physical literature, but as yet there is no basis for its being fully admitted, although it is possible that a polymerization or aggregation of several molecules into one takes place in the passage of water into a liquid or solid state, and that there is a converse depolymerization in the act of evaporation. Recently, particular attention has been drawn to this subject owing to the researches of Eötvös (1886) and Ramsay and Shields (1893) on the variation of the surface tension N with the temperature (N = the capillary constant a^2 multiplied by the specific gravity and divided by 2, for example, for water at 0° and 100° the value of $a^2 = 15\cdot41$ and $12\cdot58$ sq. mm., and the surface tension 7·92 and 6·04). Starting from the absolute boiling point (Chapter II., Note 29) and adding 6°, as was necessary from all the data obtained, and calling this temperature T, it is found that AS = kT, where S is the surface of a gram-

molecule of the liquid (if M is its weight in grams, s its sp. gr., then its sp. volume = M/s, and the surface $S = \sqrt[3]{(M/s)^2}$, A the surface tension (determined by experiment at T), and k a constant which is independent of the composition of the molecule. The equation $AS = kT$ is in complete agreement with the well-known equation for gases $vp = RT$ (p. 140) which serves for deducing the molecular weight from the vapour density. Ramsay's researches led him to the conclusion that the liquid molecules of CS_2, ether, benzene, and of many other substances, have the same value as in a state of vapour, whilst with other liquids this is not the case, and that to obtain an accordance, that is, that k shall be a constant, it is necessary to assume the molecular weight in the liquid state to be n times as great. For the fatty alcohols and acids n varies from 1½ to 3½, for water from 2¼ to 4, according to the temperature (at which the depolymerization takes place). Hence, although this subject offers a great theoretical interest, it cannot be regarded as firmly established, the more so since the fundamental observations are difficult to make and not sufficiently numerous; should, however, further experiments confirm the conclusions arrived at by Professor Ramsay, this will give another method of determining molecular weights.

[28 bis] Their variance is expressed in the same manner as was done by Van't Hoff (Chapter I., Notes 19 and 49) by the quantity i, taking it as = 1 when $k = 1·05$, in that case for KI, i is nearly 2, for borax about 4, &c.

[29] We will cite one more example, showing the direct dependence of the properties of a substance on the molecular weight. If one molecular part by weight of the various chlorides—for instance, of sodium, calcium, barium, &c.—be dissolved in 200 molecular parts by weight of water (for instance, in 3,600 grams) then it is found that the greater the molecular weight of the salt dissolved, the greater is the specific gravity of the resultant solution.

	Molecular weight	Sp. gr. at 15°		Molecular weight	Sp. gr. at 15°
HCl	36·5	1·0041	$CaCl_2$	111	1·0236
NaCl	58·5	1·0106	$NiCl_2$	130	1·0328
KCl	74·5	1·0121	$ZnCl_2$	136	1·0331
$BeCl_2$	80	1·0138	$BaCl_2$	208	1·0489
$MgCl_2$	95	1·0203			

[29 bis] With respect to the optical refractive power of substances, it must first be observed that the coefficient of refraction is determined by two methods: (*a*) either all the data are referred to one definite ray—for instance, to the Fraunhofer (sodium) line D of the solar spectrum—that is, to a ray of definite wave length, and often to that red ray (of the hydrogen spectrum) whose wave length is 656 millionths of a millimetre; (*b*) or Cauchy's formula is used, showing the relation between the coefficient of refraction and dispersion to the wave length $n = A + B \, \lambda$, where A and B are two constants varying for every substance but constant for all rays of the spectrum, and λ is the wave length of that ray whose coefficient of refraction is *n*. In the latter method the investigation usually concerns the magnitudes of A, which are independent of dispersion. We shall afterwards cite the data, investigated by the first method, by which Gladstone, Landolt, and others established the conception of the refraction equivalent.

It has long been known that the *coefficient of refraction n* for a given substance decreases with the density of a substance D, so that the magnitude $(n - 1) \div D = C$ is almost constant for a given ray (having a definite wave length) and for a given substance. This constant is called the *refractive energy*, and its product with the atomic or molecular weight of a substance the *refraction equivalent*. The coefficient of refraction of oxygen is 1·00021, of hydrogen 1·00014, their densities (referred to water) are 0·00143 and 0·00009, and their atomic weights, O = 16, H = 1; hence their refraction equivalents are 3 and 1·5. Water contains H_2O, consequently the sum of the equivalents of refraction is $(2 \times 1·5) + 3 = 6$. But as the coefficient of refraction of water = 1·331, its refraction equivalent = 5·958, or nearly 6. Comparison shows that, approximately, the sum of the refraction equivalents of the atoms forming compounds (or mixtures) is equal to the refraction equivalent of the compound. According to the researches of Gladstone, Landolt, Hagen, Brühl and others, the refraction equivalents of the elements are—H = 1·3, Li = 3·8, B = 4·0, C = 5·0, N = 4·1 (in its highest state of oxidation, 5·3), O = 2·9, F = 1·4, Na = 4·8, Mg = 7·0, Al = 8·4, Si = 6·8, P = 18·3, S = 16·0, Cl = 9·9, K = 8·1, Ca = 10·4, Mn = 12·2, Fe = 12·0 (in the salts of its higher oxides, 20·1), Co = 10·8, Cu = 11·6, Zn = 10·2, As = 15·4, Bi = 15·3, Ag = 15·7, Cd = 13·6, I = 24·5, Pt = 26·0, Hg = 20·2, Pb = 24·8, &c. The refraction equivalents of many elements could only be calculated from the solutions of their compounds. The composition of a solution being known it is possible to calculate the refraction equivalent of one of its component parts, those for all its other components being known. The results are founded on the acceptance of a law which cannot be strictly applied. Nevertheless the representation of the refraction equivalents gives an easy means for directly, although only approximately, obtaining the coefficient of refraction from the chemical composition of a substance. For instance, the composition of carbon bisulphide is $CS_2 = 76$, and from its density, 1.27, we find its coefficient of refraction to be 1.618 (because the refraction equivalent $= 5 + 2 \times 16 = 37$), which is very near the actual figure. It is evident that in the above representation compounds are looked on as simple mixtures of atoms, and the physical properties of a compound as the sum of the properties present in the elementary atoms forming it. If this representation of the presence of simple atoms in compounds had not existed, the idea of combining by a few figures a whole mass of data relating to the coefficient of refraction of different substances could hardly have arisen. For further details on this subject, see works on *Physical Chemistry*.

[338]

CHAPTER VIII

CARBON AND THE HYDROCARBONS

It is necessary to clearly distinguish between the two closely-allied terms, charcoal and carbon. Charcoal is well known to everybody, although it is no easy matter to obtain it in a chemically pure state. Pure charcoal is a simple, insoluble, infusible, combustible substance produced by heating organic matter, and has the familiar aspect of a black mass, devoid of any crystalline structure, and completely insoluble. Charcoal is a substance possessing a peculiar combination of physical and chemical properties. This substance, whilst in a state of ignition, combines directly with oxygen; in organic substances it is found in combination with hydrogen, oxygen, nitrogen, and sulphur. But in all these combinations there is no real charcoal, as in the same sense there is no ice in steam. What is found in such combinations is termed 'carbon'—that is, an element common to charcoal, to those substances which can be formed from it, and also to those substances from which it can be obtained. Carbon may take the form of charcoal, but occurs also as diamond and as graphite. Truly no other element has such a wide terminology. Oxygen is always called 'oxygen,' whether it is in a free gaseous state, or in the form of ozone, or oxygen in water, or in nitric acid or in carbonic anhydride. But here there is some confusion. In water it is evident that there is no oxygen in a gaseous form, such as can be obtained in a free state, no oxygen in the form of ozone, but a substance which is capable of producing both oxygen, ozone, and water. As an element, oxygen possesses a known chemical individuality, and an influence on the properties of those combinations into which it enters. Hydrogen gas is a substance which reacts with difficulty, but the element hydrogen represents in its combinations an easily displaceable component part. Carbon may be considered as an atom of carbon matter, and charcoal as a collection of such atoms forming a whole substance, or mass of molecules of the substance. The accepted atomic weight of carbon is 12, because that is the least quantity of carbon which enters[339] into combination in molecules of its compounds; but the weight of the molecules of charcoal is probably very much greater. This weight remains unknown because charcoal is capable of but few direct reactions and those only at a high temperature (when the weight of its molecules probably changes, as when ozone changes into oxygen), and it does not turn into vapour. Carbon exists in nature, both in a free and combined state, in most varied forms and aspects. Carbon in a free state is found in at least three different forms, as charcoal, graphite, and the diamond. In a combined state it enters into the composition of what are called organic substances—a multitude of substances which are found in all plants and animals. It exists as carbonic anhydride both in air and in water, and in the soil and crust of the earth as salts of carbonic acid and as organic remains.

The variety of the substances of which the structure of plants and animals is built up is familiar to all. Wax, oil, turpentine, and tar, cotton and albumin, the tissue of plants and the muscular fibre of animals, vinegar and starch, are all vegetable and animal matters, and all carbon compounds.[1] The class of carbon compounds is so vast[340] that it forms a separate branch of chemistry, known under the name of organic chemistry—that is, the chemistry of carbon compounds, or, more strictly, of the hydrocarbons and their derivatives.

[341]

If any one of these organic compounds be strongly heated without free access of air—or, better still, in a vacuum—it decomposes with more or less facility. If the supply of air be insufficient, or the temperature be too low for combustion (*see* Chapter III.), and if the first volatile products of transformation of the organic matter are subjected to condensation (for example, if the door of a stove be opened), an imperfect combustion takes place, and smoke, with charcoal or soot, is formed.[2][342] The nature of the phenomenon, and the products arising from it, are the same as those produced by heating alone, since that part which is in a state of combustion serves to heat the remainder of the fuel. The decomposition which takes place on heating a compound composed of carbon, hydrogen, and oxygen is as follows:—A part of the hydrogen is separated in a gaseous state, another part in combination with oxygen, and a third part separates in combination with carbon, and sometimes in combination with carbon and oxygen in the form of gaseous or volatile products, or, as they are also called, the products of dry distillation. If the vapours of these products are passed through a strongly heated tube, they are changed again in a similar manner and finally resolve themselves into hydrogen and charcoal. Altogether these various products of decomposition contain a smaller amount of carbon than the original organic matter; part of the carbon remains in a free state, forming charcoal.[3] It remains in that space where the decomposition took place, in the shape of the black, infusible, non-volatile charcoal familiar to all. The earthy matter and all non-volatile[343] substances (ash) forming a part of the organic matter, remain behind with the charcoal. The tar-like substances, which require a high temperature in order to decompose them, also remain mixed with charcoal. If a volatile organic substance, such as a gaseous compound containing oxygen and hydrogen, be taken, the carbon separates on passing the vapour through a tube heated to a high temperature. Organic substances when burning with an insufficient supply of air give off soot—that is, charcoal—proceeding from carbon compounds in a state of vapour, the hydrogen of which has, by combustion, been converted into water; so, for instance, turpentine, naphthalene, and other hydrocarbons which are with difficulty decomposed by heat, easily yield carbon in the form of soot during combustion. Chlorine and other substances which, like oxygen, are capable of taking up hydrogen, and also substances which are capable of taking up water, can also separate carbon from (or char) most organic substances.

Wood charcoal is prepared in large quantities in a similar manner—that is, by the partial combustion of wood.[4] In nature a similar[344] process of carbonisation of vegetable refuse takes place in its transformation under water, as shown by the marshy vegetation which forms peat.[5] In this manner doubtless the enormous masses of coal were formed[6] which, following the example set by England, are now utilised everywhere as the principal material for heating steam[345] [346] boilers, and in general for all purposes of heating and burning.[7] Russia possesses many very rich coalfields, amongst which the Donetz district is most worthy of remark.[8]

During the imperfect combustion of volatile substances containing[347] carbon and hydrogen, the hydrogen and part of the carbon first burn, and the remainder of the carbon forms soot. Tar, pitch, and similar substances for this reason burn with a smoky flame. Thus soot is finely-divided charcoal separated during the imperfect combustion of the vapours and gases of carbonaceous substances rich in carbon. Specially-prepared soot (lampblack) is very largely used as a black paint and a large quantity goes for the manufacture of printers' ink. It is prepared by burning tar, oil, natural gas, naphtha, &c. The quantity of organic matter remaining undecomposed in the charcoal depends on the temperature to which it has been submitted. Charcoal prepared at the lowest temperature still contains a considerable quantity of hydrogen and oxygen—even as much as 4 p.c. of hydrogen and 20 p.c. of oxygen. Such charcoal still preserves the structure of the substance from which it was obtained. Ordinary charcoal, for instance, in which the structure of the tree is still visible, is of this kind. On submitting it to further heating, a fresh quantity of hydrogen with carbon and oxygen (in the form of gases or volatile matter) may be separated, and the purest charcoal will be obtained on submitting it to the greatest heat.[9] If it be required to prepare pure charcoal from soot it is necessary first to wash it with alcohol and ether in order to remove the soluble tarry products, and then submit it to a powerful heat to drive off the impurities containing hydrogen and oxygen. Charcoal however when completely purified does not change in appearance. Its porosity,[10] bad conducting power for heat,[348] capability of absorbing the luminous rays (hence its blackness and opacity), and many other qualities, are familiar from everyday experience.[11] The specific gravity of charcoal varies from 1·4 to 1·9, and that it floats on water is due to the air contained in its pores. If charcoal is reduced to a powder and moistened with spirit, it immediately sinks in water. It is *infusible* in the furnace and even at the temperature of the oxyhydrogen flame. In the heat generated by means of a powerful galvanic current charcoal only softens but does not completely melt, and on cooling it is found to have undergone a complete change both in properties and appearance, and is more or less transformed into graphite. The physical stability of charcoal is without doubt allied to its chemical stability. It is evidently a substance devoid of energy, for it is insoluble in all known liquids,[349] and *at an ordinary temperature does not combine with anything*; it is an inactive substance, like nitrogen.[12] But these properties of charcoal change with a rise of temperature; thus, unlike nitrogen, charcoal, at a high temperature, combines directly with oxygen. This is well known, as charcoal burns in air. Indeed, not only does oxygen *combine with charcoal at a red heat*, but sulphur, hydrogen, silicon, and also iron and some other metals[12 bis] do so at a very high temperature—that is, when the molecules of the charcoal have reached a state of great instability—whilst at ordinary temperatures neither oxygen, sulphur, nor metals act on charcoal in any way. When burning in oxygen, charcoal forms carbonic anhydride, CO_2, whilst in the vapours of sulphur, carbon bisulphide, CS_2, is formed, and wrought iron, when acted on by carbon, becomes cast iron. At the great heat obtained by passing the galvanic current through carbon electrodes, charcoal combines with hydrogen, forming acetylene, C_2H_2. Charcoal does not combine directly with nitrogen, but in the presence of metals and alkaline oxides, nitrogen is absorbed, forming a metallic cyanide, as, for instance, potassium cyanide, KCN. From these few direct combinations which charcoal is capable of entering into, may be derived those numerous carbonaceous compounds which enter into the composition of plants and animals, and can be thus obtained artificially. Certain substances containing oxygen give up a[350] part of it to charcoal at a relatively low temperature. For instance, nitric acid when boiled with charcoal gives carbonic anhydride and nitric peroxide. Sulphuric acid is reduced to sulphurous anhydride when heated with carbon. When heated to redness charcoal absorbs oxygen from a large number of the oxides. Even such oxides as those of sodium and potassium, when heated to redness, yield their oxygen to charcoal although they do not part with it to hydrogen. Only a few of the oxides, like silica (oxide of silicon) and lime (calcium oxide) resist the reducing action of charcoal. Charcoal is capable of changing its physical condition without undergoing any alteration in its essential chemical properties—that is, it passes into *isomeric* or *allotropic forms*. The two other particular forms in which carbon appears are the *diamond* and *graphite*. The identity of composition of these with charcoal is proved by burning an equal quantity of all three separately in oxygen (at a very high temperature), when each gives the same quantity of carbonic anhydride—namely, 12 parts of charcoal, diamond, or graphite in a pure state, yield on burning 44 parts by weight of carbonic anhydride. The physical properties present a marked contrast; the densest sorts of charcoal have a density of only 1·9, whilst the density of graphite is about 2·3, and that of the diamond 3·5. A great many other properties depend on the density, for instance combustibility. The lighter charcoal is, the more easily it burns; graphite burns with considerable difficulty even in oxygen, and the diamond burns only in oxygen and at a very high temperature. On burning, charcoal, the diamond, and graphite develop different quantities of heat. One part by weight of wood charcoal converted by burning into carbonic anhydride develops 8,080 heat units; dense charcoal separated in gas retorts develops 8,050 heat units; natural graphite, 7,800 heat units; and the diamond 7,770. The greater the density the less the heat evolved by the combustion of the carbon.[13]

By means of intense heat charcoal may be transformed into graphite. If a charcoal rod 4 mm. in diameter and 5 mm. long be enclosed in an exhausted receiver and the current from 600 Bunsen's elements, placed in parallel series of 100, be passed through it, the charcoal[351] becomes strongly incandescent, partially volatilises, and is deposited in the form of graphite. If sugar be placed in a charcoal crucible and a powerful galvanic current passed through it, it is baked into a mass similar to graphite. If charcoal be mixed with wrought iron and heated, cast iron is formed, which contains as much as five per cent. of charcoal. If molten cast iron be suddenly chilled, the carbon remains in combination with the iron, forming so called white cast iron; but if the cooling proceeds slowly, the greater part of the carbon separates in the form of graphite, and if such cast iron (so called grey cast iron) be dissolved in acid, the carbon remains in the form of graphite. Graphite is met with in nature, sometimes in the form of large compact masses, sometimes permeating rocky formations like the schists or slates, and in fact is met with in those places which, in all probability, have been subjected to the action of subterranean heat.[14] The graphite in cast iron, and sometimes also natural graphite, occasionally appears in a crystalline form in the shape of six-sided plates, but more often it occurs as a compact amorphous mass having the characteristic properties of the familiar black-lead pencil.[15]

The diamond is a crystalline and transparent form of carbon. It is[352] of rare occurrence in nature, and is found in the alluvial deposits of the diamond mines of Brazil, India, South Africa, &c. It has also been found in meteorites.[15 bis] It crystallises in octahedra, dodecahedra, cubes, and other forms of the regular system.[16] The efforts which have been made to produce diamonds artificially, although they have not been fruitless, have not as yet led to the production of large-sized crystals, because those means by which crystals are generally formed are inapplicable to carbon. Indeed, carbon in all its forms being insoluble and infusible does not pass into a liquid condition by means of which crystallisation could take place. Diamonds have several times been successfully produced in the shape of minute crystals having the appearance of a black powder, but when viewed under the microscope appearing transparent, and possessing that hardness which is the peculiar characteristic of the diamond. This diamond powder is deposited on the negative electrode, when a weak galvanic current is passed through liquid chloride of carbon.[16 bis]

Moissan (Paris, 1893) produced diamonds artificially by means of the high temperature attained in the electrical furnace[17] by dissolving[353] carbon in molten cast iron, and allowing the solution with an excess of carbon, to cool under the powerful pressure exerted by rapidly cooling the metal.[17 bis] K. Chroustchoff attained the same end by means of silver, which dissolves carbon to the extent of 6 p.c.[354] at a high temperature. Rousseau, for the same purpose, heated carbide of calcium in the electric furnace. There is no doubt that all these investigators obtained the diamond as a transparent body, which burnt into CO_2, and possessed an exceptional hardness, but only in the form of a fine powder.

Judging from the fact that carbon forms a number of gaseous bodies (carbonic oxide, carbonic anhydride, methane, ethylene, acetylene, &c.) and volatile substances (for example, many hydrocarbons and their most simple derivatives), and considering that the atomic weight of carbon, C = 12, approaches that of nitrogen, N = 14, and that of oxygen, O = 16, and that the compounds CO (carbonic oxide) and N_2C_2 (cyanogen) are gases, it may be argued that if carbon formed the molecule C_2, like N_2 and O_2, it would be a gas. And as through polymerism or the combination of like molecules (as O_2 passes into O_3 or NO_2 into N_2O_4) the temperatures of ebullition and fusion rise (which is particularly clearly proved with the hydrocarbons of the C_nH_{2n} series), it ought to be considered that *the molecules of charcoal, graphite, and the diamond are very complex*, seeing that they are insoluble, non-volatile, and infusible. The aptitude which the atoms of carbon show for combining together and forming complex molecules appears in all carbon compounds. Among the volatile compounds of carbon many are well known the molecules of which contain C_5 ... C_{10} ... C_{20} ... C_{30}, &c., in general C_n where n may be very large, and in none of the other elements is this faculty of complexity so developed as in carbon.[18] Up to the present time there are no grounds for determining the degree of polymerism of the charcoal, graphite, or diamond molecules, and it can only be supposed that they contain C_n where n is a large quantity. Charcoal and those complex non-volatile organic substances which represent the gradual transitions to charcoal[19] and form the principal[355] solid substances of organisms, contain a store or accumulation of internal power in the form of the energy binding the atoms into complex molecules. When charcoal or complex compounds of carbon burn, the energy of the carbon and oxygen is turned into heat, and this fact is taken advantage of at every turn for the generation of heat from fuel.[20]

No other two elements are capable of combining together in such variety as carbon and hydrogen. The hydrocarbons of the C_nH_{2m} series in many cases differ widely from each other, although they have some properties in common. All hydrocarbons, whether gaseous, liquid or solid, are combustible substances sparingly soluble or insoluble in water. The liquefied gaseous hydrocarbons, as well as those which are liquid at ordinary temperatures, and those solid hydrocarbons which have been liquefied by fusion, have the appearance and property of oily liquors, more or less viscid, or fluid.[21] The solid hydrocarbons more or less resemble wax in their properties, although ordinary oils[356] and wax generally contain oxygen in addition to carbon and hydrogen, but in relatively small proportion. There are also many hydrocarbons which have the appearance of tar—as, for instance, metacinnamene and gutta-percha. Those liquid hydrocarbons which boil at a high temperature are like oils, and those which have a low boiling point resemble ether, whilst the gaseous hydrocarbons in many of their properties are akin to hydrogen. All this tends to show that in hydrocarbons physically considered the properties of solid non-volatile charcoal are strongly modified and hidden, whilst those of the hydrogen predominate. All hydrocarbons are neutral substances (neither basic nor acid), but under certain conditions they enter into peculiar reactions. It has been seen in those hydrogen compounds which have been already considered (water, nitric acid, ammonia) that the hydrogen in almost all cases enters into reaction, being displaced by metals. The hydrogen of the hydrocarbons, it may be said, has no metallic character that is to say, it is not directly[22] displaced by metals, even by such as sodium and potassium. On the application of more or less heat all hydrocarbons decompose[23] forming charcoal and hydrogen. The majority of hydrocarbons do not combine with the oxygen of the air or oxidise at ordinary temperatures, but under the action of nitric acid and many other oxidising substances most of them undergo oxidation, in which either a portion of the hydrogen and carbon is separated, or the oxygen enters into combination, or else the elements of hydrogen peroxide enter into combination with the hydrocarbon.[24] When heated in air, hydrocarbons[357] burn, and, according to the amount of carbon they contain, their combustion is attended more or less with a separation of soot—that is, finely divided charcoal—which imparts great brilliancy to the flame, and on this account many of them are used for the purposes of illumination—as, for instance, kerosene, coal gas, oil of turpentine. As hydrocarbons contain reducing elements (that is, those capable of combining with oxygen), they often act as reducing agents—as, for instance, when heated with oxide of copper, they burn, forming carbonic anhydride and water, and leave metallic copper. Gerhardt proved that all hydrocarbons contain an even number of hydrogen atoms. Therefore, the general formula for all hydrocarbons is C_nH_{2m} where n and m are whole numbers. This fact is known as *the law of even numbers*. Hence, the simplest possible hydrocarbons ought to be: CH_2, CH_4, CH_6 ... C_2H_2, C_2H_4, C_2H_6, C_2H_8 ... but they do not all exist, since the quantity of H which can combine with a certain amount of carbon is limited, as we shall learn directly.

Some of the hydrocarbons are capable of combination, whilst others do not show that power. Those which contain less hydrogen belong to the former category, and those which, for a given quantity of carbon, contain the maximum amount of hydrogen, belong to the latter. The composition of those last mentioned is expressed by the general formula C_nH_{2n+2}. These so-called *saturated hydrocarbons* are incapable of combination.[25] The hydrocarbons CH_6, C_2H_8, C_3H_{10}, &c.... do not exist. Those containing the maximum amount of hydrogen will be represented by CH_4 ($n = 1$, $2n + 2 = 4$), C_2H_6 ($n = 2$), C_3H_8 ($n = 3$), C_4H_{10}, &c. This may be termed the *law of limits*. Placing this in juxtaposition with the law of even numbers, it is easy to perceive that the possible hydrocarbons can be ranged in series, the terms of which may be expressed by the general formulæ C_nH_{2n+2}, C_nH_{2n}, C_nH_{2n-2}, &c.... Those hydrocarbons which belong to any one of the series[358] expressible by a general formula are said to be *homologous*0 with one another. Thus, the hydrocarbons CH_4, C_2H_6, C_3H_8, C_4H_{10}, &c.... are members of the limiting (saturated) homologous series C_nH_{2n+2}. That is, the difference between the members of the series is CH_2.[26] Not only the composition but also the properties of the members of a series tend to classification in one group. For instance, the members of the series C_nH_{2n+2} are not capable of forming additive compounds, whilst those of the series C_nH_{2n} are capable of combining with chlorine, sulphuric anhydride, &c.; and the members of the C_nH_{2n-6} group, belonging to the coal tar series, are easily nitrated (give nitro-compounds, Chapter VI.), and have other properties in common. The physical properties of the members of a given homologous series vary in some such manner as this; the boiling point generally rises and the internal friction increases as n increases[27]—that is, with an increase in the relative amount of carbon and the atomic weight; the specific gravity also regularly changes as n becomes greater.[28]

Many of the hydrocarbons met with in nature are the products of organisms, and do not belong to the mineral kingdom. A still greater number are produced artificially. These are formed by what is termed[359] the combination of residues. For instance, if a mixture of the vapours of hydrogen sulphide and carbon bisulphide be passed through a tube in which copper is heated, this latter absorbs the sulphur from both the compounds, and the liberated carbon and hydrogen combine to form a hydrocarbon, methane. If carbon be combined with any metal and this compound MC_n be treated with an acid HX, then the haloid X will give a salt with the metal and the residual carbon and hydrogen will give a hydrocarbon. Thus cast iron which contains a compound of iron and carbon gives liquid hydrocarbons like naphtha under the action of acids. If a mixture of bromo-benzene, C_6H_5Br, and ethyl bromide, C_2H_5Br, be heated with metallic sodium, the sodium combines with the bromine of both compounds, forming sodium bromide, NaBr. From the first combination the group C_6H_5 remains, and from the second C_2H_5. Having an odd number of hydrogen atoms, they, in virtue of the law of even numbers, cannot exist alone, and therefore combine together forming the compound $C_6H_5.C_2H_5$ or C_8H_{10} (ethylbenzene). Hydrocarbons are also produced by the breaking up of more complex organic or hydrocarbon compounds, especially by heating—that is, by dry distillation. For instance, gum-benzoin contains an acid called benzoic acid, $C_7H_6O_2$, the vapours of which, when passed through a heated tube, split up into carbonic anhydride, CO_2, and benzene, C_6H_6. Carbon and hydrogen only unite directly in one ratio of combination—namely, to form acetylene, having the composition C_2H_2, which, as compared with other hydrocarbons, exhibits a very great stability at a somewhat high temperature.[29]

[360]

There is one substance known among the saturated hydrocarbons composed of 1 atom of carbon and 4 atoms of hydrogen; this is a compound containing the highest percentage of hydrogen (CH_4 contains 25 per cent. of hydrogen), and at the same time it is the only hydrocarbon whose molecule contains but a single atom of carbon. This saturated hydrocarbon, CH_4, is called *marsh gas* or *methane*. If vegetable or animal refuse suffers decomposition in a space where the air has not free access, or no access at all, then the decomposition is accompanied with the formation of marsh gas, and this either at the ordinary temperature, or at a comparatively much higher one. On this account *plants*, when decomposing under water in *marshes*, give out this gas.[29 bis] It is well known that if the mud in bogs be stirred up, the act is accompanied with the evolution of a large quantity of gas bubbles; these may, although slowly, also separate of their own[361] accord. The gas which is evolved consists principally of

marsh gas.[30] If wood, coal, or many other vegetable or animal substances are decomposed by the *action of heat* without access of air—that is, are subjected to dry distillation—they, in addition to many other gaseous products of decomposition (carbonic anhydride, hydrogen, and various other substances), evolve a great deal of methane. Generally the gas which is used for lighting purposes is obtained by this means and therefore always contains marsh gas, mixed with dry hydrogen and other vapours and gases, although it is subsequently purified from many of them.[31][362]
[363]
[364] As the decomposition of the organic matter, which forms coal, is still going on underground, the evolution of large quantities of marsh gas frequently occurs in coal-mines.[32] When mixed with air it forms an explosive mixture, which forms one of the great dangers of coal mining, as subterranean work has always to be carried on by lamp-light. This danger is, however, overcome by the use of Humphry Davy's safety lamp.[33] Sir Humphry Davy observed that on introducing a piece of wire gauze into a flame, it absorbs so much heat that combustion does not proceed beyond it (the unburnt gases which pass through it may be ignited on the other side). In accordance with this, the flame of the Davy lamp is surrounded with a thick glass (as shown in the drawing), and has no communication whatever with the explosive mixture except through a wire gauze which prevents it igniting the mixture of the marsh-gas issuing from the coal with air. In some districts, particularly in those where petroleum is found—as, for instance, near Baku, where a temple of the Indian fire-worshippers was built, and in Pennsylvania, and other places—marsh gas in abundance issues from the earth, and it is used, like coal gas, for the purposes of lighting and warming.[34][365] Tolerably pure marsh gas[35] may be obtained by heating a mixture of an acetate with an alkali. Acetic acid, $C_2H_4O_2$, on being heated is decomposed into marsh gas and carbonic anhydride, $C_2H_4O_2 = CH_4 + CO_2$.

An alkali—for instance, $NaHO$—gives with acetic acid a salt, $C_2H_3NaO_2$, which on decomposition retains carbonic anhydride, forming a carbonate, Na_2CO_3, and marsh gas is given off:

$$C_2H_3NaO_2 + NaHO = Na_2CO_3 + CH_4$$

Marsh gas is difficult to liquefy; it is almost insoluble in water, and is without taste or smell. The most important point in connection with its chemical reactions is that it does not combine directly with anything, whilst the other hydrocarbons which contain less hydrogen than expressed by the formula C_nH_{2n+2} are capable of combining with hydrogen, chlorine, certain acids, &c.

If the law of substitution gives a very simple explanation of the formation of hydrogen peroxide as a compound containing two aqueous residues (OH)(OH), then on the basis of this law all hydrocarbons ought to be derived from methane, CH_4, as being the simplest hydrocarbon.[36] The increase in complexity of a molecule of methane is brought about by the faculty of mutual combination which exists in the atoms of carbon, and, as a consequence of the most detailed study of the subject, much that might have been foreseen and conjectured from the law of substitution has been actually brought about in such a manner as might have been predicted, and although this subject on account of its magnitude really belongs, as has been already stated, to the sphere of organic chemistry, it has been alluded to here in order to show, although only in part, the best investigated example of the application of the law of substitution. According to this law, a molecule of methane, CH_4, is capable of undergoing substitution in the four following ways:—(1) Methyl substitution, when the radicle, equivalent to hydrogen, called *methyl* CH_3, replaces hydrogen. In CH_4 this radicle is combined with H and therefore can replace it, as (OH) replaces H because with it it gives water; (2) methylene substitution, or the exchange between H_2 and CH_2 (this radicle is called methylene), is founded on a similar division of the molecule CH_4 into two equivalent[366] parts, H_2 and CH_2; (3) acetylene substitution, or the exchange between CH on the one hand and H_3 on the other; and (4) carbon substitution—that is, the substitution of H_4 by an atom of carbon C, which is founded on the law of substitution just as is the methyl substitution. These four cases of substitution render it possible to understand the principal relations of the hydrocarbons. For instance, the *law of even numbers* is seen from the fact that in all the cases of substitution mentioned the hydrogen atoms increase or decrease by an even number; but as in CH_4 they are likewise even, it follows that no matter how many substitutions are effected there will always be obtained an even number of hydrogen atoms. When H is replaced by CH_3 there is an increase of CH_2; when H_2 is replaced by CH_2 there is no increase of hydrogen; in the acetylene substitution CH replaces H_3, therefore there is an increase of C and a decrease of H_2; in the carbon substitution there is a decrease of H_4. In a similar way the *law of limit* may be deduced as a corollary of the law of substitution. For the largest possible quantity of hydrogen is introduced by the methyl substitution, since it leads to the addition of CH_2; starting from CH_4 we obtain C_2H_6, C_3H_8, and in general, C_nH_{2n+2}, and these contain the greatest possible amount of hydrogen. Unsaturated hydrocarbons, containing less hydrogen, are evidently only formed when the increase of the new molecule derived from methane proceeds from one of the other forms of substitution. When the methyl substitution alone takes place in methane, CH_4, it is evident that the saturated hydrocarbon formed is C_2H_6 or (CH_3)(CH_3).[37] This is called *ethane*. By means of the methylene substitution alone, *ethylene*, C_2H_4, or $(CH_2)(CH_2)$ may be directly obtained from CH_4, and by the acetylene substitution C_2H_2 or[367] $(CH)(CH)$, or *acetylene*, both the latter being unsaturated hydrocarbons. Thus we have all the possible hydrocarbons with two atoms of carbon in the molecule, C_2H_6, ethane, C_2H_4, ethylene, and C_2H_2, acetylene. But in them, according to the law of substitution, the same forms of substitution may be repeated—that is, the methyl, methylene, acetylene, and even carbon substitutions (because C_2H_6 will still contain hydrogen when C replaces H_4) and therefore further substitutions will serve as a source for the production of a fresh series of saturated and unsaturated hydrocarbons, containing more and more carbon in the molecule and, in the case of the acetylene substitution and carbon substitution, containing less and less hydrogen. Thus *by means of the law of substitution we can foresee* not only the limit C_nH_{2n+2}, but an unlimited number of unsaturated hydrocarbons, C_nH_{2n}, C_nH_{2n-2} ... $C_nH_{2(n-m)}$, where *m* varies from 0 to *n*-1,[38] and where *n* increases indefinitely. From these facts not only does the existence of a multitude of polymeric hydrocarbons, differing in molecular weight, become intelligible, but it is also seen that there is a possibility of cases of isomerism with the same molecular weight. This *polymerism* so common to hydrocarbon compounds is already apparent in the first unsaturated series C_nH_{2n}, because all the terms of this series C_2H_4, C_3H_6, C_4H_8 ... $C_{30}H_{60}$ ... have one and the same composition CH_2, but different molecular weights, as has been already explained in Chapter VII. The differences in the vapour density, boiling points, and melting points, of the quantities entering into reactions,[39] and the methods of preparation[40] also so clearly tally with the conception of polymerism, that this example will always be the clearest and most conclusive for the illustration of polymerism and molecular weight. Such a case is also met with among other hydrocarbons. Thus benzene, C_6H_6, and cinnamene, C_8H_8, correspond with the composition of acetylene or to a compound of the composition CH.[41] The first boils at 81°, the second at 144°;[368] the specific gravity of the first is 0·899; that of the second, 0·925, at 0°—that is, here also the boiling point rises with the increase of molecular weight, and so also, as might be expected, does the density.

Cases of isomerism in the restricted sense of the word—that is, when with an identity of composition and of molecular weight, the properties of the substances are different—are very numerous among the hydrocarbons and their derivatives. Such cases are particularly important for the comprehension of molecular structure and they also, like the polymerides, may be predicted from the above-mentioned conceptions, expressing the principles of the structure of the carbon compounds[42] based on the law of substitution. According to it, for example, it is evident that there can be no isomerism in the cases of the saturated hydrocarbons C_2H_6 and C_3H_8, because the former is CH_4, in which methyl has taken the place of H, and as all the hydrogen atoms of methane must be supposed to have the same relation to the carbon, it is all the same which of them be subjected to the methyl substitution—the resulting product can only be ethane, CH_3CH_3;[43] the same argument also applies in the case of propane, $CH_3CH_2CH_3$, where one compound only can be imagined. It[369] is to be expected, however, that there should be two butanes, C_4H_{10}, and this is actually the case. In one, methyl may be considered as replacing the hydrogen of one of the methyls, $CH_3CH_2CH_2CH_3$; and in the other CH_3 may be considered as substituted for H in CH_3, and there it will consist of CH_3CH CH_3 CH_3 . The latter may also be regarded as methane in which three of hydrogen are exchanged for three of methyl. On going further in the series it is evident that the number of possible isomerides will be still greater, but we have limited ourselves to the simplest examples, showing the possibility and actual existence of isomerides. C_2H_4 and CH_2CH_2 are, it is evident, identical; but there ought to be, and are, two hydrocarbons of the composition C_3H_6, propylene and trimethylene; the first is ethylene, CH_2CH_2, in which one atom of hydrogen is exchanged for methyl, CH_2CHCH_3, and trimethylene is ethane, CH_3CH_3, with the substitution of methylene for two hydrogen atoms from two methyl groups—that is, CH_2 CH_2 CH_2 ,[44] where the methylene introduced is united to both the atoms of carbon in CH_3CH_3. It is evident that the cause of isomerism here is, on the one hand, the difference of the amount of hydrogen in union with the particular atoms of carbon, and, on the other, the different connection between the several atoms of carbon. In the first case they may be said to be chained together (more usually to form an 'open chain'), and in the second case, to be locked together (to form a 'closed chai' or 'ring'). Here also it is easily understood that on increasing the quantity of carbon atoms the number of possible and existing isomerides will greatly increase. If, at the same time, in addition to the substitution of one of the radicles of methane for hydrogen a further exchange of part of the hydrogen for some of the other groups of elements X, Y ... occurs, the quantity of possible isomerides still further increases in a considerable degree. For instance, there are even two possible isomerides for the derivatives of ethane, C_2H_6: if two atoms of the hydrogen be exchanged for X_2,[370] one will have the ethylene structure, CH_2XCH_2X, and the other an ethylidene structure, CH_3CHX_2; such are, for instance, ethylene chloride, CH_2ClCH_2Cl, and ethylidene chloride, CH_3CHCl_2. And as in the place of the first atom of hydrogen not only metals may be substituted, but Cl, Br, I, OH (the water radicle), NH_2 (the ammonia radicle), NO_2 (the radicle of nitric acid), &c., so also in exchange for two atoms of hydrogen O, NH, S, &c., may be substituted; hence it will be understood that the quantity of isomerides is sometimes very great. It is impossible here to describe how the isomerides are distinguished from each other, in what reactions they occur, how and when one changes into another, &c.; for this, taken together with the description of the hydrocarbons already known, and their derivatives, forms a very extensive and very thoroughly investigated branch of chemistry, called *organic chemistry*. Enriched with a mass of closely observed phenomena and strictly deduced generalisations, this branch of chemistry has been treated separately for the reason that in it the hydrocarbon groups are subjected to transformations which are not met with in such quantity in dealing with any of the other elements or their hydrogen compounds. It was important for us to show that notwithstanding the great variety of the hydrocarbons and their products,[45] they are all of them governed by the law of substitution, and referring our readers for detailed information to works on organic chemistry, we will limit ourselves to a short exposition of the properties of the two simplest unsaturated hydrocarbons: ethylene, CH_2CH_2, and acetylene, CHCH, and a short acquaintance with petroleum as the natural source of a mass of hydrocarbons. *Ethylene, or olefiant gas,* C_2H_4,[371] is the lowest known member of the unsaturated hydrocarbon series of the composition C_nH_{2n}. As in composition it is equal to two molecules of marsh gas deprived of two molecules of hydrogen, it is evident that it might be, and it actually can be, produced, although but in small quantities, together with hydrogen, by heating marsh gas. On being heated, however, olefiant gas splits up, first into acetylene and methane ($3C_2H_4 = 2C_2H_2 + 2CH_4$, Lewes, 1894), and at a higher temperature into carbon and hydrogen; and therefore in those cases where marsh gas is produced by heating, olefiant gas, hydrogen, and charcoal will also be formed, although only in small quantities. The lower the temperature at which complex organic substances are heated, the greater the quantity of olefiant gas found in the gases given off; at a white heat it is entirely decomposed into charcoal and marsh gas. If coal, wood, and more particularly petroleum, tars, and fatty substances, are subjected to dry distillation, they give off illuminating gas, which contains more or less olefiant gas.

Olefiant gas, almost free from other gases,[46] may be obtained from ordinary alcohol (if possible, free from water) if it be mixed with five parts of strong sulphuric acid and the mixture heated to slightly above 100°. Under these conditions, the sulphuric acid removes the elements of water from the alcohol, $C_2H_5(OH)$, and gives olefiant gas; $C_2H_6O = H_2O + C_2H_4$. The greater molecular weight of olefiant gas compared with marsh gas indicates that it may be comparatively easily converted into a liquid by means of pressure or great cold; this may be effected, for example, by the evaporation of liquid nitrous oxide. Its absolute boiling point is +10°, it boils at -103° (1 atmosphere), liquefies at 0°, at a pressure of 43 atmospheres, and solidifies at -160°. Ethylene is colourless, has a slight ethereal smell, is slightly soluble in water, and somewhat more soluble in alcohol and in ether (in five volumes of spirit and six volumes of ether).[47]

[372]

Like other unsaturated hydrocarbons, olefiant gas readily enters into combination with certain substances, such as chlorine, bromine, iodine, fuming sulphuric acid, or sulphuric anhydride, &c. If olefiant gas be sealed up with a small quantity of sulphuric acid in a glass vessel, and constantly agitated (as, for instance, by attaching it to the moving part of a machine), the prolonged contact and repeated mixing causes the olefiant gas, little by little, to combine with the sulphuric acid, forming $C_2H_4H_2SO_4$. If, after this absorption, the sulphuric acid be diluted with water and distilled, alcohol separates, which is produced in this case by the olefiant gas combining with the elements of water, $C_2H_4 + H_2O = C_2H_6O$. In this reaction (Berthelot) we see an excellent example of the fact that if a given substance, like olefiant gas, is produced by the decomposition of another, then in the reverse way this substance, entering into combination, is capable of forming the original substance—in our example, alcohol. In combination with various molecules, X_2, ethylene gives saturated compounds, $C_2H_4X_2$ or CH_2XCH_2X (for example, $C_2H_4Cl_2$), which correspond with ethane, CH_3CH_3 or C_2H_6.[48]

Acetylene, $C_2H_2 = CHCH$, is a gas; it was first prepared by Berthelot (1857). It has a very pungent smell, is characterised by its great stability under the action of heat, and is obtained as the only product of the direct combination of carbon with hydrogen when a luminous arc (voltaic) is formed between carbon electrodes. This arc contains particles of carbon passing from one pole to the other. If the carbons be surrounded with an atmosphere of hydrogen, the carbon in part combines with the hydrogen, forming C_2H_2.[48 bis] Acetylene may be formed from olefiant gas if two atoms of hydrogen be taken from it. This may be effected in the following way: the olefiant gas is first made to combine with bromine, giving $C_2H_4Br_2$; from this the hydrobromic acid is removed by means of an alcoholic solution of caustic potash, leaving the volatile product C_2H_3Br; and from this yet another part of hydrobromic acid is withdrawn by passing it through anhydrous alcohol in which metallic sodium has been dissolved, or by heating it with a strong alcoholic solution of caustic potash. Under these circumstances (Berthelot, Sawitsch, Miasnikoff) the alkali takes up the hydrobromic acid from $C_nH_{2n-1}Br$, forming C_nH_{2n-2}.

[373]

Acetylene is also produced in all those cases where organic substances are decomposed by the action of a high temperature—for example, by dry distillation. On this account a certain quantity is always found in coal gas, and gives to it, at all events in part, its peculiar smell, but the quantity of acetylene in coal gas is very small. If the vapour of alcohol be passed through a heated tube a certain quantity of acetylene is formed. It is also produced by the imperfect combustion of olefiant and marsh gas—for example, if the flame of coal gas has not free access to air.[49] The inner part of every flame contains gases in imperfect combustion, and in them some amount of acetylene.

Acetylene, being further removed than ethylene from the limit C_nH_{2n+2} of hydrocarbon compounds, has a still greater faculty of combination than is shown by olefiant gas, and therefore can be more readily separated from any mixture containing it. Actually, acetylene not only combines with one and two molecules of I_2, HI, H_2SO_4, Cl_2, Br_2, &c.... (many other unsaturated hydrocarbons combine with them), but also with cuprous chloride, CuCl, forming a red precipitate. If a gaseous mixture containing acetylene be passed through an ammoniacal solution of cuprous chloride (or silver nitrate), the other gases do not combine, but the acetylene gives a red precipitate (or grey with silver), which detonates when struck with a hammer. This red precipitate gives off acetylene under the action of acids. In this manner pure acetylene may be obtained. Acetylene and its homologues also readily react with corrosive sublimate, $HgCl_2$ (Koucheroff, Favorsky). Acetylene burns with a very brilliant flame, which is accounted for by the comparatively large amount of carbon it contains.[50]

The formation and existence in nature of large masses of petroleum or a mixture of liquid hydrocarbons, principally of the series C_nH_{2n+2} and C_nH_{2n} is in many respects remarkable.[51] In some mountainous[374] districts—as, for instance, by the slopes of the Caucasian chain, on inclines lying in a direction parallel to the range—an oily liquid issues from the earth together with salt water and hot gases (methane and others); it has a tarry smell and dark brown colour, and is lighter than water. This liquid is called naphtha or rock oil (petroleum) and is obtained in large quantities by sinking wells and deep bore-holes in those places where traces of naphtha are observed, the naphtha being sometimes thrown up from the wells in fountains of considerable height.[52] The evolution of naphtha is always accompanied by salt water and marsh gas. Naphtha has from ancient times been worked in Russia in the Apsheron peninsula near Baku, and is also now worked in Burmah (India), in Galicia near the Carpathians, and in America, especially in Pennsylvania and Canada, &c. Naphtha does not consist of one definite hydrocarbon, but of a mixture of several, and its density, external appearance, and other qualities vary with the amount of the different hydrocarbons of which it is composed. The light kinds of naphtha have a specific gravity about 0·8 and the heavy kinds up to 0·98. The former are very mobile liquids, and more volatile; the latter contain less of the volatile hydrocarbons and are less mobile. When the light kinds of naphtha are distilled, the boiling point taken in the vapours constantly changes, beginning at 0° and going up to above 350°. That which passes over first is a very mobile, colourless ethereal liquid (forming gazolene, ligroin, benzoline, &c.), from which the hydrocarbons whose boiling points start from 0° may be extracted—namely, the hydrocarbons C_4H_{10}, C_5H_{12} (which boils at 30°), C_6H_{14} (boils at 62°), C_7H_{16} (boils about 90°), &c. Those fractions of the naphtha distillate which boil above 130°, and contain hydrocarbons with C_9, C_{10}, C_{11}, &c., enter into the composition of the[375] oily substance, universally used for lighting, called kerosene or photogen or photonaphthalene, and by other names. The specific gravity of kerosene is from 0·78 to 0·84, and it smells like naphtha. Those products of the distillation of naphtha which pass off below 130° and have a specific gravity below 0·75, enter into the composition of light petroleum (benzoline, ligroin, petroleum spirit, &c.); which is used as a solvent for india-rubber, for removing grease spots, &c. Those portions of naphtha (which can only be distilled without change by means of superheated steam, otherwise they are largely decomposed) which boil above 275° and up to 300° and have a specific gravity higher than 0·85, form an excellent oil,[53] safe as regards inflammability (which is very important as diminishing the risks of fire), and may be used in lamps as an effective substitute for kerosene.[54] Those portions of naphtha which pass over at a still higher temperature and have a higher specific gravity than 0·9, which are found in abundance (about 30 p.c.) in the Baku naphtha, make excellent lubricating or machine oils. Naphtha has many important applications, and the naphtha industry is now of great commercial importance, especially as naphtha[376] and its refuse may be used as fuel.[55] Whether naphtha was formed from organic matter is very doubtful, as it is found in the most ancient Silurian strata which correspond with epochs of the earth's existence when there was little organic matter; it could not penetrate from the higher to the lower (more ancient) strata as it floats on water (and water penetrates through all strata). It therefore tends to rise to the surface of the earth, and it is always found in highlands parallel to the direction of the mountains.[56] Much more probably its formation may be attributed to the action of water penetrating through the crevasses formed on the mountain slopes and reaching to the heart of the earth, to that kernel of heated metallic matter which must be accepted as existing in the interior of the earth. And as meteoric iron often contains carbon (like cast iron), so, accepting the existence of such carburetted iron at unattainable depths in the interior of the earth, it may be supposed that naphtha was produced by the action of water penetrating through the crevices of the strata during the upheaval of[377] mountain chains,[57] because water with iron carbide ought to give iron oxide and hydrocarbons.[58] Direct experiment proves that the so-called *spiegeleisen* (manganiferous iron, rich in chemically combined carbon) when treated with acids gives liquid hydrocarbons[59] which in composition,[378] appearance, and properties are completely identical with naphtha.[60]

Footnotes:

[1] Wood is the non-vital part of ligneous plants: the vital part of ordinary trees is situated between the bark and the lignin. Every year a layer of lignin is deposited on this part by the juices which are absorbed by the roots and drawn up by the leaves; for this reason the age of trees may be determined by the number of lignin layers deposited. The woody matter consists principally of fibrous tissue on to which the lignin or so-called incrusting matter has been deposited. The tissue has the composition $C_6H_{10}O_5$, the substance deposited on it contains more carbon and hydrogen and less oxygen. This matter is saturated with moisture when the wood is in a fresh state. Fresh birch wood contains about 31 p.c. of water, lime wood 47 p.c., oak 35 p.c., pine and fir about 37 p.c. When dried in the air the wood loses a considerable quantity of water and not more than 19 p.c. remains. By artificial means this loss of water may be increased. If water be driven into the pores of wood the latter becomes heavier than water, as the lignin of which it is composed has a density of about 1·6. One cubic centimetre of birch wood does not weigh more than 0·901 gram, fir 0·894, lime tree 0·817, poplar 0·765 when in a fresh state; when in a dry state birch weighs 0·622, pine 0·550, fir 0·355, lime 0·430, guaiacum 1·342, ebony 1·226. On one hectare (2·7 acres) of woodland the yearly growth averages the amount of 3,000 kilograms (or about 3 tons) of wood, but rarely reaches as much as 5,000 kilos. The average chemical composition of wood dried in air may be expressed as follows:—Hygroscopic water 15 p.c., carbon 42 p.c., hydrogen 5 p.c., oxygen and nitrogen 37 p.c., ash 1 p.c. Wood parts with its hygroscopic water at 150°, and decomposes at about 300°, giving a brown, brittle, so-called red charcoal; above 350° black charcoal is produced. As the hydrogen contained in wood requires for its combustion about forty parts by weight of oxygen, which is present to the amount of about 36 p.c., all that burns of the wood is the carbon which it contains, 100 parts of wood only giving out as much heat as forty parts of charcoal, and therefore it would be far more profitable to use charcoal for heating purposes than wood, if it were possible to obtain it in such quantities as correspond with its percentage ratio—that is forty parts per 100 parts of wood. Generally, however, the quantity produced is far less, not more than 30 p.c., because part of the carbon is given off as gas, tar, &c. If wood has to be transported great distances, or if it is necessary to obtain a very high temperature by burning it, then even as little as 25 p.c. of charcoal from 100 parts of wood may be advantageous. Charcoal (from

wood) develops on burning 8,000 heat units, whilst wood dried in air does not develop more than 2,800 units of heat; therefore seven parts of charcoal give as much heat as twenty parts of wood. As regards the temperature of combustion, it is far higher with charcoal than with wood, because twenty parts of burning wood give, besides the carbonic anhydride which is also formed together with charcoal, eleven parts of water, the evaporation of which requires a considerable amount of heat.

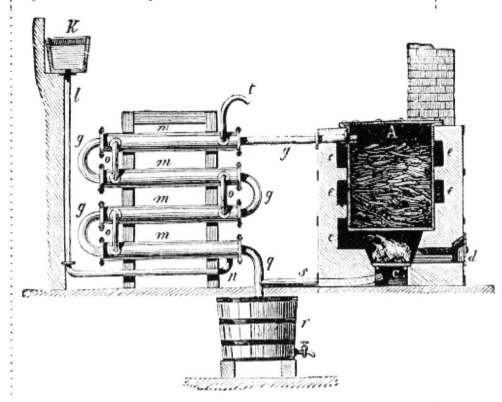

FIG. 57.—Apparatus for the dry distillation of wood. The retort a containing the wood is heated by the flues $c\ e$. The steam and volatile products of distillation pass along the tube g through the condenser m, where they are condensed. The form, distribution, and dimensions of the apparatus vary.

The composition of the growing parts of plants, the leaves, young branches, shoots, &c., differs from the composition of the wood in that these vital parts contain a considerable quantity of sap which contains much nitrogenous matter (in the wood itself there is very little), mineral salts, and a large amount of water. Taking, for example, the composition of clover and pasture hay in the green and dry state; in 100 parts of green clover there is about 80 p.c. of water and 20 p.c. of dry matter, in which there are about 3·5 parts of nitrogenous albuminous matter, about 9·5 parts of soluble and about 5 parts of insoluble non-nitrogenous matter, and about 2 p.c. of ash. In dry clover or clover-hay there is about 15 p.c. of water, 13 p.c. of nitrogenous matter, and 7 p.c. of ash. This composition of grassy substances shows that they are capable of forming the same sort of charcoal as wood itself. It also shows the difference of nutritive properties existing between wood and the substances mentioned. These latter serve as food for animals, because they contain those substances which are capable of being dissolved (entering into the blood) and forming the body of animals; such substances are proteids, starch, &c. Let us remark here that with a good harvest an acre of land gives in the form of grass as much organic substance as it yields in the form of wood.

One hundred parts of dry wood are capable of giving, on dry distillation, besides 25 p.c. of charcoal and 10 p.c. or more of tar, 40 p.c. of watery liquid, containing acetic acid and wood spirit, and about 25 p.c. of gases, which may be used for heating or lighting purposes, because they do not differ from ordinary illuminating gas, which can indeed be obtained from wood. As wood-charcoal and tar are valuable products, in some cases the dry distillation of wood is carried on principally for producing them. For this purpose those kinds of woods are particularly advantageous which contain resinous substances, especially coniferous trees, such as fir, pine, &c.; birch, oak, and ash give much less tar, but on the other hand they yield more aqueous liquor. The latter is used for the manufacture of wood spirit, CH_4O, and acetic acid, $C_2H_4O_2$. In such cases, the dry distillation is carried on in stills. The stills are nothing more than horizontal or vertical cylindrical retorts, made of boiler plate, heated with fuel and having apertures at the top and sometimes also at the bottom for the exit of the light and heavy products of distillation. The dry distillation of wood in stoves is carried on in two ways, either by burning a portion of the wood inside the stove in order to submit the remainder to dry distillation by means of the heat obtained in this manner, or by placing the wood in a stove the thin sides of which are surrounded with a flue leading from the fuel, placed in a space below.

The first method does not give such a large amount of liquid products of the dry distillation as the latter. In the latter process there is generally an outlet below for emptying out the charcoal at the close of the operation. For the dry distillation of 100 parts of wood from forty to twenty parts of fuel are used.

In the north of Russia wood is so plentiful and cheap that this locality is admirably fitted to become the centre of a general trade in the products of its dry distillation. Coal (Note 6), sea-weed, turf, animal substances (Chapter VI.), &c., are also submitted to the process of dry distillation.

[2] The result of imperfect combustion is not only the loss of a part of the fuel and the production of smoke, which in some respects is inconvenient and injurious to health, but also a low flame temperature, which means that a less amount of heat is transmitted to the object heated. Imperfect combustion is not only always accompanied by the formation of soot or unburnt particles of charcoal, but also by that of carbonic oxide, CO, in the smoke (Chapter IX.) which burns, emitting much heat. In works and factories where large quantities of fuel are consumed, many appliances are adopted to ensure perfect combustion, and to combat against such a ruinous practice as the imperfect combustion of fuel. The most effective and radical means consists in employing combustible gases (producer and water gases), because by their aid perfect combustion can be easily realised without a loss of heat-producing power and the highest temperature can be reached. When solid fuel is used (such as coal, wood, and turf), imperfect combustion is most liable to occur when the furnace doors are opened for the introduction of fresh fuel. The step furnace may often prove a remedy for this defect. In the ordinary furnace fresh fuel is placed on the burning fuel, and the products of dry distillation of the fresh fuel have to burn at the expense of the oxygen remaining uncombined with the burnt fuel. Imperfect combustion is observed in this case also from the fact that the dry distillation and evaporation of the water of the fresh fuel lying on the top of that burnt, lowers the temperature of the flame, because part of the heat becomes latent. On this account a large amount of smoke (imperfect combustion) is observed when a fresh quantity of fuel is introduced into the furnace. This may be obviated by constructing the furnace (or managing the stoking) in such a way that the products of distillation pass through the red-hot charcoal remaining from the burnt fuel. It is only necessary in order to ensure this to allow a sufficient quantity of air for perfect combustion. All this may be easily attained by the use of step fire-bars. The fuel is fed into a hopper and falls on to the fire-bars, which are arranged in the form of a staircase. The burning charcoal is below, and hence the flame formed by the fresh fuel is heated by the contact of the red-hot burning charcoal. An air supply through the fire grate, an equal distribution of the fuel on the fire-bars (otherwise the air will blow through empty spaces and lower the temperature), a proper proportion between the supply of air and the chimney draught, and a perfect admixture of air with the flame (without an undue excess of air), are the means by which we can contend against the imperfect combustion of such kinds of fuel as wood, peat, and ordinary (smoky) coal. Coke, charcoal, anthracite, burn without smoke, because they do not contain hydrogenous substances which furnish

the products of dry distillation, but imperfect combustion may occur with them also; in that case the smoke contains carbonic oxide.

[3] Under the action of air, organic substances are capable of oxidising to such an extent that all the carbon and all the hydrogen they contain will be transformed into carbonic anhydride and water. The refuse of plants and that of animals are subjected to such a change whether they slowly decompose and putrefy, or rapidly burn with direct access of air. But if the supply of air be limited, there can be no complete transformation into water and carbonic anhydride, there will be other volatile matters (rich in hydrogen), while charcoal must remain as a non-volatile substance. All organic substances are unstable, they do not resist heat, and change even at ordinary temperatures, particularly if water be present. It is therefore easy to understand that charcoal may in many cases be obtained through the transformation of substances entering into the composition of organisms, but that it is never found in a pure state.

However, water and carbonic anhydride are not the only products separated from organic substances. Carbon, hydrogen, and oxygen are capable of giving a multitude of compounds; some of these are volatile compounds, gaseous, soluble in water—they are carried off from organic matter, undergoing change without access of air. Others, on the contrary, are non-volatile, rich in carbon, unaffected by heat and other agents. The latter remain in admixture with charcoal in the place where the decomposition takes place; such, for example, are tarry substances. The quantity of those bodies which are found mixed with the charcoal is very varied, and depends on the energy and duration of the decomposing agent. The annexed table shows, according to the data of Violette, those changes which wood undergoes at various temperatures when submitted to dry distillation by means of superheated steam:—

Temperature	Residue from 100 parts of alder wood	In 100 parts of the residual charcoal			
		C	H	O and N	Ash
150°	100·0	47·5	6·1	46·3	0·1
350°	29·7	76·6	4·1	18·4	0·6
1032°	18·7	81·9	2·3	14·1	1·6
1500°	17·3	95·0	0·7	3·8	1·7

[4] The object of producing charcoal from wood has been explained in Note 1. *Wood charcoal* is obtained in so-called stacks by partially burning the wood, or by means of dry distillation (Note 1) without the access of air. It is principally manufactured for metallurgical processes, especially for smelting and forging iron. The preparation of charcoal in stacks has one advantage, and that is that it may be done on any spot in the forest. But in this way all the products of dry distillation are lost. For charcoal burning, a pile or stack is generally built, in which the logs are placed close together, either horizontally, vertically, or inclined, forming a stack of from six to fifty feet in diameter and even larger. Under the stack are several horizontal air passages, and an opening in the middle to let out the smoke. The surface of the stack is covered with earth and sods to a considerable thickness, especially the upper part, in order to hinder the free passage of air and to concentrate the heat inside. When the stack is kindled, the pile begins to settle down by degrees, and it is then necessary to look after the turf casing and keep it in repair. As the combustion spreads throughout the whole pile, the temperature rises and real dry distillation commences. It is then necessary to stop the air holes, in order as much as possible to prevent unnecessary combustion. The nature of the process is, that part of the fuel burns and develops the heat required for subjecting the remainder to dry distillation. The charring is stopped when the products of dry distillation, which are emitted, no longer burn with a brilliant flame, but the pale blue flame of carbonic oxide appears. Dry wood in stacks yields about one-fourth of its weight of charcoal.

[5] When dead vegetable matter undergoes transformation in air, in the presence of moisture and lower organisms, there remains a substance much richer in carbon—namely, humus, black earth or mould. 100 parts of humus in a dry state contain about 70 p.c. of carbon. The roots, leaves, and stems of plants which wither and fall to the ground form a soil rich in humus. The non-vital vegetable substances (ligneous tissue) first form brown matter (ulmic compounds), and then black matter (humic substances), which are both insoluble in water; after this a brown acid is produced, which is soluble in water (apocrenic acid), and lastly a colourless acid also soluble in water (crenic acid). Alkali dissolves a part of the original brown and black substances, forming solutions of a brown tint (ulmic and humic acids) which sometimes communicate their colour to springs and rivers. The proportion of humus in soil generally has a direct influence on its fertility; firstly, because putrefying plants develop carbonic anhydride and ammonia, and yield the substances forming the ashes of plants, which are necessary to vegetation; secondly, because humus is capable of attracting the moisture of the air and of absorbing water (twice its weight) and in this way keeps the soil in a damp condition, which is indispensable for nourishment; thirdly, humus renders the soil porous, and, fourthly, it

renders it more capable of absorbing the heat of the sun's rays. On this account black earth is often most remarkable for its fertility. One object of manuring is to increase the quantity of humus in the soil, and any easily changeable vegetable or any animal matter (composts) may be used. The boundless tracts of black earth soil in Russia are capable of bestowing countless wealth on the country.

The origin and extent of black earth soil are treated in detail in Professor Dokouchaeff's works.

If those substances which produce humus undergo decomposition under water, less carbonic anhydride is formed, a quantity of marsh gas, CH_4, is evolved, and the solid residue forms an acid humus found in great quantities in marshy places and called *peat*. Peat is especially abundant in the lowlands of Holland, North Germany, Ireland, and Bavaria. In Russia it is likewise found in large quantities, especially in the North-West districts. The old hard forms of peat resemble in composition and properties brown coal; the newest formations, as yet unhardened by pressure, form very porous masses which retain traces of the vegetable matter from which they have been formed. Dried (and sometimes pressed) peat is used as fuel. The composition of peat varies considerably with the locality in which it is found. When dried in air it does not contain less than 15 p.c. of water and 8 p.c. of ash; the remainder consists of 45 p.c. of carbon, 4 p.c. of hydrogen, 1 p.c. of nitrogen, and 28 p.c. of oxygen. Its heating power is about equivalent to that of wood. The brown earthy varieties of coal were probably formed from peat. In other cases they have a marked woody structure, and are then known as lignites. The composition of the brown sorts of coal resembles in a marked degree that of peat—namely, in a dried state brown coal contains on an average 60 p.c. of carbon, 5 p.c. of hydrogen, 26 p.c. of oxygen and nitrogen, and 9 p.c. of ash. In Russia brown coal is met with in many districts near Moscow, in the Governments of Toula and Tver and the neighbourhood; it is very usually used as fuel, particularly when found in thick seams. The brown coals usually burn with a flame like wood and peat, and are akin to them in heating power, which is half or a third that of the best coal.

[6] Grass and wood, the vegetation of primæval seas and similar refuse of all geological periods, must have been in many cases subjected to the same changes they now undergo—that is, under water they formed peat and lignites. Such substances, preserved or a long time underground, subjected to the action of water, compressed by the new strata formed above them, transformed by the separation of their more volatile component parts (peat and lignites, even in their last condition, still continue to evolve nitrogen, carbonic anhydride, and marsh gases) form *coal*. Coal is a dense homogeneous mass, black, with an oily or glassy lustre,

or more rarely dull without any evident vegetable structure; this distinguishes it in appearance from the majority of lignites. The density of coal (not counting the admixture of pyrites, &c.) varies from 1·25 (dry bituminous coal) to 1·6 (anthracite, flameless), and even reaches 1·9 in the very dense variety of coal found in the Olonetzky government (termed shungite), which according to the investigations of Professor Inostrantzeff may be regarded as the extreme member of the various forms of coal.

In order to explain the formation of coal from vegetable matter, Cagniard de la Tour enclosed pieces of dried wood in a tube and heated them to the boiling point of mercury, when the wood was changed into a semi-liquid black mass from which a substance exceedingly like coal separated. In this manner some kinds of wood formed coal which on being heated left caking coke, others non-caking; precisely as we find with the natural varieties of coal. Violette repeated these experiments with wood dried at 150°, and showed that when wood is decomposed in this way, a gas, an aqueous liquor, and a residue are formed. The latter at a temperature of 200° has the properties of wood charcoal incompletely burnt; at 300° and higher a homogeneous mass like coal is formed which at 340° is dense and without cavities. At 400° the residue resembles anthracite. In nature probably the decomposition was in rare cases effected by heat alone; more generally it was effected by means of water and heat, but in either case the result ought to be almost the same.

The average composition of coal compiled from many analyses, disregarding the ash, is as follows: 84 parts of carbon, 5 parts of hydrogen, 1 part of nitrogen, 8 parts of oxygen, 2 of sulphur. The quantity of ash is on an average 5 p.c., but there are coals which contain a larger quantity, and naturally they are not so advantageous for use as fuel. The amount of water does not usually exceed more than 10 p.c. The *anthracites* form a remarkable variety of coals, they do not give any volatile products, or but a very small amount, as they contain but little hydrogen compared to oxygen. In the average composition of coal we saw that for 5 parts of hydrogen there were 8 parts of oxygen; therefore 4 parts by weight of hydrogen are capable of forming hydrocarbons, because 1 part of hydrogen is necessary in order to form water with the 8 parts of oxygen. These 4 parts by weight of hydrogen can convert 48 parts of carbon into volatile products, because 1 part of hydrogen by weight in these substances combines with 12 parts of carbon. The anthracites differ essentially from this: neglecting the ash, their average composition is as follows: 94 parts of carbon, 3 of hydrogen, and 3 of oxygen and nitrogen. According to the analyses of A. A. Voskresensky, the Grousheffsky anthracite (Don district) contains: C = 93·8, H = 1·7, ash = 1·5. Therefore the anthracites contain but little hydrogen capable of combining with the carbon to form hydrocarbons which burn with a flame.

Anthracites are the oldest forms of coal. The newest and least transformed coals, which resemble some of the brown varieties, are the *dry* coals. They burn with a flame like wood, and leave a coke having the appearance of lumps of coal, half their component parts being absorbed by the flame (they contain much hydrogen and oxygen). The remaining varieties of coal (gas coal, smithy coal, coking, and anthracite) according to Grüner in all respects form connecting links between the *dry* coals and the anthracites. These coals burn with a very smoky flame, and on being heated leave *coke*, which bears the same relation to coal that charcoal does to wood. The quantity and quality of coke vary considerably with the different sorts of coal from which it is formed. In practice coals are most often distinguished by the properties and quantity of the coke which they give. In this particular the so-called bituminous coals are especially valuable, as even the slack of this kind gives on dry distillation large spongy masses of coke. If large pieces of these kinds of coal are subjected to dry distillation, they, as it were, melt, flow together, and form caking masses of coke. The best coking coals give 65 p.c. of dense caking coke. Such coal is very valuable for metallurgical purposes (*see* Note 8). Besides coke, the dry distillation of coal produces gas (*see* further, illuminating gas, p. 361), coal-tar (which gives benzene, carbolic acid, naphthalene, tar for artificial asphalt, &c.) and also an aqueous alkaline liquor (with wood and lignites the liquid is acid from acetic acid) which contains ammonium carbonate (*see* Note 6).

[7] In England in 1850 the output of coal was as much as 48 million tons, and in latter years it has risen to about 190 millions. Besides this other countries contribute 300 millions—Russia about 6 millions. The United States of America come next to England with an output of 160 million tons, then Germany 90 millions; France produces but little (25 millions), and takes about 5 million tons from England. Thus the world consumes about 500 million tons of coal yearly. Besides household purposes, coal is chiefly used as fuel for steam-engines. As every horse-power (= 75 kilogrammetres per second) of a steam-engine expends on the average more than 25 kilograms in 24 hours, or in a year (counting stoppages) not less than 5 tons per horse-power, and there are not less than 40 million horse-power at work in the world, the consumption of coal for motive-power is at least equal to half the whole production. For this reason coal serves as a criterion of the industrial development of a country. About 15 p.c. of coal is used for the manufacture of cast iron, wrought iron, steel, and articles made of them.

[8] The principal coal beds of Russia under exploitation are: The Don basin (150 million poods per annum, 62 poods = 1 ton), the Polish basin (Dombrovo and others 120 million poods per annum), the Toula and Riazan beds of the Moscow basin (up to 25 million poods), the Ural basin

(10 million poods), the Caucasian (Kviboul, near Kutais), the Khirjhis steppes, the smithy coal basin (Gov. of Tomsk), the Sahaline, &c. The Polish and Moscow basins do not give any coking coals. The presence of every variety of coal (from the dry coal near Lisichansk on the Donetz to the anthracites of the entire south-east basin), the great abundance of excellent metallurgical coal (coking, *see* Note 6) in the western part of the basin, its vast extent (as much as 25,000 sq. versts), the proximity of the seams to the surface (the shafts are now from 20 to 100 fathoms deep, and in England and Belgium as deep as 500 fathoms), the fertility of the soil (black earth), the proximity of the sea (about 100 versts from the Sea of Azoff) and of the rivers Donetz, Don, and Dneiper, the most abundant seams of excellent iron ore (Korsan Mogila, Krivoy Rog, Soulin, &c., &c.), copper ore, mercury ore (near Nikitovka, in the Bakhmouth district of the Ekaterinoslav Gov.), and other ores, the richest probably in the whole world, the beds of rock-salt (near the stations of the Stoupka and Brianzovka) the excellent clay of all kinds (china, fire-clay), gypsum, slate, sandstone, and other *wealth of the Don coal basin*, give complete assurance of the fact that with the growth of industrial activity in Russia this bountiful land of the Cossacks and New Russia will become the centre of the most extensive productive enterprise, not for the requirements of Russia alone, but of the whole world, because in no other place can be found such a concentration of favourable conditions. The growth of enterprise and knowledge, together with the extinction of the forests which compels Russia to foster the production of coal, will help to bring about this desired result. England with a whole fleet of merchant vessels exports annually about 25 million tons of coal, the price of which is higher than on the Donetz (where a pood of worked coal costs less than 5 copecks on the average), where anthracites and semi-anthracites (like Cardiff or steam coal, which burns without smoke) and coking and metallurgical coals are able both in quantity and quality to satisfy the most fastidious requirements of the industry already existing and rapidly increasing everywhere. The coal mines of England and Belgium are approaching a state of exhaustion, whilst in those of the Don basin, only at a depth of 100 fathoms, 1,200,000 million poods of coal lie waiting to be worked.

[9] As it is difficult to separate from the charcoal the admixture of ash—that is, the earthy matter contained in the vegetable substance used for producing charcoal—in order to obtain it in its purest condition it is necessary to use such organic substances as do not contain any ash, for example completely refined or purified crystallised sugar, crystallised tartaric acid, &c.

[10] The cavities in charcoal are the passages through which those volatile products formed at the same time as the charcoal have passed. The

degree of porosity of charcoal varies considerably, and has a technical significance, in different kinds of charcoal. The most porous charcoal is very light; a cubic metre of wood charcoal weighs about 200 kilograms. Many of the properties of charcoal which depend exclusively on its porosity are shared by many other porous substances, and vary with the density of the charcoal and depend on the way it was prepared. The property which charcoal has of absorbing gases, liquids, and many substances in solution, is a case in point. The densest kind of charcoal is formed by the action of great heat on sugar and other fusible substances. The lustrous grey dense coke formed in gas retorts is also of this character. This dense coke collects on the internal walls of the retorts subjected to great heat, and is produced by the vapours and gases separated from the heated coal in the retorts. In virtue of its density such coke becomes a good conductor of the galvanic current and approaches graphite. It is principally used in galvanic batteries. Coke, or the charcoal remaining from the imperfect combustion of coal and tarry substances, is also but slightly porous, brilliant, does not soil or mark paper, is dense, almost devoid of the faculty of retaining liquids and solids, and does not absorb gases. The light sorts of charcoal produced from charred wood, on the other hand, show this absorptive power in a most marked degree. This property is particularly developed in that very fine and friable charcoal prepared by heating animal substances such as hides and bones. *The absorptive power of charcoal* for gases is similar to the condensation of gases in spongy platinum. Here evidently there is a case of the adherence of gases to a solid, precisely as liquids have the property of adhering to various solids. One volume of charcoal will absorb the following volumes of gases (charcoal is capable of absorbing an immense amount of chlorine, almost equal to its own weight):—

Saussure. Boxwood Charcoal		Favre. Cocoanut Charcoal		Heat emitted per gram of gas	
NH_3	90	172	vols.	494	units
CO_2	35	97	,,	158	,,
N_2O	40	99	,,	169	,,
HCl	85	165	,,	274	,,

The quantity of gas absorbed by the charcoal increases with the pressure, and is approximately proportional to it. The quantity of heat given out by the absorption nearly approaches that set free on dissolving, or passing into a liquid condition.

Charcoal absorbs not only gases, but a number of other substances. For instance, alcohol which contains disagreeably smelling fusel oil, on being mixed with charcoal or filtered through it, loses most of the fusel oil. The practice of filtering substances through charcoal in order to get rid of foreign matters is often applied in chemical and manufacturing processes. Oils, spirits, various extracts, and vegetable and other solutions are filtered through charcoal in order to purify them. The bleaching power of charcoal may be tested by using various coloured solutions—such as aniline dyes, litmus, &c. Charcoal, which has absorbed one substance to saturation is still capable of absorbing certain other substances. Animal charcoal, produced in a very finely-divided state, especially by heating bones, makes the best sort for the purposes of absorption. Bone charcoal is used in large quantities in sugar works for filtering syrups and all saccharine solutions, in order to purify them, not only from colouring and odorous matter, but also from the lime which is mixed with the syrups in order to render them less unstable during boiling. The absorption of lime by animal charcoal depends, in all probability, in a great degree on the mineral component parts of bone charcoal.

[11] Charcoal is a very bad conductor of heat, and therefore forms an excellent insulator or packing to prevent the transmission of heat. A charcoal lining is often used in crucibles for heating many substances, as it does not melt and resists a far greater heat than many other substances.

[12] The unalterability of charcoal under the action of atmospheric agencies, which produce changes in the majority of stony and metallic substances, is often made use of in practice. For example, charcoal is frequently strewn in boundary ditches. The surface of wood is often charred to render it durable in those places where the soil is damp and wood itself would soon rot. The chambers (or in some works towers) through which acids pass (for example, sulphuric and hydrochloric) in order to bring them into contact with gases or liquids, are filled with charcoal or coke, because at ordinary temperatures it resists the action of even the strongest acids.

[12 bis] Maquenne (1892) discovered that carbon is capable of combining with the alkali metals. A 20 p.c. amalgam of the metals was heated to a red heat with charcoal powder in a stream of hydrogen. The compounds so obtained possessed, after the mercury had been driven off, the compositions BaC_2, SrC_2, CaC_2. All these compounds react with water forming acetylene, for example:

$$BaC_2 + 2H_2O = C_2H_2 + Ba(OH)_2$$

Maquenne proposes the barium carbide as a source of acetylene. He obtained this compound by heating carbonate of barium, magnesium powder, and retort carbon in a Perreau furnace ($BaCO_3 + 3Mg + C = 3MgO + BaC_2$). One hundred grams of BaC_2 evolve 5,200 to 5,400 c.c. of acetylene, mixed with about 2–3 p.c. of hydrogen.

The relation of acetylene, C_2H_2, to these metallic carbides is evident from the fact that these metals (Ca, Sr, Ba) replace 2 atoms of hydrogen, and therefore C_2Ba corresponds to C_2H_2, so that they may be regarded as metallic derivatives of acetylene. Moissan (1893) obtained similar carbides directly from the oxides by subjecting them to the action of the voltaic arc, in the presence of carbon, for instance, $BaO + 3C = CO + C_2Ba$, although at a furnace heat carbon has no action on the oxides CaO, BaO, SrO. Concerning Al_4C_5, *see* Chapter XVII. Note 38.

[13] When subjected to pressure, charcoal loses heat, hence the densest form stands to the less dense as a solid to a liquid, or as a compound to an element. From this the conclusion may be drawn that the molecules of graphite are more complex than those of charcoal, and those of the diamond still more so. The specific heat shows the same variation, and as we shall see further on, the increased complexity of a molecule leads to a diminution of the specific heat. At ordinary temperatures the specific heat of charcoal is $0·24$, graphite $0·20$, the diamond $0·147$. For retort carbon Le Chatelier (1893) found that the product of the sp. heat and atomic weight varies, between $0°$ and $250°$, according to the formula: $= 1·92 + 0·0077t$, and between $250°$ and $1000°$, $= 3·54 + 0·00246t$ (*see* Chapter XIV. Note 4).

[14] There are places where anthracite gradually changes into graphite as the strata sink. I myself had the opportunity of observing this gradual transformation in the valley of Aosta.

[15] Pencils are made of graphite worked up into a homogeneous mass by disintegrating, powdering, and cleansing it from earthy impurities; the best kinds are made of completely homogeneous graphite sawn up into the requisite sticks. Graphite is found in many places. In Russia the so-called Aliberoffsky graphite is particularly renowned; it is found in the Altai mountains near the Chinese frontier; in many places in Finland and likewise on the banks of the Little Tungouska, Sidoroff also found a considerable quantity of graphite. When mixed with clay, graphite is used for making crucibles and pots for melting metals.

Graphite, like most forms of charcoal, still contains a certain quantity of hydrogen, oxygen, and ash, so that in its natural state it does not contain more than 98 *p.c.* of carbon.

In practice, graphite is purified simply by washing it when in a finely-ground state, by which means the bulk of the earthy matter may be separated. The following process, proposed by Brodie, consists in mixing the powdered graphite with $\frac{1}{14}$ part of its weight of potassium chlorate. The mixture is then heated with twice its weight of strong sulphuric acid until no more odoriferous gases are emitted; on cooling, the mixture is thrown into water and washed; the graphite is then dried and heated to a red heat; after this it shrinks considerably in volume and forms a very fine powder, which is then washed. By acting on graphite several times with a mixture of potassium chlorate and nitric acid heated up to 60°, Brodie transformed it into a yellow insoluble acid substance which he called graphitic acid, $C_{11}H_4O_5$. The diamond remains unchanged when subjected to this treatment, whilst amorphous charcoal is completely oxidised. Availing himself of this possibility of distinguishing graphite from the diamond or amorphous charcoal, Berthelot showed that when compounds of carbon and hydrogen are decomposed by heat, amorphous charcoal is mainly formed, whilst when compounds of carbon with chlorine, sulphur, and boron are decomposed, graphite is principally deposited.

[15 bis] Diamonds are found in a particular dense rock, known by the name of itacolumite, and are dug out of the *débris* produced by the destruction of the itacolumite by water. When the *débris* is washed the diamonds remain behind; they are principally found in Brazil, in the provinces of Rio and Bahia, and at the Cape of Good Hope. The *débris* gives the black or amorphous diamond, carbonado, and the ordinary colourless or yellow translucent diamond. As the diamond possesses a very marked cleavage, the first operation consists in splitting it, and then roughly and finely polishing it with diamond powder. It is very remarkable that Professors P. A. Latchinoff and Eroféeff found (1887) diamond powder in a meteoric stone which fell in the Government of Penza, in the district of Krasnoslobodsk, near the settlement of Novo Urei (Sept. 10, 1886). Up to that time charcoal and graphite (a special variety, cliftonite) had been found in meteorites and the diamond only conjectured to occur therein. The Novo Urei meteorite was composed of siliceous matter and metallic iron (with nickel) like many other meteorites.

[16] Diamonds are sometimes found in the shape of small balls, and in that case it is impossible to cut them because directly the surface is ground or broken they fall into minute pieces. Sometimes minute diamond crystals form a dense mass like sugar, and this is generally reduced to diamond powder and used for grinding. Some known varieties of the diamond are almost opaque and of a black colour. Such diamonds are as hard as the ordinary ones, and are used for polishing diamonds and other precious stones, and also for rock boring and tunnelling.

[16 bis] Hannay, in 1880, obtained diamonds by heating a mixture of heavy liquid hydrocarbons (paraffin oils) with magnesium in a thick iron tube. This investigation, however, was not repeated.

[17] The *electrical furnace* is an invention of recent times, and gives the possibility of obtaining a temperature of 3,500°, which is not only not obtainable in ordinary furnaces, but even in the oxyhydrogen flame, whose temperature does not exceed 2,000°. The electrical furnace consists of two pieces of lime, laid one on the other. A cavity is made in the lower piece for the reception of the substance to be melted between two thick electrodes of dense carbon. On passing a current of 70 volts and 450 ampères a temperature of 3,000° is easily obtained. At a temperature of 2,500° (100 ampères and 40 volts) not only do all metals melt, but even lime and magnesia (when placed in the space between the carbon electrodes, *i.e.* in the voltaic arc) become soft and crystallise on cooling. At 3,000° lime becomes very fluid, metallic calcium partially separates out and a carbon compound, which remains liquid for a long time. At this temperature oxide of uranium is reduced to the suboxide and metal, zirconia and rock crystal fuse and partially volatilise, as also does alumina; platinum, gold, and even carbon distinctly volatilise; the majority of the metals form carbides. At such a temperature also cast iron and carbon give graphite, while according to Rousseau, between 2,000° and 3,000° the diamond passes into graphite and conversely graphite into the diamond, so that this is a kind of reversible reaction.

[17 bis] Moissan first investigated the solution of carbon in molten metals (and the formation of the carbides) such as magnesium, aluminium, iron, manganese, chromium, uranium, silver, platinum, and silicon. At the same time Friedel, owing to the discovery of the diamond in meteoric iron, admitted that the formation of the diamond is dependent upon the influence of iron and sulphur. With this object, that is to obtain the diamond, Friedel caused sulphur to react upon samples of cast iron rich in carbon, in a closed vessel at a maximum temperature of 500°, and after dissolving the sulphide of iron formed, he obtained a small quantity of a black powder which scratched corundum, i.e. diamond. Moissan's experiments (1893) were more successful, probably owing to his having employed the electrical furnace. If iron be saturated with carbon at a temperature between 1,100° and 3,000°, then at 1,100°–1,200° a mixture of amorphous carbon and graphite is formed, while at 3,000° graphite alone is obtained in very beautiful crystals. Thus under these conditions the diamond is not formed, and it can only be obtained if the high temperature be aided by powerful pressures. For this purpose Moissan took advantage of the pressure produced in the passage of a mass of molten cast iron from a liquid into a solid state. He first melted 150–200 grams of iron in the electrical furnace, and quickly introduced a cylinder of carbon into the molten iron. He then removed the crucible with the molten iron from the furnace and plunged it into a reservoir containing water. After treating with boiling hydrochloric acid, three varieties of carbon were obtained: (1) a

small amount of graphite (if the cooling be rapid); (2) carbon of a chestnut colour in very fine twisted threads, showing that it had been subjected to a very high pressure (a similar variety was met with in various samples of the Canon Diabolo), and lastly (3) an inconsiderable quantity of an exceeding dense mass which was freed from the admixture of the lighter modifications by treatment with *aqua regia*, sulphuric and hydrofluoric acids, and from which Moissan, by means of liquid bromoform (sp. gr. 2·900), succeeded in separating some small pieces, having a greater density than bromoform, which scratched the ruby and had the properties of the diamond. Some of these pieces were black, others were transparent and refracted light strongly. The dark grey tint of the former resembled that of the black diamonds (carbonado). Their density was between 3 and 3·5. The transparent specimens had a greasy appearance and seemed to be, as it were, surrounded by an envelope of carbon. At 1,050° they did not burn entirely in a current of air, so that the imperfectly burnt particles, and a peculiar form of grains of a light ochre colour, which retained their crystalline form, could be examined under the microscope. Similar grains also remain after the imperfect combustion of the ordinary diamond. Moissan obtained the same results by rapidly cooling in a stream of coal gas a piece of cast iron, saturated with carbon obtained from sugar and first heated to 2,000°. In this instance he obtained small crystals of diamonds. K. Chroustchoff showed that at its boiling point silver dissolves 6 p.c. of carbon. This silver was rapidly cooled, so that a crust formed on the surface and prevented the metal expanding, and so produced a powerful pressure. A portion of the carbon which separates out under these conditions exhibits the properties of the diamond.

[18] The existence of a molecule S_6 is known (up to 600°), and it must be held that this accounts for the formation of hydrogen persulphide, H_2S_5. Phosphorus appears in the molecule P_4 and gives P_4H_2. When expounding the data on specific heat we shall have occasion to return to the question of the complexity of the carbon molecule.

[19] The hydrocarbons poor in hydrogen and containing many atoms of carbon, like chrysene and carbopetrocene, &c., $C_nH_{2(n-m)}$, are solids, and less fusible as n and m increase. They present a marked approach to the properties of the diamond. And in proportion to the diminution of the water in the carbohydrates $C_nH_{2m}O_m$—for example in the humic compounds (Note 5)—the transition of complex organic substances to charcoal is very evident. That residue resembling charcoal and graphite which is obtained by the separation (by means of copper sulphate and sodium chloride) of iron from white cast-iron containing carbon chemically combined with the iron, also seems, especially after the researches of G. A. Zaboudsky, to be a complex substance containing $C_{12}H_6O_3$. The

endeavours which have been directed towards determining the measure of complexity of the molecules of charcoal, graphite, and the diamond will probably at some period lead to the solution of this problem and will most likely prove that the various forms of charcoal, graphite, and the diamond contain molecules of different and very considerable complexity. The constancy of the grouping of benzene, C_6H_6, and the wide diffusion and facility of formation of the carbohydrates containing C_6 (for example, cellulose, $C_6H_{10}O_5$, glucose, $C_6H_{12}O_6$) give reason for thinking that the group C_6 is the first and simplest of those possible to free carbon, and it may be hoped that some time or other it may be possible to get carbon in this form. Perhaps in the diamond there may be found such a relation between the atoms as in the benzene group, and in charcoal such as in carbohydrates.

[20] When charcoal burns, the complex molecule C_n is resolved into the simple molecules nCO_2, and therefore part of the heat—probably no small amount—is expended in the destruction of the complex molecule C_n. Perhaps by burning the most complex substances, which are the poorest as regards hydrogen, it may be possible to form an idea of the work required to split up C_n into separate atoms.

[21] The viscosity, or degree of mobility, of liquids is determined by their internal friction. It is estimated by passing the liquids through narrow (capillary) tubes, the mobile liquids passing through with greater facility and speed than the viscid ones. The viscosity varies with the temperature and nature of the liquids, and in the case of solutions changes with the amount of the substance dissolved, but is not proportional to it. So that, for example, with alcohol at 20° the viscosity will be 69, and for a 50 p.c. solution 160, the viscosity of water being taken as 100. The volume of the liquid which passes through by experiment (Poiseuille) and theory (Stokes) is proportional to the time, the pressure, and the fourth power of the diameter of the (capillary) tube, and inversely proportional to the length of the tube; this renders it possible to form comparative estimates of the coefficients of internal friction and viscosity.

As the complexity of the molecules of hydrocarbons and their derivatives increases by the addition of carbon (or CH_2), so does the degree of viscosity also rise. The extensive series of investigations referring to this subject still await the necessary generalisation. That connection which (already partly observed) ought to exist between the viscosity and the other physical and chemical properties, forces us to conclude that the magnitude of internal friction plays an important part in molecular mechanics. In investigating organic compounds and solutions, similar researches ought to stand foremost. Many observations have already been made, but not much has yet been done with them; the bare facts and some mechanical data exist, but their relation to molecular mechanics has not been cleared up in the requisite degree. It has already been seen from existing data that the viscosity at the temperature of the absolute boiling point becomes as small as in gases.

[22] In a number of hydrocarbons and their derivatives such a substitution of metals for the hydrogen may be attained by indirect means. The property shown by acetylene, C_2H_2, and its analogues, of forming metallic derivatives is in this respect particularly characteristic. Judging from the fact that carbon is an acid element (that is, gives an acid anhydride with oxygen), though comparatively slightly acid (for carbonic acid is not at all a strong acid and compounds of chlorine and carbon, even CCl_4, are not decomposed by water as is the case with phosphorus chloride and even silicic chloride and boric chloride, although they correspond with acids of but little energy), one might expect to find in the hydrogen of hydrocarbons this faculty for being substituted by metals. The metallic compounds which correspond with hydrocarbons are known under the name of organo-metallic compounds. Such, for instance, is zinc ethyl, $Zn(C_2H_5)_2$, which corresponds with ethyl hydride or ethane, C_2H_6, in which two atoms of hydrogen have been exchanged for one of zinc.

[23] Gaseous and volatile hydrocarbons decompose when passed through a heated tube. When hydrocarbons are decomposed by heating, the primary products are generally other more stable hydrocarbons, among which are acetylene, C_2H_2, benzene, C_6H_6, naphthalene, $C_{10}H_8$, &c.

[24] Wagner (1888) showed that when unsaturated hydrocarbons are shaken with a weak (1 p.c.) solution of potassium permanganate, $KMnO_4$, at ordinary temperatures, they form glycols—for example, C_2H_4 yields $C_2H_6O_2$.

[25] My article on this subject appeared in the Journal of the St. Petersburg Academy of Sciences in 1861. Up to that time, although many additive combinations with hydrocarbons and their derivatives were known, they had not been generalised, and were even continually quoted as cases of substitution. Thus the combination of ethylene, C_2H_4, with chlorine, Cl_2, was often regarded as a formation of the products of the substitution of C_2H_5Cl and HCl, which it was supposed were held together as the water of crystallisation is in salts. Even earlier than this (1857, *Journal of the Petroffsky Academy*) I considered similar cases as true compounds. In general, according to the law of limits, an unsaturated hydrocarbon, or its derivative, on combining with rX_2, gives a substance which is saturated or else approaching the limit. The investigations of Frankland with many organo-metallic compounds clearly showed the limit in the case of metallic compounds, which we shall constantly refer to later on.

[26] The conception of homology has been applied by Gerhardt to all organic compounds in his classical work, 'Traité de Chimie Organique,' finished in 1855 (4 vols.), in which he divided all organic compounds into *fatty* and *aromatic*, which is in principle still adhered to at the present time, although the latter are more often called benzene derivatives, on account of the fact that Kekulé, in his beautiful investigations on the structure of aromatic compounds, showed the presence in them all of the 'benzene nucleus,' C_6H_6.

[27] This is always true for hydrocarbons, but for derivatives of the lower homologues the law is sometimes different; for instance, in the series of saturated alcohols, $C_nH_{2n+1}(OH)$, when $n = 0$, we obtain water, $H(OH)$, which boils at 100°, and whose specific gravity at 15° = 0·9992; when $n =$ 1, wood spirit $CH_3(OH)$, which boils at 66°, and at 15° has a specific gravity = 0·7964; when $n = 2$, ordinary alcohol, $C_2H_5(OH)$, boiling at 78°, specific gravity at 15° = 0·7936, and with further increase of CH_2 the specific gravity increases. For the glycols $C_nH_{2n}(OH)_2$ the phenomenon of a similar kind is still more striking; at first the temperature of the boiling point and the density increase, and then for higher (more complex) members of the series diminish. The reason for this phenomenon, it is evident, must be sought for in the influence and properties of water, and that strong affinity which, acting between hydrogen and oxygen, determines many of the exceptional properties of water (Chapter I.).

[28] As, for example, in the saturated series of hydrocarbons C_nH_{2n+2}, the lowest member ($n = 0$) must be taken as hydrogen H_2, a gas which (*t.c.* below -190°) is liquefied with great difficulty, and when in a liquid state has doubtless a very small density. Where $n = 1, 2, 3$, the hydrocarbons CH_4, C_2H_6, C_3H_8 are gases, more and more readily liquefiable. The temperature of the absolute boiling point for CH_4 = -100°, and for ethane C_2H_6, and in the higher members it rises. The hydrocarbon C_4H_{10}, liquefies at about 0°. C_5H_{12} (there are several isomers) boils at from +9° (Lvoff) to 37°, C_6H_{14} from 58° to 78°, &c. The specific gravities in a liquid state at 15° are:—

C_5H_{12}	C_6H_{14}	C_7H_{16}	$C_{10}H_{22}$	$C_{16}H_{34}$
0·63	0·66	0·70	0·75	0·85

[29] If, at the ordinary temperature (assuming therefore that the water formed will be in a liquid state) a gram molecule (26 grams) of acetylene, C_2H_2, be burnt, 310 thousand calories will be emitted (Thomsen), and as 12 grams of charcoal produce 97 thousand calories, and 2 grams of hydrogen 69 thousand calories, it follows that, if the hydrogen and carbon of the acetylene were burnt there would be only 2 × 97 + 69, or 263 thousand

calories produced. It is evident, then, that acetylene in its formation absorbs 310–263, or 47 thousand calories.

For considerations relative to the combustion of carbon compounds, we will first enumerate the quantity of heat separated by the combustion of definite chemical carbon compounds, and then give a few figures bearing on the kinds of fuel used in practice.

For molecular quantities in perfect combustion the following amounts of heat are given out (when gaseous carbonic anhydride and liquid water are formed), according to Thomsen's data (1) for gaseous C_nH_{2n+2}: $52\cdot8 + 158\cdot8n$ thousand calories; (2) for C_nH_{2n}: $17\cdot7 + 158\cdot1n$ thousand calories; (3) according to Stohmann (1888) for liquid saturated alcohols, $C_nH_{2n+2}O$: $11\cdot8 + 156\cdot3n$, and as the latent heat of evaporation = about $8\cdot2 + 0\cdot6n$, in a gaseous state, $20\cdot0 + 156\cdot9n$; (4) for monobasic saturated liquid acids, $C_nH_{2n}O_2$:—$95\cdot3 + 154\cdot3n$, and as their latent heat of evaporation is about $5\cdot0 + 1\cdot2n$, in a gaseous form, about—$90 + 155n$; (5) for solid saturated bibasic acids, $C_nH_{2n-2}O_4$:—$253\cdot8 + 152\cdot6n$, if they are expressed as $C_nH_{2n}C_2H_2O_4$, then $51\cdot4 + 152\cdot6n$; (6) for benzene and its liquid homologues (still according to Stohmann) C_nH_{2n-6}:—$158\cdot6 + 156\cdot3n$, and in a gaseous form about—$155 + 157n$; (7) for the gaseous homologues of acetylene, C_nH_{2n-2} (according to Thomsen)—$5 + 157n$. It is evident from the preceding figures that the group CH_2, or CH_3 substituted for H, on burning gives out from 152 to 159 thousand calories. This is less than that given out by $C + H_2$, which is $97 + 69$ or 166 thousand; the reason for this difference (it would be still greater if carbon were gaseous) is the amount of heat separated during the formation of CH_2. According to Stohmann, for dextroglucose, $C_6H_{12}O_6$, it is $673\cdot7$; for common sugar, $C_{12}H_{22}O_{11}$, $1325\cdot7$; for cellulose, $C_6H_{10}O_5$, $678\cdot0$; starch, $677\cdot5$; dextrin, $666\cdot2$; glycol, $C_2H_6O_2$, $281\cdot7$; glycerine, $397\cdot2$, &c. The heat of combustion of the following solids (determined by Stohmann) is expressed per unit of weight: naphthalene, $C_{10}H_8$, 9,621; urea, CN_2H_4O, 2,465; white of egg, 5,579; dry rye bread, 4,421; wheaten bread, 4,302; tallow, 9,365; butter, 9,192; linseed oil, 9,323. The most complete collection of arithmetical data for the heats of combustion will be found in V. F. Longinin's work, 'Description of the Various Methods of Determining the Heats of Combustion of Organic Compounds' (Moscow, 1894).

The number of units of heat given out by *unit weight* during the complete combustion and cooling of the following ordinary kinds of fuel in their usual state of dryness and purity are:—(1) for wood charcoal, anthracite, semi-anthracite, bituminous coal and coke, from 7,200 to 8,200; (2) dry, long flaming coals, and the best brown coals, from 6,200 to 6,800; (3) perfectly dry wood, 3,500; hardly dry, 2,500; (4) perfectly dry peat, best kind, 4,500; compressed and dried, 3,000; (5) petroleum refuse and similar liquid hydrocarbons, about 11,000; (6) illuminating gas of the ordinary composition (about 45 vols. H, 40 vols. CH_4, 5 vols. CO, and 5 vols. N), about 12,000; (7) producer gas (*see* next Chapter), containing 2 vols. carbonic anhydride, 30 vols. carbonic oxide, and 68 vols. nitrogen *for one part by weight of the whole carbon burnt*, 5,300, and for one part by weight of the gas, 910, units of heat; and (8) water gas (*see* next chapter) containing 4 vols. carbonic anhydride, 8 vols. N_2, 24 vols. carbonic oxide, and 46 vols. H_2, for one part by weight of the carbon consumed in the *generator* 10,900, and for one part by weight of the gas, 3,600 units of heat. In these figures, as in all calorimetric observations, the water produced by the combustion of the fuel is supposed to be liquid. As regards the temperature reached by the fuel, it is important to remark that for solid fuel it is indispensable to admit (to ensure complete combustion) twice the amount of air required, but liquid, or pulverised fuel, and especially gaseous fuel, does not require an excess of air; therefore, a kilogram of charcoal, giving 8,000 units of heat, requires about 24 kilograms of air (3 kilograms of air per thousand calories) and a kilogram of producer gas requires only 0·77 kilogram of air (0·85 kilo. of air per 1,000 calories), 1 kilogram of water gas about 4·5 of air (1·25 kilo. of air per 1,000 calories).

[29 bis] Manure which decomposes under the action of bacteria gives off CO_2 and CH_4.

[30] It is easy to collect the gas which is evolved in marshy places if a glass bottle be inverted in the water and a funnel put into it (both filled with water); if the mud of the bottom be now agitated, the bubbles which rise may be easily caught by the inverted funnel.

[31]

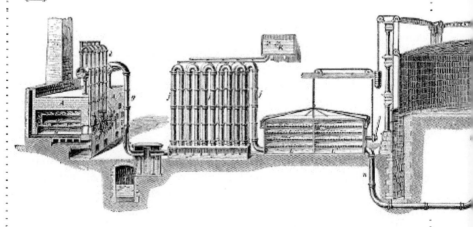

FIG. 58.—General view of gas works. *B*, retorts; *f*, hydraulic main; *H* and *I*, tar well; *i*, condensers; *L*, purifiers; *P*, gasholder.

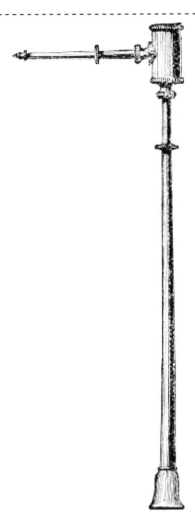

FIG. 59.—Blowpipe. Air is blown in at the trumpet-shaped
mouthpiece, and escapes in a fine stream from the platinum jet
placed at the extremity of the side tube.

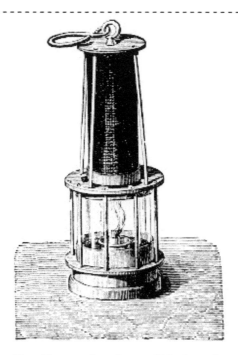

FIG. 60.—Davy safety-lamp. [Modern form.]

Illuminating gas is generally prepared by heating gas coal (*see* Note 6) in oval cylindrical horizontal cast-iron or clay retorts. Several such retorts *BB* (fig. 58) are disposed in the furnace *A*, and heated together. When the retorts are heated to a red heat, lumps of coal are thrown into them, and they are then closed with a closely fitting cover. The illustration shows the furnace, with five retorts. Coke (*see* Note 1, dry distillation) remains in the retorts, and the volatile products in the form of vapours and gases travel along the pipe *d*, rising from each retort. These pipes branch above the stove, and communicate with the receiver *f* (hydraulic main) placed above the furnace. Those products of the dry distillation which most easily pass from the gaseous into the liquid and solid states collect in the hydraulic main. From the hydraulic main the vapours and gases travel along the pipe *g* and the series of vertical pipes *j* (which are sometimes cooled by water trickling over the surface), where the vapours and gases cool from the contact of the colder surface, and a fresh quantity of vapour condenses. The condensed liquids pass from the pipes *g* and *j* and into the troughs *H*. These troughs always contain liquid at a constant level (the excess flowing away) so that the gas cannot escape, and thus they form, as it is termed, a hydraulic joint. In the state in which it leaves the condensers the gas consists principally of the following vapours and gases: (1) vapour of water, (2) ammonium carbonate, (3) liquid hydrocarbons, (4) hydrogen sulphide,

H_2S, (5) carbonic anhydride, CO_2, (6) carbonic oxide, CO, (7) sulphurous anhydride, SO_2, but a great part of the illuminating gas consists of (8) hydrogen, (9) marsh gas, (10) olefiant gas, C_2H_4, and other gaseous hydrocarbons. The hydrocarbons (3, 9, and 10), the hydrogen, and carbonic oxide are capable of combustion, and are useful component parts, but the carbonic anhydride, the hydrogen sulphide, and sulphurous anhydride, as well as the vapours of ammonium carbonate, form an injurious admixture, because they do not burn (CO_2, SO_2) and lower the temperature and brilliancy of the flame, or else, although capable of burning (for example, H_2S, CS_2, and others), they give out during combustion sulphurous anhydride which has a disagreeable smell, is injurious when inhaled, and spoils many surrounding objects. In order to separate the injurious products, the gas is washed with water, a cylinder (not shown in the illustration) filled with coke continually moistened with water serving for this purpose. The water coming into contact with the gas dissolves the ammonium carbonate; hydrogen sulphide, carbonic anhydride, and sulphurous anhydride, being only partly soluble in water, have to be got rid of by a special means. For this purpose the gas is passed through moist lime or other alkaline liquid, as the above-mentioned gases have acid properties and are therefore retained by the alkali. In the case of lime, calcium carbonate, sulphite and sulphide, all solid substances, are formed. It is necessary to renew the purifying material as its absorbing power decreases. A mixture of lime and sulphate of iron, $FeSO_4$, acts still better, because the latter, with lime, $Ca(HO)_2$, forms ferrous hydroxide, $Fe(HO)_2$ and gypsum, $CaSO_4$. The suboxide (partly turning into oxide) of iron absorbs H_2S, forming FeS and H_2O, and the gypsum retains the remainder of the ammonia, the excess of lime absorbing carbonic anhydride and sulphuric anhydride. [In English works a native hydrated ferric hydroxide is used for removing hydrogen sulphide.] This purification of the gas takes place in the apparatus L, where the gas passes through perforated trays m, covered with sawdust mixed with lime and sulphate of iron. It is necessary to remark that in the manufacture of gas it is indispensable to draw off the vapours from the retorts, so that they should not remain there long (otherwise the hydrocarbons would in a considerable degree be resolved into charcoal and hydrogen), and also to avoid a great pressure of gas in the apparatus, otherwise a quantity of gas would escape at all cracks such as must inevitably exist in such a complicated arrangement. For this purpose there are special pumps (exhausters) so regulated that they only pump off the quantity of gas formed (the pump is not shown in the illustration). The purified gas passes through the pipe n into the gasometer (gasholder) P, a dome made of iron plate. The edges of the dome dip into water poured into a ring-shaped channel g, in which the sides of the dome rise and fall. The gas is collected in this holder, and distributed to its destination by pipes communicating with the pipe o, issuing from the dome. The pressure of the dome on the gas enables it, on issuing from a long pipe, to penetrate through the small aperture of the burner. A hundred kilograms of coal give about 20 to 30 cubic metres of gas, having a density from four to nine times greater than that of hydrogen. A cubic metre (1,000 litres) of hydrogen weighs about 87 grams; therefore 100 kilograms of coal give about 18 kilograms of gas, or about one-sixth of its weight. Illuminating gas is generally lighter than marsh gas, as it contains a considerable amount of hydrogen, and is only heavier than marsh gas when it contains much of the heavier hydrocarbons. Thus olefiant gas, C_2H_4, is fourteen times, and the vapours of benzene thirty-nine times, heavier than hydrogen, and illuminating gas sometimes contains 15 p.c. of its volume of them. The brilliancy of the flame of the gas increases with the quantity of olefiant gas and similar heavy hydrocarbons, as it then contains more carbon for a given volume and a greater number of carbon particles are separated. Gas usually contains from 35 to 60 p.c. of its volume of marsh gas, from 30 to 50 p.c. of hydrogen, from 3 to 5 p.c. of carbonic oxide, from 2 to 10 p.c. heavy hydrocarbons, and from 3 to 10 p.c. of nitrogen. Wood gives almost the same sort of gas as coal and almost the same quantity, but the wood gas contains a great deal of carbonic anhydride, although on the other hand there is an almost complete absence of sulphur compounds. Tar, oils, naphtha, and such materials furnish a large quantity of good illuminating gas. An ordinary burner of 8 to 12 candle-power burns 5 to 6 cubic feet of coal gas per hour, but only 1 cubic foot of naphtha gas. One pood (36 lbs. Eng.) of naphtha gives 500 cubic feet of gas—that is, one kilogram of naphtha produces about one cubic metre of gas. The formation of combustible gas by heating coal was discovered in the beginning of the last century, but only put into practice towards the end by Le-Bon in France and Murdoch in England. In England, Murdoch, together with the renowned Watt, built the first gas works in 1805.

In practice illuminating gas is not only used for lighting (electricity and kerosene are cheaper in Russia), but also as the motive power for gas engines (*see* p. 175), which consume about half a cubic metre per horse-power per hour; gas is also used in laboratories for heating purposes. When it is necessary to concentrate the heat, either the ordinary blowpipe (fig. 59) is applied, placing the end in the flame and blowing through the mouthpiece; or, in other forms, gas is passed through the blowpipe; when a large, hot, smokeless flame is required for heating crucibles or glass-blowing, a foot-blower is used. High temperatures, which are often required for laboratory and manufacturing purposes, are most easily attained by the use of gaseous fuel (illuminating gas, producer gas, and water gas, which will be treated of in the following chapter), because complete combustion may be effected without an access of air. It is evident that in order to obtain high temperatures means must be taken to diminish the loss of heat by radiation, and to ensure perfect combustion.

[32] The gas which is set free in coal mines contains a good deal of nitrogen, some carbonic anhydride, and a large quantity of marsh gas. The best means of avoiding an explosion consists in efficient ventilation. It is best to light coal mines with electric lamps.

[33] The Davy lamp, of which an improved form is represented in the accompanying figure, is used for lighting coal and other mines where combustible gas is found. The wick of the lamp is enclosed in a thick glass cylinder which is firmly held in a metallic holder. Over this a metallic cylinder and the wire gauze are placed. The products of combustion pass through the gauze, and the air enters through the space between the cylinder and the wire gauze. To ensure greater safety the lamp cannot be opened without extinguishing the flame.

[34] In Pennsylvania (beyond the Alleghany mountains) many of the shafts sunk for petroleum only emitted gas, but many useful applications for it were found and it was conducted in metallic pipes to works hundreds of miles distant, principally for metallurgical purposes.

[35] The purest gas is prepared by mixing the liquid substance called zinc methyl, $Zn(CH_3)_2$, with water, when the following reaction occurs:

$$Zn(CH_3)_2 + 2HOH = Zn(HO)_2 + 2CH_3H.$$

[36] Methylene, CH_2, does not exist. When attempts are made to obtain it (for example, by removing X_2 from CH_2X_2), C_2H_4 or C_3H_6 are produced—that is to say, it undergoes polymerisation.

[37] Although the methods of formation and the reactions connected with hydrocarbons are not described in this work, because they are dealt with in organic chemistry, yet in order to clearly show the mechanism of those transformations by which the carbon atoms are built up into the molecules of the carbon compounds, we here give a general example of reactions of this kind. From marsh gas, CH_4, on the one hand the substitution of chlorine or iodine, CH_3Cl, CH_3I, for the hydrogen may be effected, and on the other hand such metals as sodium may be substituted for the hydrogen, e.g. CH_3Na. These and similar products of substitution serve as a means of obtaining other more complex substances from given carbon compounds. If we place the two above-named products of substitution of marsh gas (metallic and haloid) in mutual contact, the metal combines with the halogen, forming a very stable compound—namely, common salt, NaCl, and the carbon groups which were in combination with them separate in mutual combination, as shown by the equation:

$$CH_3Cl + CH_3Na = NaCl + C_2H_6.$$

This is the most simple example of the formation of a complex hydrocarbon from these radicles. The cause of the reaction must be sought for in the property which the haloid (chlorine) and sodium have of entering into mutual combination.

[38] When $m = n - 1$, we have the series C_nH_2. The lowest member is acetylene, C_2H_2. These are hydrocarbons containing a minimum amount of hydrogen.

[39] For instance, ethylene, C_2H_4, combines with Br_2, HI, H_2SO_4, as a whole molecule, as also does amylene, C_5H_{10}, and, in general, C_nH_{2n}.

[40] For instance, ethylene is obtained by removing the water from ethyl alcohol, $C_2H_5(OH)$, and amylene, C_5H_{10}, from amyl alcohol, $C_5H_{11}(OH)$, or in general C_nH_{2n}, from $C_nH_{2n+1}(OH)$.

[41] Acetylene and its polymerides have an empirical composition CH, ethylene and its homologues (and polymerides) CH_2, ethane CH_3, methane CH_4. This series presents a good example of the law of multiple proportions, but such diverse proportions are met with between the number of atoms of the carbon and hydrogen in the hydrocarbons already known that the accuracy of Dalton's law might be doubted. Thus the substances $C_{30}H_{62}$ and $C_{30}H_{60}$ differ so slightly in their composition by weight as to be within the limits of experimental error, but their reactions and properties are so distinct that they can be distinguished beyond a doubt. Without Dalton's law chemistry could not have been brought to its present condition, but it cannot alone express all those gradations which are quite clearly understood and predicted by the law of Avogadro-Gerhardt.

[42] The conception of the structure of carbon compounds—that is, the expression of those unions and correlations which their atoms have in the molecules—was for a long time limited to the representation that organic substances contained complex radicles (for instance, ethyl C_2H_5, methyl CH_3, phenyl C_6H_5, &c.); then about the year 1840 the phenomena of substitution and the correspondence of the products of substitution with the primary bodies (nuclei and types) were observed, but it was not until about the year 1860 and later when on the one hand the teaching of Gerhardt about molecules was spreading, and on the other hand the materials had accumulated for discussing the transformations of the simplest hydrocarbon compounds, that conjectures began to appear as to the mutual connection of the atoms of carbon in the molecules of the complex hydrocarbon compounds. Then Kekulé and A. M. Butleroff began to formulate the connection between the separate atoms of carbon,

regarding it as a quadrivalent element. Although in their methods of expression and in some of their views they differ from each other and also from the way in which the subject is treated in this work, yet the essence of the matter—namely, the comprehension of the causes of isomerism and of the union between the separate atoms of carbon—remains the same. In addition to this, starting from the year 1870, there appears a tendency which from year to year increases to discover the actual spacial distribution of the atoms in the molecules. Thanks to the endeavours of Le-Bel (1874), Van't Hoff (1874), and Wislicenus (1887) in observing cases of isomerism—such as the effect of different isomerides on the direction of the rotation of the plane of polarisation of light—this tendency promises much for chemical mechanics, but the details of the still imperfect knowledge in relation to this matter must be sought for in special works devoted to organic chemistry.

[43] Direct experiment shows that however CH_3X is prepared (where X = for instance Cl, &c.) it is always one and the same substance. If, for example, in CX_4, X is gradually replaced by hydrogen until CH_3X is produced, or in CH_4, the hydrogen by various means is replaced by X, or else, for instance, if CH_3X be obtained by the decomposition of more complex compounds, the same product is always obtained.

This was shown in the year 1860, or thereabout, by many methods, and is the fundamental conception of the structure of hydrocarbon compounds. If the atoms of hydrogen in methyl were not absolutely identical in value and position (as they are not, for instance, in $CH_3CH_2CH_3$ or CH_3CH_2X), then there would be as many different forms of CH_3X as there were diversities in the atoms of hydrogen in CH_4. The scope of this work does not permit of a more detailed account of this matter. It is given in works on organic chemistry.

[44] The union of carbon atoms in closed chains or rings was first suggested by Kekulé as an explanation of the structure and isomerism of the derivatives of benzene, C_6H_6, forming aromatic compounds (Note 26).

[45] The following are the most generally known of the oxygenised but non-nitrogenous hydrocarbon derivatives. (1) the alcohols. These are hydrocarbons in which hydrogen is exchanged for hydroxyl (OH). The simplest of these is methyl alcohol, $CH_3(OH)$, or wood spirit obtained by the dry distillation of wood. The common spirits of wine or ethyl alcohol, $C_2H_3(OH)$, and glycol, $C_2H_4(OH)_2$, correspond with ethane. Normal propyl alcohol, $CH_3CH_2CH_2(OH)$, and isopropyl alcohol, $CH_3CH(OH)CH_3$, propylene-glycol, $C_3H_6(OH)_2$, and glycerol, $C_3H_3(OH)_3$ (which, with stearic and other acids, forms fatty substances), correspond with propane, C_3H_8. All alcohols are capable of forming water and ethereal salts with acids, just

as alkalis form ordinary salts. (2) Aldehydes are alcohols minus hydrogen; for instance, acetaldehyde, C_2H_4O, corresponds with ethyl alcohol. (3) It is simplest to regard organic acids as hydrocarbons in which hydrogen has been exchanged for carboxyl (CO_2H), as will be explained in the following chapter. There are a number of intermediate compounds; for example, the aldehyde-alcohols, alcohol-acids (or hydroxy-acids), &c. Thus the hydroxy-acids are hydrocarbons in which some of the hydrogen has been replaced by hydroxyl, and some by carboxyl; for instance, lactic acid corresponds with C_2H_6, and has the constitution $C_2H_4(OH)(CO_2H)$. If to these products we add the haloid salts (where H is replaced by Cl, Br, I), the nitro-compounds containing NO_2 in place of H, the amides, cyanides, ketones, and other compounds, it will be readily seen what an immense number of organic compounds there are and what a variety of properties these substances have; this we see also from the composition of plants and animals.

[46] Ethylene bromide, $C_2H_4Br_2$, when gently heated in alcoholic solution with finely divided zinc, yields pure ethylene, the zinc merely taking up the bromine (Sabaneyeff).

[47] Ethylene decomposes somewhat easily under the influence of the electric spark, or a high temperature. In this case the volume of the gas formed may remain the same when olefiant gas is decomposed into carbon and marsh gas, or may increase to double its volume when hydrogen and carbon are formed, $C_2H_4 = CH_4 + C = 2C + 2H_2$. A mixture of olefiant gas and oxygen is highly explosive; two volumes of this gas require six volumes of oxygen for its perfect combustion. The eight volumes thus taken then resolve themselves into eight volumes of the products of combustion, a mixture of water and carbonic anhydride, $C_2H_4 + 3O_2 = 2CO_2 + 2H_2O$. On cooling after the explosion diminution of volume occurs because the water becomes liquid. For two volumes of the olefiant gas taken, the diminution will be equal to four volumes, and the same for marsh gas. The quantity of carbonic anhydride formed by both gases is not the same. Two volumes of marsh gas give only two volumes of carbonic anhydride, and two volumes of ethylene give four volumes of carbonic anhydride.

[48] The homologues of ethylene, C_nH_{2n}, are also capable of direct combination with halogens, &c., but with various degrees of facility. The composition of these homologues can be expressed thus: $(CH_3)\_x(CH_2)_y(CH)_zC_r$, where the sum of $x + z$ is always an even number, and the sum of $x + z + r$ is equal to half the sum of $3x + z$, whence $z + 2r = x$; by this means the possible isomerides are determined. For example, for butylenes, C_4H_8, $(CH_3)_2(CH)_2$, $(CH_3)_2(CH_2)C$, $(CH_2)(CH_2)_2CH$, and $(CH_2)_4$ are possible.

[48 bis] *See* also method of preparing C_2H_2 in Note 12 bis.

[49] This is easily accomplished with those gas burners which are used in laboratories and mentioned in the Introduction. In these burners the gas is first mixed with air in a long tube, above which it is kindled. But if it be lighted inside the pipe it does not burn completely, but forms acetylene, on account of the cooling effect of the walls of the metallic tube; this is detected by the smell, and may be shown by passing the issuing gas (by aid of an aspirator) into an ammoniacal solution of cuprous chloride.

[50] Amongst the homologues of acetylene C_nH_{2n-2}, the lowest is C_3H_4; allylene, CH_3CCH, and allene, CH_2CCH_2, are known, but the closed structure, $CH_2(CH)_2$, is little investigated.

[51] The saturated hydrocarbons predominate in American petroleum, especially in its more volatile parts; in Baku naphtha the hydrocarbons of the composition C_nH_{2n} form the main part (Lisenko, Markovnikoff, Beilstein) but doubtless (Mendeléeff) it also contains saturated ones, C_nH_{2n+2}. The structure of the naphtha hydrocarbons is only known for the lower homologues, but doubtless the distinction between the hydrocarbons of the Pennsylvanian and Baku naphthas, boiling at the same temperature (after the requisite refining by repeated fractional distillation, which can be very conveniently done by means of steam rectification—that is, by passing the steam through the dense mass), depends not only on the predominance of saturated hydrocarbons in the former, and naphthenes, C_nH_{2n}, in the latter, but also on the diversity of composition and structure of the corresponding portions of the distillation. The products of the Baku naphtha are richer in carbon (therefore in a suitably constructed lamp they ought to give a brighter light), they are of greater specific gravity, and have greater internal friction (and are therefore more suitable for lubricating machinery) than the American products collected at the same temperature.

[52] The formation of naphtha fountains (which burst forth after the higher clay strata covering the layers of sands impregnated with naphtha have been bored through) is without doubt caused by the pressure or tension of the combustible hydrocarbon gases which accompany the naphtha, and are soluble in it under pressure. Sometimes these naphtha fountains reach a height of 100 metres—for instance, the fountain of 1887 near Baku. Naphtha fountains generally act periodically and their force diminishes with the lapse of time, which might be expected, because the gases which cause the fountains find an outlet, as the naphtha issuing from the bore-hole carries away the sand which was partially choking it up.

[53] This is a so-called intermediate oil (between kerosene and lubricating oils), solar oil, or pyronaphtha. Lamps are already being manufactured for burning it but still require improvement. Above all,

however, it requires a more extended market, and this at present is wanting, owing to the two following reasons: (1) Those products of the American petroleum which are the most widely spread and almost universally consumed contain but little of this intermediate oil, and what there is is divided between the kerosene and the lubricating oils; (2) the Baku naphtha, which is capable of yielding a great deal (up to 30 p.c.) of intermediate oil, is produced in enormous quantities, about 300 million poods, but has no regular markets abroad, and for the consumption in Russia (about 25 million poods of kerosene per annum) and for the limited export (60 million poods per annum) into Western Europe (by the Trans-Caucasian Railway) those volatile and more dangerous parts of the naphtha which enter into the composition of the American petroleum are sufficient, although Baku naphtha yields about 25 p.c. of such kerosene. For this reason pyronaphtha is not manufactured in sufficient quantities, and the whole world is consuming the unsafe kerosene. When a pipe line has been laid from Baku to the Black Sea (in America there are many which carry the raw naphtha to the sea-shore, where it is made into kerosene and other products) then the whole mass of the Baku naphtha will furnish safe illuminating oils, which without doubt will find an immense application. A mixture of the intermediate oil with kerosene or Baku oil (specific gravity 0·84 to 0·85) may be considered (on removing the benzoline) to be the best illuminating oil, because it is safe (flashing point from 40° to 60°), cheaper (Baku naphtha gives as much as 60 p.c. of Baku oil), and burns perfectly well in lamps differing but little from those made for burning American kerosene (unsafe, flashing point 20° to 30°).

[54] The substitution of Baku pyronaphtha, or intermediate oil, or Baku oil (*see* Note 53), would not only be a great advantage as regards safety from fire, but would also be highly economical. A ton (62 poods) of American crude petroleum costs at the coast considerably more than 24*s.* (12 roubles), and yields two-thirds of a ton of kerosene suitable for ordinary lamps. A ton of raw naphtha in Baku costs less than 4*s.* (1 rouble 80 copecks), and with a pipe line to the shore of the Black Sea would not cost more than 8 roubles, or 16*s.* Moreover, a ton of Baku naphtha will yield as much as two-thirds of a ton of kerosene, Baku oil, and pyronaphtha suitable for illuminating purposes.

[55] Naphtha has been applied for heating purposes on a large scale in Russia, not only on account of the low cost of naphtha itself and of the residue from the preparation of kerosene, but also because the products of all the Baku naphtha do not find an outlet for general consumption. Naphtha itself and its various residues form excellent fuel, burning without smoke and giving a high temperature (steel and iron may be easily melted in the flame). A hundred poods of good coal (for instance, Don coal) used as

fuel for heating boilers are equivalent to 36 cubic feet (about 250 poods) of dry wood, while only 70 poods of naphtha will be required; and moreover there is no need for stoking, as the liquid can be readily and evenly supplied in the required quantity. The economic and other questions relating to American and Baku petroleums have been discussed more in detail in some separate works of mine (D. Mendeléeff): (1) 'The Naphtha Industry of Pennsylvania and the Caucasus,' 1870; (2) 'Where to Build Naphtha Works,' 1880; (3) 'On the Naphtha Question,' 1883; (4) 'The Baku Naphtha Question,' 1886; (5) the article on the naphtha industry in the account of the Russian industries printed for the Chicago Exhibition.

[56] As during the process of the dry distillation of wood, sea-weed, and similar vegetable *débris*, and also when fats are decomposed by the action of heat (in closed vessels), hydrocarbons similar to those of naphtha are formed, it was natural that this fact should have been turned to account to explain the formation of the latter. But the hypothesis of the formation of naphtha from vegetable *débris* inevitably assumes coal to be the chief element of decomposition, and naphtha is met with in Pennsylvania and Canada, in the Silurian and Devonian strata, which do not contain coal, and correspond to an epoch not abounding in organic matter. Coal was formed from the vegetable *débris* of the Carboniferous, Jurassic, and other recent strata, but judging more from its composition and structure, it has been subjected to the same kind of decomposition as peat; nor could liquid hydrocarbons have been thus formed to such an extent as we see in naphtha. If we ascribe the derivation of naphtha to the decomposition of fat (adipose, animal fat) we encounter three almost insuperable difficulties: (1) Animal remains would furnish a great deal of nitrogenous matter, whilst there is but very little in naphtha; (2) the enormous quantity of naphtha already discovered as compared with the insignificant amount of fat in the animal carcase; (3) the sources of naphtha always running parallel to mountain chains is completely inexplicable. Being struck with this last-mentioned circumstance in Pennsylvania, and finding that the sources in the Caucasus surround the whole Caucasian range (Baku, Tiflis, Gouria, Kouban, Tamman, Groznoe, Dagestan), I developed in 1876 the hypothesis of the mineral origin of naphtha expounded further on.

[57] During the upheaval of mountain ranges crevasses would be formed at the peaks with openings upwards, and at the foot of the mountains with openings downwards. These cracks in course of time fill up, but the younger the mountains the fresher the cracks (the Alleghany mountains are, without doubt, more ancient than the Caucasian, which were formed during the tertiary epoch); through them water must gain access deep into the recesses of the earth to an extent that could not occur on the level (on

plains). The situation of naphtha at the foot of mountain chains is the principal argument in my hypothesis.

Another fundamental reason is the consideration of the mean density of the earth. Cavendish, Airy, Cornu, Boys, and many others who have investigated the subject by various methods, found that, taking water = 1, the mean density of the earth is nearly 5·5. As at the surface water and all rocks (sand, clay, limestone, granite, &c.) have a density less than 3, it is evident (as solid substances are but slightly compressible even under the greatest pressure) that inside the earth there are substances of a greater density—indeed, not less than 7 or 8. What conclusion, then, can be arrived at? Anything heavy contained in the bosom of the earth must be distributed not only on its surface, but throughout the whole solar system, for everything tends to show that the sun and planets are formed from the same material, and according to the hypothesis of Laplace and Kant it is most probable, and indeed must necessarily be held, that the earth and planets are but fragments of the solar atmosphere, which have had time to cool considerably and become masses semi-liquid inside and solid outside, forming both planets and satellites. The sun amongst other heavy elements contains a great deal of iron, as shown by spectrum analysis. There is also much of it in an oxidised condition on the surface of the earth. Meteoric stones, carried as fragmentary planets in the solar system and sometimes falling upon the earth, consisting of siliceous rocks similar to terrestrial ones, often contain either dense masses of iron (for example, the Pallosovo iron preserved in the St. Petersburg Academy of Sciences) or granular masses (for instance, the Okhansk meteorite of 1886). It is therefore possible that the interior of the earth contains much iron in a metallic state. This might be anticipated from the hypothesis of Laplace, for the iron must have been compressed into a liquid at that period when the other component parts of the earth were still strongly heated, and oxides of iron could not then have been formed. The iron was covered with slags (mixtures of silicates like glass fused with rocky matter) which did not allow it to burn at the expense of the oxygen of the atmosphere or of water, just at that time when the temperature of the earth was very high. Carbon was in the same state; its oxides were also capable of dissociation (Deville); it is also but slightly volatile, and has an affinity for iron, and iron carbide is found in meteoric stones (as well as carbon and even the diamond). Thus the supposition of the existence of iron carbides in the interior of the earth was derived by me from many indications, which are to some extent confirmed by the fact that granular pieces of iron have been found in some basalts (ancient lava) as well as in meteoric stones. The occurrence of iron in contact with carbon during the formation of the earth is all the more probable because those elements predominate in nature which have small atomic weights, and among them the most widely diffused, the most difficultly fusible, and therefore the most easily condensed (Chapter XV.) are carbon and iron. They passed into the liquid state when all compounds were at a temperature of dissociation.

[58] The following is the typical equation for this formation:

$$3Fe_mC_n + 4_mH_2O = mFe_3O_4 \text{ (magnetic oxide)} + C_5nH_{8m} \text{ (see Chapter XVII., Note 38)}.$$

[59] Cloez investigated the hydrocarbons formed when cast-iron is dissolved in hydrochloric acid, and found C_nH_{2n} and others. I treated crystalline manganiferous cast-iron with the same acid, and obtained a liquid mixture of hydrocarbons exactly similar to natural naphtha in taste, smell, and reaction.

[60] Probably naphtha was produced during the upheaval of all mountain chains, but only in some cases were the conditions favourable to its being preserved underground. The water penetrating below formed there a mixture of naphtha and watery vapours, and this mixture issued through fissures to the cold parts of the earth's crust. The naphtha vapours, on condensing, formed naphtha, which, if there were no obstacles, appeared on the surface of land and water. Here part of it soaked through formations (possibly the bituminous slates, schists, dolomites, &c., were thus formed), another part was carried away on the water, became oxidised, evaporated, and was driven to the shores (the Caucasian naphtha probably in this way, during the existence of the Aralo-Caspian sea, was carried as far as the Sisran banks of the Volga, where many strata are impregnated with naphtha and products of its oxidation resembling asphalt and pitch); a great part of it was burnt in one way or another—that is, gave carbonic anhydride and water. If the mixture of vapours, water, and naphtha formed inside the earth had no free outlet to the surface, it nevertheless would find its way through fissures to the superior and colder strata, and there become condensed. Some of the formations (clays) which do not absorb naphtha were only washed away by the warm water, and formed mud, which we also now observe issuing from the earth in the form of mud volcanoes. The neighbourhood of Baku and the whole of the Caucasus near the naphtha districts are full of such volcanoes, which from time to time are in a state of eruption. In old naphtha beds (such as the Pennsylvanian) even these blow-holes are closed, and the mud volcanoes have had time to be washed away. The naphtha and the gaseous hydrocarbons formed with it under the pressure of the overlying earth and water impregnated the layers of sand, which are capable of absorbing a great quantity of such liquid, and if above this there were strata impermeable to naphtha (dense, clayey, damp strata) the naphtha would accumulate in them. It is thus preserved from remote geological periods up to the present day, compressed and

dissolved under the pressure of the gases which burst out in places forming naphtha fountains. If this be granted, it may be thought that in the comparatively new (geologically speaking) mountain chains, such as the Caucasian, naphtha is even now being formed. Such a supposition may explain the remarkable fact that, in Pennsylvania, localities where naphtha had been rapidly worked for five years have become exhausted, and it becomes necessary to constantly have recourse to sinking new wells in fresh places. Thus, from the year 1859, the workings were gradually transferred along a line running parallel to the Alleghany mountains for a distance of more than 200 miles, whilst in Baku the industry dates from time immemorial (the Persians worked near the village of Ballaghana) and up to the present time keeps to one and the same place. The amounts of the Pennsylvanian and Baku annual outputs are at present equal—namely, about 250 million poods (4 million tons). It may be that the Baku beds, as being of more recent geological formation, are not so exhausted by nature as those of Pennsylvania, and perhaps in the neighbourhood of Baku naphtha is still being formed, which is partially indicated by the continued activity of the mud volcanoes. As many varieties of naphtha contain in solution solid slightly volatile hydrocarbons like paraffin and mineral wax, the production of ozocerite, or mountain wax, is accounted for in conjunction with the formation of naphtha. Ozocerite is found in Galicia, also in the neighbourhood of Novorossisk, in the Caucasus, and on the islands of the Caspian Sea (particularly in the Chileken and Holy Islands); it is met with in large masses, and is used for the production of paraffin and *ceresene*, for the manufacture of candles, and similar purposes.

As the naphtha treasures of the Caucasus have hardly been exploited (near Baku and near Kouban and Grosnyi), and as naphtha finds numerous uses, the subject presents most interesting features to chemists and geologists, and is worthy of the close attention of practical men.

[379]

CHAPTER IX

COMPOUNDS OF CARBON WITH OXYGEN AND NITROGEN

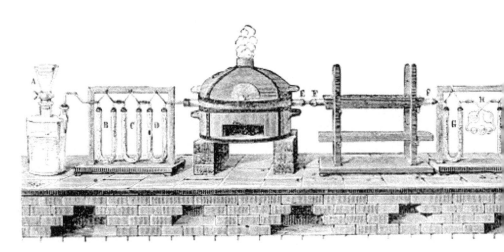

FIG. 61.—Dumas and Stas' apparatus for determining the composition of carbonic anhydride. Carbon, graphite, or a diamond is placed in the tube E in the furnace, and heated in a stream of oxygen displaced from the bottle by water flowing from A. The oxygen is purified from carbonic anhydride and water in the tubes B, C, D. Carbonic anhydride, together with a certain amount of carbon monoxide, is formed in E. The latter is converted into carbonic acid by passing the products of combustion through a tube F, containing cupric oxide heated in a furnace. The cupric oxide oxidises this CO into CO_2, forming metallic copper. The potash bulbs H and tubes I, J, K retain the carbonic anhydride. Thus, knowing the weight of carbon taken and the weight of the resultant carbonic anhydride (by weighing H, I, J, K before and after the experiment), the composition of carbonic anhydride and the equivalent of carbon may be determined.

Carbonic anhydride (or carbonic acid or carbon dioxide, CO_2) was the first of all gases distinguished from atmospheric air. Paracelsus and Van Helmont, in the sixteenth century, knew that on heating limestone a particular gas separated, which is also formed during the alcoholic fermentation of saccharine solutions (for instance, in the manufacture of wine); they knew that it was identical with the gas which is produced by the combustion of charcoal, and that in some cases it is found in nature. In course of time it was found that this gas is absorbed by alkali, forming a salt which, under the action of acid, again yields this same gas. Priestley found that this gas exists in air, and Lavoisier determined its formation during respiration, combustion, putrefaction, and during the reduction of the oxides of metals by charcoal; he determined its composition, and showed that it only contains oxygen and carbon. Berzelius, Dumas with Stas, and Roscoe, determined its composition,[380] showing that it contains twelve parts of carbon to thirty-two of oxygen. The composition by volume of this gas is determined from the fact that during the combustion of charcoal in oxygen, the volume remains unchanged; that is to say, *carbonic anhydride occupies the same volume as the oxygen which it contains*—that is, the atoms of the carbon are, so to speak, squeezed in between the atoms of the oxygen. O_2 occupies two volumes and is a molecule of ordinary oxygen; CO_2 likewise occupies two volumes, and expresses the composition and molecular weight of the gas. Carbonic anhydride exists *in nature*, both in a free state and in the most varied compounds. In a free state it is always contained (Chapter V.) in the air, and in solution is in all kinds of water. It is evolved from volcanoes, from mountain fissures, and in some caves. The well-known Dog grotto, near Agnano on the bay of Baiæ, near Naples, furnishes the best known example of such an evolution. Similar sources of carbonic anhydride are also found in other places. In France, for instance, there is a well-known poisonous fountain in Auvergne. It is a round hole, surrounded with luxurious vegetation and constantly evolving carbonic anhydride. In the woods surrounding the Lacher See near the Rhine, in the neighbourhood of extinct volcanoes, there is a depression constantly filled with this same gas. The insects which fly to this place perish, animals being unable to breathe this gas. The birds chasing the insects also die, and this is turned to profit by the local peasantry. Many mineral springs carry into the air enormous quantities of this gas. Vichy in France, Sprüdel in Germany, and Narzan in Russia (in Kislovodsk near Piatigorsk) are known for their carbonated gaseous waters. Much of this gas is also evolved in mines, cellars, diggings, and wells. People descending into such places are suffocated. The combustion, putrefaction, and fermentation of organic substances give rise to the formation of carbonic anhydride. It is also introduced into the atmosphere during the respiration of animals at all times and during the respiration of plants in darkness and also during their growth. Very simple experiments prove the formation of carbonic anhydride under these circumstances; thus, for example, if the air expelled from the lungs be passed through a glass tube into a transparent solution of lime (or baryta) in water a white precipitate will soon be formed consisting of an insoluble compound of lime and carbonic anhydride. By allowing the seeds of plants to grow under a bell jar, or in a closed vessel, the formation of carbonic anhydride may be similarly confirmed. By confining an animal, a mouse, for instance, under a bell jar, the quantity of carbonic acid which it evolves may be exactly determined, and it will he found to be many grams per day for a mouse. Such experiments on the respiration of animals have[381] been also made with great exactitude with large animals, such as men, bulls, sheep, &c. By means of enormous hermetically closed bell receivers and the analysis of the gases evolved during respiration it was found that a man expels about 900 grams (more than two pounds) of carbonic anhydride per diem, and absorbs during this time 700 grams of oxygen.[1] It must be remarked that the carbonic anhydride of the air constitutes the fundamental food of plants (Chapters III., V., and VIII.) Carbonic anhydride in a state of combination with a variety of other substances is perhaps even more widely distributed in nature than in a free state. Some of these substances are very stable and form a large portion of the earth's crust. For instance, limestones, calcium carbonate, $CaCO_3$, were formed as precipitates in the seas existing previously on the earth; this is proved by their stratified structure and the number of remains of sea animals which they frequently contain. Chalk, lithographic stone, limestone, marls (a mixture of limestone and clay), and many other rocks are examples of such sedimentary formations.[382] Carbonates with various other bases—such as, for instance, magnesia, ferrous oxide, zinc oxide, &c.—are often found in nature. The shells of molluscs also have the composition $CaCO_3$ and many limestones were exclusively formed from the shells of minute organisms. As carbonic anhydride (together with water) is produced during the combustion of all organic compounds in a stream of oxygen or by heating them with substances which readily part with their oxygen—for instance, with copper oxide—this method is employed for estimating the amount of carbon in organic compounds, more especially as the CO_2 can be easily collected and the amount of carbon calculated from its weight. For this purpose a hard glass tube, closed at one end, is filled with a mixture of the organic substance (about $0 \cdot 2$ gram) and copper oxide. The open end of the tube is fitted with a cork and tube containing calcium chloride for absorbing the water formed by the oxidation of the substance. This tube is hermetically connected (by a caoutchouc tube) with potash bulbs or other weighing apparatus (Chapter V.) containing alkali destined to absorb the carbonic anhydride. The increase in weight of this apparatus shows the amounts of carbonic anhydride formed during the combustion of the given substance, and the quantity of carbon may be determined from this, because three parts of carbon give eleven parts of carbonic anhydride.

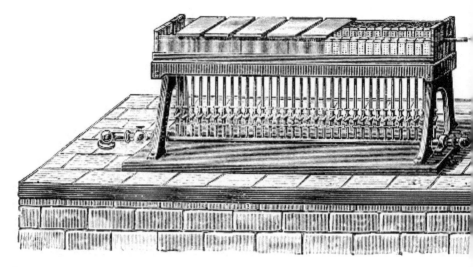

FIG. 62.—62. Apparatus for the combustion of organic substances by igniting them with oxide of copper.

For the preparation of carbonic anhydride in laboratories and often in manufactories, various kinds of calcium carbonate are used, being treated with some acid; it is, however, most usual to employ the so-called muriatic acid—that is, an aqueous solution of hydrochloric acid, HCl—because, in the first place, the substance formed, calcium chloride. $CaCl_2$, is soluble in water and does not hinder the further[383] action of the acid on the calcium carbonate, and secondly because, as we shall see further on, muriatic acid is a common product of chemical works and one of the cheapest. For calcium carbonate, either limestone, chalk, or marble is used.[2]

$$CaCO_3 + 2HCl = CaCl_2 + H_2O + CO_2.$$

The nature of the reaction in this case is the same as in the decomposition of nitre by sulphuric acid; only in the latter case a hydrate is formed, and in the former an anhydride of the acid, because the hydrate, carbonic acid, H_2CO_3, is unstable and as soon as it separates decomposes into water and its own anhydride. It is evident from the explanation of the cause of the action of sulphuric acid on nitre that not every acid can be employed for obtaining carbonic anhydride; namely, those will not set it free which chemically are but slightly energetic, or those which are insoluble in water, or are themselves as volatile as carbonic anhydride.[3] But as many acids are soluble in water and are less volatile than carbonic anhydride, the latter is evolved by the action of most acids on its salts, and this reaction takes place at ordinary temperatures.[4]

For the preparation of carbonic anhydride in laboratories, marble is generally used. It is placed in a Woulfe's bottle and treated with hydrochloric acid in an apparatus similar to the one used for the production of hydrogen. The gas evolved carries away through the tube part of the volatile hydrochloric acid, and it is therefore necessary to wash the gas by passing it through another Woulfe's bottle containing water. If it be necessary to obtain dry carbonic anhydride, it must be passed through chloride of calcium.[5]

Carbonic anhydride may also be prepared by heating many of the salts of carbonic acid; for instance, by heating magnesium carbonate, $MgCO_3$ (*e.g.*, in the form of dolomite), the separation is easily effected, particularly in the presence of the vapours of water. The acid salts of carbonic acid (for instance, $NaHCO_3$, see further on) readily and abundantly give carbonic anhydride when heated.

Carbonic anhydride is colourless, has a slight smell and a faint acid taste; its density in a gaseous state is twenty-two times as great as that of hydrogen, because its molecular weight is forty-four.[6][385] It is an example of those gaseous substances which have been long ago transformed into all the three states. In order to obtain liquid carbonic anhydride, the gas must be submitted to a pressure of thirty-six atmospheres at $0°$.[7] Its absolute boiling point = $+32°$.[8] Liquid carbonic anhydride is colourless, does not mix with water, but is soluble in alcohol, ether, and oils; at $0°$ its specific gravity is 0.83.[8 bis] The boiling point of this liquid lies at $-80°$—that is to say, the pressure of carbonic acid gas at that temperature does not exceed that of the atmosphere. At the ordinary temperature the liquid remains as such for some time under ordinary pressure, on account of its requiring a considerable amount of heat for its evaporation. If the evaporation takes place rapidly, especially if the liquid issues in a stream, such a decrease of temperature occurs that a part of the carbonic anhydride is transformed into a solid snowy mass. Water, mercury, and many other liquids freeze on coming into contact with snow-like carbonic anhydride.[9] In this form carbonic anhydride may be preserved for a long time in the open air, because it requires still more heat to turn it into a gas than when in a liquid state.[9 bis]

The capacity which carbonic anhydride has of being liquefied stands[386] in connection with its *considerable solubility in water*, alcohol, and other liquids. Its solubility in water has been already spoken of in the first chapter. Carbonic anhydride is still more soluble in alcohol than in water, namely at $0°$ one volume of alcohol dissolves 4.3 volumes of this gas, and at $20°$ 2.9 volumes.

Aqueous solutions of carbonic anhydride, under a pressure of several atmospheres, are now prepared artificially, because water saturated with this gas promotes digestion and quenches thirst. For this purpose the carbonic anhydride is pumped by means of a force-pump into a closed vessel containing the liquid, and then bottled off, taking special means to ensure rapid and air-tight corking. Various effervescing drinks and artificially effervescing wines are thus prepared. The presence of carbonic anhydride has an important significance in nature, because by its means water acquires the property of decomposing and dissolving many substances which are not acted on by pure water; for instance, calcium phosphates and carbonates are soluble in water containing carbonic acid. If the water in the interior of the earth is saturated with carbonic acid under pressure, the quantity of calcium carbonate in solution may reach three grams per litre, and on issuing at the surface, as the carbonic anhydride escapes, the calcium carbonate will be deposited.[10] Water charged with carbonic anhydride brings about the destruction of many rocky formations by removing the lime, alkali, &c., from them. This process has been going on and continues on an enormous scale. Rocks[387] contain silica and the oxides of various metals; amongst others, the oxides of aluminium, calcium, and sodium. Water charged with carbonic acid dissolves both the latter, transforming them into carbonates. The waters of the ocean ought, as the evolution of the carbonic anhydride proceeds, to precipitate salts of lime; these are actually found everywhere on the surface of the ground in those places which previously formed the bed of the ocean. The presence of carbonic anhydride in solution in water is essential to the nourishment and growth of water plants.

Although carbonic anhydride is soluble in water, yet no definite hydrate is formed;[11] nevertheless an idea of the composition of this hydrate may be formed from that of the salts of carbonic acid, because a hydrate is nothing but a salt in which the metal is replaced by hydrogen. As carbonic anhydride forms salts of the composition K_2CO_3, Na_2CO_3, $HNaCO_3$, &c., therefore carbonic acid ought to have the composition H_2CO_3—that is, it ought to contain CO_2 + H_2O. Whenever this substance is formed, it decomposes into its component parts—that is, into water and carbonic anhydride. *The acid properties* of carbonic anhydride[11 bis] are demonstrated by its being directly absorbed by alkaline solutions and forming salts with them. In distinction from nitric, HNO_3, and similar monobasic acids which with univalent metals (exchanging one atom for one atom of hydrogen) give salts such as those of potassium, sodium, and silver containing only one atom of the metal ($NaNO_3$, $AgNO_3$), and with bivalent[12] metals (such as calcium, barium, lead) salts containing two acid groups—for example, $Ca(NO_3)_2$, $Pb(NO_3)_2$—carbonic acid, H_2CO_3, *is bibasic*, that is contains two atoms of hydrogen in the hydrate or two atoms of univalent metals in their salts: for example, Na_2CO_3 is washing soda, a normal salt; $NaHCO_3$ is the bicarbonate, an acid salt. Therefore, if M' be a univalent metal, its carbonates in general are the normal carbonate M'_2CO_3 and the[388] acid carbonate, $M'HCO_3$; or if M" be a bivalent metal (replacing H_2) its normal carbonate will be $M''CO_3$; these metals do not usually form acid salts, as we shall see further on. The bibasic character of carbonic acid is akin to that of sulphuric acid, H_2SO_4,[13] but the latter, in distinction from the former, is an example of the energetic or strong acids (such as nitric or hydrochloric), whilst in carbonic acid we observe but feeble development of the acid properties; hence carbonic acid must be considered *a weak acid*. This conception must, however, be taken as only comparative, as up to this time there is no definitely established rule for measuring the energy[14] of acids. The feeble acid properties of carbonic[389] acid may, however, be judged from the joint evidence of many properties. With such energetic alkalis as soda and potash, carbonic acid forms normal salts, soluble in water, but having an alkaline reaction and in[390] many cases themselves acting as alkalis.[15] The acid salts of these alkalis, $NaHCO_3$ and $KHCO_3$, have a neutral reaction on litmus, although they, like acids, contain hydrogen, which may be exchanged for metals. The acid salts of such acids—as, for instance, of sulphuric acid, $NaHSO_4$—have a clearly defined acid reaction, and therefore carbonic acid is unable to neutralise the powerful basic properties of such alkalis as potash or soda. Carbonic acid does not even combine at all with feeble bases, such as alumina, Al_2O_3, and therefore if a strong solution of sodium carbonate, Na_2CO_3, be added to a strong solution of aluminium sulphate, $Al_2(SO_4)_3$, although according to double saline decompositions aluminium carbonate, $Al_2(CO_3)_3$, ought to be formed, the carbonic acid separates, for this salt splits up in the presence of water into aluminium hydroxide and carbonic anhydride: $Al_2(CO_3)_3 + 3H_2O = Al_2(OH)_6 + 3CO_2$. Thus feeble bases are unable to retain carbonic acid even at ordinary temperatures. For the same reason, in the case of bases of medium energy, although they form carbonates, the latter are comparatively easily decomposed by heating, as is shown by the decomposition of copper carbonate, $CuCO_3$ (*see* Introduction), and even of calcium carbonate,[391] $CaCO_3$. Only the normal (not the acid) salts of such powerful bases as potassium and sodium are capable of standing a red heat without decomposition. The acid salts—for instance, $NaHCO_3$— decompose even on heating their solutions ($2NaHCO_3 = Na_2CO_3 + H_2O + CO_2$), evolving carbonic anhydride. The amount of heat given out by the combination of carbonic acid with bases also shows its feeble acid properties, being considerably less than with energetic acids. Thus if a weak solution of forty grams of sodium hydroxide be saturated (up to the formation of a normal salt) with sulphuric or nitric acid or another powerful acid, from thirteen to fifteen thousand calories are given out, but with carbonic acid only about ten thousand calories.[16] The majority of carbonates are insoluble in water, and therefore such solutions as sodium, potassium, or ammonium carbonates form in solutions of most other salts, MX or M"X$_2$, insoluble precipitates of carbonates, M$_2$CO$_3$ or M"CO$_3$. Thus a solution of barium chloride gives with sodium carbonate a precipitate of barium carbonate, BaCO$_3$. For this reason rocks, especially those of aqueous origin, very often contain carbonates; for example, calcium, ferrous, or magnesium carbonates, &c.

Carbonic anhydride—which, like water, is formed with the development of a large amount of heat—is very stable. Only very few substances are capable of depriving it of its oxygen. However, certain metals, such as magnesium, potassium and the like, on being heated, burn in it, depositing carbon and forming oxides. If a mixture of carbonic anhydride and hydrogen be passed through a heated tube, the formation of water and carbonic oxide will be observed; $CO_2 + H_2 = CO + H_2O$.[392] But only a portion of the carbonic acid gas undergoes this change, and therefore the result will be a mixture of carbonic anhydride, carbonic oxide, hydrogen, and water, which does not suffer further change under the action of heat.[17] Although, like water, carbonic anhydride is exceedingly stable, still on being heated it partially decomposes into carbonic oxide and oxygen. Deville showed that such is the case if carbonic anhydride be passed through a long tube containing pieces of porcelain and heated to 1,300°. If the products of decomposition—namely, the carbonic oxide and oxygen—be suddenly cooled, they can be collected separately, although they partly reunite together. A similar decomposition of carbonic anhydride into carbonic oxide and oxygen takes place on passing a series of electric sparks through it (for instance, in the eudiometer). Under these conditions an increase of volume occurs, because two volumes of CO_2 give two volumes of CO and one volume of O. The decomposition reaches a certain limit (less than one-third) and does not proceed further, so that the result is a mixture of carbonic anhydride, carbonic oxide, and oxygen, which is not altered in composition by the continued action of the sparks. This is readily understood, as it is a reversible reaction. If the carbonic anhydride be removed, then the mixture explodes when a spark is passed and forms carbonic anhydride.[17 bis] If from an identical[393] mixture the oxygen (and not the carbonic anhydride) be removed, and a series of sparks be again passed, the decomposition is renewed, and terminates with the complete dissociation of the carbonic anhydride. Phosphorus is used in order to effect the complete absorption of the oxygen. In these examples we see that a definite mixture of changeable substances is capable of arriving at a state of stable equilibrium, destroyed, however, by the removal of one of the substances composing the mixture. This is one of the instances of the influence of mass.

Although carbonic anhydride is decomposed on heating, yielding oxygen, it is nevertheless, like water, an unchangeable substance at ordinary temperatures. Its decomposition, as effected by plants, is on this account all the more remarkable; in this case the whole of the oxygen of the carbonic anhydride is separated in the free state. The mechanism of this change is that the heat and light absorbed by the plants are expended in the decomposition of the carbonic anhydride. This accounts for the enormous influence of temperature and light on the growth of plants. But it is at present not clearly understood how this takes place, or by what separate intermediate reactions the whole process of decomposition of carbonic anhydride in plants into oxygen and the carbohydrates (Note 1) remaining in them, takes place. It is known that sulphurous anhydride (in many ways resembling carbonic anhydride) under the action of light (and also of heat) forms sulphur and sulphuric anhydride, SO_3, and in the presence of water, sulphuric acid. But no similar decomposition has been obtained directly with carbonic anhydride, although it forms an exceedingly easily decomposable higher oxide—percarbonic[394] acid;[18] and perhaps that is the reason the oxygen separates. On the other hand, it is known that plants always form and contain *organic acids*, and these must be regarded as derivatives of carbonic acid, as is seen by all their reactions, of which we will shortly treat. For this reason it might be thought that the carbonic acid absorbed by the plants first forms (according to Baeyer) formic aldehyde, CH_2O, and from it organic acids, and that these latter in their final transformation form all the other complex organic substances of the plants. Many organic acids are found in plants in considerable quantity; for instance, tartaric acid, $C_4H_6O_6$, found in grape-juice and in the acid juice of many plants; malic acid, $C_4H_6O_5$, found not only in unripe apples but in still larger quantities in mountain ash berries; citric acid, $C_6H_8O_7$, found in the acid juice of lemons, in gooseberries, cranberries, &c.; oxalic acid, $C_2H_2O_4$, found in wood-sorrel and many other plants. Sometimes these acids exist in a free state in the plants, and sometimes in the form of salts; for instance, tartaric acid is met with in grapes as the salt known as cream of tartar, but in the impure state called argol, or tartar, $C_4H_5KO_6$. In sorrel we find the so-called salts of sorrel, or acid potassium oxalate, C_2HKO_4. There is a very clear connection between carbonic anhydride and the above-mentioned organic acids—namely, they all, under one condition or another, yield carbonic anhydride, and can all be formed by means of it from substances destitute of acid properties. The following examples afford the best demonstration of this fact: if acetic acid, $C_2H_4O_2$, the acid of vinegar, be passed in the form of vapour through a heated tube,[395] it splits up into carbonic anhydride and marsh gas $= CO_2 + CH_4$. But conversely it can also be obtained from those components into which it decomposes. If one equivalent of hydrogen in marsh gas be replaced (by indirect means) by sodium, and the compound CH_3Na is obtained, this directly absorbs carbonic anhydride, forming a salt of acetic acid, $CH_3Na + CO_2 = C_2H_3NaO_2$; from this acetic acid itself may be easily obtained. Thus acetic acid decomposes into marsh gas and carbonic anhydride, and conversely is obtainable from them. The hydrogen of marsh gas does not, like that in acids, show the property of being directly replaced by metals; *i.e.* CH_4 does not show any acid character whatever, but on combining with the elements of carbonic anhydride it acquires the properties of an acid. The investigation of all other organic acids shows similarly that their acid character depends on their containing the elements of carbonic anhydride. For this reason there is no organic acid containing less oxygen in its molecule than there is in carbonic anhydride; every organic acid contains in its molecule at least two atoms of oxygen. In order to express the relation between carbonic acid, H_2CO_3, and organic acids, and in order to understand the reason of the acidity of these latter, it is simplest to turn to that law of substitution which shows (Chapter VI.) the relation between the hydrogen and oxygen compounds of nitrogen, and permits us (Chapter VIII.) to regard all hydrocarbons as derived from methane. If we have a given organic compound, A, which has not the properties of an acid, but contains hydrogen connected to carbon, as in hydrocarbons, then ACO_2 will be a monobasic organic acid, $A2CO_2$ a bibasic, $A3CO_2$ a tribasic, and so on—that is, each molecule of CO_2 transforms one atom of hydrogen into that state in which it may be replaced by metals, as in acids. This furnishes a direct proof that in organic acids it is necessary to recognise the group HCO_2, or carboxyl. If the addition of CO_2 raises the basicity, the removal of CO_2 lowers it. Thus from the bibasic oxalic acid, $C_2H_2O_4$, or phthalic acid, $C_8H_6O_4$, by eliminating CO_2 (easily effected experimentally) we obtain the monobasic formic acid, CH_2O_2, or benzoic acid, $C_7H_6O_2$, respectively. The nature of carboxyl is directly explained by the law of substitution. Judging from what has been stated in Chapters VI. and VIII. concerning this law, it is evident that CO_2 is CH_4 with the exchange of H_4 for O_2, and that the hydrate of carbonic anhydride, H_2CO_3, is $CO(OH)_2$, that is, methane, in which two parts of hydrogen are replaced by two parts of the water radical (OH, hydroxyl) and the other two by oxygen. Therefore the group $CO(OH)$, or carboxyl, HCO_2, is a part of carbonic acid, and is equivalent to (OH), and therefore also to H. That is, it[396] is a univalent residue of carbonic acid capable of replacing one atom of hydrogen. Carbonic acid itself is a bibasic acid, both hydrogen atoms in it being replaceable by metals, therefore carboxyl, which contains one of the hydrogen atoms of carbonic acid, represents a group in which the hydrogen is exchangeable for metals. And therefore if 1, 2 ... n atoms of non-metallic hydrogen are exchanged 1, 2 ... n times for carboxyl, we ought to obtain 1, 2 ... n-basic acids. *Organic acids are the products of the carboxyl substitution in hydrocarbons.*[18 bis] If in the saturated hydrocarbons, C_nH_{2n+2}, one part of hydrogen is replaced by carboxyl, the monobasic saturated (or fatty) acids, $C_nH_{2n+1}(CO_2H)$, will be obtained, as, for instance, formic acid, HCO_2H, acetic acid, CH_2CO_2H, ... stearic acid, $C_{17}H_{35}CO_2H$, &c. The double substitution will give bibasic acids, $C_nH_{2n}(CO_2H)(CO_2H)$; for instance, oxalic acid $n = 0$, malonic acid $n = 1$, succinic acid $n = 2$, &c. To benzene, C_6H_6 correspond benzoic acid, $C_6H_5(CO_2H)$, phthalic acid (and its isomerides), $C_6H_4(CO_2H)_2$, up to mellitic acid, $C_6(CO_2H)_6$, in all of which the basicity is equal to the number of carboxyl groups. As many isomerides exist in hydrocarbons, it is readily understood not only that such can exist also in organic acids, but that their number and structure may be foreseen. This complex and most interesting branch of chemistry is treated separately in organic chemistry.

Carbonic Oxide.—This gas is formed whenever the combustion of organic substances takes place in the presence of a large excess of[397] incandescent charcoal; the air first burns the carbon into carbonic anhydride, but this in penetrating through the red-hot charcoal is transformed into carbonic oxide, $CO_2 + C = 2CO$. By this reaction carbonic oxide is prepared by passing carbonic anhydride through charcoal at a red heat. It may be separated from the excess of carbonic anhydride by passing it through a solution of alkali, which does not absorb carbonic oxide. This reduction of carbonic anhydride explains why carbonic oxide is formed in ordinary clear fires, where the incoming air passes over a large surface of heated coal. A blue flame is then observed burning above the coal; this is the burning carbonic oxide. When charcoal is burnt in stacks, or when a thick layer of coal is burning in a brazier, and under many similar circumstances, carbonic oxide is also formed. In metallurgical processes, for instance when iron is smelted from the ore, very often the same process of conversion of carbonic anhydride into carbonic oxide occurs, especially if the combustion of the coal be effected in high, so-called blast, furnaces and ovens, where the air enters at the lower part and is compelled to pass through a thick layer of incandescent coal. In this way, also, combustion with flame may be obtained from those kinds of fuel which under ordinary conditions burn without flame: for instance, anthracite, coke, charcoal. Heating by means of a gas-producer—that is, an apparatus producing combustible carbonic oxide from fuel—is carried on in the same manner.[19] In transforming one part of charcoal[398] into carbonic oxide 2,420 heat units are given out, and on burning to carbonic anhydride 8,080 heat units. It is evident that on transforming the charcoal first into carbonic oxide we obtain a gas which in burning is capable of giving out 5,660 heat units for one part of charcoal. This preparatory transformation of fuel into carbonic oxide, or producer gas containing a mixture of carbonic oxide (about ⅓ by volume) and nitrogen (⅔ volume), in many cases presents most important advantages, as it is easy to completely burn gaseous fuel without an excess of air, which would lower the temperature.[20] In stoves where solid fuel is burnt it is impossible to effect the complete combustion of the various kinds of fuel without admitting an excess of air. Gaseous fuel, such as carbonic oxide, is easily completely mixed with air and burnt without excess of it. If, in addition to this, the air and gas required for the combustion be previously heated by means of the heat which would otherwise be uselessly carried off in the products of combustion (smoke)[21] it is easy to reach a high temperature, so high (about 1,800°) that platinum may be melted. Such an arrangement is known as a *regenerative furnace*.[22] By means of this process not only may the high temperatures indispensable in many industries be obtained (for instance,[399] glass-working, steel-melting, &c.), but great advantage also[23] is gained as regards the quantity of fuel, because the transmission of heat to the object to be heated, other conditions being equal, is determined by the difference of temperatures.

The transformation of carbonic anhydride, by means of charcoal, into carbonic oxide $(C + CO_2 = CO + CO)$ is considered a reversible reaction, because at a high temperature the carbonic oxide splits up into carbon and carbonic anhydride, as Sainte-Claire Deville showed by using the method of the 'cold and hot tube.' Inside a tube heated in a furnace another thin metallic (silvered copper) tube is fitted, through which a constant stream of cold water flows. The carbonic oxide coming into contact with the heated walls of the exterior tube forms charcoal, and its minute particles settle in the form of lampblack on the lower side of the cold tube, and, since they are cooled, do not act further on the oxygen or carbonic anhydride formed.[24] A series[400] of electric sparks also decomposes carbonic oxide into carbonic anhydride and carbon, and if the carbonic anhydride be removed by alkali complete decomposition may be obtained (Deville).[24 bis] Aqueous vapour, which is so similar to carbonic anhydride in many respects, acts, at a high temperature, on charcoal in an exactly similar way, $C + H_2O = H_2 + CO$. From 2 volumes of carbonic anhydride with charcoal 4 volumes of carbonic oxide (2 molecules) are obtained, and precisely the same from 2 volumes of water vapour with charcoal 4 volumes of a gas consisting of hydrogen and carbonic oxide $(H_2 + CO)$ are formed. This mixture of combustible gases is called *water gas*.[25][401] But aqueous vapour (and only when strongly superheated, otherwise it cools the charcoal) only acts on charcoal to form a large amount of carbonic oxide at a very high temperature (at which carbonic anhydride dissociates); it begins to react at about 500°, forming carbonic anhydride according to the equation $C + 2H_2O = CO_2 + 2H_2$. Besides this, carbonic oxide on splitting up forms carbonic anhydride, and therefore water gas always contains a mixture[26] in which hydrogen predominates, the volume of carbonic oxide being comparatively less,[402] whilst the amount of carbonic anhydride increases as the temperature of the reaction decreases (generally it is more than 3 per cent.)

Metals like iron and zinc which at a red heat are capable of decomposing water with the formation of hydrogen, also decompose carbonic anhydride with the formation of carbonic oxide; so both the ordinary products of complete combustion, water and carbonic anhydride, are very similar in their reactions, and we shall therefore presently compare hydrogen and carbonic oxide. The metallic oxides of the above-mentioned metals, when reduced by charcoal, also give carbonic oxide. Priestley obtained it by heating charcoal with zinc oxide. As free carbonic anhydride may be transformed into carbonic oxide, so, in precisely the same way, may that carbonic acid which is in a state of combination; hence, if magnesium or barium carbonates ($MgCO_3$ or $BaCO_3$) be heated to redness with charcoal, or iron or zinc, carbonic oxide will be produced—for instance, it is obtained by heating an intimate mixture of 9 parts of chalk and 1 part of charcoal in a clay retort.

Many organic substances[27] on being heated, or under the action of various agents, yield carbonic oxide; amongst these are many organic or carboxylic acids. The simplest are formic and oxalic acids. Formic acid, CH_2O_2, on being heated to 200°, easily decomposes into carbonic oxide and water, $CH_2O_2 = CO + H_2O$.[27 bis] Usually, however, carbonic oxide is prepared in laboratories, not from formic but from oxalic acid, $C_2H_2O_4$, the more so as formic acid is itself prepared from oxalic acid. The latter acid is easily obtained by the action of nitric acid on starch, sugar, &c.; it is also found in nature. Oxalic acid is easily decomposed by heat; its crystals first lose water, then partly volatilise, but the greater part is decomposed. The decomposition is of the following nature: it splits up into water, carbonic oxide, and carbonic anhydride,[28] $C_2H_2O_4 = H_2O + CO_2 + CO$. This decomposition is generally practically effected by mixing oxalic acid with strong sulphuric[403] acid, because the latter assists the decomposition by taking up the water. On heating a mixture of oxalic and sulphuric acids a mixture of carbonic oxide and carbonic anhydride is evolved. This mixture is passed through a solution of an alkali in order to absorb the carbonic anhydride, whilst the carbonic oxide passes on.[28 bis]

In its physical *properties* carbonic oxide resembles nitrogen; this is explained by the equality of their molecular weights. The absence of colour and smell, the low temperature of the absolute boiling point, -140° (nitrogen, -146°), the property of solidifying at -200° (nitrogen, -202°), the boiling point of -190° (nitrogen, -203°), and the slight solubility (Chapter I., Note 30), of carbonic oxide are almost the same as in those of nitrogen. The chemical properties of both gases are, however, very different, and in these carbonic oxide resembles hydrogen. Carbonic oxide burns with a blue flame, giving 2 volumes of carbonic anhydride from 2 volumes of carbonic oxide, just as 2 volumes of hydrogen give 2 volumes of aqueous vapour. It explodes with oxygen, in the eudiometer, like hydrogen.[29] When breathed it acts as a strong poison, being absorbed by the blood;[30] this explains the action of charcoal fumes, the products of the[404] incomplete combustion of charcoal and other carbonaceous fuels. Owing to its faculty of combining with oxygen, carbonic oxide acts as a powerful reducing agent, taking up the oxygen from many compounds at a red heat, and being itself transformed into carbonic anhydride. The reducing action of carbonic oxide, however, is (like that of hydrogen, Chapter II.) naturally confined to those oxides which easily part with their oxygen—as, for instance, copper oxide—whilst the oxides of magnesium or potassium are not reduced. Metallic iron itself is capable of reducing carbonic anhydride to carbonic oxide, just as it liberates the hydrogen from water. Copper, which does not decompose water, does not decompose carbonic oxide. If a platinum wire heated to 300°, or spongy platinum at the ordinary temperature, be plunged into a mixture of carbonic oxide and oxygen, or of hydrogen and oxygen, the mixture explodes. These reactions are very similar to those peculiar to hydrogen. The following important distinction, however, exists between them—namely: the molecule of hydrogen is composed of H_2, a group of elements divisible into two like parts, whilst, as the molecule of carbonic oxide, CO, contains unlike atoms of carbon and oxygen, in none of its reactions of combination can it give two molecules of matter containing its elements. This is particularly noticeable in the action of chlorine on hydrogen and on carbonic oxide respectively; with the former chlorine forms hydrogen chloride, and with the latter it produces the so-called carbonyl chloride, $COCl_2$: that is to say, the molecule of hydrogen, H_2, under the action of chlorine divides, forming two molecules of hydrochloric acid, whilst the molecule of carbonic oxide enters in its entirety into the molecule of carbonyl chloride. This characterises the so-called *diatomic* or *bivalent* reactions of radicles or *residues*. H is a monatomic residue or radicle, like K, Cl, and others, whilst carbonic oxide, CO, is an indivisible (undecomposable) bivalent radicle, equivalent to H_2 and not to H, and therefore combining with X_2 and interchangeable with H_2. This distinction is evident from the annexed comparison:

HH, hydrogen.   CO, carbonic oxide.

HCl, hydrochloric acid. $COCl_2$, carbonyl chloride.

HKO, potash. $CO(KO)_2$, potassium carbonate.

HNH_2, ammonia. $CO(NH_2)_2$, urea.

HCH_3, methane. $CO(CH_3)_2$, acetone.

HHO, water. $\qquad$ CO(HO)$_2$, carbonic acid.

Such monatomic (univalent) residues, X, as H, Cl, Na, NO$_2$, NH$_4$, CH$_3$, CO$_2$H (carboxyl), OH, and others, in accordance with the law of substitution, combine together, forming compounds, XX'; and with[405] oxygen, or in general with diatomic (bivalent) residues, Y—for instance, O, CO, CH$_2$, S, Ca, &c. forming compounds XX'Y; but diatomic residues, Y, sometimes capable of existing separately may combine together, forming YY' and with X$_2$ or XX', as we see from the transition of CO into CO$_2$ and COCl$_2$. This combining power of carbonic oxide appears in many of its reactions. Thus it is very easily absorbed by cuprous chloride, CuCl, dissolved in fuming hydrochloric acid, forming a crystalline compound, COCu$_2$Cl$_2$,2H$_2$O, decomposable by water; it combines directly with potassium (at 90°), forming (KCO)$_n$[31] with platinum dichloride, PtCl$_2$, with chlorine, Cl$_2$, &c.

But the most remarkable compounds are (1) the compound of CO with metallic nickel, a colourless volatile liquid, Ni(CO)$_4$, obtained by L. Mond (described in Chapter XXII.) and (2) the compounds of carbonic oxide with the alkalis, for instance with potassium or barium hydroxide, &c.— although it is not directly absorbed by them, as it has no acid properties. Berthelot (1861) showed that potash in the presence of water is capable of absorbing carbonic oxide, but the absorption takes place slowly, little by little, and it is only after being heated for many hours that the whole of the carbonic oxide is absorbed by the potash. The salt CHKO$_2$ is obtained by this absorption; it corresponds with an acid found in nature—namely, the simplest organic (carboxylic) acid, *formic acid*, CH$_2$O$_2$. It can be extracted from the potassium salt by means of distillation with dilute sulphuric acid, just as nitric acid is prepared from sodium nitrate. The same acid is found in ants and in nettles (when the stings of the nettles puncture the skin they break, and the corrosive formic acid enters into the body); it is also obtained during the action of oxidising agents on many organic substances; it is formed from oxalic acid, and under many conditions splits up into carbonic oxide and water. In the formation of formic acid from carbonic oxide we observe an example of the synthesis of organic compounds, such as are now very numerous, and are treated of in detail in works on organic chemistry.

Formic acid, H(CHO$_2$), carbonic acid, HO(CHO$_2$), and oxalic acid, (CHO$_2$)$_2$, are the simple organic or carboxylic acids, R(CHO$_2$) corresponding[406] with HH and HOH. Commencing with carbonic oxide, CO, the formation of carboxylic acids is clearly seen from the fact that CO is capable of combining with X$_2$, that is of forming COX$_2$. If, for instance, one X is an aqueous residue, OH (hydroxyl), and the other X is hydrogen, then the simplest organic acid—formic acid, H(COOH)—is obtained. As all hydrocarbons (Chapter VIII.) correspond with the simplest, CH$_4$, so all organic acids may be considered to proceed from formic acid.

In a similar way it is easy to explain the relation to other compounds of carbon of those compounds which contain nitrogen. By way of an example, we will take one of the carboxyl acids, R(CO$_2$H), where R is a hydrocarbon radicle (residue). Such an acid, like all others, will give by combination with NH$_3$ an ammoniacal salt, R(CO$_2$NH$_4$). This salt contains the elements for the formation of two molecules of water, and under suitable conditions by the action of bodies capable of taking it up, water may in fact be separated from R(CO$_2$NH$_4$), forming by the loss of one molecule of water, *amides*, RCONH$_2$, and by the loss of two molecules of water, *nitriles*, RCN, otherwise known as *cyanogen compounds* or *cyanides*.[32] If all the carboxyl acids are united not only by many common reactions but also by a mutual conversion into each other (an instance of which we saw above in the conversion of oxalic acid into formic and carbonic acids) one would expect the same for all the cyanogen compounds also. The common character of their reactions, and the reciprocity of their transformation, were long ago observed by Gay-Lussac, who recognised a common group or radicle (residue) cyanogen, CN, in all of them. The simplest compounds are *hydrocyanic* or *prussic acid*, HCN, cyanic acid, OHCN, and free cyanogen, (CN)$_2$, which correspond to the three simplest carboxyl acids: formic, HCO$_2$H, carbonic, OHCO$_2$H, and oxalic, (CO$_2$H)$_2$. Cyanogen, like carboxyl, is evidently a monatomic residue and acid, similar to chlorine. As regards the amides RCONH$_2$, corresponding to the carboxyl acids, they contain the ammoniacal residue NH$_2$, and form a numerous class of organic compounds met with in nature and obtained in many ways,[33] but not[407] distinguished by such characteristic peculiarities as the cyanogen compounds.

The reactions and properties of the amides and nitriles of the organic acids are described in detail in books on organic chemistry; we will here only touch upon the simplest of them, and to clearly explain the derivative compounds will first consider the ammoniacal salts and amides of carbonic acid.

As carbonic acid is bibasic, its ammonium salts ought to have the following composition: *acid carbonate of ammonium*, H(NH$_4$)CO$_3$, and *normal carbonate*, (NH$_4$)$_2$CO$_3$; they represent compounds of one or two molecules of ammonia with carbonic acid. The acid salt appears in the form of a non-odoriferous and (when tested with litmus) neutral substance, soluble at the ordinary temperature in six parts of water, insoluble in alcohol, and obtainable in a crystalline form either without water of crystallisation or with various proportions of it. If an aqueous solution of ammonia be saturated with an excess of carbonic anhydride, and then evaporated over sulphuric acid in the bell jar of an air-pump, crystals of this salt are separated. Solutions of all other ammonium carbonates, when evaporated under the air-pump, yield crystals of this salt. A solution of this salt, even at the ordinary temperature, gives off carbonic anhydride, as do all the acid salts of carbonic acid (for instance, $NaHCO_3$), and at 38° the separation of carbonic anhydride takes place with great rapidity. *On losing carbonic anhydride and water*, the acid salt is converted into the normal salt, $2(NH_4)HCO_3 = H_2O + CO_2 + (NH_4)2CO_3$; the latter, however, decomposes in solution, and can therefore only be obtained in crystals, $(NH_4)_2CO_3,H_2O$, at low temperatures, and from solutions containing *an excess of ammonia* as the product of dissociation of this salt: $(NH_4)_2CO_3 = NH_3 + (NH_4)HCO_3$. But the normal salt,[34] according to the general type, is[408] capable of decomposing *with separation of water*, and forming *ammonium carbamate*, $NH_4O(CONH_2) = (NH_4)_2CO_3 - H_2O$; this still further complicates the chemical transformations of the carbonates of ammonium. It is in fact evident that, by changing the ratios of water, ammonia, and carbonic acid, various intermediate salts will be formed containing mixtures or combinations of those mentioned above. Thus the ordinary commercial *carbonate of ammonia* is obtained by heating a mixture of chalk and sulphate of ammonia (Chapter VI.), or sal-ammoniac, $2NH_4Cl + CaCO_3 = CaCl_2 + (NH_4)_2CO_3$. The normal salt, however, through loss of part of the ammonia, partly forms the acid salt, and, partly through loss of water, forms carbamate, and most frequently presents the composition $NH_4O(CONH_2) + 2OH(CO_2NH_4) = 4NH_3 + 3CO_2 + 2H_2O$. This salt, in parting under various conditions with ammonia, carbonic anhydride, and water, does not present a constant composition, and ought rather to be regarded as a mixture of acid salt and amide salt. The latter must be recognised as entering into the composition of the ordinary carbonate of ammonia, because it contains less water than is required for the normal or acid salt;[35] but on being dissolved in water this salt gives a mixture of acid and normal salts.

Each of the two ammoniacal salts of carbonic acid has its corresponding amide. That of the acid salt should be acid, if the water given off takes up the hydrogen of the ammonia, as it should according to the common type of formation of the amides, so that $OHCONH_2$, or *carbamic acid*, is formed from $OHCO_3NH_4$. This acid is not known in a free state, but its corresponding ammoniacal salt or *ammonium carbamate* is known. The latter is easily and immediately formed by mixing 2 volumes of *dry* ammonia with 1 volume of dry carbonic anhydride, $2NH_3 + CO_2 = NH_4O(CONH_2)$; it is a solid substance, smells strongly of ammonia, attracts moisture from the air, and decomposes completely at 60°. The fact of this decomposition may be proved[36] by the density of its vapour, which $= 13$ ($H = 1$); this exactly corresponds with the density of a mixture of 2 volumes of ammonia and 1 volume[409] of carbonic anhydride. It is easily understood that such a combination will take place with any ammonium carbonate under the action of salts which take up the water—for instance, sodium or potassium carbonate[37]—as in an anhydrous state ammonia and carbonic anhydride only form one compound, CO_22NH_3.[38] As the normal ammonium carbonate contains two ammonias, and as the amides are formed with the separation of water at the expense of the hydrogen of the ammonias, so this salt has its symmetrical amide, $CO(NH_2)_2$. This must be termed carbamide. It is identical with urea, CN_2H_4O, which, contained in the urine (about 2 per cent. in human urine), is for the higher animals (especially the carnivorous) the ordinary product of excretion[39] and oxidation of the nitrogenous substances found in the organism. If ammonium carbamate be heated to 140° (in a sealed tube, Bazaroff), or if carbonyl chloride, $COCl_2$, be treated with ammonia (Natanson), urea will be obtained, which shows its direct connection with carbonic acid—that is, the presence of carbonic acid and ammonia in it. From this it will be understood how urea during the putrefaction of urine is converted into ammonium carbonate, CN_2H_4O + $H_2O = CO_2 + 2NH_3$.

Thus urea, both by its origin and decomposition, is an amide of carbonic acid. Representing as it does ammonia (two molecules) in which hydrogen (two atoms) is replaced by the bivalent radicle of carbonic acid, urea retains the property of ammonia of entering into combination, with acids (thus nitric acid forms CN_2H_4O,HNO_3), with bases (for instance, with mercury oxide), and with salts (such as sodium chloride, ammonium chloride), but containing an acid residue it has no alkaline properties. It is soluble in water without change, but at a red heat loses ammonia and forms *cyanic acid*, CNHO,[39 bis] which is a nitrile of carbonic acid—that is to say, is a[410] cyanogen compound, corresponding to the acid ammonium carbonate, $OH(CNH_4O_2)$, which on parting with $2H_2O$ ought to form cyanic acid, CNOH. Liquid cyanic acid, exceedingly unstable at the ordinary temperatures, gives its stable solid polymer cyanuric acid, $O_3H_3C_3N_3$. Both have the same composition, and they pass one into another at different temperatures. If crystals of cyanuric acid be heated to a temperature, t, then the vapour tension, p, in millimetres of mercury (Troost and Hautefeuille) will be:

t. 160°, 170°, 200°, 250°, 300°, 350°

p. 56,   68,   130, 220, 430, 1,200

The vapour contains cyanic acid, and, if it be rapidly cooled, it condenses into a mobile volatile liquid (specific gravity at 0° = 1·14). If the liquid cyanic acid be gradually heated, it passes into a new amorphous polymeride (cyamelide), which, on being heated, like cyanuric acid, forms vapours of cyanic acid. If these fumes are heated above 150° they pass directly into cyanuric acid. Thus at a temperature of 350°, the pressure does not rise above 1,200 mm. on the addition of vapours of cyanic acid, because the whole excess is transformed into cyanuric acid. Hence, the above-mentioned figures give the tension of dissociation of cyanuric acid, or the greatest pressure which the vapours of HOCN are able to attain at a given temperature, whilst at a greater pressure, or by the introduction of a larger mass of the substance into a given volume, the whole of the excess is converted into cyanuric acid. The properties of cyanic acid which we have described were principally observed by Wöhler, and clearly show the *faculty of polymerisation of cyanogen compounds*. This is observed in many other cyanogen derivatives, and is to be regarded as the consequence of the above-mentioned explanation of their nature. All cyanogen compounds are ammonium salts, $R(CNH_4O_2)$, deprived of water, $2H_2O$; therefore the molecules, RCN, ought to possess the faculty of combining with two molecules of water or with other molecules in exchange for it (for instance, with H_2S, or HCl, or $2H_2$, &c.), and are therefore capable of combining together. The combination of molecules of the same kind to form more complex ones is what is meant by polymerisation.[40]

[411]

Besides being a substance very prone to form polymerides, cyanic acid presents many other features of interest, expounded in greater detail in organic chemistry. However we may mention here the production of the cyanates by the oxidation of the metallic cyanides. Potassium cyanate, KCNO, is most often obtained in this way. Solutions of cyanates by the addition of sulphuric acid yield cyanic acid, which, however, immediately decomposes: $CNHO + H_2O = CO_2 + NH_3$. A solution of ammonium cyanate, $CN(NH_4)O$, behaves in the same manner, but only in the cold. On being heated it completely changes because it is transformed into urea. The composition of both substances is identical, CN_2H_4O, but the structure, or disposition of, and connection between, the elements is different: in the ammonium cyanate one atom of nitrogen exists in the form of cyanogen, CN—that is, united with carbon—and the other as ammonium, NH_4, but, as cyanic acid contains the hydroxyl radicle of carbonic acid, OH(CN), the ammonium in this salt is united with oxygen. The composition of this salt is best expressed by supposing one atom of the hydrogen in water to be replaced by ammonium and the other by cyanogen—*i.e.* that its composition is not symmetrical—whilst in urea both the nitrogen atoms are symmetrically and uniformly disposed as regards the radicle CO of carbonic acid: $CO(NH_2)_2$. For this reason, urea is much more stable than ammonium cyanate, and therefore the latter, on being slightly heated in solution, is converted into urea. This remarkable isomeric transformation was discovered by Wöhler in 1828.[41] Formamide, $HCONH_2$, and *hydrocyanic acid*, HCN, as a nitrile, correspond with formic acid, HCOOH, and therefore ammonium formate, $HCOONH_4$, and formamide, when acted on by heat and by substances which take up water (phosphoric anhydride) form hydrocyanic acid, HCN, whilst, under many conditions (for instance, on combining with hydrochloric acid in presence of water), this hydrocyanic acid forms formic acid and ammonia. Although containing hydrogen in the presence of two acid-forming elements—namely, carbon and nitrogen[42]—hydrocyanic[412] acid does not give an acid reaction with litmus (cyanic acid has very marked acid properties); *but it forms salts, MCN,* thus presenting the properties of a feeble acid, and for this reason is called an *acid*. The small amount of energy which it has is shown by the fact that the cyanides of the alkali metals—for instance, potassium cyanide (KHO + HCN = H_2O + KCN) in solution have a strongly alkaline reaction.[43] If ammonia be passed over charcoal at a red heat, especially in the presence of an alkali, or if gaseous nitrogen be passed through a mixture of charcoal and an alkali (especially potash, KHO), and also if a mixture of nitrogenous organic substances and alkali be heated to a red heat, in all these cases the alkali metal combines with the carbon and nitrogen, forming a metallic cyanide, MCN—for example, KCN.[43 bis] Potassium cyanide is much used in the arts, and is obtained, as above stated, under many circumstances—as, for instance, in iron smelting, especially with the assistance of wood charcoal, the ash of which contains much potash. The nitrogen of the air, the alkali of the ash, and the charcoal are brought into contact at a high temperature during iron smelting, and therefore, under these conditions, a considerable quantity of potassium cyanide is formed. In practice it is not usual to prepare potassium cyanide directly, but a peculiar compound of it containing potassium, iron, and cyanogen. This compound is potassium ferrocyanide, and is also known as *yellow prussiate of potash.* This saline substance (*see* Chapter XXII) has the composition $K_4FeC_6N_6$ + $2H_2O$. The name of cyanogen (κύανος) is derived from the property which this yellow prussiate possesses of forming, with a solution of a ferric salt, FeX_3, the familiar pigment Prussian blue. The yellow prussiate is manufactured[413] on a large scale, and is generally used as the source of the other cyanogen compounds.

If four parts of yellow prussiate be mixed with eight parts of water and three parts of sulphuric acid, and the mixture be heated, it decomposes, volatile hydrocyanic acid separating. This was obtained for the first time by Scheele in 1782, but it was only known to him in solution. In 1809 Ittner prepared anhydrous prussic acid, and in 1815 Gay-Lussac finally settled its properties and showed that it contains only hydrogen, carbon, and nitrogen, CNH. If the distillate (a weak solution of HCN) be redistilled, and the first part collected, the anhydrous acid may be prepared from this stronger solution. In order to do this, pieces of calcium chloride are added to the concentrated solution, when the anhydrous acid floats as a separate layer, because it is not soluble in an aqueous solution of calcium chloride. If this layer be then distilled over a new portion of calcium chloride at the lowest temperature possible, the prussic acid may be obtained completely free from water. It is, however, necessary to use the greatest caution in work of this kind, because prussic acid, besides being extremely poisonous, is exceedingly volatile.[44]

Anhydrous prussic acid is a very mobile and volatile liquid; its specific gravity is 0·697 at 18°; at lower temperatures, especially when mixed with a small quantity of water, it easily congeals; it boils at 26°, and therefore very easily evaporates, and at ordinary temperatures may be regarded as a gas. An insignificant amount, when inhaled or brought into contact with the skin, causes death. It is soluble in all[414] proportions in water, alcohol, and ether: weak aqueous solutions are used in medicine.[45]

The salts MCN—for instance, potassium, sodium, ammonium—as well as the salts $M''(CN)_2$—for example, barium, calcium, mercury—are soluble in water, but the cyanides of manganese, zinc, lead, and many others are insoluble in water. They form double salts with potassium cyanide and similar metallic cyanides, an example of which we will consider in a further description of the yellow prussiate. Not only are some of the double salts remarkable for their constancy and comparative stability, but so also are the soluble salt HgC_2N_2, the insoluble silver cyanide AgCN, and even potassium cyanide in the absence of water. The last salt,[46] when fused, acts as a reducing agent with its elements K and C, and oxidises when fused with lead oxide, forming potassium cyanate, KOCN, which establishes the connection between HCN and OHCN—that is, between the nitriles of formic and carbonic acids—and this connection is the same as that between the acids themselves, since formic acid, on oxidation, yields carbonic acid. Free cyanogen, $(CN)_2$ or CNCN, corresponds to hydrocyanic acid in the same manner as free chlorine, Cl_2 or ClCl, corresponds to hydrochloric acid. This composition, judging from what has been already stated, exactly expresses that of the nitrile of oxalic acid, and, as a matter of fact, oxalate of ammonia and the amide corresponding with it (oxamide, Note 33), on being heated with phosphoric anhydride, which takes up the water, yield *cyanogen*, $(CN)_2$. This substance is also produced by simply heating some of the[415] metallic cyanides. Mercuric cyanide is particularly adapted for this purpose, because it is easily obtained in a pure state and is then very stable. If mercuric cyanide be heated, it decomposes, in like manner to mercury oxide, into metallic mercury and cyanogen: $HgC_2N_2 = Hg + C_2N_2$.[47] When cyanogen is formed, part of it always polymerises into a dark brown insoluble substance called *paracyanogen*, capable of forming cyanogen when heated to redness.[48] Cyanogen is a colourless, poisonous gas, with a peculiar smell and easily condensed by cooling into a colourless liquid, insoluble in water and having a specific gravity of 0·86. It boils at about -21°, and therefore cyanogen may be easily condensed into a liquid by a strong freezing mixture. At -35° liquid cyanogen solidifies. The gas is soluble in water and in alcohol to a considerable extent—namely, 1 volume of water absorbs as much as 4½ volumes, and alcohol 23 volumes. Cyanogen resists the action of a tolerably high temperature without decomposing, but under the action of the electric spark the carbon is separated, leaving a volume of nitrogen equal to the volume of the gas taken. As it contains carbon it burns, and the colour of the flame is reddish-violet, which is due to the presence of nitrogen, all compounds of which impart more or less of this reddish-violet hue to the flame. During the combustion of[416] cyanogen, carbonic anhydride and nitrogen are formed. The same products are obtained in the eudiometer with oxygen or by the action of cyanogen on many oxides at a red heat.

The relation of cyanogen to the metallic cyanides is seen not only in the fact that it is formed from mercuric cyanide, but also by its forming cyanide of sodium or potassium on being heated with either of those metals, the sodium or potassium taking fire in the cyanogen. On heating a mixture of hydrogen and cyanogen to 500° (Berthelot),[49] or under the action of the silent discharge (Boilleau), hydrocyanic acid is formed, so that the reciprocity of the transitions does not leave any doubt in the matter that all the nitriles of the organic acids contain cyanogen, just as all the organic acids contain carboxyl and in it the elements of carbonic anhydride. Besides the amides,[50] the nitriles (or cyanogen compounds, RCN), and nitro-compounds (containing the radicle of nitric acid, RNO_2), there are a great number of other substances containing at the same time carbon and nitrogen, particulars of which must be sought for in special works on organic chemistry.

Footnotes:

[1] The quantity of carbonic acid gas exhaled by a man during the twenty-four hours is not evenly produced; during the night more oxygen is taken in than during the day (by night, in twelve hours, about 450 grams), and more carbonic anhydride is separated by day than during night-time and repose; thus, of the 900 grams produced during the twenty-four hours about 375 are given out during the night and 525 by day. This depends on the formation of carbonic anhydride during the work performed by the man in the day. Every movement is the result of some change of matter, for force cannot be self-created (in accordance with the law of the conservation of energy). Proportionally to the amount of carbon consumed an amount of energy is stored up in the organism and is consumed in the

various movements performed by animals. This is proved by the fact that during work a man exhales 525 grams of carbonic anhydride in twelve hours instead of 375, absorbing the same amount of oxygen as before. After a working day a man exhales by night almost the same amount of carbonic anhydride as after a day of rest, so that during a total twenty-four hours a man exhales about 900 grams of carbonic anhydride and absorbs about 980 grams of oxygen. Therefore during work the change of matter increases. The carbon expended on the work is obtained from the food; on this account the food of animals ought certainly to contain carbonaceous substances capable of dissolving under the action of the digestive fluids, and of passing into the blood, or, in other words, capable of being digested. Such food for man and all other animals is formed of vegetable matter, or of parts of other animals. The latter in every case obtain their carbonaceous matter from plants, in which it is formed by the separation of the carbon from the carbonic anhydride taken up during the day by the respiration of the plants. The volume of the oxygen exhaled by plants is almost equal to the volume of the carbonic anhydride absorbed; that is to say, nearly all the oxygen entering into the plant in the form of carbonic anhydride is liberated in a free state, whilst the carbon from the carbonic anhydride remains in the plant. At the same time the plant absorbs moisture by its leaves and roots. By a process which is unknown to us, this absorbed moisture and the carbon obtained from the carbonic anhydride enter into the composition of the plants in the form of so-called carbohydrates, composing the greater part of the vegetable tissues, starch and cellulose of the composition $C_6H_{10}O_5$ being representatives of them. They may be considered like all carbohydrates as compounds of carbon and water, $6C + 5H_2O$. In this way a *circulation* of the carbon goes on in nature by means of vegetable and animal organisms, in which changes the principal factor is the carbonic anhydride of the air.

[2] Other acids may be used instead of hydrochloric; for instance, acetic, or even sulphuric, although this latter is not suitable, because it forms as a product insoluble calcium sulphate (gypsum) which surrounds the untouched calcium carbonate, and thus prevents a further evolution of gas. But if porous limestone—for instance, chalk—be treated with sulphuric acid diluted with an equal volume of water, the liquid is absorbed and acting on the mass of the salt, the evolution of carbonic anhydride continues evenly for a long time. Instead of calcium carbonate other carbonates may of course be used; for instance, washing-soda, Na_2CO_3, which is often chosen when it is required to produce a rapid stream of carbonic anhydride (for example, for liquefying it). But natural crystalline magnesium carbonate and similar salts are with difficulty decomposed by hydrochloric and sulphuric acids. When for manufacturing purposes—for instance, in precipitating lime in sugar-works—a large quantity of carbonic

acid gas is required, it is generally obtained by burning charcoal, and the products of combustion, rich in carbonic anhydride, are pumped into the liquid containing the lime, and the carbonic anhydride is thus absorbed. Another method is also practised, which consists in using the carbonic anhydride separated during fermentation, or that evolved from limekilns. During the fermentation of sweet-wort, grape-juice, and other similar saccharine solutions, the glucose $C_6H_{12}O_6$ changes under the influence of the yeast organism, forming alcohol ($2C_2H_6O$), and carbonic anhydride ($2CO_2$) which separates in the form of gas; if the fermentation proceeds in closed bottles sparkling wine is obtained. When carbonic acid gas is prepared for saturating water and other beverages it is necessary to use it in a pure state. Whilst in the state in which it is evolved from ordinary limestones by the aid of acids it contains, besides a certain quantity of acid, the organic matters of the limestone; in order to diminish the quantity of these substances the densest kinds of dolomites are used, which contain less organic matter, and the gas formed is passed through various washing apparatus, and then through a solution of potassium permanganate, which absorbs organic matter and does not take up carbonic anhydride.

[3] Hypochlorous acid, HClO, and its anhydride, Cl_2O, do not displace carbonic acid, and hydrogen sulphide has the same relation to carbonic acid as nitric acid to hydrochloric—an excess of either one displaces the other.

[4] Thus, in preparing the ordinary effervescing powders, sodium bicarbonate (or acid carbonate of soda) is used, and mixed with powdered citric or tartaric acid. In a dry state these powders do not evolve carbonic anhydride, but when mixed with water the evolution takes place briskly, which is due to the substances passing into solution. The salts of carbonic acid may be recognised from the fact that they evolve carbonic acid with a hissing noise when treated with acids. If vinegar, which contains acetic acid, be poured upon limestone, marble, malachite (containing copper carbonate), &c., carbonic anhydride is evolved with a hissing noise. It is noteworthy that neither hydrochloric acid, nor even sulphuric acid nor acetic acid, acts on limestone except in presence of water. We shall refer to this later on.

[5] The direct observations made (1876) by Messrs. Bogouski and Kayander lead to the conclusion that the quantity of carbonic anhydride evolved by the action of acids on marble (as homogeneous as possible) is directly proportional to the time of action, the extent of surface, and the degree of concentration of the acid, and inversely proportional to the molecular weight of the acid. If the surface of a piece of Carrara marble be equal to one decimetre, the time of action one minute, and one cubic decimetre or litre contains one gram of hydrochloric acid, then about 0·02 gram of carbonic anhydride will be evolved. If the litre contains n grams of

hydrochloric acid, then by experiment the amount will be $n \times 0.02$ of carbonic anhydride. Therefore, if the litre contains 36·5 (= HCl) grams, about 0·73 gram of carbonic anhydride (about half a litre) would he evolved per minute. If nitric acid or hydrobromic acid be used instead of hydrochloric, then, with a combining proportion of the acid, the same quantity of carbonic anhydride will be evolved; thus, if the litre contains 63 (= HNO_3) grams of nitric acid, or 81 (= HBr) grams of hydrobromic acid, the quantity of carbonic anhydride evolved will still be 0·73 gram. Spring, in 1890, made a series of similar determinations.

[6] As carbonic anhydride is one and a half times heavier than air, it diffuses with difficulty, and therefore does not easily mix with air, but sinks in it. This may be shown in various ways; for instance, the gas may be carefully poured from one vessel into another containing air. If a lighted taper be plunged into the vessel containing carbonic anhydride it is extinguished, and then, after pouring the gas into the other cylinder, it will burn in the former and be extinguished in the latter. If a certain quantity of carbonic anhydride be poured into a vessel containing air, and soap-bubbles be introduced, they will only sink as far as the stratum where the atmosphere of carbonic anhydride commences, as this latter is heavier than the soap-bubbles filled with air. Naturally, after a certain lapse of time, the carbonic anhydride will be diffused throughout the vessel, and form a uniform mixture with the air, just as salt in water.

[7] This liquefaction was first observed by Faraday, who sealed up in a tube a mixture of a carbonate and sulphuric acid. Afterwards this method was very considerably improved by Thilorier and Natterer, whose apparatus is given in Chapter VI. in describing N_2O. It is, however, necessary to remark that the preparation of liquid carbonic anhydride requires good liquefying apparatus, constant cooling, and a rapid preparation of large masses of carbonic anhydride.

[8] Carbonic anhydride, having the same molecular weight as nitrous oxide, very much resembles it when in a liquid state.

[8 bis] When poured into a tube, which is then sealed up, liquefied carbonic anhydride can be easily preserved, because a thick tube easily supports the pressure (about 50 atmospheres) exerted by the liquid at the ordinary temperature.

[9] When a fine stream of liquid carbonic anhydride is discharged into a closed metallic vessel, about one-third of its mass solidifies and the remainder evaporates. In employing solid carbonic anhydride for making experiments at low temperatures, it is best to use it mixed with ether, otherwise there will be few points of contact. If a stream of air be blown through a mixture of liquid carbonic anhydride and ether, the evaporation

proceeds rapidly, and great cold is obtained. At present in some special manufactories (and for making artificial mineral waters) carbonic anhydride is liquefied on the large scale, filled into wrought-iron cylinders provided with a valve, and in this manner it can be transported and preserved safely for a long time. It is used, for instance, in breweries.

[9 bis] Solid carbonic anhydride, notwithstanding its very low temperature, can be safely placed on the hand, because it continually evolves gas which prevents its coming into actual contact with the skin, but if a piece be squeezed between the fingers, it produces a severe frost bite similar to a burn. If the snow-like solid be mixed with ether, a semi-liquid mass is obtained, which is employed for artificial refrigeration. This mixture may be used for liquefying many other gases—such as chlorine, nitrous oxide, hydrogen sulphide, and others. The evaporation of such a mixture proceeds with far greater rapidity under the receiver of an air-pump, and consequently the refrigeration is more intense. By this means many gases may be liquefied which resist other methods—namely, olefiant gas, hydrochloric acid gas, and others. Liquid carbonic anhydride in this case congeals in the tube into a glassy transparent mass. Pictet availed himself of this method for liquefying many permanent gases (*see* Chapter II.)

Bleekrode, by compressing solid CO_2 in a cylinder by means of a piston, obtained a semi-transparent stick, which contained as much as 1·3 and even 1·6 gram of CO_2 per cubic centimetre. In this form the CO_2 slowly evaporated, and could be kept for a long time.

[10] If such water trickles through crevices and enters a cavern, the evaporation will be slow, and therefore in those places from which the water drips growths of calcium carbonate will be formed, just like the icicles formed on the roof-gutters in winter-time. Similar conical and cylindrical stony growths form the so-called stalactites or pendants hanging from above and stalagmites formed on the bottom of caves. Sometimes these two kinds meet together, forming entire columns filling the cave. Many of these caves are remarkable for their picturesqueness; for instance, the cave of Antiparos, in the Grecian Archipelago. This same cause also forms spongy masses of calcium carbonate in those places where the springs come to the surface of the earth. It is therefore very evident that a calcareous solution is sometimes capable of penetrating plants and filling the whole of their mass with calcium carbonate. This is one of the forms of petrified plants. Calcium phosphate in solution in water containing carbonic acid plays an important part in the nourishment of plants, because all plants contain both lime and phosphoric acid.

[11] The crystallohydrate, $CO_2,8H_2O$ of Wroblewski (Chapter 1., Note 67), in the first place, is only formed under special conditions; in the

second place, its existence still requires confirmation; and in the third place, it does not correspond with that hydrate H_2CO_3 which should occur, judging from the composition of the salts.

[11 bis] It is easy to demonstrate the acid properties of carbonic anhydride by taking a long tube, closed at one end, and filling it with this gas; a test-tube is then filled with a solution of an alkali (for instance, sodium hydroxide), which is then poured into the long tube and the open end is corked. The solution is then well shaken in the tube, and the corked end plunged into water. If the cork be now withdrawn under water, the water will fill the tube. The vacuum obtained by the absorption of the carbonic anhydride by an alkali is so complete that even an electric discharge will not pass through it. This method is often applied to produce a vacuum.

[12] The reasons for distinguishing the uni-, bi-, tri-, and quadrivalent metals will be explained hereafter on passing from the univalent metals (Na, K, Li) to the bivalent (Mg. Ca, Ba), Chapter XIV.

[13] Up to the year 1840, or thereabout, acids were not distinguished by their basicity. Graham, while studying phosphoric acid, H_3PO_4, and Liebig, while studying many organic acids, distinguished mono-, bi-, and tribasic acids. Gerhardt and Laurent generalised these relations, showing that this distinction extends over many reactions (for instance, to the faculty of bibasic acids of forming acid salts with alkalis, KHO or NaHO, or with alcohols, RHO, &c.); but now, since a definite conception as to atoms and molecules has been arrived at, *the basicity of an acid is determined by the number of hydrogen atoms*, contained in a molecule of the acid, which can be exchanged for metals. If carbonic acid forms acid salts, $NaHCO_3$, and normal salts, Na_2CO_3, it is evident that the hydrate is H_2CO_3, a bibasic acid. Otherwise it is at present impossible to account for the composition of these salts. But when C=6 and O=8 were taken, then the formula CO_2 expressed the composition, but not the molecular weight, of carbonic anhydride; and the composition of the normal salt would be $Na_2C_2O_6$ or $NaCO_3$, therefore carbonic acid might have been considered as a monobasic acid. Then the acid salt would have been represented by $NaCO_3,HCO_3$. Such questions were the cause of much argument and difference of opinion among chemists about forty years ago. At present there cannot be two opinions on the subject if the law of Avogadro-Gerhardt and its consequences be strictly adhered to. It may, however, be observed here that the monobasic acids R(OH) were for a long time considered to be incapable of being decomposed into water and anhydride, and this property was ascribed to the bibasic acids R(OH)$_2$ as containing the elements necessary for the separation of the molecule of water, H_2O. Thus H_2SO_4 or $SO_2(OH)_2$, H_2CO_3, or $CO(OH)_2$, and other bibasic acids decompose into an

anhydride, RO, and water, H_2O. But as nitrous, HNO_2, iodic, HIO_3, hypochlorous, $HClO$, and other monobasic acids easily give their anhydrides N_2O_3, I_2O_5, Cl_2O, &c., that method of distinguishing the basicity of acids, although it fairly well satisfies the requirements of organic chemistry, cannot be considered correct. It may also be remarked that up to the present time not one of the bibasic acids has been found to have the faculty of being distilled without being decomposed into anhydride and water (even H_2SO_4, on being evaporated and distilled, gives $SO_3 + H_2O$), and the decomposition of acids into water and anhydride proceeds particularly easily in dealing with feebly energetic acids, such as carbonic, nitrous, boric, and hypochlorous. Let us add that carbonic acid, as a hydrate corresponding to marsh gas, $C(HO)_4 = CO_2 + 2H_2O$, ought to be tetrabasic. But in general it does not form such salts. Basic salts, however, such as $CuCO_3CuO$, may be regarded in this sense, for CCu_2O_4 corresponds with CH_4O_4, as Cu corresponds with H_2. Amongst the ethereal salts (alcoholic derivatives) of carbonic acid corresponding cases are, however, observed; for instance, ethylic orthocarbonate, $C(C_2H_5O)_4$ (obtained by the action of chloropicrin, $C(NO_2)Cl_3$, on sodium ethoxide, C_2H_5ONa; boiling point 158°; specific gravity, 0·92). The name *orthocarbonic acid* for CH_4O_4 is taken from *orthophosphoric acid*, PH_3O_4, which corresponds with PH_3 (*see* Chapter on Phosphorus).

[14] Long ago endeavours were made to find a *measure of affinity* of acids and bases, because some of the acids, such as sulphuric or nitric, form comparatively stable salts, decomposed with difficulty by heat and water, whilst others, like carbonic and hypochlorous acids, do not combine with feeble bases, and with most of the other bases form salts which are easily decomposed. The same may be said with regard to bases, among which those of potassium, K_2O, sodium, Na_2O, and barium, BaO, may serve as examples of the most powerful, because they combine with the most feeble acids and form a mass of salts of great stability, whilst as examples of the feeblest bases alumina, Al_2O_3, or bismuth oxide, Bi_2O_3, may be taken, because they form salts easily decomposed by water and by heat if the acid be volatile. Such a division of acids and bases into the feeblest and most powerful is justified by all evidence concerning them, and is quoted in this work. But the teaching of this subject in certain circles has acquired quite a new tone, which, in my opinion, cannot be accepted without certain reservations and criticisms, although it comprises many interesting features. The fact is that Thomsen, Ostwald, and others proposed to express the measure of affinity of acids to bases by figures drawn from data of the measure of displacement of acids in aqueous solutions, judging (1) from the amount of heat developed by mixing a solution of the salt with a solution of another acid (the avidity of acids, according to Thomsen); (2) from the change of the volumes accompanying such a mutual action of

solutions (Ostwald); (3) from the change of the index of refraction of solutions (Ostwald), &c. Besides this there are many other methods which allow us to form an opinion about the distribution of bases among various acids in aqueous solutions. Some of these methods will be described hereafter. It ought, however, to be remarked that in making investigations in aqueous solutions the affinity to water is generally left out of sight. If a base N, combining with acids X and Y in presence of them both, divides in such a way that one-third of it combines with X and two-thirds with Y, a conclusion is formed that the affinity, or power of forming salts, of the acid Y is twice as great as that of X. But the presence of the water is not taken into account. If the acid X has an affinity for water and for N it will be distributed between them; and if X has a greater affinity for water than Y, then less of X will combine with N than of Y. If, in addition to this, the acid X is capable of forming an acid salt NX_2, and Y is not, the conclusion of the relative strength of X and Y will be still more erroneous, because the X set free will form such a salt on the addition of Y to NX. We shall see in Chapter X. that when sulphuric and nitric acids in weak aqueous solution act on sodium, they are distributed exactly in this way: namely, one-third of the sodium combines with the sulphuric and two-thirds with the nitric acid; but, in my opinion, this does not show that sulphuric acid, compared with nitric acid, possesses but half the degree of affinity for bases like soda, and only demonstrates the greater affinity of sulphuric acid for water compared with that of nitric acid. In this way the methods of studying the distribution in aqueous solutions probably only shows the difference of the relation of the acid to a base and to water.

In view of these considerations, although the teaching of the distribution of salt-forming elements in *aqueous solutions* is an object of great and independent interest, it can hardly serve to determine the measure of affinity between bases and acids. Similar considerations ought to be kept in view when determining the energy of acids by means of the *electrical conductivity of their weak solutions*. This method, proposed by Arrhenius (1884), and applied on an extensive scale by Ostwald (who developed it in great detail in his *Lehrbuch d. allgemeinen Chemie*, v. ii., 1887), is founded on the fact that the relation of the so-called molecular electrical-conductivity of weak solutions of various acids (I) coincides with the relation in which the same acids stand according to the distribution, (II) found by one of the above-mentioned methods, and with the relation deduced for them from observations upon the velocity of reaction, (III) for instance, according to the rate of the splitting up of an ethereal salt (into alcohol and acid), or from the rate of the so-called inversion of sugar—that is, its transformation into glucose—as is seen by comparing the annexed figures, in which the energy of hydrochloric acid is taken as equal to 100:—

	I	II	III
Hydrochloric acid, HCl	100	100	100
Hydrobromic acid, HBr	101	98	105
Nitric acid, HNO_3	100	100	96
Sulphuric acid, H_2SO_4	65	49	96
Formic acid, CH_2O_2	2	4	1
Acetic acid, $C_2H_4O_2$	1	2	1
Oxalic acid, $C_2H_2O_4$	20	24	18
Phosphoric acid, PH_3O_4	7	—	6

The coincidence of these figures, obtained by so many various methods, presents a most important and instructive relation between phenomena of different kinds, but in my opinion it does not permit us to assert that the degree of affinity existing between bases and various acids is determined by all these various methods, because the influence of the water must be taken into consideration. On this account, until the theory of solution is more thoroughly worked out, this subject (which for the present ought to be treated of in special treatises on chemical mechanics) must be treated with great caution. But now we may hope to decide this question guided by a study of the rate of reaction, the influence of acids and bases upon indicators, &c., all of which are treated fully in works on physical and theoretical chemistry.

[15] Thus, for instance, in the washing of fabrics the caustic alkalis, such as sodium hydroxide, in weak solutions, act in removing the fatty matter just in the same way as carbonate solutions; for instance, a solution of soda crystals, Na_2CO_3. Soap acts in the same way, being composed of feeble acids, either fatty or resinous, combined with alkali. On this account all such substances are applied in manufacturing processes, and answer equally well in practice for bleaching and washing fabrics. Soda crystals or soap are preferred to caustic alkali, because an excess of the latter may have a destructive effect on the fabrics. It may be supposed that in aqueous solutions of soap or soda crystals, part of the base will form caustic alkali; that is to say, the water will compete with the weak acids, and the alkali will be distributed between them and the water.

[16] Although carbonic acid is reckoned among the feeble acids, yet there are evidently many others still feebler—for instance, prussic acid, hypochlorous acid, many organic acids, &c. Bases like alumina, or such

feeble acids as silica, when in combination with alkalis, are decomposed in aqueous solutions by carbonic acid, but on fusion—that is, without the presence of water—they displace it, which clearly shows in phenomena of this kind how much depends upon the conditions of reaction and the properties of the substances formed. These relations, which at first sight appear complex, may be best understood if we represent that two salts, MX and NY, in general always give more or less of two other salts, MY and NX, and then examine the properties of the derived substances. Thus, in solution, sodium silicate, Na_2SiO_3, with carbonic anhydride will to some extent form sodium carbonate and silica, SiO_2; but the latter, being colloid, separates, and the remaining mass of sodium silicate is again decomposed by carbonic anhydride, so that finally silica separates and sodium carbonate is formed. In a fused state the case is different; sodium carbonate will react with silica to form carbonic anhydride and sodium silicate, but the carbonic anhydride will be separated as a gas, and therefore in the residue the same reaction will again take place, and ultimately the carbonic anhydride is entirely eliminated and sodium silicate remains. If, on the other hand, nothing is removed from the sphere of the reaction, distribution takes place. Therefore, although carbonic anhydride is a feeble acid, still not for this reason, but only in virtue of its gaseous form, do all soluble acids displace it in saline solutions (*see* Chapter X.)

[17] Hydrogen and carbon are near akin to oxygen as regards affinity, but it ought to be considered that the affinity of hydrogen is slightly greater than that of carbon, because during the combustion of hydrocarbons the hydrogen burns first. Some idea of this similarity of affinity may be formed by the quantity of heat evolved. Gaseous hydrogen, H_2, on combining with an atom of oxygen, $O = 16$, develops 69,000 heat-units if the water formed be condensed to a liquid state. If the water remains in the form of a gas (steam) the latent heat of evaporation must be subtracted, and then 58,000 calories will be developed. Carbon, C, as a solid, on combining with $O_2 = 32$ develops about 97,000 calories, forming gaseous CO_2. If it were gaseous like hydrogen, and only contained C_2 in its molecule, much more heat would be developed, and judging by other substances, whose molecules on passing from the solid to the gaseous state absorb about 10,000 to 15,000 calories, it must be held that gaseous carbon on forming gaseous carbonic anhydride would develop not less than 110,000 calories—that is, approximately twice as much as is developed in the formation of water. And since there is twice as much oxygen in a molecule of carbonic anhydride as in a molecule of water, the oxygen develops approximately the same quantity of heat on combining with hydrogen as with carbon. That is to say, that here we find the same close affinity (*see* Chapter II., Note 7) determined by the quantity of heat as between hydrogen, zinc, and iron. For this reason here also, as in the case of hydrogen and iron, we ought to

expect an equal distribution of oxygen between hydrogen and carbon, if they are both in excess compared with the amount of oxygen; but if there be an excess of carbon, it will decompose water, whilst an excess of hydrogen will decompose carbonic anhydride. Even if these phenomena and similar ones have been explained in isolated cases, a complete theory of the whole subject is still wanting in the present condition of chemical knowledge.

[17 bis] The degree or relative magnitude of the dissociation of CO_2 varies with the temperature and pressure—that is, it increases with the temperature and as the pressure decreases. Deville found that at a pressure of 1 atmosphere in the flame of carbonic oxide burning in oxygen, about 40 per cent. of the CO_2, is decomposed when the temperature is about 3,000°, and at 1,500° less than 1 per cent. (Krafts); whilst under a pressure of 10 atmospheres about 34 per cent. is decomposed at 3,300° (Mallard and Le Chatelier). It follows therefore that, under very small pressures, the dissociation of CO_2 will be considerable even at comparatively moderate temperatures, but at the temperature of ordinary furnaces (about 1,000°) even under the small partial pressure of the carbonic acid, there are only small traces of decomposition which may be neglected in a practical estimation of the combustion of fuels. We may here cite the molecular specific heat of CO_2 (*i.e.* the amount of heat required to raise 44 units of weight of CO_2 1°), according to the determinations and calculations of Mallard and Le Chatelier, for a constant volume $C_v = 6\cdot26 + 0\cdot0037t$; for a constant pressure $C_p = C_v + 2$ (*see* Chapter XIV., Note 7), *i.e.* the specific heat of CO_2 increases rapidly with a rise of temperature: for example, at 0° (per 1 part by weight), it is, at a constant pressure = $0\cdot188$, at 1,000° = $0\cdot272$, at 2,000°, about $0\cdot356$. A perfectly distinct rise of the specific heat (for example, at 2,000°, $0\cdot409$), is given by a comparison of observations made by the above-mentioned investigators and by Berthelot and Vieille (Kournakoff). The cause of this must be looked for in dissociation. T. M. Cheltzoff, however, considers upon the basis of his researches upon explosives that it must be admitted that a maximum is reached at a certain temperature (about 2,500°), beyond which the specific heat begins to fall.

[18] Percarbonic acid, H_2CO_4 (= H_2CO_3 + O) is supposed by A. Bach (1893) to be formed from carbonic acid in the action of light upon plants, (in the same manner as, according to the above scheme, sulphuric acid from sulphurous) with the formation of carbon, which remains in the form of hydrates of carbon: $3H_2CO_3 = 2H_2CO_4 + CH_2O$. This substance CH_2O expresses the composition of formic aldehyde which, according to Baeyer, by polymerisation and further changes, gives other hydrates of carbon and forms the first product which is formed in plants from CO_2. And Berthelot (1872) had already, at the time of the discovery of persulphuric (Chapter

XX.) and pernitric (Chapter VI., Note 26) acids pointed out the formation of the unstable percarbonic anhydride, CO_3. Thus, notwithstanding the hypothetical nature of the above equation, it may be admitted all the more as it explains the comparative abundance of peroxide of hydrogen (Schöne, Chapter IV.) in the air, and this also at the period of the most energetic growth of plants (in July), because percarbonic acid should like all peroxides easily give H_2O_2. Besides which Bach (1894) showed that, in the first place, traces of formic aldehyde and oxidising agents (CO_3 or H_2O_2) are formed under the simultaneous action of CO_2 and sunlight upon a solution containing a salt of uranium (which is oxidised), and diethylaniline (which reacts with CH_2O), and secondly, that by subjecting BaO_2, shaken up in water, to the action of a stream of CO_2 in the cold, extracting (also in the cold) with ether, and then adding an alcoholic solution of NaHO, crystalline plates of a sodium salt may be obtained, which with water evolve oxygen and leave sodium carbonate; they are therefore probably the per-salt. All these facts are of great interest and deserve further verification and elaboration.

[18 bis] If CO_2 is the anhydride of a bibasic acid, and carboxyl corresponds with it, replacing the hydrogen of hydrocarbons, and giving them the character of comparatively feeble acids, then SO_3 is the anhydride of an energetic bibasic acid, and *sulphoxyl*, $SO_2(OH)$, corresponds with it, being capable of replacing the hydrogen of hydrocarbons, and forming comparatively energetic *sulphur oxyacids* (*sulphonic acids*); for instance, $C_6H_5(COOH)$, benzoic acid, and $C_6H_5(SO_2OH)$, benzenesulphonic acid, are derived from C_6H_6. As the exchange of H for methyl, CH_3, is equivalent to the addition of CH_2, the exchange of carboxyl, COOH, is equivalent to the addition of CO_2; so the exchange of H for sulphoxyl is equivalent to the addition of SO_3. The latter proceeds directly, for instance: $C_6H_6 + SO_3 = C_6H_5(SO_2OH)$.

As, according to the determinations of Thomsen, the heat of combustion of the *vapours* of acids RCO_2 is known where R is a hydrocarbon, and the heat of combustion of the hydrocarbons R themselves, it may be seen that the formation of acids, RCO_2, from R + CO_2, is always accompanied by a *small* absorption or development of heat. We give the heats of combustion in thousands of calories, referred to the molecular weights of the substances:—

R = H_2 CH_4 C_2H_6 C_6H_6

         68·4 212 370 777

RCO_2 = 69·4 225 387 766

Thus H_2, corresponds with formic acid, CH_2O_2; benzene, C_6H_6, with benzoic acid, $C_7H_6O_2$. The data for the latter are taken from Stohmann, and refer to the solid condition. For formic acid Stohmann gives the heat of combustion as 59,000 calories in a liquid state, but in a state of vapour, 64·6 thousand units, which is much less than according to Thomsen.

[19]

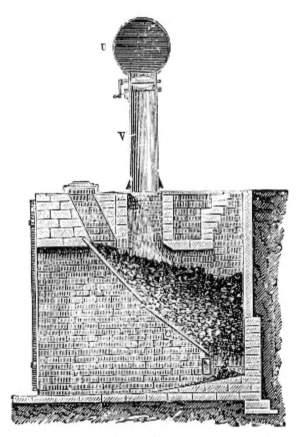

FIG. 63.—Gas-producer for the formation of carbon monoxide for heating purposes..

In gas-producers all carbonaceous fuels are transformed into inflammable gas. In those which (on account of their slight density and large amount of water, or incombustible admixtures which absorb heat) are not as capable of giving a high temperature in ordinary furnaces—for instance, fir cones, peat, the lower kinds of coal, &c.—the same gas is obtained as with the best kinds of coal, because the water condenses on cooling, and the ashes and earthy matter remain in the gas-producer. The construction of a gas-producer is seen from the accompanying drawing. The fuel lies on the fire-bars O, the air enters through them and the ash-hole (drawn by the draught of the chimney of the stove where the gas burns, or else forced by a blowing apparatus), the quantity of air being exactly regulated by means of valves. The gases formed are then led by the tube V, provided with a valve, into the gas main U. The addition of fuel ought to proceed in such a way as to prevent the generated gas escaping; hence the space A is kept filled with the combustible material and covered with a lid.

[20] An excess of air lowers the temperature of combustion, because it becomes heated itself, as explained in Chapter III. In ordinary furnaces the excess of air is three or four times greater than the quantity required for perfect combustion. In the best furnaces (with fire-bars, regulated air supply, and corresponding chimney draught) it is necessary to introduce twice as much air as is necessary, otherwise the smoke contains much carbonic oxide.

[21] If in manufactories it is necessary, for instance, to maintain the temperature in a furnace at 1,000°, the flame passes out at this or a higher temperature, and therefore much fuel is lost in the smoke. For the draught of the chimney a temperature of 100° to 150° is sufficient, and therefore the remaining heat ought to be utilised. For this purpose the flues are carried under boilers or other heating apparatus. The preparatory heating of the air is the best means of utilisation when a high temperature is desired (see Note 22).

[22] Regenerative furnaces were introduced by the Brothers Siemens about the year 1860 in many industries, and mark a most important progress in the use of fuel, especially in obtaining high temperatures. The principle is as follows: The products of combustion from the furnace are led into a chamber, I, and heat up the bricks in it, and then pass into the outlet flue; when the bricks are at a red heat the products of combustion are passed (by altering the valves) into another adjoining chamber, II, and air requisite for the combustion of the generator gases is passed through I. In passing round about the incandescent bricks the air is heated, and the bricks are cooled—that is, the heat of the smoke is returned into the furnace. The air is then passed through II, and the smoke through I. The regenerative burners for illuminating gas are founded on this same principle, the products of combustion heat the incoming air and gas, the temperature is higher, the light brighter, and an economy of gas is effected. Absolute perfection in these appliances has, of course, not yet been attained; further improvement is still possible, but dissociation imposes a limit because at a certain high temperature combinations do not ensue, possible temperatures being limited by reverse reactions. Here, as in a

number of other cases, the further investigation of the matter must prove of direct value from a practical point of view.

[23] At first sight it appears absurd, useless, and paradoxical to lose nearly one-third of the heat which fuel can develop, by turning it into gas. Actually the advantage is enormous, especially for producing high temperatures, as is already seen from the fact that fuels rich in oxygen (for instance, wood) when damp are unable, with any kind of hearth whatever, to give the temperature required for glass-melting or steel-casting, whilst in the gas-producer they furnish exactly the same gas as the driest and most carbonaceous fuel. In order to understand the principle which is here involved, it is sufficient to remember that a large amount of heat, but having a low temperature, is in many cases of no use whatever. We are unable here to enter into all the details of the complicated matter of the application of fuel, and further particulars must be sought for in special technical treatises. The following footnotes, however, contain certain fundamental figures for calculations concerning combustion.

[24] The first product of combustion of charcoal is always carbonic anhydride, and not carbonic oxide. This is seen from the fact that with a shallow layer of charcoal (less than a decimetre if the charcoal be closely packed) carbonic oxide is not formed at all. It is not even produced with a deep layer of charcoal if the temperature is not above 500°, and the current of air or oxygen is very slow. With a rapid current of air the charcoal becomes red-hot, and the temperature rises, and then carbonic oxide appears (Lang 1888). Ernst (1891) found that below 995° carbonic oxide is always accompanied by CO_2, and that the formation of CO_2 begins about 400°. Naumann and Pistor determined that the reaction of carbonic anhydride with carbon commences at about 550°, and that between water and carbon at about 500°. At the latter temperature carbonic anhydride is formed, and only with a rise of temperature is carbonic oxide formed (Lang) from the action of the carbonic anhydride on the carbon, and from the reaction $CO_2 + H_2 = CO + H_2O$. Rathke (1881) showed that at no temperature whatever is the reaction as expressed by the equation $CO_2 + C = 2CO_2$, complete; a part of the carbonic anhydride remains, and Lang determined that at about 1,000° not less than 3 p.c. of the carbonic anhydride remains untransformed into carbonic oxide, even after the action has been continued for several hours. The endothermal reactions, $C + 2H_2O = CO_2 + 2H_2$, and $CO + H_2O = CO_2 + H_2$, are just as incomplete. This is made clear if we note that on the one hand the above-mentioned reactions are all reversible, and therefore bounded by a limit; and, on the other hand, that at about 500° oxygen begins to combine with hydrogen and carbon, and also that the lower limits of dissociation of water, carbonic anhydride, and carbonic oxide lie near one another between 500° and

1,200°. For water and carbonic oxide the lower limit of the commencement of dissociation is unknown, but judging from the published data (according to Le Chatelier, 1888) that of carbonic anhydride may be taken as about 1,050°. Even at about 200° half the carbonic anhydride dissociates if the pressure be small, about 0·001 atmosphere. At the atmospheric pressure, not more than 0·05 p.c. of the carbonic anhydride decomposes. The reason of the influence of pressure is here evidently that the splitting up of carbonic anhydride into carbonic oxide and oxygen is accompanied by an increase in volume (as in the case of the dissociation of nitric peroxide. *See* Chapter VI., Note 46). As in stoves and lamps, and also with explosive substances, the temperature is not higher than 2,000° to 2,500°, it is evident that although the partial pressure of carbonic anhydride is small, still its dissociation cannot here be considerable, and probably does not exceed 5 p.c.

[24 bis] Besides which L. Mond (1890) showed that the powder of freshly reduced metallic nickel (obtained by heating the oxide to redness in a stream of hydrogen) is able, when heated even to 350°, to completely decompose carbonic oxide into CO_2 and carbon, which remains with the nickel and is easily removed from it by heating in a stream of air. Here $2CO = CO_2 + C$. It should be remarked that heat is evolved in this reaction (Note 25), and therefore that the influence of 'contact' may here play a part. Indeed, this reaction must be classed among the most remarkable instances of the influence of contact, especially as metals analogous to Ni (Fe and Co) do not effect this reaction (*see* Chapter II., Note 17).

[25] A molecular weight of this gas, or 2 volumes CO (28 grams), on combustion (forming CO_2) gives out 68,000 heat units (Thomsen 67,960 calories). A molecular weight of hydrogen, H_2 (or 2 volumes), develops on burning into *liquid* water 69,000 heat units (according to Thomsen 68,300), but if it forms aqueous vapour 58,000 heat units. Charcoal, resolving itself by combustion into the molecular quantity of CO_2 (2 volumes), develops 97,000 heat units. From the data furnished by these exothermal reactions it follows: (1) that the oxidation of charcoal into carbonic oxide develops 29,000 heat units; (2) that the reaction $C + CO_2 = 2CO$ *absorbs* 39,000 heat units; (3) $C + H_2O = H_2 + CO$ *absorbs* (if the water be in a state of vapour) 29,000 calories, but if the water be liquid 40,000 calories (almost as much as $C + CO_2$); (4) $C + H_2O = CO_2 + 2H_2$ *absorbs* (if the water be in a state of vapour) 19,000 heat units; (5) the reaction $CO + H_2O = CO_2 + H_2$ *develops* 10,000 heat units if the water be in the state of vapour; and (6) the decomposition expressed by the equation $2CO = C + CO_2$ (Note 24 bis) is accompanied by the *evolution* of 39,000 units of heat.

Hence it follows that 2 volumes of CO or H_2 burning into CO_2 or H_2O develop almost the same amount of heat, just as also the heat effects corresponding with the equations

$$C + H_2O = CO + H_2$$
$$C + CO_2 = CO + CO$$

are nearly equal.

[26] *Water gas*, obtained from steam and charcoal at a white heat, contains about 50 p.c. of hydrogen, about 40 p.c. of carbonic oxide, about 5 p.c. of carbonic anhydride, the remainder being nitrogen from the charcoal and air. Compared with producer gas, which contains much nitrogen, this is a gas much richer in combustible matter, and therefore capable of giving high temperatures, and is for this reason of the greatest utility. If carbonic anhydride could be as readily obtained in as pure a state as water, then CO might be prepared directly from $CO_2 + C$, and in that case the utilisation of the heat of the carbon would be the same as in water gas, because CO evolves as much heat as H_2, and even more if the temperature of the smoke be over 100°, and the water remains in the form of vapour (Note 25). But producer gas contains a large proportion of nitrogen, so that its effective temperature is below that given by water gas; therefore in places where a particularly high temperature is required (for instance, for lighting by means of incandescent lime or magnesia, or for steel melting, &c.), and where the gas can be easily distributed through pipes, water gas is at present held in high estimation, but when (in ordinary furnaces, re-heating, glass-melting, and other furnaces) a very high temperature is not required, and there is no need to convey the gas in pipes, producer gas is generally preferred on account of the simplicity of its preparation, especially as for water gas such a high temperature is required that the plant soon becomes damaged.

There are numerous systems for making water gas, but the American patent of T. Lowe is generally used. The gas is prepared in a cylindrical generator, into which hot air is introduced, in order to raise the coke in it to a white heat. The products of combustion containing carbonic oxide are utilised for superheating steam, which is then passed over the white hot coke. Water gas, or a mixture of hydrogen and carbonic oxide, is thus obtained.

Water gas is sometimes called '*the fuel of the future*,' because it is applicable to all purposes, develops a high temperature, and is therefore available, not only for domestic and industrial uses, but also for gas-motors and for lighting. For the latter purpose platinum, lime, magnesia, zirconia, and similar substances (as in the Drummond light, Chapter III.), are rendered incandescent in the flame, or else the gas is *carburetted*—that is, mixed with the vapours of volatile hydrocarbons (generally benzene or naphtha, naphthalene, or simply naphtha gas), which communicate to the pale flame of carbonic oxide and hydrogen a great brilliancy, owing to the high temperature developed by the combustion of the non-luminous gases. As water gas, possessing these properties, may be prepared at central works and conveyed in pipes to the consumers, and as it may be produced from any kind of fuel, and ought to be much cheaper than ordinary gas, it may as a matter of fact be expected that in course of time (when experience shall have determined the cheapest and best way to prepare it) it will not only supplant ordinary gas, but will with advantage everywhere replace the ordinary forms of fuel, which in many respects are inconvenient. At present its consumption spreads principally for lighting purposes, and for use in gas-engines instead of ordinary illuminating gas. In some cases Dowson gas is prepared in producers. This is a mixture of water and producer gases obtained by passing steam into an ordinary producer (Note 19), when the temperature of the carbon has become sufficiently high for the reaction $C + H_2O = CO + H_2$.

[27] The so-called yellow prussiate, $K_4FeC_6N_6$, on being heated with ten parts of strong sulphuric acid forms a considerable quantity of very pure carbonic oxide quite free from carbonic anhydride.

[27 bis] To perform this reaction, the formic acid is mixed with glycerine, because when heated alone it volatilises much below its temperature of decomposition. When heated with sulphuric acid the salts of formic acid yield carbonic oxide.

[28] The decomposition of formic and oxalic acids, with the formation of carbonic oxide, considering these acids as carboxyl derivatives, may be explained as follows:—The first is H(COOH) and the second (COOH)$_2$, or H_2 in which one or both halves of the hydrogen are exchanged for carboxyl; therefore they are equal to $H_2 + CO_2$ and $H_2 + 2CO_2$; but H_2 reacts with CO_2, as has been stated above, forming CO and H_2O. From this it is also evident that oxalic acid on losing CO_2 forms formic acid, and also that the latter may proceed from $CO + H_2O$, as we shall see further on.

[28 bis] Greshoff (1888) showed that with a solution of nitrate of silver, iodoform, CHI_3, forms CO according to the equation $CHI_3 + 3AgNO_3 + H_2O = 3AgI + 3HNO_3 + CO$. The reaction is immediate and is complete.

[29] It is remarkable that, according to the investigations of Dixon, perfectly dry carbonic oxide does not explode with oxygen when a spark of low intensity is used, but an explosion takes place if there is the slightest admixture of moisture. L. Meyer, however, showed that sparks of an electric discharge of considerable intensity produce an explosion. N. N.

Beketoff demonstrated that combustion proceeds and spreads slowly unless there be perfect dryness. I think that this may he explained by the fact that water with carbonic oxide gives carbonic anhydride and hydrogen, but hydrogen with oxygen gives hydrogen peroxide (Chapter VII.), which with carbonic oxide forms carbonic anhydride and water. The water, therefore, is renewed, and again serves the same purpose. But it may be that here it is necessary to acknowledge a simple contact influence. After Dixon had shown the influence of traces of moisture upon the reaction $CO + O$, many researches were made of a similar nature. The fullest investigation into the influence of moisture upon the course of many chemical reactions was made by Baker in 1894. He showed that with perfect dryness, many chemical transformations (for example, the formation of ozone from oxygen, the decomposition of AgO, $KClO_3$ under the action of heat, &c.) proceeds in exactly the same manner as in the presence of moisture; but that in many cases traces of moisture have an evident influence. We may mention the following instances: (1) Dry SO_3 does not act upon dry CaO or CuO; (2) perfectly dry sal-ammoniac does not give NH_3 with dry CaO, but simply volatilises; (3) dry NO and O do not react; (4) perfectly dry NH_3 and HCl do not combine; (5) perfectly dry sal-ammoniac does not dissociate at 350° (Chapter VII., Note 15 bis); and (6) perfectly dry chlorine does not act upon metals, &c.

[30] Carbonic oxide is very rapid in its action, because it is absorbed by the blood in the same way as oxygen. In addition to this, the absorption spectrum of the blood changes so that by the help of blood it is easy to detect the slightest traces of carbonic oxide in the air. M. A. Kapoustin found that linseed oil and therefore oil paints, are capable of giving off carbonic oxide while drying (absorbing oxygen).

[31] The molecule of metallic potassium (Scott, 1887), like that of mercury, contains only one atom, and it is probably in virtue of this that the molecules CO and K combine together. But as in the majority of cases potassium acts as a univalent radicle, the polymeride $K_2C_2O_2$ is formed, and probably $K_{10}C_{10}O_{10}$, because products containing C_{10} are formed by the action of hydrochloric acid. The black mass formed by the combination of carbonic oxide with potassium explodes with great ease, and oxidises in the air. Although Brodie, Lerch, and Joannis (who obtained it in 1873 in a colourless form by means of NH_3K, described in Chapter VI., Note 14) have greatly extended our knowledge of this compound, much still remains unexplained. It probably exists in various polymeric and isomeric forms, having the composition $(KCO)_n$ and $(NaCO)_n$.

[32] The connection of the cyanogen compounds with the rest of the hydrocarbons by means of carboxyl was enunciated by me, about the year 1860, at the first Annual Meeting of the Russian Naturalists.

[33] Thus, for instance, *oxamide*, or the amide of oxalic acid, $(CNH_2O)_2$, is obtained in the form of an insoluble precipitate on adding a solution of ammonia to an alcoholic solution of ethyl oxalate, $(CO_2C_2H_5)_2$, which is formed by the action of oxalic acid on alcohol: $(CHO_2)_2 + 2(C_2H_5)OH = 2HOH + (CO_2C_2H_5)_2$. As the nearest derivatives of ammonia, the amides treated with alkalis yield ammonia and form the salt of the acid. The nitriles do not, however, give similar reactions so readily. The majority of amides corresponding to acids have a composition RNH_2, and therefore recombine with water with great ease even when simply boiled with it, and with still greater facility in presence of acids or alkalis. Under the action of alkalis the amides naturally give off ammonia, through the combination of water with the amide, when a salt of the acid from which the amide was derived is formed: $RNH_2 + KHO = RKO + NH_3$.

The same reaction takes place with acids, only an ammoniacal salt of the acid is of course formed whilst the acid held in the amide is liberated: $RNH_2 + HCl + H_2O = RHO + NH_4Cl$.

Thus in the majority of cases amides easily pass into ammoniacal salts, but they differ essentially from them. No ammoniacal salt sublimes or volatilises unchanged, and generally when heated it gives off water and yields an amide, whilst many amides volatilise without alteration and frequently are volatile crystalline substances which may be easily sublimed. Such, for instance, are the amides of benzoic, formic, and many other organic acids.

[34] The acid salt, $(NH_4)HCO_3$, on losing water ought to form the *carbamic acid*, $OH(CNH_2O)$; but it is not formed, which is accounted for by the instability of the acid salt itself. Carbonic anhydride is given off and ammonia is produced, which gives ammonium carbamate.

[35] In the normal salt, $2NH_3 + CO_2 + H_2O$, in the acid salt, $NH_3 + CO_2 + H_2O$, but in the commercial salt only $2H_2O$ to $3CO_2$.

[36] Naumann determined the following dissociation tensions of the vapour of ammonium carbamate (in millimetres of mercury):—

-10° 0° +10° 20° 30° 40° 50° 60°

5   12   30   62 124 248 470 770

Horstmann and Isambert studied the tensions corresponding to excess of NH_3 or CO_2, and found, as might have been expected, that with such excess the mass of the salt formed (in a solid state) increases and the decomposition (transition into vapour) decreases.

[37] Calcium chloride enters into double decomposition with ammonium carbamate. Acids (for instance, sulphuric) take up ammonia, and set free carbonic anhydride; whilst alkalis (such as potash) take up carbonic anhydride and set free ammonia, and therefore, in this case for removing water only sodium or potassium carbonate can be taken. An aqueous solution of ammonium carbamate does not entirely precipitate a solution of $CaCl_2$, probably because calcium carbamate is soluble in water, and all the $(NH_3)_2CO_2$ is not converted by dissolving into the normal salt, $(NH_4O)_2CO_3$.

[38] It must be imagined that the reaction takes place at first between equal volumes (Chapter VII.); but then carbamic acid, $HO(CNH_2O)$, is produced, which, as an acid, immediately combines with the ammonia, forming $NH_4O(CNH_2O)$.

[39] Urea is undoubtedly a product of the oxidation of complex nitrogenous matters (albumin) of the animal body. It is found in the blood. It is absorbed from the blood by the kidneys. A man excretes about 30 grams of urea per day. As a derivative of carbonic anhydride, into which it is readily converted, urea is in a sense a product of oxidation.

[39 bis] Its polymer, $C_3N_3H_3O_3$, is formed together with it. Cyanic acid is a very unstable, easily changeable liquid, while cyanuric acid is a crystalline solid which is very stable at the ordinary temperature.

[40] Just as the aldehydes (such as C_2H_4O) are alcohols (like C_2H_6O) which have lost hydrogen and are also capable of entering into combination with many substances, and of polymerising, forming slightly volatile polymerides, which depolymerise on heating. Although there are also many similar phenomena (for instance, the transformation of yellow into red phosphorus, the transition of cinnamene into metacinnamene, &c.) of polymerisation, in no other case are they so clearly and simply expressed as in cyanic acid. The details relating to this must be sought for in treatises on organic and theoretical chemistry. If we touch on certain sides of this question it is principally with the view of showing the phenomenon of polymerisation by typical examples, for it is of more frequent occurrence than was formerly supposed among compounds of several elements.

[41] It has an important historical interest, more especially as at that time such an easy preparation of substances occurring in organisms without the aid of organic life was quite unexpected, for they were supposed to be formed under the influence of the forces acting in organisms, and without the latter their formation was considered impossible. And in addition to destroying this illusion, the easy transition of NH_4OCN into $CO(NH_2)_2$ is

the best example of the passage of one system of equilibrium of atoms into another more stable system.

[42] If ammonia and methane (marsh gas) do not show any acid properties, that is in all probability due to the presence of a large amount of hydrogen in both; but in hydrocyanic acid one atom of hydrogen is under the influence of two acid-forming elements. Acetylene, C_2H_2, which contains but little hydrogen, presents acid properties in certain respects, for its hydrogen is easily replaced by metals. Hydronitrous acid, HN_3, which contains little hydrogen, also has the properties of an acid.

[43] Solutions of cyanides—for instance, those of potassium or barium—are decomposed by carbonic acid. Even the carbonic anhydride of the air acts in a similar way, and for this reason these solutions do not keep, because, in the first place, free hydrocyanic acid itself decomposes and polymerises, and, in the second place, with alkaline liquids it forms ammonia and formic acid. Hydrocyanic acid does not liberate carbonic anhydride from solutions of sodium or potassium carbonates. But a mixture of solutions of potassium carbonate and hydrocyanic acid yields carbonic anhydride on the addition of oxides like zinc oxide, mercuric oxide, &c. This is due to the great inclination which the cyanides exhibit of forming double salts. For instance, $ZnK_2(CN)_4$ is formed, which is a soluble double salt.

[43 bis] The conversion of the atmospheric nitrogen into cyanogen compounds, although possible, has not yet been carried out on a large scale, and one of the problems for future research should be the discovery of a practical and economical means of converting the atmospheric nitrogen into metallic cyanides, not only because potassium cyanide has found a vast and important use for the extraction of gold from even the poorest ores, but more especially because the cyanides furnish the means for effecting the synthesis of many complex carbon compounds, and the nitrogen contained in cyanogen easily passes into other forms of combination such as ammonia, which is of great importance in agriculture.

[44] The mixture of the vapours of water and hydrocyanic acid, evolved on heating yellow prussiate with sulphuric acid, may be passed directly through vessels or tubes filled with calcium chloride. These tubes must be cooled, because, in the first place, hydrocyanic acid easily changes on being heated, and, in the second place, the calcium chloride when warm would absorb less water. The mixture of hydrocyanic acid and aqueous vapour on passing over a long layer of calcium chloride gives up water, and hydrocyanic acid alone remains in the vapour. It ought to be cooled as carefully as possible in order to bring it into a liquid condition. The method which Gay-Lussac employed for obtaining pure hydrocyanic acid consisted

in the action of hydrochloric acid gas on mercuric cyanide. The latter may he obtained in a pure state if a solution of yellow prussiate be boiled with a solution of mercuric nitrate, filtered, and crystallised by cooling; the mercuric cyanide is then obtained in the form of colourless crystals, $Hg(CN)_2$.

If a strong solution of hydrochloric acid be poured upon these crystals, and the mixture of vapours evolved, consisting of aqueous vapour, hydrochloric acid, and hydrocyanic acid, be passed through a tube containing, first, marble (for absorbing the hydrochloric acid), and then lumps of calcium chloride, on cooling the hydrocyanic acid will be condensed. In order to obtain the latter in an anhydrous form, the decomposition of heated mercury cyanide by hydrogen sulphide may be made use of. Here the sulphur and cyanogen change places, and hydrocyanic acid and mercury sulphide are formed: $Hg(CN)_2 + H_2S = 2HCN + HgS$.

[45] A weak (up to 2 p.c.) aqueous solution of hydrocyanic acid is obtained by the distillation of certain vegetable substances. The so-called laurel water in particular enjoys considerable notoriety from its containing hydrocyanic acid. It is obtained by the steeping and distillation of laurel leaves. A similar kind of water is formed by the infusion and distillation of bitter almonds. It is well known that bitter almonds are poisonous, and have a peculiar characteristic taste. This bitter taste is due to the presence of a certain substance called amygdalin, which can be extracted by alcohol. This amygdalin decomposes in an infusion of bruised almonds, forming the so-called bitter almond oil, glucose, and hydrocyanic acid:

$$C_{10}H_{27}NO_{11} + H_2O = C_7H_6O + CNH + 2C_6H_{12}O_6$$

Amygdalin in bitter almonds	Water	Bitter almond oil	Hydrocyanic acid	Glucose

If after this the infusion of bitter almonds be distilled with water, the hydrocyanic acid and the volatile bitter almond oil are carried over with the aqueous vapour. The oil is insoluble in water, or only sparingly soluble, while the hydrocyanic acid remains as an aqueous solution. Bitter almond water is similar to laurel water, and is used like the former in medicine, naturally only in small quantities because any considerable amount has poisonous effects. Perfectly pure anhydrous hydrocyanic acid keeps without change, just like the weak solutions, but the strong solutions only keep in the presence of other acids. In the presence of many admixtures these solutions easily give a brown polymeric substance, which is also formed in a solution of potassium cyanide.

[46] This salt will be described in Chapter XIII.

[47] For the preparation it is necessary to take completely dry mercuric cyanide, because when heated in the presence of moisture it gives ammonia, carbonic anhydride, and hydrocyanic acid. Instead of mercuric cyanide, a mixture of perfectly dry yellow prussiate and mercuric chloride may be used, then double decomposition and the formation of mercuric cyanide take place in the retort. Silver cyanide also disengages cyanogen, on being heated.

[48] *Paracyanogen* is a brown substance (having the composition of cyanogen) which is formed during the preparation of cyanogen by all methods, and remains as a residue. Silver cyanide, on being slightly heated, fuses, and on being further heated evolves a gas; a considerable quantity of paracyanogen remains in the residue. Here it is remarkable that exactly half the cyanogen becomes gaseous, and the other half is transformed into paracyanogen. Metallic silver will be found in the residue with the paracyanogen; it may be extracted with mercury or nitric acid, which does not act on paracyanogen. If paracyanogen be heated in a vacuum it decomposes, forming cyanogen; but here the pressure p for a given temperature t cannot exceed a certain limit, so that the phenomenon presents all the external appearance of a physical transformation into vapour; but, nevertheless, it is a complete change in the nature of the substance, though limited by the *pressure of dissociation*, as we saw before in the transformation of cyanuric into hydrocyanic acid, and as would be expected from the fundamental principles of dissociation. Troost and Hautefeuille (1868) found that for paracyanogen,

$t = 530°\ 581°\ 600°\quad 635°$

$p = 90\quad 143\quad 296\quad 1,089$ mm.

However, even at 550° part of the cyanogen decomposes into carbon and nitrogen. The reverse transition of cyanogen into paracyanogen commences at 350°, and at 600° proceeds rapidly. And if the transition of the first kind is likened to evaporation, then the reverse transition, or polymerisation, presents a likeness to the transition of vapours into the solid state.

[49] Cyanogen (like chlorine) is absorbed by a solution of sodium hydroxide, sodium cyanide and cyanate being produced: $C_2N_2 + 2NaHO = NaCN + CNNaO + H_2O$. But the latter salt decomposes relatively easily, and moreover part of the cyanogen liberated by heat from its compounds undergoes a more complex transformation.

[50] If, in general, compounds containing the radicle NH_2 are called amides, some of the *amines* ought to be ranked with them; namely, the hydrocarbons C_nH_{2m}, in which part of the hydrogen is replaced by NH_2; for

instance, methylamine, CH_3NH_2, aniline, $C_6H_5NH_2$, &c. In general the amines may be represented as ammonia in which part or all of the hydrogen is replaced by hydrocarbon radicles—as, for example, trimethylamine, $N(CH_3)_3$. They, like ammonia, combine with acids and form crystalline salts. Analogous substances are sometimes met with in nature, and bear the general name of *alkaloids*; such are, for instance, quinine in cinchona bark, nicotine in tobacco, &c.

[417]

CHAPTER X

SODIUM CHLORIDE—BERTHOLLET'S LAWS—HYDROCHLORIC ACID

In the preceding chapters we have become acquainted with the most important properties of the four elements, hydrogen, oxygen, nitrogen, and carbon. They are sometimes termed the *organogens*, because they enter into the composition of organic substances. Their mutual combinations may serve as types for all other chemical compounds—that is, they present the same atomic relations (types, forms, or grades of combinations) as those in which the other elements also combine together.

Hydrogen, HH, or, in general, HR.

Water,   H₂O,   „   „   H₂R.

Ammonia, H₃N,   „   „   H₃R.

Marsh gas, H₄C,   „   „   H₄R.

One, two, three, and four atoms of hydrogen enter into these molecules for one atom of another element. No compounds of one atom of oxygen with three or four atoms of hydrogen are known; hence the atom of oxygen does not possess certain properties which are found in the atoms of carbon and nitrogen.

The faculty of an element to form a compound of definite composition with hydrogen (or an element analogous to it) gives the possibility of foretelling the composition of many other of its compounds. Thus, if we know that an element, M, combines with hydrogen, forming, by preference, a gaseous substance such as HM, but not forming H₂M, H₃M, HₙMₘ, then we must conclude, on the basis of the law of substitution, that this element will give compounds M₂O, M₃N, MHO, MH₃C, &c. Chlorine is an example of this kind. If we know that another element, R, like oxygen, gives with hydrogen a molecule H₂R, then we may expect that it will form compounds similar to hydrogen peroxide, the metallic oxides, carbonic anhydride, or carbonic oxide, and others. Sulphur is an instance of this kind. Hence the elements may be classified according to their resemblance to hydrogen, oxygen, nitrogen, and carbon, and in conformity with this analogy it is possible[418] to foretell, if not the properties (for example, the acidity or basicity), at any rate the composition,[1] of some of their compounds. This forms the substance of *the conception of the valency or atomicity of the elements.* Hydrogen is taken as the representative of the univalent elements, giving compounds, RH, R(OH), R_2O, RCl, R_3N, R_4C, &c. Oxygen, in that form in which it gives water, is the representative of the[419] bivalent elements, forming RH_2, RO, RCl_2, RHCl, R(OH)Cl, $R(OH)_2$, R_2C, RCN, &c. Nitrogen in ammonia is the representative of the trivalent elements, giving compounds RH_3, R_2O_3, $R(OH)_3$, RCl_3, RN, RHC, &c. In carbon are exemplified the properties of the quadrivalent elements, forming RH_4, RO_2, $RO(OH)_2$, $R(OH)_4$, RHN, RCl_4, $RHCl_3$, &c. We meet with these *forms of combination*, or degrees of union of atoms, in all other elements, some being analogous to hydrogen, others to oxygen, and others to nitrogen or to carbon. But besides these quantitative analogies or resemblances, which are foretold by the law of substitution (Chapter VI.), there exist among the elements qualitative analogies and relations which are not fully seen in the compounds of the elements which have been considered, but are most distinctly exhibited in the formation of bases, acids, and salts of different types and properties. Therefore, for a complete study of the nature of the elements and their compounds it is especially important to become acquainted with the salts, as substances of a peculiar character, and with the corresponding acids and bases. Common table salt, or sodium chloride, NaCl, may in every respect be taken as a type of salts in general, and we will therefore pass to the consideration of this substance, and of hydrochloric acid, and of the base sodium hydroxide, formed by the non-metal chlorine and the metal sodium, which correspond with it.

Sodium chloride, NaCl, the familiar table salt, occurs, although in very small quantities, in all the primary formations of the earth's crust,[2] from which it is washed away by the atmospheric waters; it is contained in small quantities in all waters flowing through these formations, and is in this manner conveyed to the oceans and seas. The immense mass of salt in the oceans has been accumulated by this process from the remote ages of the earth's creation, because the water has evaporated from them while the salt has remained in solution. The salt of sea water serves as the source not only for its direct extraction, but[420] also for the formation of other masses of workable salt, such as rock salt, and of saline springs and lakes.[2 bis]

The extraction of salt *from sea water* is carried on in several ways. In southern climes, especially on the shores of the Atlantic Ocean and the Mediterranean and Black Seas, the summer heats are taken advantage of. A convenient low-lying sea shore is chosen, and a whole series of basins, communicating with each other, are constructed along it. The upper of these basins are filled with sea water by pumping, or else advantage is taken of high tides. These basins are sometimes separated from the sea by natural sand-banks (limans) or by artificial means, and in spring the water already begins to evaporate considerably. As the solution becomes more concentrated, it is run into the succeeding basins, and the upper ones are supplied with a fresh quantity of sea water, or else an arrangement is made enabling the salt water to flow by degrees through the series of basins. It is evident that the beds of the basins should be as far as possible impervious to water, and for this purpose they are made of beaten clay. The crystals of salt begin to separate out when the concentration attains 28 p.c. of salt (which corresponds to 28° of Baumé's hydrometer). They are raked off, and employed for all those purposes to which table salt is applicable. In the majority of cases only the first half of the sodium chloride which can be separated from the sea water is extracted, because the second half has a bitter taste from the presence of magnesium salts which separate out together with the sodium salt. But in certain localities—as, for instance, in the estuary of the Rhone, on the island of Camarga[3]—the evaporation is carried on to the very end, in order to obtain those magnesium and potassium salts which separate out at the end of the evaporation of sea water. Various salts are separated from sea water in its evaporation. From 100 parts of sea water there separates out, by natural and artificial evaporation, about one part of tolerably pure table salt at the very commencement of the operation; the total amount held in solution being about 2½ p.c. The remaining portion separates out intermixed[421] with the bitter salts of magnesium which, owing to their solubility and the small amount in which they are present (less than 1 p.c.), only separate out, in the first crystallisations, in traces. Gypsum, or calcium sulphate, $CaSO_4,2H_2O$, because of its sparing solubility, separates together with or even before the table salt. When about half of the latter has separated, then a mixture of table salt and magnesium sulphate separates out, and on still further evaporation the chlorides of potassium and magnesium begin to separate in a state of combination, forming the double salt $KMgCl_3,6H_2O$, which occurs in nature as *carnallite*.[4] After the separation of this salt from sea water, there remains a mother liquor containing a large amount of magnesium chloride in admixture with various other salts.[5] The extraction of sea salt is usually carried on for the purpose of procuring table salt, and therefore directly it begins to separate mixed with a considerable proportion[6] of magnesium salts (when it acquires a bitter taste) the remaining liquor is run back into the sea.

The same process which is employed for artificially obtaining salt in a crystalline form from sea water has been repeatedly accomplished during the geological evolution of the earth on a gigantic scale; upheavals of the earth have cut off portions of the sea from the remainder (as the Dead Sea was formerly a part of the Mediterranean, and the Sea of Aral of the Caspian), and their water has evaporated and formed (if the mass of the inflowing fresh water were less than that of the mass evaporated) deposits of *rock salt*. It is always accompanied by gypsum, because the latter is separated from sea water with or before the sodium chloride. For this reason rock salt may always be looked for[422] in those localities where there are deposits of gypsum. But inasmuch as the gypsum remains on the spot where it has been deposited (as it is a sparingly soluble salt), whilst the rock salt (as one which is very soluble) may be washed away by rain or fresh running water, it may sometimes happen that although gypsum is still found there may be no salt; but, on the other hand, where there is rock salt there will always be gypsum. As the geological changes of the earth's surface are still proceeding at the present day, so in the midst of the dry land salt lakes are met with, which are sometimes scattered over vast districts formerly covered by seas now dried up. Such is the origin of many of the salt lakes about the lower portions of the Volga and in the Kirghiz steppes, where at a geological epoch preceding the present the Aralo-Caspian Sea extended. Such are the Baskunchaksky (in the Government of Astrakhan, 112 square kilometres superficial area), the Eltonsky (140 versts from the left bank of the Volga, and 200 square kilometres in superficial area), and upward of 700 other salt lakes lying about the lower portions of the Volga. In those in which the inflow of fresh water is less than that yearly evaporated, and in which the concentration of the solution has reached saturation, the *self-deposited* salt is found already deposited on their beds, or is being yearly deposited during the summer months. Certain limans, or sea-side lakes, of the Azoff Sea are essentially of the same character—as, for instance, those in the neighbourhood of Henichesk and Berdiansk. The saline soils of certain Central Asian steppes, which suffer from a want of atmospheric fresh water, are of the same origin. Their salt originally proceeded from the salt of seas which previously covered these localities, and has not yet been washed away by fresh water. The main result of the above-described process of nature is the formation of masses of rock salt, which are, however, being gradually washed away by the subsoil waters flowing in their neighbourhood, and afterwards rising to the surface in certain places as *saline springs*, which indicate the presence of masses of deposited rock salt in the depths of the earth. If the subsoil water flows along a stratum of salt for a sufficient length of time it becomes saturated; but in flowing in its further course along an impervious stratum (clay) it becomes diluted by the fresh water leaking through the upper soil, and therefore the greater the distance of a saline spring from the deposit of rock salt, the poorer will it be in salt. A perfectly saturated brine, however, may be procured from the depths of the earth by means of bore-holes. The deposits of rock salt themselves, which are sometimes hidden at great depths below the earth's strata, may be discovered by the guidance of bore-holes and the direction of the strata of the district. Deposits of rock salt, about[423] 35 metres thick and 20 metres below the surface, were discovered in this manner in the neighbourhood of Brianstcheffky and Dekonoffky, in the Bakhmut district of the Government of Ekaterinoslav. Large quantities of most excellent rock salt are now (since 1880) obtained from these deposits, whose presence was indicated by the neighbouring salt springs (near Slaviansk and Bakhmut) and by bore-holes which had been sunk in these localities for procuring strong (saturated) brines. But the Stassfurt deposits of rock salt near Magdeburg in Germany are celebrated as being the first discovered in this manner, and for their many remarkable peculiarities.[7] The plentiful distribution of saline springs in this and the neighbouring districts suggested the presence of deposits of rock salt in the vicinity. Deep bore-holes sunk in this locality did in fact give a richer brine—even quite saturated with salt. On sinking to a still greater depth, the deposits of salt themselves were at last arrived at. But the first deposit which was met with consisted of a bitter salt unfit for consumption, and was therefore called refuse salt (*Abraumsalz*). On sinking still deeper vast beds of real rock salt were struck. In this instance the presence of these upper strata containing salts of potassium, magnesium, and sodium is an excellent proof of the formation of rock salt from sea water. It is very evident that not only a case of evaporation to the end—as far, for instance, as the separation of carnallite—but also the preservation of such soluble salts as separate out from sea water after the sodium chloride, must be a very exceptional phenomenon, which is not repeated in all deposits of rock salt. The Stassfurt deposits therefore are of particular interest, not only from a scientific point of view, but also because they form a rich source of potassium salts which have many practical uses.[7 bis]

[424]

A saturated brine, formed by the continued contact of subsoil water with rock salt, is extracted by means of bore-holes, as, for instance, in the Governments of Perm, Kharkoff, and Ekaterinoslav. Sometimes, as at Berchtesgaden (and at Hallein) in Austria, spring water is run on to underground beds of rock salt containing much clay.

FIG. 64.—Graduator for the evaporation of the water of saline springs.

If a saline spring, or the salt water pumped from bore-holes, contains but little salt, then the first concentration of the natural solution is not carried on by the costly consumption of fuel, but by the cheaper method of evaporation by means of the wind. For this purpose so-called graduators are constructed: they consist of long and lofty sheds, which are sometimes several versts long, and generally extend in a direction at right angles to that of the usual course of the wind in the district. These sheds are open at the sides, and are filled with brushwood as shown in fig. 64. Troughs, A B, C D, into which the salt[425] water is pumped, run along the top. On flowing from these troughs, through the openings, *a*, the water spreads over the brushwood and distributes itself in a thin layer over it, so that it presents a very large surface for evaporation, in consequence of which it rapidly becomes concentrated in warm or windy weather. After trickling over the brushwood, the solution collects in a reservoir under the graduator, whence it is usually pumped up by the pumps P P', and again run a second and third time through the graduator, until the solution reaches a degree of concentration at which it becomes profitable to extract the salt by direct heating. Generally the evaporation in the graduator is not carried beyond a concentration of 12 to 15 parts of salt in 100 parts of solution. Strong natural solutions of salt, and also the graduated solutions, are evaporated in large shallow metallic vessels, which are either heated by the direct action of the flame from below or from above. These vessels are made of boiler plate, and are called salt-pans. Various means are employed for accelerating the evaporation and for economising fuel, which are mainly based on an artificial draught to carry off the steam as it is formed, and on subjecting the saline solution to a preliminary heating by the waste heat of the steam and furnace gases. Furthermore, the first portions of the salt which crystallise out in the salt-pans are invariably contaminated with gypsum, since the waters of saline springs always contain this substance. It is only the portions of the salt which separate later that are distinguished by their great purity. The salt is ladled out as it is deposited, left to drain on inclined tables and then dried, and in this manner the so-called bay salt is obtained. Since it has become possible to discover the saline deposits themselves, the extraction of table salt from the water of saline springs by evaporation, which previously was in general use, has begun to be disused, and is only able to hold its ground in places where fuel is cheap.

In order to understand the full importance of the extraction of salt, it need only be mentioned that on the average 20 lbs. of table salt are consumed yearly per head of population, directly in food or for cattle. In those countries where common salt is employed in technical processes, and especially in England, almost an equal quantity is consumed in the production of substances containing chlorine and sodium, and especially in the manufacture of washing soda, &c., and of chlorine compounds (bleaching powder and hydrochloric acid). The yearly production of salt in Europe amounts to as much as $7\frac{1}{2}$ million tons.

Although certain lumps of rock salt and crystals of bay salt sometimes consist of almost pure sodium chloride, still the ordinary commercial salt contains various impurities, the most common of which are[426] magnesium salts. If the salt be pure, its solution gives no precipitate with sodium carbonate, Na_2CO_3, showing the absence of magnesium salts, because magnesium carbonate, $MgCO_3$, is insoluble in water. Rock salt, which is ground for use, generally contains also a considerable admixture of clay and other insoluble impurities.[8] For ordinary use the bulk of the salt obtained can be employed directly without further purification; but some salts are purified by solution and crystallisation of the solution after standing, in which case the evaporation is not carried on to dryness, and the impurities remain in the *mother liquor* or in the sediment. When perfectly pure salt is required for chemical purposes it is best obtained as follows: a saturated solution of table salt is prepared, and hydrochloric acid gas is passed through it; this precipitates the sodium chloride (which is not soluble in a strong solution of hydrochloric acid), while the impurities remain in solution. By repeating the operation and fusing the salt (when adhering hydrochloric acid is volatilised) a pure salt is obtained, which is again crystallised from its solution by evaporation.[9]

Pure sodium chloride, in well-defined crystals (slowly deposited at the bottom of the liquid) or in compact masses (in which form rock salt is sometimes met with), is a colourless and transparent substance resembling, but more brittle and less hard than, glass.[10] Common salt always crystallises in the cubic system, most frequently in *cubes*, and more rarely in octahedra. Large transparent cubes of common salt, having edges up to 10 centimetres long, are sometimes found in masses of rock salt.[11] When evaporated in the open the salt often[427] separates out on the surface[12] as cubes, which grow on to each other in the form of pyramidal square funnels. In still weather, these clusters are able to support themselves on the surface of the water for a long time, and sometimes go on increasing to a considerable extent, but they sink directly the water penetrates inside them. Salt fuses to a colourless liquid (sp. gr. 1·602, according to Quincke) at 851° (V. Meyer); if pure it solidifies to a non-crystalline mass, and if impure to an opaque mass whose surface is not smooth. In fusing, sodium chloride commences to volatilise (its weight decreases) and at a white heat it volatilises with great ease and completely; but at the ordinary temperature it may, like all ordinary salts, be considered as non-volatile, although as yet no exact experiments have been made in this direction.

A saturated[13] solution of table salt (containing 26·4 p.c.) has at the ordinary temperature a specific gravity of about 1·2. The specific gravity of the crystals is 2·167 (17°). The salt which separates out at the ordinary and higher temperatures contains no water of crystallisation;[14] but if the crystals are formed at a low temperature,[428] especially from a saturated solution cooled to -12°, then they present a prismatic form, and contain two equivalents of water, $NaCl,2H_2O$. At the ordinary temperature these crystals split up into sodium chloride and its solution.[15] Unsaturated solutions of table salt when cooled below 0° give[16] crystals of ice, but when the solution has a composition $NaCl,10H_2O$ it solidifies completely at a temperature of -23°. A solution of table salt saturated at its boiling point boils at about 109°, and contains about 42 parts of salt per 100 parts of water.

Of all its physical properties the specific gravity of solutions of sodium chloride is the one which has been the most fully investigated. A comparison of all the existing determinations of the specific gravity[429] of solutions of NaCl[17] at 15° (in vacuo, taking water at 4° as 10,000), with regard to p (the percentage amount of the salt in solution), show that it is expressed by the equation $S_{15} = 9991 \cdot 6 + 71 \cdot 17p + 0 \cdot 2140p^2$. For instance, for a solution $200H_2O + NaCl$, in which case $p = 1 \cdot 6$, $S_{15} = 1 \cdot 0106$. It is seen from the formula that the addition of water produces a contraction.[18] The specific gravity[19] at certain temperatures and concentrations in vacuo referred to water at 4° = 10,000[20] is here given for

	0°	15°	30°	110°
p = 5	10372	10353	10307	9922
10	10768	10728	10669	10278
15	11164	11107	11043	10652
20	11568	11501	11429	11043

It should be remarked that Baumé's hydrometer is graduated by taking a 10 p.c. solution of sodium chloride as 10° on the scale, and therefore it gives approximately the percentage amount of the salt in a[430] solution. Common salt is somewhat soluble in alcohol,[21] but it is insoluble in ether and in oils.

Common salt gives very few compounds[22] (double salts) and these are very readily decomposed: it is also decomposed with great difficulty and its dissociation is unknown.[23] But it is easily decomposed, both when fused and in solution, by the action of a galvanic current. If the dry salt be fused in a crucible and an electric current be passed through it by immersing carbon or platinum electrodes in it (the positive electrode is made of carbon and the negative of platinum or mercury), it is *decomposed*: the suffocating gas, chlorine, is liberated at the positive pole and metallic sodium at the negative pole. Both of them act on the excess of water at the moment of their evolution; the sodium evolves hydrogen and forms caustic soda, and the chlorine evolves oxygen and forms hydrochloric acid, and therefore on passing a current through a solution of common salt metallic sodium will not be obtained—but oxygen, chlorine, and hydrochloric acid will appear at the positive pole, and hydrogen and caustic soda at the negative pole.[23 bis] Thus salt, like other salts, is decomposed by the action of an electric current into a metal and a haloid (Chapter III.) Naturally, like all other salts, it may be formed from the corresponding base and acid with the separation of water. In fact if we mix caustic soda (base) with hydrochloric acid (acid), table salt is formed, $NaHO + HCl = NaCl + H_2O$.

[431]

With respect to the double decompositions of sodium chloride it should be observed that they are most varied, and serve as means of obtaining nearly all the other compounds of sodium and chlorine.

The double decompositions of sodium chloride are almost exclusively based on the possibility of the metal sodium being exchanged for hydrogen and other metals. But neither hydrogen nor any other metal can directly displace the sodium from sodium chloride. This would result in the separation of metallic sodium, which itself displaces hydrogen and the majority of other metals from their compounds, and is not, so far as is known, ever separated by them. The replacement of the sodium in sodium chloride by hydrogen and various metals can only take place by the transference of the sodium into some other combination. If hydrogen or a metal, M, be combined with an element X, then the double decomposition $NaCl + MX = NaX + MCl$ takes place. Such double decompositions take place under special conditions, sometimes completely and sometimes only partially, as we shall endeavour to explain. In order to acquaint ourselves with the double decompositions of sodium chloride, we will follow the methods actually employed in practice to procure compounds of sodium and of chlorine from common salt. For this purpose we will first describe the treatment of sodium chloride with sulphuric acid for the preparation of hydrochloric acid and sodium sulphate. We will then describe the substances obtained from hydrochloric acid and sodium sulphate. Chlorine itself, and nearly all the compounds of this element, may be procured from hydrochloric acid, whilst sodium carbonate, caustic soda, metallic sodium itself and all its compounds, may be obtained from sodium sulphate.

Even in the animal organism salt undergoes similar changes, furnishing the sodium, alkali, and hydrochloric acid which take part in the processes of animal life.

Its necessity as a constituent in the food both of human beings and of animals becomes evident when we consider that both hydrochloric acid and salts of sodium are found in the substances which are separated out from the blood into the stomach and intestines. Sodium salts are found in the blood and in the bile which is elaborated in the liver and acts on the food in the alimentary canal, whilst hydrochloric acid is found in the acid juices of the stomach. Chlorides of the metals are always found in considerable quantities in the urine, and if they are excreted they must be replenished in the organism; and for the replenishment of the loss, substances containing chlorine compounds must be taken in food. Not only do animals consume those small amounts of sodium chloride which are found in drinking water or in plants[432] or other animals, but experience has shown that many wild animals travel long distances in search of salt springs, and that domestic animals which in their natural condition do not require salt, willingly take it, and that the functions of their organisms become much more regular from their doing so.

The action of sulphuric acid on sodium chloride.—If sulphuric acid be poured over common salt, then even at the ordinary temperature, as Glauber observed, an odorous gas, hydrochloric acid, is evolved. The reaction which takes place consists in the sodium of the salt and the hydrogen of the sulphuric acid changing places.

$$NaCl \quad + \quad H_2SO_4 \quad = \quad HCl \quad + \quad NaHSO_4$$

Sodium chloride	Sulphuric acid	Hydrochloric acid	Acid sodium sulphate

At the ordinary temperature this reaction is not complete, but soon ceases. When the mixture is heated, the decomposition proceeds until, if there be sufficient salt present, all the sulphuric acid taken is converted into acid sodium sulphate. Any excess of acid will remain unaltered. If 2 molecules of sodium chloride (117 parts) be taken per molecule of sulphuric acid (98 parts), then on heating the mixture to a moderate temperature only one-half (58·5) of the salt will suffer change. Complete decomposition, after which neither hydrogen nor chlorine is left in the residue, proceeds (when 117 parts of table salt are taken per 98 parts of sulphuric acid) *at a red heat only.* Then—

$$2NaCl \quad + \quad H_2SO_4 \quad = \quad 2HCl \quad + \quad Na_2SO_4$$

Table salt   Sulphuric acid   Hydrochloric acid   Sodium sulphate

This double decomposition is the result of the action of the acid salt, $NaHSO_4$, first formed, on sodium chloride, for the acid salt, since it contains hydrogen, itself acts like an acid, $NaCl + NaHSO_4 = HCl + Na_2SO_4$. By adding this equation to the first we obtain the second, which expresses the ultimate reaction. Hence in the above reaction, non-volatile or sparingly volatile table salt and sparingly volatile sulphuric acid are taken, and as the result of their reaction, after the hydrogen and sodium have exchanged places, there is obtained non-volatile sodium sulphate and gaseous hydrochloric acid. The fact of the latter being a gaseous substance forms the main reason for the reaction proceeding to the very end. The mechanism of this kind of double decomposition, and the cause of the course of the reaction, are exactly the same as those we saw in the decomposition of nitre (Chapter VI.) by the action of sulphuric acid. The sulphuric acid in each case displaces the other, volatile, acid.

[433]

Not only in these two instances, but in every instance, if a volatile acid can be formed by the substitution of the hydrogen of sulphuric acid for a metal, then this volatile acid will be formed. From this it may be concluded that the volatility of the acid should be considered as the cause of the progress of the reaction; and indeed if the acid be soluble but not volatile, or if the reaction take place in an enclosed space where the resulting acid cannot volatilise, or at the ordinary temperature when it does not pass into the state of elastic vapour—then the decomposition does not proceed to the end, but only up to a certain limit. In this respect the explanations given at the beginning of this century by the French chemist Berthollet in his work 'Essai de Statique Chimique' are very important. *The doctrine of Berthollet* starts from the supposition that the chemical reaction of substances is determined not only by the degrees of affinity between the different parts, but also by the relative masses of the reacting substances and by those physical conditions under which the reaction takes place. Two substances containing the elements MX and NY, being brought into contact with each other, form by double decomposition the compounds MY and NX; but the formation of these two new compounds will not proceed to the end unless one of them is removed from the sphere of action. But it can only be removed if it possesses different physical properties from those of the other substances which are present with it. Either it must be a gas while the others are liquid or solid, or an insoluble solid while the others are liquid or soluble. The relative amounts of the resultant substances, if nothing separates out from their intermixture, depend only on the relative quantities of the substances MX and NY, and upon the degrees of attraction existing between the elements M, N, X, and Y; but however great their mass may be, and however considerable the attractions, still in any case if nothing separates out from the sphere of action the decomposition will presently cease, a state of equilibrium will be established, and instead of two there will remain four substances in the mass: namely, a portion of the original bodies MX and NY, and a certain quantity of the newly formed substances MY and NX, if it be assumed that neither MN or XY nor any other substances are produced, and this may for the present[24] be admitted in the case of[434] the double decomposition of salts in which M and X are metals and X and Y haloids. As the ordinary double decomposition here consists merely in the exchange of metals, the above simplification is applicable. The sum total of existing data concerning the double decomposition of salts leads to the conclusion that from salts MX + NY there always arises a certain quantity of NX and MY, as should be the case according to Berthollet's doctrine. A portion of the historical data concerning this subject will be afterwards mentioned, but we will at once proceed to point out the observations made by Spring (1888) which show that *even in a solid state* salts are subject to a similar interchange of metals if in a condition of sufficiently close contact (it requires time, a finely divided state, and intimate mixture). Spring took two non-hygroscopic salts, potassium nitrate, KNO_3, and well-dried sodium acetate, $C_2H_3NaO_2$, and left a mixture of their powders for several months in a desiccator. An interchange of metals took place, as was seen from the fact that the resultant mass rapidly attracted the moisture of the air, owing to the formation of sodium nitrate, $NaNO_3$, and potassium acetate, $C_2H_3KO_2$, both of which are highly hygroscopic.[24 bis]

When Berthollet enunciated his doctrine the present views of atoms and molecules had yet to be developed, and it is now necessary to submit the matter to examination in the light of these conceptions; we will therefore consider the reaction of salts, taking M and N, X and Y as equivalent to each other—that is, as capable of replacing each other 'in toto,' as Na or K,, ½Ca or ½Mg (bivalent elements) replace hydrogen.

And since, according to Berthollet's doctrine, when mMX of one salt comes into contact with nNY of another salt, a certain quantity xMY and xNX is formed, there remains $m - x$ of the salt MX, and $n - x$ of the salt NY. If m be greater than n, then the maximum interchange could lead to $x = n$, whilst from the salts taken there would be formed nMY + nNX + ($m - n$)MX—that is, a portion of one only of the salts taken would remain unchanged because the reaction could only proceed between nMX and nNY. If x were actually equal[435] to n, the mass of the salt MX would not have any influence on the *modus operandi* of the reaction, which is equally in accordance with the teaching of Bergmann, who supposed double reactions to be independent of the mass and determined by affinity only. If M had more affinity for X than for Y, and N more affinity for Y than for X, then according to Bergmann there would be no decomposition whatever, and x would equal 0. If the affinity of M for Y and of N for X were greater than those in the original grouping, then the affinity of M for X and of N for Y would be overcome, and, according to Bergmann's doctrine, complete interchange would take place—*i.e.* x would equal n. According to Berthollet's teaching, a distribution of M and N between X and Y will take place in every case, not only in proportion to the degrees of affinity, but also in proportion to the masses, so that with a small affinity and a large mass the same action can be produced as with a large affinity and a small mass. Therefore, (1) x will always be less than n and their ratio $x \boxed{n}$ less than unity—that is, the decomposition will be expressed by the equation, $mMX + nNY = (m - x)MX + (n - x)NY + xMY + xNX$; (2) by increasing the mass m we increase the decomposition—that is, we increase x and the ratio $x \boxed{(n - x)}$, until with an infinitely large quantity m the fraction $x \boxed{n}$ will equal 1, and the decomposition will be complete, however small the affinities uniting MY and NX may be; and (3) if $m = n$, by taking MX + NY or MY + NX we arrive at one and the same system *in either case*: $(n - x)MX + (n - x)NY + xMY + xNX$. These direct consequences of Berthollet's teaching are verified by experience. Thus, for example, a mixture of solutions of sodium nitrate and potassium chloride in all cases has entirely the same properties as a mixture of solutions of potassium nitrate and sodium chloride, of course on condition that the mixed solutions are of identical elementary composition. But this identity of properties might either proceed from one system of salts passing entirely into the other (Bergmann's hypothesis) in conformity with the predominating affinities (for instance, from KCl + NaNO$_3$ there might arise KNO$_3$ + NaCl, if it be admitted that the affinities of the elements as combined in the latter system are greater than in the former); or, on the other hand, it might be because both systems by the interchange of a portion of their elements give one and the same state of equilibrium, as according to Berthollet's teaching. Experiment proves the latter hypothesis to be the true one. But before citing the most historically important experiments verifying Berthollet's[436] doctrine, we must stop to consider the conception *of the mass* of the reacting substances. Berthollet understood by mass the actual relative quantity of a substance; but now it is impossible to understand this term otherwise than as the number of molecules, for they act as chemical units, and in the special case of double saline decompositions it is better to take it as the number of equivalents. Thus in the reaction NaCl + H$_2$SO$_4$ the salt is taken in one equivalent and the acid in two. If 2NaCl + H$_2$SO$_4$ act, then the number of equivalents are equal, and so on. The *influence of mass* on the amount of decomposition $x \boxed{n}$ forms the root of Berthollet's doctrine, and therefore we will first of all turn our attention to the establishment of this principle in relation to the double decomposition of salts.

About 1840 H. Rose[25] showed that water decomposes metallic sulphides like calcium sulphide, CaS, forming hydrogen sulphide, H$_2$S, notwithstanding the fact that the affinity of hydrogen sulphide, as an acid, for lime, CaH$_2$O$_2$, as a base, causes them to react on each other, forming calcium sulphide and water, CaS + 2H$_2$O. Furthermore, Rose showed that the greater the amount of water acting on the calcium sulphide, the more complete is the decomposition. The results of this reaction are evident from the fact that the hydrogen sulphide formed may be expelled from the solution by heating, and that the resulting lime is sparingly soluble in water. Rose clearly saw from this that such feeble agents, in a chemical sense, as carbonic anhydride and water, by acting in a mass and for long periods of time in nature on the durable rocks, which resist the action of the most powerful acids, are able to bring about chemical change—to extract, for example, from rocks the bases, lime, soda, potash. The influence of the mass of water on antimonious chloride, bismuth nitrate, &c., is essentially of the same character. These substances give up to the water a quantity of acid which is greater in proportion as the mass of the water acting on them is greater.[25 bis]

[437]

Barium sulphate, $BaSO_4$, which is insoluble in water, when fused with sodium carbonate, Na_2CO_3, gives, but not completely, barium carbonate, $BaCO_3$, (also insoluble), and sodium sulphate, Na_2SO_4. If a solution of sodium carbonate acts on precipitated barium sulphate, the same decomposition is also effected (Dulong, Rose), but it is restricted by a limit and requires time. A mixture of sodium carbonate and sulphate is obtained in the solution and a mixture of barium carbonate and sulphate in the precipitate. If the solution be decanted off and a fresh solution of sodium carbonate be poured over the precipitate, then a fresh portion of the barium sulphate passes into barium carbonate, and so by increasing the mass of sodium carbonate it is possible to entirely convert the barium sulphate into barium carbonate. If a definite quantity of sodium sulphate be added to the solution of sodium carbonate, then the latter will have no action whatever on the barium sulphate, because then a system in equilibrium determined by the reverse action of the sodium sulphate on the barium carbonate and by the presence of both sodium carbonate and sulphate in the solution, is at once arrived at. On the other hand, if the mass of the sodium sulphate in the solution be great, then the barium carbonate is reconverted into sulphate until a definite state of equilibrium is attained between the two opposite reactions, producing barium carbonate by the action of the sodium carbonate and barium sulphate by the action of the sodium sulphate.

Another most important principle of Berthollet's teaching is the existence of *a limit of exchange decomposition,* or *the attainment of a state of equilibrium.* In this respect the determinations of Malaguti (1857) are historically the most important. He took a mixture of solutions of equivalent quantities of two salts, MX and NY, and judged the amount of the resulting exchange from the composition of the precipitate produced by the addition of alcohol. When, for example, zinc sulphate and sodium chloride ($ZnSO_4$ and $2NaCl$) were taken, there were produced by exchange sodium sulphate and zinc chloride. A mixture of zinc sulphate and sodium sulphate was precipitated by an excess of alcohol, and it appeared from the composition of the precipitate that 72 per cent. of the salts taken had been decomposed. When, however, a mixture of solutions of sodium sulphate and zinc chloride was taken, the precipitate presented the same composition as before—that is, about 28 per cent. of the salts taken had been subjected to decomposition. In a similar experiment with a mixture of sodium chloride and magnesium sulphate, $2NaCl + MgSO_4$ or $MgCl_2 + Na_2SO_4$, about half of the metals underwent the decomposition, which may be expressed by the equation[438] $4NaCl + 2MgSO_4 = 2NaCl + MgSO_4 + Na_2SO_4 + MgCl_2 = 2Na_2SO_4 + 2MgCl_2$. A no less clear limit expressed itself in another of Malaguti's researches when he investigated the above-mentioned reversible reactions of the insoluble salts of barium. When, for example, barium carbonate and sodium sulphate ($BaCO_3 + Na_2SO_4$) were taken, then about 72 per cent. of the salts were decomposed, that is, were converted into barium sulphate and sodium carbonate. But when the two latter salts were taken, then about 19 per cent. of them passed into barium carbonate and sodium sulphate. Probably the end of the reaction was not reached in either case, because this would require a considerable time and a uniformity of conditions attainable with difficulty.

Gladstone (1855) took advantage of the colour of solutions of different ferric salts for determining the measure of exchange between metals. Thus a solution of ferric thiocyanate has a most intense red colour, and by making a comparison between the colour of the resulting solutions and the colour of solutions of known strength it was possible to judge to a certain degree the quantity of the thiocyanate formed. This colorimetric method of determination has an important significance as being the first in which a method was applied for determining the composition of a solution without the removal of any of its component parts. When Gladstone took equivalent quantities of ferric nitrate and potassium thiocyanate—$Fe(NO_3)_3 + 3KCNS$—only 13 per cent. of the salts underwent decomposition. On increasing the mass of the latter salt the quantity of ferric thiocyanate formed increased, but even when more than 300 equivalents of potassium thiocyanate were taken a portion of the iron still remained as nitrate. It is evident that the affinity acting between Fe and NO_3 and between K and CNS on the one hand, is greater than the affinity acting between Fe and CNS, together with the affinity of K for NO_3, on the other hand. The investigation of the variation of the fluorescence of quinine sulphate, as well as the variation of the rotation of the plane of polarisation of nicotine, gave in the hands of Gladstone many proofs of the entire applicability of Berthollet's doctrine, and in particular demonstrated the influence of mass which forms the chief distinctive feature of the teaching of Berthollet, teaching little appreciated in his own time.

At the beginning of the year 1860, the doctrine of the limit of reaction and of the influence of mass on the process of chemical transformations received a very important support in the researches of Berthelot and P. de Saint-Gilles on the formation of the ethereal salts RX from the alcohols ROH and acids HX, when water is also formed. This conversion is essentially very similar to the formation of salts, but[439] differs in that it proceeds slowly at the ordinary temperature, extending over whole years, and is not complete—that is, it has a distinct limit determined by a reverse reaction; thus an ethereal salt RX with water gives an alcohol ROH and an acid HX—up to that limit generally corresponding with two-thirds of the alcohol taken, if the action proceed between molecular quantities of alcohol and acid. Thus common alcohol, C_2H_5OH, with acetic acid, $HC_2H_3O_2$, gives the following system rapidly when heated, or slowly at the ordinary temperature, $ROH + HX + 2RX + 2H_2O$, whether we start from $3RHO + 3HX$ or from $3RX + 3H_2O$. The process and completion of the reaction in this instance are very easily observed, because the quantity of free acid is easily determined from the amount of alkali requisite for its saturation, as neither alcohol nor ethereal salt acts on litmus or other reagent for acids. Under the influence of an increased mass of alcohol the reaction proceeds further. If two molecules of alcohol, RHO, be taken for every one molecule of acetic acid, HX, then instead of 66 p.c., 83 p.c. of the acid passes into ethereal salt, and with fifty molecules of RHO nearly all the acid is etherised. The researches of Menschutkin in their details touched on many important aspects of the same subject, such as the influence of the composition of the alcohol and acid on the limit and rate of exchange—but these, as well as other details, must be looked for in special treatises on organic and theoretical chemistry. In any case the study of etherification has supplied chemical mechanics with clear and valuable data, which directly confirm the two fundamental propositions of Berthollet; the influence of mass, and the limit of reaction—that is, the equilibrium between opposite reactions. The study of numerous instances of dissociation which we have already touched on, and shall again meet with on several occasions, gave the same results. With respect to double saline decompositions, it is also necessary to mention the researches of Wiedemann on the decomposing action of a mass of water on the ferric salts, which could be determined by measuring the magnetism of the solutions, because the ferric oxide (soluble colloid) set free by the water is less magnetic than the ferric salts.

A very important epoch in the history of Berthollet's doctrine was attained when, in 1867, the Norwegian chemists, Guldberg and Waage, expressed it as an algebraical formula. They defined the active mass as the number of molecules contained in a given volume, and assumed, as follows from the spirit of Berthollet's teaching, that the action between the substances was equal to the product of the masses of the reacting substances. Hence if the salts MX and NY be taken in equivalent quantities ($m = 1$ and $n = 1$) and the salts MY and NX are[440] not added to the mixture but proceed from it, then if k represent the coefficient of the rate of the action of MX on NY and if k' represent the same coefficient for the pair MY and NX, then we shall have at the moment when the decomposition equals x a measure of action for the first pair: $k(1 - x)(1 - x)$ and for the second pair $k'xx$, and a state of equilibrium or limit will be reached when $k(1 - x)^2 = k'x^2$, whence the ratio $k/k' = [x/(1 - x)]^2$. Therefore in the case of the action of alcohol on an acid, when $x = ⅔$, the magnitude $k/k' = 4$, that is, the reaction of the alcohol on the acid is four times as fast as that of the ethereal salt on water. If the ratio k/k' be known, then the influence of mass may be easily determined from it. Thus if instead of one molecule of alcohol two be taken, then the equation will be $k(2 - x)(1 - x) = k'xx$, whence $x = 0·85$ or 85 percent., which is close to the result of experiment. If 300 molecules of alcohol be taken, then x proves to be approximately 100 per cent., which is also found to be the case by experiment.[26]

But it is impossible to subject the formation of salts to any process directly analogous to that which is so conveniently effected in etherification. Many efforts have, however, been made to solve the problem of the measure of reaction in this case also. Thus, for example, Khichinsky (1866), Petrieff (1885), and many others investigated the distribution of metals and haloid groups in the case of one metal and several haloids taken in excess, as acids; or conversely with an excess of bases, the distribution of these bases with relation to an acid; in cases where a portion of the substances forms a precipitate and a portion remains in solution. But such complex cases, although they in general confirm Berthollet's teaching (for instance, a solution of silver nitrate gives some silver oxide with lead oxide, and a solution of nitrate of lead precipitates some lead oxide under the action of silver oxide, as Petrieff demonstrated), still, owing to the complexity of the phenomena (for instance, the formation of basic and double salts), they cannot give simple results. But much more instructive and complete are researches like those made by Pattison Muir (1876), who took the simple case of the precipitation of calcium carbonate, $CaCO_3$, from the mixture of solutions of calcium chloride and sodium or potassium carbonate, and found in this case that not only was the[441] rate of action (for example, in the case of $CaCl_2 + Na_2CO_3$, 75 per cent. of $CaCO_3$ was precipitated in five minutes, 85 per cent. in thirty minutes, and 94 per cent. in two days) determined by the temperature, relative mass, and amount of water (a large mass of water decreases the rate), but that the limit of decomposition was also dependent on these influences. However, even in researches of this kind the conditions of reaction are complicated by the non-uniformity of the media, inasmuch as a portion of the substance is obtained or remains in the form of a precipitate, so that the system is heterogeneous. The investigation of double saline decompositions offers many difficulties which cannot be considered as yet entirely overcome. Although many efforts have long since been made, the majority of the researches were carried on in aqueous solutions, and as water is itself a saline compound and able to combine with salts and enter into double decomposition with them, such reactions taking place in solutions in reality present very complex cases.[27] In this sense the reaction between alcohols and acids[442] is much more simple, and therefore its significance in confirmation of Berthollet's doctrine is of particular importance. The only cases[443] which can be compared with these reactions for simplicity are those exchange decompositions investigated by G. G. Gustavson, which[444] take place between CCl_4 and RBr_n on the one hand, and CBr_4 and RCl_n on the other. This case is convenient for investigation inasmuch as the RCl_n and RBr_n taken (such as BCl_3, $SiCl_4$, $TiCl_4$, $POCl_3$, and $SnCl_4$) belong to those substances which are decomposed by water, whilst CCl_4 and CBr_4 are not decomposed by water; and therefore, by heating, for instance, a mixture of CCl_4 + $SiBr_4$ it is possible to arrive at a conclusion as to the amount of interchange by treating the product with water, which decomposes the $SiBr_4$ left unchanged and the $SiCl_4$ formed by the exchange, and therefore by determining the composition of the product acted on by the water it is possible to form a conclusion as to the amount of decomposition. The mixture was always formed with equivalent quantities—for instance, $4BCl_3$ + $3CBr_4$. It appeared that there was no exchange whatever on simple intermixture, but that it proceeded slowly, when the mixture was heated (for example, with the mixture above mentioned at 123° 4·86 per cent. of Cl was replaced by Br after 14 days' heating, and 6·83 per cent. after 28 days, and 10·12 per cent. when heated at 150° for 60 days). A limit was always reached which corresponded with that of the complemental system; in the given instance the system $4BBr_3$ + $3CCl_4$. In this last 89·97 per cent. of bromine in the BBr_3 was replaced by chlorine; that is, there were obtained 89·97 molecules of BCl_3 and there remained 10·02 molecules of BBr_3, and therefore the same state of equilibrium was reached as that given by the system $4BCl_3$ + $3CBr_4$. Both systems gave one and the same state of equilibrium at the limit, which is in agreement with Berthollet's doctrine.[28]

[445]

Thus we now find ample confirmation from various quarters for the following rules of Berthollet, applying them to double saline decompositions: 1. From two salts MX and NY containing different haloids and metals there result from their reaction two others, MY and NX, but such a substitution will not proceed to the end unless one product passes from the sphere of action. 2. This reaction is limited by the existence of an equilibrium between MX, NY, MY, and NX, because a reverse reaction is quite as possible as the direct reaction. 3. This limit is determined both by the measure of the active affinities and by the relative masses of the substances as measured by the number of the reacting molecules. 4. Other conditions being constant, the chemical action is proportional to the product of the chemical masses in action.[29]

[446]

Thus if the salts MX and NY after reaction partly formed salts MY and NX, then a state of equilibrium is reached and the reaction ceases; but if one of the resultant compounds, in virtue of its physical properties, passes from the sphere of action of the remaining substances, then the reaction will continue. This exit from the sphere of action depends on the physical properties of the substance and on the conditions under which the reaction takes place. Thus, for instance, the salt NX may, in the case of reaction between solutions, separate as a precipitate, an insoluble substance, while the other three substances remain in solution, or it may pass into vapour, and in this manner also pass away from the sphere of action of the remaining substances. Let us now suppose that it passes away in some form or other from the sphere of action of the remaining substances—for instance, that it is transformed into a precipitate or vapour—then a fresh reaction will set in and a re-formation of the salt NX. If this be removed, then, although the quantity of the elements N and X in the mass will be diminished, still, according to Berthollet's law, a certain amount of NX should be again formed. When this substance is again formed, then, owing to its physical properties, it will again pass away; hence the reaction, in consequence of the physical properties of the resultant substances, is able to proceed to completion notwithstanding the possible weakness of the attraction existing between the elements entering into the composition of the resultant substance NX. Naturally, if the resultant substance is formed of elements having a considerable degree of affinity, then the complete decomposition is considerably facilitated.

Such a representation of the *modus operandi* of chemical transformations is applicable with great clearness to a number of reactions studied in chemistry, and, what is especially important, the application of this aspect of Berthollet's teaching does not in any way require the determination of the measure of affinity acting between the substances present. For instance, the action of ammonia on solutions[447] of salts; the displacement, by its means, of basic hydrates insoluble in water; the separation of volatile nitric acid by the aid of non-volatile sulphuric acid, as well as the decomposition of common salt by means of sulphuric acid, when gaseous hydrochloric acid is formed—may be taken as examples of reactions which proceed to the end, inasmuch as one of the resultant substances is entirely removed from the sphere of action, but they in no way indicate the measure of affinity.[30]

As a proof that double decompositions like the above are actually accomplished in the sense of Berthollet's doctrine, the fact may be cited that common salt may be entirely decomposed by nitric acid, and nitre may be completely decomposed by hydrochloric acid, just as they are decomposed by sulphuric acid; but this only takes place when, in the first instance, an excess of nitric acid is taken, and in the second instance, an excess of hydrochloric acid, for a given quantity of the sodium salt, and when the resultant acid passes off. If sodium chloride be put into a porcelain evaporating basin, nitric acid added to it, and the mixture heated, then both hydrochloric and nitric acids are expelled by the heat. Thus the nitric acid partially acts on the sodium chloride, but on heating, as both acids are volatile, they are both converted into[448] vapour; and therefore the residue will contain a mixture of a certain quantity of the sodium chloride taken and of the sodium nitrate formed. If a fresh quantity of nitric acid be then added, reaction will again set in, a certain portion of hydrochloric acid is again evolved, and on heating is expelled together with nitric acid. If this be repeated several times, it is possible to expel all the hydrochloric acid, and to obtain sodium nitrate only in the residue. If, on the contrary, we take sodium nitrate and add hydrochloric acid to it in an aqueous solution, a certain quantity of the hydrochloric acid displaces a portion of the nitric acid, and on heating the excess of hydrochloric acid passes away with the nitric acid formed. On repeating this process, it is possible to displace the nitric acid with an excess of hydrochloric acid, just as it was possible to displace the hydrochloric acid by an excess of nitric acid. The influence of the mass of the substance in action and the influence of volatility are here very distinctly seen. Hence it may be affirmed that sulphuric acid does not displace hydrochloric acid because of an especially high degree of affinity, but that this reaction is only carried on to the end because the sulphuric acid is not volatile, whilst the hydrochloric acid which is formed is volatile.

The preparation of hydrochloric acid in the laboratory and on a large scale is based upon these data. In the first instance, an excess of sulphuric acid is employed in order that the reaction may proceed easily at a low temperature, whilst on a large scale, when it is necessary to economise every material, equivalent quantities are taken in order to obtain the normal salt Na_2SO_4 and not the acid salt, which would require twice as much acid. The hydrochloric acid evolved is a gas which is very soluble in water. It is most frequently used in practice in this state of solution under the name of *muriatic acid*.[31]

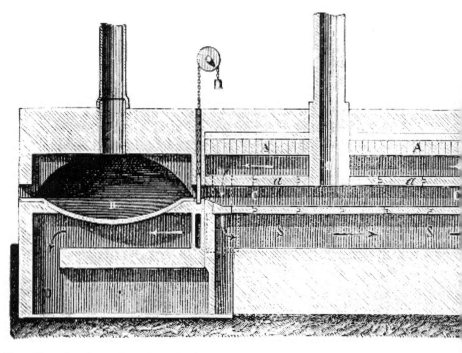

FIG. 65.—Section of a salt-cake furnace. B, pan in which the sodium chloride and sulphuric acid are first mixed and heated. C, muffle for the ultimate decomposition.

In chemical works the decomposition of sodium chloride by means of sulphuric acid is carried on on a very large scale, chiefly with a view to the preparation of normal sodium sulphate, the hydrochloric acid being a bye-product.[31 bis] The furnace employed is termed a *salt cake furnace*. It is represented in fig. 65, and consists of the following two parts: the pan B and the roaster C, or enclosed space built up of large bricks *a* and enveloped on all sides by the smoke and flames from the fire grate, F. The ultimate decomposition of the salt by the sulphuric acid is accomplished in the roaster. But the first decomposition of sodium chloride by sulphuric acid does not require so high a temperature as the ultimate decomposition, and is therefore carried on in the front and cooler portion, B, whose bottom is heated by gas flues. When the reaction in this portion ceases and the evolution of hydrochloric acid stops, then the mass, which contains about half of the sodium chloride still undecomposed, and the sulphuric acid in the form of acid sodium sulphate, is removed from B and thrown into the roaster C, where the action is completed. Normal sodium sulphate, which we shall afterwards describe, remains in the roaster. It is employed both directly in the manufacture of glass, and in the preparation of other sodium compounds—for instance, in the[450] preparation of soda ash, as will afterwards be described. For the present we will only turn our attention to the hydrochloric acid evolved in B and C.

The hydrochloric acid gas evolved is subjected to condensation by dissolving it in water.[32] If the apparatus in which the decomposition is accomplished were hermetically closed, and only presented one outlet, then the escape of the hydrochloric acid would only proceed through the escape pipe intended for this purpose. But as it is impossible to construct a perfectly hermetically closed furnace of this kind, it is necessary to increase the draught by artificial means, or to oblige the hydrochloric acid gas to pass through those arrangements in which it is to be condensed. This is done by connecting the ends of the tubes through which the hydrochloric acid gas escapes from the furnace with high chimneys, where a strong draught is set up from the combustion of the fuel. This causes a current of hydrochloric acid gas to pass through the absorbing apparatus in a definite direction. Here it encounters a current of water flowing in the opposite direction, by which it is absorbed. It is not customary to cause the acid to pass through the water, but only to bring it into contact with the surface of the water. The absorption apparatus consists of large earthenware vessels having four orifices, two above and two lateral ones in the wide central portion of each vessel. The upper orifices serve for connecting the vessels together, and the hydrochloric acid gas escaping from the furnace passes through these tubes. The water for absorbing the acid enters at the upper, and[451] flows out from the lower, vessel, passing through the lateral orifices in the vessels. The water flows from the chimney towards the furnace and it is therefore evident that the outflowing water will be the most saturated with acid, of which it actually contains about 20 per cent. The absorption in these vessels is not complete. The ultimate absorption of the hydrochloric acid is carried on in the so-called *coke towers*, which usually consist of two adjacent chimneys. A lattice-work of bricks is laid on the bottom of these towers, on which coke is piled up to the top of the tower. Water, distributing itself over the coke, trickles down to the bottom of the tower, and in so doing absorbs the hydrochloric acid gas rising upwards.

It will be readily understood that hydrochloric acid may be obtained from all other metallic chlorides.[33] It is frequently formed in other reactions, many of which we shall meet with in the further course of this work. It is, for instance, formed by the action of water on sulphur chloride, phosphorus chloride, antimony chloride, &c.

Hydrochloric acid is a colourless gas having a pungent suffocating odour and an acid taste. This gas fumes in air and attracts moisture, because it forms vapour containing a compound of hydrochloric acid and water.

Hydrochloric acid is liquefied by cold, and under a pressure of 40 atmospheres, into a colourless liquid of sp. gr. 0·908 at 0°,[34] boiling point -35° and absolute boiling point +52°. We have already seen (Chapter I.) that hydrochloric acid combines very energetically *with water*, and in so doing evolves a considerable amount of heat. The solution saturated in the cold attains a density 1·23. On heating such a solution containing about 45 parts of acid per 100 parts, the hydrochloric[452] acid gas is expelled with only a slight admixture of aqueous vapour. But it is impossible to entirely separate the whole of the hydrochloric acid from the water by this means, as could be done in the case of an ammoniacal solution. The temperature required for the evolution of the gas rises and reaches 110°–111°, and after this remains constant—that is, a solution having a constant boiling point is obtained (as with HNO_3), which, however, does not (Roscoe and Dittmar) present a constant composition under different pressures, because the hydrate is decomposed in distillation, as is seen from the determinations of its vapour density (Bineau). Judging from the facts (1) that with decrease of the pressure under which the distillation proceeds the solution of constant boiling point approaches to a composition of 25 p.c. of hydrochloric acid,[35] (2) that by passing a stream of dry air through a solution of hydrochloric acid there is obtained in the residue a solution which also approaches to 25 p.c. of acid, and more nearly as the temperature falls,[36] (3) that many of the properties of solutions of hydrochloric acid vary distinctly according as they contain more or less than 25 p.c. of hydrochloric acid (for instance, antimonious sulphide gives hydrogen sulphide with a stronger acid, but is not acted on by a weaker solution, also a stronger solution fumes in the air, &c.), and (4) that the composition $HCl,6H_2O$ corresponds with 25·26 p.c. HCl—judging from all these data, and also from the loss of tension which occurs in the combination of hydrochloric acid with water, it may be said that they form a *definite hydrate* of the composition $HCl,6H_2O$. Besides this hydrate there exists also a crystallo-hydrate, $HCl,2H_2O$,[37] which is formed by the absorption of hydrochloric acid by a saturated solution at a temperature of -23°. It crystallises and melts at -18°.[38]

The mean specific gravities at 15°, taking water at its maximum[453] density (4°) as 10,000, for solutions containing *p* per cent. of hydrogen chloride are—

p	*S*	*p*	*S*
5	10,242	25	11,266
10	10,490	30	11,522

15 10,744 35 11,773

20 11,001 40 11,997

The formula $S = 9{,}991 \cdot 6 + 49 \cdot 43p + 0 \cdot 0571p^2$, up to $p = 25 \cdot 26$, which answers to the hydrate $HCl,6H_2O$ mentioned above, gives the specific gravity. Above this percentage $S = 9{,}785 \cdot 1 + 65 \cdot 10p - 0 \cdot 240p^2$. The[454] rise of specific gravity with an increase of percentage (or the differential ds/dp) reaches a maximum at about 25 p.c.[39] The intermediate solution, $HCl,6H_2O$, is further distinguished by the fact that the variation of the specific gravity with the variation of temperature is a constant quantity, so that the specific gravity of this solution is equal to $11{,}352 \cdot 7(1 - 0 \cdot 000447t)$, where $0 \cdot 000447$ is the coefficient of expansion of the solution.[40] In the case of more dilute solutions, as with water, the specific gravity per $1°$ (or the differential $ds \, \boxed{dt}$) rises with a rise of temperature.[41]

$p =$ 0   5 10 15 20

$S_0 - S_{15} =$ $7 \cdot 2$ 23 38 52 64

$S_{15} - S_{130} =$ $34 \cdot 1$ 42 50 59 67

Whilst for solutions which contain a greater proportion of hydrogen chloride than $HCl,6H_2O$, these coefficients *decrease* with a rise of temperature; for instance, for 30 p.c. of hydrogen chloride $S_0 - S_{15} = 88$ and $S_{15} - S_{30} = 87$ (according to Marignac's data). In the case of $HCl,6H_2O$ these differences are constant, and equal 76.

Thus the formation of two definite hydrates, $HCl,2H_2O$ and $HCl,6H_2O$, between hydrochloric acid and water may be accepted upon the basis of many facts. But both of them, if they occur in a liquid state, dissociate with great facility into hydrogen chloride and water, and are completely decomposed when distilled.

All solutions of hydrochloric acid present the properties of an energetic acid. They not only transform blue vegetable colouring matter into red, and disengage carbonic acid gas from carbonates, &c., but they also entirely saturate bases, even such energetic ones as potash, lime, &c. In a dry state, however, hydrochloric acid does not alter[455] vegetable dyes, and does not effect many double decompositions which easily take place in the presence of water. This is explained by the fact that the gaso-elastic state of the hydrochloric acid prevents its entering into reaction. However, incandescent iron, zinc, sodium, &c., act on gaseous hydrochloric acid, displacing the hydrogen and leaving half a volume of hydrogen for each volume of hydrochloric acid gas; this reaction may serve for determining the composition of hydrochloric acid. Combined with water hydrochloric acid acts as an acid much resembling nitric acid[42] in its energy and in many of its reactions; however, the latter contains oxygen, which is disengaged with great ease, and so very frequently acts as an oxidiser, which hydrochloric acid is not capable of doing. The majority of metals (even those which do not displace the H from H_2SO_4, but which, like copper, decompose it to the limit of SO_2) displace the hydrogen from hydrochloric acid. Thus hydrogen is disengaged by the action of zinc, and even of copper and tin.[42 bis] Only a few metals withstand its action; for example, gold and platinum. Lead in compact masses is only acted on feebly, because the lead chloride formed is insoluble and prevents the further action of the acid on the metal. The same is to be remarked with respect to the feeble action of hydrochloric acid on mercury and silver, because the compounds of these metals, AgCl and HgCl, are insoluble in water. Metallic chlorides are not only formed by the action of hydrochloric acid on the metals, but also by many other methods; for instance, by the action of hydrochloric acid on the carbonates, oxides, and hydroxides, and also by the action of chlorine on metals and certain of their compounds. Metallic chlorides have a composition MCl; for example, NaCl, KCl, AgCl, HgCl, if the metal replaces hydrogen equivalent for equivalent, or, as it is said, if it be monatomic or univalent. In the case of bivalent metals, they have a composition MCl_2; for example, $CaCl_2$, $CuCl_2$, $PbCl_2$, $HgCl_2$, $FeCl_2$, $MnCl_2$. The composition of the haloid salts of other metals presents a further variation; for example, $AlCl_3$, $PtCl_4$, &c. Many metals, for instance Fe, give several degrees of combination with chlorine ($FeCl_2$, $FeCl_3$) as with hydrogen. In their composition the metallic chlorides differ from the corresponding oxides, in that the O is replaced by Cl_2, as should follow from the law of substitution, because oxygen gives OH_2, and is[456] consequently bivalent, whilst chlorine forms HCl, and is therefore univalent. So, for instance, ferrous oxide, FeO, corresponds with ferrous chloride, $FeCl_2$, and the oxide Fe_2O_3 with ferric chloride, which is also seen from the origin of these compounds, for $FeCl_2$ is obtained by the action of hydrochloric acid on ferrous oxide or carbonate and $FeCl_3$ by its action on ferric oxide. In a word, all the typical properties of acids are shown by hydrochloric acid, and all the typical properties of salts in the metallic chlorides derived from it. Acids and salts composed like HCl and M_nCl_{2m} without any oxygen bear the name of haloid salts; for instance, HCl is a haloid acid, NaCl a haloid salt, chlorine a halogen. The capacity of hydrochloric acid to give, by its action on bases, MO, a metallic chloride, MCl_2, and water, is limited at high temperatures by the reverse reaction $MCl_2 + H_2O = MO + 2HCl$, and the more pronounced are the basic properties of MO the feebler is the reverse action, while for feebler bases such as Al_2O_3, MgO, &c., this reverse reaction proceeds with ease. Metallic chlorides corresponding with the peroxides either do not exist, or are easily decomposed with the disengagement of chlorine. Thus there is no compound $BaCl_4$ corresponding with the peroxide BaO_2. Metallic chlorides having the general aspect of salts, like their representative sodium chloride, are, as a rule, easily fusible, more so than the oxides (for instance, CaO is infusible at a furnace heat, whilst $CaCl_2$ is easily fused) and many other salts. Under the action of heat many chlorides are more stable than the oxides, some can even be converted into vapour; thus corrosive sublimate, $HgCl_2$, is particularly volatile, whilst the oxide HgO decomposes at a red heat. Silver chloride, AgCl, is fusible and is decomposed with difficulty, whilst Ag_2O is easily decomposed. The majority of the metallic chlorides are soluble in water, but silver chloride, cuprous chloride, mercurous chloride, and lead chloride are sparingly soluble in water, and are therefore easily obtained as precipitates when a solution of the salts of these metals is mixed with a solution of any chloride or even with hydrochloric acid. The metal contained in a haloid salt may often be replaced by another metal, or even by hydrogen, just as is the case with a metal in an oxide. Thus copper displaces mercury from a solution of mercuric chloride, $HgCl_2 + Cu = CuCl_2 + Hg$, and hydrogen at a red heat displaces silver from silver chloride, $2AgCl + H_2 = Ag_2 + 2HCl$. These, and a whole series of similar reactions, form the typical methods of double saline decompositions. The measure of decomposition and the conditions under which reactions of double saline decompositions proceed in one or in the other direction are determined by the properties of the compounds which take part in the reaction, and of those capable of formation at the[457] temperature, &c., as was shown in the preceding portions of this chapter, and as will be frequently found hereafter.

If hydrochloric acid enters into double decomposition with basic oxides and their hydrates, this is only due to its acid properties; and for the same reason it rarely enters into double decomposition with acids and acid anhydrides. Sometimes, however, it combines with the latter, as, for instance, with the anhydride of sulphuric acid, forming the compound SO_3HCl; and in other cases it acts on acids, giving up its hydrogen to their oxygen and forming chlorine, as will be seen in the following chapter.

Hydrochloric acid, as may already be concluded from the composition of its molecule, belongs to the monobasic acids, and does not, therefore, give true acid salts (like $HNaSO_4$ or $HNaCO_3$); nevertheless many metallic chlorides, formed from powerful bases, are capable of *combining with hydrochloric acid*, just as they combine with water, or with ammonia, or as they give double salts. Compounds have long been known of hydrochloric acid with auric, platinic, and antimonious chlorides, and other similar metallic chlorides corresponding with very feeble bases. But Berthelot,

Engel, and others have shown that the capacity of HCl for combining with M_nCl_m is much more frequently encountered than was previously supposed. Thus, for instance, dry hydrochloric acid when passed into a solution of zinc chloride (containing an excess of the salt) gives in the cold ($0°$) a compound $HCl,ZnCl_2,2H_2O$, and at the ordinary temperature $HCl,2ZnCl_2,2H_2O$, just as it is able at low temperatures to form the crystallo-hydrate $ZnCl_2,3H_2O$ (Engel, 1886). Similar compounds are obtained with $CdCl_2,CuCl_2$, $HgCl_2,Fe_2Cl_6$, &c. (Berthelot, Ditte, Cheltzoff, Lachinoff, and others). These compounds with hydrochloric acid are generally more soluble in water than the metallic chlorides themselves, so that whilst hydrochloric acid decreases the solubility of M_nCl_m, corresponding with energetic bases (for instance, sodium or barium chlorides), it increases the solubility of the metallic chlorides corresponding with feeble bases (cadmium chloride, ferric chloride, &c.) Silver chloride, which is insoluble in water, is soluble in hydrochloric acid. Hydrochloric acid also combines with certain unsaturated hydrocarbons (for instance, with turpentine, $C_{10}H_{16},2HCl$) and their derivatives. *Sal-ammoniac*, or ammonia hydrochloride, $NH_4Cl = NH_3,HCl$, also belongs to this class of compounds.[43] If hydrogen chloride gas be mixed with ammonia gas a solid compound consisting[458] of equal volumes of each is immediately formed. The same compound is obtained on mixing solutions of the two gases. It is also produced by the action of hydrochloric acid on ammonium carbonate. Sal-ammoniac is usually prepared, in practice, by the last method.[44] The specific gravity of sal-ammoniac is $1·55$. We have already seen (Chapter VI.) that sal-ammoniac, like all other ammonium salts, easily decomposes; for instance, by volatilisation with alkalis, and even partially when its solution is boiled. The other properties and reactions of sal-ammoniac, especially in solution, fully recall those already mentioned in speaking of sodium chloride. Thus, for instance, with silver nitrate it gives a precipitate of silver chloride; with sulphuric acid it gives hydrochloric acid and ammonium sulphate, and it forms double salts with certain metallic chlorides and other salts.[45]

Footnotes:

[1] But it is impossible to foretell all the compounds formed by an element from its atomicity or valency, because the atomicity of the elements is variable, and furthermore this variability is not identical for different elements. In CO_2, COX_2, CH_4, and the multitude of carbon compounds corresponding with them, the C is quadrivalent, but in CO either the carbon must be taken as bivalent or the atomicity of oxygen be accounted as variable. Moreover, carbon is an example of an element which preserves its atomicity to a greater degree than most of the other elements. Nitrogen in NH_3, $NH_2(OH)$, N_2O_3, and even in CNH, must be

considered as trivalent, but in NH_4Cl, $NO_2(OH)$, and in all their corresponding compounds it is necessarily pentavalent. In N_2O, if the atomicity of oxygen = 2, nitrogen has an uneven atomicity (1, 3, 5), whilst in NO it is bivalent. If sulphur be bivalent, like oxygen, in many of its compounds (for example, H_2S, SCl_2, KHS, &c.), then it could not be foreseen from this that it would form SO_2, SO_3, SCl_4, $SOCl_2$, and a series of similar compounds in which its atomicity must be acknowledged as greater than 2. Thus SO_2, sulphurous anhydride, has many points in common with CO_2, and if carbon be quadrivalent then the S in SO_2 is quadrivalent. Therefore the principle of atomicity (valency) of the elements cannot be considered established as the basis for the study of the elements, although it gives an easy method of grasping many analogies. I consider the four following as the chief obstacles to acknowledging the atomicity of the elements as a primary conception for the consideration of the properties of the elements: 1. Such univalent elements as H, Cl, &c., appear in a free state as molecules H_2, Cl_2, &c., and are consequently like the univalent radicles CH_3, OH, CO_2H, &c., which, as might be expected, appear as C_2H_6, O_2H_2, $C_2O_4H_2$ (ethane, hydrogen peroxide, oxalic acid), whilst on the other hand, potassium and sodium (perhaps also iodine at a high temperature) contain only one atom, K, Na, in the molecule in a free state. Hence it follows that *free affinities* may exist. Granting this, nothing prevents the assumption that free affinities exist in all unsaturated compounds; for example, two free affinities in NH_3. If such instances of free affinities be admitted, then all the possible advantages to be gained by the application of the doctrine of atomicity (valency) are lost. 2. There are instances—for example, Na_2H—where univalent elements are combined in molecules which are more complex than R_2, and form molecules, R_3, R_4, &c.; this may again be either taken as evidence of the existence of free affinities, or else necessitates such primary univalent elements as sodium and hydrogen being considered as variable in their atomicity. 3. The periodic system of the elements, with which we shall afterwards become acquainted, shows that there is a law or rule for the variation of the forms of oxygen and hydrogen compounds; chlorine is univalent with respect to hydrogen, and septavalent with respect to oxygen; sulphur is bivalent to hydrogen, and sexavalent to oxygen; phosphorus is trivalent to hydrogen and pentavalent in respect to oxygen—the sum is in every case equal to 8. Only carbon and its analogues (for example, silicon) are quadrivalent to both hydrogen and oxygen. Hence the power of the elements to change their atomicity is an essential part of their nature, and therefore constant valency cannot he considered as a fundamental property. 4. Crystallo-hydrates (for instance, $NaCl,2H_2O$, or $NaBr,2H_2O$), double salts (such as $PtCl_4,2KCl,H_2SiF_6$, &c.), and similar complex compounds (and, according to Chap. L., solutions also) demonstrate the capacity not only of the elements themselves, but also of their saturated and limiting compounds, of entering into further combination. Therefore the admission of a definite limited atomicity of the elements includes in itself an admission of limitation which is not in accordance with the nature of chemical reactions.

[2] The primary formations are those which do not bear any distinct traces of having been deposited from water (have not a stratified formation and contain no remains of animal or vegetable life), occur under the sedimentary formations of the earth, and are everywhere uniform in composition and structure, the latter being generally distinctly crystalline. If it be assumed that the earth was originally in a molten condition, the first primary formations are those which formed the first solid crust of the earth. But even with this hypothesis of the earth's origin, it is necessary to admit that the first aqueous deposits must have caused a change in the original crust of the earth, and therefore under the head of primary formations must be understood the most ancient of the products of decomposition (mostly by atmospheric, aqueous, and organic agency, &c.), from which all the rocks and substances of the earth's surface have arisen. In speaking of the origin of one or another substance, we can only, on the basis of facts, descend to the primary formations, of which granite, gneiss, and trachyte may be taken as examples.

[2 bis] Chloride of sodium has been found to occur in the atmosphere in the form of a fine dust; in the lower strata it is present in larger quantities than in the upper, so that the rain water falling on mountains contains less NaCl than that falling in valleys. Müntz (1891) found that a litre of rain water collected on the summit of the Pic du Midi (2,877 metres above the sea level) contained $0 \cdot 34$ milligram of chloride of sodium, while a litre of rain collected from the valley contained $2 \cdot 5$–$7 \cdot 6$ milligrams.

[3] The extraction of the potassium salts (or so-called summer salts) was carried on at the Isle of Camarga about 1870, when I had occasion to visit that spot. At the present time the deposits of Stassfurt provide a much cheaper salt, owing to the evaporation and separation of the salt being carried on there by natural means and only requiring a treatment and refining, which is also necessary in addition for the 'summer salt' obtained from sea-water.

[4] The double salt $KCl,MgCl_2$ is a crystallohydrate of KCl and $MgCl_2$, and is only formed from solutions containing an excess of magnesium chloride, because water decomposes this double salt, extracting the more soluble magnesium chloride from it.

[5] Owing to the fundamental property of salts of interchanging their metals, it cannot be said that sea water contains this or that salt, but only that it contains certain amounts of certain metals M (univalent like Na and

K, and bivalent like Mg and Ca), and haloids X (univalent like Cl, Br, and bivalent like SO_4, CO_3), which are disposed in every possible kind of grouping; for instance, K as KCl, KBr, K_2SO_4, Mg as $MgCl_2$, $MgBr_2$, $MgSO_4$, and so on for all the other metals. In evaporation different salts separate out consecutively only because they reach saturation. A proof of this may be seen in the fact that a solution of a mixture of sodium chloride and magnesium sulphate (both of which salts are obtained from sea water, as was mentioned above), when evaporated, deposits crystals of these salts, but when refrigerated (if the solution be sufficiently saturated) the salt $Na_2SO_4,10H_2O$ is first deposited because it is the first to arrive at saturation at low temperatures. Consequently this solution contains $MgCl_2$ and Na_2SO_4, besides $MgSO_4$ and NaCl. So it is with sea water.

[6] The salt extracted from water is piled up in heaps and left exposed to the action of rain water, which purifies it, owing to the water becoming saturated with sodium chloride and then no longer dissolving it, but washing out the impurities.

[7] When the German savants pointed out the exact locality of the Stassfurt salt-beds and their depth below the surface, on the basis of information collected from various quarters respecting bore-holes and the direction of the strata, and when the borings, conducted by the Government, struck a salt-bed which was bitter and unfit for use, there was a great outcry against science, and the doubtful result even caused the cessation of the further work of deepening the shafts. It required a great effort to persuade the Government to continue the work. Now, when the pure salt encountered below forms one of the important riches of Germany, and when those 'refuse salts' have proved to be most valuable (as a source of potassium and magnesium), we should see in the utilisation of the Stassfurt deposits one of the conquests of science for the common welfare.

[7 bis] In Western Europe, deposits of rock salt have long been known at Wieliczka, near Cracow, and at Cardona in Spain. In Russia the following deposits are known: (a) the vast masses of rock salt (3 square kilometres area and up to 140 metres thick) lying directly on the surface of the earth at Iletzky Zastchit, on the left bank of the river Ural, in the Government of Orenburg; (b) the Chingaksky deposit, 90 versts from the river Volga, in the Enotaeffsky district of the Government of Astrakhan; (c) the Kulepinsky (and other) deposits (whose thickness attains 150 metres), on the Araks, in the Government of Erivan in the Caucasus; (d) the Katchiezmansky deposit in the province of Kars; (e) the Krasnovodsky deposit in the Trans-Caspian province; and (f) the Bardymkulsky salt mines in Kokhand.

[8] The fracture of rock salt generally shows the presence of interlayers of impurities which are sometimes very small in weight, but visible owing to their refraction. In the excellently laid out salt mines of Briansk I counted (1888), if my memory does not deceive me, on an average ten interlayers per metre of thickness, between which the salt was in general very pure, and in places quite transparent. If this be the case, then there would be 350 interlayers for the whole thickness (about 35 metres) of the bed. They probably correspond with the yearly deposition of the salt. In this case the deposition would have extended over more than 300 years. This should be observable at the present day in lakes where the salt is saturated and in course of deposition.

[9] My own investigations have shown that not only the sulphates, but also the potassium salts, are entirely removed by this method.

[10] According to the determinations of Klodt, the Briansk rock salt withstands a pressure of 340 kilograms per square centimetre, whilst glass withstands 1,700 kilos. In this respect salt is twice as secure as bricks, and therefore immense masses may be extracted from underground workings with perfect safety, without having recourse to brickwork supports, merely taking advantage of the properties of the salt itself.

[11] To obtain well-formed crystals, a saturated solution is mixed with ferric chloride, several small crystals of sodium chloride are placed at the bottom, and the solution is allowed to evaporate slowly in a vessel with a loose-fitting cover. Octahedral crystals are obtained by the addition of borax, urea, &c., to the solution. Very fine crystals are formed in a mass of gelatinous silica.

[12] If a solution of sodium chloride be slowly heated from above, where the evaporation takes place, then the upper layer will become saturated before the lower and cooler layers, and therefore crystallisation will begin on the surface, and the crystals first formed will float, having also dried from above, on the surface until they become quite soaked. Being heavier than the solution the crystals are partially immersed under it, and the following crystallisation, also proceeding on the surface, will only form crystals along the side of the original crystals. A funnel is formed in this manner. It will be borne on the surface like a boat (if the liquid be quiescent), because it will grow more from the upper edges. We can thus understand this at first sight strange funnel form of crystallisation of salt. In explanation why the crystallisation under the above conditions begins at the surface and not at the lower layers, it must be mentioned that the specific gravity of a crystal of sodium chloride = 2·16, and that of a solution saturated at 25° contains 26·7 p.c. of salt and has a specific gravity at 25°/4° of 1·2004; at 15° a saturated solution contains 26·5 p.c. of salt and

has a sp. gr. 1·203 at 15°/4°. Hence a solution saturated at a higher temperature is specifically lighter, notwithstanding the greater amount of salt it contains. With many substances *surface crystallisation* cannot take place because their solubility increases more rapidly with the temperature than their specific gravity decreases. In this case the saturated solution will always be in the lower layers, where also the crystallisation will take place. Besides which it may be added that as a consequence of the properties of water and solutions, when they are heated from above (for instance, by the sun's rays), the warmer layers being the lightest remain above, whilst when heated from below they rise to the top. For this reason the water at great depths below the surface is always cold, which has long been known. These circumstances, as well as those observed by Soret (Chapter I., Note 19), explain the great differences of density and temperature, and in the amount of salts held in the oceans at different latitudes (in polar and tropical climes) and at various depths.

[13] By combining the results of Poggiale, Müller, and Karsten (they are evidently more accurate than those of Gay-Lussac and others) I found that a saturated solution at $t°$, from 0° to 108°, contains $35·7 + 0·024t + 0·0002t^2$ grams of salt per 100 grams of water. This formula gives a solubility at 0° = 35·7 grams (= 26·3 p.c.), whilst according to Karsten it is 36·09, Poggiale 35·5, and Müller 35·6 grams.

[14] Perfectly pure *fused* salt is not hygroscopic, according to Karsten, whilst the crystallised salt, even when quite pure, attracts as much as 0·6 p.c. of water from moist air, according to Stas. (In the Briansk mines, where the temperature throughout the whole year is about +10°, it may be observed, as Baron Klodt informed me, that in the summer during damp weather the walls become moist, while in winter they are dry).

If the salt contain impurities—such as magnesium sulphate, &c.—it is more hygroscopic. If it contain any magnesium chloride, it partially deliquesces in a damp atmosphere. The crystallised and not perfectly pure salt decrepitates when heated, owing to its containing water. The pure salt, and also the transparent rock salt, or that which has been once fused, does not decrepitate. Fused sodium chloride shows a faint alkaline reaction to litmus, which has been noticed by many observers, and is due to the presence of sodium oxide (probably by the action of the oxygen of the atmosphere). According to A. Stcherbakoff very sensitive litmus (washed in alcohol and neutralised with oxalic acid) shows an alkaline reaction even with the crystallised salt.

It may be observed that rock salt sometimes contains cavities filled with a colourless liquid. Certain kinds of rock salt emit an odour like that of hydrocarbons. These phenomena have as yet received very little attention.

[15] By cooling a solution of table salt saturated at the ordinary temperature to -15°, I obtained first of all well-formed tabular (six-sided) crystals, which when warmed to the ordinary temperature disintegrated (with the separation of anhydrous sodium chloride), and then prismatic needles up to 20 mm. long were formed from the same solution. I have not yet investigated the reason of the difference in crystalline form. It is known (Mitscherlich) that $NaI,2H_2O$ also crystallises either in plates or prisms. Sodium bromide also crystallises with $2H_2O$ at the ordinary temperature.

[16] Notwithstanding the great simplicity (Chapter I., Note 49) of the observations on the formation of ice from solution, still even for sodium chloride they cannot yet be considered as sufficiently harmonious. According to Blagden and Raoult, the temperature of the formation of ice from a solution containing c grams of salt per 100 grams of water $= -0 \cdot 6c$ to $c = 10$, according to Rosetti $= -0 \cdot 649c$ to $c = 8 \cdot 7$, according to De Coppet (to $c = 10$) $= -0 \cdot 55c - 0 \cdot 006c^2$, according to Karsten (to $c = 10$) $- 0 \cdot 762c + 0 \cdot 0084c^2$, and according to Guthrie a much lower figure. By taking Rosetti's figure and applying the rule given in Chapter I., Note 49 we obtain—

$$i = 0 \cdot 649 \times 58 \cdot 5 \boxed{18 \cdot 5} = 2 \cdot 05.$$

Pickering (1893) gives for $c = 1 - 0 \cdot 603$, for $c = 2 - 1 \cdot 220$; that is (c up to $2 \cdot 7$) about $- (0 \cdot 600 + 0 \cdot 005c)c$.

The data for strong solutions are not less contradictory. Thus with 20 p.c. of salt, ice is formed at $-14 \cdot 4°$ according to Karsten, $-17°$ according to Guthrie, $-17 \cdot 6°$ according to De Coppet. Rüdorff states that for strong solutions the temperature of the formation of ice descends in proportion to the contents of the compound, $NaCl,2H_2O$ (per 100 grams of water) by $0° \cdot 342$ per 1 gram of salt, and De Coppet shows that there is no proportionality, in a strict sense, for either a percentage of NaCl or of $NaCl,2H_2O$.

[17] A collection of observations on the specific gravity of solutions of sodium chloride is given in my work cited in Chapter I., Note 50.

Solutions of common salt have also been frequently investigated as regards rate of *diffusion* (Chapter I.), but as yet there are no complete data in this respect. It may be mentioned that Graham and De Vries demonstrated that diffusion in gelatinous masses (for instance, gelatin jelly, or gelatinous silica) proceeds in the same manner as in water, which may probably lead to a convenient and accurate method for the investigation of the phenomena of diffusion. N. Umoff (Odessa, 1888) investigated the diffusion of common salt by means of glass globules of definite density. Having poured water into a cylinder over a layer of a solution of sodium chloride, he observed during a period of several months the position (height) of the globules, which floated up higher and higher as the salt permeated upwards. Umoff found that at a constant temperature the distances of the globules (that is, the length of a column limited by layers of definite concentration) remain constant; that at a given moment of time the concentration, q, of different layers situated at a depth z is expressed by the equation B - Kz = log.(A - q), where A, B, and K are constants; that at a given moment the rate of diffusion of the different layers is proportional to their depth, &c.

[18] If S_0 be the specific gravity of water, and S the specific gravity of a solution containing p p.c. of salt, then by mixing equal weights of water and the solution, we shall obtain a solution containing $\frac{1}{2}p$ of the salt, and if it be formed without contraction, then its specific gravity x will be determined by the equation $2\boxed{x} = 1\boxed{S_0} + 1\boxed{S}$, because the volume is equal to the weight divided by the density. In reality, the specific gravity is always found to be greater than that calculated on the supposition of an absence of contraction.

[19] Generally the specific gravity is observed by weighing in air and dividing the weight in grams by the volume in cubic centimetres, the latter being found from the weight of water displaced, divided by its density at the temperature at which the experiment is carried out. If we call this specific gravity S_1, then as a cubic centimetre of air under the usual conditions weighs about $0\cdot0012$ gram, the sp. gr. in a vacuum $S = S_1 + 0\cdot0012$ $(S_1 - 1)$, if the density of water = 1.

[20] If the sp. gr. S_2 be found directly by dividing the weight of a solution by the weight of water at the same temperature and in the same volume, then the true sp. gr. S referred to water at 4° is found by multiplying S_2 by the sp. gr. of water at the temperature of observation.

[21] According to Schiff 100 grams of alcohol, containing p p.c. by weight of C_2H_6O, dissolves at 15°—

p = 10 20 40 60   80

28·5 22·6 13·2 5·9 1·2 grams NaCl.

[22] Amongst the double salts formed by sodium chloride that obtained by Ditte (1870) by the evaporation of the solution remaining after heating sodium iodate with hydrochloric acid until chlorine ceases to be liberated, is a remarkable one. Its composition is $NaIO_3,NaCl,14H_2O$. Rammelsberg obtained a similar (perhaps the same) salt in well-formed crystals by the direct reaction of both salts.

[23] But it gives sodium in the flame of a Bunsen's burner (see Spectrum Analysis), doubtless under the reducing action of the elements carbon and

hydrogen. In the presence of an excess of hydrochloric acid in the flame (when the sodium would form sodium chloride), no sodium is formed in the flame and the salt does not communicate its usual coloration.

[23 bis] There is no doubt, however, but that chloride of sodium is also decomposed in its aqueous solutions with the separation of sodium, and that it does not simply enter into double decomposition with the water (NaCl + H₂O = NaHO + HCl). This is seen from the fact that when a saturated solution of NaCl is rapidly decomposed by an electric current, a large amount of chlorine appears at the anode and a sodium amalgam forms at the mercury cathode, which acts but slowly upon the strong solution of salt. Castner's process for the electrolysis of brine into chlorine and caustic soda is an application of this method which has been already worked in England on an industrial scale.

[24] If MX and NY represent the molecules of two salts, and if there be *no third substance* present (such as water in a solution), the formation of XY would also be possible; for instance, cyanogen, iodine, &c. are capable of combining with simple haloids, as well as with the complex groups which in certain salts play the part of haloids. Besides which the salts MX and NY or MY with NX may form double salts. If the number of molecules be unequal, or if the valency of the elements or groups contained in them be different, as in NaCl + H₂SO₄, where Cl is a univalent haloid and SO₄ is bivalent, then the matter may be complicated by the formation of other compounds besides MY and NX, and when a solvent participates in the action, and especially if present in large proportion, the phenomena must evidently become still more complex; and this is actually the case in nature. Hence while placing before the reader a certain portion of the existing store of knowledge concerning the phenomena of double saline decompositions, I cannot consider the theory of the subject as complete, and have therefore limited myself to a few data, the completion of which must be sought in more detailed works on the subject of theoretical chemistry, without losing sight of what has been said above.

[24 bis] When the mixture of potassium nitrate and sodium acetate was heated by Spring to 100°, it was completely fused into one mass, although potassium nitrate fuses at about 340° and sodium nitrate at about 320°.

[25] H. Rose is more especially known for his having carefully studied and perfected several methods for the exact chemical analysis of many mineral substances. His predecessor in this branch of research was Berzelius, and his successor Fresenius.

[25 bis] Historically the influence of the mass of water was the first well-observed phenomenon in support of Berthollet's teaching, and it should not now be forgotten. In double decompositions taking place in dilute

solutions where the mass of water is large, its influence, notwithstanding the weakness of affinities, must he great, according to the very essence of Berthollet's doctrine.

As explaining the action of the mass of water, the experiments of Pattison Muir (1879) are very instructive. These experiments demonstrate that the decomposition of bismuth chloride is the more complete the greater the relative quantity of water, and the less the mass of hydrochloric acid forming one of the products of the reaction.

[26] From the above it follows that an excess of acid should influence the reaction like an excess of alcohol. It is in fact shown by experiment that if two molecules of acetic acid be taken to one molecule of alcohol, 84 p.c. of alcohol is etherified. If with a large preponderance of acid or of alcohol certain discrepancies are observed, their cause must be looked for in the incomplete correspondence of the conditions and external influences.

[27] As an example two methods may be mentioned, Thomsen's and Ostwald's. Thomsen (1869) applied a thermochemical method to exceedingly dilute solutions without taking the water into further consideration. He took solutions of caustic soda containing $100H_2O$ per $NaHO$, and sulphuric acid containing $\frac{1}{2}H_2SO_4 + 100H_2O$. In order that these solutions may be mixed in such quantities that atomic proportions of acid and alkali would act, for forty grams of caustic soda (which answers to its equivalent) there should be employed 49 grams of sulphuric acid, and then $+15,689$ heat units would be evolved. If the normal sodium sulphate so formed be mixed with n equivalents of sulphuric acid, a certain amount of heat is absorbed, namely a quantity equal to $n.1650 \boxed{(n + 0\cdot8)}$ heat units. An equivalent of caustic soda, in combining with an equivalent of nitric acid, evolves $+13,617$ units of heat, and the augmentation of the amount of nitric acid entails an absorption of heat for each equivalent equal to -27 units; so also in combining with hydrochloric acids $+13,740$ heat units are absorbed, and for each equivalent of hydrochloric acid beyond this amount there are absorbed -32 heat units. Thomsen mixed each one of three neutral salts, sodium sulphate, sodium chloride and sodium nitrate, with an acid which is not contained in it; for instance, he mixed a solution of sodium sulphate with a solution of nitric acid and determined the number of heat units then absorbed. An absorption of heat ensued because a normal salt was taken in the first instance, and the mixture of all the above normal salts with acid produces an absorption of heat. The amount of heat absorbed enabled him to obtain an insight into the process taking place in this mixture, for sulphuric acid added to sodium sulphate absorbs a considerable quantity of heat, whilst hydrochloric and nitric acids absorb a very small amount of heat in this case. By mixing an equivalent of sodium sulphate with various numbers of equivalents of nitric acid, Thomsen

observed that the amount of heat absorbed increased more and more as the amount of nitric acid was increased; thus when HNO_3 was taken per $\frac{1}{2}Na_2SO_4$, 1,752 heat units were absorbed per equivalent of soda contained in the sodium sulphate. When twice as much nitric acid was taken, 2,026 heat units, and when three times as much, 2,050 heat units were absorbed. Had the double decomposition been complete in the case where one equivalent of nitric acid was taken per equivalent of Na_2SO_4 then according to calculation from similar data there should have been absorbed -2,989 units of heat, while in reality only -1,752 units were absorbed. Hence Thomsen concluded that a displacement of only about two-thirds of the sulphuric acid had taken place—that is, the ratio $k : k'$ for the reaction $\frac{1}{2}Na_2SO_4 + HNO_3$ and $NaNO_3 + \frac{1}{2}H_2SO_4$ is equal, as for ethereal salts, to 4. By taking this figure and admitting the above supposition, Thomsen found that for all mixtures of soda with nitric acid, and of sodium nitrate with sulphuric acid, the amounts of heat followed Guldberg and Waage's law; that is, the limit of decomposition reached was greater the greater the mass of acid added. The relation of hydrochloric to sulphuric acid gave the same results. Therefore the researches of Thomsen fully confirm the hypotheses of Guldberg and Waage and the doctrine of Berthollet.

Thomsen concludes his investigation with the words: (*a*) 'When equivalent quantities of NaHO, HNO_3 (or HCl) and $\frac{1}{2}H_2SO_4$ react on one another in an aqueous solution, then two-thirds of the soda combines with the nitric and one-third with the sulphuric acid; (*b*) this subdivision repeats itself, whether the soda be taken combined with nitric or with sulphuric acid; (*c*) and therefore nitric acid has double the tendency to combine with the base that sulphuric acid has, and hence in an aqueous solution it is a stronger acid than the latter.'

'It is therefore necessary,' Thomsen afterwards remarks, 'to have an expression indicating the tendency of an acid for the saturation of bases. This idea cannot be expressed by the word *affinity*, because by this term is most often understood that force which it is necessary to overcome in order to decompose a substance into its component parts. This force should therefore be measured by the amount of work or heat employed for the decomposition of the substance. The above-mentioned phenomenon is of an entirely different nature,' and Thomsen introduces the term *avidity*, by which he designates the tendency of acids for neutralisation. 'Therefore the avidity of nitric acid with respect to soda is twice as great as the avidity of sulphuric acid. An exactly similar result is obtained with hydrochloric acid, so that its avidity with respect to soda is also double the avidity of sulphuric acid. Experiments conducted with other acids showed that not one of the acids investigated had so great an avidity as nitric acid; some had a greater avidity than sulphuric acid, others less, and in some instances the avidity =

0.' The reader will naturally see clearly that the path chosen by Thomsen deserves to be worked out, for his results concern important questions of chemistry, but great faith cannot be placed in the deductions he has already arrived at, because great complexity of relations is to be seen in the very method of his investigation. It is especially important to turn attention to the fact that all the reactions investigated are reactions of double decomposition. In them A and B do not combine with C and distribute themselves according to their affinity or avidity for combination, but reversible reactions are induced. MX and NY give MY and NX, and conversely; therefore the affinity or avidity for combination is not here directly determined, but only the difference or relation of the affinities or avidities. The affinity of nitric acid not only for the water of constitution, but also for that serving for solution, is much less than that of sulphuric acid. This is seen from thermal data. The reaction $N_2O_5 + H_2O$ gives +3,600 heat units, and the solution of the resultant hydrate, $2NHO_3$, in a large excess of water evolves +14,986 heat units. The formation of SO_3 + H_2O evolves +21,308 heat units, and the solution of H_2SO_4 in an excess of water 17,860—that is, sulphuric acid gives more heat in both cases. The interchange between Na_2SO_4 and $2HNO_3$ is not only accomplished at the expense of the production of $NaNO_3$, but also at the expense of the formation of H_2SO_4, hence the affinity of sulphuric acid for water plays its part in the phenomena of displacement. Therefore in determinations like those made by Thomsen the water does not form a medium which is present without participating in the process; it also takes part in the reaction. (Compare Chapter IX., Note 14.)

Whilst retaining essentially the methods of Thomsen, Ostwald (1876) determined the variation of the sp. gr. (and afterwards of volume), proceeding in the same dilute solutions, on the saturation of acids by bases, and in the decomposition of the salts of one acid by the other, and arrived at conclusions of just the same nature as Thomsen's. Ostwald's method will be clearly understood from an example. A solution of caustic soda containing an almost molecular (40 grams) weight per litre had a specific gravity of 1·04051. The specific gravities of solutions of equal volume and equivalent composition of sulphuric and nitric acids were 1·02970 and 1·03084 respectively. On mixing the solutions of NaHO and H_2SO_4 there was formed a solution of Na_2SO_4 of sp. gr. 1·02959; hence there ensued a decrease of specific gravity which we will term Q, equal to 1·04051 + 1·02970 - 2(1·02959) = 0·01103. So also the specific gravity after mixture of the solutions of NaHO and HNO_3 was 1·02633, and therefore Q = 0·01869. When one volume of the solution of nitric acid was added to two volumes of the solution of sodium sulphate, a solution of sp. gr. 1·02781 was obtained, and therefore the resultant decrease of sp. gr.

$$Q_1 = 2(1 \cdot 02959) + 1 \cdot 03084 - 3(1 \cdot 02781) = 0 \cdot 00659.$$

Had there been no chemical reaction between the salts, then according to Ostwald's reasoning the specific gravity of the solutions would not have changed, and if the nitric acid had entirely displaced the sulphuric acid Q_2 would be $= 0 \cdot 01869 - 0 \cdot 01103 = 0 \cdot 00766$. It is evident that a portion of the sulphuric acid was displaced by the nitric acid. But the measure of displacement is not equal to the ratio between Q_1 and Q_2, because a decrease of sp. gr. also occurs on mixing the solution of sodium sulphate with sulphuric acid, whilst the mixing of the solutions of sodium nitrate and nitric acid only produces a slight variation of sp. gr. which falls within the limits of experimental error. Ostwald deduces from similar data the same conclusions as Thomsen, and thus reconfirms the formula deduced by Guldberg and Waage, and the teaching of Berthollet.

The participation of water is seen still more clearly in the methods adopted by Ostwald than in those of Thomsen, because in the saturation of solutions of acids by alkalis (which Kremers, Reinhold, and others had previously studied) there is observed, not a contraction, as might have been expected from the quantity of heat which is then evolved, but an expansion, of volume (a decrease of specific gravity, if we calculate as Ostwald did in his first investigations). Thus by mixing 1,880 grams of a solution of sulphuric acid of the composition $SO_3 + 100H_2O$, occupying a volume of 1,815 c.c., with a corresponding quantity of a solution $2(NaHO + 5H_2O)$, whose volume $= 1,793$ c.c., we obtain not 3,608 but 3,633 c.c., an expansion of 25 c.c. per gram molecule of the resulting salt, Na_2SO_4. It is the same in other cases. Nitric and hydrochloric acids give a still greater expansion than sulphuric acid, and potassium hydroxide than sodium hydroxide, whilst a solution of ammonia gives a contraction. The relation to water must be considered as the cause of these phenomena. When sodium hydroxide and sulphuric acid dissolve in water they develop heat and give a vigorous contraction; the water is separated from such solutions with great difficulty. After mutual saturation they form the salt Na_2SO_4, which retains the water but feebly and evolves but little heat with it, i.e., in other words, has little affinity for water. In the saturation of sulphuric acid by soda the water is, so to say, displaced from a stable combination and passes into an unstable combination; hence an expansion (decrease of sp. gr.) takes place. It is not the reaction of the acid on the alkali, but the reaction of water, that produces the phenomenon by which Ostwald desires to measure the degree of salt formation. The water, which escaped attention, itself has affinity, and influences those phenomena which are being investigated. Furthermore, in the given instance its influence is very great because its mass is large. When it is not present, or only present in small quantities, the attraction of the base to the acid leads to contraction, and not expansion. Na_2O has a sp. gr. 2·8, hence its molecular volume = 22; the sp. gr. of SO_3 is 1·9 and volume 41, hence the sum of their volumes is 63; for Na_2SO_4 the sp. gr. is 2·65 and volume 53·6, consequently there is a contraction of 10 c.c. per gram-molecule of salt. The volume of H_2SO_4 = 53·3, that of $2NaHO$ = 37·4; there is produced $2H_2O$, volume = 36, + Na_2SO_4, volume = 53·6. There react 90·7 c.c., and on saturation there result 89·6 c.c.; consequently contraction again ensues, although less, and although this reaction is one of substitution and not of combination. Consequently the phenomena studied by Ostwald depend but little on the measure of the reaction of the salts, and more on the relations of the dissolved substances to water. In substitutions, for instance $2NaNO_3$ + H_2SO_4 = $2HNO_3$ + Na_2SO_4, the volumes vary but slightly: in the above example they are 2(38·8) + 53·3 and 2(41·2) + 53·6; hence 131 volumes act, and 136 volumes are produced. It may be concluded, therefore, on the basis of what has been said, that on taking water into consideration the phenomena studied by Thomsen and Ostwald are much more complex than they at first appear, and that this method can scarcely lead to a correct interpretation as to the distribution of acids between bases. We may add that P. D. Chroustcheff (1890) introduced a new method for this class of research, by investigating the electro-conductivity of solutions and their mixtures, and obtained remarkable results (for example, that hydrochloric acid almost entirely displaces formic acid and only ⅔ of sulphuric acid), but details of these methods must be looked for in text-books of theoretical chemistry.

[28] G. G. Gustavson's researches, which were conducted in the laboratory of the St. Petersburg University in 1871–72, are among the first in which the measure of the affinity of the elements for the halogens is recognised with perfect clearness in the limit of substitution and in the rate of reaction. The researches conducted by A. L. Potilitzin (of which mention will be made in Chapter XI., Note 66) in the same laboratory touch on another aspect of the same problem which has not yet made much progress, notwithstanding its importance and the fact that the theoretical side of the subject (thanks especially to Guldberg and Van't Hoff) has since been rapidly pushed forward. If the researches of Gustavson took account of the influence of mass, and were more fully supplied with data concerning velocities and temperatures, they would be very important, because of the great significance which the case considered has for the understanding of double saline decompositions in the absence of water.

Furthermore, Gustavson showed that the greater the atomic weight of the element (B, Si, Ti, As, Sn) combined *with chlorine* the greater the amount of chlorine replaced by bromine by the action of CBr_4, and consequently the less the amount of bromine replaced by chlorine by the action of CCl_4 on bromine compounds. For instance, for chlorine compounds the percentage of substitution (at the limit) is—

BCl_3 $SiCl_4$ $TiCl_4$ $AsCl_3$ $SnCl_4$

10·1 12·5 43·6 71·8 77·5

It should be observed, however, that Thorpe, on the basis of his experiments, denies the universality of this conclusion. I may mention one conclusion which it appears to me may be drawn from the above-cited figures of Gustavson, if they are subsequently verified even within narrow limits. If CBr_4 be heated with RCl_4, then an exchange of the bromine for chlorine takes place. But what would be the result if it were mixed with CCl_4? Judging by the magnitude of the atomic weights, B = 11, C = 12, Si = 28, about 11 p.c. of the chlorine would be replaced by bromine. But to what does this point? I think that this shows the existence of a motion of the atoms in the molecule. The mixture of CCl_4 and CBr_4 does not remain in a condition of static equilibrium; not only are the molecules contained in it in a state of motion, but also the atoms in the molecules, and the above figures show the measure of their translation under these conditions. The bromine in the CBr_4 is, *within the limit*, substituted by the chlorine of the CCl_4 in a quantity of about 11 out of 100: that is, a portion of the atoms of bromine previously to this moment in combination with one atom of carbon pass over to the other atom of carbon, and the chlorine passes over from this second atom of carbon to replace it. Therefore, also, in the homogeneous mass CCl_4 all the atoms of Cl do not remain constantly combined with the same atoms of carbon, and *there is on exchange of atoms between different molecules in a homogeneous medium also*. This hypothesis may in my opinion explain certain phenomena of dissociation, but though mentioning it I do not consider it worth while to dwell upon it. I will only observe that a similar hypothesis suggested itself to me in my researches on solutions, and that Pfaundler enunciated an essentially similar hypothesis, and in recent times a like view is beginning to find favour with respect to the electrolysis of saline solutions.

[29] Berthollet's doctrine is hardly at all affected in principle by showing that there are cases in which there is no decomposition between salts, because the affinity may be so small that even a large mass would still give no observable displacements. The fundamental condition for the application of Berthollet's doctrine, as well as Deville's doctrine of dissociation, lies in the reversibility of reactions. There are practically irreversible reactions (for instance, $CCl_4 + 2H_2O = CO_2 + 4HCl$), just as there are non-volatile substances. But while accepting the doctrine of reversible reactions and retaining the theory of the evaporation of liquids, it

is possible to admit the existence of non-volatile substances, and in just the same way of reactions, without any visible conformity to Berthollet's doctrine. This doctrine evidently comes nearer than the opposite doctrine of Bergmann to solving the complex problems of chemical mechanics for the successful solution of which at the present time the most valuable help is to be expected from the working out of data concerning dissociation, the influence of mass, and the equilibrium and velocity of reactions. But it is evident that from this point of view we must not regard a solvent as a non-participant space, but must take into consideration the chemical reactions accompanying solution, or else bring about reactions without solution.

[30] Common salt not only enters into double decomposition with acids but also *with every salt*. However, as clearly follows from Berthollet's doctrine, this form of decomposition will only in a few cases render it possible for new metallic chlorides to be obtained, because the decomposition will not be carried on to the end unless the metallic chloride formed separates from the mass of the active substances. Thus, for example, if a solution of common salt be mixed with a solution of magnesium sulphate, double decomposition ensues, but not completely, because all the substances remain in the solution. In this case the decomposition must result in the formation of sodium sulphate and magnesium chloride, substances which are soluble in water; nothing is disengaged, and therefore the decomposition $2NaCl + MgSO_4 = MgCl_2 + Na_2SO_4$ cannot proceed to the end. However, the sodium sulphate formed in this manner may be separated by freezing the mixture. The complete separation of the sodium sulphate will naturally not take place, owing to a portion of the salt remaining in the solution. Nevertheless, this kind of decomposition is made use of for the preparation of sodium sulphate from the residues left after the evaporation of sea-water, which contain a mixture of magnesium sulphate and common salt. Such a mixture is found at Stassfurt in a natural form. It might be said that this form of double decomposition is only accomplished with a change of temperature; but this would not be true, as may be concluded from other analogous cases. Thus, for instance, a solution of copper sulphate is of a blue colour, while a solution of copper chloride is green. If we mix the two salts together the green tint is distinctly visible, so that by this means the presence of the copper chloride in the solution of copper sulphate is clearly seen. If now we add a solution of common salt to a solution of copper sulphate, a green coloration is obtained, which indicates the formation of copper chloride. In this instance it is not separated, but it is immediately formed on the addition of common salt, as it should be according to Berthollet's doctrine.

The complete formation of a metallic chloride from common salt can only occur, judging from the above, when it separates from the sphere of action. The salts of silver are instances in point, because the silver chloride is insoluble in water; and therefore if we add a solution of sodium chloride to a solution of a silver salt, silver chloride and the sodium salt of that acid which was in the silver salt are formed.

[31] The apparatus shown in fig. 46 (Chapter VI., Note 12) is generally employed for the preparation of small quantities of hydrochloric acid. Common salt is placed in the retort; the salt is generally previously fused, as it otherwise froths and boils over in the apparatus. When the apparatus is placed in order sulphuric acid mixed with water is poured down the thistle funnel into the retort. Strong sulphuric acid (about half as much again as the weight of the salt) is usually taken, and it is diluted with a small quantity of water (half) if it be desired to retard the action, as in using strong sulphuric acid the action immediately begins with great vigour. The mixture, at first without the aid of heat and then at a moderate temperature (in a water-bath), evolves hydrochloric acid. Commercial hydrochloric acid contains many impurities; it is usually purified by distillation, the middle portions being collected. It is purified from arsenic by adding $FeCl_2$, distilling, and rejecting the first third of the distillate. If free hydrochloric acid gas be required, it is passed through a vessel containing strong sulphuric acid to dry it, and is collected over a mercury hath.

Phosphoric anhydride absorbs hydrogen chloride (Bailey and Fowler, 1888; $2P_2O_3 + 3HCl = POCl_3 + 3HPO_3$) at the ordinary temperature, and therefore the gas cannot he dried by this substance.

[31 bis] In chemical works where sulphuric acid of 60° Baumé (22 p.c. of water) is employed, 117 parts of sodium chloride are taken to about 125 parts of sulphuric acid.

[32] As in works which treat common salt in order to obtain sodium sulphate, the hydrochloric acid is sometimes held to be of no value, it might be allowed to escape with the waste furnace gases into the atmosphere, which would greatly injure the air of the neighbourhood and destroy all vegetation. In all countries, therefore, there are laws forbidding the factories to proceed in this manner, and requiring the absorption of the hydrochloric acid by water at the works themselves, and not permitting the solution to be run into rivers and streams, whose waters it would spoil. It may be remarked that the absorption of hydrochloric acid presents no particular difficulties (the absorption of sulphurous acid is much more difficult) because hydrochloric acid has a great affinity for water and gives a hydrate which boils above 100°. Hence, even steam and hot water, as well as weaker solutions, can be used for absorbing the acid. However, Warder (1888) showed that weak solutions of composition $H_2O + nHCl$ when boiled (the residue will be almost $HCl,8H_2O$) evolve (not water but) a

solution of the composition $H_2O + 445n^4HCl$; for example, on distilling HCl,10H$_2$O, HCl,23H$_2$O is first obtained in the distillate. As the strength of the residue becomes greater, so also does that of the distillate, and therefore in order to completely absorb hydrochloric acid it is necessary in the end to have recourse to water.

As in Russia the manufacture of sodium sulphate from sodium chloride has not yet been sufficiently developed, and as hydrochloric acid is required for many technical purposes (for instance, for the preparation of zinc chloride, which is employed for soaking railway sleepers), therefore salt is often treated mainly for the manufacture of hydrochloric acid.

[33] Thus the metallic chlorides, which are decomposed to a greater or less degree by water, correspond with feeble bases. Such are, for example, $MgCl_2$, $AlCl_3$, $SbCl_3$, $BiCl_3$. The decomposition of magnesium chloride (and also carnallite) by sulphuric acid proceeds at the ordinary temperature; water decomposes $MgCl_2$ to the extent of 50 p.c. when aided by heat, and *may be employed* as a convenient *method for the production of hydrochloric acid.* Hydrochloric acid is also produced by the ignition of certain metallic chlorides in a stream of hydrogen, especially of those metals which are easily reduced and difficultly oxidised—for instance, silver chloride. Lead chloride, when heated to redness in a current of steam, gives hydrochloric acid and lead oxide. The multitude of the cases of formation of hydrochloric acid are understood from the fact that it is a substance which is comparatively very stable, resembling water in this respect, and even most probably more stable than water, because, at a high temperature and even under the action of light, chlorine decomposes water, with the formation of hydrochloric acid. The combination of chlorine and hydrogen also proceeds by their direct action, as we shall afterwards describe.

[34] According to Ansdell (1880) the sp. gr. of liquid hydrochloric acid at $0° = 0·908$, at $11·67° = 0·854$, at $22·7° = 0·808$, at $33° = 0·748$. Hence it is seen that the expansion of this liquid is greater than that of gases (Chapter II., Note 34).

[35] According to Roscoe and Dittmar at a pressure of three atmospheres the solution of constant boiling point contains 18 p.c. of hydrogen chloride, and at a pressure of one-tenth atmosphere 23 p.c. The percentage is intermediate at medium pressures.

[36] At 0° 25 p.c., at 100° 20·7 p.c.; Roscoe and Dittmar.

[37] This crystallo-hydrate (obtained by Pierre and Puchot, and investigated by Roozeboom) is analogous to NaCl,2H$_2$O. The crystals HCl,2H$_2$O at -22° have a specific gravity 1·46; the vapour tension (under dissociation) of the solution having a composition HCl,2H$_2$O at -24° =

760, at -19° = 1,010, at -18° = 1,057, at -17° = 1,112 mm. of mercury. In a solid state the crystallo-hydrate at -17·7° has the same tension, whilst at lower temperatures it is much less: at -24° about 150, at -19° about 580 mm. A mixture of fuming hydrochloric acid with snow reduces the temperature to -38°. If another equivalent of water be added to the hydrate $HCl,2H_2O$ at -18°, the temperature of solidification falls to -25°, and the hydrate $HCl,3H_2O$ is formed (Pickering, 1893).

[38] According to Roscoe at 0° one *hundred* grams of water at a pressure p (in millimetres of mercury) dissolves—

$$p = 100 \quad 200 \quad 300 \quad 500 \quad 700 \quad 1000$$

Grams HCl   65·7 70·7 73·8 78·2 81·7 85·6

At a pressure of 760 millimetres and temperature t, one *hundred* grams of water dissolves

$$t = \quad 0 \quad 8° \quad 16° \quad 24° \quad 40° \quad 60°$$

Grams HCl   82·5 78·3 74·2 70·0 63·3 56·1

Roozeboom (1886) showed that at p solutions containing c grams of hydrogen chloride per 100 grams of water may (with the variation of the pressure p) be formed together with the crystallo-hydrate $HCl,2H_2O$:

$t = $ -28°·8 -21° -19° -18°

$c = $ 84·2 86·8 92·6 98·4   101·4

$p = $ —   334 580 900 1,073 mm.

The last combination answers to the melted crystallo-hydrate $HCl,2H_2O$, which splits up at temperatures above -17°·7, and at a constant atmospheric pressure when there are no crystals—

$t = $ -24° -21° -18° -10° -0°

$c = $ 101·2 98·3 95·7 89·8 84·2

From these data it is seen that the hydrate $HCl,2H_2O$ can exist in a liquid state, which is not the case for the hydrates of carbonic and sulphurous anhydrides, chlorine, &c.

According to Marignac, the specific heat c of a solution HCl + mH₂O (at about 30°, taking the specific heat of water = 1) is given by the expression—

$$C(36·5 + m18) = 18m - 28·39 + 140/m - 268/m^2$$

if m be not less than 6·25. For example, for HCl + 25H$_2$O, C = 0·877.

According to Thomsen's data, the amount of heat Q, expressed in thousands of calories, evolved in the solution of 36·5 grams of gaseous hydrochloric acid in mH$_2$O or 18m grams of water is equal to—

m =   2   4   10   50   400

Q = 11·4 14·3 16·2 17·1 17·3

In these quantities the latent heat of liquefaction is included, which must be taken as 5–9 thousand calories per molecular quantity of hydrogen chloride.

The researches of Scheffer (1888) on the rate of diffusion (in water) of solutions of hydrochloric acid show that the coefficient of diffusion k decreases with the amount of water n, if the composition of the solution is HCl,nH$_2$O at 0°:—

n =   5   6·9   9·8   14   27·1 129·5

k = 2·31 2·08 1·86 1·67 1·52 1·39

It also appears that strong solutions diffuse more rapidly into dilute solutions than into water.

[39] If it be admitted that the maximum of the differential corresponds with HCl,6H$_2$O, then it might be thought that the specific gravity is expressed by a parabola of the third order; but such an admission does not give expressions in accordance with fact. This is all more fully considered in my work mentioned in Chapter I., Note 19.

[40] As in water, the coefficient of expansion (or the quantity k in the expression S$_t$ = S$_0$ - kS$_0$$t$, or V$t$ = 1/(1 - $k$$t$)) attains a magnitude 0·000447 at about 48°, it might be thought that at 48° all solutions of hydrochloric acid would have the same coefficient of expansion, but in reality this is not the case. At low and at the ordinary temperatures the coefficient of expansion of aqueous solutions is greater than that of water, and increases with the amount of substance dissolved.

[41] The figures cited above may serve for the direct determination of that variation of the specific gravity of solutions of hydrochloric acid with the temperature. Thus, knowing that at 15° the specific gravity of a 10 p.c. solution of hydrochloric acid = 10,492, we find that at $t°$ it = 10,530 - t(2·13 + 0·027t). Whence also may be found the coefficient of expansion (Note 40).

[42] Thus, for instance, with feeble bases they evolve in dilute solutions (Chapter III., Note 53) almost equal amounts of heat; their relation to sulphuric acid is quite identical. They both form fuming solutions as well as hydrates; they both form solutions of constant boiling point.

[42 bis] Pybalkin (1891) found that copper begins to disengage hydrogen at 100°, and that chloride of copper begins to give up its chlorine to hydrogen gas at 230°; for silver these temperatures are 117° and 260°—that is, there is less difference between them.

[43] When an unsaturated hydrocarbon, or, in general, an unsaturated compound, assimilates to itself the molecules Cl_2, HCl, SO_3, H_2SO_4, &c., the cause of the reaction is most simple. As nitrogen, besides the type NX_3 to which NH_3, belongs, gives compounds of the type NX_5—for example, $NO_2(OH)$—the formation of the salts of ammonium should be understood in this way. NH_3 gives NH_4Cl because NX_3 is capable of giving NX_5. But as saturated compounds—for instance, SO_3,H_2O, NaCl, &c.— are also capable of combination even between themselves, it is impossible to deny the capacity of HCl also for combination. SO_3 combines with H_2O, and also with HCl and the unsaturated hydrocarbons. It is impossible to recognise the distinction formerly sought to be established between atomic and molecular compounds, and regarding, for instance, PCl_3 as an atomic compound and PCl_5 as a molecular one, only because it easily splits up into molecules PCl_3 and Cl_2.

[44] Sal-ammoniac is prepared from ammonium carbonate, obtained in the dry distillation of nitrogenous substances (Chapter VI.), by saturating the resultant solution with hydrochloric acid. A solution of sal-ammoniac is thus produced, which is evaporated, and in the residue a mass is obtained containing a mixture of various other, especially tarry, products of dry distillation. The sal-ammoniac is generally purified by sublimation. For this purpose iron vessels covered with hemispherical metallic covers are employed, or else simply clay crucibles covered by other crucibles. The upper portion, or head, of the apparatus of this kind will have a lower temperature than the lower portion, which is under the direct action of the flame. The sal-ammoniac volatilises when heated, and settles on the cooler portion of the apparatus. It is thus freed from many impurities, and is obtained as a crystalline crust, generally several centimetres thick, in which form it is commonly sold. The solubility of sal-ammoniac rises rapidly with the temperature: at 0°, 100 parts of water dissolve about 28 parts of NH_4Cl, at 50° about 50 parts, and at the ordinary temperature about 35 parts. This is sometimes taken advantage of for separating NH_4Cl from solutions of other salts.

[45] The solubility of sal-ammoniac in 100 parts of water (according to Alluard) is—

0°	10°	20°	30°	40°	60°	80°	100°	100°
28·40	32·48	37·28	41·72	46	55	64	73	77

A saturated solution boils at 115°·8. The specific gravity at 15°/4° of solutions of sal-ammoniac (water 4° = 10,000) = 9,991·6 - 31·26p - 0·085p^2, where p is the amount by weight of ammonium chloride in 100 parts of solution. With the majority of salts the differential ds/dp increases, but here it decreases with the increase of p. For (unlike the sodium and potassium salts) a solution of the alkali *plus* a solution of acid occupy a greater volume than that of the resultant ammonium salt. In the solution of *solid* ammonium chloride a contraction, and not expansion, generally takes place. It may further be remarked that solutions of sal-ammoniac have an acid reaction even when prepared from the salt remaining after prolonged washing of the sublimed salt with water (A. Stcherbakoff).

[459]

CHAPTER XI

THE HALOGENS: CHLORINE, BROMINE, IODINE, AND FLUORINE

Although hydrochloric acid, like water, is one of the most stable substances, it is nevertheless decomposed not only by the action of a galvanic current,[1] but also by a high temperature. Sainte-Claire Deville showed that decomposition already occurs at 1,300°, because a cold tube (as with CO, Chapter IX.) covered with an amalgam of silver absorbs chlorine from hydrochloric acid in a red-hot tube, and the escaping gas contains hydrogen. V. Meyer and Langer (1885) observed the decomposition of hydrochloric acid at 1,690° in a platinum vessel; the decomposition in this instance was proved not only from the fact that hydrogen diffused through the platinum (p. 142), owing to which the volume was diminished, but also from chlorine being obtained in the residue (the hydrogen chloride was mixed with nitrogen), which liberated iodine from potassium iodide.[2] The usual method for the preparation of chlorine consists in the abstraction of the hydrogen by oxidising agents.[2 bis]

[460]

An aqueous solution of hydrochloric acid is generally employed for the evolution of chlorine. The hydrogen has to be abstracted from the hydrochloric acid. This is accomplished by nearly all oxidising substances, and especially by those which are able to evolve oxygen at a red heat (besides bases, such as mercury and silver oxides, which are able to give salts with hydrogen chloride); for example, manganese peroxide, potassium chlorate, chromic acid, &c. The decomposition essentially consists in the oxygen of the oxidising substance displacing the chlorine from 2HCl, forming water, H_2O, and setting the chlorine free, 2HCl + O (disengaged by the oxidising substances) = H_2O + Cl_2. Even nitric acid partially produces a like reaction; but as we shall afterwards see its action is more complicated, and it is therefore not suitable for the preparation of pure chlorine.[3] But other oxidising substances which do not give any other volatile products with hydrochloric acid may be employed for the preparation of chlorine. Among these may be mentioned: potassium chlorate, acid potassium chromate, sodium manganate, manganese peroxide, &c. Manganese peroxide is commonly employed in the laboratory, and on a large scale, for the preparation of chlorine. The chemical process in this case may be represented as follows: an exchange takes place between 4HCl and MnO_2, in which the manganese takes the place of the four atoms of hydrogen, or the chlorine and oxygen exchange places—that is, $MnCl_4$ and $2H_2O$ are produced. The chlorine compound, $MnCl_4$, obtained is very unstable; it splits up into chlorine, which as a gas passes from the sphere of action, and a lower compound containing less chlorine than the substance first formed, which remains in the apparatus in which the mixture is heated, $MnCl_4 = MnCl_2 + Cl_2$.[3 bis] The action of hydrochloric acid requires a temperature of[461] about 100°. In the laboratory the *preparation of chlorine* is carried on in flasks, heated over a water-bath, by acting on manganese peroxide[462] with hydrochloric acid or a mixture of common salt and sulphuric acid[4] and washing the gas with water to remove hydrochloric acid.[5] Chlorine cannot be collected over mercury, because it combines with it as with many other metals, and it is soluble in water; however, it is but slightly soluble in hot water or brine. Owing to its great weight, chlorine may be directly collected in a dry vessel by carrying the gas-conducting tube down to the bottom of the vessel. The chlorine will lie in a heavy layer at the bottom of the vessel, displace the air, and the extent to which it fills the vessel may be followed by its colour.[6]

[463]

Chlorine is a *gas* of a yellowish green colour, and has a very suffocating and characteristic odour. On lowering the temperature to -50° or increasing the pressure to six atmospheres (at 0°) chlorine condenses[7] into a liquid which has a yellowish-green colour, a density of 1·3, and boils at -34°. The density and atomic weight of chlorine is 35·5 times greater than that of hydrogen, hence the molecule contains Cl_2[8]. At 0° one volume of water dissolves about 1½ volume of chlorine, at 10° about 3 volumes, at 50° again 1½ volume.[9] Such[464] a solution of chlorine is termed 'chlorine water;' and is employed in a diluted form in medicine and as a laboratory reagent. It is prepared by passing chlorine through a series of Woulfe's bottles or into an inverted retort filled with water. Under the action of light, chlorine water gives oxygen and hydrochloric acid. At 0° a saturated solution of chlorine yields a crystallo-hydrate, $Cl_2,8H_2O$, which easily splits up into chlorine and water when heated, so that if it be sealed up in a tube and heated to 35°, two layers of liquid are formed—a lower stratum of chlorine containing a small quantity of water, and an upper stratum of water containing a small quantity of chlorine.[10]

Chlorine explodes *with hydrogen*, if a mixture of equal volumes be exposed to the direct action of the sun's rays[11] or brought into contact[465] with spongy platinum, or a strongly heated substance, or when subjected to the action of an electric spark. The explosion in this case takes place for exactly the same reasons—*i.e.* the evolution of heat and expansion of the resultant product—as in the case of detonating gas (Chapter III.) Diffused light acts in the same way, but slowly, whilst direct sunlight causes an explosion.[12] The hydrochloric acid gas produced by the[466] reaction of chlorine on hydrogen occupies (at the original temperature and pressure) a volume equal to the sum of the original volumes; that is, a reaction of substitution here takes place: $H_2 + Cl_2 = HCl + HCl$. In this reaction twenty-two thousand heat units are evolved for one part by weight [1 gram] of hydrogen.[13]

These relations show that the affinity of chlorine for hydrogen is very great and analogous to the affinity between hydrogen and oxygen. Thus[14] on the one hand by passing a mixture of steam and chlorine through a red-hot tube, or by exposing water and chlorine to the sunlight, oxygen is disengaged, whilst on the other hand, as we saw above, oxygen in many cases displaces chlorine from its compound with hydrogen, and therefore the reaction $H_2O + Cl_2 = 2HCl + O$ belongs to the number of reversible reactions, and hydrogen will distribute itself between oxygen and chlorine. This determines the relation of Cl to substances containing hydrogen and its reactions in the presence of water, to which we shall turn our attention after having pointed out the relation of chlorine to other elements.

Many *metals* when brought into contact with chlorine immediately combine with it, and form those metallic chlorides which correspond with hydrogen chloride and with the oxide of the metal taken. This combination may proceed rapidly with the evolution of heat and light; that is, metals are able to burn in chlorine. Thus, for example, sodium[15] burns in chlorine, synthesising common salt. Metals in the form of powders burn without the aid of heat, and become highly incandescent in the process; for instance, antimony, which is a metal easily converted into a powder.[16] Even such metals as gold and[467] platinum,[17] which do not combine directly with oxygen and give very unstable compounds with it, unite directly with chlorine to form metallic chlorides. Either chlorine water or aqua regia may be employed for this purpose instead of gaseous chlorine. These dissolve gold and platinum, converting them into metallic chlorides. *Aqua regia* is a mixture of 1 part of nitric acid with 2 to 3 parts of hydrochloric acid. This mixture converts into soluble chlorides not only those metals which are acted on by hydrochloric and nitric acids, but also gold and platinum, which are insoluble in either acid separately. This action of aqua regia depends on the fact that nitric acid in acting on hydrochloric acid evolves chlorine. If the chlorine evolved be transferred to a metal, then a fresh quantity is formed from the remaining acids and also combines with the metal.[18] Thus the aqua regia acts by virtue of the chlorine which it contains and disengages.

The majority of *non-metals* also react directly on chlorine; hot sulphur and phosphorus burn in it and combine with it at the ordinary temperature.

Only nitrogen, carbon, and oxygen do not combine directly with it. The chlorine compounds formed by the non-metals—for instance, phosphorus trichloride, PCl_3, and sulphurous chloride, &c., do not have the properties of salts, and, as we shall afterwards see more fully, correspond to acid anhydrides and acids; for example, PCl_3—to phosphorous acid, $P(OH)_3$:

$NaCl \quad FeCl_2 \quad SnCl_4 \quad PCl_3 \quad HCl$

$Na(HO) \quad Fe(HO)_2 \quad Sn(HO)_4 \quad P(HO)_3 \quad H(HO)$

[468]

As the above-mentioned relation in composition—*i.e.* substitution of Cl by the aqueous residue—exists between many chlorine compounds and their corresponding hydrates, and as furthermore some (acid) hydrates are obtained from chlorine compounds by the action of water, for instance,

$$PCl_3 \quad + 3H_2O = \quad P(HO)_3 \quad + \quad 3HCl$$

Phosphorus   Water   Phosphorus   Hydrochloric
   trichloride   acid   acid

whilst other chlorine compounds are formed from hydroxides and hydrochloric acid, with the liberation of water, for example,

$$NaHO + HCl = NaCl + H_2O$$

we endeavour to express this intimate connection between the hydrates and chlorine compounds by calling the latter *chloranhydrides*. In general terms, if the hydrate be basic, then,

$$M(HO) + \quad HCl \quad = \quad MCl \quad + H_2O$$

hydrate   hydrochloric acid   chloranhydride   water

and if the hydrate ROH be acid, then,

$$RCl \quad + H_2O = R(HO) + \quad HCl$$

Chloranhydride   water   hydrate   hydrochloric acid

The chloranhydrides MCl corresponding to the bases are evidently metallic chlorides or salts corresponding to HCl. In this manner a distinct equivalency is marked between the compounds of chlorine and the so-called hydroxyl radicle (HO), which is also expressed in the analogy existing between chlorine, Cl_2, and hydrogen peroxide, $(HO)_2$.

As regards the chloranhydrides corresponding to acids and non-metals, they bear but little resemblance to metallic salts. They are nearly all volatile, and have a powerful suffocating smell which irritates the eyes and respiratory organs. They react on water like many anhydrides of the acids, with the evolution of heat and liberation of hydrochloric acid, forming acid hydrates. For this reason they cannot usually be obtained from hydrates—that is, acids—by the action of hydrochloric acid, as in that case water would be formed together with them, and water decomposes them, converting them into hydrates. There are many intermediate chlorine compounds between true saline metallic chlorides like sodium chloride and true acid chloranhydrides, just as there are all kinds of transitions between bases and acids. Acid chloranhydrides are not only obtained from chlorine and non-metals, but also from many lower oxides, by the aid of chlorine. Thus, for example, CO, NO, NO_2, SO_2, and other lower oxides which are capable of combining with oxygen may also combine with a corresponding[469] quantity of chlorine. Thus $COCl_2$, $NOCl$, NO_2Cl, SO_2Cl_2, &c., are obtained. They correspond with the hydrates $CO(OH)_2$, $NO(OH)$, $NO_2(OH)$, $SO_2(OH)_2$, &c., and to the anhydrides CO_2, N_2O_3, N_2O_5, SO_3, &c. Here we should notice two aspects of the matter: (1) chlorine combines with that with which oxygen is able to combine, because it is in many respects equally if not more energetic than oxygen and replaces it in the proportion Cl_2: O; (2) that highest limit of possible combination which is proper to a given element or grouping of elements is very easily and often attained by combination with chlorine. If phosphorus gives PCl_3 and PCl_5, it is evident that PCl_5 is the higher form of combination compared with PCl_3. To the form PCl_5, or in general PX_5, correspond PH_4I, $PO(OH)_3$, $POCl_3$, &c. If chlorine does not always directly give compounds of the highest possible forms for a given element, then generally the lower forms combine with it in order to reach or approach the limit. This is particularly clear in hydrocarbons, where we see the limit C_nH_{2n+2} very distinctly. The unsaturated hydrocarbons are sometimes able to combine with chlorine with the greatest ease and thus reach the limit. Thus ethylene, C_2H_4, combines with Cl_2, forming the so-called Dutch liquid or ethylene chloride, $C_2H_4Cl_2$, because it then reaches the limit C_nX_{2n+2}. In this and all similar cases the combined chlorine is able by reactions of substitution to give a hydroxide and a whole series of other derivatives. Thus a hydroxide called glycol, $C_2H_4(OH)_2$, is obtained from $C_2H_4Cl_2$.

Chlorine *in the presence of water* very often acts directly *as an oxidising agent*. A substance A combines with chlorine and gives, for example, ACl_2, and this in turn a hydroxide, $A(OH)_2$, which on losing water forms AO. Here the chlorine has oxidised the substance A. This frequently happens in the simultaneous action of water and chlorine: $A + H_2O + Cl_2 = 2HCl + AO$. Examples of this oxidising action of chlorine may frequently be observed both in practical chemistry and technical processes. Thus, for instance, chlorine in the presence of water oxidises sulphur and metallic sulphides. In this case the sulphur is converted into sulphuric acid, and the chlorine into hydrochloric acid, or a metallic chloride if a metallic sulphide be taken. A mixture of carbonic oxide and chlorine passed into water gives carbonic anhydride and hydrochloric acid. Sulphurous anhydride is oxidised by chlorine in the presence of water into sulphuric acid, just as it is by the action of nitric acid: $SO_2 + 2H_2O + Cl_2 = H_2SO_4 + 2HCl$.

The oxidising action of chlorine in the presence of water is taken advantage of in practice for the rapid bleaching of tissues and fibres. The colouring matter of the fibres is altered by oxidation and converted[470] into a colourless substance, but the chlorine afterwards acts on the tissue itself. Bleaching by means of chlorine therefore requires a certain amount of technical skill in order that the chlorine should not act on the fibres themselves, but that its action should be limited to the colouring matter only. The fibre for making writing paper, for instance, is bleached in this manner. The bleaching property of chlorine was discovered by Berthollet, and forms an important acquisition to the arts, because it has in the majority of cases replaced that which before was the universal method of bleaching—namely, exposure to the sun of the fabrics damped with water, which is still employed for linens, &c. Time and great trouble, and therefore money also, have been considerably saved by this change.[19]

The power of chlorine for combination is intimately connected with its capacity for substitution, because, according to the law of substitution, if chlorine combines with hydrogen, then it also replaces hydrogen, and furthermore the combination and substitution are accomplished in the same quantities. Therefore *the atom of chlorine* which combines with the atom of hydrogen is also able *to replace the atom of hydrogen*. We mention this property of chlorine not only because it illustrates the application of the law of substitution in clear and historically important examples, but more especially because reactions of this kind explain those *indirect methods* of the formation of many substances which we have often mentioned and to which recourse is had in many cases in chemistry. Thus chlorine does not act on carbon,[20] oxygen, or nitrogen, but nevertheless its compounds with these elements may be obtained by the indirect method of the substitution of hydrogen by chlorine.

As chlorine easily combines with hydrogen, and does not act on carbon, it decomposes hydrocarbons (and many of their derivatives) at a high temperature, depriving them of their hydrogen and liberating the carbon, as, for example, is clearly seen when a lighted candle is placed in a vessel containing chlorine. The flame becomes smaller, but[471] continues to burn for a certain time, a large amount of soot is obtained, and hydrochloric acid is formed. In this case the gaseous and incandescent substances of the flame are decomposed by the chlorine, the hydrogen combines with it, and the carbon is disengaged as soot.[21] This action of chlorine on hydrocarbons, &c., proceeds otherwise at lower temperatures, as we will now consider.

A very important epoch in the history of chemistry was inaugurated by the discovery of Dumas and Laurent that chlorine is able to displace and *replace hydrogen*. This discovery is important from the fact that chlorine proved to be an element which combines with great ease simultaneously with both the hydrogen and the element with which the hydrogen was combined. This clearly proved that there is no opposite polarity between elements forming stable compounds. Chlorine does not combine with hydrogen because it has opposite properties, as Dumas and Laurent stated previously, accounting hydrogen to be electro-positive and chlorine electro-negative; this is not the reason of their combining together, for the same chlorine which combines with hydrogen is also able to replace it without altering many of the properties of the resultant substance. This substitution of hydrogen by chlorine is termed *metalepsis*. The mechanism of this substitution is very constant. If we take a hydrogen compound, preferably a hydrocarbon, and if chlorine acts directly on it, then there is produced on the one hand hydrochloric acid and on the other hand a compound containing chlorine in the place of the hydrogen—so that the chlorine divides itself into two equal portions, one portion is evolved as hydrochloric acid, and the other portion takes the place of the hydrogen thus liberated. *Hence this metalepsis is always accompanied by the formation of hydrochloric acid.*[22] The scheme of the process is as follows:

$$C_nH_mX \quad + \quad Cl_2 \quad = \quad C_{nm-1}ClX \quad + \quad HCl$$

Hydrocarbon   Free chlorine   Product of metalepsis   Hydrochloric acid

Or, in general terms—

$$RH + Cl_2 = RCl + HCl.$$

The conditions under which metalepsis takes place are also very constant. In the dark chlorine does not usually act on hydrogen compounds,[472] but the action commences under the influence of light. The direct action of the sun's rays is particularly propitious to metalepsis. It is also remarkable that the presence of traces of certain substances,[23] especially of iodine, aluminium chloride, antimony chloride, &c., promotes the action. A trace of iodine added to the substance subjected to metalepsis often produces the same effect as sunlight.[24]

If marsh gas be mixed with chlorine and the mixture ignited, then the hydrogen is entirely taken up from the marsh gas and hydrochloric acid and carbon formed, but there is no metalepsis.[25] But if a mixture of equal volumes of chlorine and marsh gas be exposed to the action of diffused light, then the greenish yellow mixture gradually becomes colourless, and hydrochloric acid and the first product of metalepsis—namely, methyl chloride—are formed:

$$CH_4 \quad + \quad Cl_2 \quad = \quad CH_3Cl \quad + \quad HCl$$

Marsh gas   Chlorine   Methyl chloride   Hydrochloric acid

The volume of the mixture remains unaltered. The methyl chloride which is formed is a gas. If it be separated from the hydrochloric acid (it is soluble in acetic acid, in which hydrochloric acid is but sparingly soluble) and be again mixed with chlorine, then it may be[473] subjected to a further metalepsical substitution—the second atom of hydrogen may be substituted by chlorine, and a liquid substance, CH_2Cl_2, called methylene chloride, will be obtained. In the same manner the substitution may be carried on still further, and $CHCl_3$, or chloroform, and lastly carbon tetrachloride, CCl_4, will be produced. Of these substances the best known is chloroform, owing to its being formed from many organic substances (by the action of bleaching powder) and to its being used in medicine as an anæsthetic; chloroform boils at 62° and carbon tetrachloride at 78°. They are both colourless odoriferous liquids, heavier than water. The progressive substitution of hydrogen by chlorine is thus evident, and it can be clearly seen that the double decompositions are accomplished between molecular quantities of the substance—that is, between equal volumes in a gaseous state.

Carbon tetrachloride, which is obtained by the metalepsis of marsh gas, cannot be obtained directly from chlorine and carbon, but it may be obtained from certain compounds of carbon—for instance, from carbon bisulphide—if its vapour mixed with chlorine be passed through a red-hot tube. Both the sulphur and carbon then combine with the chlorine. It is evident that by ultimate metalepsis a corresponding carbon chloride may be obtained from any hydrocarbon—indeed, the number of chlorides of carbon C_nCl_{2m} already known is very large.

As a rule, the fundamental chemical characters of hydrocarbons are not changed by metalepsis; that is, if a neutral substance be taken, then the product of metalepsis is also a neutral substance, or if an acid be taken the product of metalepsis also has acid properties. Even the crystalline form not unfrequently remains unaltered after metalepsis. The metalepsis of acetic acid, $CH_3 \cdot COOH$, is historically the most important. It contains three of the atoms of the hydrogen of marsh gas, the fourth being replaced by carboxyl, and therefore by the action of chlorine it gives three products of metalepsis (according to the amount of the chlorine and conditions under which the reaction takes place), mono-, di-, and tri-chloracetic acids—$CH_2Cl \cdot COOH$, $CHCl_2 \cdot COOH$, and $CCl_3 \cdot COOH$; they are all, like acetic acid, monobasic. The resulting products of metalepsis, in containing an element which so easily acts on metals as chlorine, possess the possibility of attaining a further complexity of molecules of which the original hydrocarbon is often in no way capable. Thus on treating with an alkali (or first with a salt and then with an alkali, or with a basic oxide and water, &c.) the chlorine forms a salt with its metal, and the hydroxyl radicle takes the place of the chlorine—for example, $CH_3 \cdot OH$ is obtained from CH_3Cl. By the action of metallic derivatives of hydrocarbons—for example, CH_3Na— the chlorine also gives a salt, and the hydrocarbon radicle—for instance,[474] CH_3—takes the place of the chlorine. In this, or in a similar manner, $CH_3 \cdot CH_3$, or C_2H_6 is obtained from CH_3Cl and $C_6H_5 \cdot CH_3$ from C_6H_6. The products of metalepsis also often react on ammonia, forming hydrochloric acid (and thence NH_4Cl) and an amide; that is, the product of metalepsis, with the ammonia radicle NH_2, &c. in the place of chlorine. Thus by means of metalepsical substitution methods were found in chemistry for an artificial and general means of the formation of complex carbon compounds from more simple compounds which are often totally incapable of direct reaction. Besides which, this key opened the doors of that secret edifice of complex organic compounds into which man had up to then feared to enter, supposing the hydrocarbon elements to be united only under the influence of those mystic forces acting in organisms.[26]

It is not only hydrocarbons which are subject to metalepsis. Certain other hydrogen compounds, under the action of chlorine, also give corresponding chlorine derivatives in exactly the same manner; for instance, ammonia, caustic potash, caustic lime, and a whole series of *alkaline* substances.[27] In fact, just as the hydrogen in marsh gas can be replaced by chlorine and form methyl chloride, so the hydrogen in caustic potash, KHO, ammonia, NH_3, and calcium hydroxide,[475] CaH_2O_2 or $Ca(OH)_2$, may be replaced by chlorine and give potassium hypochlorite, KClO, calcium hypochlorite, $CaCl_2O_2$, and the so-called chloride of nitrogen, NCl_3. For not only is the correlation in composition the same as in the substitution in marsh gas, but the whole mechanism of the reaction is the same. Here also two atoms of chlorine act: one takes the place of the hydrogen whilst the other is evolved as hydrochloric acid, only in the former case the hydrochloric acid evolved remained free, and in the latter, in presence of alkaline substances, it reacts on them. Thus, in the action of chlorine on caustic potash, the hydrochloric acid formed acts on another quantity of caustic potash and gives potassium chloride and water, and therefore not only $KHO + Cl_2 = HCl + KClO$, but also $KHO + HCl = H_2O + KCl$, and the result of both simultaneous phases will be $2KHO + Cl_2 = H_2O + KCl + KClO$. We will here discuss certain special cases.

The action of chlorine on ammonia may either result in the entire breaking up of the ammonia, with the evolution of gaseous nitrogen, or in a product of metalepsis (as with CH_4). With an excess of chlorine and the aid of heat the ammonia is decomposed, with the disengagement of free nitrogen.[28] This reaction evidently results in the formation of sal-ammoniac, $8NH_3 + 3Cl_2 = 6NH_4Cl + N_2$. But if the ammonium salt be in excess, then the reaction takes the direction of the replacement of the hydrogen in the ammonia by chlorine. The principal result is that $NH_3 + 3Cl_2$ forms $NCl_3 + 3HCl$.[29][476] The resulting product of metalepsis, or *chloride of nitrogen*, NCl_3, discovered by Dulong, is a liquid having the property of decomposing with excessive ease not only when heated, but even under the action of mechanical influences, as by a blow or by contact with certain solid substances. The explosion which accompanies the decomposition is due to the fact that the liquid chloride of nitrogen gives gaseous products, nitrogen and chlorine.[29 bis]

[477]

Chloride of nitrogen is a yellow oily liquid of sp. gr. 1·65, which boils at 71°, and breaks up into $N + Cl_3$ at 97°. The contact of phosphorus, turpentine, india-rubber, &c. causes an explosion, which is sometimes so violent that a small drop will pierce through a thick board. The great ease with which chloride of nitrogen decomposes is dependent upon the fact that it is formed with an absorption of heat, which it evolves when decomposed, to the amount of about 38,000 heat units for NCl_3, as Deville and Hautefeuille determined.

Chlorine, when absorbed by a solution of caustic soda (and also of other alkalis) at the ordinary temperature, causes the replacement of the hydrogen in the caustic soda by the chlorine, with the formation of sodium chloride by the hydrochloric acid, so that the reaction may be represented in two phases, as described above. In this manner, sodium hypochlorite, $NaClO$, and sodium chloride are simultaneously formed: $2NaHO + Cl_2 = NaCl + NaClO + H_2O$. The resultant solution contains $NaClO$ and is termed 'eau de Javelle.' An exactly similar reaction takes place when chlorine is passed over dry hydrate of lime at the ordinary temperature: $2Ca(HO)_2 + 2Cl_2 = CaCl_2O_2 + CaCl_2 + 2H_2O$. A mixture of the product of metalepsis with calcium chloride is obtained. This mixture is employed in practice on a large scale, and is termed 'bleaching powder,' owing to its acting, especially when mixed with acids, as a bleaching agent on tissues, so that it resembles chlorine in this respect. It is however preferable to chlorine, because the destructive action of the chlorine can be moderated in this case, and because it is much more convenient to deal with a solid substance than with gaseous chlorine. Bleaching powder is also called *chloride of lime*, because it is obtained from chlorine and hydrate of lime, and contains[30] both these substances. It[478] may be prepared in the laboratory by passing a current of chlorine through a cold mixture of water and lime (milk of lime). The mixture must be kept cold, as otherwise $3Ca(ClO)_2$ passes into $2CaCl_2 + Ca(ClO_3)_2$. In the manufacture of bleaching powder in large quantities at chemical works, the purest possible slaked lime is taken and laid in a thin layer in large flat chambers, M (whose walls are made of Yorkshire flags or tarred wood, on which chlorine has no action), and into which chlorine gas is introduced by lead tubes. The distribution of the plant is shown in the annexed drawing (fig. 67).

FIG. 67.—Apparatus for the manufacture of bleaching powder (on a small scale) by the action of chlorine, which is generated in the vessels C, on lime, which is charged into M.

The products of the metalepsis of alkaline hydrates, NaClO and $Ca(ClO)_2$, which are present in solutions of 'Javelle salt' and bleaching[479] powder (they are not obtained free from metallic chlorides), must be counted as salts, because their metals are capable of substitution. But the hydrate HClO corresponding with these salts, or *hypochlorous acid*, is not obtained in a free or pure state, for two reasons: in the first place, because this hydrate, as a very feeble acid, splits up (like H_2CO_3 or HNO_3) into water and the anhydride, or *chlorine monoxide*, $Cl_2O = 2HClO - H_2O$; and, in the second place, because, in a number of instances, it evolves oxygen with great facility, forming hydrochloric acid: $HClO = HCl + O$. Both hypochlorous acid and chlorine monoxide may be regarded as products of the metalepsis of water, because HOH corresponds with ClOH and ClOCl. Hence in many instances bleaching salts (a mixture of hypochlorites and chlorides) break up, with the evolution of (1) *chlorine*, under the action of an excess of a powerful acid capable of evolving hydrochloric acid from sodium or calcium chlorides, and this takes place most simply under the action of hydrochloric acid itself, because (p. 462) NaCl + NaClO + 3HCl = 2NaCl + HCl + Cl$_2$ + H$_2$O; (2) *oxygen*, as we saw in Chapter III.—The bleaching properties and, in general, *oxidising action* of bleaching salts is based on this evolution of oxygen (or chlorine); oxygen is also disengaged on heating the dry salts—for instance, NaCl + NaClO = 2NaCl + O; (3) and, lastly, *chlorine monoxide*, which contains both chlorine and oxygen. Thus, if a little sulphuric, nitric, or similar acid (not enough to liberate hydrochloric acid from the CaCl$_2$) be added to a solution of a bleaching salt (which has an alkaline reaction, owing either to an excess of alkali or to the feeble acid properties of HClO), then the hypochlorous acid set free gives water and chlorine monoxide. If carbonic anhydride (or boracic or a similar very feeble acid) act on the solution of a bleaching salt, then hydrochloric acid is not evolved from the sodium or calcium chlorides, but the hypochlorous acid is displaced and gives chlorine monoxide,[31] because hypochlorous acid is one of the most feeble acids. Another method for the preparation of chlorine monoxide is based on these feeble acid properties of hypochlorous acid. Zinc oxide and mercury oxide, under the action of chlorine in the presence of water, do not give a salt of hypochlorous acid, but form a chloride and hypochlorous acid, which fact shows the incapacity of this acid to[480] combine with the bases mentioned. Therefore, if such oxides as those of zinc or mercury be shaken up in water, and chlorine be passed through the turbid liquid,[32] a reaction occurs which may be expressed in the following manner: 2HgO + 2Cl$_2$ = Hg$_2$OCl$_2$ + Cl$_2$O. In this case, a compound of mercury oxide with mercury chloride, or the so-called mercury oxychloride, is obtained: Hg$_2$OCl$_2$ = HgO + HgCl$_2$. This is insoluble in water, and is not affected by hypochlorous anhydride, so that the solution will contain hypochlorous acid only, but the greater part of it splits up into the anhydride and water.[32 bis]

Chlorine monoxide, which corresponds to bleaching and hypochlorous salts, containing as it does the two elements oxygen and chlorine, forms a characteristic example of a compound of elements which, in the majority of cases, act chemically in an analogous manner. Chlorine monoxide, as prepared from an aqueous solution by the abstraction of water or by the action of dry chlorine on cold mercury oxide, is, at the ordinary temperature, a gas or vapour which condenses into a red liquid boiling at +20° and giving a vapour whose density (43 referred to hydrogen) shows that 2 vols. of chlorine and 1 vol. of oxygen give 2 vols. of chlorine monoxide. In an anhydrous form the gas or liquid easily explodes, splitting up into chlorine and oxygen. This explosiveness is determined by the fact that heat is *evolved* in the decomposition to the amount of about 15,000 heat units for Cl$_2$O.[33] The explosion may even take place spontaneously, and also[481] in the presence of many oxidisable substances (for instance, sulphur, organic compounds, &c.), but the solution, although unstable and showing a strong oxidising tendency, does not explode.[34] It is evident that the presence of hypochlorous acid, HClO, may be assumed in an aqueous solution of Cl_2O, since $Cl_2O + H_2O = 2HClO$.

Hypochlorous acid, its salts, and chlorine monoxide serve as a transition between hydrochloric acid, chlorides, and chlorine, and a whole series of compounds containing the same elements combined with a still greater quantity of oxygen. The higher oxides of chlorine, as their origin indicates, are closely connected with hypochlorous acid and its salts:

Cl_2 NaCl   HCl   hydrochloric acid.

Cl_2O NaClO HClO hypochlorous acid.

Cl_2O_3 $NaClO_2$ $HClO_2$ chlorous acid.[35]

Cl_2O_5 $NaClO_3$ $HClO_3$ chloric acid.

Cl_2O_7 $NaClO_4$ $HClO_4$ perchloric acid.

When heated, solutions of hypochlorites undergo a remarkable change. Themselves so unstable, they, without any further addition, yield two fresh salts which are both much more stable; one contains more oxygen than MClO, the other contains none at all.

$3MClO = MClO_3 + 2MCl$

hypochlorite   chlorate   chlorate

[482]

Part of the salt—namely, two-thirds of it—parts with its oxygen in order to oxidise the remaining third.[36] From an intermediate substance, RX, two extremes, R and RX_3 are formed, just as nitrous anhydride splits up into nitric oxide and nitric anhydride (or nitric acid). The resulting salt, $MClO_3$, corresponds with *chloric acid* and potassium chlorate, $KClO_3$. It is evident that a similar salt may be obtained directly by the action of chlorine on an alkali if its solution be heated, because RClO will be first formed, and then $RClO_3$; for example, $6KHO + 3Cl_2 = KClO_3 + 5KCl + 3H_2O$. Chlorates are so prepared; for instance, *potassium chlorate*, which is easily separated from potassium chloride, being sparingly soluble in cold water.[37]

[483]

If dilute sulphuric acid be added to a solution of potassium chlorate, *chloric acid* is liberated, but it cannot be separated by distillation, as it is decomposed in the process. To obtain the free acid, sulphuric acid must be added to a solution of barium chlorate.[38] The sulphuric acid gives a precipitate of barium sulphate, and free chloric acid remains in solution. The solution may be evaporated under the receiver of an air-pump. This solution is colourless, has no smell, and acts as a powerful acid (it neutralises sodium hydroxide, decomposes sodium carbonate, gives hydrogen with zinc, &c.); when heated above 40°, however, it decomposes, forming chlorine, oxygen, and perchloric acid: $4HClO_3 = 2HClO_4 + H_2O + Cl_2 + O_3$. In a concentrated condition the acid acts as an exceedingly energetic oxidiser, so that organic substances brought into contact with it burst into flame. Iodine, sulphurous acid, and similar oxidisable substances form higher oxidation products and reduce the chloric acid to hydrochloric acid. Hydrochloric acid gas gives chlorine with chloric acid[484] (and consequently with $KClO_3$ also) acting in the same manner as it acts on the lower acids: $HClO_3 + 5HCl = 3H_2O + 3Cl_2$.

By cautiously acting on potassium chlorate with sulphuric acid, the *dioxide* (*chloric peroxide*), ClO_2,[39] is obtained (Davy, Millon). This gas is easily liquefied in a freezing mixture, and boils at $+10°$. The vapour density (about 35 if H = 1) shows that the molecule of this substance is ClO_2.[40] In a gaseous or liquid state it very easily explodes (for instance, at 60°, or by contact with organic compounds or finely divided substances, &c.), forming Cl and O_2, and in many instances[41] therefore it acts as an oxidising agent, although (like nitric peroxide) it may itself be further oxidised.[42] In dissolving in water or alkalis chloric peroxide gives chlorous and hypochlorous acids—$2ClO_2 + 2KHO = KClO_3 + KClO_2 + H_2O$— and therefore, like nitric peroxide, the dioxide may be regarded as an intermediate oxide between the (unknown) anhydrides of chlorous and chloric acids: $4ClO_2 = Cl_2O_3 + Cl_2O_5$.[43]

As the salts of chloric acid, $HClO_3$, are produced by the splitting up of the salts of hypochlorous acid, so in the same way the salts of[485] perchloric acid, $HClO_4$, are produced from the salts of chloric acid, $HClO_3$. But this is the highest form of the oxidation of HCl. *Perchloric acid*, $HClO_4$, is the most stable of all the acids of chlorine. When fused potassium chlorate begins to swell up and solidify, after having parted with one-third of its oxygen, potassium chloride and potassium perchlorate have been formed according to the equation $2KClO_3 = KClO_4 + KCl + O_2$.

The formation of this salt is easily observed in the preparation of oxygen from potassium chlorate, owing to the fact that the potassium perchlorate fuses with greater difficulty than the chlorate, and therefore appears in the molten salt as solid grains (*see* Chapter III. Note 12). Under the action of certain acids—for instance, sulphuric and nitric—potassium chlorate also gives potassium perchlorate. This latter may be easily purified, because it is but sparingly soluble in water, although all the other salts of perchloric acid are very soluble and even deliquesce in the air. The perchlorates, although they contain more oxygen than the chlorates, are decomposed with greater difficulty, and even when thrown on ignited charcoal give a much feebler deflagration than the chlorates. Sulphuric acid (at a temperature not below $100°$) evolves volatile and to a certain extent stable perchloric acid from potassium perchlorate. Neither sulphuric nor any other acid will further decompose perchloric acid as it decomposes chloric acid. Of all the acids of chlorine, perchloric acid alone can be distilled.[44] The pure hydrate $HClO_4$[45] is a colourless and exceedingly caustic substance[486] which fumes in the air and has a specific gravity $1·78$ at $15°$ (sometimes, after being kept for some time, it decomposes with a violent explosion). It explodes violently when brought into contact with charcoal, paper, wood, and other organic substances. If a small quantity of water be added to this hydrate, and it be cooled, a crystallo-hydrate, $ClHO_4,H_2O$, separates out. This is much more stable, but the liquid hydrate $HClO_4,2H_2O$ is still more so. The acid dissolves in water in all proportions, and its solutions are distinguished for their stability.[46] When ignited both the acid and its salts are decomposed, with the evolution of oxygen.[47]

[487]

On comparing chlorine as an element not only with nitrogen and carbon but with all the other non-metallic elements (chlorine has so little analogy with the metals that a comparison with them would be superfluous), we find in it the following fundamental properties of *the halogens* or salt-producers. With metals chlorine gives salts (such as sodium chloride, &c.); with hydrogen a very energetic and monobasic acid HCl, and the same quantity of chlorine is able by metalepsis to replace the hydrogen; with oxygen it forms unstable oxides of an acid character. These properties of chlorine are possessed by three other elements, bromine, iodine, and fluorine. They are members of one natural family. Each representative has its peculiarities, its individual properties and points of distinction, in combination and in the free state—otherwise they would not be independent elements; but the repetition in all of them of the same chief characteristics of the family enables one more quickly to grasp all their various properties and to classify the elements themselves.

In order to have a guiding thread in forming comparisons between the elements, attention must however be turned not only to their points of resemblance but also to those of their properties and characters in which they differ most from each other. And the atomic weights of the elements must be considered as their most elementary property, since this is a quantity which is most firmly established, and must be taken account of in all the reactions of the element. The halogens have the following atomic weights—

$$F = 19, Cl = 35·5, Br = 80, I = 127.$$

All the properties, physical and chemical, of the elements and their corresponding compounds must evidently be in a certain dependence[488] on this fundamental point, if the grouping in one family be natural.[47 bis] And we find in reality that, for instance, the properties of bromine, whose atomic weight is almost the mean between those of iodine and chlorine, occupy a mean position between those of these two elements. The second measurable property of the elements is their equivalence or their capacity for forming *compounds of definite forms*. Thus carbon or nitrogen in this respect differs widely from the halogens. Although the form ClO_2 corresponds with NO_2 and CO_2, yet the last is the highest oxide of carbon, whilst that of nitrogen is N_2O_5, and for chlorine, if there were an anhydride of perchloric acid, its composition would be Cl_2O_7, which is quite different from that of carbon. In respect to the forms of their compounds the halogens, like all elements of one family or group, are perfectly analogous to each other, as is seen from their hydrogen compounds:

HF, HCl, HBr, HI.

Their oxygen compounds exhibit a similar analogy. Only fluorine does not give any oxygen compounds. The iodine and bromine compounds corresponding with $HClO_3$ and $HClO_4$ are $HBrO_3$ and $HBrO_4$, HIO_3 and HIO_4. On comparing the properties of these acids we can even predict that fluorine will not form any oxygen compound. For iodine is easily oxidised—for instance, by nitric acid—whilst chlorine is not directly oxidised. The oxygen acids of iodine are comparatively more stable than those of chlorine; and, generally speaking, the affinity of iodine for oxygen is much greater than that of chlorine. Here also bromine occupies an intermediate position. In fluorine we may therefore expect a still smaller affinity for oxygen than in chlorine—and up to now it has not been combined with oxygen. If any oxygen compounds of fluorine should be obtained, they will naturally be exceedingly unstable. The relation of these elements to hydrogen is the reverse of the above. Fluorine has so great an affinity for hydrogen that it decomposes water at the ordinary temperature; whilst iodine[489] has so little affinity for hydrogen that hydriodic acid, HI, is formed with difficulty, is easily decomposed, and acts as a reducing agent in a number of cases.

From the form of their compounds the halogens are *univalent elements* with respect to hydrogen and septivalent with respect to oxygen, N being trivalent to hydrogen (it gives NH_3) and quinqui-valent to oxygen (it gives N_2O_5), and C being quadrivalent to both H and O as it forms CH_4 and

CO_2. And as not only their oxygen compounds, but also their hydrogen compounds, have acid properties, the halogens are *elements* of an exclusively *acid character*. Such metals as sodium, potassium, barium only give basic oxides. In the case of nitrogen, although it forms acid oxides, still in ammonia we find that capacity to give an alkali with hydrogen which indicates a less distinctly acid character than in the halogens. In no other elements is the acid-giving property so strongly developed as in the halogens.

In describing certain peculiarities characterising the halogens, we shall at every step encounter a confirmation of the above-mentioned general relations.

As *fluorine* decomposes water with the evolution of oxygen, $F_2 + H_2O = 2HF + O$, for a long time all efforts to obtain it in free state by means of methods similar to those for the preparation of chlorine proved fruitless.[48] Thus by the action of hydrofluoric acid on manganese peroxide, or by decomposing a solution of hydrofluoric acid by an electric current, either oxygen or a mixture of oxygen and fluorine were obtained instead of fluorine. Probably a certain quantity of fluorine[48 bis] was set free by the action of oxygen or an electric current on incandescent and fused calcium fluoride, but at a high temperature fluorine acts even on platinum, and therefore it was not obtained. When chlorine acted on silver fluoride, AgF, in a vessel of natural fluor spar, CaF_2, fluorine was also liberated; but it was mixed[490] with chlorine, and it was impossible to study the properties of the resultant gas. Brauner (1881) also obtained fluorine by igniting cerium fluoride, $2CeF_4 = 2CeF_3 + F_2$; but this, like all preceding efforts, only showed fluorine to be a gas which decomposes water, and is capable of acting in a number of instances like chlorine, but gave no possibility of testing its properties. It was evident that it was necessary to avoid as far as possible the presence of water and a rise of temperature; this Moissan succeeded in doing in 1886. He decomposed anhydrous hydrofluoric acid, liquefied at a temperature of -23° and contained in a U-shaped tube (to which a small quantity of potassium fluoride had been added to make it a better conductor), by the action of a powerful electric current (twenty Bunsen's elements in series). Hydrogen was then evolved at the negative pole, and fluorine appeared at the positive pole (of iridium platinum) as a pale green gas which decomposed water with the formation of ozone and hydrofluoric acid, and combined directly with silicon (forming silicon fluoride, SiF_4), boron (forming BF_3), sulphur, &c. Its density (H = 1) is 18, so that its molecule is F_2. But the action of fluorine on metals at the ordinary temperature is comparatively feeble, because the metallic fluoride formed coats the remaining mass of the metals; it is, however, completely absorbed by iron. Hydrocarbons (such as naphtha), alcohol, &c.,

immediately absorb fluorine, with the formation of hydrofluoric acid. Fluorine when mixed with hydrogen can easily be made to explode violently, forming hydrofluoric acid.[49]

In 1894, Brauner obtained fluorine directly by igniting the easily[491] formed[49 bis] double lead salt HF,3KF,PbF$_4$, which first, at 230°, decomposes with the evolution of HF, and then splits up forming 3KF,PbF$_2$ and fluorine F$_2$, which is recognised by the fact that it liberates iodine from KI and easily combines with silicon, forming SiF$_4$. This method gives chemically pure fluorine, and is based upon the breaking up of the higher compound—tetrafluoride of lead, PbF$_4$, corresponding to PbO$_2$, into free fluorine, F$_2$, and the lower more stable form—bifluoride of lead, PbF$_2$, which corresponds to PbO; that is, this method resembles the ordinary method of obtaining chlorine by means of MnO$_2$, as MnCl$_4$ here breaks up into MnCl$_2$ and chlorine, just as PbF$_4$ splits up into PbF$_2$ and fluorine.

Among the compounds of fluorine, calcium fluoride, CaF$_2$, is somewhat widely distributed in nature as fluor spar,[50] whilst *cryolite*, or aluminium sodium fluoride, Na$_3$AlF$_6$, is found more rarely (in large masses in Greenland). Cryolite, like fluor spar, is also insoluble in water, and gives hydrofluoric acid with sulphuric acid. Small quantities of fluorine have also in a number of cases been found in the bodies of animals, in the blood, urine, and bones. If fluorides occur in the bodies of animals, they must have been introduced in food, and must occur in plants and in water. And as a matter of fact river, and especially sea, water always contains a certain, although small, quantity of fluorine compounds.

Hydrofluoric acid, HF, cannot be obtained from fluor spar in glass retorts, because glass is acted on by and destroys the acid. It is[492] prepared in lead vessels, and when it is required pure, in platinum vessels, because lead also acts on hydrofluoric acid, although only very feebly on the surface, and when once a coating of fluoride and sulphate of lead is formed no further action takes place. Powdered fluor spar and sulphuric acid evolve hydrofluoric acid (which fumes in the air) even at the ordinary temperature, CaF$_2$ + H$_2$SO$_4$ = CaSO$_4$ + 2HF. At 130° fluor spar is completely decomposed by sulphuric acid. The acid is then evolved as vapour, which may be condensed by a freezing mixture into an anhydrous acid. The condensation is aided by pouring water into the receiver of the condenser, as the acid is easily soluble in cold water.

In the liquid anhydrous form hydrofluoric acid boils at +19°, and its specific gravity at 12·8° = 0·9849.[51] It dissolves in water with the evolution of a considerable amount of heat, and gives a solution of constant boiling point which distils over at 120°; showing that the acid is able to combine with water. The specific gravity of the compound is $1·15$, and its composition $HF,2H_2O$.[52] With an excess of water a dilute solution distils over first. The aqueous solution and the acid itself must be kept in platinum vessels, but the dilute acid may be conveniently preserved in vessels made of various organic materials, such as gutta-percha, or even in glass vessels having an interior coating of paraffin. Hydrofluoric acid does not act on hydrocarbons and many other substances, but it acts in a highly corrosive manner on metals, glass, porcelain, and the majority of rock substances.[53] It also attacks the skin,[493] and is distinguished by its poisonous properties, so that in working with the acid a strong draught must be kept up, to prevent the possibility of the fumes being inhaled. The non-metals do not act on hydrofluoric acid, but all metals—with the exception of mercury, silver, gold, and platinum, and, to a certain degree, lead— decompose it with the evolution of hydrogen. With bases it gives directly metallic fluorides, and behaves in many respects like hydrochloric acid. There are, however, several distinct individual differences, which are furthermore much greater than those between hydrochloric, hydrobromic, and hydriodic acids. Thus the silver compounds of the latter are insoluble in water, whilst silver fluoride is soluble. Calcium fluoride, on the contrary, is insoluble in water, whilst calcium chloride, bromide, and iodide are not only soluble, but attract water with great energy. Neither hydrochloric, hydrobromic, nor hydriodic acid acts on sand and glass, whilst hydrofluoric acid corrodes them, forming gaseous silicon fluoride. The other halogen acids only form normal salts, KCl, NaCl, with Na or K, whilst hydrofluoric acid gives acid salts, for instance HKF_2 (and by dissolving KF in liquid HF, KHF_22HF is obtained). This latter property is in close connection with the fact that at the ordinary temperature the vapour density of hydrofluoric acid is nearly 20, which corresponds with a formula H_2F_2, as Mallet (1881) showed; but a depolymerisation occurs with a rise of temperature, and the density approaches 10, which answers to the formula HF.[54]

The analogy between chlorine and the other two halogens, bromine and iodine, is much more perfect. Not only have their hydrates or halogen acids much in common, but they themselves resemble chlorine in many respects,[55] and even the properties of the corresponding[494] metallic compounds of bromine and iodine are very much alike. Thus, the chlorides, bromides, and iodides of sodium and potassium crystallise in the cubic system, and are soluble in water; the chlorides of calcium, aluminium, magnesium, and barium are just as soluble in water as the bromides and iodides of these metals. The iodides and bromides of silver and lead are sparingly soluble in water, like the chlorides of these metals. The oxygen compounds of bromine and iodine also present a very strong analogy to the corresponding compounds of chlorine. A hypobromous acid is known corresponding with hypochlorous acid. The salts of this acid have the same bleaching property as the salts of hypochlorous acid. Iodine was discovered in 1811 by Courtois in kelp, and was shortly afterwards investigated by Clement, Gay-Lussac, and Davy. Bromine was discovered in 1826 by Balard in the mother liquor of sea water.

Bromine and iodine, like chlorine, occur in sea water in combination with metals. However, the amount of bromides, and especially of iodides, in sea water is so small that their presence can only be discovered by means of sensitive reactions.[56] In the extraction of salt from sea water the bromides remain in the mother liquor. Iodine and bromine also occur combined with silver, in admixture with silver chloride, as a rare ore which is mainly found in America. Certain[495] mineral waters (those of Kreuznach and Staro-rossüsk) contain metallic bromides and iodides, always in admixture with an excess of sodium chloride. Those upper strata of the Stassfurt rock salt (Chapter X.) which are a source of potassium salts also contain metallic bromides,[57] which collect in the mother liquors left after the crystallisation of the potassium salts; and this now forms the chief source (together with certain American springs) of the bromine in common use. Bromine may be easily liberated from a mixture of bromides and chlorides, owing to the fact that chlorine displaces bromine from its compounds with sodium, magnesium, calcium, &c. A colourless solution of bromides and chlorides turns an orange colour after the passage of chlorine, owing to the disengagement of bromine.[58] Bromine may be extracted on a large scale by a similar method, but it is simpler to add a small quantity of manganese peroxide and sulphuric acid to the mother liquid direct. This sets free a portion of the chlorine, and this chlorine liberates the bromine.

Bromine is a *dark brown liquid*, giving brown fumes, and having a poisonous suffocating smell, whence its name (from the Greek βρῶμος, signifying evil smelling). The vapour density of bromine shows that its molecule is Br_2. In the cold bromine freezes into brown-grey scales like iodine. The melting point of pure bromine is -7°·05.[59] The density of liquid bromide at 0° is 3·187, and at 15° about 3·0. The boiling point of bromine is about 58°·7. Bromine, like chlorine, is soluble in water; 1 part of bromine at 5° requires 27 parts of water, and at 15° 29 parts of water. The aqueous solution of bromine is of[496] an orange colour, and when cooled to -2° yields crystals containing 10 molecules of water to 1 molecule of bromine.[60] Alcohol dissolves a greater quantity of bromine, and ether a still greater amount. But after a certain time products of the action of the bromine on these organic substances are formed in the solutions. Aqueous solutions of the bromides also absorb a large amount of bromine.

With respect to *iodine*, it is almost exclusively extracted from the mother liquors after the crystallisation of natural sodium nitrate (Chili saltpetre) and from the ashes of the sea-weed cast upon the shores of France, Great

Britain, and Spain, sometimes in considerable quantities, by the high tides. The majority of these sea-weeds are of the genera *Fucus, Laminaria*, &c. The fused ashes of these sea-weeds are called 'kelp' in Scotland and 'varech' in Normandy. A somewhat considerable quantity of iodine is contained in these sea-weeds. After[497] being burnt (or subjected to dry distillation) an ash is left which chiefly contains salts of potassium, sodium, and calcium. The metals occur in the sea-weed as salts of organic acids. On being burnt these organic salts are decomposed, forming carbonates of potassium and sodium. Hence, sodium carbonate is found in the ash of sea plants. The ash is dissolved in hot water, and on evaporation sodium carbonate and other salts separate, but a portion of the substances remains in solution. These mother liquors left after the separation of the sodium carbonate contain chlorine, bromine, and iodine in combination with metals, the chlorine and iodine being in excess of the bromine. 13,000 kilos of kelp give about 1,000 kilos of sodium carbonate and 15 kilos of iodine.

The liberation of the iodine from the mother liquor is effected with comparative ease, because chlorine disengages iodine from potassium iodide and its other combinations with the metals. Not only chlorine, but also sulphuric acid, liberates iodine from sodium iodide. Sulphuric acid, in acting on an iodide, sets hydriodic acid free, but the latter easily decomposes, especially in the presence of substances capable of evolving oxygen, such as chromic acid, nitrous acid, and even ferric salts.[61] Owing to its sparing solubility in water, the iodine liberated separates as a precipitate. To obtain pure iodine it is sufficient to distil it, and neglect the first and last portions of the distillate, the middle portion only being collected. Iodine passes directly from a state of vapour into a crystalline form, and settles on the cool portions of the[498] apparatus in tabular crystals, having a black grey colour and metallic lustre.[62]

The specific gravity of the crystals of iodine is 4·95. It melts at 114° and boils at 184°. Its vapour is formed at a much lower temperature, and is of a violet colour, whence iodine receives its name (ἰοειδης, violet). The smell of iodine recalls the characteristic smell of hypochlorous acid; it has a sharp sour taste. It destroys the skin and organs of the body, and is therefore frequently employed for cauterising and as an irritant for the skin. In small quantities it turns the skin brown, but the coloration disappears after a certain time, partly owing to the volatility of the iodine. Water dissolves only $\frac{1}{5000}$ part of iodine. A brown solution is thus obtained, which bleaches, but much more feebly than bromine and chlorine. Water which contains salts, and especially iodides, in solution dissolves iodine in considerable quantities, and the resultant solution is of a dark brown colour. Pure alcohol dissolves a small amount of iodine, and in so doing acquires a brown colour, but the solubility of iodine is considerably increased by the presence of a small quantity of an iodine compound—for instance, ethyl iodide—in the alcohol.[63] Ether dissolves a larger amount of iodine than alcohol; but iodine is particularly soluble in liquid hydrocarbons, in carbon bisulphide, and in chloroform. A small quantity of iodine dissolved in carbon bisulphide tints it rose-colour, but in a somewhat larger amount it gives a violet colour. Chloroform (quite free from alcohol) is also tinted rose colour by a small amount of iodine. This gives an easy means for detecting the presence of free iodine in small quantities. The blue coloration which free iodine gives with *starch* may also, as has already been frequently mentioned (*see* Chapter IV.), serve for the detection of iodine.

If we compare the four elements, fluorine, chlorine, bromine, and iodine, we see in them an example of analogous substances which arrange themselves by their physical properties in the same order as[499] they stand in respect to their atomic and molecular weights. If the weight of the molecule be large, the substance has a higher specific gravity, a higher melting and boiling point, and a whole series of properties depending on this difference in its fundamental properties. Chlorine in a free state boils at about -35°, bromine boils at 60°, and iodine only above 180°. According to Avogadro-Gerhardt's law, the vapour densities of these elements in a gaseous state are proportional to their atomic weights, and here, at all events approximately, the densities in a liquid (or solid) state are also almost in the ratio of their atomic weights. Dividing the atomic weight of chlorine (35·5) by its specific gravity in a liquid state (1·3), we obtain a volume = 27, for bromine (80/3·1) 26, and for iodine also (127/4·9) 26.[64]

The metallic bromides and iodides are in the majority of cases, in most respects analogous to the corresponding chlorides,[65] but chlorine displaces the bromine and iodine from them, and bromine liberates iodine from iodides, which is taken advantage of in the preparation of these halogens. However, the researches of Potilitzin showed that a *reverse* displacement of chlorine by bromine may occur both in solutions and in ignited metallic chlorides in an atmosphere of bromine vapour—that is, a distribution of the metal (according to Berthollet's doctrine) takes place between the halogens, although however the larger portion, still unites with the chlorine, which shows its greater affinity for metals as compared with that of bromine and iodine.[66] The latter, however,[500] sometimes behave with respect to metallic oxides in exactly the same manner as chlorine. Gay-Lussac, by igniting potassium carbonate in iodine vapour, obtained (as with chlorine) an evolution of oxygen and carbonic anhydride, $K_2CO_3 + I_2 = 2KI + CO_2 + O$, only the reactions between the halogens and oxygen are more easily reversible with bromine and iodine than with chlorine. Thus, at a red heat oxygen displaces iodine from barium iodide. Aluminium iodide burns in a current of oxygen (Deville and Troost), and a similar, although not so clearly marked, relation exists for aluminium chloride, and shows that the halogens have a distinctly smaller affinity for those metals which only form feeble bases. This is still more the case with the non-metals, which form acids and evolve much more heat with oxygen than with the halogens (Note 13). But in all these instances the affinity (and amount of heat evolved) of iodine and bromine is less than that of chlorine, probably because the atomic weights are greater.[501] The smaller store of energy in iodine and bromine is seen still more clearly in the relation of the halogens to hydrogen. In a gaseous state they all enter, with more or less ease, into direct combination with gaseous hydrogen—for example, in the presence of spongy platinum, forming halogen acids, HX—but the latter are far from being equally stable; hydrogen chloride is the most stable, hydrogen iodide the least so, and hydrogen bromide occupies an intermediate position. A very high temperature is required to decompose hydrogen chloride even partially, whilst hydrogen iodide is decomposed by light even at the ordinary temperature and very easily by a red heat. Hence the reaction $I_2 + H_2 = HI + HI$ is very easily reversible, and consequently has a limit, and hydrogen iodide easily dissociates.[67] Judging by the direct measurement of the heat evolved (22,000 heat units) in the formation of HCl, the conversion of 2HCl into $H_2 + Cl_2$ requires the expenditure[502] of 44,000 heat units. The decomposition of 2HBr into $H_2 + Br_2$ only requires, if the bromine be obtained in a gaseous state, a consumption of about 24,000 units, whilst in the decomposition of 2HI into $H_2 + I_2$ as vapour about 3,000 heat units are *evolved*;[68] these facts, without doubt, stand in causal connection with the great stability of hydrogen chloride, the easy decomposability of hydrogen iodide, and the intermediate properties of hydrogen bromide. From this it would be expected that chlorine is capable of decomposing water with the evolution of oxygen, whilst iodine has not the energy to produce this disengagement,[69] although it is able to liberate the oxygen from the oxides of potassium and sodium, the affinity of these metals for the halogens being very considerable. For this reason oxygen, especially in compounds from which it can be evolved readily (for instance, ClHO, CrO_3, &c.), easily decomposes hydrogen iodide. A mixture of hydrogen iodide and oxygen burns in the presence of an ignited substance, forming water and iodine. Drops of nitric acid in an atmosphere of hydrogen iodide cause the disengagement of violet fumes of iodine and brown fumes of nitric peroxide. In the presence of alkalis and an excess of water, however, iodine is able to effect oxidation like chlorine—that is,[503] it decomposes water; the action is here aided by the affinity of hydrogen iodide for the alkali and water, just as sulphuric acid helps zinc to decompose water. But the relative instability of hydriodic acid is best seen in comparing the acids in a gaseous state. If the halogen acids be dissolved in water, they evolve so much heat that they approach much nearer to each other in properties. This is seen from thermochemical data, for in the formation of HX in solution (in a large excess of water) from the *gaseous* elements there is *evolved* for HCl 39,000, for HBr 32,000, and for HI 18,000 heat units.[70] But it is especially evident from the fact that solutions of hydrogen bromide and iodide in water have many points in common with solutions of hydrogen chloride, both in their capacity to form hydrates and fuming solutions of constant boiling point, and in their capacity to form haloid salts, &c. by reacting on bases.

In consequence of what has been said above, it follows that *hydrobromic and hydriodic acids*, being substances which are but slightly stable, cannot be evolved in a gaseous state under many of those conditions under which hydrochloric acid is formed. Thus if sulphuric acid in solution acts on sodium iodide, all the same phenomena take place as with sodium chloride (a portion of the sodium iodide gives hydriodic acid, and all remains in solution), but if sodium iodide be mixed with strong sulphuric acid, then the oxygen of the latter decomposes the hydriodic acid set free, with liberation of iodine, $H_2SO_4 + 2HI = 2H_2O + SO_2 + I_2$. This reaction takes place in the reverse direction in the presence of a *large quantity* of water (2,000 parts of water per 1 part of SO_2), in which case not only the affinity of hydriodic acid for water is brought to light but also the action of water in directing chemical reactions in which it participates.[71] Therefore, with a halogen salt, it is easy to obtain gaseous hydrochloric acid by the action of sulphuric acid, but neither hydrobromic nor hydriodic acid can be so obtained in the free state (as gases).[72] Other methods have to be resorted to for their preparation, and recourse must not be had to compounds of oxygen, which are so easily able to destroy these acids. Therefore hydrogen sulphide, phosphorus, &c., which themselves easily take up oxygen, are introduced as means for the conversion of bromine and iodine into hydrobromic and hydriodic acids in the presence of water. For example, in the action of phosphorus the essence of the matter is that the oxygen of the water goes[504] to the phosphorus, and the union of the remaining elements leads to the formation of hydrobromic or hydriodic acid; but the matter is complicated by the reversibility of the reaction, the affinity for water, and other circumstances which are understood by following Berthollet's doctrine. Chlorine (and bromine also) directly decomposes hydrogen sulphide, forming hydrochloric acid and liberating sulphur, both in a gaseous form and in solutions, whilst iodine only decomposes hydrogen sulphide in weak solutions, when its affinity for hydrogen is aided by the affinity of hydrogen iodide for water. In a gaseous state iodine does not act on hydrogen sulphide,[73] whilst sulphur is able to decompose gaseous hydriodic acid, forming hydrogen sulphide and a compound of sulphur and iodine which with water forms hydriodic acid.[74]

If hydrogen sulphide be passed through water containing iodine, the reaction $H_2S + I_2 = 2HI + S$ proceeds so long as the solution is dilute, but when the mass of free HI increases the reaction stops, because the iodine then passes into solution. A solution having a composition approximating to $2HI + 4I_2 + 9H_2O$ (according to Bineau) does not react with H_2S, notwithstanding the quantity of free iodine. Therefore only weak solutions of hydriodic acid can be obtained by passing hydrogen sulphide into water with iodine.[74 bis]

To obtain[75] gaseous hydrobromic and hydriodic acids it is most[505] convenient to take advantage of the reactions between phosphorus, the halogens, and water, the latter being present in small quantity (otherwise the halogen acids formed are dissolved by it); the halogen is gradually added to the phosphorus moistened with water. Thus if red phosphorus be placed in a flask and moistened with water, and bromine be added drop by drop (from a tap funnel), hydrobromic acid is abundantly and uniformly disengaged.[76] Hydrogen[506] iodide is prepared by adding 1 part of common (yellow) dry phosphorus to 10 parts of dry iodine in a glass flask. On shaking the flask, union proceeds quietly between them (light and heat being evolved), and when the mass of iodide of phosphorus which is formed has cooled, water is added drop by drop (from a tap funnel) and hydrogen iodide is evolved directly without the aid of heat. These methods of preparation will be at once understood when it is remembered (p. 468) that phosphorus chloride gives hydrogen chloride with water. It is exactly the same here—the oxygen of the water passes over to the phosphorus, and the hydrogen to the iodine, thus, $PI_3 + 3H_2O = PH_3O_3 + 3HI$.[77]

In a gaseous form hydrobromic and hydriodic acids are closely analogous to hydrochloric acid; they are liquefied by pressure and cold, they fume in the air, form solutions and hydrates, of constant boiling point, and react on metals, oxides and salts, &c.[78] Only the relatively[507] easy decomposability of hydrobromic acid and especially of hydriodic acid, clearly distinguish these acids from hydrochloric acid. For this reason, hydriodic acid acts in a number of cases as a deoxidiser or reducer, and frequently even serves as a means for the transference of hydrogen. Thus Berthelot, Baeyer, Wreden, and others, by heating unsaturated hydrocarbons in a solution of hydriodic acid, obtained their compounds with hydrogen nearer to the limit C_nH_{2n+2} or even the saturated compounds. For example, benzene, C_6H_6, when heated in a closed tube with a strong solution of hydriodic acid, gives hexylene, C_6H_{12}. The easy decomposability of hydriodic acid accounts for the fact that iodine does not act by metalepsis on hydrocarbons, for the hydrogen iodide liberated with the product of metalepsis, RI, formed, gives iodine and the hydrogen compound, RH, back again. And therefore, to obtain the products of iodine substitution, either iodic acid, HIO_3 (Kekulé), or mercury oxide, HgO (Weselsky), is added, as they immediately react on the hydrogen iodide, thus: $HIO_3 + 5HI = 3H_2O + 3I_2$, or, $HgO + 2HI = HgI_2 + H_2O$. From these considerations it will be readily understood that iodine acts like chlorine (or bromine) on ammonia and sodium hydroxide, for in these cases the hydriodic acid produced forms NH_4I and NaI. With tincture of iodine or even the solid element, a solution of ammonia immediately forms a highly-explosive solid black product of metalepsis, NHI_2, generally known as *iodide* of *nitrogen*, although it still contains hydrogen (this was proved beyond doubt by Szuhay 1893), which may be replaced by silver (with the formation of $NAgI_2$): $3NH_3 + 2I_2 = 2NH_4I + NHI_2$. However, the composition of the last product is variable, and with an excess of water NI_3 seems to be formed. Iodide of nitrogen is just as explosive as nitrogen chloride.[78 bis] In the[508] action of iodine on sodium hydroxide no bleaching compound is formed (whilst bromine gives one), but a direct reaction is always accomplished with the formation of an iodate, $6NaHO + 3I_2 = 5NaI + 3H_2O + NaIO_3$ (Gay-Lussac). Solutions of other alkalis, and even a mixture of water and oxide of mercury, act in the same manner.[79] This direct formation of *iodic acid*, $HIO_3 = IO_2(OH)$, shows the propensity of iodine to give compounds of the type IX_5. Indeed, this capacity of iodine to form compounds of a high type emphasises itself in many ways. But it is most important to turn attention to the fact that iodic acid is easily and directly formed by the action of oxidising substances on iodine. Thus, for instance, strong nitric acid directly converts iodine into iodic acid, whilst it has no oxidising action on chlorine.[79 bis] This shows a greater affinity in iodine for oxygen than in chlorine, and this conclusion is confirmed by the fact that iodine displaces chlorine from[509] its oxygen acids,[80] and that in the presence of water chlorine oxidises iodine.[81] Even ozone or a silent discharge passed through a mixture of oxygen and iodine vapour is able to directly oxidise iodine[82] into iodic acid. It is disengaged from solutions as a hydrate, HIO_3, which loses water at 170°, and gives an anhydride, I_2O_5. Both these substances are crystalline (sp. gr. I_2O_5 5·037, HIO_3 4·869 at 0°), colourless and soluble in water;[83] both decompose at a red heat into iodine and oxygen, are in many cases powerfully oxidising—for instance, they oxidise sulphurous anhydride, hydrogen sulphide, carbonic oxide, &c.— form chloride of iodine and water with hydrochloric acid, and with bases form salts, not only normal MIO_3, but also acid; for example, KIO_3HIO_3, KIO_32HIO_3.[83 bis] With hydriodic acid iodic acid immediately reacts, disengaging iodine, $HIO_3 + 5HI = 3H_2O + 3I_2$.

[510]

As with chlorine, so with iodine, a *periodic acid*, HIO_4, is formed. This acid is produced in the form of its salts, by the action of chlorine on alkaline solutions of iodates, and also by the action of iodine on chloric acid.[84] It crystallises from solutions as a hydrate containing $2H_2O$ (corresponding with $HClO_4,2H_2O$), but as it forms salts containing up to 5 atoms of metals, this water must be counted as water of constitution. Therefore $IO(OH)_5 = HIO_4,2H_2O$ corresponds with the highest form of halogen compounds, IX_7.[85] In decomposing (at[511] 200°) or acting as an oxidiser, periodic acid first gives iodic acid, but it may also be ultimately decomposed.

Compounds formed between chlorine and iodine must be classed among the most interesting halogen bodies.[86] These elements combine together directly with evolution of heat, and form *iodine monochloride*, ICl, or *iodine trichloride*, ICl_3.[87] As water reacts on these substances, forming iodic acid and iodine, they have to be prepared from dry iodine and chlorine.[88] Both substances are formed in a number of reactions; for example, by the action of aqua regia on iodine, of chlorine on hydriodic acid, of hydrochloric acid on periodic acid, of iodine on potassium chlorate (with the aid of heat, &c.) Trapp obtained iodine monochloride, in beautiful red crystals, by passing a rapid current of chlorine into molten iodine. The monochloride then distils over and solidifies, melting at 27°. By passing chlorine over the[512] crystals of the monochloride, it is easy to obtain iodine trichloride in orange crystals, which melt at 34° and volatilise at 47°, but in so doing decompose (into Cl_2 and ClI). The chemical properties of these chlorides entirely resemble those of chlorine and iodine, as would be expected, because, in this instance, a combination of similar substances has taken place as in the formation of solutions or alloys. Thus, for instance, the unsaturated hydrocarbons (for example, C_2H_4), which are capable of directly combining with chlorine and iodine, also directly combine with iodine monochloride.

Footnotes:

[1] The decomposition of fused sodium chloride by an electric current has been proposed in America and Russia (N. N. Beketoff) as a means for the preparation of chlorine and sodium. A strong solution of hydrochloric acid is decomposed into equal volumes of chlorine and hydrogen by the action of an electric current. If sodium chloride and lead be melted in a crucible, the former being connected with the cathode and a carbon anode immersed in the lead, then the lead dissolves sodium and chlorine is disengaged as gas. This electrolytic method has not yet been practised on a large scale, probably because gaseous chlorine has not many applications, and because of the difficulty there is in dealing with it.

[2] To obtain so high a temperature (at which the best kinds of porcelain soften) Langer and Meyer employed the dense graphitoidal carbon from

gas retorts, and a powerful blast. They determined the temperature by the alteration of the volume of nitrogen in the platinum vessel, for this gas does not permeate through platinum, and is unaltered by heat.

[2 bis] The acid properties of hydrochloric acid were known when Lavoisier pointed out the formation of acids by the combination of water with the oxides of the non-metals, and therefore there was reason for thinking that hydrochloric acid was formed by the combination of water with the oxide of some element. Hence when Scheele obtained chlorine by the action of hydrochloric acid on manganese peroxide he considered it as the acid contained in common salt. When it became known that chlorine gives hydrochloric acid with hydrogen, Lavoisier and Berthollet supposed it to be a compound with oxygen of an anhydride contained in hydrochloric acid. They supposed that hydrochloric acid contained water and the oxide of a particular radicle, and that chlorine was a higher degree of oxidation of this radicle *muvias* (from the Latin neme of hydrochloric acid, *acidum muriaticum*). It was only in 1811 that Gay-Lussac and Thénard in France and Davy in England arrived at the conclusion that the substance obtained by Scheele does not contain oxygen, nor under any conditions give water with hydrogen, and that there is no water in hydrochloric acid gas, and therefore concluded that chlorine is an elementary substance. They named it 'chlorine' from the Greek word χλωϱός, signifying a green colour, because of the peculiar colour by which this gas is characterised

[3] However, nitric acid has been proposed as a means for obtaining chlorine, but by methods which have the drawback of being very complicated

[3 bis] This representation of the process of the reaction is most natural. However, this decomposition is generally represented as if chlorine gave only one degree of combination with manganese, $MnCl_2$, and therefore directly reacts in the following manner—$MnO_2 + 4HCl = MnCl_2 + 2H_2O + Cl_2$, in which case it is supposed that manganese peroxide, MnO_2, breaks up, as it were, into manganous oxide, MnO and oxygen, both of which react with hydrochloric acid, the manganous oxide acting upon HCl as a base, giving $MnCl_2$ and at the same time $2HCl + O = H_2O + Cl_2$. In reality, a mixture of oxygen and hydrochloric acid does give chlorine at a red heat, and this reaction may also take place at the moment of its evolution in this case.

All the oxides of manganese (Mn_2O_3, MnO_2, MnO_3, Mn_2O_7), with the exception of manganous oxide, MnO, disengage chlorine from hydrochloric acid, because manganous chloride, $MnCl_2$, is the only compound of chlorine and manganese which exists as a stable compound, all the higher chlorides of manganese being unstable and evolving chlorine.

Hence we here take note of two separate changes: (1) an exchange between oxygen and chlorine, and (2) the instability of the higher chlorine compounds. As (according to the law of substitution) in the substitution of oxygen by chlorine, Cl_2 takes the place of O, the chlorine compounds will contain more atoms than the corresponding oxygen compounds. It is not surprising, therefore, that certain of the chlorine compounds corresponding with oxygen compounds do not exist, or if they are formed are very unstable. And furthermore, an atom of chlorine is heavier than an atom of oxygen, and therefore a given element would have to retain a large mass of chlorine if in the higher oxides the oxygen were replaced by chlorine. For this reason equivalent compounds of chlorine do not exist for all oxygen compounds. Many of the former are immediately decomposed, when formed, with the evolution of chlorine. From this it is evident that there should exist such chlorine compounds as would evolve chlorine as peroxides evolve oxygen, and indeed a large number of such compounds are known. Amongst them may be mentioned antimony pentachloride, $SbCl_5$, which splits up into chlorine and antimony trichloride when heated. Cupric chloride, corresponding with copper oxide, and having a composition $CuCl_2$, similar to CuO, when heated parts with half its chlorine, just as barium peroxide evolves half its oxygen. This method may even be taken advantage of for the preparation of chlorine and cuprous chloride, CuCl. The latter attracts oxygen from the atmosphere, and in so doing is converted from a colourless substance into a green compound whose composition is Cu_2Cl_2O. With hydrochloric acid this substance gives cupric chloride ($Cu_2Cl_2O + 2HCl = H_2O + 2CuCl_2$), which has only to be dried and heated in order again to obtain chlorine. Thus, in solution, and at the ordinary temperature, the compound $CuCl_2$ is stable, but when heated it splits up. On this property is founded Deacon's process for the preparation of chlorine from hydrochloric acid with the aid of air and copper salts, by passing a mixture of air and hydrochloric acid at about 440° over bricks saturated with a solution of a copper salt (a mixture of solutions of $CuSO_4$ and Na_2SO_4). $CuCl_2$ is then formed by the double decomposition of the salt of copper and the hydrochloric acid; the $CuCl_2$ liberates chlorine, and the CuCl forms Cu_2Cl_2O with the oxygen of the air, which again gives $CuCl_2$ with 2HCl, and so on.

Magnesium chloride, which is obtained from sea-water, carnallite, &c., may serve not only as a means for the preparation of hydrochloric acid, but also of chlorine, because its basic salt (magnesium oxychloride) when heated in the air gives magnesium oxide and chlorine (Weldon-Pechiney's process, 1888). Chlorine is now prepared on a large scale by this method. Several new methods based upon this reaction have been proposed for procuring chlorine from the bye-products of other chemical processes. Thus, Lyte and Tattars (1891) obtained up to 67 p.c. of chlorine from

CaCl$_2$ in this manner. A solution of CaCl$_2$, containing a certain amount of common salt, is evaporated and oxide of magnesium added to it. When the solution attains a density of 1·2445 (at 15°), it is treated with carbonic acid, which precipitates carbonate of calcium, while chloride of magnesium remains in solution. After adding ammonium chloride, the solution is evaporated to dryness and the double chloride of magnesium and ammonium formed is ignited, which drives off the chloride of ammonium. The chloride of magnesium which remains behind is used in the Weldon-Pechiney process. The De Wilde-Reychler (1892) process for the manufacture of chlorine consists in passing alternate currents of hot air and hydrochloric acid gas through a cylinder containing a mixture of the chlorides of magnesium and manganese. A certain amount of sulphate of magnesium which does not participate in any way in the reaction, is added to the mixture to prevent its fusing. The reactions may be expressed by the following equations: (1) $3MgCl_2 + 3MnCl_2 + 8O = Mg_3Mn_3O_8 + 12Cl$; (2) $Mg_3Mn_3O_8 + 16HCl = 3MgCl_2 + 3MnCl_2 + 8H_2O + 4Cl$. As nitric acid is able to take up the hydrogen from hydrochloric acid, a heated mixture of these acids is also employed for the preparation of chlorine. The resultant mixture of chlorine and lower oxides of nitrogen is mixed with air and steam which regenerates the HNO$_3$, while the chlorine remains as a gas together with nitrogen, in which form it is quite capable of bleaching, forming chloride of lime, &c. Besides these, Solvay and Mond's methods of preparing chlorine must be mentioned. The first is based upon the reaction $CaCl_2 + SiO_2 + O(air) = CaOSiO_2 + Cl_2$, the second on the action of the oxygen of the air (heated) upon MgCl$_2$ (and certain similar chlorides) $MgCl_2 + O = MgO + Cl_2$ The remaining MgO is treated with sal-ammoniac to re-form MgCl$_2$ ($MgO + 2NH_4Cl = MgCl_2 + H_2O + 2NH_3$) and the resultant NH$_3$ again converted into sal-ammoniac, so that hydrochloric acid is the only substance consumed. The latter processes have not yet found much application.

[4] The following proportions are accordingly taken by weight: 5 parts of powdered manganese peroxide, 11 parts of salt (best fused, to prevent its frothing), and 14 parts of sulphuric acid previously mixed with an equal volume of water. The mixture is heated in a salt bath, so as to obtain a temperature above 100°. The corks in the apparatus must be soaked in paraffin (otherwise they are corroded by the chlorine), and black india-rubber tubing smeared with vaseline must be used, and not vulcanised rubber (which contains sulphur, and becomes brittle under the action of the chlorine).

The reaction which proceeds may be expressed thus: $MnO_2 + 2NaCl + 2H_2SO_4 = MnSO_4 + Na_2SO_4 + 2H_2O + Cl_2$. The method of preparation of Cl_2 from manganese peroxide and hydrochloric acid was discovered by Scheele, and from sodium chloride by Berthollet.

[5] The reaction of hydrochloric acid upon bleaching powder gives chlorine without the aid of heat, $CaCl_2O_2 + 4HCl = CaCl_2 + 2H_2O + 2Cl_2$ and is therefore also used for the preparation of chlorine. This reaction is very violent if all the acid be added at once; it should be poured in drop by drop (Mermé, Kämmerer). C. Winkler proposed to mix bleaching powder with one quarter of burnt and powdered gypsum, and having damped the mixture with water, to press and cut it up into cubes and dry at the ordinary temperature. These cubes can be used for the preparation of chlorine in the same apparatus as that used for the evolution of hydrogen and carbonic anhydride—the disengagement of the chlorine proceeds uniformly.

A mixture of potassium dichromate and hydrochloric acid evolves chlorine perfectly free from oxygen (V. Meyer and Langer).

[6]

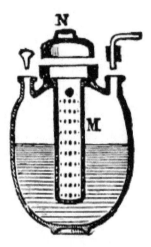

FIG. 66.—Clay retort for the preparation of chlorine on a large scale.

Chlorine is manufactured on a *large scale* from manganese peroxide and hydrochloric acid. It is most conveniently prepared in the apparatus shown in fig. 66, which consists of a three-necked earthenware vessel whose central orifice is the largest. A clay or lead funnel, furnished with a number of orifices, is placed in the central wide neck of the vessel. Roughly-ground lumps of natural manganese peroxide are placed in the funnel, which is then closed by the cover N, and luted with clay. One orifice is closed by a clay stopper, and is used for the introduction of the hydrochloric acid and withdrawal of the residues. The chlorine disengaged passes along a leaden gas-conducting tube placed in the other orifice. A row of these vessels is surrounded by a water-bath to ensure their being uniformly heated. Manganese chloride is found in the residue. In Weldon's process lime is added to the acid solution of manganese chloride. A double decomposition takes place, resulting in the formation of manganous hydroxide and calcium chloride. When the insoluble manganous hydroxide has settled, a further excess of milk of lime is added (to make a mixture $2Mn(OH)_2 + CaO + xCaCl_2$, which is found to be the best proportion, judging from experiment), and then air is forced through the mixture. The hydroxide is thus converted from a colourless to a brown substance, containing peroxide, MnO_2, and oxide of manganese, Mn_2O_3. This is due to the manganous oxide absorbing oxygen from the air. Under the action of hydrochloric acid this mixture evolves chlorine, because of all the compounds of chlorine and manganese the chloride $MnCl_2$ is the only one which is stable (*see* Note 3). Thus one and the same mass of manganese may be repeatedly used for the preparation of chlorine. The same result is attained in other ways. If manganous oxide be subjected to the action of oxides of nitrogen and air (Coleman's process), then manganese nitrate is formed, which at a red heat gives oxides of nitrogen (which are again used in the process) and manganese peroxide, which is thus renewed for the fresh evolution of chlorine.

[7] Davy and Faraday liquefied chlorine in 1823 by heating the crystallo-hydrate Cl_28H_2O in a bent tube (as with NH_3), surrounded by warm water, while the other end of the tube was immersed in a freezing mixture. Meselan condensed chlorine in freshly-burnt charcoal (placed in a glass tube), which when cold absorbs an equal weight of chlorine. The tube was then fused up, the bent end cooled, and the charcoal heated, by which means the chlorine was expelled from the charcoal, and the pressure increased.

[8] Judging from Ludwig's observations (1868), and from the fact that the coefficient of expansion of gases increases with their molecular weight (Chapter II., Note 26, for hydrogen = 0·367, carbonic anhydride = 0·373, hydrogen bromide = 0·386), it might be expected that the expansion of chlorine would be greater than that of air or of the gases composing it. V. Meyer and Langer (1885) having remarked that at 1,400° the density of chlorine (taking its expansion as equal to that of nitrogen) = 29, consider that the molecules of chlorine split up and partially give molecules Cl, but it might be maintained that the decrease in density observed only depends on the increase of the coefficient of expansion.

[9] Investigations on the solubility of chlorine in water (the solutions evolve all their chlorine on boiling and passing air through them) show many different peculiarities. First Gay-Lussac, and subsequently Pelouze, determined that the solubility increases between 0° and 8°–10° (from 1½

to 2 vols. of chlorine per 100 vols. of water at 0° up to 3 to 2¾ at 10°). In the following note we shall see that this is not due to the breaking-up of the hydrate at about 8° to 10°, but to its formation below 9°. Roscoe observed an increase in the solubility of chlorine in the presence of hydrogen—even in the dark. Berthelot determined an increase of solubility with the progress of time. Schönbein and others suppose that chlorine acts on water, forming hypochlorous and hypochloric acids, (HClO + HCl).

The equilibrium between chlorine and steam as gases and between water, liquid chlorine, ice, and the solid crystallo-hydrate of chlorine is evidently very complex. Gibbs, Guldberg (1870) and others gave a theory for similar states of equilibrium, which was afterwards developed by Roozeboom (1887), but it would be inopportune here to enter into its details. It will be sufficient in the first place to mention that there is now no doubt (according to the theory of heat, and the direct observations of Ramsay and Young) that the vapour tensions at one and the same temperature are different for the liquid and solid states of substances; secondly, to call attention to the following note; and, thirdly, to state that, in the presence of the crystallo-hydrate, water between $O°·24$ and $+28°·7$ (when the hydrate and a solution may occur simultaneously) dissolves a different amount of chlorine than it does in the absence of the crystallo-hydrate.

[10] According to Faraday's data the hydrate of chlorine contains $Cl_2,10H_2O$, but Roozeboom (1885) showed that it is poorer in water and = $Cl_2,8H_2O$. At first small, almost colourless, crystals are obtained, but they gradually form (if the temperature be below their critical point $28°·7$, above which they do not exist) large yellow crystals, like those of potassium chromate. The specific gravity is $1·23$. The hydrate is formed if there be more chlorine in a solution than it is able to dissolve under the dissociation pressure corresponding with a given temperature. *In the presence of the hydrate* the percentage amount of chlorine at $0° = 0·5$, at $9° = 0·9$, and at $20° = 1·82$. At temperatures below 9° the solubility (determined by Gay-Lussac and Pelouze, *see* Note 9) is dependent on the formation of the hydrate; whilst at higher temperatures under the ordinary pressure the hydrate cannot be formed, and the solubility of chlorine falls, as it does for all gases (Chapter I.). If the crystallo-hydrate is not formed, then below 9° the solubility follows the same rule (6° $1·07$ p.c. Cl, 9° $0·95$ p.c.). According to Roozeboom, the chlorine evolved by the hydrate presents the following tensions of dissociation: at $0° = 249$ mm., at $4° = 398$, at $8° = 620$, at $10° = 797$, at $14° = 1,400$ mm. In this case a portion of the crystallo-hydrate remains solid. At $9°·6$ the tension of dissociation is equal to the atmospheric pressure. At a higher pressure the crystallo-hydrate may form at temperatures above 9° up to $28°·7$, when the vapour tension of the

hydrate equals the tension of the chlorine. It is evident that the equilibrium which is established is on the one hand a case of a complex heterogeneous system, and on the other hand a case of the solution of solid and gaseous substances in water.

The crystallo-hydrate or chlorine water must be kept in the dark, or the access of light be prevented by coloured glass, otherwise oxygen is evolved and hydrochloric acid formed.

[11] The chemical action of light on a mixture of chlorine and hydrogen was discovered by Gay-Lussac and Thénard (1809). It has been investigated by many savants, and especially by Draper, Bunsen, and Roscoe. Electric or magnesium light, or the light emitted by the combustion of carbon bisulphide in nitric oxide, and actinic light in general, acts in the same manner as sunlight, in proportion to its intensity. At temperatures below -12° light no longer brings about reaction, or at all events does not give an explosion. It was long supposed that chlorine that had been subjected to the action of light was afterwards able to act on hydrogen in the dark, but it was shown that this only takes place with moist chlorine, and depends on the formation of oxides of chlorine. The presence of foreign gases, and even of excess of chlorine or of hydrogen, very much enfeebles the explosion, and therefore the experiment is conducted with a detonating mixture prepared by the action of an electric current on a strong solution (sp. gr. 1·15) of hydrochloric acid, in which case the water is not decomposed—that is, no oxygen becomes mixed with the chlorine.

[12] The quantity of chlorine and hydrogen which combine is proportional to the intensity of the light—not of all the rays, but only those so-termed chemical (actinic) rays which produce chemical action. Hence a mixture of chlorine and hydrogen, when exposed to the action of light in vessels of known capacity and surface, may be employed as an actinometer—that is, as a means for estimating the intensity of the chemical rays, the influence of the heat rays being previously destroyed, which may be done by passing the rays through water. Investigations of this kind (photo-chemical) showed that chemical action is chiefly limited to the violet end of the spectrum, and that even the invisible ultra-violet rays produce this action. A colourless gas flame contains no chemically active rays; the flame coloured green by a salt of copper evinces more chemical action than the colourless flame, but the flame brightly coloured yellow by salts of sodium has no more chemical action than that of the colourless flame.

As the chemical action of light becomes evident in plants, photography, the bleaching of tissues, and the fading of colours in the sunlight, and as a means for studying the phenomenon is given in the reaction of chlorine on hydrogen, this subject has been the most fully investigated in *photo-chemistry*. The researches of Bunsen and Roscoe in the fifties and sixties are the most complete in this respect. Their actinometer contains hydrogen and chlorine, and is surrounded by a solution of chlorine in water. The hydrochloric acid is absorbed as it forms, and therefore the variation in volume indicates the progress of the combination. As was to be expected, the action of light proved to be proportional to the time of exposure and intensity of the light, so that it was possible to conduct detailed photometrical investigations respecting the time of day and season of the year, various sources of light, its absorption, &c. This subject is considered in detail in special works, and we only stop to mention one circumstance, that a small quantity of a foreign gas decreases the action of light; for example, $\frac{1}{330}$ of hydrogen by 38 p.c., $\frac{1}{200}$ of oxygen by 10 p.c., $\frac{1}{100}$ of chlorine by 60 p.c., &c. According to the researches of Klimenko and Pekatoros (1889), the photo-chemical alteration of chlorine water is retarded by the presence of traces of metallic chlorides, and this influence varies with different metals.

As much heat is evolved in the reaction of chlorine on hydrogen, and as this reaction, being exothermal, may proceed by itself, the action of light is essentially the same as that of heat—that is, it brings the chlorine and hydrogen into the condition necessary for the reaction—it, as we may say, disturbs the original equilibrium; this is the work done by the luminous energy. It seems to me that the action of light on the mixed gases should be understood in this sense, as Pringsheim (1877) pointed out.

[13] In the formation of steam (from one part by weight [1 gram] of hydrogen) 29,000 heat units are evolved. The following are the quantities of heat (thousands of units) evolved in the formation of various other *corresponding* compounds of oxygen and of chlorine (from Thomsen's, and, for Na_2O, Beketoff's results):

2NaCl, 195;　$CaCl_2$, 170; $HgCl_2$, 63; 2AgCl, 59.

Na_2O, 100;　CaO, 131; HgO, 42; Ag_2O, 6.

$2AsCl_3$, 143; $2PbCl_5$, 210;　CCl_4, 21;　2HCl, 44 (gas).

As_2O_3, 155;　P_2O_5, 370;　CO_2, 97;　H_2O, 58 (gas).

With the first four elements the formation of the chlorine compound gives the most heat, and with the four following the formation of the oxygen compound evolves the greater amount of heat. The first four chlorides are true salts formed from HCl and the oxide, whilst the remainder have other properties, as is seen from the fact that they are not formed from hydrochloric acid and the oxide, but give hydrochloric acid with water.

[14] This has been already pointed out in Chapter III., Note 5.

[15] Sodium remains unaltered in perfectly dry chlorine at the ordinary temperature, and even when slightly warmed; but the combination is exceedingly violent at a red heat.

[16] An instructive experiment on combustion in chlorine may be conducted as follows: leaves of Dutch metal (used instead of gold for gilding) are placed in a glass globe, and a gas-conducting tube furnished with a glass cock is placed in the cork closing it, and the air is pumped out of the globe. The gas-conducting tube is then connected with a vessel containing chlorine, and the cock opened; the chlorine rushes in, and the metallic leaves are consumed.

[17] The behaviour of platinum to chlorine at a high temperature (1,400°) is very remarkable, because platinous chloride, $PtCl_2$, is then formed, whilst this substance decomposes at a much lower temperature into chlorine and platinum. Hence, when chlorine comes into contact with platinum at such high temperatures, it forms fumes of platinous chloride, and they on cooling decompose, with the liberation of platinum, so that the phenomenon appears to be dependent on the volatility of platinum. Deville proved the formation of platinous chloride by inserting a cold tube inside a red-hot one (as in the experiment on carbonic oxide). However, V. Meyer was able to observe the density of chlorine in a platinum vessel at 1,690°, at which temperature chlorine does not exert this action on platinum, or at least only to an insignificant degree.

[18] When left exposed to the air aqua regia disengages chlorine, and afterwards it no longer acts on gold. Gay-Lussac, in explaining the action of aqua regia, showed that when heated it evolves, besides chlorine, the vapours of two chloranhydrides—that of nitric acid, NO_2Cl (nitric acid, NO_2OH, in which HO is replaced by chlorine; see Chapter on Phosphorus), and that of nitrous acid, NOCl—but these do not act on gold. The formation of aqua regia may therefore be expressed by $4NHO_3 + 8HCl = 2NO_2Cl + 2NOCl + 6H_2O + 2Cl_2$. The formation of the chlorides NO_2Cl and NOCl is explained by the fact that the nitric acid is deoxidised, gives the oxides NO and NO_2, and they directly combine with chlorine to form the above anhydrides.

[19] Ozone and peroxide of hydrogen also bleach tissues. As the action of peroxide of hydrogen is easily controlled by taking a weak solution, and as it has hardly any action upon the tissues themselves, it is replacing

chlorine more and more as a bleaching agent. The oxidising property of chlorine is apparent in destroying the majority of organic tissues, and proves fatal to organisms. This action of chlorine is taken advantage of in quarantine stations. But the simple fumigation by chlorine must be carried on with great care in dwelling places, because chlorine disengaged into the atmosphere renders it harmful to the health.

[20] A certain propensity of carbon to attract chlorine is evidenced in the immense absorption of chlorine by charcoal (Note 7), but, so far as is at present known (if I am not mistaken, no one has tried the aid of light), no combination takes place between the chlorine and carbon.

[21] The same reaction takes place under the action of oxygen, with the difference that it burns the carbon, which chlorine is not able to do. If chlorine and oxygen compete together at a high temperature, the oxygen will unite with the carbon, and the chlorine with the hydrogen.

[22] This division of chlorine into two portions may at the same time be taken as a clear confirmation of the conception of molecules. According to Avogadro-Gerhardt's law, the molecule of chlorine (p. 310) contains two atoms of this substance; one atom replaces hydrogen, and the other combines with it.

[23] Such carriers or media for the transference of chlorine and the halogens in general were long known to exist in iodine and antimonious chloride, and have been most fully studied by Gustavson and Friedel, of the Petroffsky Academy—the former with respect to aluminium bromide, and the latter with respect to aluminium chloride. Gustavson showed that if a trace of metallic aluminium be dissolved in bromine (it floats on bromine, and when combination takes place much heat and light are evolved), the latter becomes endowed with the property of entering into metalepsis, which it is not able to do of its own accord. When pure, for instance, it acts very slowly on benzene, C_6H_6, but in the presence of a trace of aluminium bromide the reaction proceeds violently and easily, so that each drop of the hydrocarbon gives a mass of hydrobromic acid, and of the product of metalepsis. Gustavson showed that the *modus operandi* of this instructive reaction is based on the property of aluminium bromide to enter into combination with hydrocarbons and their derivatives. The details of this and all researches concerning the metalepsis of the hydrocarbons must be looked for in works on organic chemistry.

[24] As small admixtures of iodine, aluminium bromide, &c., aid the metalepsis of large quantities of a substance, just as nitric oxide aids the reaction of sulphurous anhydride on oxygen and water, so the principle is essentially the same in both cases. Effects of this kind (which should also be explained by a chemical reaction proceeding at the surfaces) only differ

from true contact phenomena in that the latter are produced by solid bodies and are accomplished at their surfaces, whilst in the former all is in solution. Probably the action of iodine is founded on the formation of iodine chloride, which reacts more easily than chlorine.

[25] Metalepsis belongs to the number of delicate reactions—if it may be so expressed—as compared with the energetic reaction of combustion. Many cases of substitution are of this kind. Reactions of metalepsis are accompanied by an evolution of heat, but in a less quantity than that evolved in the formation of the resulting quantity of the halogen acids. Thus the reaction $C_2H_6 + Cl_2 = C_2H_5Cl + HCl$, according to the data given by Thomsen, evolves about 20,000 heat units, whilst the formation of hydrochloric acid evolves 22,000 units.

[26] With the predominance of the representation of compound radicles (this doctrine dates from Lavoisier and Gay-Lussac) in organic chemistry, it was a very important moment in its history when it became possible to gain an insight into the structure of the radicles themselves. It was clear, for instance, that ethyl, C_2H_5, or the radicle of common alcohol, $C_2H_5 \cdot OH$, passes, without changing, into a number of ethyl derivatives, but its relation to the still simpler hydrocarbons was not clear, and occupied the attention of science in the 'forties' and 'fifties.' Having obtained ethyl hydride, $C_2H_5H = C_2H_6$, it was looked on as containing the same ethyl, just as methyl hydride, $CH_4 = CH_3H$, was considered as existing in methane. Having obtained free methyl, $CH_3CH_3 = C_2H_6$, from it, it was considered as a derivative of methyl alcohol, CH_3OH, and as only isomeric with ethyl hydride. By means of the products of metalepsis it was proved that this is not a case of isomerism but of strict identity, and it therefore became clear that ethyl is methylated methyl, $C_2H_5 = CH_2CH_3$. In its time a still greater impetus was given by the study of the reactions of monochloracetic acid, $CH_2Cl \cdot COOH$, or $CO(CH_2Cl)(OH)$. It appeared that metalepsical chlorine, like the chlorine of chloranhydrides—for instance, of methyl chloride, CH_3Cl, or ethyl chloride, C_2H_5Cl—is capable of substitution; for example, glycollic acid, $CH_2(OH)(CO_2H)$, or $CO(CH_2 \cdot OH)(OH)$, was obtained from it, and it appeared that the OH in the group $CH_2(OH)$ reacted like that in alcohols, and it became clear, therefore, that it was necessary to examine the radicles themselves by analysing them from the point of view of the bonds connecting the constituent atoms. Whence arose the present doctrine of the structure of the carbon compounds. (*See* Chapter VIII., Note 42.)

[27] By including many instances of the action of chlorine under metalepsis we not only explain the indirect formation of CCl_4, NCl_3, and Cl_2O by one method, but we also arrive at the fact that the reactions of the metalepsis of the hydrocarbons lose that exclusiveness which was often

ascribed to them. Also by subjecting the chemical representations to the law of substitution we may foretell metalepsis as a particular case of a general law.

[28] This may be taken advantage of in the preparation of nitrogen. If a large excess of chlorine water be poured into a beaker, and a small quantity of a solution of ammonia be added, then, after shaking, nitrogen is evolved. If chlorine act on a dilute solution of ammonia, the volume of nitrogen does not correspond with the volume of the chlorine taken, because ammonium hypochlorite is formed. If ammonia gas be passed through a fine orifice into a vessel containing chlorine, the reaction of the formation of nitrogen is accompanied by the emission of light and the appearance of a cloud of sal-ammoniac. In all these instances an excess of chlorine must be present.

[29] The hydrochloric acid formed combines with ammonia, and therefore the final result is $4NH_3 + 3Cl_2 = NCl_3 + 3NH_4Cl$. For this reason, more ammonia must enter into the reaction, but the metalepsical reaction in reality only takes place with an excess of ammonia or its salt. If bubbles of chlorine be passed through a fine tube into a vessel containing ammonia gas, each bubble gives rise to an explosion. If, however, chlorine be passed into a solution of ammonia, the reaction at first brings about the formation of nitrogen, because chloride of nitrogen acts on ammonia like chlorine. But when sal-ammoniac has begun to form, then the reaction directs itself towards the formation of chloride of nitrogen. The first action of chlorine on a solution of sal-ammoniac always causes the formation of chloride of nitrogen, which then reacts on ammonia thus: $NCl_3 + 4NH_3 = N_2 + 3NH_4Cl$. Therefore, so long as the liquid is alkaline from the presence of ammonia the chief product will be nitrogen. The reaction $NH_4Cl + 3Cl_2 = NCl_3 + 4HCl$ is reversible; with a dilute solution it proceeds in the above-described direction (perhaps owing to the affinity of the hydrochloric acid for the excess of water), but with a strong solution of hydrochloric acid it takes the opposite direction (probably by virtue of the affinity of hydrochloric acid for ammonia). Therefore there must exist a very interesting case of equilibrium between ammonia, hydrochloric acid, chlorine, water, and chloride of nitrogen which has not yet been investigated. The reaction $NCl_3 + 4HCl = NH_4Cl + 3Cl_2$ enabled Deville and Hautefeuille to determine the composition of chloride of nitrogen. When slowly decomposed by water, chloride of nitrogen gives, like a chloranhydride, nitrous acid or its anhydride, $2NCl_3 + 3H_2O = N_2O_3 + 6HCl$. From these observations it is evident that chloride of nitrogen presents great chemical interest, which is strengthened by its analogy with trichloride of phosphorus. The researches of F. F. Selivanoff (1891–94) prove that NCl_3 may be regarded as an ammonium derivative of

hypochlorous acid. Chloride of nitrogen is decomposed by dilute sulphuric acid in the following manner: $NCl_3 + 3H_2O + H_2SO_4 = NH_4HSO_4 + 3HClO$. This reaction is reversible and is only complete when some substance, combining with HClO (for instance, succinimide) or decomposing it, is added to the liquid. This is easily understood from the fact that hypochlorous acid itself, HClO, may, according to the view held in this book, be regarded as the product of the metalepsis of water, and consequently bears the same relation to NCl_3 as H_2O does to NH_3, or as RHO to RNH_2, R_2NH, and R_3N—that is to say, NCl_3 corresponds as an ammonium derivative to ClOH and Cl_2 in exactly the same manner as NR_3 corresponds to ROH and R_2. The connection of NCl_3 and other similar explosive chloro-nitrogen compounds (called chloryl compounds by Selivanoff; for example, the $C_2H_5NCl_2$ of Wurtz is chloryl ethylamine), such as $NRCl_2$ (as $NC_2H_5Cl_2$), and NR_2Cl (for instance, $N(CH_3CO)HCl$, chlorylacetamide, and $N(C_2H_5)_2Cl$, chloryl diethylamine) with HClO is evident from the fact that under certain circumstances these compounds give hypochlorous acid, with water, for instance, $NR_2Cl + H_2O = NR_2H + HClO$, and frequently act (like NCl_3 and HClO, or Cl_2) in an oxidising and chloridising manner. We may take chloryl succinimide, $C_2H_4(CO)_2NCl$ for example. It was obtained by Bender by the action of HClO upon succinimide, $C_2H_4(CO)_2NH$, and is decomposed by water with the re-formation of amide and HClO (the reaction is reversible). Selivanoff obtained, investigated, and classified many of the compounds NR_2Cl and $NRCl_2$, where R is a residue of organic acids or alcohols, and showed their distinction from the chloranhydrides, and thus supplemented the history of chloride of nitrogen, which is the simplest of the amides containing chlorine, NR_3, where R is fully substituted by chlorine.

[29 bis] In preparing NCl_3 every precaution must he used to guard against an explosion, and care should he taken that the NCl_3 remains under a layer of water. Whenever an ammoniacal substance comes into contact with chlorine great care must be taken, because it may be a case of the formation of such products and a very dangerous explosion may ensue. The liquid product of the metalepsis of ammonia may be most safely prepared in the form of small drops by the action of a galvanic current on a slightly warm solution of sal-ammoniac; chlorine is then evolved at the positive pole, and this chlorine acting on the ammonia gradually forms the product of metalepsis which floats on the surface of the liquid (being carried up by the gas), and if a layer of turpentine be poured on to it these small drops, on coming into contact with the turpentine, give feeble explosions, which are in no way dangerous owing to the small mass of the substance formed. Drops of chloride of nitrogen may with great caution be collected for investigation in the following manner. The neck of a funnel is immersed in a basin containing mercury, and first a saturated solution of

common salt is poured into the funnel, and above it a solution of sal-ammoniac in 9 parts of water. Chlorine is then slowly passed through the solutions, when drops of chloride of nitrogen fall into the salt water.

[30] Quicklime, CaO (or calcium carbonate, $CaCO_3$), does not absorb chlorine when cold, but at a red heat, in a current of chlorine, it forms calcium chloride, with the evolution of oxygen. (This was confirmed in 1893 by Wells, at Oxford.) This reaction corresponds with the decomposing action of chlorine on methane, ammonia, and water. Slaked lime (calcium hydroxide, CaH_2O_2) also, when dry, does not absorb chlorine at 100°. The absorption proceeds at the ordinary temperature (below 40°). The dry mass thus obtained contains not less than three equivalents of calcium hydroxide to four equivalents of chlorine, so that its composition is $[Ca(HO)_2]_5Cl_4$. In all probability a simple absorption of chlorine by the lime at first takes place in this case, as may be seen from the fact that even carbonic anhydride, when acting on the dry mass obtained as above, disengages all the chlorine from it, leaving only calcium carbonate. But if the bleaching powder be obtained by a wet method, or if it be dissolved in water (in which it is very soluble), and carbonic anhydride be passed into it, then chlorine is no longer disengaged, but chlorine oxide, Cl_2O, and only half of the chlorine is converted into this oxide, while the other half remains in the liquid as calcium chloride. From this it may be inferred that calcium chloride is formed by the action of water on bleaching powder, and this is proved to be the case by the fact that small quantities of water extract a considerable amount of calcium chloride from bleaching powder. If a large quantity of water act on bleaching powder an excess of calcium hydroxide remains, a portion of which is not subjected to change. The action of the water may be expressed by the following formulæ: From the dry mass $Ca_3(HO)_6Cl_4$ there is formed lime, $Ca(HO)_2$, calcium chloride, $CaCl_2$, and a saline substance, $Ca(ClO)_2$. $Ca_3H_6O_6Cl_4 = CaH_2O_2 + CaCl_2O_2 + CaCl_2 + 2H_2O$. The resulting substances are not equally soluble; water first extracts the calcium chloride, which is the most soluble, then the compound $Ca(ClO)_2$ and ultimately calcium hydroxide is left. A mixture of calcium chloride and hypochlorite passes into solution. On evaporation there remains $Ca_2O_2Cl_43H_2O$. The dry bleaching powder does not absorb more chlorine, but the solution is able to absorb it in considerable quantity. If the liquid be boiled, a considerable amount of chlorine monoxide is evolved. After this calcium chloride alone remains in solution, and the decomposition may be expressed as follows: $CaCl_2 + CaCl_2O_2 + 2Cl_2 = 2CaCl_2 + 2Cl_2O$. Chlorine monoxide may be prepared in this manner.

It is sometimes said that bleaching powder contains a substance, $Ca(OH)_2Cl_2$, that is calcium peroxide, CaO_2, in which one atom of oxygen is replaced by (OH)$_2$, and the other by Cl$_2$; but, judging from what has been said above, this can only be the case in the dry state, and not in solutions.

On being kept for some time, bleaching powder sometimes decomposes, with the evolution of oxygen (because CaCl$_2$O$_2$ = CaCl$_2$ + O$_2$, *see* p. 163); the same takes place when it is heated.

[31] For this reason it is necessary that in the preparation of bleaching powder the chlorine should be free from hydrochloric acid, and even the lime from calcium chloride. An excess of chlorine, in acting on a solution of bleaching powder, may also give chlorine monoxide, because calcium carbonate also gives chlorine monoxide under the action of chlorine. This reaction may be brought about by treating freshly precipitated calcium carbonate with a stream of chlorine in water: 2Cl$_2$ + CaCO$_3$ = CO$_2$ + CaCl$_2$ + Cl$_2$O. From this we may conclude that, although carbonic anhydride displaces hypochlorous anhydride, it may be itself displaced by an excess of the latter.

[32] Dry red mercury oxide acts on chlorine, forming dry hypochlorous anhydride (chlorine monoxide) (Balard); when mixed with water, red mercury oxide acts feebly on chlorine, and when freshly precipitated it evolves oxygen and chlorine. An oxide of mercury which easily and abundantly evolves chlorine monoxide under the action of chlorine in the presence of water may be prepared as follows: the oxide of mercury, precipitated from a mercuric salt by an alkali, is heated to 300° and cooled (Pelouze). If a salt, MClO, be added to a solution of mercuric salt, HgX$_2$, mercuric oxide is liberated, because the hypochlorite is decomposed.

[32 bis] A solution of hypochlorous anhydride is also obtained by the action of chlorine on many salts; for example, in the action of chlorine on a solution of sodium sulphate the following reaction takes place: Na$_2$SO$_4$ + H$_2$O + Cl$_2$ = NaCl + HClO + NaHSO$_4$. Here the hypochlorous acid is formed, together with HCl, at the expense of chlorine and water, for Cl$_2$ + H$_2$O = HCl + HClO. If the crystallo-hydrate of chlorine be mixed with mercury oxide, the hydrochloric acid formed in the reaction gives mercury chloride, and hypochlorous acid remains in solution. A dilute solution of hypochlorous acid or chlorine monoxide may be concentrated by distillation, and if a substance which takes up water (without destroying the acid)—for instance, calcium nitrate—be added to the stronger solution, then the anhydride of hypochlorous acid—*i.e.* chlorine monoxide—is disengaged.

[33] All explosive substances are of this kind—ozone, hydrogen peroxide, chloride of nitrogen, nitro-compounds, &c. Hence they cannot be formed directly from the elements or their simplest compounds, but, on the contrary, decompose into them. In a liquid state chlorine monoxide

explodes even on contact with powdery substances, or when rapidly agitated—for instance, if a file be rasped over the vessel in which it is contained.

[34] A solution of chlorine monoxide, or hypochlorous acid, does not explode, owing to the presence of the mass of water. In dissolving, chlorine monoxide evolves about 9,000 heat units, so that its store of heat becomes less.

The capacity of hypochlorous acid (studied by Carius and others) for entering into combination with the unsaturated hydrocarbons is very often taken advantage of in organic chemistry. Thus its solution absorbs ethylene, forming the chlorhydrin C_2H_4ClOH.

The oxidising action of hypochlorous acid and its salts is not only applied to bleaching but also to many reactions of oxidation. Thus it converts the lower oxides of manganese into the peroxide.

[35] *Chlorous acid*, $HClO_2$ (according to the data given by Millon, Brandau, and others) in many respects resembles hypochlorous acid, $HClO$, whilst they both differ from chloric and perchloric acids in their degree of stability, which is expressed, for instance, in their bleaching properties; the two higher acids do not bleach, but both the lower ones do so (oxidise at the ordinary temperature). On the other hand, chlorous acid is analogous to nitrous acid, HNO_2. The anhydride of chlorous acid, Cl_2O_3, is not known in a pure state, but it probably occurs in admixture with chlorine dioxide, ClO_2, which is obtained by the action of nitric and sulphuric acids on a mixture of potassium chlorate with such reducing substances as nitric oxide, arsenious oxide, sugar, &c. All that is at present known is that pure chlorine dioxide ClO_2 (*see* Notes 39–43) is gradually converted into a mixture of hypochlorous and chlorous acids under the action of water (and alkalis); that is, it acts like nitric peroxide, NO_2 (giving HNO_3 and HNO_2), or as a mixed anhydride, $2ClO_2 + H_2O = HClO_3 + HClO_2$. The silver salt, $AgClO_2$, is sparingly soluble in water. The investigations of Garzarolli-Thurnlackh and others seem to show that the anhydride Cl_2O_3 does not exist in a free state.

[36] Hydrochloric acid, which is an example of compounds of this kind, is a saturated substance which does not combine directly with oxygen, but in which, nevertheless, a considerable quantity of oxygen may be inserted between the elements forming it. The same may be observed in a number of other cases. Thus oxygen may be added or inserted between the elements, sometimes in considerable quantities, in the saturated hydrocarbons; for instance, in C_3H_8, three atoms of oxygen produce an alcohol, glycerin or glycerol, $C_3H_5(OH)_3$. We shall meet with similar examples hereafter. This is generally explained by regarding oxygen as a

bivalent element—that is, as capable of combining with two different elements, such as chlorine, hydrogen, &c. On the basis of this view, it may be inserted between each pair of combined elements; the oxygen will then be combined with one of the elements by one of its affinities and with the other element by its other affinity. This view does not, however, express the entire truth of the matter, even when applied to the compounds of chlorine. Hypochlorous acid, HOCl—that is, hydrochloric acid in which one atom of oxygen is inserted—is, as we have already seen, a substance of small stability; it might therefore be expected that on the addition of a fresh quantity of oxygen, a still less stable substance would be obtained, because, according to the above view, the chlorine and hydrogen, which form such a stable compound together, are then still further removed from each other. But it appears that chloric and perchloric acid, $HClO_3$ and $HClO_4$, are much more stable substances. Furthermore, the addition of oxygen has also its limit, it can only be added to a certain extent. If the above representation were true and not merely hypothetical, there would be no limit to the combination of oxygen, and the more it entered into one continuous chain the more unstable would be the resultant compound. But not more than four atoms of oxygen can be added to hydrogen sulphide, nor to hydrochloric acid, nor to hydrogen phosphide. This peculiarity must lie in the properties of oxygen itself; four atoms of oxygen seem to have the power of forming a kind of radicle which retains two or several atoms of various other substances—for example, chlorine and hydrogen, hydrogen and sulphur, sodium and manganese, phosphorus and metals, &c., forming comparatively stable compounds, $NaClO_4$, Na_2SO_4, $NaMnO_4$, Na_3PO_4, &c. *See* Chapter X. Note 1 and Chapter XV.

[37] If chlorine be passed through a *cold* solution of potash, a bleaching compound, potassium chloride and hypochlorite, $KCl + KClO$, is formed, but if it be passed through a *hot* solution potassium chlorate is formed. As this is sparingly soluble in water, it chokes the gas-conducting tube, which should therefore be widened out at the end.

Potassium chlorate is usually obtained on a large scale from calcium chlorate, which is prepared by passing chlorine (as long as it is absorbed) into water containing lime, the mixture being kept warm. A mixture of calcium chlorate and chloride is thus formed in the solution. Potassium chloride is then added to the warm solution, and on cooling a precipitate of potassium chlorate is formed as a substance which is sparingly soluble in cold water, especially in the presence of other salts. The double decomposition taking place is $Ca(ClO_3)_2 + 2KCl = CaCl_2 + 2KClO_3$. On a small scale in the laboratory potassium chlorate is best prepared from a strong solution of bleaching powder by passing chlorine through it and then adding potassium chloride. $KClO_3$ is always formed by the action of an electric current on a solution of KCl, especially at 80° (Häussermann and Naschold, 1894), so that this method is now used on a large scale.

Potassium chlorate crystallises easily in large colourless tabular crystals. Its solubility in 100 parts of water at 0° = 3 parts, 20° = 8 parts, 40° = 14 parts, 60° = 25 parts, 80° = 40 parts. For comparison we will cite the following figures showing the solubility of potassium chloride and perchlorate in 100 parts of water: potassium chloride at O° = 28 parts, 20° = 35 parts, 40° = 40 parts, 100° = 57 parts; potassium perchlorate at 0° about 1 part, 20° about 1¾ part, 100° about 18 parts. When heated, potassium chlorate melts (the melting point has been given as from 335°–376°; according to the latest determination by Carnelley, 359°) and decomposes with the evolution of oxygen, potassium perchlorate being at first formed, as will afterwards be described (*see* Note 47). A mixture of potassium chlorate and nitric and hydrochloric acids effects oxidation and chlorination in solutions. It deflagrates when thrown upon incandescent carbon, and when mixed with sulphur (⅓ by weight) it ignites it on being struck, in which case an explosion takes place. The same occurs with many metallic sulphides and organic substances. Such mixtures are also ignited by a drop of sulphuric acid. All these effects are due to the large amount of oxygen contained in potassium chlorate, and to the ease with which it is evolved. A mixture of two parts of potassium chlorate, one part of sugar, and one part of yellow prussiate of potash acts like gunpowder, but burns too rapidly, and therefore bursts the guns, and it also has a very strong oxidising action on their metal. The sodium salt, $NaClO_3$, is much more soluble than the potassium salt, and it is therefore more difficult to free it from sodium chloride, &c. The barium salt is also more soluble than the potassium salt; O° = 24 parts, 20° = 37 parts, 80° = 98 parts of salt per 100 of water.

[38] Barium chlorate, $Ba(ClO_3)_2,H_2O$, is prepared in the following way: impure chloric acid is first prepared and saturated with baryta, and the barium salt purified by crystallisation. The impure free chloric acid is obtained by converting the potassium in potassium chlorate into an insoluble salt. This is done by adding tartaric or hydrofluosilicic acid to a solution of potassium chlorate, because potassium tartrate and potassium silicofluoride are very sparingly soluble in water. Chloric acid is easily soluble in water.

[39] To prepare ClO_2 100 grams of sulphuric acid are cooled in a mixture of ice and salt, and 15 grams of powdered potassium chlorate are gradually added to the acid, which is then carefully distilled at 20° to 40°, the vapour given off being condensed in a freezing mixture. Potassium perchlorate is then formed: $3KClO_3 + 2H_2SO_4 = 2KHSO_4 + KClO_4 + 2ClO_2 + H_2O$. The reaction may result in an explosion. Calvert and Davies

obtained chloric peroxide without the least danger by heating a mixture of oxalic acid and potassium chlorate in a test tube in a water-bath. In this case $2KClO_3 + 3C_2H_2O_4,2H_2O = 2C_2HKO_4 + 2CO_2 + 2ClO_2 + 8H_2O$. The reaction is still further facilitated by the addition of a small quantity of sulphuric acid. If a solution of HCl acts upon $KClO_3$ at the ordinary temperature, a mixture of Cl_2 and ClO_2 is formed, but if the temperature be raised to 80° the greater part of the ClO_2 decomposes, and when passed through a hot solution of $MnCl_2$ it oxidises it. Gooch and Kreider proposed (1894) to employ this method for preparing small quantities of chlorine in the laboratory.

[40] By analogy with nitric peroxide it might be expected that at low temperatures a doubling of the molecule into Cl_2O_4 would take place, as the reactions of ClO_2 point to its being a mixed anhydride of $HClO_2$ and $HClO_3$.

[41] Owing to the formation of this chlorine dioxide, a mixture of potassium chlorate and sugar is ignited by a drop of sulphuric acid. This property was formerly made use of for making matches, and is now sometimes employed for setting fire to explosive charges by means of an arrangement in which the acid is caused to fall on the mixture at the moment required. An interesting experiment on the combustion of phosphorus under water may be conducted with chlorine dioxide. Pieces of phosphorus and of potassium chlorate are placed under water, and sulphuric acid is poured on to them (through a long funnel); the phosphorus then burns at the expense of the chlorine dioxide.

[42] Potassium permanganate oxidises chlorine dioxide into chloric acid (Fürst).

[43] The euchlorine obtained by Davy by gently heating potassium chlorate with hydrochloric acid is (Pebal) a mixture of chlorine dioxide and free chlorine. The liquid and gaseous chlorine oxide (Note 35), which Millon considered to be Cl_2O_3, probably contains a mixture of ClO_2 (vapour density 35), Cl_2O_3 (whose vapour density should be 59), and chlorine (vapour density 35·5), since its vapour density was determined to be about 40.

[44] If a solution of chloric acid, $HClO_3$, be first concentrated over sulphuric acid under the receiver of an air-pump and afterwards distilled, chlorine and oxygen are evolved and perchloric acid is formed: $4HClO_3 = 2HClO_4 + Cl_2 + 3O + H_2O$. Roscoe accordingly decomposed directly a solution of potassium chlorate by hydrofluosilicic acid, decanted it from the precipitate of potassium silicofluoride, K_2SiF_6, concentrated the solution of chloric acid, and then distilled it, perchloric acid being then obtained (see following footnote). That chloric acid is capable of passing

into perchloric acid is also seen from the fact that potassium permanganate is decolorised, although slowly, by the action of a solution of chloric acid. On decomposing a solution of potassium chlorate by the action of an electric current, potassium perchlorate is obtained at the positive electrode (where the oxygen is evolved). Perchloric acid is also formed by the action of an electric current on solutions of chlorine and chlorine monoxide. Perchloric acid was obtained by Count Stadion and afterwards by Serullas, and was studied by Roscoe and others.

[45] Perchloric acid, which is obtained in a free state by the action of sulphuric acid on its salts, may be separated from a solution very easily by distillation, being volatile, although it is partially decomposed by distillation. The solution obtained after distillation may be concentrated by evaporation in open vessels. In the distillation the solution reaches a temperature of 200°, and then a very constant liquid hydrate of the composition $HClO_4,2H_2O$ is obtained in the distillate. If this hydrate be mixed with sulphuric acid, it begins to decompose at 100°, but nevertheless a portion of the acid passes over into the receiver without decomposing, forming a crystalline hydrate $HClO_4,H_2O$ which melts at 50°. On carefully heating this hydrate it breaks up into perchloric acid, which distills over below 100°, and into the liquid hydrate $HClO_4,2H_2O$. The acid $HClO_4$ may also be obtained by adding one-fourth part of strong sulphuric acid to potassium chlorate, carefully distilling and subjecting the crystals of the hydrate $HClO_4,H_2O$ obtained in the distillate to a fresh distillation. Perchloric acid, $HClO_4$, itself does not distil, and is decomposed on distillation until the more stable hydrate $HClO_4, H_2O$ is formed; this decomposes into $HClO_4$ and $HClO_4,2H_2O$, which latter hydrate distils without decomposition. This forms an excellent example of the influence of water on stability, and of the property of chlorine of giving compounds of the type ClX_7, of which all the above hydrates, $ClO_3(OH)$, $ClO_2(OH)_3$, and $ClO(OH)_5$, are members. Probably further research will lead to the discovery of a hydrate $Cl(OH)_7$.

[46] According to Roscoe the specific gravity of perchloric acid $= 1·782$ and of the hydrate $HClO_4,H_2O$ in a liquid state (50°) $1·811$; hence a considerable contraction takes place in the combination of $HClO_4$ with H_2O.

[47] The decomposition of salts analogous to potassium chlorate has been more fully studied in recent years by Potilitzin and P. Frankland. Professor Potilitzin, by decomposing, for example, lithium chlorate $LiClO_3$, found (from the quantity of lithium chloride and oxygen) that at first the decomposition of the fused salt (368°) takes place according to the equation, $3LiClO_3 = 2LiCl + LiClO_4 + 5O$, and that towards the end the remaining salt is decomposed thus: $5LiClO_3 = 4LiCl + LiClO_4 + 10O$. The

phenomena observed by Potilitzin obliged him to admit that lithium perchlorate is capable of decomposing simultaneously with lithium chlorate, with the formation of the latter salt and oxygen; and this was confirmed by direct experiment, which showed that lithium chlorate is always formed in the decomposition of the perchlorate. Potilitzin drew particular attention to the fact that the decomposition of potassium chlorate and of salts analogous to it, although exothermal (Chapter III., Note 12), not only does not proceed spontaneously, but requires time and a rise of temperature in order to attain completion, which again shows that chemical equilibria are not determined by the heat effects of reactions only.

P. Frankland and J. Dingwall (1887) showed that at 448° (in the vapour of sulphur) a mixture of potassium chlorate and powdered glass is decomposed almost in accordance with the equation $2KClO_3 = KClO_4 + KCl + O_2$, whilst the salt by itself evolves about half as much oxygen, in accordance with the equation, $8KClO_3 = 5KClO_4 + 3KCl + 2O_2$. The decomposition of potassium perchlorate in admixture with manganese peroxide proceeds to completion, $KClO_4 = KCl + 2O_2$. But in decomposing by itself the salt at first gives potassium chlorate, approximately according to the equation $7KClO_4 = 2KClO_3 + 5KCl + 11O_2$. Thus there is now no doubt that when potassium chlorate is heated, the perchlorate is formed, and that this salt, in decomposing with evolution of oxygen, again gives the former salt.

In the decomposition of barium hypochlorite, 50 per cent. of the whole amount passes into chlorate, in the decomposition of strontium hypochlorite (Potilitzin, 1890) 12·5 per cent., and of calcium hypochlorite about 2·5 per cent. Besides which Potilitzin showed that the decomposition of the hypochlorites and also of the chlorates is always accompanied by the formation of a certain quantity of the oxides and by the evolution of chlorine, the chlorine being displaced by the oxygen disengaged. Spring and Prost (1889) represent the evolution of oxygen from $KClO_3$ as due to the salt first splitting up into base and anhydride, thus (1) $2MClO_3 = M_2O + Cl_2O_5$; (2) $Cl_2O_5 = Cl_2 + O_3$; and (3) $M_2O + Cl = 2MCl + O$.

I may further remark that the decomposition of potassium chlorate as a reaction evolving heat easily lends itself for this very reason to the contact action of manganese peroxide and other similar admixtures; for such very feeble influences as those of contact may become evident either in those cases (for instance, detonating gas, hydrogen peroxide, &c.), when the reaction is accompanied by the evolution of heat, or when (for instance, $H_2 + I_2$, &c.) little heat is absorbed or evolved. In these cases it is evident that the existing equilibrium is not very stable, and that a small alteration in the conditions at the surfaces of contact may suffice to upset it. In order to conceive the *modus operandi* of contact phenomena, it is enough to imagine, for instance, that at the surface of contact the movement of the atoms in the molecules changes from a circular to an elliptical path. Momentary and transitory compounds may he formed, but their formation cannot affect the explanation of the phenomena.

[47 bis] See, for example the melting point of NaCl, NaBr, NaI in Chapter II. Note 27. According to F. Freyer and V. Meyer (1892), the following are the boiling points of some of the corresponding compounds of chlorine and bromine:

BCl_3 17° BBr_3 90°

$SiCl_3$ 59° $SiBr_4$ 153°

PCl_3 76° PBr_3 175°

$SbCl_3$ 223° $SbBr_3$ 275°

$BiCl_3$ 447° $BiBr_3$ 453°

$SnCl_4$ 606° $SnBr_4$ 619°

$ZnCl_2$ 730° $ZnBr_2$ 650°

Thus for all the more volatile compounds the replacement of chlorine by bromine raises the boiling point, but in the ease of ZnX_2 it lowers it (Chapter XV. Note 19).

[48] Even before free fluorine was obtained (1886) it was evident from experience gained in the efforts made to obtain it, and from analogy, that it would decompose water (*see* first Russian edition of the *Principles of Chemistry*).

[48 bis] It is most likely that in this experiment of Fremy's, which corresponds with the action of oxygen on calcium chloride, fluorine was set free, but that a converse reaction also proceeded, $CaO + F_2 = CaF_2 + O$—that is, tbe calcium distributed itself between the oxygen and fluorine. MnF_4, which is capable of splitting up into MnF_2 and F_2, is without doubt formed by the action of a strong solution of hydrofluoric acid on manganese peroxide, but under the action of water the fluorine gives hydrofluoric acid, and probably this is aided by the affinity of the manganese fluoride and hydrofluoric acid. In all the attempts made (by Davy, Knox, Louget, Fremy, Gore, and others) to decompose fluorides (those of lead, silver, calcium, and others) by chlorine, there were doubtless also cases of distribution, a portion of the metal combined with chlorine and a portion of the fluorine was evolved; but it is improbable that any

decisive results were obtained. Fremy probably obtained fluorine, but not in a pure state.

[49] According to Moissan, fluorine is disengaged by the action of an electric current on fused hydrogen potassium fluoride, KHF_2. The present state of chemical knowledge is such that the knowledge of the properties of an element is much more general than the knowledge of the free element itself. It is useful and satisfactory to learn that even fluorine in the free state has not succeeded in eluding experiment and research, that the efforts to isolate it have been crowned with success, but the sum total of chemical data concerning fluorine as an element gains but little by this achievement. The gain will, however, be augmented if it be now possible to subject fluorine to a comparative study in relation to oxygen and chlorine. There is particular interest in the phenomena of the distribution of fluorine and oxygen, or fluorine and chlorine, competing under different conditions and relations. We may add that Moissan (1892) found that free fluorine decomposes H_2S, HCl, HBr, CS_2, and CNH with a flash; it does not act upon O_2, N_2, CO, and CO_2; Mg, Al, Ag, and Ni, when heated, burn in it, as also do S, Se, P (forms PF_5); it reacts upon H_2 even in the dark, with the evolution of 366·00 units of heat. At a temperature of -95°, F_2 still retains its gaseous state. Soot and carbon in general (but not the diamond) when heated in gaseous fluorine form *fluoride of carbon*, CF_4 (Moissan, 1890); this compound is also formed at 300° by the double decomposition of CCl_4 and AgF; it is a gas which liquefies at 10° under a pressure of 5 atmospheres. With an alcoholic solution of KHO, CF_4 gives K_2CO_3, according to the equation $CF_4 + 6KHO = K_2CO_3 + 4KF + 3H_2O$. CF_4 is not soluble in water, but it is easily soluble in CCl_4 and alcohol.

[49 bis] T. Nikolukin (1885) and subsequently Friedrich and Classen obtained $PbCl_4$ and a double ammonium salt of tetrachloride of lead (starting from the binoxide), $PbCl_42NH_4Cl$; Hutchinson and Pallard obtained a similar salt of acetic acid (1893) corresponding to PbX_4 by treating red lead with strong acetic acid; the composition of this salt is $Pb(C_2H_3O_2)_4$; it melts (and decomposes) at about 175°. Brauner (1894) obtained a salt corresponding to tetrafluoride of lead, PbF_4, and the acid corresponding to it, H_4PbF_8. For example, by treating potassium plumbate (Chapter XVIII. Note 55) with strong HF, and also the above-mentioned tetra-acetate with a solution of KHF_2, Brauner obtained crystalline HK_3PbF_8—i.e. the salt from which he obtained fluorine.

[50] It is called spar because it very frequently occurs as crystals of a clearly laminar structure, and is therefore easily split up into pieces bounded by planes. It is called fluor spar because when used as a flux it renders ores fusible, owing to its reacting with silica, $SiO_2 + 2CaF_2 = 2CaO + SiF_4$; the silicon fluoride escapes as a gas and the lime combines with a

further quantity of silica, and gives a vitreous slag. Fluor spar occurs in mineral veins and rocks, sometimes in considerable quantities. It always crystallises in the cubic system, sometimes in very large semi-transparent cubic crystals, which are colourless or of different colours. It is insoluble in water. It melts under the action of heat, and crystallises on cooling. The specific gravity is 3·1. When steam is passed over incandescent fluor spar, lime and hydrofluoric acid are formed: $CaF_2 + H_2O = CaO + 2HF$. A double decomposition is also easily produced by fusing fluor spar with sodium or potassium hydroxides, or potash, or even with their carbonates; the fluorine then passes over to the potassium or sodium, and the oxygen to the calcium. In solutions—for example, $Ca(NO_3)_2 + 2KF = CaF_2$ (precipitate) $+ 2KNO_3$ (in solution)—the formation of calcium fluoride takes place, owing to its very sparing solubility. 26,000 parts of water dissolve one part of fluor spar.

[51] According to Gore. Fremy obtained anhydrous hydrofluoric acid by decomposing lead fluoride at a red heat, by hydrogen, or by beating the double salt HKF_2, which easily crystallises (in cubes) from a solution of hydrofluoric acid, half of which has been saturated with potassium hydroxide. Its vapour density corresponds to the formula HF.

[52] This composition corresponds to the crystallo-hydrate $HCl,2H_2O$. All the properties of hydrofluoric acid recall those of hydrochloric acid, and therefore the comparative ease with which hydrofluoric acid is liquefied (it boils at $+19°$, hydrochloric acid at $-35°$) must be explained by a polymerisation taking place at low temperatures, as will be afterwards explained, H_2F_2 being formed, and therefore in a liquid state it differs from hydrochloric acid, in which a phenomenon of a similar kind has not yet been observed.

[53] The corrosive action of hydrofluoric acid on glass and similar siliceous compounds is based upon the fact that it acts on silica, SiO_2, as we shall consider more fully in describing that compound, forming gaseous silicon fluoride, $SiO_2 + 4HF = SiF_4 + 2H_2O$. Silica, on the other hand, forms the binding (acid) element of glass and of the mass of mineral substances forming the salts of silica. When it is removed the cohesion is destroyed. This is made use of in the arts, and in the laboratory, for etching designs and scales, &c., on glass. In *engraving on glass* the surface is covered with a varnish composed of four parts of wax and one part of turpentine. This varnish is not acted on by hydrofluoric acid, and it is soft enough to allow of designs being drawn upon it whose lines lay bare the glass. The drawing is made with a steel point, and the glass is afterwards laid in a lead trough in which a mixture of fluor spar and sulphuric acid is placed. The sulphuric acid must be used in considerable excess, as otherwise transparent lines are obtained (owing to the formation of hydrofluosilicic

acid). After being exposed for some time, the varnish is removed (melted) and the design drawn by the steel point is found reproduced in dull lines. The drawing may be also made by the direct application of a mixture of a silicofluoride and sulphuric acid, which forms hydrofluoric acid.

[54] Mallet (1881) determined the density at 30° and 100°, previous to which Gore (1869) had determined the vapour density at 100°, whilst Thorpe and Hambly (1888) made fourteen determinations between 26° and 88°, and showed that within this limit of temperature the density gradually diminishes, just like the vapour of acetic acid, nitrogen dioxide, and others. The tendency of HF to polymerise into H_2F_2 is probably connected with the property of many fluorides of forming acid salts—for example, KHF_2 and H_2SiF_6. We saw above that HCl has the same property (forming, for instance, H_2PtCl_6, &c., p. 457), and hence this property of hydrofluoric acid does not stand isolated from the properties of the other halogens.

[55] For instance, the experiment with Dutch metal foil (Note 16) may be made with bromine just as well as with chlorine. A very instructive experiment on the direct combination of the halogens with metals maybe made by throwing a small piece (a shaving) of aluminium into a vessel containing liquid bromine; the aluminium, being lighter, floats on the bromine, and after a certain time reaction sets in accompanied by the evolution of heat, light, and fumes of bromine. The incandescent piece of metal moves rapidly over the surface of the bromine in which the resultant aluminium bromide dissolves. For the sake of comparison we will proceed to cite several thermochemical data (Thomsen) for analogous actions of (1) chlorine, (2) bromine, and (3) iodine, with respect to metals; the halogen being expressed by the symbol X, and the plus sign connecting the reacting substances. All the figures are given in thousands of calories, and refer to molecular quantities in grams and to the ordinary temperature:—

	1	2	3
K_2 + X_2	211	191	160
Na_2 + X_2	195	172	138
Ag_2 + X_2	59	45	28
Hg_2 + X_2	83	68	48
Hg + X_2	63	51	34
Ca + X_2	170	141	—
Ba + X_2	195	170	—

Zn + X_2 97 76 49

Pb + X_2 83 64 40

Al + X_2 161 120 70

We may remark that the latent heat of vaporisation of the molecular weight Br_2 is about 7·2, and of iodine 6·0 thousand heat units, whilst the latent heat of fusion of Br_2 is about 0·3, and of I_2 about 3·0 thousand heat units. From this it is evident that the difference between the amounts of heat evolved does not depend on the difference in physical state. For instance, the vapour of iodine in combining with Zn to form ZnI_2 would give 48 + 8 + 3, or about sixty thousand heat units, or 1½ times less than Zn + Cl_2.

[56] One litre of sea-water contains about 20 grams of chlorine, and about 0·07 gram of bromine. The Dead Sea contains about ten times as much bromine.

[57] But there is no iodine in Stassfurt carnallite.

[58] The chlorine must not, however, be in large excess, as otherwise the bromine would contain chlorine. Commercial bromine not unfrequently contains chlorine, as bromine chloride; this is more soluble in water than bromine, from which it may thus be freed. To obtain pure bromine the commercial bromine is washed with water, dried by sulphuric acid, and distilled, the portion coming over at 58° being collected; the greater part is then converted into potassium bromide and dissolved, and the remainder is added to the solution in order to separate iodine, which is removed by shaking with carbon bisulphide. By heating the potassium bromide thus obtained with manganese peroxide and sulphuric acid, bromine is obtained quite free from iodine, which, however, is not present in certain kinds of commercial bromine (the Stassfurt, for instance). By treatment with potash, the bromine is then converted into a mixture of potassium bromide and bromate, and the mixture (which is in the proportion given in the equation) is distilled with sulphuric acid, bromine being then evolved: $5KBr + KBrO_3 + 6H_2SO_4 = 6KHSO_4 + 3H_2O + 3Br_2$. After dissolving the bromine in a strong solution of calcium bromide and precipitating with an excess of water, it loses all the chlorine it contained, because chlorine forms calcium chloride with $CaBr_2$.

[59] There has long existed a difference of opinion as to the melting point of pure bromine. By some investigators (Regnault, Pierre) it was given as between -7° and -8°, and by others (Balard, Liebig, Quincke, Baumhauer) as between -20° and -25°. There is now no doubt, thanks more especially to the researches of Ramsay and Young (1885), that pure

bromine melts at about -7°. This figure is not only established by direct experiment (Van der Plaats confirmed it), but also by means of the determination of the vapour tensions. For solid bromine the vapour tension p in mm. at t was found to be—

$p =$ 20 25 30 35 40 45 mm.

$t =$ -16°·6 -14° -12° -10° -8·5° -7°

For liquid bromine—

$p =$ 50 100 200 400 600 760 mm.

$t =$ -5°·0 +8°·2 23°·4 40°4 51°·9 58°·7

These curves intersect at -7°·05. Besides which, in comparing the vapour tension of many liquids (for example, those given in Chapter II., Note 27), Ramsay and Young observed that the ratio of the absolute temperatures $(t + 273)$ corresponding with equal tension *varies* for every pair of substances in rectilinear proportion in dependence upon t, and, therefore, for the above pressure p, Ramsay and Young determined the ratio of $t + 273$ for water and bromine, and found that the straight lines expressing these ratios for liquid and solid bromine intersect also at 7°·05; thus, for example, for solid bromine—

$p =$	20	25	30	35	40	45
$273 + t =$	256·4	259	261	263	264·6	266
$273 + t =$	295·3	299	302·1	304·8	307·2	309·3
$c =$	1·152	1·154	1·157	1·159	1·161	1·163

where t indicates the temperature of water corresponding with a vapour tension p, and where c is the ratio of $273 + t$ to $273 + t$. The magnitude of c is evidently expressed with great accuracy by the straight line $c = 1·1703 + 0·0011t$. In exactly the same way we find the ratio for liquid bromine and water to be $c_1 = 1·1585 + 0·00057t$. The intersection of these straight lines in fact corresponds with -7°·06, which again confirms the melting point given above for bromine. In this manner it is possible with the existing store of data to accurately establish and *verify* the melting point of substances. Ramsay and Young established the thermal constants of iodine by exactly the same method.

[60] The observations made by Paterno and Nasini (by Raoult's method, Chapter I. Note 49) on the temperature of the formation of ice (-1°·115, with 1·391 gram of bromine in 100 grams of water) in an aqueous solution

of bromine, showed that bromine is contained in solutions as the molecule Br_2. Similar experiments conducted on iodine (Kloboukoff 1889 and Beckmann 1890) show that in solution the molecule is I_2.

B. Roozeboom investigated the hydrate of bromine as completely as the hydrate of chlorine (Notes 9, 10). The temperature of the complete decomposition of the hydrate is $+6°·2$; the density of $Br_2,10H_2O = 1·49$.

[61] In general, $2HI + O = I_2 + H_2O$, if the oxygen proceed from a substance from which it is easily evolved. For this reason compounds corresponding with the higher stages of oxidation or chlorination frequently give a lower stage when treated with hydriodic acid. Ferric oxide, Fe_2O_3, is a higher oxide, and ferrous oxide, FeO, a lower oxide; the former corresponds with FeX_3, and the latter with FeX_2, and this passage from the higher to the lower takes place under the action of hydriodic acid. Thus hydrogen peroxide and ozone (Chapter IV.) are able to liberate iodine from hydriodic acid. Compounds of copper oxide, CuO or CuX_2, give compounds of the suboxide Cu_2O, or CuX. Even sulphuric acid, which corresponds to the higher stage SO_3, is able to act thus, forming the lower oxide SO_2. The liberation of iodine from hydriodic acid proceeds with still greater ease under the action of substances capable of disengaging oxygen. In practice, many methods are employed for liberating iodine from acid liquids containing, for example, sulphuric acid and hydriodic acid. The higher oxides of nitrogen are most commonly used; they then pass into nitric oxide. Iodine may even be disengaged from hydriodic acid by the action of iodic acid, &c. But there is a limit in these reactions of the oxidation of hydriodic acid because, under certain conditions, especially in dilute solutions, the iodine set free is itself able to act as an oxidising agent—that is, it exhibits the character of chlorine, and of the halogens in general, to which we shall again have occasion to refer. In Chili, where a large quantity of iodine is extracted in the manufacture of Chili nitre, which contains $NaIO_3$, it is mixed with the acid and normal sulphites of sodium in solution; the iodine is then precipitated according to the equation $2NaIO_3 + 3Na_2SO_3 + 2NaHSO_3 = 5Na_2SO_4 + I_2 + H_2O$. The iodine thus obtained is purified by sublimation.

[62] For the final purification of iodine, Stas dissolved it in a strong solution of potassium iodide, and precipitated it by the addition of water (*see* Note 58).

[63] The solubility of iodine in solutions containing iodides, and compounds of iodine in general, may serve, on the one hand, as an indication that solution is due to a similarity between the solvent and dissolved substance, and, on the other hand, as an indirect proof of that view as to solutions which was cited in Chapter I., because in many

instances unstable highly iodised compounds, resembling crystallo-hydrates, have been obtained from such solutions. Thus iodide of tetramethylammonium, $N(CH_3)_4I$, combines with I_2, and I_4. Even a solution of iodine in a saturated solution of potassium iodide presents indications of the formation of a definite compound KI_3. Thus, an alcoholic solution of KI_3 does not give up iodine to carbon bisulphide, although this solvent takes up iodine from an alcoholic solution of iodine itself (Girault, Jörgensen, and others). The instability of these compounds resembles the instability of many crystallo-hydrates, for instance of $HCl,2H_2O$.

[64] The equality of the atomic volumes of the halogens themselves is all the more remarkable because in all the halogen compounds the volume augments with the substitution of fluorine by chlorine, bromine, and iodine. Thus, for example, the volume of sodium fluoride (obtained by dividing the weight expressed by its formula by its specific gravity) is about 15, of sodium chloride 27, of sodium bromide 32, and of sodium iodide 41. The volume of silicon chloroform, $SiHCl_3$, is 82, and those of the corresponding bromine and iodine compounds are 108 and 122 respectively. The same difference also exists in solutions; for example, $NaCl + 200H_2O$ has a sp. gr. (at $15°/4°$) of $1\cdot0106$, consequently the volume of the solution $3,658\cdot5/1\cdot0106 = 3,620$, hence the volume of sodium chloride in solution $= 3,620–3,603$ (this is the volume of 200 H_2O) $= 17$, and in similar solutions, $NaBr = 26$ and $NaI = 35$.

[65] But the density (and also molecular volume, Note 64) of a bromine compound is always greater than that of a chlorine compound, whilst that of an iodine compound is still greater. The order is the same in many other respects. For example, an iodine compound has a higher boiling point than a bromine compound, &c.

[66] A. L. Potilitzin showed that in heating various metallic chlorides in a closed tube, with an equivalent quantity of bromine, a distribution of the metal between the halogens always occurs, and that the amounts of chlorine replaced by the bromine in the ultimate product are proportional to the atomic weights of the metals taken and inversely proportional to their equivalence. Thus, if $NaCl + Br$ be taken, then out of 100 parts of chlorine, $5\cdot54$ are replaced by the bromine, whilst with $AgCl + Br$ $27\cdot28$ parts are replaced. These figures are in the ratio $1 : 4\cdot9$, and the atomic weights Na : Ag = $1 : 4\cdot7$. In general terms, if a chloride MCl_n be taken, it gives with nBr a percentage substitution $= 4M/n^2$ where M is the atomic weight of the metal. This law was deduced from observations on the chlorides of Li, K, Na, Ag ($n = 1$), Ca, Sr, Ba, Co, Ni, Hg, Pb ($n = 2$), Bi ($n = 3$), Sn ($n = 4$), and Fe_2 ($n = 6$).

In these determinations of Potilitzin we see not only a brilliant confirmation of Berthollet's doctrine, but also the first effort to directly determine the affinities of elements by means of displacement. The chief object of these researches consisted in proving whether a displacement occurs in those cases where heat is absorbed, and in this instance it should be absorbed, because the formation of all metallic bromides is attended with the evolution of less heat than that of the chlorides, as is seen by the figures given in Note 55.

If the mass of the bromine be increased, then the amount of chlorine displaced also increases. For example, if masses of bromine of 1 and 4 equivalents act on a molecule of sodium chloride, then the percentages of the chlorine displaced will be 6·08 p.c. and 12·46 p.c.; in the action of 1, 4, 25, and 100 molecules of bromine on a molecule of barium chloride, there will be displaced 7·8, 17·6, 35·0, and 45·0 p.c. of chlorine. If an equivalent quantity of hydrochloric acid act on metallic bromides in closed tubes, and in the absence of water at a temperature of 300°, then the percentages of the substitution of the bromine by the chlorine in the double decomposition taking place between univalent metals are inversely proportional to their atomic weights. For example, NaBr + HCl gives at the limit 21 p.c. of displacement, KCl 12 p.c. and AgCl 4¼ p.c. Essentially the same action takes place in an aqueous solution, although the phenomenon is complicated by the participation of the water. The reactions proceed spontaneously in one or the other direction at the ordinary temperature but at different *rates*. In the action of a dilute solution (1 equivalent per 5 litres) of sodium chloride on silver bromide at the ordinary temperature the amount of bromine replaced in six and a half days is 2·07 p.c., and with potassium chloride 1·5 p.c. With an excess of the chloride the magnitude of the substitution increases. These conversions also proceed with the absorption of heat. The reverse reactions evolving heat proceed incomparably more rapidly, but also to a certain limit; for example, in the reaction AgCl + RBr the following percentages of silver bromide are formed in different times:

hours	2	3	22	96	120
K	79·82	87·4	88·22	—	94·21
Na	83·63	90·74	91·70	95·49	—

That is, the conversions which are accompanied by an evolution of heat proceed with very much greater rapidity than the reverse conversions.

[67] The *dissociation of hydriodic acid* has been studied in detail by Hautefeuille and Lemoine, from whose researches we extract the following

information. The decomposition of hydriodic acid is decided, but proceeds slowly at 180°; the rate and limit of decomposition increase with a rise of temperature. The reverse action—that is, $I_2 + H_2 = 2HI$—proceeds not only under the influence of spongy platinum (Corenwinder), which also accelerates the decomposition of hydriodic acid, but also by itself, although slowly. The limit of the reverse reaction remains the same with or without spongy platinum. An increase of pressure has a very powerful accelerative effect on the rate of formation of hydriodic acid, and therefore spongy platinum by condensing gases has the same effect as increase of pressure. At the atmospheric pressure the decomposition of hydriodic acid reaches the limit at 250° in several months, and at 440° in several hours. The limit at 250° is about 18 p.c. of decomposition—that is, out of 100 parts of hydrogen previously combined in hydriodic acid, about 18 p.c. may be disengaged at this temperature (this hydrogen may be easily measured, and the measure of dissociation determined), but not more; the limit at 440° is about 26 p.c. If the pressure under which 2HI passes into $H_2 + I_2$ be $4\frac{1}{2}$ atmospheres, then the limit is 24 p.c.; under a pressure of $\frac{1}{6}$ atmosphere the limit is 29 p.c. The small influence of pressure on the dissociation of hydriodic acid (compared with N_2O_4, Chapter VI. Note 46) is due to the fact that the reaction $2HI = I_2 + H_2$ is not accompanied by a change of volume. In order to show the influence of time, we will cite the following figures referring to 350°: (1) Reaction $H_2 + I_2$; after 3 hours, 88 p.c. of hydrogen remained free; 8 hours, 69 p.c.; 34 hours, 48 p.c.; 76 hours, 29 p.c.; and 327 hours, 18·5 p.c. (2) The reverse decomposition of 2HI; after 9 hours, 3 p.c. of hydrogen was set free, and after 250 hours 18·6 p.c.—that is, the limit was reached. The addition of extraneous hydrogen diminishes the limit of the reaction of decomposition, or increases the formation of hydriodic acid from iodine and hydrogen, as would be expected from Berthollet's doctrine (Chapter X.). Thus at 440° 26 p.c. of hydriodic acid is decomposed if there be no admixture of hydrogen, while if H_2 be added, then at the limit only half as large a mass of HI is decomposed. Therefore, if an infinite mass of hydrogen be added there will be no decomposition of the hydriodic acid. Light aids the decomposition of hydriodic acid very powerfully. At the ordinary temperature 80 p.c. is decomposed under the influence of light, whilst under the influence of heat alone this limit corresponds with a very high temperature. The distinct action of light, spongy platinum, and of impurities in glass (especially of sodium sulphate, which decomposes hydriodic acid), not only render the investigations difficult, but also show that in reactions like $2HI = I_2 + H_2$, which are accompanied by slight heat effects, all foreign and feeble influences may strongly affect the progress of the action (Note 47).

[68] The thermal determinations of Thomsen (at 18°) gave in thousands of calories, $Cl + H = +22$, $HCl + Aq$ (that is, on dissolving HCl in a large amount of water) $= +17\cdot3$, and therefore $H + Cl + Aq = +39\cdot3$. In taking molecules, all these figures must be doubled. $Br + H = +8\cdot4$; $HBr + Aq = 19\cdot9$; $H + Br + Aq = +28\cdot3$. According to Berthelot $7\cdot2$ are required for the vaporisation of Br_2, hence $Br_2 + H_2 = 16\cdot8 + 7\cdot2 = +24$, if Br_2 be taken as vapour for comparison with Cl_2. $H + I = -6\cdot0$, $HI + Aq = 19\cdot2$; $H + I + Aq = +13\cdot2$, and, according to Berthelot, the heat of fusion of $I_2 = 3\cdot0$, and of vaporisation $6\cdot0$ thousand heat units, and therefore $I_2 + H_2 = -2(6\cdot0) + 3 + 6 = -3\cdot0$, if the iodine be taken as vapour. Berthelot, on the basis of his determinations, gives, however, $+0\cdot8$ thousand heat units. Similar contradictory results are often met with in thermochemistry owing to the imperfection of the existing methods, and particularly the necessity of depending on indirect methods for obtaining the fundamental figures. Thus Thomsen decomposed a dilute solution of potassium iodide by gaseous chlorine; the reaction gave $+26\cdot2$, whence, having first determined the heat effects of the reactions $KHO + HCl$, $KHO + HI$ and $Cl + H$ in aqueous solutions, it was possible to find $H + I + Aq$; then, knowing $HI + Aq$, to find $I + H$. It is evident that unavoidable errors may accumulate.

[69] One can believe, however, on the basis of Berthollet's doctrine, and the observations of Potilitzin (Note 66), that a certain slow decomposition of water by iodine takes place. On this view the observations of Dossios and Weith on the fact that the solubility of iodine in water increases after the lapse of several months will be comprehensible. Hydriodic acid is then formed, and it increases the solubility. If the iodine be extracted from such a solution by carbon bisulphide, then, as the authors showed, after the action of nitrous anhydride iodine may be again detected in the solution by means of starch. It can easily be understood that a number of similar reactions, requiring much time and taking place in small quantities, have up to now eluded the attention of investigators, who even still doubt the universal application of Berthollet's doctrine, or only see the thermochemical side of reactions, or else neglect to pay attention to the element of time and the influence of mass.

[70] On the basis of the data in Note 68.

[71] A number of similar cases confirm what has been said in Chapter X.

[72] This is prevented by the reducibility of sulphuric acid. If volatile acids be taken they pass over, together with the hydrobromic and hydriodic acids, when distilled; whilst many non-volatile acids which are not reduced by hydrobromic and hydriodic acids only act feebly (like phosphoric acid), or do not act at all (like boric acid).

[73] This is in agreement with the thermochemical data, because if all the substances be taken in the gaseous state (for sulphur the heat of fusion is 0·3, and the heat of vaporisation 2·3) we have $H_2 + S = 4·7$; $H_2 + Cl_2 = 44$; $H_2 + Br_2 = 24$, and $H_2 + I_2 = -3$ thousand heat units; hence the formation of H_2S gives less heat than that of HCl and HBr, but more than that of HI. In dilute solutions $H_2 + S + Aq = 9·3$, and consequently less than the formation of all the halogen acids, as H_2S evolves but little heat with water, and therefore in dilute solutions chlorine, bromine, and iodine decompose hydrogen sulphide.

[74] Here there are three elements, hydrogen, sulphur, and iodine, each pair of which is able to form a compound, HI, H_2S, and SI, besides which the latter may unite in various proportions. The complexity of chemical mechanics is seen in such examples as these. It is evident that only the study of the simplest cases can give the key to the more complex problems, and on the other hand it is evident from the examples cited in the last pages that, without penetrating into the conditions of chemical equilibria, it would be impossible to explain chemical phenomena. By following the footsteps of Berthollet the possibility of unravelling the problems will be reached; but work in this direction has only been begun during the last ten years, and much remains to be done in collecting experimental material, for which occasions present themselves at every step. In speaking of the halogens I wished to turn the reader's attention to problems of this kind.

[74 bis] The same essentially takes place when sulphurous anhydride, in a dilute solution, gives hydriodic acid and sulphuric acid with iodine. On concentration a reverse reaction takes place. The equilibrated systems and the part played by water are everywhere distinctly seen.

[75] Methods of formation and preparation are nothing more than particular cases of chemical reaction. If the knowledge of chemical mechanics were more exact and complete than it now is it would be possible to foretell all cases of preparation *with every detail* (of the quantity of water, temperature, pressure, mass, &c.) The study of practical methods of preparation is therefore one of the paths for the study of chemical mechanics. The reaction of iodine on phosphorus and water is a case like that mentioned in Note 74, and the matter is here further complicated by the possibility of the formation of the compound PH_3 with HI, as well as the production of PI_2, PI_3, and the affinity of hydriodic acid and the acids of phosphorus for water. The theoretical interest of equilibria in all their complexity is naturally very great, but it falls into the background in presence of the primary interest of discovering practical methods for the isolation of substances, and the means of employing them for the requirements of man. It is only after the satisfaction of these requirements that interests of the other order arise, which in their turn must exert an

influence on the former. For these reasons, whilst considering it opportune to point out the theoretical interest of chemical equilibria, the chief attention of the reader is directed in this work to questions of practical importance.

[76] Hydrobromic acid is also obtained by the action of bromine on paraffin heated to 180°. Gustavson proposed to prepare it by the action of bromine (best added in drops together with traces of aluminium bromide) on anthracene (a solid hydrocarbon from coal tar). Balard prepared it by passing bromine vapour over moist pieces of common phosphorus. The liquid tribromide of phosphorus, directly obtained from phosphorus and bromine, also gives hydrobromic acid when treated with water. Bromide of potassium or sodium, when treated with sulphuric acid in the presence of phosphorus, also gives hydrobromic acid, but hydriodic acid is decomposed by this method. In order to free hydrobromic acid from bromine vapour it is passed over moist phosphorus and dried either by phosphoric anhydride or calcium bromide (calcium chloride cannot be used, as hydrochloric acid would be formed). Neither hydrobromic nor hydriodic acids can be collected over mercury, on which they act, but they may be directly collected in a dry vessel by leading the gas-conducting tube to the bottom of the vessel, both gases being much heavier than air. Merz and Holtzmann (1889) proposed to prepare HBr directly from bromine and hydrogen. For this purpose pure dry hydrogen is passed through a flask containing boiling bromine. The mixture of gas and vapour then passes through a tube provided with one or two bulbs, which is heated moderately in the middle. Hydrobromic acid is formed with a series of flashes at the part heated. The resultant HBr, together with traces of bromine, passes into a Woulfe's bottle into which hydrogen is also introduced, and the mixture is then carried through another heated tube, after which it is passed through water which dissolves the hydrobromic acid. According to the method proposed by Newth (1892) a mixture of bromine and hydrogen is led through a tube containing a platinum spiral, which is heated to redness after the air has been displaced from the tube. If the vessel containing the bromine be kept at 60°, the hydrogen takes up almost the theoretical amount of bromine required for the formation of HBr. Although the flame which appears in the neighbourhood of the platinum spiral does not penetrate into the vessel containing the bromine, still, for safety, a tube filled with cotton wool may be interposed.

Hydriodic acid is obtained in the same manner as hydrobromic. The iodine is heated in a small flask, and its vapour is carried over by hydrogen into a strongly heated tube, The gas passing from the tube is found to contain a considerable amount of HI, together with some free iodine. At a low red heat about 17 p.c. of the iodine vapour enters into combination; at a higher temperature, 78 p.c. to 79 p.c.; and at a strong heat about 82 p.c.

[77] But generally more phosphorus is taken than is required for the formation of PI$_3$, because otherwise a portion of the iodine distils over. If less than one-tenth part of iodine be taken, much phosphonium iodide, PH$_4$I, is formed. This proportion was established by Gay-Lussac and Kolbe. Hydriodic acid is also prepared in many other ways. Bannoff dissolves two parts of iodine in one part of a previously prepared strong (sp. gr. 1·67) solution of hydriodic acid, and pours it on to red phosphorus in a retort. Personne takes a mixture of fifteen parts of water, ten of iodine, and one of red phosphorus, which, when heated, disengages hydriodic acid mixed with iodine vapour; the latter is removed by passing it over moist phosphorus (Note 76). It must be remembered however that reverse reaction (Oppenheim) may take place between the hydriodic acid and phosphorus, in which the compounds PH$_4$I and PI$_2$ are formed.

It should be observed that the reaction between phosphorus, iodine and water must be carried out in the above proportions and with caution, as they may react with explosion. With red phosphorus the reaction proceeds quietly, but nevertheless requires care.

L. Meyer showed that with an excess of iodine the reaction proceeds without the formation of bye-products (PH$_4$I), according to the equation P + 5I + 4H$_2$O = PH$_3$O$_4$ + 5HI. For this purpose 100 grams of iodine and 10 grams of water are placed in a retort, and a paste of 5 grams of red phosphorus and 10 grams of water is added little by little (at first with great care). The hydriodic acid may be obtained free from iodine by directing the neck of the retort upwards and causing the gas to pass through a shallow layer of water (respecting the formation of HI, *see* also Note 75).

[78] The specific gravities of their solutions as deduced by me on the basis of Topsöe and Berthelot's determinations for 15°/4° are as follows:—

	10	20	30	40	50	60 p.c.
HBr	1·071	1·156	1·258	1·374	1·505	1·650
HI	1·075	1·164	1·267	1·399	1·567	1·769

Hydrobromic acid forms two hydrates, HBr,2H$_2$O and HBr,H$_2$O, which have been studied by Roozeboom with as much completeness as the hydrate of hydrochloric acid (Chapter X. Note 37).

With metallic silver, solutions of hydriodic acid give hydrogen with great ease, forming silver iodide. Mercury, lead, and other metals act in a similar manner.

[78 bis] Iodide of nitrogen, NHI_2 is obtained as a brown pulverulent precipitate on adding a solution of iodine (in alcohol, for instance) to a solution of ammonia. If it be collected on a filter-paper, it does not decompose so long as the precipitate is moist; but when dry it explodes violently, so that it can only be experimented upon in small quantities. Usually the filter-paper is torn into bits while moist, and the pieces laid upon a brick; on drying an explosion proceeds not only from friction or a blow, but even spontaneously. The more dilute the solution of ammonia, the greater is the amount of iodine required for the formation of the precipitate of NHI_2. A low temperature facilitates its formation. NHI_2 dissolves in ammonia water, and when heated the solution forms HIO_3 and iodine. With KI, iodide of nitrogen gives iodine, NH_3 and KHO. These reactions (Selivanoff) are explained by the formation of HIO from $NHI_2 + 2H_2O = NH_3 + 2HIO$—and then $KI + HIO = I_2 + KHO$. Selivanoff (see Note 29) usually observed a temporary formation of hypoiodous acid, HIO, in the reaction of ammonia upon iodine, so that here the formation of NHI_2 is preceded by that of HIO—i.e. first $I_2 + H_2O = HIO + HI$, and then not only the HI combines with NH_3, but also $2HIO + NH_3 = NHI_2 + 2H_2O$. With dilute sulphuric acid iodide of nitrogen (like NCl_3) forms hypoiodous acid, but it immediately passes into iodic acid, as is expressed by the equation $5HIO = 2I_2 + HIO_3 + 2H_2O$ (first $3HIO = HIO_3 + 2HI$, and then $HI + HIO = I_2 + H_2O$). Moreover, Selivanoff found that iodide of nitrogen, NHI_2, dissolves in an excess of ammonia water, and that with potassium iodide the solution gives the reaction for hypoiodous acid (the evolution of iodine in an alkaline solution). This shows that HIO participates in the formation and decomposition of NHI_2, and therefore the condition of the iodine (its metaleptic position) in them is analogous, and differs from the condition of the halogens in the haloid-anhydrides (for instance, NO_2Cl). The latter are tolerably stable, while (the haloid being designated by X) NHX_2, NX_3, XOH, RXO (see Chapter XIII. Note 43), &c., are unstable, easily decomposed with the evolution of heat, and, under the action of water, the haloid is easily replaced by hydrogen (Selivanoff), as would be expected in true products of metalepsis.

[79] Hypoiodous acid, HIO, is not known, but organic compounds, RIO, of this type are known. To illustrate the peculiarities of their properties we will mention one of these compounds, namely, iodosobenzol, C_6H_5IO. This substance was obtained by Willgerodt (1892), and also by V. Meyer, Wachter, and Askenasy, by the action of caustic alkalis upon phenoldiiodochloride, $C_6H_5ICl_2$ (according to the equation, $C_6H_5ICl_2 +$

2MOH = C_6H_5IO + 2MCl + H_2O). Iodosobenzol is an amorphous yellow substance, whose melting point could not be determined because it explodes at 210°, decomposing with the evolution of iodine vapour. This substance dissolves in hot water and alcohol, but is not soluble in the majority of other neutral organic solvents. If acids do not oxidise C_6H_5IO, they give saline compounds in which iodosobenzol appears as a basic oxide of a diatomic metal, C_6H_5I. Thus, for instance, when an acetic acid solution of iodosobenzol is treated with a solution of nitric acid, it gives large monoclinic crystals of a nitric acid salt having the composition $C_6H_5I(NO_3)_2$ (like $Ca(NO_3)_2$). In appearing as the analogue of basic oxides, iodosobenzol displaces iodine from potassium iodide (in a solution acidulated with acetic or hydrochloric acid)—*i.e.* it acts with its oxygen like HClO. The action of peroxide of hydrogen, chromic acid, and other similar oxidising agents gives iodoxybenzol, $C_6H_5IO_2$, which is a neutral substance—*i.e.* incapable of giving salts with acids (compare Chapter XIII. Note 43).

[79 bis] The oxidation of iodine by strong nitric acid was discovered by Connell; Millon showed that it is effected, although more slowly, by the action of the hydrates of nitric acid up to HNO_3,H_2O, but that the solution $HNO_3,2H_2O$, and weaker solutions, do not oxidise, but simply dissolve, iodine. The participation of water in reactions is seen in this instance. It is also seen, for example, in the fact that dry ammonia combines directly with iodine—for instance, at 0° forming the compound $I_2,4NH_3$—whilst iodide of nitrogen is only formed in presence of water.

[80] Bromine also displaces chlorine—for instance, from chloric acid, directly forming bromic acid. If a solution of potassium chlorate be taken (75 parts per 400 parts of water), and iodine be added to it (80 parts), and then a small quantity of nitric acid, chlorine is disengaged on boiling, and potassium iodate is formed in the solution. In this instance the nitric acid first evolves a certain portion of the chloric acid, and the latter, with the iodine, evolves chlorine. The iodic acid thus formed acts on a further quantity of the potassium chlorate, sets a portion of the chloric acid free, and in this manner the action is kept up. Potilitzin (1887) remarked, however, that not only do bromine and iodine displace the chlorine from chloric acid and potassium chlorate, but also chlorine displaces bromine from sodium bromate, and, furthermore, the reaction does not proceed as a direct substitution of the halogens, but is accompanied by the formation of free acids; for example, $5NaClO_3 + 3Br_2 + 3H_2O = 5NaBr + 5HClO_3 + HBrO_3$.

[81] If iodine be stirred up in water, and chlorine passed through the mixture, the iodine is dissolved; the liquid becomes colourless, and contains, according to the relative amounts of water and chlorine, either

IHCl$_2$, or ICl$_3$, or HIO$_3$. If there be a small amount of water, then the iodic acid may separate out directly as crystals, but a complete conversion (Bornemann) only occurs when not less than ten parts of water are taken to one part of iodine—ICl + 3H$_2$O + 2Cl$_2$ = IHO$_3$ + 5HCl.

[82] Schönbein and Ogier proved this. Ogier found that at 45° ozone immediately oxidises iodine vapour, forming first of all the oxide I$_2$O$_3$, which is decomposed by water or on heating into iodic anhydride and iodine. Iodic acid is formed at the positive pole when a solution of hydriodic acid is decomposed by a galvanic current (Riche). It is also formed in the combustion of hydrogen mixed with a small quantity of hydriodic acid (Salet).

[83] Kämmerer showed that a solution of sp. gr. 2·127 at 14°, containing 2HIO$_3$,9H$_2$O, solidified completely in the cold. On comparing solutions HI + mH$_2$O with HIO$_3$ + mH$_2$O, we find that the specific gravity increases but the volume decreases, whilst in the passage of solutions HCl + mH$_2$O to HClO$_3$ + mH$_2$O both the specific gravity and the volume increase, which is also observed in certain other cases (for example, H$_3$PO$_3$ and H$_3$PO$_4$).

[83 bis] Ditte (1890) obtained many iodates of great variety. A neutral salt, 2(LiIO$_3$)H$_2$O, is obtained by saturating a solution of lithia with iodic acid. There is an analogous ammonium salt, 2(NH$_4$IO$_3$)H$_2$O. He also obtained hydrates of a more complex composition, such as 6(NH$_4$IO$_3$)H$_2$O and 6(NH$_4$IO$_3$)2H$_2$O. Salts of the alkaline earths, Ba(IO$_3$)$_2$H$_2$O and Sr(IO$_3$)$_2$H$_2$O, may be obtained by a reaction of double decomposition from the normal salts of the type 2(MeIO$_3$)H$_2$O. When evaporated at 70° to 80° with nitric acid these salts lose water. A mixture of solutions of nitrate of zinc and an alkaline iodate precipitates Zn(IO$_3$)$_2$2H$_2$O. An anhydrous salt is thrown out if nitric acid be added to the solutions. Analogous salts of cadmium, silver, and copper give compounds of the type 2Me'IO$_3$4NH$_3$ and Me''(IO$_3$)$_2$4NH$_3$, with gaseous ammonia (Me' and Me'' being elements of the first (Ag) and second (Cd, Zn, Cu) groups). With an aqueous solution of ammonia the above salts give substances of a different composition, such as Zn(IO$_3$)$_2$(NH$_4$)$_2$O, Cd(IO$_3$)$_2$(NH$_4$)$_2$O. Copper gives Cu(IO$_3$)$_2$4(NH$_4$)$_2$O and Cu(IO$_3$)$_2$(NH$_4$)$_2$O. These salts may be regarded as compounds of I$_2$O$_5$, and MeO and (NH$_4$)$_2$O; for example, Zn(IO$_3$)$_2$(NH$_4$)$_2$O may be regarded as ZnO(NH$_4$)$_2$OI$_2$O$_5$, or, as derived from the hydrate, I$_2$O$_5$2H$_2$O = 2(HIO$_3$)H$_2$O.

[84] If sodium iodate be mixed with a solution of sodium hydroxide, heated, and chlorine passed through the solution, a sparingly soluble salt separates out, which corresponds with periodic acid, and has the composition Na$_4$I$_2$O$_9$,3H$_2$O.

$$6NaHO + 2NaIO_3 + 4Cl = 4NaCl + Na_4I_2O_9 + 3H_2O.$$

This compound is sparingly soluble in water, but dissolves easily in a very dilute solution of nitric acid. If silver nitrate be added to this solution a precipitate is formed which contains the corresponding compound of silver, $Ag_4I_2O_9,3H_2O$. If this sparingly soluble silver compound be dissolved in hot nitric acid, orange crystals of a salt having the composition $AgIO_4$ separate on evaporation. This salt is formed from the preceding by the nitric acid taking up silver oxide—$Ag_4I_2O_9 + 2HNO_3 = 2AgNO_3 + 2AgIO_4 + H_2O$. The silver salt is decomposed by water, with the re-formation of the preceding salt, whilst iodic acid remains in solution—

$$4AgIO_4 + H_2O = Ag_4I_2O_9 + 2HIO_4.$$

The structure of the first of these salts, $Na_4I_2O_9,3H_2O$, presents itself in a simpler form if the water of crystallisation is regarded as an integral portion of the salt; the formula is then divided in two, and takes the form of $IO(OH)_3(ONa)_2$—that is, it answers to the type IOX_5, or IX_7, like $AgIO_4$ which is $IO_3(OAg)$. The composition of all the salts of periodic acids are expressed by this type IX_7. Kimmins (1889) refers all the salts of periodic acid to four types—the meta-salts of HIO_4 (salts of Ag, Cu, Pb), the meso-salts of H_3IO_5 (PbH, Ag_2H, CdH), the para-salts of H_5IO_6 (Na_2H_3, Na_3H_2), and the di-salts of $H_4I_2O_9$ (K_4, Ag_4, Ni_2). The three first are direct compounds of the type IX_7, namely, $IO_3(OH)$, $IO_2(OH)_3$, and $IO(OH)_5$, and the last are types of diperiodic salts, which correspond with the type of the meso-salts, as pyrophosphoric salts correspond with orthophosphoric salts—*i.e.* $2H_3IO_5-H_2O = H_4I_2O_9$.

[85] Periodic acid, discovered by Magnus and Ammermüller, and whose salts were afterwards studied by Langlois, Rammelsberg, and many others, presents an example of hydrates in which it is evident that there is not that distinction between the water of hydration and of crystallisation which was at first considered to be so clear. In $HClO,2H_2O$ the water, $2H_2O$, is not displaced by bases, and must be regarded as water of crystallisation, whilst in $HIO_4,2H_2O$ it must be regarded as water of hydration. We shall afterwards see that the system of the elements obliges us to consider the halogens as substances giving a highest saline type, GX_7, where G signifies a halogen, and X oxygen ($O = X_2$), OH, and other like elements. The hydrate $IO(OH)_5$ corresponding with many of the salts of periodic acid (for example, the salts of barium, strontium, mercury) does not exhaust all the possible forms. It is evident that various other pyro-, meta-, &c., forms are possible by the loss of water, as will be more fully explained in speaking of phosphoric acid, and as was pointed out in the preceding note.

[86] With respect to hydrogen, oxygen, chlorine, and other elements, bromine occupies an intermediate position between chlorine and iodine, and therefore there is no particular need for considering at length the

compounds of bromine. This is the great advantage of a natural grouping of the elements.

[87] They were both obtained by Gay-Lussac and many others. Recent data respecting iodine monochloride, ICl, entirely confirm the numerous observations of Trapp (1854), and even confirm his statement as to the existence of two isomeric (liquid and crystalline) forms (Stortenbeker). With a small excess of iodine, iodine monochloride remains liquid, but in the presence of traces of iodine trichloride it easily crystallises. Tanatar (1893) showed that of the two modifications of ICl, one is stable, and melts at 27°; while the other, which easily passes into the first, and is formed in the absence of ICl_3, melts at 14°. Schützenberger amplified the data concerning the action of water on the chlorides (Note 88), and Christomanos gave the fullest data regarding the trichloride.

After being kept for some time, the liquid monochloride of iodine yields red deliquescent octahedra, having the composition ICl_4, which are therefore formed from the monochloride with the liberation of free iodine, which dissolves in the remaining quantity of the monochloride. This substance, however, judging by certain observations, is impure iodine trichloride. If 1 part of iodine be stirred up in 20 parts of water, and chlorine be passed through the liquid, then all the iodine is dissolved, and a colourless liquid is ultimately obtained which contains a certain proportion of chlorine, because this compound gives a metallic chloride and iodate with alkalis without evolving any free iodine: $ICl_5 + 6KHO = 5KCl + KIO_3 + 3H_2O$. The existence of a pentachloride ICl_5 is, however, denied, because this substance has not been obtained in a free state.

Stortenbeker (1888) investigated the equilibrium of the system containing the molecules I_2, ICl, ICl_3, and Cl_2, in the same way that Roozeboom (Chapter X. Note 38) examined the equilibrium of the molecules HCl, $HCl,2H_2O$, and H_2O. He found that iodine monochloride appears in two states, one (the ordinary) is stable and melts at 27°·2, whilst the other is obtained by rapid cooling, and melts at 13°·9, and easily passes into the first form. Iodine trichloride melts at 101° only in a closed tube under a pressure of 16 atmospheres.

[88] By the action of water on iodine monochloride and trichloride a compound $IHCl_2$ is obtained, which does not seem to be altered by water. Besides this compound, iodine and iodic acid are always formed, $10ICl + 3H_2O = HIO_3 + 5IHCl_2 + 2I_2$; and in this respect iodine trichloride may be regarded as a mixture, $ICl + ICl_5 = 2ICl_3$, but $ICl_5 + 3H_2O = IHO_3 + 5HCl$; hence iodic acid, iodine, the compound $IHCl_2$, and hydrochloric acid are also formed by the action of water.

[513]

CHAPTER XII

SODIUM

The neutral salt, sodium sulphate, Na_2SO_4, obtained when a mixture of sulphuric acid and common salt is strongly heated (Chapter X.),[1] forms a colourless saline mass consisting of fine crystals, soluble in water. It is the product of many other double decompositions, sometimes carried out on a large scale; for example, when ammonium sulphate is heated with common salt, in which case the sal-ammoniac is volatilised, &c. A similar decomposition also takes place when, for instance, a mixture of lead sulphate and common salt is heated; this mixture easily fuses, and if the temperature be further raised heavy vapours of lead chloride appear. When the disengagement of these vapours ceases, the remaining mass, on being treated with water, yields a solution of sodium sulphate mixed with a solution of undecomposed common salt. A considerable quantity, however, of the lead sulphate remains unchanged during this reaction, $PbSO_4 + 2NaCl = PbCl_2 + Na_2SO_4$, the vapours will contain lead chloride, and the residue will contain the mixture of the three remaining salts. The cause and nature of the reaction are just the same as were pointed out when considering the action of sulphuric acid upon NaCl. Here too it may be shown that the double decomposition is determined by the removal of $PbCl_2$ from the sphere of the action of the remaining substances. This is seen from the fact that sodium sulphate, on being dissolved in water and mixed with a solution of any lead salt (and even with a solution of lead chloride, although this latter is but sparingly soluble in water), immediately gives a white precipitate of lead sulphate. In this case the lead takes up the elements of sulphuric acid from the sodium sulphate in the solutions.[514] On heating, the reverse phenomenon is observed. The reaction in the solution depends upon the insolubility of the lead sulphate, and the decomposition which takes place on heating is due to the volatility of the lead chloride. Silver sulphate, Ag_2SO_4, in solution with common salt, gives silver chloride, because the latter is insoluble in water, $Ag_2SO_4 + 2NaCl = Na_2SO_4 + 2AgCl$. Sodium carbonate, mixed in solution with the sulphates of iron, copper, manganese, magnesium, &c., gives in solution sodium sulphate, and in the precipitate a carbonate of the corresponding metal, because these salts of carbonic acid are insoluble in water; for instance, $MgSO_4 + Na_2CO_3 = Na_2SO_4 + MgCO_3$. In precisely the same way sodium hydroxide acts on solutions of the majority of the salts of sulphuric acid containing metals, the hydroxides of which are insoluble in water—for instance, $CuSO_4 + 2NaHO = Cu(HO)_2 + Na_2SO_4$. Sulphate of magnesium, $MgSO_4$, on being mixed in solution with common salt, forms, although not completely, chloride of magnesium, and sodium sulphate. On cooling the mixture of such (concentrated) solutions sodium sulphate is deposited, as was shown in Chapter $\underline{X}$. This is made use of for preparing it on the large scale in works where sea-water is treated. In this case, on cooling, the reaction $2NaCl + MgSO_4 = MgCl_2 + Na_2SO_4$ takes place.

Thus where sulphates and salts of sodium are in contact, it may be expected that sodium sulphate will be formed and separated if the conditions are favourable; for this reason it is not surprising that sodium sulphate is often found in the native state. Some of the springs and salt lakes in the steppes beyond the Volga, and in the Caucasus, contain a considerable quantity of sodium sulphate, and yield it by simple evaporation of the solutions. Beds of this salt are also met with; thus at a depth of only 5 feet, about 38 versts to the east of Tiflis, at the foot of the range of the 'Wolf's mane" (Voltchia griva) mountains, a deep stratum of very pure Glauber's salt, $Na_2SO_4,10H_2O$, has been found.[2] A layer two metres thick of the same salt lies at the bottom of several lakes (an area of about 10 square kilometres) in the Kouban district near Batalpaschinsk, and here its working has been commenced (1887). In Spain, near Arangoulz and in many parts of the Western States of North America, mineral sodium sulphate has likewise been found, and is already being worked.

The methods of obtaining salts by means of double decomposition[515] from others already prepared are so general, that in describing a given salt there is no necessity to enumerate the cases hitherto observed of its being formed through various double decompositions.[3] The possibility of this occurrence ought to be foreseen according to Berthollet's doctrine from the properties of the salt in question. On this account it is important to know the properties of salts; all the more so because up to the present time those very properties (solubility, formation of crystallo-hydrates, volatility, &c.) which may be made use of for separating them from other salts have not been generalised.[4] These properties as yet remain subjects for investigation, and are rarely to be foreseen. The crystallo-hydrate of the normal sodium sulphate, $Na_2SO_4,10H_2O$, very easily parts with water, and may be obtained in an anhydrous state if it be carefully heated until the weight remains constant; but if heated further, it partly loses the elements of sulphuric anhydride. The normal salt fuses at 843° (red heat), and volatilises to a slight extent when very strongly heated, in which case it naturally decomposes with the evolution of SO_3. At 0° 100 parts of water dissolve 5 parts of the anhydrous salt, at 10° 9 parts, at 20° 19·4, at 30° 40, and at 34° 55 parts, the same being the case in the presence of an excess of crystals of $Na_2SO_4,10H_2O$.[5] At 34° the latter fuses, and the solubility decreases at higher temperatures.[6] A concentrated solution at 34° has a composition nearly approaching to $Na_2SO_4 + 14H_2O$,[516] and the decahydrated salt contains 78·9 of the anhydrous salt combined with 100 parts of water. From the above figures it is seen that the decahydrated salt cannot fuse without decomposing,[7] like hydrate of chlorine, $Cl_2,8H_2O$ (Chapter XI., Note 10). Not only the fused decahydrated salt, but also the concentrated solution at 34° (not all at once, but gradually), yields the monohydrated salt, Na_2SO_4,H_2O. The heptahydrated salt, $Na_2SO_4,7H_2O$, also splits up, even at low temperatures, with the formation of this monohydrated salt, and therefore from 35° the solubility can be given only for the latter. For 100 parts of water this is as follows: at 40° 48·8, at 50° 46·7, at 80° 43·7, at 100° 42·5 parts of the anhydrous salt. If the decahydrated salt be fused, and the solution allowed to cool in the presence of the monohydrated salt, then at 30° 50·4 parts of anhydrous salt are retained in the solution, and at 20° 52·8 parts. Hence, with respect to the anhydrous and monohydrated salts, the solubility is identical, and falls with increasing temperature, whilst with respect to decahydrated salt, the solubility rises with increasing temperature. So that if in contact with a solution[517] of sodium sulphate there are only crystals of that heptahydrated salt (Chapter I., Note 54), $Na_2SO_4,7H_2O$, which is formed from saturated solutions, then saturation sets in when the solution has the following composition per 100 parts of salt: at 0° 19·6, at 10° 30·5, at 20° 44·7, and at 25° 52·9 parts of anhydrous salt. Above 27° the heptahydrated salt, like the decahydrated salt at 34°, splits up into the monohydrated salt and a saturated solution. Thus sodium sulphate has three curves of solubility: one for $Na_2SO_4,7H_2O$ (from 0° to 26°), one for $Na_2SO_4,10H_2O$ (from 0° to 34°), and one for Na_2SO_4,H_2O (a descending curve beginning at 26°), because there are three of these crystallo-hydrates, and the solubility of a substance only depends upon the particular condition of that portion of it which has separated from the solution or is present in excess.[8]

Thus solutions of sodium sulphate may give crystallo-hydrates of three kinds on cooling the saturated solution: the unstable heptahydrated salt is obtained at temperatures below 26°, the decahydrated salt forms under ordinary conditions at temperatures below 34°, and the monohydrated salt at temperatures above 34°. Both the latter crystallo-hydrates present a stable state of equilibrium, and the heptahydrated salt decomposes into them, probably according to the equation $3Na_2SO_4,7H_2O = 2Na_2SO_4,10H_2O + Na_2SO_4,H_2O$. The ordinary decahydrated salt is called *Glauber's salt*. All forms of these crystallo-hydrates lose their water entirely, and give the anhydrous salt when dried over sulphuric acid.[9]

Sodium sulphate, Na_2SO_4, only enters into a few reactions of combination with other salts, and chiefly with salts of the same acid, forming double sulphates. Thus, for example, if a solution of sodium[518] sulphate be mixed with a solution of aluminium, magnesium, or ferrous sulphate, it gives crystals of a double salt when evaporated. Sulphuric acid itself forms a compound with sodium sulphate, which is exactly like these double salts. It is formed with great ease when sodium sulphate is dissolved in sulphuric acid and the solution evaporated. On evaporation, crystals of the acid salt separate, $Na_2SO_4 + H_2SO_4 = 2NaHSO_4$. This separates from hot solutions, whilst the crystallo-hydrate, $NaHSO_4,H_2O$,[10] separates from cold solutions. The crystals when exposed to damp air decompose into H_2SO_4, which deliquesces, and Na_2SO_4 (Graham, Rose); alcohol also extracts sulphuric acid from the acid salt. This shows the feeble force which holds the sulphuric acid to the sodium sulphate.[11] Both acid sodium sulphate and all mixtures of the normal salt and sulphuric acid lose water when heated, and are converted into sodium *pyrosulphate*, $Na_2S_2O_7$, at a low red heat.[11 bis] This anhydrous salt, at a bright red heat, parts with the elements of sulphuric anhydride, the normal sodium sulphate remaining behind—$Na_2S_2O_7 = Na_2SO_4 + SO_3$. From this it is seen that the normal salt is able to combine with water, with other sulphates, and with sulphuric anhydride or acid, &c.

Sodium sulphate may by double decomposition be converted into a sodium salt of any other acid, by means of heat and taking advantage of the volatility, or by means of solution and taking advantage of the different degree of solubility of the different salts. Thus, for instance, owing to the insolubility of barium sulphate, sodium hydroxide or caustic soda may be prepared from sodium sulphate, if barium hydroxide be added to its solution, $Na_2SO_4 + Ba(HO)_2 = BaSO_4 + 2NaHO$. And by taking any salt of barium, BaX_2, the corresponding salt of sodium may be obtained, $Na_2SO_4 + BaX_2 = BaSO_4 + 2NaX$. Barium[519] sulphate thus formed, being a very sparingly-soluble salt, is obtained as a precipitate, whilst the sodium hydroxide, or salt, NaX, is obtained in solution, because *all salts of sodium are soluble*. Berthollet's doctrine permits all such cases to be foreseen.

The reactions of *decomposition* of sodium sulphate are above all noticeable by the separation of oxygen. Sodium sulphate by itself is very stable, and it is only at a temperature sufficient to melt iron that it is possible to separate the elements SO_3 from it, and then only partially. However, the oxygen may be separated from sodium sulphate, as from all other sulphates, by means of many substances which are able to combine with oxygen, such as charcoal and sulphur, but hydrogen is not able to produce this action. If sodium sulphate be heated with charcoal, then carbonic oxide and anhydride are evolved, and there is produced, according to the circumstances, either the lower oxygen compound, sodium sulphite, Na_2SO_3 (for instance, in the formation of glass); or else the decomposition proceeds further, and sodium sulphide, Na_2S, is formed, according to the equation $Na_2SO_4 + 2C = 2CO_2 + Na_2S$.

On the basis of this reaction the greater part of the sulphate of sodium prepared at chemical works is converted into *soda ash*—that is, *sodium carbonate*, Na_2CO_3, which is used for many purposes. In the form of carbonates, the metallic oxides behave in many cases just as they do in the state of oxides or hydroxides, owing to the feeble acid properties of carbonic acid. However, the majority of the salts of carbonic acid are insoluble, whilst sodium carbonate is one of the few soluble salts of this acid, and therefore reacts with facility. Hence sodium carbonate is employed for many purposes, in which its alkaline properties come into play. Thus, even under the action of feeble organic acids it immediately parts with its carbonic acid, and gives a sodium salt of the acid taken. Its solutions exhibit an alkaline reaction on litmus. It aids the passage of certain organic substances (tar, acids) into solution, and is therefore used, like caustic alkalis and soap (which latter also acts by virtue of the alkali it contains), for the removal of certain organic substances, especially in bleaching cotton and similar fabrics. Besides which a considerable quantity of sodium carbonate is used for the preparation of sodium hydroxide or caustic soda, which has also a very wide application. In large chemical works where sodium carbonate is manufactured from Na_2SO_4, it is usual first to manufacture sulphuric acid, and then by its aid to convert common salt into sodium sulphate, and lastly to convert the sodium sulphate thus obtained into carbonate and caustic soda. Hence these works prepare both alkaline substances (soda ash and caustic[520] soda) and acid substances (sulphuric and hydrochloric acids), the two classes of chemical products which are distinguished for the greatest energy of their reactions and are therefore most frequently applied to technical purposes. Factories manufacturing soda are generally called alkali works.

The process of the conversion of sodium sulphate into sodium carbonate consists in strongly heating a mixture of the sulphate with charcoal and calcium carbonate. The following reactions then take place: the sodium sulphate is first deoxidised by the charcoal, forming sodium sulphide and carbonic anhydride, $Na_2SO_4 + 2C = Na_2S + 2CO_2$. The sodium sulphide thus formed then enters into double decomposition with the calcium carbonate taken, and gives calcium sulphide and sodium carbonate, $Na_2S + CaCO_3 = Na_2CO_3 + CaS$.

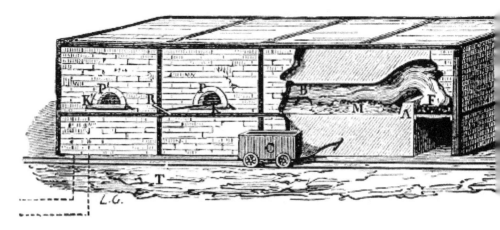

FIG. 68.—Reverberatory furnace for the manufacture of sodium
carbonate. F, grate. A, bridge. M, hearth for the ultimate calcination
of the mixture of sodium sulphate, coal, and calcium carbonate,
which is charged from above into the part of the furnace furthest
removed from the fire F. P, P, doors for stirring and bringing the
mass towards the grate F by means of stirrers R. At the end of the
operation the semifused mass is charged into trucks C.

Besides which, under the action of the heat, a portion of the excess of
calcium carbonate is decomposed into lime and carbonic anhydride, $CaCO_3$
$= CaO + CO_2$, and the carbonic anhydride with the excess of charcoal
forms carbon monoxide, which towards the end of the operation shows
itself by the appearance of a blue flame. Thus from a mass containing
sodium sulphate we obtain a mass which includes sodium carbonate,
calcium sulphide, and calcium oxide, but none of the sodium sulphide
which was formed on first heating the mixture. The entire process, which
proceeds at a high temperature, may be expressed by a combination of the
three above-mentioned formulæ, if it be considered that the product
contains one equivalent of calcium oxide to two equivalents of calcium
sulphide.[12] The sum of the reactions may then be expressed thus: $2Na_2SO_4$
$+ 3CaCO_3 + 9C = 2Na_2CO_3 + CaO,2CaS + 10CO$. Indeed, the quantities
in which the substances are mixed together at chemical works approaches
to the proportion required by this equation. The entire process of
decomposition is carried on in reverberatory furnaces, into which a mixture
of 1,000 parts of sodium sulphate, 1,040 parts of calcium carbonate (as a
somewhat porous limestone), and 500 parts of small coal is introduced
from above. This mixture is first heated in the portion of the furnace which
is[521] furthest removed from the fire-grate; it is then brought to the
portion nearest to the fire-grate, when it is stirred during heating. The
partially fused mass obtained at the end of the process is cooled, and then

subjected to methodical lixiviation[13] to extract the sodium carbonate,[522] the mixture of calcium oxide and sulphide forming the so-called 'soda waste' or 'alkali waste.'[14]

[523]

The above-mentioned process for making soda was discovered in the year 1808 by the French doctor Leblanc, and is known as the Leblanc process. The particulars of the discovery are somewhat remarkable. Sodium carbonate, having a considerable application in industry, was for a long time prepared exclusively from the ash of marine plants (Chapter XI., page 497). Even up to the present time this process is carried on in Normandy. In France, where for a long time the manufacture of large quantities of soap (so-called Marseilles soap) and various fabrics required a large amount of soda, the quantity prepared at the coast was insufficient to meet the demand. For this reason during the wars at the beginning of the century, when the import of foreign goods into France was interdicted, the want of sodium carbonate was felt. The French Academy offered a prize for the discovery of a profitable method of preparing it from common salt. Leblanc then proposed the above-mentioned process, which is remarkable for its great simplicity.[15]

[524]

Of all other industrial processes for manufacturing sodium carbonate, the *ammonia process* is the most worthy of mention.[16] In this the vapours of ammonia, and then an excess of carbonic anhydride, are directly introduced into a concentrated solution of sodium chloride in order to form the acid ammonium carbonate, NH_4HCO_3. Then, by means of the double saline decomposition of this salt, sodium chloride is decomposed, and in virtue of its slight solubility acid sodium carbonate, $NaHCO_3$, is precipitated and ammonium chloride, NH_4Cl, is obtained in solution (with a portion of the sodium chloride and acid sodium carbonate). The reaction proceeds in the solution owing to the sparing solubility of the $NaHCO_3$ according to the equation $NaCl + NH_4HCO_3 = NH_4Cl + NaHCO_3$. The ammonia is recovered from the solution by heating with lime or magnesia,[16 bis] and the precipitated acid sodium carbonate is converted into the normal salt by heating. It is thus obtained in a very pure state.[17]

[525]

Sodium carbonate, like sodium sulphate, loses all its water on being heated, and when anhydrous fuses at a bright-red heat (1098°). A small quantity of sodium carbonate placed in the loop of a platinum wire volatilises in the heat of a gas flame, and therefore in the furnaces of glass works part of the soda is always transformed into the condition of vapour.

Sodium carbonate resembles sodium sulphate in its relation to water.[18] Here also the greatest solubility is at the temperature of 37°; both salts, on crystallising at the ordinary temperature, combine with ten molecules of water, and such crystals of soda, like crystals of Glauber's salt, fuse at 34°. Sodium carbonate also forms a supersaturated solution, and, according to the conditions, gives various combinations with water of crystallisation (mentioned on page 108), &c.

At a red heat superheated steam liberates carbonic anhydride from sodium carbonate and forms caustic soda, $Na_2CO_3 + H_2O = 2NaHO + CO_2$. Here the carbonic anhydride is replaced by water; this depends on the feebly acid character of carbonic anhydride. By direct heating, sodium carbonate is only slightly decomposed into sodium oxide and carbonic anhydride; thus, when sodium carbonate is fused, about 1 per cent. of carbonic anhydride is disengaged.[19] The carbonates of many other metals—for instance, of calcium, copper, magnesium, iron, &c.—on being heated lose all their carbonic anhydride. This shows[526] the considerable basic energy which sodium possesses. With the soluble salts of most metals, sodium carbonate gives precipitates either of insoluble carbonates of the metals, or else of the hydroxides (in this latter case carbonic anhydride is disengaged); for instance, with barium salts it precipitates an insoluble barium carbonate ($BaCl_2 + Na_2CO_3 = 2NaCl + BaCO_3$) and with the aluminium salts it precipitates aluminium hydroxide, carbonic anhydride being disengaged: $3Na_2CO_3 + Al_2(SO_4)_3 + 3H_2O = 3Na_2SO_4 + 2Al(OH)_3 + 3CO_2$. Sodium carbonate, like all the salts of carbonic acid, evolves carbonic anhydride on treatment with all acids which are to any extent energetic. But if an acid diluted with water be gradually added to a solution of sodium carbonate, *at first* such an evolution does not take place, because the excess of the carbonic anhydride forms acid sodium carbonate (sodium bicarbonate), $NaHCO_3$.[20] The acid sodium carbonate is an unstable salt. Not only when heated alone, but even on being slightly heated in solution, and also at the ordinary temperature in damp air, it loses carbonic anhydride and forms the normal salt. And at the same time it is easy to obtain it in a pure crystalline form, if a strong solution of sodium carbonate be cooled and a stream of carbonic anhydride gas passed through it. The acid salt is less soluble in water than the normal,[21] and therefore a strong[527] solution of the latter gives crystals of the acid salt if carbonic anhydride be passed through it. The acid salt may be yet more conveniently formed from effloresced crystals of sodium carbonate, which, on being considerably heated, very easily absorb carbonic anhydride.[22] The acid salt crystallises well, but not, however, in such large crystals as the normal salt; it has a brackish and not an alkaline taste like that of the normal salt; its reaction is feebly alkaline, nearly neutral. At 70° its solution begins to lose carbonic anhydride, and on boiling the evolution becomes very abundant.

From the preceding remarks it is clear that in most reactions this salt, especially when heated, acts similarly to the normal salt, but has, naturally, some distinction from it. Thus, for example, if a solution of sodium carbonate be added to a normal magnesium salt, a turbidity (precipitate) is formed of magnesium carbonate. $MgCO_3$. No such precipitate is formed by the acid salt, because magnesium carbonate is soluble in the presence of an excess of carbonic anhydride.

Sodium carbonate is used for the preparation of *caustic soda*[23]—that is, the hydrate of sodium oxide, or the alkali which corresponds to sodium. For this purpose the action of lime on a solution of sodium carbonate is generally made use of. The process is as follows: a weak, generally 10 per cent., solution of sodium carbonate is taken,[24][528] and boiled in a cast-iron, wrought-iron, or silver boiler (sodium hydroxide does not act on these metals), and lime is added, little by little, during the boiling. This latter is soluble in water, although but very slightly. The clear solution becomes turbid on the addition of the lime because a precipitate is formed; this precipitate consists of calcium carbonate, almost insoluble in water, whilst caustic soda is formed and remains in solution. The decomposition is effected according to the equation: $Na_2CO_3 + Ca(HO)_2 = CaCO_3 + 2NaHO$. On cooling the solution the calcium carbonate easily settles as a precipitate, and the clear solution or alkali above it contains the easily soluble sodium hydroxide formed in the reaction.[25] After the necessary quantity of lime has been added, the solution is allowed to stand, and is then decanted off and evaporated in cast or wrought iron boilers, or in silver pans if a perfectly pure product is required.[26] The evaporation cannot[529] be conducted in china, glass, or similar vessels, because caustic soda attacks these materials, although but slightly. The solution does not crystallise on evaporation, because the solubility of caustic soda when hot is very great, but crystals containing water of crystallisation may be obtained by cooling. If the evaporation of the alkali be conducted until the specific gravity reaches $1\cdot38$, and the liquid is then cooled to $0°$, transparent crystals appear containing $2NaHO,7H_2O$; they fuse at $+6°$.[27] If the evaporation be conducted so long as water is disengaged, which requires a considerable amount of heat, then, on cooling, the hydroxide, $NaHO$, solidifies in a semi-transparent crystalline mass,[28] which eagerly absorbs moisture and carbonic anhydride from the air.[29] Its specific gravity is $2\cdot13$;[30] it is easily soluble in water, with disengagement of a considerable quantity of heat.[31] A saturated solution at the ordinary temperature has a specific gravity of about $1\cdot5$, contains about 45 per cent. of sodium hydroxide, and boils at $130°$; at $55°$ water dissolves an equal weight of it.[32] Caustic soda is not only soluble in[530] water but in alcohol, and even in ether. Dilute solutions of sodium hydroxide produce a soapy feeling on the skin because the active base of soap consists of caustic soda.[33] Strong solutions have a corroding action.

The chemical *reactions of sodium hydroxide* serve as a type for those of a whole class of alkalis—that is, of soluble basic hydroxides, MOH. The solution of sodium hydroxide is a very caustic liquid—that is to say, it acts in a destructive way on most substances, for instance on most organic tissues—hence caustic soda, like all soluble alkalis, is a poisonous substance; acids, for example hydrochloric, serve as antidotes. The action of caustic soda on bones, fat, starch, and similar vegetable and animal substances explains its action on organisms. Thus bones, when plunged into a weak solution of caustic soda, fall to powder,[34][531] and evolve a smell of ammonia, owing to the caustic soda changing the gelatinous organic substance of the bones (which contains carbon, hydrogen, nitrogen, oxygen, and sulphur, like albumin), dissolving it and in part destroying it, whence ammonia is disengaged. Fats, tallow, and oils become saponified by a solution of caustic soda—that is to say, they form with it *soaps* soluble in water, or sodium salts of the organic acids contained in the fats.[35] The most characteristic reactions of sodium hydroxide are determined by the fact that it *saturates all acids, forming salts with them*, which are almost all soluble in water, and in this respect caustic soda is as characteristic amongst the bases as nitric acid is among the acids. It is impossible to detect sodium by means of the formation of precipitates of insoluble sodium salts, as may be done with other metals, many of whose salts are but slightly soluble. The powerful alkaline properties of caustic soda determine its capacity for combining with even the feeblest acids, its property of disengaging ammonia from ammonium salts, its faculty of forming precipitates from solutions of salts whose bases are insoluble in water, &c. If a solution of the salt of almost any metal be mixed with caustic soda, then a soluble sodium salt will be formed, and an insoluble hydroxide of the metal will be separated—for instance, copper nitrate yields copper hydroxide, $Cu(NO_3)_2 + 2NaHO = Cu(HO)_2 + 2NaNO_3$. Even many *basic oxides* precipitated by caustic soda *are capable* of *combining* with it and forming soluble compounds, and therefore caustic soda in the presence of salts of such metals first forms a precipitate of hydroxide, and then, employed in excess, dissolves this precipitate. This phenomenon occurs, for example, when caustic soda is added to the salts of aluminium. This shows the property of such an alkali as caustic soda of combining not only with acids, but also with feeble basic oxides. For this reason caustic soda *acts on most elements* which are capable of forming acids or oxides similar to them; thus the metal aluminium gives hydrogen with caustic soda in consequence of the formation of alumina, which combines with the caustic soda—that is, in this case, the caustic alkali acts on the metal just as sulphuric acid does on Fe or Zn. If caustic soda acts in this manner on a metalloid capable of combining with the hydrogen evolved (aluminium does not give a compound with hydrogen), then it forms such a hydrogen compound. Thus, for instance, phosphorus acts in this way on caustic soda, yielding hydrogen phosphide. When the hydrogen compound disengaged is capable of combining[532] with the alkali, then, naturally, a salt of the corresponding acid is formed. For example, chlorine and sulphur act in this way on caustic soda. Chlorine, with the hydrogen of the caustic soda, forms hydrochloric acid, and the latter forms common salt with the sodium hydroxide, whilst the other atom in the molecule of chlorine, Cl_2, takes the place of the hydrogen, and forms the hypochlorite, $NaClO$. In the same way, by the action of sodium hydroxide on sulphur, hydrogen sulphide is formed, which acts on the soda forming sodium *sulphide*, in addition to which sodium thiosulphate is formed (*see* Chapter XX.) By virtue of such reactions, sodium hydroxide acts on many metals and non-metals. Such action is often accelerated by the presence of the oxygen of the air, as by this means the formation of acids and oxides rich in oxygen is facilitated. Thus many metals and their lower oxides, in the presence of an alkali, absorb oxygen and form acids. Even manganese peroxide, when mixed with caustic soda, is capable of absorbing the oxygen of the air, and forming sodium manganate. Organic acids when heated with caustic soda give up to it the elements of carbonic anhydride, forming sodium carbonate, and separating that hydrocarbon group which exists, in combination with carbonic anhydride, in the organic acid.

Thus sodium hydroxide, like the soluble alkalis in general, ranks amongst the most active substances in the chemical sense of the term, and but few substances are capable of resisting it. Even siliceous rocks, as we shall see further on, are transformed by it, forming when fused with it vitreous slags. Sodium hydroxide (like ammonium and potassium hydroxides), as a typical example of the basic hydrates, in distinction from many other basic oxides, easily *forms acid salts* with acids (for instance, $NaHSO_4$, $NaHCO_3$), and does not form any basic salts at all; whilst many less energetic bases, such as the oxides of copper and lead, easily form basic salts, but acid salts only with difficulty. This capability of forming acid salts, particularly with polybasic acids, may be explained by the energetic basic properties of sodium hydroxide, contrasted with the small development of these properties in the bases which easily form basic salts. An energetic base is capable of retaining a considerable quantity of acid, which a slightly energetic base would not have the power of doing. Also, as will be shown in the subsequent chapters, sodium belongs to the univalent metals, being exchangeable for hydrogen atom for atom—that is, amongst metals sodium may, like chlorine amongst the non-metals, serve as the representative of the univalent properties. Most of the elements which are not capable of forming acid salts are bivalent. Whence it may be understood that in a bibasic acid—for instance, carbonic,[533] H_2CO_3, or sulphuric, H_2SO_4—the hydrogen may be exchanged, atom for atom, for sodium, and yield an acid salt by means of the first substitution, and a normal salt by means of the second—for instance, $NaHSO_4$, and Na_2SO_4, whilst such bivalent metals as calcium and barium do not form acid salts because one of their atoms at once takes the place of both hydrogen atoms, forming, for example, $CaCO_3$ and $CaSO_4$.[35 bis]

We have seen the transformation of common salt into sodium sulphate, of this latter into sodium carbonate, and of sodium carbonate into caustic soda. Lavoisier still regarded sodium hydroxide as an element, because he was unacquainted with its decomposition with the formation of metallic sodium, which separates the hydrogen from water, reforming caustic soda.

The preparation of *metallic sodium* was one of the greatest discoveries in chemistry, not only because through it the conception of elements became broader and more correct, but especially because in sodium, chemical properties were observed which were but feebly shown in the other metals more familiarly known. This discovery was made in 1807 by the English chemist *Davy* by means of the galvanic current. By connecting with the positive pole (of copper or carbon) a piece of caustic soda (moistened in order to obtain electrical conductivity), and boring a hole in it filled with mercury connected with the negative pole of a strong Volta's pile, Davy observed that on passing the current a peculiar metal dissolved in the mercury, less volatile than mercury, and capable of decomposing water, again forming caustic soda. In this way (by analysis and synthesis) Davy demonstrated the compound nature of alkalis. On being decomposed by the galvanic current, caustic soda disengages hydrogen and sodium at the[534] negative pole and oxygen at the positive pole. Davy showed that the metal formed volatilises at a red heat, and this is its most important physical property in relation to its extraction, all later methods being founded on it. Besides this Davy observed that sodium easily oxidises, its vapour taking fire in air, and the latter circumstance was for a long time an obstacle to the easy preparation of this metal. The properties of sodium were subsequently more thoroughly investigated by Gay-Lussac and Thénard, who observed that metallic iron at a high temperature was capable of reducing caustic soda to sodium.[36] Brunner latterly discovered that not only iron, but also charcoal, has this property, although hydrogen has not.[37] But still the methods of extracting sodium were very troublesome, and consequently it was a great rarity. The principal obstacle to its production was that an endeavour was made to condense the easily-oxidising vapours of sodium in vacuo in complicated apparatus. For this reason, when Donny and Maresca, having thoroughly studied the matter, constructed a specially simple condenser, the production of sodium was much facilitated. Furthermore, in practice the most important epoch in the history of the production of sodium is comprised in the investigation of Sainte-Claire Deville, who avoided the complex methods in vogue up to that time, and furnished those simple means by which the production of sodium is now rendered feasible in chemical works.

For the production of sodium according to Deville's method, a mixture of anhydrous sodium carbonate (7 parts), charcoal (two parts), and lime or chalk (7 parts) is heated. This latter ingredient is only added in order that the sodium carbonate, on fusing, shall not separate[535] from the charcoal.[38] The chalk on being heated loses carbonic anhydride, leaving infusible lime, which is permeated by the sodium carbonate and forms a thick mass, in which the charcoal is intimately mixed with the sodium carbonate. When the charcoal is heated with the sodium carbonate, at a white heat, carbonic oxide and vapours of sodium are disengaged, according to the equation:

$$Na_2CO_3 + 2C = Na_2 + 3CO$$

On cooling the vapours and gases disengaged, the vapours condense into molten metal (in this form sodium does not easily oxidise, whilst in vapour it burns) and the carbonic oxide remains as gas.

FIG. 70.—Manufacture of sodium by Deville's process. A C, iron tube containing a mixture of soda, charcoal, and chalk. B, condenser.

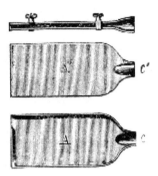

FIG. 71.—Donny and Maresca's sodium condenser, consisting of two cast-iron plates screwed together.

In sodium works an iron tube, about a metre long and a decimeter in diameter, is made out of boiler plate. The pipe is luted into a furnace having a strong draught, capable of giving a high temperature, and the tube is charged with the mixture required for the preparation of sodium. One end of the tube is closed with a cast-iron stopper A with clay luting, and the other with the cast-iron stopper C provided[536] with an aperture. On heating, first of all the moisture contained in the various substances is given off, then carbonic anhydride and the products of the dry distillation of the charcoal, then the latter begins to act on the sodium carbonate, and carbonic oxide and vapours of sodium appear. It is easy to observe the appearance of the latter, because on issuing from the aperture in the stopper C they take fire spontaneously and burn with a very bright yellow flame. A pipe is then introduced into the aperture C, compelling the vapours and gases formed to pass through the condenser B. This condenser consists of two square cast-iron trays, A and A', fig. 71, with wide edges firmly screwed together. Between these two trays there is a space in which the condensation of the vapours of sodium is effected, the thin metallic walls of the condenser being cooled by the air but remaining hot enough to preserve the sodium in a liquid state, so that it does not choke the apparatus, but continually flows from it. The vapours of sodium, condensing in the cooler, flow in the shape of liquid metal into a vessel containing some non-volatile naphtha or hydrocarbon. This is used in order to prevent the sodium oxidising as it issues from the condenser at a somewhat high temperature. In order to obtain sodium of a pure quality it is necessary to distil it once more, which may even be done in porcelain retorts, but the distillation must be conducted in a stream of some gas on which sodium does not act, for instance in a stream of nitrogen; carbonic anhydride is not applicable, because sodium partially decomposes it, absorbing oxygen from it. Although the above described methods of preparing sodium by chemical means have proved very convenient in practice, still it is now (since 1893) found profitable in England to obtain it (to the amount of several tons a week) by Davy's classical method, *i.e.* by the action of an electric current at a moderately high temperature, because the means for producing an electric current (by motors and dynamos) now render this quite feasible. This may be regarded as a sign that in process of time many other technical methods for producing various substances by *decomposition* may be profitably carried on by electrolysis.

Pure sodium is a lustrous metal, white as silver, soft as wax; it becomes brittle in the cold. In ordinary moist air it quickly tarnishes[537] and becomes covered with a film of hydroxide, NaHO, formed at the expense of the water in the air. In perfectly dry air sodium retains its lustre for an indefinite time. Its density at the ordinary temperature is equal to 0.98, so that it is lighter than water; it fuses very easily at a temperature of 95°, and distils at a bright red heat (742° according to Perman, 1889). Scott (1887) determined the density of sodium vapour and found it to be nearly 12 (if H = 1). This shows that its molecule contains one atom (like mercury and cadmium) Na.[38 bis] It forms alloys with most metals, combining with them, heat being sometimes evolved and sometimes absorbed. Thus, if sodium (having a clean surface) be thrown into mercury, especially when heated, there is a flash, and such a considerable amount of heat is evolved that part of the mercury is transformed into vapour.[39] Compounds or solutions of sodium in mercury, or *amalgams* of sodium, even when containing 2 parts of sodium to 100 parts of mercury, are solids. Only those amalgams which are the very poorest in sodium are liquid. Such alloys of sodium with mercury are often used instead of sodium in chemical investigations, because in combination with mercury sodium is not easily acted on by air, and is heavier than water, and therefore more convenient to handle, whilst at the same time it retains the principal properties of sodium,[40] for instance it decomposes water, forming NaHO.

It is easy to form an alloy of mercury and sodium having a crystalline structure, and a definite atomic composition, $NaHg_5$. The alloy of sodium with hydrogen or *sodium hydride*, Na_2H, which has the external[538] appearance of a metal,[41] is a most instructive example of the characteristics of alloys. At the ordinary temperature sodium does not absorb hydrogen, but from 300° to 421° the absorption takes place at the ordinary pressure (and at an increased pressure even at higher temperatures), as shown by Troost and Hautefeuille (1874). One volume of sodium absorbs as much as 238 volumes of hydrogen. The metal increases in volume, and when once formed the alloy can be preserved for some time without change at the ordinary temperature. The appearance of sodium hydride resembles that of sodium itself; it is as soft as this latter, when heated it becomes brittle, and decomposes above 300°, evolving hydrogen. In this decomposition all the phenomena of dissociation are very clearly shown—that is, the hydrogen gas evolved has a definite tension[42] corresponding with each definite temperature. This confirms the fact that the formation of substances capable of dissociation can only be accomplished within the dissociation limits. Sodium hydride melts more easily than sodium itself, and then does not undergo decomposition if it is in an atmosphere of hydrogen. It oxidises easily in air, but not so easily as potassium hydride. The chemical reactions of sodium are retained in its hydride, and, if we may so express it, they are even increased by the addition of hydrogen. At all events, in the properties of sodium hydride[43] we see other properties than in such hydrogen compounds as HCl, H_2O, H_3N, H_4C, or even in the gaseous metallic hydrides AsH_3, TeH_2. Platinum, palladium, nickel, and iron, in absorbing hydrogen form compounds in which hydrogen is in a similar state. In them, as in sodium hydride, the hydrogen is compressed, absorbed, occluded (Chapter II.)[43 bis]

[539]

The most important chemical property of sodium is its power of easily decomposing water and *evolving hydrogen* from the majority of the hydrogen compounds, and especially from all acids, and hydrates in which hydroxyl must be recognised. This depends on its power of combining with the elements which are in combination with the hydrogen. We already know that sodium disengages hydrogen, not only from water, hydrochloric acid,[44] and all other acids, but also from ammonia,[44 bis] with the formation of sodamide NH_2Na, although it does not displace hydrogen from the hydrocarbons.[45] Sodium burns[540] both in chlorine and in oxygen, evolving much heat. These properties are closely connected with its power of taking up oxygen, chlorine, and similar elements from most of their compounds. Just as it removes the oxygen from the oxides of nitrogen and from carbonic anhydride, so also does it decompose the majority of oxides at definite temperatures. Here the action is essentially the same as in the decomposition of water. Thus, for instance, when acting on magnesium chloride the sodium displaces the magnesium, and when acting on aluminium chloride it displaces metallic aluminium. Sulphur, phosphorus, arsenic and a whole series of other elements, also combine with sodium.[46]

With *oxygen* sodium unites in three degrees of combination, forming a suboxide Na_4O,[46 bis] an oxide, Na_2O, and a peroxide, NaO. They are thus termed because Na_2O is a stable basic oxide (with water it forms a basic hydroxide), whilst Na_4O and NaO do not form corresponding saline hydrates and salts. The suboxide is a grey inflammable substance which easily decomposes water, disengaging hydrogen; it is formed by the slow oxidation of sodium at the ordinary temperature. The peroxide is a greenish yellow substance, fusing at a bright red heat; it is produced by burning sodium in an excess of oxygen, and it yields oxygen when treated with water:

Suboxide: $Na_4O + 3H_2O = 4NaHO + H_2$[47]

Oxide: $\quad Na_2O + H_2O = 2NaHO$[48]

Peroxide: $Na_2O_2 + H_2O = 2NaHO + O$[49]

[541]

All three oxides form sodium hydroxide with water, but only the oxide Na_2O is directly transformed into a hydrate. The other oxides liberate either hydrogen or oxygen; they also present a similar distinction with reference to many other agents. Thus carbonic anhydride combines directly with the oxide Na_2O, which when heated in the gas burns, forming sodium carbonate, whilst the peroxide yields oxygen in addition. When treated with acids, sodium and all its oxides only form the salts corresponding with sodium oxide—that is, of the formula or type NaX. Thus the oxide of sodium, Na_2O, is *the only salt-forming*[542] *oxide* of this metal, as water is in the case of hydrogen. Although the peroxide H_2O_2 is derived from hydrogen, and Na_2O_2 from sodium, yet there are no corresponding salts known, and if they are formed they are probably as unstable as hydrogen peroxide. Although carbon forms carbonic oxide, CO, still it has only one salt-forming oxide—carbonic anhydride, CO_2. Nitrogen and chlorine both give several salt-forming oxides and types of salts. But of the oxides of nitrogen, NO and NO_2 do not form salts, as do N_2O_3, N_2O_4, and N_2O_5, although N_2O_4 does not form special salts, and N_2O_5 corresponds with the highest form of the saline compounds of nitrogen. Such distinctions between the elements, according to their power of giving one or several saline forms, is a radical property of no less importance than the basic or acid properties of their oxides. Sodium as a typical metal does not form any acid oxides, whilst chlorine, as a typical non-metal, does not form bases with oxygen. Therefore sodium *as an element* may be thus characterised: it forms one very stable salt-forming oxide, Na_2O, having powerful basic properties, and its salts are of the general formula, NaX, therefore in its compounds it is, like hydrogen, a basic and univalent element.

On comparing sodium and its analogues, which will be described later with other metallic elements, it will be seen that these properties, together with the relative lightness of the metal itself and its compounds, and the magnitude of its atomic weight comprise the most essential properties of this element, clearly distinguishing it from others, and enabling us easily to recognise its analogues.

Footnotes:

[1] Whilst describing in some detail the properties of sodium chloride, hydrochloric acid, and sodium sulphate, I wish to impart, by separate examples, an idea of the properties of saline substances, but the dimensions of this work and its purpose and aim do not permit of entering into particulars concerning every salt, acid, or other substance. The fundamental object of this work—an account of the characteristics of the elements and an acquaintance with the forces acting between atoms—has nothing to gain from the multiplication of the number of as yet ungeneralised properties and relations.

[2] Anhydrous (ignited) sodium sulphate, Na_2SO_4, is known in trade as 'sulphate' or salt-cake, in mineralogy *thenardite*. Crystalline decahydrated salt is termed in mineralogy *mirabilite*, and in trade Glauber's salt. On fusing it, the monohydrate $Na_2SO_4H_2O$ is obtained, together with a supersaturated solution.

[3] The salts may be obtained not only by methods of substitution of various kinds, but also by many other combinations. Thus sodium sulphate may be formed from sodium oxide and sulphuric anhydride, by oxidising sodium sulphide, Na_2S, or sodium sulphite, Na_2SO_3, &c. When sodium chloride is heated in a mixture of the vapours of water, air, and sulphurous anhydride, sodium sulphate is formed. According to this method (patented by Hargreaves and Robinson), sodium sulphate, Na_2SO_4, is obtained from NaCl without the preliminary manufacture of H_2SO_4. Lumps of NaCl pressed into bricks are loosely packed into a cylinder and subjected, at a red heat, to the action of steam, air and SO_2. Under these conditions, HCl, sulphate, and a certain amount of unaltered NaCl are obtained. This mixture is converted into soda by Gossage's process (*see* Note 15) and may have some practical value.

[4] Many observations have been made, but little general information has been obtained from particular cases. In addition to which, the properties of a given salt are changed by the presence of other salts. This takes place not only in virtue of mutual decomposition or formation of double salts capable of separate existence, but is determined by the influence which some salts exert on others, or by forces similar to those which act during solution. Here nothing has been generalised to that extent which would render it possible to predict without previous investigation, if there be no close analogy to help us. Let us state one of these numerous cases: 100 parts of water at 20° dissolve 34 parts of potassium nitrate but on the addition of sodium nitrate the solubility of potassium nitrate

increases to 48 parts in 10 of water (Carnelley and Thomson). In general, in all cases of which there are accurate observations it appears that the presence of foreign salts changes the properties of any given salt.

[5] The information concerning solubility (Chapter I.) is given according to the determinations of Gay-Lussac, Lovell, and Mulder.

[6] In Chapter I., Note 24, we have already seen that with many other sulphates the solubility also decreases after a certain temperature is passed. Gypsum, $CaSO_4,2H_2O$, lime, and many other compounds present such a phenomenon. An observation of Tilden's (1884) is most instructive; he showed that on raising the temperature (in closed vessels) above 140° the solubility of sodium sulphate again begins to increase. At 100° 100 parts of water dissolve about 43 parts of anhydrous salt, at 140° 42 parts, at 160° 43 parts, at 180° 44 parts, at 230° 46 parts. According to Étard (1892) the solubility of 30 parts of Na_2SO_4 in 100 of solution (or 43 per 100 of water) corresponds to 80°, and above 240° the solubility again falls, and very rapidly, so that at 320° the solution contains 12 per 100 of solution (about 14 per 100 of water) and a further rise of temperature is followed by a further deposition of the salt. It is evident that the phenomenon of saturation, determined by the presence of an excess of the dissolved substance, is very complex, and therefore that for the theory of solutions considered as liquid indefinite chemical compounds, many useful statements can hardly be given.

[7] Already referred to in Chapter I., Note 56.

The example of sodium sulphate is historically very important for the theory of solutions. Notwithstanding the number of investigations which have been made, it is still insufficiently studied, especially from the point of the vapour tension of solutions and crystallo-hydrates, so that those processes cannot be applied to it which Guldberg, Roozeboom, Van't Hoff, and others applied to solutions and crystallo-hydrates. It would also be most important to investigate the influence of pressure on the various phenomena corresponding with the combinations of water and sodium sulphate, because when crystals are separated—for instance, of the decahydrated salt—an increase of volume takes place, as can be seen from the following data:—the sp. gr. of the anhydrous salt is 2·66, that of the decahydrated salt = 1·46, but the sp. gr. of solutions at 15°/4° = 9,992 + $90·2p + 0·35p^2$ where p represents the percentage of anhydrous salt in the solution, and the sp. gr. of water at 4° = 10,000. Hence for solutions containing 20 p.c. of anhydrous salt the sp. gr. = 1·1936; therefore the volume of 100 grams of this solution = 83·8 c.c., and the volume of anhydrous salt contained in it is equal to 20/2·66, or = 7·5 c.c., and the volume of water = 80·1 c.c. Therefore, the solution, on decomposing into anhydrous salt and water, increases in volume (from 83·8 to 87·6); but in the same way 83·8 c.c. of 20 p.c. solution are formed from (45·4/1·46 =) 31·1 c.c. of the decahydrated salt, and 54·6 c.c. of water—that is to say, that during the formation of a solution from 85·7 c.c., 83·8 c.c. are formed.

[8] From this example it is evident the solution remains unaltered until from the contact of a solid it becomes either saturated or supersaturated, crystallisation being determined by the attraction to a solid, as the phenomenon of supersaturation clearly demonstrates. This partially explains certain apparently contradictory determinations of solubility. The best investigated example of such complex relations is cited in Chapter XIV., Note 50 (for $CaCl_2$).

[9] According to Pickering's experiments (1886), the molecular weight in grams (that is, 142 grams) of anhydrous sodium sulphate, on being dissolved in a large mass of water, at 0° absorbs (hence the - sign) -1,100 heat units, at 10°–700, at 15°–275, at 20° gives out +25, at 25° +300 calories. For the decahydrated salt, $Na_2SO_4,10H_2O$, 5° - 4,225, 10° - 4,000, 15° - 3,570, 20° - 3,160, 25° - 2,775. Hence (just as in Chapter I., Note 56) the heat of the combination $Na_2SO_4,10H_2O$ at 5° = +3,125, 10° = +3,250, 20° = +3,200, and 25° = +3,050.

It is evident that the decahydrated salt dissolving in water gives a decrease of temperature. Solutions in hydrochloric acid give a still greater decrease, because they contain the water of crystallisation in a solid state— that is, like ice—and this on melting absorbs heat. A mixture of 15 parts of $Na_2SO_4,10H_2O$ and 12 parts of strong hydrochloric acid produces sufficient cold to freeze water. During the treatment with hydrochloric acid a certain quantity of sodium chloride is formed.

[10] The very large and well-formed crystals of this salt resemble the hydrate H_2SO_4,H_2O, or $SO(OH)_4$. In general the replacement of hydrogen by sodium modifies many of the properties of acids less than its replacement by other metals. This most probably depends on the volumes being nearly equal.

[11] In solution (Berthelot) the acid salt in all probability decomposes most in the greatest mass of water. The specific gravity (according to the determinations of Marignac) of solutions at 15°/4° = 9,992 + 77·92p + 0·231p^2 (see Note 7). From these figures, and from the specific gravities of sulphuric acid, it is evident that on mixing solutions of this acid and sodium sulphate *expansion* will always take place; for instance, H_2SO_4 + 25H_2O with Na_2SO_4 + 25H_2O increases from 483 volumes to 486. In addition to which, in weak solutions heat is absorbed, as shown in Chapter X., Note 27. Nevertheless, even more acid salts may be formed and obtained in a crystalline form. For instance, on cooling a solution of 1 part of sodium

sulphate in 7 parts of sulphuric acid, crystals of the composition $NaHSO_4,H_2SO_4$ are separated (Schultz, 1868). This compound fuses at about 100°; the ordinary acid salt, $NaHSO_4$, at 149°.

[11 bis] On decreasing the pressure, sodium hydrogen sulphate, $NaHSO_4$, dissociates much more easily than at the ordinary pressure; it loses water and forms the pyrosulphate, $Na_2S_2O_7$; this reaction is utilised in chemical works.

[12] Calcium sulphide, CaS, like many metallic sulphides which are soluble in water, is decomposed by it (Chapter X.), $CaS + H_2O = CaO + H_2S$, because hydrogen sulphide is a very feeble acid. If calcium sulphide be acted on by a large mass of water, lime may be precipitated, and a state of equilibrium will be reached, when the system $CaO + 2CaS$ remains unchanged. Lime, being a product of the action of water on CaS, limits this action. Therefore, if in black ash the lime were not in excess, a part of the sulphide would be in solution (actually there is but very little). In this manner in the manufacture of sodium carbonate the conditions of equilibrium which enter into double decompositions have been made use of (*see above*), and the aim is to form directly the unchangeable product $CaO,2CaS$. This was first regarded as a special insoluble compound, but there is no evidence of its independent existence.

[13]

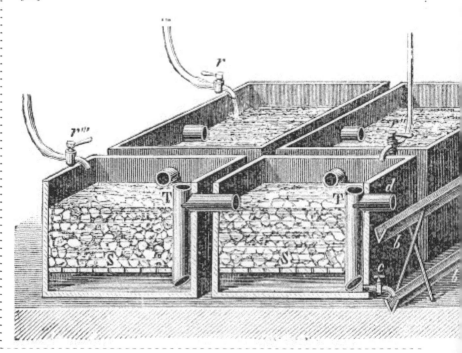

FIG. 69.—Apparatus for the methodical lixiviation of black ash, &c. Water flows into the tanks from the pipes *r, r,* and the saturated liquid is drawn off from *c, c.*

Methodical lixiviation is the extraction, by means of water, of a soluble substance from the mass containing it. It is carried on so as not to obtain weak aqueous solutions, and in such a way that the residue shall not contain any of the soluble substance. This problem is practically of great importance in many industries. It is required to extract from the mass all that is soluble in water. This is easily effected if water be first poured on the mass, the strong solution thus obtained decanted, then water again poured on, time being allowed for it to act, then again decanted, and so on until fresh water does not take up anything. But then finally such weak solutions are obtained that it would be very disadvantageous to evaporate them. This is avoided by pouring the fresh hot water destined for the lixiviation, not onto the fresh mass, but upon a mass which has already been subjected to a first lixiviation by weak solutions. In this way the fresh water gives a weak solution. The strong solution which goes to the evaporating pan flows from those parts of the apparatus which contain the fresh, as yet unlixiviated, mass, and thus in the latter parts the weak alkali formed in the other parts of the apparatus becomes saturated as far as possible with the soluble substance. Generally several intercommunicating vessels are constructed (standing at the same level) into which in turn the fresh mass is charged which is intended for lixiviation; the water is poured in, the alkali drawn off, and the lixiviated residue removed. The illustration represents such an apparatus, consisting of four communicating vessels. The water poured into one of them flows through the two nearest and issues from the third. The fresh mass being placed in one of these boxes or vessels, the stream of water passing through the apparatus is directed in such a manner as to finally issue from this vessel containing the fresh unlixiviated mass. The fresh water is added to the vessel containing the material which has been almost completely exhausted. Passing through this vessel it is conveyed by the pipe (syphon passing from the bottom of the first box to the top of the second) communicating with the second; it finally passes (also through a syphon pipe) into the box (the third) containing the fresh material. The water will extract all that is soluble in the first vessel, leaving only an insoluble residue. This vessel is then ready to be emptied, and refilled with fresh material. The levels of the liquids in the various vessels will naturally be different, in consequence of the various strengths of the solutions which they contain.

It must not, however, be thought that sodium carbonate alone passes into the solution; there is also a good deal of caustic soda with it, formed by the action of lime on the carbonate of sodium, and there are also certain sodium sulphur compounds with which we shall partly become acquainted hereafter. The sodium carbonate, therefore, is not obtained in a very pure state. The solution is concentrated by evaporation. This is conducted by means of the waste heat from the soda furnaces, together with that of the gases given off. The process in the soda furnaces can only be carried on at a high temperature, and therefore the smoke and gases issuing from them are necessarily very hot. If the heat they contain was not made use of there would be a great waste of fuel; consequently in immediate proximity to these furnaces there is generally a series of pans or evaporating boilers, under which the gases pass, and into which the alkali solution is poured. On evaporating the solution, first of all the undecomposed sodium sulphate separates, then the sodium carbonate or soda crystals. These crystals as they separate are raked out and placed on planks, where the liquid drains away from them. Caustic soda remains in the residue, and also any sodium chloride which was not decomposed in the foregoing process.

Part of the sodium carbonate is recrystallised in order to purify it more thoroughly. In order to do this a saturated solution is left to crystallise at a temperature below 30° in a current of air, in order to promote the separation of the water vapour. The large transparent crystals (efflorescent in air) of $Na_2CO_3,10H_2O$ are then formed which have already been spoken of (Chapter I.).

[14] The whole of the sulphur used in the production of the sulphuric acid employed in decomposing the common salt is contained in this residue. This is the great burden and expense of the soda works which use Leblanc's method. As an instructive example from a chemical point of view, it is worth while mentioning here two of the various methods of recovering the sulphur from the soda waste. Chance's process is treated in Chapter XX., Note 6.

Kynaston (1885) treats the soda waste with a solution (sp. gr. 1·21) of magnesium chloride, which disengages sulphuretted hydrogen: $CaS + MgCl_2 + 2H_2O = CaCl_2 + Mg(OH)_2 + H_2S$. Sulphurous anhydride is passed through the residue in order to form the insoluble calcium sulphite: $CaCl_2 + Mg(OH)_2 + SO_2 = CaSO_3 + MgCl_2 + H_2O$. The solution of magnesium chloride obtained is again used, and the washed calcium sulphite is brought into contact at a low temperature with hydrochloric acid (a weak aqueous solution) and hydrogen sulphide, the whole of the sulphur then separating:

$$CaSO_3 + 2H_2S + 2HCl = CaCl_2 + 3H_2O + 3S.$$

But most efforts have been directed towards avoiding the formation of soda waste.

[15] Among the drawbacks of the Leblanc process are the accumulation of 'soda waste' (Note 14) owing to the impossibility at the comparatively low price of sulphur (especially in the form of pyrites) of finding employment for the sulphur and sulphur compounds for which this waste is sometimes treated, and also the insufficient purity of the sodium carbonate for many purposes. The advantages of the Leblanc process, besides its simplicity and cheapness, are that almost the whole of the acids obtained as bye-products have a commercial value; for chlorine and bleaching powder are produced from the large amount of hydrochloric acid which appears as a bye-product; caustic soda also is very easily made, and the demand for it increases every year. In those places where salt, pyrites, charcoal, and limestone (the materials required for alkali works) are found side by side—as, for instance, in the Ural or Don districts—conditions are favourable to the development of the manufacture of sodium carbonate on an enormous scale; and where, as in the Caucasus, sodium sulphate occurs naturally, the conditions are still more favourable. A large amount, however, of the latter salt, even from soda works, is used in making glass. The most important soda works, as regards the quantity of products obtained from them, are the English works.

As an example of the other numerous and varied methods of manufacturing soda from sodium chloride, the following may be mentioned: Sodium chloride is decomposed by oxide of lead, PbO, forming lead chloride and sodium oxide, which, with carbonic anhydride, yields sodium carbonate (Scheele's process). In Cornu's method sodium chloride is treated with lime, and then exposed to the air, when it yields a small quantity of sodium carbonate. In E. Kopp's process sodium sulphate (125 parts) is mixed with oxide of iron (80 parts) and charcoal (55 parts), and the mixture is heated in reverberatory furnaces. Here a compound, $Na_6Fe_4S_3$, is formed, which is insoluble in water absorbs oxygen and carbonic anhydride, and then forms sodium carbonate and ferrous sulphide; this when roasted gives sulphurous anhydride, the indispensable material for the manufacture of sulphuric acid, and ferric oxide which is again used in the process. In Grant's method sodium sulphate is transformed into sodium sulphide, and the latter is decomposed by a stream of carbonic anhydride and steam, when hydrogen sulphide is disengaged and sodium carbonate formed. Gossage prepares Na_2S from Na_2SO_4 (by heating it with carbon), dissolves it in water and subjects the solution to the action of an excess of CO_2 in coke towers, thus obtaining H_2S (a gas which gives SO_2 under perfect combustion, or sulphur when incompletely burnt, Chapter XX., Note 6) and bicarbonate of sodium; $Na_2S + 2CO_2 + 2H_2O = H_2S + 2HNaCO_3$. The latter gives soda and CO_2 when ignited. This process quite eliminates the formation of soda-waste (see Note 3) and should in my opinion be suitable for the treatment of native

Na$_2$SO$_4$, like that which is found in the Caucasus, all the more since H$_2$S gives sulphur as a bye-product.

Repeated efforts have been made in recent times to obtain soda (and chlorine, *see* Chapter II., Note 1) from strong solutions of salt (Chapter X., Note 23 bis) by the action of an electric current, but until now these methods have not been worked out sufficiently for practical use, probably partly owing to the complicated apparatus needed, and the fact that the chlorine given off at the anode corrodes the electrodes and vessels and has but a limited industrial application. We may mention that according to Hempel (1890) soda in crystals is deposited when an electric current and a stream of carbonic acid gas are passed through a saturated solution of NaCl.

Sodium carbonate may likewise be obtained from cryolite (Chapter XVII., Note 23) the method of treating this will be mentioned under Aluminium.

[16] This process (Chapter XVII.) was first pointed out by Turck, worked out by Schloesing, and finally applied industrially by Solvay. The first (1883) large soda factories erected in Russia for working this process are on the banks of the Kama at Berezniak, near Ousolia, and belong to Lubimoff. But Russia, which still imports from abroad a large quantity of bleaching powder and exports a large amount of manganese ore, most of all requires works carrying on the Leblanc process. In 1890 a factory of this kind was erected by P. K. Oushkoff, on the Kama, near Elagoubi.

[16 bis] Mond (*see* Chapter XI., Note 3 bis) separates the NH$_4$Cl from the residual solutions by cooling (Chapter X., Note 44); ignites the sal-ammoniac and passes the vapour over MgO, and so re-obtains the NH$_3$, and forms MgCl$_2$: the former goes back for the manufacture of soda, while the latter is employed either for making HCl or Cl$_2$.

[17] Commercial soda ash (calcined, anhydrous) is rarely pure; the crystallised soda is generally purer. In order to purify it further, it is best to boil a concentrated solution of soda ash until two-thirds of the liquid remain, collect the soda which settles, wash with cold water, and then shake up with a strong solution of ammonia, pour off the residue, and heat. The impurities will then remain in the mother liquors, &c.

Some numerical data may be given for sodium carbonate. The specific gravity of the anhydrous salt is 2·48, that of the decahydrated salt 1·46. Two varieties are known of the heptahydrated salt (Löwel, Marignac, Rammelsberg), which are formed together by allowing a saturated solution to cool under a layer of alcohol; the one is less stable (like the corresponding sulphate) and at 0° has a solubility of 32 parts (of anhydrous salt) in 100 water; the other is more stable, and its solubility 20 parts (of anhydrous salt) per 100 of water. The solubility of the decahydrated salt in 100 water = at 0°, 7·0; at 20°, 21·7; at 30°, 37·2 parts (of anhydrous salt). At 80° the solubility is only 46·1, at 90° 45·7, at 100°, 45·4 parts (of anhydrous salt). That is, it falls as the temperature rises, like Na_2SO_4. The specific gravity (Note [7]) of the solutions of sodium carbonate, according to the data of Gerlach and Kohlrausch, at 15°/4° is expressed by the formula, $s = 9,992 + 104·5p + 0·165p^2$. Weak solutions occupy a volume not only less than the sum of the volumes of the anhydrous salt and the water, but even less than the water contained in them. For instance, 1,000 grams of a 1 p.c. solution occupy (at 15°) a volume of 990·4 c.c. (sp. gr. 1·0097), but contain 990 grams of water, occupying at 15° a volume of 990·8 c.c. A similar case, which is comparatively rare occurs also with sodium hydroxide, in those dilute solutions for which the factor A is greater than 100 if the sp. gr. of water at 4° = 100,000, and if the sp. gr. of the solution be expressed by the formula $S = S_0 + Ap + Bp^2$, where S_0 is the specific gravity of the water. For 5 p.c. the sp. gr. 15°/4° = 1·0520; for 10 p.c. 1·1057; for 15 p.c. 1·1603. The changes in the sp. gr. with the temperature are here almost the same as with solutions of sodium chloride with an equal value of p.

[18] The resemblance is so great that, notwithstanding the difference in the molecular composition of Na_2SO_4 and Na_2CO_3, they ought to be classed under the type $(NaO)_2R$, where R = SO_2 or CO. Many other sodium salts also contain 10 mol. H_2O.

[19] According to the observations of Pickering. According to Rose, when solutions of sodium carbonate are boiled a certain amount of carbonic anhydride is disengaged.

[20] The composition of this salt, however, may be also represented as a combination of carbonic acid, H_2CO_3, with the normal salt, Na_2CO_3, just as the latter also combines with water. Such a combination is all the more likely because (1) there exists another salt, $Na_2CO_3,2NaHCO_3,2H_2O$ (sodium sesquicarbonate), obtained by cooling a boiling solution of sodium bicarbonate, or by mixing this salt with the normal salt; but the formula of this salt cannot be derived from that of normal carbonic acid, as the formula of the bicarbonate can. At the same time the sesqui-salt has all the properties of a definite compound; it crystallises in transparent crystals, has a constant composition, its solubility (at 0° in 100 of water, 12·6 of anhydrous salt) differs from the solubility of the normal and acid salts; it is found in nature, and is known by the names of *trona* and *urao*. The observations of Watts and Richards showed (1886) that on pouring a strong solution of the acid salt into a solution of the normal salt saturated by heating, crystals of the salt $NaHCO_3,Na_2CO_3,2H_2O$ may be easily

obtained, as long as the temperature is above 35°. The natural urao (Boussingault) has, according to Laurent, the same composition. This salt is very stable in air, and may be used for purifying sodium carbonate on the large scale. Such compounds have been little studied from a theoretical point of view, although particularly interesting, since in all probability they correspond with ortho-carbonic acid, $C(OH)_4$, and at the same time correspond with double salts like astrakhanite (Chapter XIV., Note 25). (2) Water of crystallisation does not enter into the composition of the crystals of the acid salt, so that on its formation (occurring only at low temperatures, as in the formation of crystalline compounds with water) the water of crystallisation of the normal salt separates and the water is, as it were, replaced by the elements of carbonic acid. If anhydrous sodium carbonate be mixed with the amount of water requisite for the formation of Na_2CO_3,H_2O, this salt will, when powdered, absorb CO_2 as easily at the ordinary temperature as it does water.

[21] 100 parts of water at 0° dissolve 7 parts of the acid salt, which corresponds with 4·3 parts of the anhydrous normal salt, but at 0° 100 parts of water dissolve 7 parts of the latter. The solubility of the bi- or acid salt varies with considerable regularity; 100 parts of water dissolves at 15° 9 parts of the salt, at 30° 11 parts.

The ammonium, and more especially the calcium, salt, is much more soluble in water. The ammonia process (*see* p. 524) is founded upon this. Ammonium bicarbonate (acid carbonate) at 0° has a solubility of 12 parts in 100 water, at 30° of 27 parts. The solubility therefore increases very rapidly with the temperature. And its saturated solution is more stable than a solution of sodium bicarbonate. In fact, saturated solutions of these salts have a gaseous tension like that of a mixture of carbonic anhydride and water—namely, at 15° and at 50°, for the sodium salt 120 and 750 millimetres, for the ammonium salt 120 and 563 millimetres. These data are of great importance in understanding the phenomena connected with the ammonia process. They indicate that with an increased pressure the formation of the sodium salt ought to increase if there be an excess of ammonium salt.

[22] Crystalline sodium carbonate (broken into lumps) also absorbs carbonic anhydride, but the water contained in the crystals is then disengaged: $Na_2CO_3,10H_2O + CO_2 = Na_2CO_3,H_2CO_3 + 9H_2O$, and dissolves part of the carbonate; therefore part of the sodium carbonate passes into solution together with all the impurities. When it is required to avoid the formation of this solution, a mixture of ignited and crystalline sodium carbonate is taken. Sodium bicarbonate is prepared chiefly for medicinal use, and is then often termed *carbonate of soda*, also, for instance, in the so-called soda powders, for preparing certain artificial mineral

waters, for the manufacture of digestive lozenges like those made at Essentuki, Vichy, &c.

[23] In chemistry, sodium oxide is termed 'soda,' which word must be carefully distinguished from the word sodium, meaning the metal.

[24] With a small quantity of water, the reaction either does not take place, or even proceeds in the reverse way—that is, sodium and potassium hydroxides remove carbonic anhydride from calcium carbonate (Liebig, Watson, Mitscherlich, and others). The influence of the mass of water is evident. According to Gerberts, however, strong solutions of sodium carbonate are decomposed by lime, which is very interesting if confirmed by further investigation.

[25] As long as any undecomposed sodium carbonate remains in solution, excess of acid added to the solution disengages carbonic anhydride, and the solution after dilution gives a white precipitate with a barium salt soluble in acids, showing the presence of a carbonate in solution (if there be sulphate present, it also forms a white precipitate, but this is insoluble in acids). For the decomposition of sodium carbonate, milk of lime—that is, slaked slime suspended in water—is employed. Formerly pure sodium hydroxide was prepared (according to Berthollet's process) by dissolving the impure substance in alcohol (sodium carbonate and sulphate are not soluble), but now that metallic sodium has become cheap and is purified by distillation, *pure caustic soda* is prepared by acting on a small quantity of water with sodium. Perfectly pure sodium hydroxide may also be obtained by allowing strong solutions to crystallise (in the cold) (Note 27).

In alkali works where the Leblanc process is used, caustic soda is prepared directly from the alkali remaining in the mother liquors after the separation of the sodium carbonate by evaporation (Note 14). If excess of lime and charcoal have been used, much sodium hydroxide maybe obtained. After the removal as much as possible of the sodium carbonate, a red liquid (from iron oxide) is left, containing sodium hydroxide mixed with compounds of sulphur and of cyanogen (*see* Chapter IX.) and also containing iron. This red alkali is evaporated and air is blown through it, which oxidises the impurities (for this purpose sometimes sodium nitrate is added, or bleaching powder, &c.) and leaves fused caustic soda. The fused mass is allowed to settle in order to separate the ferruginous precipitate, and poured into iron drums, where the sodium hydroxide solidifies. Such caustic soda contains about 10 p.c. of water in excess and some saline impurities, but when properly manufactured is almost free from carbonate and from iron. The greater part of the caustic soda, which forms so important an article of commerce, is manufactured in this manner.

[26] Löwig gave a method of preparing sodium hydroxide from sodium carbonate by heating it to a dull red heat with an excess of ferric oxide. Carbonic anhydride is given off, and warm water extracts the caustic soda from the remaining mass. This reaction, as experiment shows, proceeds very easily, and is an example of contact action similar to that of ferric oxide on the decomposition of potassium chlorate. The reason of this may be that a small quantity of the sodium carbonate enters into double decomposition with the ferric oxide, and the ferric carbonate produced is decomposed into carbonic anhydride and ferric oxide, the action of which is renewed. Similar explanations expressing the *reason* for a reaction really adds but little to that elementary conception of contact which, according to my opinion, consists in the change of motion of the atoms in the molecules under the influence of the substance in contact. In order to represent this clearly it is sufficient, for instance, to imagine that in the sodium carbonate the elements CO_2 move in a circle round the elements Na_2O, but at the points of contact with Fe_2O_3 the motion becomes elliptic with a long axis, and at some distance from Na_2O the elements of CO_2 are parted, not having the faculty of attaching themselves to Fe_2O_3.

[27] By allowing strong solutions of sodium hydroxide to crystallise in the cold, impurities—such as, for instance, sodium sulphate—may be separated from them. The fused crystallo-hydrate $2NaHO,7H_2O$ forms a solution having a specific gravity of $1 \cdot 405$ (Hermes). The crystals on dissolving in water produce cold, while $NaHO$ produces heat. Besides which Pickering obtained hydrates with 1, 2, 4, 5, and 7 H_2O.

[28] In solid caustic soda there is generally an excess of water beyond that required by the formula $NaHO$. The caustic soda used in laboratories is generally cast in sticks, which are broken into pieces. It must be preserved in carefully closed vessels, because it absorbs water and carbonic anhydride from the air.

[29] By the way it changes in air it is easy to distinguish caustic soda from caustic potash, which in general resembles it. Both alkalis absorb water and carbonic anhydride from the air, but caustic potash forms a deliquescent mass of potassium carbonate, whilst caustic soda forms a dry powder of efflorescent salt.

[30] As the molecular weight of $NaHO = 40$, the volume of its molecule $= 40/2 \cdot 13 = 18 \cdot 5$, which very nearly approaches the volume of a molecule of water. The same rule applies to the compounds of sodium in general—for instance, its salts have a molecular volume approaching the volume of the acids from which they are derived.

[31] The molecular quantity of sodium hydroxide (40 grams), on being dissolved in a large mass (200 gram molecules) of water, develops,

according to Berthelot 9,780, and according to Thomsen 9,940, heat-units, but at 100° about 13,000 (Berthelot). Solutions of NaHO + nH$_2$O, on being mixed with water, evolve heat if they contain less than 6H$_2$O, but if more they absorb beat.

[32] The specific gravity of solutions of sodium hydroxide at 15°/4° is given in the short table below:—

NaHO, p.c.	5	10	15	20	30	40
Sp. gr.	1·057	1·113	1·169	1·224	1·331	1·436

1,000 grams of a 5 p.c. solution occupies a volume of 946 c.c.; that is, less than the water serving to make the solution (*see* Note 18).

[33] Sodium hydroxide and some other alkalis are capable of hydrolysing—saponifying, as it is termed—the compounds of acids with alcohols. If RHO (or R(HO)$_n$) represent the composition of an alcohol— that is, of the hydroxide of a hydrocarbon radicle—and QHO an acid, then the compound of the acid with the alcohol or ethereal salt of the given acid will have the composition RQO. Ethereal salts, therefore, present a likeness to metallic salts, just as alcohols resemble basic hydroxides. Sodium hydroxide acts on ethereal salts in the same way that it acts on the majority of metallic salts—namely, it liberates alcohol, and forms the sodium salt of that acid which was in the ethereal salt. The reaction takes place in the following way:—

RQO + NaHO = NaQO + RHO

Ethereal salt   Caustic soda   Sodium salt   Alcohol

Such a decomposition is termed saponification; similar reactions were known very long ago for the ethereal salts corresponding with glycerin, C$_3$H$_5$(OH)$_3$ (Chapter IX.), found in animals and plants, and composing what are called fats or oils. Caustic soda, acting on fat and oil, forms glycerin, and sodium salts of those acids which were in union with the glycerin in the fat, as Chevreul showed at the beginning of this century. The sodium salts of the fatty acids are commonly known as soaps. That is to say, soap is made from fat and caustic soda, glycerin being separated and a sodium salt or soap formed. As glycerin is usually found in union with certain acids, so also are the sodium salts of the same acids found in soap. The greater part of the acids found in conjunction with glycerin in fats are the solid palmitic and stearic acids, C$_{16}$H$_{32}$O$_2$ and C$_{18}$H$_{38}$O$_2$, and the liquid oleic acid, C$_{18}$H$_{34}$O$_2$. In preparing soap the fatty substances are mixed with a solution of caustic soda until an emulsion is formed; the proper quantity of caustic soda is then added in order to produce saponification on heating, the soap being separated from the solution either by means of an excess of caustic soda or else by common salt, which displaces the soap from the aqueous solution (salt water does not dissolve soap, neither does it form a lather). Water acting on soap partly decomposes it (because the acids of the soap are feeble), and the alkali set free acts during the application of soap. Hence it may be replaced by a very feeble alkali. Strong solutions of alkali corrode the skin and tissues. They are not formed from soap, because the reaction is reversible, and the alkali is only set free by the excess of water. Thus we see how the teaching of Berthollet renders it possible to understand many phenomena which occur in every-day experience (*see* Chapter IX., Note 15).

[34] On this is founded the process of Henkoff and Engelhardt for treating bones. The bones are mixed with ashes, lime, and water; it is true that in this case more potassium hydroxide than sodium hydroxide is formed, but their action is almost identical.

[35] As explained in Note 33.

[35 bis] It might be expected, from what has been mentioned above, that bivalent metals would easily form acid salts with acids containing more than two atoms of hydrogen—for instance, with tribasic acids, such as phosphoric acid, H_3PO_4—and actually such salts do exist; but all such relations are complicated by the fact that the character of the base very often changes and becomes weakened with the increase of valency and the change of atomic weight; the feebler bases (like silver oxide), although corresponding with univalent metals, do not form acid salts, while the feeblest bases (CuO, PbO, &c.) easily form basic salts, and notwithstanding their valency do not form acid salts which are in any degree stable—that is, which are undecomposable by water. Basic and acid salts ought to be regarded rather as compounds similar to crystallo-hydrates, because such acids as sulphuric form with sodium not only an acid and a normal salt, as might be expected from the valency of sodium, but also salts containing a greater quantity of acid. In sodium sesquicarbonate we saw an example of such compounds. Taking all this into consideration, we must say that the property of more or less easily forming acid salts depends more upon the energy of the base than upon its valency, and the best statement is that *the capacity of a base for forming acid and basic salts is characteristic*, just as the faculty of forming compounds with hydrogen is characteristic of elements.

[36] Deville supposes that such a decomposition of sodium hydroxide by metallic iron depends solely on the dissociation of the alkali at a white heat into sodium, hydrogen, and oxygen. Here the part played by the iron is only that it retains the oxygen formed, otherwise the decomposed elements would again reunite upon cooling, as in other cases of dissociation. If it be

supposed that the temperature at the commencement of the dissociation of the iron oxides is higher than that of sodium oxide, then the decomposition may be explained by Deville's hypothesis. Deville demonstrates his views by the following experiment:—An iron bottle, filled with iron borings, was heated in such a way that the upper part became red hot, the lower part remaining cooler; sodium hydroxide was introduced into the upper part. The decomposition was then effected—that is, sodium vapours were produced (this experiment was really performed with potassium hydroxide). On opening the bottle it was found that the iron in the upper part was not oxidised, but only that in the lower part. This may be explained by the decomposition of the alkali into sodium, hydrogen, and oxygen taking place in the upper part, whilst the iron in the lower part absorbed the oxygen set free. If the whole bottle be subjected to the same moderate heat as the lower extremity, no metallic vapours are formed. In that case, according to the hypothesis, the temperature is insufficient for the dissociation of the sodium hydroxide.

[37] It has been previously remarked (Chapter II. Note 9) that Beketoff showed the displacement of sodium by hydrogen, not from sodium hydroxide but from the oxide Na_2O; then, however, only one half is displaced, with the formation of NaHO.

[38] Since the close of the eighties in England, where the preparation of sodium is at present carried out on a large commercial scale (from 1860 to 1870 it was only manufactured in a few works in France), it has been the practice to add to Deville's mixture iron, or iron oxide which with the charcoal gives metallic and carburetted iron, which still further facilitates the decomposition. At present a kilogram of sodium may be purchased for about the same sum (2/-) as a gram cost thirty years ago. Castner, in England, greatly improved the manufacture of sodium in large quantities, and so cheapened it as a reducing agent in the preparation of metallic aluminium. He heated a mixture of 44 parts of NaHO, and 7 parts of carbide of iron in large iron retorts at 1,000° and obtained about 6½ parts of metallic sodium. The reaction proceeds more easily than with carbon or iron alone, and the decomposition of the NaHO proceeds according to the equation: $3NaHO + C = Na_2CO_3 + 3H + Na$. Subsequently, in 1891, aluminium was prepared by electrolysis (*see* Chapter XVII.), and metallic sodium found two new uses; (1) for the manufacture of peroxide of sodium (see later on) which is used in bleaching works, and (2) in the manufacture of potassium and sodium cyanide from yellow prussiate (Chapter XIII., Note 12).

[38 bis] This is also shown by the fall in the temperature of solidification of tin produced by the addition of sodium (and also Al and Zn). Heycock and Neville (1889).

[39] By dissolving sodium amalgams in water and acids, and deducting the heat of solution of the sodium, Berthelot found that *for each atom of the sodium* in amalgams containing a larger amount of mercury than $NaHg_5$, the amount of heat evolved increases, after which the heat of formation falls, and the heat evolved decreases. In the formation of $NaHg_5$ about 18,500 calories are evolved; when $NaHg_3$ is formed, about 14,000; and for $NaHg$ about 10,000 calories. Kraft regarded the definite crystalline amalgam as having the composition of $NaHg_6$, but at the present time, in accordance with Grimaldi's results, it is thought to be $NaHg_5$. A similar amalgam is very easily obtained if a 3 p.c. amalgam be left several days in a solution of sodium hydroxide until a crystalline mass is formed, from which the mercury may be removed by strongly pressing in chamois leather. This amalgam with a solution of potassium hydroxide forms a potassium amalgam, KHg_{10}. It may be mentioned here that the latent heat of fusion (of atomic quantities) of $Hg = 360$ (Personne), $Na = 730$ (Joannis), and $K = 610$ calories (Joannis).

[40] Alloys are so similar to solutions (exhibiting such complete parallelism in properties) that they are included in the same class of so-called indefinite compounds. But in alloys, as substances passing from the liquid to the solid state, it is easier to discover the formation of definite chemical compounds. Besides the alloys of Na with Hg, those with tin (Bailey 1892 found Na_2Sn), lead ($NaPb$), bismuth (Na_3Bi), &c. (Joannis 1892 and others) have been investigated.

[41] Potassium forms a similar compound, but lithium, under the same circumstances, does not.

[42] The tension of dissociation of hydrogen p, in millimetres of mercury, is:—

$t =$	330°	350°	400°	430°
for Na_2H $p =$	28	57	447	910
for K_2H	45	72	548	1100

[43] In general, during the formation of alloys the volumes change very slightly, and therefore from the volume of Na_2H some idea may be formed of the volume of hydrogen in a solid or liquid state. Even Archimedes concluded that there was gold in an alloy of copper and gold by reason of its volume and density. From the fact that the density of Na_2H is equal to $0\cdot959$, it may be seen that the volume of 47 grams (the gram molecule) of this compound $= 49\cdot0$ c.c. The volume of 46 grams of sodium contained in the Na_2H (the density under the same conditions being $0\cdot97$) is equal to $47\cdot4$ c.c. Therefore the volume of 1 gram of hydrogen in Na_2H is equal to

1·6 c.c., and consequently the density of metallic hydrogen, or the weight of 1 c.c., approaches 0·6 gram. This density is also proper to the hydrogen alloyed with potassium and palladium. Judging from the scanty information which is at present available, liquid hydrogen near its absolute boiling point (Chapter II.) has a much lower density.

[43 bis] We may remark that at low temperatures Na absorbs NH₃ and forms (NH₃Na)₂ (*see* Chapter VI., Note 14); this substance absorbs CO and gives (NaCO)n (Chapter IX., Note 31), although by itself Na does not combine directly with CO (but K does).

[44] H. A. Schmidt remarked that perfectly dry hydrogen chloride is decomposed with great difficulty by sodium, although the decomposition proceeds easily with potassium and with sodium in moist hydrogen chloride. Wanklyn also remarked that sodium burns with great difficulty in dry chlorine. Probably these facts are related to other phenomena observed by Dixon, who found that perfectly dry carbonic oxide does not explode with oxygen on passing an electric spark.

[44 bis] Sodamide, NH₂Na, (Chapter IV., Note 14), discovered by Gay-Lussac and Thénard, has formed the object of repeated research, but has been most fully investigated by A. W. Titherley (1894). Until recently the following was all that was known about this compound:—

By heating sodium in dry ammonia, Gay-Lussac and Thénard obtained an olive-green, easily-fusible mass, *sodamide*, NH₂Na, hydrogen being separated. This substance with water forms sodium hydroxide and ammonia; with carbonic oxide, CO, it forms sodium cyanide, NaCN, and water, H₂O; and with dry hydrogen chloride it forms sodium and ammonium chlorides. These and other reactions of sodamide show that the metal in it preserves its energetic properties in reaction, and that this compound of sodium is more stable than the corresponding chlorine amide. When heated, sodamide, NH₂Na, only partially decomposes, with evolution of hydrogen, the principal part of it giving ammonia and sodium nitride, Na₃N, according to the equation $3NH_2Na = 2NH_3 + NNa_3$. The latter is an almost black powdery mass, decomposed by water into ammonia and sodium hydroxide.

Titherley's researches added the following data:—

Iron or silver vessels should be used in preparing this body, because glass and porcelain are corroded at 300°–400°, at which temperature ammonia gas acts upon sodium and forms the amide with the evolution of hydrogen. The reaction proceeds slowly, but is complete if there be an excess of NH₃. Pure NH₂Na is colourless (its colouration is due to various impurities), semi-transparent, shows traces of crystallisation, has a conchoidal fracture, and melts at 145°. Judging from the increase in weight of the sodium and the quantity of hydrogen which is disengaged, the composition of the amide is exactly NH_2Na. It partially volatilises (sublimes) in vacuo at 200°, and breaks up into $2Na + N_2 + 2H_2$ at 500°. The same amide is formed when oxide of sodium is heated in NH_3: $Na_2O + 2NH_3 = 2NaH_2N + H_2O$. NaHO is also formed to some extent by the resultant H_2O. Potassium and lithium form similar amides. With water, alcohol, and acids, NH_2Na gives NH_3 and NaHO, which react further. Anhydrous CaO absorbs NH_2Na when heated without decomposing it. When sodamide is heated with SiO_2, NH_3 is disengaged, and silicon nitride formed. It acts still more readily upon boric anhydride when heated with it: $2NH_2Na + B_2O_3 = 2BN + 2NaHO + H_2O$. When slightly heated, $NH_2Na + NOCl = NaCl + N_2 + H_2O$ ($NHNa_2$ and NNa_3 are apparently not formed at a higher temperature). The halogen organic compounds react with the aid of heat, but with so much energy that the reaction frequently leads to the ultimate destruction of the organic groups and production of carbon.

[45] As sodium does not displace hydrogen from the hydrocarbons, *it may be preserved* in liquid hydrocarbons. Naphtha is generally used for this purpose, as it consists of a mixture of various liquid hydrocarbons. However, in naphtha sodium usually becomes coated with a crust composed of matter produced by the action of the sodium on certain of the substances contained in the mixture composing naphtha. In order that sodium may retain its lustre in naphtha, secondary octyl alcohol is added. (This alcohol is obtained by distilling castor oil with caustic potash.) Sodium keeps well in a mixture of pure benzene and paraffin.

[46] If sodium does not directly displace the hydrogen in hydrocarbons, still by indirect means compounds may be obtained which contain sodium and hydrocarbon groups. Some of these compounds have been produced, although not in a pure state. Thus, for instance, zinc ethyl, $Zn(C_2H_5)_2$, when treated with sodium, loses zinc and forms sodium ethyl, C_2H_5Na, but this decomposition is not complete, and the compound formed cannot be separated by distillation from the remaining zinc ethyl. In this compound the energy of the sodium is clearly manifest, for it reacts with substances containing haloids, oxygen, &c., and directly absorbs carbonic anhydride, forming a salt of a carboxylic acid (propionic).

[46 bis] It is even doubtful whether the suboxide exists (*see* Note 47).

[47] A compound, Na_2Cl, which corresponds with the suboxide, is apparently formed when a galvanic current is passed through fused common salt; the sodium liberated dissolves in the common salt, and does not separate from the compound either on cooling or on treatment with

mercury. It is therefore supposed to be Na_2Cl; the more so as the mass obtained gives hydrogen when treated with water: $Na_2Cl + H_2O = H + NaHO + NaCl$, that is, it acts like suboxide of sodium. If Na_2Cl really exists as a salt, then the corresponding base Na_4O, according to the rule with other bases of the composition M_4O, ought to be called a quaternary oxide. According to certain evidence, a suboxide is formed when thin sheets or fine drops of sodium slowly oxidise in moist air.

[48] According to observations easily made, sodium when fused in air oxidises but does not burn, the combustion only commencing with the formation of vapour—that is, when considerably heated. Davy and Karsten obtained the oxides of potassium, K_2O, and of sodium, Na_2O, by heating the metals with their hydroxides, whence $NaHO + Na = Na_2O + H$, but N. N. Beketoff failed to obtain oxides by this means. He prepared them by directly igniting the metals in dry air, and afterwards heating with the metal in order to destroy any peroxide. The oxide produced, Na_2O, when heated in an atmosphere of hydrogen, gave a mixture of sodium and its hydroxide: $Na_2O + H = NaHO + Na$ (*see* Chapter II., Note 9). If both the observations mentioned are accurate, then the reaction is reversible. Sodium oxide ought to be formed during the decomposition of sodium carbonate by oxide of iron (*see* Note 26), and during the decomposition of sodium nitrite. According to Karsten, its specific gravity is 2·8, according to Beketoff 2·3. The difficulty in obtaining it is owing to an excess of sodium forming the suboxide, and an excess of oxygen the peroxide. The grey colour peculiar to the suboxide and oxide perhaps shows that they contain metallic sodium. In addition to this, in the presence of water it may contain sodium hydride and $NaHO$.

[49] Of the oxides of sodium, that easiest to form is the peroxide, NaO or Na_2O_2; this is obtained when sodium is burnt in an excess of oxygen. If $NaNO_3$ be melted, it gives Na_2O_2 with metallic Na. In a fused state the peroxide is reddish yellow, but it becomes almost colourless when cold. When heated with iodine vapour, it loses oxygen: $Na_2O_2 + I_2 = Na_2OI_2 + O$. The compound Na_2OI_2 is akin to the compound Cu_2OCl_2 obtained by oxidising CuCl. This reaction is one of the few in which iodine directly displaces oxygen. The substance Na_2OI_2 is soluble in water, and when acidified gives free iodine and a sodium salt. Carbonic oxide is absorbed by heated sodium peroxide with formation of sodium carbonate: $Na_2CO_3 = Na_2O_2 + CO$, whilst carbonic anhydride liberates oxygen from it. With nitrous oxide it reacts thus: $Na_2O_2 + 2N_2O = 2NaNO_2 + N_2$; with nitric oxide it combines directly, forming sodium nitrite, $NaO + NO = NaNO_2$. Sodium peroxide, when treated with water, does not give hydrogen peroxide, because the latter in the presence of the alkali formed ($Na_2O_2 + 2H_2O = 2NaHO + H_2O_2$) decomposes into water and oxygen. In the

presence of dilute sulphuric acid it forms H_2O_2 ($Na_2O_2 + H_2SO_4 = Na_2SO_4 + H_2O_2$). Peroxide of sodium is now prepared on a large scale (by the action of air upon Na at 300°) for bleaching wool, silk &c. (when it acts in virtue of the H_2O_2 formed). The oxidising properties of Na_2O_2 under the action of heat are seen, for instance, in the fact that when heated with I it forms sodium iodate; with PbO, Na_2PbO_3; with pyrites, sulphates, &c. When peroxide of sodium comes into contact with water, it evolves much heat, forming H_2O_2, and decomposing with the disengagement of oxygen; but, as a rule, there is no explosion. But if Na_2O_2 be placed in contact with organic matter, such as sawdust, cotton, &c., it gives a violent explosion when heated, ignited, or acted on by water. Peroxide of sodium forms an excellent oxidising agent for the preparation of the higher product of oxidation of Mn, Cr, W, &c., and also for oxidising the metallic sulphides. It should therefore find many applications in chemical analysis. To prepare Na_2O_2 on a large scale, Castner melts Na in an aluminium vessel, and at 300° passes first air deprived of a portion of its oxygen (having been already once used), and then ordinary dry air over it.

[543]

CHAPTER XIII

POTASSIUM, RUBIDIUM, CÆSIUM, AND LITHIUM. SPECTRUM ANALYSIS

Just as the series of halogens, fluorine, bromine and iodine correspond with the chlorine contained in common salt, so also there exists a corresponding series of elements: lithium, Li = 7, potassium, K = 39, rubidium, Rb = 85, and cæsium, Cs = 133, which are analogous to the sodium in common salt. These elements bear as great a resemblance to sodium, Na = 23, as fluorine, F = 19, bromine, Br = 80, and iodine, I = 127, do to chlorine, Cl = 35·5. Indeed, in a free state, these elements, like sodium, are soft metals which rapidly oxidise in moist air and decompose water at the ordinary temperature, forming soluble hydroxides having clearly-defined basic properties and the composition RHO, like that of caustic soda. The resemblance between these metals is sometimes seen with striking clearness, especially in compounds such as salts.[1] The corresponding salts of nitric, sulphuric, carbonic, and nearly all acids with these metals have many points in common. The metals which resemble sodium so much in their reactions are termed the *metals of the alkalis*.

[544]

Among the metals of the alkalis, the most widely distributed in nature, after sodium, is *potassium*. Like sodium, it does not appear either in a free state or as oxide or hydroxide, but in the form of salts, which present much in common with the salts of sodium in the manner of their occurrence. The compounds of potassium and sodium in the earth's crust occur as mineral compounds of silica. With silica, SiO_2, potassium oxide, like sodium oxide, forms saline mineral substances resembling glass. If other oxides, such as lime, CaO, and alumina, Al_2O_3, combine with these compounds, glass is formed, a vitreous stony mass, distinguished by its great stability, and its very slight variation under the action of water. It is such complex silicious compounds as these which contain potash (potassium oxide), K_2O, or soda (sodium oxide), Na_2O, and sometimes both together, silica, SiO_2, lime, CaO, alumina, Al_2O_3, and other oxides, that form the chief mass of rocks, out of which, judging by the direction of the strata, the chief mass of the accessible crust (envelope) of the earth is made up. The primary rocks, like granite, porphyry, &c.,[1 bis] are formed of such crystalline silicious rocks as these. The oxides entering into the composition of these rocks do not form a homogeneous amorphous mass like glass, but are distributed in a series of peculiar, and in the majority of cases crystalline, compounds, into which the primary rocks may be divided. Thus a felspar (orthoclase) in granite contains from 8 to 15 per cent. of potassium, whilst another variety (plagioclase) which also occurs in granite contains 1·2 to 6 per cent. of potassium, and 6 to 12 per cent. of sodium. The mica in granite contains 3 to 10 per cent. of potassium. As already mentioned, and further explained in Chapter XVII., the friable, crumbling, and stratified formations which in our times cover a large part of the earth's surface have been formed from these primary rocks by the action of the atmosphere and of water containing carbonic acid. It is evident that in the chemical alteration of the primary rocks by the action of water, the compounds of potassium, as well as the compounds of sodium, must have been dissolved by the water (as they are soluble in water), and that therefore the compounds of potassium must be accumulated together with those of sodium in sea water. And indeed compounds of potassium are always found in *sea water*, as we have already pointed out (Chapters I. and X.). This forms one of the sources from which they are extracted. After the evaporation of sea water, there remains a mother liquor, which contains potassium chloride and a large proportion of magnesium chloride. On cooling this solution crystals separate out which contain chlorides of magnesium and potassium. A double salt of this kind, called *carnallite*,[545] $KMgCl_3,6H_2O$, occurs at Stassfurt. This carnallite[2] is now employed as a material for the extraction of potassium chloride, and of all the compounds of this element.[3] Besides which, potassium chloride itself is sometimes found at Stassfurt as *sylvine*.[3 bis] By a method of[546] double saline decomposition, the chloride of potassium may be converted into all the other potassium salts,[4] some of which are of practical use. The potassium salts have, however, their greatest importance as an indispensable component of the food of plants.[5]

The primary rocks contain an almost equal proportion of potassium and sodium. But in sea water the compounds of the latter metal predominate. It may be asked, what became of the compounds of potassium in the disintegration of the primary rocks, if so small a quantity went to the sea water? They remained with the other products of the decomposition of the primary rocks. When granite or any other similar rock formation is disintegrated, there are formed, besides the soluble substances, also insoluble substances—sand and finely-divided clay, containing water, alumina, and silica. This clay is carried away by the water, and is then deposited in strata. It, and especially its admixture with vegetable remains, retain compounds of potassium in a greater quantity than those of sodium. This has been proved with absolute certainty to be the case, and is due to the *absorptive power of the soil*. If a dilute solution of a potassium compound be filtered through common mould used for growing plants, containing clay and the remains of vegetable decomposition, this mould will be[547] found to have retained a somewhat considerable percentage of the potassium compounds. If a salt of potassium be taken, then during the filtration an equivalent quantity of a salt of calcium—which is also found, as a rule, in soils—is set free. Such a process of filtration through finely divided earthy substances proceeds in nature, and the compounds of potassium are everywhere retained by the friable earth in considerable quantity. This explains the presence of so small an amount of potassium salts in the water of rivers, lakes, streams, and oceans, where the lime and soda have accumulated. The compounds of potassium retained by the friable mass of the earth are absorbed as an aqueous solution by the roots of *plants*. Plants, as everyone knows, when burnt leave an ash, and this ash, besides various other substances, without exception contains compounds of potassium. Many land plants contain a very small amount of sodium compounds,[6] whilst potassium and its compounds occur in all kinds of vegetable ash. Among the generally cultivated plants, grass, potatoes, the turnip, and buckwheat are particularly rich in potassium compounds. The ash of plants, and especially of herbaceous plants, buckwheat straw, sunflower and potato leaves are used in practice for the extraction of potassium compounds. There is no doubt that potassium occurs in the plants themselves in the form of complex compounds, and often as salts of organic acids. In certain cases such salts of potassium are even extracted from the juice of plants. Thus, sorrel and oxalis, for example, contain in their juices the acid oxalate of potassium, C_2HKO_4, which is employed for removing ink stains. Grape juice contains the so-called cream of tartar, which is the acid tartrate of potassium, $C_4H_5KO_6$.[7][548] This salt also separates as a sediment from wine. When the plants, containing one or more of the salts of potassium, are burnt, the carbonaceous matter is oxidised, and in consequence the potassium is obtained in the ash as carbonate, K_2CO_3, which is generally known as *potashes*. Hence potashes occur ready prepared in the ash of plants, and therefore the ash of land plants is employed as a source for the extraction of potassium compounds. Potassium carbonate is extracted by lixiviating the ash with water.[8] Potassium carbonate[549] may also be obtained from the chloride by a method similar to that by which sodium carbonate is prepared from sodium chloride.[8 bis] There is no difficulty in obtaining any salt of potassium—for example, the sulphate,[9][550] bromide, and iodide[10]—by the action of the corresponding acid on KCl and especially on the carbonate, whilst the hydroxide, *caustic potash*, KHO, which is in many respects analogous to caustic soda, is easily obtained[551] by means of lime in exactly the same manner in which sodium hydroxide is prepared from sodium carbonate.[11] Therefore, in order to complete our knowledge of the alkali metals, we will only describe two salts of potassium which are of practical importance, and whose analogues have not been described in the preceding chapter, potassium cyanide and potassium nitrate.

Potassium cyanide, which presents in its chemical relations a certain analogy with the halogen salts of potassium, is not only formed according to the equation, $KHO + HCN = H_2O + KCN$, but also whenever a nitrogenous carbon compound—for instance, animal matter—is heated in the presence of metallic potassium, or of a compound of potassium, and even when a mixture of potash and carbon is heated in a stream of nitrogen. Potassium cyanide is obtained from yellow prussiate, which has been already mentioned in Chapter IX., and whose preparation on a large scale will be described in Chapter XXII. If the yellow prussiate be ground to a powder and dried, so that it loses its water of crystallisation, it then melts at a red heat, and decomposes into carbide of iron, nitrogen, and potassium cyanide, $FeK_4C_6N\_6 = 4KCN + FeC_2 + N_2$. After the decomposition it is found that the yellow salt has been converted into a white mass of potassium cyanide. The carbide of iron formed collects at the bottom of the vessel. If the mass thus obtained be treated with water, the potassium cyanide is partially decomposed by the water, but if it be treated with alcohol, then the cyanide is dissolved, and on cooling separates in a crystalline form.[12] A solution of potassium cyanide has a powerfully alkaline[552] reaction, a smell like that of bitter almonds, peculiar to prussic acid, and acts as a most powerful poison. Although exceedingly stable in a fused state, potassium cyanide easily changes when in solution. Prussic acid is so very feebly energetic that even water decomposes potassium cyanide. A solution of the salt, even without access of air, easily turns brown and decomposes, and when heated evolves ammonia and forms potassium formate; this is easily comprehensible from the representation of the cyanogen compounds which was developed in Chapter IX., $KCN + 2H_2O = CHKO_2 + NH_3$. Furthermore, as carbonic anhydride acts on potassium cyanide with evolution of prussic acid, and as potassium cyanate, which is also unstable, is formed by the action of air, it will be easily seen that solutions of potassium cyanide are very unstable. Potassium cyanide, containing as it does carbon and potassium, is a substance which can act in a very vigorously reducing manner, especially when fused; it is therefore used as a powerful reducing agent at a red heat.[13] The property of potassium cyanide of giving double salts with other cyanides is very clearly shown by the fact that many metals dissolve in a solution of potassium cyanide, with the evolution of hydrogen. For example, iron, copper, and zinc act in this manner. Thus—

[553]

$$4KCN + 2H_2O + Zn = K_2ZnC_4N_4 + 2KHO + H_2$$

Gold and silver are soluble in potassium cyanide in the presence of air, in which case the hydrogen, which would otherwise be evolved in the reaction, combines with the oxygen of the air, forming water (Eissler, MacLaurin, 1893), for example, $4Au + 4KCN + O + H_2O = 2AuKC_2N_2 + 2KHO$, which is taken advantage of for extracting gold from its ores (Chapter XXIV.).[13 bis] Platinum, mercury, and tin are not dissolved in a solution of potassium cyanide, even with access of air.

Potassium nitrate, or common *nitre* or *saltpetre*, KNO_3, is chiefly used as a component part of gunpowder, in which it cannot be replaced by the sodium salt, because the latter is deliquescent. It is necessary that the nitre in gunpowder should be perfectly pure, as even small traces of sodium, magnesium, and calcium salts, especially chlorides, render the nitre and the gunpowder capable of attracting moisture. Nitre may easily be obtained pure, owing to its great disposition to form crystals both large and small, which aids its separation from other salts. The considerable differences between the solubility of nitre at different temperatures aids this crystallisation. A solution of nitre saturated at its boiling point (116°) contains 335 parts of nitre to 100 parts of water, whilst at the ordinary temperature—for instance, 20°—the solution is only able to retain 32 parts of the salt. Therefore, in the preparation and refining of nitre, its solution, saturated at the boiling point, is cooled, and nearly all the nitre is obtained in the form of crystals. If the solution be quietly and slowly cooled in large quantities then large crystals are formed, but if it be rapidly cooled and agitated then small crystals are obtained. In this manner, if not all, at all events the majority, of the impurities present in small quantities remain in the mother liquor. If an unsaturated solution of nitre be rapidly cooled, so as to prevent the formation of large crystals (in whose crevices the mother liquor, together with the impurities, would remain), the very minute crystals of nitre known as saltpetre flour are obtained.

Common nitre occurs in nature, but only in small quantities in admixture with other nitrates, and especially with sodium, magnesium, and calcium nitrates. Such a mixture of salts of nitric acid is formed in nature in fertile earth, and in those localities where, as in *the soil*, nitrogenous organic remains are decomposed in the presence of alkalis or alkaline bases with free access of air. This method of the formation of nitrates requires moisture, besides the free access of air, and takes place principally during warm weather.[14] In warm countries, and in[554] temperate climates during the summer months, fertile soils produce a small quantity of nitre. In this respect India is especially known as affording a considerable supply of nitre extracted from the soil. The nitre-bearing soil after the rainy season sometimes becomes covered during the summer with crystals of nitre, formed by the evaporation of the water in which it was previously dissolved. This soil is collected, subjected to repeated lixiviations, and treated for nitre as will be presently described. In temperate climates nitrates are obtained from the lime rubbish of demolished buildings which have stood for many years, and especially from those portions which have been in contact with the ground. The conditions there are very favourable for the formation of nitre, because the lime used as a cement in buildings contains the base necessary for the formation of nitrates, while the excrement, urine, and animal refuse are sources of nitrogen. By the methodical lixiviation of this kind of rubbish a solution of nitrogenous salts is formed similar to that obtained by the lixiviation of fertile soil. A similar solution is also obtained by the lixiviation of the so-called *nitre plantations*. They are composed of manure interlaid with brushwood, and strewn over with ashes, lime, and other alkaline rubbish. These nitre plantations are set up in those localities where the manure is not required for the fertilisation of the soil, as, for example, in the south-eastern 'black earth' Governments of Russia. The same process of oxidation of nitrogenous matter freely exposed to air and moisture during the warm season in the presence of alkalis takes place in nitre plantations as in fertile soil and in the walls of buildings. From all these sources there is obtained a solution containing various salts of nitric acid mixed with soluble organic matter. The simplest method of treating this impure solution of nitre is to add a solution of potassium carbonate, or to simply treat it with ashes containing this substance. The potassium carbonate enters into double decomposition with the calcium and magnesium salts, forming insoluble carbonates of these bases and leaving the nitre in solution. Thus, for instance, $K_2CO_3 + Ca(NO_3)_2 = 2KNO_3 + CaCO_3$. Both calcium and magnesium carbonates are insoluble, and therefore after treatment with potassium carbonate the solution no longer contains salts of these metals but only the salts of sodium and potassium together with organic matter. The latter partially separates on heating in an insoluble form, and is entirely destroyed by heating the nitre to a low red heat. The nitre thus obtained is easily purified by[555] repeated crystallisation. The greater part of the nitre used for making gunpowder is now obtained from the sodium salt *Chili saltpetre* or *cubic nitre*, which occurs in nature, as already mentioned. The conversion of this salt into common nitre is also carried on by means of a double decomposition. This is done either by adding potassium carbonate (when, on mixing the strong and hot solutions, sodium carbonate is directly obtained as a precipitate), or, as is now most frequent, potassium chloride. When a mixture of strong solutions of potassium chloride and sodium nitrate is evaporated, sodium chloride first separates, because this salt, which is formed by the double decomposition $KCl + NaNO_3 = KNO_3 + NaCl$, is almost equally soluble in hot and cold water; on cooling, therefore, a large amount of potassium nitrate separates from the saturated solution, while the sodium chloride remains dissolved. The nitre is ultimately purified by recrystallisation and by washing with a saturated solution of nitre, which cannot dissolve a further quantity of nitre but only the impurities.

Nitre is a colourless salt having a peculiar cool taste. It crystallises easily in long striated six-sided rhombic prisms terminating in rhombic pyramids. Its crystals (sp. gr. 1·93) do not contain water, but their cavities generally contain a certain quantity of the solution from which they have crystallised. For this reason in refining nitre, the production of large crystals is prevented, *saltpetre flour* being prepared. At a low red heat (339°) nitre melts to a colourless liquid.[14 bis] Potassium nitrate at the ordinary temperature and in a solid form is inactive and stable, but *at a high temperature* it acts as a powerful *oxidising agent*, giving up a considerable amount of oxygen to substances[556] mixed with it.[15] When thrown on to incandescent charcoal it brings about its rapid combustion, and a mechanical mixture of powdered charcoal and nitre ignites when brought into contact with a red-hot substance, and continues to burn by itself. In this action, nitrogen is evolved, and the oxygen oxidises the charcoal, in consequence of which potassium carbonate and carbonic anhydride are formed: $4KNO_3 + 5C = 2K_2CO_3 + 3CO_2 + 2N_2$. This phenomenon depends on the fact that oxygen in combining with carbon evolves more heat than it does in combining with nitrogen. Hence, when once the combustion has been started at the expense of the nitre, it is able to go on without requiring the aid of external heat. A similar oxidation or combustion at the expense of the contained oxygen takes place when nitre is heated with different combustible substances. If a mixture of sulphur and nitre be thrown upon a red-hot surface, the sulphur burns, forming potassium sulphate and sulphurous anhydride. In this case, also, the nitrogen of the nitre is evolved as gas: $2KNO_3 + 2S = K_2SO_4 + N_2 + SO_2$. A similar phenomenon occurs when nitre is heated with many metals. The oxidation of those metals which are able to form acid oxides with an excess of oxygen is especially remarkable. In this case they remain in combination with potassium oxide as potassium salts. Manganese, antimony, arsenic, iron, chromium, &c. are instances of this kind. These elements, like carbon and sulphur, displace free nitrogen. The lower oxides of these metals when fused with nitre pass into the higher oxides. Organic substances are also oxidised when heated with nitre—that is, they burn at the expense of the nitre. It will be readily understood from this that nitre is frequently used in practical chemistry and the arts as an oxidising agent at high temperatures.[557] Its application in *gunpowder* is based on this property; gunpowder consists of a mechanical mixture of finely-ground sulphur, nitre, and charcoal. The relative proportion of these substances varies according to the destination of the powder and to the kind of charcoal employed (a friable, incompletely-burnt charcoal, containing therefore hydrogen and oxygen, is employed). Gases are formed in its combustion, chiefly nitrogen and carbonic anhydride, which create a considerable pressure if their escape be in any way impeded. This action of gunpowder may be expressed by the equation: $2KNO_3 + 3C + S = K_2S + 3CO_2 + N_2$.

It is found by this equation that gunpowder should contain thirty-six parts of charcoal (13·3 p.c.), and thirty-two parts (11·9 p.c.) of sulphur, to 202 parts (74·8 p.c.) of nitre, which is very near to its actual composition.[16]

[558]

Metallic potassium was obtained like sodium; first by the action of a galvanic current, then by reduction of the hydroxide by means of metallic iron, and lastly, by the action of charcoal on the carbonate at a high temperature. The behaviour of metallic potassium differs, however, from that of sodium, because it easily combines with carbonic oxide, forming an explosive and inflammable mass.[17]

Potassium is quite as volatile as sodium, if not more so. At the ordinary temperature potassium is even softer than sodium; its freshly-cut surfaces present a whiter colour than sodium, but, like the latter, and with even greater ease, it oxidises in moist air. It is brittle at low temperatures, but is quite soft at 25°, and melts at 58°. At a low red heat (667°, Perkin) it distils without change, forming a green vapour, whose density,[18] according to A. Scott (1887), is equal to 19 (if that of[559] hydrogen = 1). This shows that the molecule of potassium (like that of sodium, mercury, and zinc) contains but one atom. This is also the case with many other metals, judging by recent researches.[19] The specific gravity of potassium at 15° is 0·87, and is therefore less than that of sodium, as is also the case with all its compounds.[20] Potassium decomposes water with great ease at the ordinary temperature, evolving 45,000 heat units per atomic weight in grams. The heat evolved is sufficient to inflame the hydrogen, the flame being coloured violet from the presence of particles of potassium.[21]

With regard to the relation of potassium to hydrogen and oxygen, it is closely analogous to sodium in this respect. Thus, with hydrogen it forms potassium hydride, K_2H (between 200° and 411°), and with oxygen it gives a suboxide K_4O, oxide K_2O, and peroxide, only more oxygen enters into the composition of the latter than in sodium peroxide; potassium peroxide contains KO_2, but it is probable that in the combustion of potassium an oxide KO is also formed. Potassium, like sodium, is soluble in mercury.[22] In a word, the relation between sodium and potassium is as close as that between chlorine and bromine, or, better still, between fluorine and chlorine, as the atomic weight of[560] sodium, 23, is as much greater than that of fluorine, 19, as that of potassium, 39, is greater than that of chlorine, 35·5.

The resemblance between *potassium* and *sodium* is so great that *their compounds* can only be easily *distinguished* in the form of certain of their salts. For instance, the acid potassium tartrate, $C_4H_5KO_6$ (cream of tartar), is distinguished by its sparing solubility in water and in alcohol, and in a solution of tartaric acid, whilst the corresponding sodium salt is easily soluble. Therefore, if a solution of tartaric acid be added in considerable excess to the solutions of the majority of potassium salts, a precipitate of the sparingly-soluble acid salt is formed, which does not occur with salts of sodium. The chlorides KCl and NaCl in solutions easily give double salts K_2PtCl_6 and Na_2PtCl_6, with platinic chloride, $PtCl_4$, and the solubility of these salts is very different, especially in a mixture of alcohol and ether. The sodium salt is easily soluble, whilst the potassium salt is insoluble or almost so, and therefore the reaction with platinic chloride is that most often used for the separation of potassium from sodium, as is more fully described in works on analytical chemistry.

It is possible to discover the least traces of these metals in admixture together, by means of their property of imparting different colours to *a flame*. The presence of a salt of sodium in a flame is recognised by a brilliant yellow coloration, and a pure potassium salt colours a colourless flame violet. However, in the presence of a sodium salt the pale violet coloration given by a potassium salt is quite undistinguishable, and it is at first sight impossible in this case to discover the potassium salt in the presence of that of sodium. But by decomposing the light given by a flame coloured by these metals or a mixture of them, by means of a prism, they are both easily distinguishable, because the yellow light emitted by the sodium salt depends on a group of light rays having a definite index of refraction which corresponds with the yellow portion of the solar spectrum, having the index of refraction of the Fraunhofer line (strictly speaking, group of lines) D, whilst the salts of potassium give a light from which these rays are entirely absent, but which contain rays of a red and violet colour. Therefore, if a potassium salt occur in a flame, on decomposing the light (after passing it through a narrow slit) by means of a prism, there will be seen red and violet bands of light situated at a considerable distance from each other; whilst if a sodium salt be present a yellow line will also appear. If both metals simultaneously occur in a flame and emit light, the spectrum lines corresponding to the potassium and the sodium will appear simultaneously.

[561]

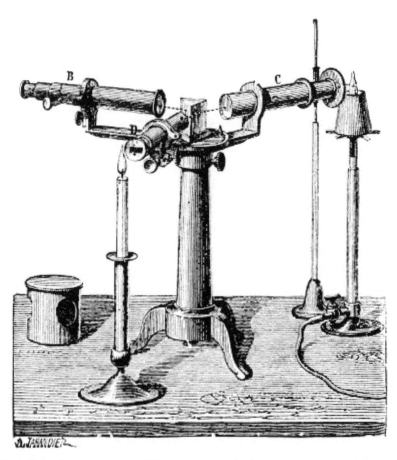

FIG. 72.—Spectroscope. The prism and table are covered with an opaque cover. The spectrum obtained from the flame coloured by a substance introduced on the wire is viewed through B. A light is placed before the scale D in order to illuminate the image of the scale reflected through B by the side of the prism.

For convenience in carrying on this kind of testing, *spectroscopes* (fig. 72) are constructed,[23] consisting of a refracting prism and three tubes placed in the plane of the refracting angle of the prism. One of the tubes, C, has a vertical slit at the end, giving access to the light to be tested, which then passes into the tube (collimator), containing a lens which gives the rays a parallel direction. The rays of light having passed through the slit, and having become parallel, are refracted and dispersed in the prism, and the spectrum formed is observed through the eye-piece of the other telescope B. The third tube D contains a horizontal transparent scale (at the outer end) which is divided into equal divisions. The light from a source such as a gas burner or candle placed before this tube, passes through the scale, and is reflected on that face of the prism which stands before the telescope B, so that the image of the scale is seen through this telescope simultaneously with the spectrum given by the rays passing through the slit of the tube C. In this manner the image of the scale and the spectrum given by the source of light under investigation are seen simultaneously. If the[562] sun's rays be directed through the slit of the tube C, then the observer looking through the eye-piece of B will see the solar spectrum, and (if the aperture of the slit be narrow and the apparatus correctly adjusted) the dark Fraunhofer lines in it.[24] Small-sized spectroscopes are usually so adjusted that (looking through B) the violet portion of the spectrum is seen to the right and the red portion to the left, and the Fraunhofer line D (in the bright yellow portion of the spectrum) is situated on the 50th division of the scale.[25] If the light emitted by an incandescent solid—for example, the Drummond light—be passed through the spectroscope, then all the colours of the solar spectrum are seen, but not the Fraunhofer lines. To observe the result given by a flame coloured by various salts a Bunsen gas burner (or the pale flame of hydrogen gas issuing from a platinum orifice) giving so pale a flame that its spectrum will be practically invisible is placed before the slit. If any compound of sodium be placed in the flame of the gas burner (for which purpose a platinum wire on whose end sodium chloride is fused is fixed to the stand), then the flame is coloured yellow, and on looking through the spectroscope the observer will see a bright *yellow* line falling upon the 50th division of the scale, which is seen together with the spectrum in the telescope. No yellow lines of other refractive index, nor any rays of any other colour, will be seen, and, therefore, the spectrum corresponding with sodium compounds consists of yellow rays of that index of refraction which belong to the Fraunhofer (black) line D of the solar spectrum. If a potassium salt be introduced into the flame instead of a sodium salt, then two bands will be seen which are much feebler than the bright sodium band—namely, one red line near the Fraunhofer line A and another violet line. Besides which, a pale, almost continuous, spectrum will be[563] observed in the central portions of the scale. If a mixture of sodium and potassium salts be now introduced into the flame, three lines will be seen simultaneously—namely, the red and pale violet lines of potassium and the yellow line of sodium. In this manner it is possible, by the aid of the spectroscope, to determine the relation between the spectra of metals and known portions of the solar spectrum. The continuity of the latter is interrupted by dark lines (that is, by an absence of light of a definite index of refraction), termed the Fraunhofer lines of the solar spectrum. It has been shown by careful observations (by Fraunhofer, Brewster, Foucault, Ångstrom, Kirchhoff, Cornu, Lockyer, Dewar, and others) that there exists an exact *agreement between the spectra* of certain *metals* and certain of the

Fraunhofer lines. Thus the bright yellow sodium line exactly corresponds with the dark Fraunhofer line D of the solar spectrum. A similar agreement is observed in the case of many other metals. This is not an approximate or chance correlation. In fact, if a spectroscope having a large number of refracting prisms and a high magnifying power be used, it is seen that the dark line D of the solar spectrum consists of an entire system of closely adjacent but definitely situated fine and wide (sharp, distinct) dark lines,[26] and an exactly similar group of bright lines is obtained when the yellow sodium line is examined through the same apparatus, so that each bright sodium line exactly corresponds with a dark line in the solar spectrum.[26 bis] This conformity of the bright lines formed by sodium with the dark lines of the solar spectrum cannot be accidental. This conclusion is further confirmed by the fact that the bright lines of other metals correspond with dark lines of the solar spectrum. Thus, for example, a series of sparks passing between the iron electrodes of a Ruhmkorff coil gives 450 very distinct lines characterising this metal. All these 450 bright lines, constituting the whole spectrum corresponding with iron, are repeated, as Kirchhoff showed, in the solar spectrum as dark Fraunhofer lines which occur in exactly the same situations as the bright lines in the iron spectrum, just as the sodium lines correspond with the band D in the solar spectrum. Many observers have in this manner studied the solar spectrum and the spectra of different metals simultaneously, and discovered in the former lines which[564] correspond not only with sodium and iron, but also with many other metals.[27] The spectra of such elements as hydrogen, oxygen, nitrogen, and other gases may be observed in the so-called Geissler's tubes—that is, in glass tubes containing rarefied gases, through which the discharge of a Ruhmkorff's coil is passed. Thus hydrogen gives a spectrum composed of three lines—a red line corresponding with the Fraunhofer line C, a green line corresponding with the line F, and a violet line corresponding with one of the lines between G and H. Of these rays the red is the brightest, and therefore the general colour of luminous hydrogen (with an electric discharge through a Geissler tube) is reddish.

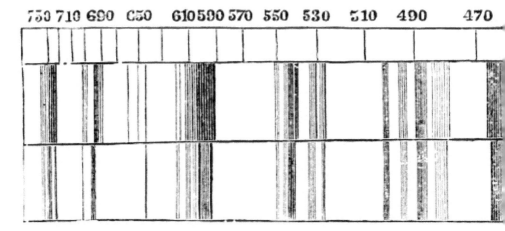

FIG. 73.—Absorption spectrum (Lecoq de Boisbaudran) of salts of didymium in concentrated and dilute solutions.

The correlation of the Fraunhofer lines with the spectra of metals depends on the phenomenon of the so-called *reversal of the spectrum*. This phenomenon consists in this, that instead of the bright spectrum corresponding with a metal, under certain circumstances a similar dark[565] spectrum in the form of Fraunhofer lines may be obtained, as will be explained directly. In order to clearly understand the phenomenon of[566] reversed spectra, it must be known that when light passes through certain transparent substances these substances retain rays of a certain refrangibility. The colour of solutions is a proof of this. Light which has passed through a yellow solution of a uranium salt contains no violet rays, and after having passed through a red solution of a permanganate, does not contain many rays in the yellow, blue, and green portions of the spectrum. Solutions of copper salts absorb nearly all red rays. Sometimes colourless solutions also absorb rays of certain definite refractive indexes, and give *absorption spectra*. Thus solutions of salts of didymium absorb rays of a certain refrangibility, and therefore an impression of black lines is received,[28] as shown in fig. 73. Many vapours (iodine) and gases (nitric peroxide) give similar spectra. Light which has passed through a deep layer of aqueous vapour, oxygen, or nitrogen also gives an absorption spectrum. For this reason the peculiar (winter) dark lines discovered by Brewster are observed in sunlight, especially in the evening and morning, when the sun's rays pass through the atmosphere (containing these substances) by a longer path than at mid-day. It is evident that the Fraunhofer[567] lines may be ascribed to the absorption of certain rays of light in its passage from the luminous mass of the sun to the earth. The remarkable progress made in all spectroscopic research dates from the investigations made by *Kirchhoff* (1859) on the relation between absorption spectra and the spectra of luminous incandescent gases. It had already been observed long before (by Fraunhofer, Foucault, Ångstrom) that the bright spectrum of the sodium flame gives two bright lines which are in exactly the same position as two black lines known as D in the solar spectrum, which evidently belong to an absorption spectrum. When Kirchhoff caused diffused sunlight to fall upon the slit of a spectroscope, and placed a sodium flame before it, a perfect superposition was observed—the bright sodium lines completely covered the black lines D of the solar spectrum. When further the continuous spectrum of a Drummond light showed the black line D on placing a sodium flame between it and the slit of the spectroscope—that is, when the Fraunhofer line of the solar spectrum was artificially produced—then there was no doubt that its appearance in the solar spectrum was due to the light passing somewhere through incandescent vapours of sodium. Hence a new theory of *reversed spectra*[29] arose—that is,[568] of the relation between the waves of light emitted and absorbed by a substance under given conditions of temperature; this is expressed by Kirchhoff's law, discovered by a careful analysis of the phenomena. This law may be formulated in an elementary way as follows: At a given temperature the relation between the intensity of the light emitted (of a definite wave-length) and the absorptive capacity with respect to the same colour (of the same wave-length) is a constant quantity.[30] As a black dull surface emits and also absorbs a considerable quantity of heat rays whilst a polished metallic surface both absorbs and emits but few, so a flame coloured by sodium emits a considerable quantity of yellow rays of a definite refrangibility, and has the property of absorbing a considerable quantity of the rays of the same refractive index. In general, the medium which emits definite rays also absorbs them.

FIG. 75.—Bright spectra of copper compounds.

Thus the bright spectral rays characteristic of a given metal may be reversed—that is, converted into dark lines—by passing light which gives a continuous spectrum through a space containing the heated vapours of the given metal. A similar phenomenon to that thus artificially produced is observed in sunlight, which shows dark lines characteristic of known metals—that is, the Fraunhofer lines form an absorption spectrum or depend on a reversed spectrum; it being presupposed that the sun itself, like all known sources of artificial light, gives a continuous spectrum without Fraunhofer lines.[31] We must[569] imagine that the sun, owing to the high temperature which is proper to it, emits a brilliant light which gives a continuous spectrum, and that this light, before reaching our eyes, passes through a space full of the vapours of different metals and their compounds. As the earth's atmosphere[32] contains very little, or no, metallic vapours, and as they cannot be supposed to exist in the celestial space,[32 bis] the only place in which the existence of such vapours can be admitted is in the *atmosphere surrounding the sun itself*. As the cause of the sun's luminosity must be looked for in its high temperature, the existence of an atmosphere containing metallic vapours is readily understood, because at that high temperature such metals as sodium, and even iron, are separated from their compounds and converted into vapour. The sun must be imagined as surrounded by an atmosphere of incandescent vaporous and gaseous matter,[33] including those elements whose reversed spectra correspond with the Fraunhofer lines—namely, sodium, iron, hydrogen, lithium, calcium, magnesium, &c. Thus in spectrum analysis we find a means of determining the composition of the inaccessible heavenly luminaries, and much has been done in this respect since Kirchhoff's theory was formulated. By observations on the spectra of many heavenly bodies, changes have been discovered going on in them,[34] and[570] many of the elements known to us have been found with certainty in them.[35] From this it must be concluded that the same elements which exist on the earth occur throughout the whole universe, and that at that degree of heat which is proper to the sun those simple substances which we accept as the elements in chemistry are still undecomposed and remain unchanged. A high temperature forms one of those conditions under which compounds most easily decompose; and if sodium or a similar element were a compound, in all probability it would be decomposed into component parts at the high temperature of the sun. This may indeed be concluded from the fact that in ordinary spectroscopic experiments the spectra obtained often belong to the metals and not to the compounds taken; this depends on the decomposition of these compounds in the heat of the flame. If[571] common salt be introduced into the flame of a gas-burner, a portion of it is decomposed, first forming, in all probability, with water, hydrochloric acid and sodium hydroxide, and the latter then becoming partially decomposed by the hydrocarbons, giving metallic sodium, whose incandescent vapour emits light of a definite refrangibility. This conclusion is arrived at from the following experiment:—If hydrochloric acid gas be introduced into a flame coloured by sodium it is observed that the sodium spectrum disappears, owing to the fact that metallic sodium cannot remain in the flame in the presence of an excess of hydrochloric acid. The same thing takes place on the addition of sal-ammoniac, which in the heat of the flame gives hydrochloric acid. If a porcelain tube containing sodium chloride (or sodium hydroxide or carbonate), and closed at both ends by glass plates, be so powerfully heated that the salt volatilises, then the sodium spectrum is not observable; but if the salt be replaced by sodium, then either the bright line or the absorption spectra is obtained, according to whether the light emitted by the incandescent vapour be observed, or light passing through the tube. Thus the above spectrum is not given by sodium chloride or other sodium compound, but is proper to the metal sodium itself. This is also the case with other analogous metals. The chlorides and other halogen *compounds* of barium, calcium, copper, &c., give independent spectra which differ from those of the metals. If barium chloride be introduced into a flame, it gives a mixed spectrum belonging to metallic barium and barium chloride. If besides barium chloride, hydrochloric acid or sal-ammoniac be introduced into the flame, then the spectrum of the metal disappears, and that of the chloride remains, which differs distinctly from the spectrum of barium fluoride, barium bromide, or barium iodide. A certain common resemblance and certain common[572] lines are observed in the spectra of two different compounds of one and the same element obtained in the above-described manner, and also in the spectrum of the metal, but they all have their peculiarities. The independent spectra of the compounds of copper are easily observed (fig. 75). Thus certain compounds which exist in a state of vapour, and are luminous at a high temperature, give their independent spectra. In the majority of cases the spectra of compounds are composed of indistinct luminous lines and complete bright bands, whilst metallic elements generally give a few clearly-defined spectral lines.[36] There is[573] no reason for supposing that the spectrum of a compound is equal to the sum of the spectra of its elements—that is, *every compound* which is not decomposed by heat *has its own proper spectrum*. This is best proved by absorption spectra, which are essentially only reversed spectra observed at low temperatures. If every salt of sodium, lithium, and potassium gives one and the same spectrum, this must be ascribed to the presence in the flame of the free metals liberated by the decomposition of their salts. Therefore *the phenomena of the spectrum are determined by molecules, and not by atoms*—that is, the molecules of the metal sodium, and not its atoms, produce those particular vibrations which determine the spectrum of a sodium salt. Where there is no free metallic sodium there is no sodium spectrum.

Spectrum analysis has not only endowed science with a knowledge of the composition of distant heavenly bodies (of the sun, stars, nebulæ, comets, &c.), but has also given a new *method* for studying the matter of the earth's surface. With its help Bunsen discovered two new elements belonging to the group of the alkali metals, and thallium, indium, and gallium were afterwards discovered by the same means. The spectroscope is employed in the study of rare metals (which in solution often give distinct absorption spectra), of dyes, and of many organic substances, &c.[37] With respect to the metals which are analogous to sodium, they all give similar very volatile[574] salts and such very characteristic spectra that the least traces of them[38] are discovered with great ease by means of the spectroscope. For instance, *lithium* gives a very brilliant red coloration to a flame and a very bright red spectral line (wave-length, 670 millionths mm.), which indicates the presence of this metal in admixture with compounds of other alkali metals.

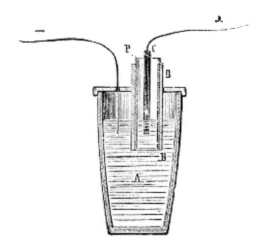

FIG. 77.—Preparation of lithium by the action of a galvanic current on fused lithium chloride.

Lithium, Li, is, like potassium and sodium, somewhat widely spread in siliceous rocks, but only occurs in small quantities and as mere traces in considerable masses of potassium and sodium salts. Only a very few rather rare minerals contain more than traces of it,[39] for example, spodumene and lithia mica. Many compounds of lithium are in all respects closely analogous to the corresponding compounds of sodium[575] and potassium; but the *carbonate* is sparingly soluble in cold water, which fact is taken advantage of for separating lithium from potassium and sodium. This salt, Li_2CO_3, is easily converted into the other compounds of lithium. Thus, for instance, the lithium hydroxide, LiHO, is obtained in exactly the same way as caustic soda, by the action of lime on the carbonate, and it is soluble in water and crystallises (from its solution in alcohol) as $LiHO,H_2O$. Metallic *lithium* is obtained by the action of a galvanic current on fused lithium chloride; for this purpose a cast-iron crucible, furnished with a stout cover, is filled with lithium chloride, heated until the latter fuses, and a strong galvanic current is then passed through the molten mass. The positive pole (fig. 77) consists of a dense carbon rod C (surrounded by a porcelain tube P fixed in an iron tube BB), and the negative pole of an iron wire, on which the metal is deposited after the current has passed through the molten mass for a certain length of time. Chlorine is evolved at the positive pole. When a somewhat considerable quantity of the metal has accumulated on the wire it is withdrawn, the metal is collected from it, and the experiment is then carried on as before.[39 bis] Lithium is the lightest of all metals, its specific gravity is 0·59, owing to which it floats even on naphtha; it melts at 180°, but does not volatilise at a red heat. Its appearance recalls that of sodium, and, like it, it has a yellow tint. At 200° it burns in air with a very bright flame, forming lithium oxide. In decomposing water it does not ignite the hydrogen. The characteristic test for lithium compounds is the *red coloration* which they impart to a colourless flame.[40]

Bunsen in 1860 tried to determine by means of the spectroscope[576] whether any other as yet unknown metals might not occur in different natural products together with lithium, potassium, and sodium, and he soon discovered two new alkali metals showing independent spectra. They are named after the characteristic coloration which they impart to the flame. One which gives a red and violet band is named *rubidium*, from *rubidius* (dark red), and the other is called *cæsium*, because it colours a pale flame sky blue, which depends on its containing bright blue rays, which appear in the spectrum of cæsium as two blue bands (table on p. 565). Both metals accompany sodium, potassium, and lithium, but in small quantities; rubidium occurs in larger quantity than cæsium. The amount of the oxides of cæsium and rubidium in lepidolite does not generally exceed one-half per cent. Rubidium has also been found in the ashes of many plants, while the Stassfurt carnallite (the mother-liquor obtained after having been treated for KCl) forms an abundant source for rubidium and also partly for cæsium. Rubidium also occurs, although in very small quantities, in the majority of mineral waters. In a very few cases cæsium is not accompanied by rubidium; thus, in a certain granite on the Isle of Elba, cæsium has been discovered, but not rubidium. This granite contains a very rare mineral called *pollux*, which contains as much as 34 per cent. of cæsium oxide. Guided by the spectroscope, and aided by the fact that the double salts of platinic chloride and rubidium and cæsium chlorides are still less soluble in water than the corresponding potassium salt, K_2PtCl_6,[41] Bunsen succeeded in separating both metals from each other and from potassium, and demonstrated the great resemblance[577] they bear to each other. The isolated metals,[42] rubidium and cæsium, have respectively the specific gravities 1·52 and 2·366, and melting points 39° and 27° as N. N. Beketoff showed (1894), he having obtained cæsium by heating $CsAlO_2$ with Mg([42 bis]).

Judging by the properties of the free metals, and of their corresponding and even very complex compounds, lithium, sodium, potassium, rubidium, and cæsium present an indubitable chemical resemblance. The fact that the metals easily decompose water, and that their[578] hydroxides RHO and carbonates R_2CO_3 are soluble in water, whilst the hydroxides and carbonates of nearly all other metals are insoluble, shows that these metals form a natural group of *alkali metals*. The halogens and the alkali metals form, by their character, the two extremes of the elements. Many of the other elements are metals approaching the alkali metals, both in their capacity of forming salts and in not forming acid compounds, but are not so energetic as the alkali metals, that is, they form less energetic bases. Such are the common metals, silver, iron, copper, &c. Some other elements, in the character of their compounds, approach the halogens, and, like them, combine with hydrogen, but these compounds do not show the energetic property of the halogen acids; in a free state they easily combine with metals, but they do not then form such saline compounds as the halogens do—in a word, the halogen properties are less sharply defined in them than in the halogens themselves. Sulphur, phosphorus, arsenic, &c. belong to this order of elements. The clearest distinction of the properties of the halogens and alkali metals is expressed in the fact that the former give acids and do not form bases, whilst the latter, on the contrary, only give bases. The first are true *acid elements*, the latter clearly-defined *basic or metallic elements*. On combining together, the halogens form, in a chemical sense, unstable compounds, and the alkali metals alloys in which the character of the metals remains unaltered, just as in the compound ICl the character of the halogens remains undisguised; thus both classes of elements on combining with members of their own class form non-characteristic compounds, which have the properties of their components. On the other hand, the halogens on combining with the alkali metals form compounds which are, in all respects, stable, and in which the original characters of the halogens and alkali metals have entirely disappeared. The formation of such compounds is accompanied by evolution of a large amount of heat, and by an entire change of both the physical and chemical properties of the substances originally taken. The alloy of sodium and potassium, although liquid at the ordinary temperature, is perfectly metallic, like both its components. The compound of sodium and chlorine has neither the appearance nor the properties of the original elements; sodium chloride melts at a higher temperature, and is more difficultly volatile, than either sodium or chlorine.

With all these qualitative differences there is, however, an important quantitative *resemblance between the halogens and the alkali metals*. This resemblance is clearly expressed by stating that both orders of elements belong to those which are univalent with respect to hydrogen. It is thus correct to say that both the above-named orders of elements[579] replace hydrogen atom for atom. Chlorine is able to take the place of hydrogen by metalepsis, and the alkali metals take the place of hydrogen in water and acids. As it is possible to consecutively replace every equivalent of hydrogen in a hydrocarbon by chlorine, so it is possible in an acid containing several equivalents of hydrogen to replace the hydrogen consecutively equivalent after equivalent by an alkali metal; hence an atom of these elements is analogous to an atom of hydrogen, which is taken, in all cases, as the unit for the comparison of the other elements. In ammonia, and in water, chlorine and sodium are able to bring about a direct replacement.

According to the law of substitution, the formation of sodium chloride, NaCl, at once shows the equivalence of the atoms of the alkali metals and the halogens. The halogens and hydrogen and the alkali metals combine with such elements as oxygen, and it is easily proved that in such compounds one atom of oxygen is able to retain two atoms of the halogens, of hydrogen, and of the alkali metals. For this purpose it is enough to compare the compounds KHO, K_2O, HClO, and Cl_2O, with water. It must not be forgotten, however, that the halogens give, with oxygen, besides compounds of the type R_2O, higher acid grades of oxidation, which the alkali metals and hydrogen are not capable of forming. We shall soon see that these relations are also subject to a special law, showing a gradual transition of the properties of the elements from the alkali metals to the halogens.[43]

The atomic weights of the alkali metals, lithium 7, sodium 23, potassium 39, rubidium 85, and cæsium 133, show that here, as in the class of halogens, the elements may be arranged according to their atomic weights in order to compare the properties of the analogous compounds of the members of this group. Thus, for example, the platinochlorides of lithium and sodium are soluble in water; those[580] of potassium, rubidium, and cæsium sparingly soluble, and the greater the atomic weight of the metal the less soluble is the salt. In other cases the reverse is observed—the greater the atomic weight the more soluble are the corresponding salts. The variation of properties with the variation in atomic weights even shows itself in the metals themselves; thus lithium volatilises with difficulty, whilst sodium is obtained by distillation, potassium volatilises more easily than sodium, and rubidium and cæsium as we have seen, are still more volatile.

Footnotes:

[1] Tutton's researches (1894) upon the analogy of the crystalline forms of K_2SO_4, Rb_2SO_4 and Cs_2SO_4 may be taken as a typical example of the comparison of analogous compounds. We cite the following data from these excellent researches: the sp. gr. at $20°/4°$ of K_2SO_4 is 2·6633 of Rb_2SO_4, 3·6113, and of Cs_2SO_4, 4·2434. The coefficient of cubical expansion (the mean between 20° and 60°) for the K salt is 0·0053, for the Rb salt 0·0052, for the Cs salt 0·0051. The linear expansion (the maximum for the vertical axis) along the axis of crystallisation is the same for all three salts, within the limits of experimental error. The replacement of potassium by rubidium causes the distance between the centres of the molecules in the direction of the three axes of crystallisation to increase equally, and less than with the replacement of rubidium by cæsium. The index of refraction for all rays and for every crystalline path (direction) is greater for the rubidium salt than for the potassium salt, and less than for the cæsium salt, and the differences are nearly in the ratio 2 : 5. The lengths of the rhombic

crystalline axes for K_2SO_4 are in the ratio $0{\cdot}5727 : 1 : 0{\cdot}7418$, for Rb_2SO_4, $0{\cdot}5723 : 1 : 0{\cdot}7485$, and for Cs_2SO_4, $0{\cdot}5712 : 1 : 0{\cdot}7521$. The development of the basic and brachy-pinacoids gradually increases in passing from K to Rb and Cs. The optical properties also follow the same order both at the ordinary and at a higher temperature. Tutton draws the general conclusion that the crystallographic properties of the isomorphic rhombic sulphates R_2SO_4 are a function of the atomic weight of the metals contained in them (*see* Chapter XV.) Such researches as these should do much towards hastening the establishment of a true molecular mechanics of physico-chemical phenomena.

[1 bis] The origin of the primary rocks has been mentioned in Chapter X., Note 2.

[2] Carnallite belongs to the number of double salts which are directly decomposed by water, and it only crystallises from solutions which contain an excess of magnesium chloride. It may be prepared artificially by mixing strong solutions of potassium and magnesium chlorides, when colourless crystals of sp. gr. $1{\cdot}60$ separate, whilst the Stassfurt salt is usually of a reddish tint, owing to traces of iron. At the ordinary temperature sixty-five parts of carnallite are soluble in one hundred parts of water in the presence of an excess of the salt. It deliquesces in the air, forming a solution of magnesium chloride and leaving potassium chloride. The quantity of carnallite produced at Stassfurt is now as much as 100,000 tons a year.

[3] The method of separating sodium chloride from potassium chloride has been described in Chapter I. On evaporation of a mixture of the saturated solutions, sodium chloride separates; and then, on cooling, potassium chloride separates, owing to the difference of rate of variation of their solubilities with the temperature. The following are the most trustworthy figures for the solubility of *potassium chloride* in one hundred parts of water (for sodium chloride, *see* Chapter X., Note 13):—

10° 20° 40° 60° 100°

32 35 40 46   57

When mixed with solutions of other salts the solubility of potassium chloride naturally varies, but not to any great extent.

[3 bis] The specific gravity of the solid salt is $1{\cdot}99$—that is, less than that of sodium chloride. All the salts of sodium are specifically heavier than the corresponding salts of potassium, as are also their solutions for equal percentage compositions. If the specific gravity of water at $4° = 10,000$, then at $15°$ the specific gravity of a solution of p p.c. potassium chloride $=$

$9,992 + 63 \cdot 29p + 0 \cdot 226p^2$, and therefore for 10 p.c. $= 1 \cdot 0647$, 20 p.c. $= 1 \cdot 1348$, &c.

Potassium chloride combines with iodine trichloride to form a compound $KCl + ICl_3 = KICl_4$, which has a yellow colour, is fusible, loses iodine trichloride at a red heat, and gives potassium iodate and hydrochloric acid with water. It is not only formed by direct combination, but also by many other methods; for instance, by passing chlorine into a solution of potassium iodide so long as the gas is absorbed, $KI + 2Cl_2 = KCl,ICl_3$. Potassium iodide, when treated with potassium chlorate and strong hydrochloric acid, also gives this compound; another method for its formation is given by the equation $KClO_3 + I + 6HCl = KCl,ICl_3 + 3Cl + 3H_2O$. This is a kind of salt corresponding with KIO_2 (unknown) in which the oxygen is replaced by chlorine. If valency be taken as the starting-point in the study of chemical compounds, and the elements considered as having a constant atomicity (number of bonds)—that is, if K, Cl, and I be taken as univalent elements—then it is impossible to explain the formation of such a compound because, according to this view, univalent elements are only able to form dual compounds with each other; such as, KCl, ClI, KI, &c., whilst here they are grouped together in the molecule $KICl_4$. Wells, Wheeler, and Penfield (1892) obtained a large number of such poly-haloid salts. They may all be divided into two large classes: the tri-haloid and the penta-haloid salts. They have been obtained not only for K but also for Rb and Cs, and partially also for Na and Li. The general method of their formation consists in dissolving the ordinary halogen salt of the metal in water, and treating it with the requisite amount of free halogen. The poly-haloid salt separates out after evaporating the solution at a more or less low temperature. In this manner, among the tri-haloid salts, may be obtained: KI_3, KBr_2I, KCl_2I, and the corresponding salts of rubidium and cæsium, for instance, CsI_3, $CsBrI_2$, $CsBr_2I$, $CsClBrI,CsCl_2I$, $CsBr_3$, $CsClBr_2$, $CsCl_2Br$, and in general MX_3 where X is a halogen. The colour of the crystals varies according to the halogen, thus CsI_3 is black, $CrBr_3$ yellowish red, $CrBrI_2$ reddish brown, $CsBr_2I$ red, $CsCl_2Br$ yellow. The cæsium salts are the most stable, and those of potassium least so, as also those which contain Br and I separately or together; for cæsium no compounds containing Cl and I were obtained. The penta-haloid salts form a smaller class; among these salts potassium forms KCl_4I, rubidium $RbCl_4I$, cæsium CsI_5, CsBr, $CsCl_4I$, lithium $LiCl_4I$ (with $4H_2O$) and sodium $NaCl_4I$ (with $2H_2O$). The most stable are those salts containing the metal with the greatest atomic weight—cæsium (*see* Chapter XI., Note 63).

[4] It is possible to extract the compounds of potassium directly from the primary rocks which are so widely distributed over the earth's surface and so abundant in some localities. From a chemical point of view this

problem presents no difficulty; for instance, by fusing powdered orthoclase with lime and fluor spar (Ward's method) and then extracting the alkali with water (on fusion the silica gives an insoluble compound with lime), or by treating the orthoclase with hydrofluoric acid (in which case silicon fluoride is evolved as a gas) it is possible to transfer the alkali of the orthoclase to an aqueous solution, and to separate it in this manner from the other insoluble oxides. However, as yet there is no profit in, nor necessity for, recourse to this treatment, as carnallite and potash form abundant materials for the extraction of potassium compounds by cheaper methods. Furthermore, the salts of potassium are now in the majority of chemical reactions replaced by salts of sodium, especially since the preparation of sodium carbonate has been facilitated by the Leblanc process. The replacement of potassium compounds by sodium compounds not only has the advantage that the salts of sodium are in general cheaper than those of potassium, but also that a smaller quantity of a sodium salt is needed for a given reaction than of a potassium salt, because the combining weight of sodium (23) is less than that of potassium (39).

[5] It has been shown by direct experiment on the cultivation of plants in artificial soils and in solutions that under conditions (physical, chemical, and physiological) otherwise identical plants are able to thrive and become fully developed in the entire absence of sodium salts, but that their development is impossible without potassium salts.

[6] If herbaceous plants contain much sodium salts, it is evident that these salts mainly come from the sodium compounds in the water absorbed by the plants.

[7] As plants always contain mineral substances and cannot thrive in a medium which does not contain them, more especially in one which is free from the salts of the four basic oxides, K_2O, CaO, MgO, and Fe_2O_3, and of the four acid oxides, CO_2, N_2O_5, P_2O_5, and SO_3, and as the amount of ash-forming substances in plants is small, the question inevitably arises as to what part these play in the development of plants. With the existing chemical data only one answer is possible to this question, and it is still only a hypothesis. This answer was particularly clearly expressed by Professor Gustavson of the Petroffsky Agricultural Academy. Starting from the fact (Chapter XI., Note 55) that a small quantity of aluminium renders possible or facilitates the reaction of bromine on hydrocarbons at the ordinary temperature, it is easy to arrive at the conclusion, which is very probable and in accordance with many data respecting the reactions of organic compounds, that the addition of mineral substances to organic compounds lowers the temperature of reaction and in general facilitates chemical reactions in plants, and thus aids the conversion of the most simple nourishing substances into the complex component parts of the

plant organism. The province of chemical reactions proceeding in organic substances in the presence of a small quantity of mineral substances has as yet been but little investigated, although there are already several disconnected data concerning reactions of this kind, and although a great deal is known with regard to such reactions among inorganic compounds. The essence of the matter may be expressed thus—two substances, A and B, do not react on each other of their own accord, but the addition of a small quantity of a third particularly active substance, C, produces the reaction of A on B, because A combines with C, forming AC, and B reacts on this new compound, which has a different store of chemical energy, forming the compound AB or its products, and setting C free again or retaining it.

It may here be remarked that all the mineral substances necessary for plants (those enumerated at the beginning of the note) are the highest saline compounds of their elements, that they enter into the plants as salts, that the lower forms of oxidation of the same elements (for instance, sulphites and phosphites) are harmful to plants (poisonous), and that strong solutions of the salts assimilated by plants (their osmotic pressure being great and contracting the cells, as De Vries showed, (*see* Chapter I., Note 19)) not only do not enter into the plants but kill them (poison them).

[8] Besides which, it will be understood from the preceding paragraph that the salts of potassium may become exhausted from the soil by long cultivation, and that there may therefore be cases when the direct fertilisation by salts of potassium may be profitable. But manure and animal excrements, ashes, and, in general, nearly all refuse which may serve for fertilising the soil, contain a considerable quantity of potassium salts, and therefore, as regards the natural salts of potassium (Stassfurt), and especially potassium sulphate, if they often improve the crops, it is in all probability due to their action on the properties of the soil. The agriculturist cannot therefore be advised to add potassium salts, without making special experiments showing the advantage of such a fertiliser on a given kind of soil and plant.

The animal body also contains potassium compounds, which is natural, since animals consume plants. For example, milk, and especially human milk, contains a somewhat considerable quantity of potassium compounds. Cow's milk, however, does not contain much potassium salt. Sodium compounds generally predominate in the bodies of animals. The excrement of animals, and especially of herbivorous animals, on the contrary, often contains a large proportion of potassium salts. Thus sheep's dung is rich in them, and in washing sheep's wool salts of potassium pass into the water.

The ash of tree stems, as the already dormant portion of the plant (Chapter VIII., Note 1), contains little potash. For the extraction of potash, which was formerly carried on extensively in the east of Russia (before the discovery of the Stassfurt salt), the ash of grasses, and the green portions of potatoes, buckwheat, &c., are taken and treated with water (lixiviated), the solution is evaporated, and the residue ignited in order to destroy the organic matter present in the extract. The residue thus obtained is composed of raw potash. It is refined by a second dissolution in a small quantity of water, for the potash itself is very soluble in water, whilst the impurities are sparingly soluble. The solution thus obtained is again evaporated, and the residue ignited, and this potash is then called refined potash, or pearlash. This method of treatment cannot give chemically pure potassium carbonate. A certain amount of impurities remain. To obtain chemically pure potassium carbonate, some other salt of potassium is generally taken and purified by crystallisation. Potassium carbonate crystallises with difficulty, and it cannot therefore be purified by this means, whilst other salts, such as the tartrate, acid carbonate, sulphate, or nitrate, &c., crystallise easily and may thus be directly purified. The tartrate is most frequently employed, since it is prepared in large quantities (as a sediment from wine) for medicinal use under the name of cream of tartar. When ignited without access of air, it leaves a mixture of charcoal and potassium carbonate. The charcoal so obtained being in a finely-divided condition, the mixture (called 'black flux'), is sometimes used for reducing metals from their oxides with the aid of heat. A certain quantity of nitre is added to burn the charcoal formed by heating the cream of tartar. Potassium carbonate thus prepared is further purified by converting it into the acid salt, by passing a current of carbonic anhydride through a strong solution. $KHCO_3$ is then formed, which is less soluble than the normal salt (as is also the case with the corresponding sodium salts), and therefore crystals of the acid salt separate from the solution on cooling. When ignited, they part with their water and carbonic anhydride, and pure potassium carbonate remains behind. The physical properties of potassium carbonate distinguish it sufficiently from sodium carbonate; it is obtained from solutions as a powdery white mass, having an alkaline taste and reaction, and, as a rule, shows only traces of crystallisation. It also attracts the moisture of the air with great energy. The crystals do not contain water, but absorb it from the air, deliquescing into a saturated solution. It melts at a red heat (1045°), and at a still higher temperature is even converted into vapour, as has been observed at glass works where it is employed. It is very soluble. At the ordinary temperature, water dissolves an equal weight of the salt. Crystals containing two equivalents of water separate from such a saturated solution when strongly cooled (Morel obtained $K_2CO_3 3H_2O$ in well-formed crystals at +10°). There is no necessity to describe its reactions, because they are all analogous to those of sodium carbonate. When manufactured sodium carbonate was but little known, the consumption of potassium carbonate was very considerable, and even now washing soda is frequently replaced for household purposes by 'lye'—*i.e.* an aqueous solution obtained from ashes. It contains potassium carbonate, which acts like the sodium salt in washing tissues, linen, &c.

A mixture of potassium and sodium carbonates fuses with much greater ease than the separate salts, and a mixture of their solutions gives well-crystallised salts—for instance (Marguerite's salt), $K_2CO_3,6H_2O,2Na_2CO_3,6H_2O$. Crystallisation also occurs in other multiple proportions of K and Na (in the above case 1 : 2, but 1 : 1 and 1 : 3 are known), and always with 6 mol. H_2O. This is evidently a combination *by similarity*, as in alloys, solutions, &c.

[8 bis] About 25,000 tons of potash annually are now prepared from KCl by this method at Stassfurt.

[9] *Potassium sulphate*, K_2SO_4, crystallises from its solutions in an anhydrous condition, in which respect it differs from the corresponding sodium salt, just as potassium carbonate differs from sodium carbonate. In general, it must be observed that the majority of sodium salts combine more easily with water of crystallisation than the potassium salts. The solubility of *potassium sulphate* does not show the same peculiarities as that of sodium sulphate, because it does not combine with water of crystallisation; at the ordinary temperature 100 parts of water dissolve about 10 parts of the salt, at 0° 8·3 parts, and at 100° about 26 parts. *The acid sulphate*, $KHSO_4$, obtained easily by heating crystals of the normal salt with sulphuric acid, is frequently employed in chemical practice. On heating the mixture of acid and salt, fumes of sulphuric acid are at first given off; when they cease to be evolved, the acid salt is contained in the residue. At a higher temperature (of above 600°) the acid salt parts with all the acid contained in it, the normal salt being re-formed. The definite composition of this acid salt, and the ease with which it decomposes, render it exceedingly valuable for certain chemical transformations accomplished by means of sulphuric acid at a high temperature, because it is possible to take, in the form of this salt, a strictly definite quantity of sulphuric acid, and to cause it to act on a given substance at a high temperature, which it is often necessary to do, more especially in chemical analysis. In this case, the acid salt acts in exactly the same manner as sulphuric acid itself, but the latter is inefficient at temperatures above 400°, because it all evaporates, while at that temperature the acid salt still remains in a fused state, and acts with the elements of sulphuric acid on the substance taken. Hence by its means the boiling-point of sulphuric acid is raised. Thus the acid potassium sulphate is employed, where for conversion

of certain oxides, such as those of iron, aluminium, and chromium, into salts, a high temperature is required.

Weber, by heating potassium sulphate with an excess of sulphuric acid at 100°, observed the formation of a lower stratum, which was found to contain a definite compound containing eight equivalents of SO_3 per equivalent of K_2O. The salts of rubidium, cæsium, and thallium give a similar result, but those of sodium and lithium do not. (*See* Note 1.)

[10] The *bromide* and *iodide* of potassium are used, like the corresponding sodium compounds, in medicine and photography. Potassium iodide is easily obtained in a pure state by saturating a solution of hydriodic acid with caustic potash. In practice, however, this method is rarely had recourse to, other more simple processes being employed although they do not give so pure a product. They aim at the direct formation of hydriodic acid in the liquid in the presence of potassium hydroxide or carbonate. Thus iodine is thrown into a solution of pure potash, and hydrogen sulphide passed through the mixture, the iodine being thus converted into hydriodic acid. Or a solution is prepared from phosphorus, iodine, and water, containing hydriodic and phosphoric acid; lime is then added to this solution, when calcium iodide is obtained in solution, and calcium phosphate as a precipitate. The solution of calcium iodide gives, with potassium carbonate, insoluble calcium carbonate and a solution of potassium iodide. If iodine is added to a slightly-heated solution of caustic potash (free from carbonate—that is, freshly prepared), so long as the solution is not coloured from the presence of an excess of iodine, there is formed (as in the action of chlorine on a solution of caustic potash) a mixture of potassium iodide and iodate. On evaporating the solution thus obtained and igniting the residue, the iodate is destroyed and converted into iodide, the oxygen being disengaged, and potassium iodide only is left behind. On dissolving the residue in water and then evaporating, cubical crystals of the anhydrous salt are obtained, which are soluble in water and alcohol, and on fusion give an alkaline reaction, owing to the fact that when ignited a portion of the salt decomposes, forming potassium oxide. The neutral salt may be obtained by adding hydriodic acid to this alkaline salt until it gives an acid reaction. It is best to add some finely-divided charcoal to the mixture of iodate and iodide before igniting it, as this facilitates the evolution of the oxygen from the iodate. The iodate may also be converted into iodide by the action of certain reducing agents, such as zinc amalgam, which when boiled with a solution containing an iodate converts it into iodide. Potassium iodide may also be prepared by mixing a solution of ferrous iodide (it is best if the solution contain an excess of iodine) and potassium carbonate, in which case ferrous carbonate $FeCO_3$, is precipitated (with an excess of iodine the precipitate is granular, and

contains a compound of the suboxide and oxide of iron), while potassium iodide remains in solution. Ferrous iodide, FeI_2, is obtained by the direct action of iodine on iron in water. Potassium iodide considerably lowers the temperature (by 24°), when it dissolves in water, 100 parts of the salt dissolve in 73·5 parts of water at 12·5°, in 70 parts at 18°, whilst the saturated solution which boils at 120° contains 100 parts of salt per 45 parts of water. Solutions of potassium iodide dissolve a considerable amount of iodine; strong solutions even dissolving as much or more iodine than they contain as potassium iodide (*see* Note 3 bis and Chapter XI., Note 64).

[11] Caustic potash is not only formed by the action of lime on dilute solutions of potassium carbonate (as sodium hydroxide is prepared from sodium carbonate), but by igniting potassium nitrate with finely-divided copper (*see* Note 15), and also by mixing solutions of potassium sulphate (or even of alum, $KAlS_2O_8$) and barium hydroxide, BaH_2O_2. It is sometimes purified by dissolving it in alcohol (the impurities, for example, potassium sulphate and carbonate, are not dissolved) and then evaporating the alcohol.

The specific gravity of potassium hydroxide is 2·04, but that of its solutions (see Chapter XII., Note 18) at 15° S = $9,992 + 90·4p + 0·28p^2$ (here p^2 is +, and for sodium hydroxide it is -). Strong solutions, when cooled, yield a crystallo-hydrate, $KHO,4H_2O$, which dissolves in water, producing cold (like $2NaHO,7H_2O$), whilst potassium hydroxide in solution develops a considerable amount of heat.

[12] When the yellow prussiate is heated to redness, all the cyanogen which was in combination with the iron is decomposed into nitrogen, which is evolved as gas, and carbon, which combines with the iron. In order to avoid this, potassium carbonate is added to the yellow prussiate while it is being fused. A mixture of 8 parts of anhydrous yellow prussiate and 3 parts of pure potassium carbonate is generally taken. Double decomposition then takes place, resulting in the formation of ferrous carbonate and potassium cyanide. But by this method, as by the first, a pure salt is not obtained, because a portion of the potassium cyanide is oxidised at the expense of the iron carbonate and forms potassium cyanate, $FeCO_3 + KCN = CO_2 + Fe + KCNO$; and the potassium cyanide very easily forms oxide, which acts on the sides of the vessel in which the mixture is heated (to avoid this iron vessels should be used). By adding one part of charcoal powder to the mixture of 8 parts of anhydrous yellow prussiate and 3 parts of potassium carbonate a mass is obtained which is free from cyanate, because the carbon absorbs the oxygen, but in that case it is impossible to obtain a colourless potassium cyanide by simple fusion, although this may be easily done by dissolving it in alcohol. Cyanide of

potassium may also be obtained from potassium thiocyanate, which is formed from ammonium thiocyanate obtained by the action of ammonia upon bisulphide of carbon (*see* works upon Organic Chemistry). Potassium cyanide is now prepared in large quantities from yellow prussiate for gilding and silvering. When fused in large quantities the action of the oxygen of the air is limited, and with great care the operation may be successfully conducted, and therefore, on a large scale, very pure salt is sometimes obtained. When slowly cooled, the fused salt separates in cubical crystals like potassium chloride.

Pure KCN is obtained by passing CNH gas into an alcoholic solution of KHO. The large amount of potassium cyanide which is now required for the extraction of gold from its ores, is being replaced by a mixture (Rossler and Gasslaker, 1892) of KCN and NaCN, prepared by heating powdered and dried yellow prussiate with metallic sodium: $K_4Fe(CN)_6 + 2Na = 4KCN + 2NaCN + Fe$. This method offers two advantages over the above methods: (1) the whole of the cyanide is obtained, and does not decompose with the formation of N_2; and (2) no cyanates are formed, as is the case when carbonate of potash is heated with the prussiate.

[13] A considerable quantity of potassium cyanide is used in the arts, more particularly for the preparation of metallic solutions which are decomposed by the action of a galvanic current; thus it is very frequently employed in electro-silvering and gilding. An alkaline solution is prepared, which is moderately stable owing to the fact that potassium cyanide in the form of certain double salts—that is, combined with other cyanides—is far more stable than when alone (yellow prussiate, which contains potassium cyanide in combination with ferrous cyanide, is an example of this).

[13 bis] A dilute solution of KCN is taken, not containing more than 1 per cent. KCN. MacLaurin explains this by the fact that strong solutions dissolve gold less rapidly, owing to their dissolving less air, whose oxygen is necessary for the reaction.

[14] Besides which Schloesing and Müntz, by employing similar methods to Pasteur, showed that the formation of nitre in the decomposition of nitrogenous substances is accomplished by the aid of peculiar micro-organisms (ferments), without which the simultaneous action of the other necessary conditions (alkalis, moisture, a temperature of 37°, air, and nitrogenous substances) cannot give nitre.

[14 bis] Before fusing, the crystals of potassium nitrate change their form, and take the same form as sodium nitrate—that is, they change into rhombohedra. Nitre crystallises from hot solutions, and in general under the influence of a rise of temperature, in a different form from that given at the ordinary or lower temperatures. Fused nitre solidifies to a radiated

crystalline mass; but it does not exhibit this structure if metallic chlorides be present, so that this method may be taken advantage of to determine the degree of purity of nitre.

Carnelley and Thomson (1888) determined the fusing point of mixtures of potassium and sodium nitrates. The first salt fuses at 339° and the second at 316°, and if p be the percentage amount of potassium nitrate, then the results obtained were—

$p = 10 \quad 20 \quad 30 \quad 40 \quad 50 \quad 60 \quad 70 \quad 80 \quad 90$

$298° \quad 283° \; 268° \; 242° \; 231° \; 231° \; 242° \; 284° \; 306°$

which confirms Shaffgotsch's observation (1857) that the lowest fusing point (about 231°) is given by mixing molecular quantities ($p = 54\cdot3$) of the salts—that is, in the formation of the alloy, $KNO_3, NaNO_3$.

A somewhat similar result was discovered by the same observers for the solubility of mixtures of these salts at 20° in 100 parts of water. Thus, if p be the weight of potassium nitrate mixed with $100 - p$ parts by weight of sodium nitrate taken for solution, and c be the quantity of the mixed salts which dissolves in 100, the solubility of sodium nitrate being 85, and of potassium nitrate 34, parts in 100 parts of water, then—

$p = 10 \quad 20 \quad 30 \quad 40 \quad 50 \; 60 \; 70 \; 80 \; 90$

$c = 110 \; 136 \; 136 \; 138 \; 106 \; 81 \; 73 \; 54 \; 41$

The maximum solubility proved not to correspond with the most fusible mixture, but to one much richer in sodium nitrate.

Both these phenomena show that in homogeneous liquid mixtures the chemical forces that act between substances are the same as those that determine the molecular weights of substances, even when the mixture consists of such analogous substances as potassium and sodium nitrates, between which there is no direct chemical interchange. It is instructive to note also that the maximum solubility does not correspond with the minimum fusing point, which naturally depends on the fact that in solution a third substance, namely water, plays a part, although an attraction between the salts, like that which exists between sodium and potassium carbonates (Note 8), also partially acts.

[15] Fused nitre, with a further rise of temperature, disengages oxygen and then nitrogen. The nitrite KNO_2 is first formed and then potassium oxide. The admixture of certain metals—for example, of finely-divided copper—aids the last decomposition. The oxygen in this case naturally passes over to the metal.

[16] In China, where the manufacture of gunpowder has long been carried on, 75·7 parts of nitre, 14·4 of charcoal, and 9·9 of sulphur are used. Ordinary powder for sporting purposes contains 80 parts of nitre, 12 of charcoal, and 8 of sulphur, whilst the gunpowder used in heavy ordnance contains 75 of nitre, 15 of charcoal, and 10 of sulphur. Gunpowder explodes when heated to 300°, when struck, or by contact with a spark. A compact or finely-divided mass of gunpowder burns slowly and has but little disruptive action, because it burns gradually. To act properly the gunpowder must have a definite rate of combustion, so that the pressure should increase during the passage of the projectile along the barrel of the fire-arm. This is done by making the powder in large granules or in the shape of six-sided prisms with holes through them (prismatic powder).

The products of combustion are of two kinds: (1) gases which produce the pressure and are the cause of the dynamical action of gunpowder, and (2) a solid residue, usually of a black colour owing to its containing unburnt particles of charcoal. Besides charcoal, the residue generally contains potassium sulphide, K_2S, and a whole series of other salts—for instance, carbonate and sulphate. It is apparent from this that the combustion of gunpowder is not so simple as it appears to be from the above formula, and hence the weight of the residue is also greater than indicated by that formula. According to the formula, 270 parts of gunpowder give 110 parts of residue—that is, 100 parts of powder give 37·4 parts of residue, K_2S, whilst in reality the weight of the residue varies from 40 p.c. to 70 p.c. (generally 52 p.c.). This difference depends on the fact that so much oxygen (of the nitre) remains in the residue, and it is evident that if the residue varies the composition of the gases evolved by the powder will vary also, and therefore the entire process will be different in different cases. The difference in the composition of the gases and residue depends, as the researches of Gay-Lussac, Shishkoff and Bunsen, Nobel and Abel, Federoff, Debus, &c., show, on the conditions under which the combustion of the powder proceeds. When gunpowder burns in an open space, the gaseous products which are formed do not remain in contact with the residue, and then a considerable portion of the charcoal entering into the composition of the powder remains unburnt, because the charcoal burns after the sulphur at the expense of the oxygen of the nitre. In this extreme case the commencement of the combustion of the gunpowder may be expressed by the equation, $2KNO_3 + 3C + S = 2C + K_2SO_4 + CO_2 + N_2$. The residue in a blank cartridge often consists of a mixture of C, K_2SO_4, K_2CO_3, and $K_2S_2O_3$. If the combustion of the gunpowder be impeded—if it take place in a cartridge in the barrel of a gun—the quantity of potassium sulphate will first be diminished, then the amount of sulphite, whilst the amount of carbonic anhydride in the gases and the amount of potassium sulphide in the residue will increase. The quantity of charcoal entering into the action will then be also increased, and hence the amount in the residue will decrease. Under these circumstances the weight of the residue will be less—for example, $4K_2CO_3 + 4S = K_2SO_4 + 3K_2S + 4CO_2$. Besides which, carbonic oxide has been found in the gases, and potassium bisulphide, K_2S_2, in the residue of gunpowder. The amount of potassium sulphide, K_2S, increases with the completeness of the combustion, and is formed in the residue at the expense of the potassium sulphite. In recent times the knowledge of the action of gunpowder and other explosives has made much progress, and has developed into a vast province of artillery science, which, guided by the discoveries of chemistry, has worked out a 'smokeless powder' which burns without leaving a residue, and does not therefore give any 'powder smoke' (to hinder the rapidity of firing and aiming), and at the same time disengages a greater volume of gas and consequently gives (under proper conditions of combustion) the possibility of communicating to the charge a greater initial velocity, and therefore greater distance, force, and accuracy of aim. Such 'smokeless powder' is prepared either from the varieties of nitrocellulose (Chapter VI., Note [37]) or from a mixture of them with nitro-glycerine (*ibid*). In burning they give, besides steam and nitrogen, generally a large amount of oxide of carbon (this is a very serious drawback in all the present forms of smokeless powder, because carbonic oxide is poisonous), and also CO_2, H_2, &c.

[17] The substances obtained in this case are mentioned in Chapter IX., Note [31].

[18] A. Scott (1887) determined the vapour densities of many of the alkali elements and their compounds in a platinum vessel heated in a furnace and previously filled with nitrogen. But these, the first data concerning a subject of great importance, have not yet been sufficiently fully described, nor have they received as much attention as could be desired. Taking the density of hydrogen as unity, Scott found the vapour densities of the following substances to be—

Na   12·75 (11·5).   KI   92 (84).

K   19   (19·5).   RbCl   70 (60).

CsCl   89·5 (84·2).   CsI   133 (130).

FeCl₃ 68.   AgCl   80 (71·7).

In brackets are given the densities corresponding with the formulæ, according to Avogadro-Gerhardt's law. This figure is not given for FeCl₃, because in all probability under these conditions (the temperature at which it was determined) a portion of the FeCl₃ was decomposed. If it was not decomposed, then a density 81 would correspond with the formula $FeCl_3$, and if the decomposition were $Fe_2Cl_6 = 2FeCl_2 + Cl_2$, then the density should be 54. With regard to the silver chloride, there is reason to think that the platinum decomposed this salt. The majority of Scott's results so closely correspond with the formulæ that a better concord cannot be expected in such determinations. V. Meyer (1887) gives 93 as the density of KI.

[19] The molecules of non-metals are more complex—for instance, H_2, O_3, Cl_2, &c. But arsenic, whose superficial appearance recalls that of metals, but whose chemical properties approach more nearly to the non-metals, has a complex molecule containing As_4.

[20] As the atomic weight of potassium is greater than that of sodium, the volumes of the molecules, or the quotients of the molecular weight by the specific gravity, for potassium compounds are greater than those of sodium compounds, because both the denominator and numerator of the fraction increase. We cite for comparison the volumes of the corresponding compounds—

Na 24 NaHO 18 NaCl 28 $NaNO_3$ 37 Na_2SO_4 54

K 45 KHO 27 KCl 39 KNO_3 48 K_2SO_4 66

[21] The same precautions must be taken in decomposing water by potassium as have to be observed with sodium (Chapter II., Note 8).

It must be observed that potassium decomposes carbonic anhydride and carbonic oxide when heated, the carbon being liberated and the oxygen taken up by the metal, whilst on the other hand charcoal takes up oxygen from potassium, as is seen from the preparation of potassium by heating potash with charcoal, hence the reaction $K_2O + C = K_2 + CO$ is reversible and the relation is the same in this case as between hydrogen and zinc.

[22] *Potassium* forms *alloys with sodium* in all proportions. The alloys containing 1 and 3 equivalents of potassium to one equivalent of sodium are *liquids*, like mercury at the ordinary temperature. Joannis, by determining the amount of heat developed by these alloys in decomposing water, found the evolution for Na_2K, NaK, NaK_2 and NaK_3 to be 44·5, 44·1, 43·8 and 44·4 thousand heat units respectively (for Na 42·6 and for K 45·4). The formation of the alloy NaK_2 is therefore accompanied by the development of heat, whilst the other alloys may be regarded as solutions of potassium or sodium in this alloy. In any case a fall of the temperature of fusion is evident in this instance as in the alloys of nitre (Note 14). The liquid alloy NaK_2 is now used for filling thermometers employed for temperatures above 360°, when mercury boils.

[23] For accurate measurements and comparative researches more complicated spectroscopes are required which give a greater dispersion, and are furnished for this purpose with several prisms—for example, in Browning's spectroscope the light passes through six prisms, and then, having undergone an internal total reflection, passes through the upper portion of the same six prisms, and again by an internal total reflection passes into the ocular tube. With such a powerful dispersion the relative position of the spectral lines may be determined with accuracy. For the absolute and exact determination of the wave lengths it is particularly important that the spectroscope should be furnished with diffraction gratings. The construction of spectroscopes destined for special purposes (for example, for investigating the light of stars, or for determining the absorption spectra in microscopic preparations, &c.) is exceedingly varied. Details of the subject must be looked for in works on physics and on spectrum analysis. Among the latter the best known for their completeness and merit are those of Roscoe, Kayser, Vogel, and Lecoq de Boisbaudran.

[24] The arrangement of all the parts of the apparatus so as to give the clearest possible vision and accuracy of observation must evidently precede every kind of spectroscopic determination. Details concerning the practical use of the spectroscope must be looked for in special works on the subject. In this treatise the reader is supposed to have a certain knowledge of the physical data respecting the refraction of light, and its dispersion and diffraction, and the theory of light, which allows of the determination of the length of the waves of light in absolute measure on the basis of observations with diffraction gratings, the distance between whose divisions may be easily measured in fractions of a millimetre; by such means it is possible to determine the wave-length of any given ray of light.

[25] In order to give an idea of the size of the scale, we may observe that the ordinary spectrum extends from the zero of the scale (where the red portion is situated) to the 170th division (where the end of the visible violet portion of the spectrum is situated), and that the Fraunhofer line A (the extreme prominent line in the red) corresponds with the 17th division of the scale; the Fraunhofer line F (at the beginning of the blue, near the green colour) is situated on the 90th division, and the line G, which is clearly seen in the beginning of the violet portion of the spectrum, corresponds with the 127th division of the scale.

[26] The two most distinct lines of D, or of sodium, have wave-lengths of 589·5 and 588·9 millionths of a millimeter, besides which fainter and fainter lines are seen whose wave-lengths in millionths of a millimeter are 588·7 and 588·1, 616·0 and 615·4, 515·5 and 515·2, 498·3 and 498·2, &c., according to Liveing and Dewar.

[26 bis] In the ordinary spectroscopes which are usually employed in chemical research, one yellow band, which does not split up into thinner lines, is seen instead of the system of sodium lines, owing to the small dispersive power of the prism and the width of the slit of the object tube.

[27] The most accurate investigations made in this respect are carried on with spectra obtained by diffraction, because in this case the position of the dark and bright lines does not depend on the index of refraction of the material of the prism, nor on the dispersive power of the apparatus. The best—that is, the most general and accurate—method of expressing the results of such determinations consists in determining the lengths of the waves corresponding to the rays of a definite index of refraction. (Sometimes instead of this the fraction of 1 divided by the square of the wave-length is given.) We will express this *wave-length* in *millionth parts of a millimetre* (the ten-millionth parts are already doubtful, and fall within the limits of error). In order to illustrate the relation between the wave-lengths and the positions of the lines of the spectrum, we will cite the wave-lengths corresponding with the chief Fraunhofer lines and colours of the spectrum.

Fraunhofer line	A	B	C	D	E	b	F	G	H
Wave-length	761·0	687·5	656·6	589·5 – 588·9	527·3	518·7	486·5	431·0	397·2
Colour		red		orange	yellow	green	blue		violet

In the following table are given the *wave-lengths* of the light rays (the longest and most distinct, *see* later) for certain elements, those in black type being the most clearly defined and distinct lines, which are easily obtained either in the flame of a Bunsen's burner, or in Geissler's tubes, or in general, by an electric discharge. These lines refer to the elements (the lines of compounds are different, as will be afterwards explained, but many compounds are decomposed by the flame or by an electric discharge), and moreover to the elements in an incandescent and rarefied gaseous state, for the spectra sometimes vary considerably with a variation of temperature and pressure.

It may be mentioned that the *red* colour corresponds with lines having a wave-length of from 780 (with a greater wave-length the lines are hardly visible, and are ultra red) to 650, the *orange* from 650 to 590, the *yellow* from 590 to 520, the *green* from 520 to 490, the *blue* from 490 to 420, and the

N₂	O₂	Cl₂	Br₂	I₂	Pb	Sn	Tl	In	Ga	Al	Ba	Sr	Ca	Mg	Zn	Cd	Hg	Mn	Fe
—	—	—	—	—	—	—	—	—	—	—	—	—	—	—	—	—	—	—	—
662													646						
632			636		645				624	649·7	641		644		636	643·8			640
620	615			621				619	623	614	606					615	602		
585				613	605·7	580					612				—	579	601		561
574		546		579	560·7	556			572	553·5					—	577	551		544
544	543	539	544	560	554·7		549		570	549	548	559				537·7	546 534		537
535	533	528	523	545	537		535	525				524				533·6			532
527	516	519	517	506										518	492	508·5			521
516	495	494	479				489			493·3				516			482		496
—	494	480	470											481			171		489
457	470	462		452				451	466		455	460		471	472	479·9	468 467·7		
442	465	454	445										115	118					441
436	447	436	437										412				436		430
426	432	431									130		121 123						427
			421				417			413						121	121		107
409				406			410	403	396		408	397	384	404				401
									394			393	383					

In the table (p. 565) which is arranged in conformity with the image of the spectrum as it is seen (the red lines on the left-hand and the violet on the right-hand side), the figures in black type correspond with lines which are so bright and distinctly visible that they may easily be made use of, both in determining the relation between the divisions of the scale and the wave-lengths, and in determining the admixture of a given element with another. Brackets join those lines between which several other lines are clearly visible if the dispersive power of the spectroscope permits distinguishing the neighbouring lines. In the ordinary laboratory spectroscopes with one prism, even with all possible precision of arrangement and with a brilliancy of light permitting the observations being made with a very narrow aperture, the lines whose wave-lengths only differ by 2–3 millionths of a millimetre, are blurred together; and with a wide aperture a series of lines differing by even as much as 20 millionths of a millimetre appear as one wide line. With a faint light (that is, with a small quantity of light entering into the spectroscope) only the most *brilliant* lines are clearly visible. The *length* of the lines does not always correspond with their brilliancy. According to Lockyer this length is determined by placing the carbon electrodes (between which the incandescent vapours of the metals are formed), not horizontally to the slit (as they are generally placed, to give more light), but vertically to it. Then certain lines appear long and others short. As a rule (Lockyer, Dewar, Cornu), the longest lines are those with which it is easiest to obtain *reversed* spectra (*see* later). Consequently, these lines are the most characteristic. Only the longest and most brilliant are given in our table, which is composed on the basis of a collection of the data at our disposal for *bright* spectra of the *incandescent and rarefied vapours of the elements.* As the spectra change with great variations of temperature and vapour density (the faint lines become brilliant whilst the bright lines sometimes disappear), which is particularly clear from Ciamician's researches on the halogens, until the method of observation and the theory of the subject are enlarged, particular theoretical importance should not be given to the wave-lengths showing the maximum brilliancy, which only possess a practical significance in the common methods of spectroscopic observations. In general the spectra of metals are simpler than those of the halogens, and the latter are variable; at an increased pressure all spectral lines become broader.

[28] The method of observing absorption spectra consists in taking a continuous spectrum of white light (one which does not show either dark lines or particularly bright luminous bands—for instance, the light of a candle, lamp, or other source). The collimator (that is, the tube with the slit) is directed towards this light, and then all the colours of the spectrum are visible in the ocular tube. A transparent absorptive medium—for instance, a solution or tube containing a gas—is then placed between the source of light and the apparatus (or anywhere inside the apparatus itself in the path of the rays). In this case either the entire spectrum is uniformly fainter, or absorption bands appear on the bright field of the continuous spectrum in definite positions along it. These bands have different lengths and positions, and distinctness and intensity of absorption, according to the properties of the absorptive medium. Like the luminous spectra given by incandescent gases and vapours, the absorption spectra of a number of substances have already been studied, and some with great precision—as, for example, the spectrum of the brown vapours of nitrogen dioxide by Hasselberg (at Pulkowa), the spectra of colouring matters (Eder and others), especially of those applied to orthochromatic photography, the spectra of blood, chlorophyll (the green constituent of leaves), and other similar substances, all the more carefully as by the aid of their spectra the presence of these substances may be discovered in small quantities (even in microscopical quantities, by the aid of special appliances on the microscope), and the changes they undergo investigated.

FIG. 74.—Absorption spectra of nitrogen dioxide and iodine.

The absorption spectra, obtained at the ordinary temperature and proper to substances in all physical states, offer a most extensive but as yet little studied field, both for the general theory of spectroscopy, and for gaining an insight into the structure of substances. The investigation of colouring matters has already shown that in certain cases a definite change of composition and structure entails not only a definite change of the colours but also a displacement of the absorption bands by a definite number of wave-lengths.

[29] A number of methods have been invented to demonstrate the reversibility of spectra; among these methods we will cite two which are very easily carried out. In Bunsen's method sodium chloride is put into an apparatus for evolving hydrogen (the spray of the salt is then carried off by the hydrogen and colours the flame with the yellow sodium colour), and the hydrogen is ignited in two burners—in one large one with a wide flame giving a bright yellow sodium light, and in another with a small fine orifice whose flame is pale: this flame will throw a dark patch on the large bright flame. In Ladoffsky's method the front tube (p. 561) is unscrewed from a spectroscope directed towards the light of a lamp (a continuous spectrum), and the flame of a spirit lamp coloured by a small quantity of NaCl is placed between the tube and the prism; a black band corresponding to sodium will then be seen on looking through the ocular tube. This experiment is always successful if only there be the requisite relation between the strength of light of the two lamps.

[30] The absorptive capacity is the relation between the intensity of the light (of a given wave-length) falling upon and retained by a substance. Bunsen and Roscoe showed by direct experiment that this ratio is a constant quantity for every substance. If A stand for this ratio for a given

substance at a given temperature—for instance, for a flame coloured by sodium—and E be the intensity of the light of the same wave-length emitted at the same temperature by the same substance, then Kirchhoff's law, the explanation and deduction of which must be looked for in text-books of physics, states that the fraction A/E is a constant quantity depending on the nature of a substance (as A depends on it) and determined by the temperature and wave-length.

[31] Heated metals begin to emit light (only visible in the dark) at about 420° (varying with the metal). On further heating, solids first emit red, then yellow, and lastly white light. Compressed or heavy gases (*see* Chapter III., Note 44), when strongly heated, also emit white light. Heated liquids (for example, molten steel or platinum) also give a white compound light. This is readily understood. In a dense mass of matter the collisions of the molecules and atoms are so frequent that waves of only a few definite lengths cannot appear; the reverse is possible in rarefied gases or vapours.

[32] Brewster, as is mentioned above, first distinguished the atmospheric, cosmical Fraunhofer lines from the solar lines. Janssen showed that the spectrum of the atmosphere contains lines which depend on the absorption produced by aqueous vapour. Egoreff, Olszewski, Janssen, and Liveing and Dewar showed by a series of experiments that the oxygen of the atmosphere gives rise to certain lines of the solar spectrum, especially the line A. Liveing and Dewar took a layer of 165 c.m. of oxygen compressed under a pressure of 85 atmospheres, and determined its absorption spectrum, and found that, besides the Fraunhofer lines A and B, it contained the following groups: 630–622, 581–568, 535, 480–475. The same lines were found for liquid oxygen.

[32 bis] If the material of the whole heavenly space formed the absorbent medium, the spectra of the stars would be the same as the solar spectrum; but Huyghens, Lockyer, and others showed not only that this is the case for only a few stars, but that the majority of stars give spectra of a different character with dark and bright lines and bands.

[33] Eruptions, like our volcanic eruptions, but on an incomparably larger scale, are of frequent occurrence on the sun. They are seen as protuberances visible during a total eclipse of the sun, in the form of vaporous masses on the edge of the solar disc and emitting a faint light. These protuberances of the sun are now observed at all times by means of the spectroscope (Lockyer's method), because they contain luminous vapours (giving bright lines) of hydrogen and other elements.

[34] The great interest and vastness of astro-physical observations concerning the sun, comets, stars, nebulæ, &c., render this new province of

natural science very important, and necessitate referring the reader to special works on the subject.

The most important astro-physical data since the time of Kellner are those referring to the *displacement* of the lines of the spectrum. Just as a musical note changes its pitch with the approach or withdrawal of the resonant object or the ear, so the pitch of the luminous note or wave-length of the light varies if the luminous (or absorbent) vapour and the earth from which we observe it approach or recede from each other; this expresses itself in a visible displacement of the spectral lines. The solar eruptions even give broken lines in the spectrum, because the rapidly moving eruptive masses of vapour and gases either travel in the direction of the eye or fall back towards the sun. As the earth travels with the solar system among the stars, so it is possible to determine the direction and velocity with which the sun travels in space by the displacement of the spectral lines and light of the stars. The changes proceeding on the sun in its mass, which must be pronounced as vaporous, and in its atmosphere, are now studied by means of the spectroscope. For this purpose, many special astro-physical observatories now exist where these investigations are carried on.

We may remark that if the observer or luminous object moves with a velocity $\pm v$, the ray, whose wave-length is λ, has an apparent wave-length $\lambda \dfrac{n\pm v}{n}$, where n is the velocity of light. Thus Tolon, Huyghens, and others proved that the star Aldebaran approaches the solar system with a velocity of 30 kilometres per second, while Arcturus is receding with a velocity of 45 kilometres. The majority of stars give a distinct hydrogen spectrum, besides which nebulæ also give the spectrum of nitrogen. Lockyer classes the stars from their spectra, according to their period of formation, showing that some stars are in a period of increasing temperature (of formation or aggregation), whilst others are in a period of cooling. Altogether, in the astro-physical investigation of the spectra of heavenly bodies we find one of the most interesting subjects of recent science.

[35] Spectrum analysis has proved the indubitable existence in the sun and stars of a number of elements known in chemistry. Huyghens, Secchi, Lockyer, and others have furnished a large amount of material upon this subject. A compilation of existing information on it has been given by Prof. S. A. Kleiber, in the Journal of the Russian Physico-chemical Society for 1885 (vol. xviii. p. 146). Besides which, a peculiar element called helium has been discovered, which is characterised by a line (whose wave-length is 587·5, situated near D), which is seen very brightly in the projections (protuberances) and spots of the sun, but which does not belong to any known element, and is not reproducible as a reversed, dark line. This may be a right conclusion—that is to say, it is possible that an element may be

discovered to which the spectrum of helium corresponds—but it may be that the helium line belongs to one of the known elements, because spectra vary in the brilliancy and position of their lines with changes of temperature and pressure. Thus, for instance, Lockyer could only see the line 423, at the very end of the calcium spectrum, at comparatively low temperatures, whilst the lines 397 and 393 appear at a higher temperature, and at a still higher temperature the line 423 becomes quite invisible.

[36]

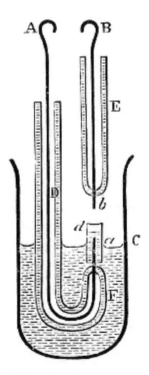

FIG. 76.—Method of showing the spectrum of substances in solution.

Spectroscopic observations are still further complicated by the fact that one and the same substance gives different spectra at different temperatures. This is especially the case with gases whose spectra are obtained by an electric discharge in tubes. Plücker, Wüllner, Schuster, and others showed that at low temperatures and pressures the spectra of iodine, sulphur, nitrogen, oxygen, &c. are quite different from the spectra of the same elements at high temperatures and pressures. This may either depend on the fact that the elements change their molecular structure with a change of temperature, just as ozone is converted into oxygen (for instance, from N_2 molecules are obtained containing only one atom of nitrogen), or else it may be because at low temperature certain rays have a greater relative intensity than those which appear at higher temperatures. If we suppose that the molecules of a gas are in continual motion, with a velocity dependent on the temperature, then it must be admitted that they often strike against each other and rebound, and thus communicate peculiar motions to each other and the supposed ether, which express themselves in luminiferous phenomena. A rise of the temperature or an increase in the density of a gas must have an influence on the collision of its molecules and luminiferous motions thus produced, and this may be the cause of the difference of the spectra under these circumstances. It has been shown by direct experiment that gases compressed by pressure, when the collision of the molecules must be frequent and varied, exhibit a more complex spectrum on the passage of an electric spark than rarefied gases, and that even a continuous spectrum appears. In order to show the variability of the spectrum according to the circumstances under which it proceeds, it may be mentioned that potassium sulphate fused on a platinum wire gives, on the passage of a series of sparks, a distinct system of lines, 583–578, whilst when a series of sparks is passed through a solution of this salt this system of lines is faint, and when Roscoe and Schuster observed the absorption spectrum of the vapour of metallic potassium (which is green) they remarked a number of lines of the same intensity as the above system in the red, orange, and yellow portions.

The spectra of solutions are best observed by means of Lecoq de Boisbaudran's arrangement, shown in fig. 76. A bent capillary tube, D F, inside which a platinum wire, A a (from 0·3 to 0·5 mm. in diameter) is fused, is immersed in a narrow cylinder, C (in which it is firmly held by a cork). The projecting end, a, of the wire is covered by a fine capillary tube, d, which extends 1–2 mm. beyond the wire. Another straight capillary tube, E, with a platinum wire, B b, about 1 mm. in diameter (a finer wire soon becomes hot), is held (by a cork or in a stand) above the end of the tube, D. If the wire A be now connected with the positive, and the wire B with the negative terminal of a Ruhmkorff's coil (if the wires be connected in the opposite order, the spectrum of air is obtained), a series of sparks rapidly following each other appear between a and b, and their light may be examined by placing the apparatus in front of the slit of a spectroscope. The variations to which a spectrum is liable may easily be observed by increasing the distance between the wires, altering the direction of the current or strength of the solution, &c.

[37] The importance of the spectroscope for the purpose of chemical research was already shown by Gladstone in 1856, but it did not become an accessory to the laboratory until after the discoveries of Kirchhoff and

Bunsen. It may be hoped that in time spectroscopic researches will meet certain wants of the theoretical (philosophical) side of chemistry, but as yet all that has been done in this respect can only be regarded as attempts which have not yet led to any trustworthy conclusions. Thus many investigators, by collating the wave-lengths of all the light vibrations excited by a given element, endeavour to find the law governing their mutual relations; others (especially Hartley and Ciamician), by comparing the spectra of analogous elements (for instance, chlorine, bromine, and iodine), have succeeded in noticing definite features of resemblance in them, whilst others (Grünwald) search for relations between the spectra of compounds and their component elements, &c.; but—owing to the multiplicity of the spectral lines proper to many elements, and (especially in the ultra-red and ultra-violet ends of the spectrum) the existence of lines which are undistinguishable owing to their faintness, and also owing to the comparative novelty of spectroscopic research—this subject cannot be considered as in any way perfected. Nevertheless, in certain instances there is evidently some relationship between the wave-lengths of all the spectral lines formed by a given element. Thus, in the hydrogen spectrum the wave-length $= 364 \cdot 542 \, m^2 / (m^2 - 4)$, if m varies as a series of whole numbers from 3 to 15 (Walmer, Hagebach, and others). For example, when $m = 3$, the wave-length of one of the brightest lines of the hydrogen spectrum is obtained ($656 \cdot 2$), when $m = 7$, one of the visible violet lines ($396 \cdot 8$), and when m is greater than 9, the ultra-violet lines of the hydrogen spectrum.

[38] In order to show the degree of sensitiveness of spectroscopic reactions the following observation of Dr. Bence Jones may be cited: If a solution of 3 grains of a lithium salt be injected under the skin of a guinea-pig, after the lapse of four minutes, lithium can be discovered in the bile and liquids of the eye, and, after ten minutes, in all parts of the animal.

[39] Thus *spodumene* contains up to 6 p.c. of lithium oxide, and *petolite*, and *lepidolite* or lithia mica, about 3 p.c. of lithium oxide. This mica is met with in certain granites in a somewhat considerable quantity, and is therefore most frequently employed for the preparation of lithium compounds. The treatment of lepidolite is carried on on a large scale, because certain salts of lithium are employed in medicine as a remedy for certain diseases (stone, gouty affections), as they have the power of dissolving the insoluble uric acid which is then deposited. Lepidolite, which is unacted on by acids in its natural state, decomposes under the action of strong hydrochloric acid after it has been fused. After being subjected to the action of the hydrochloric acid for several hours all the silica is obtained in an insoluble form, whilst the metallic oxides pass into solution as chlorides. This solution is mixed with nitric acid to convert the ferrous salts into ferric, and sodium carbonate is then added until the liquid

becomes neutral, by which means a precipitate is formed of the oxides of iron, alumina, magnesia, &c., as insoluble oxides and carbonates. The solution (with an excess of water) then contains the chlorides of the alkaline metals KCl, NaCl, LiCl, which do not give a precipitate with sodium carbonate in a dilute solution. It is then evaporated, and a strong solution of sodium carbonate added. This precipitates lithium carbonate, which, although soluble in water, is much less so than sodium carbonate, and therefore the latter precipitates lithium from strong solutions as carbonate, $2LiCl + Na_2CO_3 = 2NaCl + Li_2CO_3$. *Lithium carbonate*, which resembles sodium carbonate in many respects, is a substance which is very slightly soluble in cold water and is only moderately soluble in boiling water. In this respect lithium forms a transition between the metals of the alkalis and other metals, especially those of the alkaline earths (magnesium, barium), whose carbonates are only sparingly soluble. Oxide of lithium, Li_2O, may be obtained by heating lithium carbonate with charcoal. Lithium oxide in dissolving gives (per gram-molecule) 26,000 heat units; but the combination of Li_2 with O evolves 140,000 calories—that is, more than Na_2O (100,000 calories) and K_2O (97,000 calories), as shown by Beketoff (1887). Oeuvrard (1892) heated lithium to redness in nitrogen, and observed the absorption of N and formation of Li_3N, like Na_3N (*see* Chapter XII. Note 50).

LiCl, LiBr, and LiI form crystallo-hydrates with H_2O, $2H_2O$, and $3H_2O$. As a rule, $LiBr,2H_2O$ crystallises out, but Bogorodsky (1894) showed that a solution containing $LiBr + 3\cdot7H_2O$, cooled to -62°, separates out crystals $LiBr,3H_2O$, which decompose at +4° with the separation of H_2O. LiF is but slightly soluble (in 800 parts) in water (and still less so in a solution of NH_4F).

[39 bis] Guntz (1893) recommends adding KCl to the LiCl in preparing Li by this method, and to act with a current of 10 ampères at 20 volts, and not to heat above 450°, so as to avoid the formation of Li_2Cl.

[40] In determining the presence of lithium in a given compound, it is best to treat the material under investigation with acid (in the case of mineral silicon compounds hydrofluoric acid must be taken), and to treat the residue with sulphuric acid, evaporate to dryness, and extract with alcohol, which dissolves a certain amount of the lithium sulphate. It is easy to discover lithium in such an alcoholic solution by means of the coloration imparted to the flame on burning it, and in case of doubt by investigating its light in a spectroscope, because lithium gives a red line, which is very characteristic and is found as a dark line in the solar spectrum. Lithium was first discovered in 1817 in petolite by Arfvedson.

[41] The salts of the majority of metals are precipitated as carbonates on the addition of ammonium carbonate—for instance, the salts of calcium, iron, &c. The alkalis whose carbonates are soluble are not, however, precipitated in this case. On evaporating the resultant solution and igniting the residue (to remove the ammonium salts), we obtain salts of the alkali metals. They may he separated by adding hydrochloric acid together with a solution of platinic chloride. The chlorides of lithium and sodium give easily soluble double salts with platinic chloride, whilst the chlorides of potassium, rubidium, and cæsium form double salts which are sparingly soluble. A hundred parts of water at $0°$ dissolve $0·74$ part of the potassium platinochloride; the corresponding rubidium platinochloride is only dissolved to the amount of $0·134$ part, and the cæsium salt, $0·024$ part; at $100°$ $5·13$ parts of potassium platinochloride, K_2PtCl_6, are dissolved, $0·634$ part of rubidium platinochloride, and $0·177$ part of cæsium platinochloride. From this it is clear how the salts of rubidium and cæsium may be isolated. The separation of cæsium from rubidium by this method is very tedious. It can be better effected by taking advantage of the difference of the solubility of their carbonates in alcohol; cæsium carbonate, Cs_2CO_3, is soluble in alcohol, whilst the corresponding salts of rubidium and potassium are almost insoluble. Setterberg separated these metals as alums, but the best method, that given by Scharples, is founded on the fact that from a mixture of the chlorides of potassium, sodium, cæsium, and rubidium in the presence of hydrochloric acid, stannic chloride precipitates a double salt of cæsium, which is very slightly soluble. The salts of Rb and Cs are closely analogous to those of potassium.

[42] Bunsen obtained rubidium by distilling a mixture of the tartrate with soot, and Beketoff (1888) by heating the hydroxide with aluminium, $2RbHO + Al = RbAlO_2 + H_2 + Rb$. By the action of 85 grams of rubidium on water, 94,000 heat units are evolved. Setterberg obtained cæsium (1882) by the electrolysis of a fused mixture of cyanide of cæsium and of barium. Winkler (1890) showed that metallic magnesium reduces the hydrates and carbonates of Rb and Cs like the other alkaline metals. N. N. Beketoff obtained them with aluminium (see following note).

[42 bis] Beketoff (1888) showed that metallic aluminium reduces the hydrates of the alkaline metals at a red heat (they should be perfectly dry) with the formation of aluminates (Chapter XVII.), $RAlO_2$—for example, $2KHO + Al = KAlO_2 + K + H_2$. It is evident that in this case only half of the alkaline metal is obtained free. On the other hand, K. Winkler (1889) showed that magnesium powder is also able to reduce the alkaline metals from their hydrates and carbonates. N. N. Beketoff and Tscherbacheff (1894) prepared cæsium upon this principle by heating its aluminate $CsAlO_2$ with magnesium powder. In this case aluminate of magnesium is

formed, and the whole of the cæsium is obtained as metal: $2CsAlO_2 + Mg = MgOAl_2O_5 + 2Cs$. A certain excess of alumina was taken (in order to obtain a less hygroscopic mass of aluminate), and magnesium powder (in order to decompose the last traces of water); the $CsAlO_2$ was prepared by the precipitation of cæsium alums by caustic baryta, and evaporating the resultant solution. We may add that N. N. Beketoff (1887) prepared oxide of potassium, K_2O, by heating the peroxide, KO, in the vapour of potassium (disengaged from its alloy with silver), and showed that in dissolving in an excess of water it evolves (for the above-given molecular weight) 67,400 calories (while $2KHO$ in dissolving in water evolves 24,920 cal.; so that $K_2O + H_2O$ gives 42,480 cal.), whence (knowing that $K_2 + O + H_2O$ in an excess of water evolves 164,500) it follows that $K_2 + O$ evolves 97,100 cal. This quantity is somewhat less than that (100,260 cal.) which corresponds to sodium, and the energy of the action of potassium upon water is explained by the fact that K_2O evolves more heat than Na_2O in combining with water (*see* Chapter II. Note 9). Just as hydrogen displaces half the Na from Na_2O forming $NaHO$, so also N. N. Beketoff found from experiment and thermochemical reasonings that hydrogen displaces half the potassium from K_2O forming KHO and evolving 7,190 calories. Oxide of lithium, Li_2O, which is easily formed by igniting Li_2CO_3 with carbon (when $Li_2O + 2CO$ is formed), disengages 26,000 cals. with an excess of water, while the reaction $Li_2 + O$ gives 114,000 cals. and the reaction $Li_2 + H_2O$ gives only 13,000 cals., and metallic lithium cannot be liberated from oxide of lithium with hydrogen (nor with carbon). Thus in the series Li, Na, K, the formation of R_2O gives most heat with Li and least with K, while the formation of RCl evolves most heat with K (105,000 cals.) and least of all with Li (93,500 cals.). Rubidium, in forming Rb_2O, gives 94,000 cals. (Beketoff). Cæsium, in acting upon an excess of water, evolves 51,500 cals., and the reaction $Cs_2 + O$ evolves about 100,000 cals.—*i.e.* more than K and Rb, and almost as much as Na—and oxide of cæsium reacts with hydrogen (according to the equation $Cs_2O + H = CsHO + Cs$) more easily than any of the oxides of the alkali metals, and this reaction takes place at the ordinary temperature (the hydrogen is absorbed), as Beketoff showed (1893). He also obtained a mixed oxide, $AgCsO$, which was easily formed in the presence of silver, and absorbed hydrogen with the formation of $CsHO$.

[43] We may here observe that the halogens, and especially iodine, may play the part of metals (hence iodine is more easily replaced by metals than the other halogens, and it approaches nearer to the metals in its physical properties than the other halogens). Schützenberger obtained a compound $C_2H_3O(OCl)$, which he called chlorine acetate, by acting on acetic anhydride, $(C_2H_3O)_2O$, with chlorine monoxide, Cl_2O. With iodine this compound gives off chlorine and forms iodine acetate, $C_2H_3O(OI)$, which

also is formed by the action of iodine chloride on sodium acetate, $C_2H_3O(ONa)$. These compounds are evidently nothing else than mixed anhydrides of hypochlorous and hypoiodous acids, or the products of the substitution of hydrogen in RHO by a halogen (*see* Chapter XI., Notes 29 and 78 bis). Such compounds are very unstable, decompose with an explosion when heated, and are changed by the action of water and of many other reagents, which is in accordance with the fact that they contain very closely allied elements, as does Cl_2O itself, or ICl or KNa. By the action of chlorine monoxide on a mixture of iodine and acetic anhydride, Schützenberger also obtained the compound $I(C_2H_3O_2)_3$, which is analogous to ICl_3, because the group $C_2H_3O_2$ is, like Cl, a halogen, forming salts with the metals. Similar properties are found in iodosobenzene (Chapter XI., Note 79).

[581]

CHAPTER XIV

THE VALENCY AND SPECIFIC HEAT OF THE METALS. MAGNESIUM. CALCIUM, STRONTIUM, BARIUM, AND BERYLLIUM

It is easy by investigating the composition of corresponding compounds, to establish the *equivalent weights* of the metals compared with hydrogen— that is, the quantity which replaces one part by weight of hydrogen. If a metal decomposes acids directly, with the evolution of hydrogen, the equivalent weight of the metal may be determined by taking a definite weight of it and measuring the volume of hydrogen evolved by its action on an excess of acid; it is then easy to calculate the weight of the hydrogen from its volume.[1] The same result may be arrived at by determining the composition of the normal salts of the metal; for instance, by finding the weight of metal which combines with 35·5 parts of chlorine or 80 parts of bromine.[2] The equivalent of a metal may be also ascertained by simultaneously (*i.e.* in one circuit) decomposing an acid and a fused salt of a given metal by an electric current and determining the relation between the amounts of hydrogen and metal separated, because, according to Faraday's law, electrolytes (conductors of the second order) are always decomposed in equivalent quantities.[2 bis] The equivalent of a metal may even be found by simply[582] determining the relation between its weight and that of its salt-giving oxide, as by this we know the quantity of the metal which combines with 8 parts by weight of oxygen, and this will be the equivalent, because 8 parts of oxygen combine with 1 part by weight of hydrogen. One method is verified by another, and all the processes for the accurate determination of equivalents require the greatest care to avoid the absorption of moisture, further oxidation, volatility, and other accidental influences which affect exact weighings. The description of the methods necessary for the attainment of exact results belongs to the province of analytical chemistry.

For univalent metals, like those of the alkalis, the weight of the equivalent is equal to the weight of the atom. For bivalent metals the atomic weight is equal to the weight of two equivalents, for *n*-valent metals it is equal to the weight of *n* equivalents. Thus aluminium, $Al = 27$, is trivalent, that is, its equivalent $= 9$; magnesium, $Mg = 24$, is bivalent, and its equivalent $= 12$. Therefore, if potassium or sodium, or in general a univalent metal, M, give compounds M_2O, MHO, MCl, MNO_3, M_2SO_4,

&c., and in general MX, then for bivalent metals like magnesium or calcium the corresponding compounds will be MgO, $Mg(HO)_2$, $MgCl_2$, $Mg(NO_3)_2$, $MgSO_4$, &c., or in general MX_2.

By what are we to be guided in ascribing to some metals univalency and to others bi-, ter-, quadri-, ... n-valency? What obliges us to make this difference? Why are not all metals given the same valency—for instance, why is not magnesium considered as univalent?[583] If this be done, taking $Mg = 12$ (and not 24 as now), not only is a simplicity of expression of the composition of all the compounds of magnesium attained, but we also gain the advantage that their composition will be the same as those of the corresponding compounds of sodium and potassium. These combinations were so expressed formerly—why has this since been changed?

These questions could only be answered after the establishment of the idea of multiples of the atomic weights as the minimum quantities of certain elements combining with others to form compounds—in a word, since the time of the establishment of Avogadro-Gerhardt's law (Chapter VII.). By taking such an element as arsenic, which has many volatile compounds, it is easy to determine the density of these compounds, and therefore to establish their molecular weights, and hence to find the indubitable atomic weight, exactly as for oxygen, nitrogen, chlorine, carbon, &c. It appears that As = 75, and its compounds correspond, like the compounds of nitrogen, with the forms AsX_3, and AsX_5; for example, AsH_3, $AsCl_3$, AsF_5, As_2O_5, &c. It is evident that we are here dealing with a metal (or rather element) of two valencies, which moreover is never univalent, but tri- or quinqui-valent. This example alone is sufficient for the recognition of the existence of polyvalent atoms among the metals. And as antimony and bismuth are closely analogous to arsenic in all their compounds, (just as potassium is analogous to rubidium and cæsium); so, although very few volatile compounds of bismuth are known, it was necessary to ascribe to them formulæ corresponding with those ascribed to arsenic.

As we shall see in describing them, there are also many analogous metals among the bivalent elements, some of which also give volatile compounds. For example, zinc, which is itself volatile, gives several volatile compounds (for instance, zinc ethyl, ZnC_4H_{10}, which boils at 118°, vapour density = $61 \cdot 3$), and in the molecules of all these compounds there is never less than 65 parts of zinc, which is equivalent to H_2, because 65 parts of zinc displace 2 parts by weight of hydrogen; so that zinc is just such an example of the bivalent metals as oxygen, whose equivalent = 8 (because H_2 is replaced by O = 16), is a representative of the bivalent elements, or as arsenic is of the tri- and quinqui-valent elements. And, as we shall afterwards see, magnesium is in many respects closely analogous to zinc, which fact obliges us to regard magnesium as a bivalent metal.

Such metals as mercury and copper, which are able to give not one but two bases, are of particular importance for distinguishing univalent and bivalent metals. Thus copper gives the suboxide Cu_2O and the[584] oxide CuO—that is, the compounds CuX corresponding with the suboxide are analogous (in the quantitative relations, by their composition) to NaX or AgX, and the compounds of the oxide CuX_2, to MgX_2, ZnX_2, and in general to the bivalent metals. It is clear that in such examples we must make a distinction between atomic weights and equivalents.

In this manner the valency, that is, the number of equivalents entering into the atom of the metals may in many cases be established by means of comparatively few volatile metallic compounds, with the aid of a search into their analogies (concerning which see Chapter XV.). *The law of specific heats* discovered by Dulong and Petit has frequently been applied to the same purpose[3] in the history of chemistry, especially since the development given to this law by the researches of Regnault, and since Cannizzaro (1860) showed the agreement between the deductions of this law and the consequences arising from Avogadro-Gerhardt's law.

Dulong and Petit, having determined the specific heat of a number of solid elementary substances, observed that as the atomic weights of the elements increase, their specific heats decrease, and that *the product[585] of the specific heat Q into the atomic weight A is an almost constant quantity.* This means that to bring different elements into a known thermal state an equal amount of work is required if atomic quantities of the elements are taken; that is, the amounts of heat expended in heating equal quantities by weight of the elements are far from equal, but are in inverse proportion to the atomic weights. For thermal changes the atom is a unit; all atoms, notwithstanding the difference of weight and nature, are equal. This is the simplest expression of the fact discovered by Dulong and Petit. The specific heat measures that quantity of heat which is required to raise the temperature of *one unit of weight* of a substance by one degree. If the magnitude of the specific heat of elements be multiplied by the atomic weight, then we obtain the atomic heat—that is, the amount of heat required to raise the temperature of the atomic weight of an element by one degree. It is these products which for the majority of the elements prove to be approximately, if not quite, identical. A complete identity cannot be expected, because the specific heat of one and the same substance varies with the temperature, with its passage from one state into another, and frequently with even a simple mechanical change of density (for instance by hammering), not to speak of allotropic changes, &c. We will cite several figures[4] proving the truth of the conclusions[586] arrived at by Dulong and Petit with respect to solid elementary bodies.

	Li	Na	Mg	P
A =	7	23	24	31
Q =	0·9408	0·2934	0·245	0·202
AQ =	6·59	6·75	5·88	6·26

	Fe	Cu	Zn	Br
A =	56	63	65	80
Q =	0·112	0·093	0·093	0·0843
AQ =	6·27	5·86	6·04	6·74

	Pd	Ag	Sn	I
A =	106	108	118	127
Q =	0·0592	0·056	0·055	0·0541
AQ =	6·28	6·05	6·49	6·87

	Pt	Au	Hg	Pb
A =	196	198	200	206
Q =	0·0325	0·0324	0·0333	0·0315
AQ =	6·37	6·41	6·66	6·49

It is seen from this that the product of the specific heat of the element into the atomic weight is an almost constant quantity, which is nearly 6. Hence it is possible to determine the valency by the specific heats of the metals. Thus, for instance, the specific heats of lithium, sodium, and potassium convince us of the fact that their atomic weights are indeed those which we chose, because by[587] multiplying the specific heats found by experiment by the corresponding atomic weights we obtain the following figures: Li, 6·59, Na, 6·75 and K, 6·47. Of the alkaline earth metals the specific heats have been determined: of magnesium = 0·245 (Regnault and Kopp), of calcium = 0·170 (Bunsen), and of barium = 0·05 (Mendeléeff). If the same composition be ascribed to the compounds of magnesium as to the corresponding compounds of potassium, then the equivalent of magnesium will be equal to 12. On multiplying this atomic weight by the specific heat of magnesium, we obtain a figure 2·94, which is half that which is given by the other solid elements and therefore the atomic weight of magnesium must be taken as equal to 24 and not to 12. Then the atomic heat of magnesium = $24 \times 0.245 = 5.9$; for calcium, giving its compounds a composition CaX_2—for example $CaCl_2$, $CaSO_4$, CaO (Ca = 40)—we obtain an atomic heat = $40 \times 0.17 = 6.8$, and for barium it is equal to $137 \times 0.05 = 6.8$; that is, they must be counted as bivalent, or that their atom replaces H_2, Na_2, or K_2. This conclusion may be confirmed by a method of analogy, as we shall afterwards see. The application of the principle of specific heats to the determination of the magnitudes of the atomic weights of those metals, the magnitude of whose atomic weights could not be determined by Avogadro-Gerhardt's law, was made about 1860 by the Italian professor Cannizzaro.

Exactly the same conclusions respecting the bivalence of magnesium and its analogues are obtained by comparing the specific heats of their compounds, especially of the halogen compounds as the most simple, with the specific heats of the corresponding alkali compounds. Thus, for instance, the specific heats of magnesium and calcium chlorides, $MgCl_2$ and $CaCl_2$, are 0.194 and 0.164, and of sodium and potassium chlorides, NaCl and KCl, 0.214 and 0.172, and therefore their molecular heats (or the products QM, where M is the weight of the molecule) are 18.4 and 18.2, 12.5 and 12.8, and hence the atomic heats (or the quotient of QM by the number of atoms) are all nearly 6, as with the elements. Whilst if, instead of the actual atomic weights Mg = 24 and Ca = 40, their equivalents 12 and 20 be taken, then the atomic heats of the chlorides of magnesium and calcium would be about 4.6, whilst those of potassium and sodium chlorides are about 6.3.[5] We[588] must remark, however, that as the specific heat or the amount of heat required to raise the temperature of a unit of weight one degree[6] is a[589] complex quantity—including not only the increase of the energy of a substance with its rise in temperature, but also the external work of expansion[7] and the internal work accomplished in the molecules[590] causing them to decompose according to the rise of temperature[8]—therefore it is impossible to expect in the magnitude of the specific heat the great simplicity of relation to composition which we see, for instance, in the density of gaseous substances. Hence, although the specific heat is one of the important means for determining the atomicity of the elements, still the mainstay for a true judgment of atomicity is only given by Avogadro-Gerhardt's law, *i.e.* this other method can only be accessory or preliminary, and when possible recourse should be had to the determination of the vapour density.

Among the bivalent metals the first place, with respect to their distribution in nature, is occupied by *magnesium* and *calcium*, just as sodium and potassium stand first amongst the univalent metals. The relation which exists between the atomic weights of these four metals confirms the above comparison. In fact, the combining weight of magnesium is equal to 24, and of calcium 40; whilst the combining weights of sodium and potassium are 23 and 39—that is, the latter[591] are one unit less than the former.[9] They all belong to the number of *light metals*, as they have but a small specific gravity, in which respect they differ from the ordinary, generally known heavy, or ore, metals (for instance, iron, copper, silver, and lead), which are distinguished by a much greater specific gravity. There is no doubt that their low specific gravity has a significance, not only as a simple point of distinction, but also as a property which determines the fundamental properties of these metals. Indeed, all the light metals have a series of points of resemblance with the metals of the alkalis; thus both magnesium and calcium, like the metals of the alkalis, decompose water (without the addition of acids), although not so easily as the latter metals. The process of the decomposition is essentially one and the same; for example, $Ca + 2H_2O = CaH_2O_2 + H_2$—that is, hydrogen is liberated and a hydroxide of the metal formed. These hydroxides are bases which neutralise nearly all acids. However, the hydroxides RH_2O_2 of calcium and magnesium are in no respect so energetic as the hydroxides of the true metals of the alkalis; thus when heated they lose water, are not so soluble, develop less heat with acids, and form various salts, which are less stable and more easily decomposed by heat than the corresponding salts of sodium and potassium. Thus calcium and magnesium carbonates easily part with carbonic anhydride when ignited; the nitrates are also very easily decomposed by heat, calcium and magnesium oxides, CaO and MgO, being left behind. The chlorides of magnesium and calcium, when heated with water, evolve hydrogen chloride, forming the corresponding hydroxides, and when ignited the oxides themselves. All these points are evidence of a weakening of the alkaline properties.

These metals have been termed *the metals of the alkaline earths*, because they, like the alkali metals, form energetic bases. They are called alkaline *earths* because they are met with in nature in a state of combination, forming the insoluble mass of the earth, and because as oxides, RO, they themselves have an earthy appearance. Not a few salts of these metals are known which are insoluble in water, whilst the corresponding salts of the alkali metals are generally soluble—for example, the carbonates, phosphates, borates, and other salts of the alkaline earth metals are nearly insoluble. This enables us to separate the metals of the alkaline earths from the metals of the alkalis. For this purpose a solution of ammonium carbonate is added to a mixed solution of salts of both kinds of metals, when by a double decomposition the insoluble carbonates of the metals of the alkaline earths are formed[592] and fall as a precipitate, whilst the metals of the alkalis remain in solution: $RX_2 + Na_2CO_3 = RCO_3 + 2NaX$.

We may here remark that the oxides of the metals of the alkaline earths are frequently called by special names: MgO is called magnesia or bitter earth; CaO, lime; SrO, strontia; and BaO, baryta.

In the primary rocks the oxides of calcium and magnesium are combined with silica, sometimes in variable quantities, so that in some cases the lime predominates and in other cases the magnesium. The two oxides, being analogous to each other, replace each other in equivalent quantities. The various forms of *augite, hornblende,* or *amphibole,* and of similar minerals, which enter into the composition of nearly all rocks, contain lime and magnesia and silica. The majority of the primary rocks also contain alumina, potash, and soda. These rocks, under the action of water (containing carbonic acid) and air, give up lime and magnesia to the water, and therefore they are contained in all kinds of water, and especially in sea-water. The *carbonates* $CaCO_3$ and $MgCO_3$, frequently met with in nature, *are soluble in an excess of water saturated with carbonic anhydride,*[10] and therefore many natural waters contain these salts, and are able to yield them when evaporated. However, one kilogram of water saturated with carbonic anhydride does not dissolve more than three grams of calcium carbonate. By gradually expelling the carbonic anhydride from such water, an insoluble precipitate of calcium carbonate separates out. It may confidently be stated that the formation of the very widely distributed strata of calcium and magnesium carbonates was of this nature, because these strata are of a sedimentary character—that is, such as would be exhibited by a gradually accumulating deposit on the bottom of the sea, and, moreover, frequently containing the remains of marine plants, and animals, shells, &c. It is very probable that the presence of these organisms in the sea has played the chief part in the precipitation of the carbonates from the sea water, because the plants absorb CO_2, and many of the organisms $CaCO_3$, and after death give deposits of carbonate of lime; for instance, chalk, which is almost entirely composed of the minute remains of the calcareous shields of such organisms. These deposits of calcium and magnesium carbonates are the most important sources of these metals. Lime generally predominates, because it is present in rocks and running water in greater quantity than magnesia, and in this case these sedimentary rocks are[593] termed *limestone.* Some common flagstones used for paving, &c., and chalk may be taken as examples of this kind of formation. Those limestones in which a considerable portion of the calcium is replaced by magnesium are termed *dolomites.* The dolomites are distinguished by their hardness, and by their not parting with the whole of their carbonic anhydride so easily as the limestones under the action of acids. Dolomites[11] sometimes contain an equal number of molecules of calcium carbonate and magnesium carbonate, and they also sometimes appear in a crystalline form, which is easily intelligible, because calcium carbonate itself is exceedingly common in this form in nature, and is then known as *calc spar*, whilst natural crystalline magnesium carbonate is termed *magnesite*. The formation of the crystalline varieties of the insoluble carbonates is explained by the possibility of a slow deposition from solutions containing carbonic acid. Besides which (Chapter X.) calcium and magnesium sulphates are obtained from sea water, and therefore they are met with both as deposits and in springs. It must be observed that magnesium is held in considerable quantities in sea water, because the sulphate and chloride of magnesium are very soluble in water, whilst calcium sulphate is but little soluble, and is used in the formation of shells; and therefore if the occurrence of considerable deposits of magnesium sulphate cannot be expected in nature, still, on the other hand, one would expect (and they do actually occur) large masses of calcium sulphate or *gypsum*, $CaSO_4,2H_2O$. Gypsum sometimes forms strata of immense size, which extend over many hectometres—for example, in Russia on the Volga, and in the Donetz and Baltic provinces.

Lime and magnesia also, but in much smaller quantities (only to the amount of several fractions of a per cent. and rarely more), enter into the composition of every fertile soil, and without these bases the soil is unable to support vegetation. Lime is particularly important in this respect, and its presence in a larger quantity generally improves the harvest, although purely calcareous soils are as a rule infertile. For this reason the soil is fertilised both with lime[12] itself and with[594] marl—that is, with clay mixed with a certain quantity of calcium carbonate, strata of which are found nearly everywhere.

From the soil the lime and magnesia (in a smaller quantity) pass into the substance of *plants*, where they occur as salts. Certain of these salts separate in the interior of plants in a crystalline form—for example, calcium oxalate. The lime occurring in plants serves as the source for the formation of the various calcareous secretions which are so common in *animals* of all classes. The bones of the highest animal orders, the shells of mollusca, the covering of the sea-urchin, and similar solid secretions of sea animals, contain calcium salts; namely, the shells mainly calcium carbonate, and the bones mainly calcium phosphate. Certain limestones are almost entirely formed of such deposits. Odessa is situated on a limestone of this kind, composed of shells. Thus magnesium and calcium occur throughout the entire realm of nature, but calcium predominates.

As lime and magnesia form bases which are in many respects analogous, they were not distinguished from each other for a long time. Magnesia was obtained for the first time in the seventeenth century from Italy, and used as a medicine; and it was only in the last century that Black, Bergmann, and others distinguished magnesia from lime.

Metallic magnesium (and calcium also) is not obtained by heating magnesium oxide or the carbonate with charcoal, as the alkali metals are obtained,[13] but is liberated by the action of a galvanic current on fused magnesium chloride (best mixed with potassium chloride); Davy and Bussy obtained metallic magnesium by acting on magnesium[595] chloride with the vapours of potassium. At the present time (Deville's process) magnesium is prepared in rather considerable quantities by a similar process, only the potassium is replaced by sodium. Anhydrous magnesium chloride, together with sodium chloride and calcium fluoride, is fused in a close crucible. The latter substances only serve to facilitate the formation of a fusible mass before and after the reaction, which is indispensable in order to prevent the access and action of air. One part of finely divided sodium to five parts of magnesium chloride is thrown into the strongly heated molten mass, and after stirring the reaction proceeds very quickly, and magnesium separates, $MgCl_2 + Na_2 = Mg + 2NaCl$. In working on a large scale, the powdery metallic magnesium is then subjected to distillation at a white heat. The distillation of the magnesium is necessary, because the undistilled metal is not homogeneous[14] and burns unevenly: the metal is prepared for the purpose of illumination. Magnesium is a white metal, like silver; it is not soft like the alkali metals, but is, on the contrary, hard like the majority of the ordinary metals. This follows from the fact that it melts at a somewhat high temperature—namely, about 500°—and boils at about 1000°. It is malleable and ductile, like the generality of metals, so that it can be drawn into wires and rolled into ribbon; it is most frequently used for lighting purposes in the latter form. Unlike the alkali metals, magnesium does not decompose the atmospheric moisture at the ordinary temperature, so that it is almost unacted on by air; it is not even acted on by water at the ordinary temperature, so that it may be washed to free it from sodium chloride. Magnesium only decomposes water with the evolution of hydrogen at the boiling point of water,[15] and more rapidly at still higher temperatures. This is explained by the fact that in decomposing water magnesium forms an insoluble hydroxide, MgH_2O_2, which covers the metal and hinders the further action of the water. Magnesium easily displaces hydrogen from acids, forming magnesium salts. When ignited it *burns*, not only in oxygen but in air (and even in carbonic anhydride), forming a white powder of magnesium oxide, or magnesia; in burning it emits a white and exceedingly *brilliant light*. The strength of this light naturally depends on the fact that magnesium (24 parts by weight) in burning[596] evolves about 140 thousand heat units, and that the product of combustion, MgO, is infusible by heat; so that the vapour of the burning magnesium contains an ignited powder of non-volatile and infusible magnesia, and consequently presents all the conditions for the production of a brilliant light. The light emitted by burning magnesium contains many rays which act chemically, and are situated in the violet and ultra-violet parts of the spectrum. For this reason burning magnesium may be employed for producing photographic images.[16]

Owing to its great affinity for oxygen, magnesium *reduces* many metals (zinc, iron, bismuth, antimony, cadmium, tin, lead, copper, silver, and others) from solutions of their salts at the ordinary temperature,[17] and at a red heat finely divided magnesium takes up the oxygen from silica, alumina, boric anhydride, &c.; so that silicon and similar elements may be obtained by directly heating a mixture of powdered silica and magnesium in an infusible glass tube.[18]

The affinity of magnesium for the halogens is much more feeble than for oxygen,[19] as is at once evident from the fact that a solution of iodine acts feebly on magnesium; still magnesium burns in the vapours of iodine, bromine, and chlorine. The character of magnesium is also seen in the fact that all its salts, especially in the presence of water, are decomposable at a comparatively moderate temperature, the elements of the acid being evolved, and the magnesium oxide, which is non-volatile and unchangeable by heat, being left. This naturally refers to those acids which are themselves volatilised by heat. Even magnesium sulphate is completely decomposed at the temperature at which iron melts, oxide of magnesium remaining behind. This decomposition of magnesium salts by heat proceeds[597] much more easily than that of calcium salts. For example, magnesium carbonate is totally decomposed at 170°, magnesium oxide being left behind. This *magnesia*, or *magnesium oxide*, is met with both in an anhydrous and hydrated state in nature (the anhydrous magnesia as the mineral *periclase*, MgO, and the hydrated magnesia as *brucite*, MgH_2O_2). Magnesia is a well-known medicine (calcined magnesia—*magnesia usta*). It is a white, extremely fine, and very voluminous powder, of specific gravity 3·4; it is infusible by heat, and only shrinks or shrivels in an oxyhydrogen flame. After long contact the anhydrous magnesia combines with water, although very slowly, forming the hydroxide $Mg(HO)_2$, which, however, parts with its water with great ease when heated even below a red heat, and again yields anhydrous magnesia. This hydroxide is obtained directly as a gelatinous amorphous substance when a soluble alkali is mixed with a solution of any magnesium salt, $MgCl_2 + 2KHO = Mg(HO)_2 + 2KCl$. This decomposition is complete, and nearly all the magnesium passes into the precipitate; and this clearly shows the almost perfect insolubility of magnesia in water. Water dissolves a scarcely perceptible quantity of magnesium hydroxide—namely, one part is dissolved by 55,000 parts of water. Such a solution, however, has an alkaline reaction, and gives, with a salt of phosphoric acid, a precipitate of magnesium phosphate, which is still more insoluble. Magnesia is not only dissolved by acids, forming salts, but it also displaces certain other bases—for example, ammonia from ammonium salts when boiled; and the hydroxide also absorbs carbonic anhydride from the air. The magnesium salts, like those of calcium, potassium, and sodium, are colourless if they are formed from colourless acids. Those which are soluble have a bitter taste, whence magnesia has been termed *bitter-earth*. In comparison with the alkalis magnesia is a feeble base, inasmuch as it forms somewhat unstable salts, easily gives basic salts, forms acid salts with difficulty, and is able to give double salts with the salts of the alkalis, which facts are characteristic of feeble bases, as we shall see in becoming acquainted with the different metals.

The power of magnesium salts to form double and basic salts is very frequently shown in reactions, and is specially marked as regards ammonium salts. If saturated solutions of magnesium and ammonium sulphates are mixed together, a crystalline double salt $Mg(NH_4)_2(SO_4)_2,6H_2O$,[20] is immediately precipitated. A strong[598] solution of ordinary ammonium carbonate dissolves magnesium oxide or carbonate, and precipitates crystals of a double salt, $Mg(NH_4)_2(CO_3)_2,4H_2O$, from which water extracts the ammonium carbonate. With an excess of an ammonium salt the double salt passes into solution,[21] and therefore if a solution contain a magnesium salt and an excess of an ammonium salt—for instance, sal-ammoniac—then sodium carbonate will no longer precipitate magnesium carbonate. A mixture of solutions of magnesium and ammonium chlorides, on evaporation or refrigeration, gives a double salt, $Mg(NH_4)Cl_3,6H_2O$.[22] The salts of potassium, like those of ammonium, are able to enter into combination with the magnesium salts.[23] For instance, the double salt, $MgKCl_3,6H_2O$, which is known as *carnallite*,[24] and occurs in the salt mines of Stassfurt, may be formed by freezing a saturated solution of potassium chloride with an excess of magnesium chloride. A saturated solution of magnesium sulphate dissolves potassium sulphate, and solid magnesium sulphate is soluble in a saturated solution of potassium sulphate. A double salt, $K_2Mg(SO_4)_2,6H_2O$, which closely resembles the above-mentioned ammonium salt, crystallises from these solutions.[25][599] The nearest analogues of magnesium are able to give exactly similar double salts, both in crystalline form (monoclinic system) and composition;[600] they, like this salt (*see* Chapter XV.), are easily able (at 140°) to part with all their water of crystallisation, and correspond with the salts of sulphuric acid, whose type may be taken as *magnesium sulphate*, $MgSO_4$.[26] It occurs at Stassfurt as *kieserite*, $MgSO_4,H_2O$, and generally separates from solutions as a heptahydrated salt, $MgSO_4,7H_2O$, and from supersaturated solutions as a hexahydrated salt, $MgSO_4,6H_2O$; at temperatures below 0° it crystallises out as a dodecahydrated salt, $MgSO_4,12H_2O$, and a solution of the composition $MgSO_4,2H_2O$ solidifies completely at -5°.[27] Thus between[601] water and magnesium sulphate there may exist several definite and more or less stable degrees of equilibrium; the double salt $MgSO_4K_2SO_4,6H_2O$ may be regarded as one of these equilibrated systems, the more so since it contains $6H_2O$, whilst $MgSO_4$ forms its most stable system with $7H_2O$, and the double salt may be considered as this crystallo-hydrate in which one molecule of water is replaced by the molecule K_2SO_4.[28]

The power of forming basic salts is a very remarkable peculiarity of magnesia and other feeble bases, and especially of those corresponding with polyvalent metals. The very powerful bases corresponding with univalent metals—like potassium and sodium—do not form basic salts, and, indeed, are more prone to give acid salts, whilst magnesium easily and frequently forms basic salts, especially with feeble acids, although there are some oxides—as, for example, copper and lead oxides—which still more frequently give basic salts. If a cold solution of magnesium sulphate be mixed with a solution of sodium carbonate there is formed a gelatinous precipitate of a basic salt,[602] $Mg(HO)_2,4MgCO_3,9H_2O$; but all the magnesia is not precipitated in this case, as a portion of it remains in solution as an acid double salt. If sodium carbonate be added to a boiling solution of magnesium sulphate a precipitate of a still more basic salt is formed, $4MgSO_4 + 4Na_2CO_3 + 4H_2O = 4Na_2SO_4 + CO_2 + Mg(OH)_2,3MgCO_3,3H_2O$. This basic salt forms the ordinary drug *magnesia* (*magnesia alba*), in the form of light porous lumps. Other basic salts are formed under certain modifications of temperature and conditions of decomposition. But *the normal salt*, $MgCO_3$, which occurs in nature as magnesite in the form of rhombohedra of specific gravity $3 \cdot 056$, cannot be obtained by such a method of precipitation. In fact, the formation of the different basic salts shows the power of water to decompose the normal salt. It is possible, however, to obtain this salt both in an anhydrous and hydrated state. A solution of magnesium carbonate in water containing carbonic acid is taken for this purpose. The reason for this is easily understood—carbonic anhydride is one of the products of the decomposition of magnesium carbonate in the presence of water. If this solution be left to evaporate spontaneously the normal salt separates in a hydrated form, but in the evaporation of a heated solution, through which a stream of carbonic anhydride is passed, the anhydrous salt is formed as a crystalline mass, which remains unaltered in the air, like the natural mineral.[29] The decomposing influence of water on the salts of magnesium, which is directly dependent on the feeble basic properties of magnesia,[30] is most clearly seen in *magnesium chloride*, $MgCl_2$. This salt is contained[31] in the last mother-liquors of the evaporation of sea-water. On cooling a sufficiently concentrated solution, the crystallo-hydrate, $MgCl_2,6H_2O$, separates;[32] but if it be[603] further heated (above 106°) to remove the water, then hydrochloric acid passes off together with the latter, so that there ultimately remains magnesia with a small quantity of magnesium chloride.[33] From what has been said it is evident that anhydrous magnesium chloride cannot be obtained by simple evaporation. But if sal-ammoniac or sodium chloride be added to a solution of magnesium chloride, then the evolution of hydrochloric acid does not take place, and after complete evaporation the residue is perfectly soluble in water. This renders it possible to obtain anhydrous magnesium chloride from its aqueous solution. Indeed the mixture with sal-ammoniac (in excess) may be dried (the residue consists of an anhydrous double salt, $MgCl_2,2NH_4Cl$) and then ignited (460°), when the sal-ammoniac is converted into vapour and a fused mass of anhydrous magnesium chloride remains behind. The anhydrous chloride evolves a very considerable amount of heat on the addition of water, which shows the great affinity the salt has for water.[34] Anhydrous magnesium chloride is not only obtained by the above method, but is also formed by the direct combination of chlorine and magnesium, and by the action of chlorine on magnesium oxide, oxygen being evolved; this proceeds still more easily *by heating magnesia with charcoal in a stream of chlorine,* when the charcoal serves to take up the oxygen. This latter method is also employed for the preparation of chlorides which are formed in an anhydrous condition with still greater difficulty than magnesium chloride. Anhydrous magnesium chloride forms a colourless, transparent mass, composed of flexible crystalline plates of a pearly lustre. It fuses at a low red heat (708°) into a colourless liquid, remains unchanged in a dry state, but under the action of moisture is partially decomposed even at the ordinary temperature, with formation of hydrochloric acid. When heated in the presence of oxygen (air) it gives chlorine and the basic salt, which[604] is formed with even greater facility under the action of heat in the presence of steam, when HCl is formed, according to the equation $2MgCl_2 + H_2O = MgOMgCl_2 + 2HCl$.[34 bis]

Calcium (or the metal of lime) and its compounds in many respects present a great resemblance to magnesium compounds, but are also clearly distinguished from them by many properties.[35] In general, calcium stands to magnesium in the same relation as potassium occupies in respect to sodium. Davy obtained metallic calcium, like potassium, as an amalgam by the action of a galvanic current; but neither charcoal nor iron decomposes calcium oxide, and even sodium decomposes calcium chloride[36] with difficulty. But a galvanic current easily decomposes calcium chloride, and metallic sodium somewhat easily decomposes calcium iodide when heated. As in the case of hydrogen, potassium, and magnesium, the affinity of iodine for calcium is feebler than that of chlorine (and oxygen), and therefore it is not surprising that calcium iodide may be subjected to that decomposition, which the chloride and oxide undergo with difficulty.[37] *Metallic calcium* is of a yellow colour, and has a considerable lustre, which it preserves in dry air. Its specific gravity is 1·58. Calcium is distinguished by its great ductility; it melts at a red heat and then burns in the air with a very brilliant flame; the brilliancy is due to the formation of finely divided infusible calcium oxide. Judging from the fact that calcium in burning gives a very large flame, it is probable that this[605] metal is volatile. Calcium decomposes water at the ordinary temperature, and is oxidised in moist air, but not so rapidly as sodium. In burning, it gives its oxide or *lime*, CaO, a substance which is familiar to every one, and of which we have already frequently had occasion to speak. This oxide is not met with in nature in a free state, because it is an energetic base which everywhere encounters acid substances forming salts with them. It is generally combined with silica, or occurs as calcium carbonate or sulphate. The carbonate and nitrate are decomposed, at a red heat, with the formation of lime. As a rule, the carbonate, which is so frequently met with in nature, serves as the source of the calcium oxide, both commercial and pure. When heated, calcium carbonate dissociates: $CaCO_3 = CaO + CO_2$. In practice the decomposition is conducted at a bright red heat, in the presence of steam, or a current of a foreign gas, in heaps or in special kilns.[38]

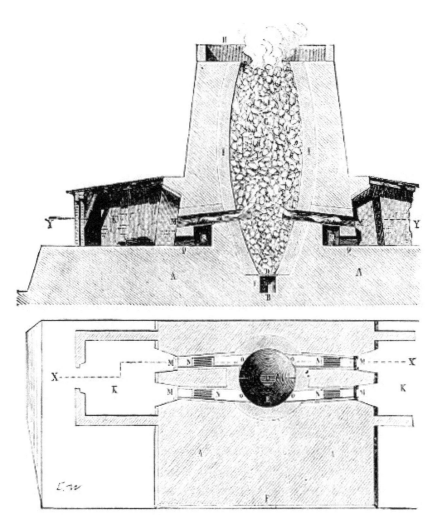

FIG. 78.—Continually-acting kiln for burning lime. The lime is charged from above and calcined by four lateral grates, R, M. D, fire-bars. B, space for withdrawing the burnt lime. K, stoke-house. M. fire grate. Q, R, under-grate.

Calcium oxide—that is, quicklime—is a substance (sp. gr. 3·15)[606] which is unaffected by heat,[39] and may therefore serve as a fire-resisting material, and was employed by Deville for the construction of furnaces in which platinum was melted, and silver volatilised by the action of the heat evolved by the combustion of detonating gas. The hydrated lime, slaked lime, or calcium hydroxide, CaH_2O_2 (specific gravity 2·07) is a most common alkaline substance, employed largely in building for making mortars or cements, in which case its binding property is mainly due to the absorption of carbonic anhydride.[40][607] Lime, like other alkalis, acts on many animal and vegetable substances, and for this reason has many practical uses—for example, for removing fats, and in agriculture for accelerating the decomposition of organic substances in the so-called *composts* or accumulations of vegetable and animal remains used for fertilising land. Calcium hydroxide easily loses its water at a moderate heat (530°), but it does not part with water at 100°. When mixed with water, lime forms a pasty mass known as *slaked lime* and in a more dilute form as *milk of lime*, because when shaken up in water it remains suspended in it for a long time and presents the appearance of a milky liquid. But, besides this, lime is directly soluble in water, not to any considerable extent, but still in such a quantity that *lime water* is precipitated by carbonic anhydride, and has clearly distinguishable alkaline properties. One part of lime requires at the ordinary temperature about 800 parts of water for solution. At 100° it requires about 1500 parts of water, and therefore lime-water becomes cloudy when boiled. If lime-water be evaporated in a vacuum, calcium hydroxide separates in six-sided crystals.[41] If lime-water be mixed with hydrogen peroxide minute crystals of *calcium peroxide*, $CaO_2,8H_2O$, separate; this compound is very unstable and, like barium peroxide, is decomposed by heat. Lime, as a powerful base, combines with all acids, and in this respect presents a transition from the true alkalis to magnesia. Many of the salts of[608] calcium (the carbonate, phosphate, borate, and oxalate) are insoluble in water; besides which the sulphate is only sparingly soluble. As a more energetic base than magnesia, lime forms salts, CaX_2, which are distinguished by their stability in comparison with the salts MgX_2; neither does lime so easily form basic and double salts as magnesia.

Anhydrous lime does not absorb dry carbonic anhydride at the ordinary temperature. This was already known by Scheele, and Prof. Schuliachenko showed that there is no absorption even at 360°. It only proceeds at a red heat,[42] and then only leads to the formation of a mixture of calcium oxide and carbonate (Rose). But if the lime be slaked or dissolved, the absorption of carbonic anhydride proceeds rapidly and completely. These phenomena are connected with the *dissociation of calcium carbonate*, studied by Debray (1867) under the influence of the conceptions of dissociation introduced into science by Henri Saint-Claire Deville. Just as there is no vapour tension for non-volatile substances, so there is no dissociation tension of carbonic anhydride for calcium carbonate at the ordinary[609] temperature. Just as every volatile substance has a maximum possible vapour tension for every temperature, so also calcium carbonate has its corresponding *dissociation tension*; this at 770° (the boiling point of cadmium) is about 85 mm. (of the mercury column), and at 930° (the boiling point of Zn) it is about 520 mm. As, if the tension be greater, there will be no evaporation, so also there will he no decomposition. Debray took crystals of calc spar, and could not observe the least change in them at the boiling point of zinc (930°) in an atmosphere of carbonic anhydride taken at the atmospheric pressure (760 mm.), whilst on the other hand calcium carbonate may be completely decomposed at a much lower temperature if the tension of the carbonic anhydride be kept below the dissociation tension, which may be done either by directly pumping away the gas with an air-pump, or by mixing it with some other gas—that is, by diminishing the partial pressure of the carbonic anhydride,[43] just as an object may be dried at the ordinary temperature by removing the aqueous vapour or by carrying it off in a stream of another gas. Thus it is possible to obtain calcium carbonate from lime and carbonic anhydride at a certain temperature above that at which dissociation begins, and conversely to decompose calcium carbonate at the same temperature into lime and carbonic anhydride.[44] At the ordinary temperature the reaction of the first order (combination) cannot proceed because the second (decomposition, dissociation)[610] cannot take place, and thus all the most important phenomena with respect to the behaviour of lime towards carbonic anhydride are explained by starting from one common basis.[45]

Calcium carbonate, $CaCO_3$, is sometimes met with in nature in a crystalline form, and it forms an example of the phenomenon termed *dimorphism*—that is, it appears in two crystalline forms. When it exhibits combinations of forms belonging to the hexagonal system (six-sided prisms, rhombohedra, &c.) it is called *calc spar*. Calc spar has a specific gravity of 2·7, and is further characterised by a distinct cleavage along the planes of the fundamental rhombohedron having an angle of 105°. Perfectly transparent Iceland spar presents a clear example of double refraction (for which reason it is frequently employed in physical apparatus). The other form of calcium carbonate occurs in crystals belonging to the rhombic system, and it is then called *aragonite*; its specific gravity is 3·0. If calcium carbonate be artificially produced by slow crystallisation at the ordinary temperature, it appears in the rhombohedral form, but if the crystallisation be aided by heat it then appears as aragonite. It may therefore be supposed that calc spar presents the form corresponding with a low temperature, and aragonite with a higher temperature during crystallisation.[46]

[611]

Calcium sulphate in combination with two equivalents of water, $CaSO_4,2H_2O$, is very widely distributed in nature, and is known as *gypsum*. Gypsum loses one and a half and two equivalents of water at a moderate temperature,[47] and anhydrous or burnt gypsum is then obtained, which is also known as *plaster of Paris*, and is employed in large quantities for modelling.[48] This use depends on the fact that burnt and finely-divided and sifted gypsum forms a paste when mixed with water; after a certain time this paste becomes slightly heated and solidifies, owing to the fact that the anhydrous calcium sulphate, $CaSO_4$, again combines with water. When the plaster of Paris and water are first made into a paste they form a mechanical mixture, but when the mass solidifies, then a compound of the calcium sulphate with two molecules of water is produced; and this may be regarded as derived from $S(OH)_6$ by the substitution of two atoms of hydrogen by one atom of bivalent calcium. Natural gypsum sometimes appears as perfectly colourless, or variegated, marble-like, masses, and sometimes in perfectly colourless crystals, *selenite*, of specific gravity 2·33. The semi-transparent gypsum, or *alabaster*, is often carved into small statues. Besides[612] which an anhydrous calcium sulphate, $CaSO_4$, called *anhydrite* (specific gravity 2·97), occurs in nature. It sometimes occurs along with gypsum. It is no longer capable of combining directly with water, and differs in this respect from the anhydrous salt obtained by gently igniting gypsum. If gypsum be very strongly heated it shrinks and loses its power of combining with water.[48 bis] One part of calcium sulphate requires at 0° 525 parts of water for solution, at 38° 466 parts, and at 100° 571 parts of water. The maximum solubility of gypsum is at about 36°, which is nearly the same temperature as that at which sodium sulphate is most soluble.[49]

As lime is a more energetic base than magnesia, so *calcium chloride*, $CaCl_2$, is not so easily decomposed by water, and its solutions only disengage a small quantity of hydrochloric acid when evaporated, and when the evaporation is conducted in a stream of hydrochloric acid it easily gives an anhydrous salt which fuses at 719°; otherwise an aqueous solution yields a crystallo-hydrate, $CaCl_2,6H_2O$, which melts at 30°.[50]

[613]
[614]

Just as for potassium, $K = 39$ (and sodium, $Na = 23$), there are the near analogues, $Rb = 85$ and $Cs = 133$, and also another, $Li = 7$, so in exactly the same manner for calcium, $Ca = 40$ (and magnesium, $Mg = 24$), there is another analogue of lighter atomic weight, beryllium, $Be = 9$, besides the near analogues strontium, $Sr = 87$, and barium, $Ba = 137$. As rubidium and cæsium are more rarely met with in nature than potassium, so also strontium and barium are rarer than calcium (in the same way that bromine and iodine are rarer than chlorine). Since they exhibit many points of resemblance with calcium, strontium and barium may be characterised after a very short acquaintance with their chief compounds; this shows the important advantages gained by distributing the elements according to their natural groups, to which matter we shall turn our attention in the next chapter.

Among the compounds of barium met with in nature the commonest is the *sulphate*, $BaSO_4$, which forms anhydrous crystals of the rhombic system, which are identical in their crystalline form with anhydrite, and generally occur as transparent and semi-transparent masses of tabular crystals having a high specific gravity, namely 4·45, for which reason this salt bears the name of *heavy spar* or *barytes*. Analogous to it is *celestine*, $SrSO_4$, which is, however, more rarely met with. Heavy spar frequently forms the gangue separated on dressing metallic ores from the vein stuff; this mineral is the source of all other barium compounds; for the carbonate, although more easily transformed into the other compounds (because acids act directly on it, evolving carbonic anhydride), is a comparatively rare mineral ($BaCO_3$ forms the mineral *witherite*; $SrCO_3$, *strontianite*; both are rare, the latter is found at Etna). The treatment of barium sulphate is rendered difficult from the fact that it is insoluble both in water and acids, and has therefore to be treated by a method of reduction.[51] Like sodium sulphate and calcium sulphate, heavy spar when heated with charcoal parts with its oxygen and forms barium sulphide, BaS. For this purpose a pasty mixture of powdered heavy spar, charcoal, and tar is subjected to the action of a strong heat, when $BaSO_4 + 4C = BaS + 4CO$. The residue is then treated with water, in which the barium sulphide is soluble.[52] When boiled with hydrochloric acid,[615] barium chloride, $BaCl_2$, is obtained in solution, and the sulphur is disengaged as gaseous sulphuretted hydrogen, $BaS + 2HCl = BaCl_2 + H_2S$. In this manner barium sulphate is converted into barium chloride,[53] and the latter by double decomposition with strong nitric acid or nitre gives the less soluble barium nitrate, $Ba(NO_3)_2$,[54] or with sodium[616] carbonate a precipitate of barium carbonate, $BaCO_3$. Both these salts are able to give *barium oxide*, or *baryta*, BaO, and the hydroxide, $Ba(HO)_2$, which differs from lime by its great solubility in water,[55] and by the ease with which it forms a crystallo-hydrate, $BaH_2O_2,8H_2O$, from its solutions. Owing to its solubility, baryta is frequently employed in manufactures and in practical chemistry as an alkali which has the very important property that it may be always entirely removed from solution by the addition of sulphuric acid, which entirely separates it as the insoluble barium sulphate, $BaSO_4$. It may also be removed whilst it remains in an alkaline state (for example, the excess which may remain when it is used for saturating acids) by means of carbonic anhydride, which also completely precipitates baryta as a sparingly soluble, colourless, and powdery carbonate. Both these reactions show that baryta has such properties as would very greatly extend its use were its compounds as widely distributed as those of sodium and calcium, and were its soluble compounds not poisonous. Barium nitrate is directly decomposed by the action of heat, barium oxide being left behind. The same takes place with barium carbonate, especially that form of it precipitated from solutions, and when mixed with charcoal or ignited in an atmosphere of steam. Barium oxide combines with water with the development of a large amount of heat, and the resultant hydroxide is very stable in its retention of the water, although it parts with it when strongly ignited.[55 bis] With oxygen the anhydrous oxide gives, as already mentioned in[617] Chapters III. and IV., a *peroxide*, BaO_2.[56] Neither calcium nor strontium oxides are able to give such a peroxide directly, but they form peroxides under the action of hydrogen peroxide.

Barium oxide is decomposed when heated with potassium; fused barium chloride is decomposed, as Davy showed, by the action of a galvanic current, forming metallic *barium*; and Crookes (1862) obtained an amalgam of barium from which the mercury could easily be driven off, by heating sodium amalgam in a saturated solution of barium chloride. Strontium is obtained by the same processes. Both metals are soluble in mercury, and seem to be non-volatile or only very slightly volatile. They are both heavier than water; the specific gravity of barium is 3·6, and of strontium 2·5. They both decompose water at the ordinary temperature, like the metals of the alkalis.

Barium and strontium as saline elements are characterised by their powerful basic properties, so that they form acid salts with difficulty, and scarcely form basic salts. On comparing them together and with calcium, it is evident that the alkaline properties in this group (as in the group potassium, rubidium, cæsium) increase with the atomic weight, and this succession clearly shows itself in many of their corresponding compounds. Thus, for instance, the solubility of the hydroxides RH_2O_2 and the specific gravity[57] rise in passing from calcium to strontium and barium, while the solubility of the sulphates[618] decreases,[58] and therefore in the case of magnesium and beryllium, as metals whose atomic weights are still less, we should expect the solubility of the sulphates to be greater, and this is in reality the case.

Just as in the series of the alkali metals we saw the metals potassium, rubidium, and cæsium approaching near to each other in their properties, and allied to them two metals having smaller combining weights—namely, sodium, and the lightest of all, lithium, which all exhibited certain peculiar characteristic properties—so also in the case of the metals of the alkaline earths we find, besides calcium, barium, and strontium, the metal magnesium and also *beryllium* or *glucinum*. In respect to the magnitude of its atomic weight, this last occupies the same position in the series of the metals of the alkaline earths as lithium does in the series of the alkali metals, for the combining weight of beryllium, Be or Gl = 9. This combining weight is greater than that of lithium (7), as the combining weight of magnesium (24) is greater than that of sodium (23), and as that of calcium (40) is greater than that of potassium (39), &c.[59] Beryllium was so named because it occurs in the mineral *beryl*. The metal is also called glucinum (from the Greek word γλυχύς, 'sweet'), because its salts have a sweet taste. It occurs in beryl, aquamarine, the emerald, and other minerals, which are generally of a green colour; they are sometimes found in considerable masses, but as a rule are comparatively rare and, as transparent crystals, form precious stones. The composition of beryl and of the emerald is as follows: $Al_2O_3,3BeO,6SiO_2$. The Siberian and Brazilian beryls are the best known. The specific gravity of beryl is about 2·7. Beryllium oxide, from the feebleness of its basic properties, presents[619] an analogy to aluminium oxide in the same way that lithium oxide is analogous to magnesium oxide.[60] Owing to its rare occurrence in nature, to the absence of any especially distinct individual properties, and to the possibility of foretelling them to a certain extent on the basis of the periodic system of the elements given in the following chapter, and owing to the brevity of this treatise, we will not discuss at any length the compounds of beryllium, and will only observe that their individuality was pointed out in 1798 by Vauquelin, and that metallic beryllium was obtained by Wöhler and Bussy. Wöhler obtained *metallic beryllium* (like magnesium) by acting on beryllium chloride, $BeCl_2$, with potassium (it is best prepared by fusing K_2BeF_4 with Na). Metallic beryllium has a specific gravity 1·64 (Nilson and Pettersson). It is very infusible, melting at nearly the same temperature as silver, which it resembles in its white colour and lustre. It is characterised by the fact that it is very difficultly oxidised, and even in the oxidising flame of the blowpipe is only superficially covered by a coating of oxide; it does not burn in pure oxygen, and does not decompose water at the ordinary temperature or[620] at a red heat, but gaseous hydrochloric acid is decomposed by it when slightly heated, with evolution of hydrogen and development of a considerable amount of heat. Even dilute hydrochloric acid acts in the same manner at the ordinary temperature. Beryllium also acts easily on sulphuric acid, but it is remarkable that neither dilute nor strong nitric acid acts on beryllium, which seems especially able to resist oxidising agents. Potassium hydroxide acts on beryllium as on aluminium, hydrogen being disengaged and the metal dissolved, but ammonia has no action on it. These properties of metallic beryllium seem to isolate it from the series of the other metals described in this chapter, but if we compare the properties of calcium, magnesium, and beryllium we shall see that magnesium occupies a position intermediate between the other two. Whilst calcium decomposes water with great ease, magnesium does so with difficulty, and beryllium not at all. The peculiarities of beryllium among the metals of the alkaline earths recall the fact that in the series of the halogens we saw that fluorine differed from the other halogens in many of its properties and had the smallest atomic weight. The same is the case with regard to beryllium among the other metals of the alkaline earths.

In addition to the above characteristics of the compounds of the metals of the alkaline earths, we must add that they, like the alkali metals, combine with nitrogen and hydrogen, and while sodium nitride (obtained by igniting the amide of sodium, Chapter XII., Note 44 bis) and lithium nitride (obtained by heating lithium in nitrogen, Chapter XIII., Note 39) have the composition R_3N, so the nitrides of magnesium (Note 14), calcium, strontium, and barium have the composition R_3N_2, for example, Ba_3N_2, as might be expected from the diatomicity of the metals of the alkaline earths and from the relation of the nitrides to ammonia, which is obtained from all of these compounds by the action of water. The *nitrides* of Ca, Sr, and Ba are formed directly (Maquenne, 1892) by heating the metals in nitrogen. They all have the appearance of an amorphous powder of dark colour; as regards their reactions, it is known that besides disengaging ammonia with water, they form cyanides when heated with carbonic oxide; for instance, $Ba_3N_2 + 2CO = Ba(CN)_2 + 2BaO$.[61]

The metals of the alkaline earths, just like Na and K, absorb hydrogen under certain conditions, and form pulverulent easily oxidisable metallic hydrides, whose composition corresponds exactly to that of Na_2H and K_2H, with the substitution of K_2 and Na_2 by the atoms[621] Be, Mg, Ca, Sr, and Ba. The *hydrides of the metals of the alkaline earths* were discovered by C. Winkler (1891) in investigating the reducibility of these metals by magnesium. In reducing their oxides by heating them with magnesium powder in a stream of hydrogen, Winkler observed that the hydrogen was absorbed (but very slowly), *i.e.* at the moment of their separation all the metals of the alkaline earths combine with hydrogen. This absorptive power increases in passing from Be to Mg, Ca, Sr, and Ba, and the resultant hydrides retain the combined hydrogen[62] when heated, so that these hydrides are distinguished for their considerable stability under heat, but they oxidise very easily.[63]

Thus the analogies and correlation of the metals of these two groups are now clearly marked, not only in their behaviour towards oxygen, chlorine, acids, &c., but also in their capability of combining with nitrogen and hydrogen.

Footnotes:

[1] Under favourable circumstances (by taking all the requisite precautions), the weight of the equivalent may be accurately determined by this method. Thus Reynolds and Ramsay (1887) determined the equivalent of zinc to be 32·7 by this method (from the average of 29 experiments), whilst by other methods it has been fixed (by different observers) between 32·55 and 33·95.

The differences in their equivalents may be demonstrated by taking equal weights of different metals, and collecting the hydrogen evolved by them (under the action of an acid or alkali).

[2] The most accurate determinations of this kind were carried on by Stas, and will be described in Chapter XXIV.

[2 bis] The amount of electricity in one coulomb according to the present nomenclature of electrical units (*see* Works on Physics and Electro-technology) disengages 0·00001036 gram of hydrogen, 0·00112 gram of silver, 0·0003263 gram of copper from the salts of the oxide, and 0·0006526 gram from the salts of the suboxide, &c. These amounts stand in the same ratio as the equivalents, *i.e.* as the quantities replaced by one part by weight of hydrogen. The intimate bond which is becoming more and more marked existing between the electrolytic and purely chemical relations of substances (especially in solutions) and the application of electrolysis to the preparation of numerous substances on a large scale, together with the employment of electricity for obtaining high temperatures, &c., makes me regret that the plan and dimensions of this book, and the impossibility of giving a concise and objective exposition of the necessary electrical facts, prevent my entering upon this province of knowledge, although I consider it my duty to recommend its study to all those who desire to take part in the further development of our science.

There is only one side of the subject respecting the direct correlation between thermochemical data and electro-motive force, which I think right to mention here, as it justifies the general conception, enunciated by Faraday, that the galvanic current is an aspect of the transference of chemical motion or reaction along the conductors.

From experiments conducted by Favre, Thomsen, Garni, Berthelot, Cheltzoff, and others, upon the amount of heat evolved in a closed circuit, it follows that the electro-motive force of the current or its capacity to do a certain work, E, is proportional to the whole amount of heat, Q, disengaged by the reaction forming the source of the current. If E be expressed in volts, and Q in thousands of units of heat referred to equivalent weights, then $E = 0·0436Q$. For example in a Daniells battery E $= 1·09$ both by experiment and theory, because in it there takes place the decomposition of $CuSO_4$ into $Cu + O$ together with the formation of $Zn + O$ and $ZnO + SO_3Aq$, and these reactions correspond to $Q = 25·06$ thousand units of heat. So also in all other primary batteries (*e.g.* Bunsen's, Poggendorff's, &c.) and secondary ones (for instance, those acting according to the reaction $Pb + H_2SO_4 + PbO_2$, as Cheltzoff showed) $E = 0·0436Q$.

[3] The chief means by which we determine the valency of the elements, or what multiple of the equivalent should be ascribed to the atom, are: (1) The law of Avogadro-Gerhardt. This method is the most general and trustworthy, and has already been applied to a great number of elements. (2) The different grades of oxidation and their isomorphism or analogy in general; for example, Fe = 56 because the suboxide (ferrous oxide) is isomorphous with magnesium oxide, &c., and the oxide (ferric oxide) contains half as much oxygen again as the suboxide. Berzelius, Marignac, and others took advantage of this method for determining the composition of the compounds of many elements. (3) The specific heat, according to Dulong and Petit's law. Regnault, and more especially Cannizzaro, used this method to distinguish univalent from bivalent metals. (4) The periodic law (*see* Chapter XV.) has served as a means for the determination of the atomic weights of cerium, uranium, yttrium, &c., and more especially of gallium, scandium, and germanium. The correction of the results of one method by those of others is generally had recourse to, and is quite necessary, because, phenomena of dissociation, polymerisation, &c., may complicate the individual determinations by each method.

It will be well to observe that a number of other methods, especially from the province of those physical properties which are clearly dependent on the magnitude of the atom (or equivalent) or of the molecule, may lead to the same result. I may point out, for instance, that even the specific gravity of solutions of the metallic chlorides may serve for this purpose. Thus, if beryllium he taken as trivalent—that is, if the composition of its chloride be taken as $BeCl_3$ (or a polymeride of it), then the specific gravity of solutions of beryllium chloride will not fit into the series of the other metallic chlorides. But by ascribing to it an atomic weight Be = 7, or taking Be as bivalent, and the composition of its chloride as $BeCl_2$, we arrive at the general rule given in Chapter VII., Note 28. Thus W. G. Burdakoff determined in my laboratory that the specific gravity at 15°/4° of the solution $BeCl_2$ + $200H_2O$ = 1·0138—that is, greater than the corresponding solution KCl + $200H_2O$ (= 1·0121), and less than the solution $MgCl_2$ + $200H_2O$ (= 1·0203), as would follow from the magnitude of the molecular weight $BeCl_2$ = 80, since KCl = 74·5 and $MgCl_2$ = 95.

[4] The specific heats here given refer to different limits of temperature, but in the majority of cases between 0° and 100°; only in the case of bromine the specific heat is taken (for the solid state) at a temperature below -7°, according to Regnault's determination. *The variation of the specific heat with a change of temperature* is a very complex phenomenon, the consideration of which I think would here be out of place. I will only cite a few figures as an example. According to Bystrom, the specific heat of iron at 0° = 0·1116, at 100° = 0·1114, at 200° = 0·1188, at 300° = 0·1267, and

at $1,400° = 0·4031$. Between these last limits of temperature a change takes place in iron (a spontaneous heating, *recalescence*), as we shall see in Chapter XXII. For quartz SiO_2 Pionchon gives $Q = 0·1737 + 394t10^{-6} - 27t^210^{-9}$ up to 400°, for metallic aluminium (Richards, 1892) at 0° 0·222, at 20° 0·224, at 100° 0·232; consequently, as a rule, the specific heat varies slightly with the temperature. Still more remarkable are H. E. Weber's observations on the great variation of the specific heat of charcoal, the diamond and boron:

	0°	100°	200°	600°	900°
Wood charcoal	0·15	0·23	0·29	0·44	0·46
Diamond		0·10	0·19	0·22	0·44	0·45
Boron		0·22	0·29	0·35	—	—

These determinations, which have been verified by Dewar, Le Chatelier (Chapter VIII., Note 13), Moissan, and Gauthier, the latter finding for boron $AQ = 6$ at 400°, are of especial importance as confirming the universality of Dulong and Petit's law, because the elements mentioned above form exceptions to the general rule when the mean specific heat is taken for temperatures between 0° and 100°. Thus in the case of the diamond the product of $A \times Q$ at 0° $= 1·2$, and for boron $= 2·4$. But if we take the specific heat towards which there is evidently a tendency with a rise of temperature, we obtain a product approaching to 6 as with other elements. Thus with the diamond and charcoal, it is evident that the specific heat tends towards 0·47, which multiplied by 12 gives 5·6, the same as for magnesium and aluminium. I may here direct the reader's attention to the fact that for solid elements having a small atomic weight, the specific heat varies considerably if we take the average figures for temperatures 0° to 100°:

$$Li = 7 \quad Be = 9 \quad B = 11 \quad C = 12$$

$$Q = \quad 0·94 \quad 0·42 \quad 0·24 \quad 0·20$$

$$AQ = \quad 6·6 \quad 3·8 \quad 2·6 \quad 2·4$$

It is therefore clear that the specific heat of beryllium determined at a low temperature cannot serve for establishing its atomicity. On the other hand, the low atomic heat of charcoal, graphite, and the diamond, boron, &c., may perhaps depend on the complexity of the molecules of these elements. The necessity for acknowledging a great complexity of the molecules of carbon was explained in Chapter VIII. In the case of sulphur the molecule contains at least S_6 and its atomic heat $= 32 \times 0·163 = 5·22$, which is distinctly below the normal. If a large number of atoms of carbon are contained in the molecule of charcoal, this would to a certain extent account for its comparatively small atomic heat. With respect to the specific heat of compounds, it will not be out of place to mention here the conclusion arrived at by Kopp, that the molecular heat (that is, the product of MQ) may be looked on as the sum of the atomic heats of its component elements; but as this rule is not a general one, and can only be applied to give an approximate estimate of the specific heats of substances, I do not think it necessary to go into the details of the conclusions described in Liebig's 'Annalen Supplement-Band,' 1864, which includes a number of determinations made by Kopp.

[5] It must be remarked that in the case of oxygen (and also hydrogen and carbon) compounds the quotient of MQ/n, where n is the number of atoms in the molecule, is always less than 6 for solids; for example, for $MgO = 5 \cdot 0$, $CuO = 5 \cdot 1$, $MnO_2 = 4 \cdot 6$, ice $(Q = 0 \cdot 504) = 3$, $SiO_2 = 3 \cdot 5$, &c. At present it is impossible to say whether this depends on the smaller specific heat of the atom of oxygen in its solid compounds (Kopp, Note 4) or on some other cause; but, nevertheless, taking into account this decrease depending on the presence of oxygen, a reflection of the atomicity of the elements may to a certain extent be seen in the specific heat of the oxides. Thus for alumina, Al_2O_3 $(Q = 0 \cdot 217)$, $MQ = 22 \cdot 3$, and therefore the quotient $MQ/n = 4 \cdot 5$, which is nearly that given by magnesium oxide, MgO. But if we ascribe the same composition to alumina, as to magnesia— that is, if aluminium were counted as divalent—we should obtain the figure $3 \cdot 7$, which is much less. In general, in compounds of identical atomic composition and of analogous chemical properties the molecular heats MQ are nearly equal, as many investigators have long remarked. For example, $ZnS = 11 \cdot 7$ and $HgS = 11 \cdot 8$; $MgSO_4 = 27 \cdot 0$ and $ZnSO_4 = 28 \cdot 0$, &c.

[6] If W be the amount of heat contained in a mass m of a substance at a temperature t, and dW the amount expended in heating it from t to $t + dt$, then the specific heat $Q = dW(m \times dt)$. The specific heat not only varies with the composition and complexity of the molecules of a substance, but also with the temperature, pressure, and physical state of a substance. Even for gases the variation of Q with t is to be observed. Thus it is seen from the experiments of Regnault and Wiedemann that the specific heat of carbonic anhydride at $0° = 0 \cdot 19$, at $100° = 0 \cdot 22$, and at $200° = 0 \cdot 24$. But the variation of the specific heat of permanent gases with the temperature is, as far as we know, very inconsiderable. According to Mallard and Le Chatelier it is $= 0 \cdot 0006$ [M] per $1°$, where M is the molecular weight (for instance, for O_2, M = 32). Therefore the specific heat of those permanent gases which contain two atoms in the molecule (H_2, O_2, N_2, CO, and NO) may be, as is shown by experiment, taken as not varying with the temperature. The constancy of the specific heat of perfect gases forms one

of the fundamental propositions of the whole theory of heat and on it depends the determination of temperatures by means of gas-thermometers containing hydrogen, nitrogen, or air. Le Chatelier (1887), on the basis of existing determinations, concludes that the molecular heat—that is, the product MQ—of all gases varies in proportion to the temperature, and tends to become equal (= 6·8) at the temperature of absolute zero (that is, at -273°); and therefore MQ = 6·8 + a(273 + t), where a is a constant quantity which increases with the complexity of the gaseous molecule and Q is the specific heat of the gas under a constant pressure. For permanent gases a almost = 0, and therefore MQ = 6·8—that is, the atomic heat (if the molecule contains two atoms) = 3·4, as it is in fact (Chapter IX., Note 17 bis. As regards liquids (as well as the vapours formed by them), the specific heat always rises with the temperature. Thus for benzene it equals 0·38 + 0·0014t. R. Schiff (1887) showed that the variation of the specific heat of many organic liquids is proportional to the change of temperature (as in the case of gases, according to Le Chatelier), and reduced these variations into dependence with their composition and absolute boiling point. It is very probable that the theory of liquids will make use of these simple relations which recall the simplicity of the variation of the specific gravity (Chapter II., Note 34), cohesion, and other properties of liquids with the temperature. They are all expressed by the linear function of the temperature, $a + bt$, with the same degree of proximity as the property of gases is expressed by the equation $pv = Rt$.

As regards the relation between the specific heats of liquids (or of solids) and of their vapours, the specific heat of the vapour (and also of the solid) is always less than that of the liquid. For example, benzene vapour 0·22, liquid 0·38; chloroform vapour 0·13, liquid 0·23; steam 0·475, liquid water 1·0. But the complexity of the relations existing in specific heat is seen from the fact that the specific heat of ice = 0·502 is less than that of liquid water. According to Regnault, in the case of bromine the specific heat of the vapour = 0·055 at (150°), of the liquid = 0·107 (at 30°), and of solid bromine = 0·084 (at -15°). The specific heat of solid benzoic acid (according to experiment and calculation, Hess, 1888) between 0° and 100° is 0·31, and of liquid benzoic acid 0·50. One of the problems of the present day is the explanation of those complex relations which exist between the composition and such properties as specific heat, latent heat, expansion by heat, compression, internal friction, cohesion, and so forth. They can only be connected by a complete theory of liquids, which may now soon be expected, more especially as many sides of the subject have already been partially explained.

[7] According to the above reasons the quantity of heat, Q, required to raise the temperature of one part by weight of a substance by one degree

may be expressed by the sum Q = K + B + D, where K is the heat actually expended in heating the substance, or what is termed the absolute specific heat, B the amount of heat expended in the internal work accomplished with the rise of temperature, and D the amount of heat expended in external work. In the case of gases the last quantity may be easily determined, knowing their coefficient of expansion, which is approximately = 0·00368. By applying to this case the same argument given at the end of Note 11, Chapter I., we find that one cubic metre of a gas heated 1° produces an external work of 10333 × 0·00368, or 38·02 kilogrammetres, on which 38·02/424 or 0·0897 heat units are expended. This is the heat expended for the external work produced by one cubic metre of a gas, but the specific heat refers to units of weight, and therefore it is necessary in order to know D to reduce the above quantity to a unit of weight. One cubic metre of hydrogen at 0° and 760 mm. pressure weighs 0·0896 kilo, a gas of molecular weight M has a density M/2, consequently a cubic metre weighs (at 0° and 760 mm.) 0·0448M kilo, and therefore 1 kilogram of the gas occupies a volume 1/0·0448M cubic metres, and hence the external work D in the heating of 1 kilo of the given gas through 1° = 0·0896/0·0448M, or D = 2/M.

Taking the magnitude of the internal work B for gases as negligible if permanent gases are taken, and therefore supposing B = 0, we find the specific heat of gases at a constant pressure Q = K + 2 M, where K is the specific heat at a constant volume, or the true specific heat, and M the molecular weight. Hence K = Q - 2/M. The magnitude of the specific heat Q is given by direct experiment. According to Regnault's experiments, for oxygen it = 0·2175, for hydrogen 3·405, for nitrogen 0·2438; the molecular weights of these gases are 32, 2, and 28, and therefore for oxygen K = 0·2175 - 0·0625 = 0·1550, for hydrogen K = 3·4050 - 1·000 = 2·4050, and for nitrogen K = 0·2438 - 0·0714 = 0·1724. These true specific heats of elements are in inverse proportion to their atomic weights—that is, their product by the atomic weight is a constant quantity. In fact, for oxygen this product = 0·155 × 16 = 2·48, for hydrogen 2·40, for nitrogen 0·7724 × 14 = 2·414, and therefore if A stand for the atomic weight we obtain the expression K × A = a constant, which may be taken as 2·45. This is the true expression of Dulong and Petit's law, because K is the true specific heat and A the weight of the atom. It should be remarked, moreover, that the product of the observed specific heat Q into A is also a constant quantity (for oxygen = 3·48, for hydrogen = 3·40), because the external work D is also inversely proportional to the atomic weight.

In the case of gases we distinguish the specific heat at a constant pressure c' (we designated this quantity above by Q), and at a constant volume c. It is evident that *the relation between the two specific heats, k, judging* from the above, is the ratio of Q to K, or equal to the ratio of $2 \cdot 45n + 2$ to $2 \cdot 45n$. When $n = 1$ this ratio $k = 1 \cdot 8$; when $n = 2$, $k = 1 \cdot 4$, when $n = 3$, $k = 1 \cdot 3$, and with an exceedingly large number n, of atoms in the molecule, $k = 1$. That is, the ratio between the specific heats decreases from $1 \cdot 8$ to $1 \cdot 0$ as the number of atoms, n, contained in the molecule increases. This deduction is verified to a certain extent by direct experiment. For such gases as hydrogen, oxygen, nitrogen, carbonic oxide, air, and others in which $n = 2$, the magnitude of k is determined by methods described in works on physics (for example, by the change of temperature with an alteration of pressure, by the velocity of sound, &c.) and is found in reality to be nearly $1 \cdot 4$, and for such gases as carbonic anhydride, nitric dioxide, and others it is nearly $1 \cdot 3$. Kundt and Warburg (1875), by means of the approximate method mentioned in Note 29, Chapter VII., determined k for mercury vapour when $n = 1$, and found it to be $= 1 \cdot 67$—that is, a larger quantity than for air, as would be expected from the above.

It may be admitted that the true atomic heat of gases $= 2 \cdot 43$, only under the condition that they are distant from a liquid state, and do not undergo a chemical change when heated—that is, when no internal work is produced in them (B = 0). Therefore this work may to a certain extent be judged by the observed specific heat. Thus, for instance, for chlorine (Q $= 0 \cdot 12$, Regnault; $k = 1 \cdot 33$, according to Straker and Martin, and therefore K $= 0 \cdot 09$, MK $= 6 \cdot 4$), the atomic heat ($3 \cdot 2$) is much greater than for other gases containing two atoms in a molecule, and it must be assumed, therefore, that when it is heated some great internal work is accomplished.

In order to generalise the facts concerning the specific heat of gases and solids, it appears to me possible to accept the following general proposition: *the atomic heat* (that is, AQ or QM/n, where M is the molecular weight and n the number of molecules) is *smaller* (in solids it attains its highest value $6 \cdot 8$ and in gases $3 \cdot 4$), *the more complex the molecule* (i.e. *the greater the number (n) of atoms forming it) and so much smaller, up to a certain point* (in similar physical states) *the smaller the mean atomic weight M/n.*

[8] As an example, it will be sufficient to refer to the specific heat of nitrogen tetroxide, N_2O_4, which, when heated, gradually passes into NO_2— that is, chemical work of decomposition proceeds, which consumes heat. Speaking generally, specific heat is a complex quantity, in which it is clear that thermal data (for instance, the heat of reaction) alone cannot give an idea either of chemical or of physical changes individually, but always depend on an association of the one and the other. If a substance be heated from t_0 to t_1 it cannot but suffer a chemical change (that is, the state of the atoms in the molecules changes more or less in one way or another) if dissociation sets in at a temperature t_1. Even in the case of the elements whose molecules contain only one atom, a true chemical change is possible

with a rise of temperature, because more heat is evolved in chemical reactions than that quantity which participates in purely physical changes. One gram of hydrogen (specific heat = 3·4 at a constant pressure) cooled to the temperature of absolute zero will evolve altogether about one thousand units of heat, 8 grams of oxygen half this amount, whilst in combining together they evolve in the formation of 9 grams of water more than thirty times as much heat. Hence the store of chemical energy (that is, of the motion of the atoms, vortex, or other) is much greater than the physical store proper to the molecules, but it is the change accomplished by the former that is the cause of chemical transformations. Here we evidently touch on those limits of existing knowledge beyond which the teaching of science does not yet allow us to pass. Many new scientific discoveries have still to be made before this is possible.

[9] As if NaH = Mg and KH = Ca, which is in accordance with their valency. KH includes two monovalent elements, and is a bivalent group like Ca.

[10] Sodium carbonate and other carbonates of the alkalis give acid salts which are less soluble than the normal; here, on the contrary, with an excess of carbonic anhydride, a salt is formed which is more soluble than the normal, but this acid salt is more unstable than sodium hydrogen carbonate, $NaHCO_3$.

[11] The formation of dolomite may be explained, if only we imagine that a solution of a magnesium salt acts on calcium carbonate. Magnesium carbonate may be formed by double decomposition, and it must be supposed that this process ceases at a certain limit (Chapter XII.), when we shall obtain a mixture of the carbonates of calcium and magnesium. Haitinger heated a mixture of calcium carbonate, $CaCO_3$, with a solution of an equivalent quantity of magnesium sulphate, $MgSO_4$, in a closed tube at 200°, and then a portion of the magnesia actually passed into the state of magnesium carbonate, $MgCO_3$, and a portion of the lime was converted into gypsum, $CaSO_4$. Lubavin (1892) showed that $MgCO_3$ is more soluble than $CaCO_3$ in salt water, which is of some significance in explaining the composition of sea water.

[12] The undoubted action of lime in increasing the fertility of soils—if not in every case, at all events, with ordinary soils which have long been under corn—is based not so much on the need of plants for the lime itself as on those chemical and physical changes which it produces in the soil, as a particularly powerful base which aids the alteration of the mineral and organic elements of the soil.

[13] Sodium and potassium only decompose magnesium oxide at a white heat and very feebly, probably for two reasons. In the first place, because

the reaction Mg + O develops more heat (about 140 thousand calories) than K_2 + O or Na_2 + O (about 100 thousand calories); and, in the second place, because magnesia is not fusible at the heat of a furnace and cannot act on the charcoal, sodium, or potassium—that is, it does not pass into that mobile state which is necessary for reaction. The first reason alone is not sufficient to explain the absence of the reaction between charcoal and magnesia, because iron and charcoal in combining with oxygen evolve less heat than sodium or potassium, yet, nevertheless, they can displace them. With respect to magnesium chloride, it acts on sodium and potassium, not only because their combination with chlorine evolves more heat than the combination of chlorine and magnesium (Mg + Cl_2 gives 150 and Na_2 + Cl_2 about 195 thousand calories), but also because a fusion, both of the magnesium chloride and of the double salt, takes place under the action of heat. It is probable, however, that a reverse reaction will take place. A reverse reaction might probably be expected, and Winkler (1890) showed that Mg reduces the oxides of the alkali metals (Chapter XIII., Note 42).

[14] Commercial magnesium generally contains a certain amount of magnesium nitride (Deville and Caron), Mg_3N_2—that is, a product of substitution of ammonia which is directly formed (as is easily shown by experiment) when magnesium is heated in nitrogen. It is a yellowish green powder, which gives ammonia and magnesia with water, and cyanogen when heated with carbonic anhydride. Pashkoffsky (1893) showed that Mg_3N_2 is easily formed and is the sole product when Mg is heated to redness in a current of NH_3. Perfectly pure magnesium may be obtained by the action of a galvanic current.

[15] Hydrogen peroxide (Weltzien) dissolves magnesium. The reaction has not been investigated.

[16] A special form of apparatus is used for burning magnesium. It is a clockwork arrangement in which a cylinder rotates, round which a ribbon or wire of magnesium is wound. The wire is subjected to a uniform unwinding and burning as the cylinder rotates, and in this manner the combustion may continue uniform for a certain time. The same is attained in special lamps, by causing a mixture of sand and finely divided magnesium to fall from a funnel-shaped reservoir on to the flame. In photography it is best to blow finely divided magnesium into a colourless (spirit or gas) flame, and for instantaneous photography to light a cartridge of a mixture of magnesium and chlorate of potassium by means of a spark from a Ruhmkorff's coil (D. Mendeléeff, 1889).

[17] According to the observations of Maack, Comaille, Böttger, and others. The reduction by heat mentioned further on was pointed out by Geuther, Phipson, Parkinson and Gattermann.

[18] This action of metallic magnesium in all probability depends, although only partially (*see* Note 13), on its volatility, and on the fact that, in combining with a given quantity of oxygen, it evolves more heat than aluminium, silicon, potassium, and other elements.

[19] Davy, on heating magnesia in chlorine, concluded that there was a complete substitution, because the volume of the oxygen was half the volume of the chlorine; it is probable, however, that owing to the formation of chlorine oxide (Chapter XI., Note 30) the decomposition is not complete and is limited by a reverse reaction.

[20] Even a solution of ammonium chloride gives this salt with magnesium sulphate. Its sp. gr. is 1·72; 100 parts of water at 0° dissolve 9, at 20° 17·9 parts of the anhydrous salt. At about 130° it loses all its water.

[21] This is an example of equilibrium and of the influence of mass; the double salt is decomposed by water, but if instead of water we take a solution of that soluble part which is formed in the decomposition of the double salt, then the latter dissolves as a whole.

[22] If an excess of ammonia be added to a solution of magnesium chloride, only half the magnesium is thrown down in the precipitate, $2MgCl_2 + 2NH_4.OH = Mg(OH)_2 + Mg.NH_4Cl_3 + NH_4Cl$. A solution of ammonium chloride reacts with magnesia, evolving ammonia and forming a solution of the same salt, $MgO + 3NH_4Cl = MgNH_4Cl_3 + H_2O + 2NH_3$.

Among the double salts of ammonium and magnesium, the phosphate, $MgNH_4PO_4,6H_2O$, is almost insoluble in water (0·07 gram is soluble in a litre), even in the presence of ammonia. Magnesia is very frequently precipitated as this salt from solutions in which it is held by ammonium salts. As lime is not retained in solution by the presence of ammonium salts, but is precipitated nevertheless by sodium carbonate, &c., it is very easy to separate calcium from magnesium by taking advantage of these properties.

[23] In order to see the nature and cause of formation of double salts, it is sufficient (although this does not embrace the whole essence of the matter) to consider that one of the metals of such salts (for instance, potassium) easily gives acid salts, and the other (in this instance, magnesium) basic salts; the properties of distinctly basic elements predominate in the former, whilst in the latter these properties are enfeebled, and the salts formed by them bear the character of acids—for example, the salts of aluminium or magnesium act in many cases like acids. By their mutual combination these two opposite properties of the salts are both satisfied.

[24] Carnallite has been mentioned in Chapter X. (Note 4) and in Chapter XIII. These deposits also contain much *kainite*, $KMgCl(SO_4),3H_2O$ (sp. gr. 2·13; 100 parts of water dissolve 79·6 parts at 18°). This double salt contains two metals and two haloids. Feit (1889) also obtained a bromide corresponding to carnallite.

[25] The component parts of certain double salts diffuse at different rates, and as the diffused solution contains a different proportion of the component salts than the solution taken of the double salt, it shows that such salts are decomposed by water. According to Rüdorff, the double salts, like carnallite, $MgK_2(SO_4)_2,6H_2O$, and the alums, all belong to this order (1888). But such salts as tartar emetic, the double oxalates, and double cyanides are not separated by diffusion, which in all probability depends both on the relative rate of the diffusion of the component salts and on the degree of affinity acting between them. Those complex states of equilibrium which exist between water, the individual salts MX and NY, and the double salt MNXY, have been already partially analysed (as will be shown hereafter) in that case when the system is heterogeneous (that is, when something separates out in a solid state from the liquid solution), but in the case of equilibria in a homogeneous liquid medium (in a solution) the phenomenon is not so clear, because it concerns that very theory of solution which cannot yet be considered as established (Chapter I., Note 9, and others). As regards the heterogeneous decomposition of double salts, it has long been known that such salts as carnallite and $K_2Mg(SO_4)_2$ give up the more soluble salt if an insufficient quantity of water for their complete solution be taken. The complete saturation of 100 parts of water requires at 0° 14·1, at 20° 25, and at 60° 50·2 parts of the latter double salt (anhydrous), while 100 parts of water dissolve 27 parts of magnesium sulphate at 0°, 36 parts at 20°, and 55 parts at 60°, of the anhydrous salt taken. Of all the states of equilibrium exhibited by double salts the most fully investigated as yet is the system containing water, sodium sulphate, magnesium sulphate, and their double salt, $Na_2Mg(SO_4)_2$, which crystallises with 4 and 6 mol. OH_2. The first crystallo-hydrate, $MgNa_2(SO_4)_2,4H_2O$, occurs at Stassfurt, and as a sedimentary deposit in many of the salt lakes near Astrakhan, and is therefore called *astrakhanite*. The specific gravity of the monoclinic prisms of this salt is 2·22. If this salt, in a finely divided state, be mixed with the necessary quantity of water (according to the equation $MgNa_2(SO_4)_2,4H_2O + 13H_2O = Na_2SO_4,10H_2O + MgSO_4,7H_2O$), the mixture solidifies like plaster of Paris into a homogeneous mass if the temperature be *below* 22° (Van't Hoff und Van Deventer, 1886; Bakhuis Roozeboom, 1887); but if the temperature be above this *transition-point* the water and double salt do not react on each other: that is, they do not solidify or give a mixture of sodium and magnesium sulphates. If a mixture (in equivalent quantities) of solutions of

these salts be evaporated, and crystals of astrakhanite and of the individual salts capable of proceeding from it be added to the concentrated solution to avoid the possibility of a supersaturated solution, then at temperatures above 22° astrakhanite is exclusively formed (this is the method of its production), but at lower temperatures the individual salts are alone produced. If equivalent amounts of Glauber's salt and magnesium sulphate be mixed together in a solid state, there is no change at temperatures below 22°, but at higher temperatures astrakhanite and water are formed. The volume occupied by $Na_2SO_4,10H_2O$ in grams = 322/1·46 = 220·5 cubic centimetres, and by $MgSO_4,7H_2O$ = 246/1·68 = 146·4 c.c.; hence their mixture in equivalent quantities occupies a volume of 366·9 c.c. The volume of astrakhanite = 334/2·22 = 150·5 c.c., and the volume of $13H_2O$ = 234 c.c., hence their sum = 380·5 c.c., and therefore it is easy to follow the formation of the astrakhanite in a suitable apparatus (a kind of thermometer containing oil and a powdered mixture of sodium and magnesium sulphates), and to see by the variation in volume that below 22° it remains unchanged, and at higher temperatures proceeds the more quickly the higher the temperature. At the transition temperature the solubility of astrakhanite and of the mixture of the component salts is one and the same, whilst at higher temperatures a solution which is saturated for a mixture of the individual salts would be supersaturated for astrakhanite, and at lower temperatures the solution of astrakhanite will be supersaturated for the component salts, as has been shown with especial detail by Karsten, Deacon, and others. Roozeboom showed that there are two limits to the composition of the solutions which can exist for a double salt; these limits are respectively obtained by dissolving a mixture of the double salt with each of its component simple salts. Van't Hoff demonstrated, besides this, that the tendency towards the formation of double salts has a distinct influence on the progress of double decomposition, for at temperatures above 31° the mixture $2MgSO_4,7H_2O$ + 2NaCl passes into $MgNa_2(SO_4)_2,4H_2O$ + $MgCl_2,6H_2O$ + $4H_2O$, whilst below 31° there is not this double decomposition, but it proceeds in the opposite direction, as may be demonstrated by the above-described methods. Van der Heyd obtained a potassium astrakhanite, $K_2SO_4MgSO_4,4H_2O$, from solutions of the component salts at 100°.

From these experiments on double salts we see that there is as close a dependence between the temperature and the formation of substances as there is between the temperature and a change of state. It is a case of Deville's principles of dissociation, extended in the direction of the passage of a solid into a liquid. On the other hand, we see here how essential a *rôle* water plays in the formation of compounds, and how the affinity for water of crystallisation is essentially analogous to the affinity between salts, and hence also to the affinity of acids for bases, because the formation of double salts does not differ in any essential point (except the degree of affinity—that is, from a quantitative aspect) from the formation of salts themselves. When sodium hydroxide with nitric acid gives sodium nitrate and water the phenomenon is essentially the same as in the formation of astrakhanite from the salts $Na_2SO_4,10H_2O$ and $MgSO_4,7H_2O$. Water is disengaged in both cases, and hence the volumes are altered.

[26] This salt, and especially its crystallo-hydrate with $7H_2O$, is generally known as Epsom salts. It has long been used as a purgative. It is easily obtained from magnesia and sulphuric acid, and it separates on the evaporation of sea water and of many saline springs. When carbonic anhydride is obtained by the action of sulphuric acid on magnesite, magnesium sulphate remains in solution. When dolomite—that is, a mixture of magnesium and calcium carbonates—is subjected to the action of a solution of hydrochloric acid until about half of the salt remains, the calcium carbonate is mostly dissolved and magnesium carbonate is left, which by treatment with sulphuric acid gives a solution of magnesium sulphate.

[27] The anhydrous salt, $MgSO_4$ (sp. gr. 2·61), attracts moisture (7 mol. H_2O) from moist air; when heated in steam or hydrogen chloride it gives sulphuric acid, and when heated with carbon it is decomposed according to the equation $2MgSO_4 + C = 2SO_2 + CO_2 + 2MgO$. The monohydrated salt (kieserite), $MgSO_4,H_2O$ (sp. gr. 2·56), dissolves in water with difficulty; it is formed by heating the other crystallo-hydrates to 135°. The hexahydrated salt is dimorphous. If a solution, saturated at the boiling-point, be prepared, and cooled without access of crystals of the heptahydrated salt, then $MgSO_4,6H_2O$ crystallises out in *monoclinic* prisms (Loewel, Marignac), which are quite as unstable as the salt, $Na_2SO_4,7H_2O$; but if prismatic crystals of the cubic system of the copper-nickel salts of the composition $MSO_4,6H_2O$ be added, then crystals of $MgSO_4,6H_2O$ are deposited on them as prisms of the *cubic* system (Lecoq de Boisbaudran). The common crystallo-hydrate, $MgSO_4,7H_2O$, Epsom salts, belongs to the *rhombic* system, and is obtained by crystallisation below 30°. Its specific gravity is 1·69. In a vacuum, or at 100°, it loses $5H_2O$, at 132° $6H_2O$, and at 210° all the $7H_2O$ (Graham). If crystals of ferrous or cobaltic sulphate be placed in a saturated solution, *hexagonal* crystals of the heptahydrated salt are formed (Lecoq de Boisbaudran); they present an unstable state of equilibrium, and soon become cloudy, probably owing to their transformation into the more stable common form. Fritzsche, by cooling saturated solutions below 0°, obtained a mixture of crystals of ice and of a dodecahydrated salt, which easily split up at temperatures above 0°. Guthrie showed that dilute solutions of magnesium sulphate, when refrigerated, separate ice until the solution attains a composition

$MgSO_4,24H_2O$, which will completely freeze into a crystallo-hydrate at -5·3°. According to Coppet and Rüdorff, the temperature of the formation of ice falls by 0·073° for every part by weight of the heptahydrated salt per 100 of water. This figure gives (Chapter I., Note 49) $i = 1$ for both the heptahydrated and the anhydrous salt, from which it is evident that it is impossible to judge the state of combination in which a dissolved substance occurs by the temperature of the formation of ice.

The solubility of the different crystallo-hydrates of magnesium sulphate, according to Loewel, also varies, like those of sodium sulphate or carbonate (*see* Chapter XII., Notes 7 and 18). At 0° 100 parts of water dissolves 40·75 $MgSO_4$ in the presence of the hexahydrated salt, 34·67 $MgSO_4$ in the presence of the hexagonal heptahydrated salt, and only 26 parts of $MgSO_4$ in the presence of the ordinary heptahydrated salt—that is, solutions giving the remaining crystallo-hydrates will be supersaturated for the ordinary heptahydrated salt.

All this shows how many diverse aspects of more or less stable equilibria may exist between water and a substance dissolved in it; this has already been enlarged on in Chapter I.

Carefully purified magnesium sulphate in its aqueous solution gives, according to Stcherbakoff, an alkaline reaction with litmus, and an acid reaction with phenolphthalein.

The specific gravity of solutions of certain salts of magnesium and calcium reduced to 15°/4° (see my work cited, Chapter I., Note 119), are, if water at 4° = 10,000,

$$MgSO_4: s = 9,992 + 99·89p + 0·553p^2$$
$$MgCl_2: s = 9,992 + 81·31p + 0·372p^2$$
$$CaCl_2: s = 9,992 + 80·24p + 0·476p^2$$

[28] Graham even distinguished the last equivalent of the water of crystallisation of the heptahydrated salt as that which is replaced by other salts, pointing out that double salts like $MgK_2(SO_4)_2,6H_2O$ lose all their water at 135°, whilst $MgSO_4,7H_2O$ only parts with $6H_2O$.

[29] The crystalline form of the anhydrous salt obtained in this manner is not the same as that of the natural salt. The former gives rhombohedra, like those in which calcium carbonate appears as calc spar, whilst the natural salt appears as rhombic prisms, like those sometimes presented by the same carbonate as aragonite, which will shortly be described.

[30] Magnesium sulphate enters into certain reactions which are proper to sulphuric acid itself. Thus, for instance, if a carefully prepared mixture of equivalent quantities of hydrated magnesium sulphate and sodium chloride

be heated to redness, the evolution of hydrochloric acid is observed just as in the action of sulphuric acid on common salt, $MgSO_4 + 2NaCl + H_2O = Na_2SO_4 + MgO + 2HCl$. Magnesium sulphate acts in a similar manner on nitrates, with the evolution of nitric acid. A mixture of it with common salt and manganese peroxide gives chlorine. Sulphuric acid is sometimes replaced by magnesium sulphate in galvanic batteries—for example, in the well-known Meidinger battery. In the above-mentioned reactions we see a striking example of the similarity of the reactions of acids and salts, especially of salts which contain such feeble bases as magnesia.

[31] As sea-water contains many salts, MCl and MgX_2, it follows, according to Berthollet's teaching, that $MgCl_2$ is also present.

[32] As the crystallo-hydrates of the salts of sodium often contain $10H_2O$, so many of the salts of magnesium contain $6H_2O$.

[33] This decomposition is most simply defined as the result of the two reverse reactions, $MgCl_2 \div H_2O = MgO + 2HCl$ and $MgO + 2HCl = MgCl_2 + H_2O$, or as a distribution between O and Cl_2 on the one hand and H_2 and Mg on the other. (With O, $MgCl_2$ gives chlorine, *see* Chapter X., Note 33, and Chapter II., Note 3 bis and others, where the reactions and applications of $MgCl_2$ are given.) It is then clear that, according to Berthollet's doctrine, the mass of the hydrochloric acid converts the magnesium oxide into chloride, and the mass of the water converts the magnesium chloride into oxide. The crystallo-hydrate, $MgCl_2,6H_2O$, forms the limit of the reversibility. But an intermediate state of equilibrium may exist in the form of basic salts. On mixing ignited magnesia with a solution of magnesium chloride of specific gravity about 1·2, a solid mass is obtained which is scarcely decomposed by water at the ordinary temperature (*see* Chapter XVI., Note 4). A similar means is employed for cementing sawdust into a solid mass, called cylolite, used for flooring, &c.

We may remark that $MgBr_2$ crystallises not only with $6H_2O$ (temperature of fusion 152°), but also with $10H_2O$ (temperature of fusion +12°, formed at -18°). (Panfiloff, 1894).

[34] According to Thomsen, the combination of $MgCl_2$ with $6H_2O$ evolves 33,000 calories, and its solution in an excess of water 36,000.

[34 bis] Hence $MgCl_2$ may be employed for the preparation of chlorine and hydrochloric acid (Chapters X. and XI.). In general magnesium chloride, which is obtained in large quantities from sea water and Stassfurt carnallite, may find numerous practical uses.

[35] There are many other methods of separating calcium from magnesium besides that mentioned above (Note 22). Among them it will be sufficient to mention the behaviour of these bases towards a solution of

sugar; hydrated *lime* is exceedingly *soluble in an aqueous solution of sugar*, whilst magnesia is but little soluble. All the lime may be extracted from dolomite by burning it, slaking the mixture of oxides thus obtained, and adding a 10 p.c. solution of sugar. Carbonic anhydride precipitates calcium carbonate from this solution. The addition of sugar (molasses) to the lime used for building purposes powerfully increases the binding power of the mortar, as I have myself found. I have been told that in the East (India, Japan) the addition of sugar to cement has long been practised.

[36] Moreover Caron obtained an alloy of calcium and zinc by fusing calcium chloride with zinc and sodium. The zinc distilled from this alloy at a white heat, leaving calcium behind (Note 50).

[37] Calcium iodide may be prepared by saturating lime with hydriodic acid. It is a very soluble salt (at 20° one part of the salt requires 0·49 part and at 43° 0·35 part of water for solution), is deliquescent in the air, and resembles calcium chloride in many respects. It changes but little when evaporated, and like calcium chloride fuses when heated, and therefore all the water may be driven off by heat. If anhydrous calcium iodide be heated with an equivalent quantity of sodium in a closely covered iron crucible, sodium iodide and metallic calcium are formed (Liés-Bodart). Dumas advises carrying on this reaction in a closed space under pressure.

[38] Kilns which act either intermittently or continuously are built for this purpose. Those of the first kind are filled with alternate layers of fuel and limestone; the fuel is lighted, and the heat developed by its combustion serves for decomposing the limestone. When the process is completed the kiln is allowed to cool somewhat, the lime raked out, and the same process repeated. In the continuously acting furnaces, constructed like that shown in fig. 78, the kiln itself only contains limestone, and there are lateral hearths for burning the fuel, whose flame passes through the limestone and serves for its decomposition. Such furnaces are able to work continuously, because the unburnt limestone may be charged from above and the burnt lime raked out from below. It is not every limestone that is suitable for the preparation of lime, because many contain impurities, principally clay, dolomite, and sand. Such limestones when burnt either fuse partially or give an impure lime, called *poor* lime in distinction from that obtained from purer limestone, which is called *rich* lime. The latter kind is characterised by its disintegrating into a fine powder when treated with water, and is suitable for the majority of uses to which lime is applied, and for which the poor lime is sometimes quite unfit. However, certain kinds of poor lime (as we shall see in Chapter XVIII., Note 25) are used in the preparation of hydraulic cements, which solidify into a hard mass under water.

In order to obtain perfectly pure lime it is necessary to take the purest possible materials. In the laboratory, marble or shells are used for this purpose as a pure form of calcium carbonate. They are first burnt in a furnace, then put in a crucible and moistened with a small quantity of water, and finally strongly ignited, by which means a pure lime is obtained. Pure lime may be more rapidly prepared by taking calcium nitrate, CaN_2O_6, which is easily obtained by dissolving limestone in nitric acid. The solution obtained is boiled with a small quantity of lime in order to precipitate the foreign oxides which are insoluble in water. The oxides of iron, aluminium, &c., are precipitated by this means. The salt is then crystallised and ignited: $CaN_2O_6 = CaO + 2NO_2 + O$.

In the decomposition of calcium carbonate the lime preserves the form of the lumps subjected to ignition; this is one of the signs distinguishing quicklime when it is freshly burnt and unaltered by air. It attracts moisture from the air and then disintegrates to a powder; if left long exposed in the air, it also attracts carbonic anhydride and increases in volume; it does not entirely pass into carbonate, but forms a compound of the latter with caustic lime.

[39] Lime, when raised to a white heat in the vapour of potassium, gives calcium, and in chlorine it gives off oxygen. Sulphur, phosphorus, &c., when heated with lime, are absorbed by it.

[40] The greater quantity of lime is used in making mortar for binding bricks or stones together, in the form of *lime* or *cement*, or the so-called *slaked lime*. For this purpose the lime is mixed with water and sand, which serves to separate the particles of lime from each other. If only lime paste were put between two bricks they would not hold firmly together, because after the water had evaporated the lime would occupy a smaller space than before, and therefore cracks and powder would form in its mass, so that it would not at all produce that complete cementation of the bricks which it is desired to attain. Pieces of stone—that is, sand—mixed with the lime hinder this process of disintegration, because the lime binds together the individual grains of sand mixed with it, and forms one concrete mass, in consequence of a process which proceeds after the desiccation or removal of the water. The process of the solidification of lime, taken as slaked lime, consists first in the direct evaporation of the water and crystallisation of the hydrate, so that the lime binds the stones and sand mixed with it, just as glue binds two pieces of wood. But this preliminary binding action of lime is feeble (as is seen by direct experiment) unless there be further alteration of the lime leading to the formation of carbonates, silicates, and other salts of calcium which are distinguished by their great cohesiveness. With the progress of time the cement is partially subjected to the action of the carbonic anhydride in the air, owing to which calcium carbonate is formed,

but not more than half the lime is thus converted into carbonate. Besides which, the lime partially acts on the silica of the bricks, and it is owing to these new combinations simultaneously forming in the cement that it gradually becomes stronger and stronger. Hence the binding action of the lime becomes stronger with the lapse of time. This is the reason (and not, as is sometimes said, because the ancients knew how to build stronger than we do) why buildings which have stood for centuries possess a very strongly binding cement. Hydraulic cements will be described later (Chapter XVIII., Note 25).

[41] Professor Glinka measured the transparent bright crystals of calcium hydroxide which are formed in common hydraulic (Portland) cement.

[42] The act of heating brings the substance into that state of internal motion which is required for reaction. It should be considered that by the act of heating not only is the bond between the parts, or cohesion of the molecules, altered (generally diminished), not only is the motion or store of energy of the whole molecule increased, but also that in all probability the motion of the atoms themselves in molecules undergoes a change. The same kind of change is accomplished by the act of solution, or of combination in general, judging from the fact that a dissolved or combined substance—for instance, lime with water—reacts on carbonic anhydride as it does under the action of heat. For the comprehension of chemical phenomena it is exceedingly useful to recognise clearly this parallelism. Rose's observation on the formation (by the slow diffusion of solutions of calcium chloride and sodium carbonate) of aragonite from dilute, and of calc spar from strong, solutions is easily understood from this point of view. As aragonite is always formed from hot solutions, it appears that dilution with water acts like heat. The following experiment of Kühlmann is particularly instructive in this sense. Anhydrous (perfectly dry) barium oxide does not react with monohydrated sulphuric acid, H_2SO_4 (containing neither free water nor anhydride, SO_3). But if either an incandescent object or a moist substance is brought into contact with the mixture a violent reaction immediately begins (it is essentially the same as combustion), and the whole mass reacts.

The influence of solution on the process of reaction is instructively illustrated by the following experiment. Lime, or barium oxide, is placed in a flask or retort having an upper orifice and connected with a tube immersed in mercury. A funnel furnished with a stopcock and filled with water is fixed into the upper orifice of the retort, which is then filled with dry carbonic anhydride. There is no absorption. When a constant temperature is arrived at, the unslaked oxide is made to absorb all the carbonic anhydride by carefully admitting water. A vacuum is formed, as is seen by the mercury rising in the neck of the retort. With water the absorption goes on to the end, whilst under the action of heat there remains the dissociating tension of the carbonic anhydride. Furthermore, we here see that, with a certain resemblance, there is also a distinction, depending on the fact that at low temperatures calcium carbonate does not dissociate; this determines the complete absorption of the carbonic anhydride in the aqueous solution.

[43] Experience has shown that by moistening partially-burnt lime with water and reheating it, it is easy to drive off the last traces of carbonic anhydride from it, and that, in general, by blowing air or steam through the lime, and even by using moist fuel, it is possible to accelerate the decomposition of the calcium carbonate. The partial pressure is decreased by these means.

[44] Before the introduction of Deville's theory of dissociation, the *modus operandi* of decompositions like that under consideration was understood in the sense that decomposition starts at a certain temperature, and that it is accelerated by a rise of temperature, but it was not considered possible that combination could proceed at the same temperature as that at which decomposition goes on. Berthollet and Deville introduced the conception of equilibrium into chemical science, and elucidated the question of reversible reactions. Naturally the subject is still far from being clear—the questions of the rate and completeness of reaction, of contact, &c., still intrude themselves—but an important step has been made in chemical mechanics, and we have started on a new path which promises further progress, towards which much has been done not only by Deville himself, but more especially by the French chemists Debray, Troost, Lemoine, Hautefeuille, Le Chatelier, and others. Among other things those investigators have shown the close resemblance between the phenomena of evaporation and dissociation, and pointed out that the amount of heat absorbed by a dissociating substance may be calculated according to the law of the variation of dissociation-pressure, in exactly the same manner as it is possible to calculate the latent heat of the evaporation of water, knowing the variation of the tension with the temperature, on the basis of the second law of the mechanical theory of heat. Details of this subject must be looked for in special works on physical chemistry. *One and the same conception* of the mechanical theory of heat *is applicable to dissociation* and *evaporation.*

[45] But the question as to the formation of a basic calcium carbonate with a rise of temperature still remains undecided. The presence of water complicates all the relations between lime and carbonic anhydride, all the more as the existence of an attraction between calcium carbonate and water is seen from its being able to give a *crystallo-hydrate*, $CaCO_3,5H_2O$ (Pelouze),

which crystallises in rhombic prisms of sp. gr. about 1·77 and loses its water at 20°. These crystals are obtained when a solution of lime in sugar and water is left long exposed to the air and slowly attracts carbonic anhydride from it, and also by the evaporation of such a solution at a temperature of about 3°. On the other band, it is probable that an *acid salt*, $CaH_2(CO_3)_2$, is formed in an aqueous solution, not only because water containing carbonic acid dissolves calcium carbonate, but more especially in view of the researches of Schloesing (1872), which showed that at 16° a litre of water in an atmosphere of carbonic anhydride (pressure 0·984 atmosphere) dissolves 1·086 gram of calcium carbonate and 1·778 gram of carbonic anhydride, which corresponds with the formation of calcium hydrogen carbonate, and the solution of carbonic anhydride in the remaining water. Caro showed that a litre of water is able to dissolve as much as 3 grams of calcium carbonate if the pressure be increased to 4 and more atmospheres. The calcium carbonate is precipitated when the carbonic anhydride passes off in the air or in a current of another gas; this also takes place in many natural springs. Tufa, stalactites, and other like formations from waters containing calcium carbonate and carbonic acid in solution are formed in this manner. The solubility of calcium carbonate itself at the ordinary temperature does not exceed 13 milligrams per litre of water.

[46] Dimorphous bodies differ from true isomers and polymers in that they do not differ in their chemical reactions, which are determined by a difference in the distribution (motion) of the atoms in the molecules, and therefore dimorphism is usually ascribed to a difference in the distribution of similar molecules, building up a crystal. Although such a hypothesis is quite admissible in the spirit of the atomic and molecular theory, yet, as in such a redistribution of the molecules a perfect conservation of the distribution of the atoms in them cannot be imagined, and in every effort of chemical reaction there must take place a certain motion among the atoms; so in my opinion there is no firm basis for distinguishing dimorphism from the general conception of isomerism, under which the cases of those organic bodies which are dextro and lævo rotatory (with respect to polarised light) have recently been brought with such brilliant success. When calcium carbonate separates out from solutions, it has at first a gelatinous appearance, which leads to the supposition that this salt appears in a colloidal state. It only crystallises with the progress of time. The colloidal state of calcium carbonate is particularly clear from the following observations made by Prof. Famintzin, who showed that when it separates from solutions it is obtained under certain conditions in the form of grains having the peculiar paste-like structure proper to starch, which fact has not only an independent interest, but presents an example of a mineral substance being obtained in a form until then only known in the

organic substances elaborated in plants. This shows that the forms (cells, vessels, &c.) in which vegetable and animal substances occur in organisms do not present in themselves anything peculiar to organisms, but are only the result of those particular conditions in which these substances are formed. Traube and afterwards Monnier and Vogt (1882) obtained formations which, under the microscope, were in every respect identical in appearance with vegetable cells, by means of a similar slow formation of precipitates (by reacting on sulphates of different metals with sodium silicate or carbonate).

[47] According to Le Chatelier (1888), $1\frac{1}{2}H_2O$ is lost at 120°—that is, $H_2O,2CaSO_4$ is formed, but at 194° all the water is expelled. According to Shenstone and Cundall (1888) gypsum begins to lose water at 70° in dry air. The semi-hydrated compound $H_2O,2CaSO_4$ is also formed when gypsum is heated with water in a closed vessel at 150° (Hoppe-Seyler).

[48] For stucco-work it is usual to add lime and sand, as the mass is then harder and does not solidify so quickly. For imitating marble, glue is added to the plaster, and the mass is polished when thoroughly dry. Re-burnt gypsum cannot be used over again, as that which has once solidified is, like the natural anhydride, not able to recombine with water. It is evident that the structure of the molecules in the crystallised mass, or in general in any dense mass, exerts an influence on the chemical action, which is more particularly evident in metals in their different forms (powder, crystalline, rolled, &c.)

[48 bis] According to MacColeb, gypsum dehydrated at 200° has a specific gravity 2·577, and heated to its point of fusion, 2·654. Potilitzin (1894) also admits the two above-named modifications of anhydrous gypsum, which, moreover, always contain the semi-hydrated hydrate (Note 47), and he explains by their relation to water the phenomena observed in the solidification of a mixture of burnt gypsum and water.

[49] As Marignac showed, gypsum, especially when desiccated at 120°, easily gives supersaturated solutions with respect to $CaSO_4,2H_2O$, which contain as much as 1 part of $CaSO_4$ to 110 parts of water. Boiling dilute hydrochloric acid dissolves gypsum, forming calcium chloride. The behaviour of gypsum towards the alkaline carbonates has been described in Chapter X. Alcohol precipitates gypsum from its aqueous solutions, because, like the sulphates in general, it is sparingly soluble in alcohol. Gypsum, like all the sulphates, when heated with charcoal, gives up its oxygen, forming the sulphide, CaS.

Calcium sulphate, like magnesium sulphate, is capable of forming double salts, but with difficulty, and they are chemically less stable. They contain, as is always the case with double salts, less water of crystallisation than the component salts. Rose, Struvé, and others obtained the salt $CaK_2(SO_4)_2,H_2O$; a mixture of gypsum with an equivalent amount of potassium sulphate and water solidifies into a homogeneous mass. Fritzsche obtained the corresponding sodium salt in a hydrated and anhydrous state, by heating a mixture of gypsum with a saturated solution of sodium sulphate. The anhydrous salt occurs in nature as *glauberite*. Fritzsche also obtained *gaylussite*, $Na_2Ca(CO_3)_2,5H_2O$, by pouring a saturated solution of sodium carbonate on to freshly-precipitated calcium carbonate. Calcium also forms basic salts, but only a few. Veeren (1892) obtained $Ca(NO_3)_2Ca(OH)_2,2\frac{1}{2}H_2O$ by leaving powdered caustic lime in a saturated solution of $Ca(NO_3)_2$ until it solidified. This salt is decomposed by water.

[50] Calcium chloride has a specific gravity 2·20, or, when fused, 2·12, and the sp. gr. of the crystallised salt $CaCl_2,6H_2O$ is 1·69. If the volume of the crystals at $0° = 1$, then at $29°$ it is 1·020, and the volume of the fused mass at the same temperature is 1·118 (Kopp) (specific gravity of solutions, *see* Note 27). The solution containing 50 p.c. $CaCl_2$ boils at $130°$, 70 p.c. at $158°$. Superheated steam decomposes calcium chloride with more difficulty than magnesium chloride and with greater ease than barium chloride (Kuhnheim). Sodium does not decompose fused calcium chloride even on prolonged heating (Liés-Bodart), but an alloy of sodium with zinc, lead, and bismuth decomposes it, forming an alloy of calcium with one of the above-named metals (Caron). The zinc alloy may be obtained with as much as 15 p.c. of calcium. Calcium chloride is soluble in alcohol and absorbs ammonia.

A gram molecular weight of calcium chloride in dissolving in an excess of water evolves 18,723 calories, and in dissolving in alcohol 17,555 units of heat, according to Pickering.

Roozeboom made detailed researches on the crystallo-hydrates of calcium chloride (1889), and found that $CaCl_2,6H_2O$ melts at $30·2°$, and is formed at low temperatures from solutions containing not more than 103 parts of calcium chloride per 100 parts of water; if the amount of salt (always to 100 parts of water) reaches 120 parts, then tabular crystals of $CaCl_2,4H_2O\beta$ are formed, which at temperatures above $38·4°$ are converted into the crystallo-hydrates $CaCl_2,2H_2O$, whilst at temperatures below $18°$ the β variety passes into the more stable $CaCl_2,4H_2O\alpha$, which process is aided by mechanical friction. Hence, as is the case with magnesium sulphate (Note 27), one and the same crystallo-hydrate appears in two forms—the β, which is easily produced but is unstable, and the α, which is stable. The solubility of the above-mentioned hydrates of chloride of calcium, or amount of calcium chloride per 100 parts of water, is as follows:—

	0°	20°	30°	40°	60°
CaCl$_2$,6H$_2$O	60	75	100		(102·8)
CaCl$_2$,4H$_2$Oα	—	90	101	117	(154·2)
CaCl$_2$,4H$_2$Oβ	—	104	114	—	
CaCl$_2$,2H$_2$O	—	—	(308·3)	128	137

The amount of calcium chloride to 100 parts of water in the crystallo-hydrate is given in brackets. The point of intersection of the curves of solubility lies at about 30° for the first two salts and about 45° for the salts with 4H$_2$O and 2H$_2$O. The crystals CaCl$_2$,2H$_2$O may, however, be obtained (Ditte) at the ordinary temperature from solutions containing hydrochloric acid. The vapour tension of this crystallo-hydrate equals the atmospheric at 165°, and therefore the crystals may be dried in an atmosphere of steam and obtained without a mother liquor, whose vapour tension is greater. This crystallo-hydrate decomposes at about 175° into CaCl$_2$,H$_2$O and a solution; this is easily brought about in a closed vessel when the pressure is greater than the atmosphere. This crystallo-hydrate is destroyed at temperatures above 260°, anhydrous calcium chloride being formed.

Neglecting the unstable modification CaCl$_2$,4H$_2$Oβ, we will give the temperatures t at which the passage of one hydrate into another takes place and at which the solution CaCl$_2$ + nH$_2$O, the two solids A and B and aqueous vapour, whose tension is given as p in millimetres, are able to exist together in stable equilibrium, according to Roozeboom's determinations:

t	n	A	B	p
-55°	14·5	ice	CaCl$_2$,6H$_2$O	0
+29·8°	6·1	CaCl$_2$,6H$_2$O	CaCl$_2$,4H$_2$O	6·8
45·3°	4·7	CaCl$_2$,4H$_2$O	CaCl$_2$,2H$_2$O	11·8
175·5°	2·1	CaCl$_2$,2H$_2$O	CaCl$_2$,H$_2$O	842
200°	1·8	CaCl$_2$,H$_2$O	CaCl$_2$	Several atmospheres

Solutions of calcium chloride may serve as a convenient example for the study of the supersaturated state, which in this case easily occurs, because different hydrates are formed. Thus at 25° solutions containing more than 83 parts of anhydrous calcium chloride per 100 of water will be supersaturated for the hydrate CaCl$_2$,6H$_2$O.

On the other hand, Hammerl showed that solutions of calcium chloride, when frozen, deposit ice if they contain less than 43 parts of salt per 100 of water, and if more the crystallo-hydrate $CaCl_2,6H_2O$ separates, and that a solution of the above composition ($CaCl_2,14H_2O$ requires 44·0 parts calcium chloride per 100 of water) solidifies as a cryohydrate at about -55°.

[51] The action of barium sulphate on sodium and potassium carbonates is given on p. 437.

[52] Barium sulphide is decomposed by water, $BaS + 2H_2O = H_2S + Ba(OH)_2$ (the reaction is reversible), but both substances are soluble in water, and their separation is complicated by the fact that barium sulphide absorbs oxygen and gives insoluble barium sulphate. The hydrogen sulphide is sometimes removed from the solution by boiling with the oxides of copper or zinc. If sugar be added to a solution of barium sulphide, barium saccharate is precipitated on heating; it is decomposed by carbonic anhydride, so that barium carbonate is formed. An equivalent mixture of sodium sulphate with barium or strontium sulphates when ignited with charcoal gives a mixture of sodium sulphide and barium or strontium sulphide, and if this mixture be dissolved in water and the solution evaporated, barium or strontium hydroxide crystallises out on cooling, and sodium hydrosulphide, NaHS, is obtained in solution. The hydroxides BaH_2O_2 and SrH_2O_2 are prepared on a large scale, being applied to many reactions; for example, strontium hydroxide is prepared for sugar works for extracting crystallisable sugar from molasses.

We may remark that Boussingault, by igniting barium sulphate in hydrochloric acid gas, obtained a complete decomposition, with the formation of barium chloride. Attention should also be turned to the fact that Grouven, by beating a mixture of charcoal and strontium sulphate with magnesium and potassium sulphates, showed the easy decomposability depending on the formation of double salts, such as SrS,K_2S, which are easily soluble in water, and give a precipitate of strontium carbonate with carbonic anhydride. In such examples as these we see that the force which binds double salts may play a part in directing the course of reactions, and the number of double salts of silica on the earth's surface shows that nature takes advantage of these forces in her chemical processes. It is worthy of remark that Buchner (1893), by mixing a 40 per cent. solution of barium acetate with a 60 per cent. solution of sulphate of alumina, obtained a thick glutinous mass, which only gave a precipitate of $BaSO_4$ after being diluted with water.

[53] Barium sulphate is sometimes converted into barium chloride in the following manner: finely-ground barium sulphate is heated with coal and manganese chloride (the residue from the manufacture of chlorine). The

mass becomes semi-liquid, and when it evolves carbonic oxide the heating is stopped. The following double decompositions proceed during this operation: first the carbon takes up the oxygen from the barium sulphate, and gives sulphide, BaS, which enters into double decomposition with the chloride of manganese, $MnCl_2$, forming manganese sulphide, MnS, which is insoluble in water, and soluble barium chloride. This solution is easily obtained pure because many foreign impurities, such as iron, remain in the insoluble portion with the manganese. The solution of barium chloride is chiefly used for the preparation of barium sulphate, which is precipitated by sulphuric acid, by which means *barium sulphate* is re-formed as a powder. This salt is characterised by the fact that it is unacted on by the majority of chemical reagents, is insoluble in water, and is not dissolved by acids. Owing to this, artificial barium sulphate forms a permanent white paint which is used instead of (and mixed with) white lead, and has been termed 'blanc fixé' or 'permanent white.'

The solution of one part of calcium chloride at 20° requires 1·36 part of water, the solution of one part of strontium chloride requires 1·88 part of water at the same temperature, and the solution of barium chloride 2·88 parts of water. The solubility of the bromides and iodides varies in the same proportion. The chlorides of barium and strontium crystallise out from solution with great ease in combination with water; they form $BaCl_2,2H_2O$ and $SrCl_2,6H_2O$. The latter (which separates out at 40°) resembles the salts of Ca and Mg in composition, and Étard (1892) obtained $SrCl_2,2H_2O$ from solutions at 90–130°. We may also observe that the crystallo-hydrates $BaBr_2,H_2O$ and $BaI_2,7H_2O$ are known.

[54] The nitrates $Sr(NO_3)_2$ (in the cold its solutions give a crystallo-hydrate containing $4H_2O$) and $Ba(NO_3)_2$ are so very sparingly soluble in water that they separate in considerable quantities when a solution of sodium nitrate is added to a strong solution of either barium or strontium chloride. They are obtained by the action of nitric acid on the carbonates or oxides. 100 parts of water at 15° dissolve 6·5 parts of strontium nitrate and 8·2 parts of barium nitrate, whilst more than 300 parts of calcium nitrate are soluble at the same temperature. Strontium nitrate communicates a crimson coloration to the flame of burning substances, and is therefore frequently used for Bengal fire, fireworks, and signal lights, for which purpose the salts of lithium are still better fitted. Calcium nitrate is exceedingly hygroscopic. Barium nitrate, on the contrary, does not show this property in the least degree, and in this respect it resembles potassium nitrate, and is therefore used instead of the latter for the preparation of a gunpowder which is called 'saxifragin powder' (76 parts of barium nitrate, 2 parts of nitre, and 22 parts of charcoal).

[55] The dissociation of the crystallo-hydrate of baryta is given in Chapter I., Note 65. 100 parts of water dissolve

0° 20° 40° 60° 80°

BaO 1·5 3·5 7·4 18·8 90·8

SrO 0·3 0·7 1·4 3   9

Supersaturated solutions are easily formed.

The anhydrous oxide BaO fuses in the oxyhydrogen flame. When ignited in the vapour of potassium, the latter takes up the oxygen; whilst in chlorine, oxygen is separated and barium chloride formed.

[55 bis] Brugellmann, by heating BaH_2O_2 in a graphite or clay crucible, obtained BaO in needles, sp. gr. 5·32, and by heating in a platinum crucible—in crystals belonging to the cubical system, sp. gr. 5·74. SrO is obtained in the latter form from the nitrate. The following are the specific gravities of the oxides from different sources:—

MgO CaO SrO

from RN_2O_6 3·38 3·25 4·75

„ RCO_3 3·48 3·26 4·45

„ RH_2O_2 3·41 3·25 4·57

[56] The property of barium oxide of absorbing oxygen when heated, and giving the peroxide, BaO_2, is very characteristic for this oxide (*see* Chapter III., Note 7). It only belongs to the anhydrous oxide. The hydroxide does not absorb oxygen. Peroxides of calcium and strontium may be obtained by means of hydrogen peroxide. Barium peroxide is insoluble in water, but is able to form a hydrate with it, and also to combine with hydrogen peroxide, forming a very unstable compound having the composition BaH_2O_4 (obtained by Professor Schöne), which in course of time evolves oxygen (Chapter IV., Note 21).

[57] Even in solutions a gradual progression in the increase of the specific gravity shows itself, not only for equivalent solutions (for instance, $RCl_2 + 200H_2O$), but even with an equal percentage composition, as is seen from the curves giving the specific gravity (water 4° = 10,000) at 15° (for barium chloride, according to Bourdiakoff's determinations):

$$BeCl_2: S = 9,992 + 67{\cdot}21p + 0{\cdot}111p^2$$
$$CaCl_2: S = 9,992 + 80{\cdot}24p + 0{\cdot}476p^2$$

$$\text{SrCl}_2: S = 9{,}992 + 85 \cdot 57 p + 0 \cdot 733 p^2$$
$$\text{BaCl}_2: S = 9{,}992 + 86 \cdot 56 p + 0 \cdot 813 p^2$$

[58] One part of calcium sulphate at the ordinary temperature requires about 500 parts of water for solution, strontium sulphate about 7,000 parts, barium sulphate about 400,000 parts, whilst beryllium sulphate is easily soluble in water.

[59] We refer beryllium to the class of the bivalent metals of the alkaline earths—that is, we ascribe to its oxide the formula BeO, and do not consider it as trivalent (Be = 13·5, Chapter VII., Note 21), although that view has been upheld by many chemists. The true atomic composition of beryllium oxide was first given by the Russian chemist, Avdéeff (1819), in his researches on the compounds of this metal. He compared the compounds of beryllium to those of magnesium, and refuted the notion prevalent at the time, of the resemblance between the oxides of beryllium and aluminium, by proving that beryllium sulphate presents a greater resemblance to magnesium sulphate than to aluminium sulphate. It was especially noticed that the analogues of alumina give alums, whilst beryllium oxide, although it is a feeble base, easily giving, like magnesia, basic and double salts, does not form true alums. The establishment of the periodic system of the elements (1869), considered in the following chapter, immediately indicated that Avdéeff's view corresponded with the truth—that is, that beryllium is bivalent, which therefore necessitated the denial of its trivalency. This scientific controversy resulted in a long series of researches (1870–80) concerning this element, and ended in Nilson and Pettersson—two of the chief advocates of the trivalency of beryllium—determining the vapour density of $\text{BeCl}_2 = 40$, (Chapter VII., Note 21), which gave an undoubted proof of its bivalency (*see* also Note 3).

[60] Beryllium oxide, like aluminium oxide, is precipitated from solutions of its salts by alkalis as a gelatinous hydroxide, BeH_2O_2, which, like alumina, is soluble in an excess of caustic potash or soda. This reaction may be taken advantage of for distinguishing and separating beryllium from aluminium, because when the alkaline solution is diluted with water and boiled, beryllium hydroxide is precipitated, whilst the alumina remains in solution. The solubility of the beryllium oxide at once clearly indicates its feeble basic properties, and, as it were, separates this oxide from the class of the alkaline earths. But on arranging the oxides of the above-described metals of the alkaline earths according to their decreasing atomic weights we have the series

BaO, SrO, CaO, MgO, BeO,

in which the basic properties and solubility of the oxides consecutively and distinctly decrease until we reach a point when, had we not known of the existence of the beryllium oxide, we should expect to find in its place an oxide insoluble in water and of feeble basic properties. If an alcoholic solution of caustic potash be saturated with the hydrate of BeO, and evaporated under the receiver of an air pump, it forms silky crystals BeK_2O_2.

Another characteristic of the salts of beryllium is that they give with aqueous ammonia a gelatinous precipitate which is soluble in an excess of ammonium carbonate like the precipitate of magnesia; in this beryllium oxide differs from the oxide of aluminium. Beryllium oxide easily forms a carbonate which is insoluble in water, and resembles magnesium carbonate in many respects. Beryllium sulphate is distinguished by its considerable solubility in water—thus, at the ordinary temperature it dissolves in an equal weight of water; it crystallises out from its solutions in well-formed crystals, which do not change in the air, and contain $BeSO_4, 4H_2O$. When ignited it leaves beryllium oxide, but this oxide, after prolonged ignition, is re-dissolved by sulphuric acid, whilst aluminium sulphate, after a similar treatment, leaves aluminium oxide, which is no longer soluble in acids. With a few exceptions, the salts of beryllium crystallise with great difficulty, and to a considerable extent resemble the salts of magnesium; thus, for instance, beryllium chloride is analogous to magnesium chloride. It is volatile in an anhydrous state, and in a hydrated state it decomposes, with the evolution of hydrochloric acid.

[61] Thus in the nitrides of the metals we have substances by means of which we can easily obtain from the nitrogen of the air, not only ammonia, but also with the aid of CO, by synthesis, a whole series of complex carbon and nitrogen compounds.

[62] As the hydrides of calcium, magnesium, &c. are very stable under the action of heat, and these metals and hydrogen occur in the sun, it is likely that the formation of their hydrides may take place there. (Private communication from Prof. Winkler, 1894.) It is probable that in the free metals of the alkaline earths hitherto obtained a portion was frequently in combination with nitrogen and hydrogen.

[63] Thus, for instance, a mixture of 56 parts of CaO and 24 parts of magnesium powder is heated in an iron pipe (placed over a row of gas burners as in the combustion furnace used for organic analysis) in a stream of hydrogen. After being heated for $\frac{1}{2}$ hour the mixture is found to absorb hydrogen (it no longer passes over the mixture, but is retained by it). The product, which is light grey, and slightly coherent, disengages a mass of hydrogen when water is poured over it, and burns when heated in air. The resultant mass contains 33 per cent. CaH, about 28 per cent. CaO, and

about 38 per cent. MgO. Neither CaH nor any other MH has yet been obtained in a pure state.

The acetylene derivatives of the metals of the alkaline earths C_2M (Chapter VIII., Note 12 bis), for instance, C_2Ba, obtained by Maquenne and Moissan, belong to the same class of analogous compounds. It must here be remarked that the oxides MO of the metals of the alkaline earths, although not reducible by carbon at a furnace heat, yet under the action of the heat attained in electrical furnaces, not only give up their oxygen to carbon (probably partly owing to the action of the current), but also combine with carbon. The resultant compounds, C_2M, evolve acetylene, C_2H_2, with HCl, just as N_2M_3 give ammonia. We may remark moreover that the series of compounds of the metals of the alkaline earths with hydrogen, nitrogen and carbon is a discovery of recent years, and that probably further research will give rise to similar unexpected compounds, and by extending our knowledge of their reactions prove to be of great interest.

Milton Keynes UK
Ingram Content Group UK Ltd.
UKHW030621061024
449204UK00004B/437

9 789362 515155